ANNUAL REVIEW OF PSYCHOLOGY

ANNUAL REVIEW OF PSYCHOLOGY

VOLUME 40, 1989

MARK R. ROSENZWEIG, *Editor*

University of California, Berkeley

LYMAN W. PORTER, *Editor*

University of California, Irvine

ANNUAL REVIEWS INC.   4139 EL CAMINO WAY   P.O. BOX 10139   PALO ALTO, CALIFORNIA 94303–0897

ANNUAL REVIEWS INC.
Palo Alto, California, USA

International Standard Serial Number: 0066–4308
International Standard Book Number: 0–8243–0240-0
Library of Congress Catalog Card Number: 50–13143

Annual Review and publication titles are registered trademarks of Annual Reviews Inc.

∞ The paper used in this publication meets the minimum requirements of American National Standard for Information Sciences—Permanence of Paper for Printed Library Materials, ANSI Z39.48-1984.

Annual Reviews Inc. and the Editors of its publications assume no responsibility for the statements expressed by the contributors to this *Review*.

Typesetting by Kachina Typesetting Inc., Tempe, Arizona; John Olson, President
Typesetting coordinator, Janis Hoffman

PRINTED AND BOUND IN THE UNITED STATES OF AMERICA

PREFACE

This year marks a first for the *Annual Review of Psychology*. This is the first time our Prefatory Chapter has been written jointly by a wife-husband team. The authors are eminent psychologists Dorothea Jameson and Leo Hurvich. Their chapter, encompassing insights gained from many years of significant contribution to their arena of scholarship, is entitled "Essay Concerning Color Constancy."

As is customary, the collection of chapters for this volume spans a wide range of topics, from "Brain Dopamine and Reward" to "Cross-Cultural Psychology," from "Comparative Psychology, Ethology, and Animal Behavior" to "Social Cognition," and from "The Intensity of Motivation" to "Psychometric Methods," among other areas. The total set of topics reflects the Master List for the *Review* as well as the evolving and expanding breadth of the very large field of science and applications we call psychology.

As is also customary, we include in this volume two "Timely Topics"— chapters not specified by the Master List and written with shorter lead-times. One is the chapter by Judith Rodin and Peter Salovey on "Health Psychology," a subject that has been reviewed only once before in this series. The other chapter, by Ray Human, is on an area never before reviewed in the *ARP*, "The Psychology of Deception."

The Editorial Committee is pleased to welcome its newest member, John M. Darley, who began his service in 1988.

L.W.P.
M.R.R.

Annual Review of Psychology
Volume 40, 1989

CONTENTS

RELATED ARTICLES OF INTEREST TO READERS OF THE *ANNUAL REVIEW OF PSYCHOLOGY*

From the *Annual Review of Anthropology,* Volume 17 (1988)

DNA and Human Origins, R. L. Cann

From the *Annual Review of Medicine,* Volume 40 (1989)

The Pathobiology of Alzheimer's Disease, G. G. Glenner
The Neuropharmacology of Attention-Deficit Hyperactivity Disorder, A. J. Zametkin and B. G. Borcherding
Cocaine Dependence, F. H. Gawin and E. H. Ellinwood, Jr.

From the *Annual Review of Neuroscience,* Volume 11 (1988)

Modulation of Ion Channels in Neurons and Other Cells, I. B. Levitan
Some Aspects of Language Processing Revealed Through the Analysis of Acquired Aphasia: The Lexical System, A. Caramazza
Behavioral Studies of Pavlovian Conditioning, R. A. Rescorla
Neuroethology of Electric Communication, C. D. Hopkins
Excitatory Amino Acid Neurotransmission: NMDA Receptors and Hebb-Type Synaptic Plasticity, C. W. Cotman, D. T., Monaghan, and A. H. Ganong
Anatomical Organization of Macaque Monkey Striate Visual Cortex, J. S. Lund
Formation of Topographical Maps, S. B. Udin and J. W. Fawcett
Transgenic Mice: Applications to the Study of the Nervous System, M. G. Rosenfeld, E. B. Crenshaw III, S. A. Lira, L. Swanson, E. Borrelli, R. Heyman, and R. M. Evans
Neurogenetic Dissection of Learning and Short-term Memory in Drosophila, Y. Dudai
Animal Solutions to Problems of Movement Control: The Role of Proprioceptors, Z. Hasan and D. G. Stuart

From the *Annual Review of Pharmacology and Toxicology,* Volume 29 (1989)

Modulation of Glutamate Receptors: Molecular Mechanisms and Functional Implications, J. T. Wroblewski and W. Danysz
Neurotransmitter Receptors and Phosphoinositide Turnover, D.-M. Chuang

From the *Annual Review of Public Health,* Volume 10 (1989)

Perspectives on Statistical Significance Testing, R. F. Woolson and J. C. Kleinman
Communicating Technological Risk: The Social Construction of Risk Perception, D. Nelkin

Prevention and the Elderly: Public Health Issues and Strategies, P. S. German and
   L. P. Fried
Literacy and Health Status, R. Grosse
Prevention and the Field of Mental Health: A Psychiatric Perspective, H. Pardes
The Role of Media Across Four Levels of Health Promotion Intervention, J. A.
   Flora, E. W. Maibach, and N. Maccoby

From the *Annual Review of Sociology*, Volume 14 (1988)

Social Structure, Psychology, and the Estimation of Risk, C. A. Heimer
Organizational Demography, S. Stewman
Structures and Processes of Social Support, J. House, D. Umberson, and K. Landis
Recent Developments in Attitudes and Social Structure, K. J. Kiecolt
Organizational Learning, B. Levitt, J. G. March

For the convenience of readers, a detachable order form/envelope is bound into the back of this volume.

Dorothea Jameson

Ann. Rev. Psychol. 1989. 40:1–22

ESSAY CONCERNING COLOR CONSTANCY*

Dorothea Jameson and Leo M. Hurvich

Department of Psychology, University of Pennsylvania, Philadelphia, Pennsylvania 19104-6196

CONTENTS

INTRODUCTION

Current Interest

Issues of constancy have arisen in the study of perception whenever the senses have been examined as information systems that mediate knowledge of the characteristics of the physical world. The kinds of constancy are manifold. They include mappings on sensory surfaces that are somehow converted into external space location maps so integrated that they serve not only as efficient and precise indicators of distance and direction information, but as mediators of sensorimotor integration and skill control as well (Guthrie et al 1983; Jay & Sparks 1984). Objects, moreover, preserve their objective identities despite a

---

*This is the tenth in a series of prefatory chapters written by eminent senior psychologists.

1

variety of changes in the energy maps projected on the sensory receiving surfaces whether these changes relate to the object (or event) sizes, shapes, intensities, or qualities. At the same time, objects are systematically dependent, in terms of their phenomenal appearances, on the different local contexts in which they are embedded in the objective environment. Emphasis on only one or the other of these factors—i.e. identity preservation or context-dependent perception—tends to ignore the richness of the total information that our sensory mechanisms contribute to the cognitive systems that fashion the so-called real world as we know it.

Some of the current resurgence of interest in the constancy problem can be attributed to the advent of the computer in its various degrees of technological sophistication and processing capacity; the computer as a tool for testing intricately detailed hypotheses, as a tool for developing simulations, and as a would-be substitute for a human perceiver—i.e. a perceptual robot or a "task" robot with "machine vision." The last use, or better, goal, is one that seems to encourage an understandable tendency toward oversimplification of the problem. We would have no quarrel with such a tendency if it were not that the oversimplification that might be useful for the machine as tool to perform specific tasks in the robot context is somehow carried over into the analysis of perception, even though the oversimplification distorts the nature of the human perceptual problem.

In a 1986 issue of the *Journal of the Optical Society,* a Feature Section was devoted to computational approaches to color vision.[1] In his introduction the feature editor explicitly recognized the focus on the machine task aspect of the approach. "If we want to address robots in higher-level languages that we understand about objects, we must make them see the way we do" (Krauskopf 1986). Eight of the twelve feature papers dealt with color constancy, and the primary aim was to find algorithms or computational approaches that would yield means for deriving constant surface reflectance properties of objects for different and initially unknown illuminants.[2] Apart from its use in the computation of surface reflectance characteristics for object recognition, perceptual information about the different conditions of illumination as relevant in its own right was largely if not totally ignored in these papers. Our own judgment is that human visual systems (including both higher- and lower-order processes) are likely to have evolved a design that provides perceptual information about change as well as constancy—about light, weather, and time of day, as well as about the relatively constant physical properties of mainly opaque objects within a scene. To what extent current technology

---

[1]The phrase "computational vision" is already gaining wide currency (e.g. Boynton 1988).

[2]Stanford University has applied for a patent based on research directed toward this goal, a fact that emphasizes its obvious relation to machine design (Maloney & Wandell 1986).

might or might not find such information relevant for the tasks of present-day or near-future robots we are not prepared to say, but that luminosity information, as well as opaque surface information, is relevant for biological organisms of human or other species is an assumption that we are prepared to make.

Historical Overview

Early experimental studies of the perceptual constancies typically examined the degree of constancy manifested under different conditions. [For an integrative theoretical discussion of the various constancies, with an emphasis on Gestalt principles, see Koffka (1935).] With respect to color (including both the chromatic and achromatic brightness or lightness properties), the central issue was the same as it is today. How can the surface reflectance characteristics of the distal object be recovered to achieve an approximately constant surface percept despite the fact that the retinal image of the object depends on both its surface reflectance (R) and the incident illumination (I), $R \times I$, when R is constant but I is both unknown and changes from one situation to the next? Helmholtz's conjecture was both best known and most widely accepted. In his text on experimental psychology, Woodworth (1938) included Helmholtz's own statement of his view, which we quote here.[3]

> Colors are mainly important for us as properties of objects and as means of identifying objects. In visual observation we constantly aim to reach a judgment on the object colors and to eliminate differences of illumination. So, we clearly distinguish between a white sheet of paper in weak illumination and a gray sheet in strong illumination. We have abundant opportunity to examine the same object colors in full sunlight, in the blue light from the clear sky, and the reddish yellow light of the sinking sun or of candlelight—not to mention the colored reflections from surrounding objects. Seeing the same objects under these different illuminations, we learn to get a correct idea of the object colors in spite of difference of illumination. We learn to judge how such an object would look in white light, and since our interest lies entirely in the object color, we become unconscious of the sensations on which the judgment rests.

Woodworth also cites Hering's views on color constancy. Hering, not surprisingly, disagreed with Helmholtz's analysis. He called attention to the various peripheral factors (pupillary changes, retinal adaptation, and physiological contrast mechanisms) that actually must alter the sensory effects of visual stimulation under different conditions of illumination, and that, with continued visual experience, Hering thought would also alter the state of the central mechanisms involved in perception—the kinds of changes we would today refer to as visual plasticity. Hering's view led directly to his concept of "memory color."

---

[3]The statement quoted here from Woodworth was abstracted by him from the first edition of Helmholtz's *Physiological Optics* (1866, p. 408). In Southall's (1924) English translation of the third edition, Helmholtz's discussion appears in Volume 2, pp. 286–87.

The color in which we have most consistently seen an external object is impressed indelibly on our memory and becomes a fixed property of the memory image. What the layman calls the real color of an object is a color of the object that has become fixed, as it were, in his memory; I should like to call it the memory color of the object. . . . Moreover, the memory color of the object need not be rigorously fixed but can have a certain range of variation depending on its derivation. . . . All objects that are already known to us from experience, or that we regard as familiar by their color, we see through the spectacles of memory color. (Hering 1920)

Woodworth's summary chapter on the perception of color captures the flavor of the experimental work on approximate color constancy during the period between 1900 and the late 1930s. Typically, the experiments were designed to determine the degree of lightness constancy for various conditions, sometimes by sample matches made to a display of surfaces of different reflectances under different levels of illumination and/or shadow conditions, sometimes by matches made between rotating disks of various average reflectances. The term "albedo" came into common use as the relative reflectance index, and the measure in these experiments was the degree to which the albedo determined the visual matches for the different conditions. Arithmetic (Brunswik) or logarithmic (Thouless) ratios were developed to express the departures of the experimental matches from those predicted for perfect lightness constancy. Ordinarily the data fell somewhere between perfect retinal image light matches and perfect object constancy, although occasionally overcompensation for illumination differences was observed. Considerable effort was devoted to determining the efficacy of various cues for judging illumination, a requirement, in the Helmholtz context, for solving the reflectance problem; and in the same context, measures were compared for children of various ages. For the most part, children did not seem very different from adults, although the results differed for different experiments and were particularly susceptible to effects of instructions. Instructions have always been recognized as crucial in such experiments (MacLeod 1932; Katz 1935; Hurvich & Jameson 1966), and they continue to recur as an experimental variable (Arend & Reeves 1986; Arend & Goldstein 1987). The extremes can best be summarized by the difference between making an adjustment to make a particular part of a display *look* identical to the same area in a differently illuminated display, as contrasted with an adjustment to make a particular surface in a display *seem identical in its surface characteristics* to the same object in a differently illuminated display. Behavioral experiments on nonhumans used "identification" as indexed by a trained response, and these results, too, suggested that fish and primates are able to identify objects in different illuminations in terms of their surface reflectances.

Not included in Woodworth's summary was the classical experiment of Hess & Pretori (1894). Although their aim was to measure the effects of brightness contrast between two (adjacent) center/surround displays, their results can readily be analyzed in constancy terms. That is, for a center area of one reflectance and a surround of different reflectance, a uniform increase in illumination would produce a proportional increase in light reflected from each surface, and the ratio of reflected light of center-to-surround in the retinal images would remain unchanged despite the proportional increase in each. The measured contrast ratio for the matched area in the center/surround comparison display would also be constant if the observers were exhibiting perfect lightness constancy. Our own replot of the Hess & Pretori data (Jameson & Hurvich 1964, 1970) shows that their observations encompass a range of findings that depend systematically on the surround-to-center contrast ratio of each test display. When this ratio is low (equivalent to surround reflectance lower than center's), the center appears to increase in perceived brightness as center and surround are both increased proportionally in illumination; as the contrast ratio is made higher (equivalent to surround reflectance higher than center's), the center appearance approaches constancy; and as the contrast ratio is made still higher (equivalent to surround reflectance much higher than center's), the dark center appears to become blacker with proportional increase in illumination of both center and surround. We have reported findings similar to these for a patterned array of different achromatic patches, and cite in our report concordant results from other laboratories (Jameson & Hurvich 1961a, 1964).

RELEVANT VARIABLES

Visual Sensitivity

Light sensitivity is so well known to be controlled by the level of illumination to which one is adapted that it hardly needs documentation here. Although it is most often illustrated by the dark-adaptation curve, for relevance to the important constancy issue, only the photopic segment of that threshold sensitivity function, the cone region, describes the course of sensitivity recovery of interest. Moreover, the reflection of this recovery function, which shows the increasing threshold energy requirement with increase in level of background light, makes clear the decrement in light sensitivity with increase in adaptation level. Because the visual response depends on the product of stimulus × sensitivity, a major part of the compensation for illumination changes (in addition to the small contribution of pupillary changes) obviously occurs at a very peripheral level, and largely in the retinal light receptors. For the range of adaptation levels within which Weber's law holds, it is often assumed that contrast sensitivity (and by extension, suprathreshold contrast perception) will be constant, and thus account for perceived lightness constancy. It is essentially another statement of the ratio hypothesis proposed by Wallach (1948). Were this a perfectly compensatory mechanism, then there would certainly be no need for experience with, or judgments of, different levels of illumination, because their effects, at least for uniform illuminations and diffuse object surfaces, would never be registered at all beyond the most peripheral level of the visual system. But the situation is not quite this simple. If contrast sensitivity is measured with sinewave stimuli as a function of spatial frequency to determine the human contrast-sensitivity function, both the level and the form of this function change with average level of illumination. This dependence on illumination has important implications for visual perception; it is one of the findings that make it most unlikely that form perception depends on a straightforward Fourier processing of a scene by the visual system (Kelly & Burbeck 1984). It also suggests that all sharply focused edges between surfaces of different reflectances will not appear equally sharp at different light levels. Kelly & Burbeck believe that at low spatial frequencies, contrast sensitivity is closely related to mechanisms of lateral inhibition, which are spatially more diffuse than the excitatory processes. The dependence of the effectiveness of such mechanisms on illumination level is consistent with our own long-held conviction that visual adaptation must involve postreceptoral changes as well as receptoral sensitivity adjustments (Hurvich & Jameson 1958, 1960, 1961, 1966; Jameson 1985; Jameson & Hurvich 1956, 1959, 1961b, 1964, 1970, 1972; Varner et al 1984).

Chromatic Sensitivity

In 1905, von Kries made an analysis of the way the visual system might compensate for changes in the spectral quality of illumination to make it possible to identify object colors, and proposed that the three different spectrally selective mechanisms of the retina (cone types) suffer relative decrements in overall light sensitivity in proportion to the relative strengths of their individual stimulation by the prevailing illumination. This analysis is qualitatively consistent with the way both the threshold and suprathreshold spectral luminosity functions vary in form with chromatic adaptation (Jameson & Hurvich 1953; Hurvich & Jameson 1954). Thus, for example, exposure to longwave light selectively reduces light sensitivity in the same region of the spectrum, as it should if the contribution of the longwave cone signal to light sensitivity were reduced in amplitude. However, von Kries's postulated changes in the balance of sensitivities would not change the forms of the three individual wavelength vs receptor sensitivity functions, but only their amplitudes; hence additive color matches that depend on the selective absorptions of the three different cone pigments would be unaffected by the sensitivity adjustments. Within reasonable limits, such matches are so unaffected, but only if the state of adaptation is uniform throughout retinal image areas of both the test and matching fields.

If this is not the case and the matches are "asymmetric" (for example between test field in one eye for one state of chromatic adaptation and matching field in the other eye for a different adaptation), then differences in responsiveness between the two states of adaptation can be registered by changes in the proportions of the matching lights. Such asymmetric color matches make it clear that the von Kries rule of linear, proportional changes in amplitude of receptor sensitivities cannot account for all the data (Hurvich & Jameson 1958; Jameson & Hurvich 1972). Departures from this rule are systematic. That is, the measured changes in proportions of the matching lights vary systematically with the luminance level of the test field relative to the surround luminance to which the eye is adapted. The departures from the proportionality rule are, moreover, in the directions that would have been predicted from a nonconstancy phenomenon known as the Helson-Judd effect (Helson 1938; Judd 1940). Spectrally nonselective surfaces seen against a spectrally nonselective background all appear achromatic (white through grays to black) in white light. When illuminated by chromatic light, samples whose reflectances are near the background level continue to appear gray, those above the background level take on the hue of the illuminant, and those below take on a hue that is complementary to that of the illuminant. Hue shifts for chromatic samples tend to behave similarly—i.e. as if intermixed with the illuminant hue or with its complementary, depending on the relative reflectances of sample and background. Such departures from perfect color constancy with changes in spectral quality of illumination are reminiscent of those described above for lightness constancy, and both sets of phenomena imply that perceived contrast between objects of different surface reflectance varies with the level and kind of illumination in which they are seen and to which the visual system is adapted.

We should emphasize that the magnitudes of these perceptual changes are not so great as usually to prevent object identification by color, particularly for distinctly colored surfaces that, under most ordinary illuminants, undergo perceived hue, saturation, or brightness shifts that still do not move them out of one color category and into another, which would certainly be the case were there no compensatory changes in visual sensitivities (Jameson 1983).

For particular kinds of arrays that contain strong colors, but with subtle color differences, however, the state of chromatic adaptation can make the difference between seeing a pattern and failing to perceive that the surface is anything but uniformly colored. This statement is based on our studies of wavelength discrimination for test lights viewed within surrounds to which the observer is adapted (Hurvich & Jameson 1961). The consequences of chromatic adaptation for such discriminations are not a priori obvious. It might be anticipated that exposure, for example, to longwave light, which reduces the sensitivity of the longwave receptor, would selectively impair discriminability between just detectably different long wavelengths. Instead, the opposite occurs. In the longwave spectral region, the threshold wavelength difference is actually decreased; thus discriminability is improved, relative to what it is for neutral adaptation. And conversely, wavelength discrimination is relatively impaired in the midwave spectral region (where light sensitivity remains high). Qualitatively, what happens in this situation is that the perceived redness is somewhat depressed in the longer wavelengths, making slight differences in the yellowness of these same lights more obvious, whereas the perceived midspectrum greenness is enhanced, and tends to mask slight differences in the yellowness of these lights that can be detected reliably in a neutral state of adaptation. Changes analogous to these occur in other spectral regions for other kinds of chromatic adaptation.

Anyone who has had the opportunity to observe paintings hung in the same surroundings in both daylight and at night under incandescent illumination is likely to be aware of the disappearance or enhancement of such subtle hue differences. In most of these situations, the state of chromatic adaptation is probably determined primarily by the spectral quality of the illuminant. This assumes that the different surfaces in the field of view will be sufficiently varied so that the space average reflectance will not be far from neutral or spectrally nonselective. Some paintings, of course, are sufficiently large so that only the gamut of reflectances within the painting itself enter, with the illuminant, to affect the adaptation state. But here too the discriminability of similar hues and saturations will be dependent on the quality as well as level of the average light reflected from the surface area within the field of view as one inspects the painting, and it will differ for different illuminants.

In connection with paintings of the sort just mentioned, it should be pointed out that even for a very large painting that is very nearly monochromatic, such as Ad Reinhart's canvas called "Red Painting" (red geometric figure against red background, 6.5 ft by 12.5 ft), which hangs in the Metropolitan Museum of Art in New York, continued inspection of the painting does not rob it of its redness and transform it into a gray painting. Fortunately for the artist, chromatic adaptation of the von Kries sort need not be complete; that is, the balance of sensitivities need not be completely compensatory so that the space average product of the reflectances × illumination yields a neutral or achromatic response. For highly selective reflectances or illuminants this is seldom the case; rather, the sensitivity balance only partially compensates for the effective adapting light rather than completely compensating for it. In brief, there are degrees of chromatic adaptation (Jameson & Hurvich 1956), as well as degrees of light and dark adaptation. Complete adaptation to strongly chromatic light is a special case; it does occur in a so-called *Ganzfeld* situation—that is, when the eye is exposed to completely uniform illumination throughout the entire surface of the retina (Hochberg et al 1951). With prolonged exposure to a *Ganzfeld,* all visual effect of light fades away and we become, as it were, sightless.

SURFACE METAMERS   Surface metamers constitute a special case of an illuminant-dependent departure from color constancy. This case comes about because the appearance of a given surface material under one illuminant can be precisely matched for the same illuminant by a variety of different dyes and paint mixtures used to color other material samples. The spectral reflectance distributions of the samples can differ markedly, but the samples are visually identical. Such surfaces are thus, by definition, all surface-color metamers for this one illuminant. If the illuminant is changed, the surface color matches no longer hold. The different samples take on different hues and saturations that deviate, one from the next, in directions and amounts that are governed by their particular spectral reflectances in relation to the spectral characteristics of the new illuminant. [For a detailed technical discussion of surface metamers, illuminants, and distortion transformations, see Wyszecki & Stiles (1967).] The color changes cannot be predicted without a priori knowledge of the spectral distributions that are involved, but, in general, they will be more significant the more irregular the spectral reflectance and illuminance distributions. With the increased use of fluorescent light sources that contain localized spectral energy peaks, the so-called "color rendering" properties of illuminants have required the increased attention of lighting engineers and illuminant manufacturers. Visual mechanisms of color adaptation do not, even in principle, solve this problem caused by illuminant energy peaks and high degrees of surface-color metamerism.

Neutral Adaptation and White Light

Chromatic adaptation is, by commonsense definition, measured as a departure from adaptation to white light. By common sense as well, white light is light that looks white or achromatic. But what looks white or achromatic is, quite obviously, any one of a variety of very different spectral distributions depending on other variables in the viewing situation. Consider only one series of such illuminants whose energy varies smoothly and systematically across the visible spectrum in a way that nearly parallels the energy output of a physicist's ideal *black body* raised to increasing temperatures. Such illuminants are characterized by so-called *color temperatures* (*kelvin,* K); lights of high color temperatures (such as light from the north sky, about 10,000 K) have their energy output more heavily weighted in the short wavelengths, whereas artificial incandescent light of the sort used for indoor illumination (2400–2800 K) is relatively impoverished in shortwave energy but has comparatively high energy output in the longwave region of the visible spectrum. Illumination that is a mixture of skylight and noonday sunlight (color temperature of about 5500 K) has a relatively balanced energy distribution. This continuum of illuminants is approximately the one referred to in Helmholtz's statement that "we have abundant opportunity to examine the same object color in full sunlight, in the blue light from the clear sky, and the reddish-yellow light of the sinking sun or of candlelight . . .", although our incandescent lights are less "reddish-yellow" than either the sinking sun or Helmholtz's candlelight. In controlled laboratory test situations, uniform light fields from this whole gamut of color temperatures can be perceived as white light, but the perception depends on a multiplicity of interacting variables that include level of total light energy, exposure duration, area of light field, and prior light exposure (Hurvich & Jameson 1951a,b; Jameson & Hurvich 1951b). The gamut of color temperatures perceived as white increases with energy level whatever the parametric value of each of the other variables. That is, at high levels the relatively desaturated blue or yellow hues seen at lower light levels are somehow veiled or weakened. Since the cone system adapts rapidly, chromatic adaptation might well be a contributing factor responsible for the neutral percept for all illuminants except the one that approximates an equal-energy distribution. The latter illuminant (with some individual variation probably due to differences in ocular media) in our experiments had no perceptible hue at any energy level for any of the exposure durations or field sizes we examined. Results of other experiments designed to test for chromatic adaptation effects were consistent with the conclusion that it is only a near equal-energy illuminant that leaves the visual system in a neutrally balanced equilibrium state (Jameson & Hurvich 1951a).

For opaque surfaces of spectrally nonselective reflectances, it is only for conditions that produce such a physiologically neutral equilibrium state of adaptation that all gray-scale levels of the nonselective surfaces can be expected to appear equally achromatic as whites through grays to blacks. Illuminants that produce other adaptation states will alter the perceived neutrality in accord with the Helson-Judd effect, tinting the lighter samples toward the illuminant hue and the darker ones toward its complementary. The extent of the perceived departures from strict neutrality of such surface colors will be minimal for illuminants very similar to the physiologically neutral one, and increasingly more noticeable for illuminants that are more heavily weighted toward one or another end of the spectrum. If the visual scene includes a variety of spectrally selective as well as nonselective surfaces, then the neutral or nonneutral appearances of the latter will further depend on the other surfaces in the array. In addition to illumination and reflectance characteristics, additional variables such as size and proximity become relevant for all the perceived surface colors.

Contrast, Assimilation, and Receptive Fields

The systematic departures from color constancy that carry information about illumination are essentially color contrast effects. They include both (a) brightness or lightness contrast that accentuates the perceived difference between the lightest and darkest objects or reflectances as mentioned above for both surfaces (Jameson & Hurvich 1961a, 1964) and sinewave gratings (Kelly & Burbeck 1984), and (b) color contrast that accentuates perceived differences in the complementary yellow-to-blue and red-to-green hue dimensions (Jameson & Hurvich 1961b). In retinal images of natural scenes that contain three-dimensional objects and surface reflectances made up of both specular and diffuse components, contrast accentuates the differences between highlight and shadow, and contributes to the three-dimensionality of the scene, even if the image is not of the scene itself but of a two-dimensional photographic display. Shadowing is so effective a cue for three-dimensional shape that even shadowing that is produced by border contrast, rather than a gradation in either illumination or reflectance, can result in perceived depth variations across a perfectly flat surface. A good example is the familiar Mach scallop or fluted effect that perceptually "curves" adjacent edges forward and back into the surface plane when one views contiguous rectangular samples of a gray scale that is regularly ordered from light to dark.

Lateral interactions are common to the anatomy and neurophysiology of visual systems. Although at least in some species there may be contact influences that spread across the retinal receptor layer itself, in primates and thus probably also in humans, the more significant lateral interactions seem to occur at postreceptoral levels. In the color processing system, the three-variable spectral analysis of retinal image light occurs, as it were, in three parallel classes of cone receptors, each with a characteristic spectral sensitivity determined by its particular cone photopigment. Light absorption is signalled by graded hyperpolarizing electrical responses in each cone class, and gives rise to synaptic changes that result, ultimately, in postreceptoral "neural images."

A significant recombination in the color processing system involves a transformation from the three different light absorption maps of the receptor mosaic that yields another set of three maps essentially based on a set of three different sums and differences governed by the signal strengths in the different receptor types. In our model based on psychophysical evidence (see Hurvich 1981), one of the neural systems is activated in accord with a difference between the weighted signal strengths of the midwave-sensitive receptor and the summed short- and longwave-sensitive receptors, a second in accord with a difference between the weighted signal strengths of the short-wave-sensitive receptor and the summed mid- and longwave-sensitive receptors, and a third in accord with the weighted signal strengths of the signals summed from all three receptor types. It should be noted here that opponent neural processing as fundamental to color vision is by now universally accepted, but the specific models proposed by different investigators differ in their detailed formulations. A recent computational proposal (not yet implemented by experiment) suggests use of sinewave spectral power distributions to most efficiently evaluate a subset of these formulations, including our own (Benzschawel et al 1986). All models require differencing mechanisms for hue processing, in accord with Hering's original hypothesis. The three overlapping spectral separations achieved by the selective photopigments are thus sharpened in the two differencing systems of the neural map, and essentially lost in the third. But since this spectral sharpening requires neural activation related to more than any single one of the adjacent cones, it comes at the expense of the spatial discreteness potentially available at the retinal receptor level. Thus the effective spatial grain in the neural maps is necessarily coarsened relative to that of the individual cones of the retinal mosaic.

Spatial, simultaneous color contrast has been a recognized characteristic of perception since at least the time of Leonardo da Vinci, and it has been exploited by artists who often exaggerate both hue and brightness contrast for pictorial effect (Jameson & Hurvich 1975). Because of contrast, any formal process expression for perceived color for a specified retinal light image array must include not only (a) the spectral sensitivities of the three classes of photopic light receptors, (b) coefficients to express the amplitude balance of these receptors brought about by adaptation of the von Kries type, and (c) the interactions that give rise to the difference and sum functions that characterize spectral opponent processing in the neural image, but also (d) the mutual lateral neural interactions that occur within each class of the triplex of processing systems at this level (Jameson & Hurvich 1959). The effects of the latter are readily measured by perceptual scaling techniques and by color matches made to individual, uniform samples within an array compared with matches to the same samples in the presence of parts or all of the remaining array. Quantitative modeling of the effects by simultaneous equations that include spatial terms can describe them to a rough approximation (Jameson & Hurvich 1961b, 1964), but a physiologically more realistic model, and one that intrinsically subsumes more spatial variables, involves filtering by a difference of Gaussians (DOG) at the opponent neural level. Such functions are idealized representations of neural receptive fields of the circularly symmetric, spatially antagonistic, center/surround type. Psychophysically determined threshold interaction effects have been used to estimate the critical spatial dimensions within which only excitatory summative effects (receptive field center effects) occur within a small central foveal region of the visual field (Westheimer 1967). When such estimates are compared with those derived from other kinds of psychophysical experiments, such as measures of sinewave contrast sensitivity that typically involve larger retinal areas, there are differences in calculated receptive field center diameters, although the shapes of the derived sensitivity profiles are very similar (Kelly & Burbeck 1984). The nonhomogeneity of the receptor mosaic—that is, the decline in numbers of cones per unit area from fovea to periphery of the retina (and corresponding decline in numbers of related postreceptoral cells)—is accompanied by expansion of receptive field center diameters with increasing distance from the foveal projection; but there is also considerable size variation within any particular projection area (Hubel & Wiesel 1960). Thus, the spatial grain of the neural maps, although coarser, follows the grain of the retinal receptor mosaic, but in a graded band, so to speak, rather than being singularly determined by retinal location.

Spatial mixture and blending of hue and/or lightness are effects that are opposite to border contrast since they reduce, rather than accentuate, differences in contiguous image areas. In our own analyses of these phenomena, the variation in receptive field size within a particular locus referred to above has seemed to provide the kind of physiological basis needed to account for the fact that both sharp edges between adjacent image areas and apparent spreading of different hues across the image boundaries can occur. Such effects, variously called *assimilation* or *spreading,* are particularly striking in repetitive patterns whether striped or curvilinear, and they can readily be observed in decorative fabrics and other motifs as well as in the paintings of some contemporary artists (Jameson & Hurvich 1975).

What is seen in such patterns depends on the sizes of the uniform elements within the pattern imaged on the retina relative to the cone diameters, and to the diameters of both the center and surround regions of the related neural receptive fields. If the image elements are small relative to the cone diameters, then true spatial light mixture occurs; if they are small relative to the receptive field centers, then some degree of spatial blending or assimilation occurs; and if they are larger, then assimilation gives way to spatial contrast. These changes can be observed most easily by decreasing or increasing viewing distance from the pattern, thus controlling the relative sizes by increasing or decreasing, respectively, the width (in the stripe example) of the pattern elements in the retinal image. In this case, color constancy fails with change in distance: For example, stripes that are seen close up as red alternating with blue become increasingly reddish purple and bluish purple stripes farther away. Complete light mixture with failure of spatial resolution requires very distant viewing. Far enough away, a striped pattern can look uniform. It is the intermediate range that is of most interest, because here there is both good pattern resolution and partial hue mixture. Also, at just the right distance within the intermediate range, it is possible to attend to the striped field as a whole and see the stripes as reddish purple and bluish purple, or, alternatively, to concentrate on the adjacent stripes at the center of gaze (where the receptive fields are smallest in the foveal region) and see them as vividly red and blue with no trace of the purple mixture hue. To the casual viewer, the nonconstancy of adjacent stripe color that can occur when scanning such a pattern at the critical viewing distance is usually not noticed as such without deliberate attention, but what is noticed is a kind of visual liveliness that fabric designers sometimes strive for.

Since resolution and mixture depend on neural receptive field center sizes, the fact that, for some retinal image dimensions, both can occur simultaneously and at the same location suggests that the two effects result from processing in different neural systems with different receptive field dimensions; and indeed, process modeling using scaled receptive field (DOG) filtering gives a good qualitative match to the perceptual effects (Jameson 1985). Receptive fields of different scales are used commonly in computational models, and their dimensions have typically been based on analyses of psychophysical data indicating that sinewave contrast sensitivity requires a number of different spatial processing "channels" for different regions of the spatial frequency dimension. [A good critical summary and relevant references can be found in Kelly & Burbeck (1984).] It is also concluded from the dependence of sinewave contrast sensitivity on luminance level that the effectiveness of the inhibitory surround region of receptive fields is decreased at low luminances and increased at higher ones. Thus, the relative effectiveness of the mutual lateral interactions that give rise to spatial contrast both at edges and across more extended retinal image areas (see von Békésy 1968) would be expected to vary with luminance in the same way and provide a physiological basis for the perceived increase in object color contrast in bright light.

Postreceptoral Adaptation or Biasing

It seems clear that change in the spectral quality and quantity of the adapting illuminant not only changes the balance of sensitivities at the receptor level, but that it also changes the balance of excitatory and inhibitory influences that are related to both spectral and spatial processing in the color related systems at the postreceptoral level. In addition to the evidence from our own studies of asymmetric color matches, perceptual scaling data, and discrimination functions discussed earlier in this essay, and the evidence from sinewave contrast functions mentioned above, additional evidence for the involvement of postreceptoral mechanisms comes from a very different experimental and analytical paradigm. This paradigm is the two-color increment threshold technique employed in the many exemplary experiments and analyses carried out by W. S. Stiles. Pugh & Kirk (1986) have published a comprehensive historical review of this work, including references to others (among whom Pugh was an important contributor), that outlines the changes in Stiles's own interpretation of such discrimination thresholds and provides the basis for the current interpretation that the mechanism for adaptation to the background light in this paradigm cannot be restricted exclusively to the triplex of retinal light receptors but must also involve postreceptoral adaptation effects in the neural differencing mechanisms—i.e. at the spectrally opponent level of neural color processing. In their review, the authors emphasize that, although Stiles had started from the hypothesis that analysis of his psychophysical data would reveal activities and adaptation effects only in the cones, by 1967 he himself pointed out that difference signals may also make an important contribution to the discriminations in his experimental paradigm.[4]

We do not intend to imply here that the postreceptoral influences envisaged by all investigators concerned with this issue are necessarily identical with those that we have hypothesized to account for a variety of different psychophysical and perceptual findings. For example, D'Zmura & Lennie (1986) postulate variable weights that are adaptation-dependent applied to the adaptation-scaled cone signals at the differencing level. Whether their specific formulation would yield effects at the cortical level equivalent to our postulated postreceptoral, incremental or decremental, equilibrium level or set-point shifts that depend on lateral opponent interactions is not directly evident. Their discussion of physiological mechanisms leaves uncertain the level (or levels) of neural processing at which the postreceptoral adaptation effects occur (as does our own model of these effects), and even includes an expression of uncertainty about whether the kinds of adjustments to scaled cone signals that they postulate for their second stage are actually made by the visual system. Clearly, independent evidence on this issue from visual neurophysiology is both lacking and needed. Some of our own psychophysical experiments that compare adaptation to steady light fields with adaptation to the same lights for an equivalent duration but with interpolated dark intervals that permit partial recovery of cone sensitivity have led us to the conclusion that postreceptoral mechanisms (at some level) recover from chromatic adaptation shifts very slowly before the neutral equilibrium level is restored (Jameson et al 1979). Such relatively long-term biasing suggests a potential contribution to the adaptation effects at processing levels as far removed from the retinal receptors as the visual projection areas of the cortex.

Visual Cortex and Double-Opponent Cells

Cells that show opponent spectral characteristics are known to exist in the primate all the way from the retina, through the lateral geniculate nucleus

---

[4]For an earlier suggestion that this might be so, see Hurvich 1963.

(LGN), to various cortical projection areas. Although cortical cells in area 17 and beyond usually have receptive fields that are organized in such a way that the cells are preferentially sensitive to lines and edges with particular orientations, some of which have been reported also to be spectrally selective and opponent, there are also cortical cells with circularly symmetric receptive fields that are characterized by spectral opponency both in the centers and in the antagonistic surrounds (De Valois et al 1982; Michael 1978a,b; Jameson 1985 for additional references). Recent work by Livingstone & Hubel (1984; Hubel & Livingstone 1987) has localized such cells, thought to be related to the parvocellular system of the LGN, in cluster-like formations, *blobs,* in area 17, and has suggested that these double-opponent blob cells feed into *thin stripe* formations in area 18, from which there are also anatomical connections back to area 17 as well as with other visual projection areas. Such double-opponent cells conveniently display characteristics similar to the difference-of-Gaussians receptive fields combined with spectral differencing for two hue systems and broadband spectral sensitivities for an achromatic system, which are consistent with our interpretations of psychophysical and perceptual data. Despite this convenient convergence, we do not intend to imply either that these are *the* relevant physiological findings for neural color processing or that our own analyses are anything but oversimplified and incomplete. It is with this caveat, and the further caveat that these are certainly not the only collections of cells or brain areas involved, that they are included in the digest shown in Table 1. The suggestion in this digest that the connections to area 17 from area 18 as well as from 17 to 18 might be related to changes in state related to the establishment of "memory color" is our own speculation, and it is no more than that. Interconnections with other subdivisions and other brain areas would certainly be required for colors of particular hue categories to be regularly associated with objects of particular forms and particular contexts.

From the point of view of understanding visual perception, or even a circumscribed aspect of the mechanism such as color processing, in terms of visual neurophysiology, we are barely at the starting line ready for the first halting step. From a perspective of 20 or more years back, progress in visual neurophysiology has been rapid and impressive. But examined from today's perspective, the missing details and the nearly totally unexplored functional specializations of the different relevant brain areas, as well as of their mutual interrelations, loom even more impressively large.

REMARKS ON COMPUTATIONAL APPROACHES

We mentioned in the introductory paragraphs of this essay that issues related to object color constancy are a common focus of computational approaches; in

Table 1   Some relevant aspects of color processing

Retinal light stimulus	Space (and time) average of: Direct light Illuminant × surface reflectances (specular and diffuse components)
von Kries adaptation (proportionality rule weighted for degree of adaptation)	Influence on: Amplitudes of three phototopic sensitivity functions Control of magnitudes of input signals to postreceptoral spectral differencing mechanisms and summative luminosity mechanism
Additional postreceptoral activation	Locally weighted space (and time) average of: Difference and sum effects within adjacent postreceptoral neural elements
Receptive field effects (control by spatial sums and differences)	Influence on: Set points of spectrally and spatially opponent mechanisms $(R+G-, R-G+, Y+B-, Y-B+, W+Bk-, W-Bk+)$
Activation of cortical sensory area 17	Inputs from parvocellular system to: Blob-like subdivisions of retinotopic organization containing cells with double-opponent receptive fields
Area 17 local cortical connections between blobs	Influence on: Spatial extent of lateral influences on individual double-opponent cells
Activation of cortical area 18	Inputs from blob cells of area 17 to: Cells segregated in thin stripe subdivisions containing cells with double-opponent, nonoriented receptive fields
Reciprocal cortical connections between area 17 and area 18	Influence on: Possible recurrent activation for hypothetical synaptic weighting in successive approximation to a "memory color"

Hurlbert's (1986) words, computations that will "extract the invariant spectral-reflectance properties of an object's surface from the varying light that it reflects." Part of the problem considered by some computational studies is the separate extraction of the illuminant properties from specular highlights in a three-dimensional scene or representation thereof (D'Zmura & Lennie 1986; Lee 1986), and another part is the separation of shadows from material changes (Gershon et al 1986). Many of these approaches are concerned to some extent with one or another version of the *retinex* algorithm proposed by Land (1983, 1986; Land & McCann 1971) to specify lightness and color in constant terms related to constant reflectances and independently of illumination (Arend & Reeves 1986; Brainard & Wandell 1986; D'Zmura & Lennie 1986; Hurlbert 1986; Worthey & Brill 1986). Land's computational procedures for describing perceived colors have undergone a number of modifications since he was first surprised by his own observation that the wide gamut of hues he was able to recognize in a photographic slide projection did not require wavelengths in the projected image that he associated with those hues, nor did they require mixtures of wavelengths from three different parts of the spectrum as he would have anticipated from the technology of colorimetry (Land 1959). Although others saw his demonstrations as instances of simultaneous color contrast, Land was not interested in contrast explanations, whether cognitive or physiological. As a physicist looking for another account from the physics of light, he proposed that the different colors seen in the *natural image* could be attributed to (and computed by) the ratios of almost any pair of longer and shorter wavelengths or wavelength distributions used to form the projected image or to illuminate the original scene. The first significant change in this anti-trichromatic, or at least nontrichromatic, idea was in the direction of traditional color theory. The two-record account was modified to a three-layer, three-light-record account in which lightness ratios were computed for each record separately, with the maximum lightness in each assigned a value of 1.0. Such a procedure yields a three-variable chromaticity and photometric lightness space normalized with respect to the maximum lightness, taken to represent "white," with hue designations assigned to various regions in the space in accord with the hue names assigned to the three different light records. We would describe this procedure as akin to the application of a von Kries adaptation rule for the normalization, and a Young-Helmholtz type of theory for the color coding. Further modifications of the specifics of the retinex procedure include the computation of each lightness ratio record across reflectance boundaries, akin to Wallach's (1948) account of achromatic lightness constancy; a reset correction to retain a maximum of 1.0; a logarithmic transformation; and the introduction of a ratio threshold. The latter serves to discount gradual lightness changes within reflectance boundaries of the sort that would be produced by an illumination gradient, thus eliminating the gradient from the computation and presumably from the perception as well. In his 1983 paper, Land includes a transformation from what we described above as a chromaticity and lightness space, which he calls the *color three-space,* to a red-green, yellow-blue, white-black opponent color three-space. This is another step in the direction of currently accepted color theory. In a still more recent report (Land 1986), an alternative algorithm is presented that involves photometric measurements of the surface pattern with a small and a large photometer aperture (the latter having a diminishing sensitivity profile), a log transform of the record at each of the two very different scales, and then a differencing operation. This alternative algorithm for the first time in retinex computations relaxes the strict coupling between computed lightness at a point on a surface and surface reflectance at that location. The procedure, although described differently, is implicitly akin to the mechanism proposed by von Békésy (1968) to account for simultaneous contrast. This most recent change in retinex formulation thus brings the computational approach closer to the center/surround receptive field based modeling that we, and many others, have been engaged in for some time. The retinex operations do not yet, however, include the receptive field dependences required to subsume the systematic departures from lightness and color constancy that occur with change in level and quality of illumination. Nor do they yet include in the photometric procedures provision for change in retinal image size with change in viewer-to-surface distance, and thus the distance-dependent departures from perceived color constancy that can vary from assimilation to contrast effects for the same reflectance pattern which we discussed above (see the section on *Contrast, Assimilation, and Receptive Fields*).

It seems predictable that computational approaches to the old issue of color constancy will not for long continue to seek direct and precise perceptual correlates of constant surface reflectances, but will increasingly embody the more realistic approach of object identification through approximate invariance of color category. As we have pointed out elsewhere, there are some colors (e.g. the colors of haystacks, concrete and other masonry) that are difficult to categorize under any illuminant and that change quite noticeably with change in viewing conditions. For objects of this sort, color identification, rather than contributing to object identification, is more likely a result of it. It also seems predictable that approaches that include computations to extract illumination information as well as surface color will probably begin to incorporate shadow, as well as highlight effects, and to recognize the biological significance of such information as such for purposes other than being discounted. We have already cited attempts to separate shadow from material changes across surfaces, but we should add here that with no change in shadow, illumination, or reflectance, perceived differences can also result from apparent differences in object shape and orientation. Thus, a surface seen as a trapezoid under glancing illumination can appear less light than it does when the observer's set is manipulated so that the same surface is seen as a normally illuminated square lying flat on a receding plane (Hochberg 1978). Effects of this sort, when they occur, are clearly not under the control of any variables in the light stimulus, but rather point to mutual influences between different specialized processing systems tempered by well-practiced adaptive behavioral responses of the individual.

In the long run, the kind of widely encompassing computational approach that seems to us to offer the most promise for modeling of perceptual effects is exemplified by Edelman's *neuronal group selection* theory (Reeke & Edelman 1988). The theory is based on biological considerations, with both variability and selection emphasized not only as evolutionary but also as developmental principles. In development, selection for neuronal connectivity is elaborated by selective mechanisms for differential cell growth and survival, and followed during early experience by selection, through modification of synaptic strengths, among diverse preexisting groups of cells to shape and adapt the behavior of the organism. An appealing feature of the computational model based on this theory is the processing in parallel of unique responses to individual stimuli (the automaton sampling system called *Darwin*), and of generic responses to stimulus class (the automaton sampling system called *Wallace*). There is high-level reciprocal connectivity between these systems, and a natural emergence of similarity-based categories that are relevant to the adaptive needs of organisms.

It seems to be agreed that surface color recognition is a useful component of object identification, and it is our judgment that such recognition is adequately accomplished by category matching and does not require precise matching-to-sample by the three color variables of hue, brightness, and saturation. It seems also to be agreed that context and instructions can modify actual experimental matching between extremes that approximate reflectance matches, on the one hand, and on the other hand, an illumination-dependent range of perceived hues, saturations, and brightnesses that include, but are not restricted to, a set of approximate reflectance matches. Both the systematic changes and the categorical constancies are perceptually available for recording in experiments, and more importantly, for adaptive responses to objects recognized in the environment and to the illumination conditions of that environment. Recognition and identification require some degree of perceived constancy, but we could cite too many examples of identification and recognition, whether of persons, objects, buildings, or landscapes, despite aging, fading, season, and illumination, to assume that the systematic changes related to such different conditions are not also perceptually informative in important ways.

Literature Cited

Arend, L., Goldstein, R. 1987. Simultaneous constancy, lightness, and brightness. *J. Opt. Soc. Am. A* 4:2281–85

Arend, L., Reeves, A. 1986. Simultaneous color constancy. *J. Opt. Soc. Am. A* 3:1743–51

Benzschawel, T., Brill, M. H., Cohn, T. E. 1986. Analysis of human color mechanisms using sinusoidal spectral power distributions. *J. Opt. Soc. Am. A* 3:1713–25

Boynton, R. M. 1988. Color vision. *Ann. Rev. Psychol.* 39:69–100

Brainard, D. H., Wandell, B. A. 1986. Analysis of the retinex theory of color vision. *J. Opt. Soc. Am. A* 3:1651–61

De Valois, R. L., Yund, E. W., Hepler, N. 1982. The orientation and direction selectivity of cells in macaque visual cortex. *Vision Res.* 22:531–44

D'Zmura, M., Lennie, P. 1986. Mechanisms of color constancy. *J. Opt. Soc. Am. A* 3:1662–72

Gershon, R., Jepson, A. D., Tsotsos, J. K. 1986. Ambient illumination and the determination of material changes. *J. Opt. Soc. Am. A* 3:1700–7

Guthrie, B. L., Porter, J. D., Sparks, D. L. 1983. Corollary discharge provides accurate eye position information to the oculomotor system. *Science* 221:1193–95

Helson, H. 1938. Fundamental problems in color vision. I. The principles governing changes in hue, saturation, and lightness of nonselective samples in chromatic illumination. *J. Exp. Psychol.* 23:439–76

Hering, E. 1920. *Outlines of a Theory of the Light Sense.* Transl. from German by L. M. Hurvich, D. Jameson, pp. 7–8. 1964. Cambridge: Harvard Univ. Press.

Hess, C., Pretori, H. 1894. Messende Untersuchungen über die Gesetzmessigkeit des simultanen Helligkeitskontrastes. *Arch. Ophthalmol.* 40:1–24

Hochberg, J. E. 1978. *Perception.* Englewood Cliffs, NJ: Prentice-Hall. 280 pp. 2nd ed.

Hochberg, J. E., Triebel, W., Seaman, G. 1951. Color adaptation under conditions of homogeneous stimulation (Ganzfeld). *J. Exp. Psychol.* 41:153–59

Hubel, D. H., Livingstone, M. S. 1987. Segregation of form, color and stereopsis in primate area 18. *J. Neurosci.* 7:3378–415

Hubel, D. H., Wiesel, T. N. 1960. Receptive fields of optic nerve fibers in the spider monkey. *J. Physiol. London* 154:572–80

Hurlbert, A. 1986. Formal connections between lightness algorithms. *J. Opt. Soc. Am. A* 3:1684–93

Hurvich, L. M. 1963. Contributions to color-discrimination theory: review, summary, and discussion. *J. Opt. Soc. Am.* 53:196–201

Hurvich, L. M. 1981. *Color Vision.* Sunderland, Mass: Sinauer. 328 pp.

Hurvich, L. M., Jameson, D. 1951a. A psychophysical study of white. I. Neutral adaptation. *J. Opt. Soc. Am.* 41:521–27

Hurvich, L. M., Jameson, D. 1951b. A psychophysical study of white. III. Adaptation as variant. *J. Opt. Soc. Am.* 41:787–80

Hurvich, L. M., Jameson, D. 1954. Spectral sensitivity of the fovea. III. Heterochromatic brightness and chromatic adaptation. *J. Opt. Soc. Am.* 44:213–22

Hurvich, L. M., Jameson, D. 1958. Further development of a quantified opponent-colours theory. In *Visual Problems of Colour,* Ch. 22. London: Her Majesty's Stationery Office

Hurvich, L. M., Jameson, D. 1960. Perceived color, induction effects, and opponent-response mechanisms. *J. Gen. Physiol.* 43(6):63–80 (Suppl.)

Hurvich, L. M., Jameson, D. 1961. Opponent chromatic induction and wavelength discrimination. In *The Visual System: Neurophysiology and Psychophysics,* ed. R. Jung, H. Kornhuber. Berlin: Springer

Hurvich, L. M., Jameson, D. 1966. *Perception of Brightness and Darkness.* Boston: Allyn & Bacon

Jameson, D. 1983. Some misunderstandings about color perception, color mixture and color measurement. *Leonardo* 16:41–42

Jameson, D. 1985. Opponent-colours theory in the light of physiological findings. In *Central and Peripheral Mechanisms of Colour Vision,* ed. D. Ottoson, S. Zeki. London: Macmillan. pp. 83–102

Jameson, D., Hurvich, L. M. 1951a. Use of spectral hue-invariant loci for the specification of white stimuli. *J. Exp. Psychol.* 41:455–63

Jameson, D., Hurvich, L. M. 1951b. A psychophysical study of white. II. Area and duration as variants. *J. Opt. Soc. Am.* 41:528–36

Jameson, D., Hurvich, L. M. 1953. Spectral sensitivity of the fovea. II. Dependence on chromatic adaptation. *J. Opt. Soc. Am.* 43:552–59

Jameson, D., Hurvich, L. M. 1956. Some quantitative aspects of an opponent colors theory. III. Changes in brightness, saturation, and hue with chromatic adaptation. *J. Opt. Soc. Am.* 46:405–15

Jameson, D., Hurvich, L. M. 1959. Perceived color and its dependence on focal, surrounding, and preceding stimulus variables. *J. Opt. Soc. Am.* 49:890–98

Jameson, D., Hurvich, L. M. 1961a. Complexities of perceived brightness. *Science* 133:174–79

Jameson, D., Hurvich, L. M. 1961b. Opponent chromatic induction: experimental evaluation and theoretical account. *J. Opt. Soc. Am.* 51:46–53

Jameson, D., Hurvich, L. M. 1964. Theory of brightness and color contrast in human vision. *Vision Res.* 4:135–54

Jameson, D., Hurvich, L. M. 1970. Improvable, yes; insoluble, no: a reply to Flock. *Percept. Psychophys.* 8:125–28

Jameson, D., Hurvich, L. M. 1972. Color adaptation: sensitivity, contrast, afterimages. In *Handbook of Sensory Physiology,* Vol. 7/4. *Visual Psychophysics,* ed. D. Jameson, L. M. Hurvich, pp. 568–81. Berlin: Springer

Jameson, D., Hurvich, L. M. 1975. From contrast to assimilation: in art and in the eye. *Leonardo* 8:125–31

Jameson, D., Hurvich, L. M., Varner, F. D. 1979. Receptoral and postreceptoral processes in recovery from chromatic adaptation. *Proc. Natl. Acad. Sci. USA* 76:3034–38

Jay, M. F., Sparks, D. L. 1984. Auditory receptive fields in primate superior colliculus shift with changes in eye position. *Nature* 309:345–47

Judd, D. B. 1940. Hue, saturation, and lightness of surface colors with chromatic illumination. *J. Opt. Soc. Am.* 30:2–32

Katz, D. 1935. *The World of Color.* Transl.

from German by R. B. MacLeod, C. W. Fox. London: Kegan Paul, Trench, Trubner. Reprinted 1970. New York: Johnson Reprint

Kelly, D. H., Burbeck, C. A. 1984. Critical problems in spatial vision. *CRC Crit. Rev. Biomed. Eng.* 10:125–77

Koffka, K. 1935. *Principles of Gestalt Psychology.* New York: Harcourt Brace. 720 pp.

Krauskopf, J. J. 1986. Computational approaches to color vision: Introduction. *J. Opt. Soc. Am. A* 3:1648

Land, E. H. 1959. Color vision and the natural image. Part 1. *Proc. Natl. Acad. Sci. USA* 45:115–29

Land, E. H. 1983. Recent advances in retinex theory and some implications for cortical computations: color vision and the natural image. *Proc. Natl. Acad. Sci. USA* 80:5163–69

Land, E. H. 1986. An alternative technique for the computation of the designator in the retinex theory of color vision. *Proc. Natl. Acad. Sci. USA* 83:3078–80

Land, E. H., McCann, J. J. 1971. Lightness and retinex theory. *J. Opt. Soc. Am.* 61:1–11

Lee, H.-C. 1986. Method for computing the scene-illuminant chromaticity from specular highlights. *J. Opt. Soc. Am. A* 3:1694–99

Livingstone, M. S., Hubel, D. H. 1984. Anatomy and physiology of a color system in the primate visual cortex. *J. Neurosci.* 4:309–56

MacLeod, R. B. 1932. An experimental investigation of brightness constancy. *Arch. Psychol.* 23(135):1–102

Maloney, L. T., Wandell, B. A. 1986. Color constancy; a method for recording surface spectral reflectance. *J. Opt. Soc. Am. A* 3:29–33

Michael, C. R. 1978a. Color vision mechanisms in monkey striate cortex: dual-opponent cells with concentric receptive fields. *J. Neurophysiol.* 41:572–88.

Michael, C. R. 1978b. Color vision mechanisms in monkey striate cortex: simple cells with dual opponent-color receptive fields. *J. Neurophysiol.* 41:1233–49

Pugh, E. N., Kirk, D. B. 1986. The *Π* mechanisms of W. S. Stiles: An historical review. *Perception* 15:705–28

Reeke, G. N. Jr., Edelman, G. M. 1988. Real brains and artificial intelligence. *Daedalus* 117:143–73

Varner, D., Jameson, D., Hurvich, L. M. 1984. Temporal sensitivities related to color theory. *J. Opt. Soc. Am. A* 1:474–81

von Békésy, G. 1968. Mach- and Hering-type lateral inhibition in vision. *Vision Res.* 8:1483–99

von Helmholtz, H. 1924 (1911). *Physiological Optics,* ed. J. P. Southall, 2:286–87. Rochester, NY: Optical Soc. Am. 3rd ed.

von Kries, J. 1905. Die Gesichtsempfindungen. In *Handbuch der Physiologie der Menschen,* ed. W. Nagel, pp. 109–282. Brunswick: Wieweg

Wallach, H. 1948. Brightness constancy and the nature of achromatic colors. *J. Exp. Psychol.* 38:310–24

Westheimer, G. 1967. Spatial interaction in human cone vision. *J. Physiol.* 190:139–54

Woodworth, R. S. 1938. *Experimental Psychology.* New York: Holt. 889 pp.

Worthey, J. A., Brill, M. H. 1986. Heuristic analysis of von Kries color constancy. *J. Opt. Soc. Am. A* 3:1708–12

Wyszecki, G., Stiles, W. S. 1967. *Color Science.* New York: Wiley

Ann. Rev. Psychol. 1989. 40:23–43
Copyright © 1989 by Annual Reviews Inc. All rights reserved

PSYCHOMETRIC METHODS

Lyle V. Jones and Mark I. Appelbaum

L. L. Thurstone Psychometric Laboratory, The University of North Carolina at Chapel Hill, Chapel Hill, North Carolina 27599-3270

CONTENTS

INTRODUCTION

Recent volumes of the *Annual Review of Psychology* include many chapters that address psychometric methodology: Anastasi (1986) on concepts of test validity; earlier chapters on test theory (Traub & Lam 1985; Weiss & Davison 1981), which focus more on technical details of latent tarif or item response theory; chapters on personnel selection (Guion & Gibson 1988; Hakel 1986; Zedeck & Cascio 1984), which review developments in testing for the prediction of occupational success; chapters on personality assessment and clinical assessment (Lanyon 1984, Robins & Helzer 1986), which discuss measurement issues, especially reliability and validity of assessment; a chapter on scaling by Young (1984), which presents a review of developments in multidimensional scaling; and a review by Gesheider (1988), which addresses scaling in the context of psychophysics. Our chapter is related to all of these, but we attempt to avoid unnecessary redundancy. Our primary focus is on psychological testing, the most visible topic within psychometrics.

23

0066-4308/89/0201-0023$02.00

A signal accomplishment pertinent to testing was the successful effort of the Joint Committee on Testing Standards to reach consensus on revised testing standards (AERA, APA, NCME 1985). The new edition of *Standards* represents the third major version of a formal statement on testing issued jointly by these three groups, with earlier editions having been published in 1966 and 1974. The massive task of preparing the revised *Standards* was born by a committee of 12 under the chairmanship of the late Melvin R. Novick. Criticisms of draft versions were solicited from 125 commentators and then were considered by the committee. The 180 standards (127 primary, 22 secondary, and 31 conditional) cover four large domains (Technical Standards, Professional Standards, Standards for Particular Applications, and Standards for Administrative Procedures) and are further subdivided into 16 specific subsections (e.g. validity, clinical testing, testing people who have handicapping conditioning, and protecting the rights of test takers). The *Standards* provide guidance for a wide range of activities from test development to test interpretation. In addition to setting standards for application, the *Standards* provide a rich nontechnical background for many of the fundamental issues in testing. Included is a concise and useful seven-page glossary of technical terms. While the authors of the *Standards* were appropriately cautious in their statements regarding the use of the standards (p. 9), this edition already has had and will continue to have a major influence on testing practices, as have the earlier editions.

For a thorough history of psychological testing up to 1930, we can highly recommend Sokal (1987). An important source of new developments in measurement as applied to research in education is Linn's *Educational Measurement* (1988).

PSYCHOLOGICAL TESTING

The introduction to the new *Standards* states that "psychological testing represents one of the most important contributions of behavioral science to our society . . . ." It "has also been the target of extensive scrutiny, criticism, and debate both outside and within the professional testing community" (p. 1). Here, we discuss areas of recent and current controversy. We feature efforts in psychometric research that are designed to improve testing and to alleviate problems encountered in the use of tests.

Models for Test Construction and Scoring

Developments in latent trait theory and, more specifically, in item response theory (IRT), have led to constructive changes in the field of psychological testing. The primary advantage of IRT over classical test theory resides in properties of invariance. When unidimensionality is assured for all items and over all groups of examinees, "item parameters are invariant across groups" and "ability parameters are invariant across items or tests from a given unidimensional pool" (Lord 1982, p. 146). Under these conditions, IRT is especially valuable for comparing ability levels of examinees or groups of examinees and for interpreting those comparisons in terms of predictions of test scores on a variety of different tests (p. 141), as exemplified in National Assessment of Educational Progress (1985), and as a framework for computer adaptive testing (e.g. Hulin et al 1983, pp. 210–34).

Bock & Mislevy (1987), drawing upon Mislevy (1983), have proposed a set of procedures based on matrix-sampling methods by which item response data may be scored on the same scale at individual as well as group levels. The development of these methods is expected to be particularly useful for assessing educational achievement, allowing scaled results to be reported by student as well as by classroom, school, district, state, and nation.

Alternative methods for parameter estimation in IRT models include the method of joint maximum likelihood (Lord 1980; Lord & Novick 1968) implemented in LOGIST (Wingersky 1983; Wood et al 1976); the method of marginal maximum likelihood (Bock & Aitkin 1981; Bock & Lieberman 1970) implemented in BILOG (Mislevy & Bock 1981); and Bayesian approaches developed for the Rasch model (Swaminathan & Gifford 1982), for the two-parameter logistic model (Swaminathan & Gifford 1985), and for the three-parameter logistic model (Swaminathan & Gifford 1986). Lord (1986) discusses the relative advantages and disadvantages of these methods, noting the practical advantages of the Bayesian methods, but also the need for more experience with those methods before they can be safely employed.

The Rasch one-parameter IRT model continues to receive attention (e.g. Anderson 1983; de Gruijter & van der Kamp 1984; van de Vijver 1986). When data fit the model, a prominent advantage of Rasch models resides in the maintenance of interval scale properties for examinees and for items (see Mislevy 1987; Roskam & Jansen 1984). This advantage, when coupled with the statistical sufficiency in the Rasch model of the unweighted sum over items of right answers (Wright 1977), is deemed sufficient by some investigators to make the Rasch model the model of choice over all competitors—e.g. Masters & Wright (1984). Unfortunately, in most testing applications, the Rasch model provides a rather poor fit to the data. To achieve a better fit of model to data for multiple-choice tests, evidence is mounting in favor of the 3-parameter IRT model when sample size is sufficient for good parameter estimation (Divgi 1986; Drasgow 1982; Green et al 1984; Hambleton 1983, 1988; Harrison 1986; Hambleton & Swaminathan 1985; Lewis 1986; Lord 1980; Mislevy 1986; Wainer & Thissen 1987).

As shown by Lord (1980, p. 84) and emphasized by Mislevy (1987) and Yen (1986), a given data set that is fit by an IRT model can be fit equally well by another model for which the form of response curves is a monotonic increasing function of the form specified in the first model. This is interpreted by some as not only violating a requisite of interval measurement, but also requiring that group comparisons be limited to comparisons of medians or percentile points. These critics argue against the use of means and score differences, the meaningfulness of which depend upon having established an interval scale of measurement (Marcus-Roberts & Roberts 1987). Note, however, that when the IRT assumptions are fulfilled, including the distributional assumption (logistic or normal), then the unit of measurement for the ability parameter, theta (θ), is invariant up to linear transformation (Lord 1982, p. 144), and an interval-scale interpretation may be warranted, albeit with an arbitrary unit of measurement.

Yen (1986) proposed that the interval IRT scale be justified on grounds other than fit of the model to the data—e.g. by a display of linear relations with variables that are theoretically related to the trait being measured. We agree that such external evidence is desirable, for it would support the uniqueness of an interval-scale interpretation of IRT results. We would also argue, however, that interval-scale properties may be accepted as useful working hypotheses whenever conclusions or generalizations are restricted to circumstances for which the same model is employed. The interval-scale properties then remain conditional on the specific measurement model that has been adopted, but are generalizable under that constraint. This argument is identical to that which allows interval-scale interpretations from applying Thurstonian scaling procedures (see Adams & Messick 1958; Messick 1983).

Yen (1986) demonstrated that a Thurstonian scaling model (traditionally employed for scaling standardized achievement tests) and an IRT model (increasingly being employed for the same purpose) yield inconsistent sets of results when applied to school achievement tests. Specifically, the Thurstonian model displays increasing variability of individual scores as a function of increasing mean scale score (and increasing age and grade), while the IRT model displays an inverse relation between variability and mean score (and grade). This finding for IRT scores is troublesome. Psychologically, it makes little sense that a group of examinees with minimal or no knowledge in a domain should exhibit a large variance of ability levels; rather, their ability levels should become homogeneous, uniformly close to zero. Variability should increase as a function of higher average achievement level, as individual levels of achievement are expected to be more diverse. In current IRT models, however, a person completely lacking in ability is presumed to have an ability level $\theta = -\infty$ rather than a $\theta = 0$ (Lord 1980, p. 12). Consequently, a group of persons of very low ability will necessarily display large variability, because their individual differences are represented by values of θ that span a wide range, from near $-\infty$ to some less extreme negative value. It appears timely to investigate alternative IRT scales for which ability level may vary only between zero and infinity rather than between minus and plus infinity, scales for which individual variation of ability level would be expected to be a positive function of mean ability, in keeping with theoretical expectation.

One of the key assumptions of IRT is that of unidimensionality of test items, which implies a state of local independence, under which a given ability level for an examinee is sufficient to yield a probability of correct response for every item on a test. Unless the items are homogeneous, on a single dimension, local independence will fail to be maintained and item parameters are unlikely to be invariant for different groups of examinees (e.g. Cook et al 1988). A number of investigators have suggested fitting separate IRT models to homogeneous subtests—e.g. Bock & Aitken (1981), Lord (1980), Reckase (1985), Takane & de Leeuw (1986), and Wainer & Kiely (1987). However, as noted by Yen (1986), "when several traits influence single items, . . . the test cannot be separated into unidimensional subtests" (p. 322).

The first large-scale empirical study based upon a multidimensional IRT approach probably is that of National Assessment of Educational Progress (1988), which presents results for several distinct components of achievement in mathematics.

In recognition of the limitations of item response theory, alternative models are receiving some attention. Tucker (1983) proposed a multiple-factor solution for dichotomously scored test items, but with weaker distributional assumptions than those required by IRT. Cliff (1983) discussed methods for analyzing dichotomous data, using no assumptions about latent-trait distributions, where interest resides in the consistency of the data, assuming a Guttman scale. The notions of consistency of individual response patterns also have been extended by others (e.g. Tatsuoka & Tatsuoka 1982). This approach might be generalized to incorporate several dimensions, if there are sufficient items for each dimension and if each dimension is approximately "scalable" in the Guttman sense.

A latent trait model quite different from IRT has been developed by Falmagne (1988). A given set of test questions is designed with a structure such that knowledge of the answer to one question implies knowledge of answers to one or more additional questions in the set. The model allows estimation of the "knowledge state" of each examinee, based on answers given to all questions in the set. Falmagne's model may prove to be especially useful for characterizing developmental growth of knowledge for groups of examinees representing different ages or different levels of opportunity to learn a content domain.

Falmagne's model exemplifies one way cognitive theory can influence the theory of psychological testing. Other examples are apparent in the books edited by Embretson (1985) and by Ronning et al (1987), and in the work of Sternberg (e.g. 1985). An especially promising approach is that of Kyllonen & Christal (1988), who are designing assessment procedures to be consonant with a model of learning ability that entails four logically distinct components: processing speed, as reflected by response times; processing capacity, or the size of working memory; declarative knowledge; and procedural knowledge or skills.

A marriage of cognitive psychology and psychometrics seems especially propitious in the area of computer adaptive testing (CAT); see, for example, Hofer & Green (1985). The success of CAT clearly depends on the integrity of the cognitive structure of items in the item pool (Wright & Bell 1984), and on the use of IRT or alternative latent trait models to select appropriate levels of item difficulty to be presented to different examinees. Butcher (1987), Eyde (1987), Forehand (1986), Weiss (1983), and Weiss & Kingsbury (1984) have presented a variety of recent developments in this domain.

Guidelines now have been developed that outline the responsibilities of developers of computer tests and of those who use computerized test results (American Psychological Association 1986). Progress has been made toward applying CAT in two major testing programs, the Armed Services Vocational Aptitude Battery (Green et al 1984) and the College Board Advanced Placement Testing Program (Ward et al 1986).

Validity and Validity Generalization

"Validity" has been subjected to relatively little restructuring as a result of empirical or theoretical work in the past few years. One major event likely, however, to have a long-term impact on the field was a conference on *Test Validity for the 1990s and Beyond* sponsored by the Air Force Human Resources Laboratories and the Educational Testing Service in May of 1986, and the subsequent publication of a book (Wainer & Braun 1988) based upon papers presented at that conference. Three of the chapters therein (Cronbach 1988; Angoff 1988; Messick 1988a) discuss classical issues of validity theory, each from a different perspective. Nevertheless, construct validity, described by Angoff (1988) as "the most fundamental and embracing of all types of validity" (p. 26), receives central attention in each of those chapters. Messick (1988b), by proposing a unified concept of validity in which content and predictive validity are subsumed under construct validity, seems to be responding to these issues.

Despite the fundamental theoretical importance of construct validity, predictive and content validity continue to be of major concern, particularly in educational and occupational testing. Based on the legal history of employment testing (e.g. Wigdor 1982), it is unlikely that a test, no matter how firm its construct validity, will go unchallenged if it cannot also be shown to predict to a desired outcome or to be sampling a relevant content.

A relatively new issue in validity theory is the interface between construct validity and the processing approach to cognition. This line of work has been explored by Embretson (1983) and by Embretson et al (1986).

Validity generalization has received considerable attention in recent years. While only mentioned in passing (as "generalizability of validity") in the earlier edition of *Standards for Educational & Psychological Tests* (APA, AERA, NCME 1974), several paragraphs of text are dedicated to this topic in the more recent edition, and the conditions under which the use of the results of validity generalization studies may be used are explicitly stated in Standard 1.16 (AERA, APA, NCME 1985). As defined in the *Standards,* validity generalization refers to "applying validity evidence obtained in one or more situations to other similar situations on the basis of simultaneous estimation, meta-analysis, or synthetic validation arguments" (pp. 94–95). By 1986, validity generalization had received enough empirical treatment to be included as a section in the *Annual Review* chapter on "Evolving Concepts of Test Validation" (Anastasi 1986). As noted there, validity generalization is of particular importance in personnel assessment because many of the individual validity studies in that field are based upon small sample sizes. Application of validity generalization in large-scale testing programs has been described (US Department of Labor 1983a,b).

In the short period since 1986, there have been substantial additions to the literature on validity generalization. Schmidt (1988) reported that more than 500 validity generalization studies have been conducted. Based on earlier critiques of validity generalization and the results of numerous studies, Schmidt et al (1985) summarized the many issues and findings. They concluded that the methods employed are valid and that the bulk of the validity generalization studies provide little evidence to sustain the importance of situational specifics in validity. Others, however, have not completely concurred with this conclusion (e.g. Sackett et al 1985).

The basic strategies employed in validity generalization are variations on more-or-less traditional meta-analytic methods (Glass et al 1981). However, the purpose of validity generalization is two-fold: (*a*) to combine results from multiple studies, each constrained by its own situational specifics, to obtain a "best estimate" of the true underlying validity (usually predictive) of an assessment instrument; and (*b*) to provide an estimate of the variability of true validities—that is, to determine the degree to which the true validities are constant across situations. To fulfill this dual purpose, some modifications of "Glassian meta-analysis" have been suggested (e.g. see Hunter et al 1982).

Hedges (1988) recently described another approach to validity generalization, essentially an empirical Bayesian method of meta-analysis that relies on the use of the EM algorithm. This approach has been described by Rubin (1988) as being "right on target," but Rubin does offer some useful cautions regarding the expected shrinkage of estimates of validity.

A technical aspect of validity generalization that has received some attention is that of deciding which coefficients should be used in performing the meta-analyses—the validity correlation coefficients or the Fisher z transformation of the coefficients. James et al (1986) and Rubin (1988) have argued that the Fisher transformation is the proper index. Hunter et al (1986) and Linn et al (1981), however, indicated that issues identified as being problematic with the direct use of the correlation coefficient are not of such large magnitude as to warrant great concern.

While most of the recent work on validity generalization has focused upon approaches utilizing meta-analysis, Trattner (1982) described the use of synthetic validity in the context of the *Uniform Guidelines for Employee Selection Procedures* (1978), and Mossholder & Arvey (1984) provide a general review of this approach.

Generalizability Theory

Generalizability theory, an elaboration of traditional reliability theory based on procedures from analysis of variance, allows the total variability in a batch of test scores to be decomposed into a number of specific variance components, each associated with a different facet of the testing situation (e.g. items, raters, occasions, etc). Through the estimation of variance components, the degree to which test results might generalize to other situations may be assessed.

Weiss & Davison (1981) noted in their *Annual Review* chapter that "because of its complexity and the lack of procedures for estimating many of its parameters, generalizability theory had not been brought to practical status prior to the period under review" (p. 634). The years since that review can be characterized as a period of consolidation and increased application of generalizability theory. Shavelson & Webb (1981) provided a detailed review of the development of the theory during the period 1978–1980. Two recent works present concise summaries and enlarged frameworks for the now complex field of generalizability theory. Cardinet & Allal (1983), in addition to summarizing the basic formulation of Cronbach et al (1972), explicitly considered the mixed-model approach to generalizability theory (e.g. subjects random but items or conditions fixed rather than random). Brennan (1983), in addition to providing a terse but technically complete theoretical treatment, devoted considerable attention to computational aspects, and provided an extensive set of examples of analysis strategies utilizing the GENOVA, BMDP8V, and SAS-ANOVA computer programs.

Recent efforts to extend the technical aspects of the theory are seen in the attempt to produce more accurate confidence interval estimates for the variance conponents that result from the application of generalizability theory (Smith 1982) as well as in the application of Khuri intervals for simultaneous confidence intervals on several such components of variance (Bell 1986). Smith (1981) considered a related technical issue—namely, the selection of methods for combining results from multiple small-sample generalizability studies.

Applications of generalizability theory (or perhaps, more accurately, random and mixed effects analysis-of-variance models) to issues of applied psychological and educational measurement have been extensive in recent years. Gillmore (1983) considered the application of generalizability theory to problems of program evaluation; Johnson & Bell (1985) to the assessment of survey efficiency; Lomax (1982) to observational research; and Macready (1983) to diagnostic testing problems. In addition, Booth et al (1979) used generalizability theory as an approach to inter- and intra-rater reliability; Boodoo (1982), as an approach to estimation of parameters in incidence sampling; and Staybrook & Corno (1979), as an approach to the disattenuation due to measurement error of correlations in path-analytic approaches.

The application of multivariate generalizability theory has also been an active area of research. Jarjoura & Brennan (1983) applied multivariate generalization theory to the situation in which multiple forms of a test are constructed with each form guided by the same table of specifications—e.g. the cognitive subtests of the ACT. Webb et al (1983) considered the use of this technique for the study of profiles of scores such as those that might be seen when considering the subtests of the WISC.

Earlier criticism of generalizability theory—e.g. Rozeboom's dual concern "that the parameters of an item cannot cogently be defined as limiting values of observable item-sample properties" and that "the domain centroid's psychonomic and psychometric importance is at best problematic" (Rozeboom 1978, p. 87)—remains essentially unanswered. An additional concern related to that of factor indeterminacy has been raised by D. Ward (1986). McDonald (1986) argued that "classical test theory is a special case of common factor theory, and that in terms of behavior-domain theory, reliability, validity, and generalizability are the same thing and may be measured by an index resulting from a common factor analysis" (p. 523). Given the complex assumption base, both conceptual and mathematical, and the basic difficulties in the definition of a domain, a cautious approach to the use of generalizability theory still appears warranted.

Differential Prediction

Among the more vexing issues regarding test use are those pertaining to test fairness for different demographic groups. However, as stated in *Standards,* test fairness is a term that "is subject to different definitions in different social and political circumstances" (AERA, APA, NCME 1985, p. 13); consequently, any analysis of test fairness is complicated, to say the least (see Shepard 1982).

A more tractable term than "test fairness" is "differential prediction," which implies "different prediction equations . . . for different demographic groups" (or for groups that differ in their prior experiences). "If different regression slopes, intercepts, or standard errors of estimate are found among different groups, selection decisions will be biased when the same interpretation is made of a given score without regard to the group from which a person comes" (AERA, APA, NCME 1985, p. 12). When a biased test is employed for making selection or placement decisions, it is imperative that separate regression solutions be used for different subgroups, to improve fairness of decisions for the members of each subgroup.

A host of journal articles and several books attest to the high level of interest in questions of differential prediction, and in methods to alleviate the problem. Notable among the books are those of Berk (1982), Jensen (1980), Reynolds & Brown (1984), and sections of Hulin et al (1983).

Related to but distinct from issues of differential prediction or test bias is the topic of differential item functioning (dif) or item bias. A review of a number of approaches to dif taken prior to 1980 are to be found in Berk (1982). In particular, Tittle (1982) discussed the use of judgmental methods; Angoff (1982) treated difficulty and discrimination indexes, including the delta index; Ironson (1982) examined chi-square and latent-trait approaches; and Burrill (1982) reviewed studies that compare these approaches with still other methods.

Shepard et al (1985) provided a useful review of research on this topic, and applied several alternative procedures both to empirical and to generated data. Their findings are consistent with those of other investigations (e.g. Ironson et al 1984), which show the 3-parameter IRT model to have performance advantages over other procedures.

Since 1982, much of the work in dif has focused upon two approaches: those based upon IRT theory and those based upon Mantel-Haenszel methods and chi square.

The IRT approach, initiated by Lord (1977) and discussed at some length in Lord (1980), is oriented towards the detection of differences between groups on item characteristic curves (ICCs) or trace lines. The approach involves a statistical comparison of the parameters estimated by IRT methods for the separate groups, using a z test for a one-parameter ICC, or the Mahalanobis distance generalization for multiparameter ICCs. More recent work by Thissen et al (1986, 1988) tested the same hypothesis but used a likelihood-ratio test. Thissen et al (1988) noted that, while the likelihood-ratio approach detects moderate parameter differences, small differences can only be detected in large samples. They also noted that the cost of computation required with these methods can be great when there are many anchor items (items that are assumed not to exhibit dif).

The second major line of attack utilizes the Mantel-Haenszel (M-H) procedure for testing the equality of proportions in matched groups, in place of the more traditional chi-square statistics (but with most of the other features of the chi-square approach remaining unchanged). Holland & Thayer (1986, 1988) discussed this work, provided illustrations of its implementation, and also developed the relationship between the Mantel-Haenszel and IRT approaches to dif, noting that the cost of utilizing the M-H procedure is relatively low. Given the findings of Thissen et al (1988) that IRT and M-H analyses yield similar results, further research on the M-H procedure may be anticipated.

Other approaches to dif have received some recent attention. Stricker (1984) attacked the problem through the use of a partial correlation index; Van der Flier et al (1984) employed an iterative logistic model.

Despite these advancements in dif, two thorny problems remain for attempts to construct tests free of item bias.

First, it is important to recognize that most dif methods are statistical hypothesis-testing approaches, constructed so that the null hypothesis is one of "no differential item functioning." Failure to reject the null hypothesis does not assure an absence of dif. Low power resulting from small sample sizes or from small parametric values of dif can lead to Type II errors, failures to reject the null hypothesis when it is false. Then, as items are amassed into tests, an instrument with considerable test bias can result, even though there is insufficient evidence of dif for any single item.

The second issue is fundamental to all dif studies and is the problem that dif can only be defined in terms of differential group performance following adjustment for possible group-to-group differences in true ability levels. IRT methods approach this issue through the use of anchor items that are *assumed* not to exhibit dif; chi-square and M-H methods use matching or the formation of matched groups with the same putative true ability levels, usually adopting the total score on the battery whose items are being examined for dif as a surrogate for "true ability." If the assumption of the "dif-freeness" of either the anchor items or of the total score as surrogate for the true score fails, so too will the methods based upon them.

Criticisms of Achievement Tests[1]

Tests are frequently used to assess achievement [which Anastasi prefers to call "developed abilities" (Anastasi 1980, p. 3)]. Recent critics of existing modes of achievement testing have forcefully called for reform in the design

[1]Portions of this section are adapted, with permission from the publisher, from Jones (1988).

of tests. A key problem is that "standardized achievement tests are probably too often saturated with aptitude" (Willingham 1980, p. 78). As noted below, other problems have been set forth by other critics.

The National Research Council Committee on Ability Tests (Wigdor & Garner 1982) considered achievement tests to be a subset of ability tests, and its report states, "Throughout the history of ability testing interest has concentrated on a limited number of cognitive skills" that leave out "many abilities important in practical activities" such as "synthesizing abilities, spatial reasoning, problem solving for which alternative strategies are necessary, . . . problems of sequential linkage, . . . creativity, . . . perseverance, insight, and the like. The few attempts to assess them have not been conspicuously successful. Walter Lippman (1922) said of test developers in the early 1920s: 'What their foot rule does not measure soon ceases to exist for them.' The years have not stilled that complaint" (Wigdor & Garner 1982, p. 211).

A recent handbook on the development and use of educational indicators (Oakes 1986) cites a "critical need for better indicators" of educational achievement than those currently available, and notes that "we have fairly good paper-and-pencil measures of the most commonly taught basic knowledge and skills. But we lack adequate measures of children's abilities to think critically, to apply their knowledge, or to solve problems" (p. 34). Clearly, some stated objectives of an educational process are hard to measure. Many involve the acquisition of active learning skills, which would be demonstrated by productive and generalized problem solving. Yet, most standardized tests demand passive recognition skills, assessed with a multiple-choice format. Not infrequently, stated objectives require that students create alternate representations of a problem in order to effect a solution. But the multiple-choice format usually explicitly incorporates a particular representation as part of the test question, thereby frustrating the effort to assess performance related to this objective.

We agree with Linn (1987) that "testing needs to be more closely linked to instruction" (p. 1159). Students have every reason to expect that the tests used to assess their performance will conform with the objectives of education. They may learn to perform well on those tests, but if the tests fail to assess key objectives of education, students are less likely to acquire the intended developed abilities.

The National Research Council Committee on Indicators of Precollege Science and Mathematics Education stressed in its final report (Murname & Raizen 1988) the need for improved tests to assess mathematics and science education, and the Committee offered a number of specific suggestions for test development: the construction of tests of cognitive processing speed, based on response latency measures; tests of pattern recognition skills, using response latency; tests of the structure of memory, based on latency measures as well as on sorting tasks and concept-similarity rating tasks; tests of ideational fluency, based on the number and quality of ideas generated by examinees; tests for the internal representation of problems, using protocol analysis, sorting tasks, and computer simulation tasks; and the use of computers to diagnose students' problem-solving skills. All of these new tests would assess productive thinking skills that have not been adequately measured in a multiple-choice format.

The Alexander-James Study Group on the nation's report card (Alexander & James 1987) also recommended the development of new methods to evaluate problem solving and higher-order skills, for adoption in the national assessment of mathematics and science. "Open-ended and free-response questions . . . require the student to generate the correct answer, not merely to recognize it. Such assessment items would . . . allow . . . inferences about the thought processes contributing to the answer" (Alexander & James 1987, p. 23).

The Commission on Precollege Education in Mathematics, Science, and Technology of the National Science Board (National Science Board Commission on Precollege Education in Mathematics, Science, and Technology 1983) called for a national assessment mechanism to cover "the ability to write for a purpose, apply higher-level problem-solving skills, and analyze and draw conclusions, rather than minimal basic skills such as the rote memorization of facts" (p. 12). The Commission report notes that "it will take time, talent and funds to develop these . . . tests. These will not be forthcoming, however, unless top priority is given to effecting these changes" (pp. 44–45).

A report from still another National Research Council committee, the Committee on Research in Mathematics, Science, and Technology Education, states that "most present classroom methods of testing what students know emphasize the recall of facts—as does most teaching. *If tests are not to trivialize instruction even further,* new approaches to assessing student achievement must be developed that aim at conceptual understanding, the ability to reason and think with scientific or mathematical subject matter, and competence in the key processes that characterize science or mathematics" (Committee on Research in Mathematics, Science, and Technology Education, National Research Council 1987, p. 20, italics added).

After having recognized the considerable success of testing, Green (1981) noted that "its weakest aspect is the relative lack of progress over past decades. With few exceptions, we are testing the same old things in the same old ways with the same moderate success" (p. 1011). Research efforts in psychometrics have concentrated on methods for analyzing test data; too little attention has been devoted to the design of less restrictive forms of test items and to the the construction of new forms of achievement tests.

In many applications, the tests that are employed influence the curriculum.

This is inevitable, for example, with state competency examinations that are used to assess both student progress and teacher effectiveness. Each teacher, then, feels compelled to "teach to the test," and instructional emphasis shifts from meeting desirable educational objectives to meeting the more trivial objectives represented by those skills that a test measures, often memory for factual knowledge. As Frederiksen (1984) remarked, the multiple-choice test format "may influence the cognitive processes involved in dealing with test items and hence the nature of the skills taught and learned" (p. 195).

Some evidence suggests that the construct validity of well-structured verbal aptitude tests may be little affected by whether multiple-choice or free-response item format is employed (Ward 1982). However, in assessing problem-solving skills, free-response tests have been shown to measure attributes distinct from those measured by the multiple-choice format (Frederiksen et al 1981; Ward et al 1980). Also, a problem-solving test with open-ended format can have greater promise of validity for important real-life criteria than standard multiple-choice tests of aptitude and achievement (Frederiksen & Ward 1978; Gay 1980). Perhaps, because multiple-choice tests typically are timed tests, they inhibit thoughtful problem solving in favor of rapid, impulsive responses, thereby compromising their validity for the solution of many real-world problems (see Sternberg 1985, pp. 301–4).

In a 1971 review of the effects on students of test format, Kirkland (1971) concluded that test format influenced the way students prepared for a test. "When students expected an objective test, they studied for details and memorization of material. When studying for an essay test, they focused attention on relationships, trends, organization, and on identifying a few major points around which they could write descriptive or expository paragraphs" (pp. 315–16). Desired educational objectives more often are in the form of mastery of "relationships, trends, organization" than of "details and memorization." New test design, then, should be utilized to develop alternatives to the multiple-choice format, so that assessment instruments may provide better incentives for student learning that is consistent with these objectives.

Linn (1986) identified two towering barriers to new test design: the relatively high predictive validity coefficients and the economic viability of existing standardized tests. Linn concluded that "we need to focus on different goals and use different standards for evaluating the effectiveness of the measures if we are to have a significant redesign of testing. At its most general level, the goal I have in mind is the effective use of tests to enhance learning and cognitive development" (Linn 1986, p. 72).

It is imperative that the testable criteria of a successful educational experience match the stated objectives of that experience. The objectives and the criteria typically are multidimensional. From this perspective, another barrier to new test design is that the most successful models for analyzing test results assume that items or tasks are homogeneous, in the sense that they all measure a single ability.

To the extent that the multiple-choice format has had a stultifying effect in education, by encouraging student mastery of factual knowledge and discouraging the development of productive thinking skills, it might be hoped that computer-aided tests would provide alternatives to the multiple-choice format of the sort envisioned by the NRC Committee on Indicators of Precollege Mathematics and Science Education. Generally, that seems not to be so. For example, a volume on new test design (Embretson 1985) gave little attention to alternatives to multiple-choice testing; the concluding chapter of that volume, on the future of testing, stipulated that "adaptive tests usually use multiple-choice items" (Bejar 1985). In an earlier chapter, however, Snow & Peterson (1985) presented a theoretical framework for developing cognitive achievement tests, using an information-processing approach, that could serve as a useful guide for future research.

D. Ward (1986) advised that we may "look for a decline in the hegemony of the multiple-choice item" (p. 31). To avoid continuing to "look for" that decline for decades to come, what steps need to be taken to foster change?

One straightforward activity, for any specified educational domain, would be the development of a battery of free-response, short-answer test questions together with rules for scoring all possible responses. An alternative line of research relates to the mapping of cognitive structures, by using concept-comparison tasks (e.g. Diekhoff 1983; Stanners et al 1983), or by recording the order in which items are produced in free recall (Reitman & Rueter 1980). From data generated by such methods, a map of cognitive structure can be estimated or recovered by multidimensional scaling methods, or by hierarchical clustering procedures (for a branching tree-structure model).

The Committee on Indicators of Precollege Mathematics and Science Education recommended "that a greatly accelerated program of research and development be undertaken aimed at the construction of free-response techniques that measure skills not measured by multiple-choice tests" (Murname & Raizen 1988, p. 5). Suggested techniques include problem-solving tasks, tests of hypothesis formulation, experimental design and productive thinking, hands-on experimental exercises, and simulations of scientific phenomena using microcomputers. The Committee also recommended "the creation of new science tests for grades K–5 . . . by teams that include personnel from the school districts that have been developing hands-on curricula to ensure that the new tests match the objectives of this type of instruction" (Murname & Raizen 1988, p. 5). The link between instruction and testing should be strengthened by engaging teachers and curriculum specialists, as well as psychometricians, in the test-construction efforts. Finally, the Committee recommended the creation of a national center for research and development for the production, evaluation, and distribution of educational assessment procedures. Through this agency, test exercises would be available for national, state, and local assessments, and also would be provided to teachers for their use in instruction. These recommendations warrant serious consideration by educators, cognitive and educational psychologists, and psychometric researchers, as well as by funding agencies. Hand in hand with educational reform, there is a critical need for reform in achievement testing. An important phase of such reform might be the launching of research programs in psychometrics to establish new test designs for the measurement of achievement.

MEASUREMENT THEORY

Formal Measurement Models

Measurement theorists have long awaited the publication of a successor volume to *Foundations of Measurement*, Volume 1 (Krantz et al 1971), to bring up to date the status of measurement theory for psychology.

Luce & Narens (1986) traced the modern history of measurement theory through the contributions of Campbell, Stevens, von Neumann & Morgenstern, Pfanzagle, Savage, Suppes, Debreu, and Luce & Tukey. They presented as the five major questions of measurement theory: 1. the definition and classification of scale types, 2. the numerical structures of each scale type, 3. the features of scale types that are necessary in order to conform with the structure of units typical of measurement in natural physics, 4. the axiomatization of qualitative systems sufficient for correspondence with measurement representations, and 5. the meaning of "meaningfulness" for a given scale type. In Narens & Luce (1986) appears a summary of recent work on these topics, with a discussion of the relation between conjoint structures and concatenation structures, and a discussion of the status of representational theory, including uniqueness and scale types. A more extensive review of these and related topics may be found in Narens (1985).

Philosophy of Measurement and Data Analysis

Psychologists have increasingly been adopting techniques of exploratory data analysis (see Tukey 1977), in addition to the more traditional methods of confirmatory analysis. Some of the more elementary exploratory techniques, such as stem-and-leaf displays and box-and-whisker plots have found a place in introductory statistics texts, and more advanced exploratory procedures are now receiving considerable attention (e.g. Hoaglin et al 1983, 1985; Jackson 1986; Lovie 1986).

The general philosophy of data analysis espoused by Tukey and his students is now presented in a two-volume collection of previously published and unpublished Tukey papers (Jones 1986a, b). Several of these papers are of particular interest to psychologists, particularly a substantial paper on data analysis and behavioral science (Tukey 1986), not earlier available in published form.

Literature Cited

Adams, E., Messick, S. 1958. An axiomatic formulation and generalization of successive intervals scaling. *Psychometrika* 23:355–68

Alexander, L., James, H. T. 1987. *The Nation's Report Card: Improving the Assessment of Student Achievement*. Cambridge, Mass: Natl. Acad. Educ.

American Educational Research Association, American Psychological Association, National Council on Measurement in Education. 1985. *Standards for Educational and Psychological Testing*. Washington, DC: Am. Psychol. Assoc.

American Psychological Association. 1986. *Guidelines for Computer-based Tests and Interpretations*. Washington, DC: Am. Psychol. Assoc.

American Psychological Association, American Educational Research Association, National Council on Measurement in Education. 1974. *Standards for Educational and Psychological Tests*. Washington, DC: Am. Psychol. Assoc.

Anastasi, A. 1980. Abilities and the measurement of achievement. See Schrader 1980, pp. 1–10

Anastasi, A. 1986. Evolving concepts of test validation. *Ann. Rev. Psychol.* 37:1–16

Andersen, E. B. 1983. Analyzing data using the Rasch model. In *On Educational Testing*, ed. S. B. Andersen, J. S. Helmick, pp. 193–223. San Francisco: Jossey-Bass

Angoff, W. H. 1982. Use of difficulty and discrimination indices for detecting item bias. See Berk 1982, pp. 96–116

Angoff, W. H. 1988. Validity: an evolving concept. See Wainer & Braun 1988, pp. 19–32

Bejar, I. I. 1985. Speculations on the future of test design. See Embretson 1985, pp. 279–94

Bell, J. F. 1986. Simultaneous confidence intervals for the linear functions of expected mean squares used in generalizability theory. *J. Educ. Stat.* 11:197–205

Berk, R. A., ed. 1982. *Handbook of Methods for Detecting Test Bias*. Baltimore: Johns Hopkins Press

Bock, R. D., Aitken, M. 1981. Marginal maximum likelihood estimation of item parameters: application of an EM algorithm. *Psychometrika* 46:443–59

Bock, R. D., Lieberman, M. 1970. Fitting a response model for *n* dichotomously scored items. *Psychometrika* 35:179–97

Bock, R. D., Mislevy, R. J. 1987. *Comprehensive Educational Assessment for the States: The Duplex Design*. Chicago: NORC, Univ. Chicago

Boodoo, G. M. 1982. On describing an incidence sample. *J. Educ. Stat.* 7:311–31

Booth, C. L., Mitchell, S. K., Solin, F. K. 1979. The generalizability study as a method of assessing intra- and interobserver reliability in observational research. *Behav. Res. Methods Instrum.* 11:491–94

Brennan, R. L. 1983. *Elements of Generalizability Theory*. Iowa City: ACT Publications

Burrill, L. E. 1982. Comparative studies of item bias methods. See Berk 1982, pp. 161–79

Butcher, J. N., ed. 1987. *Computerized Psychological Assessment: A Practitioner's Guide*. New York: Basic Books

Cardinet, J., Allal, L. 1983. Estimation of generalizability parameters. See Fyans 1983, pp. 17–48

Cliff, N. 1983. Evaluating Guttman scales: some old and new thoughts. See Wainer & Messick 1983, pp. 283–302

Committee on Research in Mathematics, Science, and Technology Education, National Research Council. 1987. *Interdisciplinary Research in Mathematics, Science, and Technology Education*. Washington, DC: Natl. Acad. Press

Cook, L. L., Eignor, D. R., Taft, H. L. 1988. A comparative study of the effects of recency of instruction on the stability of IRT and conventional item parameter estimates. *J. Educ. Meas.* 25:31–45

Cronbach, L. J. 1988. Five perspectives on the validity argument. See Wainer & Braun 1988, pp. 3–18

Cronbach, L. J., Gleser, G. C., Nanda, H., Rajaratnam, N. 1972. *The Dependability of Behavioral Measurements: Theory of*

Generalizability for Scores and Profiles. New York: Wiley

de Gruijter, D. N. M., van der Kamp, L. J. T. 1984. *Statistical Models in Psychological and Educational Testing.* Lisse, Holland: Swets & Zeitlinger

Diekhoff, G. M. 1983. Testing through relationship judgments. *J. Educ. Psychol.* 75:227–33

Divgi, D. R. 1986. Does the Rasch model really work for multiple choice items? Not if you look closely. *J. Educ. Meas.* 23:283–98

Drasgow, F. 1982. Choice of test model for appropriateness measurement. *Appl. Psychol. Meas.* 6:297–308

Educational Testing Service. 1986. *The Redesign of Testing for the 21st Century, Proceedings of the 1985 ETS Invitational Conference.* Princeton: Educ. Test. Serv.

Embretson, S. E. 1983. Construct validity: construct representation versus nomothetic span. *Psychol. Bull.* 93:179–97

Embretson, S. E., ed. 1985. *Test Design: Developments in Psychology and Psychometrics.* Orlando, Fla: Academic

Embretson, S. E., Schneider, L. M., Roth, D. L. 1986. Multiple processing strategies and the construct validity of verbal reasoning tests. *J. Educ. Meas.* 23:13–32

Eyde, L. D., ed. 1987. Computerized psychological testing (special issue). *Appl. Psychol.: Int. Rev.* 36(3–4)

Falmagne, J. C. 1988. A latent trait theory via a stochastic learning theory for a knowledge space. *Psychometrika.* In press

Forehand, G. A. 1986. *Computerized Diagnostic Testing,* ETS Res. Mem. 86–2. Princeton: Educ. Test. Serv.

Frederiksen, N. 1984. The real test bias: influences of testing on teaching and learning. *Am. Psychol.* 39:193–202

Frederiksen, N., Ward, W. C. 1978. Measures for the study of creativity in scientific problem-solving. *Appl. Psychol. Meas.* 2:1–24

Frederiksen, N., Ward, W. C., Case, S. M., Carlson, S. B., Samph, T. 1981. *Development of Methods for Selection and Evaluation in Undergraduate Medical Education.* Res. Rep. 81–4. Princeton: Educ. Test. Serv.

Fyans, L. J., ed. 1983. Generalizability theory: inferences and practical applications. *New Directions for Testing and Measurement, No. 18.* San Francisco: Jossey-Bass

Gay, L. R. 1980. The comparative effects of multiple-choice versus short-answer tests on retention. *J. Educ. Meas.* 17:45–50

Gescheider, G. A. 1988. Psychophysical scaling. *Ann. Rev. Psychol.* 39:169–200

Gillmore, G. M. 1983. Generalizability theory: applications to program evaluation. See Fyans 1983, pp. 3–16

Glass, G. V., McGaw, B., Smith, M. L. 1981. *Meta-analysis in Social Research.* Beverly Hills, Calif: Sage

Green, B. F. 1981. A primer of testing. *Am. Psychol.* 36:1001–11

Green, B. F., Bock, R. D., Humphreys, L. G., Linn, R. L., Reckase, M. D. 1984. Technical guidelines for assessing computerized adaptive testing. *J. Educ. Meas.* 21:361–75

Guion, R. M., Gibson, W. M. 1988. Personnel selection and placement. *Ann. Rev. Psychol.* 39:349–74

Hakel, M. D. 1986. Personnel selection and placement. *Ann. Rev. Psychol.* 37:351–80

Hambleton, R. K. 1983. Application of item response models to criterion-referenced assessment. *Appl. Psychol. Meas.* 7:33–44

Hambleton, R. K. 1988. Principles and applications of item response theory. See Linn 1988

Hambleton, R. K., Swaminathan, H. 1985. *Item Response Theory.* Boston: Kluwer-Nijhoff

Harrison, D. A. 1986. Robustness of the IRT parameter estimation procedures to violations of the unidimensionality assumption. 1986. *J. Educ. Stat.* 11:91–115

Hedges, L. V. 1988. The meta-analysis of test validity studies: some new approaches. See Wainer & Braun 1988, pp. 191–212

Hoaglin, D. C., Mosteller, R., Tukey, J. W., eds. 1983. *Understanding Robust and Exploratory Data Analysis.* New York: Wiley

Hoaglin, D. C., Mosteller, F., Tukey, J. W., eds. 1985. *Exploring Data Tables, Trends, and Shapes.* New York: Wiley

Hofer, P. J., Green, B. F. 1985. The challenge of competence and creativity in computerized psychological testing. *Consult. Clin. Psychol.* 53:826–38

Holland, P. W., Thayer, D. T. 1986. *Differential Item Functioning and the Mantel-Haentszel Procedure.* Res. Rep. 86–31. Princeton: Educ. Test. Serv.

Holland, P. W., Thayer, D. T. 1988. Differential item performance and the Mantel-Haenszel procedure. See Wainer & Braun 1988, pp. 129–45

Hulin, C. L., Drasgow, F., Parsons, C. K. 1983. *Item Response Theory: Application to Psychological Measurement.* Homewood, Ill: Dow Jones-Irwin

Hunter, J. E., Schmidt, F. L., Coggin, T. D. 1986. *Meta-analysis of Correlations: The Issue of Bias and Misconceptions about the Fisher z Transformation.* East Lansing: Dept. Psychol., Michigan State Univ.

Hunter, J. E., Schmidt, F. L., Jackson, G. B. 1982. *Meta-analysis: Cumulating Research Findings Across Studies.* Beverly Hills, Calif: Sage

Ironson, G. H. 1982. Use of chi-square and

latent trait approaches for detecting item bias. See Berk 1982, pp. 117–60

Ironson, G., Homan, S., Willis, R., Signer, B. 1984. The validity of item bias techniques with math word problems. *Appl. Psychol. Meas.* 8:391–96

Jackson, P. R. 1986. Robust methods in statistics. See Lovie 1986, pp. 22–43

James, L. R., Damaree, R. G., Mulaid, S. A. 1986. A note on validity generalization procedures. *J. Appl. Psychol.* 71:440–50

Jarjoura, D., Brennan, R. L. 1983. Multivariate generalizability models for test developed from tables of specification. See Fyans 1983, pp. 83–102

Jensen, A. R. 1980. *Bias in Mental Testing.* New York: Free Press

Johnson, S., Bell, J. F. 1985. Evaluating and predicting survey efficiency using generalizability theory. *J. Educ. Meas.* 22:107–19

Jones, L. V. 1986a. *The Collected Works of John W. Tukey. Vol. III, Philosophy and Principles of Data Analysis: 1949–1964.* Monterey, Calif: Wadsworth & Brooks Cole

Jones, L. V. 1986b. *The Collected Works of John W. Tukey. Vol. IV, Philosophy and Principles of Data Analysis: 1965–1986.* Monterey, Calif: Wadsworth & Brooks Cole

Jones, L. V. 1988. Educational assessment as a promising area for psychometric research. *Appl. Meas. Educ.* 1:233–41

Kirkland, M. C. 1971. The effects of tests on students and schools. *Rev. Educ. Res.* 41:303–50

Krantz, D. H., Luce, R. D., Suppes, P., Tversky, A. 1971. *Foundations of Measurement.* New York: Academic

Kyllonen, P. C., Christal, R. E. 1988. *Cognitive Modeling of Learning Abilities.* AFHRL-TP-87-66. Brooks Air Force Base, Tex: Air Force Syst. Command

Lanyon, R. I., 1984. Personality assessment. *Ann. Rev. Psychol.* 35:667–701

Lewis, C. 1986. Test theory and Psychometrika: The past twenty-five years. *Psychometrika* 51:11–22

Linn, R. L. 1986. Barriers to new test designs. See Educational Testing Sevice 1986, pp. 69–80

Linn, R. L. 1987. Educational testing and assessment: research needs and policy issues. *Am. Psychol.* 41:1153–60

Linn, R. L. 1988. *Educational Measurement.* New York: Am. Counc. Educ./Macmillan. *3rd ed.* In press

Linn, R. L., Harnisch, D. L., Dunbar, S. B. 1981. Validity generalization and situational specificity: an analysis of the prediction of first-year grades in law school. *Appl. Psychol. Meas.* 5:281–89

Lippman, W. 1922. A future for tests. *New Republic* 33 (9):9–11

Lomax, R. G. 1982. An application of generalizability theory to observational research. *J. Exp. Educ.* 51:22–30

Lord, F. M. 1977. A study of item bias using item characteristic curve theory. In *Basic Problems in Cross-cultural Research,* ed. Y. H. Poortinga. Amsterdam: Swets & Zeitlinger

Lord, F. M. 1980. *Applications of Item Response Theory to Practical Testing Problems.* Hillsdale, NJ: Lawrence Erlbaum Assoc.

Lord, F. M. 1982. Item response theory and equating—a technical summary. In *Test Equating,* ed. P. W. Holland, D. B. Rubin, pp. 141–48. New York: Academic

Lord, F. M. 1986. Maximum likelihood and Bayesian parameter estimation in item response theory. *J. Educ. Meas.* 23:157–62

Lord, F. M., Novick, M. R. 1968. *Statistical Theories of Mental Test Scores.* Reading, Mass: Addison-Wesley

Lovie, A. D., ed. 1986. *New Developments in Statistics for Psychology and the Social Sciences.* London/New York: Brit. Psychol. Soc./Methuen

Luce, R. D., Narens, L. 1986. The mathematics underlying measurement on the continuum. *Science* 236:1527–32

Macready, G. B. 1983. The use of generalizability theory for assessing relations among items within domains in diagnostic testing. *Appl. Psychol. Meas.* 7:149–57

Marcus-Roberts, H. M., Roberts, F. S. 1987. Meaningless statistics. *J. Educ. Stat.* 12:383–94

Masters, G. N., Wright, B. D. 1984. The essential process in a family of measurement models. *Psychometrika* 50:69–82

McDonald, R. P. 1986. Describing the elephant: structure and function in multivariate data. *Psychometrika* 51:513–34

Messick, S. 1983. Assessment of children. In *Handbook of Child Psychology,* ed. W. Kessen. New York: Wiley

Messick, S. 1988a. The once and future issues of validity: assessing the meaning and consequences of measurement. See Wainer & Braun 1988, pp. 33–46

Messick, S. 1988b. Validity. See Linn 1988

Mislevy, R. J. 1983. Item response models for grouped data. *J. Educ. Stat.* 8:271–88

Mislevy, R. J. 1986. Bayes modal estimation in item response models. *Psychometrika* 51:177–95

Mislevy, R. J. 1987. Recent developments in item response theory with implications for teacher certification. *Rev. Educ. Res.* 14:239–75

Mislevy, R. J., Bock, R. D. 1981. *BILOG—Maximum Likelihood Item Analysis and Test*

Scoring: LOGISTIC Model. Chicago: Int. Educ. Serv.

Mossholder, K. W., Arvey, R. D. 1984. Synthetic validity: a conceptual and comparative review. *J. Appl. Psychol.* 69:322–33

Murname, R. J., Raizen, S. A., eds. 1988. *Improving Indicators of the Quality of Science and Mathematics Education in Grades K–12.* Washington, DC: Nat. Acad. Press

Narens, L. 1985. *Abstract Measurement Theory.* Cambridge, Mass: MIT Press

Narens, L., Luce, R. D. 1986. Measurement: the theory of numerical assignment. *Psychol. Bull.* 99:166–80

National Assessment of Educational Progress. 1985. *The Reading Report Card.* NAEP Rep. 15R-01. Princeton: Educ. Test. Serv.

National Assessment of Educational Progress. 1988. *The Mathematics Report Card.* Princeton: Educ. Test. Serv. In press

National Science Board Commission on Precollege Education in Mathematics, Science and Technology. 1983. *Educating Americans for the 21st Century.* Washington, DC: Natl. Sci. Found.

Oakes, J. 1986. *Educational Indicators: A Guide for Policy Makers.* Santa Monica, Calif: Cent. Policy Res. Educ./The RAND Corp.

Reckase, M. 1985. The difficulty of test items that measure more than one ability. *Appl. Psychol. Meas.* 9:401–12

Reitman, J. S., Rueter, H. H. 1980. Organization revealed by recall orders and confirmed by pauses. *Cogn. Psychol.* 12:554–81

Reynolds, C. R., Brown, R. T. 1984. *Perspectives on Bias in Mental Testing.* New York: Plenum

Robins, L. N., Helzer, J. E. 1986. Diagnosis and clinical assessment: the current state of psychiatric diagnosis. *Ann. Rev. Psychol.* 37:409–32

Ronning, R. R., Glover, J. A., Conoley, J. C., Witt, J. C. 1987. *The Influence of Cognitive Psychology on Testing.* Hillsdale, N.J.: Lawrence Erlbaum Assoc.

Roskam, E. E., Jansen, P. G. W. 1984. A new derivation of the Rasch model. In *Trends in Mathematical Psychology*, ed. E. Degreef, J. van Buggenhaut. Amsterdam: Elsevier

Rozeboom, W. W. 1978. Domain validity—why care? *Educ. Psychol. Meas.* 38:81–88

Rubin, D. B. 1988. Discussion. See Wainer & Braun 1988, pp. 241–56

Sackett, P. R., Schmitt, N., Tenopyr, M. L., Kehoe, J., Zedeck, S. 1985. Commentary on forty questions about validity generalization and meta-analysis. *Pers. Psychol.* 38: 697–798

Schmidt, F. L. 1988. Validity generalization and the future of criterion-related validity. See Wainer & Braun 1988, pp. 173–90

Schmidt, F. L., Hunter, J. E., Pearlman, K., Hirsh, H. R. 1985. Forty questions about validity generalization and meta-analysis. *Pers. Psychol.* 38:697–798

Schrader, W. B., ed. 1980. *Measuring Achievement: Progress over a Decade.* San Francisco: Jossey-Bass

Shavelson, R. J., Webb, N. M. 1981. Generalizability theory: 1978–1980. *Brit. J. Math. Stat. Psychol.* 34:133–66

Shepard, L. A. 1982. Definitions of test bias. See Berk 1982, pp. 9–30

Shepard, L. A., Camilli, G., Williams, D. M. 1985. Validity of approximation techniques for detecting item bias. *J. Educ. Meas.* 22:77–106

Smith, P. L. 1981. Gaining accuracy in generalizability theory: using multiple designs. *J. Educ. Meas.* 18:147–54

Smith, P. L. 1982. A confidence interval approach for variance component estimates in the context of generalizability theory. *Educ. Psychol. Meas.* 42:459–66

Snow, R. E., Peterson, P. L. 1985. Cognitive analyses of tests: implications for redesign. See Embretson 1985, pp. 149–66

Sokal, M. M. 1987. *Psychological Testing and American Society, 1890–1930.* New Brunswick: Rutgers Univ. Press

Stanners, R. F., Brown, L. T., Price, J. M., Holmes, M. 1983. Concept comparisons, essay examinations, and conceptual knowledge. *J. Educ. Psychol.* 75:857–64

Staybrook, N., Corno, L. 1979. An application of generalizability theory in disattenuating a path model of teaching and learning. *J. Educ. Res.* 16:227–37

Sternberg, R. J. 1985. *Beyond IQ: A Triarchical Theory of Human Intelligence.* Cambridge: Cambridge Univ. Press

Stricker, L. J. 1984. The stability of a partial correlation index for identifying items that perform differentially in subgroups. *Educ. Psychol. Meas.* 44:831–37

Swaminathan, H., Gifford, J. A. 1982. Bayesian estimation in the Rasch model. *J. Educ. Stat.* 7:175–92

Swaminathan, H., Gifford, J. A. 1985. Bayesian estimation in the two-parameter logistic model. *Psychometrika* 50:349–64

Swaminathan, H., Gifford, J. A. 1986. Bayesian estimation in the three-parameter logistic model. *Psychometrika* 51:589–601

Takane, Y., de Leeuw, J. 1986. *The relationship between item response theory and factor analysis of discretized variables.* Presented at Ann. Meet. Psychometric Soc., Toronto

Tatsuoka, K. K., Tatsuoka, M. M. 1982. Detection of aberrant response patterns and their effect on dimensionality. *J. Educ. Stat.* 7:215–31

Thissen, D., Steinberg, L., Gerrard, M. 1986. Beyond group mean differences: the concept of item bias. *Psychol. Bull.* 99:118–28

Thissen, D., Steinberg, L., Wainer, H. 1988. Use of item response theory in the study of group differences in trace lines. See Wainer & Braun 1988, pp. 147–69

Tittle, C. K. 1982. Use of judgmental methods in item bias studies. See Berk 1982, pp. 31–63

Trattner, M. H. 1982. Synthetic validity and its applications to Uniform Guidelines validation requirements. *Pers. Psychol.* 35: 383–97

Traub, R. E., Lam, Y. R. 1985. Latent structure and item sampling models for testing. *Ann. Rev. Psychol.* 36:19–48

Tucker, L. R 1983. Searching for structure in binary data. See Wainer & Messick 1983, pp. 215–36

Tukey, J. W. 1977. *Exploratory Data Analysis.* New York: Addison-Wesley

Tukey, J. W. 1986. Data analysis and behavioral science or learning to bear the quantitative man's burden by shunning badmandments. See Jones 1986a, pp. 187–390

Uniform guidelines on employee selection procedures. 1978. *Fed. Reg.* 43:38296–309

US Department of Labor. 1983a. *Overview of Validity Generalization,* USES Test Res. Rep. No. 43. Washington, DC: US GPO

US Department of Labor. 1983b. *Test Validation for 12,000 Jobs: An Application of Job Classification and Validity Generalization Analysis to the General Aptitude Test Battery,* USES Test Res. Rep. No. 45. Washington, DC: US GPO

Van der Flier, H., Mellenbergh, G. J., Ader, H. J., Wijn, M. 1984. An iterative item bias detection method. *J. Educ. Meas.* 21:131–45

van de Vijver, F. J. 1986. The robustness of Rasch estimates. *Appl. Psychol. Meas.* 10:45–57

Wainer, H., Braun, H. I., eds. 1988. *Test Validity.* Hillsdale, NJ: Lawrence Erlbaum Assoc.

Wainer, H., Kiely, G. L. 1987. Item clusters and computerized testing: a case for testlets. *J. Educ. Meas.* 24:185–202

Wainer, H., Messick, S., eds. 1983. *Principals of Modern Psychological Measurement: A Festschrift for Frederic M. Lord.* Hillsdale, NJ: Lawrence Erlbaum Assoc.

Wainer, H., Thissen, D. 1987. Estimating ability with the wrong model. *J. Educ. Statist.* 12:339–68

Ward, D. G. 1986. Factor indeterminacy in generalizability theory. *Appl. Psychol. Meas.* 10:159–65

Ward, W. C. 1982. A comparison of free-response and multiple-choice forms of verbal aptitude tests. *Appl. Psychol. Meas.* 6:1–12

Ward, W. C. 1986. Measurement research

that will change test design for the future. See Educational Testing Service 1986, pp. 25–34

Ward, W. C., Frederiksen, N., Carlson, S. B. 1980. Construct validity of free-response and machine-scorable forms of a test. *J. Educ. Meas.* 17:11–29

Ward, W. C., Kline, R. G., Flaugher, J. 1986. *College Board Computerized Placement Tests: Validation of an Adaptive Test of Basic Skills,* Res. Rep. 86–29. Princeton: Educ. Test. Serv.

Webb, N. M., Shavelson, R. J., Maddahian, E. 1983. Multivariate generalizability theory. See Fyans 1983, pp. 67–82

Weiss, D. J., ed. 1983. *New Horizons in Testing: Latent Trait Test Theory and Computerized Adaptive Testing.* New York: Academic

Weiss, D. J., Davison, M. L. 1981. Test theory and methods. *Ann. Rev. Psychol.* 32:629–58

Weiss, D. J., Kingsbury, G. G. 1984. Application of computerized adaptive testing to educational problems. *J. Educ. Meas.* 21:361–75

Wigdor, A. K. 1982. Psychological testing and the law of employment discrimination. In *Ability Testing: Uses, Consequences, and Controversies, Part II,* ed. A. K. Wigdor, W. R. Garner, pp. 39–69. Washington, DC: Natl. Acad. Press

Wigdor, A. K., Garner, W. R., eds. 1982. *Ability Testing: Uses, Consequences, and Controversies, Part I.* Washington, DC: Natl. Acad. Press

Willingham, W. W. 1980. New methods and directions in achievement measurement. See Schrader 1980, pp. 73–80

Wingersky, M. S. 1983. LOGIST: a program for computing maximum likelihood procedures for logistic test models. In *Applications of Item Response Theory,* ed. R. K. Hambleton. Vancouver: Educ. Res. Inst. British Columbia

Wood, R. L., Wingersky, M. S., Lord, F. M. 1976. *LOGIST: a computer program for estimating examinee ability and item characteristic curve parameters.* Res. Memo. 76–6. Princeton: Educ. Test. Serv.

Wright, B. D. 1977. Solving measurement problems with the Rasch model. *J. Educ. Meas.* 14:97–116

Wright, B. D., Bell, S. R. 1984. Item banks: what, why, how. *J. Educ. Meas.* 21:331–45

Yen, W. M. 1986. The choice of scale for educational measurement: an IRT perspective. *J. Educ. Meas.* 23:299–326

Young, F. W. 1984. Scaling. *Ann. Rev. Psychol.* 35:55–81

Zedeck, S., Cascio, W. F. 1984. Psychological issues in personnel decisions. *Ann. Rev. Psychol.* 35:461–518

Ann. Rev. Psychol. 1989. 40:45–81

INTERGROUP RELATIONS

David M. Messick and Diane M. Mackie

Department of Psychology, University of California, Santa Barbara, California 93106

CONTENTS

INTRODUCTION

When people are judged, either singly or together, on the basis of group memberships, intergroup processes are involved. This review, which follows those of Tajfel (1982) and Brewer & Kramer (1985), is structured to highlight four research foci currently receiving intense attention.

The study of intergroup relations, like many other areas of research in social psychology, has acquired a distinctly cognitive tone. We accentuate this cognitive atmosphere both to portray current thinking about intergroup processes and to signal our optimism that the cognitive approach will fruitful-

45

0066-4308/89/0201-0045$02.00

ly augment traditional approaches. The backbone of the chapter is the study of the way information about groups (categories) and their members is represented mentally. This approach promises fresh ideas about improving relations between groups and may elucidate underlying processes. We review the effect of categorization on the perception of the variability or heterogeneity of group members. Also important is the effect of categorization on tendencies to differentiate behaviorally between members of different categories, particularly in-group and out-group members. We address the difficult but crucial issue of extracting principles from this research that can be applied to improve the relations among groups. We conclude by noting some inroads that intergroup theory has made in other research domains, and by listing some research questions that appear especially timely.

COGNITIVE REPRESENTATIONS OF SOCIAL CATEGORIES

Cognitive representations of groups are assumed to be multiple-element (typically a category label, attributes, and/or exemplars) structures with both horizontal links, connecting related concepts at a similar level of generality, and vertical ones, reflecting the hierarchical progression from more to less inclusive categories. The encoding and retrieval of these representations is assumed to underlie judgments about groups and group members, which in turn guide intergroup behavior. In this section we review recent models of the information stored in category representations, progress in uncovering their cognitive and affective content, and the implications for intergroup perception of classification at subordinate compared to superordinate categories.

Models of Category Representation

Category representations have traditionally been conceptualized as a category label linked to an abstracted prototype or list of the features assumed to be true of the group as a whole (the group stereotype). Such group-level information is assumed to derive from social learning or from multiple experiences with individual category members, about whom information is not stored (Posner & Keele 1968; Reed 1972).

Prototype models of social stereotypes have been widely used in social psychology, and the storage of knowledge about a group as central-tendency information has been assumed to play a major role in stereotyped judgments. However, people can make estimates about how variable a group is, so prototype models must be complemented or supplanted by models that include variability information (E. E. Smith & Medin 1981; Posner & Keele 1968). Mixed models (Estes 1986; Hayes-Roth & Hayes-Roth 1977; Fried & Holyoak 1984; Flannagan et al 1986), in which both central-tendency and frequency information are stored, and pure exemplar models (Hintzman 1986; Medin & Schaffer 1978; Elio & Anderson 1981), in which only information about individual category members is stored, have recently been proposed as better representations of social categories (Linville et al 1986, 1988; Park & Hastie 1987; Rothbart & John 1985; Smith & Zarate 1988).

Linville's (Linville et al 1986, 1988) multiple-exemplar model includes both specific instances of the category and abstracted subtypes. In contrast to the use of prototypes, in which a single abstracted set of features is stored about a category, this approach suggests that individual exemplars as well as abstracted subtypes might be stored. Judgments about the group as a whole (including variability judgments) are made by retrieving and integrating information about exemplars. Rothbart (1988; Rothbart & John 1985) also proposed that judgments about a group's attributes may be made by integrating those "episodes" from memory most strongly associated with the category label (Wilder & Shapiro 1984; Lord et al 1984).

Although pure exemplar models have proven useful for studying group variability, mixed models seem more appropriate for several reasons (Lingle et al 1984; Smith & Zarate 1988). First, strict prototype and strict exemplar models both predict a substantial relation between judgments of the group as a whole and judgments of individual group members. However, Park & Hastie (1987) found judgments about the variability of individual (out)group members to be unrelated to judgments about the group as a whole (Allison & Messick 1985; Judd & Park 1988; although there are problems in comparing judgments at the different levels).

Second, whereas variability judgments pose problems for strict prototype models, strong versions of exemplar models are inconsistent with the possibility that at least some judgments about groups are made and stored as information is received (on-line), rather than on the basis of retrieval alone (Park & Hastie 1987). When perceivers form coherent impressions of targets as information is received, incongruent information is likely to receive extra processing and thus be differentially recalled (Hastie 1980; Srull 1981). Such effects have been found when information about cohesive, close-knit groups (such as political caucuses and fraternities) is received, but not when information about loosely related groups or aggregates is processed (Srull et al 1985; Wyer et al 1984; see also Stern et al 1984).

These findings suggest that on-line processing of coherent group-level impressions might occur for cohesive groups perceived as a unit, but not for aggregates. Group-level judgments about aggregates, in which consistency is not expected, are therefore more likely to be memory based and subject to retrieval biases. For example, distinctiveness-based illusory correlations [the perception of a relationship between, for example, category membership and a particular feature, when no such relationship exists (Hamilton & Sherman

1988)] appear to be based on the overrecall of cooccurrences of distinctive targets and distinctive events [such as minority group members performing infrequent behaviors (Acorn et al 1988; Arkes & Rothbart 1985; Hamilton et al 1985; Regan & Crawley 1984)]. These findings suggest that coherent impressions of laboratory groups labelled merely Group A or Group B are not formed on-line. However, illusory correlations do not develop when subjects are explicitly told to form an impression of the group (Pryor 1986; Sanbonmatsu et al 1987). These findings suggest that group judgments are not always based on exemplar retrieval, but can occur via on-line processing.

Third, pure exemplar models cannot explain the social learning of group-level information ("big boys don't cry," "boys will be boys") in contrast to learning from direct experience. Smith & Zarate (1988, Exp. 2) showed that learning a group prototype before encountering individual exemplars increased use of prototype information in later judgments, while subjects who received information in the opposite order were more likely to use exemplars. Similarly, Park & Hastie (1987, Exp. 2) found lower estimates of group variability when subjects received prototype before exemplar information than when the same information was presented in the opposite order.

Some evidence regarding the factors that determine storage and use of exemplar compared to group-level information has appeared. In general, categorization cues, which highlight the group as a unit, appear to reduce incorporation of individual exemplar information into representations (Taylor et al 1978; Nesdale et al 1987; Miller 1986), whereas drawing attention to individual members increases their inclusion. McCann et al (1985) found that heterogeneous stimulus groups (differing on gender and race and thus interfering with perception of the group as a unit) produced more clustering of recall by person (suggesting the presence of exemplar structures in the representation) than homogeneous groups. Smith & Zarate (1988) found that instructions to form an impression of each individual member increased use of exemplar information (compared to memory instructions), although all subjects showed equally good learning of the group's prototypical attributes. Familiarity with particular targets might also be expected to increase inclusion of exemplar information in representations (Hampson 1983; Pryor & Ostrom 1981; Pyror et al 1982). On the other hand, processing constraints such as time pressure or information overload are likely to increase formation of category-level representations (Medin et al 1984; Rothbart et al 1978).

As noted above, exemplar-based representations produce memory-based judgments of greater variability, are more easily elaborated and differentiated than prototype representations, and are thus more likely to produce veridical social perception. However because exceptions or inconsistent exemplars are easily dealt with by subclassification in exemplar-based representations, exceptional features may be less likely to become closely associated with the category label (Rothbart & Lewis 1988). In addition, on-line estimates of group variability may be more accurate than judgments based on exemplar retrieval; if this is the case, a reduction in on-line group-level judgments caused by the increased processing of exemplars necessary to produce exemplar-based representations may reduce accurate perception.

Content of Group Representations

Investigation of the content of group representations has always been hindered by the possibility of response biases, particularly in post–Civil Rights Movement American society. For example, recent evidence from survey studies suggests that white Americans' stereotypes of Blacks are becoming less prejudiced in content and less negative in affect (see Dovidio & Gaertner 1986). These results have been challenged by the argument that, although white Americans comply with egalitarian norms in rejecting blatant stereotypes, their underlying attitudes and stereotypes are at worst unchanged and at best marked by unacknowledged ambivalence. Whites' attitudes toward Blacks have been portrayed as marked by conflict between egalitarian values and unacknowledged negative feelings (Gaertner & Dovidio 1986b), between beliefs that racism is bad and beliefs that Blacks are making unfair demands now that most inequalities have been addressed (Kinder 1986; McConahay 1986), and between the positive and negative affect about them that has been internalized (Katz et al 1986).

Social cognition techniques hold some promise of eliciting information about category content in a manner that is relatively nonreactive. For example, subjects may make evaluative (How good is this?) or nonevaluative (Is this a real word?) judgments or simple responses (Name this word aloud) about trait words (AMBITIOUS, LAZY) displayed after presentation of a category label (WHITES, BLACKS). Faster response times of such judgments indicate greater associative strength between category labels and traits varying in stereotypicality and affect (Gaertner & McLaughlin 1983; Dovidio et al 1986). These studies have shown that traits traditionally associated with Black and White stereotypes (Katz & Braly 1933) are still associated with category labels, suggesting that attitudes and beliefs have not changed markedly. In addition, positive adjectives are more closely associated with the category Whites, although evidence that negative traits are still more closely associated with the category Blacks is mixed (Gaertner & McLaughlin 1983; Dovidio et al 1986).

Despite these indications that for white students traditionally related adjectives are still closely associated with Black and White categories and that the category White is the more positive, these techniques have methodological and conceptual problems. Tasks differ in the extent to which they are reactive, and delays between presentation of prime words and presentation of target words (stimulus onset asynchrony, SOA) plus the repetitive nature of the tasks might provide ample opportunity for respondents to pre-manage their responses. Manipulation of SOA may help distinguish automatic and attentional consequences of category activation on responding (Neely 1977; Fazio et al 1986), as a more sensitive indicant of response management. In a paradigm that reduces response management concerns, Devine (1986) found that subjects primed (outside of conscious awareness) with the content of their Black stereotypes (musical, ostentatious, but not including hostility-related words) were more likely to interpret a later ambiguous act as aggressive, suggesting that the idea of aggression is elicited by activation of the Black category. On the other hand, finding that activation of traditionally stereotypic attributes facilitates some responses may show only that the cultural stereotype is known, but not necessarily endorsed (Devine 1986). Multiple representations of groups may exist, any or all of which may be activated under different circumstances. If some category labels automatically activate particular content, but other material is available to override it attentionally, the cognitive, motivational, and contextual factors that inhibit or override activation of one category in favor of another become important. In this regard, Gaertner & Dovidio (1986b) note that clear normative pressures can produce either discrimination (Larwood et al 1984) or the lack of it; but when situational norms are vague, discrimination increases (Frey & Gaertner 1986). Similarly, stereotypic judgments increase under conditions of task difficulty or complexity (Bodenhausen & Wyer 1985; Bodenhausen & Lichtenstein 1987; cf Futoran & Wyer 1986) and time pressure (Freund et al 1985; Kruglanski & Freund 1983).

Definitive interpretation of response latency studies also awaits more judicious choice of both category (prime) and attribute (target) words. The latter need to be chosen so that affective valence and degree of association with a particular category can be independently manipulated if possible. Use of multiple target and multiple subject groups is important both to distinguish such effects as in-group/out-group bias (although see Sagar & Schofield 1980) and majority/minority status from the effects of specific representations, and because some colors (black) elicit associations that are similar to those produced by the corresponding group name (Blacks; Frank & Gilovich 1988).

Other work continues to explore the possibility that the content of stereotypes consists not only of abstract trait concepts but includes visual images (Brewer 1988; Brewer et al 1981; Lynn et al 1985), behavioral associations, physical features, typical beliefs, attitudes, and feelings (Andersen & Klatzky 1987; Hymes 1986). For example, Deaux & Lewis (1983, 1984) identified four components of gender stereotypes—traits, role behaviors, physical characteristics, occupational preferences—and traced the inferential links among them. Traits continue to be of interest because, like typical beliefs, preferences, etc, they are unobserved inferences (Rothbart & Park 1986) that perceivers seem prone to make about groups even when external constraints are present (Allison & Messick 1985; Mackie & Allison 1987; Worth et al 1987).

Recent research has also investigated how affect is associated with category structures. Fiske & Pavelchak (1986) have argued that summary affect (derived previously from integrating affectively laden category features) is stored with category labels and is activated when the category is activated: Activation of affect thus depends on the degree to which a stimulus fits a stored category. Fazio (Fazio et al 1986) has shown that some categories (especially those with which we have extensive direct experience) automatically activate the linked positive or negative affect. These developments may help integrate contradictory findings about whether and when affective reactions to groups overwhelm or are overwhelmed by cognitive content and whether affect influences judgments independently of or in concert with cognition (Bodenhausen 1988; Brown & Geis 1984; Jackson & Sullivan 1987; Jackson et al 1987; Taylor & Falcone 1982; Triplet & Sugarman 1987).

The automatic activation of affective material associated with a group category may have both cognitive and motivational influences on further processing, resulting in the increased use of heuristics and biases (Isen & Daubman 1984; Stephan & Stephan 1985; Wilder & Shapiro 1988). Stephan & Stephan (1985; Dijker 1987) have suggested that intergroup interactions accompanied by negative affect [such as anxiety resulting from ignorance and scant previous contact (Stephan & Stephan 1985)] will involve greater reliance on heuristics that promote category-level rather than individualized judgments [as might arousal (Kim & Baron 1988)]. Stephan & Stephan present data indicating that the anxiety expressed by Hispanic college students about interaction with Anglos is negatively related to the frequency of intergroup contacts and positively related to assumed dissimilarity, stereotyping, and xenophobia. Affect can also influence which of several features will be utilized by the perceiver in making initial judgments (Forgas & Bower 1987) as well as further recategorizations (Erber 1985), and it can act as a cue in making other evaluative judgments (Schwarz & Clore 1988).

Superordinate and Subordinate Categories

Despite suggestions that the simultaneous activation of horizontally linked concepts (such as gender, race, and age) might produce interactive effects on judgments (Deaux & Lewis 1984; Futoran & Wyer 1986), little is known about relationships among horizontal structures. There has been increased interest in whether category representations include diagnostic attributes that distinguish the group from other categories at the same level of generality (particularly groups with which the target category is frequently contrasted), rather than only typical traits [(Klayman & Ha 1987; Trope & Bassok 1982; Trope & Mackie 1987); see also the role of the social frame of reference in ascertaining the prototypical member of a category (Turner 1987)]. For example, the attributes thought to be prototypical of university professors may be different depending on whether they are compared to research scientists or to high school teachers. This possibility has important implications for categorization. First, match of a target to a category prototype or exemplar might not be sufficient for categorization if alternative categories have similar features or members. In this case, the importance of nonprototypical but diagnostic features increases (Trope & Mackie 1987). Second, it may be that prototypes are more flexible than earlier use of the concept connoted; rather than a prototype being a constant array of features equally activated by the category label, certain features or particular exemplars may be differentially activated by alternative categories considered for classification. Such ideas are consistent with notions of gender and ethnic identity as socially negotiated (Deaux & Major 1987).

More attention has been paid to the nature and organization of vertically linked category structures. Most current conceptualizations assume some hierarchical progression from broad social categories (such as Blacks, Whites, females, males) through increasingly specific subcategories (such as streetwise Black, Connecticut Yankee, career woman, macho man) with individualized structures of particular individuals as the lowest level of the hierarchy [although exemplar information can of course be associated with category labels at any level in the structure (Billig 1985; Fiske 1988; Miller & Brewer 1986; Rothbart 1988; cf Brewer 1988)]. Considerable attention has been paid to the nature of subtypes, for at least two reasons.

First, the possibility that middle-level structures might constitute a basic level of categorization [as in the nonsocial domain (Rosch 1978)] and thus carry the burden of social prediction has generated a focus on subtypes (Andersen & Klatzky 1987; Ashmore et al 1984; Brewer et al 1981; Deaux & Kite 1988; Deaux & Lewis 1984; Deaux et al 1985a,b; Hamilton & Trolier 1986; Trzebinski 1985; Trzebinski et al 1985; Weber & Crocker 1983). Social subtypes are easily activated (even by indirect instructions), easily generated, and organize category-relevant information in memory [as shown by clustering in recall (Martin 1987; Noseworthy & Lott 1984; Walker & Antaki 1986)]. It has been suggested that subtypes are richer [although Deaux et al (1985b) found no evidence for this; see also Rothbart & John (1985)], more visualizable (Brewer 1988), more internally coherent, and characterized by closer associations between category labels and associated attributes (Crocker & Park 1988) and affect (Fiske 1988) than broader social categories.

On the other hand, vertically related social structures are not strictly hierarchical (Deaux et al 1985b; Lingle et al 1984), unless only prototypical exemplars are considered (Hampson et al 1986). "Subordinate" categories ("business woman") are often distinct from generic superordinate concepts ("woman") and perhaps from logical conjunctions of superordinate categories [such as "woman" and "business executive" (Brewer 1988)]. They exhibit numerous idiosyncratic and distinctive associations (Andersen & Klatzky 1987; see also Pryor et al 1984), domain specific effects (Linville et al 1986, 1988; Weber & Crocker 1983), and between-category overlap (Deaux & Lewis 1983, 1984; Deaux et al 1985b). For example, because many generic labels, like "American," are male oriented (Eagly & Kite 1987), the degree of overlap between these generic and subordinate categories ("American athlete," for example) may be higher for male categories than for female categories (Deaux et al 1985b); and categorization of women might be more easily influenced by context than is categorization of men (Deaux & Major 1987; Eagly & Steffen 1984). Similar effects might be expected in the category structures of dominant versus minority groups. All of these features suggest that no basic level of categorization exists for social stimuli: The level of social categorization that maximizes within-category similarity and between-category differences and thus has descriptive and predictive superiority for a particular task will vary across social situations and contexts (Lingle et al 1984; Turner 1987).

A second reason for interest in subtypes is the assumption that the most detailed subtyping results in individualization of the target, "accurate" social perception, and by implication, improved intergroup relations. Rothbart & John (1985; Hampson et al 1986) have argued that there is a trade-off between the number of attributes that a category predicts and how well it predicts them. Broad categories (such as gender stereotypes) link many traits to the category label but only loosely, so that the certainty that any member of a category has the trait is reduced. In contrast, members of more specific subcategories are more certain to have the (fewer) attributes associated with category membership. Subordinate categories are therefore seen as more accurate predictors of fewer attributes (see also Andersen & Klatzky 1987), and beliefs about these attributes' association with the category may be hard to change (Miller & Turnbull 1986). Both Rothbart & John (1985) and Sears (1983) note that individual members of groups are reacted to more positively than the group as a whole, suggesting the benefits of individualized processing. Locksley et al (1982) argued that stereotypic beliefs might be overridden by individuating information about a single target (Heilman 1984; Miller 1986) because perceivers fall prey to the base-rate fallacy and underutilize prior probabilities. However Rasinski et al (1985) demonstrated that subjects in fact underrevised their own prior probabilities in the face of the new information, particularly diagnostic information (Bodenhausen & Wyer 1985; Deaux & Lewis 1984; Jackson & Cash 1985; Nisbett et al 1983; Wyer

& Martin 1986). Krueger & Rothbart (1988) demonstrated that the diagnostic strength of both category and target information combine additively in judgments: Target information overrode initial categorization only when category information was nondiagnostic for the required judgment *and* individuating information was both stable and diagnostic (see also Hinsz et al 1988). Given the difficulty of eliminating category effects from information processing completely, categorizations of the target at increasingly specific sublevels may have the best chance of reducing any prejudicial effects of category-based processing.

Despite any benefits that subcategorization might have for intergroup perception, there is increasing agreement that social targets initially activate primary or primitive generic categories such as race, gender, and age [although there is little direct evidence of this (Brewer 1988; Bruner 1957a,b; Fiske & Neuberg 1988; Taylor 1981)]. For example, gender identification apparently requires less extensive processing than trait judgments (Bower & Karlin 1974), and it interferes with subject-target similarity judgments on other dimensions (Brewer 1988). Such primitive categorization has considerable influence in that it constrains the range of subcategories that may subsequently be activated (Brewer 1988). It may inhibit subtype activation entirely (Rothbart & John 1985) unless motivation and capacity for increased processing are present (Fiske & Neuberg 1988; Langer et al 1985; Rodin 1987). Frequent activation of these primitive categories increases their likelihood of subsequent activation (Higgins et al 1985), further enhancing the priority of superordinate categorization over subtype classification.

When subcategorization does occur, the level at which it ceases has been studied in terms of fit or match between target features and category features (Bruner 1957a,b; see Fiske & Neuberg 1988, Oakes 1987 for reviews) and the perceiver's motivation (Fiske & Neuberg 1988; Neuberg & Fiske 1987; Omoto & Borgida 1988). Categories are activated and become salient when they are matched by behaviors and attributes present in the target, relative to other targets and other categories available. Oakes (1987) has highlighted the importance of the perceivers' social goals in determining fit, arguing that immediate goals sometimes undermine the influence of features such as infrequency, rarity, and novelty that reportedly make some categories automatically distinctive (Oakes & Turner 1986; Nesdale & Dharmalingam 1986; Nesdale et al 1987; cf McGuire et al 1978; Taylor 1981). In general, the presence of category-consistent features in the target confirms categorization at the initial level, whereas the presence of inconsistent features makes recategorization or subtyping more probable (Fiske & Neuberg 1988; Fiske et al 1987; Heilman 1984; Rothbart 1988; Rothbart & John 1985; see also Hoffman 1986).

THE OUT-GROUP HOMOGENEITY EFFECT

When asked to judge the variability of social groups, people judge groups to which they do not belong to be more homogeneous than in-groups (Linville et al 1986, 1988; Mullen & Hu 1989; Quattrone 1986; Wilder 1984b). Even when the perceived group is held constant (Judd & Park 1988; Worth et al 1987), it is seen as more variable by its own members than by members of other groups.

Evidence for this effect has been found with different conceptualizations and measurements of homogeneity (see Linville et al 1986, 1988; Mullen & Hu 1989; Quattrone 1986 for reviews), with real and minimal groups (Simon & Brown 1987; Judd & Park 1988; Worth et al 1987). Perceived homogeneity has been associated with polarized evaluative judgments about group members [(Linville & Jones 1980); although this may hold only when the dimensions of evaluation are correlated (Judd & Lusk 1984)], with more confident member-to-group and group-to-member inferences (Quattrone & Jones 1980; Nisbett et al 1983), and with increased intergroup bias (Wilder 1978). Considerable effort has therefore been directed at understanding how the cognitive representations of in-groups and out-groups differ so as to influence judged variability.

In-group vs Out-group Representations

Linville (Linville et al 1986, 1988) used an exemplar model of group representations to explain why in-groups are seen as more variable than out-groups. In this view, variability judgments depend on (*a*) the retrieval of individual exemplars from memory, and (*b*) the use of an availability heuristic to estimate the shape of the group distribution. Linville distinguishes between variability (the degree to which group members are seen as being dispersed) and differentiation (the likelihood of distinguishing among group members on a particular attribute). Whereas variability reflects the spread of a distribution, differentiation reflects the number of attribute levels and their likelihood. Because increased contact with a group increases the number of exemplars as well as the number of ways in which they differ, such contact should increase both perceived variability and differentiation. Because people have more contact with in-group than out-group members, according to Linville, the former are seen as more differentiated and variable.

There is evidence from computer simulations of the model that exposure to multiple exemplars increases perceived differentiation, and to a lesser extent, variability (Linville et al 1988, Exp. 1). These results are consistent with the known statistical relationships among variability, dimensional complexity, and sample size. In addition, Linville et al (1988 Exp. 2) showed out-group homogeneity effects in groups where more in-group than out-group members were known (such as with age cohorts and nationality), but not when acquaintance included approximately equal numbers of in-group and out-group members (genders). More importantly, increased familiarity over time with the same in-group (college class) resulted in greater differentiation (Exp. 3).

There are reasons to suspect that the number of in-group and out-group exemplars known is not the sole mediator of the homogeneity effect. First, with no knowledge, perceivers seem to assume homogeneity in minimal out-groups (Judd & Park 1988; Quattrone 1986; Worth et al 1987) compared to minimal in-groups, although the difference appears primarily due to exaggerations of out-group homogeneity (Mullen & Hu 1989). One could argue that there is always one known in-group exemplar, the self. Second, group size contributes to subjects' judgments of variability independently of exemplar retrieval. For example, subjects' estimates of the variability of minimal in-groups and out-groups of various sizes (where the self was the only exemplar that could be retrieved) show a positive relationship to size of the group (Simon & Brown 1987). A group of 50 seems more variable than a group of 5. Third, there is no simple relationship between the number of group members reportedly known and variability estimates (Jones et al 1981; Linville 1982). Fourth, out-group homogeneity effects have been reported with gender groups, where equal familiarity is assumed (Carpenter & Ostrom 1985; Park & Rothbart 1982).

For these reasons it appears that *how* information about in-group and out-group members is processed may be as important as *how many* members from each group are encountered. In particular, variability estimates are sensitive to whether information about individual exemplars is distinguished and differentiated in the group representation (see section above; Linville et al 1986). Representations of in-groups, for instance, involve more differentiation of individual members than representations of the out-group. Park & Rothbart (1982) have demonstrated that more information about distinctive (sub)category memberships of individual in-group, compared to out-group, members can be recalled. Whereas women recall the gender of male and female targets equally well, for example, they are more likely to remember also the occupation of the female (in-group) than the male (out-group) targets. It is not clear whether this reflects encoding or retrieval differences (Judd & Park 1988; Park & Rothbart 1982; Rothbart 1988; Rothbart & John 1985), although both imply differences in in-group and out-group representations. Information about in-group members is also more likely than information about out-group members to be organized by individuals (as measured by clustering of individual items in recall) (Carpenter & Ostrom 1985; Sedikides & Ostrom 1987). Thus factors that influence individuation of group members should influence perceived homogeneity, independently of the number of exemplars known.

Motivational Factors

Several plausible motivations to differentiate among individuals are conceptually independent of group membership. First, the possibility of future interaction has been shown to lead to more complex representations, and if future interaction is more likely with the in-group than the out-group, differences in complexity should result (Fiske & Neuberg 1988). However, this seems more relevant to laboratory groups, for example, than to gender groups, since men have ample incentive to distinguish among women, and vice versa.

Second, targets upon whom one is dependent are likely to be more differentiated. Although dependency is also often associated with in-group members, less powerful or minority groups must often depend on specific knowledge of the majority out-group's preferences, behaviors, values, etc. Thus more complex representations about a majority out-group might be formed by members of a minority in-group, not only because the majority is greater in number, but also because the in-group minority is dependent on them (Linville et al 1986). At the same time, perceived in-group homogeneity might be an adaptive response to boost solidarity for a threatened minority ingroup (Simon & Brown 1987). Simon & Brown assigned subjects to groups (based ostensibly on performance of perceptual tasks) and manipulated the majority and minority numerical status of the in-group and the out-group. Subjects made estimates of the range of in-group and out-group scores (a measure of variability that is positively correlated with group size) on dimensions that differed in their relevance to the classification task. Out-group homogeneity was perceived only when the in-group was a majority: When the in-group was a minority, in-group homogeneity was found. Although the minimal nature of the situation reduced true dependency, a dependency interpretation of these results is consistent with other findings. Sedikides & Ostrom (1986) found more individualized representation of a high-status group (sophomores) by both in-group and lower status out-group (freshmen) members. [A status interpretation may also help explain the increased differentiation of male, compared to female, targets noted by Linville et al (1988).]

Interactions involving competition and cooperation may also influence differentiation of the in-group and out-group (Quattrone 1986; Wilder 1981). Although competition is usually associated with increased perception of out-group homogeneity [(Judd & Park 1988); and perhaps of in-groups as well (Simon & Brown 1987)], it need not always result in undifferentiated views of the out-group. Consider a situation of high intergroup conflict in which the best strategy for preservation of the in-group involves differentiating the out-group. The enemy troops make one last desperate charge towards one's own line. Under such conditions, motivation would be high to identify a commanding officer, whose death will maximally undermine success of the attack. Intergroup competition could thus increase incentives for out-group differentiation. Consistent with this possibility, Judd & Park found that intergroup competition actually increased the amount of information recalled about individual out-group members.

The self as a member of the in-group ensures that there is always at least one in-group exemplar for whom a detailed and differentiated cognitive structure exists. As noted above, this fact provides an explanation of out-group homogeneity effects in minimal groups because one in-group exemplar is always available, even if no out-group exemplars are. The self is also a readily accessible exemplar, and thus may have disproportionate influence on group judgments (Rothbart et al 1984; Judd & Park 1988). In addition, Park & Rothbart (1982) suggest that differentiation of in-group members at more specific levels occurs in order that other in-group members may be distinguished from the self, although this idea awaits direct testing. The contribution of the self to increased heterogeneity of the in-group may thus be mediated by both cognitive and motivational processes.

Other Processing Effects

In criticizing exemplar models, Park & Hastie (1987) have argued that variability judgments about a group can be made on-line and thus may not depend totally on recall of exemplars. [Linville et al (1988) acknowledge that group judgments made frequently might be stored and retrieved without recalculation.] This raises the issue of whether variability judgments about in-groups or out-groups are more likely to be made on-line, and if so, whether on-line judgments are any more likely to reflect greater variability than memory-based judgments. If on-line judgments are more likely for in-groups than out-groups, and if on-line judgments reflect greater variability than memory-based judgments, this would provide a processing explanation for the out-group homogeneity effect. Currently, there is no definitive evidence for either of these suppositions. There may be more at stake in processing in-group than out-group information, and this might lead to more on-line processing. On the other hand, on-line variability judgments about nonmembership groups has also been reported under laboratory conditions (Park & Hastie 1987). Similarly, it is not clear whether on-line or memory-based judgments are more accurate indicators of actual group variability. As noted above, on-line judgments are not influenced by retrieval biases and, for this reason, might be more accurate. On the other hand, the exemplars that are likely to have a recall advantage (consistent, salient, or extreme ones, for example) are also the ones likely to receive on-line attention and to over-contribute to on-line judgments. In addition, it is possible that expectations that in-groups are variable and out-groups homogeneous directs attention towards differentiating information about the in-group and away from such information about the out-group (Worth 1988). Under many conditions, therefore, on-line judgments may not differ markedly from memory-based judgments.

INTERGROUP BIAS

Tajfel et al (1971) discovered that the mere categorization of a group of boys into two subgroups, subgroups that were randomly determined by trivial preferences, was sufficient to elicit behavior from the boys that favored members of their newly defined in-group over out-group members (intergroup bias). This discovery challenged the idea that intergroup discrimination re-sulted from a real conflict of interest between the two groups (Sherif 1967). It also initiated a voluminous research effort to replicate and clarify the bias. Brewer (1979), Tajfel (1982), and Brewer & Kramer (1985) have reviewed much of this work, leaving little doubt that the trivial or random classification of a group of people into two subgroups is sufficient to induce people in one of the subgroups to favor others in that group relative to those in the other group. In this summary of recent work on the intergroup bias, we focus first on theoretical and then on methodological issues.

Theoretical Issues

The most prominent theory guiding research on intergroup bias is social identity theory (SIT) (e.g. Tajfel & Turner 1986). In brief, social identity theory proposes that people's self-evaluations are shaped in part by their group memberships. Furthermore, as part of a pervasive need to maintain positive self-regard, people want to view the groups to which they belong in a positive light. Because it is the relative position of one's own group in contrast to another that is important, self-esteem can be enhanced if people can make a favorable comparison of their own group to another. Intergroup bias or discrimination, according to SIT, is such a favorable comparison.

The SIT interpretation of intergroup bias is difficult to test. It may be true that people want to maintain positive self-esteem and that they view member-ship groups positively, but it remains to be shown that these are the causes of intergroup bias. A direct test of such a causal relation is, in fact, hard to imagine. However, SIT does indirectly imply that an act of intergroup discrimination should increase the actor's self-esteem. Oakes & Turner

(1980) report an experiment that claims to demonstrate just this. Subjects who were categorized into two subgroups and who had a chance to make allocations that favored in-group members, manifested higher subsequent self-esteem scores than subjects who were similarly categorized, but who had no opportunity to make a group-favoring choice (cf Wagner et al 1986). Noting that this experiment lacked some essential controls, Lemyre & Smith (1985) attempted to test the self-esteem hypothesis more adequately. Subjects were either categorized into two subgroups or not, and roughly half the members of each group were given a chance to make intergroup point allocations before measures of self-esteem were collected. For the other half of the subjects, measures of self-esteem were taken before the subjects were given the opportunity to discriminate. The results indicated that subjects who had been categorized and who had displayed intergroup discrimination had higher self-esteem scores than subjects who had been categorized but who had not had the chance to discriminate. While this finding provides support for SIT, an additional finding was unexpected. Subjects who were simply categorized showed lower self-esteem scores than noncategorized subjects. As Lemyre & Smith note, mere categorization in these minimal-group studies may threaten self-esteem and intergroup discrimination may restore it. If minimal categorization creates a challenge to self-esteem, and if intergroup bias is a consequence of that threat, the generalizability of studies using such categorization manipulations will be severely restricted [although similar effects of trivial and important categorization have been found (Moghaddam & Stringer 1986)].

Numerous studies using SIT as an interpretive framework have provided only mixed evidence for other key derivations from the theory. Brown et al (1986) found little evidence of a positive association between the degree of in-group identification and the extent of positive intergroup differentiation. Such results can be explained by hypothesizing that the relationship will be mediated by the saliency of group membership and the security of in-group identity (Smith 1985). However, studies examining the idea that discrimination would be greater to the extent that group memberships were made salient did not discover much support for SIT. Both Ng (1986) and Sachdev & Bourhis (1985) found bias for nonsalient groups only, and Sachdev & Bourhis (1987) found no salience effects. Similarly, studies investigating the effects of status on discrimination have yielded conflicting results. Sachdev & Bourhis (1987) found that high- and equal-status groups discriminated more than low-status groups, whereas Finchilescu (1986) found that groups assigned low status were more discriminatory. Ng (1985) found no differences in bias as a function of group status. Espinoza & Garza (1985) report that minority group members (Hispanics) who are in a numerical minority in a group, discriminate more (are more competitive) than majority group members or

Hispanics in a majority. Simon & Brown (1987) claim that a group in a numerical minority discriminates by enhancing its perception of its relative homogeneity [although Park & Rothbart (1982) and Linville & Jones (1980) found no relationship between perceptions of homogeneity and evaluation]. Simon & Brown failed to find evidence of direct discrimination by the minority.

An important study that failed to find support for SIT was reported by Vanbeselaere (1987). At issue in this study was the effect of cross-categorizing subjects into two different sets of subcategories. SIT offers no obvious reason why such cross-categorization should reduce intergroup bias, but Deschamps & Doise (1978) reported data suggesting that it did. Vanbeselaere's experiment, designed to correct possible flaws that Brown & Turner (1979) noted in the Deschamps & Doise procedures, closely replicated the original results: Simultaneously categorizing subjects on two crossed dimensions eliminated intergroup bias, measured both by performance evaluations and by general attitude questions. Although Vanbeselaere offers no theoretical rationale for this result, it is clearly incompatible with SIT, since in-group members apparently feel no need to make their own group positively distinct from any of the others. Although SIT has been responsible for almost single-handedly reviving intergroup research, invoking the concept of self-esteem has not provided a definitive understanding of in-group discrimination (see also Taylor & Moghaddam 1987).

More recently Turner (1987) has described a self-categorization theory (SCT) that is broader than SIT and from which SIT may be derived. SCT appears to place greater emphasis than SIT on the nature of categorization processes per se. In this sense the theory reflects an earlier concern with the effects of perceptual accentuation (Tajfel & Wilkes 1963; Doise 1978; Eiser & Stroebe 1972). According to Turner, people perceive themselves to be members of some groups within a hierarchical structure of categories. Humans are distinguished from nonhumans. Within humans, different groupings are distinguished on the basis of relative intraclass similarities and interclass differences. Finally, within groups, the unique properties of individuals are differentiated.

Categorization leads to perceptual distortions in that objects in the same category appear more similar to one another and more different from objects in another category than they would if not categorized (see Wilder 1986a for a review; Herringer & Garza 1987). In addition, groupings that contain the self are special. Not only are they easily activated, they are also positively regarded. They possess "positive distinctiveness." Ethnocentrism at the group level is analogous to self-esteem at the individual level.

Perceptual accentuation effects coupled with positive regard for the in-group might well contribute to ethnocentrism. Perceptual accentuation effects on distinguishing dimensions may generalize to evaluative dimensions, or evaluative judgments might be accentuated or polarized when distinguishing and evaluative dimensions are correlated (Doise 1978; Eiser & Stroebe 1972; Judd & Lusk 1984). Such an interpretation might explain Vanbeselaere's 1987 results by arguing that cross-classifying people simultaneously on two dimensions reduces or eliminates the perceptual distortion that simple categorization induces, and that without the perceptual distortion, the evaluative gradient disappears.

In summary, nearly 20 years after the discovery that mere categorization produced intergroup bias, an adequate theory of the phenomenon has yet to be developed. Both perceptual accentuation effects and self-esteem maintenance seem likely to be part of the story, but empirical findings have not definitively clarified their necessary or sufficient roles.

Another factor, discovered in a different paradigm, is the extent to which people behave, or expect to behave, in terms of their group memberships. McCallum et al (1985) discovered that when dyads played a Prisoners' Dilemma Game (PDG), they made more competitive choices than individuals playing the same game. The competitive choice in the PDG not only maximizes the chooser's payoff, it also maximizes the chooser's competitive advantage, the difference between the chooser's payoff and that of the other. McCallum et al (1985) reported a second experiment that ruled out the possibility that groups were simply trying to maximize their own gains. Thus groups seemed to have a more competitive orientation than individuals.

Insko et al (1987) asked whether the increased group competitiveness was due to the interdependence of the payoffs of the group members or to the fact that the groups in the McCallum et al study had met only through group representatives. They found that neither of these features could account for the enhanced group competitiveness.

Insko et al (1988) next reported that neither mere intragroup contact nor intragroup discussion was sufficient to produce the group competitiveness. However, having to reach an intragroup consensus about the choice that the group members would make, even though the intergroup contact was individual, did produce the competitive group effect. At this point, the evidence suggests that the major factor involved with this so-called "discontinuity" in competitiveness between individuals and groups (Brown 1954) is whether the choices are made individually (with or without discussion, visual contact, or payoff sharing), or whether they are made for the group (i.e. whether on each interaction trial, only one choice is made by the group or group members). Enhanced competition appears to characterize situations in which the group members act in lockstep. These results are consistent with Turner's argument that group formation is an antecedent rather than a consequence of such effects, although Insko & Schopler (1987) offer other interpretations.

Methodological Issues

The central issue to be discussed in this section has to do with the variety of dependent variables that have been used to measure intergroup bias. Before reviewing these measures, however, we note a pervasive but problematic characteristic of nearly all of the experiments that have investigated this phenomenon. This common element is a symmetry in the manipulation of the independent variable. In research with categorization the symmetry is that the subjects are typically categorized into 2 (or more) groups, making it impossible to determine if the bias emanates from individuals who have been categorized in a common group, or if it is directed toward others who have been so categorized, or, of course, both. In the PDG experiments summarized above, the symmetry is that both groups of subjects in an experimental condition are governed by the same rules (e.g. there are no conditions in which individuals play against group representatives). Thus it is impossible to say whether the increased level of competition associated with group responding results from the fact that the *others* are responding as a unit, or because one's own group is doing so. Of some relevance to this issue is the study of Rehm et al (1987), who found that handball teams composed of 11-year-old boys who were given bright orange jerseys to wear during the game were more aggressive than their opponents who wore only their personal street clothes. Enhancing the group identity of one of the groups appeared to increase the competitiveness of the boys in that group. This kind of study, in which membership in a single group is spotlighted, is much needed.

Intergroup bias has been observed with an impressive array of dependent variables. Rating measures include performance evaluations (see Hinkle & Schopler 1986 for a review; Sachdev & Bourhis 1987; Vanbeselaere 1987), attributions (Bond et al 1985; Brown & Wade 1987; Stewart et al 1985), general evaluative ratings (Brewer & Silver 1978), and trait ratings (Rosenbaum & Holtz 1985). Behavioral measures have included direct money or point allocations (Ng 1985, 1986), allocations made using the Tajfel matrixes (TMs), which Bourhis & Sachdev (1986) have carefully explained (Brewer & Silver 1978; Finchilescu 1986; Sachdev & Bourhis 1985), allocations made using the Brewer & Silver matrixes (BSMs) (Brewer & Silver 1978; Herringer & Garza 1987), allocations made using the multiple alternative matrixes (MAMs) (Bornstein et al 1983a,b), and choices in the PDG and MDG (McCallum et al 1985; Insko et al 1987, 1988). This broad spectrum of dependent measures would be reassuring about the pervasive nature of the intergroup bias if the evidence suggested that these measures all assessed the same thing. Unfortunately, this is not the case.

Brewer & Silver (1978), for instance, used the BSMs, TMs, and general evaluative ratings to assess bias as a result of categorization and intergroup orientation. While both of the behavioral measures indicated less bias with a cooperative than with a competitive or independent orientation, the evaluative ratings showed a small bias that was constant across orientations. Ng (1985) found no evidence of bias with direct monetary allocations to in-group and out-group members, but when subjects were asked how to weight two tasks to determine payments, they tended to place a greater weight on the task on which the in-group was superior. The most controversial divergence of measures is with the use of the TMs and the MAMs (see Bornstein et al 1983a,b and Turner 1983a,b). Typical results with the TMs suggest that intergroup bias results from trying to achieve an in-group payment that is as large as possible (*maximum in-group profit* or MIP) and trying to achieve a payment that is larger than the payment to the out-group regardless of absolute size (*maximizing* the *difference* or MD). The typical MAM findings show a prevalence of maximizing the joint payoff for the two groups, so long as the in-group gets more than the out-group (*maximizing joint* gain with *own* group ahead, or MJO), and very little MIP and MD.

The experimental study of intergroup discrimination faces the basic chore of developing a comprehensive theory of its dependent variables, and of determining what the various indexes measure and how they relate to one another and to other theoretical concepts. Here we mention a few ideas that may be useful in this pursuit.

One of the first studies indicating that there might be important differences between methods of measuring intergroup bias was reported by LaPiere (1934). While this study is frequently cited in research on the connection between attitudes and behavior (see, for instance, Ajzen 1987), it is rarely seen in contemporary studies of intergroup bias. This classic study should serve as a reminder that measures of attitudes toward a group do not necessarily predict behavior toward that group.

As we noted in a previous section, recent research suggests that attitudes toward racial or ethnic out-groups may now be more complicated than they once were. Gaertner & Dovidio's (1986b) concept of aversive racism, implies that although people may hold negative views of racial minorities, they also condemn racial prejudice and shun overtly racist behavior. Similarly, subjects in mere categorization experiments rarely discriminate maximally against the out-group—their choices are "tempered with fairness" (Wilder 1986a:312)— suggesting either an ambivalence toward discrimination or the presence of normative controls on the magnitude of discrimination. In both the attitude and behavioral domains, therefore, there appear to be impediments to the direct assessment of intergroup bias that would argue in favor of the use of more indirect unobtrusive measures. Ng (1985) attributed to such factors the failure to find discrimination with direct allocations when he did find it with an indirect measure.

In allocation studies, people may not only be reluctant to discriminate overtly, their allocations may be influenced by a variety of factors other than group membership (Leventhal 1976). Ng (1986) has shown equity effects, larger allocations to groups that performed better, that tend to override intergroup bias. When group performance is equal, direct allocations also tend to be equal (Ng 1985). Moreover, when a variable like status is manipulated by varying perceived performance (e.g. Sachdev & Bourhis 1987), self-assigned performance (e.g. Finchilescu 1986), or actual performance (e.g. Ng 1986), allocations may reflect performance distinctions rather than group discrimination. Thus, if a high-status group (which is always paired with a low-status group) shows intergroup discrimination and a low-status group shows a "negative" bias (see Sachdev & Bourhis 1987), the implication is simply that both groups give more to the group that did better than to the group that did worse. In cases like this, techniques are needed that allow for the simultaneous assessment of tendencies to reward good performance and tendencies to overreward one's own group.

Bourhis & Sachdev (1986) persuasively argue that the TMs are sensitive to the subtle effects of mere categorization. However, in the studies reported by McCallum et al (1985), Insko et al (1987), and Insko et al (1988), manipulations that would have had the effect of categorizing the subjects into those on one side of the corridor and those on the other did not result in increased competition. When competition did occur in these studies it was more blatant and overt than that manifested in simple categorization experiments. So, just as it is necessary to use different instruments to measure temperatures from widely different sections of the temperature scale, it may be that the TMs and the PDG are most appropriate for studying intergroup orientations that differ in their intensity. The cultivation of this idea would require that the situations and manipulations, as well as dependent variables, be ordered on a scale of severity or intensity. It would then be possible to test the proposal that certain kinds of measures are more appropriate for some kinds of situations than for others.

Finally, we applaud the kind of exchange that occurred between Bornstein et al (1983a,b) and Turner (1983a,b). It can only be beneficial to examine in such detail the possible goals or strategies of subjects in categorization experiments and the relationship of these goals to the set of choices available. The issues that were raised in these papers run deeper than those raised in many recent articles because they deal with the bedrock questions of how theoretical concepts (like discrimination) are expressed in behavior. One reason why the relative superiority of the MAMs and TMs was not definitively resolved stems from different assumptions that Bornstein et al and Turner make about the set of motives, goals, or strategies that subjects can pursue in minimal-group experiments. Both Bornstein et al and Turner seem to accept the premise that subjects will choose the option that best satisfies their goals. They seem to differ with regard to assumptions that they make about what those goals can be. Bornstein et al appear to hold that the goals must be one of seven orientations that include MIP, MD, and MJO. While Turner is somewhat vague, he views these goals as "continuous variables" (Turner 1983a:358), which we take to mean evaluative strategies in which trade-offs can be made between one pure strategy and others (e.g. a willingness to exchange some amount of in-group payoff for an increase in relative advantage, or to give up some relative advantage to gain something in fairness). This dispute is not about the connection of underlying theoretical states (strategies or orientations) to choices, but rather about the possible theoretical states themselves. In view of the complexity that has been observed in studies of people's choices of payoffs for themselves and others (MacCrimmon & Messick 1976; Messick & Sentis 1985; Lurie 1987), we see no reason to restrict the set of theoretically possible goals to the finite set proposed by Bornstein et al. Trade-offs among "pure" states are surely possible.

The exchange between Turner and Bornstein et al illustrates the major point of this section: Careful thought about dependent variables often leads to central conceptual issues.

IMPROVING INTERGROUP RELATIONS

From its very inception, the study of intergroup relations has aimed not only to understand but also to improve intergroup relationships. In this section, we review recent contributions toward this goal. Our first focus is on the role that intergroup contact may play, after which we mention contributions made by other approaches.

Intergroup Contact

The contact hypothesis is the proposal that under the right circumstances, direct interpersonal contact between members of two antagonistic groups will lead to a reduction in the negativity of intergroup attitudes (Allport 1954). While this principle "aspired to the role of dragon slayer" (Stephan 1987:15) early on, it has acquired the qualities of a "bag lady . . . encumbered with excess baggage" (Stephan 1987:17) or of a "laundry list" (Pettigrew 1986:171). This metamorphosis appears to have resulted from the accumulation of facts about the conditions under which intergroup contact does or does not have beneficial consequences, with little parallel development of theory (Hewstone & Brown 1986b). Several authors have recently attempted to redress this imbalance. Indeed, the last few years have witnessed an explosion of theoretical articles about intergroup contact (Brewer & Miller 1984; Hewstone & Brown 1986b; Pettigrew 1986; Rothbart & John 1985; Stephan 1985, 1987; Stephan & Stephan 1985; Wilder 1986a,b; Worchel 1986).

Pettigrew (1986) has noted that the theoretical frailty of the contact hypothesis is common to other social psychological theories. It is logically loose, narrowly cognitive, statically focused on isolated rather than cumulative impacts, and mute about generality. Pettigrew documents these charges by reference to the chapters in Hewstone & Brown's (1986) important volume and, in so doing, he maps fruitful directions for conceptual development.

At a minimum, theoretical development requires the organization of the multitude of variables that are known to influence the effectiveness of intergroup contact. Two independent but similar efforts have recently appeared (Hewstone & Brown 1986b; Stephan 1987). Both of these highlight broader contextual factors, situational details, and the kinds of psychological processes that are evoked. Hewstone & Brown attribute great significance to whether the contact is interpersonal or intergroup, and they further examine the perceptual and attributional consequences of the contact as well as outcome judgments. Both the intergroup-interpersonal distinction and the relatively detailed attention afforded to outcomes underscore the importance of the issue of generalizing from interpersonal contact to changes in intergroup attitudes.

The process of generalizing from interpersonal contacts to intergroup attitudes is a central issue for theory and research. Brewer & Miller (1984) propose that intergroup contact will be maximally successful when the group or category memberships of the participants are as inconspicuous as possible and when the interaction is intimate. Decategorization, according to these authors, is promoted by differentiation among out-group members as well as the personalization of intergroup contact. Miller et al (1985) and Miller & Brewer (1986) summarize research supporting this position. The objective of decategorization would appear to be a society that is devoid of cultural, racial, or other intergroup differences—a colorblind society. A number of theorists have questioned the desirability of this as a societal goal. Schofield (1986) notes that suppressing race as a meaningful topic in a biracial public school in the United States not only obscured real differences between black and white children—so that when classes were organized according to performance level, for instance, the groupings tended to be racially homogeneous—but also created an atmosphere in which it was taboo for children as well as teachers to discuss racial similarities and differences. Berry (1984) and Hewstone & Brown (1986b) note that intergroup homogenization may be not only impossible but also undesirable: impossible because the activation of primitive categories like race or gender may be automatic, and undesirable because of the attendant loss of subcultural differences that enrich the texture of society. These theorists take the position that positive beliefs derived from interpersonal encounters will not generalize to the group level unless the intergroup character of the interaction is made salient (Hewstone & Brown 1986). Suppressing intergroup categorization thus impedes generalization. Rothbart & John (1985) and Wilder (1986b) attack the generalization problem from somewhat different cognitive perspectives. The former view the problem as one of associating new features with a category stereotype. Perhaps because "poor" exemplars of a category are less accessible through the category label—for a prejudiced person, a black scientist is more likely to be stored with the category "scientist" than "black"—they seem to have less impact on judgments about the group. Wilder (1986b) employs information-processing concepts to isolate various ways generalization could fail. Both, however, discuss the paradox that for an impression of a person to generalize to that person's group, the person must be perceived as a "typical" group member, which implies that the person may be encumbered with negative stereotypical connotations that will retard the formation of a positive impression in the first place (Rothbart & Lewis 1988; Wilder 1984a).

As a final illustration of the recent permeation of theory in studies of intergroup contact, we note the chapter by Miller & Davidson-Podgorny (1987). These authors focus on classroom learning situations like Jigsaw (Aronson et al 1978), Learning Together (Johnson & Johnson 1975), and Teams Games Tournament (Edwards et al 1972) that are designed to promote intergroup cooperative learning [see Slavin (1985) for an assessment of these efforts]. The authors tease out implications of three different theoretical positions—expectation states theory (Cohen 1982), the ignorance model (Stephan & Stephan 1984), and the social categorization model developed by Brewer & Miller (1984)—and then compare these implications to the metaanalytic findings of a number of pertinent studies. A major contribution of the chapter is the application of social psychological theory to this area.

Despite the conceptual progress made in the last few years, Pettigrew (1986) warns that we may have created unreasonably high expectations for the good that intergroup contact can achieve. What can be expected of programs to bring Catholic and Protestant children together briefly in Northern Ireland when both denominations insist on separate schools (Trew 1986)? Foster & Finchilescu (1986) argue that the Black-White contact that does occur in South Africa will do little to alter interracial attitudes so long as an explicitly racial status hierarchy, *apartheid,* is the law of the land. Reicher (1986:164) espouses the extreme position that research on interracial contact not only offers no hope but is itself "part of the problem" to the extent that it accepts racial categories, themselves symptoms of racism, as valid. [In a similar vein, Stein (1988) claims that the odious racial views of the Third Reich were simply lifted from contemporary scientific thought and not invented by the

National Socialists.] If intergroup contact per se offers only modest hope of improving intergroup relations, what other alternatives are available?

Other Approaches

INSTITUTIONAL AND LEGISLATIVE CHANGE   In societies that allocate privileges differentially to different groups, be they Whites versus Blacks, Anglophone versus Francophone, Jewish versus Arab, or Protestant versus Catholic, efforts must be made to change the social structure in ways that will promote intergroup harmony. These changes are probably the most important of all since other efforts to promote intergroup peace are unlikely to succeed in societies that condone institutional discrimination. The elimination of societal barriers between groups usually entails the replacement of one set of rules, procedures, and institutions with another set; and it is here that social psychological research can be useful in illuminating the strengths and weaknesses of various alternatives (see, for instance, Gerard & Miller 1975; Brewer & Miller 1984).

CONFLICT RESOLUTION, BARGAINING, AND NEGOTIATION   To the extent that there is a real conflict of interest between two groups, attempts to settle the dispute fairly and efficiently may prevent the disagreement from escalating into intergroup hostility (Pruitt & Rubin 1986). It strikes us as curious that the immense literature on conflict management, a literature large enough to support two scholarly journals—*The Journal of Conflict Resolution* and *The Negotiation Journal*—remains by and large apart from the literature on intergroup relations and vice versa. An inspection of the reference lists of two recently published texts—*Social Conflict* (Pruitt & Rubin 1986) and *Theories of Intergroup Relations* (Taylor & Moghaddam 1987)—reveals little common content, despite the fact that dispute management techniques like those described by Fisher & Ury (1981) or Raiffa (1982) may be thought of as "preventive" intergroup relations when applied to intergroup conflicts (Fisher 1983). Recent books on negotiation and conflict management have been published by Lewicki & Litterer (1985), Lewicki et al (1986), Rangarajan (1985), and Roth (1985). Notable exceptions to this insularity are the volume on intergroup conflict edited by Stroebe et al (1988), particularly the chapter by Morley et al (1988), and Worchel & Austin's edited book (1986).

   Conflict management at the international level may involve efforts to understand the causes, pitfalls, and consequences of foreign policies (Tetlock 1986). Psychologists can contribute to policy formation by studying the psychological consequences of various policy options. Gergen (1974), for example, showed why it was naive to expect countries receiving US foreign aid to feel unadulterated gratitude for the aid. Allison & Messick (1985, 1987) have shown that group decisions, such as are made by governments, are assumed to reflect the views of the citizens, even in situations where citizens are perceived to have little influence on government decisions. Government policies and decisions may therefore become important determinants of people's beliefs about the compatibility of their interests with those of other nations. Bar-Tal & Geva (1986) pinpoint such belief incompatibility as a necessary condition for international conflict.

Our position is that the principles of dispute management and conflict resolution need to be explicitly woven into the fabric of intergroup relations.

CATEGORIZATION   Previous research on intergroup contact has failed to generate great optimism. If the consequences of contact are unreliable, and if it is not feasible or desirable to eliminate intergroup categories as Brewer & Miller (1984) recommend, what options are left? We mention several approaches that derive from the emerging focus on categorization. Wilder's (1986b) excellent review is recommended for more detail.

Changing the out-group stereotype   As mentioned earlier, direct efforts to change beliefs and attitudes toward out-groups, either through direct contact or information campaigns, have been carefully analyzed by Rothbart & John (1985) and Wilder (1986a). Both of these analyses focus on the difficulty of generalizing from a positive interaction with an out-group member to the out-group itself. Rothbart & Park (1986) further argue that the nature of trait adjectives associated with stereotypes may make stereotypes differentially resistant to change. Negative traits in particular are easy to confirm but difficult to disconfirm. Disconfirming evidence may not be available if contact with outgroup members is avoided.

Weakening intergroup boundaries   To the extent that intergroup boundaries are blurred or weakened, intergroup interaction will be more likely to occur in terms of personal characteristics than category labels, and intergroup bias will be reduced. Intergroup boundaries can be weakened in many ways, including, for instance, by cross-cutting category memberships so that an out-group member in one categorization is an in-group member on another (Vanbeselaere 1987), by reducing cues to category membership (Worchel 1979), by disrupting the assumed belief dissimilarity to the out-group (Wilder 1986b), and by highlighting superordinate categories (Kramer 1988). Gaertner (1985; cited in Gaertner & Dovidio 1986a) reports a study in which the seating pattern of A and B group members was varied from segregated (AAAABBBB), through partially integrated (BAAABABBA), to fully integrated (ABABABAB). Members of the more integrated groups experienced their merged groups as a unit, showed less intergroup bias in leader choice, expressed more satisfaction with group membership, and cooperated more than members of segregated groups.

However, even the assimilation of new members into a single group may evoke categorization. Moreland (1985) found that in the initial stages of integration, new members perceived themselves as an in-group and saw the old members as an out-group, with many of the attendant consequences of intergroup categorization.

Diminishing the intensity of ingroup identification Intergroup boundaries are likely to be more salient when one's membership in the in-group serves important personal goals, including the maintenance of positive self-regard (Tajfel & Turner 1986). Thus reducing the instrumental importance of group membership, perhaps by providing alternative routes to goal achievement, may decrease the tendency to perceive and to interact with others in categorical terms. We know of little experimental research on this point.

CONCLUDING COMMENTS

Space constraints prevent us from covering all of the important research that has been conducted in recent years. In these concluding remarks we first note three such domains that deserve attention.

Intergroup theory, and particularly social identity theory, has helped forge a new subdiscipline at the interface of language, communication, and social psychology (for reviews see Clark 1985; Giles & Wiemann 1988; Giles et al 1987). The predominant guiding framework in the area has been speech accommodation theory (SAT), which deals with the cognitive, motivational, and affective processes that underlie speech convergence (adaptation to others' speech) and divergence (accentuation of linguistic differences). Speech divergence, which can be viewed as a symbolic tactic for maintaining intergroup distinctiveness, might be usefully considered as a more subtle measure in studies of in-group bias.

An intergroup perspective has also provided an impetus to theory development in social influence. Moscovici's (1980) treatment of the issue of minority influence as an intergroup problem and Mugny's (1982) application of SIT to minority persuasion attempts injected social influence research with a vigor it has lacked since the 1950s. This work is thoroughly reviewed in Chaiken & Stangor (1987), Levine & Russo (1987), Maass et al (1987), Moscovici & Mugny 1987), and Wolf (1987). Referent identity theory (Turner 1982, 1987), which posits that recognition of group membership is a necessary condition for influence, has had less impact but has been successfully applied to an integrative understanding of group polarization (Mackie 1986; Wetherell 1987) and conformity (Hogg & Turner 1987).

Finally, ideas from intergroup relations have begun to seep into the study of group decision-making, in particular in social dilemma situations (Messick & Brewer 1983). While the typical focus in this research area is on intragroup behavior, Rapoport & Bornstein (1987) and Bornstein & Rapoport (1988) have examined situations in which two groups explicitly compete with regard to the extent of self-sacrificial cooperation their members display. Kramer & Brewer (1984) and Brewer & Kramer (1986) maintained the focus on intragroup behavior and found evidence that subjects displayed more cooperative choices when a superordinate common identity was made salient than when subordinate subcategories were highlighted. Likewise, Kramer (1988) reports that subjects are less defensive when their common category membership (Stanford students) is emphasized than when subordinate categories (Stanford undergraduates and MBA students) are spotlighted. Finally, Dawes (1987) reports very high levels of self-sacrificial cooperation among groups in which (a) discussion of the decision problem is possible and (b) the cooperative benefit goes to members who were randomly chosen to be in the decision-makers' group. If there is no discussion or if the benefits go to the (randomly selected) members of the other group, the level of cooperation drops sharply. These studies, which focus on intragroup cooperation, must eventually be melded with research on intergroup discrimination to provide a complete picture of relations among and within groups.

Our review of research on intergroup relations leaves us impressed with the vigor and creativity of the enterprise. We conclude by offering an idiosyncratic and admittedly incomplete list of research questions that seem especially ripe. Are there primitive categories (race, gender, age) that are always activated automatically, and, if so, what are their consequences? How do attentional and intentional processes interact with the automatic activation of social categories? Must the fact of categorization imply out-group prejudice or bias? Is intergroup bias a defensive reaction to categorized others or an offensive initiative of those categorized? What are the interrelationships among various measures of intergroup discrimination and what is their conceptual significance? How can research on conflict management be fused with intergroup research to promote social harmony? If progress is made on only a few of these questions, the next few years of research on intergroup relations will be as fruitful as the last few have been.

ACKNOWLEDGMENTS

The preparation of this chapter was supported in part by a grant, No.MH43041, from NIMH to Diane M. Mackie. We are grateful to David L. Hamilton for his comments on sections of the chapter, to Terry Boles and Holly Schroth for their help in assembling the references, and to the graduate students in the Intergroup Relations seminar for their summaries, insights, and criticisms.

Literature Cited

Acorn, D. A., Hamilton, D. L., Sherman, S. J. 1988. Generalization of biased perceptions of groups based on illusory correlations. *Soc. Cognit.* In press

Ajzen, I. 1987. Attitudes, traits, and actions: dispositional prediction of behavior in personality and social psychology. *Adv. Exp. Soc. Psychol.* 20:1–63

Allison, S. T., Messick, D. M. 1985. The group attribution error. *J. Exp. Soc. Psychol.* 21:563–79

Allison, S. T., Messick, D. M. 1987. From individual inputs to group outputs and back again: group processes and inferences about members. See Hendrick 1987a, pp. 111–43

Allport, G. W. 1954. *The Nature of Prejudice.* Cambridge, Mass: Addison-Wesley

Andersen, S. M., Klatzky, R. L. 1987. Traits and social stereotypes: levels of categorization in person perception. *J. Pers. Soc. Psychol.* 53:235–46

Arkes, H. R., Rothbart, M. 1985. Memory retrieval and contingency judgments. *J. Pers. Soc. Psychol.* 49:598–606

Aronson, E., Blaney, N., Stephan, C., Sikes, J., Snapp, M. 1978. *The Jigsaw Classroom.* Newbury Park, Calif: Sage

Ashmore, R. D., Del Boca, F. K., Titus, D. 1984. Types of women and men: yours, mine, and ours. Presented at Ann. Meet. Am. Psychol. Assoc., Toronto

Bar-Tal, D., Geva, N. 1986. A cognitive basis of international conflicts. See Worchel & Austin 1986, pp. 118–33

Berry, J. W. 1984. Cultural relations in plural societies: alternatives to segregation and their sociopsychological implications. See Miller & Brewer 1984, pp. 11–27

Billig, M. 1985. Prejudice, categorization and particularization: from a perceptual to a rhetorical approach. *Eur. J. Soc. Psychol.* 15:79–103

Bodenhausen, G. V. 1988. Effects of social stereotypes on evidence processing: the cognitive basis of discrimination in juridic decision making. *J. Pers. Soc. Psychol.* In press

Bodenhausen, G. V., Lichtenstein, M. 1987. Social stereotypes and information processing strategies: the impact of task complexity. *J. Pers. Soc. Psychol.* 52:871–80

Bodenhausen, G. V., Wyer, R. S. Jr. 1985. Effects of stereotypes on decision making and information processing strategies. *J. Pers. Soc. Psychol.* 48:267–82

Bond, M. H., Hewstone, M., Wan, K.-C., Chiu, C.-K. 1985. Group-serving attributions across intergroup contexts: cultural differences in the explanation of sex-type behaviors. *Eur. J. Soc. Psychol.* 15:435–51

Bornstein, G., Crum, L., Wittenbraker, J., Harring, K., Insko, C. A. 1983a. On measurement of social orientations in the minimal group paradigm. *Eur. J. Soc. Psychol.* 13:321–50

Bornstein, G., Crum, L., Wittenbraker, J., Harring, K., Insko, C. A. 1983b. Reply to Turner's comments. *Eur. J. Soc. Psychol.* 13:369–82

Bornstein, G., Rapoport, A. 1988. Intergroup competition for the provision of step-level public goods: effects of preplay communication. *Eur. J. Soc. Psychol.* In press

Bourhis, R. Y., Sachdev, I. 1986. *The Tajfel Matrices as an Instrument for Conducting Intergroup Research.* Hamilton, Ontario: McMaster Univ. Mimeo

Bower, G. H., Karlin, M. B. 1974. Depth of processing pictures of faces and recognition memory. *J. Exp. Psychol.* 103:751–57

Brewer, M. B. 1979. In-group bias in the minimal intergroup situation: a cognitive-motivational analysis. *Psychol. Bull.* 86:307–24

Brewer, M. B. 1988. A dual process model of impression formation. *Adv. Soc. Cognit.* 1:1–36

Brewer, M. B., Kramer, R. M. 1985. The psychology of intergroup attitudes and behavior. *Ann. Rev. Psychol.* 36:219–43

Brewer, M. B., Kramer, R. M. 1986. Choice behavior in social dilemmas: effects of social identity, group size, and decision framing. *J. Pers. Soc. Psychol.* 50:543–49

Brewer, M. B., Miller, N. 1984. Beyond the contact hypothesis: theoretical perspectives on desegregation. See Miller & Brewer 1984, pp. 281–302

Brewer, M. B., Silver, M. 1978. Ingroup bias as a function of task characteristics. *Eur. J. Soc. Psychol.* 8:393–400

Brewer, M. B., Dull, V., Lui, L. 1981. Perceptions of the elderly: stereotypes as prototypes. *J. Pers. Soc. Psychol.* 41:656–70

Brown, R. J. 1954. Mass phenomena. In *Handbook of Social Psychology*, ed. G. Lindzey, 2:833–76. Cambridge, Mass: Addison-Wesley

Brown, R. J., Turner, J. C. 1979. The crisscross categorization effect in intergroup discrimination. *Brit. J. Soc. Clin. Psychol.* 18:371–83

Brown, R. J., Wade, G. 1987. Superordinate goals and intergroup behavior: the effect of role ambiguity and status on intergroup attitudes and task performance. *Eur. J. Soc. Psychol.* 17:131–42

Brown, R. J., Condor, S., Mathews, A., Wade, G., Williams, J. 1986. Explaining intergroup differentiation in an industrial organization. *J. Occup. Psychol.* 59:273–86

Brown, V., Geis, F. L. 1984. Turning lead into gold: evaluations of men and women leaders and the alchemy of social consensus. *J. Pers. Soc. Psychol.* 46:811–24

Bruner, J. S. 1957a. Going beyond the information given. In *Contemporary Approaches to Cognition*, ed. H. Gruber, G. Terrell, M. Wertheimer, pp. 41–74. Cambridge, Mass: Harvard Univ. Press

Bruner, J. S. 1957b. On perceptual readiness. *Psychol. Rev.* 64:123–52

Carpenter, S. L., Ostrom, T. M. 1985. *The perception of outgroup homogeneity: differential information organization.* Presented at Midwest Psychol. Assoc., Chicago

Chaiken, S., Stangor, S. 1987. Attitudes and attitude change. *Ann. Rev. Psychol.* 38:575–630

Clark, H. H. 1985. Language use and language users. See Lindzey & Aronson 1985, 1:179–231

Cohen, E. G. 1982. Expectation states and interracial interaction in school settings. *Ann. Rev. Sociol.* 8:209–35

Crocker, J., Park, B. 1988. The consequences of social stereotypes. In *The Buffalo Symposium on Decision Making and Information Processing*, ed. R. Cardy, J. M. Newman, S. Puffer. In press

Dawes, R. M. 1987. *Not me or thee but we.* Paper presented at 11th SPUDM Conf., Cambridge, England

Deaux, K., Kite, M. E. 1988. Gender and cognition. In *Woman and Society: Social Science Research Perspectives*, ed. B. B. Hess, M. M. Ferree. Beverly Hills, Calif: Sage. In press

Deaux, K., Lewis, L. L. 1983. Components of gender stereotypes. *Psychol. Doc.* 13:25–34

Deaux, K., Lewis, L. L. 1984. The structure of gender stereotypes: interrelationships among components and gender label. *J. Pers. Soc. Psychol.* 46:991–1004

Deaux, K., Major, B. 1987. Putting gender into context: an interactive model of gender-related behavior. *Psychol. Rev.* 94:369–89

Deaux, K., Kite, M. E., Lewis, L. L. 1985a. Clustering and gender schemata: an uncertain link. *Pers. Soc. Psychol. Bull.* 11:387–98

Deaux, K., Winton, W., Crowley, M., Lewis, L. L. 1985b. Level of categorization and content of gender stereotypes. *Soc. Cognit.* 3:145–67

Deschamps, J.-C., Doise, W. 1978. Crossed category memberships in intergroup relations. In *Differentiation Between Social Groups*, ed. H. Tajfel. London: Academic

Devine, P. G. 1986. *Automatic and controlled processes in stereotyping and prejudice.* PhD thesis. Ohio State Univ.

Dijker, A. G. M. 1987. Emotional reactions to ethnic minorities. *Eur. J. Soc. Psychol.* 17:305–26

Doise, W. 1978. *Groups and Individuals: Explanations in Social Psychology.* Cambridge: Cambridge Univ. Press

Dovidio, J. F., Gaertner, S. L., eds. 1986. *Prejudice, Discrimination, Racism: Theory and Research.* New York: Academic. 337 pp.

Dovidio, J. F., Evans, N., Tyler, R. B. 1986. Racial stereotypes: the contents of their cognitive representation. *J. Exp. Soc. Psychol.* 22:22–37

Eagly, A. H., Kite, M. E. 1987. Are stereotypes of nationalities applied to both women and men? *J. Pers. Soc. Psychol.* 53:451–62

Eagly, A. H., Steffen, V. 1984. Gender stereotypes stem from the distribution of women and men into social roles. *J. Pers. Soc. Psychol.* 46:735–54

Edwards, K. J., DeVries, D. L., Snyder, J. P. 1972. Games and teams: a winning combination. *Simulation and Games* 3:247–69

Eiser, J. T., Stroebe, W. 1972. *Categorization and Social Judgment.* London: Academic

Elio, R., Anderson, J. R. 1981. Effects of category generalizations and instance similarity on schema abstraction. *J. Exp. Psychol. Hum. Learn. Mem.* 7:397–417

Erber, R. 1985. *Choosing among multiple categories: the effects of moods on category accessibility, inference, and interpersonal affect.* PhD thesis. Carnegie-Mellon Univ.

Espinoza, J. A., Garza, R. T. 1985. Social group salience and interethnic cooperation. *J. Exp. Soc. Psychol.* 21:380–92

Estes, W. K. 1986. Array models for category learning. *Cogn. Psychol.* 18:500–49

Fazio, R. H., Sanbonmatsu, D. M., Powell, M. C., Kardes, F. R. 1986. On the automatic activation of attitudes. *J. Pers. Soc. Psychol.* 50:229–38

Finchilescu, G. 1986. Effect of incompatibility between internal and external group membership criteria on intergroup behavior. *Eur. J. Soc. Psychol.* 16:83–87

Fisher, R. J. 1983. Third party consultation as a method of intergroup conflict resolution. *J. Conflict Resolut.* 27:301–34

Fisher, R., Ury, W. 1981. *Getting to Yes: Negotiating Agreement Without Giving In.* Boston: Houghton Mifflin

Fiske, S. T. 1988. Brewer's dual process model and Fiske et al's continuum model. *Adv. Soc. Cogn.* 1:65–76

Fiske, S. T., Neuberg, S. L. 1988. A continuum model of impression formation: from category-based to individuating processes as a function of information, motivation, and attention. *Adv. Exp. Soc. Psychol.* 23:1–108

Fiske, S. T., Pavelchak, M. A. 1986. Category-based versus piecemeal-based affective responses: developments in schema-triggered affect. See Sorrentino & Higgins 1986, pp. 167–203

Fiske, S. T., Neuberg, S. L., Beattie, A. E., Milberg, S. J. 1987. Category-based and attribute-based reactions to others: some informational conditions of stereotyping and individuating processes. *J. Exp. Soc. Psychol.* 23:399–427

Flannagan, M. J., Fried, L. S., Holyoak, K. J. 1986. Distributional expectations and the induction of category structure. *J. Exp. Psychol. Learn. Mem. Cogn.* 12:241–56

Forgas, J. P., Bower, G. H. 1987. Mood effects on person-perception judgments. *J. Pers. Soc. Psychol.* 53:53–60

Foster, D., Finchilescu, G. 1986. Contact in a 'non-contact' society: the case of South Africa. See Hewstone & Brown 1986a, pp. 119–36

Frank, M. G., Gilovich, T. 1988. The dark side of self- and social perception: black uniforms and aggression in professional sports. *J. Pers. Soc. Psychol.* 54:74–85

Freund, T., Kruglanski, A. W., Schpitzajzen, A. 1985. The freezing and unfreezing of impression primacy: effects of the need for structure and the fear of invalidity. *Pers. Soc. Psychol. Bull.* 11:479–87

Frey, D., Gaertner, S. L. 1986. Helping and the avoidance of inappropriate interracial behavior: a strategy that can perpetuate a non-prejudice self-image. *J. Pers. Soc. Psychol.* 50:1083–90

Fried, L. S., Holyoak, K. J. 1984. Induction of category distributions: a framework for classification learning. *J. Exp. Psychol. Learn. Mem. Cogn.* 10:234–57

Futoran, G. C., Wyer, R. S. Jr. 1986. The effects of traits and gender stereotypes on occupational suitability judgments and the recall of judgment relevant information. *J. Exp. Soc. Psychol.* 22:475–503

Gaertner, S. L., Dovidio, J. F. 1986a. Prejudice, discrimination, and racism: problems, progress, and promise. See Dovidio & Gaertner 1986, pp. 315–32

Gaertner, S. L., Dovidio, J. F. 1986b. The aversive form of racism. See Dovidio & Gaertner 1986, pp. 61–89

Gaertner, S. L., McLaughlin, J. P. 1983. Racial stereotypes: associations and ascriptions of positive and negative characteristics. *Soc. Psychol. Q.* 46:23–30

Gerard, H., Miller, N. 1975. *School Desegregation.* New York: Plenum

Gergen, K. J. 1974. Toward a psychology of receiving help. *J. Appl. Soc. Psychol.* 4:187–93

Giles, H., Wiemann, J. 1988. Language, social comparison, and power. In *Handbook of Communication,* ed. C. R. Berger, S. Chaffee, pp. 350–84. Newbury Park: Sage

Giles, H., Mulac, A., Bradac, J. J., Johnson, P. 1987. Speech accommodation theory: the first decade and beyond. In *Communication Yearbook,* ed. M. L. McLaughlin, 10:13–48. Beverly Hills: Sage

Hamil, R., Wilson, T. D., Nisbett, R. E. 1980. Insensitivity to sample bias: generalizing from atypical cases. *J. Pers. Soc. Psychol.* 39:578–89

Hamilton, D. L., ed. 1981. *Cognitive Processes in Stereotyping and Intergroup Behavior.* Hillsdale, NJ: Erlbaum

Hamilton, D. L., Sherman, S. J. 1988. Illusory correlations: implications for stereotype theory and research. In *Stereotypes and Prejudice: Changing Conceptions,* ed. D. Bar-Tal, C. F. Graumann, A. W. Kruglanski, W. Stroebe. New York: Springer-Verlag. In press

Hamilton, D. L., Trolier, T. K. 1986. Stereotypes and stereotyping: an overview of the cognitive approach. See Dovidio & Gaertner 1986, pp. 127–63

Hamilton, D. L., Dugan, P. M., Trolier, T. K. 1985. The formation of stereotypic beliefs: further evidence for distinctiveness-based illusory correlation. *J. Pers. Soc. Psychol.* 48:5–17

Hampson, S. E. 1983. Trait ascription and depth of acquaintance: the preference for traits in personality descriptions and its relation to target familiarity. *J. Res. Pers.* 17:398–411

Hampson, S. E., John, O. P., Goldberg, L. R. 1986. Category breadth and hierarchical structure in personality: studies of asymmetries in judgments of trait implications. *J. Pers. Soc. Psychol.* 51:37–54

Hastie, R. 1980. Memory for behavioral information that confirms or contradicts a personality impression. In *Person Memory: The Cognitive Basis of Social Interaction,* ed. R. Hastie, T. Ostrom, E. Ebbesen, R. Wyer, D. Hamilton, D. Carlston, pp. 155–77. Hillsdale, NJ: Erlbaum

Hayes-Roth, B., Hayes-Roth, F. 1977. Concept learning and the recognition and classification of exemplars. *J. Verb. Learn. Verb. Behav.* 16:321–38

Heilman, M. E. 1984. Information as a deterrent against sex discrimination: the effects of applicant sex and information type on preliminary employment decisions. *Org. Behav. Hum. Perform.* 33:174–86

Hendrick, C., ed. 1987a. *Review of Personality and Social Psychology,* Vol. 8. Newbury Park: Sage. 294 pp.

Hendrick, C., ed. 1987b. *Review of Personality and Social Psychology,* Vol. 9. Newbury Park: Sage. 256 pp.

Herringer, L. G., Garza, R. T. 1987. Perceptual accentuation in minimal groups. *Eur. J. Soc. Psychol.* 17:347–52

Hewstone, M., Brown, R., eds. 1986a. *Con-

tact and Conflict in Intergroup Encounters. Oxford/New York: Basil Blackwell. 231 pp.

Hewstone, M., Brown, R. 1986b. Contact is not enough: an intergroup perspective on the 'contact hypothesis'. See Hewstone & Brown 1986a, pp. 1–44

Higgins, E. T., Bargh, J. A., Lombardi, W. 1985. Nature of priming effects on categorization. *J. Exp. Psychol. Learn. Mem. Cogn.* 11:59–69

Hinkle, S., Schopler, J. 1986. Bias in the evaluation of in-group and out-group performance. See Worchel & Austin 1986, pp. 196–212

Hinsz, V. B., Tindale, R. S., Nagao, D. H., Davis, J. H., Robertson, B. A. 1988. The influence of the accuracy of individuating information on the use of baserate information in probability judgment. *J. Pers. Soc. Psychol.* 24:127–45

Hintzman, D. L. 1986. "Schema abstraction" in a multiple-trace memory model. *Psychol. Rev.* 93:411–28

Hoffman, M. L. 1986. Affect, cognition, motivation. See Sorrentino & Higgins 1986, pp. 244–80

Hogg, M. A., Turner, J. C. 1987. Social identity and conformity: a theory of referent informational influence. In *Current Issues in European Social Psychology,* ed. W. Doise, S. Moscovici, Vol. 2:110–41 Cambridge: Cambridge Univ. Press

Hymes, R. W. 1986. Political attitudes as social categories: a new look at selective memory. *J. Pers. Soc. Psychol.* 51:233–41

Insko, C. A., Schopler, J. 1987. Categorization, competition, and collectivity. See Hendrick 1987a, pp. 213–51

Insko, C. A., Hoyle, R. H., Pinkley, R. L., Hong, G., Slim, R. M. 1988. Individual-group discontinuity: the role of a consensus rule. *J. Exp. Soc. Psychol.* In press

Insko, C. A., Pinkley, R. L., Hoyle, R. H., Dalton, B., Hong, G. 1987. Individual versus group discontinuity: the role of intergroup contact. *J. Exp. Soc. Psychol.* 23:250–67

Isen, A. M., Daubman, K. A. 1984. The influence of affect on categorization. *J. Pers. Soc. Psychol.* 47:1206–17

Jackson, L. A., Cash, T. F. 1985. Components of gender stereotypes: their implications for inferences on stereotypic and nonstereotypic dimensions. *Pers. Soc. Psychol. Bull.* 11:326–44

Jackson, L. A., Sullivan, L. A. 1987. *Cognition and affect in evaluations of stereotyped group members.* Presented at Soc. Exp. Soc. Psychol., Charlottesville, Va.

Jackson, L. A., MacCoun, R. J., Kerr, N. L. 1987. Stereotypes and nonstereotypic

judgments: the effects of gender role attitudes on ratings of likability, adjustment, and occupational potential. *Pers. Soc. Psychol. Bull.* 13:45–52

Johnson, D. W., Johnson, R. 1975. *Learning Together and Alone: Cooperation, Competition and Individualization.* Englewood Cliffs, NJ: Prentice-Hall

Jones, E. E., Wood, G. C., Quattrone, G. A. 1981. Perceived variability of person characteristics in in-groups and out-groups: the role of knowledge and evaluation. *Pers. Soc. Psychol. Bull.* 7:523–28

Judd, C. M., Lusk, C. M. 1984. Knowledge structures and evaluative judgments. *J. Pers. Soc. Psychol.* 46:1193–1207

Judd, C. M., Park, B. 1988. Outgroup homogeneity: judgments of variability at the individual and group levels. *J. Pers. Soc. Psychol.* 54:778–88

Katz, D., Braly, K. W. 1933. Racial stereotypes of one hundred college students. *J. Abnorm. Psychol.* 28:280–90

Katz, I., Wackenhut, J., Hass, R. G. 1986. Racial ambivalence, value duality, and behavior. See Dovidio & Gaertner 1986, pp. 35–60

Kim, H.-S., Baron, R. S. 1988. Exercise and the illusory correlation: does arousal heighten stereotypic processing? *J. Exp. Soc. Psychol.* 24:366–80

Kinder, D. R. 1986. The continuing American dilemma: white resistance to racial change 40 years after Myrdal. *J. Soc. Issues* 42:151–71

Klayman, J., Ha, V. W. 1987. Confirmation, disconfirmation, and information in hypothesis testing. *Psychol. Rev.* 94:211–28

Kramer, R. M. 1988. Windows of vulnerability or cognitive illusions? Cognitive processes and the nuclear arms race. *J. Exp. Soc. Psychol.* In press

Kramer, R. M., Brewer, M. B. 1984. Effects of group identity on resource use in a simulated commons dilemma. *J. Pers. Soc. Psychol.* 46:1044–57

Krueger, J., Rothbart, M. 1988. The use of categorical and individuating information in making inferences about personality. *J. Pers. Soc. Psychol.* In press

Kruglanski, A. W., Freund, T. 1983. The freezing and unfreezing of lay-inferences: effects of impressional primacy, ethnic stereotyping, and numerical anchoring. *J. Exp. Soc. Psychol.* 19:448–68

Langer, E. J., Bashner, R. S., Chanowitz, B. 1985. Decreasing prejudice by increasing discrimination. *J. Pers. Soc. Psychol.* 49:113–20

LaPiere, R. T. 1934. Attitudes versus actions. *Soc. Forces* 13:230–37

Larwood, L., Gutek, B., Gattiker, U. E. 1984. Perspectives on institutional discrimination and resistance to change. *Group Organ. Stud.* 9:333–52

Lemyre, L., Smith, P. M. 1985. Intergroup discrimination and self-esteem in the minimal group paradigm. *J. Pers. Soc. Psychol.* 49:660–70

Leventhal, G. S. 1976. Fairness in social relationships. In *Contemporary Social Psychology*, ed. J. Thibaut, J. Spence, R. Carson, pp. 209–39. Morristown NJ: General Learning Press

Levine, J. M., Russo, E. M. 1987. Majority and minority influence. See Hendrick 1987a, pp. 13–54

Lewicki, R. J., Litterer, J. A. 1985. *Negotiation.* Homewood, Ill: Richard D. Irwin, Inc.

Lewicki, R. J., Sheppard, B. H., Bazerman, M. H. 1986. *Research in Negotiation in Organizations*, Vol. 1. Greenwich, Conn: JAI Press

Lindzey, G., Aronson, E., eds. 1985. *Handbook of Social Psychology*, Vols. 1, 2. New York: Random House

Lingle, J. H., Altom, M. W., Medin, D. L. 1984. Of cabbages and kings: assessing the extendibility of natural object concept models to social things. In *Handbook of Social Cognition*, ed. R. Wyer, T. Srull, 1:71–117. Hillsdale, NJ: Erlbaum

Linville, P. W. 1982. Self-complexity as a cognitive buffer against stress-related illness and depression. *J. Pers. Soc. Psychol.* 52:663–76

Linville, P. W., Jones, E. E. 1980. Polarized appraisals of out-group members. *J. Pers. Soc. Psychol.* 38:689–703

Linville, P. W., Fischer, G. W., Salovey, P. 1988. Perceived distributions of the characteristics of ingroup and outgroup members. *J. Pers. Soc. Psychol.* In press

Linville, P. W., Salovey, P., Fischer, G. W. 1986. Stereotyping and perceived distributions of social characteristics: an application to ingroup-outgroup perception. See Dovidio & Gaertner 1986, pp. 165–208

Locksley, A., Hepburn, C., Ortiz, V. 1982. On the effect of social stereotypes on judgments of individuals: a comment on Grant and Holmes's "The integration of implicit personality theory, schemas and stereotypic images". *Soc. Psychol. Q.* 45:270–73

Lord, C. G., Lepper, M. R., Mackie, D. 1984. Attitude prototypes as determinants of attitude-behavior consistency. *J. Pers. Soc. Psychol.* 46:1254–66

Lurie, S. 1987. A parametric model of utility for two-person distributions. *Psychol. Rev.* 94:42–60

Lynn, M., Shavitt, S., Ostrom, T. 1985. Effects of pictures on the organization and recall of social information. *J. Pers. Soc. Psychol.* 49:1160–68

Maass, A., West, S. G., Cialdini, R. B. 1987.

Minority influence and conversion. See Hendrick 1987a, pp. 55–79

MacCrimmon, K. R., Messick, D. M. 1976. A framework for social motives. *Behav. Sci.* 21:86–100

Mackie, D. 1986. Social identification effects in group polarization. *J. Pers. Soc. Psychol.* 50:720–28

Mackie, D. M., Allison, S. T. 1987. Group attribution errors and the illusion of group attitude change. *J. Exp. Soc. Psychol.* 23:460–80

Martin, C. L. 1987. A ratio measure of sex stereotyping. *J. Pers. Soc. Psychol.* 52:489–99

McCallum, D. M., Harring, K., Gilmore, R., Drenan, S., Chase, J. P. 1985. Competition and co-operation between groups and individuals. *J. Exp. Soc. Psychol.* 21:301–20

McCann, C. D., Ostrom, T. M., Tyner, L. K., Mitchell, M. L. 1985. Person perception in heterogeneous groups. *J. Pers. Soc. Psychol.* 49:1449–59

McConahay, J. B. 1986. Modern racism, ambivalence, and the modern racism scale. See Dovidio & Gaertner 1986, pp. 91–126

McGuire, W. J., McGuire, C. V., Child, P., Fujioka, T. 1978. Salience of ethnicity in the spontaneous self-concept as a function of one's ethnic distinctiveness in the social environment. *J. Pers. Soc. Psychol.* 36:511–20

Medin, D. L., Schaffer, M. M. 1978. Context theory of classification learning. *Psychol. Rev.* 85:207–38

Medin, D. L., Altom, M. W., Murphy, T. D. 1984. Given versus induced category representations: use of prototype and exemplar information in classification. *J. Exp. Psychol. Learn. Mem. Cogn.* 10:333–52

Messick, D. M., Brewer, M. B. 1983. Solving social dilemmas: a review. In *Review of Personality and Social Psychology*, ed. L. Wheeler, P. Shaver, 4:11–44. Beverly Hills: Sage

Messick, D. M., Sentis, K. P. 1985. Estimating social and nonsocial utility functions from ordinal data. *Eur. J. Soc. Psychol.* 15:389–99

Miller, C. T. 1986. Categorization and stereotypes about men and women. *Pers. Soc. Psychol. Bull.* 12:502–12

Miller, D. T., Turnbull, W. 1986. Expectancies and interpersonal processes. *Ann. Rev. Psychol.* 37:233–56

Miller, N., Brewer, M. B., eds. 1984. *Groups in Contact: The Psychology of Desegregation.* New York: Academic. 316 pp.

Miller, N., Brewer, M. B. 1986. Categorization effects on ingroup and outgroup perception. See Dovidio & Gaertner 1986, pp. 209–30

Miller, N., Davidson-Podgorny, G. 1987.

Theoretical models of intergroup relations and the use of cooperative teams as an intervention for desegregated settings. See Hendrick 1987b, pp. 41–67

Miller, N., Brewer, M. B., Edwards, K. 1985. Cooperative interaction in desegregated settings: a laboratory analogue. *J. Soc. Issues* 41(3):63–81

Moghaddam, F. M., Stringer, P. 1986. "Trivial" and "important" criteria for social categorization in the minimal group paradigm. *J. Soc. Psychol.* 126:345–54

Moreland, R. 1985. Social categorization and the assimilation of "new" group members. *J. Pers. Soc. Psychol.* 48:1173–90

Morley, I. E., Webb, J., Stephenson, G. M. 1988. The resolution of conflict. See Stroebe et al 1988, pp. 117–34

Moscovici, S. 1980. Toward a theory of conversion behavior. *Adv. Exp. Soc. Psychol.* 13:209–39

Moscovici, S., Mugny, G., eds. 1987. *Psychologie de la Conversion.* Delval: Cousset

Mugny, G. 1982. *The Power of Minorities.* London: Academic

Mullen, B., Hu, L.-T. 1989. Perceptions of ingroup and outgroup variability: a meta-analytic integration. In *Basic and Applied Social Psychology.* In press

Neely, J. H. 1977. Semantic priming and retrieval from lexical memory: roles of memory, inhibitionless spreading activation and limited-capacity attention. *J. Exp. Psychol.* 106:226–54

Nesdale, A. R., Dharmalingam, S. 1986. Category salience, stereotyping and person memory. *Aust. J. Psychol.* 38:145–51

Nesdale, A. R., Dharmalingam, S., Kerr, G. K. 1987. Effect of subgroup ratio on stereotyping. *Eur. J. Soc. Psychol.* 17:353–56

Neuberg, S. L., Fiske, S. T. 1987. Motivational influences on impression formation: outcome dependency, accuracy driven attention, and individuating processes. *J. Pers. Soc. Psychol.* 53:431–44

Ng, S. H. 1985. Biases in reward allocation resulting from personal status, group status, and allocation procedure. *Aust. J. Psychol.* 37:297–307

Ng, S. H. 1986. Equity, intergroup bias and interpersonal bias in reward allocation. *Eur. J. Soc. Psychol.* 16:239–55

Nisbett, R. E., Krants, D. H., Jepson, C., Kunda, Z. 1983. The use of statistical heuristics in everyday intuitive reasoning. *Psychol. Rev.* 90:339–63

Noseworthy, C. M., Lott, A. J. 1984. The cognitive organization of gender-stereotypic categories. *Pers. Soc. Psychol. Bull.* 10:474–81

Oakes, P. J. 1987. The salience of social categories. See Turner 1987, pp. 117–41

Oakes, P. J., Turner, J. C. 1980. Social categorization and intergroup behaviour: does minimal intergroup discrimination make social identity more positive? *Eur. J. Soc. Psychol.* 10:295–301

Oakes, P. J., Turner, J. C. 1986. Distinctiveness and the salience of social category memberships: is there an automatic perceptual bias towards novelty. *Eur. J. Soc. Psychol.* 16:325–44

Omoto, A. M., Borgida, E. 1988. Guess who might be coming to dinner? Personal involvement and racial stereotypes. *J. Exp. Soc. Psychol.* In press

Park, B., Hastie, R. 1987. Perception of variability in category development: instance-versus abstraction-based stereotypes. *J. Pers. Soc. Psychol.* 53:621-35

Park, B., Rothbart, M. 1982. Perception of out-group homogeneity and levels of social categorization: memory for the subordinate attributes of in-group and out-group members. *J. Pers. Soc. Psychol.* 42:1051–68

Pettigrew, T. F. 1986. The intergroup contact hypothesis reconsidered. See Hewstone & Brown 1986a, pp. 169–95

Posner, M. I., Keele, S. W. 1968. On the genesis of abstract ideas. *J. Exp. Psychol.* 77:353–63

Pruitt, D. G., Rubin, J. Z. 1986. *Social Conflict: Escalation, Stalemate, and Settlement.* New York: Random House. 213 pp.

Pryor, J. B. 1986. The influence of different encoding sets upon the formation of illusory correlations and group impressions. *Pers. Soc. Psychol. Bull.* 12:216–26

Pryor, J. B., Ostrom, T. M. 1981. The cognitive organization of social information: a converging operations approach. *J. Pers. Soc. Psychol.* 41:628–41

Pryor, J. B., Kott, T. L., Bovee, G. R. 1984. The influence of information redundancy upon the use of traits and persons as organizing categories. *J. Exp. Soc. Psychol.* 20:246–62

Pryor, J. B., Simpson, D. D., Mitchell, M., Ostrom, T. M., Lydon, J. 1982. Structural selectivity in the retrieval of social information. *Soc. Cognit.* 1:336–57

Quattrone, G. A. 1986. On the perception of a group's variability. See Worchel & Austin 1986, pp. 25–48

Quattrone, G. A., Jones, E. E. 1980. The perception of variability within ingroups and outgroups: implications for the law of small numbers. *J. Pers. Soc. Psychol.* 38:141–52

Raiffa, H. 1982. *The Art and Science of Negotiation.* Cambridge Mass: Harvard Univ. Press

Rangarajan, L. M. 1985. *The Limitation of Conflict: A Theory of Bargaining and Negotiation.* New York: St. Martin's Press

Rapoport, A., Bornstein, G. 1987. Intergroup competition for the provision of binary public goods. *Psychol. Rev.* 94:291–99

Rasinki, K. A., Crocker, J., Hastie, R. 1985. Another look at sex stereotypes and social judgments: an analysis of the social perceiver's use of subjective probabilities. *J. Pers. Soc. Psychol.* 49:317–26

Reed, S. K. 1972. Pattern recognition and categorization. *Cognit. Psychol.* 3:382–407

Regan, D. T., Crawley, D. M. 1984. *Illusory correlation and stereotype formation: Replication and extension.* Presented at Ann. Meet. Am. Psychol. Assoc., Toronto, Canada

Rehm, J., Steinleitner, J., Lilli, W. 1987. Wearing uniforms and aggression: a field experiment. *Eur. J. Soc. Psychol.* 17:357–60

Reicher, S. 1986. Contact, action and racialization: some British evidence. See Hewstone & Brown 1986a, pp. 152–68

Rodin, M. J. 1987. Who is memorable to whom: a study of cognitive disregard. *Soc. Cognit.* 5:144–65

Rosch, E. 1978. Principles of categorization. In *Cognition and Categorization*, ed. E. Rosch, B. B. Lloyd, pp. 27-48. Hillsdale, NJ: Erlbaum

Rosenbaum, M. E., Holtz, R. 1985. *The minimal intergroup discrimination effect: out-group derogation, not in-group favorability.* Presented at Ann. Meet. Am. Psychol. Assoc., Los Angeles

Roth, A. E. 1985. *Game Theoretic Models of Bargaining.* New York: Cambridge Univ. Press

Rothbart, M. 1988. Categorization and impression formation: capturing the mind's flexibility. *Adv. Soc. Cognit.* 1:139–44

Rothbart, M., John, O. P. 1985. Social categorization and behavioral episodes: a cognitive analysis of the effects of intergroup contact. *J. Soc. Issues* 41:81–104

Rothbart, M., Lewis, S. Inferring category attributes from exemplar attributes: geometric shapes and social categories. *J. Pers. Soc. Psychol.* In press

Rothbart, M., Park, B. 1986. On the confirmability and disconfirmability of trait concepts. *J. Pers. Soc. Psychol.* 50:131–42

Rothbart, M., Dawes, R. M., Park, B. 1984. Stereotyping and sampling biases in intergroup perception. In *Attitudinal Judgment*, ed. J. R. Eiser, pp. 109–33. New York: Springer-Verlag

Rothbart, M., Fulero, S., Jensen, C., Howard, J., Birrell, B. 1978. From individual to group impressions: availability heuristics in stereotype formation. *J. Exp. Soc. Psychol.* 14:237–55

Sachdev, I., Bourhis, R. Y. 1985. Social categorization and power differentials in group relations. *Eur. J. Soc. Psychol.* 15:415–34

Sachdev, I., Bourhis, R. Y. 1987. Status differentials and intergroup behavior. *Eur. J. Soc. Psychol.* 17:277–93

Sagar, H. A., Schofield, J. W. 1980. Racial behavioral cues in black and white children's perceptions of ambiguously aggressive acts. *J. Pers. Soc. Psychol.* 39:590–98

Sanbonmatsu, D. M., Sherman, S. J., Hamilton, D. L. 1987. Illusory correlation in the perception of individual and groups. *Soc. Cognit.* 5:1–25

Schofield, J. W. 1986. Causes and consequences of the colorblind perspective. See Dovidio & Gaertner 1986, pp. 231–53

Schwarz, N., Clore, G. L. 1988. How do I feel about it? The information function of affective state. In *Affect, Cognition, and Social Behavior*, ed. K. Fiedler, J. Forgas. Toronto: Hogrefe International, pp. 44–62

Sears, D. O. 1983. The person-positivity bias. *J. Pers. Soc. Psychol.* 44:233–50

Sedikides, C., Ostrom, T. M. 1986. *Status and ingroup/outgroup membership as determinants of person organization.* Presented at Ann. Meet. Midwest Psychol. Assoc., Chicago

Sedikides, C., Ostrom, T. M. 1987. *Familiarity as a mediator of the outgroup homogeneity effect.* Presented at Ann. Meet. Midwest Psychol. Assoc., Chicago

Sherif, M. 1967. *Group Conflict and Cooperation.* London: Routledge & Kegan Paul

Simon, B., Brown, R. 1987. Perceived homogeneity in minority-majority contexts. *J. Pers. Soc. Psychol.* 53:703–11

Slavin, R. E. 1985. Cooperative learning: applying contact theory in desegregated schools. *J. Soc. Issues* 41(3):45–62

Smith, E. E., Medin, D. L. 1981. *Categories and Concepts.* Cambridge, Mass: Harvard Univ. Press

Smith, E. R., Zarate, M. 1988. Exemplar-based models of social categorization. *J. Exp. Soc. Psychol.* In press

Smith, P. 1985. *Language, the Sexes and Society.* Oxford: Basil Blackwell

Sorrentino, R. M., Higgins, E. T., eds. 1986. *The Handbook of Motivation and Cognition: Foundations of Social Behavior.* New York: Guilford Press

Srull, T. K. 1981. Person memory: some tests of associative storage and retrieval models. *J. Exp. Psychol.: Hum. Learn. Cogn.* 9:550–59

Srull, T. K., Lichtenstein, M., Rothbart, M. 1985. Associative storage and retrieval processes in person memory. *J. Exp. Psychol.: Learn. Mem. Cogn.* 11:316–45

Stein, G. J. 1988. Biological science and the roots of Nazism. *Am. Sci.* 76:50–58

Stephan, W. G. 1985. Intergroup relations. See Lindzey & Aronson 1985, 2:599–658

Stephan, W. G. 1987. The contact hypothesis in intergroup relations. See Hendrick 1987b, pp. 13–40

Stephan, W. G., Stephan, C. W. 1984. The role of ignorance in intergroup relations. See Miller & Brewer 1984, pp. 229–55

Stephan, W. G., Stephan, C. W. 1985. Intergroup anxiety. J. Soc. Issues 41:157–75

Stern, L. D., Marrs, S., Millar, M. G., Cole, E. 1984. Processing time and the recall of inconsistent and consistent behaviors of individuals and groups. J. Pers. Soc. Psychol. 47:253–62

Stewart, M. S., Ryan, E. B., Giles, H. 1985. Accent and social class effects on status and solidarity evaluations. Pers. Soc. Psychol. Bull. 11:98–105

Stroebe, W., Kruglanski, A. W., Bar-Tal, D., Hewstone, M., eds. 1988. The Social Psychology of Intergroup Conflict. New York: Springer-Verlag. 198 pp.

Tajfel, H. 1982. Social psychology of intergroup relations. Ann. Rev. Psychol. 33:1–39

Tajfel, H., Turner, J. C. 1986. An integrative theory of intergroup relations. See Worchel & Austin 1986, pp. 7-24

Tajfel, H., Wilkes, A. L. 1963. Classification and quantitative judgement. Brit. J. Psychol. 54:101–13

Tajfel, H., Flament, C., Billig, M. G., Bundy, R. F. 1971. Social categorization and intergroup behavior. Eur. J. Soc. Psychol. 1:149–77

Taylor, D. M., Moghaddam, F. M. 1987. Theories of Intergroup Relations: International Social Psychological Perspectives. New York: Praeger. 223 pp.

Taylor, S. E. 1981. A categorization approach to stereotyping. See Hamilton 1981, pp. 83–114

Taylor, S. E., Falcone, H. T. 1982. Cognitive bases of stereotyping: the relationship between categorization and prejudice. Pers. Soc. Psychol. Bull. 8:426–32

Taylor, S. E., Fiske, S. T., Etcoff, N. L., Ruderman, A. J. 1978. Categorical bases of person memory and stereotyping. J. Pers. Soc. Psychol. 36:778–93

Tetlock, P. E. 1986. Psychological advice on foreign policy: What do we have to contribute? Am. Psychol. 41:557–67

Trew, K. 1986. Catholic-Protestant contact in Northern Ireland. See Hewstone & Brown 1986a, pp. 93–106

Triplet, R. G., Sugarman, D. B. 1987. Reactions to AIDS victims: Ambiguity breeds contempt. Pers. Soc. Psychol. Bull. 13: 265–74

Trope, Y., Bassok, M. 1982. Confirmatory and diagnosing strategies in social information gathering. J. Pers. Soc. Psychol. 43: 22–34

Trope, Y., Mackie, D. M. 1987. Sensitivity to alternatives in social hypothesis testing. J. Exp. Soc. Psychol. 23:445–59

Trzebinski, J. 1985. Action-oriented representations of implicit personality theories. J. Pers. Soc. Psychol. 48:1266–78

Trzebinski, J., McGlynn, R. P., Gray, G., Tubbs, D. 1985. The role of categories of an actor's goals in organizing inferences about a person. J. Pers. Soc. Psychol. 48:1387–97

Turner, J. C. 1982. Towards a cognitive redefinition of the social group. In Social Identity and Intergroup Relations, ed. H. Tajfel, pp. 15–40. Cambridge: Cambridge Univ. Press

Turner, J. C. 1983a. Some comments on . . . 'the measurement of social orientations in the minimal group paradigm'. Eur. J. Soc. Psychol. 13:351–67

Turner, J. C. 1983b. A second reply to Bornstein, Crum, Wittenbraker, Harring, Insko, and Thibaut on the measurement of social orientations. Eur. J. Soc. Psychol. 13:383–87

Turner, J. C. 1987. Rediscovering the Social Group: A Self-categorization Theory. New York: Basil Blackwell

Vanbeselaere, N. 1987. The effects of dichotomous and crossed social categorization upon intergroup discrimination. Eur. J. Soc. Psychol. 17:143–56

Wagner, U., Lampen, L., Syllwasschy, J. 1986. In-group inferiority, social identity and out-group devaluation in a modified minimal group study. Brit. J. Soc. Psychol. 25:15–23

Walker, P., Antaki, C. 1986. Sexual orientation as a basis for categorization in recall. Brit. J. Soc. Psychol. 25:337–39

Weber, R., Crocker, J. 1983. Cognitive processes in the revision of stereotypic beliefs. J. Pers. Soc. Psychol. 45:961–77

Wetherell, M. 1987. Social identity and group polarization. See Turner 1987, pp. 142–70

Wilder, D. A. 1978. Perceiving persons as a group: effects on attributions of causality and beliefs. Soc. Psychol. 13:253–58

Wilder, D. A. 1981. Perceiving persons as a group: categorization and intergroup relations. See Hamilton 1981, pp. 213–58

Wilder, D. A. 1984a. Intergroup contact: the typical member and the exception to the rule. J. Exp. Soc. Psychol. 20:177–94

Wilder, D. A. 1984b. Predictions of belief homogeneity and similarity following social categorization. Brit. J. Soc. Psychol. 23: 323–33

Wilder, D. A. 1986a. Social categorization: implications for creation and reduction of intergroup bias. *Adv. Exp. Soc. Psychol.* 19:291–355

Wilder, D. A. 1986b. Cognitive factors affecting the success of intergroup contact. See Worchel & Austin 1986, pp. 49–66

Wilder, D. A., Shapiro, P. N. 1984. Role of outgroup cues in determining social identity. *J. Pers. Soc. Psychol.* 47:342–48

Wilder, D. A., Shapiro, P. N. 1988. A role of competition induced anxiety in limiting the beneficial impact of positive behavior by an outgroup member. *J. Pers. Soc. Psychol.* In press

Wolf, S. 1987. Majority and minority influence: a social impact analysis. In *Social Influence: The Ontario Symposium*, ed. M. P. Zanna, J. M. Olson, C. P. Herman, 5:207–35. Hillsdale, NJ: Erlbaum

Worchel, S. 1979. Cooperation and the reduction of intergroup conflict: some determining factors. In *The Social Psychology of Intergroup Relations*, ed. W. G. Austin, S. Worchel, pp. 262–73. Monterey, Calif: Brooks/Cole

Worchel, S. 1986. The role of cooperation in reducing intergroup conflict. See Worchel & Austin 1986, pp. 288–304

Worchel, S., Austin, W. G., eds. 1986. *Psychology of Intergroup Relations*. Chicago: Nelson-Hall. 429 pp.

Worth, L. T. 1988. *The role of prior expectations and selective information processing in outgroup homogeneity*. PhD thesis. Univ. Calif., Santa Barbara

Worth, L. T., Allison, S. T., Messick, D. M. 1987. Impact of a group's decision on the perception of one's own and other's attitudes. *J. Pers. Soc. Psychol.* 53:673–82

Wyer, R. S. Jr., Martin, L. L. 1986. Person memory: the role of traits, group stereotypes, and specific behaviors in the cognitive representations of persons. *J. Pers. Soc. Psychol.* 50:661–75

Wyer, R. S., Bodenhausen, G. V., Srull, T. K. 1984. The cognitive representation of persons and groups and its effect on recall and recognition memory. *J. Exp. Soc. Psychol.* 20:445–69

Ann. Rev. Psychol. 1989. 40:83–108

DIAGNOSIS AND CLINICAL ASSESSMENT: Current Status and Major Issues

Paul McReynolds

Department of Psychology, University of Nevada, Reno, Nevada 89557

CONTENTS

INTRODUCTION

Diagnosis and assessment are crucial in clinical practice and research. In the clinic, diagnostic assessment facilitates treatment, and the success or failure of particular treatments in turn illuminates the diagnostic process. In research on psychopathology, groupings, however tentative, of persons having similar problems and characteristics are essential to the testing of theoretical positions. The area of diagnosis and assessment is currently very active, with notable advances being made on several fronts, and with a number of significant controversies—spiced by the involvement of several disciplines and varying perspectives—enlivening the scene.

0066-4308/89/0201-0083$02.00

The purpose of this chapter is to bring to the reader a general picture of the state of the area, with a focus on recent developments, trends, and outstanding issues. The chapter is organized into two major sections. The first section examines the diagnostic process in psychopathology, and includes a review of the new DSM-III-R, the major current diagnostic taxonomy. The second section considers the present status of the tools for clinical assessment, including checklists and rating scales, interviews, and psychological tests.

The term "diagnosis," here as elsewhere, is employed in two different senses—first, to refer to the *process* of determining that an individual has characteristics that fit a particular category, and second, as a name or *label* for that category. I use the phrase "clinical assessment" in a broader sense, to designate the process of systematically learning about a patient or client; the expression thus encompasses diagnosis, but also includes the detailed understanding of an individual.

THE DIAGNOSTIC PROCESS

The last review of the area covered in this chapter appeared three years ago (Robins & Helzer 1986). Since then the renaissance of interest in psychopathological diagnosis noted in that chapter has continued, and the literature has grown enormously. There are three recent books to which I particularly wish to call the reader's attention. The first is the revision of DSM-III (American Psychiatric Association 1980), appropriately titled DSM-III-R (American Psychiatric Association 1987), which is discussed below. The second is *Contemporary Directions in Psychopathology: Toward the DSM-IV* (Millon & Klerman 1986); this is a veritable feast of historical perspectives, divergent viewpoints, and important systematic proposals. The third volume is *Issues in Diagnostic Research* (Last & Hersen 1987), which contains a number of searching examinations of relevant conceptual issues.

The Logic of Diagnosis

Classifications of mental disturbances have a long and interesting history, reaching back into antiquity, but modern approaches derive largely from the pioneering work of Kraepelin (Blashfield 1984; Stengel 1959). The development of an adequate taxonomy in psychopathology can be seen as one facet of the generic science of classification, as also represented, for example, in biological and disease taxonomies. Recently a number of authors (including Achenbach 1985a; Blashfield 1984, 1986; Feinstein 1977; Millon 1987a) have provided sophisticated examinations of the taxonomic problem in psychopathology. The best introduction is that by Millon (1987a), and the best treatment in depth is the book by Blashfield (1984).

In considering the logic of psychopathological classification the obvious first question is, What should it include? Or to put it differently, what are the defining features of psychopathology? Thus, before we can meaningfully classify the units of a domain we need to know what it encompasses. One approach to this problem is to include within the domain those mental disturbances that have been recognized by society at large over the centuries and in different cultures. Such an approach is based on the assumption that constellations surviving such a cultural winnowing process would reflect at least part of reality. This societal orientation would clearly include the depressions, mania, and the schizophrenia spectrum, and probably psychopathy. The approach would have to be employed with great care, however, since cultures vary considerably (Butcher 1987; Westermeyer 1985) with respect to what they consider deviant—as witnessed, for example, by the recent transition in our own culture in the general attitude toward homosexuality. Nevertheless, the rough boundaries of psychopathology demarcated by society-at-large should not be depreciated, since no taxonomy devised by professionals can long maintain its credibility if it flies counter to societal values.

A second possible approach to the delineation of psychopathology would be to utilize some sort of self-determination, say by construing as being within its compass the problems of all individuals voluntarily seeking treatment. Such a plan, however, is deficient in two respects—first, some persons recognized by society as disturbed (e.g. paranoid schizophrenics) do not consider themselves disturbed; and second, some individuals (e.g. persons suffering bereavement or marital discord) may seek temporary professional help even when their problem is clearly not pathological. Despite these limitations, it is obvious that considerable caution should be exercised in classing as psychopathological conditions that are routinely seen as within the normal range by people so afflicted.

This analysis leaves some sort of professional judgment as the primary method for determining what behavior patterns are to be included within a psychopathological taxonomy. Such judgments are made difficult by the facts that unlike most diseases, behavioral problems have—for the most part—no identifiable pathogenic agents, and that normal problems in living merge imperceptibly into clearly disturbed behaviors. The issue of what behaviors are to be considered pathological is complex and for the present can best be served by a conservative approach.

The next systematic question is, What are to be the units of a taxonomy of psychopathology? The unit employed in DSM-III and DSM-III-R, as well as in DSM-II (American Psychiatric Association 1968), is *mental disorder*. A mental disorder is defined as a clinically significant behavioral or psychological pattern that is associated with personal distress, impairment, or risk. Ideally, such patterns should be identified and distinguished on the basis of empirical criteria, and indeed there have been important advances in this direction; but for the present most mental disorders are delineated on the grounds of accumulated clinical judgment and consensus.

Though the DSM-III-R manual notes that deviant behaviors may sometimes be manifested in conflicts between individuals and society, its clear assumption is that a mental disorder is an inner condition of an individual. No doubt this is typically true to a significant degree; yet it should be noted that the assumption is dissonant with psychosociological assertions that the very definition of mental disturbances involves society, with the underlying behaviorist claim that behaviors are under the control of the prevailing stimuli, and with the influential interactional perspective (see Magnusson & Öhman 1987). To put it differently, DSM-III-R, from the personological perspective, is strictly a state-trait conceptualization. Thus, as Walton (1986) has observed, relatively transient, state-like signs and symptoms are crucial in diagnosing most of the clinical syndromes (Axis I), whereas enduring trait-like characteristics are central in diagnosing personality disorders (Axis II).

The issue of categorical vs dimensional approaches in assessment is an old one, but is still topical (Achenbach 1985a; Blashfield 1984; Eysenck 1986; Frances 1982; Millon 1987a; Robins & Helzer 1986; Walton 1986). In the categorical approach (the orientation traditionally used in psychiatric taxonomies, including DSM-III-R) a person is assigned a given diagnosis, whereas in the dimensional approach the individual receives separate values on different relevant dimensions, which together constitute a personality profile. The categorical approach assumes that the various mental disorders are qualitatively different, at least to a degree that justifies considering them as distinct; in contrast, the dimensional approach assumes that the various disorders reflect different profiles on the same underlying subject variables. The categorical approach is simpler to use and facilitates communication. However, except where there are specific diagnostic markers—very rare in the present state of knowledge—its underlying assumption of distinct categories is moot at best; and by reducing masses of data to a limited number of categories, it is wasteful of information. The dimensional approach, on the other hand, is in principle more accurate and informative. However, unreduced profile data tend to strain the cognitive capacity of the human processors, which inherently tend to group data, and are more difficult to communicate or to use in outcome studies. It should be emphasized that the categorical and dimensional approaches are not mutually exclusive, and may in some instances serve complementary functions.

A recent important development in taxonomic theory is the notion that categories in the natural world (e.g. classifications of objects) tend to have indistinct (i.e. fuzzy) boundaries, and to be best represented by prototypes.

First discussed by Wittgenstein, this concept was systematically developed by Rosch (1978) and others, and later applied to psychiatric diagnosis (Cantor & Genero 1986). A number of other authors (including Achenbach 1985a; Blashfield 1984; Millon 1987a) have further developed the prototypic notion for psychopathological categories. The implication of these analyses is that many (but perhaps not all; see Widiger 1982) psychiatric diagnoses are best conceived as fuzzy categories delineated by prototypic examples, rather than by strict borders.

The last point to be considered here is, What kinds of information should go into diagnostic decisions? The possibilities, briefly, are (*a*) current behavioral and patient-report data; (*b*) etiological (historical) data; and (*c*) laboratory data. The last of these is currently of little help for the bulk of behavioral problems. Multidimensional approaches (e.g. symptom ratings) are for practical reasons largely limited to the first class. The categorical approach can, in principle, utilize both classes *a* and *b*. Usage of etiological data, however, entails major theoretical assumptions; and since different positions (e.g. psychoanalytic, social learning) make different assumptions, the authors of DSM-III and DSM-III-R eschewed the general diagnostic use of etiological data. This decision seems to me appropriate, but it should be recognized as a temporary state of affairs. Thus, the full understanding of a psychopathological condition clearly requires insight into its etiology. Exclusive dependence on presenting signs and symptoms involves obvious risks, as can be illustrated by the analogy of considering two diseases (e.g. influenza and pneumonia) basically the same because they both present high fever. An illustration in psychopathology is the distinction between process and reactive schizophrenia, which at certain stages present similar clinical pictures, but which have dissimilar histories and courses.

Reactions to DSM-III

The widespread use of DSM-III has led to a large number of studies and critiques. Most of these articles are still relevant, since relatively few systematic changes were made in DSM-III-R. I therefore selectively review the recent literature on DSM-III. First, though, a brief resumé of its background and nature.

Modern American psychiatry has been characterized by two somewhat incongruent paradigms—the descriptive, derived from Kraepelin, and the dynamic, derived primarily, though not entirely, from Freud (other orientations also exist in psychiatry, but are less influential). Up into the 1950s the dynamic position, with its emphasis on early life etiological factors, and on the general theme that intrapsychic conflicts may lead to various defensive (neurotic) conditions, tended to be dominant. In that period, however, the newly developed psychopharmacologic agents—which led to drastic changes in treatment methods—stimulated a resurgence of the Kraepelinian tradition. This was because systematic evidence began to suggest that certain drugs were at least somewhat specific to particular diagnoses.

It is understandable, then, that the new diagnostic manual was tilted in a neo-Kraepelinian direction. Another significant influence was the notoriously low reliability of psychiatric diagnosis, which it was felt would be enhanced by a diagnostic system based primarily on descriptive data. Still another relevant factor was the beginning development of more specific diagnostic criteria and interview schedules (reviewed by Robins & Helzer 1986). The actual construction of DSM-III involved the efforts of a large number of committees and consultants, and despite the scientific commitment of the participants, the process included numerous compromises and internecine struggles (Millon 1986), and can fruitfully be examined from the perspective of the sociology of science (Bayer & Spitzer 1985). The dispute between the descriptive and dynamic groups has not subsided (Klerman et al 1984) and will likely arise again in the deliberations for DSM-IV, scheduled to appear in the early 1990s.

The chief innovative characteristics of DSM-III, all carried over into DSM-III-R, were the following. There were five diagnostic axes: Axis I included the psychiatric syndromes, Axis II developmental and personality disorders, and Axis III relevant physical disorders. Axis IV concerned possible predisposing stressors, and Axis V the individual's level of functioning. DSM-III provided detailed descriptive criteria for each disorder, and specified the number of criteria that a person must meet in order to be assigned to that category. This polythetic approach, with its implications that different patients with the same diagnosis may be noticeably different, means that DSM-III (and DSM-III-R) is already largely a prototypic system; this trend will probably be increased in DSM-IV (Cantor & Genero 1986).

The emphasis in DSM-III on descriptive criteria has led many authors to refer to it as being "atheoretical" and as having "operational" criteria. The effort to state the various defining criteria as clearly and objectively as possible—which is presumably what is meant by "operational"—is highly commendable; but Faust & Miner (1986) are correct in arguing that it is ultimately impossible to separate fact and theory. Further, many of the most salient criteria for some of the disorders are extremely judgmental (Taylor 1983). It may also be noted that the concept of operationism, if meant in its technical sense, has been passé in the philosophy of science for several decades.

Commentaries on DSM-III included both positive (e.g. Klerman 1984; Millon 1986; Robins & Helzer 1986) and negative (e.g. Eysenck 1986; Garfield 1986; Vaillant 1984) evaluations. Two surveys gauged reactions among professional users. Smith & Kraft (1983) surveyed the members of

Division 29 (Psychotherapy) of the American Psychological Association. Overall, the orientations preferred by the 546 respondents were, in order of preference: social-interpersonal, nondiagnostic, behavioral, and DSM-III. Only 13 % of the respondents favored DSM-III, with 58% opposed, and 29% unsure. Jampala et al (1986) surveyed 557 practicing psychiatrists and 498 senior residents. Most respondents were in settings that required use of DSM-III, but about 56% of the practitioners and 75% of the residents reported that they would continue to use DSM-III even if it were not required. The residents were more positively oriented toward the multiaxial system than were the practitioners, but both groups were strongly opposed to the inclusion of additional axes.

The reservations about DSM-III by psychoanalysts (Vaillant 1984) have already been indicated. Frances & Cooper (1981), however, argued that the taxonomy is compatible with a dynamic approach. I would add that the descriptive (Kraepelinian) and psychodynamic views have more in common than their adherents may think, in that both, in contradistinction to the behavioral and interactional perspectives, place the disorder strictly within the person. The attitude of behaviorists toward DSM-III is ambivalent (Nelson 1987; Taylor 1983). On the negative side the fundamental DSM-III internality assumption is completely counter to the behavioral premise of stimulus control. On the positive side, however, behaviorists are attracted by the attempts of DSM-III authors to devise objective diagnostic defining criteria. Humanistically oriented therapists, such as Rogerians, tend to feel that all diagnostic systems are counterproductive.

The taxonomy for disorders of childhood and adolescence in DSM-III received strong criticism (Bemporad & Schwab 1986; Garfield 1986; Quay 1986; Quay et al 1987). A basic concern was that the diagnostic categorizations appear to have been developed with insufficient attention to empirical data (Achenbach 1980; Quay 1986). It was also felt by some that DSM-III inappropriately brought certain transient developmental problems under the umbrella of "disorder." Bemporad & Schwab (1986) argued that parts of DSM-III are based on the fallacious assumption that children are just little adults, and that what is needed is a separate classification system for child psychopathology.

One of the hopes of those who developed DSM-III and its revision was that these would stimulate increased research in psychopathology. This expectation appears to have been realized, though space permits only a limited accounting here. There have been a number of reliability studies, mostly focusing on interrater agreement; fewer studies have concerned temporal consistency of diagnoses—a method relevant in some instances (e.g. personality disorders). Overall data, reviewed by Grove (1987) and Matarazzo (1983), indicate generally acceptable levels of reliability obtained with the new criterion-based systems. The situation is spotty, however, with the lowest reliability coefficients found for the Axis II personality disorders. Mellsop et al (1982), in their comparisons of the diagnoses assigned by three psychiatrists, obtained kappa coefficients ranging from .01 to .49 for specific personality disorders, with an overall value of .41 (in contrast to .54 reported for the initial trials) for the presence or absence of a personality disorder. Whether the changes in the descriptors for the personality disorders in DSM-III-R will improve the reliability values remains to be seen. Another area in which serious questions concerning DSM-III reliability were raised was the childhood section (Bemporad & Schwab 1986; Quay 1986); analogous data for DSM-III-R were not available at the time of this writing.

The issue of diagnostic validity is crucial, but it is difficult to assess adequately because of the problem of a criterion. Nevertheless, some progress has been made. Coryell & Zimmerman (1987) compared the validity of DSM-III diagnostic criteria with the earlier Feighner criteria and Research Diagnostic Criteria (reviewed by Robins & Helzer 1986) for 98 psychotic patients against follow-up criteria. Results were positive, and essentially equal for all three systems. Drake & Vaillant (1985), in an outstanding longitudinal study of 86 men, obtained solid support for the validity of the overall diagnosis of personality disorder, but less for the subcategories. Zimmerman et al (1985) reported strong evidence for the validity of DSM-III Axis IV (stressors) in a sample of 130 depressed patients. A study of 257 psychiatric hospital admissions (Schrader et al 1986) supported the utility of both Axes IV and V. A problem noted was that the clinician, in completing the rating for Axis IV, was instructed to include only stressors considered to have significantly contributed to the current disorder—a judgment difficult to make. This requirement is softened somewhat in DSM-III-R.

The above review took a broad, overall perspective. However, extensive empirical research—beyond the scope of this chapter—has been and is being performed on specific disorders, particularly the personality disorders.

DSM-III-R

The revision of DSM-III was published in 1987. Like the earlier version, this was developed under the leadership of Robert L. Spitzer. As already noted, the overall format of DSM-III was retained in DSM-III-R. I here note some of the more significant changes (American Psychiatric Association 1987, pp. 409–30; Nathan 1987; Williams 1986).

DSM-III listed two types of substance-use disorders—substance abuse and substance dependence. This distinction has been largely eliminated in DSM-III-R (by greatly increasing the scope of substance dependence) because practitioners had difficulty differentiating them reliably (Landry 1988; Rounsaville et al 1987; Schuckit et al 1985). DSM-III, in contradistinction to DSM-II (American Psychiatric Association 1968), did not designate homosexuality a disorder, but it did list "Ego-dystonic homosexuality." Even this category is omitted in DSM-III-R, which instead includes "persistent and marked distress about one's sexual orientation" as one example of a "Sexual Disorder Not Otherwise Specified." Among the other changes in the adult taxonomy are the addition of a category of sleep disorders (described tentatively in an Appendix in DSM-III), more detailed criteria for the personality disorders, and minor alterations for anxiety disorders.

A proposal to add three new diagnostic categories—Late Luteal Phase Dysphoric Disorder, Self-Defeating (Masochistic) Personality Disorder, and Sadistic Personality Disorder—aroused strong opposition, especially from women's groups. The first of these, termed Premenstrual Stress Disorder in an earlier draft, was strongly objected to on the ground that it should not be considered psychopathological and could be used in a way unfair to women. The second proposed category was also seen as possibly being applied primarily—and unfairly—to women, especially those caught in abusive relationships. The proposed sadistic category also aroused criticism, on the basis that it might be used as a legal defense by rapists and other perpetrators of violence. Even before the concerns just noted about the prospective DSM-III-R, questions about possible sex bias in DSM-III had been raised (Kaplan 1983a,b) and responded to (Williams & Spitzer 1983; Kass et al 1983). These instances testify to the complex interrelationships between psychiatric diagnoses and societal values that were noted earlier and about which I comment further below.

The question of the legitimacy of the three proposed new diagnoses was resolved for the present by assigning them to the Appendix of the DSM-III-R manual as "categories needing further study." A recent empirical study (Reich 1987a) casts considerable doubt on the validity and utility of the category "self-defeating" as currently defined.

DSM-III, in its taxonomy of childhood disorders, divided Attention Deficit Disorder into two types—ADD with hyperactivity and ADD without hyperactivity. However, field trials for DSM-III-R failed to support this distinction, and it has been dropped in the revised manual.

The most salutary changes appearing in DSM-III-R are improvements in Axes IV (stressors) and V (level of functioning). The Axis IV 6-point rating scale is more clearly delineated than in DSM-III, and separates stress due to acute events (e.g. a divorce) from that due to enduring circumstances (e.g. chronic illness). The DSM-III Axis V scale has been discarded entirely and replaced by a Global Assessment of Functioning scale (GAF). This is a 90-point scale (with 9 descriptive levels) designed to provide for numerical representation of the individual's placement on a hypothetical continuum of mental health-illness. The GAF requires the clinician to rate both the patient's current level of functioning and the highest level during the past year.

At the time of this writing only a few articles (Landry 1988; Nathan 1987; Reich 1987a; Rounsaville et al 1987) on DSM-III-R have appeared. An early judgment from the behavioral perspective is highly reserved (Nathan 1987), and presumably dynamic and interpersonal theorists will be no more enthusiastic about DSM-III-R than about its predecessor. My own evaluation is that the revision represents a modest improvement.

Alternatives to DSM-III-R

At present there is no viable taxonomic alternative—on the criteria of breadth of coverage and detailed exposition—to DSM-III-R. This is not to say that broad alternatives to DSM-III-R cannot or will not be developed, or that more limited psychopathological taxonomies do not exist. Further, it needs to be emphasized that many clinicians, while they may utilize the DSM-III-R taxonomy for practical and legal reasons, will continue, in their everyday clinical work as well as in their research, to follow those paradigms they have already found useful—the psychodynamic, the social-learning, the behavioral, the psychometric, and so on. Nor is such a double accounting to be decried; indeed, there is reason to believe that it is by such a mixing of metaphors that science most typically advances.

In other words, DSM-III-R is not the only game in town. One hopes that its descriptive, atheoretical stance will enable it to serve as a kind of lingua franca among the various diagnostic perspectives, and to some extent this has already occurred. Because of its breadth and format DSM-III-R does not provide the idiographic detail necessary for treatment of most individual patients. For this purpose, depending on the treatment context, many therapists will find it most useful to classify (i.e. diagnose) the patient in terms of level of psychosexual development, MMPI profile type, functional behavioral analysis, systems theory, or other diagnostic paradigms. Jungian therapists will continue to utilize the Jungian personality typology, and therapists working with the mentally retarded will employ more detailed diagnostic procedures than those indicated in DSM-III-R. And so on.

The above comments concern the relevance of particular theoretical schematizations in working with individual patients. I now briefly examine several classificatory possibilities that can be considered as serious alternatives or supplements to certain psychopathological areas covered by DSM-III-R.

I begin with a brief survey of empirically based approaches to the major clinical syndromes in adults. These approaches are primarily dimensional rather than categorical, and the chief research methodology has been factor analysis. A number of investigators, of whom the most prominent has been Maurice Lorr (1971, 1986; Lorr et al 1966), have been involved in this research (reviewed by Blashfield 1984; Lorr 1986) over the past several decades. In 1966 Lorr et al published the Inpatient Multidimensional Psychiatric Scale (IMPS), a research-based interview procedure for assigning patients quantitative values on 12 psychotic dimensions (e.g. Excitement, Hostile belligerence, Paranoid projection). More recent studies, using other data sources (reviewed by Lorr 1986), tend to confirm and extend the earlier results and suggest that a profile including 14–16 dimensions can adequately describe functional psychotic behavior. There are a number of other techniques, including the Brief Psychiatric Rating Scale (BPRS) (Overall & Gorham 1962; Overall & Hollister 1982), that can be employed to yield dimensional ratings of clinical syndromes.

Analogous proposals for dimensionalizing the personality disorders (Axis II), based on interview data, have also been proposed. One method, suggested by Frances (1982) and others, would be to simply rate the subject on all of the 11 DSM-III personality disorders. Widiger et al (1987), employing a multidimensional scaling technique, proposed three key dimensions (affiliation, assertion, and anxious rumination-vs-acting out) for describing individuals with personality disturbances.

Clinical self-report inventories provide another avenue for factor analyses to reveal basic psychopathological variables. The three scales of the Eysenck Personality Questionnaire (EPQ) (Eysenck & Eysenck 1975) and the 12 clinical scales of the Clinical Analysis Questionnaire (CAQ) (Krug 1980) are all factor based. This is not true of the scales in the Minnesota Multiphasic Personality Inventory (MMPI); but a recent replicated factor analysis of MMPI items (Johnson et al 1984), involving over 11,000 cases, provides an excellent basis for a dimensional taxonomy.

I next consider several theory-based approaches to psychopathological taxonomy, though this is not to imply that they lack empirical support. The interpersonal orientation, derived from Leary's 1957 conceptualization, holds (a) that personality—and by implication, personality disorders—can best be rationalized in terms of interpersonal concepts, and (b) that the various interpersonal transactions can be accurately represented in a circle having two intersecting motivations—the need for dominance and the need for affiliation. A number of investigators, of whom Wiggins (1982, 1988; Wiggins & Broughton 1985) has been particularly active, have contributed to the theoretical development of this conception. A somewhat more complex interpersonal system, known as the Structural Analysis of Social Behavior (SASB), has been put forward by Benjamin (1986). Several methods, including interpersonal adjective checklists (Leary 1957; Wiggins & Broughton 1985) and questionnaires (Benjamin 1986; Horowitz et al 1988; Kiesler 1986) have been developed to assess interpersonal attitudes. Kiesler (1986), Benjamin (1987), and McLemore & Brokaw (1987) have utilized the interpersonal approach in rationalizing personality disorders.

Vaillant (1985), working in the psychoanalytic tradition, has developed a method, based on interview material, for ranking a patient's defense mechanisms in terms of maturity-immaturity. This scale is designed primarily for use with personality disorders (Vaillant & Drake 1985).

There has been a great deal of activity addressed to the development of an accurate taxonomy of psychological disturbances in childhood and adolescence. Quay (1986; see also Quay et al 1987) has summarized evidence from 55 multivariate studies implicating 9 dimensions (e.g. attention problems, social ineptness) in childhood psychopathology. Two recent books, by Achenbach (1985a) and Achenbach & McConaughy (1987), represent major advances in conceptualizing disorders in early life. Extensive research by Achenbach and his associates (Achenbach 1985a; Achenbach et al 1987) utilizing the Child Behavior Checklist (Achenbach & Edelbrock 1983) supports the division of childhood disturbances into internalizing (e.g. anxious) and externalizing (e.g. aggressive) categories, and suggests the possibility of five axes (parent perceptions, teacher perceptions, cognitive measures, physical conditions, clinician's assessment) for the evaluation of child psychopathology.

Another instrument that has a role to play in the development of an improved taxonomy for child behavior problems is the Personality Inventory for Children (PIC) (Wirt et al 1984). The study by Gdowski et al (1985), based on cluster analyses of PIC Profiles, suggests 11 different profile types.

Though it has not been possible to examine in detail the various alternatives noted above, I believe they all show considerable promise, and should figure prominently in the development of DSM-IV. In terms of present levels of development, systematic rating scales, based on interview or observational data, appear to provide the best candidates to supplement DSM-III-R.

Societal and Professional Implications

Psychiatric diagnoses are not simply entries in a clinician's case notes, nor is the prevailing diagnostic classification system of interest only to mental health professionals. On the contrary, such a psychopathological taxonomy is a social document, with important and widespread implications for the larger society. This is true in a number of ways. First, the particular behaviors classed as disorders determine to a large extent the kinds of behaviors that the society deems deviant, or abnormal, and by extension the particular individuals who are perceived as abnormal or mentally ill. Second, the diagnostic labels attached to an individual may have significant socio-legal implications for the degree of responsibility of an individual in antisocial or criminal acts. And third, diagnostic categorizations may directly influence an individual's perception of his or her status, condition, or worth.

If we think the main functions of diagnostic statements are to facilitate treatment, research, and communication, then the effects just noted can be thought of as side effects. This is not the place for an examination of such side effects, but it is obvious that they merit careful consideration and call for great caution and circumspection in extending the range of behaviors encompassed by the term "mental disorder."

In particular, it is important to recognize the danger of iatrogenic effects of diagnostic labeling. While some individuals may be relieved to learn that their distress has a technical name—with the implications that many other people have had the same distress and that there may be a cure for it—others are even more upset to learn that they are considered mentally ill. The magnitude of this problem—one effect of which is to discourage people from seeking needed professional help—should not be underestimated. It is made more pressing by the strong trend toward third-party payments for psychiatric and psychological services, and the fact that these payments are typically made only for the treatment of diagnosed mental disorders. This fact means that serious crises in ordinary living—e.g. bereavement or post-divorce distress (V codes in DSM-III-R)—which might benefit from professional attention but are clearly not pathological, are typically not covered by insurance plans. This trend urgently needs to be changed, since society is the loser when persons highly distressed but not technically mentally ill are denied insurance coverage for professional help. The restriction may seem justified by thinking of mental disorders as analogous to diseases, but it should be remembered that physicians who treat diseases also treat nondisease problems of living, such as pregnancies, broken bones, and burns, which are covered in insurance plans.

Though the concept of mental disorder need not imply a medical model in the full sense of the term, it at least suggests a limited medical analogue, as reflected in such terms as "mental health," "psychopathology," and "treatment," now employed routinely in all mental health disciplines. Though some authorities reject any medical analogue in its entirety, most clinicians, as well as the public at large, find some kind of psychopathological concept appropriate for the more serious disturbances. The problem is where to draw the line between (a) disorders and (b) personal concerns that can better be conceptualized as problems in living.

The entire health delivery system in the United States is undergoing rapid change, and these changes interact in various ways with the prevailing diagnostic system. For one thing, the increasing prevalence of Health Maintenance Organizations (HMOs) (Cheifetz & Salloway 1984) and insurance plans based on the DSM-III-R nosology greatly increases both the professional and societal impact of that system. Another development is the rise of prospective payment plans, the most common of which is the DRG (Diagnosis Related Group) model. This approach, in which funding for hospitals is calculated on the assumption that patient diagnoses furnish an accurate gauge of treatment expenses, has proved relatively successful for medical, especially surgical, procedures, but works very poorly for psychiatric diagnoses (Binner 1986; English et al 1986). What effect, if any, this fact will have on diagnostic practices in psychopathology remains to be seen.

Comments and Suggestions

How shall we evaluate DSM-III and DSM-III-R? My impression is that most users find them reasonably satisfactory, the revision being somewhat better received than its predecessor. Very few if any users are completely satisfied, but their reservations vary greatly. My own view is that even with all their limitations these systems represent a significant advance in psychopathological taxonomy. Their main positive characteristics are an increased emphasis on specific, relatively discrete diagnostic criteria, and the implicit adoption of a polythetic, prototypic mode. The separation of the clinical syndromes and the personality disorders (Axes I & II) is clearly a step forward. The most lasting effect of the new taxonomic system, however, is likely to be in its stimulation and facilitation of fundamental research on psychopathology.

Along with these positive points a number of serious problems in DSM-III-R can be discerned. While the general outline of the clinical syndromes appears to be fairly well established, the systematic portrayal of children's developmental problems and the personality disorders is much less so. Difficult issues in reliability and validity, especially with the personality disorders, remain. On a global level my chief reservation about the DSM process is that it does not always appear to be sufficiently committed to a hard-nosed dependence on basic empirical data, with the result that diagnostic categories sometimes tend to be framed without adequate supporting data. However, rather than focus here on limitations in DSM-III-R, I prefer to offer suggestions for its further development.

First, I urge caution in extending the range of human distresses and difficulties construed as mental disorders. Indeed, consideration should be given to declassifying as mental illnesses certain problems now so considered. For example, it seems highly inappropriate (Garfield 1986) to conceive of children's problems in reading, spelling, and arithmetic—which are routinely handled by educational specialists—as psychiatric disorders.

Second, a way should be found to modify DSM-III-R's insistence that psychological problems are always *in individuals*. This view, which may have been inherited from the disease model background and implies that only individuals are treated psychologically, has long been obsolete, and is incongruent with the obvious fact that in modern practice the focus of treatment is often on couples and families—i.e. on interpersonal relationships. It is also contradicted by the universally recognized fact that the problems that bring children to clinics are frequently not so much in the children as in their families (or lack of families) and living environments.

My third suggestion concerns the issue of categories vs dimensions. I do not favor giving up the categorical system, but I strongly recommend, following Lorr (1986) and others, that it be routinely supplemented by dimensional profiles. Separate dimensional scales should be provided for the clinical syndromes, the personality disorders, and child behavior problems. The evidence for the validity and utility of the dimensional procedure is overwhelming.

Fourth, I recommend that consideration be given to the development of a separate taxonomical approach, with its own manual, for childhood problems. While there is a certain attractive symmetry in forcing the disturbances of childhood into the format used for adults, this precision is probably illusory, since the contexts in which children's problems arise differ greatly from those of adults.

TOOLS FOR CLINICAL ASSESSMENT

Clinical assessment encompasses all of the systematic professional approaches that contribute to the deeper understanding of a patient or client. The area overlaps with the broader field of personality assessment but is more specifically concerned with psychopathology. For most clinicians the determination of a formal diagnosis is only a part, and frequently the lesser part, of the overall assessment process. This is particularly true for individuals treated by psychotherapy. The present highly selective treatment examines, in turn, checklists and rating scales, interviews, and psychological tests. Among the recent survey books in the area are the volumes edited by Burdock et al (1982), Corcoran & Fischer (1987), Goldstein & Hersen (1984), Harrington (1987), Swiercinsky (1985), Weaver (1984), and the continuing series of McReynolds et al (1988) and Butcher & Spielberger (1987).

Checklists and Rating Scales

Abnormality in an individual has traditionally been detected in the way he or she acts. Behaviors so bizarre or moods so extreme as to appear outside the widest ken of normality have conventionally been interpreted as suggestive of psychopathology. During the last several decades—roughly, since WWII, though the antecedents can be traced back further—there has been a concerted effort to systematize and objectify the observational approach to abnormal behavior. This movement has been most prominent in inpatient settings, and I first consider methods developed in that context. These are of two general types: first, checklists or ratings to be completed by nurses or trained technicians concerning the patient's everyday behavior (reviewed in Raskin 1982); and second, ratings based on interviews by clinicians.

The forerunner of most current instruments of the first type was the Hospital Adjustment Scale (HAS) developed in 1952 (reviewed in McReynolds 1968; Raskin 1982), a 180-item checklist designed to assess the patient's level of functioning independent of diagnosis. The 30-item Nurses Observation Scale for Inpatient Evaluation (NOSIE-30) (Honigfeld et al 1966) is still widely used to assess overall patient ward behavior. The Psychotic Inpatient Profile (PIP) (Lorr & Vestre 1985) includes 96 items and is widely employed to assess 12 syndromes of psychotic behaviors. A recent instrument with excellent credentials is the Missouri Inpatient Behavior Scale (MIBS) (Evenson & Cho 1987). This 91-item inventory includes 7 symptom scales and 5 other relevant indices. Factor analytic data are based on 12,106 patients. Montgomery et al (1987) have reported the factorial structure of 4 psychiatric rating scales. Paul (1987) has developed a more complex set of procedures for recording patient behaviors in residential settings.

The above instruments follow the format of having the observer rate actual patient behaviors. Two scales provide for direct rating of psychopathological dimensions by nursing personnel: the French & Heninger (1970) Short Clinical Rating Scale (SCRS), which provides 13 pathological scales; and the Nurses Evaluation Rating Scale (NERS) (Overall et al 1986), which includes scales for 14 clinical variables. Ellsworth (1975) developed several scales for use by relatives in rating psychiatric patients. There are a number of instruments for obtaining patient self-ratings of symptomatology; probably the best known of these is Derogatis's 90-item Symptom Check List (SCL-90) (reviewed in Cyr et al 1985), which yields an overall measure of distress and can be scored on a number of different dimensions.

I turn now to clinical rating scales designed to be completed by clinicians on the basis of interviews. The IMPS (Lorr et al 1966) is perhaps the premier procedure of this type. Probably the most extensively employed broad-gauged symptom-oriented rating procedure, however, is the Brief Psychiatric Rating Scale (BPRS) (Overall & Gorham 1962; reviewed in Hedlund & Vieweg 1980; see also Gabbard et al 1987; Overall & Hollister 1982). This useful instrument evaluates the inpatients on 18 salient variables, ranging from somatic concern to disorientation. An analogous form, the Brief Outpatient Psychopathology Scale (BOPS) (Free & Overall 1977), is also available. Another relevant rating scale in the present context is the 65-item Comprehensive Psychopathological Rating Scale of Åsberg et al (1978).

Currently, the most active area for the development of new assessment techniques is child psychopathology (Achenbach & Edelbrock 1984; Quay et al 1987). Perhaps the most widely used instrument is the Child Behavior Checklist and Profile (Achenbach & Edelbrock 1983). This is typically completed by parents, and includes 118 items reflective of child behavior problems. Factor analyses have identified 9 clinical syndromes (e.g. depressed, hyperactive) from Checklist data, and cluster analyses have revealed 6 profile types (summarized in Achenbach 1985a). Achenbach, Conners & Quay (personal communication from T. M. Achenbach) have developed an impressive new instrument, the ACQ Behavior Checklist, and a large-scale norming project is nearing completion.

The Personality Inventory for Children (PIC) (Wirt et al 1984; Gdowski et al 1985) is a 600-item instrument to be completed by an informant, usually the mother. The inventory, which has excellent psychometric qualities, includes 12 clinical and a number of supplementary scales. Recent research (Lachar et al 1987) indicates that scores are not significantly biased by mothers' psychopathology. Another increasingly used assessment device with children is the Brief Psychiatric Rating Scale for Children (BPRS-C) (Gale et al 1986; Mullins et al 1986), which is analogous to the BPRS described above.

Interview Schedules

The central role of interviews in clinical assessment is axiomatic (Ginsberg 1985; Wiens 1983). In interviewing the subject, the clinician not only learns how the individual preceives his or her problem situation, but also benefits from observing the person's behavior during the interview. Interviews vary from the largely unstructured, in which only a general agenda is utilized, to the highly structured, in which a precise schedule for the wording and order of questions to be asked is followed [for reviews of structured interviews for children see Edelbrock & Costello (1984); for adults, Spiker & Ehler (1984)]. In the recent period there has been a strong movement in psychiatry, in keeping with the increasing emphasis on diagnosis, to make diagnostic interviews more structured, and hopefully more reliable. The history of this movement has received several excellent reviews (Robins & Helzer 1986; Helzer & Robins 1988; Spitzer 1983) and need not be recapitulated here. Instead, I concentrate on more recent developments, especially on the new Structured Clinical Interview for DSM-III-R (SCID) (Spitzer et al 1987).

The purpose of the SCID is to enable a clinician interviewer to arrive at DSM-III-R diagnoses. There are slightly separate forms for diagnosing psychiatric inpatients, outpatients, and nonpatients, and a form for personality disorders. The latter schedule includes a 120-item self-report (test) questionnaire to be completed by the patient. Though highly structured, the format of the SCID includes a number of open-ended questions, and requires continual clinical judgment on the part of the interviewer. Like most other structured interview schedules, there are a number of transition or branching points at which certain questions are skipped depending on the subject's answers to previous questions. In completing the interview form the clinician is encouraged to utilize whatever additional clinical data are available.

The SCID, if administered in its entirety, is a broad-spectrum diagnostic instrument. The Diagnostic Interview Schedule (DIS), intended for lay interviewers and designed primarily for epidemiological studies (Helzer & Robins 1988; see also Spitzer 1983), is also of this type. A number of more focal interview schedules have also been developed. The best known and one of the earliest of these is the Schedule of Affective Disorders and Schizophrenia (SADS) (Endicott & Spitzer 1978). Other limited-range schedules include the Structured Interview for the DSM-III Personality Disorders (SIDP) (Stangl et al 1985), the Personality Assessment Schedule (PAS) (Tyrer & Alexander 1979), the Diagnostic Interview for Borderlines (DIB) (Kolb & Gunderson 1980), and the Personality Disorder Examination (PDE) (Loranger et al 1987). The SCID can also be modified, by omitting certain modules, into special-purpose interviews.

A reservation that many workers have had about highly structured interviews is that their formality would tend to inhibit the development of rapport. The evidence (reviewed by Helzer & Robins 1988), however, indicates that this need not be the case. Data (reviewed by Matarazzo 1983) also support the expectation of increased reliability for structured-interview diagnostic categorizations. Nevertheless, the structured-interview approach to diagnosis is not without its problems. Brockington & Meltzer (1982) argue, very plausibly, that it is in itself too dependent on the patient's perceptual and descriptive capacities, and should be supplemented by ongoing clinical observations. Zimmerman et al (1986) reported that almost 20% of diagnoses based on the SIDP were changed after additional information was obtained from informants.

Psychological Tests

In this section I present a brief overview of the recent literature on psychopathological assessment through the use of psychological tests. I do not imply comprehensiveness, and authors whose favorite instruments are not included should not feel slighted. There are dozens of relevant instruments, of which only a few can be noted here.

The past two years constituted a banner period for new editions of standard clinical inventories and the emergence of new ones. Leading the list is the Minnesota Multiphasic Inventory (MMPI). First published in 1943, this venerable instrument has recently been revised and restandardized by Butcher, Dahlstrom & Graham (personal communication from J. N. Butcher). The new version, termed MMPI-2 and in final preparation at the time of this writing, will in all probability be available by the time this chapter is published. MMPI-2 includes an updating and revision of the item pool, and the addition of several new scales. Two test forms, one for adults and one for adolescents, are provided. Perhaps the major advance is the development of new norms based on 2,600 normals randomly sampled in seven US communities. In addition, extensive data have been collected by the developers of MMPI-2 on numerous clinical groups.

In 1987 a revision of the Millon Clinical Multiaxial Inventory instrument, known as MCMI-II (Millon 1987b), became available. Scales on the revision are designed to coordinate with the DSM-III-R personality disorders and clinical syndromes. Like its predecessor, MMCI-II includes 175 items, of which 45 are replacement items. The MCMI-II is intended for use only with clinical populations, and the selected normative sample (n = 1292) includes only psychiatric cases. Considerable research, which is generally supportive, has accumulated on the MCMI-II; much of this is summarized in the test manual.

A new inventory on the assessment scene is the Basic Personality Inventory (BPI) (Jackson 1988), which, despite its name, is designed to assess clinical variables. The BPI has been in research use for several years, and its formal appearance is expected well before this chapter is published. The test includes 240 items and 12 scales somewhat similar to the MMPI variables, and has excellent psychometric characteristics.

The California Psychological Inventory, though long a favorite in personality assessment, has not usually been considered a clinical instrument. The new revision (Gough 1987) should change that perception. Like its earlier format the new CPI contains 18 basic personality variables, plus two additional ones (independence and empathy). The main change is the development of three structural variables which when considered together yield a capsule picture of the subject's life-style and the degree to which his or her potential is being realized. The clinical significance of this model is that the same overall personality structure may appear in both highly adequate and disturbed individuals, with the difference being in the level of functioning.

Clinicians emphasizing interpersonal factors in their therapeutic and diagnostic functions should find the newly published Interpersonal Style Inventory (Lorr & Youniss 1986), which assesses 15 important interpersonal variables, a useful instrument. Another recently developed inventory that appears to have important potential for clinical applications is the NEO Personality Inventory (Costa & McCrae 1985; McCrae & Costa 1986). There has recently been a great deal of interest in theoretical personology in the hypothesis of five basic personality factors, and the NEO-PI is designed to assess each of these posited factors.

The above comments focus on several major new or recently revised inventories. There are of course a number of other widely used inventories in clinical assessment, among which may be mentioned the Clinical Analysis

Questionnaire (Krug 1980) and the Psychiatric Screening Inventory (Lanyon 1978; Vieweg & Hedlund 1984). Projective tests, especially the Rorschach, continue to be widely used in clinical settings, though there have been no recent major new directions. The Exner (Wiener-Levy & Exner 1981) Comprehensive System, because of its objectivity, is the most popular Rorschach scoring method and has led to extensive research on the major syndromes and personality disorders. The alternative inkblot instrument, the Holtzman (1988) Inkblot Test, has outstanding qualities and is represented by over 650 publications, many of them concerning psychopathological and cross-cultural comparisons.

Comments and Suggestions

The above discussion considers the different methods of assessment—rating scales, interviews, and tests—separately. This division, however, is somewhat artificial, since in good clinical practice the three approaches are integrated whenever possible. While all treatment decisions involve interviews, the other two modalities are less frequently employed. Observational ratings are largely restricted to inpatient settings. Tests are employed with both outpatients and inpatients, and are especially suitable for detailed studies of individuals. The relation between assessment and clinical practice has been examined by McReynolds (1985) and Hayes et al (1987).

In closing this section, I call attention to several additional assessment resources. I have so far discussed types of assessment technique, but an alternate approach is to focus on the clinical problem or variable being assessed. In the key clinical area of anxiety there are numerous assessment methods. The most widely used instrument is probably the State-Trait Anxiety Inventory (STAI) (Spielberger 1983). Recent reviews of anxiety assessment include for adults those by Finney (1985) and Tellegen (1985), and for children those by Achenbach (1985b) and Dudding (1988). McReynolds and associates (McReynolds 1987) have developed an inventory for differentiating cognitive and conditioned anxiety.

An outstanding recent book (Marsella et al 1987), edited from an interdisciplinary perspective, reviews many of the techniques available to assess depression. Probably the most widely used objective approach is the Beck Depression Inventory (reviewed by Beck et al 1988). Recently developed instruments include the Depressive Experiences Questionnaire (Welkowitz et al 1985), the Reynolds (1986) Adolescent Depression Scale and the Inventory to Diagnose Depression (Zimmerman & Coryell (1987). In the area of anger and hostility several recent assessment approaches merit attention. These include the State-Trait Anger Scale and the State-Trait Anger Expression Scale (Spielberger et al 1988), Siegel's (1986) Multidimensional Anger

Inventory, and the Overt Aggression Scale (Yudofsky et al 1986). Widiger & Frances (1987) and Reich (1987b) review the various available methods for assessment of personality disorders.

Space limitations bar the examination of assessment in other focal areas of psychopathology, but relevant review data may be found in the general sources noted at the beginning of this main section. For advances in computer-assisted interviews and diagnosis see Hedlund & Vieweg (1987). An area of great potential importance in psychiatric diagnosis, but which is beyond the scope of this chapter, is biological markers. For an introduction to this topic see Rea et al (1987).

SUMMARY

This chapter presented an overview of the current scene in the classification and assessment of psychopathology. Recent research on DSM-III and DSM-III-R was reviewed, and potential alternatives for, or supplements to DSM-III-R were examined. DSM-III-R was seen as a modest improvement over its predecessor, and several suggestions for its improvement were put forward. The societal and professional implications of the concept of mental disorder were considered, and the desirability of health insurance being extended to cover nonpathological personal crises was emphasized. Recent advances in clinical assessment methods, subdivided into checklists and rating scales, interview schedules, and psychological tests, were reviewed. The recent period was remarkable for the revision of important psychological tests, including the MMPI, CPI, and MCMI, and for the emergence of new inventories, including the BPI and the ISI.

It is important to see all present diagnostic taxonomies, including the DSM-III-R, as tentative systems, due to be altered or replaced as additional research accumulates. The great need in the field reviewed is for additional, inspired research to further dispel the darkness that currently limits our understanding of the basic nature of human distresses and abnormal behaviors.

Acknowledgments

I thank John Altrocchi, David Antonuccio, Patricia Chatham, Georgia Dudding, Gerald Ginsburg, Grant Miller, and Richard Weiher for providing valuable suggestions during the preparation of this chapter. My thanks also to the many authors who furnished me with relevant papers, and my regrets that space limitations precluded citing many of these.

Literature Cited

Achenbach, T. M. 1980. DSM-III in the light of empirical research on the classification of child psychopathology. *J. Am. Acad. Child Psychiatry* 19:395–412

Achenbach, T. M. 1985a. *Assessment and Taxonomy of Child and Adolescent Psychopathology*. Newbury Park, CA: Sage

Achenbach, T. M. 1985b. Assessment of anxiety in children. In *Anxiety and the Anxiety Disorders*, ed. A. H. Tuma, J. D. Maser, pp. 707–34. Hillsdale, NJ: Erlbaum

Achenbach, T. M., Edelbrock, C. S. 1983. *Manual for the Child Behavior Checklist and Revised Child Behavior Profile*. Burlington VT: Dept. Psychiatry, Univ. Vermont

Achenbach, T. M., Edelbrock, C. S. 1984. Psychopathology of childhood. *Ann. Rev. Psychol.* 35:227–56

Achenbach, T. M., McConaughy, S. H. 1987. *Empirically Based Assessment of Child and Adolescent Psychopathology*. Newbury Park, CA: Sage

Achenbach, T. M., McConaughy, S. H., Howell, C. T. 1987. Child/adolescent behavioral and emotional problems: implications of cross-informant correlations for situational specificity. *Psychol. Bull.* 101:213–32

American Psychiatric Association. 1968. *Diagnostic and Statistical Manual of Mental Disorders*. Washington, DC: Am. Psychiatr. Assoc. 2nd ed. 134 pp.

American Psychiatric Association. 1980. *Diagnostic and Statistical Manual of Mental Disorders*. Washington, DC: Am. Psychiatr. Assoc. 494 pp. 3rd ed.

American Psychiatric Association. 1987. *Diagnostic and Statistical Manual of Mental Disorders*. Washington, DC: Am. Psychiatr. Assoc. 567 pp. 3rd ed. rev.

Åsberg, M., Montgomery, S. A., Peris, C., Schalling, D., Sedvall, G. 1978. A comprehensive psychopathological rating scale. *Acta Psychiatr. Scand. Suppl.* 271:5–27

Bayer, R., Spitzer, R. L. 1985. Neurosis, psychodynamics, and DSM-III: a history of the controversy. *Arch. Gen. Psychiatry* 42: 187–96

Beck, A. T., Steer, R. A., Garbin, M. G. 1988. Psychometric properties of the Beck Depression Inventory: twenty-five years of evaluation. *Clin. Psychol. Rev.* 8:77–100

Bemporad, J. R., Schwab, M. E. 1986. The DSM-III and child clinical psychiatry. See Millon & Klerman 1986, pp. 135–50

Benjamin, L. S. 1986. Adding social and intrapsychic descriptors to Axis I of DSM-III. See Millon & Klerman 1986, pp. 599–638

Benjamin, L. S. 1987. Use of the SASB dimensional model to develop treatment plans for personality disorders. I: Narcissism. *J. Pers. Disorders* 1:43–70

Binner, P. R. 1986. DRGs and the administration of mental health services. *Am. Psychol.* 41:64–69

Blashfield, R. K. 1984. *The Classification of Psychopathology*. New York: Plenum

Blashfield, R. K. 1986. Structural approaches to classification. See Millon & Klerman 1986, pp. 363–80

Brockington, I. F., Meltzer, H. Y. 1982. Documenting an episode of psychiatric illness: need for multiple information sources, multiple raters, and narrative. *Schizophrenia Bull.* 8:485–92

Burdock, E. I., Sudilovsky, A., Gershon, S., eds. 1982. *The Behavior of Psychiatric Patients: Quantitative Techniques for Evaluation*. New York: Marcel Dekker

Butcher, J. N., ed. 1987. Special series: cultural factors in understanding and assessing psychology. *J. Consult. Clin. Psychol.* 55:459–512

Butcher, J. N., Spielberger, C. D., eds. 1987. *Advances in Personality Assessment*, Vol. 6. Hillsdale, NJ: Erlbaum

Cantor, N., Genero, N. 1986. Psychiatric diagnosis and natural categorization: a close analogy. See Millon & Klerman 1986, pp. 233–54

Cheifetz, D. I., Salloway, J. C. 1984. Patterns of mental health services provided by HMOs. *Am. Psychol.* 39:495–502

Corcoran, K., Fischer, J. 1987. *Measures for Clinical Practice: A Sourcebook*. New York: Free Press

Coryell, W., Zimmerman, M. 1987. Progress in the classification of functional psychoses. *Am. J. Psychiatry* 144:1471–73

Costa, P., McCrae, R. 1985. *NEO-Personality Inventory Manual*. Odessa, FL: Psychol. Assess. Resources

Cyr, J. J., McKenna-Foley, J. M., Peacock, E. 1985. Factor structure of the SCL-90-R. Is there one? *J Pers. Assess.* 49:571–78

Drake, R. E., Vaillant, G. E. 1985. A validity study of Axis II of DSM-III. *Am. J. Psychiatry* 142:553–58

Dudding, G. 1988. Assessment of anxiety and depression in children. See McReynolds et al 1988. In press

Edelbrock, C., Costello, A. J. 1984. Structured psychiatric interviews for children and adolescents. See Goldstein & Hersen 1984, pp. 276–90

Ellsworth, R. B. 1975. Consumer feedback in measuring the effectiveness of mental health programs. In *Handbook of Evaluation Re-*

search, ed. M. Guttentag, E. L. Struening, 2:239–74. Beverly Hills: Sage

Endicott, J., Spitzer, R. L. 1978. A diagnostic interview: the schedule for affective disorders and schizophrenia. Arch. Gen. Psychiatry 35:837–44

English, J. T., Sharfstein, S. S., Scherl, D. J., Astrachan, B., Muszynski, I. L. 1986. Diagnosis-related groups and general hospital psychiatry: the APA study. Am. J. Psychiatry 143:131–39

Evenson, R. C., Cho, D. W. 1987. The Missouri Inpatient Behavior Scale. J. Clin. Psychol. 43:100–10

Eysenck, H. J. 1986. A critique of contemporary classification and diagnosis. See Millon & Klerman 1986, pp. 73–98

Eysenck, H. J., Eysenck, S. B. G. 1975. Manual for Eysenck Personality Questionnaire. San Diego: Educ. Ind. Test. Serv.

Faust, D., Miner, R. A. 1986. The empiricist and his new clothes: DSM-III in perspective. Am. J. Psychiatry 143:962–67

Feinstein, A. R. 1977. A critical overview of diagnosis in psychiatry. In Psychiatric Diagnosis, ed. V. M. Rakoff, H. D. Stancer, H. B. Kedward, pp. 189–206. New York: Brunner/Mazel

Finney, J. C. 1985. Anxiety: its measurement by objective personality tests and self-report. See Achenbach 1985b, pp. 645–73

Frances, A. 1982. Categorical and dimensional systems of personality diagnosis: a comparison. Compr. Psychiatry 23:516–27

Frances, A., Cooper, A. M. 1981. Descriptive and dynamic psychiatry: a perspective on DSM-III. Am. J. Psychiatry 138:1198–1202

Free, S. M., Overall, J. E. 1977. The Brief Outpatient Psychopathology Scale (BOPS). J. Clin. Psychol. 33:677–88

French, N. H., Heninger, G. R. 1970. A short clinical rating scale for use by nursing personnel. Arch. Gen. Psychiatry 23:233–48

Gabbard, G. O., Coyne, L., Kennedy, L. L., Beasley, C., Deering, C. D. et al. 1987. Interrater reliability in the use of the Brief Psychiatric Rating Scale. Bull. Menninger Clinic 51:519–31

Gale, J., Pfefferbaum, B., Suhr, M. A., Overall, J. E. 1986. The Brief Psychiatric Rating Scale for Children: a reliability study. J. Clin. Child Psychol. 15:341–45

Garfield, S. L. 1986. Problems in diagnostic classification. See Millon & Klerman 1986, pp. 99–114

Gdowski, C. L., Lachar, D., Kline, R. B. 1985. A PIC profile typology of children and adolescents: I. Empirically derived alternative to traditional diagnosis. J. Abnorm. Psychol. 94:346–61

Ginsberg, G. L. 1985. Psychiatric interview. In Comprehensive Textbook of Psychiatry, ed. H. I. Kaplan, B. J. Sadock, 1:482–87. Baltimore: Williams & Wilkins. 4th ed.

Goldstein, G., Hersen, M., eds. 1984. Handbook of Psychological Assessment. New York: Pergamon

Gough, H. 1987. California Psychological Inventory: Administrator's Guide. Palo Alto: Consulting Psychologists Press

Grove, W. M. 1987. The reliability of psychiatric diagnosis. See Last & Hersen 1987, pp. 99–119

Harrington, R. G., ed. 1987. Testing Adolescents: A Reference Guide for Comprehensive Psychological Assessments. Kansas City: Test Corp. Am.

Hayes, S. C., Nelson, R. O., Jarrett, R. B. 1987. The treatment utility of assessment: A functional approach to evaluating assessment quality. Am. Psychol. 42:963–74

Hedlund, J. L., Vieweg, B. W. 1980. The Brief Psychiatric Rating Scale (BPRS): a comprehensive review. J. Oper. Psychiatry 11:48–65

Hedlund, J. L., Vieweg, B. W. 1987. Computer generated diagnosis. See Last & Hersen 1987, pp. 241–69

Helzer, J. E., Robins, L. N. 1988. The Diagnostic Interview Schedule: its development, evolution and use. Soc. Psychiatry. In press

Holtzman, W. H. 1988. Beyond the Rorschach. J. Pers. Assess. In press

Honigfeld, G., Gillis, R. D., Klett, C. J. 1966. NOSIE-30: A treatment-sensitive ward behavior scale. Psychol. Rep. 19:180–92

Horowitz, L. M., Rosenberg, S. E., Baer, B. A., Ureño, G., Villaseñor, V. S. 1988. The Inventory of Interpersonal Problems. J. Consult. Clin. Psychol. In press

Jackson, D. N. 1988. Basic Personality Inventory. Port Huron, MI: Research Psychologists Press. In press

Jampala, V. C., Sierles, F. S., Taylor, M. A. 1986. Consumers' views of DSM-III: attitudes and practices of U.S. psychiatrists and 1984 graduating psychiatric residents. Am. J. Psychiatry 143:148–52

Johnson, J. H., Null, C., Butcher, J. N., Johnson, K. N. 1984. Replicated item level factor analysis of the full MMPI. J. Pers. Soc. Psychol. 47:105–14

Kaplan, M. 1983a. A woman's view of DSM-III. Am. Psychol. 38:786–92

Kaplan, M. 1983b. The issue of sex bias in DSM-III: comment on the articles by Spitzer, Williams, and Kass. Am. Psychol. 38:802–3

Kass, F., Spitzer, R. L., Williams, J. B. W. 1983. An empirical study of the issue of sex bias in the diagnostic criteria of DSM III

Axis II personality disorders. *Am. Psychol.* 38:799–801

Kiesler, D. J. 1986. The 1982 interpersonal circle: an analysis of DSM-III personality disorders. See Millon & Klerman 1986, pp. 571–97

Klerman, G. L. 1984. The advantages of DSM-III. *Am. J. Psychiatry* 141:539–42

Klerman, G. L., Vaillant, G. E., Spitzer, R. L., Michels, R. 1984. A debate on DSM-III. *Am. J. Psychiatry* 141:539–53

Kolb, J. E., Gunderson, J. S. 1980. Diagnosing borderline patients with a semistructured interview. *Arch. Gen. Psychiatry* 37:37–41

Krug, S. E. 1980. *Clinical Analysis Questionnaire Manual.* Champaign, IL: Inst. Pers. Ability Test.

Lachar, D., Kline, R. B., Gdowski, C. L. 1987. Respondent psychopathology and interpretive accuracy of the Personality Inventory for Children: the evaluation of a "most reasonable" assumption. *J. Pers. Assess.* 51:165–77

Landry, M. 1988. Psychoactive substance use disorders: the DSM-III revisions. *Prof. Counselor* 2:26–28

Lanyon, R. I. 1978. *Psychological Screening Inventory: Manual.* Port Huron, MI: Research Psychologists Press. 2nd ed.

Last, C. G., Hersen, M., eds. 1987. *Issues in Diagnostic Research.* New York: Plenum

Leary, T. 1957. *Interpersonal Diagnosis of Personality.* New York: Ronald

Loranger, A. W., Susman, V. L., Oldham, J. M., Russakoff, L. M. 1987. The Personality Disorder Examination: a preliminary report. *J. Pers. Disorders* 1:1–13

Lorr, M. 1971. Dimensions and categories for assessment of psychotics. In *Advances in Psychological Assessment,* ed. P. McReynolds, 2:198–215. Palo Alto: Science & Behavior Books

Lorr, M. 1986. Classifying psychotics: dimensional and categorical approaches. See Millon & Klerman 1986, pp. 331–45

Lorr, M., McNair, D. M., Klett, C. J. 1966. *Inpatient Multidimensional Psychiatric Scale.* Palo Alto: Consulting Psychologists Press

Lorr, M., Vestre, N. D. 1985. *Psychotic Inpatient Profile Manual,* rev. Los Angeles: Western Psychol. Serv.

Lorr, M., Youniss, R. P. 1986. *Interpersonal Style Inventory (ISI): Manual.* Los Angeles: Western Psychol. Serv.

Magnusson, D., Öhman, A., eds. 1987. *Psychopathology: an Interactional Perspective.* Orlando, FL: Academic

Marsella, A. J., Hirshfeld, R. M. A., Katz, M. M., eds. 1987. *The Measurement of Depression.* New York: Guilford

Matarazzo, J. D. 1983. The reliability of psy-chiatric and psychological diagnosis. *Clin. Psychol. Rev.* 3:103–45

McCrae, R. R., Costa, P. T. 1986. Clinical assessment can benefit from recent advances in personality psychology. *Am. Psychol.* 41:1001–3

McLemore, C. W., Brokaw, D. W. 1987. Personality disorders as dysfunctional interpersonal behavior. *J. Pers. Disorders* 1:270–85

McReynolds, P. 1968. The Hospital Adjustment Scale: research and clinical applications. *Psychol. Rep.* 23:823–35

McReynolds, P. 1985. Psychological assessment and clinical practice: problems and prospects. In *Advances in Personality Assessment,* ed. J. N. Butcher, C. D. Spielberger, 4:1–30. Hillsdale NJ: Erlbaum

McReynolds, P. 1987. Self-theory, anxiety and intrapsychic conflicts. In *Self, Symptoms and Psychotherapy,* ed. N. Cheshire, H. Thomae, pp. 197–223. New York: Wiley

McReynolds, P. 1989. Motives and metaphors: a case study in scientific creativity. In *Metaphors in the History of Psychology,* ed. D. E. Leary. New York: Cambridge Univ. Press. In press

McReynolds, P., Rosen, J., Chelune, G., eds. 1989. *Advances in Psychological Assessment,* Vol 7. New York: Plenum. In press

Mellsop, G., Varghese, F., Joshua, S., Hicks, A. 1982. The reliability of Axis II of DSM-III. *Am. J. Psychiatry* 139:1360–61

Millon, T. 1986. On the past and future of the DSM-III: personal recollections and projections. See Millon & Klerman 1986, pp. 29–70

Millon, T. 1987a. On the nature of taxonomy in psychopathology. See Last & Hersen 1987, pp. 3–85

Millon, T. 1987b. *Millon Clinical Multiaxial Inventory-II.* Minneapolis: National Computer Systems

Millon, T., Klerman, G. L., eds. 1986. *Contemporary Directions in Psychopathology: Toward the DSM IV.* New York: Guilford

Montgomery, L. M., Shadish, W. R., Orwin, R. G., Bootzin, R. R. 1987. Psychometric structure of psychiatric rating scales. *J. Abnorm. Psychol.* 96:167–70

Mullins, D., Pfefferbaum, B., Schultz, H., Overall, J. E. 1986. Brief Psychiatric Rating Scale for Children: quantitative scoring of medical records. *Psychiatry Res.* 19:43–49

Nathan, P. E. 1987. DSM-III-R and the behavior therapist. *Behav. Ther.* 10:203–5

Nelson, R. O. 1987. DSM-III and behavioral assessment. See Last & Hersen 1987, pp. 303–27

Overall, J. E., Gorham, D. R. 1962. The Brief

Psychiatric Rating Scale. *Psychol. Rep.* 10:799–812

Overall, J. E., Hollister, L. E. 1982. Decision rules for phenomenological classification of psychiatric patients. *J. Consult. Clin. Psychol.* 50:535–45

Overall, J. E., Rhoades, H. M., Moreschi, E. 1986. The Nurses Evaluation Rating Scale (NERS). *J. Clin. Psychol.* 42:454–66

Paul, G. 1987. Rational operations in residential treatment settings through ongoing assessment of client and staff functioning. In *Assessment for Decision,* ed. D. R. Peterson, D. B. Fishman, pp. 145–203. New Brunswick, NJ: Rutgers Univ. Press

Quay, H. C. 1986. A critical analysis of DSM-III as a taxonomy of psychopathology in childhood and adolescence. See Millon & Klerman 1986, pp. 151–65

Quay, H. C., Routh, D. K., Shapiro, S. K. 1987. Psychopathology of childhood: from description to validation. *Ann. Rev. Psychol.* 38:491–532

Raskin, A. 1982. Assessment of psychopathology by the nurse or psychiatric aide. See Burdock et al 1982, pp. 143–75

Rea, W. S., Extein, I. L., Gold, M. S. 1987. Biological markers. See Last & Hersen 1987, pp. 161–78

Reich, J. H. 1987a. Prevalence of DSM-III-R self-defeating (masochistic) personality disorder in normal and outpatient populations. *J. Nerv. Ment. Dis.* 175:52–54

Reich, J. H. 1987b. Instruments measuring DSM-III and DSM-III-R personality disorders. *J. Pers. Disorders* 1:220–40

Reynolds, W. M. 1986. *Manual for the Reynolds Adolescent Depression Scale.* Odessa, FL: Psychol. Assoc. Resources

Robins, L. N., Helzer, J. E. 1986. Diagnosis and clinical assessment: the current state of psychiatric diagnosis. *Ann. Rev. Psychol.* 37:409–32

Rosch, E. H. 1978. Principles of categorization. In *Cognition and Categorization,* ed. E. H. Rosch, B. B. Lloyd, pp. 27–48. Hillsdale, NJ: Erlbaum

Rounsaville, B. J., Kosten, T. R., Williams, J. B. W., Spitzer, R. L. 1987. A field trial of DSM-III-R psychoactive substance dependence disorders. *Am. J. Psychiatry* 144:351–55

Schrader, G., Gordon, M., Harcourt, R. 1986. The usefulness of DSM-III Axis IV and Axis V assessments. *Am. J. Psychiatry* 143:904–7

Schuckit, M. A., Zisook, S., Mortola, J. 1985. Clinical implications of DSM-III diagnoses of alcohol abuse and alcohol dependence. *Am. J. Psychiatry* 142:1403–8

Siegel, J. M. 1986. The Multidimensional

Anger Inventory. *J. Pers. Soc. Psychol.* 51:191–200

Smith, D., Kraft, W. A. 1983. DSM-III: Do psychologists really want an alternative? *Am. Psychol.* 38:777–85

Spielberger, C. D. 1983. *State-Trait Anxiety Inventory (Form Y) Manual.* Palo Alto: Consulting Psychologists Press

Spielberger, C. D., Krasner, S. S., Solomon, E. P. 1988. The experience, expression and control of anger. In *Health Psychology: Individual Differences and Stress,* ed. M. P. Janisse. New York: Springer-Verlag. In press

Spiker, D. G., Ehler, J. G. 1984. Structured psychiatric interviews for adults. See Goldstein & Hersen 1984, pp. 291–304

Spitzer, R. L. 1983. Psychiatric diagnosis: Are clinicians still necessary? *Compr. Psychiatry* 24:399–411

Spitzer, R. L., Williams, J. B. W., Gibbon, M. 1987. *Instruction Manual for the Structured Clinical Interview for DSM-III-R* (SCID, 4/1/87 Revis.). New York: NY State Psychiatr. Inst.

Stangl, D., Pfohl, B., Zimmerman, M., Bowers, W., Corenthal, C. 1985. A structured interview for the DSM-III personality disorders. *Arch. Gen. Psychiatry* 42:591–96

Stengel, E. 1959. Classification of mental disorders. *Bull. WHO* 21:601–63

Swiercinsky, D. P., ed. 1985. *Testing Adults: A Reference Guide for Special Psychodiagnostic Assessments.* Kansas City: Test Corp. America

Taylor, C. B. 1983. DSM-III and behavioral assessment. *Behav. Assess.* 5:5–14

Tellegen, A. 1985. Structures of mood and personality and their relevance to assessing anxiety, with an emphasis on self-report. See Achenbach 1985b, pp. 681–706

Tyrer, P., Alexander, J. 1979. Classification of personality disorders. *Br. J. Psychiatry* 135:163–67

Vaillant, G. E. 1984. The disadvantages of DSM-III outweigh its advantages. *Am. J. Psychiatry* 141:542–45

Vaillant, G. E. 1985. An empirically derived hierarchy of adaptive mechanisms and its usefulness as a potential diagnostic axis. *Acta Psychiatr. Scand.* 71:171–80

Vaillant, G. E., Drake, R. E. 1985. Maturity of ego defenses in relation to DSM-III Axis II personality disorder. *Arch. Gen. Psychiatry* 42:597–601

Vieweg, B. W., Hedlund, J. L. 1984. Psychological Screening Inventory: a comprehensive review. *J. Clin. Psychol.* 40:1382–93

Walton, H. J. 1986. The relationship between personality disorder and psychiatric illness. See Millon & Klerman 1986, pp. 553–69

Weaver, S. J., ed. 1984. *Testing Children: A Reference Guide for Effective Clinical and Psychoeducational Assessments*. Kansas City: Test Corp. America

Weiner, I. B. 1983. *Clinical Methods in Psychology*. New York: Wiley. 2nd ed.

Welkowitz, J., Lish, J. D., Bond, R. N. 1985. The Depressive Experiences Questionnaire: revision and validation. *J. Pers. Assess.* 49:89–94

Westermeyer, J. 1985. Psychiatric diagnosis across cultural boundaries. *Am. J. Psychiatry* 142:798–805

Widiger, T. A. 1982. Prototypic typology and borderline diagnoses. *Clin. Psychol. Rev.* 2:115–35

Widiger, T. A., Frances, A. 1987. Interviews and inventories for the measurement of personality disorders. *Clin. Psychol. Rev.* 7:49–75

Widiger, T. A., Trull, T. J., Hurt, S. W., Clarkin, J., Frances, A. 1987. A multidimensional scaling of the DSM-III personality disorders. *Arch. Gen. Psychiatry* 44:557–63

Wiener-Levy, D., Exner, J. E. 1981. The Rorschach Comprehensive System: an overview. In *Advances in Psychological Assessment*, ed. P. McReynolds, 5:236–93. San Francisco: Jossey-Bass

Wiens, A. N. 1983. The assessment interview. See Weiner 1983, pp. 3–57

Wiggins, J. S. 1982. Circumplex models of interpersonal behavior in clinical psychology. In *Handbook of Research Methods in Clinical Psychology*, ed. P. C. Kendall, J. N. Butcher, pp. 183–221. New York: Wiley

Wiggins, J. S., Broughton, R. 1985. The interpersonal circle; a structural model for the integration of personality research. In *Perspectives in Personality*, ed. R. Hogan, W. H. Jones, 1:1–47. Greenwich, CT: JAI Press

Wiggins, J. S., Phillips, N., Trapnell, P. 1988. Circular reasoning about interpersonal behavior: evidence concerning some untested assumptions underlying diagnostic classification. *J. Pers. Soc. Psychol.* In press

Williams, J. B. W. 1986. DSM-III-R: What's all the fuss about? *Hosp. Commun. Psychiatry* 37:549–50

Williams, J. B. W., Spitzer, R. L. 1983. The issue of sex bias in DSM-III: a critique of "A woman's view of DSM-III" by Marcie Kaplan. *Am. Psychol.* 38:793–98

Wirt, R. D., Lachar, D., Klinedinst, J. K., Seat, P. D. 1984. *Multidimensional Description of Child Personality: A Manual for the Personality Inventory for Children*. Los Angeles: Western Psychol. Serv.

Yudofsky, S. C., Silver, J. M., Jackson, W., Endicott, J., Williams, D. 1986. The overt aggression scale for the objective rating of verbal and physical aggression. *Am. J. Psychiatry* 143:35–39

Zimmerman, M., Coryell, W. 1987. The Inventory to Diagnose Depressionve (IDD): a self-report scale to diagnose major depressive disorder. *J. Consult. Clin. Psychol.* 55:55–59

Zimmerman, M., Pfohl, B., Stangl, D., Corenthal, C. 1986. Assessment of DSM-III personality disorders: the importance of interviewing an informant. *J. Clin. Psychiatry* 47:261–63

Zimmerman, M., Pfohl, B., Stangl, D., Coryell, W. 1985. The validity of DSM-III Axis IV. *Am. J. Psychiatry* 142:1437–41

Ann. Rev. Psychol. 1989. 40:109–31

THE INTENSITY OF MOTIVATION

Jack W. Brehm and Elizabeth A. Self

Department of Psychology, University of Kansas, Lawrence, Kansas 66045

CONTENTS

INTRODUCTION

The idea that motivational arousal should increase with difficulty was suggested by Ach (discussed in Kuhl & Beckmann 1985), who focused on the will to overcome task distractions, and by Hillgruber (discussed by e.g. Heckhausen et al 1985), who noted that motivation must increase to match required effort. More recently, Kukla (1972) hypothesized that the intention to try is a function of a cost-benefit analysis, and, with benefits (e.g. outcomes) held constant, would be an increasing function of task difficulty up to the point at which the individual decides the potential outcome is not worth the effort. In a somewhat different arena, Kahneman (1973) offered the hypothesis that attentional effort rises as a direct function of attentional demand, but increasingly falls short; and more recently, Eysenck (1982) has explored the effects of motivation on attention. These previous formulations

0066-4308/89/0201-0109$02.00

offer only a partial explanation for the bulk of data now available. At the same time, current investigators, with a few exceptions, have failed to note the significance of the difficulty of instrumental behavior in the understanding of motivated behavior. For example, in their otherwise excellent review of the literature on social motivation, Pittman & Heller (1987) distinguished between the states of "control" and "no control." In the following pages we hope to show, among other things, why an understanding of the psychological effects of control must take note of the difficulty of exerting control.

POTENTIAL MOTIVATION AND MOTIVATIONAL AROUSAL

Intensity of motivation may be thought of as the momentary magnitude of motivational arousal. Where the magnitude of motivational arousal concerns the total amount of effort a person would make to satisfy a motive, and this effort could be spread over time, the intensity is the magnitude at a point in time. Thus, where a high level of motivational arousal is spread over a long period, the intensity of motivation could always be low. However, where the magnitude of motivational arousal is high and must be concentrated within a brief period, the intensity of motivation must be great. It is the difference, for example, between moving 100 pounds of books one book at a time or all at once.

Potential Motivation

While the factors that determine the magnitude of motivation, or the total effort one is willing to make, are not the central concern of this review, they nevertheless must be understood because they set a boundary on the intensity of motivation. Here we adopt the simple position that whatever factors affect the effort one is willing to make to satisfy a motive are in fact the determinants of the magnitude of motivation. In general, these factors are internal states such as needs (e.g. food deprivation), potential outcomes (e.g. acquisition of food, experience of pain), and the perceived probability that some behavior, if successfully executed, will satisfy the need, produce or avoid the outcome. As in typical expectancy-value models of motivation, we assume that needs and/or potential outcomes vary in magnitude or value, and that the magnitude of motivation is a multiplicative function of need, value of the potential outcome, and the perceived probability that a properly executed behavior will produce the desired effect. This model, which will be recognized as a simple version of many present-day theories of motivation, depicts what we call *potential motivation*. The reason it is called potential as opposed to actual motivation is that it is not a sufficient set of conditions for the specification of motivational arousal.

Motivational Arousal

The direct function of motivational arousal is not the satisfaction of needs or the avoidance or acquisition of potential outcomes. Rather, it is the production of instrumental behavior. The effort required for that instrumental behavior is not simply proportional to needs and/or outcome values. If we assume that the organism conserves energy, then motivational arousal, or the mobilization of energy, should be no greater than is necessary to produce the needed instrumental behavior. Thus, when little effort is needed, motivational arousal should be low no matter how great the need or how valuable the potential outcome.

There is an upper limit, of course, on what one can or will do. As long as one is able to perform the required instrumental behavior, the upper limit is determined by whether or not potential motivation justifies the amount of effort required. A person who has just had dinner will do little to obtain a hamburger, while a person who has gone without food for a day may be willing to do quite a lot. In other cases, the required instrumental behavior may call for abilities or skills beyond the individual's capacities, in which case there should be no energization regardless of the level of potential motivation. No matter how worthwhile it might be for people to jump 20 feet in the air, they do not energize to carry out that action.

In summary, potential motivation is created by needs and/or potential outcomes and the expectation that performance of a behavior will affect those needs and outcomes. Motivational arousal occurs, however, only to the extent that the required instrumental behavior is difficult, within one's capacity, and is justified by the magnitude of potential motivation. When the difficulty of instrumental behavior surpasses one's capacities or outweighs the value of the potential gain (need reduction, outcome attainment, or outcome avoidance), there will be little or no mobilization of energy. The greater the potential motivation, the greater is the amount of energy that a person will be willing to mobilize. For further discussion of theoretical issues, see Wright & Brehm (1988).

EVIDENCE ON THE JOINT EFFECTS OF POTENTIAL MOTIVATION AND DIFFICULTY

There are three arenas of evidence for the joint effects of potential motivation and the difficulty of instrumental behavior. They are (a) physiological data on arousal, (b) behavioral effects, and (c) subjective appraisals of motivational factors.

Effects on Cardiovascular Reactivity

Because the function of motivational arousal is the production of instrumental behavior, measures of arousal deemed most reflective of motivation involve the sympathetic nervous system, which prepares the organism for activity. Specifically, cardiovascular changes in response to beta-adrenergic stimulation have been linked with effortful coping (Obrist et al 1978). Laboratory attempts to document the relationship between task difficulty and motivational arousal have focused on cardiovascular reactivity as measured by changes in heart rate (HR) and systolic and diastolic blood pressure (SBP and DBP). These changes have been noted not only during coping behavior, but also immediately prior to instrumental activity, indicating that motivational arousal varies in anticipation of task demand.

ANTICIPATORY AROUSAL   A recent study by Wright et al (1988a) varied the difficulty of a memory task required to prevent exposure to an aversive noise. In the easy condition, subjects were told they must memorize two nonsense trigrams within two minutes in order to avoid the noise, while in the difficult condition, subjects were told they must memorize seven trigrams. Subjects in a third condition were told they had been assigned to hear the noise, and no instrumental avoidance behavior was provided.

Immediately after subjects indicated they were ready to begin the memorization (or, in the third condition, to hear the noise), HR and blood pressure readings were taken. These measures were intended to provide evidence of variations in anticipatory motivational arousal.

Both HR- and SBP-change scores varied nonmonotonically with the difficulty of the avoidance task. Heart rate reactivity was greater when subjects expected to memorize seven trigrams than when they expected two or when there was nothing they could do to avoid the noise. Changes in SBP followed the same pattern.

However, DBP-change scores decreased linearly as the difficulty of avoidance increased. Diastolic blood pressure had been described in previous research as mediated by interactions between the inhibitory and excitatory aspects of vascular stimulation (Obrist 1981); therefore, these results were not unexpected.

The effects of task difficulty on HR and SBP in the above study thus provide evidence that anticipatory motivational arousal is a function of energy mobilization in accordance with what is needed for instrumental behavior to avoid an aversive outcome. Two studies indicate that the relationship also holds in an appetitive context.

The first of these (Contrada et al 1984) offered subjects $3.00 for mentally solving eight out of ten arithmetic problems within five minutes, ostensibly as part of a national test standardization procedure. The difficulty of this task was varied by presenting different groups of subjects with problems that were labeled either "high school freshman level" or "second year college level," and that indeed were simple or difficult for the average undergraduate to solve. Measures of blood pressure were taken immediately before the five-minute period was to start, revealing greater SBP increases in the difficult condition than in the easy condition.

The second study (Wright et al 1986) changed the cognitive task and added an impossible condition. Subjects in this study were promised their choice of several pens in a display case if they correctly memorized either 2, 6, or 20 nonsense trigrams within two minutes. Those in the 20-trigram condition were told that this was impossible for most people. Manipulation checks revealed that subjects in this condition reported, on an 11-point scale from 0 to 10, a mean likelihood of success of 0.86.

Measures of HR, SBP, and DBP were taken immediately before subjects expected to begin the memorization. Change scores for SBP showed the predicted effect of task difficulty, with the greatest increase in the difficult (6-trigram) condition. However, HR and DBP were unaffected.

Wright (1984) examined cardiovascular reactivity in preparation for a motor task to avoid shock. In this study, reactivity was assessed by measuring pulse rate and finger pulse volume (greater volume indicating lower reactivity). Some subjects were told they could avoid assignment to a punishment learning session, where they would be shocked for incorrect answers, by first successfully performing a qualifying task. For some subjects the task involved a difficult squeeze on a dynamometer, while for other subjects the task was an easy flip of a toggle switch. Subjects in an impossible-avoidance condition were told that they had been assigned to the punishment group and would receive shocks.

In addition, within the easy and difficult task conditions, subjects were given treatments designed to produce variations in their certainty concerning what response should be made. These manipulations were intended to distinguish between two theoretical types of difficulty in exerting control over outcomes: (*a*) control difficulty due to effortfulness of instrumental behavior, and (*b*) control difficulty due to uncertainty about what behavior should be performed. The former difficulty was varied by assigning subjects to the toggle switch or dynamometer grip tasks. The latter difficulty was varied within these tasks by presenting subjects with a choice between two toggle switches or two dynamometers, and telling them that they could distinguish the correct one to use by performing a color discrimination task. This involved detecting the darker of two squares associated with the two instruments. For some subjects one square was made clearly darker; they could see they would easily know which toggle switch or dynamometer to choose. However, the squares provided for the rest of the subjects were identical. Those in the high-response-uncertainty condition were told that most people could distinguish the squares if they tried long enough. In a third condition, where determining the correct response was intended to be perceived as impossible, subjects were faced with the identical squares and told that only those with a rare visual trait could distinguish them.

Comparisons between easy-response-discrimination subjects facing either the low-effort toggle-switch task or the high-effort dynamometer task indicated that expected effort influenced pulse rate and finger pulse volume. This effect occurred as well for subjects in the impossible discrimination conditions. Furthermore, subjects in the impossible-task condition, who had no instrumental task for which to mobilize energy, showed lower reactivity than those in the high-effort condition. Thus the predicted nonmonotonic pattern was found as a result of variations in the effortfulness of instrumental behavior. (However, within the high-effort condition, response-discrimination difficulty did not produce a similar pattern. On the contrary, subjects in the high-response-uncertainty condition evinced lower rather than greater cardiovascular arousal. Wright suggested that perhaps those subjects facing the combination of the difficult response discrimination and the difficult dynamometer grip may have given up. If so, their motivational arousal should indeed have been low.)

The above studies demonstrate that anticipatory motivational arousal occurs in proportion to the difficulty of an instrumental task and is reduced when no effective instrumental behavior is available. The effects on cardiovascular reactivity were found whether the goal was appetitive or aversive, and whether the task to be performed involved motor or cognitive effort.

AROUSAL DURING PERFORMANCE   Studies examining cardiovascular arousal during task performance have found similar results. Elliott (1969) measured HR in subjects who either could avoid shocks by lifting their hands off a shock plate, or could not lift their hands because they were strapped down. When the shocks were impossible to avoid, mean HR was lower than when subjects were actively attempting to avoid the shock. In a second experiment, subjects were given an appetitive goal (money) for correctly performing a tone-discrimination task. The tones to be discriminated varied in distinctiveness so that in the easy condition they were quite distinctive, in the moderate condition they were somewhat distinctive, and in the very hard condition, they were barely distinctive. It should be noted that subjects in this study *learned* the difficulty of their task as they performed it, rather than being informed ahead of time as in the anticipatory arousal studies described above. For subjects in the easy and very hard conditions, there was a decrease in HR over trials, but for subjects in the moderate condition, HR increased over trials.

Obrist et al (1978) gave subjects a reaction-time vigilance task that was instrumental in avoiding shock. Subjects were to release a telegraph key when they detected a tone. Difficulty was varied by imposing different reaction-time criteria. In the easy condition, subjects were to release the key within 400 msec (achieved on 671 out of 680 trials), while in the impossible condition, subjects were required to react within 200 msec (achieved on 30 of 646 trials). Subjects in the hard condition were told to release the key as fast as they could on the first trial (if they didn't, they would be shocked), and to increase their speed on each of the following trials.

Increases in HR and SBP across trials were greater for subjects in the hard condition as opposed to the easy and impossible conditions. DBP was not differentiated across conditions, a finding consistent with reasoning reported above.

A similar study (Light & Obrist 1983) used the same reaction-time task in an appetitive context. Subjects were promised $.20 each time they met the assigned criterion, which was again either easy, difficult, or impossible. Both HR and blood pressure were measured during a separate relaxation period and during performance. While adjusted SBP and DBP scores were lower in the impossible than in the easy or difficult conditions, the scores in the latter did not differ. A manipulation check revealed that subjects reported trying harder in the easy and difficult conditions combined than in the impossible condition, and roughly half of the subjects in the easy condition reported "trying their hardest" throughout the trials. Apparently the easy condition was not appraised as requiring less effort than the difficult condition, resulting in similar arousal levels. (Adjusted HRs also failed to differ between the easy and difficult conditions; and although they were slightly lower in the impossible condition, the difference was not significant.).

A purely cognitive avoidance task was employed in research by Scher et al (1984) designed to test cardiovascular responsiveness under conditions of varying difficulty and instrumentality. Subjects were given a test that required single-digit numbers to be mentally rearranged before they were repeated in reverse sequence. Electrocardiographic T-wave amplitude (TWA) and HR changes were monitored during a 15-sec anticipatory phase, as well as during each 15-second mental manipulation phase. (This ensured that the measures would reflect cognitive rather than physical effort; the digit recitation period was not included in the analysis.) Difficulty was varied for each subject by presenting either the maximum number of digits he or she had been able to rearrange during preliminary trials (easy trials) or presenting this maximum number plus two more digits (hard trials). Incentive (instrumentality) was varied by declaring that some trials would determine the administration of aversive noise while others were merely for practice.

Both HR and TWA responsiveness were more pronounced on difficult than on easy trials. Furthermore, the incentive factor produced even more pronounced effects: Subjects' reactivity was greater on trials thought to affect noise administration than on practice trials.

Cardiovascular changes during the anticipatory phase preceding each trial indicated that subjects were indeed more motivationally aroused before the test trials than before the practice trials. (Since subjects knew during the anticipatory phase whether they were facing a test or practice trial, but not how difficult that trial was to be, the latter factor was irrelevant in the analysis of anticipatory effects.)

The authors observed that in an earlier experiment (Heslegrave & Furedy 1979), a strikingly different pattern of HR and TWA change had occurred in anticipation of the possible administration of aversive noise. This anticipation period, however, had followed rather than preceded performance; subjects had already acted and were merely waiting for the results of their actions. Under these circumstances, TWA returned toward baseline, while HR decelerated below baseline. Scher et al argued that the differences in responsiveness during the two anticipatory periods were due to the difference between awaiting an "unmodifiable event" as opposed to "active preparation for performance."

The anticipatory effects in this study and the care taken to ensure that the task would be purely cognitive argue against the idea that differences in arousal are primarily due to differences in physical exertion during performance of easy or difficult tasks. Further evidence against this idea was found in research by Fowles and his associates (Fowles et al 1982; Tranel et al 1982). Subjects in the latter study were promised either no reward, $.02, or $.05 for every five button-pressing responses. Heart rate increased with increasing incentive, but response rate stabilized across trials such that there were no significant differences found between groups. The authors noted that the average subject in this experiment was moving his or her hand approximately 85 ft per minute. One might conclude that although subjects were differentially motivated, they reached a ceiling on response rate and were not able to perform any faster. The fact that HR did differ in this study and during the mental rearrangement period of the Scher et al (1984) study described above supports the view that cardiovascular reactivity occurs in response to differences in motivational intensity rather than differences in exertion.

Intended Effort

The difficulty of satisfying a motive can be operationalized in numerous ways, and many operations not intended to affect difficulty can be interpreted as doing so. Here we review evidence in research specifically designed to examine the role of motivational intensity (or at least satisfies the requirements of doing so). Generally, potential motivation and a variation of task difficulty must be involved, and dependent effects must be examined during or immediately before or after performance of instrumental behavior.

A variable that affects intensity but that may not itself depend on the immediacy of task performance is intended effort. Kukla (1972) offered an analysis of achievement behavior in terms of a cost-benefit judgment. As long as the individual believes an effort is worthwhile, the intended effort should be inversely proportional to the perceived probability of success (directly proportional to the perceived difficulty of the task). A somewhat different view has been offered by Meyer & Hallermann (1977) in which intended effort is said to be a function not only of perceived probability of success but also of perceived task skills. Meyer found that when probability of success (Ps) was defined in terms of a social norm, intended effort increased with Ps for those with low self-judged ability, and decreased with Ps for those with high self-judged ability. Regardless of level of self-judged ability, the peak of intended effort appeared to be at about .5 Ps. As we saw in regard to physiological evidence, and as we shall see in the remainder of this chapter, a variety of behavioral and subjective effects are consistent with the general proposition that intended effort increases as task difficulty increases, up to the point where successful performance becomes unlikely.

Behavioral Effects

DIFFICULTY NOT FIXED   When the structure of instrumental behavior is such that the organism can determine the level of effort to be exerted, the intensity of motivation should vary directly with the magnitude of potential motivation. This is simply a formal statement of the obvious point that both human and subhuman animals tend to try harder when the stakes are great. But factors that interfere with goal consumption, such as delay of reinforcement, greatly moderate this relationship. For example, Wike & McWilliams (1967), Wike et al (1967), and Wike et al (1968) have shown that delay of reinforcement during training trials for rats running a runway for food grossly reduces the rate of running speed whether the delay is long or short, introduced early or late in training (but a delay frequency of less than 100% leaves running speed unaffected). There is no benefit to the rat that hurries, if it must nevertheless always wait.

A goal-setting study by Mowen et al (1981) makes a similar point in regard to human behavior. In this type of study, the goal is a performance level. Locke (1968) and his associates have shown that setting high goals for individuals produces better performance than, for example, instructing individuals to do their best. Mowen et al offered certain subjects a monetary piece rate and assigned them goals of low, medium, or high performance. Other subjects could earn a monetary bonus only if they reached their assigned performance goal. Those on the piece rate performed much better at the high performance-goal level than did those who had to make the set level in order to obtain the bonus. A piece rate allows the individual to determine how much of an effort to make, while the bonus for a certain level of performance promotes an all-or-none decision and the possibility that the individual will decide not to try.

GOAL PREFERENCES   The achievement literature is rife with studies that demonstrate the preference of humans for performance levels of intermediate difficulty. While the reasons for this preference are disputed (Heckhausen et al 1985), a plausible reason not yet noted is that motivational intensity, which should be maximal at intermediate levels of task difficulty (depending on potential motivation), may make goals appear more attractive. This issue is discussed at length in the section on subjective effects, below. Here we describe one study done with rats simply to demonstrate the behavioral goal preferences that can occur.

Friedman et al (1968) reported an experiment in which rats were trained in a Y maze that had a difficult hurdle in the right arm. On half of the training trials the rats were forced to go to the right, on the other half, to the left. The goal box at the end of each arm contained either of two foods equal in weight and acceptability but disciminably different. For one group of rats there was no correlation between maze arm and type of food; for the other two groups the food associated with the difficult arm was always the same (food A for one group, food B for the other). Subsequent to training, test trials consisted of a free choice between the two arms of the maze with the same relationship between arm and food that had held for the animal during training. The rats that always found the same food associated with the difficult arm tended to continue to select that arm, while the rats that had experienced no correlation between arm and food tended to choose the easy arm. This result is consistent with the idea that the rats found the difficult-to-attain food (the goal) more attractive.

AMPLITUDE OF NONINSTRUMENTAL RESPONSES   In order to examine the effects of energization on responses irrelevant to goal attainment, Esqueda (1985) confronted subjects with mathematical problems that were easy, difficult, or impossible. Successful completion of the problems would earn each subject a record album. Subjects wore earphones with an attached microphone in order to communicate with the experimenter, who was in a different room. In addition, they were required to write an identification number on each experimental form, and just before task performance, they had to push a button to notify the experimenter that they were ready. Measures of voice amplitude and time to write the identification number were taken before subjects learned the difficulty of their task as well as just before they were to commence the task. While there were experimenter differences on changes in voice amplitude, precluding use of those data, subjects who confronted a difficult math test wrote the number faster than did those who confronted either an easy or an impossible math test. Similarly, those who confronted the difficult test pushed the button harder than did those who confronted the easy or impossible test. Apparently, the motivational intensity produced in anticipation of performing a difficult task increases the amplitude of irrelevant responses.

The Yerkes-Dodson law (1908), which holds that performance is an inverted-U-shaped function of motivation, implies that motivational intensity can become great enough so that it interferes with performance. This would be particularly true of a complex task such as solving difficult anagrams. Ford et al (1985) tested this implication by giving subjects up to 100 sec to solve each of 20 anagrams, where the correct solution for each anagram would earn ten cents. Performance was measured in terms of the mean latency required to solve, failures to solve, and the number of trials required to learn that all anagrams were scrambled in the same pattern. On the assumption that subjects' rating of the attractiveness of the goal would indicate how motivated they were, subjects were divided into groups with low, moderate, and high motivation. As anticipated, those who were most highly motivated performed worse than did those who were moderately motivated.

AMPLITUDE OF RELEVANT RESPONSES   Ach was particularly concerned with how people maintain their behavioral concentration (see Kuhl & Beckmann 1985). Düker (1963) tested Ach's notion that people try harder when their performance is hindered. In the first of two studies in which subjects practiced writing zeros daily until performance was automatic, during a 40-min experimental session subjects were asked to read a light philosophical work while doing the middle 20 min of writing zeros. In the second study, subjects were asked to simultaneously do mental arithmetic problems (addition and subtraction of three numbers) from the 5- to the 15-min mark, and from the 20- to the 30-min mark of a 35-min session of writing zeros. During the first period of mental arithmetic, the problems were done every 5 sec (relatively easy), while during the second period, problems were done every 3 sec (relatively difficult). In both studies subjects wrote zeros faster during the distracting task than during the pre- and postdistraction periods. Furthermore, the more difficult (3-sec) distraction task of the second study produced faster writing than did the easier one. Postexperimental interviews indicated that the subjects were unaware of their increased speed of writing during distraction. While these studies involved very few subjects (2 in the first, 4 in the second), the results are sufficiently dramatic and uniform to convince one of their replicability. Of course, the difficulty manipulation of the second study is confounded with order and time.

A study by Kukla (1974) provides additional evidence of the energizing effects of task difficulty. Kukla assumed that resultant achievement motivation can be interpreted as perceived own ability, with high achievers perceiving high ability, and low, low. Subjects classified as high, intermediate, or low in resultant achievement motivation were given complex mental arithmetic to perform, and were informed that the task was easy (95% should succeed) or moderately difficult (50% should succeed). They were then given 20 min to do as many problems as they could from a set of 252. Kukla reasoned that performance in this case should depend on self-perceived ability: high need-achievement subjects should find the "difficult" task more challenging and perform better on it than on the "easy" task, while low subjects should see the "easy" task as challenging and perform better on it, seeing the "difficult" task as impossible. The results accorded completely with these expectations. From the present perspective, however, either the differential achievement motive (potential motivation) or self-perceived ability, which would affect perceptions of task difficulty, could have produced this pattern of results. When the task is difficult, high potential motivation can make it worthwhile to try; low potential motivation can result in giving up.

LATENT LEARNING   The learning of incidental or irrelevant material has frequently been used to demonstrate drive-like states. For example, Pallak et al (1967) and Pallak (1970) used latent learning to show the drive-like character of cognitive dissonance. The same technique might reasonably be used, therefore, to reflect states of energization that result from task difficulty. Hill et al (1985) had subjects copy familiar and unfamiliar first names, ostensibly for use in a sentence completion task, which in turn was made to look easy, difficult, or impossible. An unforewarned test of recall for the names produced the expected pattern of results. Subjects who confronted a difficult task, relative to those confronting an easy or impossible task, tended to recall more familiar (dominant response) and fewer unfamiliar (nondominant response) names.

PROTECTION OF THE SELF   Effort to protect private self-esteem is seen in a study by Sigall & Gould (1977). The self-esteem of subjects was raised or lowered by false feedback on a supposed personality test. Subjects were then sent to another research room for what was advertised as a separate study. While the subject waited in the hall outside the research room, an ostensible other subject emerged from the research room and remarked to the subject either that the experimenter was very easy to please or that the experimenter was very difficult to please. Subjects were informed by the second experimenter that they were to solve a concept-formation problem, and they were given ten practice problems and told they could do as few or as many as they liked. The experimenter left the room, and the subject was surreptitiously observed. The high-self-esteem subjects were observed to do more practice problems for the difficult- than for the easy-to-please experimenter. In contrast, the low-self-esteem subjects did more practice problems for the easy-to-please experimenter. The pattern of results is strikingly similar to that for the solution of mental arithmetic problems by subjects in Kukla's (1974) experiment with high- and low-need achievers. It seems apparent in both studies that subjects with high self-perceived ability or esteem mobilize more energy for a difficult than for an easy task, while those with low self-perceived ability or esteem mobilize energy for the easy task, which they see as difficult, and not for the difficult task, which they see as impossible.

HELPLESSNESS   Another topic of current interest is how people respond to situations subsequent to an experience of helplessness. The conceptual analysis presented in this review implies that helplessness experiences must affect either potential motivation or perceived task difficulty in order to generalize. For example, failure at some concept-formation problems is not likely to affect either food deprivation or the value of a chef's salad for relief of that state of deprivation. Only if the failure affects the perceived difficulty of obtaining the chef's salad (or otherwise reducing the state of deprivation) will there be some "generalization." Even then, the effect could just as well be intensified effort as depressed effort. The interested reader is referred to Ford & Brehm (1987) for a review and analysis of the helplessness literature.

Subjective Appraisals of Motivational Factors

Lewin (1938) stated that the strength of a goal's valence is a function of the amount of a person's need. While situational qualifying factors were noted, a general example is that an item of food looks more attractive to a hungry than to a satiated person. However, in a study performed in order to validate the use of the Thematic Apperception Test (TAT) as a measure of motivation, Atkinson & McClelland (1948) failed to find the anticipated supporting evidence. They had subjects go without food for 1, 4, or 16 hr before responding to a set of TAT pictures. Surprisingly, increased hours of deprivation had no effect on food imagery or thema, reduced thoughts about food consumption, and increased thoughts about instrumental activity. In the terms of the present review, increasing potential motivation results in thought not about the goal or goal consumption, but about instrumental behavior that would lead to the goal. Presumably, if a TAT measure were taken in immediate anticipation of instrumental behavior, goal and goal consummation thema would be a joint function of the difficulty of the instrumental behavior and the magnitude of potential motivation.

More recently, Mischel & Mischel (1983) examined the thoughts of children concerning delay of gratification. They found two basic rules that the children learned for effective delay: (*a*) cover rather than expose the reward and (*b*) engage in task-oriented rather than in consummatory ideation. We would conjecture that concentrating on the problem of delay rather than on the act of consummation is to focus on the fact that nothing can be done, which avoids motivational arousal.

The proposition of interest in the following sections is that the subjective appraisal of the strength of motivational factors such as desire or goal attractiveness is a direct function of relevant motivational arousal. Thus, food should look attractive to a deprived person only to the extent that the person is engaged in or about to engage in relatively difficult instrumental behavior to attain the food.

APPETITIVE OUTCOMES   The first empirical investigations of goal attractiveness using appetitive paradigms were described in Brehm et al (1983). An experiment conducted by Solomon & Silka promised subjects $1.00 for correctly solving 8 out of 10 mathematics problems within 10 min. This experimental procedure was similar to that used in the Contrada et al (1984) research described above. As in that study, the problems were either at a high school freshman level or second year college level of difficulty, but there was also an impossible condition where problems were at the level of a PhD in mathematics. Subjects were informed of their difficulty level before they expected the 10-min trial to begin.

Measures of goal attractiveness were embedded in a questionnaire handed to subjects immediately before they expected to work on the mathematics problems. Subjects who expected to work on the difficult (college level) problems reported that the dollar prize for success was more desirable than did subjects in either the easy or impossible task conditions.

The researchers included in their questionnaire some items measuring mood states. Subjects in the impossible condition might have reported that the dollar was less attractive because they resented being offered a chance at the dollar and then given an impossible task. However, these subjects did not report anger. Furthermore, the correlation between perceived unfairness and goal attractiveness was .29, indicating that feelings of unfairness were not the major factor determining lowered ratings of the goal.

This experiment demonstrated a nonmonotonic effect of task difficulty on goal attractiveness. Of particular note is the methodology used to obtain subjective measures of attractiveness: Subjects were interrupted just before they expected to begin work on the task. Like the anticipatory arousal found in the studies reviewed above, goal attractiveness effects were expected to occur prior to commencement of instrumental activity. When there is something to be done, the organism should mobilize energy accordingly. Furthermore, the organism should become motivationally aroused only in proportion to task demands, and only when the task is imminent. The degree of this preparatory motivational arousal should correspond to the degree of subjective goal attractiveness.

This point becomes important when considering a dissonance-theoretic (Festinger 1957) explanation for the above results. To the extent subjects felt dissonance after deciding to expend effort to solve difficult problems, dissonance theory predicts that they would try to justify the effort required, perhaps by magnifying the attractiveness of the goal. For subjects who felt dissonance after deciding to work on problems that were impossible to solve, however, one way to reduce this dissonance would be to minimize the importance of failure by reducing the attractiveness of the goal.

However, such dissonance-reduction effects should occur at least as strongly after actual performance of the task in question. In contrast, the present discussion maintains that differences in goal attractiveness correspond to anticipatory mobilization of energy for instrumental behavior. Such differences should not persist after task performance.

An experiment designed to resolve this question was reported in Brehm et al (1983). Investigators Solomon & Greenberg again offered subjects $1.00 for successful completion of 8 out of 10 mathematics problems, labeled at either a high school freshman or second year college level of difficulty. One group of subjects was given the dependent measures questionnaire immediately before attempting the problems, while another group completed the questionnaire after performance.

While both the pretask and posttask groups reported perceiving the college level problems as more difficult and requiring more effort than the high school level problems, only the pretask group reported the expected differences in goal attractiveness. The pretask group facing difficult problems appraised the goal as more attractive than did those who were to attempt easy problems. The posttask group did not magnify goal attractiveness to justify their effort. Brehm et al (1983) concluded that the effects of task difficulty on goal attractiveness were indeed linked to anticipatory motivational arousal for instrumental task behavior.

As an example of a study that deliberately varied task difficulty in an interpersonal context, Wright et al (1984) told male subjects that each would have the opportunity to work with an attractive female if he qualified by memorizing a list of trigrams (three letter nonsense syllables) within two minutes. Subjects were told that they would be required to memorize either two, five, or eight trigrams. This was intended to create easy, moderately difficult, or very difficult task conditions. It was expected that an attractive female would provide sufficient potential motivation so that subjects would not give up even when the task was very difficult.

Manipulation checks revealed that subjects perceived these tasks as differing in difficulty, significantly so between the two- and five-trigram conditions. Unexpectedly, a nonmonotonic relationship was found between task difficulty and goal attractiveness, such that subjects viewed the female as more attractive in the moderately difficult condition than in either the easy or the very difficult conditions.

This pattern had been predicted for another target female who had been rated in pretesting as less attractive, and who was introduced as a goal to a similar group of subjects given varying levels of trigram list length. Instead, subjects rated this female as uniformly unattractive regardless of task difficulty.

These results can be interpreted with reference to the concept of potential motivation. Subjects who were promised the chance to work with the "attractive" female (moderate potential motivation) apparently viewed this chance as fairly attractive when they faced memorizing five trigrams, but not worth the effort of memorizing eight. Those whose goal was to interact with a less attractive female (low potential motivation) probably saw this opportunity as not worth energizing for, even in the five-trigram condition.

A subsequent study by Roberson (1985) also used a female target person and male subjects, but this time the subjects thought they were competing with another male to be selected by the female as a work partner. The male with whom the subject was to compete appeared to be socially inadequate (easy competition) or socially skilled (difficult competition). To create an impossible condition, some subjects were told that the other had already been randomly selected. As predicted, subjects who confronted difficult competition rated the target person as more attractive than did those who confronted easy competition or no possibility of being chosen.

A direct test of the effects of reaching the limit of potential motivation was carried out by Biner (1987). Here, potential motivation was deliberately varied by providing goals with differing objective incentive values; specifically, one group of subjects intended to work for a record album (high value), while the other group was promised $1.00 (low value) for successful task completion. Biner predicted that a very difficult task would require more effort than the dollar was worth, surpassing potential motivation and resulting in low goal attractiveness. However, the same level of task difficulty should be within the limits of what a person would be willing to do for a more objectively attractive goal, i.e. a record album.

Subjects within the two goal conditions were told they must memorize either 3, 8, or 45 trigrams to attain their goal. It was expected that attractiveness ratings of the record would be a linear function of task difficulty, because the very difficult task still would not exceed subjects' willingness to exert effort. Thus intensity of motivation and goal attractiveness should be highest in this condition. In contrast, ratings of the dollar were expected to decrease from the difficult to the very difficult task, since the latter was expected to exceed subjects' potential motivation.

These hypotheses were partially confirmed. Subjects rated the dollar as more attractive in the difficult than in the easy or very difficult conditions. They rated the record as more attractive in the difficult and very difficult conditions than in the easy condition, but not more attractive in the very difficult than in the difficult condition.

This evidence supports the assumption, described above, that a task may be viewed as possible, but as exceeding the amount of effort justified by the goal, and that subjective goal attractiveness will reflect this. Furthermore, the lack of a linear effect on attractiveness of the record may indicate that subjects intended to exert the maximum effort warranted by potential motivation in both the difficult and very difficult conditions.

Another implication to be drawn from potential motivation and the assumption of energy conservation is that when the difficulty of instrumental behavior is ambiguous or unknown, an individual should mobilize the maximum amount of energy provided by potential motivation. Thus, for example, when a person anticipates performing a task in order to attain a positive goal, but knows nothing about the difficulty of the task, motivational arousal and goal attractiveness should be as great as if the task were known to be difficult. Indeed, this effect was obtained in a condition in the above-reported experiment by Roberson (1985). Some of the male subjects who were competing with another male to be selected by an attractive female were told nothing about the social skills of the competitor. These subjects rated the target just as attractive as did those who thought the competition difficult. Similar results have been reported by R. A. Wright, A. Heaton, and B. Bushman (unpublished research).

An interesting extension of the effect of task difficulty on the appraisal of goals or desires is that a variation in difficulty may allow the assessment of what motives are producing behavior. In the controversy over whether helping is produced by egoistic or altruistic motives (e.g. Batson 1987), making it more or less difficult to help should produce differences only in the appraisal of whichever motive is operating. A study to demonstrate this implication was carried out by Fultz (1984), who tried to compare empathy-produced guilt avoidance with empathy-produced altruism. Because of weak manipulations, Fultz did a correlational analysis of his results. He found a weak but consistent pattern of subjective appraisals that suggests empathy produces altruism rather than guilt avoidance.

A further extension of the present analysis applies to the evaluations of choice alternatives. The selection of an alternative can produce anticipatory arousal if the alternative itself requires an immediate expenditure of effort. The obvious prediction, of course, is that the attractiveness of the chosen alternative will rise with anticipation of performance of the difficult task. If performance were to be delayed after the choice, then no rise in attractiveness would be expected. Just such an experiment has been carried out by White & Gerard (1981). They led subjects to expect to perform two different difficult discrimination tasks, and then, on the pretext that time was running short, asked subjects to choose between the two tasks. Following the choice, some subjects were informed that they would immediately start the chosen task, some were told there would be a 10-min delay, and others were told there would be a 30-min delay. Another group of subjects received the same information except that instead of being allowed to choose a task, they were assigned their preferred task. Ratings of task attractiveness demonstrated that the chosen task was rated relatively high in attractiveness, but only when it was to be started immediately. We would have expected the assigned task to show a similar increase in attractiveness, but there was only a slight trend in support of this expectation. Overall, however, these data suggest that the evaluation of an alternative can depend in part on the energy requirements of the alternative.

AVERSIVE OUTCOMES   The studies described above demonstrate that variations in subjective goal attractiveness are linked to variations in the difficulty of attaining a *positively* valued goal. As with the physiological arousal studies, subjective effects corresponding to energy mobilization should occur regardless of whether the goal valence is positive or negative. As the difficulty of performing instrumental behavior to avoid an aversive outcome varies, the energy mobilized should also vary, within the limits provided by potential motivation. Subjective estimates of the aversiveness of the outcome should reflect the degree of motivational arousal.

The above study by Biner (1987) manipulated potential motivation by varying the objective incentive value of the goal offered. Since potential motivation is assumed to be a multiplicative function of need, incentive value, and perceived likelihood that successful performance will be rewarded, it is also theoretically possible to manipulate potential motivation by varying the latter. This should have the effect of creating situations where it is no longer worthwhile to mobilize energy for an outcome that may not be obtained. Subjective appraisals should be depressed under these circumstances.

Expectancy of motive satisfaction was varied in a recent study by Wright et al (1988b). This study threatened subjects with an aversive outcome that was milder than most of the preceding research had used. Subjects were told that they could avoid reading and being tested on their comprehension of scientific articles if they first successfully memorized some nonsense trigrams, *and* if they were lucky enough to choose a qualifying card from a deck offered to all who correctly memorized the trigrams. Thus even successful task completion did not guarantee avoidance of the aversive goal, but rather provided subjects with a chance at avoidance. This chance was varied by describing the qualifying card as any of 14 cards in the deck of 15 (high potential motivation) or as only one of the 15 (low potential motivation). In addition, task difficulty was varied by requiring either 2 trigrams (easy task) or 5 trigrams (difficult task) to be memorized in 2 min. When subjects announced they were ready to begin the memorization task, the experimenter instead handed them a questionnaire measuring their perceptions of task difficulty, likelihood of choosing the qualifying card if they performed successfully, and unpleasantness of the reading comprehension task. Results of these measures indicated that task difficulty and expectancy of motive satisfaction were successfully manipulated. Furthermore, the two factors interacted such that the reading rask was thought to be more aversive in the difficult condition, but only when potential motivation was high due to high expectancy. In the low-potential-motivation condition, both the 2- and the 5-trigram task produced relatively low task unpleasantness ratings. In other words, subjects with low potential motivation due to low probability of motive satisfaction did not mobilize energy to avoid the aversive task, and their subjective appraisals reflected this.

Wright (Exp. 2, reported in Brehm et al 1983) told subjects that they could avoid assignment to a punishment learning group where they would be shocked for each incorrect answer, if they first correctly memorized some trigrams within a specified time. In the easy-task condition, subjects prepared to memorize 2 trigrams in 2 min. Subjects in the difficult-task condition were given 6 trigrams to memorize in 2 min. In a task condition that was intended to be perceived as impossible, subjects were told they must memorize 20 trigrams within 15 sec.

It was predicted that there would be a nonmonotonic effect of task difficulty on ratings of the potential unpleasantness of receiving shocks. Energy mobilized to avoid shock would be greater in the difficult (6-trigram) condition, and thus the shock would be subjectively more aversive than in the easy (2-trigram) condition. If subjects perceived the 20-trigram task as impossible, they should mobilize little energy to avoid the shock, and unpleasantness ratings should be low.

In addition, providing a direct test of the assumption that energy mobilization and goal valence effects occur only in immediate anticipation of instrumental behavior, half of the subjects in each of the above groups were told that the memorization task was about to begin, while the rest were told that there would be a waiting period of about 25 min. All subjects were then given a "departmental form" asking their opinion, among other things, of how unpleasant it would be for them to receive a shock.

As expected, when subjects anticipated immediate task performance, there was a nonmonotonic effect of task difficulty on ratings of shock unpleasantness. Furthermore, the effect was found only in subjects preparing to memorize the trigrams immediately; no significant rating differences were found between task difficulty levels when subjects were told they must wait 25 min.

A further study assessing the effects of task difficulty upon goal valence in an avoidance context was conducted by Wright & Brehm (1984). In this case, the instrumental activity to be performed was a motor task; subjects were to squeeze a dynamometer. The experimenters told subjects that they must either (a) merely move the dynamometer dial (easy task), (b) exceed their maximum practice grip by 5 points (difficult task), or (c) double their maximum practice grip (impossible task). Failure at these tasks would result in exposure to a 2-sec blast of 108-decibel noise. All subjects were given a sample of the noise prior to the assignment of task difficulty.

This experiment was unique among those involving aversive outcomes in that it provided subjects prior experience with the negative outcome, attempting to reduce ambiguity about its objective incentive value. Furthermore, the dependent measures included self-reports on perceived arousal (Thayer's Activation-Deactivation Adjective Checklist; Thayer 1967, 1978).

Results indicated that subjects rated the loud noise as more unpleasant when they faced a difficult task than when they faced an easy task. This provided further evidence that task difficulty mediates subjective appraisal of aversive outcomes, and also evidence that the effects are found with motor tasks. In addition, on the Thayer ADACL subjects reported feeling greater vigor and energy, and less drowsiness, in the difficult than in the easy or impossible task conditions.

However, there was no significant decrease in noise aversiveness between the difficult and the impossible conditions. Furthermore, subjects in the impossible condition did not report significantly fewer feelings of tension or anxiety. Possibly these subjects had not reduced their motivational arousal due to a belief that instrumental behavior was useless, but instead were still searching for a way to avoid the noise.

Subjective judgments of arousal do not reliably correlate with objective measures of arousal (Elliott 1969; Houston 1972; Manuck et al 1978). Apparently, one's body can be preparing for instrumental behavior in the service of a goal while one remains relatively insensitive to the degree of change occurring. More direct evidence of the relationship between task difficulty and subsequent physiological arousal has been provided by studies assessing cardiovascular reactivity (discussed above).

Two that should be reviewed here are the experiments by Contrada et al

(1984) and Wright et al (1986). These studies examined *both* cardiovascular reactivity and subjective goal appraisals. While the former study failed to find any valence effects due to task difficulty, the authors reasoned that subjects may have been distracted from evaluating the goal by the presence of unfamiliar physiological recording equipment.

Wright et al (1986) attempted to prevent distraction by keeping a small light trained on the display case of pens offered as an incentive in their experiment. Both valence effects, as well as effects on SBP, were found. However, measures of subjective perceptions of arousal were taken, and these failed to reveal any effect of task difficulty. Once again, subjects were not particularly sensitive to their cardiovascular responses.

Although the research documenting the effects of task difficulty on goal attractiveness could be taken to be even more indirect than are self-reports as a measure of motivational arousal, this research is compelling because of its consistency. Goal-valence effects have been found, as described above, in both appetitive and avoidance contexts, and for a number of different types of goals. These effects interact with the limits of potential motivation such that subjective goal appraisal is *not* increased when a task requires more effort than the goal is worth.

CONCLUSIONS

Mounting evidence indicates that the analysis of motivational phenomena is aided by distinguishing between potential motivation (e.g. deprivation, the value of positive or negative outcomes) on the one hand, and actual motivational arousal, which is a joint function of the magnitude of potential motivation and the difficulty of the instrumental behavior necessary to satisfy the motive. Motivational arousal rises with increasing difficulty of instrumental behavior up to the point where the required effort is greater than is justified by the motive, or the required effort surpasses the individual's skills and abilities, at which point arousal drops to a low level. Evidential support comes from measures of cardiovascular reactivity, effort, and subjective appraisals of needs and/or potential outcomes. Conceptually, the present analysis applies to all kinds of motivations and all kinds of motivated behaviors.

ACKNOWLEDGMENTS

We thank B. K. Houston, G. Kellas, R. A. Wicklund, and R. A. Wright for help in tracking down relevant work, and J. Mooney for comments on a draft of the manuscript.

Literature Cited

Atkinson, J. W., McClelland, D. C. 1948. The projective expression of needs. II: The effect of different intensities of the hunger drive on thematic apperception. *J. Exp. Psychol.* 38:643–58

Batson, C. D. 1987. Prosocial motivation: is it ever truly altruistic? *Adv. Exp. Soc. Psychol.* 20:65–122

Biner, P. M. 1987. Effects of difficulty and goal value on goal valence. *J. Res. Pers.* 21:395–404

Brehm, J. W., Wright, R. A., Solomon, S., Silka, L., Greenberg, J. 1983. Perceived difficulty, energization, and the magnitude of goal valence. *J. Exp. Soc. Psychol.* 19:21–48

Contrada, R. J., Wright, R. A., Glass, D. C. 1984. Task difficulty, Type A behavior pattern, and cardiovascular response. *Psychophysiology* 21:638–46

Düker, H. 1963. Über reaktive Anspannungssteigerung. *Z. Exp Angew Psychol* 10:46–72

Elliott, R. 1969. Tonic heart rate: Experiments on the effect of collative variables lead to a hypothesis about its motivational significance. *J. Pers. Soc. Psychol.* 12:211–28

Esqueda, L. S. 1985. *Behavior intensity as a function of task difficulty.* PhD thesis. Univ. Kansas, Lawrence. 58 pp.

Eysenck, M. W. 1982. *Attention and arousal.* Berlin/Heidelberg/New York: Springer-Verlag. 209 pp.

Festinger, L. 1957. *A Theory of Cognitive Dissonance.* Stanford: Stanford Univ. Press

Ford, C. E., Brehm, J. W. 1987. Effort expenditure following failure. In *Coping with Negative Life Events: Clinical and Social Psychological Perspectives,* ed. C. R. Snyder, C. E. Ford, pp. 81–104. New York: Plenum. 420 pp.

Ford, C. E., Wright, R. A., Haythornthwaite, J. 1985. Task performance and magnitude of goal valence. *J. Res. Pers.* 19:253–60

Fowles, D. C., Fisher, A. E., Tranel, D. T. 1982. The heart beats to reward: the effect of monetary incentives on heart rate. *Psychophysiology* 19:506–13

Friedman, H., Tarpy, R. M., Kamelski, P. 1968. The preference of rats for a more difficult task. *Psychon. Sci.* 13:157–58

Fultz, J. 1984. *Guilt-avoidance versus altruistic motivation as mediators of the empathy-helping relationship.* PhD thesis. Univ. Kansas, Lawrence. 89 pp.

Heckhausen, H., Schmalt, H.-D., Schneider, K. 1985. *Achievement Motivation in Perspective.* Trans. M. Woodruff, R. Wicklund. New York: Academic. 337 pp.

Heslegrave, R. J., Furedy, J. J. 1979. Sensitivities of HR and T-wave amplitude for detecting cognitive and anticipatory stress. *Physiol. Behav.* 22: 17–23

Hill, T., Fultz, J., Biner, P. M. 1985. Incidental learning as a function of anticipated task difficulty. *Motiv. Emotion* 9:71–85

Houston, B. K. 1972. Control over stress, locus of control, and responses to stress. *J. Pers. Soc. Psychol.* 21:249–55

Kahneman, D. 1973. *Attention and Effort.* Englewood Cliffs, NJ: Prentice-Hall

Kuhl, J., Beckmann, J. 1985. *Action Control.* Berlin/Heidelberg/New York/Tokyo: Springer-Verlag. 286 pp.

Kukla, A. 1972. Foundations of an attributional theory of performance. *Psychol. Rev.* 79:454–70

Kukla, A. 1974. Performance as a function of resultant achievement motivation (perceived ability) and perceived difficulty. *J. Res. Pers.* 7:374–83

Lewin, K. 1938. *The Conceptual Representation and the Measurement of Psychological Forces.* Durham, NC: Duke Univ. 247 pp.

Light, K. C., Obrist, P. A. 1983. Task difficulty, heart rate reactivity, and cardiovascular responses to an appetitive reaction time task. *Psychophysiology* 20:301–11

Locke, E. A. 1968. Toward a theory of task motivation and incentives. *Organ. Behav. Hum. Perform.* 3:157–89

Manuck, S. B., Harvey, S. H., Lechleiter, S. L., Neal, K. S. 1978. Effects of coping on blood pressure responses to threat of aversive stimulation. *Psychophysiology* 15:544–49

Meyer, W.-U., Hallermann, R. 1977. Intended effort and informational value of task outcome. *Arch. Psychol.* 129:131–40

Mischel, H. N., Mischel, W. 1983. The development of children's knowledge of self-control strategies. *Child Dev.* 54:603–19

Mowen, J. C., Middlemist, R. D., Luther, D. 1981. Joint effects of assigned goal level and incentive structure on task performance: A laboratory study. *J. Appl. Psychol.* 66: 598–603

Obrist, P. A., Gaebelein, C. J., Teller, E. S., Langer, A. W., Grignolo, A., Light, K. C., McCubbin, J. A. 1978. The relationship among heart rate, carotid dP/dt, and blood pressure in humans as a function of type of stress. *Psychophysiology* 15:102–15

Pallak, M. S. 1970. Effects of expected shock and relevant or irrelevant dissonance on incidental retention. *J. Pers. Soc. Psychol.* 14:271–80

Pallak, M. S., Brock, T. C., Kiesler, C. A.

1967. Dissonance arousal and task performance in an incidental verbal learning paradigm. *J. Pers. Soc. Psychol.* 7:11–20

Pittman, T. S., Heller, J. F. 1987. Social
motivation. *Ann. Rev. Psychol.* 38:461–
89

Roberson, B. F. 1985. *The effects of task
characteristics and motivational arousal on
the perceived valence of multiple outcomes.*
PhD thesis. Univ. Kansas, Lawrence. 94
pp.

Scher, H., Furedy, J. J., Heslegrave, R. J.
1984. Phasic T-wave amplitude and heart
rate changes as indices of mental effort and
task incentive. *Psychophysiology* 21:326–
33

Sigall, H., Gould, R. 1977. The effects of
self-esteem and evaluator demandingness of
effort expenditure. *J. Pers. Soc. Psychol.*
35:12–20

Thayer, R. E. 1967. Measurement of activation through self-report. *Psychol. Rep.*
20:663–78

Thayer, R. E. 1978. Factor analytic and
reliability studies on the Activation-Deactivation Adjective Check-List. *Psychol. Rep.*
42:747–56

Tranel, D. T., Fisher, A. E., Fowles, D. C.
1982. Magnitude of incentive effects upon
the heart. *Psychophysiology* 19:514–19

White, G. L., Gerard, H. B. 1981. Postdeci-
sion evaluation of choice alternatives as a
function of valence of alternatives, choice,
and expected delay of choice consequences.
J. Res. Pers. 15:371–82

Wike, E. L., McWilliams, J., Cooley, J. D.
1967. Delay patterns, delay-box confinement, and instrumental performance. *Psychol. Rep.* 21:873–78

Wike, E. L., McWilliams, J. 1967. Duration

of delay, delay-box confinement, and runway performance. *Psychol. Rep.* 21:865–70

Wike, E. L., Mellgren, R. L., Wike, S. S.
1968. Runway performance as a function of
delayed reinforcement and delay box confinement. *Psychol. Rec.* 18:9–18

Wright, R. A. 1984. Motivation, anxiety, and
the difficulty of avoidant control. *J. Pers.
Soc. Psychol.* 46:1376–88

Wright, R. A., Brehm, J. W. 1984. The impact of task difficulty upon perceptions of
arousal and goal attractiveness in an avoidance paradigm. *Motiv. Emotion* 8:171–181

Wright, R. A., Toi, M., Brehm, J. W. 1984.
Difficulty and interpersonal attraction.
Motiv. Emotion 8:327–41

Wright, R. A., Brehm, J. W. 1988. Energization and goal attractiveness. In *Goal Concepts in Personality and Social Psychology,*
ed. L. Pervin. Hillsdale, NJ: Erlbaum. In
press

Wright, R. A., Contrada, R. J., Patane, M. J.
1986. Task difficulty, cardiovascular response, and the magnitude of goal valence.
J. Pers. Soc. Psychol. 51:837–43

Wright, R. A., Brehm, J. W., Bushman, B. J.
1988a. Cardiovascular responses to threat:
effects of the difficulty and availability of a
cognitive avoidant task. *Basic Appl. Soc.
Psychol.* In press

Wright, R. A., Kelley, C. L., Bramwell, A.
1988b. Difficulty and effectiveness of immediately anticipated avoidant behavior as
determinants of subjective evaluations of a
potential aversive outcome. *Pers. Soc. Psych. Bull.* In press

Yerkes, R. M., Dodson, J. D. 1908. The relation of strength of stimulus to rapidity of
habit-formation. *J. Comp. Neurol. Psychol.*
18:459–82

Ann. Rev. Psychol. 1989. 40:133–54

THE PSYCHOLOGY OF DECEPTION

Ray Hyman

Department of Psychology, University of Oregon, Eugene, Oregon 97403

CONTENTS

INTRODUCTION

Deception implies that an agent acts or speaks so as to induce a false belief in a target or victim. Even if we restrict the definition to cases of deliberate or intentional deception by the agent, the domain of activities and situations covered by deception is enormous and heterogeneous. Deception includes practical jokes, forgery, imposture, conjuring, confidence games, consumer and health fraud, military and strategic deception, white lies, feints and ploys in games and sports, gambling scams, psychic hoaxes, and much more.

These varied examples can be categorized as deception because they share *formal* properties. But when we speak about a psychology of deception, we

133

raise the possibility that these examples also might share coherent psychological properties. When we refer to the psychology of perception or the psychology of memory we have in mind the possibility of a discipline that promises to hold together conceptually. Thus in one sense—what I will call the strong sense—"the psychology of deception" would be a field of inquiry that deals with coherent psychological phenomena.

No psychology of deception exists in this strong sense. Psychologists and other scholars do study, and speculate about, aspects of deception. Some have even offered preliminary theories about deception. But no one has managed so far to demonstrate that a single, coherent framework can meaningfully account for the psychological issues involved in the various types of deception.

Although we do not know if a psychology of deception in the strong sense is feasible, it is a likely possibility in a weak sense—i.e. a psychology of deception analogous to a psychology of work or psychology of law. In the latter cases, "psychology of" does not imply that either work or law can be characterized in terms of a coherent set of interrelated psychological propositions. Instead, the implication is that various aspects of work, for example, can be illuminated or understood in terms of various subfields of psychology. Employee selection and placement can be dealt with in terms of individual differences and psychometrics; training can be related to the psychology of learning; and other aspects can be related to principles and theories from such subareas as motivation, decision-making, problem-solving, and social psychology. Many aspects of deception can also be treated in terms of psychology's subareas. Indeed, such work is already taking place, especially in lie detection.

In this chapter I do not attempt to provide either systematic or comprehensive coverage of the domain of deception. Right up to the deadline for submission of this chapter, I kept discovering new caches of literature on deception. I have managed to read only a fraction of the articles I gathered in preparation for this task. Thus my objectives are to provide a preliminary overview of the domain and to suggest some of the questions and issues that might occupy a future psychology of deception.

HISTORICAL APPROACHES TO A PSYCHOLOGY OF DECEPTION

The Early Promise for a Psychology of Deception

The early years of psychology's existence as an independent science offered the strong possibility for a psychology of deception. During the late 1800s four major psychologists published articles on the topic. All four—Jastrow, Dessoir, Binet, and Triplett—used the conjurer as their model. Although those early accounts relied heavily on the prevailing associationistic psychology, the principles they illustrate have aged surprisingly well and harmonize with the contemporary view of cognitive psychology.

After 1900, however, the psychology of deception disappeared. A good guess is that it disappeared for the same reasons that attention, imagery, and other mentalistically oriented topics did. A psychology of deception is, of necessity, a mentalistic psychology. Human deception deals with the correspondences between internal representations and external reality. The behavioristic psychology that dominated American psychology from the early 1900s until the cognitive revolution in the late 1950s had no room for mentalism of any kind, including the intentionalism inherent in a psychology of deception.

Jastrow's Psychology of Deception

Joseph Jastrow (1900) included a chapter on "The Psychology of Deception" in his book *Fact and Fable in Psychology*. Jastrow pointed to the obvious illusory nature of knowledge based on sensory information. Helmholtz's controversial doctrine of unconscious inference formed the basis for much of Jastrow's argument. Our perceptions, according to this doctrine, are not based directly on sensory inputs, but rather on inferences that we unconsciously make from these inputs. Such a doctrine can easily accommodate illusory perceptions. Most contemporary cognitive psychologists and cognitive scientists accept, as almost axiomatic, that perception is highly inferential. However, the later Gestalt psychologists vigorously rejected the idea of unconscious inference. Today, those psychologists who call themselves neo-Gibsonians also strongly reject the idea that perception is indirect and inferential.

Those who reject the doctrine of unconscious inference do so because, among other things, they believe it fails to account for why perception, under most everyday conditions, is typically veridical. Whether or not the doctrine fails to account for veridical cognitions, it does provide a good account of nonveridical perception. In contemporary terms, Jastrow's position assumes that every cognition involves a contribution of the observer. The sensory input provides some constraints, but the perceiver automatically corrects for any deficiencies in the data by interpreting the inputs in terms of strong assumptions and expectations. Under ordinary and familiar circumstances these unconscious inferences serve as veridical guides to what is actually the case. But under special conditions they can badly lead us astray. This, in a nutshell, is Jastrow's argument. It accords well with contemporary cognitive accounts.

Jastrow explained illusions within this framework. He wrote that "we are creatures of the average; we are adjusted for the most probable event; our organism has acquired the habits impressed upon it by the most frequent experiences; and this has induced an inherent logical necessity to interpret a new experience by the old, an unfamiliar by the familiar." Jastrow here anticipated the ideas of both adaptation-level and schema theory.

Although many illusions result from the inferential nature of perception, Jastrow realized that unconscious inferences, unlike conscious ones, are inevitable. Even when we are aware that what we are experiencing is illusory, we are still subject to the illusion. However, our knowledge and experience enable us consciously to correct for such errors. But the ability to correct for such errors comes from having previously acquired the correct knowledge. This is why, according to Jastrow, children cannot adequately separate appearance from reality. He pointed out that when children view a spoon half immersed in water they believe it is really bent. It is only fairly recently that psychologists (such as Flavell) have begun studying the development of the distinction between appearance and reality.

Jastrow devoted the bulk of his chapter to the analysis of conjuring tricks. To some degree their success depends upon the audience's ignorance of the tricks' technical details, but it depends much more upon such psychological factors as misdirected attention, controlled expectations, and suggestiveness.

The conjurer's victims know, of course, that they are being deceived by skill and illusion. They also have nothing to lose. Jastrow contrasted this situation with the fraudulent spiritualistic practices of his day. "Spiritualistic phenomena present a perfect mine for illustrations of the psychology of deception." Unlike the conjurer's audience, the sitters at a seance believe that what they are witnessing may truly be paranormal. Jastrow believed it is this attitude that enables the medium to produce "miracles".

After presenting careful analyses of how the conjurer and spiritualistic medium succeed with their deceptions, Jastrow admitted that these deceptions may differ in important ways from con games and other deceptions. He suggested that the latter may be too varied and complex to be comprehended easily within the same framework. Jastrow ended on a note of optimism. He predicted that the spread of education, the increase in technical and other knowledge, and the understanding of the psychology of deception will greatly diminish the possibilities for deception.

Dessoir and Binet

Dessoir (1893) and Binet (1896) provided accounts similar to Jastrow's. All three psychologists carefully studied conjurers and their art. Both Binet and Jastrow enlisted the active cooperation of the most famous magicians of the period. Dessoir pointed out that anyone could purchase books and instructions from magic dealers. But knowing the mechanics and details of the trick neither protects you from being fooled by it nor enables you successfully to perform it. The real secret, according to Dessoir, lies in what he calls the "psychological kernel." Among other things this involves the ability to convince spectators that you really hold an orange in your left hand when it actually remains in your right. Dessoir claimed that this ability is at least partly inherited. The successful conjurer guides the thoughts of the onlookers to the desired conclusions. Today, we might call this the invited inference.

Dessoir, Jastrow, Binet, and Triplett acknowledged implicitly what many contemporary magicians make explicit. A conjurer should lead spectators into the desired inference rather than assert directly what he or she wants them to believe. For example, the amateur magician's statement, "I have here an ordinary deck of cards," violates the principle of the invited inference. Experienced magicians avoid calling attention to the "ordinariness" of the prepared deck. Instead, they simply produce it and handle it as if it were ordinary. Their onlookers spontaneously infer that it is what it seems to be.

Dessoir made one claim that Triplett (1900) questioned. He suggested that uneducated spectators were more difficult to deceive than the educated. Dessoir reasoned that the uneducated person, on guard against being presumed unintelligent, actively resists deception. The educated person, on the other hand, has no need to be defensive and therefore surrenders to the illusion. Triplett countered that uneducated persons might be more readily tricked because they lacked the technical knowledge to understand how the illusion was accomplished.

Regardless of who is right in this regard, the issue of whether some categories of people are more easily fooled than others has occupied both deceivers and scholars of deception. Conjurers, for example, believe that children below the age of five cannot be deceived with the same effects that succeed with adults. This belief is consistent with the findings and theories of contemporary developmental psychology.

Following Jastrow, Dessoir applied the principles of successful conjuring to an analysis of the successes achieved by fraudulent spiritualistic mediums.

Binet (1896) also based his analysis upon the laws of association and the doctrine that the mind interprets the information it gets from the senses. He argued that the study of prestidigitation was an important way to learn how the mind perceives. Using Sully's distinction between active and passive illusions, Binet classified conjuring illusions as passive. By this he meant that they were experienced in the same way by all normal minds.

In another sense, however, conjuring illusions require the cooperation of the public. The public attend the conjuring performance expecting to be deceived. Like Jastrow and Dessoir, Binet recognized that sleight-of-hand succeeds not by quickness but by misdirection. Binet pioneered in the use of photography to analyze sleight-of-hand.

Triplett

Triplett (1900) did his doctoral dissertation on the psychology of conjuring deceptions. A few years ago, Triplett's claim that conjuring originated in a universal instinct of deception would have appeared quaint. However, with the advent of sociobiology and the renewed interest in nonhuman deception, Triplett's discussion of deception in the context of natural selection no longer seems out of place.

Triplett believed that conjuring developed to help primitive man impress and gain control over his contemporaries. He characterized the instinct of deception as "grafted" upon the religious instinct. Human deception, according to Triplett, traces its roots back to such things as a protective mimicry in nature. He points out that there can be no mimicry without a creature to be deceived.

Triplett collected more than 300 observations of spontaneous fooling or deceiving by children, most by children under three years of age. Unfortunately Triplett supplied no details, so we do not know how sophisticated these deceptions were or if they would be classified as true deceptions by today's standards. Triplett also referred to "animistic tendencies of savage people" and to the power, wealth, and self-importance that deception provided the priest-conjurer.

Having shed its original priestly and supernatural context, modern conjuring is, according to Triplett, motivated by the same elements found in other types of play. His analysis of why conjuring succeeds relies on the same arguments used by Dessoir, Binet, and Jastrow. Triplett, however, sets out his analysis in a more systematic manner. He discusses the principles under the rubrics of Attention, Perception, and Suggestions and Association.

Under Attention, Triplett spells out the classic rules of conjuring: Never reveal in advance the nature of the effect, and never repeat the same trick twice on the same occasion (at least not using the same method). Both these rules recognize the fact that if spectators do not know in advance how to direct their attention then their chances of detecting how the trick was done are greatly lessened. Although the basis for these two rules seems obvious, we will see how they consistently play an important role in enabling fraudulent psychics to fool otherwise competent scientists.

Triplett concluded his discussion of the role of attention with a comment that surprisingly suits contemporary approaches to the psychology of deception. "We may summarize this section," he wrote, "with the observation that the fixed mental habits, evolved for useful purposes, to avoid being surprised and deceived, are the very agents employed by the conjurer to this end."

With slight changes in terminology several of the points made by Jastrow, Binet, Dessoir, and Triplett are consistent with the ideas of contemporary cognitive psychology. These include the role of attention and ways to control that attention, the role of expectations and suggestions, the difference between passive and active attention (today's top-down and bottom-up processing), schema theory, priming, and the idea that children before the age of five lack the cognitive structures and knowledge to understand the difference between appearance and reality.

Triplett and others, by the way, tested some of their ideas experimentally. Triplett performed an experiment in which he tossed a silver dollar, a tennis ball, or an apple into the air. This was done before pupils in grades four, five, and seven. The experimenter sat behind the teacher's desk, threw the ball into the air, caught it, and let his/her hands sink behind the desk. On the first trial the ball was tossed three feet in the air. On the second trial, it was tossed four to five feet. On the return of the ball after the second toss, it was dropped between the experimenter's legs and a third toss was mimed. The students were asked to write down what they saw on the third trial. Of the 165 subjects, 78 (47%) wrote that they had seen the ball go up on the third toss and then disappear. Triplett obtained even greater deception when he repeated the experiment under less brilliant lighting conditions.

Although these early forerunners of a psychology of deception focused on conjuring, in many ways their analyses anticipated other aspects of the contemporary scene, attempting to place deception in both biological and developmental contexts. Like some current researchers, too, they applied their findings to account for the success of fraudulent psychics.

THE CONTEMPORARY SCENE

The Psychological Data Base

My computer search of the APA data base under the topic of "deception" gleaned 722 references covering the period 1966–1986. Because this data base excludes books and articles in chapters, and because many journals are not covered, this outcome underestimates the number of relevant publications.

Using abstracts, I categorized the articles. Pieces on lying and lie-detection constituted 39% of the total. Articles dealing with the ethical and methodological issues involved in using deception in psychological experiments comprised 16% of the total. Other categories with relatively large representation involved developmental approaches to deception, evaluation of lie scales on personality inventories, and self-deception (mostly philosophical treatments). The remaining articles dealt with animal deception, legal matters, therapy, the Machiavellian Scale, cheating on tests, and the pathology of lying. The number of articles in the ethics-of-deception-in-experiments category hit a peak of approximately 15 per year in the middle 1970s and has subsequently declined to approximately 3–5 per year. The number of articles on lying and lie detection has tended to increase each year during this period.

Informal Survey of the Remaining Literature on Deception

The psychological data base contains only a small fraction of the literature on deception. Many important psychological articles on deception have appeared in sources not covered by the data base. Many major categories of deception (e.g. military and strategic deception) are not represented or are poorly represented (e.g. nonhuman deception). Several publications on swindles and confidence games, medical and psychiatric aspects of deception, fraud in psychical research, sociology of deviance, and self-deception escaped inclusion in the psychology data base. Indeed, I keep finding new sources for references on deception.

CATEGORIES AND EXAMPLES OF DECEPTION

In the absence of a systematic framework for, or a theory of, deception I cannot formally justify including the examples below and the exclusion of others. Nevertheless, I hope my choices fairly sample the varieties of deception and highlight a representative set of questions and issues.

Nonhuman Deception

Some authors might argue that nonhuman deception is a contradiction in terms because deception is uniquely human. Such a position depends partly on definition and partly on assumptions about animal cognition. A minimal definition of deception (cf Mitchell 1986) might include the following: an organism S emits a signal (behavior or communication) that is registered by an organism R. R believes that the signal indicates that X is the case and behaves appropriately, when in fact X is not the case. Mitchell would add that S should desire or benefit from $R's$ behaving as if X were the case. In this form, Mitchell's definition easily accommodates many kinds of nonhuman activity. However, many writers insist that S should *intend* that R falsely believe that X is the case.

For many, the requirement that the false belief be intentionally created would rule out nonhuman forms of "deception"—e.g. mimicry, deceptive signaling among fireflies, and the like. Most of us would not concede to infrahuman creatures the required level of cognitive complexity. But what about pongoid apes such as chimpanzees? Here the situation is not so clear. Chevalier-Skolnikoff (1986) among others has argued that adult chimpanzees develop the cognitive capacity for at least some forms of intentional deception. Investigators have reported many examples of apparent deception among nonhumans (cf Mitchell & Thompson 1986). So far, however, determined skeptics have managed to account for the observed behavior without resort to intention (Lewin 1987). On the other hand, philosophers such as Dennett, working closely with naturalists, believe they can devise criteria that will detect intentional deception if it occurs among nonhumans (Dennett 1987).

Regardless of whether nonhumans can intentionally deceive, they do engage in intricate forms of behavior that function as deceptions. Do these deceit-like behaviors have any relation to human deception? If not, what makes human deception unique? What is the biological basis, if any, of human deception?

In this chapter I can only supply a few examples to suggest the nature and scope of the problem.

ASHLEY'S DOG   The philosopher Dennett (1978) wanted to know if animals other than humans were second-order intentional systems. An intentional system in the philosophical sense is one that has mental states (such as desires and beliefs) about things other than themselves. Dennett has little doubt that many nonhumans are first-order intentional systems in this sense. A second-order intentional system is one that can have beliefs, desires, and other intentions about other beliefs, desires, and intentions. To *intentionally* deceive someone, for example, the deceiver must be a second-order intentional system (I use "intentionally," here, in both the philosophical and everyday senses.) The deceiver must have beliefs about the intended victim's beliefs.

Dennett requested friends to supply him with examples of nonhuman second-order intentional systems. Peter Ashley provided this compelling instance:

> One evening I was sitting in a chair at my home, the *only* chair my dog is allowed to sleep in. The dog was lying in front of me, whimpering. She was getting nowhere in her tyring to "convince" me to give up the chair to her. Her next move is the most interesting, nay, the *only* interesting part of the story. She stood up, and went to the front door where I could still easily see her. She scratched the door, giving me the impression that she had given up trying to get the chair and had decided to go out. However, as soon as I reached the door to let her out, she ran back across the room and climbed into her chair, the chair she had "forced" me to leave (Dennett 1978, pp. 274–75).

If we attribute to the dog the *intention* that Ashley *believe* she *wants* to go out, then we are dealing not merely with a second-order, but with at least a third-order intentional system. Dennett concedes, however, that we can provide a lower-level account of the dog's behavior. The dog might simply be a behaviorist, associating her trip to the door with Ashley's leaving the seat. The dog might have this first-order belief without harboring intentions or beliefs about Ashley's mental states.

A simpler account might be as follows. The dog has a hierarchy of desires. Her currently strongest desire is to get into her chair, but this is blocked because her master is sitting in it. Consequently, her next highest desire is activated; she tries to get outside. When Ashley vacates the chair to let her out, however, she suddenly becomes aware that her first desire can now be fulfilled.

THE BROKEN-WING DISPLAY   Dennett compares the preceding example with the case of low-nesting shore birds such as the plover, which appear to feign a broken wing to lure a predator away from the nest. If anything, such deceptive behavior appears more sophisticated than that exhibited by Ashley's dog. Even more intricate and devious is the "deception" that occurs both within and between species of fireflies (Lloyd 1986).

No one suggests that plovers or fireflies intentionally conceive and carry out their "deceptions," using cognitive operations similar to those of humans. Indeed, we tend to dismiss such seemingly complicated social interactions as instinctive. But as Dennett (1987) suggests, the behavior of these nonhumans is in some sense no less intelligent. The sophisticated deceptions work and contribute to the survival of the species. In these instances the "intelligence" is not located in the individual cognitive system of each plover and each firefly. Rather, it originates in the fine-tuning of inherited capacities by natural selection over thousands or millions of generations.

The preceding paragraph implies that we do not need intention—at least not higher-order intention—for successful deception. If this is so, can human deception be explained without recourse to intention? Or is human deception qualitatively different from the deceptions that pervade the nonhuman animal world?

DECEPTION AMONG CHIMPANZEES   One place to look for continuity between nonhuman and human deception is among the pongoid apes, our closest animal relatives. Those who study chimpanzees have looked for examples of intentional deception. As De Waal (1986) acknowledges, however, it is almost impossible to prove unequivocally that a given act was intentional. Investigators have observed apparently deceptive behaviors that seem intentional. De Waal (1986) classifies such behaviors as: (a) camouflage, (b) feigning interest, (c) feigning a mood, (d) signal correction, and (e) falsification.

De Waal (1986) supplies a typical example of chimpanzee deception observed at the Arnhem zoo. Dandy, a young male, was seen walking over a spot where some grapefruits had been buried. Because Dandy did not stop or look around as he passed the spot, the observers thought he had not noticed the grapefruits. However, some three hours later, when the other chimpanzees were asleep, Dandy ran directly to the spot, dug the grapefruits up, and ate them.

De Waal acknowledges that alternative scenarios can account for such behavior without attributing deceptive intent to the chimpanzee. He makes the interesting observation, however, that those investigators who spend the most time working with apes are the ones most likely to attribute intentional deception to them.

Chevalier-Skolnikoff (1986) believes that adult apes achieve at least the sixth stage of Piaget's sensorimotor intelligence. Among other things, this stage implies cognitive capacities such as self-awareness and the ability to take the perspective of the other. Chevalier-Skolnikoff and others (Vasek 1986) believe that these capacities should suffice for successful deception. However, Chevalier-Skolnikoff, in over 800 hr of observations of captive apes, observed only three instances of what she could describe as intentional deception (1986). None of her three cases convinces me.

De Waal (1986) concludes that "deception seems to permeate all aspects of chimpanzee social life." Yet, earlier in the same article, he writes that, after spending approximately 6,000 hr observing the social interactions among the chimpanzees at the Arnhem colony, "striking instances of possible deception among the apes were rare."

We do not know the extent to which apes practice deception. Cases that seem to implicate intention are neither plentiful nor intricate. Indeed, the nonintentional deceptions among birds and insects appear more sophisticated.

This might imply that human deception does not have evolutionary roots in nonhuman deception. However, if deception has adaptive value, then it may have arisen independently several times in evolutionary history. Human intentional deception and nonhuman forms of deception may be products of convergent evolution.

Children and Deception

Another place to look for the origins of human deception is in the social and cognitive development of children. Triplett (1900), as we have seen, claimed to observe frequent deceptions among very young children. DePaulo et al (1985) agree that very young children frequently (and unsuccessfully) lie. When first-graders tell lies, they do not fool their peers. Third-graders also do poorly at fooling their peers. Fifth-graders, however, not only successfully deceive other fifth-graders but also fool adult strangers. In some cases, they fool their parents.

The evidence indicates, then, that children become reasonably skilled in deception just before adolescence. Thus some investigators believe that children as young as five or six possess the necessary cognitive tools for successful deception (Chevalier-Skolnikoff 1986; Vasek 1986). Other analyses (Newman 1986; Chandler 1988) suggest that the necessary cognitive structures for successful deception do not develop until adolescence. Flavell (personal communication) suggests that children do possess the required cognitive competence around age five, but several years of experience and practice are needed before they can apply their deceptive competence effectively.

Jastrow (1900) and Triplett (1900), in agreement with conjurers, wrote that magicians could not fool young children in the same way that they could fool adults. They suggested this was because children had not yet developed notions of causality. When the conjurer appears to remove and then restore an assistant's head, older children and adults are baffled. Younger children, however, lacking both causal structures and knowledge of physiology, do not realize that a genuine decapitation would be fatal. The conjurer's problem is not that young children cannot be fooled, but that they cannot recognize and appreciate being fooled.

Young children, as we have seen, do attempt deceptions, but these are transparent and do not succeed. Presumably this is because they cannot fully appreciate how the situation appears to their intended victim. To deceive successfully, the deceiver must be able to take the perspective of the victim.

Both the appearance-reality distinction and the capacity for perspective-taking have been investigated by developmental psychologists. The evidence indicates that children of three years and younger cannot distinguish appearance from reality or take the perspective of another (Flavell et al 1983; Taylor & Flavell 1984). The same evidence suggests that children have acquired both of these cognitive skills by the time they reach the first grade. Indeed, Flavell et al (1983) show that these two abilities are intercorrelated and develop together.

However, the total set of cognitive tools needed for deception may be much larger and not in place until early adolescence. Newman (1986) argues that investigators may have failed to distinguish between cooperative communication, based on shared knowledge, and perspective-taking. To communicate successfully on the basis of assumed mutual knowledge, he suggests, does not require the child actively to represent the situation as perceived by the other. However, to deceive intentionally, the child must actively represent the victim's situation and keep it separate from the true situation.

Chandler (1988) believes that first-graders can appreciate that others may interpret a *situation* differently from the way they themselves do, but this need not imply a full recognition that two individuals can construe the *same information* differently. The first-grader might assume that another individual lacks the information needed to interpret the situation properly, and that if the missing information became available the other would, of necessity, find the single true interpretation. According to Chandler, only in early adolescence does the child fully appreciate the possibility that, given the same information, the other person can still construe the situation differently. Chandler's analysis seems to imply that it is not until early adolescence that children achieve the capacity for intentional deception.

The theory that children achieve the cognitive structures necessary for intentional deception in early adolescence may help account for the many and striking instances of psychic fraud by young teenagers. Nicol (1979) reviews many examples of such adolescent fraud, ranging from the fraudulent pretense to being manipulated by witches to the creation of poltergeist phenomena. I describe once such case in the next section.

Psychic Fraud

From its inception, psychical research has been plagued by problems of fraud (Hyman 1981a, 1985). When we read about how a fraudulent medium or psychic fooled an investigator (often a trained scientist), the success of the trick seems incredible. We react similarly to tales of confidence swindles and scientific hoaxes. But our assumption that we, unlike the victimized investigator, would have seen through the trick is based on hindsight and is probably unwarranted. Reading about the swindle differs essentially from being involved at the time of its occurrence.

Zimbardo et al (1977) refer to this attitude as "the illusion of personal invulnerability" or the "not me syndrome." We express it when we disparage the victims of deception and hoaxes as gullible.

> Such an orientation is dangerous because it alienates us from the human condition. By setting ourselves apart from others, we do not learn the important message from their experience—namely, that the source of their suffering, loss of face, or fall from grace may lie not in their personal weaknesses nor in the stars, but in *the power of the situation* (p. 3).

Rather than dismiss cases of successful deception as due to naiveté, we should look upon them as opportunities for discovering those situational and other factors that enabled the deception to succeed. Delanoy (1987) provides some valuable insights into factors that make the psychic pretender's task easier than it might otherwise be. She supplies us with an unusually frank account of her experiences in testing an alleged psychic who participated in over 20 testing sessions at the University of Edinburgh.

Tim was 17 years old at the time of the tests. He claimed that he had begun bending metal with the power of his mind at age four. Delanoy describes him as "an almost ideal subject." He was cooperative, seemed willing to submit to any controls, and even suggested additional controls. During the first few sessions, which were deliberately informal so as to allow the subject to acclimate to the laboratory conditions, Tim managed to bend several objects, but never when he was being carefully observed. For the next four sessions, the investigators employed controls suggested to them by the magician James Randi. The results were similar. Tim produced bent objects but never when the strict controls were in force.

During sessions 9 and 10 a visiting parapsychologist tested Tim on a special PK (psychokinesis) machine alleged to be fraud-proof. Tim succeeded on some trials. Although the parapsychologist had failed to verify that all the machine's controls had been operative during Tim's successes, he deemed the results promising. Once Tim brought a sealed plastic cube to the laboratory. He claimed to have psychically altered a metal band inside the cube. The investigators mailed the cube to Randi. Randi returned the cube with a description of how it had obviously been tampered with.

Further sessions with Tim produced similar inconclusive results.

After having experienced several sessions with Tim, Delanoy listed several reasons for being suspicious of his abilities. He had never bent metal under controlled conditions. Not only did the evidence suggest that he had tampered with the plastic cube, but, in relation to the same incident, he had apparently lied about his witnesses. In addition, he had shown no interest in trying his abilities with a similar, but fraud-proofed cube. He also had shown suspicious behavior in connection with some other tests.

Despite these reasons, Delanoy was reluctant to give up on the possibility that Tim had real powers.

However, there were also several factors which would point towards the subject's genuineness. He had succeeded in producing positive results on JI's piezo-electric crystal organ machine, at a time when the artifact controls were activated (although they had not been adequately tested for proper functioning). Indeed, JI did find the subject's results to be most promising. Other factors included: (1) he had suggested a method of metal-bending (placing a cupped hand over a small object placed on a flat surface) which was approved by Mr. Randi as being "fraud-proof"; (2) he had suggested filming his metal-bending in the ganzfeld using an infrared camera; (3) he was always very willing to work with any controls which we suggested; (4) he had invested a great deal of time in working with us and seemed quite willing to continue doing so; and (5) his general demeanor was consistently cooperative and openly friendly. This last factor requires some elaboration. During the time we had worked together I felt I had come to know Tim fairly well. We had established what appeared to be an honest, friendly and trusting rapport. If he was fraudulent I thought he either deserved an Academy Award for a most convincing performance or that he was prone to severe self-delusions, at the least (p. 252).

Delanoy refers to the generally accepted ideal in psychical research of having "a friendly and open rapport" with the subjects. She points out that parapsychologists "need" their subjects. Without them, of course, they have no basis for collecting evidence. Finally, she acknowledges she was probably biased towards believing Tim.

Although the Edinburgh parapsychologists devoted 20 sessions and approximately 60 hr to investigating Tim, they were spared the embarrassment of endorsing his "powers." They had sought and followed the advice of magician and psychic investigator Randi about how to control for possible trickery. Tim never managed to produce results under the strictly controlled conditions.

During the final sessions, the Edinburgh investigators decided to try to resolve their doubts about Tim. Up to that point they had never hidden anything in their procedures from Tim. But for these sessions they set up a hidden camera. The hidden camera produced evidence of blatant trickery on Tim's part. When confronted with this evidence, Tim confessed. He explained how he had practiced conjuring since childhood and had deliberately offered his services to the parapsychologists to see if he could trick them.

Delanoy believes her experiences with Tim are typical. Many believe they can judge the honesty of their subjects. The evidence, however, indicates that despite such confidence, humans cannot accurately distinguish honest from dishonest communications (DePaulo et al 1985; Zuckerman et al 1986). Although she had several objective reasons for suspecting Tim's claims, she managed to find even more compelling reasons to believe them. She could not believe, for example, that a 17-year-old student could dissimulate so convincingly, and she'd been misled by Tim's suggesting fraud-proof tests, even though he never succeeded at them.

Tim's metal-bending "talents" had been stimulated by the highly publicized feats of the alleged psychic Uri Geller in the 1970s. Geller was investigated and endorsed by many prominent scientists (for useful accounts see Marks & Kammann 1980; Panati 1976; Randi 1982). Yet, not one of these scientists ever observed Geller to bend metal under controlled conditions (Hyman 1976). Why were otherwise competent scientists willing to endorse the paranormal powers of Geller when he, like Tim, could not perform under properly controlled conditions?

Insights into how this could happen come from an article published in *Nature* by a team of prestigious British physicists who had observed Geller and were obviously impressed (Hasted et al 1975). They admitted that they had not observed Geller's feats under rigorous, fraud-proof conditions, but pointed out that in investigating paranormal phenomena it was counterproductive to insist upon rigor at all costs. Unlike the typical physical phenomena of the scientific laboratory, the alleged psychokinetic powers of Geller emanated from a human mind. This implied that the relationship between the experimenter and the "psychic" was very important. Indeed, this was why they rejected having a magician present during the experiments: Magicians tended to be skeptical and generated a negative attitude that blocked the occurrence of psychic phenomena.

These same investigators also found that it was important for all present to be relaxed and to seriously want the "psychic" to succeed. Just as important, they added, was open-mindedness. They found phenomena more likely to happen when no one was looking attentively for any specific outcome. "In addition, matters seem to be greatly facilitated when the experimental arrangement is aesthetically or imaginatively appealing to the person with apparent psychokinetic powers."

Hasted et al conceded that such conditions make it difficult to prevent trickery. But they optimistically believed this could nevertheless be done.

> How, then, are we to avoid the possibility of being tricked? It should be possible to design experimental arrangements which are beyond any reasonable possibility of trickery, and which magicians will generally acknowledge to be so. In the first stages of our work we did in fact present Mr. Geller with several such arrangements, but these proved aesthetically unappealing to him (Hasted et al 1976, p. 194).

Cynics may note how convenient it was for Geller that fraud-proofing turned out to be "aesthetically unappealing," and that the conditions Hasted et al listed as conducive to Geller's success are just those conditions that, according to Binet, Dessoir, Jastrow, and Triplett, enable the conjurer to fool onlookers.

To comprehend how such prominent scientists can paint themselves into such a corner we must view the situation from their perspective. When they wrote their article, they had already become convinced of Geller's paranormal powers. They realized that no such powers had ever yet survived scrutiny by scientific methods. From their perspective, then, the major task was to find a way to keep the powers they credited from fading under investigation. If they could find conditions that enabled the "psychic" to produce his phenomena reliably in the laboratory, then they could later bring in the skeptics and use more traditional scientific methods.

The flaw in this strategy, of course, is that if the alleged psychic is a fraud, the investigators have played into his or her hand.

Other Cases

I briefly mention a few other types of deceptions in this section.

DECEPTION IN SCIENCE   Deception in science has recently become a topic of interest (Bechtel & Pearson 1985; Broad & Wade 1982; Kohn 1986). The focus tends be on the possible causes of data manufacturing, plagiarism, and other deceptions by seemingly talented scientists. But an equally interesting question is how deceptions—originating within science or without—succeed in fooling competent scientists. The preceding section discussed how scientists have been fooled by fraudulent psychics.

An interesting example of another sort is that of Piltdown Man (Blinderman 1986; Gould 1980; Millar 1974; Weiner 1980). Who carried out this hoax? The obvious suspect is Charles Dawson, the man who originally "discovered" the fossils and, along with Sir Arthur Smith Woodward, announced the discovery of an ancient fossil man with a very human braincase and a decidedly ape-like jaw. From 1912 until 1953, Piltdown Man was accepted as a legitimate fossil and, at least in the earlier period, was considered the likely ancestor of modern man. Many writers, unable to believe that a country solicitor and amateur scientist could so successfully have fooled the greatest archaeologists, continue to look for a suspect with the knowledge and skills to carry out the hoax. This search for a more worthy deceiver seems motivated by the same elitism that refuses to accept Shakespeare as the author of great literature.

In fact, though, the Piltdown hoax was not skillfully executed. When Weiner first raised the question that fraud might have been involved, he asked himself on what evidence everyone had accepted the association of the ape-like jaw with the Piltdown skull. As an anatomist, he decided that the only basis for accepting this match was the fact that the molars were worn flat—a feature never previously witnessed in ape's teeth. Weiner and Le Gros Clark made a list of the features that would be exhibited by molars that had been worn flat naturally. When they went to London to examine the Piltdown jaw, they found that the molars deviated from the criteria on every count (Le Gros Clark 1956). For example, under natural stresses the first molar is normally more severely worn than the second. The first and second molars of the Piltdown jaw were worn to the same degree. The molar teeth of the lower jaw normally wear down more severely on the outer than the inner side. The Piltdown molars were worn down in exactly the opposite direction. Because enamel and dentine wear at different rates, the worn molars normally exhibit shallow concavities. The surfaces of the Piltdown molars were worn flat without any differences between the enamel and the dentine. With normal wear, the edges of the molars are rounded and beveled. The Piltdown molars had edges that were sharp and unbeveled. In addition, microscopic inspection revealed that the surfaces of the molars were scored with telltale crisscross scratches.

These and other obviously artifactual signs were glaringly obvious to Weiner and Le Gros Clark.

> Indeed, so obvious did they seem that it may well be asked—how was it that they had escaped notice before? The answer is really quite simple—they had never been looked for. The history of scientific discovery is replete with examples of the obvious being missed because it had not been looked for, and the present instance is just one more example; nobody previously ever examined the Piltdown jaw with the idea of a possible forgery in mind (Le Gros Clark 1956, p. 145).

The Piltdown forgery succeeded not so much because of the skill of the forger, but because scientists, like other humans, are heuristic systems. They focus on what matters and do not waste time on what can be taken for granted. Such a heuristic works well most of time. But when scientists deal with a nature that is intelligent and responsive to their activities, then their normal mode of operation makes them especially vulnerable to deception.

SWINDLES AND CONFIDENCE GAMES   The literature on swindling and confidence games is enormous and rich in instructive examples. The classic work on confidence games is Maurer's *The American Confidence Man* (1974), a slightly updated version of his 1944 book *The Big Con*. Additional sources of information include Henderson (1985), Nash (1976), and Ortiz (1984). Hankiss (1980) and Leff (1976) attempt to provide theoretical frameworks for understanding confidence swindles. Leff's little-known book is particularly successful in using dramaturgical, social psychological, and microeconomic theory to provide a coherent account of con games, swindling, and deceptive selling techniques.

Accounts of confidence games, because of their often bizarre characteristics, frequently elicit variants of the "not me syndrome." Listeners or readers cannot believe they can be victimized by such scams. Yet the victims are often bankers, successful business people, and even con artists themselves. In 1925 the famous confidence man Victor Lustig managed to sell the Eiffel Tower to successful Parisians not once, but twice. How he did this is particularly instructive (Mason 1978).

LYING AND LIE-DETECTION   I cannot attempt here to review the literature on lying and lie-detection. The research and the literature on this topic contribute by far the largest number of articles to the psychological data base. The issues are important and relevant to many ethical, legal, and other societal concerns. For this reason the topic is characterized by vigorous controversies. The issues are complex, and this topic deserves a chapter of its own in some future volume. The following references provide an introduction to this literature: Ben-Shakhar et al 1982; DePaulo et al 1985; Ekman 1985; Lykken 1981, 1985, 1987a,b; Raskin 1988; Raskin & Kricher 1987; Waid & Orne 1982; Zuckerman et al 1986.

ADDITIONAL TOPICS   Practical jokes (Smith 1956), self-deception (Krebs et al 1988; Sackeim & Gur 1985; Quattrone & Tversky 1984), the Munchausen Syndrome (Pankratz 1981), and strategic and military deception (Daniel & Herbig 1982; Gooch & Perlmutter 1982) are among a number of additional topics that provide instructive examples of deception.

BORDERLINE AND RELATED CASES

Without a theoretical framework, it is difficult to decide what elucidates deception. Many types of deception are interesting because they occur both as deliberate deceptions and as innocent mistakes or self-deceptions. Most character readers, for example, are as much victims of subjective validation as are their clients (Hyman 1977, 1981). But a subset of these practitioners deliberately employ deception to gain information and convince their clients of their powers. The metal bending of Uri Geller and his many imitators is the result of deliberate trickery. But the metal bending that occurs at spoon-bending parties (Houck 1984) typically results from self-delusion. The owner of the famous horse Clever Hans (Pfungst 1911) apparently was unconsciously cuing his horse, but most owners of allegedly intelligent or mind-reading animals deliberately use deceptive cuing. In addition to these ambiguous cases, there is the enormous class of human errors, mistakes, delusions, and self-deceptions.

SUMMARY AND CONCLUSIONS

When I undertook to write this chapter, I thought hopes for a psychology of deception in the strong sense were unrealistic. A psychology of deception in the weak sense, however, seemed well within reach. One value of trying to apply contemporary psychological theories to the understanding of deception could be the testing and sharpening of the theories.

I tried not to prejudge the issue. I avoided providing a systematic framework for organizing the material in this chapter, instead, simply discussing salient topics in deception. My purpose was to display the richness of the domain and the heterogeneity of issues that a potential theory of deception might have to deal with.

Although I have managed to read only a small fraction of the literature, I have become optimistic about the possibility of a coherent psychology of deception in the strong sense. (This optimism may itself be a form of self-deception.) I have discovered articles that go beyond their specific area of deception and attempt to generalize to other areas—e.g. DePaulo et al (1985), Krebs et al (1988), Flavell et al (1983), Chandler (1988), Heuer (1982), Whaley (1982), Leff (1976), and the collection edited by Mitchell & Thompson (1986). The works of philosophers such as Dennett (1987) and Freyd's (1983) study of the consequences for cognitive structures of shared knowledge are examples of theoretical efforts highly relevant to a future psychology of deception.

A more theoretical chapter than mine might have discussed the fact that most of what we know about deception belongs to "folk psychology." Some contemporary philosophers have expressed doubts about constructing a psychology on the basis of such information (Churchland 1984). Other philosophers believe that using folk psychology as our point of departure may not be such a bad idea (Flanagan 1984; Goldman 1986). Such an issue matters for a psychology of deception, because the folk psychologies of deceivers in various domains might well be what a psychology of deception might be trying to explain.

What would a psychology of deception in the strong sense look like? Would it be biologically based? Or would it be functional and close to existing folk psychologies? Deception is obviously interpersonal in nature. At one level the units would be individuals interacting in a social context. Does this mean that a theoretical account of deception has to use concepts and units from social sciences that focus on levels of function broader than those psychologists deal with?

Perhaps it is premature to try to answer such questions. But it does seem that some aspects of successful deception can be explained in terms of concepts that are basically biological. Other aspects seem to require cognitively oriented accounts. Many of the more interesting deceptions (e.g. confidence games) seem to require accounts at a social level. Whether a single coherent theory can provide an adequate account of this range of phenomena remains to be seen. One possibility is that such a theory will develop concepts and structures of its own that will cut across levels currently kept separate by existing disciplines.

Literature Cited

Bechtel, H. K., Pearson, W. 1985. Deviant scientists and scientific deviance. *Deviant Behav.* 6:237–52

Ben-Shakhar, G., Lieblich, I., Bar-Hillel, M. 1982. An evaluation of polygraphers' judgments: a review from a decision theoretic perspective. *J. Appl. Psychol.* 67:701–13

Blinderman, C. 1986. *The Piltdown Inquest.* Buffalo, NY: Prometheus Books

Binet, A. 1896. Psychology of prestidigitation. *Annual Report of the Board of Regents of the Smithsonian Institution, 1894,* pp. 555–71. Washington, DC: GPO

Broad, W., Wade, N. 1982. *Betrayers of the Truth.* New York: Simon & Schuster

Chandler, M. 1988. Doubt and developing theories of mind. In *Developing Theories of Mind,* ed. J. Astington, P. Harris, D. Olson. New York: Cambridge Univ. Press. In press

Chevalier-Skolnikoff, S. 1986. An exploration of the ontogeny of deception in human beings and nonhuman primates. See Mitchell & Thompson 1986, pp. 205–20

Churchland, P. 1984. *Matter and Consciousness.* Cambridge, MA: MIT Press

Daniel, D. C., Herbig, K. L., eds. 1982. *Strategic Military Deception.* New York: Pergamon

De Waal, F. 1986. Deception in the natural communication of chimpanzees. See Mitchell & Thompson 1986, pp. 221–44

Delanoy, D. L. 1987. Work with a fraudulent PK metal-bending subject. *J. Soc. Psychical Res.* 54:247–56

Dennett, D. C. 1978. *Brainstorms: Philosophical Essays on Mind and Psychology.* Montgomery, VT: Bradford Books

Dennett, D. C. 1987. *The Intentional Stance.* Cambridge, MA: MIT Press

DePaulo, B. M., Stone, J. I., Lassiter, G. D. 1985. Deceiving and detecting deceit. In *The Self in Social Life,* ed. B.R. Schlenker, pp. 323–70. New York: McGraw-Hill

Dessoir, M. 1893. The psychology of legerdemain. *The Open Court,* 7:3599–3602, 3608–11, 3616–19, 3626–27, 3633–34

Ekman, P. 1985. *Telling Lies: Clues to Deceit in the Marketplace, Politics, and Marriage.* New York: W. W. Norton & Co.

Flanagan, O. J. 1984. *The Science of The Mind.* Cambridge, MA: MIT Press

Flavell, J. H., Green, F. L., Flavell, E. R. 1983. Development of knowledge about the appearance-reality distinction. *Monogr. Soc. Res. Child Dev.,* Ser. 212, p. 51 (1)

Freyd, J. J. 1983. Shareability: the social psychology of epistemology. *Cognit. Sci.* 7: 191–210

Goldman, A. I. 1986. *Epistemology and Cognition.* Cambridge, MA: Harvard Univ. Press

Gooch, J., Perlmutter, A., eds. 1982. Military deception and strategic surprise. *The J. Strategic Stud.* 5 (1):(Spec. iss.)

Gould, S. J. 1980. The Piltdown conspiracy. *Nat. Hist.* 89:8, 10–11, 14, 16, 18, 20, 22, 25–26, 28

Hankiss, A. 1980. Games con men play: the semiosis of deceptive interaction. *J. Commun.* 30:104–12

Hasted, J. B., Bohm, D. J., Bastin, E. W., O'Regan, B., Taylor, J. G. 1975. Scientists confronting the paranormal. *Nature* 254:470–73. Reprinted 1976 in *The Geller Papers,* ed. C. Panati, pp. 183–96. Boston, MA: Houghton-Mifflin

Henderson, M. A. 1985. *How Con Games Work.* Secaucus, NY: Citadel

Heuer, R. J. 1982. Cognitive factors in deception and counterdeception. See Daniel & Herbig 1982, pp. 31–69

Houck, J. 1984. PK party history. In *Proceedings of the Symposium on Applications of Anomalous Phenomena*, ed. C. B. S. Jones, pp. 501–14. Alexandria, VA: Kaman Tempo

Hyman, R. 1976. [Review of *The Geller papers.] The Zetetic (The Skeptical Inquirer)* 1:73–80

Hyman, R. 1977. Cold reading: how to convince strangers that you know all about them. *The Zetetic (The Skeptical Inquirer)* 1:18–37

Hyman, R. 1981a. Scientists and psychics. In *Science and the Paranormal: Probing the Essence of the Supernatural*, ed. G. O. Abell, B. Singer, pp. 119–41. New York: Charles Scribner's Sons

Hyman, R. 1981b. The psychic reading. In *The Clever Hans Phenomenon: Communication with Horses, Whales, Apes and People*, ed. T. A. Sebeok, R. Rosenthal, pp. 169–81. New York: The NY Acad. Sci.

Hyman, R. 1985. A critical historical overview of parapsychology. In *A Skeptic's Handbook of Parapsychology*, ed. P. Kurtz, pp. 3–96. Buffalo, NY: Prometheus Books

Jastrow, J. 1900. *Fact and Fable in Psychology*. Cambridge, MA: Riverside Press

Kohn, A. 1986. *False Prophets: Fraud and Error in Science and Medicine*. New York: Blackwell

Krebs, D., Denton, K., Higgins, N. C. 1988. On the evolution of self-knowledge and self-deception. In *Sociobiological Perspectives on Human Development*, ed. K. McDonald, pp. 105–29. New York: Springer-Verlag. In press

Leff, A. A. 1976. *Swindling and Selling*. New York: The Free Press

Le Gros Clark, W. 1956. The exposure of the Piltdown forgery. *Proc. R. Inst. GB* 36:138–51

Lewin, R. 1987. Do animals read minds, tell lies? *Science* 238:1350–51

Lloyd, J. E. 1986. Firefly communication and deception: "Oh, what a tangled Web." See Mitchell & Thompson 1986, pp. 113–28

Lykken, D. T. 1981. *A Tremor in the Blood: Uses and Abuses of the Lie Detector*. New York: McGraw-Hill

Lykken, D. T. 1985. The probity of the polygraph. In *The Psychology of Evidence and Trial Procedure*, ed. S. M. Kassin, L. S. Wrightsman, pp. 95–123: Beverly Hills, CA: Sage

Lykken, D. T. 1987a. The validity of tests: caveat emptor. *Jurimetrics* 27:263–70

Lykken, D. T. 1987b. Reply to Raskin & Kircher. *Jurimetrics* 27:278–82

Marks, D., Kammann, R. 1980. *The Psychology of the Psychic*. Buffalo, NY: Prometheus Books

Mason, E. J. 1978. Victor Lustig—the man who sold the Eiffel Tower. In *The World's Greatest Rip-offs: the Extraordinary Inside Story of the Biggest, Most Inventive Confidence Tricks of Recent Times*, ed. C. Rose, pp. 33–56. New York: Sterling

Maurer, D. W. 1974. *The American Confidence Man*. Springfield, IL: Charles C. Thomas

Millar, R. 1974. *The Piltdown Men*. New York: Ballantine

Mitchell, R. W. 1986. A framework for discussing deception. See Mitchell & Thompson 1986, pp. 3–40

Mitchell, R, W., Thompson, N. S., eds. 1986. *Deception: Perspective on Human and Nonhuman Deceit*. Albany, NY: SUNY

Nash, J. R. 1976. *Hustlers and Con Men*. New York: Evans

Newman, D. 1986. The role of mutual knowledge in the development of perspective taking. *Dev. Rev.* 6:122–45

Nicol, J. F. 1979. Fraudulent children in psychical research. *Parapsychol. Rev.* 10(1): 16–21

Ortiz, D. 1984. *Gambling Scams*. New York: Dodd, Mead & Co.

Panati, C., ed. 1976. *The Geller papers: Scientific Observations on the Paranormal Powers of Uri Geller*. Boston, MA: Houghton Mifflin

Pankratz, L. 1981. A review of the Munchausen syndrome. *Clin. Psychiatry Rev.* 1:65–78

Pfungst, O. 1911. *Clever Hans: A Contribution to Experimental, Animal and Human Psychology*. New York: Holt

Quattrone, G. A., Tversky, A. 1984. Causal versus diagnostic contingencies: on self-deception and on the voter's illusion. *J. Pers. Soc. Psychol.* 46:237–48

Randi, J. 1982. *The Truth about Uri Geller*. Buffalo, NY: Prometheus Books

Raskin, D. C. 1987. Does science support polygraph testing? In *The Polygraph Test: Lies, Truth and Science*, ed. A. Gale. London: Sage. In press

Raskin, D. C., Kircher, J. C. 1987. The validity of Lykken's criticisms: fact or fancy? *Jurimetrics* 27:271–77

Sackeim, H. A., Gur, R. C. 1985. Voice recognition and the ontological status of self-deception. *J. Pers. Soc. Psychol.* 48: 1365–68

Smith, H. A. 1956. *The Compleat Practical Joker*. New York: Pocket Books, Inc.

Taylor, M., Flavell, J. H. 1984. Seeing and believing: children's understanding of the distinction between appearance and reality. *Child Dev.* 55: 1710–20

Triplett, N. 1900. The psychology of conjuring deceptions. *Am. J. Psychol.* 11:439–510

Vasek, M. E. 1986. Lying as a skill: the development of deception in children. See Mitchell & Thompson 1986, pp. 271–92

Waid, W. M., Orne, M. T. 1982. The physiological detection of deception. *Am. Sci.* 70:402–9

Weiner, J. S. 1980. *The Piltdown Forgery.* New York: Dover

Whaley, B. 1982. Toward a general theory of deception. *J. Strategic Stud.* 5:178–92

Zimbardo, P. G., Ebbesen, E. B., Maslach, C. 1977. *Influencing Attitudes and Changing Behavior.* Reading, MA: Addison-Wesley. (2nd ed.)

Zuckerman, M., DePaulo, B. M., Rosenthal, R. 1986. Humans as deceivers and lie detectors. In *Nonverbal Communication in the Clinical Context,* ed. P. D. Blanck, R. Buck, R. Rosenthal, pp. 13–35. University Park, PA: Penn. State Univ. Press

Ann. Rev. Psychol. 1989. 40:155–89

ANIMAL COGNITION: The Representation of Space, Time and Number

C. R. Gallistel

Department of Psychology, University of Pennsylvania, Philadelphia, Pennsylvania 19104-6196

CONTENTS

INTRODUCTION

Experimental investigations of animal behavior suggest that many animal brains routinely deal with the basic abstractions underlying scientific and lay discourse—space, time, and number.

Space. When a foraging ant leaves the nest, it winds this way and that in a tortuous search for fodder, but when it finds something, it turns and runs more or less directly back toward its nest (Harkness & Maroudas 1985; Wehner &

155

0066-4308/89/0201-0155$02.00

Wehner 1986), a 1-mm hole in the ground as much as 200 m away (Wehner 1985a). It does not retrace its outward path. If the ant is displaced at the start of its homeward run, it nonetheless runs straight in the predisplacement direction of the nest for a distance approximately equal to the predisplacement distance to the nest, then breaks into a search pattern (Wehner & Srinivasan 1981). It is hard to resist the inference that the foraging ant possesses a continually updated representation of its spatial position relative to its starting point—a moment-to-moment representation of the direction in which the nest lies and how far away it is.

When one displaces the landmarks that immediately surround either a bee's feeding source or the nest hole of a digger wasp, the position to which the animal flies is systematically displaced (Tinbergen & Kruyt 1938; Cartwright & Collett 1983). It is hard to resist the inference that the animal represents something about the spatial relationship between the landmarks and its goal and uses this representation to direct its flight toward the goal.

Time. When rats are fed once or twice per day at a fixed time, they develop anticipatory running behavior: A few hours before each feeding, they begin to run, and their running activity reaches a peak just when food is due. If food fails to appear on schedule, the running and other anticipatory activities subside, only to resume again a few hours before the next scheduled feeding (Bolles & Moot 1973). If the rats are returned to ad libitum feeding, the anticipatory activity ceases immediately, but it reappears whenever their food is again removed. The anticipatory peaks reappear at the correct times on the first day of renewed deprivation, before renewed experience of the scheduled feeding.

If the rats are kept under constant light conditions in the intervening period of ad libitum feeding, the endogenous approximately 24-hr rhythm in their daily activity is no longer synchronized to the local day-night cycle and they "free-run." Their internal circadian clock runs systematically faster (or slower) than the correct time; hence subjective dusk, when activity abruptly begins, occurs progressively sooner (or later) every day. Under these conditions, renewed food deprivation also leads immediately to peaks of anticipatory activity, but these peaks do not occur at the correct local time (the time of day of the earlier regular feedings); rather, they occur at the correct phase of the animal's activity cycle, that is, at the correct time on the animal's internal clock (Coleman et al 1982; Honmah et al 1983; Rosenwasser et al 1984). It is difficult to resist the inference that animals represent the time of day (circadian phase) at which events occur and use this representation to adapt their behavior to the daily regularities in their environment.

Temporal intervals. Rats may be taught to press a lever when the appearance of a stimulus (such as a steady light or noise) signals that pressing may be rewarded by the delivery of food (typically, on 50% of the trials, pressing is eventually rewarded). If there is a fixed latency between the onset of the signal and the (probabilistic) arming of the feeder, then the rat's rate of pressing the lever reaches a peak at a latency that approximately coincides with the arming latency (Church & Gibbon 1982; Roberts 1981). This simple result suggests that the brain of the rat also represents elapsed temporal intervals and can compare the magnitude of the currently elapsed interval to a standard stored in memory.

Number. Rats may be taught to press a lever a certain number of times in order to produce the unsignalled arming of a photocell-activated food delivery system (Platt & Johnson 1971). When the delivery system is armed, interrupting the light beam in front of the food hopper triggers the delivery of food. When the delivery system is not armed and the rat interrupts the beam prematurely, there is a penalty: the lights go out and everything shuts down for 10 seconds and/or the response counter is reset to 0, requiring the rat to start over again. The number of presses the rat has to make to arm the delivery system is varied from 4 to 24 in blocked training sessions. For each value of N, the required number of presses, the experimenter plots the frequency at which an animal breaks off pressing and tries the feeder, as a function of n, the number of presses the rat has made since the last resetting of the response counter. Under the right penalty conditions, the value at which this function peaks—the count at which the rat is maximally likely to break off and try the feeder—exactly corresponds to N, the required number of presses. These results are invariant under motivational manipulations that alter the rate of pressing and hence the time it takes to make the requisite number of presses (Mechner & Guevrekian 1962). This suggests that the brain of the rat can keep a running estimate (count) of the number of presses the rat has made and compare this to a standard stored in memory.

Rate. Rate is number divided by time. It is well established that the relative distribution of foraging time among various foraging sites (or "foraging keys") accurately reflects the relative rates of food occurrence at those sites or during those activities—over a wide range of relative and absolute rates [Baum & Rachlin 1969 (pigeon); Godin & Keenleyside 1984 (cichlid fish); Harper 1982 (ducks); Herrnstein 1961; Herrnstein & Loveland 1975 (pigeon); Milinski 1979 (stickleback fish)]. The assumption that animals like rats, pigeons, ducks, and fish can represent both number and temporal intervals and perform with these representations operations that are formally analogous to division would explain the fine tuning of their behavior to the observed rate of prey occurrence. It has proved difficult to account for the apportionment of behavior on the basis of relative rate using models that assume an animal cannot really represent rate per se but behaves as though it did by virtue of the dynamics of an associative process (Lea & Dow 1984). On the other hand, the behavior is elegantly accounted for by a simple model, a central postulate of which is that an animal's rate of switching to any given "patch" (or response key) is a Poisson process whose rate parameter is proportionate to the rate at which food has been observed to occur in or at that "patch" (Myerson & Miezin 1980). An implication of this postulate would seem to be that the animal has a representation of the rate.

In this review, I examine some of the experimental evidence that animals represent space, time, and number. I consider computational models of the processes by which a brain might arrive at these representations.

THE DEFINITION OF REPRESENTATION

A brain is said to represent an aspect of the animal's environment when there is a *functioning isomorphism* between that aspect of the environment and some of the brain processes that adapt the animal's behavior to that aspect of the environment. The term isomorphism is employed in the mathematical sense of a utilizable formal correspondence between systems. The best known isomorphism is the one discovered by Descartes and Fermat between geometry and algebra. The use of Cartesian coordinates maps the entities studied by geometers—points, lines, curves, and surfaces—into the entities of algebra—vectors (strings of numbers) and equations. The discovery of a formal correspondence between, for example, a straight line and a "linear" equation enabled mathematicians to represent geometric problems algebraically and thereby bring algebraic methods of proof to bear on geometric problems (and vice versa). It is the *use* of the formal correspondence that makes isomorphisms powerful engines of mathematical development rather than analytic curiosities. Similarly, it is the exploitation of formal correspondences between its internal processes and external reality that makes brain-world isomorphisms into *functioning* isomorphisms. The functional importance of these isomorphisms makes their identification a key to understanding higher brain function.

An isomorphism exists if there is a procedure or process that maps entities, relations, and operations in the represented system into entities, relations, and operations in the representing system *in such a way that* a given relation holds within the represented system if and only if (written *iff*) it holds among the corresponding entities, operations, and relations within the representing system. For example, under the Cartesian procedure for mapping points on a plane into number pairs (2-dimensional vectors), two lines intersect (geometric relation) *iff* there is a common solution to their corresponding equations (algebraic relation).

In a neuroscientific context, an isomorphism exists when there is a sensory-perceptual process that maps aspects of the environment (entities in the represented system) into neural activities (entities in the representing system) in such a way that brain processes formally isomorphic to corresponding environmental processes may operate on these neural activities to produce behavioral outputs that correctly anticipate *implicit* relations among the perceived entities—relations not directly given in the original sensory input. The homeward-bound ant's turning in the direction of the nest and running approximately the right distance before starting its search pattern is an example of a behavioral output that anticipates or corresponds to a spatial relationship not directly given in sensory input. The spatial relationship between the ant and its nest must be computed from sensory inputs received over the course of the ant's tortuous outward journey.

The concept of a functioning isomorphism between arithmetic and selected aspects of reality plays a central role in the modern theory of measurement (Krantz et al 1971). Measurement is the art of devising procedures that map nonnumerical entities into numbers in such a way that some arithmetic relations and operations may be validly employed with the resulting numbers (employed to draw correct conclusions about relations among the measured entities). The theory of measurement makes clear the important point that representations come in varying degrees of richness, depending on how many operations and relations within the representing system may be employed to draw valid conclusions about the represented system.

Representation is commonly used in psychology and neuroscience in the sense of a mental or neural entity (for example, the activity of a feature detector) that is imagined simply to "stand for" some nonneural entity (such as a horizontal line). This is a maximally impoverished use of the term (or else it confuses the notion of a representative with the notion of a representation). Such a representation is nominal in both senses of the word. It functions only as a unique naming device. There is only one relation in the representing system that may validly be employed, the identity or equals relation. The standard example is the representation of athletes by the numbers on their jerseys. If it is only in this limited sense that the brain "represents" the world, then the skeptics of representational approaches to brain function (e.g. Freeman & Skarda 1988) are justified in their skepticism.

There is substance to the claim that the brain represents reality only if combinatorial processes in the brain operate on the results of sensory/perceptual mappings in ways that mirror processes and relations in the mapped system. If the only sense in which the brain represents number is that there is a sensory/perceptual mapping from numerosity to brain states (the activities of detectors for specific numerosities), which make possible simple numerical discriminations, then the brain's representation of number is a representation in name only. Only if the brain brings combinatorial processes to bear on the neural entities that represent numerosities may we say that the brain represents number in an interesting sense of the term representation.

Thus, I will be particularly attentive to evidence that suggests the operation of such processes.

The computation of a signal representating a rate by a process in which a signal representating a numerosity is divided by a signal representating a temporal interval would be an instance of the sought-for kind of combinatorial process. At the neurophysiological level of analysis, this would require finding a neural process in which a signal that was a scalar function of the numerosity of some set of rewards combined with a signal that was a scalar function of the temporal interval over which those rewards were experienced to generate a signal that was a scalar function of the ratio between the two input signals (thus a scalar function of the rate of reward occurrence). One would then need to show that the animal's rate-dependent behavior was appropriately influenced by experimental manipulation of the output signal (the signal that represents rate). The day when such experiments are done will not come until the community of experimentalists is convinced that processes like this are to be found in the brains of animals, even quite lowly animals.

THE REPRESENTATION OF SPACE IN ANIMAL NAVIGATION

Navigation is the process of (*a*) *determining* and (*b*) *maintaining* a course or trajectory from place to place. It is a fundamental behavioral process for any animal that departs from and returns to fixed points in its environment, such as nutrient sources, mating spots, and nests or resting places. The range of animals whose behavior patterns include returning to fixed points is large, including many if not most insects and other arthropods, as well as most if not all vertebrates.

In the absence of a beacon emanating from the destination, determining or setting a course requires a spatial representation, a representation of geometric relationships between the animal's position in space and the position of the points to which it directs its movements. Maintaining a course, on the other hand, requires a directional stimulus or directional signal. The distal stimuli used in determining one's position and orientation during the process of setting a course are often not important in the process of maintaining the course, and vice versa, as for example, when one takes a positional fix from star sightings in order to determine what course to steer, then steers by the magnetic compass (a directional stimulus).

Setting a course requires positional information. There are two quite distinct processes for obtaining the requisite information. One, *dead reckoning,* is carried on more or less continuously; while the other, *taking a positional fix,* is episodic.

Dead reckoning is the process of determining the change in position (from a known starting point) by integrating velocity with respect to time. It gives a continuous representation of one's position in the world, but it is inherently subject to a cumulative error; the indication of position becomes more and more inaccurate the longer the interval of integration.

To correct the cumulative error in the "reckoning," one must occasionally obtain a fix of one's position by means of *sightings* on points that have a known position, that is, points whose positions relative to one's goal are represented on a *map* (or on an *ephemeris,* in the case of a celestial object, whose position relative to the goal is a function of time). A map, in the most general sense, is a representation of some or all of the geometric relations among points, lines, and surfaces. A sighting is the determination by some means (not necessarily visual) of the direction (bearing) of a charted point—a point whose position is represented on the map. More rarely—because it is more difficult—a sighting may also involve the determination of one's distance from the sighted point. The taking of a positional fix by sightings on charted points corrects the value of the integral that represents one's position in the "known" (charted) world.

The processes of animal navigation appear analogous to formalized marine navigation in that (*a*) Many mobile animals maintain a representation of their position in the world by means of a process analogous to dead reckoning. In the literature on animal navigation, this process is called path integration. (*b*) They also make a map of the terrain surrounding points of interest like nests and food sources and they use this map and sightings of charted points to correct the errors in their path integration. (*c*) The taking of fixes appears to be episodic; most of the time the animal's representation of its position in the world is based on its map and its reckoning, not on moment-to-moment fix-taking. The result is sometimes comically inappropriate behavior, when the spatial reality to which the animal is "reacting" no longer corresponds to the map upon which its "reactions" are based. (*d*) In maintaining a course, animals often use the sun or the wind, or inertial or kinesthetic input as sources of directional information, none of which is used in taking fixes. Thus, the process of taking a fix is quite distinct from the process of holding a course, even though both processes depend upon directional inputs. Animals look to the terrain to tell where they are, but they steer by the sun, the stars, and the wind. (*e*) The sun is a principal source of directional input in the holding of a course, which is remarkable because the sun's direction is a function of the time of day and the season of the year. To use the sun as a source of directional information requires an *ephemeris,* a representation of its position as a function of time.

In reviewing the literature relevant to these conclusions, I consider most extensively a few well-designed experiments with ants and bees for two reasons: (*a*) Some of the most elegant and compelling experiments have been

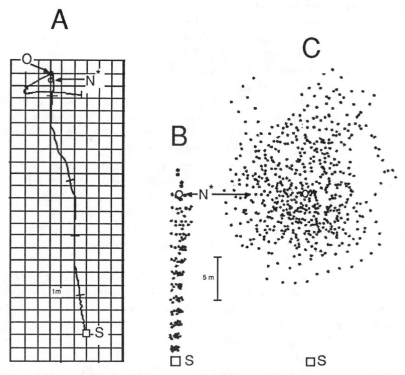

Figure 1   Course holding by dead-reckoning in the ant. *A. (above)* Tracing of an ant's course from its release point (S) to the sharp turn (O) that marks the onset of its search for the (fictive) nest (N*). Crossbars on tracing mark 10-sec intervals. *B. (above)* Superimposed plots of the positions of 10 ants at 10-sec intervals from their release to the onset of their search patterns. The larger dots surrounding the fictive nest mark the onsets of searching. *C. (above)* Superimposed plots of the positions of the 10 ants at 10-sec intervals during the first 15 min of their search. (Redrawn from Figure 2, p. 318 of Wehner & Srinivasan 1981, by permission of the authors and the publisher.) *D. (opposite)* Tracing of an ant's course during minutes 22–60 of its search. The fictive nest was between the open circle with which the trace commences and the filled circle with which it concludes. (Reproduced from Figure 3b, p. 320, of Wehner & Srinivasan 1981, by permission of the authors and the publisher.)

done with these animals. Because they make many journeys every day between their nest or hive and one or more food sources and because they are relatively unperturbed by quite drastic experimental manipulations—for example, displacement in mid-trip into completely unfamiliar territory—they make excellent subjects. (*b*) If we are persuaded that these conclusions are true for insects, then we are more likely to find explanations of vertebrate behavior in these terms plausible. In the realm of higher brain function, we are reluctant to deny to the rat and the pigeon what we concede to the bee and the ant.

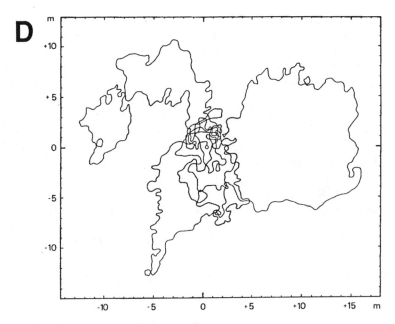

Dead Reckoning (Path Integration)

Wehner & Srinivasan (1981) set up feeding stations 20–40 m away from the nest of a colony of large fast-moving desert ants *(Cataglyphis bicolor)*. On the desert 600 m away (well beyond the foraging range of this species), they painted a gridwork of lines at 1-m intervals. They captured foragers as they left the feeding station, released them at a fictive feeding station in the area with the gridwork, and traced their subsequent movements on a data sheet with a 100:1 reduction of the grid, marking the tracing of the course with crossmarks on the beep of a timer that signalled 10-sec intervals. Figure 1A shows a typical run, from the release site to a point within a few meters of the fictive nest, where the ant broke off its straight homeward run to begin a systematic search for the entrance. Figure 1B is a superimposed display of the positions of each of 10 ants every 10 sec from release to commencement of the search pattern. Figure 1C is a superimposed display of the positions of the 10 ants every 10 sec after the start of the search pattern. Figure 1D is the tracing of a representative search pattern from minutes 22 through 60 of the (necessarily futile) search for the (fictive) nest.

When released in unfamiliar territory, where there was no nest to be found, ants homeward bound at capture followed a straight course within a degree or two of the correct homeward course from the capture point to the real nest for a distance within 10% of the correct distance. This implies: (*a*) There were in the nervous system of the ant at the time of its capture neural activities representative of the bearing of its nest from the site of its capture and of the linear distance between the capture site and the nest. Similar neural activities find behavioral expression in the well-known dance by which the successful honeybee forager indicates to other foragers the direction and distance of the food source (von Frisch 1967). (*b*) In moving along its homeward course, the ant updated its position— for example, by decrementing the activity representative of its linear distance from the nest. (*c*) The ant has a directional reference accurate and steady enough to permit it to hold a straight course for 40 m (more than 4000 body lengths). It has long been known that the sun is the preferred source of this directional input in the ant (Jander 1957; Santchi 1913) and most other diurnally active animals (Emlen 1975; Mittelstaedt 1962; Wehner 1985b), including the free-swimming Brazilian *Aplysia* (Hamilton & Russell 1982).

The focus of Wehner & Srinivasan's analysis was not the homeward run but the search pattern. The searching ant follows an extraordinarily tortuous course, full of twists and turns, big loops and small (Figure 1D), but the spatial probability density function for its position at any moment after the commencement of the search pattern approximates the bivariate Gaussian distribution (Figure 1C). The distribution remains centered on the starting point of the search no matter what postsearch interval is chosen for its determination. What changes is the standard deviation of the distribution; the more time has elapsed since the start of the search, the greater the standard deviation. What this means is that the ant ranges farther and farther from its starting point, making ever bigger loops, but it returns time and again to that starting point, so that the most densely searched area remains the area immediately around the starting point, no matter how long it has searched. This makes sense if the starting point is taken to be the best estimate of where the nest is and if there is some probability of having missed the nest in a given area no matter how densely the area has been searched.

What is most remarkable is that the search is conducted by dead reckoning. The ant does not take a fix on the terrain around its starting point and return to the starting point by reference to the terrain; rather, it keeps track of its position relative to the starting position of the search by path integration. The path integration system is sufficiently accurate that after an hour's search following the kind of course portrayed in Figure 1D, the ant's representation of its position relative to the starting position of the search is accurate to within a meter or two. Further displacement experiments showed that the repeated returns to the starting position are effected by path integration: Midway in the search, the ant was recaptured and released on the periphery of the area it had so far searched, a displacement of about 10 m. In continuing its search, the ant now often traversed portions of the territory it had already traversed, but the center of the search, the point to which it returned most often, was displaced by a vector equal to the midsearch experimental displacement. One might explain this by supposing that the ants started over "from scratch" after the second displacement, taking a new fix, and so on. However, the size of the loops they made after the second displacement were characteristic of the later stages of a search, not the early stages.

Computational models of the path-integration process have been elaborated (Gallistel 1989; Mittelstaedt 1978, 1985; Mittelstaedt & Mittelstaedt 1982; Müller & Wehner 1988), but space does not permit a critical review of them. What they have in common is what any model of path integration would seem to require—the additive combination of successive angular and linear displacement signals. Müller & Wehner propose stride-by-stride summation of linear and angular changes; whereas Mittelstaedt and Gallistel favor continuous models—that is, the integration of velocity signals. The integration of a velocity signal with respect to time is the limiting case of adding successive small displacement signals, so the models are alike in assuming the additive combination of displacement/velocity signals. Path integration, then, is our first example of a combinatorial process in the nervous system that mirrors a process external to the nervous system in a functional manner—a functioning isomorphism.

Homing by path integration has been experimentally investigated in the spider (Mittelstaedt 1985), in the gerbil (Mittelstaedt & Mittelstaedt 1980), and in passively transported geese (von Saint Paul 1982). It appears to be ubiquitous in vertebrate and arthropod behavior.

The Ephemeris Function

In marine navigation, an ephemeris table gives the data and equations necessary to compute the geographical position of the sun and commonly used stellar references as a function of year, day, and time. Animals that steer by the sun must construct their own ephemeris function. The ephemeris function enables the nervous system to compute the current azimuthal position of the sun from the time indicated by the internal clock. The azimuthal position of the sun is the angular deviation from due south (or from some other geostable reference direction) of the perpendicular from the sun to the horizon. Moment-to-moment knowledge of this ever-changing position is a prerequisite for using the sun to hold a straight course.

One of the more engaging of the many experimental demonstrations that the sun-compass mechanism depends on an internal timekeeping mechanism was done by Renner (1960). He trained honeybees to find artificial nectar at a certain time of day on a table located to the northwest of their hive in a nondescript field on Long Island, New York. One night, he packed up the hive and flew to California, where he opened the hive the next day in a nondescript field near Davis. He had arrayed tables at 45° intervals in a circle around the reopened hive, with observers at each table to tally the bees that came and when they came. The time difference between Davis and Long Island is slightly more than 3 hr, so the azimuthal position of the sun for an observer at Davis is on average 45° counterclockwise from its contemporaneous position for an observer on Long Island. When a bee from Long Island uses an internal clock synchronized to Long Island solar time to compute from its Long Island ephemeris function the azimuthal position of the sun, in order to steer a northwesterly course, it will fly a westerly course if it happens to be in California, which is what Renner's bees did. [They also came to the tables 3 hr early—see the section below on *Time of Occurrence (Circadian Phase)*.]

An ephemeris function is a representation of the position of a celestial body like the sun *with respect to the terrain surrounding the point of observation,* as a function of the time of day. Since the azimuthal position and velocity of the sun at a given time of day change with the seasons, an animal that steers by the sun must have a process that permits the continual recalibration of its ephemeris function. Gould (1980, 1984) has shown that the recalibration process involves combining the records from several successive determinations of the azimuthal position of the sun. The combining of the results of several successive sightings of the sun's azimuthal position to obtain a representation of its time-dependent azimuthal velocity is another instance of a combinatorial process in the nervous system that mirrors an external process in a functionally useful manner—another functioning isomorphism.

The sightings from which a bee calibrates its ephemeris function are separated by intervals during which the bee is in the hive out of sight of the sun. A sighting of the sun is a measurement of its azimuthal angle with respect to a direction defined by the local terrain or a geostable directional signal like the signal from a magnetic compass. To combine the results from separate sightings, the bee must be able to orient itself reproducibly with respect to the earth, which implies that it has a terrain map, a magnetic compass, and/or some other process for determining a geostable direction (Dyer & Gould 1983).

Dyer & Gould (1981) showed that the bee's ephemeris function gives the azimuthal position of the sun with respect to a map of the local terrain by displacing beehives on heavily overcast days to fields with terrain similar to the terrain in the home field, but with the salient features running in a different compass direction (say, an east-to-west treeline in the new field in place of the south-to-north treeline in the home field). Before displacement, the bees had been trained to forage at a source, say, to the west of the hive. When the bees emerged from the displaced hive under complete overcast, they flew to the south (the direction that was correct if one took the treeline in the new field to be the treeline in the old field). When they returned to the hive, their dance had the orientation with respect to the current position of the (invisible) sun that one would follow to reach a source to the west of the hive—the solar heading they "thought" they had just flown rather than the solar heading they had in fact just flown. The bees that responded to this dance, however, flew to the south, which was the direction from which the dancing bees had in fact returned. What these results show is that neither the dancing bees nor the responding bees could see the sun through the heavy overcast. The dancing bees signalled the solar bearings of the food by indicating the direction of the food relative to an ephemeris representation of the sun's current position, a representation rendered erroneous by the displacement; and the responding bees interpreted the dance in terms of a similar representation of where the sun supposedly was in relation to the local terrain. Evidently, this representation of the sun's current azimuthal position—the ephemeris function—uses prominent directional features of the terrain (e.g. the treeline) as the geostable directional reference.

The Cognitive Map

A cognitive map is a representation of the relative positions of points in the environment. The map makes it possible for an animal to orient toward or approach a point that has no currently perceived distinguishing characteristics by reference to (a) currently perceivable points that can be identified with points on its map (currently recognizable charted points) and (b) geometric relationships between the currently recognizable charted points and the goal (geometric relationships recoverable from the map). In navigational terminology, piloting is orienting toward or away from various points (for example, hidden shoals) by adopting an appropriate orientation with respect to recognizable features of the terrain with a known (charted) spatial relationship to the goal.

It is widely assumed that animals orient toward points primarily on the basis of distinctive sensory cues emanating from those points (beacon homing), rather than orienting toward a position in a larger spatial framework. However, evidence is accumulating that orienting toward a point by virtue of the position it occupies in the larger environmental framework is the rule rather than the exception. Hence, cognitive maps, which make possible this kind of orientation, may play a ubiquitous role in animal behavior, coming into play whenever the animal moves toward or away from any goal.

Map-based orientation is most convincingly demonstrated when the point to which the animal moves has no distinctive features of its own, when "there is no there there" (to quote Gertrude Stein's mot about Oakland, California). The hoverfly's station, for example, is a position in mid-air, where it hovers for minutes at a time, darting away now and then to chase passing flies, but resuming its station when the foray is over. Collett & Land (1975) showed that the hoverfly's return to its station is guided by the geometric relationship between the station and surrounding landmarks. When the landmark is an isolated, experimentally provided, patterned board, displacement of the board displaces the station. Their studies of station finding and holding in the hoverfly reveal a number of properties of map use that appear to be quite general in the animal kingdom.

Hoverflies approach their station from any angle, and their orientation with respect to the landmark upon arrival varies greatly from occasion to occasion. Thus, the hoverfly recognizes a landmark from different distances and angles, regardless of the portion of its retina upon which the image of the landmark falls. The hoverfly's fix-taking—that is, its computation of its position relative to the landmark—is episodic. The fly takes a fix on the landmark when it resumes its station after a foray, but it does not continue to monitor its position relative to the landmark while on station; rather it relies on global image motion to hold its position (an optomotor position-holding mechanism). The fix-taking mechanism does not rely on image motion, but upon static properties of the image—its size and shape relative to a presumed memory image. The optomotor position-holding mechanism does not assign a special significance to any segment of the environmental image, whereas the fix-taking mechanism assigns special significance to the segment or segments of the environmental image that correspond to the objects or terrain on which the fix is taken.

A paradigm that has been used to demonstrate that rats can find points solely on the basis of their position relative to the larger environmental framework is the Morris water maze (Morris 1981; Rudy et al 1987; Whishaw & Mittleman 1986), which is a circular or rectangular pool filled with opacified water, with a submerged platform located somewhere in it. Once they have found the submerged platform, rats dropped into any point in the pool set a course more or less directly toward the platform.

Even when the goal has distinctive remotely perceivable sensory features, animals seem to prefer to find it by means of its geometric relationship to the larger environment rather than by beacon homing. *Amphiprion* are a genus of fish that live within the tentacles of sea anemone, venturing out for distances of only a meter or so. In aquarium experiments, when an amphiprion's home anemone is displaced (either while the fish is within its tentacles or when the fish is away on a foray), the fish returns to the position in the tank previously occupied by the anemone, even though the fish is a highly visual animal and "its" anemone is among the more salient objects in the tank (Mariscal 1972).

THE LOCAL MAP OF THE HONEYBEE   The use of surrounding landmarks to localize a nectar source has been extensively studied by Collett and his collaborators (Cartwright & Collett 1983; Cheng et al 1987). They used cylindrical landmarks within an otherwise featureless room. They trained the bees to find a nectar source by reference to these landmarks, then examined the pattern of the bee's search flight on trials when the nectar source was absent. When the nectar had been at a fixed distance from a single cylinder, the bee's search was rather imprecise but clearly centered at the correct distance and direction from the cylinder. This result implies that the bee learns the compass bearing of the landmarks from the nectar source,[1] rather than simply the appearance of the landmark. A cylindrical landmark appears the same from every direction; if finding the nectar source by reference to the cylinder were based solely on the cylinder's appearance, the bee would search in an annulus around the cylinder.

Increasing the size of the cylinder increased the distance at which the bee's search was centered, which implies that the bee takes up the appropriate distance from the landmark by means of triangulation, rather than by, for example, "flying it off." In other words, the bee finds the distance at which the apparent (proximal) size of the landmark matches its remembered apparent size. It should not be concluded from this that the bee does not represent the distance between the landmark and the source or the true (distal) size of the landmark. Triangulation is the principal means of determining position in most navigational schemes and positioning by apparent size is a form of triangulation. Under natural circumstances, the use of apparent size is a *means of determining distance* and is taught as such in manuals on navigation. This method, of course, presumes that the true size of the landmark being used is fixed!

Adding landmarks (additional cylinders at other compass points) greatly narrowed the focus of the bee's search. When there was more than one cylinder, increasing their size had no effect on the locus of search, which is to be expected, since triangulation is much more accurate when it is based on sighted contours with wide angular separations (the different cylinders) rather than on sighted contours with narrow angular separations (the contours of a single cylinder). When the bee was confronted with two configurations of cylinders on test trials, which varied in how closely they conformed to the training configuration, the bee preferred the configuration that conformed more closely. Thus, the bee's triangulation process is an error-minimizing one, not an all-or-nothing match-or-mismatch process.

Even with configurations of three or more cylinders, which were rich enough to define a unique search point without reference to compass bearings,

[1]The compass bearing of Point B from a Point A is the angle measured at A between the point B and a line passing through A with a known direction on the surface of the earth, e.g., the direction of the sun's culmination (maximum elevation). There is no necessary connection between the determination of a compass bearing and the use of a magnetic indicator of geophysical direction.

the bees nonetheless required that the landmarks have approximately the correct compass bearings. This means that the coordinate framework within which the bee utilizes the landmarks is anchored to the room (a geocentric system of coordinates) rather than to the landmark configuration.[2] This surprising and important conclusion derives from experiments in which Cartwright and Collett rotated the landmark configuration, pitting coordinate frameworks anchored to the landmarks against geocentric frameworks. When the bee was at the correct point within a coordinate framework anchored to the landmarks, then the compass bearings of the landmarks were wrong; the landmarks lay in the wrong direction in a geocentric framework. When the landmark configuration was rotated by 90° or more, the bees rejected the landmark identifications and searched at random in the room. The parallel to marine practice is striking. A mariner generally knows at least approximately where he is, by dead reckoning from his last known position, and which way is north. Hence, the mariner knows the approximate compass bearing a sought-for landmark must have. A headland that resembles what the mariner is looking for will not be accepted as such if its compass bearing is too far out.

The use of a map to find a position in the world requires establishing a correspondence between what is currently perceived and what is preserved on the map (the "memory image"). An obvious question is the level of abstraction at which this comparison operation is carried out. Put another way, how much image processing precedes the comparison stage? The lowest level of abstraction would involve storing retinal "snapshots" of the landmarks and comparing the current image of the landmarks with the memory image point for point. Replacing opaque square landmarks with frame outlines would defeat a mechanism based on point-by-point matching, a mechanism in which there was negligible image processing prior to the matching of current input with remembered input. It does not, however, defeat the bee. Cartwright and Collett (1983) showed that the bee would accept a frame outline in lieu of the solid landmark it was trained with, suggesting that the matching operation occurs after a contour extraction process (or high-pass filtering of the retinal image, an operation that produces an image in which contours predominate). Beusekom (1948) showed that the digger wasp would tolerate replacement of a triangular array of pine cones with an open plastic triangle, which suggests that the matching operation may also follow a stage of low-pass image filtering. (The images of the pine cone array and of the plastic triangle would resemble each other more and more strongly as one blurred the focus of an imaging lense, which is a low-pass filtering operation.)

[2]A coordinate system is said to be anchored to a point if the coordinates of the point are always the same within that coordinate system.

Gould (1987) confronted honeybees with choices between landmarks that matched the training configuration in shape and area versus ones that matched it only in area and found that they strongly preferred the configuration with the correct shape. In elegantly designed parametric experiments, he measured the angular resolution of the memory images used in fixing a food source, revealing a horizontal resolution of about 3° and a vertical resolution of 5–6°. This resolution is poorer than the 1° visual resolution established for the honeybee using optomotor tests (Wehner 1981), indicating that the remembered "sketch" of the environment does not include all the detail that the bee's visual system is capable of resolving. On the other hand, this resolution is better than the 8–10° limit of resolution that Gould (1986b) has demonstrated in the bee's memory for the optical pattern of the source itself. The bee would appear to make a higher-resolution map of the terrain surrounding the source than it does of the source itself. Incidentally, it has also been found that the bee learns the pattern of the source itself primarily while hovering over the source prior to landing on it (Gould 1988a), while it learns the relation between the source and the surrounding landmarks while hovering over it prior to departure (Gould 1988b).

At the opposite extreme from the matching of unprocessed retinal images is the matching of a representation of the currently perceived 3-dimensional shape of the environment with a record of its previously perceived 3-dimensional shape (the map). Matching carried out at this level of abstraction requires that the images and other relevant sensory inputs (e.g. velocity signals) received over time have been processed to the point of extracting from them a coding of the macroscopic shape of the environment. Thus, it implies that the bee has a map in the ordinary sense of the term, since the lay meaning of map is a representation of the macroscopic shape of the environment.

Whether the bee has a map in the ordinary sense of the term depends in part on the extent to which metric geometric relationships are incorporated into its record of the terrain (its map) and used in navigation, since metric relationships are fundamental determinants of shape as we ordinarily conceive it. Metric relationships are geometric relationships involving distances and angles. We have already seen that the compass bearings of the landmarks from the food source are incorporated into the bee's representation of the geometric relationship between the source and the landmarks and are used in relocating the source. Compass bearings are metric relationships. Cheng et al (1987) have shown that in triangulating the location of the food source, the bee relies on nearby landmarks more than remote landmarks, even when the remote landmarks have been made larger than the nearby landmarks so that the two pairs of landmarks produce matching retinal images. This result implies that the bee incorporates into its map of the food locale a representation of both the compass bearings of, and the distances to, surrounding terrain contours and uses this information in positioning itself relative to those contours. This conclusion is equivalent to the conclusion that the bee's record of the terrain contains all the information required to construct a map in the ordinary sense of the term, an explicit representation of the shape of the environment.

One formally elegant way to demonstrate that the spatial representation an animal uses in finding a position contains metric information is to subject the local environment to an affine transformation (Cheng & Gallistel 1984). Nonmetric geometric relationships are invariant under affine transformation; hence, any navigational scheme based on nonmetric spatial relations will perform equally well in an affinely transformed environment and will, in fact, not recognize the difference between the transformed and untransformed environments. Cartwright & Collett (1983) trained bees to find nectar in the center of a square configuration of cylinders, then offered them choices between the square configuration and rectangular configurations produced by compressing the square along an axis parallel to one of its sides. A rectangle is an affine transformation of a square. A navigation system like the "qualitative" system proposed by Levitt et al (1987), which relies only on records of paired landmarks, would have no basis for choosing a rectangle over a square. [This also applies to other nonmetric models of animal cognitive maps—e.g. Deutsch (1960); Lieblich & Arbib (1982).] Cartwright & Collett found, however, that the greater the compression of the rectangle, the more the bees preferred the square array. Thus, the bee's local map preserves metric relationships among the sought-for point and the surrounding terrain.

Either the bee's nervous system contains a map of the terrain in the ordinary sense of the term or it contains the equivalent of a surveyor's field notes—the contour sketches, bearings, and distances from which a cartographer constructs a map. Cartwright & Collett (1987; see also Collett 1987) favor a model along the latter lines. In their model, the bee navigates from the equivalent of the surveyor's field notes, not from the cartographic reworking of those notes. Since the information content of the surveyor's notes and a cartographic product based on those notes are the same, it is going to be difficult to decide unequivocally from behavioral work alone what actually occurs inside the bee's nervous system. Cartwright & Collett's preference for a noncartographic model seems to rest on intuitions to the effect that such models are computationally simpler than models based on a cartographic representation of environmental shape, which, it has been argued, is why Portolan charts with rhumb-line sailing instructions antedate projective maps in the history of marine chart making (Wehner & Wehner 1986). Those whose intuitions about what is neurobiologically plausible are influenced more by mathematical considerations of elegance, simplicity, and ease of computational implementation may prefer cartographic models.

THE GLOBAL MAP OF THE HONEYBEE   Rhumb-line sailing maps (and modern piloting manuals) give course and distance directions linking one port to another and, sometimes, sketches of headlands near each port. Thus, they closely resemble a surveyor's field notes. They are easy to use in navigation, provided that all one wants to do is follow one of the courses given. Since they contain the information required to construct a cartographic representation of the spatial relations among the ports, they may also, in principle, be used to steer from any port to any other, but they are not easily used for this more general purpose, which explains the universal marine preference for true maps, representations that give the relative positions of all the represented points in a manner that permits easy computation of the compass bearing and distance of any charted point from any other. Experiments in which animals are captured, transported to arbitrary release points within a familiar territory, and induced to home to different destinations are relevant to judging the plausibility of the "cartographic" model of the bee's Euclidean representation of the terrain versus the "surveyor's-notes" model favored by Cartwright & Collett (1987) and Wehner & Wehner (1986).

It has long been known that wasps and honeybees released at arbitrary points within their foraging range set "bee-line" courses back toward the hive or nest (Fabre 1919; Romanes 1885), and there are numerous similar results with birds (Papi & Wallraff 1982) and bats (Mueller 1966; Gunier & Elder 1971). An elegant series of experiments of this kind with the honeybee has recently been reported by Gould (1986a). He trained bees to fly from their hive at the bottom of a field to a feeding station in a small opening in the woods that bordered the field (Site A in Figure 2A). While the bees could be expected to be familiar with all of the terrain shown in Figure 2A, they were trained in such a way that it was unlikely that any bee ever flew from the hive to the feeding station at A by way of the Site B. Gould then captured marked foragers known to be regularly shuttling between the hive and the station at A, as they emerged from the hive en route to A, carried them around for a while in a dark box, then released them either at B or at H. He also captured unmarked foragers, shuttling between the hive and some feeding source other than A. These he captured either as they emerged from the hive en route to their diverse destinations or as they returned to the hive from diverse directions. Both groups were released at B. Site B was downhill from the woods that surrounded A. The tree-top horizon in the direction of Site A was 24–28 m above the elevation of B, preventing any view of A from B.

Gould recorded the departure bearings of each released bee. These are plotted as filled circles, open triangles, and open squares on the unit circle in Figure 2B. The thin lines without arrowheads indicate the bearing of the various destinations from the various release sites. The lines with arrowheads give the mean departure vectors for the four different categories of released

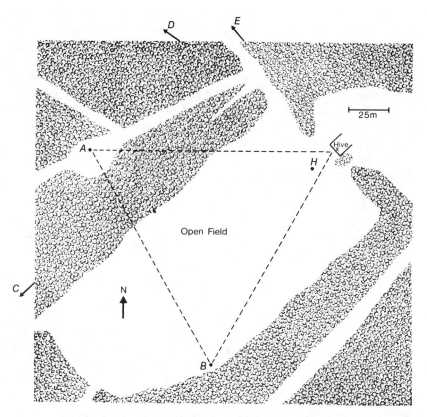

Figure 2   A. (above) Plan of Gould's test area. X=hive; A= feeding station; B=out of the way release site; H=release site near hive. *B. (opposite)* Departure bearings. Each symbol is the departure bearing of one released bee. Open triangles = bees destined for A, captured at the hive and released at H (Mean Vector 2). Filled circles = bees destined for A, captured at the hive and released at B (Mean Vector 1). Open squares = unmarked bees returning from diverse and unknown sources, captured on arrival at the hive and released at B (Mean Vector 3). The thin lines give the correct bearings of the destinations (hive or A) from the release sites (B or H). The heavy arrows give the mean vectors for the three groups whose symbols are plotted, plus a fourth group of unmarked bees with diverse and unknown destinations captured as they left the hive and released at B (Mean Vector 4, symbols not plotted). [Adapted from Gould (1986a,) by permission of the author and the publisher.]

bees: (*a*) those released at B and bound for A; (*b*) those released at H bound for A; (*c*) those released at B bound for the hive; (*d*) those released at B bound for diverse and unknown feeding sources. For the first three groups, the mean departure vectors have highly significant lengths (the r's in Figure 2B), which means that there is a statistically significant clustering of departure bearings. The directions (θ's) of the statistically significant mean departure vectors do not deviate significantly from the correct bearing of the bees' destinations

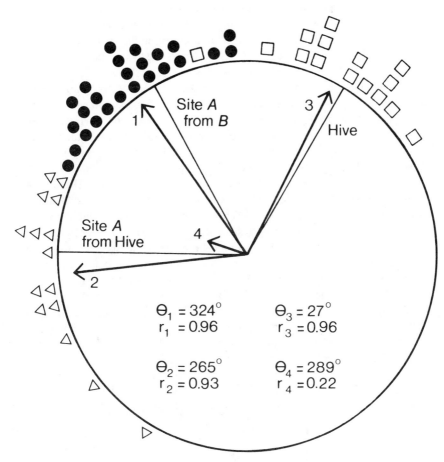

$$\Theta_1 = 324^\circ$$
$$r_1 = 0.96$$

$$\Theta_3 = 27^\circ$$
$$r_3 = 0.96$$

$$\Theta_2 = 265^\circ$$
$$r_2 = 0.93$$

$$\Theta_4 = 289^\circ$$
$$r_4 = 0.22$$

from their release sites. For the fourth group, those with diverse destinations, there is no significant clustering of departure bearings; they flew off in all directions.

Gould ran a number of interesting variations and further controls, but space does not permit a full account of this important series of experiments. What the experiments establish is the important conclusion that one and the same honeybee can quickly set approximately correct courses to different destinations from arbitrary release points within familiar terrain (when released in unfamiliar terrain, the bees never return to the hive). This is what one might expect if bees process the metric spatial information they demonstrably acquire into a unified coding of the macroscopic shape of their environment and use this unified metric representation of the shape of their environment in setting courses, plotting their ephemeris function, finding local feeding sources, and interpreting the dances of returning foragers (see below). This kind of performance is not what one might expect from an animal that kept its knowledge of the spatial relations in its environment in the disjointed form of surveyor's field notes, although it is probably possible to account for this kind of behavior with such a model (Cartwright & Collett 1987).

The integrated-map, or cartographic, model of the bee's cognitive map would also appear more consistent with the results of an experiment reported by Gould & Gould (1988). By setting up feeding stations on rowboats, they trained some marked bees from a hive to fly to a feeding station in the middle of a lake. By keeping the quality of the artificial nectar low, they induced these marked foragers not to dance during the training period when the rowboat was moved by small steps to the middle of the lake. (Returning foragers do not signal the location of their source to other foragers when the sugar content of the nectar is low.) When the marked foragers were regularly shuttling between the rowboat in the middle of the lake and the hive, the Goulds increased the sweetness, so that the returning foragers now danced vigorously. However, the other foragers generally refused to heed their dance, even though the other foragers would heed a dance signalling a source on the far side of the lake or at any point along the shore of the lake. This result suggests that a bee's reaction to the dance of a returning forager is mediated by its map of the terrain. If the position of the source on the map, as indicated by the dance, falls where there cannot ordinarily be food, the dance is ignored. This result seems to favor the hypothesis that an integrated metric map of the shape of the environment is linked to other environmental characteristics and forms a foundation for the bee's behavior, entering into every aspect of the behavior that involves moving from place to place.

Dead Reckoning and the Map

Animals possess sophisticated sensory/perceptual processes for determining the distances and directions of distal stimuli—that is, for forming an egocentric representation of the spatial positions of distal stimuli (Brownell 1984; Collett 1978; Collett & Harkness 1982; Ellard et al 1984; Lock & Collett 1979; Simmons & Kick 1984; Wallace 1959). Gallistel (1989) sketches the computations by which the representations of the animal's geocentric position (provided by the dead-reckoning module) may be integrated with the egocentric representations of the terrain surrounding a given viewpoint to yield a geocentric representation of the terrain, a representation built up from observations made at different places and different times.

Gallistel goes on to suggest that the dead-reckoning system is linked to the map in such a way that the animal has a moment-to-moment representation of its position on the map, which it uses to govern its movements. The hypothesis is that the course of an animal's movements through its environment is governed by a continuously updated representation of its position on its map, not by its immediate perceptions of the environment. The velocity components of its immediate percepts are used in the updating process (path integration). Static components of the percepts are used episodically to confirm and correct the representation of position on the map by taking a fix. Simply put, the hypothesis is that routine animal movements are governed by a navigational process closely analogous to everyday marine practice. This practice rests on an extensive isomorphism between the geometry of motion and position and the computational processes that underlie navigation. At the neurophysiological level of analysis, the hypothesis implies that the mathematical description of the processes in the animal brain that function during animal navigation parallels the mathematical description of the computations a human or computerized navigation system makes.

One attraction of the hypothesis is that it explains the many instances of "stupid" behavior in the face of a transformed environment, as when bats continue to avoid wires that are no longer there (Neuweiler & Möhres 1967), rats run into the walls of shortened segments of familiar corridors, turn into nonexistent branches of lengthened corridors (Carr & Watson 1908), run off the end of shortened planks in elevated mazes (Dennis 1932), and run right over large piles of food placed in the middle of an alley they have learned to run for a food reward at the end (Stoltz & Lott 1964). It also explains why clock-shifted homing pigeons released within sight of their home loft initially depart on an erroneous compass bearing, which is predictable from the extent of the clock shifting (Foa & Albonetti 1980; Graue 1963; Matthews 1968; Schmidt-Koenig 1972). They steer by their sun compass even when they are within sight of their destination.

Is Position-Fixing a Purely Geometric Congruence-Finding Process?

Cheng (1986; see also Gallistel 1989) ran rats in a variety of tasks in a rectangular environment where they had to find hidden food after being shown its location. The rats were kept in the dark between trials and carried to and from the experimental box in the dark, in an effort (not entirely successful) to disorient them with respect to the world at large, so that they would get their orientation while in the box entirely from the box itself, rather than carrying with them by dead reckoning during passive transport an orientation obtained outside the experimental environment (Carr 1917; Carr & Watson 1908; von Saint Paul 1982). Cheng provided very prominent and distinctive landmarks in each of the four corners of his boxes: panels that looked, felt, and smelled distinctively different from each other. He even made one wall of the enclosure of white Styrofoam, which contrasted strongly with the matte black plywood of the other three walls. Nonetheless, his rats persistently made rotational confusions; half the time they looked for the food at the spot that was the rotational equivalent of the correct location. They behaved as if they took their orientation within the box from its shape alone, ignoring the distinctive properties of the surfaces that composed that shape. Since the shape was axially symmetric, orientations based solely on the finding of a congruence between the remembered shape of the environment (the map) and the currently perceived shape would be erroneous by 180° half the time.

Margules & Gallistel (1988) showed that when the rats were trained in a lit room where they could easily assess their orientation to the extramaze environment, one did not see these rotational confusions, but when these same rats were then run under Cheng's conditions (disoriented with respect to the extramaze environment), they made rotational confusions on 50% of the trials, despite the presence of salient corner landmarks, which were present and fixed in their given corners during all phases of training, both initially when the rats were oriented to the extramaze environment and later when they were not.

Cheng (1986; see also Gallistel 1989) suggests that there is a module that encodes the shape and only the shape of the environment. Properties of environmental surfaces other than their relative positions—the smells, reflectance characteristics, textures, etc of a surface—are stored in other memory modules and linked to the representation of environmental shape (the map proper) by means of addresses, the equivalent of the latitude and longitude or number and letter addresses that link the cities or streets in a map index to positions on the map. Gallistel (1989) suggests that in taking a fix the animal brain computes shape parameters for the currently perceived locale (for example, the centroid and principal axes of an enclosed space like the rectangular box) and matches these to the corresponding shape parameters for regions on its map. Because shape parameters are a function solely of the relative positions of the surfaces that define a shape, such a process would be impenetrable to the distinctive properties of surfaces—their smells, reflectance characteristics, and so on.

THE REPRESENTATION OF TIME

Time of Occurrence (Circadian Phase)

Living systems contain self-sustaining biochemical and biophysical oscillations, whose periods range from fractions of a second to a year and perhaps more (for reviews, see Aschoff 1981; Connor 1985; Farner 1985; Jacklet 1985; Turek 1985). These endogenous oscillations play a ubiquitous role in behavior and physiology, because they provide the foundation for timekeeping and time-utilizing processes in the nervous system. We have already seen the role the internal time sense plays in the sun-compass mechanism. In this section, we review some of the experimental evidence that in storing informa-tion about events, part of what gets stored is the time of occurrence or circadian phase of the event—that is, a time-stamp derived from a reading of the internal clock.

Naturalistic and experimental observations early in this century established that bees learn the time of day at which food is to be found at a given source and time their visits accordingly (von Stein Beling 1923; von Buttel-Reepen 1915; Forel 1910; Kleber 1935). After a few days' experience with a food source where artificial nectar is only available during the same 2-hr period each day, there is a sharp increase in the visits of marked foragers an hour to a half-hour *before* the beginning of the feeding period (Wahl 1932, 1933). One and the same bee learns to visit different feeding stations at different times of the day (Wahl 1932). If there is a distinctive color or odor present at certain times and a different color or odor at other times, the bee's learned preference between the colors and odors becomes a function of the time of day: It prefers one odor or color at one time of day and the other odor or color at the other time of day (Kolterman 1971). These learned behavioral dependencies on the time of day are cued by the bee's internal clock, not by external cues (Renner 1959; Wahl 1932)—that is, they are based on the momentary phase of an endogenous circadian oscillation, not on some time-varying environmental variable, such as the elevation of the sun.

In the course of a single day, a foraging honeybee may learn to distinguish 19 different times of day (19 different momentary phases of an endogenous oscillation). Kolterman (1971) did a painstaking experiment, working with only one bee at a time to avoid the complications that might arise from communication in the hive among bees simultaneously trained. His individual foragers shuttled between the hive and the station every 5 min. On the training day, each forager experienced a geraniol odor at the food source for three visits from a quarter past to a half past each hour between 09:00 and 18:00. The next day, the test day, Kolterman repeatedly probed the bee's response to two empty beakers, only one of which smelled of geraniol. On this day, the bee found a single odorless beaker filled with sugar water, except on the probes, which were made on single visits at 20-after and 10-to each hour. The probes at 20-after coincided with the times at which the bee had smelled geraniol at this source the previous day, while the probes at 10-to coincided with times when it had not. On a probe visit, the bee was confronted with two beakers, both empty, one smelling of geraniol, the other of thyme. (Untrained bees had no preference between the geraniol and thyme odors.) The beakers were so constructed that the bee had to enter them to discover they were empty. In the course of a single visit to an empty beaker, the bee landed on and entered it repeatedly ("double-checking" that the beaker was empty). The number of such landings before the bee gave up provided a measure of search intensity. Kolterman found that a trained bee always overwhelmingly preferred the beaker smelling of geraniol to the beaker smelling of thyme. Thus, its memory for which odor had been associated with nectar in that locale was active at all times of day. However, the intensity of its searching in the beaker smelling of geraniol was significantly higher on every probe run at 20 min after the hour and significantly lower on every probe run at 10 before the hour. There were 19 different probes, alternating between 20-after and 10-to the hour, and the search intensity on each probe differed very significantly from the probe preceding and the probe following it.

The rat, like the bee, learns the time at which it finds food (Bolles & Moot 1973). It, too, can learn more than one feeding time per day (Bolles & Moot 1973; Edmonds & Adler 1977), and for it, too, the temporal cue comes from an internal endogenous circadian oscillator (Aschoff et al 1983; Boulos et al 1980; Coleman et al 1982; Edmonds & Adler 1977; Gibbs 1979; Honmah et al 1983; Rosenwasser et al 1984). Other experiences are also stamped with the time of day: In the one-trial passive avoidance paradigm, there is a strong dependence of avoidance performance upon the time of training; the rat's hesitancy to enter the chamber where it has once been shocked, while strong regardless of the time of testing, is strongest when the time of testing coincides with the time of day at which it had the one training trial (Holloway & Wansley 1973a,b). A similar effect is seen in a one-trial appetitive learning task (Wansley & Holloway 1975). When a rat is given conflicting aversive and appetitive reinforcements for entering a compartment, the extent to which the appetitive reinforcement counteracts the effect of the aversive reinforcement depends upon the relative times of day at which it has had the conflicting experiences; it is greatest when the appetitive experience is given at the same time of day as the aversive experience (Hunsicker & Melgren 1977). In an escape task, extinction is slowest when the extinction trials occur at the same time of day as the training trials (Holloway & Sturgis 1976).

While many animals are known to have an internal clock with a period of about a year (Farner 1985), there is, surprisingly, almost no literature addressed to the question whether animals can learn temporal intervals or periods measured in days. When bees are fed at the same time every other day, they show no sign of learning the 48-hr feeding schedule (Wahl 1932). In birds, however, Gallistel (1989) gives an account of an unpublished experiment by M. Denise Caubisens and Susan Edmonds. In January and February, they went out every day to a bird feeder in a wooded area in Purchase, New York. They carried a sack of seed with them to the feeder every day, but they only used it to stock the feeder every other day. After a while, the mixed flock of chickadees, titmice, and nuthatches that frequented the feeder was there waiting for them only every other day, suggesting that birds can learn an every-other-day schedule.

Whether animals can distinguish one day from the next remains to be determined, but it is now well established that many of the records that animals keep of their experiences are stamped with, at least, the time of day at which the experience occurred. Gallistel (1989) suggests that the time stamp and the address stamp (record of where the experience occurred) play a unique role as index variables in memory, variables that permit one record to be linked to another.

Temporal Intervals

The capacity of rats and pigeons to remember the duration of stimuli and the latencies from the onset of a stimulus to the (probabilistic) occurrence of a reward have been extensively studied by Church, Gibbon, Meck, and Roberts. Their work has been reviewed in Gibbon & Allan (1984). For more recent work, see Holder & Roberts (1985), Meck (1988), Meck & Church (1984, 1987), Meck et al (1984, 1987), and Olton (1987).

This work demonstrates a rich representation of time in that the animals respond to the *ratio* between a currently elapsed interval and the remembered latency at which reward occurs [in the peak procedure (Gibbon et al 1984)]. Or, still more complexly, in the time-left procedure, they respond to the *ratio* of the *difference* between a currently elapsed interval and a remembered comparison interval (the numerator) and yet another comparison interval (the denominator). In timing the duration of a stimulus that is interrupted by gaps, the animals do not normally time the gap; they respond to the first segment of the stimulus plus the second segment. However, they may be taught to respond to the first segment, plus the gap, plus the second segment (Roberts & Church 1978). These results may indicate either variable use of the switch that gates pulses to an accumulator (Church 1984), or they may indicate the addition of temporal intervals computed by subtracting times of onset and times of offset (Gallistel 1989). Rats can also process two elapsing intervals simultaneously, making a ratio comparison of each elapsing interval to a different remembered standard (Meck & Church 1984). In short, there exist in the brains of birds and rodents (at least) time-measuring processes that enable them to store variables that represent temporal intervals. These variables enter into combinatorial response-determining processes isomorphic to arithmetic addition, subtraction, and division.

THE REPRESENTATION OF NUMBER

Many vertebrates can be taught a discrimination based on the number of items or stimuli in a set, whether the set is presented simultaneously [Davis 1984 (raccoon); Davis & Bradford 1986 (rat); Matsuzawa 1985; Rumbaugh et al 1987 (chimpanzee); Pepperberg 1987 (parrot)] or sequentially (Capaldi &

Miller 1988; Davis & Albert 1986; Davis & Memmott 1983; Fernandes & Church 1982—all with rats). For a review of earlier number-discrimination work see Davis & Memmott (1982).

While most work has used small numerosities, rats and pigeons discriminate the numbers of responses they have made in the range 16–50 (Mechner 1958; Mechner & Guevrekian 1962; Platt & Johnson 1971; Rilling 1967; Rilling & McDiarmid 1965). The upper limit on the numerosities common lab animals can discriminate has yet to be established. The accuracy with which animals discriminate numerosity (the extent to which they generalize to neighboring numerosities) is a function of the magnitude of the numerosity. As with other scalar dimensions of experience, the generalization function gets wider as the number gets bigger (Mechner 1958; Platt & Johnson 1971). Even when the numbers are large, however, the discriminative capacity is reasonably good: The pigeon discriminates 45 pecks from 50 pecks with about 70% accuracy and 40 from 50 with close to 90% accuracy (Rilling & McDiarmid 1965).

When, as is commonly the case, the duration of a sequence covaries with its numerosity during discriminative training, rats learn both the numerical cue and the temporal cue and use either dimension alone to discriminate when the other is held constant (Meck & Church 1983). Pigeons are more disposed to use the numerosity of the responses they have made in tasks that require a discrimination based on temporal interval than they are to use the temporal interval as a discriminative cue in tasks requiring a discrimination based on number (Rilling 1967), when the numbers of responses being counted are in the 30–50 range and the intervals being timed are in the 30–45 sec range. Thus, the pigeon's capacity to represent large numerosities and use these representations as a basis for discriminative responding would appear to be on a par with, or superior to, its capacity to utilize its representations of temporal intervals measured in tens of seconds.

The results of number-discrimination experiments imply that there is a systematic mapping from the numerosities of simultaneously and sequentially presented sets to states of the nervous system. It seems likely that this mapping process is a counting process of some kind. Gelman & Gallistel (1978) give a formal analysis of counting. Meck & Church (1983) show that a modification of the switch control mechanism in their timing model yields a counting mechanism [whose formal properties conform to the analysis of Gelman & Gallistel; see Gallistel (1989)]. In several ingenious experiments, they have obtained extensive experimental evidence that the counting and timing mechanisms are closely related (Church & Meck 1984; Meck et al 1985). Capaldi & Miller (1988) have applied the Gelman & Gallistel analysis of counting in systematic tests of the hypothesis that rats count rewarded and unrewarded trials in runway experiments.

However, it continues to be argued that the mapping process in the discrimination of small numbers by animals must be a nonserial perceptual process called subitizing (Davis & Pérusse 1988; Rumbaugh et al 1987). In this view, twoness is discriminated from threeness by perceptual processes analogous to those by which we discriminate cowness from treeness. The persistence of this view is puzzling given the experimental evidence that "there is no such thing as 'the immediate cognition of number' " in adult human subjects (Mandler & Shebo 1982, p. 2; Kaufman et al 1949, p. 525): In humans, the reaction-time function for the estimation of the numerosity of visual arrays has a significant positive slope over its entire range, including from one to two (Mandler & Shebo 1982).

Given the existence of a mapping from numerosities to neural representatives of numerosities, the question whether animals have a concept of number would appear to turn on the answers to the following two questions: (*a*) Do they represent numerosity as a distinct property of a set, separable from the properties of the items that compose the set? (*b*) Do they perform with the representatives of numerosity combinatorial operations isomorphic to the arithmetic operations that define the number system $(=, <, +, -, \times, \div)$? The answer to both questions appears to be "yes."

If the numerosity of a set is represented as a property that is separable from the properties of the items that compose the set, then an animal taught a numerical discrimination with one set should respond appropriately and without further training when the same numerosities are instantiated with sets composed of items with properties different from the properties of the items in the training sets. The immediate generalization of numerical discriminations from the training sets to other sets composed of different types of items, or stimuli in other modalities, has been demonstrated in the chimpanzee (Matsuzawa 1985) and the rat (Capaldi & Miller 1988; Church & Meck 1984).

The chimpanzee presented with a choice between two trays, each having two wells, with various numbers of chocolate bits in each well, reliably chooses the tray with the greater total (Rumbaugh et al 1987). This may mean that the chimpanzee is adding separate estimates of number (one for each well of a tray). On the other hand, it may mean only that the chimpanzee continues its count as it shifts its attention from one well to the next. In any event, the chimpanzee's systematic preference for the greater number implies a relational decision process isomorphic to the ">" operator in arithmetic. The best evidence for a combinatorial process isomorphic to subtraction comes from experiments in which the rat must press a lever a certain number of times prior to trying the food-delivery system, with a penalty for premature attempts. The value of n, the number of responses made, at which the rat is maximally likely to break off pressing and try the feeder, is greater than N, the required number of presses, by a fixed amount (a fixed difference), and the magnitude of this difference is a function of the penalty: the greater the penalty, the bigger the difference (Mechner 1958; Platt & Johnson 1971). This result would seem to imply a decision process based on the size of the *difference* between the animal's current count and a learned comparison value. On the other hand, when a rat is trained to discriminate 2 from 8 and then presented with intermediate numerosities, it makes a *ratio* comparison of the intermediate numerosities to the learned discriminant values: The intermediate numerosity at which the rat is equally likely to choose either of the alternatives is the logarithmic (equiratio) midpoint not the arithmetic (equidifference) midpoint (Meck & Church 1983).

Given the evidence that animal brains perform operations isomorphic to addition, subtraction, and division with the representatives of temporal intervals and the evidence that they have a closely related system for representing numerosity, it may reasonably be conjectured that their well-documented ability to match the allocation of their foraging behavior to the relative rates of prey occurrence (see Introduction) depends upon a representation of rate obtained by dividing representatives of numerosities by representatives of temporal intervals. It is not clear how else they obtain their representation of rate, since models based on temporally decaying "running averages" do not work at all well (Lea & Dow 1984; Gallistel 1989). If rate estimates are obtained in the suggested manner, then the animal representation of number is a rich one.

CONCLUSIONS

The empiricist view of mind has been the dominant view in behavioral and neural science since their inceptions as experimental disciplines. Very roughly, this is Locke's view that "there is nothing in the mind that was not first in the senses." From this perspective, the primitives in the brain's representation of the world are simple sensory signals, which are functions of first-, second-, or third-order properties of proximal stimuli (wavelength, intensity, position on the sensory surface, the spatio-temporal intensity distribution, and so on). Representations of such abstract properties of the world as space, time, and number are arrived at, if at all, by some poorly understood process of inference from regular patterns observed in the simple sense data. And, it has often been argued, such abstract representations play no role in the behavior of the many animals that we imagine to be in some sense substantially simpler creatures than ourselves.

An alternative view is again very roughly captured by Leibnitz's rejoinder that "there is nothing in the mind that was not first in the senses, except the mind itself." By "mind itself," a modern behavioral or neuroscientist might understand brain circuits that are tuned to the location of objects in egocentric space (Knudsen 1982; Sparks & Nelson 1987; Suga 1982), or to the animal's position and orientation in geocentric space (Muller et al 1987; Ranck 1984), and endogenous rhythmic processes that indicate the time (Connor 1985; Farner 1985; Jacklet 1985). The experimental data just reviewed are consistent with the view that natural selection has shaped brains in such a way that there exists the kind of brain-world parallelism of formal structure that Leibnitz seems to have envisaged. The formal (mathematical) descriptions of many brain processes appear to mirror the formal descriptions of the external realities to which those processes adapt the animal's behavior. Because space, time, and number are such fundamental aspects of an animal's environment, their formal characteristics are mirrored in the formal characteristics of basic brain processes. The formal similarity between these aspects of the environment and the brain processes that adapt the animal's behavior to them is what justifies a computational-representational approach to the behavioral and neurobiological analysis of higher brain function.

Literature Cited

Aschoff, J., ed. 1981. *Biological Rhythms. Handbook of Behavioral Neurobiology, Vol. 4.* New York: Plenum. 563 pp.

Aschoff, J., Goetz, C. von, Honmah, K. I. 1983. Restricted feeding in rats: effects of varying feeding cycle. *Z. Tierpsychol.* 63:91–111

Baum, W. M., Rachlin, H. C. 1969. Choice as time allocation. *J. Exp. Anal. Behav.* 12:861–74

Beusekom, G. van. 1948. Some experiments on the optical orientation in *Philanthus Triangulum* Fabr. *Behaviour* 1:195–225

Bolles, R. C., Moot, S. A. 1973. Rats anticipation of diurnal and adiurnal feeding. *J. Comp. Physiol. Psychol.* 83:510–14

Boulos, Z. A., Rossenwasser, A. M., Terman, M. 1980. Feeding schedules and the circadian organization of behavior in the rat. *Behav. Brain Res.* 1:39–65

Brownell, P. H. 1984. Prey detection by the sand scorpion. *Sci. Am.* 251(6):86–97

Capaldi, E. J., Miller, D. J. 1988. Counting in rats: its functional significance and the independent cognitive processes which comprise it. *J. Exp. Psychol.: Anim. Behav. Proc.* 14:3–17

Carr, H. 1917. Maze studies with the white rat. *J. Anim. Behav.* 7:259–305

Carr, H., Watson, J. B. 1908. Orientation of the white rat. *J. Comp. Neurol. Psychol.* 18:27–44

Cartwright, B. A., Collett, T. S. 1987. Landmark maps for honey bees. *Biol. Cybern.* 57:85–93

Cartwright, B. A., Collett, T. S. 1983. Landmark learning in bees: experiments and models. *J. Comp. Physiol.* 151:521–43

Cheng, K. 1986. A purely geometric module in the rat's spatial representation. *Cognition* 23:149–78

Cheng, K., Collett, T. S., Pickhard, A., Wehner, R. 1987. The use of visual landmarks by honey bees: bees weight landmarks according to their distance from the goal. *J. Comp. Physiol.* 161:469–75

Cheng, K., Gallistel, C. R. 1984. Testing the geometric power of an animal's spatial representation. See Roitblatt et al 1984, pp. 409–23

Church, R. M. 1984. Properties of the internal clock. See Gibbon & Allan 1984, pp. 567–82

Church, R. M., Gibbon, J. 1982. Temporal generalization. *J. Exp. Psychol.: Anim. Behav. Proc.* 8:165–86

Church, R. M., Meck, W. H. 1984. The numerical attribute of stimuli. See Roitblatt et al 1984, pp. 445–64

Coleman, G. J., Harper, S., Clarke, J. D., Armstrong, S. 1982. Evidence for a separate meal-associated oscillator in the rat. *Physiol. Behav.* 29:107–15

Collett, T., Harkness, L. 1982. Depth vision in animals. In *The Analysis of Visual Behavior,* ed. D. J. Ingle, M. A. Goodale, R. J. W. Mansfield, pp. 111–76. Cambridge, Mass: MIT Press. 834 pp.

Collett, T. S. 1978. Peering—a locust behavior for obtaining motion parallax information. *J. Exp. Biol.* 76:237–41

Collett, T. S. 1987. Insect maps. *Trends Neurosci.* 10:139–41

Collett, T. S., Land, M. F. 1975. Visual spatial memory in a hoverfly. *J. Comp. Physiol.* 100:59–84

Connor, J. A. 1985. Neural pacemakers and rhythmicity. *Ann. Rev. Physiol.* 47:17–28

Davis, H. 1984. Discrimination of the number three by a raccoon *(Procyon lotor). Anim. Learn. Behav.* 12:409–13

Davis, H., Albert, M. 1986. Numerical discrimination by rats using sequential auditory stimuli. *Anim. Learn. Behav.* 14:57–59

Davis, H., Bradford, S. A. 1986. Counting behavior by rats in a simulated natural environment. *Ethology* 73:265–80

Davis, H., Memmott, J. 1982. Counting behavior in animals: a critical evaluation. *Psychol. Bull.* 92:547–71

Davis, H., Memmott, J. 1983. Autocontingencies: rats count to three to predict safety from shock. *Anim. Learn. Behav.* 11:95–100

Davis, H., Pérusse, R. 1988. Numerical competence in animals. *Behav. Brain Sci:* In press

Dennis, W. 1932. Multiple visual discrimination in the block elevated maze. *J. Comp. Physiol. Psychol.* 13:391–96

Deutsch, J. A. 1960. *The Structural Basis of Behavior.* Chicago: Univ. Chicago Press. 186 pp.

Dyer, F. C., Gould, J. L. 1981. Honey bee orientation: a backup system for cloudy days. *Science* 214:1041–42

Dyer, F. C., Gould, J. L. 1983. Honey bee navigation. *Am. Sci.* 71:587–97

Edmonds, S. C., Adler, N. T. 1977. Multiplicity of biological oscillators in the control of circadian running activity in the rat. *Physiol. Behav.* 18:921–30

Ellard, C. G., Goodale, M. A., Timney, B. 1984. Distance estimation in the Mongolian gerbil: the role of dynamic depth cues. *Behav. Brain Res.* 14:29–39

Emlen, S. T. 1975. Migration: orientation and navigation. In *Avian Biology,* ed. D. S. Farner, J. R. King, 5:129–219. New York: Academic

Fabre, J. H. C. 1919. *The Hunting Wasps.* New York: Hodder & Stoughton. 427 pp.

Farner, D. S. 1985. Annual rhythms. *Ann. Rev. Physiol.* 47:65–82

Fernandes, D. M., Church, R. M. 1982. Discrimination of the number of sequential events by rats. *Anim. Learn. Behav.* 10:171–76

Foa, A., Albonetti, E. 1980. Does familiarity with the release site influence the initial orientation of homing pigeons? Experiments with clock-shifted birds. *Z. Tierpsychol.* 54:327–38

Forel, A. 1910. *Das Sinnesleben der Insekten.* München: E. Reinhardt. 393 pp.

Freeman, W. J., Skarda, C. A. 1988. Representations: Who needs them? In *Third Conference on the Neurobiology of Learning and Memory,* ed. J. L. McGaugh. In press.

Gallistel, C. R. 1989. *The Organization of Learning.* Cambridge, Mass: Bradford Books/MIT Press. In press.

Gelman, R., Gallistel, C. R. 1978. *The Child's Understanding of Number.* Cambridge, Mass: Harvard Univ. Press. 260 pp.

Gibbon, J., Allan, L., eds. 1984. *Timing and time perception. Ann. NY Acad. Sci.* Vol. 423: 654 pp.

Gibbon, J., Church, R. M., Meck, W. H. 1984. Scalar timing in memory. See Gibbon & Allan 1984, pp. 52–77

Gibbs, F. P. 1979. Fixed interval feeding does not entrain the circadian pacemaker in blind rats. *Am. J. Physiol.* 236:R249–53

Godin, J.-G. J., Keenleyside, M. H. A. 1984. Foraging on patchily distributed prey by a cichlid fish *(Teleosti, Cichlidae):* a test of the ideal free distribution theory. *Anim. Behav.* 32:120–31

Gould, J., Gould, C. G. 1988. *The Honey Bee.* New York: Freeman. In press

Gould, J. L. 1980. Sun compensation by bees. *Science* 207:545–47

Gould, J. L. 1984. Processing of sun-azimuth information by bees. *Anim. Behav.* 32:149–52

Gould, J. L. 1986a. The locale map of honey bees: Do insects have cognitive maps? *Science* 232:861–63

Gould, J. L. 1986b. Pattern learning by honey bees. *Anim. Behav.* 34:990–97

Gould, J. L. 1987. Landmark learning by honey bees. *Anim. Behav.* 35:26–34

Gould, J. L. 1988a. Resolution of pattern learning by honey bees. *J. Insect Behav.* 1:225–33

Gould, J. L. 1988b. Timing of landmark learning by honey bees. *J. Insect Behav.* In press

Graue, L. C. 1963. The effects of phase shifts in the day-night cycle on pigeon homing at distances of less than one mile. *Ohio J. Sci.* 63:214–17

Gunier, W. J., Elder, W. H. 1971. Experimental homing of gray bats to a maternity colony in a Missouri barn. *Am. Midl. Nat.* 86:502–6

Hamilton, P. V., Russell, B. J. 1982. Celestial orientation by surface swimming *Aplysia braziliana* (Mollusca: Gastropoda). *J. Exp. Mar. Biol. Ecol.* 56:145–52

Harkness, R. D., Maroudas, N. G. 1985. Central place foraging by an ant *(Cataglyphis bicolor* Fab.): a model of searching. *Anim. Behav.* 33:916–28

Harper, D. G. C. 1982. Competitive foraging in mallards: ideal free ducks. *Anim. Behav.* 30:575–84

Herrnstein, R. J. 1961. Relative and absolute strength of response as a function of frequency of reinforcement. *J. Exp. Anal. Behav.* 4:267–72

Herrnstein, R. J., Loveland, D. H. 1975. Maximizing and matching on concurrent ratio schedules. *J. Exp. Anal. Behav.* 24:107–16

Holder, M. D., Roberts, S. 1985. Comparison of timing and classical conditioning. *J. Exp. Psychol.: Anim. Behav. Proc.* 11:172–93

Holloway, F. A., Sturgis, R. D. 1976. Periodic decrements in retrieval of the memory of nonreinforcement as reflected in resistance to extinction. *J. Exp. Psychol.: Anim. Behav. Proc.* 2:335–41

Holloway, F. A., Wansley, R. 1973a. Multiphasic retention deficits at periodic intervals after passive avoidance learning. *Science* 180:208–10

Holloway, F. A., Wansley, R. 1973b. Multiple retention deficits at periodic intervals after active and passive avoidance learning. *Behav. Biol.* 9:1–14

Honmah, K.-I., Goetz, C. von, Aschoff, J. 1983. Effects of restricted daily feeding on freerunning circadian rhythms in rats. *Physiol. Behav.* 30:905–13

Hunsicker, J. P., Melgren, R. L. 1977. Multiple deficits in the retention of an appetitively motivated behavior across a 24-h period in rats. *Anim. Learn. Behav.* 5:14–26

Jacklet, J. W. 1985. Neurobiology of circadian rhythms generators. *Trends Neurosci.* 8:69–72

Jander, R. 1957. Die optische Richtungsorientierung der roten Waldameise (*Formica rufa* L). *Z. Vergl. Physiol.* 40:162–238

Kaufman, E. L., Lord, M. W., Reese, T. W., Volkman, J. 1949. The discrimination of visual number. *Am. J. Psychol.* 62:498–525

Kleber, E. 1935. Hat das Zeitgedächtnis der Bienen biologische Bedeutung? *Z. Vergl. Physiol.* 22:221–62

Knudsen, E. I. 1982. Auditory and visual maps of space in the optic tectum of the owl. *J. Neurosci.* 2:1177–94

Kolterman, R. 1971. 24-Std-Periodik in der Langzeiterinnerung an Duft- und Farbsignalen bei der Honigbiene. *Z. Vergl. Physiol.* 75:49–68

Krantz, D. H., Luce, R. D., Suppes, P., Tversky, A. 1971. *The Foundations of Measurement.* New York: Academic. 577 pp.

Lea, S. E. G., Dow, S. M. 1984. The integration of reinforcements over time. See Gibbon & Allan 1984, pp. 269–77

Levitt, T., Lawton, D., Chelberg, D., Nelson,

P. 1987. Qualitative landmark-based path planning and following. In *Proc. AAAI Natl. Conf. Artif. Intell.*, Seattle, 1987

Lieblich, I., Arbib, M. A. 1982. Multiple representations of space underlying behavior. *Behav. Brain Sci.* 5:627–59

Lock, A., Collett, T. 1979. A toad's devious approach to its prey: a study of some complex uses of depth vision. *J. Comp. Physiol.* 131:179–89

Mandler, G., Shebo, B. J. 1982. Subitizing: an analysis of its component processes. *J. Exp. Psychol. Gen.* 11:1–22

Margules, J., Gallistel, C. R. 1988. Heading in the rat: determination by environmental shape. *Anim. Learn. Behav.* In press

Mariscal, R. N. 1972. The behavior of symbiotic fish and anemones. In *The Behavior of Marine Animals,* ed. H. E. Winn, B. L. Olla, pp. 335–36. New York: Plenum. 503 pp.

Matsuzawa, T. 1985. Use of numbers by a chimpanzee. *Nature* 315:57–59

Matthews, G. V. T. 1968. *Bird Navigation.* Cambridge: Cambridge Univ. Press. 2nd ed. 197 pp.

Mechner, F. 1958. Probability relations within response sequences under ratio reinforcement. *J. Exp. Anal. Behav.* 1:109–22

Mechner, F., Guevrekian, L. 1962. Effects of deprivation upon counting and timing in rats. *J. Exp. Anal. Behav.* 5:463–66

Meck, W. H. 1988. Hippocampal function is required for feedback control of an internal clock's criterion. *Behav. Neurosci.* 102:54–60

Meck, W. H., Church, R. M. 1983. A mode control model of counting and timing processes. *J. Exp. Psychol.: Anim. Behav. Proc.* 9:320–34

Meck, W. H., Church, R. M. 1984. Simultaneous temporal processing. *J. Exp. Psychol.: Anim. Behav. Proc.* 10:1–29

Meck, W. H., Church, R. M. 1987. Cholinergic modification of the content of temporal memory. *Behav. Neurosci.* 101:457–64

Meck, W. H., Church, R. M., Gibbon, J. 1985. Temporal integration in duration and number discrimination. *J. Exp. Psychol.: Anim. Behav. Proc.* 11:591–97

Meck, W. H., Church, R. M., Olton, D. S. 1984. Hippocampus time and memory. *Behav. Neurosci.* 98:3–22

Meck, W. H., Church, R. M., Wenk, G. L., Olton, D. S. 1987. Nucleus basalis magnocellularis and medial septal area lesions differentially impair temporal memory. *J. Neurosci.* 7:3505–11

Milinski, M. 1979. An evolutionarily stable strategy in stickelbacks. *Z. Tierpsychol.* 51:36–40

Mittelstaedt, H. 1962. Control systems of orientation in insects. *Ann. Rev. Entomol.* 7:177–98

Mittelstaedt, H. 1978. Kybernetische Analyse von Orientierungsleistungen. In *Kybernetik,* ed. G. Hauske, E. Butenandt, pp. 144–95. Munich/Vienna: Oldenbourg. 424 pp.

Mittelstaedt, H. 1985. Analytic cybernetics of spider navigation. In *Neurobiology of Arachnids,* ed. F. G. Barth, pp. 298–316. Berlin/Heidelberg/New York: Springer. 385 pp.

Mittelstaedt, M. L., Mittelstaedt, H. 1980. Homing by path integration in a mammal. *Naturwissenschaft* 67:566

Mittelstaedt, H., Mittelstaedt, M. L. 1982. Homing by path integration. See Papi & Wallraff 1982, pp. 290–97

Morris, R. G. M. 1981. Spatial localization does not require the presence of local cues. *Learn. Motiv.* 12:239–60

Mueller, H. 1966. Homing and distance-orientation in bats. *Z. Tierpsych.* 23:403–21

Müller, M., Wehner, R. 1988. Path integration in desert ants, *Cataglyphis fortis. Proc. Natl. Acad. Sci. USA.* In press

Muller, R. A., Kubie, J. L., Ranck, J. B. Jr. 1987. Spatial firing patterns of hippocampal complex-spike cells in a fixed environment. *J. Neurosci.* 7:1935–50

Myerson, J., Miezin, F. M. 1980. The kinetics of choice: an operant systems analysis. *Psychol. Rev.* 87:160–74

Neuweiler, G., Möhres, F. P. 1967. Die Rolle des Ortgedächtnisses bei Orientierung der Grossblatt-Fledermaus *Megaderma lyra. Z. Vergl. Physiol.* 57:147–71

Olton, D. S. 1987. Separation of hippocampal and amygdaloid involvement in temporal memory dysfunctions. *Brain Res.* 404:180–88

Papi, F., Wallraff, H. G., eds. 1982. *Avian Navigation.* New York: Springer. 380 pp.

Pepperberg, I. M. 1987. Evidence for conceptual quantitative abilities in the African grey parrot: labeling of cardinal sets. *Ethology* 75:37–61

Platt, J. R., Johnson, D. M. 1971. Localization of position within a homogeneous behavior chain: effects of error contingencies. *Learn. Motiv.* 2:386–414

Ranck, J. B. Jr. 1984. Head direction cells in the deep layer of dorsal presubiculum in freely moving rats. *Soc. Neurosci. Abstr.* 10(Pt. 1):599

Renner, M. 1959. Über ein weiteres Versetzungs-Experiment zur Analyse des Zeitsinns und der Sonnenorientierung der Honigbiene. *Z. Vergl. Physiol.* 42:449–83

Renner, M. 1960. Contribution of the honey bee to the study of time sense and astronomical orientation. *Cold Springs Harbor Symp. Quant. Biol.* 25:361–67

Rilling, M. 1967. Number of responses as a stimulus in fixed interval and fixed ratio schedules. *J. Comp. Physiol. Psychol.* 63:60–65

Rilling, M., McDiarmid, C. 1965. Signal detection in fixed ratio schedules. *Science* 148:526–27

Roberts, S. 1981. Isolation of an internal clock. *J. Exp. Psychol.: Anim. Behav. Proc.* 7:242–68

Roberts, S., Church, R. M. 1978. Control of an internal clock. *Exp. Psychol.: Anim. Behav. Proc.* 4:318–37

Roitblatt, H. L., Bever, T. G., Terrace, H. S., eds. 1984. *Animal Cognition.* Hillsdale, NJ: Erlbaum. 682 pp.

Romanes, G. J. 1885. Homing faculty of hymenoptera. *Nature* 32:630

Rosenwasser, A. M., Pelchat, R. J., Adler, N. T. 1984. Memory for feeding time: possible dependence on coupled circadian oscillators. *Physiol. Behav.* 32:25–30

Rudy, J. W., Stadler-Morris, S., Peter, A. 1987. Ontogeny of spatial navigation behaviors in the rat: dissociation of "proximal"- and "distal"-cue-based behaviors. *Behav. Neurosci.* 101:62–73

Rumbaugh, D. M., Savage-Rumbaugh, S., Hegel, M. T. 1987. Summation in the chimpanzee *(Pan troglodytes). J. Exp. Psychol.: Anim. Behav. Proc.* 13:107–15

Santchi, F. 1913. Comment s'orient les fourmis. *Rev. Suisse Zool.* 21:347–426

Schmidt-Koenig, K. 1972. New experiments on the effect of clock shifts on homing in pigeons. *NASA Spec. Publ. SP-262,* pp. 275–82

Simmons, J. A., Kick, S. A. 1984. Physiological mechanisms for spatial filtering and image enhancement in the sonar of bats. *Ann. Rev. Physiol.* 46:599–614

Sparks, D. L., Nelson, J. S. 1987. Sensory and motor maps in the mammalian superior colliculus. *Trends Neurosci.* 10:312–17

Stoltz, S. P., Lott, D. F. 1964. Establishment in rats of a persistent response producing net loss of reinforcement. *J. Comp. Physiol. Psychol.* 57:147–49

Suga, N. 1982. Functional organization of the auditory cortex: representation beyond tonotopy in the bat. In *Multiple Auditory Areas,* Vol. 3, *Cortical Sensory Organization,* ed. C. N. Woolsey, pp. 157–218. Clifton, NJ: Humana Press.

Tinbergen, N., Kruyt, W. 1938. Über die Orientierung des Bienenwolfes *(Philanthus triangulum* Fabr.). III. Die Bevorzugung bestimmter Wegmarken. *Z. Vergl. Physiol.* 25:292–334

Turek, F. W. 1985. Circadian neural rhythms in mammals. *Ann. Rev. Physiol.* 47:49–64

von Buttel-Reepen, H. B. 1915. *Leben und*

Wesen der Bienen. Braunschweig: Vieweg 300 pp.

von Frisch, K. 1967. *The Dance-Language and Orientation of Bees.* Cambridge, Mass: Harvard Univ. Press. 566 pp.

von Saint Paul, U. 1982. Do geese use path integration for walking home? See Papi & Wallraff 1982, pp. 298–307

von Stein Beling, I. 1923. Über das Zeitgedächtnis der Bienen. *Z. Vergl. Physiol.* 9:259–338

Wahl, O. 1932. Neue Untersuchungen über das Zeitgedächtnis der Bienen. *Z. Vergl. Physiol.* 16:529–89

Wahl, O. 1933. Beitrag zur Frage der biologischen Bedeutung des Zeitgedächtnisses der Bienen. *Z. Vergl. Physiol.* 18:709–17

Wallace, G. R. 1959. Visual scanning in the desert locust *Schistocerca gregaria. J. Exp. Biol.* 36:512–25

Wansley, R. A., Holloway, F. A. 1975. Multiple retention deficits following one-trial appetitive training. *Behav. Biol.* 14:135–49

Wehner, R. 1981. Spatial vision in arthropods. In *Comparative Physiology and Evolution of Vision in Invertebrates, Handbook of Sensory Physiology,* ed. H. Autrum, VII/6C:287–617. Berlin/Heidelberg/New York: Springer. 697 pp.

Wehner, R. 1985a. Spatial organization of foraging behavior in individually searching desert ants, *Cataglyphis* (Sahara Desert) and *Ocymyrex* (Namib Desert). In *Experientia Supplementum,* Vol. 54: *Behavior in Social Insects.* Basel: Birhaüser

Wehner, R. 1985b. Astronavigation in insects. *Ann. Rev. Entomol.* 29:277–98

Wehner, R., Srinivasan, M. V. 1981. Searching behavior of desert ants, genus *Cataglyphis* (Formicidae, Hymenoptera). *J. Comp. Physiol.* 142:315–38

Wehner, R., Wehner, S. 1986. Path integration in desert ants. Approaching a long-standing puzzle in insect navigation. *Monitore Zool. Ital.* 20:309–31

Whishaw, I. Q, Mittleman, G. 1986. Visits to starts, routes, and places by rats *(Rattus norvegicus)* in a swimming pool navigation task. *J. Comp. Psychol.* 100:422–31

Ann. Rev. Psychol. 1989. 40:191–225

BRAIN DOPAMINE AND REWARD

R. A. Wise and P.-P. Rompre

Center for Studies in Behavioral Neurobiology, Department of Psychology
Concordia University, Montreal, Canada, H3G 1M8

CONTENTS

Rewards can exert powerful control over our thoughts and our behavior. It is assumed that the mechanism of these effects is in the brain, and physiological psychologists have been tempted by the possibility that there is as much to be learned about reward from the study of its mechanisms as from the study of its behavioral phenomenology. The mechanisms of reward are not easily examined, however, as they are to be found in the tangle of associational systems deep in the brain, rather than in the sensory or motor systems more accessible to the periphery.

Among the most powerful of rewards, however, are two that activate central reward circuitry directly, rather than through the peripheral nerves. These are the rewards of direct electrical stimulation and of habit-forming drugs. Electrical stimulation offers an anatomically selective tool; while it is indiscriminate about what kind of neurons it excites, its potency decreases with the square of the distance from the electrode tip and falls to trivial levels

191

within fractions of a millimeter. Drugs, on the other hand, are neurochemically selective tools; while they are carried by the circulation to all regions of the brain, many drugs act on specific receptors that are restricted to particular classes of neuron. When drugs are injected directly into the brain, they can (depending on how rapidly they are metabolized and how readily they diffuse into the blood and the surrounding tissue) have both anatomical and neurochemical specificity. It is drug reward and brain stimulation reward that have taught us most about the anatomy and neurochemistry of brain reward mechanisms. But it is assumed that the circuits studied with these laboratory rewards did not evolve merely as a curiosity for the physiological psychologist. Under certain circumstances rats will forgo food to the point of starvation while working for brain stimulation or intravenous cocaine; presumably this is because the drug or stimulation can exert more powerful activation of central reward mechanisms than can peripheral rewards necessary for survival.

Studies involving these two classes of laboratory reward have implicated dopamine-containing neurons in a number of reward phenomena. Dopamine is one of the catecholamine neurotransmitters, and the implicated dopaminergic cell groups project forward from the head of the midbrain to several forebrain structures. Subsets of these neurons are also implicated in other aspects of motivated behavior, and abnormal functioning of dopaminergic neurons has variously been suggested to account for aspects of Parkinson's disease, schizophrenia, mania, and depression. An understanding of the role of dopaminergic neurons in reward can be seen as one step toward understanding the more general roles of dopamine in mood and movement.

The present paper is a selective review of evidence implicating dopaminergic neurons in reward. Its aims are to familiarize the reader with the major findings which have established the hypothesis that dopamine plays a critical role in reward; to indicate the complexity of the brain circuitry within which dopamine serves as a single, though very important link; and to suggest a somewhat broader motivational perspective for what was initially termed a "pleasure center" in the brain. For more detailed reviews see Wise & Bozarth (1987) or Wise (1982, 1987a).

BRAIN STIMULATION REWARD: THE ANATOMICALLY SELECTIVE PROBE

Paradigmatic Considerations

The study of brain stimulation reward has come to be a highly specialized undertaking. Several technical advances over early studies must be outlined if the reader is to appreciate recent work. The technical advances are not difficult to understand, and they reflect application of well-known and basic principles of psychophysics and pharmacology.

DEFINITIONS: REWARD VS REINFORCEMENT   Gallistel et al (1974) have confirmed Deutsch's observation that there are two effects of rewarding brain stimulation, only one of which fits Skinner's definition of operant reinforcement. First, stimulation energizes performance even when it is not given in a response-contingent manner. This is a drive-like or incentive-motivational effect of stimulation which cannot be eliminated from the traditional lever-press paradigm. Second, response-contingent stimulation increases or maintains the probability of response repetition. This is a reinforcing effect consistent with Skinner's definition. The two effects—the "priming" or "energizing" effect and the "reinforcing" effect—are jointly implied by the term "reward." Thus, contrary to widely held belief, the term "reward"—as used by physiological psychologists—is not merely the lay term for "reinforcement." A second reason to prefer the term reward to the term reinforcement is that the physiological psychologist usually studies the steady-state behavior of animals that are already well trained, rather than the developing behavior of animals that are undergoing the changes in the probability of responding that supposedly accompany Thorndike's "stamping in" of a new habit.

THE REWARD-PERFORMANCE DISTINCTION   The function relating rate of bar pressing to stimulation intensity or frequency approaches the form of an ogive which rises steeply in individual animals (Figure 1). Response rate rises rapidly over a "dynamic range" of stimulation values and then remains relatively constant over a subsequent "static range" of stimulation values. Response rates in the dynamic and static ranges were not usually distinguished in early studies, but it is now realized that rate measures are meaningful only when this distinction is made.

Rate of responding in the static range (known as "asymptotic" rate) is subject to different controlling factors that contribute interestingly to rate of responding in the dynamic range. Asymptotic rate does not reflect major differences in the rewarding value of the stimulation, as can be demonstrated by offering animals choices between low and high frequencies (Miliaressis & Malette 1987; Waraczynski et al 1987) in the static range or by examining the strength of responding for access to the reward lever (Hawkins & Pliskoff 1964). Despite the fact that they do not produce different rates of response in single-lever tests, higher stimulation parameters are always chosen over lower ones and produce more responding for access. The contemporary interpretation of asymptotic responding is that it reflects constraints on performance rather than motivational indifference to more stimulation. It is very unlikely that asymptotic performance reflects the absolute limits of responding, however, as stimulation at different brain sites can often produce higher response rates (Prado-Alcala & Wise 1984; Rompre & Miliaressis 1985). It is

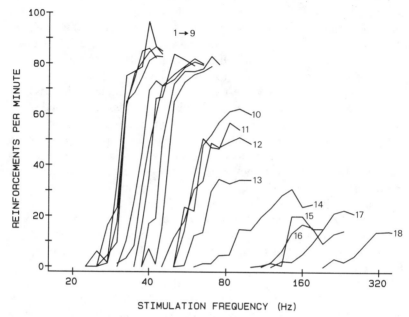

Figure 1 A family of rate-frequency functions reflecting responses for stimulation at 18 different sites on the midline of the mesencephalon in the same animal. Numbers indicate the stimulation sites; the successive sites were 0.16 mm apart.

more likely that asymptotic performance reflects limits of performance capacity associated with a particular stimulation site, and that these limits reflect reward-irrelevant side effects of stimulation specific to that site. It has been demonstrated, for example, that the addition of motoric side effects (produced by stimulating concurrently at a second site) can dramatically alter the asymptotic response rate (Miliaressis & Rompre 1987).

Rate of responding in the dynamic range, on the other hand, is quite sensitive to changes in the rewarding impact of stimulation (for example, changes in the effectiveness of various intensities when stimulation frequency is the independent variable). Moreover, rate in the dynamic range is sensitive to drugs of abuse and to drugs that reduce the rewarding impact of stimulation. For this reason, changes in response rate associated with the dynamic range of stimulation parameters are viewed as reflecting changes in the reward magnitude. Various rate criteria in the dynamic range are defined, by different investigators, as "reward threshold." Traditional psychophysics defined threshold as the value of signal intensity that was detected half the time, and this definition has led some investigators (Edmonds & Gallistel 1974) to define the self-stimulation threshold as the value of stimulation that sustains responding at half-maximal (asymptotic) levels. Others have attempted to define an absolute threshold measure in terms of the minimal stimulation value needed to sustain higher than baseline levels of responding; typically the criterion is less than 10% of asymptotic rates. Regardless of whether minimal levels or half-maximal levels are used to define threshold, threshold measures are not "rate-free"; they are, in each case, a measure of self-stimulation that reflects response rate at a single level of stimulation somewhere within the dynamic range.

It has been suggested that response rate and threshold measures of self-stimulation can be dissociated, and this is clearly true when rate is sampled from the static range of stimulation parameters that produce asymptotic performance. Figure 1 shows data involving several stimulation sites in the same animal; clearly there are sites where thresholds are high and asymptotic rates are low (curves 15–18). It is impossible, however, to have a change in threshold that is not accompanied by a change in rate if rate is sampled within the dynamic range where it bears any relevance to reward impact. It is only when asymptotic rates are considered that there can be a dissociation between threshold and rate. For this reason, it is absolutely essential that any discussion of response rate identifies whether the rates in question come from the dynamic or the static range. The fact that much of the old literature involved response rate determinations based on a single set of stimulation parameters—with no distinction made between parameters that induced asymptotic performance and parameters that induced intermediate performance—makes this literature difficult to interpret.

MEASUREMENT: THE CRITICAL VARIABLES   Since Valenstein's early criticism of rate measures, there has been a good deal of work on better paradigms for assessing the rewarding impact of stimulation. Choice measures, response-pattern analysis, and threshold measures are of obvious utility and have been used by some workers for a number of years. Recently, much analytic attention has been focused on the "curve-shift" measure which has evolved as the most powerful psychometric tool. In this approach, functions ("curves") such as those in Figure 1 are determined under experimental and control conditions; interest is in whether the experimental treatment "shifts" the function. Significant shifts to the right (to higher stimulation values) or left (to lower stimulation values) are interpreted as reflecting changes in the rewarding impact of the stimulation, and shifts up or down (to higher or lower asymptotic performance levels) are interpreted as reflecting changes in the performance capacity of the animals. The specification of *significant* in this context refers to biological significance; a small degree of left-right shift can reflect an artifact of changes in asymptote (Miliaressis et al 1986b).

One obvious advantage of this procedure is that the reader is given data across the entire dynamic and part of the static range of stimulation values. This constitutes a "dose-response" curve in which it is the "dose" of stimulation—rather than the dose of a drug—which is examined. With this procedure it is easy to see whether the effect of a treatment was general or parameter-specific; it is also easy to determine the range of interesting stimulation parameters. Threshold measures that do not reflect testing across the entire dynamic range do not give information as to where the threshold criterion falls within the range of behaviorally relevant stimulation parameters. The more important benefit of the curve-shift method—which makes it superior to all others—is that it offers a method for quantitative estimation of the impact of a reward-altering treatment. Just as Fechners's law related change in the perceived value of a stimulus to the log of the intensity of that stimulus, so does modern measurement theory relate the perceived value of rewarding stimulation to a log function. Equal changes in the log of the stimulation intensity or stimulation frequency (assuming that these parameters are in their dynamic ranges) can be taken as equal changes in the perceived impact of the stimulation. Drug treatments that produce the same size (in log units) rightward shift in the rate-frequency or rate-intensity function can be assumed to have equal reward-decreasing impact. According to the model of Gallistel et al (1981), treatments that cause a 0.3 log shift in the rate-frequency or rate-intensity function double the stimulation requirement for a given level of responding. If short pulses of stimulation (each pulse sufficient to produce one and only one action potential in each stimulated axon) are used, this would appear to reflect the need to trigger, under the treatment in question, twice the normal number of action potentials in the stimulated reward fibers. The very powerful metrics of dose-response analysis in pharmacology apply to the curve-shift paradigm as currently used in physiological psychology, and one of the current tasks of physiological psychology is to redo important experiments that were based on response-rate measures that did not distinguish dynamic-range data from static-range data. It has been demonstrated that weak or wrong conclusions have been drawn in mapping studies (Miliaressis et al 1982), refractory period estimates (Yeomans 1975), and pharmacological experiments (Edmonds & Gallistel 1974) involving simple response rate measures; consequently little is to be learned from most early studies which did not make the distinction or utilize one or another form of threshold paradigm; for this reason, most of the results that originated from such experiments are not reviewed in the present paper.

Anatomical Studies

One of the major axes of studies of brain stimulation reward involves the attempt to relate the phenomenon to what can be seen in the microscope. Mapping studies are designed to localize the regions at the tip of the stimulating electrode where there are reward-relevant neurons. Lesion studies are usually designed to identify fibers or cell groups somewhat distant from the electrode tip that carry the reward signal onward from the site where voltage-gated membrane channels are directly affected by the stimulation. Autoradiographic and neurochemical studies are designed to identify the cells most directly influenced by the stimulating current.

MAPPING STUDIES   Early suggestions that catecholamine fibers are involved in brain stimulation reward derived from evidence that many reward sites were near the trajectories of the ascending catecholamine fiber systems (the catecholamine neurotransmitters include dopamine, noradrenaline, and adrenaline). Since one or another of the ascending catecholamine systems can be found in every major forebrain region, it is not surprising that they are often identified with reward sites. Over the past decade several studies have been designed to determine whether there are any precise relationships between the boundaries or sensitivities of brain stimulation reward sites and the boundaries or regional densities of any of the catecholamine systems.

Such studies require estimates of the rewarding efficacy of the stimulation. As discussed earlier, one should study the whole dynamic and part of the static range of the rate-intensity or rate-frequency function. A second objective is to attain the highest possible histological resolution; this is best done when a number of closely adjacent sites are tested within each animal. The use of movable electrodes and low current intensities allows a level of anatomical resolution that cannot be approached in fixed-electrode studies and that gives evidence about the boundaries and relative densities of different systems and different levels of the same system. Our selective review is restricted to such studies.

Schmitt et al (1974) were the first to use movable electrodes and curve-shift methodology to map brain stimulation reward substrates. They found a column of reward sites in the mesencephalon, on the midline between the cerebral aqueduct and the interpeduncular nucleus. Most of the sites they tested in the dorsal central gray were aversive. The positive sites identified by these workers were caudal to the known dopamine cell groups and were thought most likely to represent activation of serotonergic or noradrenergic systems.

Corbett & Wise (1979, 1980) mapped the brainstem reward substrates more extensively, with specific attention to the ascending noradrenergic fiber systems and the dopamine cell groups. In no area tested did they find a consistent correlation between the quality of self-stimulation and the degree of noradrenergic fiber density or cellular aggregation; nor did they find any correspondence between the boundaries of the reward system and the boundaries of the noradrenergic fiber systems. They found no evidence of rewarding effects of stimulation of the noradrenergic nucleus locus coeruleus; rather, stimulation was clearly rewarding only when applied to sites anterior, lateral, and ventral to this nucleus. Stimulation was also rewarding in or near the dorsal raphe nucleus, the superior cerebellar peduncle, and the mesencephalic and motor nuclei of the trigeminal nerve. While the results of Corbett & Wise did not identify reward systems with any of these specific structures, they did appear to rule out the ascending noradrenergic pathways as substrates of rewarding stimulation.

In their second study, Corbett & Wise (1980; Wise 1981) were more successful in localizing rewarding stimulation to the region of specific cells and fibers. Reward sites in the ventral portion of the tegmentum were found to be closely tied to the region of the dopaminergic cell layer of the ventral tegmental area and substantia nigra. The lowest self-stimulation thresholds were found in the areas where the dopamine fiber bundles collect and begin to project forward up the medial forebrain bundle. Self-stimulation thresholds were a function of the density of dopaminergic elements surrounding the electrode tip; the lowest thresholds were associated with the densest regions of dopaminergic neurons. Their study revealed little evidence of rewarding effects of stimulation when the electrode tips were in the most caudal regions of the dopamine cell groups. Corbett & Wise interpreted their data as suggesting that direct activation of the ascending dopamine pathways was rewarding, and that the hypothesized dopaminergic reward system was discontinuous with the more caudal system mapped in their earlier study and that of Schmitt et al. While the data of Corbett & Wise have continued importance for the dopamine theory, neither interpretation proved fully accurate.

One question arose from more extensive and sensitive mapping on the midline behind the dopamine cell groups. Rompre & Miliaressis (1985) identified a large and sensitive reward system which appears to be continuous with that mapped by Corbett & Wise (1980). The region of positive sites extends 4 mm in the anterior-posterior axis, between the rostral mesencephalon and the caudal pons. In the pons, all positive sites were found on the midline between the cerebral aqueduct and the pontine nuclei. The reward threshold was lowest in the ventral region of the dorsal raphe, near the junction with the decussation of the superior cerebellar peduncle. In the rostral mesencephalon, a large column of positive sites were found up to 1 mm lateral to the midline, between the dorsal level of the central gray and the ventral tegmental area. When going from caudal to rostral, the low-threshold sites shift from dorsal to ventral and from medial to lateral along the trajectory of the tegmental radiations. High-threshold reward sites, not detected by Corbett & Wise, were also found above the A10 dopamine cell group in two animals. With the higher frequencies of the Rompre & Miliaressis study, it was clear that the midline mesencephalic reward system was either continuous with or overlapping with the ventral tegmental system.

Rompre & Boye (1986) extended this mapping to more caudal pontine regions and found that the positive sites and low-threshold region were shifted laterally to a small area near the locus coeruleus and mesencephalic trigeminal nerve. Because the inferred density of reward neurons in the caudal pontine regions was much lower than the inferred density in the rostral pontine region, they suggested that the majority of brainstem reward neurons originate or terminate at the more rostral midline pontine levels.

There are several additional brainstem neural structures where stimulation is rewarding but where the boundaries of the systems have not yet been explored with powerful mapping procedures. These include the regions of the deep cerebellar nuclei, the nucleus solitary tract, the dorsolateral region of the medulla, and the motor nucleus of the trigeminal nerve. It remains to be determined how many brainstem reward systems exist and which brainstem reward sites are connected by common systems or networks.

By far the most frequently studied brain stimulation reward sites are those of the diencephalic medial forebrain bundle (MFB). Stimulation along this bundle produces strong reward with few aversive or motoric side effects; lateral hypothalamic MFB stimulation is the standard against which other rewarding stimulation is traditionally compared. Olds et al (1960) performed the first mapping study using rate-intensity functions (with fixed stimulation electrodes) to map the entire diencephalon between the anterior hypothalamic area and the mesencephalon. They distinguished between a dorsal and a ventral system; the descriptions of these two systems fit well with the anatomy of the dorsal diencephalic bundle (DDB) and the MFB. While these facts were not known at the time, the MFB is the main pathway for the ascending dopamine fibers, and there is important dopaminergic innervation of the habenula, a way-station in the dorsal diencephalic bundle.

However, movable-electrode mapping of MFB reward sites at the level of the lateral hypothalamus (Gratton & Wise 1983) failed to identify the boundaries of the reward system with the boundaries of the ascending dopamine fibers. The main region of positive sites was found to extend ventrally from the zona incerta to the base of the brain and laterally from the fornix to the medial tip of the internal capsule; that is, reward sites were found to extend for the full width and depth of the MFB. The lowest thresholds were found in the middle of the MFB, at the dorsoventral level of the fornix. Two clusters of positive sites were observed near the midline, one ventral between the fornix and the third ventricle, and one dorsal, just lateral to the mammillothalamic tract. The system was more dispersed than the ascending dopamine fibers, and Gratton & Wise concluded that the boundaries of the reward system did not correspond to the boundaries of the dopamine fibers systems.

Mapping more rostrally in the anterior hypothalamic MFB, Blander & Wise (in press) found three clusters of reward sites. A large cluster of negative sites was observed along the edge of the third ventricle. Immediately lateral to this region was a large cluster of positive sites mainly located in the stria medullaris; interestingly, stimulation was not rewarding when the electrode was either just above or just below the fibers of the stria. Lateral to the stria medullaris was another cluster of negative sites mainly located in the internal capsule. These negative sites were bounded laterally by another column of positive sites, extending ventrally from the middle part of the globus pallidus to the base of the forebrain. Lowest thresholds were found in the dorsolateral globus pallidus.

The presence of clusters of positive sites indicates a compartmental organization of the reward substrates in the anterior hypothalamic area. Blander & Wise suggested that the more medial group of positive sites contains reward fibers of the DDB while the more lateral group contains fibers of the caudal MFB; the middle group may contain reward fibers belonging to both bundles, each of which connects forebrain regions to brainstem regions. The reward fibers that have been localized in other forebrain regions may contribute importantly to these projections and could play a role in the rewarding effect of diencephalic and brainstem stimulation. Again, the reward sites did not correspond in any straightforward way to the location of the ascending dopamine fibers.

Early studies have shown that electrical stimulation of several regions of the forebrain is rewarding; generally, the regions innervated by dopaminergic fibers contain the positive reward sites. As in the case of the MFB, however, the boundaries of the reward systems do not correspond closely to the boundaries of the regions of dopaminergic innervation (Prado-Alcala & Wise 1984; Prado-Alcala et al 1984). For example, the dopaminergic innervation of the septum forms a well-defined and dense diagonal band, with regions of sparsely (dopaminergic) innervated septal tissue above and below. Stimulation in the intensively innervated band is no more rewarding than stimulation of the sparsely innervated tissue on either side of it, and the self-stimulation threshold does not increase as stimulation is given at sites more and more distal from the dopamine terminals. In none of the regions of dopamine terminals (frontal, sulcal, and cingulate cortex; caudate; nucleus accumbens; septum; amygdala; and olfactory tubercle) was the threshold for reward related to the density of dopaminergic innervation.

The current picture of the anatomy of reward sites is that there are several brain regions where stimulation is rewarding, that at least some of these regions are interconnected, and that the diencephalic reward system is coextensive with the dopamine systems at the level of the dopamine cell bodies but not at the level of the ascending dopamine fibers or the level of the forebrain dopamine terminal fields. The anatomy of the reward systems is inconsistent with the old hypothesis that brain stimulation was rewarding when it directly activated one or another of the catecholamine pathways. Stronger evidence, reviewed below, suggests that rewarding brain stimulation seldom activates catecholamine systems directly. On the other hand, it is still possible that rewarding stimulation activates the dopamine systems trans-synaptically. The most likely explanation of why nondopaminergic MFB reward fibers would have the exact dispersion of the dopamine cell bodies is that the reward substrate involves fibers descending to make synaptic contact with the dopamine cells. That the dopamine fibers play some role—though perhaps an indirect or "second-stage" role—is more directly addressed by lesion studies and pharmacological studies. That the dopamine fibers are not usually directly activated with the traditional electrodes and parameters of rewarding MFB stimulation is more firmly established by electrophysiological studies.

LESION STUDIES   If the dopamine systems or other components of the MFB were critical for the rewarding effects of MFB stimulation, one would expect lesions of the MFB or its afferents or efferents to eliminate self-stimulation. If only one of the dopamine projection systems were important for reward, it would be lesion studies, rather than pharmacological studies, that would tell us which projection was important. However, while there have been many attempts to eliminate the rewarding effects of stimulation by focal brain lesions, the results of this work are, thus far, disappointing.

Part of the problem is that few investigators have used methods adequate for discriminating lesion-induced changes in the rewarding efficacy of the brain stimulation from changes in the performance capacity of the animal. Another problem is that it is difficult to damage one behavioral mechanism without damaging others that are adjacent or interwoven with it. Another is that each lesion is different, and finding the common denominator of a group of lesions is not easy. Just determining the limits of the damaged area and the degree of damage to different systems within that area is a difficult matter. Moreover, the brain often reacts to damage by increasing the effectiveness of undamaged neurons and by growing new connections from those that are injured but not destroyed. Whatever the reason, it is clear that it is not easy to critically damage the reward system.

The most direct test of the dopamine hypothesis involving lesion studies would be to selectively damage the dopamine systems with a neurotoxin. Most studies of the effects of such lesions have utilized simple rate measures and are difficult to interpret. In one of the stronger studies of this type, Fibiger et al (1987) measured the changes in ventral tegmental self-stimulation rate-intensity functions caused by unilateral neurotoxin lesions of the ascending dopaminergic neurons. Ipsilateral lesions decreased asymptotic rates of responding without a significant lateral shift of the functions. Fibiger et al reported significant changes in intensity threshold as defined by the current intensity required to sustain an average of 20 lever-presses per minute, but this definition of threshold is not satisfactory, as responding at such a high criterion can easily be influenced by the kind of performance impairments that are suggested by the asymptotic performance of Fibiger et al's animals (Miliaressis et al 1986b). When the data of Fibiger et al are reassessed using the "theta zero" threshold criterion which Miliaressis et al demonstrate to be least influenced by performance impairment, there is no clear evidence that the lesions of Fibiger et al altered the rewarding impact of the stimulation.

A second serious problem with the Fibiger et al study is that rate-intensity functions rather than rate-frequency functions were used. While it is true that the two functions have similar shapes, the two manipulations are not equivalent. In a lesion study, it is hoped that the reward fibers near the electrode tip are thinned. If half the fibers are killed, and if the stimulation intensity is not altered, then twice the normal frequency of stimulation will be needed to sustain normal performance. If frequency is held constant and stimulation intensity is increased, it is not clear how large an increase will be needed. The degree of thinning of the reward substrate need not be uniform; moreover, stimulation intensity may already be such that the boundaries of the stimulation field are reached. Thus changes in current spread may cause unpredictable changes in the number of reward fibers recruited. If the reward system is successfully thinned and if the stimulation field approaches the boundaries of the system, then no increase in intensity will compensate fully, and normal asymptotic rates may never be reached. The confounding of unknown locus and density of reward fibers with changes in the size of the stimulation field makes rate-intensity data difficult to interpret, whereas the interpretation of shifts in the rate-frequency function is straightforward.

In any case, how are we to interpret the study of Fibiger et al in light of evidence that pharmacological blockade of dopamine systems causes complete cessation of responding for similar stimulation? Neurochemical assays confirmed depletion of over 95% of the dopamine in each of the major projection areas on the lesioned side of the brain in the Fibiger study. Both the nigrostriatal system (which is associated, in many minds, with motor function) and the mesolimbic system (which is most frequently associated with reward function) were depleted. The depletion of the striatum suggests a ready explanation of the asymptotic performance deficit, but there is no ready explanation for the lack of shift to the right of the rate-intensity functions following this degree of dopamine depletion. If one of the dopamine projections plays an important role in the rewarding effects of the stimulation, and if this lesion causes functional inactivation of each of these projections, then there should have been a shift to the right of the rate-intensity functions in this experiment.

Other lesion studies do not improve the picture. Few studies have been designed to compare rate-frequency functions in lesioned and unlesioned rats, and those that were so designed have not involved selective damage to the dopamine systems. Still, several studies have shown minimal effects of lesions that clearly cause major dopaminergic damage. The most radical lesions are those of Huston and his colleagues; these investigators remove the entire cerebral and limbic cortex, yet this damage leaves their animals capable of at least rudimentary responses for stimulation. With more modest and unilateral ablation of the forebrain, Stellar et al (1982) saw apparently normal self-stimulation in animals with lateral hypothalamic stimulating electrodes. In this study it was not clear how much of the mesolimbic dopamine system was damaged (much of the nucleus accumbens might have been spared), and animals' performance was compared to that of animals in other labs rather than to pre-lesion data or control data from the same experiment. Still, Colle & Wise (1987) found only 30% shifts in rate-frequency functions in a similar study with larger lesions and confirmed ablation (some of Colle & Wise's animals were studied using fluorescence histochemical methods that allow direct visualization of the dopamine fibers) of most dopamine terminals of the frontal cortex, the striatum, the nucleus accumbens, the septum, and the olfactory tubercle. Within six weeks of the lesions, the animals had recovered to normal or near-normal responding for ipsilateral stimulation. Interestingly, Colle & Wise found a 30% improvement in contralateral rate-frequency functions, and there was no change in the improved thresholds over the 6-week "recovery" period. These data again suggest that performance for contralateral stimulation cannot be used as a simple yardstick of performance capability.

The important finding here, however, is that removal of most of the dopamine terminals in the brain caused only a 30% increase in self-stimulation threshold, and that even this increase was not permanent. One of the advantages of lesion studies over drug studies is that, while drug effects are transitory and can only be inferred from behavior, the effects of lesions are permanent and can be confirmed histologically. Yet when permanent damage to the dopamine system is caused (and later confirmed) it has only minor effects on self-stimulation, whereas when the dopamine system is blocked pharmacologically much more profound effects are seen. One possibility is that whereas the drugs block all dopamine terminals, lesions only reach some of the dopamine fibers. This explanation is difficult to accept in light of the levels of depletion reported by Fibiger et al or the degree of dopamine terminal damage reported by Colle & Wise. Thus at the present time there is little support from lesion studies for the hypothesis that dopamine plays a critical role in brain stimulation reward.

Knife cuts of the MFB have also been used in attempts to disrupt MFB self-stimulation. Here, the attempt has been to cut descending fibers that are thought to carry the reward signal toward the region of the dopamine cell bodies. Janas & Stellar (1987) have studied the effect of basal forebrain knife cuts on the rate-frequency functions obtained with MFB stimulation. They found no significant shift in the functions unless the cuts were made in the anterior MFB just in front of the optic chiasm. Waraczynski (1988) has done a more extensive study of the same type; she made knife cuts at several anterior-posterior levels of the basal forebrain and measured the effect on the rewarding efficacy of MFB stimulation. Unlike Janas & Stellar, she did not find systematic increases in thresholds following transections of the anterior MFB. She explained this discrepancy by differences in the extent of rostro-caudal tissue damage, which she suggested to be more extensive in Janas & Stellar's study. Again, however, dopamine fibers should have been damaged by Waraczynski's knife cuts, yet most of her lesions had no appreciable effect on self-stimulation.

In summary, lesion studies have not only failed (thus far) to indicate which of the various dopamine projections are important for brain stimulation reward; they have failed to clearly implicate *any* dopamine system in mediation of the rewarding effects of brain stimulation. One conclusion that might be drawn—were it not for pharmacological evidence—would be that the dopamine system is not involved in brain stimulation reward, though it may be involved in the performance capacity of the animal. Another possibility is, however, that the dopamine system is resilient, and that it can compensate for all but total damage to its fibers. In point of fact, the dopamine system *is* resilient, and it can compensate a great deal for lesion damage (Stricker & Zigmond 1976); whether this can account for the ineffectiveness of lesions in brain stimulation reward studies remains to be determined.

AUTORADIOGRAPHIC STUDIES   Brain cells use glucose for energy, and they take up increased levels of glucose when they are active. Sokoloff has developed a method for identifying brain regions with elevated glucose uptake; it utilizes a radiolabeled form of glucose (2-DG) that cannot be utilized or metabolized (as is glucose itself) within neurons. The labeled substance is taken up and accumulated by active neurons, where it can be detected autoradiographically. The technique has been used to identify brain regions that are significantly activated by drugs and by rewarding brain stimulation.

Using this method, Yadin et al (1982) found an extensive overlap in the neural structures unilaterally activated by stimulation of the anterior and the posterior MFB, but no overlap between the structures activated by MFB stimulation and the structures activated by stimulation of the medial prefrontal cortex or the locus coeruleus. This suggests that forebrain, brainstem, and MFB stimulation reward are mediated by different neural substrates. Gallistel et al (1985) found that rewarding MFB stimulation failed to alter glucose utilization in any of the dopamine terminal fields. Porrino et al (1984) observed increased glucose utilization in the nucleus accumbens of animals responding for ventral tegmental stimulation, but similar utilization was not seen in animals that did not have to perform any motor response for the stimulation; this would implicate nucleus accumbens in motor but not reward function.

The 2-DG data suggest—if taken at face value—that rewarding brain stimulation has little effect on brain dopamine systems. However, one very critical problem with the 2-DG method—as pointed out by Gallistel et al (1985)—is that the autoradiographic analysis does not distinguish stimulation-induced activation of reward-relevant systems from stimulation-induced activation of adjacent or intercalated tissue irrelevant to the rewarding effect of the stimulation. When the MFB is stimulated, neurons in many of the 50–60 distinct components of that bundle are likely to be activated; only a small portion of them are likely to carry reward-relevant information. The 2-DG uptake relevant to reward signals is likely to be lost in the "noise" of irrelevant signals. Moreover, the relative contributions of cells with low glucose uptake are unlikely to be noticed in total 2-DG accumulations. Finally, the 2-DG method does not distinguish changes in glucose uptake that reflect the direct actions from the feedback consequences of stimulation. As is discussed below, the feedback effects of stimulating or blocking the dopamine system can have great significance for behavioral studies.

REGIONAL NEUROCHEMICAL STUDIES   If the dopamine pathway carries reward-related signals, then neurochemical studies should be able to document dopaminergic activation. While it is clear that the dopamine system can be activated by strong levels of rewarding stimulation (Fibiger et al 1987; Phillips et al 1987), such demonstrations are not convincing when they involve stimulation levels well above threshold. If dopaminergic activation is essential for stimulation to be rewarding, then such activation should be demonstrable with the lowest levels of stimulation that are reliably rewarding. The fact that dopaminergic activation has not been directly confirmed by neurochemical measures may, however, simply reflect the insensitivity of available measures. When animals are decapitated for neurochemical analysis, stress effects may mask any dopamine metabolites that have built up from previous reward experience. We hope that the sensitive microdialysis method and the rapid voltammetry method will soon be brought to bear on this problem. Until they are, the methods currently available might be suspected of being inadequate to the task.

SUMMARY   The bulk of our useful information about the anatomy of brain stimulation reward systems comes from anatomical mapping studies. These studies reveal dozens of brain sites where stimulation is rewarding. Lesion studies, which should help determine which of these sites are anatomically connected to each other, have not yet begun to fulfill this promise. Part of the problem has to do with the resilience of the brain, and part may have to do with redundancy in the reward circuitry.

Neurophysiological Studies

Another—perhaps more useful (though more difficult)—approach to the question of which reward sites are connected to one another comes from neurophysiological studies. A major challenge in brain stimulation studies is to determine which neurons located in the stimulation field are responsible for the behavioral effect of stimulation. The fact that some 50–60 fiber bundles are interwoven to form the MFB makes this a particularly difficult problem in the case of the diencephalic reward system. Differences in the excitability characteristics of different types of MFB fibers offer some ways to begin to differentiate reward-relevant from reward-irrelevant fibers. A second problem is that the stimulated neurons represent one stage of a presumably multi-stage system (or set of systems); differences in the excitability characteristics of the directly activated or "first-stage" system have also allowed partial characterization of the first stage neurons in MFB, frontal cortex, and brainstem self-stimulation. (Note that when the term "first-stage" is used to designate one level of the reward circuitry, that term must be qualified; the "first-stage" neurons for MFB reward may be in synaptic contact with earlier or later stage neurons as defined by stimulation at other brain sites.)

The neurophysiological approach for distinguishing characteristics of the various stages of the reward system consists of studying trade-off functions relating stimulation parameters required to maintain designated rates of responding. The hypothesis is that the rules governing the trade-off functions reflect unique physiological characteristics of the neurons that are responsible for the behavior under study. These experiments have allowed a partial characterization of directly stimulated reward neurons that support self-stimulation; they constitute a major step towards the identification of central elements in the reward substrate.

REFRACTORY PERIOD ESTIMATES   The time needed for a neuron to repolarize following the axonal impulse by which neuronal messages are coded has been termed the "refractory period" of the neuron; differences in refractory period are correlated with differences in axon size and insulation. Refractory periods are determined for single neurons by stimulating the neuron with pairs of pulses with different inter-pulse intervals. Deutsch was the first to suggest that the distribution of refractory periods for a *population* of reward-relevant neurons can also be estimated; the method involves trains of pairs of pulses, since behavioral responses involving populations of stimulated neurons always require more than a single pulse for their activation. The need for trains of stimulation pulses does not change the essence of the procedure, however; when the inter-pulse interval is too short, each pulse pair has the effectiveness of a single pulse. The range of interpulse intervals over which increases alter the strength of behavior represents the range of refractory periods of the directly stimulated axons. Once further increases in inter-pulse interval no longer increase response strength, it is clear that all axons in the relevant population are responding to each of the two pulses in each pulse pair. Inter-pulse intervals halfway through this range would be interpreted as exceeding the refractory periods of half the population of relevant axons if we could assume all axons to make equal contributions to the behavior in question.

Yeomans (1975) improved the psychophysical scaling of Deutsch's original method and obtained reliable refractory period estimates of the first-stage neurons in brain stimulation reward studies. Yeomans's data showed that most MFB reward neurons have refractory periods shorter than 1.4 msec; this finding has now been confirmed several times. Since electrophysiological studies suggest the refractory periods of catecholaminergic neurons to be longer than 2 msec, these studies provide strong evidence in support of Wise's (1978) suggestion that MFB rewarding stimulation does not result from the *direct* activation of catecholaminergic neurons.

The function relating changes in response strength or self-stimulation threshold to inter-pulse interval is not always continuous, and discontinuities suggest subpopulations of first-stage fibers with different refractory period characteristics. Using Yeomans's approach with more closely spaced inter-pulse intervals, Gratton & Wise (1985) found evidence for at least two subpopulations of MFB reward neurons, having different pharmacological sensitivity in addition to different refractory periods: an atropine-sensitive population with short (0.4–0.6 msec) refractory periods and an atropine-insensitive population with longer (0.6–2.0 msec) refractory periods.

Reward neurons in different brain regions can have considerably different refractory periods. Rompre & Miliaressis (1987) characterized the directly stimulated neurons in the brainstem. In the metencephalon, the most excitable reward neurons have absolute refractory periods of less than 0.6 or 0.8 msec; these estimates agree with the earlier estimates of Bielajew and colleagues (1981) for central gray reward neurons and suggest that diencephalic and metencephalic reward neurons have similar physiological properties. Mesencephalic reward neurons were found to have more heterogeneous physiological characteristics. The most excitable neurons have absolute refractory periods of less than 0.4 msec. At some mesencephalic sites, Rompre & Miliaressis found evidence of the contribution of two subpopulations of reward neurons with different refractory periods: one population with refractory periods of 0.35–0.5 msec and one with refractory periods ≥ 0.6 msec. Because the pattern of recovery of the second population overlapped with the pattern of recovery seen in the metencephalon, they suggested that the rewarding effects at the two sites could be due to the activation of common fibers. The estimates obtained for the most excitable neurons appear to exclude the participation of the monoaminergic neurons of the brainstem.

In general, different refractory period estimates are taken to indicate different classes of first-stage axons. Thus one of the important implications drawn from refractory period experiments is that there are several classes of reward neuron associated with different brain regions and even with a single brain region. For example, Schenk & Shizgal (1982) have inferred that rewarding stimulation of the MFB and medial prefrontal cortex are due to the activation of different fibers, a finding consistent with the lesion data reported earlier.

CONNECTIVITY STUDIES   The pulse-pair technique has been modified by Shizgal et al (1980) in order to assess the conduction velocities of first-stage reward neurons. Their technique is similar to Yeomans's single-electrode method, but in this case the two pulses of each pulse pair are delivered through different electrodes to different stimulation sites. In those cases where the two stimulation fields reach common fibers that extend between (and usually beyond) the two stimulation sites, the effectiveness of paired pulses again depends on the inter-pulse interval. In this case, the critical inter-pulse interval reflects the time necessary for the first impulse to travel to the region of the second electrode plus the time necessary for the membrane to repolarize after the impulse passes. Subtraction of the refractory period estimate from the critical inter-pulse interval gives an estimate of the conduction time; dividing by the distance between the electrodes gives an estimate of the conduction velocity. The estimated conduction velocities for MFB reward fibers are greater than those of catecholaminergic neurons (Shizgal et al 1980).

The reason that stimulation at shorter inter-pulse intervals will be no more effective than single-pulse stimulation is that impulses that "collide" between stimulation sites neutralize one another. This collision occurs only if action potentials are triggered at two points on the same fibers; thus the method for estimating conduction velocities is also a test of connectivity between two stimulation sites. While knowing the conduction velocities of first-stage neurons is useful (Gallistel et al 1981), knowing which reward sites are connected to one another is, perhaps, more important (Phillips 1984; Wise & Bozarth 1984). Such studies indicate that MFB reward fibers connect the lateral preoptic area with the lateral hypothalamic areas (Bielajew et al 1987) and the lateral hypothalamic area with the ventral tegmental area (Shizgal et al 1980).

Of potentially great significance are recent findings of Boye & Rompre (1987), who found evidence that common reward fibers link the posterior hypothalamus and ventral tegmental area (VTA) with the medial pontine system. This finding is the first to seriously challenge the suggestion of Corbett & Wise (1980) that the mesencephalic and diencephalic reward systems were not continuous with one another. The mapping of Rompre & Miliaressis suggests that Corbett & Wise missed midline sites where reward fibers link the VTA with more caudal sites, and the findings of Boye & Rompre appear to confirm this possibility. Pharmacological evidence will also be seen to link the midline mesencephalic reward system with the ventral tegmental dopamine system.

DIRECTIONALITY STUDIES   In cases where connectivity between two reward sites can be demonstrated by collision effects, the major direction of impulse conduction can be determined. The demonstration rests on the fact that anodal stimulation locally hyperpolarizes neurons, and normal impulse flow fails in the hyperpolarized region. By comparing the effects of depolarization at one electrode tip and hyperpolarization at the other, it can be determined which electrode lies between the other electrode and the nerve terminals at which reward impulses are propagated. If the MFB electrode were between the VTA electrode and the terminals of the first stage neurons, then MFB hyperpolarization would degrade the reward signal triggered by VTA stimulation, while VTA hyperpolarization would not affect reward signals triggered by MFB stimulation. This is not the case; rather, VTA hyperpolarization degrades MFB stimulation effectiveness, suggesting that at least some of the MFB reward signal descends the MFB toward the region of the dopamine neurons (Bielajew & Shizgal 1986). The work of Boye & Rompre suggests that at least some of that signal continues past the VTA, travelling with the fibers of the tegmental radiations or perhaps the decussations of the cerebellar peduncle. Meanwhile, Malette & Miliaressis (1987) have used a modified version of Bielajew & Shizgal's hyperpolarization technique and found evidence that some ascending fibers also contribute to the rewarding effects of MFB stimulation.

Pharmacological Studies

While the neurophysiological experiments indicate that monoaminergic neurons are not part of the directly stimulated or "first-stage" neurons of MFB brain stimulation reward, pharmacological experiments suggest that dopamine plays an important role in reward function. Much of the old evidence involved simple rate measures, but the curve-shift approach has now confirmed that dopamine-blocking drugs (neuroleptics) reduce the rewarding impact of MFB stimulation.

DOPAMINE AGONISTS AND ANTAGONISTS   The ability of dopamine block-ers to reduce the rewarding impact of stimulation is generally correlated with their affinity for the dopamine D-2 receptor (Gallistel & Davis 1983), but the selective D-1 antagonist, SCH 23390, also attenuates the rewarding effects of MFB stimulation (Nakajima & McKenzie 1986). These findings are not discrepant, as it now appears that D-1 receptor blockade disables postsynaptic D-2 receptor function; it does so, however, without important secondary effects on D-2 autoreceptor function (the implications of this fact are dis-cussed below).

Gallistel & Karras (1984) took full advantage of the curve-shift paradigm, and quantified the effect of pimozide (a dopamine antagonist) and amphet-amine (a dopamine agonist) on MFB rewarding stimulation. Pimozide caused dose-dependent shifts to the right in the rate frequency function, whereas amphetamine caused dose-dependent shifts to the left; the combined effects of pimozide and amphetamine canceled one another, with the resulting behavior essentially normal. These results, confirmed by Gallistel & Freyd (1987), offer strong evidence that pimozide and amphetamine exert their effects on reinforcing efficacy via one and the same set of dopaminergic synapses.

The question of which dopaminergic synapses might be involved—remaining unanswered on the grounds of lesion evidence—can be addressed by central drug injection studies. It is injections of amphetamine into the nucleus accumbens (L. Colle & R. A. Wise, in press) and injections of morphine into the VTA (Jenck et al 1987) that facilitate the rewarding effects of MFB stimulation; and it is injections of neuroleptics into nucleus accum-bens (Stellar et al 1983) that attenuate it. Amphetamine presumably facilitates brain stimulation reward by augmenting nucleus accumbens dopamine release and blocking its inactivation by reuptake; morphine presumably facilitates brain stimulation reward by increasing dopamine cell firing.

Ventral tegmental morphine not only facilitates MFB reward; it reverses—up to a point—the suppressive effects of neuroleptics (Rompre 1986). Neuroleptics also suppress midline mesencephalic reward, and, again, ventral tegmental morphine reverses this effect (Rompre & Wise 1988). This finding underscores the importance of VTA dopamine systems for rewarding effects of stimulation that does not activate VTA dopamine neurons directly. In this case, the rewarding stimulation is caudal to the midbrain dopamine neurons. The facts that neuroleptics attenuate midline mesencephalic reward and that VTA morphine can reverse this attenuation add credibility to the conclusion from neurophysiological studies that MFB reward can be dopamine-dependent even if the stimulation does not activate dopaminergic neurons directly.

The nature of the interaction of VTA morphine with neuroleptics becomes very interesting when higher doses of morphine are given. Whereas low doses of morphine tend to reverse the effects of neuroleptics, higher doses summate with the neuroleptic, causing complete failure of the behavior (Rompre & Wise 1988). This failure appears to result from depolarization-inactivation of the mesolimbic dopamine system.

Depolarization-inactivation of the dopamine systems is known to result when they are overstimulated (Grace & Bunney 1986). Since dopamine neurons are stimulated both by morphine (Matthews & German 1984) and by neuroleptics (Grace & Bunney 1986; White & Wang 1983), and since each can cause depolarization-inactivation by itself, it is not surprising that the combination should do so. The test of the depolarization-inactivation hypothesis involves the use of agents that hyperpolarize the dopaminergic cells; despite the fact that such agents normally inhibit these neurons, they restore their ability to generate action potentials after depolarization-inactivation (Grace & Bunney 1986). Ventral tegmental muscimol injections, which mimic the action of the hyperpolarizing transmitter GABA and which normally inhibit self-stimulation, restored responding in animals that had ceased responding under the combination of pimozide and high-dose VTA morphine. This complex drug interaction is difficult to explain without the assumption that the dopamine system plays a critical role in the rewarding effects of MFB and mesencephalic brain stimulation.

These findings are important because they provide even more subtle evidence than that of simple postsynaptic blockade in support of the hypothesis that dopamine plays an important role in brain stimulation reward. Gallistel (1986) and Miliaressis et al (1986a) have recently argued that the dopamine system does not carry the reward signal proper, but rather serves to modulate reward signals carried by other circuitry. Their hypotheses are based primarily on the observation that increases in the number of rewarding pulses are not able to compensate for neuroleptic treatment to anywhere near the degree that they are able to compensate for reduced stimulation intensity. Dopamine antagonists can shift the rate-frequency function by about 0.3 log units, effectively doubling the number of stimulation pulses required to sustain normal responding; after that point the behavior fails completely. By contrast, decreasing the stimulation field by decreasing the current levels can shift the curves much further before behavior fails. If neuroleptics merely decrease reward, then increasing frequency might be expected to compensate over a greater range.

Gallistel & Freyd (1987) argued that if the dopaminergic neurons themselves carry the reward signal, then pimozide must cause some abrupt and dramatic failure of the system, and that since the postsynaptic effects of pimozide were not known to have such characteristics, the dopamine system must modulate the reward pathway rather than serving as a primary carrier of the reward signal. Our recent data, however, suggest a likely alternative to the hypotheses of Gallistel & Freyd; our data call attention to the fact that neuroleptics can, indeed, cause a complete failure of the system (Hand et al 1987a). In the case of brain stimulation reward, the neuroleptic-induced activation of dopaminergic cell firing—which can, in and of itself, cause depolarization-inactivation—may well be summating with trans-synaptic activation from the first-stage neurons. The combination of increased levels of rewarding stimulation with relatively moderate neuroleptic doses could cause complete failure of the system just as morphine appeared to do in combination with moderate stimulation and pimozide in our study; this could explain the failure of pimozide to shift the rate-frequency function more than 0.3 log units without producing total failure of the behavior.

In the first stages of testing this hypothesis, we have found that the selective D-1 antagonist, SCH 23390, is capable of shifting the rate-frequency function by 0.6 log units or more (Rompre & Wise 1988). This fact fits with the hypothesis that depolarization-inactivation of the dopamine system accounts for the failure of D-2 antagonists to shift the function by more than half this amount: SCH 23390 differs from the D-2 antagonists in that it does not accelerate dopamine cell firing (Hand et al 1987b) and thus should not share with the D-2 antagonists the ability to cause depolarization-inactivation.

NORADRENERGIC AGENTS   Other than dopamine antagonists, the only drugs known to cause shifts in reward functions that clearly reflect reward reduction are the alpha-2 noradrenergic agonist clonidine and the alpha-2 noradrenergic antagonist yohimbine (Gallistel & Freyd 1987). Yohimbine shifts the curve somewhat to the left at low (0.5 mg/kg) doses, but shifts it to the right at higher (5–10 mg/kg) doses. Clonidine shifts the curve to the right at moderate (30–400 μg/kg) doses. These effects are not easy to interpret, since these drugs have complex effects on noradrenergic function. Clonidine inhibits noradrenergic auto-inhibition at very low doses—doses below the effective range of Gallistel & Freyd's study. Yohimbine antagonizes these autoreceptor effects at the doses studied by Gallistel & Freyd. Clonidine can also inhibit transmitter release from noradrenergic nerve terminals; this effect is not blocked by yohimbine. To complicate matters further, clonidine may interact with the dopamine system. While clonidine has little affinity for dopamine receptors, the VTA is innervated by noradrenergic fibers; thus clonidine may act to inhibit noradrenergic effects—presumably inhibitory—on dopamine systems. Clonidine is known to alter dopamine turnover by some means or another, at least in some systems. Whatever the mechanism, clonidine has effects on brain stimulation reward that are both qualitatively and quantitatively similar to those of the dopamine antagonists.

DRUGS OF ABUSE   It has been hypothesized that many if not all drugs of abuse may share with brain stimulation reward the ability to activate the MFB reward circuitry. Thus far, the evidence for this hypothesis is weak, except in the cases of the psychomotor stimulants and the opiates, as discussed in relation to their known interactions with the dopamine systems (Wise & Bozarth 1987). What evidence there is relies heavily on rate or threshold measures; little work has been done with the curve-shift paradigm. While there is neurochemical evidence that ethanol, nicotine, caffeine, cannabis, and phencyclidine activate, in one way or another, the dopamine systems, barbiturates and benzodiazepines appear to inhibit them. Robust and replicable facilitation of brain stimulation reward is not yet established in the case of any of these drugs, and some clearly decrease performance under some circumstances. We hope that clarification of the interaction of these drugs with brain stimulation reward will follow the development and extension of the curve-shift paradigm as a quantitative tool for assessing drug effects.

DRUG REWARD: THE NEUROCHEMICALLY SELECTIVE PROBE

Paradigmatic Considerations

As in the case of brain stimulation reward, the study of drug reward raises important questions about the definitions of the terms "reward" and "reinforcement." In this case the problem arises because drug reward has been studied in two paradigms: the paradigm of Skinner and a variation of the paradigm of Pavlov. In the paradigm of Skinner, reinforcement is defined as an event—in this case a drug injection—that increases the probability of a given response—often a lever-press—when it is given in a response-contingent manner. Drugs are also said to be rewarding or reinforcing when animals develop increasing preference for portions of the environment that have been associated with drug injections given in the absence of any response contingency. Since it was Pavlov (or his translator) who first coined the term reinforcement, and since Pavlov's definition contained no specification of response-contingency, it is not clear that the term "reinforcement" should apply to the operant paradigm at all. This is a problem for the physiological psychologist who might naturally be drawn to search for the structures whose relationship is reinforced or "stamped in" during the learning that gives rise to the concept of "reinforcement." However, whether or not the two definitions can be integrated semantically, it seems generally true that the same brain mechanisms are implicated in drug reward by each of the two paradigms.

Psychomotor Stimulants

It is now firmly established that cocaine and amphetamine are rewarding because of their actions in dopaminergic synapses. It is clear that central actions are involved because the *dextro*, (D) isomer of amphetamine is more rewarding than the *levo* (L) isomer (Yokel & Pickens 1974); the two amphetamine isomers are equally potent in their peripheral, autonomic actions but differentially potent in their central dopaminergic actions. It is clear that actions in dopaminergic synapses are involved because selective dopamine receptor blockers and selective dopaminergic lesions attenuate the rewarding actions of amphetamine and cocaine. While these drugs also have effects in noradrenergic and serotonergic synapses, blockade or damage to noradrenergic systems do not alter stimulant reward and serotonergic lesions seem, if anything, to enhance it.

The question of whether a pharmacological or lesion challenge increases or decreases the rewarding impact of drugs is not simply answered by examination of their effects on response rate. Whereas decreases in the frequency or intensity of rewarding brain stimulation always causes decreases in self-stimulation rate, decreases in the rewarding dose of self-administered drugs generally cause an increase in rate. An understanding of the control of response rate is essential to the interpretation of drug self-administration data. The key to such an understanding is an appreciation of the fact that, while it is reward *intensity* that appears primarily affected by changes in brain stimulation, it is reward *duration* that appears primarily affected by manipulations of drug reward (Wise 1987b).

The strongest evidence for this assertion comes from amphetamine self-administration studies, where it has been shown that, over the normal working range of doses and response requirements, rats adjust their response rate to maintain a relatively constant hourly drug intake. The initiation of a new drug response appears to be a fall in drug concentration to nonrewarding levels (Yokel & Pickens 1974). Animals usually respond for more D-amphetamine when their blood levels fall to approximately $0.2\mu g/ml$ of blood (responding for L-amphetamine is initiated at a higher threshold; this is the basis for the inference that the two amphetamine isomers are differentially potent in their rewarding actions). If amphetamine metabolism is speeded or slowed, rate of amphetamine self-administration changes proportionally (Dougherty & Pickens 1974).

When amphetamine or cocaine self-administration is challenged by neuroleptic (dopamine blocker) treatment, compensatory increases in responding are seen over a broad range of neuroleptic doses, with eventual response cessation (following an initial period of compensatory increase) in the case of high neuroleptic doses. Such compensatory increases, typical of neuroleptic challenge of amphetamine (Yokel & Wise 1975) and cocaine (de Wit & Wise 1977; Ettenberg et al 1982) self-administration, have become the widely accepted signature of attenuated drug reward, but it should be noted that self-administration of apomorphine—a selective dopamine agonist—simply drops out when challenged with neuroleptics (Yokel & Wise 1978). In this case there is no evidence of compensatory rate increases; the lowest dose of neuroleptic that affects apomorphine self-administration causes relatively rapid cessation of responding without the persistent accelerated "frustration" responding that is seen when nonrewarding saline is substituted for rewarding amphetamine. Thus compensatory response increases are suggestive of drug reward-attentuation, but they are not the sine qua non of drug reward-attenuation. The importance of this point is stressed in the discussion of opiate self-administration below.

There are several groups of dopamine neurons, and it is not yet clearly established how many of them contribute to the mechanism of stimulant reward. The short-axon midline dopamine systems of the hypothalamus and thalamus do not appear to be involved, as these systems appear to have no uptake mechanism and thus appear unresponsive to cocaine-like drugs (Lookingland et al 1987). Of the two long-axon systems—the A9 and A10 dopamine projection systems—the A10 system is most clearly implicated. Selective lesions or receptor blockade of one of the terminal fields of this system—the nucleus accumbens—block or attenuate the rewarding effects of amphetamine and cocaine (Roberts & Zito 1987), while lesions of other regions have been found ineffective. Rats will work for direct nucleus accumbens injections of amphetamine (Hoebel et al 1983). Rats and monkeys will also work for cocaine injections into the frontal cortex (Phillips et al 1981; Goeders & Smith 1983), which is another terminal field of the A10 system; thus psychomotor stimulant reward is not a phenomenon localized to only the nucleus accumbens. Paradoxically, rats have been reported unwilling to work for nucleus accumbens cocaine injections; this finding is not yet fully understood, as cocaine and amphetamine would be expected to act in the same synapses, though not at the same receptor sites within those synapses.

Studies using the conditioned place-preference paradigm generally support the same conclusions as have been advanced on self-administration studies. Place preferences induced by association of one portion of the testing apparatus with amphetamine do not develop if the animals are treated with dopamine blockers before the conditioning trials (Spyraki et al 1982). While it originally appeared that cocaine-induced place preference might be different, it now seems clear that this was due to a procedural problem. Amphetamine-induced place preference can be established with microinjections of amphetamine into nucleus accumbens (Carr & White 1983); thus the place-preference paradigm, like the self-administration paradigm, suggests dopaminergic synapses of the mesolimbic system as the site, or at least one of the sites, at which the psychomotor stimulants initiate their rewarding actions.

Opiates

Opiate reward appears to involve at least two sites of opiate action, one at either end of the mesolimbic dopamine projection. Our understanding of the mechanisms of opiate reward derives from early studies of the mechanism of brain stimulation reward. The fact that opiates can potentiate the rewarding effects of hypothalamic stimulation (Esposito & Kornetsky 1978) led to the early speculation that a common mechanism might mediate the rewarding effects of the stimulation and the rewarding effects of opiates themselves (Olds & Travis 1960). This, in turn, led to attempts to localize the brain sites at which opiates had their reward-facilitating and their direct rewarding effects.

When direct, low-dose morphine injections into the brain were studied, it was initially found that reward-facilitating effects of morphine were restricted to sites in or near the ventral tegmental area (Broekkamp et al 1976). Injections into more rostral regions were reported to be ineffective, and injections into more caudal regions were found to inhibit self-stimulation. In apparent confirmation of the hypothesis that a common mechanism mediated the reward-enhancing and the direct rewarding effects of opiates, it was found that direct morphine injections into the ventral tegmental area were rewarding as demonstrated by the self-administration (Bozarth & Wise 1981) and place-preference (Phillips & LePiane 1980) paradigms. That the mechanism of these actions involved activation of the dopaminergic cells was implied by the facts that morphine injections into this region activate dopamine cell firing, cause increased extracellular dopamine concentrations in the nucleus accumbens, and induce dopamine-dependent locomotion (Wise & Bozarth 1987).

The notion that a common reward pathway mediates the rewarding effects of psychomotor stimulants, opiates, and hypothalamic brain stimulation was challenged by Ettenberg et al (1982), however, on the grounds that neuroleptics did not cause the compensatory increases in heroin self-administration that were caused by the opiate blocker naloxone and that were seen when stimulant self-administration was challenged by neuroleptics. The data of Ettenberg et al did reflect a compensatory increase in heroin self-administration under their lowest tested dose of neuroleptic, but the effect was small (statistically unreliable) and was not seen over the same range of neuroleptic doses that cause compensatory increases in stimulant self-administration. Ettenberg et al argued that the mechanisms of stimulant and opiate self-administration were independent of one another, despite the contribution of this group to the literature suggesting psychomotor stimulation actions of opiates in the nucleus accumbens.

The demonstration, discussed earlier, that opiates can amplify the ability of neuroleptics to drive dopaminergic neurons to depolarization-inactivation (Rompre & Wise 1988) provides a possible explanation of the absence of neuroleptic-induced compensatory increases in heroin self-administration which is consistent with the hypothesis that opiates are rewarding, at least in part, because of their ability to stimulate the mesolimbic dopamine system. Since the neuroleptics are competitive dopamine antagonists, their effects can be attenuated or reversed by dopamine agonists or by treatments that increase dopamine concentrations at the receptor. Amphetamine and cocaine increase synaptic dopamine concentrations by local actions. VTA morphine increases synaptic dopamine concentrations by stimulating (or, more likely, disinhibiting) dopamine cell firing. However, the ability of morphine to antagonize neuroleptic actions in the mesolimbic dopamine system is limited by the ability of the neurons to maintain accelerated firing in response to VTA morphine. The facts that the dopaminergic neurons cease firing altogether if overstimulated and that neuroleptics, like opiates, stimulate cell firing mean that there is a limited capacity for opiates to compensate for postsynaptic neuroleptic effects. This explains (Rompre & Wise 1988) the limited ability of VTA morphine to compensate for neuroleptics in the self-stimulation paradigm (as compared to the robust ability of amphetamine to do so: Gallistel & Karras 1984) and it would appear to explain the limited ability of intravenous heroin to compensate for neuroleptics in the self-administration paradigm. This explanation seems confirmed by the effects of SCH 23390 on intravenous heroin self-administration; SCH 23390—a dopamine antagonist that has no effect on the feedback-regulation of dopamine cell firing (Hand et al 1987b)—does cause the robust compensatory increase in heroin self-administration that was originally sought with traditional neuroleptics, and it does so over the broad range of doses that are effective in the stimulant self-administration experiments (Nakajima & Wise 1987).

These data suggest that a significant portion of the rewarding effects of intravenous opiates are due to opiate activation of the mesolimbic dopamine system. Present data suggest, however, that this is not the only site of opiate rewarding actions. Opioids have been reported to be self-administered into the nucleus accumbens (Goeders et al 1984; M. Olds 1982) and lateral hypothalamus (Stein & Olds 1976) as well as the ventral tegmental area, and they have also been reported to cause conditioned place preference when injected into these sites and also into the periaqueductal gray (van der Kooy et al 1982). Of these, the nucleus accumbens, at least, appears to be a bona fide opiate reward site.

Several lines of evidence suggest this conclusion. First, rats will work for direct microinjections of opiates into nucleus accumbens. Second, nucleus accumbens injections of opiate antagonists are reported by some (but not all: Britt & Wise 1983) investigators to cause compensatory increases in heroin self-administration (Vaccarino et al 1985). Third, nucleus accumbens dopamine terminal lesions and ventral tegmental dopamine cell body lesions disrupt cocaine self-administration far more effectively than they disrupt heroin self-administration (Bozarth & Wise 1986; Pettit et al 1984). Finally, nucleus accumbens injections of opiates stimulate locomotor activity, and they do so even in dopamine-depleted or -blocked animals (Stinus et al 1985, 1986). Since the locomotor mechanism of nucleus accumbens is activated or disinhibited by dopamine itself, it is presumed that nucleus accumbens morphine activates or disinhibits the next synaptic link in the circuitry that it activates in the VTA. These findings suggest that nucleus accumbens opiates act at a second entry point into a reward (and forward locomotion mechanism) that has the mesolimbic dopamine system as one of its synaptic inputs (Wise & Bozarth 1987).

The evidence linking other brain sites to opioid rewarding actions is not so strong. For example, conditioned place preference can be established by opioid injections into the periaqueductal gray matter, but it seems doubtful that opiates have rewarding actions at that locus. Periaqueductal gray injections inhibit brain stimulation reward (Broekkamp et al 1976), and the doses needed to produce conditioned place preference were orders of magnitude larger than are needed in the case of the VTA. Whereas low-dose injections just dorsal (Phillips & LePiane 1980), ventral, rostral, or caudal (Bozarth 1987) to the VTA are not rewarding, similar localization of the place-preference effects of periaqueductal gray, lateral hypothalamic, or nucleus accumbens injections have not been attempted.

Similarly, the putative reward sites of the lateral hypothalamus have not been localized within a zone where similar injections are ineffective. Since it is well known that drugs injected into the brain can act at considerable distance from the injection site, any attempt to localize drug effects to a central injection site must be accompanied by the demonstration that injections at adjacent loci are ineffective or at least less effective (require higher doses or act with longer latency). Ineffective sites have not been demonstrated, and it has been established that posterior hypothalamic morphine injections probably facilitate brain stimulation reward by diffusion to the ventral tegmental area (Broekkamp et al 1976); such diffusion is also a likely possibility in the case of rewarding hypothalamic morphine injections, since neurotoxic lesions of the intrinsic cells of the lateral hypothalamus have no effect on intravenous heroin self-administration (Britt & Wise 1981).

Other Drugs of Abuse

The brain sites at which other drugs of abuse have their rewarding actions are not known, but there is evidence that nicotine, caffeine, cannabis, phencyclidine, and ethanol activate the mesolimbic dopamine system and that these substances and barbiturates and benzodiazepines have psychomotor stimulant actions. Since it is the psychomotor stimulant actions, rather than the analgesic, sedative, or dependence-producing actions of opiates that are associated with identified opiate rewarding actions, it has been suggested that psychomotor stimulant actions are common to all drugs of abuse and are associated with all positive reinforcement (Wise & Bozarth 1987); this notion has yet to receive extensive experimental validation.

FOOD AND WATER: NATURAL REWARDS

Students of brain stimulation reward generally share the conviction that this phenomenon is not merely a laboratory artifact, but rather represents the central activation of an endogenous reward system—a system that evolved to serve some natural reward or rewards like food for hungry animals, water for thirsty animals, or copulation for sexually receptive animals. While this conviction is wide-spread, it has rarely been put to empirical test. The two "tests" that have been attempted involve the effects of lesions or pharmacological blockade of the mesolimbic dopamine system.

Lesions of the mesolimbic dopamine system have thus far seemed to spare the rewarding effects of food even when they eliminate the rewarding effects of stimulants or opiates (Bozarth & Wise 1986). While mesolimbic dopamine lesions can impair responding for brain stimulation and drug reward, it is lesions of the nigrostriatal system that are thought to be necessary to impair feeding and drinking (Ungerstedt 1971). Neuroleptic treatments, which attenuate both mesolimbic and nigrostriatal dopamine function, do seem to attenuate the rewarding impact of food.

When neuroleptics are tested in simple lever-press tasks, response rate decreases with increasing neuroleptic dose. There is no compensatory increase in feeding to indicate that neuroleptics reduce reward rather than motoric capability. Several paradigms have now been developed, however, that can discriminate the effects of reward attenuation from the effects of motoric impairment, and each indicates that neuroleptics attenuate food reward. One of these paradigms involves analysis of response rate on a day-to-day and moment-to-moment basis. This paradigm shows that neuroleptic-induced response deficits in food-rewarded animals develop over repeated experience with the food, and normal response capacity can be reliably demonstrated in the early moments and on the early days of testing (Beninger et al 1987; Nakajima 1986; Wise et al 1978). Free-feeding studies show that while normal responses are still seen under neuroleptic treatment, they are less frequent and are not normally sustained by the taste of food even when it is consumed (Wise & Colle 1984).

Perhaps the most interesting paradigm for examining this question involves animals that are trained to run an alleyway for food or water on a one-trial-per-day basis for 21 days (Ettenberg & Camp 1986a,b). One group of animals just receives normal training each day. A second group receives no rewarding food (or water) on seven of the 21 training days. The third group receives normal reward on each training day, but seven of the 21 training days occur after neuroleptic pretreatment. All animals are then tested for an additional 21 days in the runway under conditions of nonreward. The partial reinforcement animals (reward on only 14 of the 21 test days) run longer and faster in extinction than do the animals rewarded on every training trial; the animals given neuroleptic on seven of the training days similarly perform better than the normal training group. This "partial reinforcement extinction effect" suggests that neuroleptic treatment nullified the effects of food or water reward during training; the increased responding under extinction after partial training under neuroleptic has no other simple explanation and defies explanation in terms of the presumption that neuroleptics merely disrupt performance capability.

These studies taken together suggest that it is not the push of internal drives or motives that is lost under neuroleptic treatment, but rather the pull of external incentives. Moreover, the pull of external incentives does not fail until the animal has had considerable commerce with them. Thus it seems that blockade of dopamine receptors with neuroleptics attenuates the response-maintaining effectiveness of food and water rewards. There is evidence to suggest that sexual rewards are similarly affected.

SUMMARY AND CONCLUSIONS

While the evidence is strong that dopamine plays some fundamental and special role in the rewarding effects of brain stimulation, psychomotor stimulants, opiates, and food, the exact nature of that role is not clear. One thing is clear: Dopamine is not the only reward transmitter, and dopaminergic neurons are not the *final* common path for all rewards. Dopamine antagonists and lesions of the dopamine systems appear to spare the rewarding effects of nucleus accumbens and frontal cortex brain stimulation (Simon et al 1979) and certainly spare the rewarding effects of apomorphine (Roberts & Vickers 1988). It is clear that reward circuitry is multisynaptic, and since dopamine cells do not send axons to each other or receive axons from each other, dopamine can at best serve as but a single link in this circuitry.

If dopamine is not a final common path for all rewards, could it be an intermediate common path for most rewards? Some workers have argued against such a view, but at present they must do so on incomplete evidence. For example, Phillips (1984) has argued that there must be multiple reward systems, functionally independent and organized in parallel with one another. His primary evidence, however, is the fact that brain stimulation is rewarding at different levels of the nervous system. As we have seen in the case of midline mesencephalic stimulation, the location of the electrode tip in relation to the dopamine cells and fibers tells us little about the role of dopamine in brain stimulation reward. It seems clear that the ventral tegmental dopamine system plays a critical role in midline mesencephalic reward, despite the distance from the electrode tip to the dopamine cells where morphine causes its dopamine-dependent facilitory effects or to the dopamine terminals where low-dose neuroleptics presumably cause theirs. Until pharmacological challenge has been extended to the cases discussed by Phillips, we can only speculate as to the role of dopamine in each of those cases. In the cases where pharmacological challenge has been examined, only nucleus accumbens and frontal cortex have been found to have dopamine-independent reward sites. It is not inconsistent with the dopamine hypothesis that dopamine-independent reward sites should exist in these areas, since any reward signals carried to nucleus accumbens or frontal cortex by dopamine fibers would—unless we are to believe that reward "happens" at these sites—have to be carried to the next stage of the circuit by nondopaminergic fibers (there are no dopaminergic cell bodies in any of the dopamine terminal areas). On the other hand, until pharmacological challenge has been extended, arguments that dopamine does play a role in other cases of brain stimulation reward are equally speculative.

Even more speculative would be the suggestion that a dopamine system is specialized for reward function per se. Ventral tegmental activation of the dopamine system by opiates influences consummatory activities (Jenck et al 1986; J. B. Mitchell, 1988, unpublished PhD thesis, Concordia University) as well as instrumental activities (Jenck et al 1987), and dopamine antagonists attenuate consummatory (Wise & Colle 1984) as well as instrumental (Wise 1982) or preparatory (Blackburn et al 1987) behaviors. Both manipulations alter general arousal as reflected in locomotor activity. In all likelihood, the dopamine systems play some very general role in mood and movement, a role that is essential to reward function as well as to other aspects of motivated behavior.

ACKNOWLEDGMENTS

Preparation of this paper was supported in part by a Chercheur-Boursier award to P.-P. R. from Fonds de la Recherche en Santé, Québec.

Literature Cited

Beninger, R. J., Cheng, M., Hahn, B. L., Hoffman, D. C., Mazurski, E. J., et al. 1987. Effects of extinction, pimozide, SCH 23390, and metoclopramide on food-rewarded operant responding of rats. *Psychopharmacology* 92:343–49

Bielajew, C., Jordan, C., Ferme-Enright, J., Shizgal, P. 1981. Refractory periods and anatomical linkage of the substrates for lateral hypothalamic and periaqueductal gray self-stimulation. *Physiol. Behav.* 27:95–104

Bielajew, C., Shizgal, P. 1986. Evidence implicating descending fibers in self-stimulation of the medial forebrain bundle. *J. Neurosci.* 6:919–29

Bielajew, C., Thrasher, A., Fouriezos, G. 1987. Self-stimulation sites in the lateral hypothalamic and lateral preoptic areas are functionally connected. *Can. Psychol.* 28:36

Blackburn, J. R., Phillips, A. G., Fibiger, H. C. 1987. Dopamine and preparatory behavior: I. Effects of pimozide. *Behav. Neurosci.* 101:352–60

Boye, S., Rompre, P.-P. 1987. Evidence for a

direct axonal link between reward-relevant neurons in the ventral tegmental area-posterior hypothalamus and the medial mesencephalon. *Soc. Neurosci. Abstr.* 13:1544 (Abstr.)

Bozarth, M. A. 1987. Neuroanatomical boundaries of the reward-relevant opiate-receptor field in the ventral tegmental area as mapped by the conditioned place preference method in rats. *Brain Res.* 414:77–84

Bozarth, M. A., Wise, R. A. 1981. Intracranial self-administration of morphine into the ventral tegmental area of rats. *Life Sci.* 28:551–55

Bozarth, M. A., Wise, R. A. 1986. Involvement of the ventral tegmental dopamine system in opioid and psychomotor stimulant reinforcement. In *Problems of Drug Dependence, 1985 (Natl. Inst. Drug Abuse Res. Monogr. 67)*, ed. L. S. Harris, pp. 190–96. Washington, DC: USGPO

Britt, M. D., Wise, R. A. 1981. Opiate rewarding action: independence of the cells of the lateral hypothalamus. *Brain Res.* 222:213–17

Britt, M. D., Wise, R. A. 1983. Ventral tegmental site of opiate reward: antagonism by a hydrophilic opiate receptor blocker. *Brain Res.* 258:105–8

Broekkamp, C. L. E., Van den Bogaard, J. H., Heijnen, H. J., Rops, R. H., Cools, A. R., Van Rossum, J. M. 1976. Separation of inhibiting and stimulating effects of morphine on self-stimulation behavior by intracerebral microinjections. *Eur. J. Pharmacol.* 36:443–46

Carr, G. D., White, N. M. 1983. Conditioned place preference from intra-accumbens but not intra-caudate amphetamine injections. *Life Sci.* 33:2551–57

Colle, L. M., Wise, R. A. 1987. Opposite effects of unilateral forebrain ablations on ipsilateral and contralateral hypothalamic self-stimulation. *Brain Res.* 407:285–93

Corbett, D., Wise, R. A. 1979. Intracranial self-stimulation in relation to the ascending noradrenergic fiber systems of the pontine tegmentum and caudal midbrain: a moveable electrode mapping study. *Brain Res.* 177:423–36

Corbett, D., Wise, R. A. 1980. Intracranial self-stimulation in relation to the ascending dopaminergic systems of the midbrain: a moveable electrode mapping study. *Brain Res.* 185:1–15

de Wit, H., Wise, R. A. 1977. Blockade of cocaine reinforcement in rats with the dopamine receptor blocker pimozide but not with the noradrenergic blockers phentolamine or phenoxybenzamine. *Can. J. Psychol.* 31:195–203

Dougherty, J. D., Pickens, R. 1974. Effects of phenobarbital and SKR 525A on cocaine self-administration in rats. *Drug Addict.* 3:135–43

Edmonds, D. E., Gallistel, C. R. 1974. Parametric analysis of brain stimulation reward in the rat: III. Effect of performance variables on the reward summation function. *J. Comp. Physiol. Psychol.* 87:876–83

Esposito, R. U., Kornetsky, C. 1978. Opioids and rewarding brain stimulation. *Neurosci. Biobehav. Rev.* 2:115–22

Ettenberg, A., Camp, C. H. 1986a. A partial reinforcement extinction effect in water-reinforced rats intermittently treated with haloperidol. *Pharmacol. Biochem. Behav.* 25:1231–35

Ettenberg, A., Camp, C. H. 1986b. Haloperidol induces a partial reinforcement extinction effect in rats: implications for a dopamine involvement in food reward. *Pharmacol. Biochem. Behav.* 25:813–21

Ettenberg, A., Pettit, H. O., Bloom, F. E., Koob, G. F. 1982. Heroin and cocaine intravenous self-administration in rats: mediation by separate neural systems. *Psychopharmacology* 78:204–9

Fibiger, H. C., LePiane, F. G., Jakubovic, A., Phillips, A. G. 1987. The role of dopamine in intracranial self-stimulation of the ventral tegmental area. *J. Neurosci.* 7:3888–96

Gallistel, C. R. 1986. The role of the dopaminergic projections in MFB self-stimulation. *Behav. Brain Res.* 20:313–21

Gallistel, C. R., Davis, A. J. 1983. Affinity for the dopamine D2 receptor predicts neuroleptic potency in blocking the reinforcing effect of MFB stimulation. *Pharmacol. Biochem. Behav.* 19:867–72

Gallistel, C. R., Freyd, G. 1987. Quantitative determination of the effects of catecholaminergic agonists and antagonists on the rewarding efficacy of brain stimulation. *Pharmacol. Biochem. Behav.* 26:731–42

Gallistel, C. R., Gomita, Y., Yadin, E., Campbell, K. A. 1985. Forebrain origins and terminations of the medial forebrain bundle metabolically activated by rewarding stimulation or by reward-blocking doses of pimozide. *J. Neurosci.* 5:1246–61

Gallistel, C. R., Karras, D. 1984. Pimozide and amphetamine have opposing effects on the reward summation function. *Pharmacol. Biochem. Behav.* 20:73–77

Gallistel, C. R., Shizgal, P., Yeomans, J. 1981. A portrait of the substrate for self-stimulation. *Psychol. Rev.* 88:228–73

Gallistel, C. R., Stellar, J. R., Bubis, E. 1974. Parametric analysis of brain stimulation reward in the rat: I. The transient process and the memory-containing process. *J. Comp. Physiol. Psychol.* 87:848–59

Goeders, N. E., Lane, J. D., Smith, J. E. 1984. Self-administration of methionine enkephalin into the nucleus accumbens. *Pharmacol. Biochem. Behav.* 20:451–55

Goeders, N. E., Smith, J. E. 1983. Cortical dopaminergic involvement in cocaine reinforcement. *Science* 221:773–75

Grace, A. A., Bunney, B. S. 1986. Induction of depolarization block in midbrain dopamine neurons by repeated administration of haloperidol: analysis using in vivo intracellular recording. *J. Pharmacol. Exp. Ther.* 238:1092–1100

Gratton, A., Wise, R. A. 1983. Brain stimulation reward in the lateral hypothalamic medial forebrain bundle: mapping of boundaries and homogeneity. *Brain Res.* 274:25–30

Gratton, A., Wise, R. A. 1985. Hypothalamic reward mechanism: two first-stage fiber populations with a cholinergic component. *Science* 227:545–48

Hand, T. H., Hu, X.-T., Wang, R. Y. 1987a. Differential effects of acute clozapine and haloperidol on the activity of ventral tegmental (A10) and nigrostriatal (A9) dopamine neurons. *Brain Res.* 415:257–69

Hand, T. H., Kasser, R. J., Wang, R. Y. 1987b. Effects of acute thioridazine, metoclopramide and SCH 23390 on the basal activity of A9 and A10 dopamine cells. *Eur. J. Pharmacol.* 137:251–55

Hawkins, T. D., Pliskoff, S. S. 1964. Brain stimulation intensity, rate of self-stimulation, and reinforcement strength: an analysis through chaining. *J. Exp. Anal. Behav.* 7:285–88

Hoebel, B. G., Monaco, A. P., Hernandez, L., Aulisi, E. F., Stanley, B. G., Lenard, L. 1983. Self-injection of amphetamine directly into the brain. *Psychopharmacology* 81:158–63

Janas, J. D., Stellar, J. R. 1987. Effects of knife-cut lesions of the medial forebrain bundle in self-stimulating rats. *Behav. Neurosci.* 101:832–45

Jenck, F., Gratton, A., Wise, R. A. 1986. Opposite effects of ventral tegmental and periaqueductal gray morphine injections on lateral hypothalamic stimulation-induced feeding. *Brain Res.* 399:24–32

Jenck, F., Gratton, A., Wise, R. A. 1987. Opioid receptor subtypes associated with ventral tegmental facilitation of lateral hypothalamic brain stimulation reward. *Brain Res.* 423:34–38

Lookingland, K. J., Jarry, H. D., Moore, K. E. 1987. The metabolism of dopamine in the median eminence reflects the activity of tuberinfundibular neurons. *Brain Res.* 419:303–10

Malette, J., Miliaressis, E. 1987. Evidence for ascending and descending rewarding axons in the medial forebrain bundle. *Can. Psychol.* 28:364

Matthews, R. T., German, D. C. 1984. Elec-

trophysiological evidence for excitation of rat ventral tegmental area dopaminergic neurons by morphine. *Neuroscience* 11:617–26

Miliaressis, E., Malette, J. 1987. Summation and saturation properties in the rewarding effect of brain stimulation. *Physiol. Behav.* 41:595–604

Miliaressis, E., Malette, J., Coulombe, D. 1986a. The effects of pimozide on the reinforcing efficacy of central grey stimulation in the rat. *Behav. Brain Res.* 21:95–100

Miliaressis, E., Rompre, P.-P., Laviolette, L. P., Philippe, L., Coulombe, D. 1986b. The curve-shift paradigm in self-stimulation. *Physiol. Behav.* 37:85–91

Miliaressis, E., Rompre, P.-P., Durivage, A. 1982. Psychophysical method for mapping behavioral substrates using a moveable electrode. *Brain Res. Bull.* 8:693–701

Miliaressis, E., Rompre, P.-P. 1987. The effects of concomitant motoric reactions on the measurement of rewarding efficacy of brain stimulation. *Behav. Neurosci.* 101:827–31

Nakajima, S. 1986. Suppression of operant responding in the rat by dopamine D1 receptor blockade with SCH 23390. *Physiol. Psychol.* 14:111–14

Nakajima, S., McKenzie, G. M. 1986. Reduction of the rewarding effect of brain stimulation by blockade of dopamine D1 receptor with SCH 23390. *Pharmacol. Biochem. Behav.* 24:919–23

Nakajima, S., Wise, R. A. 1987. Heroin self-administration in the rat suppressed by SCH 23390. *Soc. Neurosci. Abstr.* 13:1545 (Abstr.)

Olds, J., Travis, R. P. 1960. Effects of chlorpromazine, meprobamate, pentobarbital and morphine on self-stimulation. *J. Pharmacol. Exp. Ther.* 128:397–404

Olds, J., Travis, R. P., Schwing, R. C. 1960. Topographic organization of hypothalamic self-stimulation functions. *J. Comp. Physiol. Psychol.* 53:23–32

Olds, M. E. 1982. Reinforcing effects of morphine in the nucleus accumbens. *Brain Res.* 237:429–40

Pettit, H. O., Ettenberg, A., Bloom, F. E., Koob, G. F. 1984. Destruction of dopamine in the nucleus accumbens selectively attenuates cocaine but not heroin self-administration in rats. *Psychopharmacology* 84:167–73

Phillips, A. G. 1984. Brain reward circuitry: a case for separate systems. *Brain Res. Bull.* 12:195–201

Phillips, A. G., Jakubovic, A., Fibiger, H. C. 1987. Increased in vivo tyrosine hydroxylase activity in rat telencephalon produced by self-stimulation of ventral tegmental area. *Brain Res.* 402:109–16

Phillips, A. G., LePiane, F. G. 1980. Reinforcing effects of morphine microinjection into the ventral tegmental area. *Pharmacol. Biochem. Behav.* 12:965–68

Phillips, A. G., Mora, F., Rolls, E. T. 1981. Intracerebral self-administration of amphetamine by rhesus monkeys. *Neurosci. Lett.* 24:81–86

Porrino, L. J., Esposito, R. U., Seeger, T. F., Crane, A. M., Pert, A., Sokoloff, L. 1984. Metabolic mapping of the brain during rewarding self-stimulation. *Science* 224:306–9

Prado-Alcala, R., Streather, A., Wise, R. A. 1984. Brain stimulation reward and dopamine terminal fields. II. Septal and cortical projections. *Brain Res.* 301:209–19

Prado-Alcala, R., Wise, R. A. 1984. Brain stimulation reward and dopamine terminal fields. I. Caudate-putamen, nucleus accumbens and amygdala. *Brain Res.* 297:265–73

Roberts, D. C. S., Vickers, G. 1988. Increased motivation to self-administer apomorphine following 6-hydroxydopamine lesions of the nucleus accumbens. *Ann. NY Acad. Sci.* In press

Roberts, D. C. S., Zito, K. A. 1987. Interpretation of lesion effects on stimulant self-administration. In *Methods of Assessing the Reinforcing Properties of Abused Drugs,* ed. M. A. Bozarth, pp. 87–104. New York: Springer-Verlag. 658 pp.

Rompre, P.-P. 1986. Diminution du seuil d'autostimulation intracérébrale après injection de morphine dans le mesencéphale médian: implications des cellules dopaminergiques du noyau A10. *L'Union Médicale du Canada* 115:599

Rompre, P.-P., Boye, S. 1986. Localization of brain stimulation reward sites in the pontine tegmentum: a moveable electrode mapping study. *Soc. Neurosci. Abstr.* 12: 931 (Abstr.)

Rompre, P.-P., Miliaressis, E. 1985. Pontine and mesencephalic substrates of self-stimulation. *Brain Res.* 359:246–59

Rompre, P.-P., Miliaressis, E. 1987. Behavioral determination of refractory periods of the brainstem substrates of self-stimulation. *Behav. Brain Res.* 23:205–19

Rompre, P.-P., Wise, R. 1988. A study of the interactions of pimozide, morphine and muscimol on brain stimulation reward: behavioral evidence for depolarization inactivation of A10 dopaminergic neurons. *Ann. NY Acad. Sci.* In press

Schenk, S., Shizgal, P. 1982. The substrates for lateral hypothalamic and medial prefrontal cortex self-stimulation have different refractory periods and show poor spatial summation. *Physiol. Behav.* 28:133–38

Schmitt, P., Eclancher, F., Karli, P. 1974. Etude des systèmes de renforcement négatif et de renforcement positif au niveau de la substance grise centrale chez le rat. *Physiol. Behav.* 12:271–79

Shizgal, P., Bielajew, C., Corbett, D., Skelton, R., Yeomans, J. 1980. Behavioral methods for inferring anatomical linkage between rewarding brain stimulation sites. *J. Comp. Physiol. Psychol.* 94:227–37

Simon, H., Stinus, L., Tassin, J. P., Lavielle, S., Blanc, G., et al. 1979. Is the dopaminergic mesocorticolimbic system necessary for intracranial self-stimulation? *Behav. Neural Biol.* 27:125–45

Spyraki, C., Fibiger, H. C., Phillips, A. G. 1982. Dopaminergic substrates of amphetamine-induced place preference conditioning. *Brain Res.* 253:185–93

Stein, E. A., Olds, J. 1976. Direct, intracerebral self-administration of opiates in the rat. *Soc. Neurosci. Abstr.* 3:302 (Abstr.)

Stellar, J., Illes, J., Mills, L. E. 1982. Role of ipsilateral forebrain in lateral hypothalamic stimulation reward in rats. *Physiol. Behav.* 29:1089–97

Stellar, J. R., Kelley, A. E., Corbett, D. 1983. Effects of peripheral and central dopamine blockade on lateral hypothalamic self-stimulation: evidence for both reward and motor deficits. *Pharmacol. Biochem. Behav.* 18:433–42

Stinus, L., Nadaud, D., Jauregui, J., Kelley, A. E. 1986. Chronic treatment with five different neuroleptics elicits behavioral supersensitivity to opiate infusion into the nucleus accumbens. *Biol. Psychiatr.* 21:34–48

Stinus, L., Winnock, M., Kelley, A. E. 1985. Chronic neuroleptic treatment and mesolimbic dopamine denervation induce behavioural supersensitivity to opiates. *Psychopharmacology* 85:323–28

Stricker, E. M., Zigmond, M. J. 1976. Recovery of function after damage to central catecholamine-containing neurons: a neurochemical model for the lateral hypothalamic syndrome. In *Progress in Psychobiology and Physiological Psychology,* ed. J. M. Sprague, A. N. Epstein, pp. 121–88. New York: Academic

Ungerstedt, U. 1971. Adipsia and aphagia after 6-hydroxydopamine induced degeneration of the nigro-striatal dopamine system. *Acta Physiol. Scand.* 367:95–122

Vaccarino, F. J., Bloom, F. E., Koob, G. F. 1985. Blockade of nucleus accumbens opiate receptors attenuates intravenous heroin reward in the rat. *Psychopharmacology* 86:37–42

van der Kooy, D., Mucha, R. F., O'Shaughnessy, M., Bucenieks, P. 1982. Reinforcing effects of brain microinjections of morphine revealed by conditioned place preference. *Brain Res.* 243:107–17

Waraczynski, M., Stellar, J. R., Gallistel, C. R. 1987. Reward saturation in medial forebrain bundle self-stimulation. *Physiol. Behav.* 41:585–93

Waraczynski, M. A. 1988. Basal forebrain knife cuts and medial forebrain bundle self-stimulation. *Brain Res.* 438:8–22

White, F. J., Wang, R. Y. 1983. Comparison of the effects of chronic haloperidol treatment on A9 and A10 dopamine neurons in the rat. *Life Sci.* 32:983–93

Wise, R. A. 1978. Catecholamine theories of reward: a critical review. *Brain Res.* 152:215–47

Wise, R. A. 1981. Intracranial self-stimulation: mapping against the lateral boundaries of the dopaminergic cells of the substantia nigra. *Brain Res.* 213:190–94

Wise, R. A. 1982. Neuroleptics and operant behavior: the anhedonia hypothesis. *Behav. Brain Sci.* 5:39–87

Wise, R. A. 1987a. Intravenous drug self-administration: a special case of positive reinforcement. In *Methods of Assessing the Reinforcing Properties of Abused Drugs,* ed. M. A. Bozarth, pp. 117–41. New York: Springer-Verlag. 658 pp.

Wise, R. A. 1987b. The role of reward pathways in the development of drug dependence. *Pharmacol. Ther.* 35:227–63

Wise, R. A., Bozarth, M. A. 1984. Brain reward circuitry: four circuit elements "wired" in apparent series. *Brain Res. Bull.* 12:203–8

Wise, R. A., Bozarth, M. A. 1987. A psychomotor stimulant theory of addiction. *Psychol. Rev.* 94:469–92

Wise, R. A., Colle, L. 1984. Pimozide attenuates free feeding: "best scores" analysis reveals a motivational deficit. *Psychopharmacologia* 84:446–51

Wise, R. A., Spindler, J., de Wit, H., Gerber, G. J. 1978. Neuroleptic-induced "anhedonia" in rats: pimozide blocks the reward quality of food. *Science* 201:262–64

Yadin, E., Guarini, V., Gallistel, C. R. 1983. Unilaterally activated systems in rats self-stimulating at sites in the medial forebrain bundle, medial prefrontal cortex, or locus coeruleus. *Brain Res.* 266:39–50

Yeomans, J. S. 1975. Quantitative measurement of neural post-stimulation excitability with behavioral methods. *Physiol. Behav.* 15:593–602

Yokel, R. A., Pickens, R. 1974. Drug level of D- and L-amphetamine during intravenous self-administration. *Psychopharmacologia* 34:255–64

Yokel, R. A., Wise, R. A. 1975. Increased lever pressing for amphetamine after pimozide in rats: implications for a dopamine theory of reward. *Science* 187:547–49

Yokel, R. A., Wise, R. A. 1978. Amphetamine-type reinforcement by dopamine agonists in the rat. *Psychopharmacology* 58:289–96

Ann. Rev. Psychol. 1989. 40:227–48

PERSONALITY

Robert C. Carson

Department of Psychology, Duke University, Durham, North Carolina 27706

CONTENTS

INTRODUCTION

In the last general review of personality for this series, Lawrence Pervin (1985) directed his attention chiefly to "controversies, issues, and directions" in the field. He began by noting the widespread impression that all was not well with respect to genuine progress in personality research, notwithstanding a few optimistic voices here and there: and—if I read him correctly—he concluded his impressive analysis largely in the pessimist camp himself. In a somewhat plaintive coda, he referred to the "gap" between the richness of persons he experiences as a clinician and the paler and decidedly simpler human organisms he encounters in the research literature.

Being also a clinician, and having spent the past year rather more immersed than usual in that literature, my appreciation of Pervin's difficulty has a poignant edge. I have lately been troubled about what Meehl (1978) felicitously termed "the slow progress of soft psychology." Meehl noted the

227

0066-4308/89/0201-0227$02.00

faddishness of topics that dominate the personality scene for a while only to "fade away," unresolved yet lacking in any current investigative appeal. To put it plainly, much of what passes as research in personality in the current era is patently trivial and noncumulative, and inspires nothing so much as boredom. As West (1987) notes, the "prototype" article appearing in the *Journal of Personality* continues to describe an empirical study involving self-report measures with college subjects in a single-occasion laboratory or classroom setting. The likelihood of discovering nonobvious, important, enduring truths about humankind by such means must be judged small, at best. I have more to say about these frustrating circumstances, and about what appear to be substantial exceptions to the rule, in what follows.

I begin with an update on the controversies and issues Pervin identified. No attempt is made either here or in later sections to include all pertinent work. In general, my selection criteria have emphasized recency, pertinence to current salient issues in the field, judged importance, and imaginativeness of approach. I have selected topics based chiefly on current activity levels in the most germane primary journals.

ISSUES, PERSISTENT AND OTHERWISE

Pervin (1985) focused on (*a*) the person-situation "controversy"; (*b*) information-processing models in personality; and (*c*) questions of research strategy. He might have added (*d*) various issues and controversies surrounding sex and gender, but that topic was thoroughly and competently addressed by Deaux (1985) in the same volume. All four of these matters are updated and critically reviewed below.

The So-Called Person-Situation Controversy

I have been baffled for two decades by the debate about whether internal dispositions and external circumstances exclude and oppose each other in determining behavior. At the most fundamental level, it has been argued for many years that these two classes of entities are not mutually independent either conceptually (e.g. Merleau-Ponty 1963) or empirically (e.g. Zener 1937) at the point of behavior. We attempt to separate them in the design of studies chiefly for reasons of convenience and clarity.

In initiating the contemporary version of this debate—and it does have predecessors (Ekehammar 1974)—it appears that Mischel (1968) confused potency of effects with relative psychometric efficiency. Within the observational limits he employed, imputed "traits" (notoriously difficult to measure) were of course no match for "situations," whose "reliability" (as measured, for example, by manipulation checks) normally approaches unity. In any event, many, including this reviewer, thought the debate was effectively—

and mercifully—ended in an interactional draw with the publication in 1973 of Bowers's superb analysis of the issues. Alas, it was not to be—a fact that compelled Pervin to rehash them 12 years later.

This unfortunate era in personality research may again be drawing to a close. Studies specifically addressing the controversy are rare in recent literature, and Kenrick & Funder (1988) have published a summary statement that reads like an epitaph. These authors suggest that the debate taught positive lessons. Curiously, these lessons support the empirical reality and potency of personality traits—the position from which most personologists began in 1968. A less charitable appraisal is offered by Kihlstrom (1987), who terms the debate "fruitless" and to a large extent ascribable to antipathy and power struggles between social (i.e. situationist) and personality (i.e. trait) psychologists.

Mischel himself abandoned years ago any radical situationist propensities (e.g. Mischel 1973) in favor of what appears to be a frankly interactionist perspective. He now thinks of traits as conditional probabilities that a particular action will be evoked by a particular environmental state (Wright & Mischel 1987)—still a somewhat mechanical notion, but definitely interactionist.

Information Processing

The cognitive revolution throughout psychology continues to reverberate in the personality domain. In fact, Neisser's (1980) warning against overextension of information-processing models in this domain, reminiscent of Oppenheimer's (1956) caveat against overuse in psychology of the classical-physics model, threatens likewise to go as unheeded. If Neisser's barely disguised contempt for the "passive" and "artificial" model of the person portrayed in much of the earlier (circa 1980) work is still deserved, and if it is shared by outsiders generally, then contemporary personality psychology is indeed in serious trouble. My impression, however, is that the situation has improved appreciably—for example, by increased incorporation of motivational and other dynamic variables into the conception and design of cognitively oriented studies.

Consistent with the trend just noted, much of the recent work conjoining personality and cognitive psychology has been done within the specialized and decidedly affect-involving topics of gender roles and psychological depression, the latter in particular having become an exceedingly popular topic among personality researchers. Consideration of these studies is postponed to later sections. What follows immediately is a sampling of otherwise difficult to classify work at the cognitive/personality interface.

One intriguing recent paper in the cognitive area has a developmental focus and deals less with content than with the structure of the cognitive apparatus. Assume that a prime developmental task of early childhood is that of learning to appreciate reality through the achievement of an adequate system of mental representation. How is it, then, asks Leslie (1987), that this task is not hopelessly undermined by a concurrent and often substantial investment in pretending? Leslie posits a separate representation system capable of differentiating continuously between "real" and "pretend." He then argues elegantly that such a system depends on the child's discerning that pretending is, in essence, the representation of representation, or *metarepresentation*. The additional observation that pretend play is frequently collaborative leads to the somewhat startling conclusion that the typical child has a generalized "theory of mind" by the time he/she is emerging from infancy.

Pretend-play may thus be seen as a primordial form of the ability to conceptualize (i.e. objectify) mental states—one's own or those of others, and this would appear to be its chief significance for a psychology of personality and personality development. It is conceivable, for example, that our understanding of concepts like self, ego identity, dissociation, "splitting," projection, etc, not to mention some significant perplexities in social cognition, might be enhanced by analysis in terms of the developmental history of representation, an idea whose essential features were advanced by Sullivan (1953) many years ago. It seems clear that any progress in this area would depend on use of a more richly elaborated (hierarchically ordered?) cognitive model than is thus far customary in personality research.

The theme of hierarchical representation may also be pertinent to how adults cognize emotions. Shaver et al (1987), taking a prototype approach to the knowledge of emotions, present evidence that people's conceptions of emotions are in fact organized in this way. If confirmed, such a finding renders inappropriate certain types of data analysis, such as multidimensional scaling, in exploring the domain. The authors comment on the implications of their thesis for the acquisition of knowledge about emotions in childhood, but they do not speculate about effects on the child's developing "theory of mind" as it pertains to the mental states of others. This may be a fruitful area for future investigation.

Finally, recent work has explored the dynamics of cognitive functioning, including selective retrieval from memory and the effects of intentional suppression of mental contents.

Larsen et al (1987) provide an interesting demonstration of a relationship between emotional and cognitive functioning. Hypothesizing that individual differences in affect intensity would be associated with differences in the cognitive processing of emotional stimuli, they in fact found that high-affect-intensity subjects reacted to both positive and negative emotional stimuli with relatively high levels of personalizing/empathic and generalizing/elaborative cognitive operations; emotionally neutral stimuli failed to elicit this effect.

Courtroom judges sometimes instruct juries to disregard information to which they have become privy, an admonition more easily issued than obeyed. Wegner et al (1987) report two demonstrations of involuntary intrusive thoughts about a "white bear" provoked by attempts to suppress such intrusions. Some success was achieved in controlling these "obsessional" phenomena by teaching subjects to use a specific distracter. Wyer & Budesheim (1987) have studied a related process in the area of person memory. Subjects were provided descriptive information on target persons and then told to disregard some of it. While the accessibility of the presumably suppressed information in a subsequent memory test varied with the experimental conditions, it was generally substantial.

The notion that memory retrieval processes are influenced by personal concerns, motives, and the like is venerable. Defining as "repressors" subjects who scored high and low on the Marlow-Crowne and Manifest Anxiety scales, respectively, Davis (1987) has shown (again) that this type of defensiveness is associated with diminished access to personal memories, especially unpleasant ones. The effect appears limited (as it should) to events involving the self, and appears especially notable for experiences that threaten or provide negative evaluations of the self. The other side of the coin is demonstrated in a recent study by Katz (1987). Here, selectively enhanced retrieval by "creative" subjects for creativity-relevant trait terms occurred only when instructions involved self-concept/schema arousal.

Research Strategies

Explicit attention to fruitful methodology appears to have waned following the period covered by Pervin's (1985) review. That review emphasized the reemergence of an idiographic perspective, continuing questions about the status of self-report, and the trend toward data aggregation (e.g. meta-analysis) as a means of differentiating robust and reliable from conditional and setting-specific findings. Suffice to say, none of these issues has been resolved in the interim. This is hardly surprising, since all of them go to the epistemological heart of a still nascent science of personality.

Another venerable problem, that of identifying the elements or dimensional units comprising "personality," has surfaced again in the contemporary literature. According to one account, the quarry are nothing less than "the biological bases of personality" (Zuckerman et al 1988)! The factorially derived *Big Five* have attracted the most attention. These presumed basic dimensions are, roughly: Introversion–Extraversion; Friendly Compliance–Hostile Noncompliance; Will (sometimes Conscientiousness); Neuroticism (sometimes Emotionality); and Openness to Experience (see, for example, Noller et al 1987). Apparently convinced of the primacy of these variables in personality functioning, McCrae & Costa (1986) urge they be adopted in clinical assessment, whose more typical instruments are said to lack comprehensive coverage of these purportedly basic organizing components.

A much needed caution on such enthusiasms has been offered by Waller & Ben-Porath (1987), who point out that the alleged robustness of the five factors pertains more to their reliability (in paper-and-pencil tests) than to their validity. I would add that, given the taxonomic absurdities of psychiatric diagnosis as represented by DSM-III and its recent revision (but cf McReynolds, this volume), clinicians need to avoid elevating observational reliability above substance observed. It is possible to become too "operational," a strategy that tends to degenerate into arbitrariness. It is not clear that mere number crunching of responses to preselected items on personality inventories, as in many factor-analytic studies, has burst its own confines to make a general contribution to the cause.

If I were to bet on what sort of "basic dimensions" we will eventually settle on in personality research, I would *still* (Carson 1969) expect variables with an interpersonal referent to provide a large share of the successful candidates. To my mind Leary (1957) and his colleagues staked out the basic territory— now generally known as the interpersonal circle. This circumplex space, meaningful both conceptually and mathematically, and defined by bipolar, orthogonal dimensions of "power" and "love," continues to show remarkable resilience. Using the pertinent adjective scales developed by Wiggins (1979), Gifford & O'Connor (1987) present evidence that the circle does more than merely summarize our collective implicit personality theory; it actually does a good job of mapping objective behavioral output. Meanwhile, Wiggins (Wiggins et al 1988) continues to refine and develop the geometric properties inherent in the model and to show its potential for subsuming other purportedly central personality dimensions, such as introversion–extraversion. It may also help clarify some problems in gender-related behavior (Wiggins et al 1988; Wiggins & Holzmuller 1978, 1981), the next topic on our agenda.

Recent Research on Sex and Gender

Little new ground has been broken in the area of sex and gender since Deaux's (1985) review. Themes already well developed in the literature, and for which she provided expert perspective, have been consolidated or elaborated. Unfortunately, much confusion remains. The "tension" she described as pervading the area seems to have diminished, possibly because the evidence for nontrivial sex differences in behavior (in terms of central tendency) has gained acceptance.

The problem of how masculinity and femininity are to be conceptualized as organized trait complexes within personality and the related problem of how to measure them continue to be debated. The original notions of Bem (1974) on gender schemata, the unidimensionality of sex typing, and the mid-dimension (i.e. nontyped) psychological gender equivalence of "undifferentiated" and "androgynous" persons seem to have lost credibility as investigators become increasingly analytic in approach. In three well-conceived studies, Edwards & Spence (1987) found little evidence for either the unidimensional or bidimensional (i.e. orthogonal instrumental and communal dimensions) views, and only weak suggestions of the operation of gender schemata (see below) in cognitive processing; their data are most consistent with a multifactor model of the organization of psychological gender. The gender schemata hypothesis also fared poorly in a cognitive processing study by Payne et al (1987). Perhaps most damaging is the observation by Paulhus (1987) that the median split method of subject allocation into (psychological) gender-related quadrants produces internally based artifacts with respect to theoretically central dependent variables. Moreover, Paulhus argues that Bem's primary data actually measure the two principal dimensions of the interpersonal circumplex mentioned above, noting the irony that both are bipolar.

It would be premature, however, to conclude (a) that individuals do not use biological sex as an important organizing principle in the way they think about persons, or (b) that the standard measures of psychological gender typing hopelessly lack construct validity. The intuitive appeal of an appropriately limited version of the gender schemata notion found support in a study by Frable (1987), in which many potentially "noisy" variables were ingeniously controlled—specifically by videotaping target persons garbed in dark clothing marked with refective tape at the joints as they walked before a dark background. In this study, sex-typed (per Bem) individuals used more gender terms and were more accurate in their guesses as to the sex of targets than nontyped subjects. In the role of target, moreover, the movements of sex-typed individuals were judged by observers to be more distinctively masculine or feminine than those of the nontyped. Interestingly, cross-typed subjects (i.e. those having a disparity of biological sex and psychological gender) moved the way the nontyped did, but were closer to typed subjects in their perceptions of targets.

Among the trait ascriptions assuming prominence in the psychology of gender are those of dominance/submission and achievement striving. Concerning the former, Sadalla et al (1987) report four studies that in the aggregate demonstrate enhanced heterosexual attractiveness of males who engage in (nonaggressive) dominant behavior, whereas similar behaviors do not affect attractiveness ratings of females. Male dominance affected sexual attractiveness, not general likeability. Halberstadt & Saitta (1987) attempted to identify nonverbal cues communicating dominance and submission between the sexes in public settings and in various media materials, focusing on such supposedly submissive gestures as canting the head and body and smiling. Few reliable sex differences emerged, suggesting either that dominance stereotypes in this area are erroneous (a conclusion contrary to much other evidence) or that the intuitive appeal of the meaning assigned to the canting and smiling behaviors observed is largely mistaken.

As for achievement, Gaeddert (1987) has added an important qualification to the common finding that women more than men tend to attribute their objectively real accomplishments to causes (such as luck) that do not enhance their self-esteem. This investigator found that, in permitting subjects to choose their own accomplishments (as opposed to standard ones provided by the experimenter) as the backdrop for reporting goals, standards of performance, and analyses of reasons for success, the previously reported gender bias is reduced to insignificance. Conventional notions of accomplishment may not apply to individuals or groups that do not fully share the values implicit in them.

In any case, the primary observations continue to be supported—in some instances with qualifications. For example, in a psychometrically sophisticated study Marsh et al (1987) present evidence that typical measures of "masculinity" may be interpreted as directly assessing self-esteem. Partialling out social desirability, which was more strongly correlated with femininity than masculinity, did not substantially diminish the masculinity/self-esteem association. Thus self-esteem and social desirability seemed to function here as forms of stereotypic masculinity and femininity, respectively. Continuing the theme, Orlofsky & O'Heron (1987) demonstrated for both sexes, the positive associations of measured masculinity with adjustment and self-esteem. Here, however, femininity also correlated significantly with self-esteem, albeit more weakly. The authors attributed the latter association to the "communal self-esteem" component of femininity, which I suspect is indistinguishable from Marsh et al's (1987) social desirability. Overall, questions of gender typing (as normally measured) and its meaning with respect to self-esteem, adjustment, and related matters remain amorphous. As Deaux & Major (1987) have recently suggested, gender-related behavior may be far more variable and context-dependent than we have realized.

On the other hand, the relationship is clear between biological sex and the incidence and prevalence of diagnosable depression: Female depressives outnumber male on the order of two to one (Wing & Bebbington 1985), a difference not readily attributable to artifacts or diagnostic biases (Nolen-Hoeksema 1987; Amenson & Lewinsohn 1981). While the general topic is discussed in the section on the psychology of depression, below, some pertinent work on this disorder and its relationship to sex and gender-roles is best considered here.

The enhanced risk of depression among women is apparently attributable in part to the (now increasingly weakly) associated factor of being a nonworking homemaker with exclusive responsibility for the care of young children (Wing & Bebbington 1985); thus traditional gender roles are directly implicated.

Longitudinal data reported by Schaefer & Burnett (1987) cast some light on the possible influence of the spouse upon the likelihood of unfortunate outcomes for such women. This study found a high correlation between wives' perceptions of how well their husbands met their needs for autonomy and relatedness, on the one hand, and the women's sense of well-being, on the other; these correlations tended to increase over time.

What aspect of the traditional female role might correlate with depression? Learned helplessness appears not to be the critical link, according to a searching analysis by Nolen-Hoeksema (1987), who believes that trait-like qualities supposedly differentiating the sexes are more likely to explain the imbalance in the occurrence of serious depression. Specifically, she suggests that men are more likely to cope with depressive feelings by an active type of distraction, whereas women tend to amplify the effects of the mood by ruminating about its causes. It seems to me that this conclusion leads us back to square one.

EMERGENT PREOCCUPATIONS: DEPRESSION AND HEALTH

The current interests of personality researchers in the phenomena of human psychological depression extend far beyond the interface with sex and gender roles. Concern with these phenomena and with relationships between personality variables and physical health has dominated the personality research literature of the past two or three years. This trend has been facilitated by the development of individual assessment instruments that appear (often deceptively) to type persons easily and reliably according to some theoretically or pragmatically attractive variable. We consider first the more general work on depression.

The Psychology of Depression

Some 20 percent of the raw material I assembled for this review dealt explicitly with depression. It appears to be a topic whose time has come. Research has been stimulated in particular by the cognitive work of Beck (Beck et al 1979) and the eventually related directions taken by Seligman's (1975; Abramson et al 1978) learned helplessness theory of depression. The convenience of the Beck Depression Inventory (BDI), widely used to select "depressed" subjects, has doubtless also contributed.

I begin by reviewing recent work on the cognitive variables purportedly underlying the experience of depression.

DYSFUNCTIONAL CAUSAL ATTRIBUTIONS   According to the revised form of the learned helplessness theory of depression, the disorder occurs consequent to "negative events" *only* for individuals having the propensity to attribute such events to factors that are internal ("it's something in me"), global ("the problem is pervasive in my life"), and stable ("and it will always be thus"). The dysfunctional triad is described in the current literature as an attributional or explanatory "style," and there is even available an Attributional Style Questionnaire (ASQ) said to permit identification of persons who view things this way (Seligman et al 1979). Whether individuals with this "style" could not be said to be depressed already, independent of any experimental manipulations performed on them, has been seriously debated for some time (e.g. Peterson et al 1985) and continues to be (e.g. Wollert & Rowley 1987), without resolution. Nevertheless, researchers persistently explore the unquestioned association (by definition?) between negative thoughts and depressed mood.

Riskind et al (1987) report a study fairly typical for the area. Here an interaction between previously assessed attributional style and expectations of future outcomes predicted BDI-measured depression in college students six weeks later. Complicating matters, however, was a significant effect for attributional style in interaction with initial level of depression. A more straightforward interpretation of results was possible in a comparable study by Peterson & Barrett (1987), where the internal-global-stable explanatory style predicted relatively poor freshman grades and certain other college difficulties independent of initial BDI scores and SAT-assessed academic ability. Of course, such outcomes are not necessarily attributable to depression. Also, it would be interesting to know how these students fared after a failure. A study by Follette & Jacobson (1987) showed "facilitation" (e.g. planning-enhanced attention to studies) following poor academic performance among students with negative attributional styles.

Given the evident perplexities and inconsistencies, it is likely that more can be learned only from correlational studies that attend to process. Ingram et al (1987) took a step in this more analytical direction by examining the "cognitive specificity" of depressed (and anxious) college students on measures of information processing, attributions, automatic thinking, and cognitive interference. They found that depressed students did indeed show distinctive thinking aberrations that seemed likely to produce further maladaptive consequences, but the causal relationships between the cognitive and affective phenomena remained unknown. If one accepts acutely induced moods as comparable to the more naturally occurring variety, there is evidence that depression may affect the cognitive processing involved in person perception (Forgas & Bower 1987).

The issue of causal direction is complicated further by findings that successful treatment of depression by other than cognitive modes (e.g. by antidepressant medication) results in improvement of dysfunctional attributions. This certainly suggests depressive mood primacy. However, Hollon et al (1987) argue that such a conclusion is unjustified because it confounds a treatment mediator role (which various therapies might produce) with the potential causal role of dysfunctional cognitions. This argument seems strained. In any event, recent work has failed to resolve the causal-direction dilemma, inherent in the revised formulation of the learned helplessness model, now a decade old.

DEPRESSION AND THE SELF   Any cognitive role in the inducement of depressive affect involves at some point the historically rich but ephemeral and elusive concept of self. One investigation linking depression with the self, that of Tennen et al (1987), directly targets the dysfunctional-attributions hypothesis discussed above. These investigators assessed college students via the ASQ and multiple measures of depression and self-esteem, and found that self-esteem was a better predictor of attributional style than was depression. In a second study involving psychiatric inpatients, self-esteem and depression proved (not surprisingly) to be highly inversely correlated, both of them predicting ASQ performance well. Even with statistical elimination of social desirability and depth of depression, a significant inverse association remained between self-esteem and the internal-global-stable style of interpreting negative events. Finally, statistical control of self-esteem essentially eliminated the depression-ASQ correlation. Given the character of the field, it would be premature to suggest that these results deliver a mortal blow to the etiologic primacy of dysfunctional cognitions as envisaged in contemporary learned helplessness theory. The image of an outsized coffin nail does suggest itself, however.

Results generally supportive of the role of self-esteem in mitigating depressive affect has also been reported by Pagel & Becker (1987) and Strauman & Higgins (1987; see also Higgins 1987). In the former study, self-esteem exerted its antidepressant effect among spouse caregivers of Alzheimer's patients by inhibiting depressive cognitions. One cannot help reflecting, however, that such effects of the self-esteem variable are hardly unprecedented and that the precise (and otherwise satisfactory) measurement of self-esteem poses its own obduracies.

Meanwhile, other aspects of the self have also figured in recent work on depression. Pyszczynski & Greenberg (1987) offer a self-awareness theory of ("reactive") depression according to which negative self-image is the product of cyclical dysregulation in response to loss and the enhanced self-focusing it brings. The theory is provided some empirical backing in two studies reported by Pyszczynski et al (1987) in which (a) depression (again as measured by questionnaire) was shown to be associated with pessimism about personal outcomes, attributed by the authors to excessive self-focus; and (b) this pessimism could be reduced to the level of nondepressed subjects by inducements to focus externally. Self-regulatory mechanisms also figure prominently in another theoretical treatise on depression offered by Hyland (1987).

OTHER DEPRESSION-RELEVANT WORK   The interpersonal context of depressive behavior continues to stimulate useful observations about the dynamics of depression. Returning for a moment to the depression/helplessness connection, a study by Sacks & Bugental (1987) demonstrates the sometimes considerable interpersonal ramifications entailed in depressive (or helpless) functioning. In this study helpless and nonhelpless (ASQ-defined) women were subjected to contrived social failure and subsequently interacted with "naive" partners. Relative to the nonhelpless, helpless women became depressed and hostile, had elevated voice tension, and engaged in more unpleasant nonverbal behaviors in these second interactions. The partners in these second interactions who were themselves helpless (relative to nonhelpless counterparts) spoke less and were more hostile to partners who had had a prior failure experience, but conversely were less hostile to partners whose prior experience had been (again by contrivance) successful.

The induction hypothesis—i.e. that the depressed person tends to generate depressive affect in others and thereby becomes aversive to those others, perhaps compounding the original difficulty (Coyne 1976)—has amassed sufficient empirical support (see also, e.g., Howes et al 1985) to merit inclusion in any comprehensive theory of depression. At the same time, however, the phenomenon is not so robust as to be routinely replicable, suggesting, as is so often the case in personality research, that we have not yet isolated the controlling variables. At any rate, Stephens et al (1987) report another disconfirmation of the strong version of the induction hypothesis, although the target persons of depressed-acting confederates did reject these confederates. In an interesting twist, the rejection was registered only in subsequent questionnaire responses; overtly, these rejecting subjects were quite responsive to the help-seeking efforts of their "depressed" interaction partners. One wonders, of course, how persistent this responsiveness would be if it failed to have a depression-relieving effect over time—a highly likely scenario in the "real world."

Doubtless there would be individual differences in such persistence, and in this connection Clark et al (1987) report the development of a new "communal orientation scale" that appears to predict especially strong helping responses to "sad" others. The other side of the coin, the sometimes enhanced helpfulness to others of (mildly) depressed persons, is a product of situational factors that increase a sense of responsibility and heighten objective self-awareness, according to an aggregational analysis of the pertinent literature by Carlson & Miller (1987).

Experienced clinicians are careful not to provide too much help to depressed persons because such support may increase the guilt that commonly accompanies serious depressions, thereby producing a negative outcome. Possibly related to the phenomenon of guilt in depression is a recent finding by McGraw (1987): Contrary to intuition, unintended harm-doing produced more guilty feelings in "normal" subjects than did the intentional variety. Using an attributional model, McGraw argues that self-blame (rather than notions of cause or responsibility per se) is the critical element in the experience of guilt, the intentional harm doer typically having "worked through" any associated guilt *prior* to commission of the culpable act.

Personality and Health

Recently an entire issue of the *Journal of Personality* (Vol. 55, No. 2, June, 1987) was given over to reports and commentaries on relations between personality variables and sundry aspects of physical health—one measure of the exploding interest in this area manifested by personality researchers. Interest has been stimulated by the establishment of a linkage between the so-called Type A Behavior Pattern (TABP) and coronary heart disease (CHD), still the most lethal of the diseases affecting the population of the United States. As expected, the availability of easily used assessment instruments for the TABP has been contributory, and, as has also become customary, the "second wave" of related research has included much questioning of the adequacy of these instruments.

TYPE A AND CORONARY HEART DISEASE   Some stage-setting comments are in order for nonspecialist readers. In the wake of the impressive longitudinal findings of the Western Collaborative Group Study (Rosenman et al 1975) and the Framingham Heart Study (Haynes et al 1980) linking TAPB with CHD, there appeared seemingly well-executed studies that unexpectedly failed to confirm this linkage. Disagreements and difficulties arose regarding how the TAPB should be measured (Fischman 1987). It became clear that Type A, as originally described, was a composite of several not necessarily strongly intercorrelated behavioral characteristics, not all of which—e.g. high levels of achievement motivation—predicted CHD.

Further complicating the picture, different assessments have differentially weighted such components of TABP as time urgency, job involvement, competitiveness, achievement striving, and generalized hostility. To make a long and complicated story short, a plurality of experts in the area now finds the structured interview (SI) method to be the surest way of assessing TABP (Dembroski et al 1978), and suggests that one or another form of hostility is its most CHD-predictive component (Fischman 1987; Wood 1986). At the level of primary assessment many researchers have settled for less, having been especially attracted to the convenience of the Jenkins Activity Survey

(JAS; Jenkins et al 1979). The JAS is a questionnaire that deals minimally with hostility and (see below) seems not to predict CHD.

Much recent research on the A-B typology has sought to identify and differentiate more precisely the supposedly lethal personality factor(s) involved in the TABP. A thorough "quantitative review" by Booth-Kewley & Friedman (1987) of work in this area published through about 1985 shows that some progress has been made. In addition to demonstrating the superiority of the SI over the JAS for predicting CHD, the data reviewed by these authors clearly implicate the negative emotions of depression and anxiety as well as anger/hostility in the correlational network that includes the development of CHD. They suggest that the concept of the coronary-prone behavior pattern be on the one hand broadened to encompass these additional negative affect features, and on the other narrowed to eliminate noncontributory components such as impatience, pressured drive, and workaholism—characteristics strongly represented in the JAS measuring instrument. These conclusions were generally confirmed in a study of 50 post–myocardial infarct men by the same authors (Friedman & Booth-Kewley 1987a), who also describe an expressive variant of the TABP that apparently is not associated with enhanced CHD risk. Type A American and Indian bus drivers who have high accident, reprimand, and absenteeism rates and perhaps blow their horns excessively (Evans, et al 1987) should be reassured by this finding.

The Booth-Kewley & Friedman (1987) review reveals substantial gaps in our information concerning the interrelations among the psychological predictors of CHD, their developmental origins, and the manner in which they may contribute to coronary (or other) arterial blockage. While the last of these remains a near-total mystery, we may be gaining some ground with respect to the other two. Dembroski & Costa (1987), also arguing for component analysis of the TABP, suggest that both the TABP and its apparently critical hostility component are multidimensional in character. Noting that the hostility involved here seems to be of a decidedly antagonistic variety, unmitigated by conflicting tendencies toward agreeableness, they reason that neuroticism as usually conceived and measured may have little contributory role in the "toxic" pattern, and could in some instances be associated with reduced CHD risk.

Meanwhile, Ward & Eisler (1987) have provided a clue to the sources of negative affect in coronary-prone persons. Identifying Type A subjects according to a JAS-like questionnaire developed by the Framingham investigators, they found that these subjects tended (a) to set personal goals at a level that invited failure, and (b) to use achievement strategies that produced low levels of self-evaluated performance. These findings seem consistent with the self-appraisal model of TABP proposed by Strube et al (1987), according to which Type As are excessively concerned with gaining information (reducing uncertainty) about their abilities, thereby risking objective failure. JAS-defined Type A subjects generally performed in accord with these expectations. Unfortunately, the meaning of both studies for CHD risk is clouded by their reliance on equivocal measures of the Type A construct.

A similar reservation applies to a newly published longitudinal study of Type A individuals by MacEvoy et al (1988), one of the very few such studies to appear. Using data obtained in repeated evaluations of Swedish children and their mothers over 25 years, and a Swedish, shortened version of the JAS administered at mean age 26.5, these investigators found notable evidence of temperamental precursors to the adult TABP, as measured, and some maternal behavior correlates of the latter such as orderliness and intelligence. Irritability, the JAS factor in this study most closely associated with independent evidence of CHD toxicity, was preceded by lively, sociable (not shy) child behavior, and with having had a poor appetite. The authors acknowledge the evident lack of face validity in these findings.

Overall, we have made genuine progress in this area—notably in sharpening the concept of coronary-proneness beyond the original formulation of the intuitively attractive but unduly inclusive TABP. Should the role of negative affect in general continue to prove to be of primary significance, the field sometimes labeled psychocardiology will doubtless merge with the larger effort under way to understand the influences of personality in all aspects of health and its maintenance.

PERSONALITY, ILLNESS-PRONENESS, AND HEALTH   The notion that personality influences health originated centuries if not millennia prior to the Holmes & Rahe (1967) demonstration that reported life-change events were associated with the occurrence of illness. The Holmes & Rahe work, however, stimulated psychologists to take a closer look at the nonphysical parameters of physical pathogenesis. And while this early work on the stress-illness relationship was later subjected to withering and to an extent deserved criticism, it seems to have emerged with its essentials more or less intact (Maddi et al 1987). Stressful events increase the likelihood of subsequent disease. This is not to say, of course, that stress plays a causative role in all diseases.

All persons experience stress, within generally accepted definitions of the term, and their health is variously compromised in undergoing such experiences. It is precisely this variance—insofar as it cannot be accounted for by reference to measurable physical properties of the organism—that justifies the intervention of psychologists in the health arena, an arena whose psychological dimensions are currently expanding at a rate that threatens to exceed the supply of appropriately trained psychological personnel.

If we exclude the classic "neurotic" medical patient, whose often multiple complaints are not apt to be matched by objectively determined health status (Costa & McCrae 1987; see also Miller et al 1988), issues of personality concern both the "disease-prone" personality and the "hardy" one (to use terms common in the literature). Concerning the former, Friedman & Booth-Kewley (1987b) provided a recent quantitative overview of the field to recent times. Focusing on asthma, arthritis, ulcers, and headaches, in addition to coronary heart disease, they find evidence of a generic disease-prone personality type. The major constituent traits are depression, anger/hostility, and anxiety. Another recent review by Jemmott (1987) suggests the addition of excessive power motives to the list. With the exception of CHD, however, the evidence, though consistent, is not strong. Friedman & Booth-Kewley appropriately caution against overinterpreting their meta-analytic results, especially in view of the fact that in most of the aggregated studies negative affective states may have followed from rather than helped to cause the diseases studied.

As several commentators (e.g. Holroyd & Coyne 1987; Krantz & Hedges 1987; Suls & Rittenhouse 1987) have suggested, we are unlikely to discover (and reliably measure) personality traits and trait-like states that will account for large outcome variances in health status. We may achieve predictive power approaching that of other known risk factors for a given disease, which typically proves less than impressive. Global traits are in this respect far less good bets than more sharply delimited personality variables, especially when the latter can be tied conceptually to the outcomes of interest on a priori theoretical grounds. Some work more nearly approaching this ideal is considered below.

Because psychological depression may increase risk of illness, it is significant that explanatory style (described above) appears itself to be directly associated with an increased likelihood of contracting disease. This finding is the product of an ingenious study by Peterson & Seligman (1987) that made use of the CAVE (Content Analysis of Verbatim Explanations) variation of the Attributional Style Questionnaire on decidedly nonstandard subject materials, such as the media-reported remarks of Baseball Hall of Famers and official records on health status and survival. One is reminded here of the long-standing but to a large extent anecdotal linking of feelings of hopelessness/helplessness to the occurrence and progression of cancer. The latter hypothesis was in fact confirmed in a recent study of breast cancer progression reported by Jensen (1987). Other results of this study, however, seem inconsistent with the suggested portrait of the victim as a ruminative pessimist; rather, tumor growth was associated with a "repressive" personal style that included, among other manifestations, an attraction to comforting daydreams. This finding is also consistent with certain classic views regarding host susceptibility and cancer progression. A more comprehensive understanding of the psychology involved may eventually resolve this apparent contradiction.

Fortunately, the negative side of the personality-health connection is only part of the story. At least since Kobasa's (1979) introduction of the notion of hardiness, researchers have sought to identify aspects of personality that protect against illness or buffer the pathogenesis of stress (Suls & Rittenhouse 1987). The path of discovery has not proved smooth, as illustrated in Funk & Houston's (1987) scathing review of research using the Hardiness Scale. This device may turn out to be another (inverse) measure of general psychological maladjustment—what is often termed "neuroticism." As we have seen, the latter's relationship to medical illness is suspect (Costa & McCrae 1987). Hull et al (1987) also offer a critique of both the concept and the measurement of hardiness, and question whether "buffering" effects have been demonstrated.

If hardiness exists, it will likely be factorially complex. A better research strategy might therefore be to focus on simpler and more precisely measurable variables or processes. Linville (1987), for example, measured self-complexity by means of a sorting task and demonstrated its substantial buffering effect for flu and other illnesses following stressful events. Affleck et al (1987) reported the benefits of a sense of control and of disease-course predictability among chronic rheumatoid arthritic patients. In line with both the positive health correlates of a nondysfunctional explanatory style (Peterson & Seligman 1987) and the potency of placebos, the trait of optimism should have buffering qualities, as seems indeed to be the case (Scheier & Carver 1987). Of course, undue optimism in the health domain can also be disastrous (Tennen & Affleck 1987).

RELATED PHENOMENA   While we do not know how psychological variables may increase the risk of physical illnesses (including infectious and neoplastic ones), a growing body of evidence suggests that the immune system may be functionally compromised by negative emotional states and events that produce them (Jemmott & Locke 1984; Schleifer et al 1985). Exactly such an effect was recently demonstrated in an exceptionally well-done study by Stone et al (1987). Here, dental students on oral doses of a harmless foreign protein recorded their mood and donated specimens of parotid saliva thrice weekly over a period of 8⅓ weeks. Secretory immunoglobulin A was assayed from the saliva samples as a measure of immune system response to the antigen analogue. The magnitude of an antigen-specific antibody response was positively correlated with variations in daily mood; the immune systems of these students responded more vigorously to foreign-substance invasion the more they enjoyed a sense of well-being. This interface between immunocompetence and personality functioning deserves maximum attention in future health-related research.

Finally, some recent work on pain control should briefly be noted. Bandura et al (1987) report an elegant experiment on cognitive (self-efficacy) control of the experience of pain that included exogenous manipulation of endogenous opioid action. Self-efficacy training increased pain tolerance with or without inhibition by naloxone of endogenous opioid action, and opioid activation itself was enhanced by a sense of efficacy concerning pain management. Complementing these findings is a demonstration by Litt (1988) that changes in self-efficacy to manage pain are accompanied by corresponding changes in pain tolerance. In this study self-efficacy and perceived control made separable but additive contributions to tolerance.

To summarize the personality/health venture is "on a roll." Problems of intimidating magnitude, some unsuspected, remain to be solved; but the thrust of efforts in this area and the progress already made predict an important and exciting future. A past Surgeon General once remarked that the future and perhaps final cutting edge of medical innovation will reside in human personality and behavior. That forecast seems more credible now than it did only a decade ago.

ADDITIONAL NOTEWORTHY AREAS SHOWING PROGRESS

Space constraints permit only the briefest of comments in three other areas of activity that strike me as especially important: genetic influences on personality, the development and outcomes of childhood peer difficulties, and the self-perpetuating nature of personal dispositions. Concerning the first of these, both Loehlin et al (1987) and Rose et al (1988) present additional compelling evidence on the modest heritability of some personality traits. Interestingly, the latter study estimated separately the concordance effects due to within-twinship social contact (which are typically confounded with genetic ones), and these proved not to be negligible.

Parker & Asher (1987) reviewed the adult sequelae of childhood peer problems, concluding that low social acceptance and excessive aggressiveness, particularly, predict such negative outcomes as dropping out and criminality. Meanwhile, Dodge & Coie (1987) have added to the evidence of information-processing aberrations in reactively aggressive youngsters; specifically, these children assign to signals from the social environment a hostile or threatening meaning that is not consensually valid. But, of course, such autistic expectations may mediate the enactment of behaviors that *do* provoke a hostile environmental response, thus confirming (and presumably strengthening future activation of) the original expectations.

In this manner a maladaptive "fix" becomes self-perpetuating, a process I have described in more general terms as crucial to remediation efforts (Carson

1982). Jones (1986) has recently offered a detailed theoretical treatment of trait-related expectancies as self-fulfilling prophecies in interpersonal behavior generally. This rich idea deserves far more attention from researchers than it has yet received. Meanwhile Buss (1987; Buss et al 1987) has been exploring the apparently considerable tactical efforts persons make to control their interpersonal environments, possibly because of the personal identity issues at stake (Swann 1987).

The field's prospects are somewhat happier than they were when Pervin wrote (1985). There is good and exciting work being done, and one can with effort find it among the barren entities that litter the scene.

Literature Cited

Abramson, L. Y., Seligman, M. E. P., Teasdale, J. D. 1978. Learned helplessness in humans: critique and reformulation. *J. Abnorm. Psychol.* 87: 49–74

Affleck, G., Tennen, H., Pfeifer, C., Fifield, J. 1987. Appraisals of control and predictability in adapting to a chronic disease. *J. Pers. Soc. Psychol.* 53: 273–79

Amenson, C. S., Lewinsohn, P. M. 1981. An investigation into the observed sex difference in prevalence of unipolar depression. *J. Abnorm. Psychol.* 90: 1–13

Bandura, A., O'Leary, A., Taylor, C. B., Gauthier, J., Gossard, D. 1987. Perceived self-efficacy and pain control: Opioid and nonopioid mechanisms. *J. Pers. Soc. Psychol.* 53: 563–71

Beck, A. T., Rush, A. J., Shaw, B. F., Emery, G. 1979. *Cognitive Therapy of Depression.* New York: Guilford Press

Bem, S. L. 1974. The measurement of psychological androgyny. *J. Consult. Clin. Psychol.* 42: 155–62

Booth-Kewley, S., Friedman, H. S. 1987. Psychological predictors of heart disease: a quantative review. *Psychol. Bull.* 101: 343–62

Bowers, K. S. 1973. Situationism in psychology: an analysis and critique. *Psychol. Rev.* 80: 307–36

Buss, D. M. 1987. Selection, evocation, and manipulation. *J. Pers. Soc. Psychol.* 53: 1214–21

Buss, D. M., Gomes, M., Higgins, D. S., Lauterbach, K. 1987. Tactics of manipulation. *J. Pers. Soc. Psychol* 53: 1219–29

Carlson, M., Miller, N. 1987. Explanation of the relation between negative mood and helping. *Psychol. Bull.* 102: 91–108

Carson, R. C. 1969. *Interaction Concepts of Personality.* Chicago: Aldine

Carson, R. C. 1982. Self-fulfilling prophecy, maladaptive behavior, and psychotherapy. In *Handbook of Interpersonal Psycho-*

therapy, ed. J. C. Anchin, D. J. Kiesler, 4: 64–77. New York: Pergamon

Carson, R. C., Butcher, J. N., Coleman, J. C. 1988. *Abnormal Psychology and Modern Life.* Glenview, IL: Scott, Foresman. 8th ed.

Clark, M. S., Ouellette, R., Powell, M. C., Milberg, S. 1987. Recipient's mood, relationship type, and helping. *J. Pers. Soc. Psychol.* 53: 94–103

Costa, P. T. Jr., McCrae, R. R. 1987. Neuroticism, somatic complaints, and disease: Is the bark worse than the bite? *J. Pers.* 55: 299–316

Coyne, J. C. 1976. Depression and the response of others. *J. Abnorm. Psychol.* 55: 186–93

Davis, P. J. 1987. Repression and the inaccessibility of affective memories. *J. Pers. Soc. Psychol.* 53: 585–93

Deaux, K. 1985. Sex and gender. *Ann. Rev. Psychol.* 36: 49–82

Deaux, K., Major, B. 1987. Putting gender into context: an interactive model of gender-related behavior. *Psychol. Rev.* 94: 369–89

Dembroski, T. M., Costa, P. T. 1987. Coronary prone behavior: components of the Type A pattern and hostility. *J. Pers.* 55: 211–35

Dembroski, T. M., Weiss, S., Shields, J., Haynes, S. G., Feinleib, M., eds. 1978. *Coronary-Prone Behavior.* New York: Springer-Verlag

Dodge, K. A., Coie, J. D. 1987. Social-information-processing factors in reactive and proactive aggression in children's peer groups. *J. Pers. Soc. Psychol.* 53: 1146–58

Edwards, V. J., Spence, J. T. 1987. Gender-related traits, stereotypes, and schemata. *J. Pers. Soc. Psychol.* 53: 146–54

Ekehammar, B. 1974. Interactionism in personality from a historical perspective. *Psychol. Bull.* 81: 1026–48

Evans, G. W., Palsane, M. N., Carrere, S.

1987. Type A behavior and occupational distress: a cross-cultural study of blue-collar workers. *J. Pers. Soc. Psychol.* 52: 1002–7

Fischman, J. 1987. Type A on trial. *Psychol. Today* 21: 42–50

Follette, V. M., Jacobson, N. S. 1987. Importance of attributions as a predictor of how people cope with failure. *J. Pers. Soc. Psychol.* 52: 1205–11

Forgas, J. P., Bower, G. H. 1987 Mood effects on person-perception judgments. *J. Pers. Soc. Psychol.* 53: 53–60

Frable, D. E. S. 1987. Sex-typed execution and perception of expressive movement. *J. Pers. Soc. Psychol.* 53: 391–96

Freidman, H. S., Booth-Kewley, S. 1987a. Personality, Type A behavior, and coronary heart disease: the role of emotional expression. *J. Pers. Soc. Psychol.* 53: 783–92

Friedman, H. S., Booth-Kewley, S. 1987b. The "disease-prone personality:" a meta-analytic view of the construct. *Am. Psychol.* 42: 539–55

Funk, S. C., Houston, B. K. 1987. A critical analysis of the Hardiness Scale's validity and utility. *J. Pers. Soc. Psychol.* 53: 572–78

Gaeddert, W. P. 1987. The relationship of gender, gender-related traits, and achievement orientation to achievement attributions: a study of subject-selected accomplishments. *J. Pers.* 55: 687–710

Gifford, R., O'Connor, B. 1987. The interpersonal circumplex as a behavioral map. *J. Pers. Soc. Psychol.* 52: 1019–26

Halberstadt, A. G., Saitta, M. B. 1987. Gender, nonverbal behavior, and perceived dominance: a test of the theory. *J. Pers. Soc. Psychol.* 53: 257–72

Haynes, S. G., Feinleib, M., Kannel, W. B. 1980. The relationship of psychosocial factors to coronary heart disease in the Framingham study. III. Eight-year incidence of coronary heart disease. *Am. J. Epidemiol.* 111: 37–58

Higgins, E. T. 1987. Self-discrepancy: a theory relating self and affect. *Psychol. Rev.* 94: 319–40

Hollon, S. D., DeRubeis, R. J., Evans, M. D. 1987. Causal mediation of change in treatment for depression: discriminating between nonspecificity and noncausality. *Psychol. Bull.* 102:139–49

Holmes, T. H., Rahe, R. H. 1967. The social readjustment rating scale. *J. Psychosomatic Res.* 11: 213–18

Holroyd, K. A., Coyne, J. 1987. Personality and health in the 1980s: psychosomatic medicine revisited? *J. Pers.* 55: 359–75

Howes, M. J., Hokanson, J. E., Loewenstein, D. A. 1985. Induction of depressive affect after prolonged exposure to a mildly depressed individual. *J. Pers. Soc. Psychol.* 49: 1110–13

Hull, J. G., Van Treuren, R. R., Virnelli, S. 1987. Hardiness and health: a critique and alternative approach. *J. Pers. Soc. Psychol.* 53: 518–30

Hyland, M. E. 1987. Control theory interpretation of psychological mechanisms of depression: comparison and integration of several theories. *Psychol. Bull.* 102: 109–21

Ingram, R. E., Kendall, P. C., Smith, T. W., Donnell, C., Ronan, K. 1987. Cognitive specificity in emotional distress. *J. Pers. Soc. Psychol.* 53: 734–42

Jemmott, J. B. III. 1987. Social motives and susceptibility to disease: Stalking individual differences in health risks. *J. Pers.* 55: 267–98

Jemmott, J. B. III, Locke, S. E. 1984. Psychosocial factors, immunologic mediation, and human susceptibility to infectious diseases: How much do we know? *Psychol. Bull.* 95: 78–108

Jenkins, C. D., Zyzansk, S. J., Rosenman, R. H. 1979. *Jenkins Activity Survey.* New York: The Psychological Corp.

Jensen, M. R. 1987. Psychobiological factors predicting the course of breast cancer. *J. Pers.* 55: 317–42

Jones, E. E. 1986. Interpreting interpersonal behavior: the effects of expectancies. *Science* 234: 41–46

Katz, K. N. 1987. Self-reference in the encoding of creative-relevant traits. *J. Pers.* 55: 97–120

Kenrick, D. T., Funder, D. C. 1988. Profiting from controversy: lessons from the person-situation debate. *Am. Psychol.* 43:23–34

Kihlstrom, J. F. 1987. Introduction to the special issue: integrating personality and social psychology. *J. Pers. Soc. Psychol.* 53: 989–92

Kobasa, S. C. 1979. Stressful life events, personality, and health: an inquiry into hardiness. *J. Pers. Soc. Psychol.* 37: 1–11

Krantz, D. S., Hedges, S. M. 1987. Some cautions for research on personality and health. *J. Pers.* 55: 351–57

Larsen, R. J., Diener, E., Cropanzano, R. S. 1987 Cognitive operations associated with individual differences in affect intensity. *J. Pers. Soc. Psychol.* 53:767–74

Leary, T. 1957. *Interpersonal Diagnosis of Personality.* New York: Ronald

Leslie, A. M. 1987. Pretense and representation: the origins of "Theory of Mind." *Psychol. Rev.* 94: 412–26

Linville, P. W. 1987. Self-complexity as a cognitive buffer against stress-related illness and depression. *J. Pers. Soc. Psychol.* 52: 663–76

Litt, M. D. 1988. Self-efficacy and perceived control: cognitive mediators of pain tolerance. *J. Pers. Soc. Psychol.* 54: 149–60

Loehlin, J. C., Willerman, L., Horn, J. M. 1987. Personality resemblances in adoptive families: a 10-year follow–up. *J. Pers. Soc. Psychol.* 53: 961–69

MacEvoy, B., Lambert, W. W., Karlberg, P., Karlberg, J., Klackenberg-Larsson, I., Klackenberg, G. 1988. Early affective antecedents of adult Type A behavior. *J. Pers. Soc. Psychol.* 54: 108–16

Maddi, S. R., Bartone, P. T., Puccetti, M. C. 1987. Stressful events are indeed a factor in physical illness: reply to Schroeder and Costa (1984). *J. Pers. Soc. Psychol.* 52: 833–43

Marsh, H. W., Antill, J. K., Cunningham, J. D. 1987. Masculinity, femininity, and androgyny: relations to self-esteem and social desirability. *J. Pers.* 55: 661–83

McCrae, R. R., Costa, P. T. 1986. Clinical assessment can benefit from recent advances in personality psychology. *Am. Psychol.* 41: 1001–2

McGraw, K. M. 1987. Guilt following transgression: an attribution of responsibility approach. *J. Pers. Soc. Psychol.* 53: 247–56

Meehl, P. E. 1978. Theoretical risks and tabular asterisks: Sir Karl, Sir Ronald, and the slow progress of soft psychology. *J. Consult. Clin. Psychol.* 46: 806–34

Merleau-Ponty, M. 1963. *The Structure of Behavior.* Boston: Beacon Press

Miller, S. M., Brody, D. S., Summerton, J. 1988. Styles of coping with threat: implications for health. *J. Pers. Soc. Psychol.* 54: 142–48

Mischel, W. 1968. *Personality and Assessment.* New York: Wiley

Mischel, W. 1973. Toward a cognitive social learning reconceptualization of personality. *Psychol. Rev.* 80: 252–83

Neisser, U. 1980. On "social knowing." *Pers. Soc. Psychol. Bull.* 6: 601–5

Nolen-Hoeksema, S. 1987. Sex differences in unipolar depression: evidence and theory. *Psychol. Bull.* 101: 259–82

Noller, P., Law, H., Comrey, A. L. 1987. Cattell, Comrey, and Eysenck personality factors compared: more evidence for the five robust factors? *J. Pers. Soc. Psychol.* 53: 775–82

Oppenheimer, R. 1956. Analogy in science. *Am. Psychol.* 11: 127–35

Orlofsky, J. L., O'Heron, C. A. 1987. Stereotypic and nonstereotypic sex role trait and behavior orientations: implications for personal adjustment. *J. Pers. Soc. Psychol.* 52: 1034–42

Pagel, M., Becker, J. 1987. Depressive thinking and depression: relations with personality and social resources. *J. Pers. Soc. Psychol.* 52: 1043–52

Parker, J. G., Asher, S. R. 1987. Peer relations and later personal adjustment: are low-accepted children at risk? *Psychol. Bull.* 102: 357–89

Paulhus, D. L. 1987. Effects of group selection on correlations and factor patterns in sex role research. *J. Pers. Soc. Psychol.* 53: 314–17

Payne, T. J., Connor, J. M., Coletti, G. 1987. Gender-based schematic processing: an empirical investigation and reevaluation. *J. Pers. Soc. Psychol.* 52: 937–45

Pervin, L. A. 1985. Personality: current controversies, issues, and directions. *Ann. Rev. Psychol.* 36: 83–114

Peterson, C., Barrett, L. C. 1987. Explanatory style and academic performance among university freshmen. *J. Pers. Soc. Psychol.* 53: 603–7

Peterson, C., Seligman, M. E. P. 1987. Explanatory style and illness. *J. Pers.* 55: 237–65

Peterson, C., Villanova, P., Raps, C. S. 1985. Depression and attributions: factors responsible for inconsistent results in the published literature. *J. Abnorm. Psychol.* 94: 165–68

Pyszczynski, T., Greenberg, J. 1987. Self-regulatory perseveration and the depressive self-focusing style: a self-awareness theory of reactive depression. *Psychol. Bull.* 102: 122–38

Pyszczynski, T., Holt, K., Greenberg, J. 1987. Depression, self-focused attention, and expectancies for positive and negative future life events for self and others. *J. Pers. Soc. Psychol.* 52: 994–1001

Riskind, J. H., Rholes, W. S., Brannon, A. M., Burdick, C. A. 1987. Attributions and expectations: a confluence of vulnerabilities in mild depression in a college student population. *J. Pers. Soc. Psychol.* 53: 349–54

Rose, R. J., Koskenvuo, M., Kaprio, J., Seppo, S., Langinvainio, H. 1988. Shared genes, shared experiences, and similarity of personality: data from 14,288 adult Finnish co-twins. *J. Pers. Soc. Psych.* 54: 161–71

Rosenman, R. H., Brand, R. J., Jenkins, C. D., Friedman, M., Straus, R. 1975. Coronary heart disease in the Western Collaborative Group Study: final follow-up experience of 8-1/2 years. *J. Am. Med. Assoc.* 233: 872–77

Sacks, C. H., Bugental, D. B. 1987. Attributions as moderators of affective and behavioral responses to social failure. *J. Pers. Soc. Psychol.* 53: 939–47

Sadalla, E. K., Kenrick, D. T., Vershure, B.

1987. Dominance and heterosexual attraction. *J. Pers. Soc. Psychol.* 52: 730–38

Schaefer, E. S., Burnett, C. K. 1987. Stability and predictability of women's marital relationships and demoralization. *J. Pers. Soc. Psychol.* 53: 1129–36

Scheier, M. F., Carver, C. S. 1987. Dispositional optimism and physical well-being: the influence of generalized outcome expectancies on health. *J. Pers.* 55: 169–210

Schleifer, S. J., Keller, S. E., Stein, M. 1985. Central nervous system mechanisms and immunity: implications for tumor response. In *Behavior and Cancer*, S. M. Levy, pp. 120–33. San Francisco: Jossey-Bass

Seligman, M. E. P. 1975. *Helplessness: On Depression, Development, and Death.* San Francisco: W. H. Freeman

Seligman, M. E. P., Abramson, L. Y., Semmel, A., von Baeyer, C. 1979. Depressive attributional style. *J. Abnorm. Psychol.* 88: 242–47

Shaver, P., Schwartz, J., Kirson, D., O'Connor, C. 1987. Emotion knowledge: further exploration of a prototype approach. *J. Pers. Soc. Psychol.* 52: 1061–86

Stephens, R. S., Hokanson, J. E., Welker, R. 1987. Responses to depressed interpersonal behavior: mixed reactions in a helping role. *J. Pers. Soc. Psychol.* 52: 1274–82

Stone, A. A., Cox, D. S., Valdimarsdottir, H., Jandorf, N., Neale, J. M. 1987. Evidence that secretory IgA antibody is associated with daily mood. *J. Pers. Soc. Psychol.* 52: 988–93

Strauman, T. J., Higgins, E. T. 1987. Automatic activation of self-discrepancies and emotional syndromes: when cognitive structures influence affect. *J. Pers. Soc. Psychol.* 53: 1004–14

Strube, M. J., Boland, S. M., Manfredo, P. A., Abdulrahman, A-F. 1987. Type A behavior pattern and the self-evaluation of abilities: empirical tests of the self-appraisal model. *J. Pers. Soc. Psychol.* 52: 956–74

Sullivan, H. S. 1953. *The Interpersonal Theory of Psychiatry.* New York: Norton

Suls, J., Rittenhouse, J. D. 1987. Personality and physical health: an introduction. *J. Pers.* 55: 155–67

Swann, W. B. Jr. 1987. Identity negotiation: where two roads meet. *J. Pers. Soc. Psychol.* 53: 1038–51

Tennen, H., Affleck, G. 1987. The costs and benefits of optimistic explanations and dispositional optimism. *J. Pers.* 55: 377–93

Tennen, H., Herzberger, S., Nelson, H. F. 1987. Depressive attributional style: the role of self-esteem. *J. Pers.* 55: 631–60

Waller, N. G., Ben-Porath, Y. S. 1987. Is it time for clinical psychology to embrace the five-factor model of personality? *Am. Psychol.* 42: 887–89

Ward, C. H., Eisler, R. M. 1987. Type A behavior, achievement striving, and a dysfunctional self-evaluation system. *J. Pers. Soc. Psychol.* 53: 318–26

Wegner, D. M., Schneider, D. J., Carter, S. R. III, White, T. L. 1987. Paradoxical effects of thought suppression. *J. Pers. Soc. Psychol.* 53: 5–13

West, S. G. 1987. An editorial transition. *J. Pers.* 55: iii–vi

Wiggins, J. S. 1979. A psychological taxonomy of trait-descriptive terms: the interpersonal domain. *J. Pers. Soc. Psychol.* 37: 395–412

Wiggins, J. S., Holzmuller, A. 1978. Psychological androgyny and interpersonal behavior. *J. Consult. Clin. Psychol.* 46: 40–52

Wiggins, J. S., Holzmuller, A. 1981. Further evidence on androgyny and interpersonal flexibility. *J. Res. Pers.* 15: 67–80

Wiggins, J. S., Phillips, N., Trapnell, P. 1988. Circular reasoning about interpersonal behavior: evidence concerning some untested assumptions underlying diagnostic classification. *J. Pers. Soc. Psychol.* In press

Wing, J. K., Bebbington, P. 1985. Epidemiology of depression. In *Handbook of Depression: Treatment, Assessment, and Research*, ed. E. E. Beckham, W. R. Leber, pp. 765–94, Homewood, IL: Dorsey Press

Wollert, R., Rowley, J. 1987. Concurrent and longitudinal patterns among sanctions, mood, and attributions. *J. Pers. Soc. Psychol.* 53: 608–13

Wood, C. 1986. The hostile heart. *Psychol. Today* 20: 10–12

Wright, J. C., Mischel, W. 1987. A conditional approach to dispositional constructs: the local predictability of social behavior. *J. Pers. Soc. Psychol.* 53: 1159–77

Wyer, R. S., Budesheim, T. L. 1987. Person memory and judgments: the impact of information that one is told to disregard. *J. Pers. Soc. Psychol.* 53: 14–29

Zener, K. 1937. The significance of behavior accompanying conditioned salivary secretion for theories of the conditioned response. *Am. J. Psychol.* 50: 384–403

Zuckerman, M., Kuhlman, M., Camac, K. 1988. What lies beyond E and N? Factor analysis of scales believed to measure basic dimensions of personality. *J. Pers. Soc. Psychol.* 54: 96–107

Ann. Rev. Psychol. 1989. 40:249–80

FACIAL EFFERENCE AND THE EXPERIENCE OF EMOTION

Pamela K. Adelmann and R. B. Zajonc

Department of Psychology and the Research Center for Group Dynamics, The University of Michigan, Ann Arbor, Michigan 48109

CONTENTS

INTRODUCTION

In this review, we consider the nature and role of facial expression in emotional processes. We examine the recent theoretical and empirical literature for its bearing on the questions of the proximal and distal correlates of facial emotional actions, particularly on the question of their modulating and initiating functions in the experience of emotion. We emphasize the role of emotional facial action in the subjective experience of emotion.

We avoid in this paper the convention of referring to emotional facial action as "expression" since that term imposes an a priori theory, implying that

249

0066–4308/89/0201–0249$02.00

emotional facial action (facial efference) has as its major role the manifestation of internal states. This as the primary role of facial action has not been established as an empirical fact, and thus it is best for now to employ a term that does not prejudge the outcome of empirical and theoretical analysis. While the term "facial efference" is less agile and less common, it has the advantage of being neutral with respect to the kind of principles that would be called upon to explain it.

Before examining the empirical evidence on facial efference and its correlates, we briefly review the major theoretical perspectives on facial efference: sensory, evolutionary, and facial feedback.

Pre-Darwinian Sensory Theories of Emotion

Two physiologists working at the second half of the 19th century, Theodor Piderit (1858, 1888) and Pierre Gratiolet (1865), based the explanation of facial emotional action on the sensory system. According to both theories, facial movements are generalizations of peripheral muscular actions elicited in the course of the sensory and perceptual process. Thus, the facial action accompanying the emotion of disgust is similar to that occurring when the individual reacts to an unsavory taste. Both theories point out that peripheral movements can also be elicited by imagination; for example, ocular accommodation and convergence show different patterns when one thinks of threading a needle than when one imagines a ship on the horizon. Gratiolet (1865) noted the close affinity between *sensation* and *sentiment,* where the former dealt with stimuli that came from the exterior whereas the latter with those that came from the interior. Sentiment, or *sens intime* is an experience that originates within the organism, and as such it constitutes the basic element of emotion. He also distinguished *symbolic* and *metaphoric* movements, where the former is illustrated by a bowler's movement following his bowling ball and the latter by the gesture of contempt that is a metaphor for a reaction to an unpleasant odor.

Gratiolet held that "no sensation, image, or thought . . . can occur without evoking a correlated sentiment which translates itself directly . . . into all spheres of external organs . . . " (1865, p. 65). More interestingly, however, he insisted that the converse is equally true. "The movements and bodily attitudes," he wrote (p. 66), "even if they arise from fortuitous causes, evoke correlated sentiments, which in turn influence imagination, feeling, and thought."

Gratiolet did not refer to Piderit, whose theory was strikingly similar, although Piderit (1888) claims to have presented his ideas in Paris in 1859 at a meeting of the Biological Society, of which Gratiolet was a member and which publishes the *Gazette Médicale,* which printed Piderit's presentation in issue #46.

Evolutionary Theory of Emotion

Darwin's views on the communicative and adaptive function of facial efference, being well known, need not be described here. It is worth noting,
however, that he rejected both Piderit's and Gratiolet's writings. He says of
the latter, "Although Gratiolet emphatically denies that any muscle has been
developed solely for the sake of expression, he seems never to have reflected
on the principle of evolution" (1896, p. 11). And to Piderit, who sent his book
to Darwin, the latter wrote:

> I have a copy and know of your work on Mimic, etc. which I have found very useful and
> often quote. But I am a poor German scholar and your style. . . . I find very difficult to
> understand. Accordingly I employed a man to translate for me several pages. These I have
> given in my introduction, in order to state, as far as possible by a few sentences, your
> views. I fear that I may not do you full justice, but assuredly I tried my best to do it (Piderit
> 1888, pp. 7–8).

In reference to this letter, Piderit says that even if Darwin had known German
better he would not have paid more attention to the sensory theory of
emotional expression because, as in other work, Darwin was only interested
in discovering new evidence for his theory of evolution ["Darwin ne cherche
ici, comme dans tous ses autres travaux, qu'à découvrir de nouveaux documents en faveur de sa théorie de l'évolution" (1888, pp. 7–8).] Piderit's
perception of Darwin's motives seems accurate, as Darwin concludes his
book by asserting that emotional expression is indeed a further demonstration
of how "man is derived from some lower animal form" (1896, p. 365).

Despite Darwin's preeminent interest in promoting evolutionary theory in
his work on emotion, his admission of a possible causal role of efference in
the emotional experience foreshadowed the development of the facial feedback hypothesis. "The free expression by outward signs of an emotion
intensifies it," he wrote. "On the other hand, the repression, as far as this is
possible, of all outward signs softens our emotions" (1896, p. 365).

Development of the Facial Feedback Hypothesis

JAMESIAN THEORY   The facial feedback theory of emotional efference derives in part from William James, who in proposing his famous theory of
emotion in 1884 introduced the possibility of a causal role of the face in the
experience of emotion. His often quoted statement that "the bodily changes
follow directly the perception of the exciting fact, and that our feeling of the
same changes as they occur is the emotion" (p. 13, 1922) was frequently
construed later by critics to include only, or primarily, visceral changes as
feedback. Yet in his original formulation of the feedback theory he named not
only visceral but respiratory, cutaneous, and circulatory alterations. In addition, he wrote, "what is really equally prominent, but less likely to be

admitted until special attention is drawn to the fact, is the continuous cooperation of the voluntary muscles in our emotional states. Even when no change of outward attitude is produced, their inward tension alters to suit each varying mood, and is felt as a difference of tone or of strain" (p. 15). Even in his somewhat revised statement in *The Principles of Psychology* (1890), the role of muscles in the experience of emotion was not discounted as thoroughly as his critics contended (e.g. Cannon 1927, 1931). He continued to refer to the "indefinitely numerous" and "the immense number" of bodily reverberations corresponding to each emotion, including among them visceral, muscular, and cutaneous effects.

As for the facial musculature, although he did not specifically distinguish it from the skeletal musculature as a source of feedback in emotional experience, virtually every example James employed to illustrate his hypothesis included some reference to facial efference. "Smooth the brow, brighten the eye, contract the dorsal rather than the ventral aspect of the frame, and speak in a major key, pass the genial compliment, and your heart must be frigid indeed if it does not gradually thaw!" he wrote (p. 1078). And, he asked, "Can one fancy the state of rage and picture no ebullition in the chest, no flushing of the face, no dilatation of the nostrils, no clenching of the teeth . . ." (p. 1067–68)?

Even so, in his most specific reference to facial efference in *The Principles,* James admitted that its influence in the generation of feeling was overshadowed by the corresponding visceral and organic components of emotion. Anticipating the criticism that among actors and others with extensive practice in posing facial emotional actions, voluntary efference does not always produce subjective feeling, he argued that these highly trained individuals may have learned to suppress the "natural association" between efference and the visceral and organic components of emotion, on the latter of which "it is probable that the chief part of the felt emotion depends" (p. 1080). For less practiced individuals, he seemed to believe that voluntarily effecting the "so-called manifestations" of an emotion ought to give rise to that emotion. He also admitted, "We may catch the trick with the voluntary muscles, but fail with the skin, glands, heart, and other viscera. Just as an artificially initiated sneeze lacks something of the reality, so the attempt to imitate an emotion in the absence of its normal instigating cause is apt to be rather 'hollow'" (p. 1066).

Although James ascribed to the skeletal musculature a lesser role in initiating emotion than other organs, he nevertheless clearly included this source of feedback as an integral component of his theory. In 1890 as in his earlier formulation, he proposed four steps in the generation of subjective experience of emotion: a sensory stimulus (of either external or internal origin) is transmitted to the cortex and perceived; reflex impulses travel to muscle, skin, and viscera; the resulting alterations in these targets are transmitted via afferent pathways back to the brain; these return impulses are then cortically perceived, and when combined with the original stimulus perception, produce the "object-emotionally-felt."

Sherrington (1900) and Cannon (1915, 1927, 1931), however, seized on James's admission that felt emotion may rely more heavily on visceral and organic than other components as the basis of their attacks on his theory. Drawing on animal research, they built a convincing argument that visceral feedback was an inadequate determinant of emotion. Sherrington (1900) cited his research on animals in which the autonomic nervous system afferent pathways from the shoulders down were destroyed, thus eliminating feedback from the viscera. When presented with an emotion stimulus, the dogs reacted with all appearance of a normal "emotional psychosis," including facial efference, head and foreleg movements, and vocalizations. His recommendation was therefore to "accept visceral and organic sensations and the memories and associations of them as contributory to primitive emotion, but we must regard them as reenforcing rather than initiating the psychosis" (p. 258).

Cannon (1927) developed a five-point attack on the Jamesian theory. Like Sherrington, he named the animal research showing an unimpaired emotional reaction in the absence of visceral feedback (Cannon 1915). He also argued that visceral changes—heart rate acceleration, inhibition of digestive activity, sweating, and others—occur uniformly across a variety of emotional states and are too diffuse to discriminate among them. The viscera are relatively insensitive structures, he continued, and changes in them are much slower than the average latent period of an affective reaction. Finally, he argued that artificial induction by adrenalin of emotion-like visceral changes does not produce the subjective experience of an emotion unless a mood is already present.

The attacks by Sherrington and Cannon brought a stream of response from people such as Angell (1916), Floyd Allport (1924), and Perry (1926), who in rising to James's defense offered theoretical interpretations placing more emphasis on the role of the skeletal musculature in emotion. Angell, for example, declared that James "nowhere set himself the task of attempting to differentiate emotions on exactly the basis suggested by Dr. Cannon's statement" (1916, p. 259). James would have agreed, he contended, that in some emotions identical patterns of visceral excitement might occur, but might have then argued that "their distinction from one another in such cases may be found in extra-visceral conditions, and particularly in the tonus of the skeletal muscles" (p. 260). He further argued, of Sherrington's head-and-shoulder dogs, that "no evidence which left facial and cranial muscles unimpaired would ever have seemed to him very convincing as ground for conclusions unfavorable to his theory" (p. 261). Perry (1926), in a similar vein, responded to Cannon that distinctions among emotions "may lie in the proprioceptive rather than in their interoceptive patterns; that is to say, in the motor set rather than in the visceral reverberation" (pp. 300–1).

Allport (1924) argued that although the autonomic nervous system may not discriminate among discrete emotions, it does differentiate the class of positive emotions from the negative. He assigned to the cranio-sacral division responsibility for the "conscious quality of pleasantness," and to the sympathetic division the "visceral responses which are represented in consciousness as unpleasant" (p. 90). Further, Allport proposed that within a single affective class "the differentiating factor arises from the stimulation of the proprioceptors in the muscles, tendons, and joints of the somatic part of the organism; and that afferent impulses from these somatic patterns of response add to the autonomic core of affectivity the characteristic sensory complexes by which one emotion is distinguished from another" (pp. 91–92). To this he added that "the facial expressions as well as bodily movements are strongly differential" (p. 92).

Indeed, Cannon had a more difficult time in dismissing the muscular component of James's theory. He claimed simply that "sensations which underlie the appreciation of posture are entirely lacking feeling-tone" (1927, p. 119). He acknowledged that motor attitude seems to influence subjective experience, but argued that instead of providing sensory feedback, certain postures remove the usual motor cortex inhibition of the thalamus, the structure at the center of his theory of emotion, thus facilitating subjective experience.

Neither James's critics nor his defenders defined a specific role of the facial muscles in emotion, a definition that was not to appear for several decades. But in the interim, Nina Bull proposed her Attitude Theory of Emotion (Bull 1951; Pasquarelli & Bull 1951), which revived and extended the muscular aspect of Jamesian theory.

THE ATTITUDE THEORY   In the *Attitude Theory,* Bull argued that confusion about whether bodily change or subjective experience comes first was due to a failure to separate emotional efference into its component parts. James was mistaken, she explained, only in that he focused on the action component rather than on the preparatory motor attitude: "We feel angry as a result of readiness to strike, and feel afraid as a result of readiness to run away, and not because of actually hitting out or running, as James explained the sequence" (1951, p. 6).

Bull postulated that the involuntary postural attitudes preparatory to action are accompanied by appropriate organic changes, and that "feelings of these organic changes combine with the feelings of the orienting posture itself—and with some awareness of the original exciting stimulus—to produce the familiar experience known as an 'emotion'" (p. 5). She further suggested that feeling "may follow and accompany a motor attitude, but does not necessarily do so; and cannot possibly precede it—cannot in fact appear at all without an antecedent motor attitude to fire the afferent pathways from the muscles and viscera to the brain" (p. 19).

To test the Attitude Theory, Pasquarelli & Bull (1951) first induced in subjects an emotion and its corresponding motor attitude through hypnosis, using such directions as these (for anger): "Your hands are getting tense and your arms are getting tense. You can feel your jaw tightening." They then "locked" this attitude, and suggested the feeling, but not the attitude, of a contrasting emotion. In some trials an unpleasant emotion (disgust, anger, fear, or depression) was locked and a pleasant one (joy, triumph) suggested and on the others the reverse sequence was followed.

Without exception, subjects reported they could not successfully "feel" the suggested emotion while locked in the contrasting attitude. Those who changed their feeling to the new emotion could do so only by disobeying the suggestion prohibiting changes in efference or organic sensation.

Like those who preceded her, Bull did not assign a special role to the face, although the hypnotic suggestions to subjects included instructions for facial as well as bodily motor attitude. But within the next decade, emotion theorists began to postulate a specific and central role of the facial musculature in the experience of emotion. These postulates, embedded within comprehensive theories of emotion, came to be known as the facial feedback hypotheses.

FACIAL FEEDBACK HYPOTHESES   First among these theorists was Silvan Tomkins, who in a wide-ranging two-volume set of books (1962, 1963) introduced the notion of facial feedback. "Most contemporary investigators have pursued the inner bodily responses, after the James-Lange theory focused attention on their significance," he explained. "Important as these undoubtedly are, we regard them as of secondary importance to the expression of emotion through the face. . . . the face expresses affect, both to others, and to the self, via feedback, which is more rapid and more complex than any stimulation of which the slower moving visceral organs are capable" (1962, pp. 205–6). As providing feedback from the face he listed the tongue and facial muscles, the sound of one's own voice in the ears, and changes in blood-flow and temperature of the face. He futher regarded the facial muscles as more informative of affective state than those of the trunk and extremities, thereby making a clear statement about the face apart from the other skeletal muscles.

Tomkins built his case for the primacy of the face upon several arguments. First, he argued the face is the most sensitive and dominant part of the body, with a high density of "neural representation and firing" (1962, p. 208). He noted that in contrast to other responses, involuntary facial responses are highly resistant to habituation. In addition, the facial muscles lack a fascial cover that binds muscles elsewhere in the body together into groups, so that in the face, "smaller muscle portions or even single muscle bundles may contract independently of the rest of the muscle" (p. 225) in a variety of complex patterns.

In the Tomkins feedback cycle, a stimulus activates an innate, subcortical "affect program," which emits messages through the motor and circulatory pathways to the entire body. The responses of the affected motor and glandular targets—the face primarily, other sites secondarily—supply sensory feedback to the brain, which, if it reaches consciousness, is subjectively experienced as emotion. Tomkins argued that this feedback may be acted upon whether or not it reaches awareness, that voluntary facial efference may not accurately duplicate the innate pattern, and that the sequence may be initiated by retrieved conscious affect or central imagery as well as by an external emotion stimulus.

He later modified his theory somewhat to downplay the facial muscles ["Muscles appear to be specialized for action and not for affect" (1980, p. 149)] and focused instead on the facial skin as playing the greatest role in producing feelings of affect. He specifically argued that in an expressive face, receptors normally hidden in the skin change position in response to the facial muscle patterns; the feedback is therefore from these cutaneous receptors rather than from the muscles of the face.

Both muscles and skin played important roles in Gellhorn's (1964) view of facial feedback, and both bodily and facial muscles were assigned important roles. Gellhorn argued that body posture influences affective arousal through the proprioceptive discharges feeding back to alter hypothalamic balance. But because such diverse states as happiness and tenseness are both associated with increased proprioceptive postural discharges, while low muscle tone accompanies sadness as well as "postprandial happiness," he considered the proprioceptive feedback provided by bodily posture to be insufficient to distinguish among discrete emotions. For this differentiating information he turned to the face.

"The great density of the cutaneous receptors in the face and the considerable variety of the patterns of contraction of the facial muscles suggest that the resulting patterns of neocortical excitation and hypothalamic-cortical discharges will match in diversity that of the emotional expression," he wrote (1964, p. 465). He argued that the proprioceptive facial-muscle discharges arouse the hypothalamic-cortical system, while tactile impulses are conveyed to sensorimotor cortex. In combination, these two sources of feedback "play an important role in the development of the emotions and a subsidiary role in their reinforcement after they have been established," he claimed (p. 468).

Izard voiced a similar view in his Differential Emotions Theory (1971). He contended that the primary components of emotion are neural activity, striate muscle or facial-postural activity, and subjective experience, augmented by the brain stem reticular system and the glandular-visceral system. In his sequence of events, a stimulus perception activates central neural activity (in an unknown order to the brain stem, hypothalamus, and limbic cortex), producing a global pleasant or unpleasant feeling. The hypothalamus signals the smooth and striate muscles (perhaps in a discrete emotion-specific pattern to the face). The specificity of the facial muscle feedback to the brain stem, hypothalamus, limbic system, thalamus, and possibly cortex determines the specificity of the felt emotion. Feedback from the auxiliary systems (including visceral, glandular, cardiovascular, and respiratory) helps sustain and amplify the subjective experience. He added that for a specific facial pattern to match subjective experience, it must correspond to the original efferent pattern, the neural message must travel innate pathways for the emotion, and the feedback must be reasonably complete (e.g. slight or micromomentary efference may produce only fleeting awareness).

In sum, although their ideas varied somewhat in the particulars, these three theorists in quick succession proposed a specific and central role of the face in the experience of emotion. Their thoughts inspired a wealth of empirical research on the facial feedback hypothesis.

INVESTIGATING FACIAL FEEDBACK

In the course of empirical investigation of facial feedback, several versions of the hypothesis have evolved. The most basic, drawn directly from the theories of Tomkins, Gellhorn, and Izard, is considered first. It proposes simply that in the process of a naturally occurring emotional experience, there will be a correspondence between facial efference and subjective experience. Implicit in this version are the notions that strength of efference and intensity of subjective experience covary, and that specific efference patterns correspond with specific subjective states.

Although in the original facial feedback hypotheses autonomic arousal was assigned only an auxiliary role, at most amplifying or sustaining an emotional experience, others have pursued the Jamesian notion that facial efference patterns correspond with patterns of autonomic arousal as well. Thus, research has also addressed whether facial efference and arousal covary in intensity and whether arousal patterns are differential, at the least, for positive versus negative emotional efference patterns, and, at most, for a variety of discrete facial efference patterns. The correlational literature on facial efference, physiological arousal, and subjective experience addresses these questions arising from the original facial feedback hypotheses.

Correlational Studies of Facial Efference and Emotional Experience

In the correlational literature on facial feedback, external stimuli such as films, electric shock, and slides are most typically used as elicitors of facial emotional efference, but some researchers have had success using other techniques such as imagery and reinforcement. In general, only physiological or subjective correlates of facial efference have been measured, but in a few studies both types of information have been collected from the same subjects.

PHYSIOLOGICAL EXPERIENCE   The literature on emotional efference and physiological arousal preceding the facial feedback hypotheses suggested that any correlation between facial expressivity and arousal would be negative. In most of this research (Prideaux 1920; Landis 1932; Jones 1948; Block 1957; Learmonth et al 1959), subjects who were most expressive showed little autonomic arousal, and those least expressive showed the most autonomic activity.

As a logical extension of this early research, initial studies on facial efference and physiological arousal adopted the same between-subjects methodology. Lanzetta & Kleck (1970), for example, were among the first to examine the association between facial efference and arousal in the context of a study on encoding and decoding ability. In their study, subjects undergoing shock trials were unknowingly videotaped. Their degree of facial expressiveness was determined by the ability of a set of judges to accurately discriminate shock from nonshock trials from the subjects' faces. Subjects with the highest galvanic skin responses (GSR), indicating sympathetic autonomic nervous system activity, were the least facially expressive, paralleling the inverse relationship between emotional expressivity and GSR reported by the earlier researchers.

Notarius & Levenson (1979), on the other hand, found no significant association between GSR responses and expressiveness of response to the threat of shock. But consistent with the general pattern, less facially expressive subjects showed greater heart rate and respiration rate responses to the threat than did more expressive subjects.

Buck et al (1972), in the context of research on nonverbal communication accuracy, looked at GSR and heart rate correlates of facial efference elicited by sexual, scenic, maternal, disgusting, unusual, and ambiguous slides. Expressivity of subjects was measured by how well observers could guess, from subjects' facial efference, the category and pleasantness of slides being viewed. Expressive subjects showed lower GSR than less expressive ones, but heart rates did not differ. Buck and colleagues (Buck et al 1974) replicated this study using male-female pairs of senders and observers as well as same-sex pairs. They again found lower GSR among more expressive subjects (this time for men only) and no differences in heart rate in between-subjects comparisons. More recently, Buck (1977) found a negative association between indicators of expressivity and skin conductance in both male and female preschoolers in response to slides.

Why the degree of an individual's emotional expressivity, facial or otherwise, should inversely vary with autonomic arousal, has been explained in a number of ways. The basic discharge or cathartic-hydraulic view is that emotion must find an exit, and if it cannot be vented outwardly through efference, it must be routed inward. Jones (1948) labeled individuals who outwardly display emotion but show little arousal "externalizers;" those who behaviorally manifest little emotion but show substantial autonomic activity he called "internalizers." Lanzetta & Kleck (1970) proposed that individuals who are socialized to inhibit their outward emotional displays evidence increased arousal from the combination of redirected emotion and conflict experienced over competing tendencies to express and to inhibit emotion. Buck et al (1974) suggested that during the emotional socialization of such individuals, the stress of parental rebukes becomes associated with emotion-eliciting situations, and that the arousal they show may arise from this association rather than from evoked emotion. Buck also later suggested (1977) that innate determinants may play a role in whether an individual is an internalizer or externalizer.

What is important for the facial feedback hypothesis, however, is that the inverse relationship found between subjects does not rule out the possibility of a positive correlation between expressivity and arousal within subjects, as would be predicted by the hypothesis. In fact, in nearly all within-subjects analyses, that is the association that has been found.

Vaughan & Lanzetta (1980) recorded both autonomic arousal and facial expressivity as judged by activity in muscles around the eyes and jaw (indicating pain) of subjects watching a model's reactions to shocks. On shock trials, subjects showed both greater facial activity (resembling pain) and increased GSR, compared to nonshock trials.

Contradictory results have been reported in two studies with infants. Brock et al (1986) found that 3-month-old infants' smiles in reaction to a female experimenter corresponded with an increase in heart rate. But Cohen et al (1986) found in a study of 4-month-old infants' facial efference in response to their mothers' facial poses that infants' heart rate increased during anger efference but decreased when their faces showed interest and joy. Skin temperature was highest during angry faces and lower during joy.

Dimberg (1982) used photographs of emotional faces as stimuli and measured both heart rate and skin conductance responses. Happy face photographs produced increased zygomatic activity and angry photographs increased corrugator activity, indicating that subjects adopted happy and angry facial patterns, respectively. Heart rate and skin conductance dropped in both patterns of emotional efference (and did not vary by emotion).

In the studies by Buck and colleagues noted earlier, greater facial activity in response to the stimulus slides corresponded with higher GSR reactivity within subjects (Buck et al 1972, 1974). In addition, GSR increased with the unpleasantness of an individual's facial reaction to slides (Buck 1977; Buck et al 1972, 1974), as did heart rate (Buck et al 1972, 1974).

The within-subjects research on physiological correlates of spontaneous facial efference is mixed. Indicators such as GSR and heart rate do not seem to consistently discriminate positive from negative facial affect, but they do appear to generally increase with intensity of facial efference.

SUBJECTIVE EXPERIENCE   More directly pertinent to facial feedback hypotheses is whether subjective experience corresponds with facial efference. In contrast to the research on physiological correlates, greater facial expressivity is uniformly associated with greater subjective experience both between and within subjects, and the reported emotion tends to match the particular facial efference pattern in both valence and category.

In two between-subjects studies, Cupchik & Leventhal reported associations between facial expressive behavior and evaluations of cartoons in research on audience and sex effects. In one (1974), the intensity of spontaneous smiling and laughing at cartoons (manipulated by playing canned laughter) was correlated with higher funniness ratings by women but only for poor-quality cartoons for men. These results were replicated in a second study (Leventhal & Cupchik 1975) in which type of canned laughter was varied.

Kleinke & Walton (1982) manipulated subjects' spontaneous facial efference of happiness using reinforcement techniques. Subjects were not aware that this was influencing the amount they smiled, nor could they accurately guess how often they smiled during the study. Those who were reinforced to smile frequently reported more positive feelings and rated the interview and interviewer higher than did those not reinforced.

Ekman et al (1980) examined both positive and negative affect in a study using films as stimuli. Facial efference patterns were coded using their Facial Action Coding System (FACS). Subjects who showed a happiness facial action while watching positive films reported themselves as happier than those who did not show it, and the frequency, duration, and intensity of this action were positively correlated with self-reported happiness. On the other hand, subjects who showed facial actions of anger, fear, disgust, sadness, or contempt to a negative film reported more negative affect than those who did not, and frequency and duration of expressed negative emotion were correlated with greater self-reported negative affect. In particular, expressed and felt disgust were significantly related.

In several within-subjects analyses, facial efference patterns as assessed by electromyography (EMG) corresponded with self-reported mood. Teasdale & Bancroft (1977) compared corrugator EMG and depressed mood in a small sample of depressed subjects during happy and unhappy thoughts. The unhappy imagery increased both depressed mood and corrugator activity (negative facial efference) compared to happy thoughts, and depressed mood and corrugator activity were highly correlated. McHugo (1983) found that activity of the zygomatic muscles (happy facial efference) while watching positive films was correlated with positive self-reports, while corrugator activity during a negative film was linked to higher self-reported anger. In a third study (Cacioppo et al 1986), although observers could not discriminate the valence and intensity of subjects' facial displays to slides, EMG activity reliably did so; corrugator activity (anger) was higher for negative than positive self-reported affect, and the more the corrugator activity, the more negative the affect. Similarly, zygomatic responses corresponded with greater pleasant than unpleasant affect. In two experiments, Dimberg (1987b) also found that subjects' corrugator and zygomatic activity in reaction to pictured stimuli corresponded to negative and positive self-reports, respectively.

Schwartz and colleagues have published a number of studies on facial efference generated by imagery-induced affect and assessed with EMG. In a 1976 study, depressed and normal subjects imagining happy, sad, and angry situations generally showed the corresponding facial efference patterns and subjective reports for each emotion, although the magnitude of each response differed for depressed and normal subjects. In a normal student sample, Brown & Schwartz (1980) found increased self-reported happiness and happy facial patterns (zygomatic) following standardized happy imagery, and greater reported sadness and sad facial patterns (corrugator) following sadness imagery. Anger and corrugator activity, and fear and zygomatic activity followed the corresponding imagery for anger and fear. Differing intensities of imagery evoked parallel intensity of both facial activity and subjective experience. In another sample, self-reported happiness and zygomatic activity both increased with happy imagery, and self-reported sadness and corrugator activity resulted from sadness imagery (Schwartz et al 1980). Similar results were reported using self-referent statements to generate affect (Sirota et al 1987).

An imagery paradigm was also used by Sutherland et al (1984) in a sample of black women. Imagining fearful and racially derogatory scenes increased corrugator activity and reduced pleasantness ratings compared to imagining a neutral scene.

Only one report departed from this consistent positive association between facial efference and subjective experience. Kleinke & Walton (1982) found in a within-subjects analysis of their data (for both subjects who were reinforced for smiling and nonreinforced subjects) that amount of smiling was not significantly correlated with self-reported positive feelings.

PHYSIOLOGICAL AND SUBJECTIVE EXPERIENCE   Finally, in several studies both physiological and self-report correlates of facial efference were assessed in the same subjects. Three of these involved between-subjects tests. In the first, researchers divided their sample into groups varying in rated facial expressivity (Notarius et al 1982). In reaction to an angry scolding by an experimenter, minimally expressive subjects showed a significant heart rate increase compared to both nonexpressive and highly expressive subjects, and reported significantly higher guilt feelings (but did not differ on nine other affect scales). In the second, Winton et al (1984) found no significant correlations of facial expressivity with heart rate or skin conductance in between-subjects analysis. Ridgeway & Waters (1987) found that children asked to think about exciting experiences showed more facial pleasure and heart rate variability than children in a calm-imagery group, and a sad-imagery group showed less facial pleasure and slightly less heart rate change than in the calm group.

When the relationship between facial efference and its correlates is examined within subjects, the picture again changes. Kleck and colleagues (1976) measured subjective and autonomic responses in a study on the impact of an observer on expressiveness. The presence of another reduced the expressive response to shock, and both subjective and autonomic responses decreased as well.

Subjects in a study by Dimberg (1987a) showed greater corrugator activity and skin conductance responses and more rated unpleasantness to a high-intensity tone than to one of low intensity. Heart rate decelerated to the low–but not the high-intensity tone.

As part of a larger study, McHugo et al (1985) showed subjects taped silent television segments of Ronald Reagan expressing happiness, fear, or anger. Subjects imitated the facial patterns, with elevated zygomatic activity during happy segments, elevated corrugator and reduced zygomatic activity during anger segments, and both moderately raised corrugator and moderately lowered zygomatic activity during the fear segments. Corresponding to their happy facial imitations, subjects' self-reported joy and warmth were high and skin conductance was low. For anger, reported negative affect and GSR responses were high. When producing fearful faces, both positive and negative self-reported affect were moderately high, and the same was true of GSR. Heart rate dropped for all three facial patterns, but more so for the negative ones.

Winton et al (1984), using slides as stimuli, found that heart rate increased linearly with pleasantness of subjective report and facial efference, while skin conductance increased with the intensity of facial efference and self-report, regardless of valence.

Finally, in a 1981 study, Schwartz and colleagues used the imagery technique to examine the blood pressure and heart rate correlates of happiness, sadness, anger, and fear in comparison to relaxed and control trials. Fear and happiness both were linked with increased heart rate and systolic blood pressure; but in fear, heart rate increased more. Sadness and happiness produced similar heart rate and systolic blood pressure levels, but sadness produced lower diastolic blood pressure. Anger, like fear, was associated with high heart rate and systolic blood pressure, but it produced higher diastolic blood pressure. Self-reported affect corresponded appropriately with each pattern of facial efference.

IMPLICATIONS FOR THE FEEDBACK HYPOTHESIS   From the correlational literature it is clear that in between-subjects tests, facial expressiveness is negatively correlated with autonomic arousal. More crucial for the feedback hypothesis, however, are within-subjects comparisons. These show convincingly that increased facial expressiveness of emotion is correlated with increased physiological arousal, as the hypothesis predicts. Generally, it appears that facial efference of either positive or negative affect is associated with autonomic arousal, although there is some evidence that increased GSR is linked specifically to negative facial affect (Buck 1977; Buck et al 1972, 1974; Dimberg 1987a; Kleck et al 1976; McHugo et al 1985; Vaughan & Lanzetta 1980) and that increased heart rate is specific to pleasantness of the facial efference pattern (Brock et al 1986; McHugo et al 1985; Ridgeway & Waters 1987; Winton et al 1984), although the reverse has also been noted for heart rate (Buck et al 1972, 1974; Cohen et al 1986; Schwartz et al 1981).

As for subjective experience, specific affective self-reports increase almost without exception with facial efference patterns of the corresponding emotion. This is not surprising given that in most research paradigms the accompanying emotional stimulus could easily inform subjects of the appropriate feeling even if facial efference did not. But in studies where spontaneous facial efference was intensified without subject awareness (i.e. by using reinforcement, canned laughter, or the presence of an observer), self-reported affect increased correspondingly above the level reported to the emotional stimulus alone. These results suggest the possibility not only of a correspondence, but of a modulating influence of facial efference in the experience of emotion, a hypothesis explored more thoroughly in research using experimentally manipulated facial efference.

Experimental Studies of Facial Efference and Emotional Experience: the Modulating Function

The possibility that facial efference plays a causal role in emotion has long been a subject of theoretical speculation (Gratiolet 1865; Darwin 1896; James 1890, 1922). Although the original facial feedback hypotheses restrict consideration of this role to the context of ongoing, spontaneous emotion, research in which facial emotional action is experimentally manipulated has mushroomed in the past decade. Part of the reason is undoubtedly the inability of research using spontaneous efference to separate correlation from causality. Interest in the possibility of modulating, and, perhaps, initiating effects of facial efference is such that the term "facial feedback hypothesis" is now commonly defined in these terms (Buck 1980; Laird 1984; Matsumoto 1987).

Most work examining the role of voluntary facial efference focuses on its modulating function in emotional experience. Typically, an emotional stimulus (in the form of an external stimulus, such as a film, or an internal one, such as imagery) is introduced, and the effects on emotional experience of exaggerating or inhibiting a congruent facial efference pattern or simulating an incongruent pattern are examined.

PHYSIOLOGICAL EXPERIENCE   In the literature relating facial efference to other components of emotional experience, correlational studies have focused largely on the physiological correlates while experimental studies have tended to focus on subjective experience. True to this split, only a few experimental studies on facial efference examine only physiological correlates.

In the first, Colby et al (1977) required subjects to facially pose high, moderate, and no pain on different shock trials. They found that as intensity of posed pain to a shock increased, so did subjects' GSR responses, but in the absence of shock, posed pain did not affect skin conductance. In the second study, a variant of their 1980 correlational study using spontaneous expressions, Vaughan & Lanzetta (1981) measured autonomic responses of subjects watching a model's display of pain in response to electric shock. The subjects were instructed either to inhibit their own facial patterns, to display pain when the model did so, or were given no instructions. The display group showed increased skin conductance and heart rate compared to the other two groups, which did not differ from each other.

Two recent studies used imagery to generate emotions. Ianni et al (1986) compared voluntary facial anger, disgust, neutral, and control conditions during anger imagery. Facial anger augmented cardiovascular activity compared to the other facial actions, particularly reducing finger blood flow; but skin conductance and heart rate were not significantly affected. Lanzetta, Kleck, and colleagues (Kappas et al 1987) reported that adding matching overt facial action to self-generated emotions (happiness, sadness, anger, peacefulness) increased heart rate but did not change skin conductance.

SUBJECTIVE EXPERIENCE   In contrast to the physiological data, a number of studies have focused on the effects of suppressing, exaggerating, or dissimulating facial efference on subjective experience during an emotional stimulus. One of the earliest was the Leventhal & Mace between-subjects experiment (1970) in which the evaluations of a comedy film by school children asked to smile and laugh as much as they could were compared with those of children asked not to laugh. Among girls, positive ratings of the film were higher in the exaggeration than the inhibition group, but the opposite was true for boys, although they laughed more.

Rhodewalt & Comer (1979) manipulated smiling, frowning, or neutral patterns using Laird's (1974) technique while subjects wrote a counterattitudinal essay. Subjects' mood was most positive in the smile and least positive in the frown conditions, with neutral in between. Mood was most negative in the frowning group, least negative in the smiling group, and in between for the neutral group. Attitude change was also greatest in the smiling and least in the frowning groups.

Laird and colleagues have made several within-subjects investigations of facial efference and mood. Laird (1974) first induced subjects to display smiles and angry frowns by manipulating muscle contraction patterns, and then exposed them to pictures of children and of the Ku Klux Klan. Aggression scores were higher on the frowning than smiling trials, and scores on elation and surgency scales were higher on smiling than frowning trials. (Anxiety, remorse, and social affection were not differentially affected by efference.) The difference between self-reported mood on smiling versus frowning trials was significantly larger for manipulated than for nonmanipulated observer subjects, suggesting an effect of efference above the effects of the slides. In a second experiment, subjects rated cartoons as funnier when in the smiling than in the frowning condition; elation was also higher (but not significantly) and aggression lower while smiling than when frowning. Laird & Crosby (1974) reported one successful and one unsuccessful replication of this work using humorous cartoons as stimuli.

Again using a technique similar to Lairds's, McArthur et al (1980) induced smiles, sad frowns, and neutral patterns while subjects viewed positive, negative, or neutral slides. Self-reported mood of normal-weight but not overweight subjects was less happy when frowning but not significantly happier when smiling compared to neutral across stimuli. In a replication reported in the same article the same pattern was found.

Rutledge & Hupka (1985) also used Laird's technique to pose joy and anger in subjects viewing neutral slides and high and low anger and joy slides. In a within-subjects comparison, subjects reported feeling more joyous and less angry when posing joy, and more angry and less joyous when in an anger pose. The difference held across all stimulus intensities. The researchers also compared the self-reported affect of posed subjects with that of observers who had undergone the same experimental session but were instructed to keep facial muscles relaxed. The subjects when posing joy reported greater feelings of joy than their paired counterparts across stimuli, and when posing anger reported greater anger.

Kraut (1982) varied the experimental paradigm by using pleasant and unpleasant odors as affective stimuli in a within-subjects experiment. Posing a pleasant reaction increased the evaluated pleasantness of the odors while posing disgust decreased it compared to the ratings made while spontaneously reacting to the odors.

Three experiments have tested for modulating influences of facial efference during self-generated emotion. McCanne & Anderson (1987) asked subjects first to imagine a positive or negative situation, then to imagine the scene while enhancing either zygomatic or corrugator tension. In a third trial, they were instructed to suppress tension in that muscle during imagery. The muscle changes were verified by EMG but were otherwise not readily detectable. Suppressed zygomatic activity during positive affective scenes decreased self-reported enjoyment and increased distress; no other effects of muscle activity were significant. Klions and Dale (Riccelli et al 1984; Antila et al 1988) used self-referent statements to induce mood and posed facial actions monitored by EMG in two studies. In the first, positive and negative emotional facial actions (zygomatic and corrugator) increased self-reported elation and depression, respectively, compared to the reports of nonmanipulated subjects reading the statements. In the second, facial actions incongruent with the statements reduced the contrasting self-reported mood compared to reports of unmanipulated subjects, but the differences were not significant.

Rutledge and colleagues (1987) reported effects on felt emotion from isolated facial muscle contractions while viewing slides used in their earlier study. Across all slides, contraction of forehead muscles (occipitofrontalis) was associated with greater reported surprise; contraction of the corrugator (brow) was linked with feelings of anger. Triangularis contraction (pulling the mouth down) and zygomaticus contraction (creating a smile) were linked respectively with sadness and joy. This study was unusual in moving beyond a positive/negative (dimensional) distinction by linking specific forms of facial emotional efference with reported changes in discrete (categorical) emotions.

Strack and Martin (Strack et al 1988; L. L. Martin, T. F. Harlow, F. Strack, in preparation) have also tested dimensional versus categorical effects of facial efference using a technique requiring subjects to hold a pen in their mouths in different ways. In two initial experiments (Strack et al 1988), subjects held the pen either in their teeth (simulating a smile) or in their lips (simulating a frown). Their ratings of cartoon funniness were higher during the "smile" and lower during ther "frown" patterns compared to ratings in a control condition. Using the pen technique to simulate smiling, angry, and frowning efference (L. L. Martin, T. F. Harlow, F. Strack, in preparation), they first found evidence only for a dimensional perspective: "smiling" subjects reacted more positively to stories than did "frowning" or "angry"-faced subjects; but when stories were changed so that only angry (not sad) evaluations were appropriate, angry poses produced more angry evaluations but sad facial efference did not. The researchers also found that adding physiological arousal that could not readily be attributed to exercise increased negative and reduced positive ratings of stories for anger-posing subjects and produced the reverse effects for smile-posing subjects.

The data in this section are largely consistent in showing that voluntary facial efference, whether produced by direct request to express or inhibit or by more subtle muscle manipulation, changes subjective experience. Exaggeration of facial efference congruent with an emotional stimulus increases corresponding subjective experience of an emotion while inhibition reduces it. Simulating efference incongruent to a stimulus also reduces stimulus-consistent subjective experience. In the only study looking at more than two emotions, the results suggest that manipulation of emotion-specific efference increases the corresponding emotion-specific subjective experience.

PHYSIOLOGICAL AND SUBJECTIVE EXPERIENCE   Two early studies dealt with the modulating effects of facial pose on subjective and physiological reactions to electric shock. In a between-subjects experiment by Kopel & Arkowitz (1974) subjects role-played either a calm or upset reaction or did not role-play during shock. Subjects posing an upset reaction reported feeling more pain and had a lower pain threshold than the neutral controls, while those posing calm reported less pain and a higher threshold. The calm facial pattern looked no different to observers than did the control, although the upset pattern did. Pulse rate was not affected by the role-playing. Lanzetta et al (1976) asked subjects to conceal or clearly reveal their reactions to shocks of varying intensity. Independent judges confirmed that facial displays for hiding and exaggerating trials differed in the appropriate directions from baseline patterns. Compared to the baseline (previously collected spontaneous reactions), hiding a facial response to shock reduced both GSR and the subjective report of shock painfulness; exaggerating the facial reaction increased both GSR and self-reported pain.

Subjects also suppressed or exaggerated the congruent patterns for pleasant, unpleasant, and neutral film segments or reacted spontaneously in another study (Zuckerman et al 1981). Finger blood volume, skin conductance, and heart rate were measured, and subjects made self-reports. These researchers reported greatest autonomic arousal across stimuli in the exaggeration group, followed by the spontaneous expressers, and the lowest arousal among the suppressors. The differences were greater in groups viewing affect-laden films than in those viewing neutral films. Films were rated as more pleasant for pleasant scenes and more unpleasant for unpleasant scenes by the exaggerators than by the suppressors or spontaneous reactors, although the differences were not significant. Reported intensity of reactions was higher for the affective films when reactions were exaggerated. Higher levels of facial expressivity were associated with greater autonomic arousal and subjective experience within as well as between subjects.

In two studies, the effects of spontaneous reactions were compared to only one other posing condition. In the first, Ochsmann & Henrich (1984) found that female subjects (but not males) rated accident pictures as more frightening and showed increased physiological arousal when they exaggerated their reactions. (In men, self-reported frightfulness did not differ, and physiological response was lower when efference was amplified.) In the second, self-reports and autonomic responses corresponding with spontaneously occurring facial efference to pleasant, neutral, and unpleasant slides were compared to responses of subjects asked to display an incongruent pose (Putnam et al 1982). Self-reported pleasantness corresponded to pleasantness of facial efference in the unmanipulated condition, but decreased in the posed condition. Skin conductance was higher for affective than neutral slides among the spontaneous reactors, while heart rate accelerated more for pleasant than unpleasant slides. Posing incongruent efference increased skin conductance responses but not heart rate.

Tourangeau & Ellsworth (1979) compared the effects of congruent and incongruent posed faces, spontaneous efference, and nonemotional poses on self-reports and physiological responses to fearful, sad, and neutral stimulus films. When watching a neutral film, subjects posing fear reported higher subjective fear and subjects posing sadness reported greater sadness than did subjects in other face conditions, but the differences were not significant. For fearful and sad films, a congruent facial pose did not increase self-reports of the matching emotion above the levels reported by the unmanipulated and nonemotional-faced groups, and incongruent poses did not decrease self-reports of the filmed emotion. On the physiological measures, both fear-posing and sorrow-posing subjects showed greater drops in heart rate than did the nonemotional-faced group across all films, but less decrease than the spontaneous expressers. The spontaneous expressers showed the biggest GSR response, the fear-posing subjects the least.

IMPLICATIONS FOR THE MODULATING HYPOTHESIS   Although the original facial feedback hypothesis would not have considered voluntarily modulated facial efference to be a theoretical equal to spontaneously produced efference (Tomkins 1962, 1981; Izard 1971, 1981), many researchers have nevertheless relied on manipulated efference in an attempt to clarify whether facial efference can play a modulating role in ongoing emotional experience. In general, in the subjective experience of emotion, it may; with only a few nonsignificant results (Laird & Crosby 1974; McCanne & Anderson 1987; Tourangeau & Ellsworth 1979) and one contradictory effect (Putnam et al 1982), the literature suggests that intensification of a congruent facial pattern enhances subjective experience, while an inhibited congruent pose or the pose of an incongruent emotion reduces subjective experience.

Exaggeration of facial efference generally increases GSR and inhibition reduces it, regardless of valence of efference. Only four attempts have addressed heart rate effects, with three revealing nondifferentiating increases for any efference pattern (Tourangeau & Ellsworth 1979; Vaughan & Lanzetta 1981; Zuckerman et al 1981) and one showing no significant change (Putnam et al 1982).

Experimental Studies of Facial Efference and Emotional Experience: the Initiating Function

A final and more difficult question to answer is whether facial efference can initiate emotional experience in the absence of an emotional stimulus. Some evidence relevant to this issue can be gleaned from conditions included in studies mentioned above, and in recent years a few attempts have been made to focus specifically on this question. In these studies, subjects are sometimes asked simply to pose a particular emotional face, are trained to contract particular muscles or combinations of muscles, or perform tasks that involve the facial muscles in ways approximating emotional postures.

PHYSIOLOGICAL AND SUBJECTIVE EXPERIENCE   Evidence of the initiating potential of facial efference can be found in those studies mentioned above where one of the conditions involved posed efference during a neutral stimulus. (For these studies, unless otherwise noted, only trends can be ascertained because significance levels were not reported.)

Colby et al (1977) found no significant effects of posing pain facial patterns on GSR in the absence of actual shock. When presented with neutral pictures, subjects in McArthur et al's study (1980) reported slightly higher happiness when smiling than with a neutral face, and lower happiness when frowning. In the Rutledge & Hupka study (1985), in a neutral-stimulus condition, subjects posing joy reported slightly higher joy (but also slightly higher anger) than subjects with a neutral pose; when posing anger they reported more felt anger and less felt joy than neutral posers. Fear posers reported more fear, and sadness posers more sadness, during a neutral film in the Tourangeau & Ellsworth study (1979), but the differences were not statistically significant. And, in response to a neutral slide in the Rutledge et al (1987) research, subjects contracting forehead muscles (resembling surprise) reported significantly more surprise than unposed subjects, and those posing joy (mouth up) and fear (mouth down) reported significantly more joy and fear, respectively, than unposed subjects.

Other studies have focused specifically on the potential initiating function of facial posture. McCaul et al (1982) asked subjects on different trials either to portray fear, to portray calm, or to show their usual face. In a first experiment, subjects showed higher pulse rates and skin conductance when they were portraying fear than for either the calm or normal expressions. Self-reported anxiety was not affected, a result that led the researchers to conclude that physiological changes were due to effort rather than change in emotion. To test this, in a second experiment they added trials in which happiness was portrayed. They also added noise as a situational manipulation of negative affect. Subjects rated the noise as less loud while portraying happiness (self-reported emotion was not directly assessed in this study). Pulse rate increased under both happiness and fear portrayals, but skin conductance did not change. The researchers believed the greater movement involved in these expressions as compared to calm or normal expressions accounted for pulse changes.

In two studies, Duncan & Laird manipulated facial posture to differentiate self-produced cue users from situational cue users for other purposes. In the context of a first study on self-attribution and attitude change (1977), they induced muscle poses of smiles, frowns, and neutral faces. Manipulated smiles corresponded to higher and frowns to lower elation and surgency than neutral (relaxed) efference in the presence of a neutral stimulus. A frowning face produced higher aggression scores than a neutral one, but smiling did not lower aggression compared to a neutral expression. In a later study on placebo effects (1980), the researchers successfully replicated this effect using slides of geometric forms as stimuli and using a group manipulation. Elation-surgency was significantly higher on smiling than frowning trials, and aggression was higher for frowning than for smiling trials; both smiles and frowns produced mood scores significantly different from those of a neutral facial pattern.

Four studies on biofeedback training as asthma treatment also fit within the consideration of facial efference and physiological consequences (Glaus & Kotses 1983; Harver & Kotses 1984; Kotses & Glaus 1981; Miller & Kotses 1987). This research involves relaxation or tensing of the frontalis muscle in the forehead, with dependent variables including respiratory expiration flow rate, respiration rate, and heart rate. Relaxation of the frontalis muscle produced an increase in peak expiration flow rate and tension decreased flow rate; no changes in respiration rate or heart rate have been found. In comparison, forearm muscle tension or relaxation had no effect on any measure.

Ekman et al (1983) used facial poses of six different emotions and collected five physiological measures. Facial surprise, disgust, sadness, anger, fear, and happiness were manipulated using both directed facial action (a muscle contraction technique similar to those used by others) and relived emotion (resembling imagery techniques). In the posed efference condition, three subgroups of emotions were discriminated based on physiological measures: poses of happiness, disgust, and surprise were associated with low heart rate; fear and sadness were linked with high heart rate and low skin temperature; and anger was accompanied by high heart rate and high skin temperature. Forearm muscle tension did not vary. Of importance to the facial feedback hypothesis is the finding that autonomic changes were more clear-cut in the facial action condition than in the relived emotion (imagery) task.

Smith et al (1986) also used both posed and imagery-induced efference (happy, sad, angry, and neutral) and measured skin conductance and heart rate. As determined by EMG magnitudes, stronger efference patterns were produced by voluntarily posing, but the patterns were similar to the imagery-induced patterns. They split their sample into expressive and nonexpressive posers. The nonexpressives produced similar levels of facial activity when happiness was posed and when it was induced by imagery, but less activity when posing the negative emotions of sadness and anger compared to spontaneous efference. Skin conductance did not significantly differ by emotion when posed. Heart rate increased over the neutral condition for all three emotions; there was no difference in heart rate increase between expressives and nonexpressives, even though the latter showed less facial activity for negative emotions than did expressives.

In two recent studies, subjects performed tasks involving facial muscles in ways that approximate emotional facial efference patterns, and thereby allow the experimenter to examine the effects of facial efference alone, independently of its emotional content. Strack et al (1988) using the pen-holding technique, noted evidence of an effect of facial posture on self-reports even in the absence of their cartoon stimuli. And Zajonc and colleagues (R. B. Zajonc, S. Murphy, M. Inglehart, submitted), in the context of research on the vascular theory of emotional efference (Zajonc 1985), compared the subjective experience of subjects pronouncing or listening to various phonemes, some of which involve the action of muscles that are dominant in emotional expressions. For example, the production of the phoneme e resembles the smile. Photographers elicit smiles from their subjects by requiring them to say "cheese". The German phoneme ü, on the other hand, has just the opposite action. Repeated pronunciation of *e* resulted in positive subjective reports as measured by ratings of liking, pleasantness, and preferences for the sound, whereas *ü* was judged unpleasant and was disliked, not only by American but by German subjects as well.

IMPLICATIONS FOR THE INITIATING FUNCTION   The evidence in this section suggests that facial efference may play an emotion-specific initiating role as well as a modulating role in the subjective experience of emotion. Some significant results support this conclusion (Duncan & Laird 1977, 1980; Rutledge et al 1987; Strack et al 1988; R. B. Zajonc, S. Murphy, M. Inglehart, submitted), and trends apparent in the nonsignificant results are at least consistent with the hypothesis (McArthur et al 1980; Rutledge & Hupka 1985; Tourangeau & Ellsworth 1979; but not McCaul et al 1982).

As in most of the research on facial efference and physiological arousal, little autonomic differentiation by the particular form of efference has been apparent. Either no significant effects on arousal are produced by efference alone or it increases uniformly across different emotions (Colby et al 1977; Glaus & Kotses 1983; Smith et al 1986). The exceptions are the Ekman et al (1983) study, and the Zajonc-Murphy-Inglehart research. In the first, enough different physiological indexes were used to detect three differentiating patterns: one for happiness, disgust, and surprise, characterized by low heart rate; one for fear and sadness, with high heart rate and low skin temperature; and one for anger, with high heart rate and high skin temperature. In the second, temperature of the forehead showed clear distinction between positive and negative affect, cooling being associated with pleasant states and warming with unpleasant hedonic states. Thus, temperature—unlike GSR, heart rate, and similar autonomic indicators that do not discriminate hedonic polarity—offers a new, important, physiological index of emotion.

SUMMARY OF THE LITERATURE ON FACIAL FEEDBACK

We have divided our discussion of the literature of facial feedback into two classes: that which examines the correlates of facial efference under conditions that elicit it spontaneously, and that in which the modulating and initiating functions of facial efference can be examined through experimental manipulation.

In the correlational literature, we drew, as Buck (1980) did in his review, a distinction between within- and between-subjects tests of association between facial efference and emotional experience. We argued that the former are more pertinent to the original facial feedback hypothesis as variously proposed by Tomkins (1962), Gellhorn, (1964), and Izard (1971), and that they generally support the hypothesis. Not only does intensity of facial efference correspond with greater subjective emotional experience in general, but particular facial efference patterns are positively correlated with subjective experience of the same emotions. Physiological arousal does not appear to vary differentially with the nature of the efference pattern but seems to increase with any increase in emotional efference.

More interest has been displayed recently in the modulating and initiating potentials of facial efference, explored through experimental manipulation of the face. The term "facial feedback hypothesis" has come to be defined by these functions, although the original proponents of the hypothesis disavow this usage (Tomkins 1981; Izard 1981). Although the experimental evidence is less unanimous than the correlational data, it appears to us that the literature supports these versions of the hypothesis, perhaps more convincingly for subjective experience than for physiological arousal.

It should be noted that in going from spontaneous efference to posing an emotion, contracting muscles in an emotion-like face, or performing other facial motor tasks, two things are likely to decrease simultaneously: the inferences subjects can consciously make about their feelings from the situation and from what their faces are doing, and the closeness of the facial efference to a spontaneous display. The first is an advantage in that it minimizes self-perception interpretations (Laird 1974) and has the strongest causal implications, while the second poses a clear disadvantage in attempting to generalize to naturally occurring facial emotional efference. Some evidence suggests that voluntarily posed efference patterns and spontaneous ones are innervated through different pathways (Monrad-Krohn 1924, 1939). However, compared to spontaneous efference, posed faces tend to be quite similar both in appearance (Borod et al 1986a, b) and EMG patterns for each emotion (Schwartz et al 1979) and thus, perhaps, in their feedback patterns to the brain. One of the main differences between spontaneous and posed efference seems to be the greater asymmetry of the latter (Ekman et al 1981).

To the extent that voluntarily produced efference can be assumed to adequately correspond to spontaneous emotional efference, the experimental evidence suggests that facial efference may play an important causal role in the subjective experience of emotion. In this, other reviewers at least partially agree. Laird (1984) concluded that these experimental studies "have demonstrated effects of varying the magnitude of expressive behavior on both self-reports of emotional experience and on various measures of physiological arousal such as heart rate and skin conductance" (p. 910). Winton (1986) agreed that the literature supports the modern facial feedback hypothesis, but cautioned that it only supports a "dimensional" view, in that almost all studies compare only one positive to one negative emotion. The exception at that time was the Tourangeau & Ellsworth study (1979), which in comparing the two negatively valenced emotions of fear and sadness failed to support a "categorical" feedback hypothesis; their study was criticized, however, on both theoretical and methodological grounds (Hager & Ekman 1981; Izard 1981; Tomkins 1981). The more recent studies by Rutledge et al (1988) and Strack et al (1988) do support a categorical version, but more studies in this vein are clearly called for. Finally, Matsumoto (1987) moved beyond a conventional review by submitting the studies reviewed by Laird (1984) to meta-analysis, and concluded that "the meta-analytic procedures indicate that the effect of facial manipulation on self-reported emotional experience is of moderate value" (p. 772).

CONTEMPORARY THEORETICAL ISSUES IN FACIAL FEEDBACK: WHAT IS FED BACK?

The empirical literature bearing on the facial feedback hypothesis strongly suggests that facial emotional efference is not only correlated with emotional experience but may modulate and initiate it. The evidence on the physiological component of that experience is weaker. If facial efference plays a causal role in the subjective experience of emotion, as the empirical literature suggests it does, it is likely to do so directly rather than by first initiating physiological arousal that is then subjectively experienced as emotion. Perhaps the most interesting contemporary theoretical question in this domain, therefore, is how facial efference may play a causal role in the subjective experience of emotion.

In general, theory has lain dormant on this question since the original facial feedback hypotheses, in which muscular proprioceptive patterns (Gellhorn 1964; Izard 1971; Tomkins 1962) and cutaneous sensation (Gellhorn 1964; Tomkins 1980) were proposed as mechanisms. Ekman (1984) has suggested that motor cortex directing facial muscle activity simultaneously connects with hypothalamic areas to stimulate ANS activity, but his model does not directly address subjective experience. Laird (1974, 1984), drawing on self-perception as a possible mechanism, does specifically focus on subjective experience; but the most recent facial feedback studies using mechanical manipulations of the face now make his position less tenable.

One exception to the current dearth of theoretical progress on facial efference in the experience of emotion is a recently reclaimed theory (Zajonc 1985) that links emotional efference to vascular processes. The author of the vascular theory of emotional efference (VTEE), Israel Waynbaum (1907), argued that facial movements in general, and emotional efference in particular, have regulatory and restorative functions for the vascular system of the head. He noted the intimate relationship between facial and cerebral blood flow (CBF), and suggested that facial muscular movements contribute to the regulation of CBF by pressing against facial veins and arteries and thus shunting blood to the brain when needed or diverting it away when the brain is threatened with excess. The face, according to Waynbaum, acts as a safety valve for the brain, where blood supply can vary only within very narrow limits. He also suggested that these regulatory muscular actions of the face have subjective consequences: Changes in CBF caused by facial motor movement are reflected as changes in feeling states. He did not disagree with Darwin (1896) that the function of emotional facial gestures is to communicate the individual's internal states to others, but he held that the communicative function was secondary.

Several of Waynbaum's assumptions are questionable and others are wrong (Burdett 1985; Fridlund & Gilbert 1985; Izard 1985; Zajonc 1986). For instance, arterial flow is unlikely to be much affected by muscular action of the face. Furthermore, arterial blood flow is under the control of so many other central factors that peripheral action could only have negligible direct effects. Facial muscles, however, can affect venous flow. Regardless of the particular physiological processes that may be involved, it is both plausible and theoretically important that facial efferents may have direct regulatory functions and subjective consequences. If true, VTEE organizes diverse findings such as biofeedback, placebo effects, unconscious preferences and aversions, growth of preference with repeated exposure, empathy, etc (Zajonc 1986). The particular neurophysiological and neurochemical processes are yet to be specified by empirical investigations. Useful speculations about such processes that would guide future research, however, can be made.

A testable hypothesis that follows from VTEE is that facial efferents can produce changes in brain blood temperature which, in turn, can facilitate and inhibit the release and synthesis of a variety of neurotransmitters. Thus, if a certain facial muscle action changes the temperature in a brain region where serotonin is released, for example, then the resulting serotonin regulation might cause the individual to experience joyful or depressive affect. Not all neurochemicals that have subjective effects are region specific. Peptides, for example, are found in profusion throughout the entire brain, and a change in temperature might change the threshold of the enzymatic actions that release them. R. B. Zajonc, Sheila Murphy, and Marita Inglehart (submitted) observed systematic correlations between changes in temperature and hedonic tone as simultaneous reactions to uttering various phonemes. They explained the results by assuming that the production of various phonemes may facilitate or impair the air cooling of the venous blood that enters the cavernous sinus. The latter is a venous structure that cools arterial blood as it enters the brain. In an experiment which subjects thought involved the psychophysics of olfaction, cool (19° C) and warm (32° C) air was introduced into subjects' nostrils and ratings of the odors were collected. On some trials no odor was present, yet subjects rated cool air as decidedly pleasant and warm air as decidedly unpleasant. To be sure, the conjecture that brain temperature changes can influence the release and synthesis of neurohormones and neuroenzymes associated with subjective emotional states still needs empirical documentation.

CONCLUSIONS

1.   There are no sufficient grounds thus far to reject *any* theory of the role of facial efference in the experience of emotion. The neglected early theories based on the sensory process have a great deal to offer given that emotional experience depends heavily on sensory input and its derivatives; the neuroanatomical connections and processes indicate a powerful role of the sensory process in emotion (LeDoux 1987). Hence, the work of Piderit and Gratiolet deserves greater attention in contemporary research. In addition, there is no conflict among the sensory theories of emotional efference, Darwin's evolutionary perspective on efference, and the facial feedback hypotheses. Clearly, nothing prevents a facial emotional action from depending on a peripheral process that is allied to sensation, having adaptive communicative value, and also arousing in the actor the subjective experience of emotion.

2.   The correlational evidence reviewed here clearly indicates a positive association between facial efference and emotional experience within subjects, particularly for the subjective component of emotion, in support of the facial feedback hypothesis. Intensity of facial efference of a specific emotion corresponds with increasing subjective experience of the same emotion.

3.   Although the experimental evidence on facial feedback is less conclusive than the correlational literature, it tends to support the notion that facial efference plays not only a modulating function but an initiating function in the experience of emotion, particularly for subjective experience. Some initial evidence suggests that facial efference may causally differentiate not only positive from negative subjective experience, but may produce emotion-specific effects. More research comparing facial efference patterns for two or more emotions of the same valence is needed.

4.   The facial feedback hypothesis does not explain why some facial actions "feel" good and others "feel" unpleasant. There is some promise in this respect from the vascular theory of emotional efference, which attributes changes in subjective hedonic states to changes in neurochemistry of the brain caused by changes in temperature reaching the hypothalamus via the cavernous sinus. If facial action can influence the thermoregulatory action of the cavernous sinus it might thereby influence the release and synthesis of some peptides and neurotransmitters that are highly temperature dependent

and have been found to produce hedonic changes. The most significant finding here is that for the first time a physiological indicator, forehead temperature, has been found to discriminate reliably between positive and negative affect.

5. The mounting evidence that facial efference under some conditions may modulate or even initiate subjective emotional experience suggests that a theoretical position that clings to the term "expression" misrepresents the complex and varied roles of the face in the experience of emotion.

Literature Cited

Allport, F. H. 1924. *Social Psychology*. Chicago: Houghton Mifflin

Angell, J. R. 1916. A reconsideration of James' theory of emotion in the light of recent criticisms. *Psychol. Rev.* 23:251–61

Antila, C. E., Dale, J. A., Klions, H. L. 1988. *Depressive and elative mood induction as a function of antagonistic facial expressions*. Presented at Ann. Meet. Eastern Psychol. Assoc., Buffalo, NY

Block, J. 1957. A study of affective responsiveness in a lie detection situation. *J. Abnorm. Soc. Psychol.* 55:11–15

Borod, J. C., Koff, E., Buck, R. 1986a. The neuropsychology of facial expression: data from normal and brain-damaged adults. In *Nonverbal Communication in the Clinical Context*, ed. R. Blanck, R. Buck, N. Rosenthal, pp. 196–222. University Park, PA: Penn. State Univ. Press

Borod, J. C., Koff, E., Lorch, M. P., Nicholas, M. 1986b. The expression and perception of facial emotion in brain-damaged patients. *Neuropsychologia* 24:169–80

Brock, S. E., Rothbart, M. K., Derryberry, D. 1986. Heart-rate deceleration and smiling in 3-month-old infants. *Infant Behav. Dev.* 9:403–14

Brown, S., Schwartz, G. E. 1980. Relationships between facial electromyography and subjective experience during affective imagery. *Biol. Psychol.* 11:49–62

Buck, R. 1977. Nonverbal communication of affect in preschool children: relationships with personality and skin conductance. *J. Pers. Soc. Psychol.* 35:225–36

Buck, R. 1980. Nonverbal behavior and the theory of emotion: the facial feedback hypothesis. *J. Pers. Soc. Psychol.* 38:811–24

Buck, R., Miller, R. E., Caul, W. F. 1974. Sex, personality, and physiological variables in the communication of affect via facial expression. *J. Pers. Soc. Psychol.* 30:587–96

Buck, R., Savin, V., Miller, R., Caul, W. 1972. Communication of affect through facial expressions in humans. *J. Pers. Soc. Psychol.* 23:362–71

Bull, N. 1951. The attitude theory of emotion. *J. Nerv. Mental Dis. Monogr.* 81. New York

Burdett, A. 1985. Emotion and facial expression. *Science* 230:608

Cacioppo, J. T., Petty, R. E., Losch, M. E., Kim, H. S. 1986. Electromyographic activity over facial muscle regions can differentiate the valence and intensity of affective reactions. *J. Pers. Soc. Psychol.* 50:260–68

Cannon, W. B. 1915. *Bodily Changes in Pain, Hunger, Fear, and Rage*. New York: Appleton

Cannon, W. B. 1927. The James-Lange theory of emotions: a critical examination and an alternative theory. *Am. J. Psychol.* 39:106–12

Cannon, W. B. 1931. Again the James-Lange and the thalamic theories of emotion. *Psychol. Rev.* 38:281–95

Cohen, B., Izard, C. E., Simons, R. F. 1986. Facial and physiological indices of emotions in mother-infant interactions. *Psychophysiology* 23: 429 (Abstr.)

Colby, C., Lanzetta, J., Kleck, R. 1977. Effects of the expression of pain on autonomic and pain tolerance responses to subject-controlled pain. *Psychophysiology* 14: 537–40

Cupchik, G. C., Leventhal, H. 1974. Consistency between expressive behavior and the evaluation of humorous stimuli: the role of sex and self-observation. *J. Pers. Soc. Psychol.* 30:429–42

Darwin, C. R. 1896. *The Expression of Emotions in Man and Animals*. New York: Appleton

Dimberg, U. 1982. Facial reactions to facial expressions. *Psychophysiology* 19:643–47

Dimberg, U. 1987a. Facial reactions and autonomic activity to auditory stimuli with high and low intensity. *Psychophysiology* 24:586 (Abstr.)

Dimberg, U. 1987b. Facial reactions and experienced emotion to visual emotional stimuli. *Psychophysiology* 24:586 (Abstr.)

Duncan, J., Laird, J. D. 1977. Cross-modality consistencies in individual differences in self-attribution. *J. Pers.* 45:191–206

Duncan, J., Laird, J. D. 1980. Positive and reverse placebo effects as a function of differences in cues used in self-perception. *J. Pers. Soc. Psychol.* 39:1024–36

Ekman, P. 1984. Expression and the nature of emotion. In *Approaches to Emotion*, ed. K. R. Scherer, P. Ekman, pp. 319–43. Hillsdale, NJ: Erlbaum

Ekman, P., Friesen, W. V., Ancoli, S. 1980. Facial signs of emotional experience. *J. Pers. Soc. Psychol.* 39:1125–34

Ekman, P., Hager, J., Friesen, W. 1981. The symmetry of emotional and deliberate facial actions. *Psychophysiology* 18:101–6

Ekman, P., Levenson, R. W., Friesen, W. V. 1983. Autonomic nervous system activity distinguishes among emotions. *Science* 221:1208–10

Fridlund, A. J., Gilbert, A. N. 1985. Emotion and facial expression. *Science* 230:607–8

Gellhorn, E. 1964. Motion and emotion: the role of proprioception in the physiology and pathology of the emotions. *Psychol. Rev.* 71:457–72

Glaus, K., Kotses, H. 1983. Facial muscle tension influences lung airway resistance; limb muscle tension does not. *Biol. Psychol.* 17:105–20

Gratiolet, P. 1865. *De la physionomie et des mouvements d'expression.* Paris: Hetzel

Hager, J. C., Ekman, P. 1981. Methodological problems in Tourangeau and Ellsworth's study of facial expression and experience of emotion. *J. Pers. Soc. Psychol.*, 40:358–62

Harver, A., Kotses, H. 1984. Pulmonary changes induced by frontal EMG training. *Biol. Psychol.* 18:3–10

Ianni, P., Stettner, L., Freedman, R. R. 1986. Voluntary facial actions modulate cardiovascular responses during angry emotion. *Psychophysiology* 23:443 (Abstr.)

Izard, C. E. 1971. *The Face of Emotion.* New York: Appleton-Century-Crofts

Izard, C. E. 1981. Differential emotions theory and the facial feedback hypothesis of emotion activation: comments on Tourangeau and Ellsworth's "The role of facial response in the experience of emotion." *J. Pers. Soc. Psychol.* 40:350–54

Izard, C. E. 1985. Emotion and facial expression. *Science* 230:608

James, W. 1890. *The Principles of Psychology.* New York: Holt

James, W. 1922. What is an emotion? In *The Emotions*, ed. K. Dunlap, pp. 11–30. Baltimore, MD: Williams & Wilkins Co. (original work published 1884)

Jones, H. E. 1935. The galvanic skin reflex as related to overt emotional expression. *Am. J. Psychol.* 47:241–51

Jones, H. E. 1948. The study of patterns of emotional expression. In *Feelings and Emotions: The Mooseheart Symposium,* ed. M. L. Reymert, pp. 161–68. New York: McGraw-Hill

Kappas, A., Hess, U., McHugo, G. J., Lanzetta, J. T., Kleck, R. E. 1987. The facilitative effects of facial expression on self-generated emotion. *Psychophysiology* 24:595 (Abstr.)

Kleck, R. E., Vaughan, R. C., Cartwright-Smith, J., Vaughan, K. B., Colby, C. Z., et al. 1976. Effects of being observed on expressive subjective, and physiological responses to painful stimuli. *J. Pers. Soc. Psychol.* 34:1211–18

Kleinke, C. L., Walton, J. H. 1982. Influence of reinforced smiling on affective responses in an interview. *J. Pers. Soc. Psychol.* 42:557–65

Kopel, S., Arkowitz, H. 1974. Role playing as a source of self-observation and behavior change. *J. Pers. Soc. Psychol.* 29:677–86

Kotses, H., Glaus, K. D. 1981. Applications of biofeedback to the treatment of asthma: a critical review. *Biofeedback Self-Reg.* 6: 573–93

Kraut, R. E. 1982. Social presence, facial feedback, and emotion. *J. Pers. Soc. Psychol.* 42:853–63

Laird, J. D. 1974. Self-attribution of emotion: the effects of expressive behavior on the quality of emotional experience. *J. Pers. Soc. Psychol.* 29:475–86

Laird, J. 1984. The real role of facial response in the experience of emotion: a reply to Tourangeau and Ellsworth, and others. *J. Pers. Soc. Psychol.* 47:909–17

Laird, J., Crosby, M. 1974. Individual differences in self-attribution of emotion. In *Thinking and Feeling: The Cognitive Alteration of Feeling States,* ed. H. London, R. Nisbett, pp. 44–59. Chicago: Aldine

Landis, C. 1932. An attempt to measure emotional traits in juvenile delinquency. In *Studies in the Dynamics of Behavior,* ed. K. S. Lashley, pp. 265–323. Chicago: Univ. Chicago Press

Lanzetta, J. T., Cartwright-Smith, J., Kleck, R. E. 1976. Effects of nonverbal dissimulation on emotional experience and autonomic arousal. *J. Pers. Soc. Psychol.* 33:354–70

Lanzetta, J., Kleck, R. 1970. Encoding and decoding of nonverbal affect in humans. *J. Pers. Soc. Psychol.* 16:12–19

Learmonth, G., Ackerly, W., Kaplan, M. 1959. Relationships between palmar skin potential during stress and personality variables. *Psychosom. Med.* 21:150–57

LeDoux, J. E. 1987. Emotion. In *Handbook of*

Physiology—The Nervous System V, ed. F. Plum, pp. 419–59. Washington, DC: Am. Physiol. Soc.

Levenson, R. W. 1989. Emotion and the autonomic nervous system: a prospectus for research on autonomic specificity. In *Social Psychophysiology: Theory and Clinical Applications*, ed. H. Wagner. London: Wiley. In press

Leventhal, H., Cupchik, G. C. 1975. The informational and facilitative effects of an audience upon expression and the evaluation of humorous stimuli. *J. Exp. Soc. Psychol.* 11:363–80

Leventhal, H., Mace, W. 1970. The effect of laughter on evaluation of a slapstick movie. *J. Pers.* 38:16–30

McArthur, L. Z., Solomon, M. R., Jaffe, R. H. 1980. Weight differences in emotional responsiveness to proprioceptive and pictorial stimuli. *J. Pers. Soc. Psychol.* 39:308–19

McCanne, T. R., Anderson, J. A. 1987. Emotional responding following experimental manipulation of facial electromyographic activity. *J. Pers. Soc. Psychol.* 52:759–68

McCaul, K. D., Holmes, D. S., Solomon, S. 1982. Voluntary expressive changes and emotion. *J. Pers. Soc. Psychol.* 42:145–52

McHugo, G. J. 1983. *Facial EMG and self-reported emotion*. Presented at Ann. Meet. Soc. Psychophysiol. Res., 23rd, Asimilomar, CA

McHugo, G. J., Lanzetta, J. T., Sullivan, D. G., Masters, R. D., Englis, B. G. 1985. Emotional reactions to a political leader's expressive displays. *J. Pers. Soc. Psychol.* 49:1513–29

Matsumoto, D. 1987. The role of facial response in the experience of emotion: more methodological problems and a meta-analysis. *J. Pers. Soc. Psychol.* 52:769–74

Miller, D. J., Kotses, H. 1987. The effects of facial muscle tension changes upon total respiratory resistance determined by the forced oscillations technique. *Psychophysiology* 24:601 (Abstr.)

Monrad-Krohn, G. H. 1924. On the dissociation of voluntary and emotional innervation in facial paresis of central origin. *Brain* 47:22–35

Monrad-Krohn, G. H. 1939. On facial dissociation. *Acta Psychiatr. Neurol. Scand.* 14:557–66

Notarius, C. I., Wemple, C., Ingraham, L. J., Burns, T. J., Kollar, E. 1982. Multichannel responses to an interpersonal stressor: interrelationships among facial display, heart rate, self-report of emotion, and threat appraisal. *J. Pers. Soc. Psychol.* 43:400–8

Notarius, C., Levenson, R. 1979. Expressive tendencies and physiological response to stress. *J. Pers. Soc. Psychol.* 37:1204–10

Ochsmann, R., Henrich, R. 1984. Erregungsniveau, expressives Verhalten und die Bemertung aversives Stimulation. (Physiological arousal, expressive behavior). *Z. Exp. Angew. Psychol.* 31:287–307

Pasquarelli, B., Bull, N. 1951. Experimental investigation of the body-mind continuum in affective states. *J. Nerv. Ment. Dis.* 113:512–21

Perry, R. B. 1926. *General Theory of Value: Its Meaning and Basic Principles Contrasted in Terms of Interest*. New York: Longmans, Green

Piderit, T. 1858. *Grundzüge der Mimik und Physiognomik*. Braunschweig: Vieweg und Sohn

Piderit, T. 1888. *La Mimique et la physiognomie*. Paris: Alcan

Prideaux, E. 1920. The psychogalvanic reflex: a review. *Brain* 43:50–73

Putnam, L., Winton, W., Krauss, R. 1982. Effects of nonverbal affective dissimulation on phasic autonomic and facial responses. *Psychophysiology* 19:580–81

Rhodewalt, F., Comer, R. 1979. Induced compliance attitude change: once more with feeling. *J. Exp. Soc. Psychol.* 15:35–47

Riccelli, P., Klions, H., Dale, A. 1984. Induced depression and elation enhanced by experimenter-demanded facial expression: physiological measures. *Psychophysiology* 21: 594 (Abstr.)

Ridgeway, D., Waters, E. 1987. Induced mood and preschoolers' behavior: Isolating the effects of hedonic tone and degree of arousal. *J. Pers. Soc. Psychol.* 52:620–25

Rutledge, L. L., Hupka, R. B. 1985. The facial feedback hypothesis: methodological concerns and new supporting evidence. *Motiv. Emotion* 9:219–40

Rutledge, L. L., Garvey, J., Johnson, C., Sheldon, B. 1987. *Interaction of facial muscle contractions, subjective emotion, and emotion context*. Presented at Ann. Conv. Am. Psychol. Assoc., 98th, New York

Schwartz, G. E., Ahern, G. L., Brown, S. 1979. Lateralized facial muscle responses to positive and negative emotional stimuli. *Psychophysiology* 16:561–71

Schwartz, G. E., Brown, S., Ahern, G. L. 1980. Facial muscle patterning and subjective experience during affective imagery: sex differences. *Psychophysiology* 17:75–82

Schwartz, G. E., Fair, P. L., Salt, P., Mandel, M. R., Klerman, G. L. 1976. Facial muscle patterning to affective imagery in depressed and nondepressed subjects. *Science* 192:489–91

Schwartz, G. E., Weinberger, D. A., Singer, J. A. 1981. Cardiovascular differentiation of happiness, sadness, anger, and fear following imagery and exercise. *Psychosom. Med.* 43:343–64

Sherrington, C. S. 1900. Experiments on the value of vascular and visceral factors for the genesis of emotion. *Proc. R. Soc. London* 56:390–403

Sirota, A. D., Schwartz, G. E., Kristeller, J. L. 1987. Facial muscle activity during induced mood states: differential growth and carryover of elated versus depressed patterns. *Psychophysiology* 24:691–99

Smith, C. A., McHugo, G. J., Lanzetta, J. T. 1986. The facial muscle patterning of posed and imagery-induced expressions of emotion by expressive and nonexpressive posers. *Motiv. Emotion* 10:133–57

Strack, F., Martin, L. L., Stepper, S. 1988. Inhibiting and facilitating conditions of facial expressions: a non-obtrusive test of the facial feedback hypothesis. *J. Pers. Soc. Psychol.* 54:768–77

Sutherland, M. E., Rasayon, K. B., Harrell, J. P., Neita, D., Fields, C. 1984. Physiological and affective responses to emotional imagery in a black population. *Psychophysiology* 21:596

Teasdale, J., Bancroft, J. 1977. Manipulation of thought content as a determinant of mood and corrugator EMG activity in depressed patients. *J. Abnorm. Psychol.* 86:235–41

Tomkins, S. S. 1962. *Affect, Imagery, Consciousness:* Vol. 1. *The Positive Affects.* New York: Springer

Tomkins, S. S. 1963. *Affect, Imagery, Consciousness:* Vol. 2. *The Negative Affects.* New York: Springer

Tomkins, S. S. 1980. Affect as amplification: some modifications in theory. In *Emotion: Theory, Research and Experience,* ed. R. Plutchik, H. Kellerman, pp. 141–64. New York: Academic

Tomkins, S. S. 1981. The role of facial response in the experience of emotion: a reply to Tourangeau and Ellsworth. *J. Pers. Soc. Psychol.* 40:355–57

Tourangeau, R., Ellsworth, P. C. 1979. The role of facial response in the experience of emotion. *J. Pers. Soc. Psychol.* 37:1519–31

Vaughan, K., Lanzetta, J. 1980. Vicarious instigation and conditioning of facial expressive and autonomic responses to a model's expressive display of pain. *J. Pers. Soc. Psychol.* 38:909–23

Vaughan, K., Lanzetta, J. 1981. The effect of modification of expressive displays on vicarious emotional arousal. *J. Exp. Soc. Psychol.* 17:16–30

Waynbaum, I. 1907. *La Physionomie Humaine: Son Mécanisme et son Rôle Social.* Paris: Alcan

Winton, W. 1986. The role of facial response in self-reports of emotion: a critique of Laird. *J. Pers. Soc. Psychol.* 50:808–12

Winton, W. M., Putnam, L. E., Krauss, R. M. 1984. Facial and autonomic manifestations of the dimensional structure of emotion. *J. Exp. Soc. Psychol.* 20:195–216

Zajonc, R. B. 1985. Emotion and facial efference: a theory reclaimed. *Science* 228:15–21

Zajonc, R. B. 1986. *The face as a primary instrument of social process.* Presented at Symp. "Social Psychology and the Emotions," Maison des Sciences de l'Homme, Paris

Zuckerman, M. K., Corman, R., Larrance, D. T., Spiegel, N. H. 1981. Facial, autonomic, and subjective components of emotion: the facial feedback hypothesis versus the externalizer-internalizer distinction. *J. Pers. Soc. Psychol.* 41:929–44

Ann. Rev. Psychol. 1989. 40:281–326

SOCIAL COGNITION

Steven J. Sherman

Department of Psychology, Indiana University, Bloomington, Indiana 47405

Charles M. Judd and Bernadette Park

Department of Psychology, University of Colorado, Boulder, Colorado 80309

CONTENTS

INTRODUCTION

For us, social cognition represents not a domain of inquiry within social psychology but an approach or set of assumptions guiding research in a variety of traditional substantive domains. Here we will illustrate the approach with reference to recent literatures in various subareas of social psychology. The approach deals with three fundamental questions, regardless of the particular social behavior that is the object of study: First, what exactly

281

is stored in memory that may mediate social behavior? What type of social information is stored, and how is it organized in memory? We believe that both the information and its organization influence how social behavior is cognitively mediated. Second—the crux of social cognition research—how does social information stored in memory affect subsequent information processing, judgments, choices, and behaviors? What factors determine the probability that particular social data are used in making judgments and behavioral choices, and how does stored information affect the processing and interpretation of new information? Third, how is stored information changed both by new information and by reflection, reappraisal, and similar processes?

Our discussion of recent literature relevant to these questions bridges a variety of traditional substantive concerns within social psychology. We have chosen to review recent literatures in the areas of attitudes and attitude change, person perception, social stereotypes, judgment and decision making, and the self. We explore how research in these areas has progressed by taking a social cognition approach, demonstrating commonalities in the issues raised across the substantive domains: A focus on the cognitive mediation of various social behaviors reveals similarities in both the questions asked and the answers obtained across diverse substantive areas.

For broader treatments of research in these substantive areas, not limited to research conducted within the social cognition approach, we refer the reader to excellent reviews on attitudes and attitude change (Chaiken & Stangor 1987), person perception (Fiske & Neuberg 1988; Hamilton 1988; Wyer & Srull 1986), social stereotypes (Brewer & Kramer 1985), judgment and decision making (Abelson & Levi 1985), and the self (Markus & Wurf 1987).

THE NATURE AND ORGANIZATION OF INFORMATION STORED IN MEMORY

Heavily influenced by the theories and methods of cognitive psychologists, researchers have wondered what types of social knowledge we possess and how that knowledge is organized. Such questions contrast sharply with earlier research that looked simply at the contents of social knowledge [e.g. in stereotyping (Katz & Braly 1933)].

Type of Information Stored

At least two types of information are stored in memory. The first consists of abstracted judgments, summaries, or inferences about a social domain. These abstractions may result from constructive processing of bits of information to form a summary (or prototype) of the domain. Such abstractions may be produced on-line, as the bits of information are presented, or they may be computed later as a memory-based judgment from retrieved information. Alternatively, summary information may come to the perceiver in an already abstracted form, which he or she may simply learn. The second type of information comprises the raw data from which summary judgments are made. These instances or exemplars may take a variety of forms in the different domains.

In stereotypes, abstracted information corresponds to category-level attributes ascribed to the group. Women, for example, are seen as less aggressive than men. At times these attributes are constructed from the behavior of group members, but they may also simply be learned from socializing agents. Information about specific exemplars or members of the group is stored in memory as well.

Park and Hastie (1987) demonstrated that when presented with a series of behaviors by members of a group, subjects abstracted central tendency and variability information. They argued that these category-level attributes were calculated as the behaviors were presented, because subjects' recall of specific behaviors was uncorrelated with category-level perceptions. Both the category-level judgments and memory for specific instances influenced subsequent judgments about the group. Linville et al (1986, 1987) developed an exemplar-based computer simulation of category representation (Hintzman 1986; Medin & Schaffer 1978). In the model, categories are represented by a set of exemplars acquired through previous experience with group members. A sample of the exemplars is retrieved as the basis for subsequent category-level judgments. Category-level information has no special status relative to exemplars in such exemplar models. Smith & Zarate (1987) argued that social categories based predominantly on either category-level or exemplar information both exist, and that what type of information dominates depends in part on the subjects' goals when the category is formed. For example, as US residents construct certain categories (e.g. "Nicaraguans") their knowledge representation contains primarily category-level attributes, whereas in forming others (e.g. "Californians" or "New Yorkers") the structure is largely instance-based.

The field of person perception has been built around the assumption that information about others includes both instances and abstractions. The abstract or summary judgment in impression formation can either be an overall evaluation of the target derived from trait attributes, or it can be a trait inference derived from behaviors performed by the target. Anderson & Hubert (1963) explicitly addressed the representation of both raw data and summary abstractions. They argued that the two types of information are stored in somewhat separate memory systems (the "two-memory hypothesis") such that each can be retrieved independently. When subjects were shown a list of traits describing a target, their impression judgments showed a primacy effect; but when they were asked to recall the traits on which the impression was based, their performance showed a recency effect. Lingle, Ostrom, and their colleagues also presented evidence that both traits and summary judgments are stored in memory (Carlston 1980; Lingle et al 1983).

Burnstein & Schul (1982, 1983) have written a great deal on this issue, arguing for four phases of impression formation: initial encoding of the trait (perceptual recognition), elaborative encoding (understanding the semantic meaning of the trait), integration (forming a summary evaluation from the traits), and making a decision (e.g. occupational suitability). Set size (the number of traits presented) affected the time spent on initial encoding and (to a lesser extent) on elaborative encoding but had relatively little effect on integration and decision. The affective consistency of the presented traits, on the other hand, had little effect on initial and elaborative encoding but a large effect on time to integrate and decide. Schul (1983) argued that an abstraction follows naturally from the integration process and that the traits and the abstraction are stored separately.

Researchers have also looked at whether the summary abstraction process occurs spontaneously during social interaction. (A process is spontaneous if it is engaged in frequently and without an external request.) Winter & Uleman (1984) argued that trait inferences are in large part spontaneous. Subjects read sentences describing an action performed by an actor. Recall for the sentences was better when cued with a trait relevant to the action than when cued with a word semantically related to the actor or when not cued at all. According to the encoding specificity hypothesis (Tulving & Thomson 1973), the trait words were likely thought about and encoded with the behavior at the time the behavior was presented, resulting in their effectiveness as retrieval cues. Smith & Miller (1983) found that a judgment about whether a behavior indicated a trait was made as quickly as a judgment of the gender of the actor. Attributional judgments of dispositional and situational causes of the behavior, and judgments of liking, all took longer than the trait judgment. These studies suggest that trait inferences from behaviors are made relatively spontaneously as part of the comprehension process.

Bassili & Smith (1986) questioned the conclusions of Winter & Uleman. In their research they further enhanced the effectiveness of the trait as a retrieval cue by giving subjects impression rather than memory instructions prior to the experimental task (Gordon & Wyer 1987). They argued that if trait inferences are spontaneous, instructing subjects to form an impression should have no effect on the impression-formation process. Although it is possible to influence the extent to which behaviors are processed with their relevance to trait concepts in mind (Hastie 1984; Higgins et al 1982b; Hoffman et al 1984), Winter & Uleman (1984) and Smith & Miller (1983) do demonstrate that under very minimal conditions there is evidence of at least some degree of spontaneous trait inference.

The suggestion that attitudes are evaluations stored in long-term memory has marked a fundamental shift in how attitudes are defined and assessed (Fazio 1986; Judd & Krosnick 1988; Sherman 1987; Zanna & Rempel 1987). More traditionally an attitude has been defined as the set of overt responses an individual provides on attitude rating scales or in response to an attitude questionnaire. Researchers are now devoting attention to the issue of what gets retrieved from memory as subjects respond to attitude scale items (Tourangeau & Rasinski 1988).

Attitudes as stored evaluations are not always abstracted at the time stimuli are encountered. However, many social situations encourage us to form evaluations spontaneously and to store those evaluations in long-term memory for future retrieval and use (Fazio et al 1983–1984).

Along with an evaluation we may also store information about the attributes of the attitude object, about affective responses that the object elicits, about how we have behaved toward the object in the past, and about how significant others evaluate the object. All of these may be more specific bits of information upon which an attitude (as an abstracted judgment) is based. Attitudes, then, may vary as a function of the type of information stored with them (Zanna & Rempel 1987).

In the area of decision making, specifically juror decision making, the assumption of Bayesian or information-integration models of decision making has been that relevant information is encoded by updating a judgment stored in memory. Thus, a given judgment—e.g. whether a defendant is guilty—is updated continuously as evidence is encountered during a trial. At the point of deliberation, the juror reports the final updated judgment and recalls whatever evidence in support of that judgment has been stored in memory.

Recently, a different model of how information relevant to judgments is stored in memory has been put forward by Pennington & Hastie (1988). They assume that jurors store evidence in an episodic or story schema. Such a story schema has a relatively formal structure, into which new evidence is incorporated as the trial progresses. No summary judgment is necessarily formed on-line as the information is encountered. Rather, when a verdict is called for, the juror simply finds one whose story matches most closely the story that has been formulated in memory from the evidence presented.

Much of the early work concerning the self-concept was devoted to specifying its contents (e.g. James 1890; Allport 1943; Wylie 1979). More recently, attention has turned to the structure of the self and how it is cognitively represented.

Psychologists have long argued that the self has many different facets

(Erikson 1950; Sullivan 1953)—even inconsistent facets (Cantor & Kihlstrom 1987; Harter 1986a). Theory and empirical evidence have now been offered in support of an even more multifaceted, diverse, and complex concept of the self (see Cantor et al 1986, Greenwald & Pratkanis 1984, and Markus & Wurf 1987 for reviews). According to these views, the self is a collection of schemas, conceptions, prototypes, goals, or images that are arranged in a space (McGuire & McGuire 1982; Markus & Nurius 1986) or a system (Martindale 1980). As such, the self is no different from other concepts and mental representations (Kihlstrom & Cantor 1984; Markus & Sentis 1982).

More specific ideas about the cognitive structure of the self have been put forth. Markus (1977; Markus & Sentis 1982) conceives of the self as a system of schemata. These schemata (self as teacher, self as jogger, self as independent person) are connected to the self in varying degrees, and a person may be aschematic with respect to certain roles or traits. Each schema is a generalization about what the self is like and contains trait information, behavioral information, and inferences (Kuiper & Derry 1981; Dance & Kuiper 1987). Pratkanis & Greenwald (1985) view the self as a schema that contains not only descriptive information but also rules and procedures for its own functioning and development (see also Kihlstrom & Cantor 1984). Markus & Sentis (1982) claim, however, that the self is a special kind of schema owing to its size, complexity, connectedness, and affect (see Higgins & Bargh 1987 for a discussion of the self as a unique structure).

Rhodewalt & Agustsdottir (1986; see also Jones et al 1981) have recently suggested viewing the various selves as latitudes rather than as discrete points. That is, for every self-conception there is a latitude of acceptable ideas (traits, behaviors, etc) and a latitude of rejection (characteristics unacceptable to the self-concept). This view has proven useful for understanding how the self processes information and how it might be subject to change.

In another structural model of self-conception, Hoelter (1985) has argued against a one-dimensional view of the self (e.g. Wylie 1979) and has adopted a role-identity model (Burke & Tully 1977). In this model, roles and attributes are the key elements of the self-concept. The self is differentiated into identities, which are further differentiated into personal attributes. This allows for a general self that differs from the self in its various roles (see also Breckler & Greenwald 1982; Breckler et al, unpublished). Bower & Gilligan (1979) conceive of the self as an associative memory network where information is stored in the form of propositions relating the self to specific episodes or characteristics.

With regard to more specific characteristics of the self, the differentiated parts of the self have been thought of in terms of roles (Hoelter 1985) as well as in terms of relevant traits and characteristics (Markus & Wurf 1987).

People differ in the components of their subselves and differ in the relative importance of these components.

Greenwald (1982; Breckler & Greenwald 1986) points out different ego tasks that can be thought of as corresponding to important structural characteristics of the self. There is, at the lowest level, a diffuse or primitive self concerned only with feeling good. In addition, there is a private self (where self-concerns come into play), a public self (concerned with others' evaluations), and a collective self (concerned with reference groups).

Finally, there is a temporal component to the self—a past self and a future self as well as a here-and-now self. What one decides that one is at present and how one feels about it is determined in part by one's view of one's past self. This happens in part because the past self is seen as having some continuity and unity with the present self and in part because the past can serve as an anchor or reference point for judging the present (Strack et al 1985).

Michael Ross (McFarland & Ross 1987; Ross & Conway 1986), who has studied people's constructions and reconstructions of the past, holds that people rewrite their autobiographies whenever their present conditions change. The present is used as a reference point from which to reevaluate the past (see also Hirt 1987). Work on hindsight bias (Baron & Hershey 1988; Fischhoff 1982; Fischhoff & Beyth 1975) also concerns how knowledge of the present guides memories of the past.

Hierarchical Representation of Stored Information

Realizing that information exists in memory at different levels of abstraction, numerous researchers have wondered about the organization of the levels. Many have argued for a hierarchical organization, with the most abstract information at the top of the hierarchy, and instances or exemplars at the bottom. For some domains, an intermediate level of abstraction is thought to exist as well.

It is not always clear what is meant by a hierarchical representation of abstraction levels. For example, based on work by Rosch (1981), some researchers argue that there is a "basic level" of abstraction for a given domain at an intermediate point in the hierarchy. This level is the most likely to be accessed and used because it is the most functional, providing some detail but not too much. What defines a basic level of abstraction is controversial. Our position is that the level of information used is determined by the context in which the domain is being thought about, the subject's goals and characteristics, and the subject's past experience (Barsalou 1987).

Social psychologists interested in stereotyping have been quick to argue that social categories are hierarchically organized with stereotype attributes (e.g. "domineering") at the top of the hierarchy and instances of the group at the bottom (Miller & Brewer 1986). Researchers have also argued for an intermediate level of abstraction analogous to the basic-level concept (Brewer et al 1981; Brewer & Lui 1984; Deaux et al 1985; Noseworthy & Lott 1984; Weber & Crocker 1983). Identifiable clusters of group members, or subtypes, make up this intermediate level. Brewer et al (1981) argued that stereotypes of the elderly consist of distinct subtypes such as the elder statesman and the grandmotherly type. Brewer & Lui (1984) extended the research to old peoples' perceptions of themselves and found that subjects were particularly likely to make distinctions among subgroups to which they belonged as opposed to other subgroups and young people.

In the field of person perception there is an implied hierarchy of the types of information stored: Behaviors are at the most specific level, trait attributes are at an intermediate level, and a global evaluation of the target is at the most general level. Neither this ordering nor the strength of such relations has been directly examined using, for example, priming studies. Hampson et al (1986) provided evidence that some trait concepts are hierarchically ordered such that more inclusive traits subsume more specific traits (e.g. "artistic" subsumes "musical"), but the findings were not applied to representations of specific individuals. Hampson et al presented an excellent discussion of the difficulties of applying the basic-level concept to personality traits. A number of researchers have challenged the notion that person information is organized by traits, arguing instead that at least under some conditions the goals of the target provide the basis of organization (Hoffman et al 1981; Trzebinski et al 1985; Trzebinski & Richards 1986).

With respect to the organization of information regarding multiple targets, there is a substantial body of work that looks at alternatives to person organization. One such alternative is organization by trait attributes (Herstein et al 1980; Pryor et al 1984; for a related study, see Cafferty et al 1986), such that all individuals who are intelligent are stored together in memory. Bond & Brockett (1987) argued against organization by traits, suggesting instead that the individuals' social context serves as the basis for organization (e.g. "*college* professors"). McCann et al (1985) demonstrated that gender and race are likely to be used as bases for organizing individuals. Mayer & Bower (1986) found that person prototypes could easily be learned, and that distinctions between instances that fit or did not fit the prototype were readily made even though the prototype consisted only of a set of uncorrelated, probabilistic features. Andersen & Klatzky (1987) argued that such person prototypes, rather than trait concepts, serve as the basis for organizing information about others.

With regard to the self, Cantor & Kihlstrom (1987) and Shavelson & Marsh (1986) posited a general self at the top of a hierarchy of more specific selves, each with its prototypic representations as well as episodic exemplars (see Marsh 1986 for a review of various multidimensional models of the self). These multiple self-aspects have their own sets of associations among features, affect, and propositions. A synthesis of such views might suggest that the self comprises a core and many peripheral parts. Kelly (1955) orginally proposed such a view. Cantor & Kihlstrom (1987) supported the notion of a core self that is experienced as unitary because the various other selves of which it is constituted resemble one another and "overlap." Some of these selves are thought to be more central and are more likely to be the focus of self-reflection. Likewise, Rosenberg & Gara (1985) see patterns of family resemblance among the different contextualized selves. In addition, a self abstracted from all the different subselves may exist at the highest level of the hierarchy. Each of the subselves will have its own prototypic representation (e.g. a typical representation of the self as father) as well as behavioral episodes and exemplars of subself-relevant behaviors.

Relations Between Information Stored at the Same and Different Levels

There are likely both domain differences and individual differences in the tightness of the connections among (*a*) the various levels of abstraction and (*b*) the multiple exemplars stored at the same level of abstraction. In knowledge structures with loose associations one can access information at one level without necessarily retrieving information at another. Information at the exemplar level can differ from that at the abstract level, and two conflicting attributes can exist at the same abstract level. Such dissociations are unlikely for tightly connected structures.

How much attitude-relevant information is stored in memory (Linville 1982; Kallgren & Wood 1986), and to what degree is it evaluatively consistent with itself and with the summary evaluative judgment that is the attitude (Chaiken & Yates 1985; Lusk & Judd 1988; Millar & Tesser 1986a,b; Tetlock 1983, 1984; Wilson & Dunn 1986)? Substantial differences exist between both individuals and domains in the degree to which the overall evaluation of an attitude object is consistent with the more specific bits of stored information about the object. Chaiken & Yates (1985) and Millar & Tesser (1986a) have focused on between-individuals differences in the degree to which the evaluative connotations of an object's attributes are consistent with one's affective response to it. Lusk & Judd (1988) have shown that, in the political domain, greater evaluative consistency of what is stored in memory about an attitude object is associated with greater political knowledge and experience; this difference in turn is associated with more extreme evaluative judgments. Finally, Judd & Krosnick (1988) and Tourangeau et al (1988) have both argued that differences in the consistency of information stored in memory about an attitude object are associated with differences in the centrality of the attitude or the degree to which it is espoused with conviction.

The differences in attitude accessibility that Fazio has documented presumably derive from differences in strength of the connections between the stored attitude and other stored bits of information likely to bring the attitude to mind. More accessible attitudes are more highly integrated with other information in memory and therefore more likely to be primed by situational events. Recently Judd et al (1988) have shown that giving an attitude response on one political issue can prime or facilitate responses on other linked attitude issues, thus demonstrating the interconnections among political attitudes stored in memory.

Dissociations between attitude-relevant bits of information stored in memory are perhaps most apparent in the literature on attitude response consistency (Converse 1964) and the effects of item wording or context on attitude responses (Schuman & Presser 1981; Tourangeau & Rasinski 1988). Substantially different attitude responses can result from relatively minor changes in item wording or the context in which an item is embedded. Thus retrieval of at least some attitude-relevant bits of information does not bring forth all of the other relevant information from memory.

In the stereotyping domain, researchers have begun to develop a method for measuring the tightness of associations between a category label and attributes stored with the category (Devine 1987; Gaertner & Dovidio 1986; Gaertner & McLaughlin 1983). In a study by Dovidio et al (1986), subjects (all white) were asked to decide whether an attribute could ever characterize members of two groups, blacks and whites. The attributes varied in their evaluative nature and their relevance to the group stereotype. Responses were faster to attributes when primed with the stereotypically consistent group. They were also faster for positive items when primed by "white," and for negative items when primed by "blacks." Such a method could be extended to look at associations between general attributes of the categories, and subtypes, or specific exemplars stored in memory.

Judd & Park (1988) offered an explanation of out-group homogeneity based on patterns of retrieving information at the different levels of abstraction. They argued that when thinking about the out-group, only category-level attributes are brought to mind. When thinking about the in-group, both category attributes and specific exemplars are retrieved; and this leads to the perception of greater variability. Moreover, they find a dissociation between judgments made of the group as a whole versus those of individual group members. Anticipated competition led to views of the out-group as homogeneous, but this effect was not present under anticipated cooperation. However, memory for the subordinate attributes of out-group members was actually superior under anticipated competition than cooperation. Such dissociations, they argued, imply unique representations of group- and individual-level information. Thus judgments of the group as a whole need not equal the aggregate of perceptions of the individuals.

Within person perception, Anderson & Hubert (1963), Burnstein & Schul (1982, 1983; Schul 1983), and Posner & Snyder (1975) all refer to two memory stores in impression formation, one for the traits themselves, and one for a summary impression or evaluation. The precise meaning of "separate stores" is unclear, but certainly it is meant to account for such dissociations as that reported by Anderson & Hubert, who found a primacy effect in impressions but a recency effect in trait recall. Many researchers have also argued that one type of information (typically the trait data) is accessed and used in subsequent judgments to the exclusion of the other (see the section below on the use of stored information in processing new information). Investigators have not yet looked at how retrieval of one sort of information influences activation of the other, nor at how discrepancies between the two stores might arise. A list of factors influencing the tightness of associations could include the importance and familiarity of the target and the information presentation format. It appears that when an information discrepancy is present at initial learning, perceivers will attempt to resolve it before storing the information (Asch & Zukier 1984).

The existence of many hierarchically arrayed subselves, exemplars, prototypes, and abstractions means that different aspects of the self can be accessible at any given time. The part active at any moment is called the "phenomenal self" by Jones et al (1981), the "working self" by Markus & Kunda (1986).

Recent work has called into question this view of self as a highly integrated and organized structure. Higgins et al (1988) found that when self-related prime words and target words were used in a Stroop paradigm, reactions were not slower. Because relatedness between the prime and the target typically increases reaction time, Higgins et al had reason to doubt the structural interconnectedness among self-attributes. Raynor & McFarlin (1986) argued that the assumption of an organized set of self-perceptions is unnecessary—people can and do function quite well without such a systematic representation.

Nevertheless, the belief that the various aspects of one's self-concept constitute a well-developed and integrated cognitive structure has held sway for many years (e.g. Epstein 1973; Kelly 1955; Lecky 1945; Rogers 1951; Snygg & Combs 1949). This view has been supported by various empirical studies that have predicted the effects of organized self-knowledge on various aspects of information processing (Greenwald 1981b; Greenwald & Pratkanis 1984; Markus 1980; Markus & Sentis 1982; Rogers 1981). The self-reference effect (discussed below), the finding that material is better recalled when encoded with reference to the self (Rogers et al 1977), is typically taken as support for structural interconnectedness of the self (but see Higgins & Bargh 1987 for an opposing view). In perhaps the strongest demonstration of this, Klein & Loftus (1988) and Klein & Kihlstrom (1986) demonstrated that self-referencing is effective for recall in part because it involves organizational processing, a perception of the relations among self-referenced words.

Steele & Liu (1983; Liu & Steele 1986) reported that bolstering one part of the self can compensate for tensions, anxieties, and self-doubts about another part. Using an individual difference approach, Linville (1985, 1987) focused on the importance of the complexity of self-representation as a structural property. Complexity is defined by both the number of selves represented and their degree of mutual independence. High-complexity individuals (many independent selves) seem protected from the general negative effects of stress. Self-complexity acts as a buffer against the spillover effects of negative emotions. Dance & Kuiper (1987) supported this role of self-complexity in protecting individuals against depression.

IMPLICATIONS OF STORED INFORMATION FOR JUDGMENTS AND BEHAVIORS

Beyond the question of content, organization, and structure, the social cognition approach is an attempt to understand (*a*) what aspects or dimensions of stored social knowledge influence our judgments, inferences, decisions, and acts, and (*b*) the psychological processes through which mental representations have their impact.

Factors That Influence Which Stored Information Is Used

Not every piece of stored information relevant to a judgment is used in making it. What determines which stored items of knowledge do play a role?

ACCESSIBILITY   Accessibility—the ease with which a bit of knowledge can be brought to consciousness—matters most. Whether this accessibility derives from the cognitive structure of the individual or is due to such situational factors as priming or context, more accessible information has an advantage in the determination of acts and decisions.

The role of information accessibility has been most thoroughly explored in the area of judgment and decision-making. In proposing that simplifying rules or heuristic principles commonly serve as a basis of judgment, Tversky & Kahneman (1973) identified availability as one such general heuristic. In judging the frequency of a category, the likelihood of an event, or the frequency of cooccurrence of two or more events, people tend to use the number of specific instances that can be brought to mind and the ease with which they can be brought to mind as primary bases for judgment. Because the accessibility (availability) of represented instances is employed to judge frequency or probability, whatever affects this accessibility affects such judgments.

Availability has subsequently been used as a way of understanding many social psychological phenomena (see Sherman & Corty 1984 for a review). Recent work has directly manipulated accessibility in order to see its effects on judgment. Gabrielcik & Fazio (1984) subliminally primed subjects with words beginning with the letter T in order to increase the accessibility of such words. This priming had significant effects on judgments of the frequency of the letter T. Similarly, Lewandowsky & Smith (1983) made certain names on a list more accessible by repetition or by salience. Recallability and frequency estimates for these names increased.

Reyes et al (1980) found that vivid information in a criminal case was recalled better than nonvivid information and guided judgments of innocence or guilt, although it had no more probative value than nonvivid information. However, Shedler & Manis (1986) concluded that this effect of vividness on judgments is not necessarily due to the increased accessibility of such information. They found that vividness affected both information availability and judgments, but causal modeling analysis showed no mediational role of accessibility on judgments.

The field of social cognition has also used the availability heuristic to account for the cognitive effects of imagining and explaining hypothetical future events. When people imagine a particular future, judgments about the likelihood of such a future increase—presumably because various speculative routes to such a future become cognitively accessible (Campbell & Fairey 1985; Hirt & Sherman 1985; Sherman et al 1985; Sherman et al 1983). Another fruitful area of research into the construction and modification of scenarios involves how counterfactual thinking—the mutation of events or generation of alternatives to reality—can affect judgments and affective reactions (Johnson 1986; Kahneman & Miller 1986; Landman 1987; Wells & Gavanski 1988; Wells et al 1987).

The False Consensus Effect (in which one's own positions or characteristics are judged to be more widespread than they really are) has also been interpreted within an accessibility context. Although other cognitive and motivational explanations have been suggested, the extent to which one's own attributes and beliefs are accessible remains a principal factor in the FCE (Dawes 1988; Hoch 1987; Marks & Miller 1987; Sherman et al 1984a). Jonides & Naveh-Benjamin (1987), for example, demonstrated that frequency estimates in general are based less on a direct coding of frequency information than on indirect mechanisms involving the strength or availability of memory traces. Likewise, Williams & Durso (1986) concluded that frequency judgments are based on availability rather than on automatically made frequency estimates (contra Alba et al 1980).

Finally, the effects of priming on social judgments involve construct accessibility. Ambiguously presented social stimuli are typically interpreted as instances of highly available categories (Higgins et al 1977; Smith & Branscombe 1987, 1988; Srull & Wyer 1980). Priming has also been shown to affect problem-solving strategies (Higgins & Chaires 1980; LaRue & Olejnik 1980) as well as more complex social judgments and behaviors (Wilson & Capitman 1982).

As stored, abstracted, evaluative judgments, attitudes differ in how easily and spontaneously they can be accessed or retrieved from memory (Fazio et al 1983; Fazio et al 1986). Attitudes seem relatively accessible when based on direct experience of the attitude object (Fazio et al 1982, Fazio & Zanna 1981) and when they have been expressed repeatedly in the past (Powell & Fazio 1984). Fazio (1986; Fazio & Williams 1986; Fazio & Zanna 1981) showed that attitudes that come readily and perhaps spontaneously to mind are more typically related to behavioral choices than are less accessible attitudes. Kallgren & Wood (1986) likewise showed that attitudes affect behavior in proportion to the sheer amount of attitude-relevant information subjects can retrieve from memory.

A number of studies have argued that individual differences in the extent to which attitudes guide behavior result from differences in attitude accessibility. Cacioppo et al (1986), for instance, suggested that subjects higher in "need for cognition" evidence greater attitude-behavior consistency because their attitudes have been thought about in great detail previously and so, presumably, come to mind more readily when confronted with a behavioral choice. Quite a number of studies have indicated that low-self-monitoring individuals show greater attitude-behavior consistency than do high-self-monitors (Ajzen et al 1982; Snyder & Kendzierski 1982; Zanna et al 1980). Kardes et al (1986) showed that low-self-monitors have attitudes that are more accessible than those of high-self-monitors, presumably clarifying the mediating variable responsible for these differences in attitude-behavior consistency.

Within stereotyping, one of the clearest determinants of accessibility is the physical salience of category membership (Crocker et al 1984). Race, gender, and age are all easily identifiable and, as a result, highly accessible categories. Chumbley (1986) argued that the speed with which a stimulus can be verified as a member of a category depends on the probability with which that category is mentioned in response to the stimulus. This is even more important than the typicality per se of the stimulus to the cateogory.

Devine (1987) suggested that the accessibility of information in the knowledge structure depends on the perceiver's level of prejudice. She argued that both high- and low-prejudice subjects know of negative attributes that comprise the stereotype, and that such information is automatically activated in response to the category label. Low-prejudice subjects have in addition positive attributes stored with the category, and these are accessed through controlled processes. This is an example of differential accessibility of information in the structure as a function of subject characteristics. Stangor (1988) presented evidence that individuals differ in the accessibility of gender stereotypes.

There is a substantial body of literature in person perception on accessibility of trait constructs and the influence of these on impressions of new targets. Higgins et al (1982a) identified trait constructs for individuals that were very likely to be used in describing others, arguing that these were chronically accessible constructs. These constructs influenced subsequent perceptions of a target, such that information relevant to the trait construct was very likely to be remembered and to be mentioned in a written impression. A given trait construct can be accessible either because of momentary priming or because of long-term individual differences in construct usage. Bargh et al (1986) presented evidence that chronic and temporary sources of accessibility combine additively to influence perceptions of a target. Bargh & Pratto (1986) argued that individuals have a readiness to perceive stimulus information relevant to chronically accessible trait dimensions. On a Stroop color naming task, traits that were chronically accessible showed greater interference than those that were not.

Although studies of accessibility effects typically find that perceptions are assimilated to the primed construct, contrast effects sometimes occur. Lombardi et al (1987) looked at the effects of priming as a function of whether the prime could be recalled. In such a case, judgments were actually contrasted with the prime (perhaps because the consciously recalled prime acted as a standard in the judgment task), and only if the prime could not be recalled did assimilation effects obtain. In a second study they found that if the priming task was interrupted, assimilation effects obtained regardless of ability to recall the prime. These findings are consistent with those reported by Martin (1986). His task involved primes that were processed in a deliberate fashion, and that subjects were likely to remember. If the priming task was interrupted, assimilation effects occurred, and otherwise contrast effects occurred. Herr (1986; Herr et al 1983) found that if moderately extreme primes were presented, or if unambiguous stimuli were presented, assimilation effects occurred. However, if extreme primes were presented, contrast effects occurred.

Self structures have important effects on processing information about the self, about other people, and about situations and events. The self is an active and directing agent (Greenwald & Pratkanis 1984). However, the degree to which the self is involved in information processing and behavioral determination is not constant. An important reason for this is that the self-concept is not equally accessible at all times. The more accessible the self is in general, the more will self-relevant ideas and beliefs guide behavior. The role of increasing self-awareness by the use of mirrors or internal focus is certainly consistent with this. Mirrors seem to increase self-consistent behaviors and behaviors that correspond to self-ideals (Carver 1975; Gibbons 1978; Pryor et al 1977). Similarly, self-regulation is most efficient when the person is self-focused (Carver & Scheier 1981). The self must be reflected upon if it is to guide behavior (Wicklund 1982). Fenigstein & Levine (1984) showed that priming the self by having subjects use the first person in story construction has important effects on attributions and inferences. Thus, the accessibility of the self-concept is important in determining the extent to which the self guides information processing.

As we have seen, however, the self is a large, complex, and multifaceted structure. Thus not all aspects of the self will be accessible at all times. Making various aspects of the self-concept more accessible will have predictable effects. Thus, we can think of making the past self or the present self more accessible, or the good self or the bad self, or the self as parent or the self as child. Factors that increase the relative accessibility of some aspect of the self should lead to information processing and behavior more consistent with that particular aspect. Supportive of this view are the findings from previously cited studies where subjects are induced to imagine and explain hypothetical situations in which they might find themselves. For example, in one set of studies (Campbell & Fairey 1985; Sherman et al 1981), subjects were asked to imagine failure or success on a upcoming task. Such imaginings and explanations require the subjects to access either the effective or in-effective parts of themselves. In subsequent performance on the task, subjects who explained success generally did well, and those who explained failure did poorly. Likewise, Salancik & Conway's work (1975) demonstrates that making accessible certain past behaviors and events in one's life can influence current self-relevant judgments.

REPRESENTATIVENESS   A second reason why some stored information has an advantage over other information in the determination of judgments and behavior is that some information may match certain requirements of the situation better than others. When there is a high degree of similarity between the features of a stored knowledge structure and the features of the definition or prototype of the current object or situation, that knowledge structure is likely to be used in categorization and other kinds of judgments or behaviors.

Representativeness of constructs has been an important principle in the field of judgment and decision-making. Kahneman & Tversky (1972) held that in judging the probability that object A belongs to class B or that event A originates from process B, people judge by the extent to which the object or event represents (or is similar to) the essential features of the parent population or the generating process. Such a principle often leads to quick and accurate judgments. For instance, in the area of juror decision making, Pennington & Hastie (1986, 1988) suggested that jurors may simply match the evidence story they have constructed in memory to the stories that seem to be associated with each verdict possibility. Verdict judgments are then generated by the best match. However, because decision making based on such a representativeness heuristic involves the use of a limited amount of information, it is also associated with characteristic errors of judgment (see Sherman & Corty 1984 for a review). For example, in the area of hypothesis testing and information seeking, people are not interested in information about the alternatives to a hypothesis. They seem to seek out and use only information about the likelihood of the datum given the hypothesis rather than about the datum given the alternative (Baron et al 1988; Beyth-Marom & Fischhoff 1983; Skov & Sherman 1986). One reason for such biased search and use is that information that mentions the hypothesis under scrutiny is more similar to the kind of information that subjects have in mind to collect and more representative of useful information.

One factor that is often ignored when representativeness is used as a basis for judgment is the base-rate of the object or event. This is because base-rate (the prior probabilities) can have a large effect on the likelihood of an event or its category membership but little or no effect on the representativeness of that event. When judgments are made primarily on the basis of representativeness, outcomes that "look like" a target category will be judged as likely members even when the prior probability of an outcome being a member of the category is extremely small.

A good deal of work has documented the "base-rate fallacy" and specified the limits of such errors of judgment. Judges do not always use case information to the exclusion of base-rate information. When base-rate information has some meaningful causal relation to the outcome, it is not ignored (Ajzen 1977; Tversky & Kahneman 1980). When the base-rate information has specificity, salience, or relevance to the problem, it tends to be used (Bar-Hillel 1980; Kassin 1979; Wells & Harvey 1977). When the individuating or case information is ambiguous, inconsistent, or clearly nondiagnostic, judges focus heavily on base-rate information (Fischhoff & Bar-Hillel 1984; Ginosar & Trope 1980).

Ginosar & Trope (1987) outlined some general principles of base-rate use. They suggested a problem-solving approach to judgment that involves a goal-directed sequence of cognitive operations. Within this framework, the information that is used more heavily, whether it be base-rate information or case information, depends upon its relation to the goal, its level of activation, and its applicability to the givens of the problem.

Use of the representativeness heuristic produces another characteristic error of judgment: the conjunction fallacy. Here, the probability of a conjunction is mistakenly judged to be higher than the probability of at least one of its components. Tversky & Kahneman (1983) initially interpreted this fallacy in terms of the representativeness heuristic. Judgments were influenced by the match between the specific stimulus and a set of general background characteristics. One of the characteristics might be especially representative of the description, and thus the conjunction would seem far more similar to the representation than would the single unrepresentative characteristic alone. Thus, "a tennis player and a democrat" seems more representative of the description "wealthy, country club member, banker, sporty," than does "democrat" alone.

Recent work in social cognition has extended demonstrations of the conjunction fallacy to new areas and has provided new and different interpretations of this cognitive bias. Markus & Zajonc (1985) suggested that the conjunction fallacy was due to a misunderstanding on the part of subjects rather than to a basic problem of heuristic use or decision-making strategy. Morier & Borgida (1984) employed a debiasing approach to determine whether the conjunction fallacy was due to a specific misunderstanding of particular problems. They found that debiasing did decrease the error rate, but not for problems that strongly implicated representativeness as a possible approach (see also Crandall & Greenfield 1986). Wells (1985) found no conjunction error when the component events were both unrepresentative (Contra Abelson et al 1987).

A set of studies has examined the conjunction fallacy in attributions and judgments of social causality and social explanation. Kun & Weiner (1973) reported that conjunction errors were prevalent in judgments of causality (i.e. the probability of a conjunction of causes was seen as more likely than the probability of one of the components), but only for successes and completed actions. Leddo et al (1984) reported similar findings and proposed that subjects employ schema-based information to explain activity. That is, subjects extract from the schema the goals that the activity satisfies, and some actions (especially successes) are represented as having multiple necessary reasons. Negative events and failures to act, on the other hand, have multiple sufficient causes and are not subject to conjunction effects. This interpretation of the conjunction fallacy in terms of the perceived sufficiency of explanations is also supported by the work of Abelson et al (1987), Jaspars (1983), and Read (1987), and is also consistent with work by Locksley & Stangor (1984).

In a different interpretation of the conjunction fallacy in social explanation, Zuckerman et al (1986) maintained that in estimating the probability of an interpretation for an event, judges may either assess whether the event can give rise to the interpretation (an inference set) or whether the interpretation can give rise to the event (an explanation set). They find that only an explanation set produces consistent conjunction effects. Finally, McClure et al (1988) investigated conjunction effects for explanations of successes and failures. These authors proposed that the key to conjunction effects for successes and failures lies in the type of causes used in the measures. When internal causes and action-related goals were employed, conjunction effects were higher for successes than for failures. However, when more failure-related causes (e.g. external causes and competing goals) were used, conjunction effects were more evident for explanations of failure.

The use of the representativeness heuristic involves a matching process. A judgment of similarity is made between an object and some representation. Tversky (1977) developed a feature-matching model to account for judgments of similarity. The model is especially interesting in that it predicts an asymmetry for judgments of similarity (i.e. the degree of similarity of A to B is not necessarily the same as the similarity of B to A). Such a feature-matching approach has been adopted recently to help explain certain social judgmental phenoma. For example, Holyoak & Gordon (1983) and Srull & Gaelick (1983) found that the self is judged as less similar to others than others are to the self. Such conclusions about social similarity could prove to be extremely important for theories of self-perception (for example, when we compare past selves to present selves or vice versa) or social comparison. Similar feature-matching models have been used to understand the detection of change (Agostinelli et al 1986) and preference judgments (Houston et al 1988).

Turning to the attitude domain, recent work has shown that feature similarity or representativeness increases the use of stored information in judgment and behavior. Lord et al (1984) suggested that attitudes can be thought of as stored evaluations of prototypic attitude objects, whose features are also stored. When confronted by a particular object toward which one must act, the closer the match between the particular object and the stored prototype, the more likely the stored evaluation will be accessed from memory and the greater the probability that behaviors toward the object will be guided by the attitude.

In the stereotyping area, researchers have looked at inferences about other group members as a function of the typicality of an observed instance. Wilder (1984) reported that when subjects had a positive interaction with a member of an out-group who was typical of that out-group in dress and political orientation, their evaluations of the entire out-group were more positive than when the member was atypical. Subjects also saw the target's behavior as more predictive of other group members' behavior if she was typical, and believed that others' personalities would be similar to hers. Rothbart & Lewis (1988) demonstrated that when making judgments about the voting behavior of a fraternity, subjects were more likely to generalize from the behavior of a typical fraternity member than from the behavior of an atypical member. Typical members of a group were also more likely than atypical members to be used in making novel judgments about the frequency of an attribute dimension.

Research on the self has shown that certain aspects of the self have an advantage over others in the processing of information and the determination of behavior because they better match the requirements of the situation. For example, behaviors that have trait implications in line with certain aspects of one's self-image are likely to be adopted. Thus, nonsmokers whose self-images matched the prototype of the typical smoker were more likely to state intentions to smoke than were nonsmokers whose self-images did not match that prototype (Barton et al 1982; Chassin et al 1981).

People choose arenas of activity representative of their self-activity. They seek out environments that allow them to "be who they are" (Niedenthal et al 1985). This selectivity in situational choice has been demonstrated by Snyder in the area of self-monitoring, where low-self-monitors seek situations where they can express their beliefs and high-self-monitors choose situations where the behavioral norms are clear (Snyder & Gangestad 1982; Snyder & Kendzierski 1982).

This tendency to choose behaviors representative and expressive of one's self-concept increases when important aspects of the self-concept are threatened. Sherman & Gorkin (1980) found that when feminist subjects had their self-concepts in this domain threatened, they became more likely subsequently to engage in profeminist behavior. Likewise, Mori et al (1987) showed that female subjects who had had their femininity threatened by false feedback from the experimenter behaved in a manner consistent with their image of femininity in front of a male audience—they ate less than did control subjects. (See also Baumeister & Jones 1978; Greenberg & Pyszczynski 1985; Markus & Kunda 1986). Research by Swann and his colleagues (Swann & Hill 1982; Swann & Ely 1984) also demonstrated that when information inconsistent with important aspects of self-identity is presented to subjects, they resist and engage in acts that reaffirm their important self-concepts.

People may select behaviors and situations not only to express and confirm what they are but also to manage an impression of who they are. Thus, both private and public identities can guide behavior (Tetlock & Manstead 1985). Perhaps people even adopt behavior in order to become what they would like to be. In the Chassin et al (1981) study, intentions to smoke were predictable not only from the degree of match between subjects' actual selves and the prototype of the smoker, but also from the match between their ideal self-images and the prototype of the smoker.

In an interesting demonstration of people's willingness to adopt a behavior in order to achieve a desired self-image, Quattrone & Tversky (1984) told subjects that a particular behavior (keeping one's hand in cold water for either a short or long time) predicted a healthy heart. Subjects altered their behavior so as to achieve the desired self-image, even though this behavior could not cause cardiac health.

PREDICTIVE UTILITY   Some kinds of information are simply more useful than other kinds in making the required judgment. In selecting the information to use for any task, a person determines (implicitly or explicitly) how useful the various kinds of information are.

The issue of predictive utility has generated controversy within research on stereotyping. Many studies have looked at the use of attributes associated with the stereotype versus individuating information when making some judgment about a target. Locksley and her colleagues (e.g. Locksley et al 1982) argued that individuating information will entirely override a stereotype. Rasinski et al (1985) criticized this work on methodological grounds. Specifically, they argued that the normative criterion against which subjects' judgments were compared should have been constructed on an individual basis for each subject, rather than using estimates for the entire group, in order to claim that subjects violated normative standards. They also challenged the mathematical formulation of the normative criterion. They claimed from their research that once these issues were corrected, base-rate information (i.e. the stereotype) did influence judgments.

Krueger & Rothbart (1988) suggested that the trait used in Locksley's research ("assertive") is not, in fact, a component of gender stereotypes. Using the trait "aggressive," Krueger & Rothbart found that both information about the individual and group membership influenced expectations of future aggressive behavior. Specifically, men were expected to behave more aggressively than women, as were targets who performed behaviors that were highly diagnostic of aggressiveness. These two effects did not interact. Moreover, as the strength of the stereotype increased (male construction workers versus female homemakers), so did the magnitude of the effect due to category membership. If the temporal stability of the individuating information was increased (the target was described as consistently behaving in an aggressive manner, or was characterized by a trait suggesting aggressiveness), the effect of category membership was eliminated, as in the Locksley work. Krueger & Rothbart suggested that the dominance of category versus individuating information depends on the relative predictive value of each.

Glick et al (1988) looked at the use of individuating information by asking subjects to evaluate male and female job applicants for typically feminine, masculine, and neutral jobs. Individuating information about each target indicated that the target possessed masculine, feminine, or neutral attributes that were unrelated to the job qualifications. Glick et al found, like Locksley, that the individuating information determined trait ratings of the targets. The individuating information also influenced judgments of whether to interview the candidate, but so did the gender information. Futoran & Wyer (1986) argued that gender affected occupational suitability judgments, and that it is used in combination with traits. Bodenhausen & Lichtenstein (1987; Bodenhausen & Wyer 1985) argued that stereotype use depends on task complexity. When a task is sufficiently complex, the stereotype will be used to generate a judgment. For less complex tasks, subjects will rely primarily on individuating information.

Work by Manis et al (1986; Manis et al 1988; Jussim et al 1987) suggests that although judgments of group members are often biased by assimilation to the stereotype, under certain conditions a contrast effect may emerge. If a moderately assertive behavior is performed by both a male and a female, and subjects are asked which is more aggressive, the female is likely to be chosen. Compared to females as a whole, this one is quite aggressive, whereas compared to males as a whole, this one is not particularly aggressive. This suggests subjects make an implicit comparison to the norm for each group— what Manis et al call "local norms"—rather than thinking about absolute levels of aggression.

Many researchers in person perception have looked at the tendency to retrieve previous inferences or judgments rather than the data on which these judgments were based when making a second judgment (e.g. Lingle et al 1983; Wyer et al 1984). Predictive utility is at least implicity one of the several factors that influence the information retrieved. Schul & Burnstein (1985) argued that when a previous judgment was easily accessible, the extent to which it (rather than the presented information) was used in making a new judgment increased with the similarity of the first judgment to the second. Lingle (1983) looked at the activation of information when making a judgment. He compared priming effects for previously presented traits relevant and irrelevant to the judgment, nonpresented traits that were likely inferred from the first traits, and nonpresented irrelevant traits. Priming effects were obtained for all but the latter and the effects were equally large for presented and inferred traits. Carlston & Skowronski (1986) pointed out that the likelihood of using a previous inference decreases to some extent if relevant behavioral information has been thought about and activated recently. Certainly there is evidence that behaviors or "raw data" can be and are used in subsequent judgments (Schul 1986). For example, Neuberg & Fiske (1987) argued that if a perceiver is outcome dependent on a target, category-based processing is less likely to occur, and individuating information is highly likely to be used. The use of individuating information can also be increased by stressing the importance of accuracy in the impression-formation task.

Both previous inferences and the information on which they were based are used in subsequent judgments. The accessibility of these, their predictive utility, and the goals of the perceiver all affect how much each type of information influences the second judgment.

How Does Stored Information Affect the Processing of New Information?

Old categories, knowledge, and constructs are always brought to bear on and determine the meaning of new information. Here we discuss how stored structure influences the depth to which new information is processed and the interpretation that is given to it.

DEPTH OF PROCESSING   Not all new information is processed to the same extent. Depth of processing is a function of both stable and temporary characteristics of the person, features of the new information, and aspects of the knowledge structure employed.

In the attitude domain, there has been an abundance of recent research on the depth with which persuasive communications are processed. Petty & Cacioppo (1986) distinguished between central and peripheral processing of persuasive communication, examining the variables that encourage more detailed central processing. Similarly, Chaiken (1980, 1987; Eagly & Chaiken 1984) distinguished between systematic and heuristic processing of persuasive communications, suggesting that only the former involves detailed consideration of the content of a communication.

Central or systematic processing of a persuasive communication tends to occur when issue involvement is high (Axsom et al 1987; Leippe & Elkin 1987; Petty & Cacioppo 1986); when dealing with subjects high in the need for cognition (Cacioppo et al 1985) or subjects who have a relative abundance of attitude-relevant information stored in memory (Wood et al 1985); when listening to communications that come from multiple, as opposed to single, sources (Harkins & Petty 1987); and when attitudes are based on direct, rather than indirect, experience with the attitude object (Wu & Shaffer 1987). In these cases, the individual is likely to process persuasive communications deeply and thoroughly.

Stored information in the form of an existing expectation affects ability to remember new information. [This work has been reviewed extensively elsewhere (Hastie et al 1984; Higgins & Bargh 1987) and is only briefly summarized here.] If the expectation concerns an individual, information that is inconsistent with the expectation is deeply processed and most likely to be remembered. Consistent information is better remembered than irrelevant. If the expectation concerns a group, consistent information is most likely to be remembered. The former effect occurs because inconsistent information about an individual is surprising. Inconsistency is less surprising in a group, where consistent items gain from the strong retrieval cue provided by the stereotype.

The influence of stored information on the processing of new information may also be observed in the self-reference effect. Recall is enhanced for words processed with respect to self-reference ("Does __ describe you?") rather than for their semantic, phonemic, or structural properties (Rogers et al 1977). This effect has been replicated many times (see Higgins & Bargh 1987 for a recent review). Information processed with respect to the self was at first believed to be processed deeply and elaborately because of the large and complex structure of the self. Recent work has been aimed at verifying the depth of processing, identifying additional underlying processes, and discovering the boundary conditions for this effect (Ferguson et al 1983; Wells et al 1984).

Lord (1980) indicated that the advantage for self-referent recall disappeared and was even reversed when subjects were instructed to use images rather than verbal propositional processing. More recently, Brown et al (1986) contradicted these results and reported a self-reference effect even with imagery. They suggested the advantages of self-referent encoding as due to the episodic instances that such encoding usually involves. Lord (1987) responded by arguing that Brown et al (1986) used self-images that were highly interactive in nature.

Klein & Kihlstrom (1986) noted that the self-referent task involved an organization of the words into two categories ("describes me" and "does not describe me"). The other tasks (e.g. semantic or phonemic) did not involve such organization. Klein & Kihlstrom showed that other tasks that encouraged organization of the words facilitated recall just as well as self-reference tasks. More recently, Klein & Loftus (1988) tested for the two most often proposed mechanisms underlying the self-reference effect—(a) elaborate processing due to the richness of the self-structure and (b) organizational processing. They found evidence for both kinds of processes.

INTERPRETATION   A situation can be interpreted in as many different ways as there are people viewing the situation. Moreover, the same situation can be interpreted differently by the same person at different times. These differences are due in large part to differences in the content, structure, and accessibility of the prior knowledge and stored representations of the perceivers. Old knowledge determines the meaning given to new knowledge, especially when the new information is ambiguous. Two aspects of stored knowledge affect the interpretation of new information—its content and its structure.

In the attitude domain, Lord et al (1979) showed that subjects who encountered ambiguous attitude-relevant information interpreted that information in support of their prior attitude positions and became even more convinced of the appropriateness of their views. Interestingly, however, when one is strongly committed on a social or political issue, one will interpret media coverage of that issue as biased against one's position (Vallone et al 1985).

Within the area of stereotyping, Darley & Gross (1983) looked at biased interpretation of new information as a factor in the phenomenon of self-fulfilling prophecies. Subjects were told that a child they were about to observe came from either a high or low socioeconomic background. This label alone was not sufficient to produce biased judgments of the child's ability. However, when subjects were given ambiguous information about the child's performance, judgments of the child's ability were biased to be consistent with the initial expectation. Sagar & Schofield (1980) found that drawings of ambiguously aggressive behaviors were seen as more aggressive when performed by a black child than a white child. In both of these studies, interpretation of the ambiguous information was biased in support of prior expectation.

In person perception, researchers have looked at how previously stored information guides attention to new information. Forgas & Bower (1987) reported that subjects in a good mood spent more time processing positive information about a target and made positive trait judgments about the target more quickly. The target was seen more positively overall, and memory was better for the positive attributes of the target. The reverse was true of subjects in a negative mood. Hoffman (1985) found that following a decision, the target was misremembered as having attributes consistent with the decision outcome. Thus following a positive judgment of the suitability of the target for a role, the target was misremembered as having attributes consistent with the role, and the rejected target was misremembered as lacking those attributes.

As the self (a structure filled with stored information) provides a sense of identity, continuity, and well-being, it necessarily becomes involved in attention to, encoding, and interpreting new information. The self affects the stimulus dimensions that are most likely to be processed, and it does this for both motivational and cognitive reasons. Many excellent discussions are available of the biasing role of the self in various kinds of information processing (Kihlstrom & Cantor 1984; Greenwald & Pratkanis 1984; Higgins & Bargh 1987; Markus & Sentis 1982). The self especially affects the seeking and interpreting of information about other people (see Bargh 1982; Kuiper 1981; Markus & Sentis 1982). For example, people seek out information about others that fits with their own self-schemas. Thus, extravert subjects learn about people by asking questions about issues relevant to extraversion, and introverts ask about introversion (Fong & Markus 1982; see Markus 1980 and Markus et al 1985 for interpretations of this effect).

Thus the existing self-concept determines what new knowledge is sought and how knowledge is interpreted. By implication, then, the self has inertia. As self-relevant information is attended to and interpreted in light of current self-beliefs, the self is likely to remain unchanged.

Two principles have been proposed to account for the general inertia of the self-concept—self-verification and self-enhancement. In its simplest form, self-verification (or self-consistency) approaches assume that people act to maintain and affirm their self-concepts—whether they like these self-perceptions or not (e.g. Swann 1983, 1987). Self-verification is achieved in part through hypothesis-confirming tendencies (Skov & Sherman 1986; Snyder & Swann 1978; Swann & Read 1981a).

Self-verification is also achieved when people choose settings, interaction partners, and interaction strategies that allow them the best opportunities for self-expression (Pelham & Swann 1988). Even depressed people seek out interaction partners who will provide them with image-consistent feedback (Swann & Predmore 1985), and individuals with negative self-images prefer negative feedback to flattering positive feedback (Swann & Predmore 1985). Wicklund & Gollwitzer's (1982) theory of symbolic self-completion suggests similar ideas about self-verification.

Reconstruction of one's past to accord with present self-concepts is yet another way to achieve stability of the self (Bem & McConnell 1970; Goethals & Reckman 1973; Ross & Conway 1986; Ross et al 1981). In a nice demonstration of this principle, McFarland & Ross (1987) had subjects rate themselves, their dating partners, and their relationship on a number of dimensions. Two months later, subjects made current evaluations and also recalled their previous ratings. Recall was very much distorted toward current feelings and perceptions.

Biasing perceptions and interpretations is another major way of achieving self-verification. We selectively attend to and selectively interpret and encode information (Kulik et al 1986; Swann & Ely 1984; Swann et al 1987; see Swann 1984 for a review). Even when self-images are based on bogus information, they persist as subjects draw unwarranted inferences about their abilities and interpret situations as confirming their self-concept (Lepper et al 1986).

Finally, the strategy of self-handicapping can be instrumental in verifying one's self-concept. Positive but tenuous self-images can be sustained by avoiding situations that would disconfirm them (Berglas & Jones 1978; Harris & Snyder 1986; see Arkin & Baumgardner 1985 for a recent review).

The second process behind the self's inertia, self-enhancement, is a desire to do whatever it takes to feel good about oneself, either by maximizing positive self-evaluation or by minimizing negative self-evaluation. According to Tesser's self-evaluation-maintenance model (SEM) (Campbell & Tesser

1985; Tesser 1986), people are motivated to maintain positive self-evaluation. The successes and failures of others affect self-evaluation as the self either "reflects" (identifies with) or compares itself against others. Identification and comparison act in opposition to each other, and both depend upon the closeness of the other and the quality of the other's performance.

Although the two processes work in opposite directions with respect to self-evaluation, they are not always weighted equally. If the self-aspect involved is self-relevant (one for which the person is schematic), comparison processes will be important. When the dimension is not self-relevant, reflection processes predominate. Tesser and his colleagues have garnered much support for the role of self-enhancement in guiding judgments and interpretations of information (Campbell & Tesser 1985; Tesser & Campbell 1983; Tesser et al 1984; Tesser & Paulhus 1983).

Additional evidence suggests that people engage in self-enhancement as they exhibit biases in information-processing in perception (Erdelyi 1974), memory (Greenwald & Pratkanis 1984), attributions of responsibility (Miller & Ross 1975), and social comparison (Pyszczynski et al 1985). Strategic self-presentation (Greenwald 1980) can also aid in self-enhancement. Moreover, when self-esteem is threatened, people reestablish it by engaging in compensatory self-enhancement, even in other parts of the self-system (Baumeister & Jones 1978; Liu & Steele 1986; Steele & Liu 1983). Kunda (1987) demonstrated that people both generate and evaluate causal theories in a self-serving manner. They generate theories that allow them to view their own attributes as predictive of desirable outcomes, and they are reluctant to believe in theories that link their own attributes to undesirable outcomes. Pyszczynski & Greenberg (1987) presented an integration of cognitive and motivational biases that serve the self.

CHANGES IN CONTENT AND STRUCTURE OF REPRESENTATIONS

What factors influence change in the stored representation of social categories? We distinguish here between (a) short-term changes based on temporary differences in accessibility of knowledge and (b) relatively permanent changes in either the content or structure of represented knowledge.

Formation of New Representations

Before considering changes in represented knowledge, we discuss how attitudes, stereotypes, impressions of others, and selves are formed in the first place.

The origins of stereotypes have long been studied from a social cognition perspective. The most active research has been on the illusory correlation effect (Acorn et al 1988; Hamilton et al 1985; Hamilton & Sherman 1988; Sanbonmatsu et al 1987a,b)—i.e. the tendency to see a (nonexistent) correlation between low-frequency items, such as members of a minority group, and negative behaviors. Evidence suggests that the effect is due to the manner in which distinctive information is processed at encoding, and to subsequent retrieval processes, rather than to biased judgment processes at the time the judgment is made (Arkes & Rothbart 1985; Hamilton et al 1985). Sanbonmatsu et al (1987b) suggest that both the encoding and judgment processes involved in illusory correlations differ when the target is an individual rather than a group. When the target is an individual, an impression is formed on-line and the majority behaviors are most strongly associated with salient targets. Salient targets are judged to have more of the frequent behaviors, in contrast to effects when the target is a group.

Eagly & Steffen (1984) argued that stereotypes derive in part from a biased distribution of group members into social roles. These roles have associated characteristics, and eventually those characteristics come to be linked to the group itself. Eagly & Steffen demonstrated that evaluations of targets were determined more by the role they occupied than by their gender. Thus a male and female homemaker were evaluated similarly, while both were evaluated differently from a male and female corporate executive.

Some of the most frequently looked at impression formation processes are primacy effects. Belmore (1987) reported that subjects spend more time reading information presented early in the impression. Reading times were also longer for information that was inconsistent with the impression, but only when this information appeared relatively late. Belmore argued that the importance of disconfirming information depends on the state of the evolving impression. Stangor & Ruble (1988) applied a similar argument when the stimulus is a group rather than an individual. In a study of impressions of real people, Park (1986) found evidence of a "passive" primacy effect. Over a seven-week period, attributes mentioned in subjects' first descriptions were more likely to be repeated in later descriptions than attributes mentioned at later weeks. The effect was labelled passive because it was due to few new attributes being reported at later time periods rather than new attributes being reported and then ignored. Early information dominates the impression in part because of its diagnosticity or informational value, given that no impression currently exists. Skowronski & Carlston (1987) similarly argued that negative information has a high information value and is therefore weighted heavily in the overall impression. This is true for moral attributes (e.g. honesty). For abilities, however, such as intelligence, positive behavior is more diagnostic. Everyone can be stupid, but only smart people can behave intelligently (Reeder & Brewer 1979).

Primacy effects can be mitigated in a number of ways—e.g. by forewarning subjects that they will be held accountable for judgments of a target, or that they will be asked to justify them (Tetlock 1983). Tetlock & Kim (1987) reported that under such conditions impressions were more integratively complex, behavior predictions were more accurate, and subjects reported more appropriate levels of confidence in their judgments (contra Wetzel et al 1981 for halo effects). Freund et al (1985; Kruglanski & Freund 1983) reported greater primacy effects for subjects high in need for cognitive structure, and when fear of invalidity was low.

Finally, Gilovich (1987) presented evidence that impressions formed simply from hearing about a target are more extreme than first-hand impressions. This appears to be due in part to the informant's failure to report to the impression forming subject the full situational constraints on the target's behavior.

Investigators of the self ask whether the self-concept is stable over time and across situations or whether it is easily changed. Some have depicted the self as relatively stable and integrated (Kihlstrom & Cantor 1984, 1988; Lecky 1945; Markus & Sentis 1982; Shrauger 1975); others have portrayed it as more malleable (Bem 1972; Natale & Hantas 1982; Jones et al 1981).

Recent work indicates that the self is best conceived as having a hierarchical and multifaceted structure. Given this representation, the question of the self's stability involves the accessibility of the various parts of the self. The various aspects of the self may be quite stable and consistent, while their relative accessibility is variable. Accessibility of the self in general or of the various aspects of the self can be based on chronic accessibility (Markus 1977, Higgins et al 1982a) or by priming or contextual factors. Andersen et al (1986) manipulated the salience of past proreligious or antireligious thoughts and feelings in their subjects, which strongly affected present self-perceptions of religiosity (see also Andersen & Williams 1985 and Nurius 1984 for issues involving priming various aspects of the self-concept).

An individual's self-evaluation may depend upon which self-aspect one is accessing at the time of judgment. Even random and arbitrary factors can affect momentary self-perception. We have already seen how imagining and explaining hypothetical events about the self can lead to particular kinds of self-perceptions based on accessibility (Campbell & Fairey 1985; Sherman et al 1983); and these self-perceptions can persevere until other parts of the self-concept become accessible (Ross et al 1975; Wegner et al 1985). In addition, giving a subject a random anchor value of high or low performance (Cervone & Peak 1986) or arbitrarily assigning status labels to people (Sande et al 1986) can affect self-perceptions. Interestingly, even affecting the accessibility of an imagined audience can cause momentary changes in the experience of the self. Baldwin & Holmes (1987) had college subjects visualize a group of peers or visualize their older family members. Later, subjects were asked to rate the enjoyableness of a piece of sexually explicit fiction. Ratings correlated with the kinds of imagined audience.

This view that the self possesses both a stable core and a phenomenal self (Jones et al 1981) or working self (Cantor et al 1986) that shifts from moment to moment is consistent with recent thinking (see Cantor et al 1986; Greenwald & Pratkanis 1984; Rhodewalt & Agustsdottir 1986; Swann 1987; and Tesser & Campbell 1983). There is no single or average self-image continuously changing, but rather a collection of self-images whose relative accessibilities change.

However, the self may change in ways other than through alterations in momentary accessibility of its various aspects. For one thing, chronic accessibility can change as one part of the self is frequently activated (Higgins et al 1982a). In addition, frequent behavioral episodes can alter the prototype of any sub-self. New subselves can also be added as one becomes a jogger, a parent, or a retired person. Systematic changes in subselves can ultimately lead to changes in self-representations at higher levels in the hierarchy.

The self clearly changes during self-concept development. We cannot present here the various theories of self-concept acquisition. Suffice it to say that whether one adopts a Piagetian approach, an Eriksonian approach (Erikson 1950), a social perception approach (Bem 1967), a social constructionist approach (Mead 1934), or a symbolic interactionist perspective (Stryker 1980), the role of social cognition principles is apparent.

Recent approaches to self-concept development have in fact adopted a cognitive-analytic model based on social-cognitive-developmental principles (Damon & Hart 1982; Harter 1983; 1986a,b; Rosenberg 1986). Self-concept development is tied to cognitive development in general and is concerned with developmental changes both in the content and the structure of the self.

Harter (1986b) proposed that the various domains of the self (scholastic and athletic competence, social acceptance, physical appearance, and behavioral conduct) differentiate with age; they are then integrated into a higher-level structure (see also Rosenberg 1986). According to Harter, the self shifts its focus from behavioral characteristics, to trait-like constructs, to more abstract, psychological constructs (see also Dweck & Elliott 1983). Adolescence is a time of significant self-concept development. Rosenberg (1986) provided an excellent summary. He identified five key developmental changes during adolescence—an increased view of the self as psychological interior; a greater focus on interpersonal sentiments and relationships; a more abstract and conceptual view; greater complexity and differentiation; and a greater use of logic and evidence in self-constructions rather than arbitrary and external bases. Early stages of self-development may be based on the reflected appraisals of others, while later stages involve self-perception.

Self-concept development continues throughout the life span. Similar social cognitive processes are no doubt involved as individuals take on new roles, develop new subselves, or develop an area of expertise.

Changes Due to New Information

Knowledge representations change primarily through encountering new information. New information is typically assimilated to existing structures. However, upon occasion the new information may be so discrepant from the existing structures and/or so compelling that accommodation is called for. Such accommodation can take a variety of forms. Change can occur in the content of represented knowledge (e.g. attitude change in response to a persuasive message) or in the structure of the representation (e.g. changes in complexity or degree of differentiation, subtyping, etc). Although structural changes in response to new information are typically conservative, we also note cases where structures change more than they should.

The literature on attitude change in response to persuasive communications has been dominated by the distinction between central and peripheral (Petty & Cacioppo 1986) or systematic and heuristic (Chaiken 1980; Eagly & Chaiken 1984) routes to persuasion. Under central or systematic processing, the quality of arguments in the persuasive communication is relatively carefully evaluated, and attitude change results to the extent that cognitive responses to those arguments are favorable.

In other situations, where subjects are less committed to carefully processing the arguments, heuristic cues may be used to determine shifts in attitude. Thus, for instance, among low-involvement subjects, the number of arguments seems to affect attitude change, regardless of their quality, while among high-involvement subjects the reverse is true (Petty & Cacioppo 1986). Presumably, the number of arguments cues subjects heuristically when they have neither the time nor the inclination to process the contents of the communication carefully. Other persuasive heuristic cues include source attractiveness, source expertise, audience approval of the position espoused, and the length of the communication (Axsom et al 1987; Chaiken & Eagly 1983; Chaiken & Stangor 1987; Mackie 1987; Pallak 1983; Pallak et al 1983; Wu & Shaffer 1987).

One of the most important issues in the study of stereotypes is the integration of new information, particularly disconfirming information, into the existing stereotype. Weber & Crocker (1983) found that disconfirming information affected the stereotype more if it derived from many stereotype-group members than if it derived from only a few. When disconfirming information was concentrated among a few group members, these were subtyped and their behavior was less likely to change the group stereotype. Moreover, disconfirming information was more effective if it came from "typical" than if it came from "atypical" members of the group. The extent to which the source of new information is seen as typical of the group appears to play a key role in determining whether the stereotype's structure will change (Rothbart & John 1985).

There is surprisingly little work in person perception on the evolving or changing impressions of others. Silka (1984) looked at subjects' perceptions of change in target individuals as a function of the time elapsed between two observations of varying behavior. If the episodes were separated by a long interval (e.g. high school and college), the target was viewed as having changed rather than as being inconsistent. Wyer & Budesheim (1987) presented subjects with information and then told them that some of the information was incorrect and should be disregarded. The ability to disregard was greater if the information had been communicated late rather than early in the presentation. The authors argued that impressions were formed on-line, as the data were presented. When told to disregard some of the information, the subjects tried to adjust their impressions. If it was negative information that was to be disregarded, an overadjustment toward the positive was likely (Wyer & Unverzagt 1985).

We considered above two processes (self-verification and self-enhancement) that generally operate to maintain the self-concept and inhibit change. We now consider a process that is more likely to lead to changes in self-perception: the concern with accurate self-assessment.

Trope (1986) posited a human motivation to seek realistic self-assessment, even at the expense of appearing inconsistent and ineffective. Self-assessment theory implies that people seek situations where performance successes may inform them about their own positive characteristics or where performance failures inform them about their negative characteristics. Self-enhancement theory maintains that people prefer to perform in areas where they expect to do well, while self-assessment theory predicts a preference to perform in areas of greatest uncertainty. The new information obtained through such self-assessment must often lead to changes in self-perceptions.

By independently manipulating the diagnostic value of tasks and outcomes for both success and failure, Trope separated enhancement from accurate assessment (e.g. 1982, 1983, Trope & Brickman 1975). In most cases, self-assessment predominated, even at the expense of finding out negative things about the self or things that were inconsistent with current self-perceptions. Strube et al (1986) also separated self-enhancement tendencies from self-assessment. They found evidence for both motives, but concluded that self-assessment was stronger. However, Tesser (1986) reported evidence that self-enhancement predominates over self-assessment.

There may be individual differences in preferences for diagnostic information about the self as well. Sorrentino & Short (1986) reported that subjects high in certainty orientation (those who prefer to avoid confusion) do not seek out information that may give accurate assessments at the expense of reducing clarity. Strube & Roemmele (1985) found that the combination of self-esteem and the tendency to use self-protective strategies predicted a preference for informative tasks. All groups preferred self-assessment except for low-esteem subjects who had a tendency to self-protect. The latter preferred self-enhancement.

Recent work identified other conditions under which new self-relevant information can lead to changes in the self-concept. Rhodewalt & Agustsdottir (1986) found that when role-playing (or strategic self-presentation) is within the latitude of one's self-image, momentary change based on accessibility [self-perception processes (Bem 1967)] takes place. When role-playing involves an unacceptable self-position, more permanent changes based on cognitive dissonance are seen.

In addition to situational factors affecting changes in the phenomenal self, individual differences may also moderate the kinds and levels of changes expected. High-complexity individuals are less subject to variations in self-perception because of the buffering effect of their independent representations of self (Linville 1985, 1987). Low self-monitors are less likely to change their momentary self-perceptions because they are less likely than high self-monitors to alter their behaviors or self-expressions across situations (Snyder 1987; Snyder & DeBono 1985). Finally, Nasby (1985) has indicated that high-self-consciousness individuals have extremely well-articulated self-schemas, and thus their self-concepts are likely more stable than those of low-self-consciousness people.

Changes Due to Reflection

Extended attention may also change the content and structure of knowledge representations. If one reflects upon a judgment or a bit of represented knowledge, that object may become more tightly organized, more accessible, and more developed. This may be seen as self-induced change in knowledge structures, rather than as change induced by new information.

The evidence is now fairly abundant that devoting thought to an attitude increases its extremity (Tesser 1978; Tesser & Leone 1977). Millar & Tesser (1986a) showed that thought about an attitude object increases its extremity by increasing the evaluative consistency of information about it stored in memory. Chaiken & Yates (1985) focused on the consistency of affective reactions to the attitude object with cognitive appraisals of it, arguing that thought-induced polarization occurs only when consistency is relatively high.

Thought thus seems to induce more evaluative consistency among the bits of information that one stores in memory about the attitude object. It should also make the attitude more accessible. Thought devoted to an attitude should thus increase subsequent attitude-behavior consistency. Substantial evidence for this hypothesis exists (e.g. Carver & Scheier 1981; Snyder & Swann 1976; Wicklund 1982). Surprisingly, however, Wilson and colleagues (Wilson & Dunn 1986; Wilson et al 1984) showed that when subjects are asked to analyze the reasons they hold an attitude, attitude-behavior consistency is reduced. These apparently contradictory results can be explained (Wilson & Dunn 1986; Millar & Tesser 1986b) by identifying differences in thought instructions. Thinking about one's attitude should increase its accessibility and thereby increase attitude-behavior consistency. On the other hand, if attitudes as stored evaluations are not necessarily consistent with the attribute information that one has also stored about the attitude object, then thinking about that attribute information (focusing on "reasons") may decrease attitude-behavior consistency.

CONCLUSION

In our view, social cognition is not a substantive domain within social psychology but an approach that guides research and thinking in a variety of domains. The approach has been useful in several areas—person perception, attitudes, stereotypes, decision making, and the self. In each of these, we have discussed recent work that has helped advance the areas by proposing and testing ideas about cognitive mediators of judgments and behaviors. In focusing on the cognitive mediators of social behavior, we have dealt with the issues of what is stored in memory that serves to mediate behavior, how such stored information affects subsequent processing and behaviors, and finally how changes in the stored information are achieved.

On the positive side, a social cognition approach helps to identify the mental structures and processes involved in the formation and maintenance of stereotypes, in forming impressions of people, in decision making, in forming and changing attitudes, and in the development and change of the self-concept. Common structural and process principles operate across these areas. Perhaps it is time for social psychology as a discipline to be organized by process and mechanism principles rather than by the dependent variable measured. Current textbooks in social psychology are typically divided into chapters on conformity, stereotypes, attitudes, etc, rather than on the basis of the various cognitive, motivational, and learning principles that operate across all kinds of responses.

On the cautionary side, we suggest that social cognition should not be viewed as the only approach to the important questions about social behavior and interaction. Other approaches involving motivation, social interaction and group dynamics, learning theory, and individual differences have much to add in clarifying the processes involved in social behavior. Once each approach is well specified, it will be possible to integrate them, as Sorrentino & Higgins (1986) have begun to do with respect to motivational and cognitive approaches.

ACKNOWLEDGMENT

The first author acknowledges support from National Institute of Health grants MH 40058 and HD13449. The second author appreciates the support of the Center for Advanced Study in the Behavioral Sciences and National Science Foundation grant BNS-8700864. Support to the third author was generously provided by National Science Foundation grant BNS-8606595.

Literature Cited

Abelson, R. P., Leddo, J., Gross, P. H. 1987. The strength of conjunctive explanations. *Pers. Soc. Psychol. Bull.* 13:141–55

Abelson, R. P., Levi, A. 1985. Decision making and decision theory. See Lindzey & Aronson 1985

Acorn, D. A., Hamilton, D. L., Sherman, S. J. 1988. Generalization of biased perceptions of groups based on illusory correlations. *Soc. Cognit.* In press

Agostinelli, G., Sherman, S. J., Fazio, R. H., Hearst, E. S. 1986. Detecting and identifying change: additions versus deletions. *J. Exp. Psychol.: Hum. Percept. Perform.* 12:445–54

Ajzen, I. 1977. Intuitive theories of events and the effects of base-rate information on prediction. *J. Pers. Soc. Psychol.* 35:303–14

Ajzen, I., Timko, C., White, J. B. 1982. Self-monitoring and the attitude-behavior relation. *J. Pers. Soc. Psychol.* 42:426–35

Alba, J. W., Chromiak, W., Hasher, L., Attig, M. S. 1980. Automatic encoding of category size information. *J. Exp. Psychol.: Hum. Learn. Mem.* 6:370–78

Allport, G. W. 1943. The ego in contemporary psychology. *Psychol. Rev.* 50:451–78

Andersen, S. M., Klatzky, R. L. 1987. Traits and social stereotypes: levels of categorization in person perception. *J. Pers. Soc. Psychol.* 53:235–46

Andersen, S. M., Lazowski, L. E., Donisi, M. 1986. Salience and self-inference: the role of biased recollections in self-inference processes. *Soc. Cognit.* 4:75–95

Andersen, S. M., Williams, M. 1985. Cognitive/affective reactions in the improvement of self-esteem: when thoughts and feelings make a difference. *J. Pers. Soc. Psychol.* 49:1086–97

Anderson, N. H., Hubert, S. 1963. Effects of concomitant verbal recall on order effects in personality impression formation. *J. Verb. Learn. Verb. Behav.* 2:379–91

Arkes, H., Rothbart, M. 1985. Memory, retrieval, and contingency judgments. *J. Pers. Soc. Psychol.* 49:598–606

Arkin, R. M., Baumgardner, A. H. 1985. Self-handicapping. In *Attribution: Basic Issues and Applications,* ed. J. H. Harvey, G. Weary, pp. 169–202. London: Academic

Asch, S. E., Zukier, H. 1984. Thinking about persons. *J. Pers. Soc. Psychol.* 46:1230–40

Axsom, D., Yates, S., Chaiken, S. 1987. Audience responses as a heuristic cue in persuasion. *J. Pers. Soc. Psychol.* 53:30–40

Baldwin, M. W., Holmes, J. G. 1987. Salient private audiences and awareness of the self. *J. Pers. Soc. Psychol.* 52:1087–98

Bargh, J. A. 1982. Attention and automaticity in the processing of self-relevant information. *J. Pers. Soc. Psychol.* 43:425–36

Bargh, J. A., Bond, R. N., Lombardi, W. J., Tota, M. E. 1986. The additive nature of chronic and temporary sources of construct accessibility. *J. Pers. Soc. Psychol.* 50: 869–78

Bargh, J. A., Pratto, F. 1986. Individual construct accessibility and perceptual selection. *J. Exp. Soc. Psychol.* 22:293–311

Bar-Hillel, M. 1980. The base-rate fallacy in probability judgments. *Acta Psychol.* 44: 211–33

Baron, J., Beattie, J., Hershey, J. C. 1988. Heuristics and biases in diagnostic reasoning: II. Congruence, information, and certainty. *Organ. Behav. Hum. Decis. Processes.* In press

Baron, J., Hershey, J. C. 1988. Outcome bias in decision evaluation. *J. Pers. Soc. Psychol.* 54:569–79

Barsalou, L. W. 1987. The instability of graded structure: implications for the nature of concepts. In *Concepts and Conceptual Development: Ecological and Intellectual Factors in Categorization,* ed. U. Neisser, pp. 101–40. Cambridge: Cambridge Univ. Press

Barton, J., Chassin, L., Presson, C. C., Sherman, S. J. 1982. Social image factors as motivators of smoking initiation in early and middle adolescence. *Child Dev.* 53:1499–511

Bassili, J. N., Smith, M. C. 1986. On the spontaneity of trait attribution: converging evidence for the role of cognitive strategy. *J. Pers. Soc. Psychol.* 50:239–45

Baumeister, R. F., Jones, E. E. 1978. When self presentation is constrained by the target's knowledge: consistency and compensation. *J. Pers. Soc. Psychol.* 36:608–18

Belmore, S. M. 1987. Determinants of attention during impression formation. *J. Exp. Psychol.; Learn. Mem. Cognit.* 13:480–89

Bem, D. J. 1967. Self-perception: an alternative interpretation of cognitive dissonance phenomena. *Psychol. Rev.* 74:183–200

Bem, D. J. 1972. Self-perception theory. *Adv. Exp. Soc. Psychol.* 6:1–62.

Bem, D. J., McConnell, H. K. 1970. Testing the self-perception explanation of dissonance phenomena: on the salience of premanipulation attitudes. *J. Pers. Soc. Psychol.* 14:23–31

Berglas, S., Jones, E. E. 1978. Drug choice as a self-handicapping strategy in response to noncontingent success. *J. Pers. Soc. Psychol.* 36:405–17

Beyth-Marom, R., Fischhoff, B. 1983. Diagnosticity and pseudodiagnosticity. *J. Pers. Soc. Psychol.* 45:1185–95

Bodenhausen, G. V., Lichtenstein, M. 1987. Social stereotypes and information-processing strategies: the impact of task complexity. *J. Pers. Soc. Psychol.* 52:871–80

Bodenhausen, G. V., Wyer, R. S. Jr. 1985. Effects of stereotypes on decision making and information-processing strategies. *J. Pers. Soc. Psychol.* 48:267–82

Bond, C. F., Brockett, D. R. 1987. A social context-personality index theory of memory for acquaintances. *J. Pers. Soc. Psychol.* 52:1110–21

Bower, G. H., Gilligan, S. G. 1979. Remembering information related to one's self. *J. Res. Pers.* 13:420–32

Breckler, S. J., Greenwald, A. G. 1982. *Charting coordinates for the self-concept in multidimensional trait space.* Presented at Symp. Funct. Meas. Self-Esteem, Am. Psychol. Assoc., Washington, DC

Breckler, S. J., Greenwald, A. G. 1986. Motivational facets of the self. See Sorrentino & Higgins 1986, pp. 145–64

Brewer, M. B., Dull, V., Lui, L. 1981. Perceptions of the elderly: stereotypes as prototypes. *J. Pers. Soc. Psychol.* 41:656–70

Brewer, M. B., Kramer, R. M. 1985. The psychology of intergroup attitudes and behavior. *Ann. Rev. Psychol.* 36:219–43

Brewer, M. B., Lui, L. 1984. Categorization of the elderly by the elderly: effects of perceiver's category membership. *Per. Soc. Psychol. Bull.* 10:585–95

Brown, P., Keenan, J. M., Potts, G. R. 1986. The self-reference effect with imagery encoding. *J. Pers. Soc. Psychol.* 51:897–906

Burke, P. J., Tully, J. 1977. The measurement of role/identity. *Soc. Forces* 55:881–97

Burnstein, E., Schul, Y. 1982. The informational basis of social judgments: operations in forming an impression of another person. *J. Exp. Soc. Psychol.* 18:217–34

Burnstein, E., Schul, Y. 1983. The informational basis of social judgments: memory for integrated and nonintegrated trait descriptions. *J. Exp. Soc. Psychol.* 19:49–57

Byrne, B. 1984. The general/academic self-concept nomological network: a review of construct validation research. *Rev. Educ. Res.* 54:427–56

Cacioppo, J. T., Petty, R. E., Kao, C. F., Rodriguez, R. 1986. Central and peripheral routes to persuasion: an individual difference perspective. *J. Pers. Soc. Psychol.* 51:1032–43

Cacioppo, J. T., Petty, R. E., Stoltenberg, C. D. 1985. Processes of social influence: the elaboration likelihood model of persuasion. *Adv. Cogn. Behav. Res. Ther.* 4:215–74

Cafferty, T. P., DeNisi, A. S., Williams, K. J. 1986. Search and retrieval patterns for performance information: effects on evaluations of multiple targets. *J. Pers. Soc. Psychol.* 50:676–83

Campbell, J. D., Fairey, P. J. 1985. Effects of self-esteem, hypothetical explanations, and verbalizations of expectancies on future performance. *J. Pers. Soc. Psychol.* 48:1097–1111

Campbell, J. D., Tesser, A. 1985. Self-evaluation maintenance processes in relationships. In *Personal Relationships,* Vol. 1, ed. S. Duck, D. Perlman. London: Sage

Cantor, N., Kihlstrom, J. F. 1987. *Personality and Social Intelligence.* Englewood Cliffs, NJ: Prentice Hall

Cantor, N., Markus, H., Niedenthal, P., Nurius, P. 1986. On motivation and the self-concept. See Sorrentino & Higgins 1986, pp. 96–121.

Carlston, D. E., Skowronski, J. J. 1986. Trait memory and behavior memory: the effects of alternative pathways on impression judgment response times. *J. Pers. Soc. Psychol.* 50:5–13

Carver, C. S. 1975. Physical aggression as a function of objective self-awareness and attitudes toward punishment. *J. Exp. Soc. Psychol.* 11:510–19

Carver, C. S., Scheier, M. F. 1981. *Attention and Self-Regulation: A Control Theory Approach to Human Behavior.* New York: Springer-Verlag. 403 pp.

Cervone, D., Peake, P. K. 1986. Anchoring, efficacy, and action: the influence of judgmental heuristics on self-efficacy judgments and behavior. *J. Pers. Soc. Psychol.* 50:492–501

Chaiken, S. 1980. Heuristic versus systematic information processing and the use of source versus message cues in persuasion. *J. Pers. Soc. Psychol.* 39:752–66

Chaiken, S. 1987. The heuristic model of persuasion. In *Social Influence: The Ontario Symposium,* ed. M. Zanna, J. Olson, C. Herman, Vol. 5. NJ: Erlbaum

Chaiken, S., Eagly, A. H. 1983. Communication modality as a determinant of persuasion: the role of communicator salience. *J. Pers. Soc. Psychol.* 45:241–56

Chaiken, S., Stangor, C. 1987. Attitudes and attitude change. *Ann. Rev. Psychol.* 38:575–630

Chaiken, S., Yates, S. 1985. Affective-cognitive consistency and thought-induced attitude polarization. *J. Pers. Soc. Psychol.* 49:1470–81

Chassin, L., Presson, C. C., Sherman, S. J., Corty, E., Olshavsky, R. W. 1981. Self-images and cigarette smoking in adolescence. *Pers. Soc. Psychol. Bull.* 7:670–76

Chumbley, J. I. 1986. The roles of typicality, instance dominance, and category dominance in verifying category membership. *J. Exp. Psychol.: Learn. Mem. Cognit.* 12:257–67

Converse, P. E. 1964. The nature of belief systems in the mass public. In *Ideology and Discontent,* ed. D. E. Apter. New York: Free Press

Crandall, C. S., Greenfield, B. 1986. Understanding the conjunction fallacy: a conjunction of effects? *Soc. Cognit.* 4:408–19

Crocker, J., Fiske, S. T., Taylor, S. E. 1984. Schematic bases of belief change. In *Attitudinal Judgment,* ed. J. R. Eiser, pp. 197–226. New York: Springer

Damon, W., Hart, D. 1982. The development of self-understanding from infancy through adolescence. *Child Dev.* 53:841–64

Dance, K. A., Kuiper, N. A. 1987. Self-schemata, social roles, and a self-worth contingency model of depression. *Motiv. Emot.* 11:251–68

Darley, J. M., Gross, P. G. 1983. A hypothesis-confirming bias in labeling effects. *J. Pers. Soc. Psychol.* 44:20–33

Dawes, R. M. 1988. Statistical criteria for establishing a truly false consensus effect. *J. Exp. Soc. Psychol.* In press

Deaux, K., Winton, W., Crowley, M., Lewis, L. L. 1985. Level of categorization and content of gender stereotypes. *Soc. Cognit.* 3:145–67

Devine, P. G. 1987. Stereotypes and prejudice: their automatic and controlled components. Univ. of Wisconsin. Unpublished

Dovidio, J. F., Evans, N., Tyler, R. B. 1986. Racial stereotypes: the contents of their cognitive representations. *J. Exp. Soc. Psychol.* 22:22–37

Dovidio, J. F., Gaertner, S. L., ed. 1986. *Prejudice, Discrimination, and Racism.* Orlando, FL: Academic

Dweck, C., Elliott, E. S. 1983. Achievement motivation. In *Handbook of Child Psychology: Socialization, Personality, and Social Development,* Vol. 4, ed. E. M. Hetherington. New York: Wiley

Eagly, A. H., Chaiken, S. 1984. Cognitive theories of persuasion. *Adv. Exp. Soc. Psychol.* 17:268–359

Eagly, A. H., Steffen, V. J. 1984. Gender stereotypes stem from distribution of women and men into social roles. *J. Pers. Soc. Psychol.* 46:735–54

Epstein, S. 1973. The self-concept revisited: or a theory of a theory. *Am. Psychol.* 28:404–16

Erdelyi, M. H. 1974. A new look at the new look: perceptual defense and vigilance. *Psychol. Rev.* 81:1–25

Erikson, E. H. 1950. Identification as the basis for a theory of motivation. *Am. Psychol. Rev.* 26:14–21

Fazio, R. H. 1986. How do attitudes guide behavior? See Sorrentino & Higgins 1986, pp. 204–43

Fazio, R. H., Chen, J., McDonel, E. C., Sherman, S. J. 1982. Attitude accessibility, attitude-behavior consistency, and the strength of the object-evaluation association. *J. Exp. Soc. Psychol.* 18:339–57

Fazio, R. H., Lenn, T. M., Effrein, E. A. 1983–1984. Spontaneous attitude formation. *Soc. Cognit.* 2:217–34

Fazio, R. H., Powell, M. C., Herr, P. M. 1983. Toward a process model of the attitude-behavior relation: accessing one's attitude upon mere observation of the attitude object. *J. Pers. Soc. Psychol.* 44:723–35

Fazio, R. H., Sanbonmatsu, D. M., Powell, M. C., Kardes, F. R. 1986. On the automatic activation of attitudes. *J. Pers. Soc. Psychol.* 50:229–38

Fazio, R. H., Williams, C. J. 1986. Attitude accessibility as a moderator of the attitude-perception and attitude-behavior relations: an investigation of the 1984 presidential election. *J. Pers. Soc. Psychol.* 51:505–14

Fazio, R. H., Zanna, M. P. 1981. Direct experience and attitude-behavior consistency. *Adv. Exp. Soc. Psychol.* 14:161–202

Fenigstein, A., Levine, M. P. 1984. Self-attention, concept activation, and the causal self. *J. Exp. Soc. Psychol.* 20:231–45

Ferguson, T. J., Rule, G. R., Carlson, D. 1983. Memory for personally relevant information. *J. Pers. Soc. Psychol.* 44:251–61

Fischhoff, B. 1975. Hindsight ≠ foresight: the effect of outcome knowledge on judgment under uncertainty. *J. Exp. Psychol.: Hum. Percept. Perform.* 1:288–99

Fischhoff, B. 1982. For those condemned to study the past: heuristics and biases in hindsight. In *Judgment under Uncertainty: Heuristics and Biases*, ed. D. Kahneman, P. Slovic, A. Tversky, pp. 335–54. New York: Cambridge Univ. Press

Fischhoff, B., Bar-Hillel, M. 1984. Diagnosticity and the base-rate effect. *Mem. Cognit.* 12:402–20

Fischhoff, B., Beyth, R. 1975. "I knew it would happen"—remembered probabilities of once-future things. *Org. Behav. Hum. Perform.* 13:1–16

Fishbein, M., Ajzen, I. 1975. *Belief, Attitude, Intention, and Behavior: An Introduction to Theory and Research.* Reading, MA: Addison-Wesley

Fiske, S. T., Neuberg, S. L. 1988. A continuum of impression formation from category-based to individuating processes: influences of information and motivation on attention and interpretation. *Adv. Exp. Soc. Psychol.* 23: In press

Fong, G. T., Markus, H. 1982. Self-schemas and judgments about others. *Soc. Cognit.* 1:191–204

Forgas, J. P., Bower, G. H. 1987. Mood effects on person-perception judgments. *J. Pers. Soc. Psychol.* 53:53–60

Freund, T., Kruglanski, A. W., Shpitzajzen, A. 1985. The freezing and unfreezing of impressional primacy: effects of the need for structure and the fear of invalidity. *Pers. Soc. Psychol. Bull.* 11:479–87

Futoran, G. C., Wyer, R. S. Jr. 1986. The effects of traits and gender stereotypes on occupational suitability judgments and the recall of judgment-relevant information. *J. Exp. Soc. Psychol.* 22:475–503

Gabrielcik, A., Fazio, R. H. 1984. Priming and frequency estimation: a strict test of the availability heuristic. *Pers. Soc. Psychol. Bull.* 10:85–90

Gaertner, S. L., Dovidio, J. F. 1986. The aversive form of racism. See Dovidio & Gaertner 1986, pp. 61–89.

Gaertner, S. L., McLaughlin, J. P. 1983. Racial stereotypes: associations and ascriptions

of positive and negative characteristics. *Soc. Psychol. Q.* 46:23–30

Gergen, K. J. 1971. *The Concept of Self.* New York: Holt, Rinehart and Winston

Gibbons, F. X. 1978. Sexual standards and reactions to pornography: enhancing behavioral consistency through self-focused attention. *J. Res. Pers.* 36:976–87

Gilovich, T. 1987. Secondhand information and social judgment. *J. Exp. Soc. Psychol.* 22:59–74

Ginosar, Z., Trope, Y. 1980. The effects of base rates and individuating information on judgments about another person. *J. Exp. Soc. Psychol.* 16:228–42

Ginosar, Z., Trope, Y. 1987. Problem solving in judgment under uncertainty. *J. Pers. Soc. Psychol.* 52:464–74

Glick, P., Zion, C., Nelson, C. 1988. What mediates sex discrimination in hiring decisions? *J. Pers. Soc. Psychol.* In press

Goethals, G. R., Reckman, R. F. 1973. The perception of consistency in attitudes. *J. Exp. Soc. Psychol.* 9:491–501

Gordon, S. E., Wyer, R. S. Jr. 1987. Person memory: the organization of behaviors in terms of traits and situations. *J. Pers. Soc. Psychol.* 53:648–62

Greenberg, J., Pyszczynski, T. 1985. Compensatory self-inflation: a response to the threat to self regard of public failure. *J. Pers. Soc. Psychol.* 49:273–80

Greenwald, A. G. 1980. The totalitarian ego: fabrication and revision of personal history. *Am. Psychol.* 35:603–18

Greenwald, A. G. 1981a. Is anyone in charge? Personalysis versus the principle of personal utility. See Suls 1982, pp. 151–84

Greenwald, A. G. 1981b. Self and memory. In *The Psychology of Learning and Motivation*, Vol. 15, ed. G. H. Bower. New York: Academic

Greenwald, A. G., Pratkanis, A. R. 1984. The self. In *Handbook of Social Cognition*, Vol. 3, ed. R. S. Wyer, T. K. Srull. Hillsdale, NJ: Erlbaum

Hamilton, D. L. 1988. Understanding impression formation: What has memory research contributed? In *Memory—An Interdisciplinary Approach*, ed. P. R. Solomon, G. R. Goethals, C. M. Kelley, B. Stephens. New York: Springer-Verlag. In press

Hamilton, D. L., Dugan, P. M., Trolier, T. K. 1985. The formation of stereotypic beliefs: further evidence for distinctiveness-based illusory correlation. *J. Pers. Soc. Psychol.* 48:5–17

Hamilton, D. L., Sherman, S. J. 1988. Illusory correlation: implications for stereotype theory and research. In *Stereotypes and Prejudice: Changing Conceptions*, ed. D.

Bar-Tal, C. F. Graumann, A. W. Kruglanski, W. Stroebe. In press

Hampson, S. E., John, O. P., Goldberg, L. R. 1986. Category breadth and hierarchical structure in personality: studies of asymmetries in judgments of trait implications. *J. Pers. Soc. Psychol.* 51:37–54

Harkins, S. G., Petty, R. E. 1987. Information utility and the multiple source effect. *J. Pers. Soc. Psychol.* 52:260–68

Harris, R. N., Snyder, C. R. 1986. The role of uncertain self-esteem in self-handicapping. *J. Pers. Soc. Psychol.* 51:451–58

Harter, S. 1983. Developmental perspectives on the self-system. In *Handbook of Child Psychology: Socialization, Personality and Social Development*, Vol. 4, ed. E. M. Hetherington, New York: Wiley

Harter, S. 1986a. Cognitive-developmental processes in the integration of concepts about emotions and the self. *Soc. Cognit.* 4:119–51

Harter, S. 1986b. Processes underlying the construction, maintenance, and enhancement of the self-concept in children. See Suls & Greenwald 1986, pp. 136–82

Hastie, R. 1984. Causes and effects of causal attribution. *J. Pers. Soc. Psychol.* 46:44–56

Hastie, R., Park, B., Weber, R. 1984. Social memory. See Wyer & Srull 1984, 2:151–212

Herr, P. M. 1986. Consequences of priming: judgment and behavior. *J. Pers. Soc. Psychol.* 51:1106–15

Herr, P. M., Sherman, S. J., Fazio, R. H. 1983. On the consequences of priming: assimilation and contrast effects. *J. Exp. Soc. Psychol.* 19:323–40

Herstein, J. A., Carroll, J. S., Hayes, J. R. 1980. The organization of knowledge about people and their attributes in long-term memory. *J. Rep. Res. Soc. Psychol.* 11:17–37

Higgins, E. T., Bargh, J. A. 1987. Social cognition and social perception. *Ann. Rev. Psychol.* 38:369–425

Higgins, E. T., Chaires, W. M. 1980. Accessibility of interrelational constructs: implications for stimulus encoding and creativity. *J. Exp. Soc. Psychol.* 16:248–61

Higgins, E. T., King, G. A., Mavin, G. H. 1982a. Individual construct accessibility and subjective impressions and recall. *J. Pers. Soc. Psychol.* 43:35–47

Higgins, E. T., McCann, C. D., Fondacaro, R. 1982b. The "communication game": Goal-directed encoding and cognitive consequences. *Soc. Cognit.* 1:21–37

Higgins, E. T., Rholes, W. S., Jones, C. R. 1977. Category accessibility and impression formation. *J. Exp. Soc. Psychol.* 13:141–54

Higgins, E. T., Van Hook, E., Dorfman, D.

1988. Do self attributes form a cognitive structure? *Soc. Cognit.* In press

Hintzman, D. G. 1986. "Schema abstraction" in a multiple-trace memory model. *Psychol. Rev.* 93:411–28

Hirt, E. R. 1987. *Techniques of reconstructing the past: implications for the accuracy of memories.* PhD thesis. Indiana Univ.

Hirt, E. R., Sherman, S. J. 1985. The role of prior knowledge in explaining hypothetical events. *J. Exp. Soc. Psychol.* 21:519–43

Hoch, S. J. 1987. Perceived consensus and predictive accuracy: the pros and cons of projection. *J. Pers. Soc. Psychol.* 53:221–34

Hoelter, J. W. 1985. The structure of self-conception: conceptualization and measurement. *J. Pers. Soc. Psychol.* 49:1392–1407

Hoffman, C. 1985. A descriptive bias in trait attributions following decisions favoring one role candidate over another. *Soc. Cognit.* 3:296–312

Hoffman, C., Mischel, W., Baer, J. S. 1984. Language and person cognition: effects of communicative set on trait attribution. *J. Pers. Soc. Psychol.* 46:1029–43

Hoffman, C., Mischel, W., Mazze, K. 1981. The role of purpose in the organization of information about behavior: trait-based versus goal-based categories in person cognition. *J. Pers. Soc. Psychol.* 40:211–25

Holyoak, K. J., Gordon, P. C. 1983. Social reference points. *J. Pers. Soc. Psychol.* 44:881–87

Houston, D. A., Sherman, S. J., Baker, S. M. 1988. The influence of unique features and direction of comparison on preferences. *J. Exp. Soc. Psychol.* In press

James, W. 1890. *The Principles of Psychology.* New York: Holt

Jaspers, J. 1983. The process of attribution in common sense. In *Attribution Theory: Social and Functional Extensions*, ed. M. Hewstone. Oxford: Basil Blackwell

Johnson, J. T. 1986. The knowledge of what might have been: affective and attributional consequences of near outcomes. *Pers. Soc. Psychol. Bull.* 12:51–62

Jones, E. E., Rhodewalt, F., Berglas, S., Skelton, J. A. 1981. Effects of strategic self-presentation on subsequent self-esteem. *J. Pers. Soc. Psychol.* 41:407–21

Jonides, J., Naveh-Benjamin, M. 1987. Estimating frequency of occurrence. *J. Exp. Psychol.: Learn. Mem. Cognit.* 13:230–40

Judd, C. M., Drake, R., Downing, J., Krosnick, J. A. 1988. Some dynamic properties of attitude structures: context induced response facilitation and polarization. Univ. of Col. Unpublished

Judd, C. M., Krosnick, J. A. 1988. The structural bases of consistency among political attitudes: effects of political expertise and attitude importance. In *Attitude Structure and Function*, ed. A. R. Pratkanis, S. J. Breckler, A. G. Greenwald. Hillsdale, NJ: Erlbaum

Judd, C. M., Park, B. 1988. Outgroup homogeneity: judgments of variability at the individual and group levels. *J. Pers. Soc. Psychol.* 54:778–88

Jussim, L., Coleman, L. M., Lerch, L. 1987. The nature of stereotypes: a comparison and integration of three theories. *J. Pers. Soc. Psychol.* 52:536–46

Kahneman, D., Miller, D. T. 1986. Norm theory: comparing reality to its alternatives. *Psychol. Rev.* 93:136–53

Kahneman, D., Tversky, A. 1972. Subjective probability: a judgment of representativeness. *Cogn. Psychol.* 3:430–54

Kahneman, D., Tversky, A. 1973. On the psychology of prediction. *Psychol. Rev.* 80:237–51

Kallgren, C. A., Wood, W. 1986. Access to attitude-relevant information in memory as a determinant of attitude-behavior consistency. *J. Exp. Soc. Psychol.* 22:328–38

Kardes, F. R., Sanbonmatsu, D. M., Voss, R. T., Fazio, R. H. 1986. Self-monitoring and attitude accessibility. *Pers. Soc. Psychol. Bull.* 12:468–74

Kassin, S. 1979. Consensus information, prediction, and causal attribution: a review of the literature and issues. *J. Pers. Soc. Psychol.* 37:1966–81

Katz, D., Braly, K. 1933. Racial stereotypes in one hundred college students. *J. Abnorm. Soc. Psychol.* 28:280–90

Kelly, G. A. 1955. *A Theory of Personality: The Psychology of Personal Constructs*. New York: Norton. 190 pp.

Kihlstrom, J. F., Cantor, N. 1984. Mental representations of the self. *Adv. Exp. Soc. Psychol.* 17:1–47

Kihlstrom, J. F., Cantor, N. 1988. Information processing and the study of the self. *Adv. Exp. Soc. Psychol.* In press

Klein, S. B., Kihlstrom, J. F. 1986. Elaboration, organization, and the self-reference effect in memory. *J. Exp. Psychol.: Gen.* 115:26–38

Klein, S. B., Loftus, J. B. 1988. The nature of self-referent encoding: the contributions of elaborative and organizational processes. *J. Pers. Soc. Psychol.* In press.

Krueger, J., Rothbart, M. 1988. The use of categorical and individuating information in making inferences about personality. *J. Pers. Soc. Psychol.* In press

Kruglanski, A. W., Freund, T. 1983. The freezing and unfreezing of lay inferences: effects on impressional primacy, ethnic stereotyping, and numerical anchoring. *J. Exp. Soc. Psychol.* 19:448–68

Kuiper, N. A. 1981. Convergent evidence for the self as a prototype: the "inverted-U RT effect" for self and other judgments. *Pers. Soc. Psychol. Bull.* 7:438–43

Kuiper, N. A., Derry, P. A. 1981. The self as a cognitive prototype: an application to person perception and depression. See Cantor & Kihlstrom 1981, pp. 215–32

Kulik, J. A., Sledge, P., Mahler, H. I. M. 1986. Self-confirmatory attribution, egocentrism, and the perpetuation of self-beliefs. *J. Pers. Soc. Psychol.* 50:587–94

Kun, A., Weiner, B. 1973. Necessary versus sufficient causal schemata for success and failure. *J. Res. Pers.* 7:197–207

Kunda, Z. 1987. Motivated inference: self-serving generation and evaluation of causal theories. *J. Pers. Soc. Psychol.* 53:636–47

Landman, J. 1987. Regret and elation following action and inaction. *Pers. Soc. Psychol. Bull.* 13:524–36

LaRue, A., Olejnik, A. B. 1980. Cognitive priming and principled moral thought. *Pers. Soc. Psychol. Bull.* 6:413–16

Lecky, P. 1945. *Self-Consistency: A Theory of Personality*. New York: Island Press

Leddo, J., Abelson, R. P., Gross, P. H. 1984. Conjunctive explanations: when two reasons are better than one. *J. Pers. Soc. Psychol.* 47:933–43

Leippe, M. R., Elkin, R. A. 1987. When motives clash: issue involvement and response involvement as determinants of persuasion. *J. Pers. Soc. Psychol.* 52:269–78

Lepper, M. R., Ross, L., Lau, R. R. 1986. Persistence of inaccurate beliefs about the self: perseverance in the classroom. *J. Pers. Soc. Psychol.* 50:482–91

Lewandowsky, S., Smith, P. W. 1983. The effect of increasing the memorability of category instances on estimates of category size. *Mem. Cognit.* 11:347–50

Lingle, J. H. 1983. Tracing memory-structure activation during person judgments. *J. Exp. Soc. Psychol.* 19:480–96

Lingle, J. H., Dukerich, J. M., Ostrom, T. M. 1983. Accessing information in memory-based impression judgments: incongruity versus negativity in retrieval selectivity. *J. Pers. Soc. Psychol.* 37:674–87

Linville, P. W. 1982. The complexity-extremity effect and age-based stereotyping. *J. Pers. Soc. Psychol.* 42:193–211

Linville, P. W. 1985. Self-complexity and affective extremity: Don't put all of your eggs in one cognitive basket. *Soc. Cognit.* 3:94–120

Linville, P. W. 1987. Self-complexity as a cognitive buffer against stress-related illness and depression. *J. Pers. Soc. Psychol.* 52:663–76

Linville, P. W., Fischer, G. W., Salovey, P. 1987. The PDIST model of ingroup/outgroup perceptions. Paper presented at the Society of Experimental Social Psychology, Charlottesville, VA

Linville, P. W., Salovey, P., Fischer, G. W. 1986. Stereotyping and perceived distributions of social characteristics: an application to ingroup-outgroup perception. See Dovidio & Gaertner 1986, pp. 165–208

Liu, T. J., Steele, C. M. 1986. Attributional analysis as self-affirmation. *J. Pers. Soc. Psychol.* 51:531–40

Locksley, A., Hepburn, C., Ortiz, V. 1982. Social stereotypes and judgments of individuals: an instance of the base-rate fallacy. *J. Exp. Soc. Psychol.* 18:23–42

Locksley, A., Stangor, C. 1984. Why versus how often: causal reasoning and the incidence of judgmental bias. *J. Exp. Soc. Psychol.* 20:470–83

Lombardi, W. J., Higgins, E. T., Bargh, J. A. 1987. The role of consciousness in priming effects on categorization: assimilation versus contrast as a function of awareness of the priming task. *Pers. Soc. Psychol. Bull.* 13:411–29

Lord, C. G. 1980. Schemas and images as memory aids: two modes of processing social information. *J. Pers. Soc. Psychol.* 38:257–69

Lord, C. G. 1987. Imagining self and others: reply to Brown, Keenan, and Potts. *J. Pers. Soc. Psychol.* 53:445–50

Lord, C. G., Lepper, M. R., Mackie, D. 1984. Attitude prototypes as determinants of attitude-behavior consistency. *J. Pers. Soc. Psychol.* 46:1254–66

Lord, C. G., Ross, L., Lepper, M. R. 1979. Biased assimilation and attitude polarization: the effects of prior theories on subsequently considered evidence. *J. Pers. Soc. Psychol.* 37:2098–109

Lusk, C. M., Judd, C. M. 1988. Political expertise and the structural mediators of candidate evaluations. *J. Exp. Soc. Psychol.* 24:105–26

Mackie, D. M. 1987. Systematic and nonsystematic processing of majority and minority persuasive communications. *J. Pers. Soc. Psychol.* 53:41–52

Manis, M., Paskewitz, J., Cotler, S. 1986. Stereotypes and social judgment. *J. Pers. Soc. Psychol.* 50:461–73

Manis, M., Nelson, T., Shedler, J. 1988. Stereotypes and social judgment: extremity, assimilation, and contrast. *J. Pers. Soc. Psychol.* 55:28–36

Marks, G., Miller, N. 1987. Ten years of research on the false-consensus effect: an

empirical and theoretical review. *Psychol. Bull.* 102:72–90

Markus, H. 1977. Self-schemata and processing information about the self. *J. Pers. Soc. Psychol.* 35:63–78

Markus, H. 1980. The self in thought in memory. In *The Self in Social Psychology,* ed. D. M. Wegner, R. R. Vallacher. New York: Oxford Press

Markus, H., Kunda, Z. 1986. Stability and malleability of the self-concept. *J. Pers. Soc. Psychol.* 51:858–66

Markus, H., Nurius, P. 1986. Possible selves. *Am. Psychol.* 41:954–69

Markus, H., Sentis, K. 1982. The self in social information processing. See Suls 1982, pp. 41–70

Markus, H., Smith, J. 1981. The influence of self-schema on the perception of others. See Cantor & Kihlstrom 1981, pp. 233–62

Markus, H., Smith, J., Moreland, R. L. 1985. Role of the self-concept in the perception of others. *J. Pers. Soc. Psychol.* 49:1494–1512

Markus, H., Wurf, E. 1987. The dynamic self-concept: a social psychological perspective. *Ann. Rev. Psychol.* 38:299–337

Markus, H., Zajonc, R. B. 1985. The cognitive perspective in social psychology. In *Handbook of Social Psychology,* ed. G. Lindzey, E. Aronson. New York: Random House. 3rd ed.

Marsh, H. W. 1986. Global self-esteem: its relation to specific facets of self-concept and their importance. *J. Pers. Soc. Psychol.* 51:1224–36

Martin, L. L. 1986. Set/reset: use and disuse of concepts in impression formation. *J. Pers. Soc. Psychol.* 51:493–504

Martindale, C. 1980. Subselves: the internal representation of situational and personal dispositions. In *Review of Personality and Social Psychology,* ed. L. Wheeler, 1:193–218. Beverly Hills, CA: Sage

Mayer, J. D., Bower, G. H. 1986. Learning and memory for personality prototypes. *J. Pers. Soc. Psychol.* 51:473–92

McCann, C. D., Ostrom, T. M., Tyner, L. K., Mitchell, M. L. 1985. Person perception in heterogeneous groups. *J. Pers. Soc. Psychol.* 49:1449–59

McClure, J., Lalljee, M., Jaspars, J., Abelson, R. P. 1988. Conjunctive explanations of success and failure: the effect of different types of causes. *J. Pers. Soc. Psychol.* In press

McFarland, C., Ross, M. 1987. The relation between current impressions and memories of self and dating partners. *Pers. Soc. Psychol. Bull.* 13:228–38

McGuire, W. J., McGuire, C. V. 1982. Significant others in self-space: sex differences and developmental trends in the social self. See Suls 1982, pp. 71–96

Mead, G. H. 1934. *Mind, Self, and Society.* Chicago: Univ. Chicago Press

Medin, D. L., Schaffer, M. M. 1978. Context theory of classification learning. *Psychol. Rev.* 85:207–38

Millar, M. G., Tesser, A. 1986a. Thought-induced attitude change: the effects of schema structure and commitment. *J. Pers. Soc. Psychol.* 51:259–69

Millar, M. G., Tesser, A. 1986b. Effects of affective and cognitive focus on the attitude-behavior relation. *J. Pers. Soc. Psychol.* 51:270–76

Miller, D. T., Ross, M. 1975. Self-serving biases in attribution of causality: fact or fiction? *Psychol. Bull.* 82:213–25

Miller, N., Brewer, M. B. 1986. Categorization effects on ingroup and outgroup perception. See Dovidio & Gaertner 1986, pp. 209–30

Mori, D., Chaiken, S., Pliner, P. 1987. "Eating lightly" and the self-presentation of femininity. *J. Pers. Soc. Psychol.* 53:693–702

Morier, D. M., Borgida, E. 1984. The conjunction fallacy: a task specific phenomenon? *Pers. Soc. Psychol. Bull.* 10:243–52

Nasby, W. 1985. Private self-consciousness, articulation of the self-schema, and recognition memory of trait adjectives. *J. Pers. Soc. Psychol.* 49:704–9

Natale, M., Hantas, M. 1982. Effects of temporary mood states on selective memory about the self. *J. Pers. Soc. Psychol.* 42:927–34

Neuberg, S. L., Fiske, S. T. 1987. Motivational influences on impression formation: outcome dependency, accuracy-driven attention, and individuating processes. *J. Pers. Soc. Psychol.* 53:431–44

Niedenthal, P. M., Cantor, N., Kihlstrom, J. F. 1985. Prototype matching: a strategy for social decision making. *J. Pers. Soc. Psychol.* 48:575–84

Noseworthy, C. M., Lott, A. J. 1984. The cognitive organization of gender-stereotypic categories. *Pers. Soc. Psychol. Bull.* 10:474–81

Nurius, P. 1984. *A dynamic view of self-concept and its relation to behavioral self-regulation.* PhD thesis. Univ. Mich.

Pallak, S. R. 1983. Salience of a communicator's physical attractiveness and persuasion: a heuristic versus systematic processing interpretation. *Soc. Cognit.* 2:158–70

Pallak, S. R., Murroni, E., Koch, J. 1983. Communicator attractiveness and expertise, emotional versus rational appeals, and persuasion: a heuristic versus systematic processing interpretation. *Soc. Cognit.* 2:122–41

Park, B. 1986. A method for studying the development of impressions of real people. *J. Pers. Soc. Psychol.* 51:907–17

Park, B., Hastie, R. 1987. The perception of variability in category development: instance- versus abstraction-based stereotypes. *J. Pers. Soc. Psychol.* 53:621–35

Pelham, B. W., Swann, W. B. Jr. 1988. From self-conceptions to self-worth: the sources and structure of self-esteem. Univ. Texas at Austin. Unpublished

Pennington, N., Hastie, R. 1986. Evidence evaluation in complex decision making. *J. Pers. Soc. Psychol.* 51:242–58

Pennington, N., Hastie, R. 1988. Explanation-based decision making: the effects of memory structure on judgment. *J. Exp. Psychol.: Learn. Mem. Cognit.* In press

Petty, R. E., Cacioppo, J. T. 1986. The elaboration likelihood model of persuasion. *Adv. Exp. Soc. Psychol.* 19:123–205

Posner, M. I., Snyder, C. R. R. 1975. Attention and cognitive control. In *Information Processing and Cognition: The Loyola Symposium,* ed. R. Solso. Potomac, MD: Erlbaum

Powell, M. C., Fazio, R. H. 1984. Attitude accessibility as a function of repeated attitude expression. *Pers. Soc. Psychol. Bull.* 10:139–48

Pratkanis, A. R., Greenwald, A. G. 1985. How shall the self be conceived? *J. Theory Soc. Behav.* 15:311–29

Pryor, J. B., Gibbons, F. X., Wicklund, R. A., Fazio, R. H., Hood, R. 1977. Self-focused attention and self-report. *J. Pers.* 45:514–27

Pryor, J. B., Kott, T. L., Bovee, G. R. 1984. The influence of information redundancy upon the use of traits and persons as organizing categories. *J. Exp. Soc. Psychol.* 20:246–62

Pyszczynski, T., Greenberg, J. 1987. Toward an integration of cognitive and motivational perspectives on social inference: a biased hypothesis-testing model. *Adv. Exp. Soc. Psychol.* 20:297–340

Pyszczynski, T., Greenberg, J., La Prelle, J. 1985. Social comparison after success and failure: biased search consistent with a self-serving conclusion. *J. Exp. Soc. Psychol.* 21:195–211

Quattrone, G. A., Tversky, A. 1984. Causal versus diagnostic contingencies: on self-deception and on the voter's illusion. *J. Pers. Soc. Psychol.* 46:237–48

Rasinski, K. A., Crocker, J., Hastie, R. 1985. Another look at sex stereotypes and social judgments: an analysis of the social perceiver's use of subjective probabilities. *J. Pers. Soc. Psychol.* 49:317–26

Raynor, J. O., McFarlin, D. B. 1986. Motivation and the self-system. See Sorrentino & Higgins 1986, pp. 315–49

Read, S. 1987. Constructing causal scenarios: a knowledge structure approach to causal reasoning. *J. Pers. Soc. Psychol.* 52:288–302

Reeder, G. D., Brewer, M. B. 1979. A schematic model of dispositional attribution in interpersonal perception. *Psychol. Rev.* 86:61–79

Reyes, R. M., Thompson, W. C., Bower, G. H. 1980. Judgmental biases resulting from differing availabilities of arguments. *J. Pers. Soc. Psychol.* 39:2–12

Rhodewalt, F., Agustsdottir, S. 1986. The effects of self-presentation on the phenomenal self. *J. Pers. Soc. Psychol.* 50:47–55

Rogers, C. 1951. *Client-Centered Therapy: Its Current Practice, Implications, and Theory.* Boston, MA: Houghton Mifflen

Rogers, T. B. 1981. A model of the self as an aspect of the human information processing system. See Cantor & Kihlstrom 1981, pp. 193–214

Rogers, T. B., Kuiper, N. A., Kirker, W. S. 1977. Self-reference and the encoding of personal information. *J. Pers. Soc. Psychol.* 35:677–88

Rosch, E. 1981. Principles of categorization. In *Cognition and Categorization,* ed. E. Rosch, B. B. Lloyd, pp. 23–48. Hillsdale, NJ: Erlbaum

Rosenberg, M. 1986. Self-concept from middle childhood through adolescence. See Suls & Greenwald 1986, pp. 107–35

Rosenberg, S., Gara, M. A. 1985. The multiplicity of personal identity. In *Review of Personality and Social Psychology,* ed. P. Shaver, 6:87–113. Beverly Hills, CA: Sage

Ross, L., Lepper, M. K., Hubbard, M. 1975. Perseverance in self-perception and social perception: biased attributional processes in the debriefing paradigm. *J. Pers. Soc. Psychol.* 32:880–92

Ross, M., Conway, M. 1986. Remembering one's own past: the construction of personal histories. See Sorrentino & Higgins 1986, pp. 122–44

Ross, M., McFarland, C., Fletcher, G. J. O. 1981. The effect of attitude on the recall of personal histories. *J. Pers. Soc. Psychol.* 40:627–34

Rothbart, M., John, O. P. 1985. Social categorization and behavioral episodes: a cognitive analysis of the effects of intergroup contact. *J. Soc. Issues* 41:81–104

Rothbart, M., Lewis, S. 1988. Inferring category attributes from exemplar attributes:

geometric shapes and social categories. *J. Pers. Soc. Psychol.* In press

Sagar, H. A., Schofield, H. W. 1980. Racial and behavioral cues in black and white children's perceptions of ambiguously aggressive acts. *J. Pers. Soc. Psychol.* 39:590–98

Salancik, G. R., Conway, M. 1975. Attitude inference from salient and relevant cognitive content about behavior. *J. Pers. Soc. Psychol.* 32:829–40

Sanbonmatsu, D. M., Shavitt, S., Sherman, S. J., Roskos-Ewoldsen, D. R. 1987a. Illusory correlation in the perception of performance by self or a salient other. *J. Exp. Soc. Psychol.* 23:518–43

Sanbonmatsu, D. M., Sherman, S. J., Hamilton, D. L. 1987b. Illusory correlation in the perception of individuals and groups. *Soc. Cognit.* 5:1–25

Sande, G. N., Ellard, J. H., Ross, M. 1986. Effect of arbitrarily assigned status labels on self-perceptions and social perceptions: the mere position effect. *J. Pers. Soc. Psychol.* 50:684–89

Schul, Y. 1983. Integration and abstraction in impression formation. *J. Pers. Soc. Psychol.* 44:45–54

Schul, Y. 1986. The effect of the amount of information and its relevance on memory-based and stimulus-based judgments. *J. Exp. Soc. Psychol.* 22:355–73

Schul, Y., Burnstein, E. 1985. The informational basis of social judgments: using past impression rather than the trait description in forming a new impression. *J. Exp. Soc. Psychol.* 21:421–39

Schuman, H., Presser, S. 1981. *Questions and Answers in Attitude Surveys.* New York: Academic

Shavelson, R. J., Marsh, H. W. 1986. On the structure of self-concept. In *Anxiety and Cognitions,* ed. R. Schwarzer, pp. 305–30. Hillsdale, NJ: Erlbaum

Shedler, J., Manis, M. 1986. Can the availability heuristic explain vividness effects? *J. Pers. Soc. Psychol.* 51:26–36

Sherman, S. J. 1987. Cognitive processes in the formation, change, and expression of attitudes. In *Social Influence: The Ontario Symposium,* Vol. 5, ed. M. P. Zanna, J. M. Olson, C. P. Herman, pp. 75–106. Hillsdale NJ: Erlbaum

Sherman, S. J., Chassin, L., Presson, C. C., Agostinelli, G. 1984a. The role of the evaluation and similarity principles in the false consensus effect. *J. Pers. Soc. Psychol.* 47:1249–62

Sherman, S. J., Cialdini, R. B., Schwartzman, D. F., Reynolds, K. D. 1985. Imagining can heighten or lower the perceived likelihood of contracting a disease. *Pers. Soc. Psychol. Bull.* 11:118–27

Sherman, S. J., Corty, E. 1984. Cognitive heuristics. See Wyer & Srull 1984, Vol. 1, pp. 189–286

Sherman, S. J., Gorkin, L. 1980. Attitude bolstering when behavior is inconsistent with central attitudes. *J. Exp. Soc. Psychol.* 16:388–403

Sherman, S. J., Presson, C. C., Chassin, L. 1984. Mechanisms underlying the false consensus effect: the special role of threats to the self. *Pers. Soc. Psychol. Bull.* 10:127–38

Sherman, S. J., Skov, R. B., Hervitz, E. F., Stock, C. B. 1981. The effects of explaining hypothetical future events: from possibility to probability to actuality and beyond. *J. Exp. Soc. Psychol.* 17:142–58

Sherman, S. J., Zehner, K. S., Johnson, J., Hirt, E. R. 1983. Social explanation: the role of timing, set, and recall on subjective likelihood estimates. *J. Pers. Soc. Psychol.* 44:1127–43

Shrauger, J. S. 1975. Responses to evaluation as a function of initial self-perceptions. *Psychol. Bull.* 82:581–96

Silka, L. 1984. Intuitive perceptions of change: an overlooked phenomenon in person perception? *Pers. Soc. Psychol. Bull.* 10:180–90

Skov, R. B., Sherman, S. J. 1986. Information-gathering processes: diagnosticity, hypothesis confirmatory strategies, and perceived hypothesis confirmation. *J. Exp. Soc. Psychol.* 22:93–121

Skowronski, J. J., Carlston, D. E. 1987. Social judgment and social memory: the role of cue diagnosticity in negativity, positivity, and extremity biases. *J. Pers. Soc. Psychol.* 52:689–99

Smith, E. R., Branscomb, N. R. 1987. Procedurally mediated social inferences: the case of category accessibility effects. *J. Exp. Soc. Psychol.* 23:361–82

Smith, E. R., Branscomb, N. R. 1988. Category accessibility as implicit memory. *J. Exp. Soc. Psychol.* In press

Smith, E. R., Miller, F. D. 1983. Mediation among attributional inferences and comprehension processes: initial findings and a general method. *J. Pers. Soc. Psychol.* 44:492–505

Smith, E. R., Zarate, M. A. 1987. Exemplar models of person memory and categorization. Purdue Univ. Unpublished

Snyder, M. 1987. *Public Appearances/Private Realities: The Psychology of Self-Monitoring.* New York: W. H. Freeman

Snyder, M., DeBono, K. G. 1985. Appeals to image and claims about quality: understanding the psychology of advertising. *J. Pers. Soc. Psychol.* 49:586–97

Snyder, M., Gangestad, S. 1982. Choosing social situations: two investigations of self-monitoring processes. *J. Pers. Soc. Psychol.* 43:123–35

Snyder, M., Gangestad, S., Simpson, J. A. 1983. Choosing friends as activity partners: the role of self-monitoring. *J. Pers. Soc. Psychol.* 45:1061–72

Snyder, M., Kendzierski, D. 1982. Acting on one's attitudes: procedures for linking attitudes and behavior. *J. Exp. Soc. Psychol.* 18:165–83

Snyder, M., Simpson, J. A. 1984. Self-monitoring and dating relationships. *J. Pers. Soc. Psychol.* 47:1281–91

Snyder, M., Simpson, J. A. 1986. Orientations toward romantic relationships. In *Intimate Relationships: Development, Dynamics, and Deterioration,* ed. S. Duck, D. Perlman. Beverly Hills, CA: Sage

Snyder, M., Swann, W. B. Jr. 1976. When actions reflect attitudes: the politics of impression management. *J. Pers. Soc. Psychol.* 34:1034–42

Snyder, M., Swann, W. B. Jr. 1978. Behavioral confirmation in social interaction: from social perception to social reality. *J. Exp. Soc. Psychol.* 14:148–62

Snygg, D., Combs, A. W. 1949. *Individual Behavior.* New York: Harper & Row

Sorrentino, R. M., Higgins, E. T. 1986. *Handbook of Motivation and Cognition: Foundations of Social Behavior.* New York: Guilford

Sorrentino, R. M., Short, J. A. C. 1986. Uncertainty orientation, motivation, and cognition. See Sorrentino & Higgins 1986, pp. 379–403

Srull, T. K., Gaelick, L. 1983. General principles and individual differences in the self as a habitual reference point: an examination of self-other judgments of similarity. *Soc. Cognit.* 2:108–21

Srull, T. K., Wyer, R. S. Jr. 1980. Category accessibility and social perception: some implications for the study of person memory and interpersonal judgments. *J. Pers. Soc. Psychol.* 38:841–56

Stangor, C. 1988. Stereotype accessibility and information processing. *Pers. Soc. Psychol. Bull.* In press

Stangor, C., Ruble, D. N. 1988. Strength of expectancies and memory of social information: what we remember depends on how much we know. *J. Exp. Soc. Psychol.* In press

Steele, C. M., Liu, T. J. 1983. Dissonance processes as self-affirmation. *J. Pers. Soc. Psychol.* 45:5–19

Strack, F., Schwarz, N., Gschneidinger, E. 1985. Happiness and reminiscing: the role of time perspective, affect, and mode of thinking. *J. Pers. Soc. Psychol.* 49:1460–69

Strube, M. J., Lott, C. L., Le-Xuan-Hy, G. M., Oxenberg, J., Deichmann, A. K. 1986. Self-evaluation of abilities: accurate self-assessment versus biased self-enhancement. *J. Pers. Soc. Psychol.* 51:16–26

Strube, M. J., Roemmele, L. A. 1985. Self-enhancement, self-assessment, and self-evaluative task choice. *J. Pers. Soc. Psychol.* 49:981–93

Stryker, S. 1980. *Symbolic Interactionism.* Menlo Park, CA: Benjamin/Cummings

Sullivan, H. S. 1953. *The Interpersonal Theory of Psychiatry.* New York: Norton

Suls, J., ed. 1982. *Psychological Perspectives on the Self,* Vol. 1. Hillsdale, NJ: Erlbaum 273 pp.

Suls, J., Greenwald, A. G., eds. 1983. *Psychological Perspectives on the Self,* Vol. 2. Hillsdale, NJ: Erlbaum. 287 pp.

Suls, J., Greenwald, A. G., eds. 1986. *Psychological Perspectives on the Self,* Vol. 3. Hillsdale, NJ: Erlbaum

Swann, W. B. Jr. 1983. Self-verification: bringing social reality into harmony with the self. See Suls & Greenwald 1983, pp. 33–66

Swann, W. B. Jr. 1984. Quest for accuracy in person perception: a matter of pragmatics. *Psychol. Rev.* 475–77

Swann, W. B. Jr. 1987. Identity negotiation: where two roads meet. *J. Pers. Soc. Psychol.* 53:1038–51

Swann, W. B. Jr., Ely, R. J. 1984. A battle of wills: self-verification versus behavioral confirmation. *J. Pers. Soc. Psychol.* 46:1287–1302

Swann, W. B. Jr., Griffin, J. J. Jr., Predmore, S. C., Gaines, B. 1987. The cognitive-affective crossfire: when self-consistency confronts self-enhancement. *J. Pers. Soc. Psychol.* 52:881–89

Swann, W. B. Jr., Hill, C. A. 1982. When our identities are mistaken: reaffirming self-conceptions through social interaction. *J. Pers. Soc. Psychol.* 43:59–66

Swann, W. B. Jr., Predmore, S. C. 1985. Intimates as agents of social support: sources of consolation or despair? *J. Pers. Soc. Psychol.* 49:1609–17

Swann, W. B. Jr., Read, S. J. 1981a. Acquiring self-knowledge: the search for feedback that fits. *J. Pers. Soc. Psychol.* 41:1119–28

Swann, W. B. Jr., Read, S. J. 1981b. Self-verification processes: how we sustain our self-conceptions. *J. Exp. Soc. Psychol.* 17:351–72

Tesser, A. 1978. Self-generated attitude change. *Adv. Exp. Soc. Psychol.* 11:289–338

Tesser, A. 1986. Some effects of self-evaluation maintenance on cognition and action. See Sorrentino & Higgins 1986, pp. 435–64

Tesser, A., Campbell, J. 1983. Self-definition and self-evaluation maintenance. See Suls & Greenwald 1983, pp. 1–31

Tesser, A., Campbell, J., Smith, M. 1984. Friendship choice and performance: self-evaluation maintenance in children. *J. Pers. Soc. Psychol.* 46:561–74

Tesser, A., Leone, C. 1977. Cognitive schemas and thought as determinants of attitude change. *J. Exp. Soc. Psychol.* 13:340–56

Tesser, A., Paulhus, D. 1983. The definition of self: private and public self-evaluation management strategies. *J. Pers. Soc. Psychol.* 44:672–82

Tetlock, P. E. 1983. Accountability and the perseverance of first impressions. *Soc. Psychol. Q.* 46:285–92

Tetlock, P. E. 1984. Cognitive style and political belief systems in the British House of Commons. *J. Pers. Soc. Psychol.* 46:365–75

Tetlock, P. E. 1986. A value pluralism model of ideological reasoning. *J. Pers. Soc. Psychol.* 50:819–27

Tetlock, P. E., Kim, J. 1987. Accountability and judgment processes in a personality prediction task. *J. Pers. Soc. Psychol.* 52:700–9

Tetlock, P. E., Manstead, A. S. R. 1985. Impression management versus intrapsychic explanations in social psychology: a useful dichotomy? *Psychol. Rev.* 92:59–77

Tourangeau, R., Rasinski, K. A. 1988. Cognitive processes underlying context effects in attitude measurement. *Psychol. Bull.* 103:299–314

Tourangeau, R., Rasinski, K. A., Abelson, R. P. 1988. Conviction, conflict, and consistency: The coherence of survey responses. Unpublished

Trope, Y. 1982. Self-assessment and task performance. *J. Exp. Soc. Psychol.* 18:201–15

Trope, Y. 1983. Self-assessment in achievement behavior. See Suls & Greenwald 1983, pp. 93–121

Trope, Y. 1986. Self-enhancement and self-assessment in achievement behavior. See Sorrentino & Higgins 1986, pp. 350–78

Trope, Y., Brickman, P. 1975. Difficulty and diagnosticity as determinants of choice among tasks. *J. Pers. Soc. Psychol.* 31:918–25

Trzebinski, J., McGlynn, R. P., Gray, G., Tubbs, D. 1985. The role of categories of an actor's goals in organizing inferences about a person. *J. Pers. Soc. Psychol.* 48:1387–97

Trzebinski, J., Richards, K. 1986. The role of categories in person impression. *J. Exp. Soc. Psychol.* 22:216–27

Tulving, E., Thomson, D. M. 1973. Encoding

specificity and retrieval processes in episodic memory. *Psychol. Rev.* 80:352–73

Tversky, A. 1977. Features of similarity. *Psychol. Rev.* 84:327–52

Tversky, A., Kahneman, D. 1973. Availability: a heuristic for judging frequency and probability. *Cogn. Psychol.* 5:207–32

Tversky, A., Kahneman, D. 1980. Causal schemas in judgments under uncertainty. In *Progress in Social Psychology,* Vol. 1, ed. M. Fishbein. Hillsdale, NJ: Erlbaum

Tversky, A., Kahneman, D. 1983. Extensional versus intuitive reasoning: the conjunction fallacy in probability judgment. *Psychol. Rev.* 90:293–315

Vallone, R. P., Ross, L., Lepper, M. R. 1985. The hostile media phenomenon: biased perception and perceptions of media bias in coverage of the Beirut massacre. *J. Pers. Soc. Psychol.* 49:577–85

Weber, R., Crocker, J. 1983. Cognitive processes in the revision of stereotypic beliefs. *J. Pers. Soc. Psychol.* 45:961–77

Wegner, D. M., Coulter, G. F., Wenzlaff, R. 1985. The transparency of denial: briefing in the debriefing paradigm. *J. Pers. Soc. Psychol.* 49:338–46

Wells, G. L. 1985. The conjunction error and the representativeness heuristic. *Soc. Cognit.* 3:266–79

Wells, G. L., Harvey, J. H. 1977. Do people use consensus information in making causal attributions? *J. Pers. Soc. Psychol.* 35:279–93

Wells, G. L., Gavanski, I. 1988. Mental simulation of causality. *J. Pers. Soc. Psychol.* In press

Wells, G. L., Hoffman, C., Enzle, M. E. 1984. Self versus other referent processing at encoding and retrieval. *Pers. Soc. Psychol. Bull.* 10:574–84

Wells, G. L., Taylor, B. R., Turtle, J. W. 1987. The undoing of scenarios. *J. Pers. Soc. Psychol.* 53:421–30

Wetzel, C. G., Wilson, T. D., Kort, J. 1981. The halo effect revisited: forewarned is not forearmed. *J. Exp. Soc. Psychol.* 17:427–39

Wicklund, R. A. 1982. Self-focused attention and the validity of self-reports. In *Consistency in Social Behavior: The Ontario Symposium,* Vol. 2, ed. M. P. Zanna, E. T. Higgins, C. P. Herman, pp. 149–72. Hillsdale, NJ: Erlbaum

Wicklund, R. A., Gollwitzer, P. M. 1982. *Symbolic Self-Completion.* Hillsdale, NJ: Erlbaum. 243 pp.

Wilder, D. A. 1984. Intergroup contact: the typical member and the exception to the rule. *J. Exp. Soc. Psychol.* 20:177–94

Williams, K. W., Durso, F. T. 1986. Judging category frequency: automaticity or availability? *J. Exp. Psychol.: Learn. Mem.*

Cognit. 12:387–96

Wilson, T. D., Capitman, J. A. 1982. Effects of script availability on social behavior. *Pers. Soc. Psychol. Bull.* 8:11–20

Wilson, T. D., Dunn, D. S. 1986. Effects of introspection on attitude-behavior consistency: analyzing reasons versus focusing on feelings. *J. Exp. Soc. Psychol.* 22:249–63

Wilson, T. D., Dunn, D. S., Bybee, J. A., Hyman, D. B., Rotondo, J. A. 1984. Effects of analyzing reasons on attitude-behavior consistency. *J. Pers. Soc. Psychol.* 47:5–16

Winter, L., Uleman, J. S. 1984. When are social judgments made? Evidence for the spontaneousness of trait inferences. *J. Pers. Soc. Psychol.* 47:237–52

Wood, W., Kallgren, C. A., Preisler, R. M. 1985. Access to attitude-relevant information in memory as a determinant of persuasion: the role of message attributes. *J. Exp. Soc. Psychol.* 21:73–85

Wu, C., Shaffer, D. R. 1987. Susceptibility to persuasive appeals as a function of source credibility and prior experience with the attitude object. *J. Pers. Soc. Psychol.* 52:677–88

Wyer, R. S. Jr., Budesheim, T. L. 1987. Person memory and judgments: the impact of information that one is told to disregard. *J. Pers. Soc. Psychol.* 53:14–29

Wyer, R. S., Jr., Srull, T. K., eds. 1984. *Handbook of Social Cognition,* Vols. 1–3. Hillsdale, NJ: Erlbaum

Wyer, R. S. Jr., Srull, T. K. 1986. Human cognition in its social context. *Psychol. Rev.* 93:322–59

Wyer, R. S. Jr., Srull, T. K., Gordon, S. 1984. The effects of predicting a person's behavior on subsequent trait judgments. *J. Exp. Soc. Psychol.* 20:29–46

Wyer, R. S. Jr., Unverzagt, W. H. 1985. Effects of instructions to disregard information on its subsequent recall and use in making judgments. *J. Pers. Soc. Psychol.* 48:533–49

Wylie, R. C. 1974. *The Self Concept.* Lincoln: Univ. Nebr. Press

Wylie, R. C. 1979. *The Self Concept,* Vol. 2. Lincoln: Univ. Nebr. Press

Zanna, M. P., Olson, J. M., Fazio, R. H. 1980. Attitude-behavior consistency: an individual difference perspective. *J. Pers. Soc. Psychol.* 38:432–40

Zanna, M. P., Rempel, J. K. 1987. In *Social Psychology of Knowledge,* ed. D. Bar-Tal, A. Kruglanski. New York: Cambridge Univ. Press

Zuckerman, M., Eghrari, H., Lambrecht, M. R. 1986. Attributions as inferences and explanations: conjunction effects. *J. Pers. Soc. Psychol.* 51:1144–53

Ann. Rev. Psychol. 1988. 40:327–51
Copyright © 1988 by Annual Reviews Inc. All rights reserved

ORGANIZATIONAL BEHAVIOR

Daniel R. Ilgen

Departments of Psychology and Management, Michigan State University, East Lansing, Michigan 48824

Howard J. Klein

Faculty of Management and Human Resources, The Ohio State University, Columbus, Ohio 43210

CONTENTS

327

0066-4308/89/0201-0327$02.00

INTRODUCTION

McGrath (1976) depicted the field of organizational behavior (OB) as the intersection of three systems: the physical-technical/structural, the social-interpersonal, and the system of the persons who populate the organization. The field of OB addresses issues in all three systems, but in practice it has not been limited to their intersection. Rather, explanation or understanding is typically gained by inferences drawn from covariance among elements either within the same domain or from a combination within and across domains.

All past reviews of OB have addressed the literature related to constructs from one or more of the three domains described by McGrath; we do the same for the period 1984 through 1987. Past reviews have concentrated on topics not covered by reviews in other areas of psychology (Mitchell 1979), those not reviewed previously (Cummings 1982), important outcomes in organizations (Staw 1984), topics sampled from all three subsystem domains described earlier (Schneider 1985), and new directions for the field (House & Singh 1987). We focus on the impact of what some have described as a shift of near revolutionary proportions in the behavioral sciences (Markus & Zajonc 1985; Wyer & Srull 1986). This is what has become known as the cognitive perspective. We first discuss the cognitive perspective in general and its relevance to OB, particularly at the micro level, then review the recent OB literature that has employed cognitive approaches. [However, we do not treat the individual and group decision-making literature, which is sufficiently large and distinct to warrant separate chapters in the *Annual Review of Psychology* (e.g. Pitz & Sachs 1984).] Admittedly, this focus greatly restricts the OB literature that is reviewed, but we believe that it provides an indication of the impact of major behavioral science perspective on the field of organizational behavior.

The Cognitive Perspective

If [people] define situations as real, they are real in their consequences.

W. I. Thomas [quoted in Volkart (1951), p. 81]

Markus & Zajonc (1985) described the history of the current dominance of cognitive views in social psychology. Their description is also relevant for OB. They pointed out that many of the early approaches to understanding human behavior were dominated by the classical stimulus-response (S-R) model. Cognitive views (e.g. Tolman 1935) developed as a reaction to the mechanistic, passive, and unthinking construal of individuals' behavior represented by the S-R model. According to cognitive theories, individuals are active processors of information received from their environments, and they respond to their construals of that information. Insistence upon a more active role for the perceiver led to a modification of the S-R model to one of S-O-R where the O represented the *organism* in the link between environmental conditions and responses. Much of OB research today operates under this S-O-R model, which affords cognitive processes a major role in the behavioral sequence (Naylor, et al 1980). Investigators no longer question that internal processes mediate between stimuli and responses; in fact, many claim these mediating cognitive processes dominate the behavioral sequence. They assume that behavior can be understood if and only if the intervening processes are understood.

Cognitive variables have recently been afforded even greater importance with the recognition that the nature of the environment to which the individual responds is at least partially constructed by that individual. Strictly speaking, the most recent model is that of O-S-O-R (Markus & Zajonc 1985). In this case, interest shifts from the contribution of the stimulus to that of the "cognizing organism." In OB, socially constructed realities, "cause maps," and shared meaning are just a few examples consistent with an O-S-O-R model of behavior.

All cognitive views share the assumption that people think and that their thoughts play a major role in human behavior. The specific cognitive processes emphasized or focused upon, however, vary a great deal. We review five orientations toward cognitive processes that have dominated the OB literature. These theoretical views have much in common but have been treated relatively independently in the OB literature.

The most comprehensive of these is *social cognition*. Models of social cognition emphasize the processing and representation of information concerning individuals, groups, or actors themselves (Wyer & Srull 1986). Treating the individual in a true systems sense, the models develop representations of the inputs, processing, and outputs of a cognitive system where inputs are stimuli received by some sensor, process involves the coding, storage, and recall of information, and outputs are the behaviors, attitudes, and/or beliefs that result from the process and may be recycled back into the system. Basic to all models of social cognition are structural constructs that order and influence information processing. These unobservable structures are both (*a*) consciously and unconsciously constructed (involving controlled and automatic processing, respectively) and (*b*) hierarchically clustered. For example, one such perspective, schema theory, posits the existence of a cognitive structure, labeled a schema, that represents the organization of knowledge about a stimulus (e.g. the self) and about the rules for which information about the stimulus will be processed (Foti & Lord 1987). General models of social cognition attempt both to describe the nature and the development of cognitive systems and to understand their impact on beliefs, attitudes, and behaviors (Sims & Gioia 1986; Wyer & Srull 1986).

A special case of social cognition, *social information processing* (SIP), was introduced to OB by Salancik & Pfeffer (1977, 1978) in the mid-1970s. Whereas social cognition defines its boundaries in terms of the types of information on which the processing is focused (i.e. information about the self, other individuals, or groups), SIP accepts a broader domain of social and nonsocial elements (e.g. task characteristics) but limits the source of that information to other persons.

The cognitive model that has dominated OB is that of *expectancy* X *value*. First introduced into the work motivation literature with the now classic book by Vroom (1964), the model has been modified (e.g. Porter & Lawler 1968), expanded (e.g. Naylor et al 1980), and qualified (e.g. Staw 1977) on a number of occasions; but its basic tenets have been maintained. In all cases, individuals are viewed as decision-makers choosing among alternatives. Frequently these alternatives involve the investment of time and effort in particular behaviors; in other cases they involve the choice of one alternative over another. According to all expectancy X value theories, choices are guided by the cognitive evaluation of subjective expected utilities (SEUs) associated with alternatives. The nature of the elements that go into the determination of the SEUs, the function used to combine the elements, and the cognitive processes involved in linking SEUs to choices vary across expectancy X value theories.

Another cognitively oriented approach to OB issues is that of *attribution theory*. This theory is limited primarily to achievement situations where perceived causes of success or failure are believed to influence behavior. Weiner (1985) described the sources of performance attributions with a three-dimensional classification system consisting of the source of the performance cause, the permanence of that source, and the control or intent of the performer over the cause. According to the theory, performance attributions affect responses toward the performing individual, expectations for future performance, and many other important beliefs, behaviors, and attitudes.

A final cognitive approach appearing in OB is *control theory*. Introduced into the OB literature by Campion & Lord (1982) primarily adapted from social psychology (e.g. Carver & Scheier 1981), control theory is not new (see e.g. Hayek 1952; Miller et al 1960; Wiener 1948). The theory holds that feedback loops are the fundamental building blocks of action. In the feedback loop, an input is perceived and compared or "tested" against a standard. If the comparison process reveals a discrepancy, an error is signaled and the system responds to reduce the discrepancy. This process of sensing, comparing, and responding is repeated until the discrepancy no longer exists. The key cognitive components consist of internal goals (referent standards) as well as the cognitive processes of perceiving inputs, matching perceived inputs to those standards, and selecting responses to evaluations resulting from the matching process.

SOCIAL COGNITION

Social cognition addresses the processing and representation of information about individuals, including the self, and about groups (Wyer & Srull 1986). The richness of the social cognitive models has been adapted most frequently to the OB topic of leadership.

Leadership

Much of the cognitive focus in leadership has been on the way leaders are perceived by others. The most comprehensive cognitive approach to this question is the work of Lord and his colleagues (Cronshaw & Lord 1987; Lord 1985; Lord & Alliger 1985; Lord et al 1984). They argue that people hold implicit theories of leadership and that these theories create the structure and content of cognitive categories affecting whether group members are viewed as leaders or nonleaders (Lord et al 1984) and how leaders are evaluated (Lord 1985). There was greater support for a model of leader perception based upon cognitive categories that influence the encoding, storage, and retrieval of information about leader behavior than for one that relied primarily upon the influence of performance attributions (Cronshaw & Lord 1987).

Implicit theories of leadership were also found to influence the emergence of leaders in leaderless groups. A meta-analysis showed that traits of intelligence, dominance, and masculinity-femininity affected the emergence of leaders (Lord et al 1986). The authors' explanation for the emergence process relied on the cognitive process of group members sharing perceptions of the characteristics of a good leader (a shared prototype) and then selecting as leaders those who fit shared prototypes.

Focusing on the content of information rather than the process, success or failure of the group has been shown to bias the evaluations of group leaders in the direction of group performance (Binning et al 1986; Larson et al 1984). In one case, however, group performance influenced the recall of leader behaviors (Binning et al 1986) and in another it simply elevated (or deflated) the level of the behavior evaluations (Larson et al 1984). When performance information was provided specifically about the leader, recall was biased toward prototypically successful or unsuccessful behavior (Phillips 1984).

Finally, two major theories of leadership, Vroom & Yetton's (1973) decision-making model and Fiedler's (Fiedler & Chemers 1974), both now ascribe a role to cognition or cognitive elements in the leadership process. Decision-making, a cognitive process by definition, was the focus of the 1973 Vroom & Yetton model and remains so in a recent update (Vroom & Jago

1988). Fiedler & Garcia (1987) introduce cognitive elements by treating leader skills and abilities as resources that leaders bring to the situation and that, in combination with situational conditions, influence the likelihood of leader effectiveness. However, neither theory gives much attention to the cognitive processes themselves.

Person Perception

OB research on the perceptions of persons other than leaders has been concentrated on a particular organizational practice—that of appraising performance. During the period covered by this review, the model presented by DeNisi et al (1984) captured the issues clearly by raising both theoretical and practical hypotheses. Major issues were also addressed by Wexley & Klimoski (1984); Nathan & Alexander (1985) provided an insightful discussion of the limitations of performance-rating instruments and the need to shift attention to the cognitive processes and implicit theories of the raters.

Empirical research on appraisal accuracy has approached the problem from a number of perspectives. Some have looked at situational conditions that surround appraisals from a cognitive perspective. Ratings are influenced by the degree of liking or familiarity between the rater and the ratee (Cardy & Dobbins 1986; Kozlowski et al 1986), performance level of the ratee (Padgett & Ilgen 1988), intervening task performance (Murphy et al 1986), prior expectations (Hogan 1987), and rating purpose (Williams et al 1985). Others have approached the problem from the theoretical side, addressing the effects predicted from the cognitive models, such as the distortion of information when stored in memory and its contribution to rating errors (Kozlowski & Kirsch 1987; Murphy & Balzer 1986; Murphy & Constans 1987). Three major problems facing the cognitive research on performance appraisal are the extent to which research in the laboratory will generalize to the field (Ilgen & Favero 1985), motivational factors at work that bias ratings (Banks & Murphy 1985), and the methods used to measure primary criteria—particularly accuracy, although Lord's (1985) suggestions regarding measures derived from signal detection theory should prove helpful, as should Weldon's (Weldon & Gargano 1988) measure of cognitive effort.

Motivation

Social cognition has also been offered as a perspective for work motivation (Landy & Becker 1987; Lord & Kernan 1987). Focusing on purposeful behavior in familiar settings, Lord & Kernan (1987) suggested that schemas of people at work are cognitive sets of means-ends chains that guide the way these people perceive work demands, structure beliefs about outcomes, and guide choices. Thus, understanding the schemas and the way that persons derive meaning and feedback from work offers a framework for predicting the commitment of time and effort to particular courses of action. Similarly Salancik & Porac (1986), after making the provocative observation that the more complex the environment, the more simplified is its representation in causal reasoning, suggested that simplified structures, analogous to schema, serve as the motivational structures for guiding future action.

Finally, Beach & Mitchell's image theory (Beach & Mitchell 1987; Beach et al 1988; Mitchell et al 1986) provides a descriptive view of behavioral choices. A number of extremely interesting hypotheses are presented about how decisions are made, assuming limited cognitive abilities and a central role for self-images—images of the past, present, and future. The theory should prove a rich source of ideas for subsequent research.

Careers and Roles

Careers, viewed as a series of roles held by individuals over a lifetime (Super & Hall 1978), have generated a great deal of recent interest in OB, particularly career development. An excellent book edited by Hall (1986) provides a number of chapters on current issues and future concerns related to careers, while a book by London (1985) offers a comprehensive look at the career development of managers.

The cognitive viewpoint contributes to the career literature by treating a career as a developing schema that guides career-related decisions. Nevill et al (1986) proposed that differentiation (the number of different dimensions of judgment contained in vocational schema) and integration (the degree of organization among dimensions) affect vocational development and influence how people interpret, regulate, and anticipate vocational events. Nevill et al (1986) found that college students with career schema that were well integrated and limited in differentiation made better choices when presented with a number of vocational decisions.

Super (1984, 1986) proposed a schematic view of career development rich in content and a suggestion for the role of cognitive processes. According to his model, five developmental life stages (growth, exploration, establishment, maintenance, and decline) interact with six roles (child, student, leisurite, citizen, worker, and homemaker) encountered by most people over the course of their lives. The roles were seen as modified and shaped by the life stages, and individuals' cognitive representations of the roles were described as influencing important career-related decisions. Combining the process-directed focus of Nevill et al (1986) with content-referenced models such as Super's (1984, 1986) should prove interesting for addressing the way career decisions are balanced with life-role demands.

While careers deal with broad-based schema encompassing individual life spans, roles are the building blocks of careers and are schema in themselves. The literature on roles is of two types. The first addresses the role process itself. Much of this is directed toward theory construction. The other focuses upon one or more role constructs and addresses the nature and consequences of the constructs. The former is conceptually rich and data poor; the latter tends to be the reverse.

A recent trend in role theory is to focus on the dynamic nature of roles. Nicholson (1984) viewed roles as a series of transitions from one role to another. Central to his model is the more emotionally loaded construct of adjustment. Individuals were seen as needing to adjust to forces impinging on them from past expectations, socialization pressures, and role requirements on the job. The combination of motivational and cognitive literatures led to predictions about modes of adjustment that would be cued up in the person, and about resulting behaviors.

Graen & Scandura (1987) offer an interesting dynamic model of role-making between superiors and subordinates. They posit a three-stage model in which the supervisor and subordinate try out and evaluate each other as the supervisor sends a role for the subordinate to assume. Soon the process shifts to a negotiation phase in which the subordinate and supervisor attempt to make a role for the subordinate that is mutually beneficial. The process reaches a temporary permanence with the completion of role-making when both settle into a routine. This routine is enacted with few modifications until the time when events force the pair to reevaluate the routine.

Although the intellectual heritage of all the role theory models is that of socialization, career development, and organizational psychology with little reference to cognitive or cognitive social psychology, the constructs used in the theories are compatible with the latter. With little or no modifications, roles can be construed as job-related schema. Then the role theories just described can be viewed as theories that address the learning of such schema and behavior in response to the schema. Attentional and recall issues important from a cognitive perspective should also be important for the acquisition and response to roles, although the role view has paid little attention to these. Some intriguing exceptions to this are the work of Ashford & Cummings (1985), which explored features of role relationships influencing informational search in the form of performance feedback; and the work of Cohen (1985), which suggested that levels of participation in decision-making created an organizing schema around procedural justice. Introducing a cognitive perspective has the possibility of suggesting interesting and important issues in these domains.

Organization-Level Variables

"At their essence, organizations are products of the thought and action of their members" (Sims & Gioia 1986, p. 1). Although most organizational theorists (including the ones just quoted) would not want to reduce organizations to the products of the cognitive processes of their members, the widespread recognition of the importance of human thoughts and actions in shaping the nature of organizations provides more than sufficient justification for exploring cognitive implications for organization-level constructs or the impact of organizational phenomena on individuals.

A significant contribution to some of the organizational implications of a cognitive perspective on organizations is a book edited by Sims & Gioia (1986). Chapters address from a cognitive perspective issues of organizational structure (Downey & Brief 1986); control systems through shared cause maps, values, and meaning (Weick & Bougon 1986; Salancik & Porac 1986; Gioia 1986, respectively). Organizational consequences are also explored (Finney & Mitroff 1986).

In an interesting treatise on organizational culture and change, Moch and his colleagues (Bartunek & Moch 1988; Moch & Fields 1985) present organizational cultures as shared schema that develop through storytelling and other means of enacting metaphors to create shared norms. Extending this to organizational change, Bartunek & Moch (1988) propose (*a*) that organizational development (OD) is a process of aiding organizational members to change their schemas and (*b*) that OD consultants should learn more about the processing of information from a schema point of view in order to improve their ability to make meaningful OD changes.

SOCIAL INFORMATION PROCESSING

Social information processing, (SIP) as introduced into the OB literature by Salancik & Pfeffer (1977, 1978), was meant to capture much of the theoretical complexities of the cognitive models appearing in the psychological literature at that time. The two primary differences between SIP and the social cognitive models just discussed are a focus on stimuli from interpersonal sources and an interest in the effects of interpersonal stimuli on perceptions of conditions at work that are not necessarily social in nature.

Unfortunately, owing in part to Salancik & Pfeffer's use of job characteristics as a means for developing and illustrating a model of SIP, almost all of the research stimulated by Salancik & Pfeffer's work has been limited to investigating the effects of social cues on perceptions of job characteristics. The primary conclusion to be drawn from this work is that social cues do affect perceptions of job characteristics and affective responses to jobs (Griffin 1987; Griffin et al 1987). Attempts to ascertain whether social cues or known task characteristics were more important sources of task perceptions failed because the samples were far too limited to permit generalization from them to populations of jobs and people of interest.

More recently, research has moved beyond demonstrating an effect of social cues to (*a*) looking more closely at the nature of the social cues, (*b*) expanding the set of variables affected by the cues, and (c) exploring individual differences in susceptibility to social influence. Research has addressed the credibility or power of the sources of social information (Blau 1985; Park et al 1987; Schnake & Dumler 1987), the means of transmission of the cues (Bateman et al 1987; Zalesny & Farace 1986), the methods for assessing SIP effects (Glick et al 1986), group norms and cohesiveness as sources of social influence (O'Reilly & Caldwell 1985), and individual differences affecting and affected by social information (Blau 1985). In general, this work provides few surprises. Social cues tend to have greater impact when they originate from credible sources, and they can be transmitted by means other than face-to-face interaction. Griffin (1987) offers a summary model integrating SIP into task-characteristics models for a combined view of job design.

Zalesny & Ford (unpublished) attempted to break SIP out of the grasp of job characteristics by returning to some of the initial intentions of Salancik & Pfeffer (1977, 1978). Zalesny & Ford reviewed the OB literature on SIP since the late 1970s and compared it to a model based upon many of Salancik & Pfeffer's original propositions. Research purportedly driven by Salancik & Pfeffer's model has been extremely narrow in focus. By restating a broader model, Zalesny & Ford hope to refocus SIP research on a number of important behaviors in organizations, avoiding simple demonstrations that social stimuli influence how people in organizations think, feel, and act.

EXPECTANCY × VALUE THEORIES

Expectancy × value theories are still frequently and widely employed in OB. While most articles using an expectancy × value approach concern motivation, such theories have been used to examine several other OB constructs.

Motivation

A number of articles have aimed at refining or modifying current models. One refinement addressed the issue of positive vs negative outcomes. Mathieu (1987) examined the validity of predictions using negative and positive outcomes with a between-subjects design. Positive outcomes correlated significantly higher with performance than negative outcomes in one of two samples of ROTC cadets, supporting earlier contentions (Leon 1981) that positive and negative outcomes are processed differently. Guzzo & Katzell (1987) suggested that the primary benefit of incentives (a positive outcome) is to make contingencies between performance and outcomes salient.

Uncertainty regarding the appropriate combination rule for the theory's elements led to a series of five studies by Harrell & Stahl (1986) which suggested that subjects did not use multiplicative combination rules in decision-making. Motivation in these studies was reasonably high even when expectancies approached zero. In addition, increases in expectancies resulted in declines in motivation rather than increases. On the other hand, two laboratory studies by Fusilier et al (1984) supported the multiplicative model. The issue is not resolved; at some level, it is unresolvable, given the scale properties of the variables, the limited ranges frequently encountered on these variables, and the lack of discrimination among the models for the ranges of variables normally encountered.

Sussmann & Vecchio (1985) presented a model using four subjective conditional probabilities based on the presence and absence of an alternative and the occurrence and nonoccurrence of an outcome. They argued that this model is more consistent with behavioral decision theory (Edwards 1954), from which most expectancy × value theories in use were derived, and resolves many of the criticisms of those theories.

A number of recent articles have employed expectancy × value theories in combination with goal-setting (e.g. Garland 1984; Kanfer 1988; Naylor & Ilgen 1984). Locke et al (1984a) found that the expectancy of attaining a goal assigned for a first trial was negatively related both to performance on that trial and to the personal goals chosen for a second trial. A goal × expectancy interaction was also observed: Expectancy was positively related to performance at higher, but not at lower, goal levels. However, instructions to these subjects not to exceed their goals may have influenced these results.

Garland (1984) addressed the supposed conflict between expectancy × value theory predictions that performance and expectancies of success covary positively (when the outcomes are valued) and the goal-setting finding that performance with difficult but attainable goals (low-expectancy conditions) is higher than with easy goals. He predicted that the difference may result from the use of between-person expectancies to define goal difficulty. Huber & Neale (1986) found some support for this, but only with moderate goals. Others have suggested that the difference may be in commitment to performance levels. Since goal-setting studies tend to include only those who express commitment to the goal by stating that they accept it, and since commitment is positively associated with expectancies (Hollenback & Brief 1987; Huber & Neale 1986; Matsui et al 1987), those with difficult goals (low expectancies) would not have the lower levels of commitment that typically accompany the lower expectancies. This issue along with others has led to increased interest in commitment to goals (Hollenbeck & Klein 1987: Hollenbeck et al 1988; Locke et al 1988).

Pritchard et al (1987) united goal-setting, incentives, and feedback within the context of the expectancy × value theory of Naylor et al (1980) to produce an integrated productivity-enhancement intervention system. In this system, the products and subproducts of the employees' acts are identified and the expectancy and value constructs are developed with the employees in their own framework and terms. This information is then mapped into a series of curves that indicate how the subproducts (and hence products) produced by the workers relate to measures of effectiveness. These graphs allow employees to visualize the results of their actions and then make decisions about whether or not to change their present distributions of time and effort. The clarification of contingencies, along with goal-setting and feedback, led to an average productivity increase of 74% above baseline for the five Air Force units receiving the intervention.

Turnover

Although often not operationalized in expectancy × value constructs, much of the turnover research is based on models that include expectancy × value concepts such as ease and desirability of movement (e.g. March & Simon 1958; Mobley 1977). Jackofsky (1984) presented a model of *job* turnover in which ease and desirability of movement were operationalized as job satisfaction and the number of perceived job alternatives. Mobley's (1977) model was tested by Hom et al (1984) with subjective expected utilities (SEUs) assessed for search, alternatives, and comparisons with present job. Cognitive variables, SEUs, and comparisons related primarily to other cognitions, including thinking of quitting, rather than to behaviors.

Dalessio et al (1986) reanalyzed several data sets testing the Mobley et al (1978) simplified turnover model using path analysis. Little or no evidence was found for the predicted relationship between tenure in a position and the expectancy of finding an acceptable alternative job. In a military sample, Motowidlo & Lawton (1984) did find that expectancies of receiving favorable outcomes from a military career were related to reenlistment.

Absenteeism

Fichman (1988) provides a comprehensive view of absence behavior that should serve as a model not only for absences but for other behaviors as well. His dynamic model of absence behavior assumes that attendance results from the combination of forces to attend and to be absent. These forces are believed to be cognitively determined, in large part, by processes consistent with expectancy × value models of motivation and are affected by each day that the person is present or absent. To understand behavior at any one time, it is necessary to understand the stream of behavior leading up to that time. Using a time-series analysis on attendance data from coal miners, he tested the assumption of this complex and interesting model. The data offer partial support for the hypotheses.

Self-Efficacy

While there are subtle differences between efficacy expectations and outcome expectancies (Bandura 1986), the concept of self-efficacy can also be considered as part of the set of expectancy × value theories. Furthermore, in the OB literature, self-efficacy and expectancies have often been indistinguishable operationally.

Bandura's book (1986) and a review by Gist (1987) elucidate the construct and review an abundant literature, mostly from laboratory and clinical settings, indicating direct relationships between (a) self-efficacy and performance and (b) such OB constructs as goals. In the OB literature, significant main effects have been reported between self-efficacy, on the one hand and, on the other, performance and goals (Earley 1986; Locke et al 1984b; Taylor et al 1984b), the complexity of career schema (Nevill et al 1986), and adaptability to new technology (Hill et al 1987). Effects on performance have been shown to hold even when ability, goal acceptance, and personal goals were controlled (Earley 1986). In another study, self-efficacy acted as a moderator between socialization practices and their effectiveness, suggesting that individuals low in self-efficacy more readily conform to definitions of situations offered by others (Jones 1986). Self-efficacy has also been the objective of an absenteeism intervention (Frayne & Latham 1987). Those trained in self-management had higher self-efficacy scores, and, interestingly, the difference between the trained and untrained groups increased over time. In addition, attendance was higher for those trained.

Conclusion

Despite the number of criticisms directed at expectancy × value theories, refinements and applications of this perspective continue unabated. While it is arguable that the theories do not describe exactly how a person makes choices, the concepts of expectancy and value are clearly relevant, both theoretically and practically. It is also apparent from reviewing the literature that many recent studies employing these theories have more carefully defined and measured their constructs.

ATTRIBUTIONS

Attributions are beliefs about the causes of behavior, particularly behavior that affects performance. Attributional research generally focuses on the nature of attributions or their effects on the persons making them.

Gender Differences

Some interest still remains in Deaux & Emswiller's (1974) early finding that both males and females attribute the performance of males more to ability and that of females more to luck, although this effect does not always replicate (e.g. Adams et al 1984). Dobbins (1985) explored gender differences in responses to poor performers from the perspective of Green & Mitchell's (1979) attributional model of leadership. In a laboratory study, males responded more punitively when poor performance was attributed to internal causes than external ones, while females did not vary their responses as a function of internality. Male leaders equally supported both male and female subordinates, whereas females were more supportive of female subordinates. Finally, males felt that support should vary according to cause, whereas females were equally supportive across attributions.

Social Settings

Dienesch & Liden (1986) proposed an interesting model in which attributions played a central role in determining the nature of dyadic exchange relationships in Graen's Leader Member Exchange model (Graen 1976; Graen & Scandura 1987). Cronshaw & Lord (1987) compared causal attributions with another cognitive theory, that of categorization, with respect to effects on the perceptions of leaders. Previous work on impression formation suggested that attributions precede impression formation and affect the nature of the categories used to judge others (DeNisi et al 1984), while other work with in-group and out-group members suggested that attributions followed from categorization (Wilder 1981). Cronshaw & Lord compared three models for the sources of impressions of leaders: attributions, categorization, and an additive combination of the two. The categorization model received the most support.

Individuals

At the individual level, concern has been both with the sources of attributions (Arnold 1985; Dorfman & Stephan 1984; Walton et al 1985), and with their consequences on beliefs (Arnold 1985; Dorfman & Stephan 1984), effort expenditure (Dorfman & Stephan 1984), performance (Arnold 1985), turnover (Parsons et al 1985), and reactions to performance feedback (Bannister 1986; Liden & Mitchell 1985). With respect to sources, Arnold (1985) found no support for the prediction from cognitive evaluation theory that extrinsic rewards decrease the likelihood that individuals will attribute behavior to intrinsic sources. These data were consistent with earlier findings (Fisher 1978). McElroy (1985) reasoned that extrinsic rewards may actually increase internal attributions through their effect on performance; extrinsic rewards might increase the likelihood of response through reinforcement, such that as the person observes his or her resulting behavior, attributions to internal sources of ability or effort follow.

Motivationally, attributions appear to affect behavior through their effect on perceptions of competency. Dorfman & Stephan (1984) found expectancies of success were related to attributions in a way consistent with the notion that individuals' impressions of their own self-efficacy are influenced by attributions.

Conclusion

Attributional research in OB has two shortcomings. First, there is a tendency to take as a given the four-fold model of attribution sources (i.e. performance is attributed to ability, effort, task difficulty, or luck). As early as the late 1970s (Abramson et al 1978; Weiner 1979) the deficiencies in this attributional model were pointed out. Weiner subsequently (1985) reiterated some of these concerns and made a strong case for a three-dimensional model that adds the actor's intentions to source and stability. In general, the attributional research in OB has not kept pace with the changing views on attributions themselves.

A second problem is the measurement of attributions. In spite of the frequent use of the construct, far too frequently the assessment of attributions is limited to a single item for each of the four attributions. The dubious psychometric quality of attributional measures may account for the lack of strong and consistent findings in some of the research.

CONTROL THEORY

While the primary focus of control theory was initially on motivation, it has recently been extended to broader models of organizational behavior.

Motivation

Campion & Lord (1982) provided one of the earliest expositions of control theory in the OB literature with a model and data using student performance in classes over a semester. Lord & Hanges (1987) elaborated on this model by discussing the advantages of a control-theory perspective and identifying boundary conditions for its use. Lord & Kernan (1987) further extended the theory by introducing the notion of scripts for goal-directed behavior and suggesting that scripts, in combination with goal-directed feedback, direct attention, expedite learning, and regulate behavior.

Taylor et al (1984a) focused more on the role of feedback in control theory and vice versa as they addressed the acquisition, processing, and response to performance feedback. Podsakoff & Farh (unpublished) tested hypotheses derived from control theory regarding the effects of feedback sign and source credibility on goal-setting and performance in a laboratory study. Consistent with the theory, they found subjects who received negative feedback set higher goals and performed better than those given positive feedback. In addition, an interaction of the sign of the feedback with its credibility showed that source credibility amplified the observed effects of negative feedback.

While not explicitly working from a control-theory perspective, Bandura & Cervone (1986) examined the effect of self-reactive influences (i.e. perceived self-efficacy, self-evaluation, and self-set goals) on motivation as a function of level and direction of the discrepancy between goals and performance. The discrepancy construct is very similar to the control-theory process of comparing outcomes with a standard. They found these influences had differential effects for different discrepancies. Perceived self-efficacy influenced motivation regardless of the sign or magnitude of the discrepancy. Self-set goals influenced motivation at all discrepancy levels except very large negative discrepancies, and self-evaluation (dissatisfaction) impacted on motivation only for moderate and large negative discrepancies.

Advocates of control theory point out that goals must be closely regulated if they are to influence performance. In a retail sales setting, Hollenbeck & Williams (1987) examined the role of two factors thought to increase goal regulation—self-focus and goal importance. They found a strong effect for goal level on performance; this was especially the case for subjects high in self-focus and goal importance.

Affect

The study by Podsakoff & Farh (unpublished), discussed earlier, also examined the effects of feedback sign and source credibility on satisfaction. Subjects receiving negative feedback were less satisfied than subjects given positive feedback. In addition, there was a significant feedback sign × credibility interaction similar to that observed regarding motivation and performance; subjects were most satisfied or dissatisfied when the source was credible. Hollenbeck (1988) investigated the effect of self-focus on satisfaction and found that self-focus moderated the relationship between control-theory elements and affective responses among a sample of department store salespersons. Job satisfaction was more closely associated with the expectation of desirable outcomes for those high in self-focus than for those who were low. Similar results were obtained regarding organizational commitment.

Leadership

Manz (1986) expanded his earlier work on self-management as a substitution for leadership by using the hierarchical notion of control loops to focus on how self-management strategies such as self-observation, self-goal-setting, and self-reinforcement can be controlled. In the process, he explicitly adopted a control theory perspective which had only been implicit in his earlier work. He defined self-leadership as "a self-influence perspective that concerns leading oneself toward performance of naturally motivating tasks as well as managing oneself to do work that must be done but is not naturally motivating" (p. 589). Working under the assumption that organizational control systems influence employees through their influence on self-control systems and that individual control systems are hierarchical in nature, Manz posited several mechanisms (e.g. intrinsic motivation) and strategies (e.g. work context, thought patterns) that influence superordinate standards—that is, those standards that control or provide the reasons for engaging in self-management activities.

Conclusion

Perhaps the most common criticism of control theory is that it is too mechanical and rigid, due to the overreliance of early theorists on the mechanical analogy (Powers 1973). Lord & Hanges (1987) argue that the perceived rigidity of earlier works is a misinterpretation and that control theory can represent a flexible, nonmechanical view of behavior. In human systems, feedback involves much more than the mechanical sensing of the environment; goals are not merely predetermined inflexible standards; and only under some circumstances are actions to reduce discrepancies programmed, automatic responses (Lord & Hanges 1987).

Actually, the differences between mechanical and human systems raise several interesting research questions. For example, different authors have offered different predictions regarding the "overshooting" of standards. A mechanical model would hold that errors on either side of the standard are equally serious. Carver & Scheier (1981) and Hollenbeck (1988) hold that reactions to negative deviations will be more extreme than positive deviations, but they still differentiated "overshooting the target" from being "on target." Taylor et al (1984a) make no such distinction. This is essentially an empirical issue, but one that has not been directly assessed.

The primary advantages of a control-theory perspective are its ability to parsimoniously integrate other theories, its range in applicability across numerous concepts, and the fact that it is a fluid model, allowing the conceptualization and investigation of dynamic processes (Campion & Lord 1982; Lord & Hanges 1987). As evidence of its widespread potential for applicaton, control theory has often been used to explain processes even though it is often not discussed or even acknowledged. Mihal et al's model (1984), for example, holds that the career decision-making process is initiated when career discrepancy (the perceived gap between expected and actual career role outcomes) exceeds a threshold level.

METHODOLOGICAL ISSUES

Two methodological issues arise regarding cognitive research in OB. The first deals with the research methods for studying cognitive issues; the second addresses the contribution of knowledge about cognitive processing to research methods regardless of content focus.

If you accept the position that all research methods are flawed (Runkel & McGrath 1972), then knowledge is best advanced when a field of study uses a number of methods to address research issues, thus compensating for the limitations of any one method. Over time, it is desirable to obtain a balance across methods, samples, and settings as a field of knowledge matures.

At present, there is an imbalance in the literature on cognitive processes in OB, with a predominance of laboratory studies and theoretical papers that do not include empirical data. Authors typically adapt what is known from basic research and theory on cognitive processes in other fields to issues of importance in OB. The imbalance across settings and methods is due in part to the state of development of the knowledge base on cognitive topics and in part to the nature of cognitive issues themselves. The shift to a cognitive focus in the behavioral sciences is a relatively recent phenomenon, and the involvement of OB in this shift is even more recent because it has followed the other developments. In addition, the very nature of cognitive constructs often demands more control over variables of interest than many research methods provide. Therefore, it could be argued that controlled experimentation has been the method of choice because of its appropriateness not simply because of convenience.

Regardless of the reasons for the limited scope of the methods applied to cognitive topics to date, in the long run there needs to be an expansion of the methods and the settings for research. Several methodological suggestions have been offered. Moch et al (1988) make an excellent case for the role of business simulations in understanding ongoing decisions and choices of managers over time. Ford et al (1988) provide a review and critique process tracing methods and comment on policy-capturing and verbal-protocol methods for understanding the processes that people use when making decisions. Although the above are more controlled methods than typical field studies, they also allow for more flexibility with regard to setting and participants than is the case with the typical laboratory studies that dominate the literature to date. Of particular interest for field data is Fichman's (1988) monograph on absence behavior, which incorporates time-series designs and cognitive processes. It deserves special attention as a model for future research on other topic areas that posit changing cognitions over time and face the problems of autocorrelation present in most time-series data. Finally, LISREL and other causal-modeling procedures should be useful for exploring the structure of cognitive systems influencing individuals in organizations, although the cautions raised by Feldman & Lynch (1988) and addressed in the next paragraph should not be ignored.

Feldman & Lynch's (1988) provocative discussion of the implications of cognitive processing on all research that employs questionnaires/surveys for the assessment of variables highlights a second methodological issue. In particular, they address the problem of reactivity, arguing that beliefs, attitudes, or intentions can be created by the measurement instrument if the constructs do not already exist in long-term memory. In addition, constructs already existing in memory may be altered in content or saliency by the measurement instrument. Feldman & Lynch use timing, order, and method of measurement to develop a rudimentary theory of a measure's effect on questionnaire data, discussing the implications of such effects for research. Of particular interest are their words of caution for those who would base causal modeling research primarily upon questionnaire data.

CONCLUDING COMMENTS

In reviewing the organizational behavior literature that reflects the recent cognitive wave in the behavioral sciences, we were both impressed and disappointed. The strengths of the work lie in the development of interesting research and theory in a few specific areas of importance to the field. The work in person perception with respect to leadership is an example where both the theory and the research have explored problems from a cognitive perspective in a systematic and thorough fashion. A second strength is the way authors have presented well-thought-through developments of the implications of cognitive constructs for organizationally relevant issues at both the individual and the organizational level.

Several major weaknesses, however, stand out. First, the "cognitive revolution" has influenced very few topics in the field of OB and has often had a narrow impact within those that have been studied. In leadership, for example, the cognitive impact has been limited almost exclusively to the study of perceptions of leaders. In one sense, the limited penetration results from a failure to employ cognitive perspectives to topics to which they could contribute. For example, as we pointed out earlier, roles are just beginning to be addressed from a schema perspective. At the same time, it should be cautioned that, for a number of important topics in OB, cognitive perspectives may not be appropriate or may be unlikely to make major contributions. One has to be careful not to get caught up in the zeitgeist and stretch the perspective beyond usefulness.

A second and potentially more debilitating limitation of the cognitive literature in OB deals with the empirical research. In our opinion, applying constructs and concepts from one discipline advances the knowledge base of another in three primary ways. Early in the adaptation or incorporation of a perspective from one discipline into another, research is demonstrative: Attempts are made to show that constructs and concepts from the one discipline are indeed appropriate to the other. Although useful and necessary, such demonstrations often do not advance knowledge in either discipline much.

Second, advances can be made if the research in the new area contributes to knowledge about the constructs under investigation regardless of the discipline. Thus, for example, research on organizationally relevant schema is valuable if it contributes to the understanding of such schema in organizations or if it contributes to basic knowledge about the nature and function of cognitive schema regardless of setting. Finally, research contributes by generating knowledge that can usefully be applied in organizations. For example, knowledge about how people store and recall information for use in reports on performance-appraisal scales may suggest ways to improve recall at the time of the appraisal. Research can be assessed in terms of the extent to which the new knowledge contributes to improvements over-and-above practices currently available. In our opinion, contributions to the basic science knowledge base and to improvements of practices are valuable and equally valid undertakings.

The cognitive literature in OB at this item is almost exclusively demonstrative. The non-empirical articles focus primarily on translating cognitive terms into the organizational environment; empirical pieces often offer little more than demonstrations that cognitive variables make sense for interpreting particular events that occur in organizational settings. The contributions to date can be justified when it is recognized that the cognitive focus has only recently been brought to OB. However, if the field is to avoid becoming stagnated at the demonstrative level, greater efforts must be made to conduct research and develop theory that begins to contribute more to the understanding of cognitive processes, to practice, or to both. Without such advances, cognitive processes will join a long list of passing fads in OB.

ACKNOWLEDGMENTS

We thank Janet Simkin for her help in the preparation of the manuscript and the John A. Hannah Fund for partial support of its preparation. We also thank Kevin Ford for his comments on earlier drafts and Marcy Schafer for her careful work preparing the manuscript. Requests for reprints should be sent to Daniel R. Ilgen, Department of Psychology, Michigan State University, East Lansing, MI 48824-1117.

Literature Cited

Abramson, L. Y., Seligman, M.E.P., Teasdale, J. 1978. Learned helplessness in humans: critique and reformulation. *J. Abnorm. Psychol.* 87:49–74

Adams, J., Rice, R. W., Instone, D. 1984. Follower attitudes toward women and judgments concerning performance by female and male leaders. *Acad. Manage. J.* 27:636–43

Arnold, H. J. 1985. Task performance, perceived competence, and attributed causes of performance as determinants of intrinsic motivation. *Acad. Manage. J.* 28:876–88

Ashford, S. J., Cummings, L. L. 1985. Proactive feedback seeking: the instrumental use of the information environment. *J. Occup. Psychol.* 58:67–79

Bandura, A. 1986. *Social Foundations of Thought and Action: A Social-Cognitive View.* Englewood Cliffs, NJ: Prentice-Hall

Bandura, A., Cervone, D. 1986. Differential engagement of self-reactive mechanisms governing the motivational effects of goal systems. *Organ. Behav. Hum. Decis. Processes* 38:92–113

Banks, C. G., Murphy, K. R. 1985. Toward narrowing the research-practice gap in performance appraisal. *Personnel Psychol.* 38:335–45

Bannister, B. D. 1986. Performance outcome feedback and attributional feedback: interactive effects of recipient responses. *J. Appl. Psychol.* 71:203–10

Bartunek, J. M., Moch, M. K. 1988. First, second and third order organization development interventions: a cognitive approach. *J. Appl. Behav. Sci.* 23:483–500

Bateman, T. S., Griffin, R. W., Rubinstein, D. 1987. Social information processing and group-induced shifts in responses to task design. *Group Organ. Stud.* 12:88–108

Beach, L. R., Mitchell, T. R. 1987. Image theory: principles, goals, and plans in decision strategies. *Acta Psychol.* 66:201–20

Beach, L. R., Smith, B., Lundell, J., Mitchell, T. R. 1988. Image theory in organization decision making: an expert system simulation of compatibility assessment. *J. Behav. Decision Theory* 1:117–31

Binning, J. F., Zaba, A. J., Whattam, J. C. 1986. Explaining the biasing effects of performance cues in terms of cognitive categorization. *Acad. Manage. J.* 29:521–35

Blau, G. J. 1985. Source-related determinants of perceived job scope. *Hum. Commun. Res.* 11:536–53

Campion, M. A., Lord, R. G. 1982. A control systems conceptualization of the goal setting and changing process. *Organ. Behav. Hum. Perform.* 30:265–87

Cardy, R. L., Dobbins, G. H. 1986. Affect and appraisal accuracy: liking as an integral dimension in evaluating performance. *J. Appl. Psychol.* 71:672–78

Carver, C. S., Scheier, M. F. 1981. *Attention and Self-Regulation: A Control Theory Approach to Human Behavior.* New York: Springer-Verlag

Cohen, R. L. 1985. Procedural justice and participation. *Hum. Relat.* 38:643–63

Cronshaw, S. F., Lord, R. G. 1987. Effects of categorization, attribution, and encoding processes on leadership perceptions. *J. Appl. Psychol.* 72:97–106

Cummings, L. L. 1982. Organizational behavior. *Ann. Rev. Psychol.* 33:541–80

Dalessio, A., Silverman, W. H., Schuck, J. R. 1986. Paths to turnover: a re-analysis and review of existing data on the Mobley, Horner, and Hollingsworth turnover model. *Hum. Relat.* 39:245–63

Deaux, K., Emswiller, T. 1974. Explanations of successful performance on sex-linked tasks: What is skill for the male is luck for the female. *J. Person. Soc. Psychol.* 29:80–85

DeNisi, A. S., Cafferty, T. P., Meglino, B. M. 1984. A cognitive view of the performance appraisal process: a model and research propositions. *Organ. Behav. Hum. Perform.* 33:360–96

Dienesch, R. M., Liden, R. C. 1986. Leader-member exchange model of leadership: a critique and further development. *Acad. Manage. Rev.* 11:618–34

Dobbins, G. H. 1985. Effects of gender on leaders' responses to poor performers: an attributional interpretation. *Acad. Manage. J.* 28:587–98

Dorfman, P. W., Stephan, W. G. 1984. The effects of group performance on cognitions, satisfaction, and behavior: a process model. *J. Manage.* 10:173–92

Downey, H. K., Brief, A. P. 1986. How cognitive structures affect organizational design: implicit theories of organizing. See Sims & Gioia 1986, pp. 165–90

Earley, P. C. 1986. Supervisors and shop stewards as sources of contextual information in goal setting: a comparison of the United States with England. *J. Appl. Psychol.* 71:111–17

Edwards, W. 1954. The theory of decision making. *Psychol. Bull.* 51:380–417

Feldman, J. M., Lynch, J. G. Jr. 1988. Self-generated validity: effects of measurement on belief, attitude, intention, and behavior. *J. Appl. Psychol.* In press

Fichman, M. 1988. Motivational consequences of absence and attendance: proportional hazard estimation of a dynamic motivation model. *J. Appl. Psychol.* 73:119–34

Fiedler, F. E., Chemers, M. M. 1974. *Leadership and Effective Management.* Glenview, Ill: Scott, Foresman

Fiedler, F. E., Garcia, J. E. 1987. *New Approaches to Effective Leadership: Cognitive Resources and Organizational Performance.* New York: Wiley

Finney, M., Mitroff, I. I. 1986. Strategic plan failures: the organization as its own worst enemy. See Sims & Gioia 1986, pp. 317–35

Fisher, C. D. 1978. The effects of personal control, competence, and extrinsic rewards on intrinsic motivation. *Organ. Behav. Hum. Perform.* 21:273–88

Ford, J. K., Schmitt, N., Schechtman, S. L., Hults, B. M., Doherty, M. L. 1988. Process tracing methods: contributions, problems, and neglected research questions. *Organ. Behav. Hum. Decis. Processes.* In press

Foti, R. S., Lord, R. G. 1987. Prototypes and scripts: the effects of alternative methods of processing information on rating accuracy. *Organ. Behav. Hum. Decis. Processes* 39:318–40

Frayne, C. A., Latham, G. P. 1987. Application of social learning theory to employee self-management of attendance. *J. Appl. Psychol.* 72:387–92

Fusilier, M. R., Ganster, D. C., Middlemest, R. D. 1984. A within-person test of the form of the expectancy theory model in a choice context. *Organ. Behav. Hum. Decis. Processes* 34:323–42

Garland, H. 1984. Relation of effort-performance expectancy to performance in goal-setting experiments. *J. Appl. Psychol.* 69:79–84

Gioia, D. A. 1986. Symbols, scripts, and sensemaking: creating meaning in the organizational experience. See Sims & Gioia 1986, pp. 49–74

Gist, M. E. 1987. Self-efficacy: implications for organizational behavior and human resource management. *Acad. Manage. Rev.* 12:472–85

Glick, W. H., Jenkins, G. D. Jr., Gupta, N. 1986. Methods versus substance: How strong are the underlying relationships between task characteristics and attitudinal outcomes. *Acad. Manage. J.* 29:441–64

Graen, G. 1976. Role-making processes within complex organizations. In *Handbook of Industrial and Organizational Psychology*, ed. M. D. Dunnette, pp. 1201–45. Chicago, Ill: Rand McNally

Graen, G., Scandura, T. 1987. Toward a psychology of dyadic organizing. *Res. Org. Behav.* 9:175–208

Green, S. G., Mitchell, T. R. 1979. Attributional processes of leaders in leader-member interactions. *Organ. Behav. Hum. Perform.* 23:429–58

Griffin, R. W. 1987. Toward an integrated theory of task design. *Res. Org. Behav.* 9:79–120

Griffin, R. W., Bateman, T. S., Wayne, S. J., Head, T. C. 1987. Objective and social factors as determinants of task perceptions and responses: an integrated perspective and empirical investigation. *Acad. Manage. J.* 30:501–23

Guzzo, R. A., Katzell, R. A. 1987. Effects of economic incentive on productivity: a psychological perspective. In *Incentives, Cooperation, and Risk Sharing*, ed. H. Nalbantian. Totowa, NJ: Littlefield Allan

Hall, D. T., ed. 1986. *Career Development in Organizations*. San Francisco: Jossey-Bass

Harrell, A., Stahl, M. 1986. Additive information processing and the relationship between expectancy of success and motivational force. *Acad. Manage. J.* 29:424–33

Hayek, F. 1952. *The Sensory Order*. Chicago, Ill: Univ. Chicago Press

Hill, T., Smith, N. D., Mann, M. F. 1987. Role of efficacy expectations in predicting the decision to use advanced technologies:

the case of computers. *J. Appl. Psychol.* 72:307–14

Hogan, E. A. 1987. Effects of prior expectations on performance ratings: a longitudinal study. *Acad. Manage. J.* 30:354–68

Hollenbeck, J. R. 1988. Control theory and the perception of work environments: the effects of focus of attention on affective and behavioral reactions to work. *Organ. Behav. Hum. Decis. Processes*. In press

Hollenbeck, J. R., Brief, A. P. 1987. The effects of individual differences and goal origin on goal setting and performance. *Organ. Behav. Hum. Decis. Processes* 40:392–414

Hollenbeck, J. R., Klein, H. J. 1987. Goal commitment and the goal setting process: problems, prospects, and proposals for future research. *J. Appl. Psychol.* 72:212–20

Hollenbeck, J. R., Williams, C. R. 1987. Goal importance, self-focus, and the goal setting process. *J. Appl. Psychol.* 72:204–11

Hollenbeck, J. R., Williams, C. R., Klein, H. J. 1988. An empirical investigation of the antecedents of goal commitment. *J. Appl. Psychol.* In press

Hom, P. W., Griffin, R. W., Sellaro, C. L. 1984. The validity of Mobley's (1977) model of employee turnover. *Organ. Behav. Hum. Decis. Processes* 34:141–74

House, R. J., Singh, J. V. 1987. Organizational behavior: some new directions for I/O psychology. 38:669–718

Huber, V. L., Neale, M. A. 1986. Effects of cognitive heuristics and goals on negotiator performance and subsequent goal setting. *Organ. Behav. Hum. Decis. Processes* 38:342–56

Ilgen, D. R., Favero, J. L. 1985. Methodological limitations of social psychological literatures for the understanding of performance appraisal processes. *Acad. Manage. J.* 10:311–21

Jackofsky, E. F. 1984. Turnover and job performance: an integrated process model. *Acad. Manage Rev.* 9:74–83

Jones, G. R. 1986. Socialization tactics, self-efficacy, and newcomers' adjustments to organizations. *Acad. Manage J.* 29:262–79

Kanfer, R. 1988. Task specific motivation: an integrative approach to issues of measurement, mechanisms, processes, and determinants. *J. Soc. Clin. Psychol.* 5:237–64

Kozlowski, S.W.J., Kirsch, M. J. 1987. The systematic distortion hypothesis, halo and accuracy: an individual level of analysis. *J. Appl. Psychol.* 72:252–61

Kozlowski, S.W.J., Kirsch, M. J., Chao, G. T. 1986. Job knowledge, ratee familiarity, conceptual similarity, and halo error: an exploration. *J. Appl. Psychol.* 71:45–49

Landy, F. J., Becker, W. S. 1987. Motivation theory reconsidered. *Res. Org. Behav.* 9:1–38

Larson, J. R. Jr., Lingle, J. H., Scerbo, M. M. 1984. The impact of performance cues on leader-behavior ratings: the role of selective information availability and probabilistic response bias. *Organ. Behav. Hum. Perform.* 33:323–49

Leon, F. R. 1981. The role of positive and negative outcomes in the causation of motivational forces. *J. Appl. Psychol.* 66:45–53

Liden, R. C., Mitchell, T. R. 1985. Reactions to feedback: the role of attributions. *Acad. Manage. J.* 28:291–308

Locke, E. A., Frederick, E., Buckner, E., Bobko, P. 1984a. Effect of previously assigned goals on self-set goals and performance. *J. Appl. Psychol.* 69:694–99

Locke, E. A., Frederick, E., Lee, C., Bobko, P. 1984b. Effect of self-efficacy, goals, and task strategy on task performance. *J. Appl. Psychol.* 69:241–51

Locke, E. A., Latham, G. P., Erez, M. 1988. Determinants of goal commitment. *Acad. Manage. J.* 13:23–39

London, M. 1985. *Developing Managers: A Guide to Motivating and Preparing People for Successful Managerial Careers.* San Francisco: Jossey-Bass

Lord, R. G. 1985. An information processing approach to social perceptions, leadership and behavioral measurement in organizations. *Res. Org. Behav.* 7:87–128

Lord, R. G., Alliger, G. M. 1985. A comparison of four information processing models of leadership and social perceptions. *Hum. Relat.* 38:47–65

Lord, R. G., DeVader, C. L., Alliger, G. M. 1986. A meta-analysis of the relationship between personality traits and leader perceptions: an application of validity generalization procedures. *J. Appl. Psychol.* 71:402–10

Lord, R. G., Foti, R. J., DeVader, C. L. 1984. A test of leadership categorization theory: internal structure, information processing, and leadership perceptions. *Organ. Behav. Hum. Perform.* 34:343–78

Lord, R. G., Hanges, P. J. 1987. A control systems model of organizational motivation: theoretical development and applied implications. *Behav. Sci.* 32:161–78

Lord, R. G., Kernan, M. C. 1987. Scripts as determinants of purposeful behavior in organizations. *Acad. Manage. Rev.* 12:265–77

McElroy, J. C. 1985. Inside the teaching machine: integrating attribution and reinforcement theories. *J. Manage.* 11:123–41

McGrath, J. 1976. Stress and behavior in organizations. See Graen 1976, pp. 1351–96

Manz, C. 1986. Self-leadership: towards an expanded theory of self-influence processes in organizations. *Acad. Manage. Rev.* 11:585–600

March, J., Simon, H. 1958. *Organizations.* New York: Wiley

Markus, H., Zajonc, R. B. 1985. The cognitive perspective in social psychology. In *Handbook of Social Psychology*, ed. G. Lindzey, E. Aronson. New York: Random House

Mathieu, J. E. 1987. The influence of positive and negative outcomes on force model expectancy predictions: mixed results from two samples. *Hum. Relat.* 40:817–32

Matsui, T., Kakuyama, T., Onglatco, M. 1987. Effects of goals and feedback in groups. *J. Appl. Psychol.* 72:407–15

Mihal, W. L., Sorce, P. A., Comte, T. E. 1984. A process model of individual career decision making. *Acad. Manage. Rev.* 9:95–103

Miller, G. A., Galanter, E., Pribram, K. H. 1960. *Plans and the Structure of Behavior.* New York: Holt, Rinehart & Winston

Mitchell, T. R. 1979. Organizational behavior. *Ann. Rev. Psychol.* 30:234–82

Mitchell, T. R., Rediker, K. J., Beach, L. R. 1986. Image theory and its implications for policy and strategic decision making. See Sims & Gioia 1986, pp. 293–316

Mobley, W. 1977. Intermediate linkages in the relationship between job satisfaction and employee turnover. *J. Appl. Psychol.* 62:237–40

Mobley, W., Horner, S., Hollingsworth, A. 1978. An evaluation of precusors of hospital turnover. *J. Appl. Psychol.* 63:408–14

Moch, M., Buchko, A., Rubin, P. 1988. A simulation based time-series policy-capturing methodology for studying recurring decision making in organizations. *Advances in Information Processing in Organizations*, ed. J. Newsome, R. Cardy, S. Puffer. Greenwich, Conn: JAI. In press

Moch, M. K., Fields, W. C. 1985. Developing a content analysis for interpreting language in organizations. *Res. Sociol. Org.* 4:81–126

Motowidlo, S. J., Lawton, G. W. 1984. Affective and cognitive factors in soldiers' reenlistment decisions. *J. Appl. Psychol.* 69:157–66

Murphy, K. R., Balzer, W. K. 1986. Systematic distortion in memory-based behavior ratings and performance evaluations: consequences for rating accuracy. *J. Appl. Psychol.* 71:39–44

Murphy, K. R., Constans, J. I. 1987. Behavioral anchors as a source of bias in rating. *J. Appl. Psychol.* 72:573–77

Murphy, K. R., Gannett, B. A., Herr, B. M., Chen, J. A. 1986. Effects of subsequent performance on the evaluations of previous performance. *J. Appl. Psychol.* 71:427–31

Nathan, B. R., Alexander, R. A. 1985. The role of inferential accuracy in performance rating. *Acad. Manage. Rev.* 10:109–15

Naylor, J. C., Ilgen, D. R. 1984. Goal Setting: a theoretical analysis of a motivational technology. *Res. Org. Behav.* 6:95–140

Naylor, J. D., Pritchard, R. D., Ilgen, D. R. 1980. *A Theory of Behavior in Organizations.* New York: Academic

Nevill, D. D., Neimeyer, G. J., Probert, B., Fukuyama, M. 1986. Cognitive structures in vocational information processing and decision making. *J. Vocat. Behav.* 28:110–22

Nicholson, N. 1984. A theory of work role transitions. *Adm. Sci. Q.* 29:172–91

O'Reilly, C. A. III, Caldwell, D. F. 1985. The impact of normative social influence and cohesiveness on task perceptions and attitudes: a social processing approach. *J. Occup. Psychol.* 58:207–16

Padgett, M. Y., Ilgen, D. R. 1988. The impact of ratee performance characteristics on rater cognitive processes and alternative measures of rater accuracy. *Organ. Behav. Hum. Decis. Processes.* In press

Park, S. R., Binning, J. F., Pryor, J. B. 1987. *Social influences on task perceptions; the moderating effects of source attributions.* Presented at Ann. Conf. Soc. Indust. Organ. Psychol., 2nd, Atlanta

Parsons, C. K., Herold, D. M., Leatherwood, M. L. 1985. Turnover during initial employment: a longitudinal study of the role of causal attributions. *J. Appl. Psychol.* 70:337–41

Phillips, J. S. 1984. The accuracy of leadership ratings: a cognitive categorization perspective. *Organ. Behav. Hum. Perform.* 33:125–38

Pitz, G. F., Sachs, N. J. 1984. Judgment and decision: theory and application. *Ann. Rev. Psychol.* 35:139–65

Podsakoff, P. M., Farh, J. 1986. *Effects of feedback sign and credibility on goal setting and task performance: a preliminary test of some control theory propositions.* Unpublished manuscript, Indiana University

Porter, L. W., Lawler, E. E. III. 1968. *Managerial Attitudes and Performance.* Homewood, Ill: Dorsey Press

Powers, W. T. 1973. *Behavior: The Control of Perception.* Chicago: Aldine

Pritchard, R. D., Jones, S. D., Roth, P. L., Struebing, K. K., Ekeberg, S. E. 1987. *Organizational productivity measurement: the development and evaluation of an integrated approach. Rep. No. 86–64.* Brooks Air Force Base, Tex.

Runkel, P. L., McGrath, J. E. 1972. *Research on Human Behavior: A Systematic Guide to Method.* New York: Holt Rinehart & Winston

Salancik, G. R., Pfeffer, J. 1977. An examination of need-satisfaction models of job attitudes. *Adm. Sci. Q.* 22:427–56

Salancik, G. R., Pfeffer, J. 1978. A social information processing approach to job attitudes and task design. *Adm. Sci. Q.* 23:224–53

Salancik, G. R., Porac, J. F. 1986. Distilled ideologies: values derived from causal reasoning in complex environments. See Sims & Gioia 1986, pp. 75–101

Schnake, M. E., Dumler, M. P. 1987. The social information processing model of task design. *Group Organ. Stud.* 12:221–40

Schneider, B. 1985. Organizational behavior. *Ann. Rev. Psychol.* 36:573–611

Sims, H. P. Jr., Gioia, D. A., eds. 1986. *The Thinking Organization.* San Francisco: Jossey-Bass

Staw, B. M. 1977. Motivation in organizations: toward a synthesis and redirection. In *New Directions in Organizational Behavior,* ed. B. M. Staw, G. R. Salancik. Chicago, Ill: St. Clair Press

Staw, B. M. 1984. Organizational behavior: a review and reformulation of the field's outcome variables. *Ann. Rev. Psychol.* 35:627–66

Super, D. E. 1984. Career life and development. In *Career Choice and Development,* ed. D. Brown, L. Brooks, pp. 217–41. San Francisco: Jossey-Bass

Super, D. E. 1986. Life career roles: self-realization in work and leisure. See Hall 1986, pp. 95–119

Super, D. E., Hall, D. T. 1978. Career development: exploration and planning. *Ann. Rev. Psychol.* 29:257–93

Sussmann, M., Vecchio, R. P. 1985. Conceptualizations of valence and instrumentality: a fourfold model. *Organ. Behav. Hum. Decis. Processes* 36:96–112

Taylor, M. S., Fisher, C. D., Ilgen, D. R. 1984a. Individuals' reactions to performance feedback in organizations: a control theory perspective. In *Research in Personnel and Human Resources Management,* ed. K. M. Rowland, G. R. Ferris, 2:81–124. Greenwich, Conn: JAI

Taylor, M. S., Locke, E. A., Lee, C., Gist, M. 1984b. Type A behavior and faculty research productivity: What are the mechanisms? *Organ. Behav. Hum. Decis. Processes* 34:402–18

Tolman, E. C. 1935. Purpose and cognition: the determinants of animal learning. *Psychol. Rev.* 32:285–97

Volkart, E. H. 1951. *Social Behavior and Personality.* New York; Soc. Sci. Res. Council

Vroom, V. H. 1964. *Work and Motivation.* New York: Wiley

Vroom, V. H., Jago, A. G. 1988. *The New Leadership: Managing Participation in Organizations.* Englewood Cliffs, NJ: Prentice-Hall

Vroom, V. H., Yetton, P. W. 1973. *Leadership and Decision Making.* Pittsburgh, PA: Univ. Pittsburgh Press

Walton, E. J., Brief, A. P., Austin, E. J. 1985. Cognitive and organizational structures: an empirical analysis. *Hum. Relat.* 38:723–28

Weick, K. E., Bougon, M. G. 1986. Organizations as cognitive maps: charting ways to success and failure. See Sims & Gioia 1986, pp. 102–35

Weiner, B. 1979. A theory of motivation for some classroom experiences. *J. Educ. Psychol.* 71:3–25

Weiner, B. 1985. An attributional theory of achievement motivation and emotion. *Psychol. Rev.* 92:548–73

Wiener, N. 1948. *Cybernetics: Control and Communication in the Animal and the Machine.* Cambridge, Mass: MIT Press

Weldon, E., Gargano, G. M. 1988. Accountability discourages cognitive loafing: the effects of accountability and shared responsibility on cognitive effort. *Person. Soc. Psychol. Bull.* In press

Wexley, K. N., Klimoski, R. 1984. Performance appraisal: an update. In *Research in Personnel and Human Resources Management,* ed. K. M. Rowland, G. R. Ferris, 2:35–79. Greenwich, Conn: JAI

Wilder, D. A. 1981. Perceiving persons as a group: categorization and intergroup relations. In *Cognitive Processes in Stereotyping and Intergroup Behavior,* ed. D. L. Hamilton, pp. 213–57. Hillsdale, NJ: Erlbaum

Williams, K. J., DeNisi, A. S., Blencoe, A. G., Cafferty, T. P. 1985. The effects of appraisal purpose on information acquisition and utilization. *Organ. Behav. Hum. Perform.* 36:314–39

Wyer, R. S. Jr., Srull, T. K. 1986. Human cognition in its social context. *Psychol. Rev.* 93:322–59

Zalesny, M. D., Farace, R. V. 1986. A field study of social information processing: mean differences and variance differences. *Hum. Commun. Res.* 13:268–90

Zalesny, M. V., Ford, J. K. 1988. Towards understanding information processing within its social context: a look at links to attitudes, behaviors, and contexts. Unpublished paper, Univ. Missouri, St. Louis

Ann. Rev. Psychol. 1989. 40:353–79

MECHANISMS OF COGNITIVE DEVELOPMENT

Robert S. Siegler

Department of Psychology, Carnegie-Mellon University, Pittsburgh, Pennsylvania, 15213

CONTENTS

To develop is to change. Without a good understanding of the mechanisms that produce change, no comprehensive understanding of development is possible. The difficulty of identifying such mechanisms is well known and has often been noted (e.g. Flavell 1984; Kuhn 1984; Miller 1983). Not as well known or as often noted, however, is the substantial progress that has been made in the past few years in establishing the effects that particular mechanisms produce and in specifying how the mechanisms operate.

Here I review some of the most promising recent ideas about change mechanisms that contribute to cognitive development. I hope that bringing together in a single context a number of these relatively well-worked-out examples will facilitate further advances in theorizing about change mechanisms.

353

0066-4308/89/0201-0353$02.00

The progress of developmental theories depends critically on improving our grasp of how change occurs (Flavell 1984; Klahr 1984; MacWhinney 1987; Miller 1983; Siegler 1983; Sternberg 1984).Well-specified change mechanisms can increase the generality of theories by revealing that seemingly unrelated acquisitions are products of the same process. They also can help explain within a single framework how early concepts can be acquired quickly while advanced forms of the same concepts can take years to attain. Improved understanding of change mechanisms also offers accurate prediction of nonintuitive empirical phenomena.

What do we mean by a "mechanism of cognitive development"? Broadly defined, a cognitive-developmental mechanism is any mental process that improves children's ability to process information. I intend all terms within this definition to be interpreted inclusively. Mental processes include perceptual and linguistic processes, as well as conceptual, reasoning, and problem-solving ones. The improvements in children's ability to process information that are of interest include large and small ones, long-term and short-term ones, qualitative and quantitative ones. Neural, associative, and higher-level change mechanisms are all included, because all interact to produce cognitive development.

I consider five types of mechanisms: neural mechanisms, associative competition, encoding, analogy, and strategy choice. I chose these because of their documented importance in producing cognitive growth in a wide variety of domains and over a wide age range, because they include a variety of types and levels of change, and because recent progress toward understanding them has been especially rapid. The particular labels used should not obscure the fact that many of them are best thought of as families of related mechanisms, rather than as a single one. For example, encoding is a member of a family that includes such relatives as differentiation, feature discrimination, perceptual learning, representation, and assimilation. Analogy is clearly related to induction, transfer, metaphor and simile, schema formation, and generalization. As a greater number of well-worked-out models of mechanisms become available, there will be a better basis for determining which within-family distinctions make a difference.

Perhaps the basic issue raised by the review is whether these mechanisms are best thought of as five distinct entities or as five facets of a single underlying mechanism. Among the arguments for viewing the five as separate mechanisms are that they operate in different contexts, vary greatly in grain of detail and generality of scope, and accomplish distinct cognitive functions. The main argument for viewing them as separate manifestations of a single change mechanism is that all share a core similarity. As described in greater detail in the discussion section, this core similarity involves each mechanism appearing to operate through competition among diverse cognitive entities. Here I do not resolve whether the five are best viewed as singular or as distinct mechanisms. However, the fact that we can even raise the question and have a reasonable data base from which to discuss it attests to the value of thinking hard about mechanisms of development.[1]

NEURAL MECHANISMS

Recent advances in neuroscience have provided much stronger evidence than previously existed for contributions for specific aspects of brain maturation to specific cognitive acquisitions (Crnic & Pennington 1987). Several types of neural change appear to exert especially large influences.

Synaptogenesis

The number of synapses within numerous parts of the brain follows a distinctive developmental course, in which there is initial overproduction and later pruning of synaptic connections. Such connections are produced in especially great numbers during the late prenatal and early postnatal periods. For example, Huttenlocher (1979) found that the average number of synaptic connections in the third layer of the middle frontal gyrus grew from 10,000 to 100,000 between birth and 12 months of age. The density of synapses increased until age 2, after which it gradually decreased to adult levels. These adult levels were reached by about age 7; from age 6 months to age 7 years, synaptic density in the children's brains exceeded adult levels.

Recent studies have linked cognitive and synaptic change. Turner & Greenough (1985) reported that rats housed in large complexes of cages that the animals were free to explore and that were filled with diverse objects formed 20–25% more synapses per neuron in the upper visual cortex than animals raised in impoverished environments. Chang & Greenough (1982) severed the corpus callosa of rats and then provided them with monocular experience running a maze. More extensive dendritic fields were found within a month in the occipital cortex of the hemisphere that received the input relative to the one that did not.

Advances in understanding of synaptogenesis have led to new perspectives on classic problems in cognitive development. For example, Goldman-Rakic (1987) suggested that early synaptic overproduction is critical to the development of ability to solve A-not-B object-permanence and delayed-response problems. With both monkey and human infants, ability to perform these tasks follows soon after the age at which synaptic density first exceeds adult levels, roughly age 2 months in monkeys and 6 months in humans. This

---

[1]The strict page constraints of this volume precluded examination of several other important mechanisms. Among these are processing efficiency (e.g. Case 1985; Kail 1986), conceptual constraints (Gelman 1988; Pinker 1987), and social scaffolding (e.g. Palincsar & Brown 1984; Rogoff 1986). Future, more complete discussions of cognitive-developmental mechanisms should definitely include consideration of these ideas.

synaptic overproduction affects the prefrontal cortex and a number of areas to which the prefrontal cortex is strongly connected and that may be critical for performing such visuo-spatial memory tasks (Rakic et al 1986). Further, surgically produced lesions in the prefrontal cortex resulted in adult rhesus monkeys' showing the same pattern of performance as infant humans and monkeys: consistent success when the object was hidden in the previously rewarded location, and near-chance performance when the location was changed (Diamond 1985). Similar-size lesions in the parietal lobe did not produce such interference on these tasks.

Goldman-Rakic (1987) theorized that the high density of synapses in the prefrontal cortex and connected areas is needed for infant monkeys and humans to initially form enduring representations capable of overcoming associative habits. She noted that the lesioned monkeys did not show per-severative errors with delay periods below 2 sec. However, at all delays equal to or greater than 2 sec, when working-memory representations would pre-sumably be necessary for success, their performance was seriously disrupted. Performance with 2-sec delays was disrupted almost as much as performance with 10-sec delays. Overall, the monkeys with prefrontal lesions appeared unable to use working-memory representations to regulate their performance so as to transcend the effects of the previous reinforcement pattern.

Goldman-Rakic suggested that ability to form enduring representations is also crucial for other types of competence that develop substantially in the period between 6 and 18 months. In particular, she hypothesized that ability to form, access, and use on-line such representations is critical to the marked progress that children show in walking and speaking during this period. Brody's (1981) explanation of changes in short-term cued recall between 8 and 16 months; Fox et al's (1979) explanation of object permanence, stranger distress, and separation anxiety; and Fischer's (1987) explanation of complex means-ends variation in actions, use of single words, and general stage transitions in infancy have also emphasized the types of changes in brain function in general and synaptogenesis in particular that occur in this period of infancy.

Segregation of Neuronal Input

Synaptogenesis is not the only type of neural change that influences early development. Held and his colleagues have linked segregation of neural input from the two eyes to the development of stereopsis. Stereopsis is the percep-tion of depth based on disparity of images impinging on each eye. The onset of stereopsis within individual infants is sudden, often developing from no detectable presence to high levels within a few weeks (Birch et al 1982).

Held (1985) suggested that the mechanism that leads to stereopsis involves segregation of neural pathways, so that axons from the two eyes do not synapse on the same cortical neuron. Prior to the segregation of neurons into ocular dominance columns in Layer IV of the visual cortex, axons from the two eyes often synapse on the same cells (LeVay et al 1980). When this occurs, there is no obvious way for the visual system to distinguish which information came from which eye. Held hypothesized that absence of discriminating information inhibits formation of cells sensitive to binocular disparity, since such cells would lack the information on which to operate.

Based on this view of the neural mechanism leading to stereopsis, Held and his colleagues developed an intriguing idea concerning infants' perceptual experience. They hypothesized that prestereoptic infants nonselectively combine whatever pattern of stimulation comes into the two eyes, essentially overlaying one eye's input on the other's. To test this prediction, Shimojo et al (1986) longitudinally followed infants' performance from 3 to 34 weeks on a preferential looking task. The infants wore polarizing goggles, which allowed them to receive different inputs to the two eyes. The stimulus on one side projected identical vertical lines to both eyes. The stimulus on the other side projected vertical lines to one eye and horizontal lines to the other. Due to binocular rivalry, adults see this latter combination as a constantly shifting and rather unpleasant set of line segments without intersections. Stereoptic infants were expected to experience the display similarly. On the other hand, if, as hypothesized, prestereoptic infants essentially overlayed the vertical lines presented to one eye and the horizontal lines presented to the other, they would see a checkerboard grid pattern. Infants are known to prefer checkerboard grids to vertical lines. Therefore, if prestereoptic infants experienced the vertical and horizontal lines as a grid, they would look more at them than at the vertical lines. Infants who possessed stereopsis, in contrast, would prefer the stable vertical lines to the constantly shifting line segments they would presumably experience when presented the horizontal and vertical lines.

This theoretical prediction was dramatically confirmed. When the infants were below 13 weeks, almost all of them (25 of 27) preferred the side where one eye received horizontal and the other side vertical lines. By the end of the experiment, every infant significantly preferred the side where both eyes received vertical lines. The mean age of onset for the significant preference for the vertical lines was 14 weeks, the mean age at which stereopsis also emerges. The change in preference was dramatic within individual infants. Many infants changed within 1 or 2 weeks from a significant preference for one eye receiving horizontal and the other receiving vertical lines to a significant preference for both eyes receiving the vertical lines. It seems unlikely that this difference in the visual experience of prestereoptic and stereoptic infants would have been discovered, much less predicted, without the hypothesis concerning the type of neural change that produces stereopsis.

Experience-Expectant and Experience-Dependent Processes

Hypotheses about change mechanisms can also lead to new perspectives on quite general issues about cognitive development. Based on their analysis of synaptic change, Greenough et al (1987) distinguished between experience-expectant processes and experience-dependent processes. Their analysis has interesting implications both for the frequently made distinction between development and learning (Liben 1987) and for analyses of sensitive periods (Hinde 1983).

Experience-expectant processes illustrate the development end of the development-learning continuum. These processes are hypothesized to be based on the synaptic overproduction and pruning described above. Greenough et al suggested that the initial overproduction of synapses is maturationally regulated, but that which ones are pruned depends on experience. Normal experience at the normal time results in neural activity that maintains typical connections; abnormal experience, or lack of experience at the usual time, results in atypical connections. The type of experience relevant to such experience-expectant processes is experience that has been widely available throughout the evolutionary history of the species. Such experience-expectant processes tend to develop early in life and to be relatively invariant across individuals.

Greenough et al suggested that one advantage of such processes is that they allow both efficient acquisition in normal environments and reasonable adaptation to abnormal environments. In particular, the genes provide a rough outline of the eventual form of the process, thus allowing quite rapid acquisition under usual circumstances. Unusual environments or physical deficiencies, however, lead to unusual neural activity, which creates alternative neural organizations that are adaptive given the unusual circumstances.

The usefulness of this concept of experience-expectant processes for understanding sensitive periods can be illustrated in the context of the segregation of neural input from each eye, described above. In young cats and monkeys, sewing shut one eye during an early sensitive period results in a severe visual impairment when the eye is later reopened (Wiesel & Hubel 1965). Instead of the usual process, in which terminal fields of axons from both eyes are cut back equally from the visual cortex columns dominated by the other eye, the terminal fields of the deprived eye are cut back from a larger area, and those from the nondeprived eye from a smaller area, than usual. The abnormal experience leads to neurons from the nondeprived eye winning competitions that these neurons are predisposed to lose when both eyes receive typical input.

The timing of the sensitive period seems to be a function both of when synaptic overproduction occurs and when the organism receives relevant experience. In kittens, the greatest damage from monocular deprivation occurs when the deprivation is in the first two months of life, overlapping substantially with the beginning of the period of synaptic overproduction. Conversely, even small amounts of binocular experience in the first two months are sufficient to protect the kitten from harmful effects of later monocular deprivation (Hubel & Wiesel 1970; Mower et al 1983). However, dark-reared kittens who do not receive any early visual experience are still harmed by monocular deprivation when it is introduced at 10 months (Cynader & Mitchell 1980).

To explain both the age-relatedness of the sensitive period and the lack of rigidity of its age boundaries, Greenough et al suggested that visual experience has the effect of committing a set of synapses to a particular organization. Once this commitment has occurred, synapses not needed for that organization are pruned away. If no relevant experience is encountered, the synaptic pruning is forestalled for a number of months. As Bertenthal & Campos (1987) noted, this analysis of sensitive periods advances understanding beyond the usual criteria of age-dependency and irreversibility. It indicates what produces the sensitive periods, why they usually occur when they do, and how, under certain circumstances, they can be prolonged.

The other side of Greenough et al's dichotomy involves experience-*dependent* processes. These are the neural substrate of what is usually thought of as learning. With experience-dependent processes, formation of synaptic connections depends on experiences that vary widely among individuals in whether and when they occur. The experience-dependent processes appear to operate through the formation of synapses in response to specific neural activity caused by partially or totally unsuccessful attempts to process information. Such synapses can be generated as rapidly as 10–15 min after a new experience (Chang & Greenough 1984). Synapse production under such circumstances appears to be fairly localized to the site of the previous information processing. However, as with experience-expectant processes, more synapses than will later be present may be produced. The synapses that are maintained are those involved in subsequent neural activity.

These analyses suggest both similarities and differences between experience-expectant and experience-dependent processes. In both, the change mechanism involves a cycle of synaptic increase and pruning. Also in both, neural activity determines which synapses are maintained. However, the events that trigger the synaptogenesis, its degree of localization, the ages at which it occurs, and the behavioral domains influenced all distinguish the two types of process. Overall, the emphasis on neural change mechanisms allows a considerably more differentiated approach to the relation between learning and development than has previously been possible.

ASSOCIATIVE COMPETITION

Synaptic connections that are used are maintained; those that are not used are pruned. This phenomenon has provided an analogy from which a variety of hypotheses about associative competition have been drawn. The basic idea of the outcomes of cognitive competitions leading to changes in children's associative networks, and therefore in their thinking, has been hypothesized to contribute to language development (Bates & MacWhinney 1987; Mac-Whinney 1987; Rumelhart & McClelland 1986), changes in the organization of free recall (Bjorklund & Jacobs 1985), acquisition of arithmetic and reading skills (Ashcraft 1987; Seidenberg & McClelland 1988), and improvements in problem solving (Anderson 1987; McClelland 1989). Some of the best-worked-out ideas about how associative competition might operate have been developed in the context of connectionist models. Therefore, these are emphasized in the present discussion.

Connectionist Models

Connectionist models, emphasizing distributed representations, parallel processing, and interactions among large numbers of simple processing units, have greatly influenced recent thinking about many aspects of adult cognition (Hinton & Anderson 1981; McClelland & Rumelhart 1986; Palmer 1987). Not surprisingly, such models are beginning to influence ideas about cognitive development as well.

Most current connectionist models involve an input level, one or more hidden levels, and an output level. Each of these levels contains a number of discrete units. For example, in MacWhinney and colleagues' (Taraban et al 1989) model of how German children acquire the set of articles used in their native language ("der", "die", "das", etc), the input level includes 39 units, the output level contains 6 units, and the two hidden levels have 30 and 7 units, respectively. The 39 input units represent individual auditory, lexical, case, and semantic features of the input noun. The 2 levels of hidden units represent a variety of combinations of these input-level features. The 6 output units represent the 6 articles in the German language. Each input-level unit is connected to each of the units in the hidden level immediately above it, each of these units is connected to each of the units at the next higher hidden level, and each unit at that level is connected to each output unit.

The processing that goes on within connectionist models can also be described in the context of the Taraban et al simulation. The simulation represents the noun that is presented in terms of a subset of the 39 input-level units. Those input-level units that are active feed activation into the units of the hidden level immediately above it. The activation that a given hidden-level unit receives from a given input-level unit is a function of whether the input-level unit is active and of the strength of the connection between input and hidden unit. The total activation received by a given hidden unit is the sum of the positive and negative activations contributed to it by all of the input units that are connected to it. The activation of each output-level unit is produced in the same way, except that the immediate source of the activation is hidden-level rather than input-level units.

Now consider how learning occurs in such models. The particular learning algorithm used by Taraban et al and in most other recent connectionist models involves backward propagation of error corrections. Such "back propagation" begins by the activations of the output units being compared to those of a target that is intended to represent feedback from the environment. For example, on a given trial, the simulation's processing might result in "der" receiving an activation of .4, and "die" an activation of .5, when "der", the correct article for that noun, would ideally have received an activation of 1, and "die," an incorrect article, an activation of 0. For each output-level unit, the value of the desired and actual activations would be compared to obtain a measure of the degree of error. The strengths of connections from all units that sent activation to higher level units would then be adjusted so that on subsequent presentations of the stimulus they would produce values of the output unit that more closely approximated the desired state. For example, strong connections between a hidden-level unit and an incorrect output-level unit would be decremented, whereas weak connections between a hidden-level unit and the correct output-level unit would be strengthened.

Associative Competition and Language Development

What can such associative competitions accomplish? Taraban et al chose to test the ability of the MacWhinney (1987) competition model to acquire the article system of German. This task was of interest precisely because the German article system is so difficult. The appropriate article varies with several properties of the noun: gender (masculine, feminine, or neuter), case (nominative, genitive, dative, or accusative), and number (singular or plural). To make matters worse, assignment of nouns to gender categories is often nonintuitive: For example, the word for "fork" is feminine, the word for "spoon" is masculine, and the word for "knife" is neuter. Maratsos (1982) argued that neither semantic nor phonological cues predict which article accompanies a given noun, and that only purely syntactic cues could allow correct choices to be made.

In contrast, Taraban et al sought to demonstrate that available lexical, semantic, phonological, and case cues were sufficient for children to learn the German article system. Input to the system was 102 common German nouns, each presented a number of times. The system needed to choose which article to use with that noun in the particular case-and-number context.

After experience with this training set, the Taraban et al simulation chose the correct article for 98% of the nouns. This could not be attributed simply to rote learning of the possible article-noun combinations. When the simulation was presented a previously encountered noun in a novel case role, it chose the correct article on 89% of trials. The simulation also proved able to generalize to entirely novel nouns. The 48 most frequent nouns in German that had not been included in the original input set were presented in all possible case roles. On this completely novel set, the simulation chose the correct article from among the 6 possibilities on 63% of trials, versus 17% expected by chance. Thus, the system's learning mechanism allowed it to make a good guess about what article would accompany a given noun, even when the noun was entirely unfamiliar.

The simulation's learning resembled children's in a number of ways. Early in acquisition, it, like children, tended to overuse the article that accompanies feminine nouns. Similarly, both the simulation and children tended to acquire the connection between the -e noun ending and feminine articles early in learning. Further, the same article-noun combinations that are the most difficult for children proved the most difficult for the simulation.

MacWhinney (1989; Bates & MacWhinney 1987) proposed that two key determiners of the difficulty of acquisition in such a system are cue availability (the frequency with which a cue is present) and cue reliability (the predictive accuracy of the cue when it is present). Results obtained from the Taraban et al simulation indicated that cue availability is a good predictor of relative speed of learning early in the learning process, but that cue reliability becomes the best predictor later in learning. Very late in learning, conflict-validity, the reliability of a cue when other cues point to different answers, may become an even better predictor of difficulty than general cue reliability (McDonald & MacWhinney 1989). The pattern suggests that as learners obtain increasing amounts of input, they rely increasingly on specifically relevant information, at the expense of less-relevant but more easily available information. This seems a plausible sequence for many aspects of cognitive growth, both in language and in other areas.

ENCODING

Although connectionist accounts are very promising, existing connectionist models also have certain limitations as explanations of development (Pinker & Prince 1988). One main limitation is that they assume veridical encoding of stimuli at the input level from the beginning of learning. For example, as described above, the Taraban et al simulation assumes that from trial 1, nouns are encoded on the 39 input features involving gender, case roles, phonology, and meaning. In human development, however, children often fail to encode relevant features; much of cognitive growth involves the acquisition of increasingly adequate encodings. Comprehensive accounts of development must explain these changes in encoding, as well as changes in how encoded information is used.

Encoding is the process by which stimuli are represented in a particular situation. In almost any context, some information is encoded and used to operate on the environment; other information is encoded but not used; yet other information is not encoded. When existing strategies fail, information that is encoded but not used provides a kind of reserve capital for constructing new, potentially superior approaches. For example, a boy approaching a playground on his first day at school may encode the presence of a friend and use this information in deciding to go over to play with the friend; may encode the presence of a playground monitor in another part of the playground but make no use of the information; and may not encode the fact that all of the older children are playing near his friend and all of the other young children are playing in a different part of the playground. If the older children started bothering the boy, he could use his encoding of the playground monitor's location to go over to her for safety, and could learn to stay near her in the future. However, not until he encoded that the older and younger children generally played in different parts of the playground could he learn to avoid playing where the older children were, and thus free himself of the need to monitor the monitor. Thus, encoding potentially relevant information can facilitate learning, and failing to encode relevant information can hinder or preclude learning.

Recent Empirical Findings

Changes in encoding have been found to underlie a variety of age-related changes in children's thinking. When presented balance scale problems, 5-year-olds encode only the weight dimension whereas 8-year-olds encode both weight and distance; teaching the 5-year-olds to encode distance as well as weight allows them to learn new rules from experiences that previously were not helpful (Siegler 1976). Adults spend more time than 7-year-olds encoding analogical reasoning problems; this lengthier encoding is more than compensated for, however, by the much more rapid execution of other components that the more extensive initial encoding makes possible (Sternberg & Rifkin 1979). Older children encode transitive inference problems in relative terms ("A is greater than B") whereas 6- and 7-year-olds encode them in absolute terms ("A is long and B is short"); the younger children may have difficulty solving transitive inference problems because their absolute encodings lead to inconsistencies, such as B being encoded as long on one trial but short on another (Perner & Mansbridge, 1983; Riley & Trabasso 1974). Across a wide range of tasks, older children's encoding has been found to be both more selective and more exhaustive of the relevant features than that of younger children (Sophian 1984; Sternberg & Powell 1983).

Differences in encoding are also related to individual differences in the thinking of children of a single age. Differences between high-IQ and average-IQ 7-year-olds' analogical reasoning parallel those between adults and 7-year-olds. The higher-IQ children take more time to encode but then solve the problem more quickly (Sternberg & Rifkin 1979). Gifted 9- to 11-year-olds are more likely than age peers to focus their encoding on the critical parts of insight problems and to ignore irrelevant parts (Davidson 1986; Marr &

Sternberg 1986). Independent of IQ, musically gifted 12- and 13-year-olds encode verbal material more efficiently than do artistically gifted peers, whereas the artistically gifted children encode visual material more efficiently (O'Connor & Hermelin 1983). Word encoding of 11-year-olds with learning disabilities, like that of typical 6-year-olds, emphasizes acoustic features, whereas word encoding of typical 11-year-olds emphasizes semantic features (Lorsbach & Gray 1985). The importance of encoding also extends to social domains; for example, aggressive 7- to 9-year-olds encode other children's intentions less accurately than do less aggressive peers (Dodge et al 1986).

How New Encodings Are Formed

Holland and his colleagues (Holland 1986; Holland et al 1986) suggested a genetic algorithm by which new encodings, and hence new opportunities to learn, might be generated. Within Holland's model, a learner's knowledge is represented as a set of rules. Each rule is a condition-action pairing, much like a production in a production system. Within a rule, a string of 1s, 0s, and neutral values on the condition side indicates the rule's encoding of the environment. Another string of 1s, 0s, and neutral values on the action side indicates what changes occur when that rule fires. Each rule also has a strength, which determines its probability of firing when several rules are applicable. Rule strengths change as a function of how often the rule is used and how consistently its use is followed by attainment of the system's goal.

Within Holland's genetic algorithm, new encodings and rules are produced when, periodically, two rules with different condition sides but identical action sides are selected to be "parents." For example, two parent rules might be: 101→010 and 000→010. New rules are produced by making a cut at an arbitrary point in the condition side of each parent, combining the part of the condition to the left of one cut with the part of the condition to the right of the other cut, and linking that new condition side to the action side of the parent productions. In the above example, making a cut between the second and third symbol on the condition side of each parent rule would give rise to the new rules: 100→010 and 001→010.

The probability of a given rule's being chosen to be a parent is proportional to its strength. This assures that rules more closely linked with goal attainment more often contribute to new encodings. It also assures that other rules have some chance of doing so, which provides potentially useful variability in the rules that are formed. Whenever new rules are created, they replace the weakest of the existing rules. The set of rules is thus driven by increasingly useful encodings.

Although this approach does not seem to have been applied yet to modeling children's thinking, it has illustrated how improved encodings could contribute to cognitive change in a number of interesting contexts, among them poker playing, Prisoner's Dilemma games, and gas-pipeline transmission problems (Holland et al 1986). Its learning to solve the pipeline problems is particularly impressive, because the system's initial encodings and rules were generated randomly and thus did not assume any prior knowledge of the environment. Input to this simulation was hourly information from a simulated gas transmission system concerning inflow and outflow of gas, input and output pressure of gas, rate and direction of changes in pressure, date, time, and current temperature. The system's task was to deliver gas at the minimum pressure needed to meet demand and to locate any leaks that were present. The genetic algorithm formed new encodings and rules after every 200 hours of experience.

Despite the initial random generation of rules (and encodings), the system progressed to near optimal performance in detecting gasoline leaks and compensating for them by sending additional gas through that part of the pipeline. It eliminated unreasonable rules, restricted the range of overly general rules, and produced new rules that were more useful than any of the previous ones. For example, it eventually produced the rule "If input and output pressure are low and the rate of change in pressure is very negative, then send a 'leak' message." This rule gained considerable strength once it was generated, because the simultaneous presence of the three encoded states was very predictive of actual leaks. The simulation demonstrates how a "mindless" mechanism for generating new encodings can come to encode the environment in new and useful ways.

ANALOGY

Analogy produces progress in children's thinking by allowing them to interpret poorly understood situations in terms of better-understood ones. It can be especially helpful in problem solving, where a novel (target) problem is often understood in terms of a familiar (base) problem. For example, people are more likely to solve Duncker's famous X-ray problem (focusing separate X-rays at the location of a tumor) if they have already learned the solution to a parallel problem in which an attacking army must divide into separate attack units and travel from different directions to converge at the enemy's location (Gick & Holyoak 1980).

Recent Empirical Findings

Knowledge about the development of analogical reasoning has expanded rapidly in the past few years. Children as young as 3–5 years have been found to solve new problems more effectively if they had previously solved analogous problems (Brown et al 1986; Chen & Daehler 1988; Crisafi & Brown 1986; Holyoak et al 1984). This is true even when there is little perceptual similarity between the base and target problems (Brown et al 1986; Crisafi & Brown 1986). Having the experimenter and the child state the common solution principle that unites the two problems (Crisafi & Brown 1986), presenting problems in an order where the causal structures proceed from most to least obvious (Crisafi & Brown 1986), and prompting children to recall key elements of the original problem's causal structure (Brown et al 1986) all help 3- to 5-year-olds to analogize from familiar to novel problems. Even 2-year-olds show analogical transfer when they understand the causal relations in both situations (Brown 1989).

Whether children detect potentially useful analogies depends on a variety of characteristics of the problem situation and of the child's cognitive activities. Among the potentially helpful aspects of the problem situation are similar base and target problems (Brown & Campione 1984; Gentner & Landers 1985; Holyoak et al 1984), presentation of multiple base problems with the same solution principle (Crisafi & Brown 1986; Gholson et al 1987), and provision of visual representations diagramming the essential aspects of the problem (Beveridge & Parkins 1987). Among the key aspects of children's cognitive activities are completeness of encoding (Chen & Daehler 1988; Sternberg & Nigro 1980; Sternberg & Rifkin 1979) and amount of knowledge of the base problem (Inagaki & Hatano 1987). These features seem to be influential at all ages.

Young children's ability to draw analogies, and their sensitivity to many of the same problem characteristics that influence the analogical reasoning of older children and adults, should not obscure the profound developmental changes that occur in analogical reasoning. Young children require explicit hints to draw analogies that older children draw without such hints (Crisafi & Brown 1986; Brown et al 1986). They at times draw unsound analogies to just-presented problems at alarmingly high rates (Chen & Daehler 1988). Their analogizing is hindered by superficial perceptual dissimilarities that do not influence the analogizing of older children and adults (Gentner & Toupin 1986; Goldman et al 1982; Holyoak et al 1984). Their execution of processes involved in analogizing, such as encoding, mapping, and inference, is less efficient than that of older children (Bisanz 1979; Pellegrino & Goldman 1983; Sternberg & Rifkin 1979). Thus, satisfactory models of analogical reasoning must account for a variety of age-related differences, as well as a variety of similarities.

How Analogies Are Generated

Gentner's structure-mapping engine (Falkenhainer et al 1986; Gentner 1989) illustrates how well-worked-out models of performance can yield interesting insights about development. The model's focus is on how children establish correspondences between a base domain and a target. The central idea is that children, like adults, strive to form analogies where the system of relations in the target domain resembles the system of relations in the base. The objects being related need not have any particular resemblance. Instead, the key is the similarity of the corresponding relations in the two situations.

Gentner (1989) used Carnot's analogy "heat flow is like water flow" to illustrate the workings of the structure-mapping model. The concrete situation she used to illustrate heat flow involved a cup of hot coffee, an ice cube, and a silver bar connecting the two. The situation used to illustrate water flow involved a large beaker with a tall liquid column, a small vial with a short liquid column, and a pipe running between the bottom of the beaker and the bottom of the vial. The task was to map the relations involved in how temperature differences influence the flow of heat between coffee and ice cube onto the relations involved in how pressure differences influence the flow of water between the two containers. Thus, the coffee cup needed to be mapped onto the large beaker, the ice cube onto the vial, the silver bar onto the pipe, and heat onto water.

Falkenhainer et al (1986) implemented a computer simulation to illustrate how the theory would draw this, and a number of other, analogies. Figure 1 illustrates the simulation's initial representation of the base and target situations in the "Heat flow is like water flow" analogy. The simulation first tries to establish local matches, then assigns evidence scores to each of the local matches, then constructs global matches, and finally evaluates the global matches.

To construct local matches, the simulation examines each object and relation in the base (better-known situation) and identifies a set of objects and relations in the target (less-well-known situation) that it could plausibly match. For example, if relations in the base and target have identical names, then a match hypothesis is created. Each match hypothesis leads to checking corresponding arguments of the relations; if they are of the same type (e.g. both are functions), then a match hypothesis between them is created. This

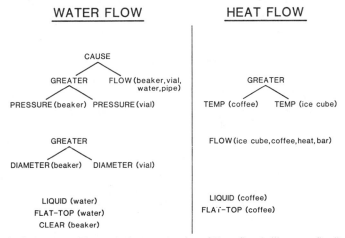

Figure 1 Structure-mapping engine's representation of "heat flow is like water flow" analogy (from Gentner 1989).

often leads to a large number of local matches, some of which prove useful and others not. For example, in Figure 1, the relation GREATER places into correspondence "pressure" in the water flow situation and "temperature" in the heat flow situation (a relation that is part of a high-quality analogy) and also "diameter" in the water flow and "temperature" in the heat flow situations (a relation that is not).

Rules assign evidence scores to these local matches. One such rule is to increase the score if corresponding relations in the base and target have the same name. Another is to increase the score for a given local match if the relation immediately higher in each hierarchy also matches. This second rule leads to the preference for the GREATER relation involving pressure over that involving diameter. The higher-level "CAUSES" relation (Figure 1) adds to the evaluation of the pressure-temperature relation but not to that of the diameter-temperature relation.

To construct global matches, the structure-mapping engine combines match hypotheses into the largest possible systems whose object mappings are internally consistent. These systems are possible interpretations of the analogy. Each system also includes a set of possible inferences about how additional, unmatched parts of the base could be mapped onto the target. For example, the CAUSE relation between pressure and water flow in the base analogy leads to an inference that there may be a CAUSE relation between temperature and heat flow in the target analogy. The global matches are evaluated on the basis of the sum of the evidence from the local matches.

This structure-mapping model has proved useful for understanding how analogical reasoning develops. Falkenhainer et al described three variants of the structure-mapping engine: one that operated solely on object matches, one that operated solely on relational matches, and one that used both. These alternative versions seemed to correspond to developmental differences in analogical reasoning. Gentner & Toupin (1986) found that 4- to 6-year-olds saw situations as analogous only when corresponding objects were similar. Their behavior was like that of the object-matching simulation. In contrast, 8- to 10-year-olds did not require such similarities between objects to draw the analogies; parallel sets of relations were sufficient for them to do so. Thus, their performance was more like that of the programs that relied on relations.

Gentner (1988) found a similar developmental trend in interpretation of metaphors. Children could correctly interpret metaphors based on similarity of objects before they could interpret metaphors where only relational structures were parallel. Further, with age, children became increasingly likely to interpret relationally those metaphors that could be viewed either in terms of similarities between objects or similarities between relations. In sum, the structure-mapping engine illustrates how a variety of characteristics of analogical reasoning and its development could arise. [See Bakker & Halford (1988) for a related model of the development of analogical reasoning; this model has the additional virtue of accounting for the age-related trend toward detecting increasingly less obvious analogies.]

STRATEGY CHOICE

People can approach almost any task in multiple ways. For example, the majority of first graders have been found to use at least three strategies in solving a set of simple addition problems (Siegler 1987). Typically, children counted from one on some problems, counted from the larger addend on other problems, and retrieved an answer from memory on yet other problems. For children, such use of multiple strategies has great advantages; it allows them to fit their strategies to constantly changing knowledge and situational demands. For researchers, however, it raises a great many questions: in particular, when do children use various strategies, how do children decide to use one strategy rather than another, and what developments lead to changes in strategy use with age and experience?

Recent Empirical Findings

From quite young ages, children choose among strategies in ways that yield desirable combinations of speed and accuracy. This adaptive quality can be seen in choices between retrieval and *backup* strategies (approaches other than retrieval, such as looking up words in a dictionary in spelling, counting from the hour by 5s in time-telling, repeatedly adding in multiplication, and sounding out words in reading). Both retrieval and backup strategies have clear, though different, advantages. Retrieval can be executed more quickly; backup strategies can yield correct answers on problems where retrieval would be inaccurate.

Siegler & Shrager (1984) found that in simple addition, even preschoolers chose between stating a retrieved answer and using a backup strategy in a very reasonable way. On easy problems, the 4- and 5-year-olds relied primarily on retrieval; on more difficult problems, they relied primarily on backup strategies. This allowed them to answer the easier items quickly and accurately, and to answer the more difficult items accurately, though not so quickly. Similarly strong relations between problem difficulty and strategy choices have been found for 4- to 12-year-olds in subtraction, multiplication, word identification, time-telling, and spelling (Geary & Burlingham-Dubree 1989; Goldman et al 1989; Siegler 1986, 1988a).

The fact that individual children of a wide range of ages use multiple strategies and choose among the strategies in adaptive ways does not mean that the particular strategy choices that children make remain constant. Children continually learn new strategies and change their frequency of use of existing strategies (Goldman et al 1989). Age-related differences are also apparent in children's transfer of recently learned strategies to new situations. Adults are more likely than fifth and sixth graders to transfer strategies, especially under conditions where no specific information about the relevance of the strategy is given (Pressley et al 1984a). This is true even when both children and adults explicitly recognize that the new strategy is more effective (Pressley et al 1984b). Older children are also more likely than younger ones to try additional strategies when their initial strategy does not produce entirely correct performance (Ceci & Howe 1978).

The Siegler (1988b) strategy-choice model illustrates how a single mechanism can give rise to both the adaptive quality of children's strategy choices at any one time and the changes in their speed, accuracy, and strategy choices that take place over time. The simulation can be divided into a representation of knowledge and a process that operates on that representation to produce performance and learning.

The representation includes knowledge of problems, of strategies, and of the interaction between problems and strategies. Knowledge of problems is represented as associations between each problem and possible answers to that problem, both correct and incorrect. For example, $5+3$ would be associated not only with 8 but also with 6, 7, and 9. These representations of knowledge of each problem can be classified along a dimension of the peakedness of the distribution of associations. In a peaked distribution, most strength is concentrated in the correct answer. At the other extreme, in a flat distribution, strength is dispersed among several answers, with none of them forming a strong peak. For example, in Figure 2, the strengths for answers to $2+1$ form a peaked distribution (with the strength for 3 at the peak) and those for $3+5$ form a flat distribution.

The simulation's representation also includes knowledge about strategies. Each time a strategy is used, the simulation gains information about that strategy's speed and accuracy. This information generates a strength for each strategy, both in general and on particular problems. The strategies modeled in the current version of the addition simulation are the three most common approaches that young children use to add: counting from one, counting from the larger number, and retrieval.

One further feature of the new simulation's representation should be mentioned. Newly generated strategies possess "novelty points" that temporarily add to their strength and thus allow them to be tried even when they have little or no track record. The strength conferred by these novelty points is gradually lost as experience with the strategy provides an increasingly informative data base about it. This feature was motivated by the view that people are often interested in exercising newly developed cognitive capabilities (Piaget 1951), and by the realization that without a track record, a newly developed strategy would be unlikely to be chosen if previously acquired strategies worked reasonably well.

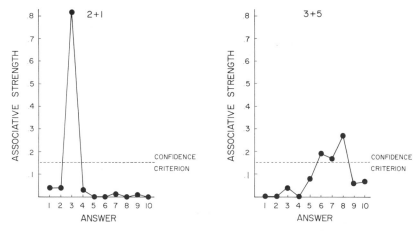

Figure 2   A peaked (*left*) and a flat (*right*) distribution of associations. The values for each answer reflect the percentage of children who stated that answer in an experiment in which children needed to state the first answer to the problem that they thought of (the retrieval-required experiment reported in Siegler 1986).

Now consider the process that operates on this representation to produce performance. First, a strategy is chosen. The probability of a given strategy being chosen is proportional to its strength relative to the strength of all strategies. (Recall that this strength reflects the speed and accuracy the strategy has generated in previous uses.) If a strategy other than retrieval is chosen, that strategy is executed. If retrieval is chosen, the simulation retrieves a specific answer (e.g. 4). Just as the probability of a given strategy being chosen is proportional to its strength relative to the strength of all strategies, the probability of any given answer being retrieved is proportional to its strength relative to the strength of all answers to the problem. Thus, in Figure 2, the connection between "2+1" and "3" has a strength of .80, the strength of connections between "2+1" and all answers is 1.00, so the probability of retrieving "3" is 80%. If the strength of whichever answer is chosen exceeds the confidence criterion (a threshold for stating a retrieved answer), the simulation states that answer. Otherwise, the simulation again cycles through the strategy-choice process; it does so until a strategy is chosen and an answer stated.

At any one time, the simulation generates patterns of accuracy, solution times, and strategy use much like those of children. For example, it counts on from the larger number most often on problems where the smaller of the two addends is small and where the difference between the two addends is large. Siegler (1987) found the same pattern in kindergarteners', first graders', and second graders' performance. Also as with children, the simulation uses retrieval most often on problems where both addends are small and uses counting from one primarily on problems where both addends are large. Relative problem difficulty and particular errors that the simulation makes also parallel those of children.

How Strategy Choices Change

The simulation learns a great deal through its experience with strategies and problems. As it gains experience, it produces faster and more accurate performance, more frequent use of retrieval, less frequent use of counting from one, and closer fitting of when strategies are used to their advantages and disadvantages on each problem. For example, the simulation's accuracy improves from 55% correct relatively early in its run to 99% correct by the end. Similarly, it progresses from using retrieval on 16% of trials at the earlier point to 99% at the end. Such learning is produced entirely through children associating strategies with the speed and accuracy that they have produced and associating answers with the problems on which those answers have been stated.

The way that this learning mechanism operates can be illustrated in the context of how some strategies come to be chosen on some problems more often than others. Consider two problems, 9+1 and 5+5. Kindergarteners and first graders count on from the larger number considerably more often on 9+1, yet count from one more often on 5+5. The simulation generates similar choices between the strategies and illustrates how such a pattern might emerge. On 9+1, counting from the larger number has a very large advantage in both speed and accuracy over counting from one. It requires only 1/10 as many counts. In contrast, the numbers of counts required to execute the two strategies are more comparable on 5+5, where counting on from the larger number requires 1/2 as many counts. If the number of counts were the only consideration, children might be expected to consistently count from the larger number on both problems (and on all problems) from the time they learned how to do so. However, for any given number of counts, counting on from an arbitrary number is considerably more difficult for young children (in terms of time and errors per count) than counting from one. The simulation's probability of erring on each count and its time per count reflect this greater difficulty of counting on from a number larger than one. Thus, the simulation learns that although counting from the larger number is generally more effective, there are some problems, such as 5+5, where counting from one works better. This leads to counting from one being the most frequent strategy on such problems for a period of time.

Eventually both counting from one and counting from the larger number are overtaken by retrieval. At the outset of the simulation, all answers to each problem have similar, minimal associations with the problem; the distribution of associations is flat. The more often that children encounter problems, and the more accurate the execution of backup strategies (strategies other than retrieval), the more the strength of the correct answer grows relatively to the strength of incorrect answers. Thus, as the simulation gains experience, the distribution becomes increasingly peaked. As discussed in detail in Siegler & Shrager (1984), the more peaked a distribution of associations, the more likely the child is to retrieve the correct answer and the more likely that answer is to exceed the confidence criterion and therefore to be stated. Thus, as children generate the correct answers to problems increasingly often, they become increasingly likely to solve the problems through retrieval.

In addition to illustrating how children in general may choose strategies, the strategy-choice model also has proved useful for analyzing individual differences. Siegler (1988c) examined first graders' consistency of strategy choices across addition, subtraction, and word-identification tasks. Cluster analyses of the children's performance suggested that they fell into three groups: "good students," "not-so-good students," and "perfectionists."

The contrast between good and not-so-good students was evident along all of the dimensions that might be expected from the names. The good students were faster and more accurate on both retrieval and backup strategy trials on all three tasks, and also used retrieval more often on all of them.

Whereas the differences between good and not-so-good students could be ascribed to simple differences in knowledge, the differences between good students and perfectionists could not be. The two groups were equally fast and accurate on both retrieval and nonretrieval trials. However, the perfectionists used retrieval significantly less often than not only the good students but even the not-so-good students.

The differences among good students, not-so-good students, and perfectionists could be interpreted in terms of two key variables within the model: the peakedness of distributions of associations, and the stringency of confidence criteria. In particular, perfectionists appeared to be children who possessed peaked distributions and who set very high confidence criteria; good students appeared to be children who also possessed peaked distributions but who set somewhat lower confidence criteria; not-so-good students appeared to be children who possessed flat distributions and set low confidence criteria. Within the computer simulation, these combinations of distributions of associations and confidence criteria produced performance much like that of the three groups of children. For example, the perfectionists' peaked distributions and high confidence criteria would lead to fast and accurate performance when they used retrieval, but also to relatively little use of retrieval.

Subsequent achievement test scores and class placements provided external validation for the experimental analysis (Siegler 1988c). Perfectionists and good students scored equally highly on standardized mathematics and reading achievement tests that were given four months after the experimental sessions; perfectionists' scores averaged at the 81st percentile, good students' at the 80th percentile. Children in both groups scored much higher than children classified as not-so-good students, whose achievement test scores averaged at the 43rd percentile. Further, 4 of the 9 children in the not-so-good students group either were assigned the next year to a learning disabilities class or retained in the first grade, versus 0 of 27 perfectionists and good students. Thus, the differences between not-so-good students and the other two groups were apparent in conventional measures of individual differences as well as within the analyses suggested by the model. However, the differences between good students and perfectionists would probably have gone undetected without the analysis of the strategy choice mechanism.

CONCLUSIONS

These ideas and results illustrate how detailed analyses of change mechanisms can contribute to understanding of cognitive development. The findings of Held and his colleagues about the perceptual experience of prestereoptic infants; those of MacWhinney and his colleagues about the learnability of the German article system on the basis of phonological, case, and lexical cues; and my own findings about the strategy choices of good students, not-so-good students, and perfectionists illustrate the nonintuitive empirical findings that can arise from such analyses. Gentner's distinction between analogies based on object and relational correspondences, Greenough's concepts of ex-perience-expectant and experience-dependent processes, and Holland's genet-ic algorithm illustrate how children can quickly acquire initial understanding of phenomena, yet take a very long time to acquire advanced understanding of them. Many of these analyses, as well as Goldman-Rakic's analysis of the development of ability to form enduring representations, illustrate how a single mechanism can contribute to a large variety of behavioral changes.

If we think about these five change mechanisms as a group, and ask what they have in common, a single theme keeps on recurring. This theme is competition. The competitions are sometimes among synaptic connections, other times among associative processing units, other times among problem-solving strategies. Sometimes they occur in the context of perceptual develop-ment, other times in language development, other times in the development of analogical reasoning and problem solving. Constant across the hypothesized mechanisms, however, are two essential features of competition: multiple competing entities and a means for choosing among them.

Consider the types of competitions that characterize the mechanisms re-viewed in this chapter. With regard to synaptogenesis, the competition in-volves an early density of synapses greater than that in mature brains. Normal experience at the normal time results in typical connections' being maintained. Abnormal experience, or lack of relevant experience, results in atypical patterns, in which synaptic connections win competitions that they ordinarily would lose. The view that neural activity determines the outcomes of synaptic competitions is evident in Greenough's experience-expectant and experience-dependent processes, and also in Held's model of the development of binocular-disparity detection cells.

Competition plays a similarly central role in connectionist models. Such models include huge numbers of connections among processing units. Back propagation provides a way of raising the strength of connections that provide useful input to units at the next higher level, and reducing the strength of connections that do not. Thus, MacWhinney (1987) had good reason to label his connectionist model of language development "The Competition Model."

Competition also plays a prominent role in ideas about how encoding might be accomplished. At any one time, a number of aspects of situations are encoded, both ones currently being used and ones that are not. Over time, encodings that prove advantageous come to be used increasingly often. For example, within Holland et al's genetic algorithm, numerous encodings compete to be the parents from which new encodings are formed. The likelihood that a given encoding becomes a parent is determined by the strength of the rule of which that encoding is a part. Rules (and encodings) that do not lead to attainment of goals lose competitions and are eventually deleted; those that prove useful are employed increasingly often.

Alternative analogies seem to compete much as alternative encodings do. An infinite number of analogies can be drawn, but only the ones that create systematic correspondences are highly evaluated. Consistent with this view, Gentner's structure-mapping engine detects a wide range of parallels between relations in base and target domains, but selects only those mappings that create the most systematic correspondences between relations in the two situations.

The whole idea of strategy choice is based on the notion of competition among multiple strategies. Rather than consistently using one strategy at an earlier age and a different strategy at a later one, children often use multiple strategies at both earlier and later ages. The Siegler strategy-choice model describes how the speed, accuracy, and answers previously generated by each strategy shape strategy choices at any one time and also lead to changes over time in which strategies are chosen.

Competition may also be at the core of another developmental mechanism not discussed here: Piaget's concept of equilibration. Within the equilibration construct, there is continuous competition between representations of new events and longer-term cognitive structures. At times of stage transition, preexisting and emerging cognitive structures also compete. The goodness of fit between the inherent structure of the environment and the child's alternative representations of the environment determines which cognitive structures prevail.

In all of these cases, competition seems to serve the same function. The multiple competing entities provide the variability needed to adapt to changing environments, contextual demands, and organismic capabilities. The selection methods produce cognitive growth by leading to greater use of those processing units that have proved useful under the particular circumstances encountered by the child. These variability and selection functions seem essential to any developing system. Thus, they may be a basic part of many, if not most, mechanisms of cognitive development.

ACKNOWLEDGMENTS

This research was supported in part by grant HD-19011 from the National Institutes of Health, in part by a grant from the Spencer Foundation, and in part by a grant from the McDonnell Foundation. Thanks are due to Robert Glaser, Patricia Goldman-Rakic, Carl Granrud, William Greenough, David Klahr, Brian MacWhinney, Jay McClelland, Mitchell Rabinowitz, and James Staszewski for comments on earlier versions of the manuscript. Request for reprints should be sent to Dr. Robert Siegler, Psychology Department, Carnegie-Mellon University, Pittsburgh, PA 15213.

Literature Cited

Anderson, J. R. 1987. Skill acquisition: Compilation of weak-method problem solutions. *Psychol. Rev.* 94:192–210

Ashcraft, M. H. 1987. Children's knowledge of simple arithmetic: A developmental model and simulation. In *Formal Methods in Developmental Psychology*, ed. J. Bisanz, C. J. Brainerd, R. Kail, pp. 302–338. New York: Springer-Verlag

Bakker, P. E., Halford, G. S. 1988. A basic computational theory of structure-mapping in analogy and transitive inference. Tech. Rep. 88/1. Australia: Univ. Queensland, Centre for Human Information Processing and Problem Solving

Bates, E., MacWhinney, B. 1987. Competition, variation, and language learning. See MacWhinney 1987, pp. 157–93

Bertenthal, B. I., Campos, J. J. 1987. New directions in the study of early experience. *Child Dev.* 58:560–67

Beveridge, M., Parkins, E. 1987. Visual representation in analogical problem solving. *Mem. Cognit.* 15:230–37

Birch, E. E., Gwiazda, J., Held, R. 1982. Stereoacuity development for crossed and uncrossed disparities in human infants. *Vis. Res.* 22:507–13

Bisanz, J. 1979. Processes and strategies in children's solutions of geometric analogies. Unpublished doctoral dissertation, Univ. Pittsburgh

Bjorklund, D. F., Jacobs, J. W. III. 1985. Associative and categorical processes in children's memory: The role of automaticity in the development of organization in free recall. *J. Exp. Child Psychol.* 39:599–617

Brody, L. R. 1981. Visual short-term cued recall memory in infancy. *Child Dev.* 52:242–50

Brown, A. L. 1989. Analogical learning and transfer: What develops? In *Similarity and Analogical Reasoning*, ed. S. Vosniadou, A. Ortony. London: Cambridge Univ. Press

Brown, A. L., Campione, J. C. 1984. Three faces of transfer: Implications for early competence, individual differences, and instruction. In *Advances in Developmental Psychology*, ed. M. Lamb, A. Brown, B. Rogoff, pp. 143–92. Hillsdale, NJ: Erlbaum

Brown, A. L., Kane, M. J., Echols, K. 1986. Young children's mental models determine analogical transfer across problems with a common goal structure. *Cognit. Dev.* 1: 103–22

Case, R. 1985. *Intellectual Development:*

Birth to Adulthood. New York: Academic

Ceci, S. J., Howe, M. 1978. Age-related differences in free recall as a function of retrieval flexibility. *J. Exp. Child Psychol.* 26:432–42

Chang, F. L., Greenough, W. T. 1982. Lateralized effects of monocular training on dendritic branching in adult split-brain rats. *Brain Res.* 232:283–92

Chang, F. L., Greenough, W. T. 1984. Transient and enduring morphological correlates of synaptic activity and efficacy change in the rat hippocampal slice. *Brain Res.* 309:35–46

Chen, Z., Daehler, M. W. 1988. Positive and negative analogical transfer in young children. Unpublished. Univ. Mass., Amherst

Crisafi, M. A., Brown, A. L. 1986. Analogical transfer in very young children: Combining two separately learned solutions to reach a goal. *Child Dev.* 57:953–68

Crnic, L. S., Pennington, B. F. 1987. Developmental psychology and the neurosciences: An introduction. *Child Dev.* 58:533–38

Cynader, M., Mitchell, D. E. 1980. Prolonged sensitivity to monocular deprivation in darkreared cats. *J. Neurophysiol.* 43:1026–1040

Davidson, J. E. 1986. The role of insight in giftedness. In *Conceptions of Giftedness,* ed. R. J. Sternberg, J. E. Davidson, pp. 201–22. New York: Cambridge Univ. Press

Diamond, A. 1985. Development of the ability to use recall to guide action, as indicated by infants' performance on AB. *Child Dev.* 56:868–83

Dodge, K. A., Pettit, G. S., McCloskey, C. L., Brown, M. M. 1986. Social competence in children. *Monogr. Soc. Res. Child Dev.* 51: Whole No. 213

Falkenhainer, B., Forbus, K. D., Gentner, D. 1986. The structure-mapping engine. In *Proceedings of the American Association for Artificial Intelligence.* Philadelphia, PA: Am. Assoc. Artificial Intelligence

Fischer, K. W. 1987. Relations between brain and cognitive development. *Child Dev.* 58:623–32

Flavell, J. H. 1984. Discussion. See Sternberg 1984, pp. 187–209

Fox, N., Kagan, J., Weiskopf, S. 1979. The growth of memory during infancy. *Genet. Psychol. Monogr.* 99:91–130

Geary, D. C., Burlingham-Dubree, M. 1989. External validation of the strategy choice model for addition. *J. Exp. Child Psychol.*

Gelman, S. 1988. The development of induction within natural kind and artifact categories. *Cogn. Psychol.* 20:65–95

Gentner, D. 1988. Metaphor as structure mapping: The relational shift. *Child Dev.* 59:47–59

Gentner, D. 1989. The mechanisms of analogical transfer. In *Similarity and Analogical Reasoning,* ed. S. Vosniadou, A. Ortony. London: Cambridge Univ. Press

Gentner, D., Landers, R. 1985. Analogical reminding: A good match is hard to find. In Proc. Int. Conf. Syst., Man, Cybernet., Tucson, AZ

Gentner, D., Toupin, C. 1986. Systematicity and similarity in the development of analogy. *Cognit. Sci.* 10:277–300

Gholson, B., Emyard, L. A, Morgan, D., Kamhi, A. G. 1987. Problem solving, recall, and isomorphic transfer among third-grade and sixth-grade children. *J. Exp. Child Psychol.* 43:227–43

Gick, M. L., Holyoak, K. J. 1980. Schema induction and analogical transfer. *Cognit. Psychol.* 15:1–38

Goldman, S. R., Pellegrino, J. W., Mertz, D. L. 1989. Extended practice of basic addition facts: Strategy changes in learning disabled students. *Cognit. Instr.* 5.

Goldman, S. R., Pellegrino, J. W., Parseghian, P. E., Sallis, R. 1982. Developmental and individual differences in verbal analogical reasoning. *Child Dev.* 53:550–59

Goldman-Rakic, P. S. 1987. Development of cortical circuitry and cognitive function. *Child Dev.* 58:601–22

Greenough, W. T., Black, J. E., Wallace, C. S. 1987. Experience and brain development. *Child Dev.* 58:539–59

Hamann, M. S., Ashcraft, M. H. 1986. Textbook presentations of the basic addition facts. *Cognit. Instr.* 3:173–92

Held, R. 1985. Binocular vision-behavioral and neuronal development. In *Neonate Cognition: Beyond the Blooming Confusion,* ed. J. Mehler, R. Fox, pp. 37–44. Hillsdale, NJ: Erlbaum.

Hinde, R. A. 1983. Ethology and child development. In *Handbook of Child Psychology,* ed. M. M. Haith, J. J. Campos, pp. 27–93. New York: Wiley

Hinton, G. E., Anderson, J. A. 1981. *Parallel Models of Associative Memory.* Hillsdale, NJ: Erlbaum

Holland, J. H. 1986. Escaping brittleness: The possibilities of general purpose machine learning algorithms applied to parallel rule-based systems. In *Machine Learning: An Artificial Intelligence Approach,* ed. R. S. Michalski, J. G. Carbonell, T. M. Mitchell, pp. 593–624. Los Altos, CA: Kaufmann

Holland, J. H., Holyoak, K. J., Nisbett, R. E., Thagard, P. R. 1986. *Induction: Processes of Inference, Learning, and Discovery.* Cambridge, MA: MIT Press

Holyoak, K. J., Junn, E. N., Billman, D. O. 1984. Development of analogical problem-solving skill. *Child Dev.* 55:2042-2055

Hubel, D. H., Wiesel, T. N. 1970. The period of susceptibility to the physiological effects of unilateral eye closure in kittens. *J. Physiol.* 206:419-36

Huttenlocher, P. R. 1979. Synaptic density in human frontal cortex-developmental changes and effects of aging. *Brain Res.* 163:195-205

Inagaki, K., Hatano, G. 1987. Young children's spontaneous personification as analogy. *Child Dev.* 58:1013-1020

Kail. R. 1986. Sources of age differences in speed of processing. *Child Dev.* 57:969-87

Klahr, D. 1984. Transition processes in quantitative development. See Sternberg 1984, pp. 101-39

Kuhn, D. 1984. Cognitive development. In *Developmental Psychology: An Advanced Textbook,* ed. M. H. Bornstein, M. E. Lamb, pp. 133-80. Hillsdale, NJ: Erlbaum

LeVay, S., Wiesel, T. N., Hubel, D. H. 1980. The development of ocular dominance columns in normal and visually deprived monkeys. *J. Comp. Neurol.* 191:1-51

Liben, L. S. 1987. *Development and Learning: Conflict or Congruence?* Hillsdale, NJ: Erlbaum

Lorsbach, T. C., Gray, J. W. 1985. The development of encoding processes in learning disabled children. *J. Learn. Disabil.* 18:222-27

MacWhinney, B., ed. 1987. *Mechanisms of Language Acquisition.* Hillsdale, NJ: Erlbaum

MacWhinney, B. 1989. Competition and teachability. In *Teachability of Language,* ed. M. Rice. London: Cambridge Univ. Press

Maratsos, M. P. 1982. The child's construction of grammatical categories. In *Language Acquisition: The State of the Art,* ed. E. Wanner, L. Gleitman, pp. 240-66. New York: Cambridge Univ. Press

Marr, D. B., Sternberg, R. J. 1986. Analogical reasoning with novel concepts: Differential attention of intellectually gifted and nongifted children to relevant and irrelevant novel stimuli. *Cognit. Dev.* 1:53-72

McClelland, J. L. 1989. Parallel distributed processing: implications for cognition and development. In *Parallel Distributed Processing: Implications for Psychology and Neurobiology,* ed. R. Morris. London: Oxford Univ. Press

McClelland, J. L., Rumelhart, D. E. 1986. *Parallel Distributed Processing: Explorations in the Microstructure of Cognition.* Cambridge, MA: MIT Press

McDonald, J. L., MacWhinney, B. 1989. Levels of learning: A comparison of concept formation and language acquisition. Un-

published manuscript, Carnegie-Mellon Univ.

Miller, P. H. 1983. *Theories of Developmental Psychology.* San Francisco: Freeman

Mower, G. D., Christen, W. G., Caplan, C. J. 1983. Very brief visual experience eliminates plasticity in the cat visual cortex. *Science* 221:178-80

O'Connor, N., Hermelin, B. 1983. The role of general ability and specific talents in information processing. *Br. J. Dev. Psychol.* 1:389-403

Palincsar, A. S., Brown, A. L. 1984. Reciprocal teaching of comprehension-monitoring activities. *Cognit. Instruct.* 1:117-75

Palmer, S. E. 1987. PDP: A new paradigm for cognitive theory. *Contemp. Psychol.* 32:925-28

Pellegrino, J. W., Goldman, S. R. 1983. Developmental and individual differences in verbal and spatial reasoning. In *Individual Differences in Cognition,* ed. R. F. Dillon, R. R. Schmeck, pp. 137-80. New York: Academic

Perner, J., Mansbridge, D. G. 1983. Developmental differences in encoding length series. *Child Dev.* 54:710-19

Piaget, J. 1951. *Play, Dreams, and Imitation in Childhood.* New York: Norton

Pinker, S. 1987. The bootstrapping problem in language acquisition. See MacWhinney 1987, pp. 399-442

Pinker, S., Prince, A. 1988. On language and connectionism: Analysis of a parallel distributed processing model of language acquisition. *Cognition* 28:73-193

Pressley, M., Levin, J. R., Ghatala, E. S. 1984. Memory strategy monitoring in adults and children. *J. Verbal Learn. Verbal Behav.* 23:270-88

Pressley, M., Ross, K. A., Levin, J. R., Ghatala, E. S. 1984. The role of strategy utility knowledge in children's strategy decision making. *J. Exp. Child Psychol.* 38:491-504

Rakic, P., Bourgeois, J.-P., Eckenhoff, M. F., Zecevic, N., Goldman-Rakic, P. S. 1986. Concurrent overproduction of synapses in diverse regions of the primate cerebral cortex. *Science* 232:232-35

Riley, C. A., Trabasso, T. 1974. Comparatives, logical structures and encoding in a transitive inference task. *J. Exp. Child Psychol.* 17:187-203

Rogoff, B. 1986. The joint socialization of development by young children and adults. In *Context of School Based Literacy,* ed. T. E. Raphael, pp. 27-40. New York: Random House

Rumelhart, D. E., McClelland, J. L. 1986. *Parallel Distributed Processing: Explorations in the Microstructure of Cognition.* Cambridge, MA: MIT Press

Seidenberg, M. S., McClelland, J. L. 1988. A distributed, developmental model of visual word recognition and naming. Unpublished manuscript.

Shimojo, S., Bauer, J. Jr., O'Connell, K. M., Held, R. 1986. Pre-stereoptic binocular vision in infants. *Vis. Res.* 26:501–10

Siegler, R. S. 1976. Three aspects of cognitive development. *Cognit. Psychol.* 8:481–520

Siegler, R. S. 1983. Five generalizations about cognitive development. *Am. Psychol.* 38:263–77

Siegler, R. S. 1986. Unities in strategy choices across domains. In *Minnesota Symposium on Child Development,* ed. M. Perlmutter, 19:1–48. Hillsdale, NJ: Erlbaum

Siegler, R. S. 1987. The perils of averaging data over strategies: An example from children's addition. *J. Exp. Psychol.: Gen.* 116:250–64

Siegler, R. S. 1988a. Strategy choice procedures and the development of multiplication skill. *J. Exp. Psychol.: Gen.* 117:258–75

Siegler, R. S. 1988b. Transitions in strategy choices. In *10th Annu. Conf. Cognit. Sci. Soc.,* pp. 11–19. Hillsdale, NJ: Erlbaum

Siegler, R. S. 1988c. Individual differences in strategy choices: Good students, not-so-good students, and perfectionists. *Child Dev.* 59:833–51

Siegler, R. S. 1989. How domain-general and domain-specific knowledge interact to produce strategy choices. *Merrill-Palmer Q.*

Siegler, R. S., Shrager, J. 1984. Strategy choices in addition and subtraction: How do children know what to do. In *Origins of Cognitive Skills,* ed. C. Sophian, pp. 229–93. Hillsdale, NJ: Erlbaum

Sophian, C. 1984. Developing search skills in infancy and early childhood. In *Origins of Cognitive Skills,* ed. C. Sophian, pp. 27–56. Hillsdale, NJ: Erlbaum

Sternberg, R. J. 1984. *Mechanisms of Cognitive Development.* New York: Freeman

Sternberg, R. J., Nigro, G. 1980. Developmental patterns in the solution of verbal analogies. *Child Dev.* 51:27–38

Sternberg, R. J., Powell, J. S. 1983. The development of intelligence. In *Handbook of Child Psychology, Vol. III,* ed. J. H. Flavell, E. M. Markman, pp. 341–419. New York: Wiley

Sternberg, R. J., Rifkin, B. 1979. The development of analogical reasoning processes. *J. Exp. Child Psychol.* 27:195–232

Taraban, R. M., McDonald, J. L., MacWhinney, B. 1989. Category learning in a connectionist model: learning to decline the German definite article. In *Milwaukee Conference on Categorization,* ed. R. Corrigan. Philadelphia: John Benjamins

Turner, A. M., Greenough, W. T. 1985. Differential rearing effects on rat visual cortex synapses. I. Synaptic and neuronal density and synapses per neuron. *Brain Res.* 329:195–203

Wiesel, T. N., Hubel, D. H. 1965. Comparison of the effects of unilateral and bilateral eye closure on cortical unit responses in kittens. *J. Neurophysiol.* 28:1029–1040

Ann. Rev. Psychol. 1989. 40:381–404

NEUROBIOLOGICAL ASPECTS OF LEARNING AND MEMORY

H. Matthies

Institute of Neurobiology and Brain Research, Academy of Sciences of the German Democratic Republic, 3090 Magdeburg, German Democratic Republic

CONTENTS

Following closely upon recent progress in the neurosciences, research on learning and memory is now experiencing a renaissance. This is at least partly due to the increasing accessibility of the cellular and molecular dimensions of life. The accumulation of new experimental results during the last decade increased the frequency of reviews in this topic that have also extended and renewed conceptual considerations (e.g. see Thompson 1986; Woody 1986; Goelet et al 1986; Bear et al 1987; Kandel 1987; Black et al 1987).

The confluence of abundant results from a broad interdisciplinary area precludes consideration of all relevant data. Therefore, I have selected for review directions of this research significant from the viewpoint of my own investigations and conceptual background.

SOME THEORETICAL PREMISES

Learning and memory exhibit several different phenomenological aspects according to the level of biological organization considered by the observer,

0066–4308/89/0201–0381$02.00

who may focus either on complex behavior and informational interaction with the environment, interneuronal communications and relationships of brain structures, or on signal processing and transduction at the cellular and molecular level. At present, the best-supported conceptual joining of these different approaches is probably connectionist theory, even if it does not meet all theoretical requirements or solve all contradictions. Such a connectivistic conception is based on premises originating from views more general and abstract than the topic of this treatise. One of these is systems theory, in which the functional structure of a system is defined by the number and properties of its elements as well as by the number and properties of their mutual relations or connections. A change of the input-output relations or behavior of a system supposes the alteration of its functional structure. However, not every change in the system necessarily results in altered behavior: The same input-output relation can be realized by different functional structures of the system.

Reifying these general rules, neuronal cells can be regarded as the main elements of the nervous system (without completely disregarding the glial cells). The synapses represent the main relations or connections of these elements of the functional structure (without neglecting other mutual interactions). Assuming that the number of neurons does not change during learning and memory formation, and that their main properties are held constant after differentiation by genomic control, a change in the functional structure to which we attribute an altered behavior after learning may be due to a change of synaptic properties or numbers.

A further consideration is related to the principal architecture of a self-organizing complex system possessing adaptive functions. With an increasing number of variable inputs from outside and an increasing number of outputs due to the increasing complexity of the system, the demands as well as the means for adaptation will exponentially develop. A corresponding addition or sequence of independent regulatory subsystems would endanger the adaptiveness of the whole organism by reason either of their mutual inhibition or of unsuitable time constants. Such problems can be overcome (a) by development of hierarchic levels of control, and (b) by formation of a multistable functional structure connecting ultrastable subsystems by means of variable relations. In terms of the nervous system, we would thus expect there to be both (a) well-controlled stable connections among neuronal elements, enabling the formation of ultrastable subprograms at different hierarchic levels of input and output control and coordination; and (b) variable connective links regulated and controlled by the activity of the system itself during signal processing. During evolution the number of such variable links considerably increased. A concomitant increase may also have occurred in the number and properties of particular mechanisms enabling such variability of connection, thus meeting the increasing demands of adaptation. It is the challenge of memory researchers to consider both general principles of information storage in the nervous system and the huge diversity of real mechanisms.

A further problem concerns the application of such terms as *information* and *signal* to different levels of biological organization. A signal as a physical or chemical entity only gains the character of information upon interaction with an individual system: The signal of a transmitter molecule conveys intercellular information when it reacts with a transmitter-sensitive cell; it obtains a qualitatively different informational content with respect to the nervous system as a whole. Information at the level of the nervous system or of the whole organism is based on the still poorly understood activity of its functional structures and cannot be reduced to the level of single elements or their specific relations. For example, memory in a behavioral sense has no neurobiological equivalent in a neuronal cell culture, which lacks the functional structure of the nervous system, even if such a preparation offers considerable advantages for examination of specific mechanisms underlying information storage in the complete system. The morphology of the brain or of partial networks no more represents a memory trace than does a biochemical event in a neuron.

Information arises only from the systemic structure in operation. But it seems dangerous and confusing to speak of "the flow of learned information from membrane to genome" (Kandel 1987). Memory formation as a result of associative learning concerns mainly the pairing of two specific signals and their quantitative and time-dependent relations. However, the resulting storage highly depends on additional influences that considerably determine its strength and duration—e.g. attention, motivation, emotion, and reward. These probably not only gradually "modulate" the specific signals, but also exert gating functions in the course of memory formation, thus enabling or avoiding the occurrence of qualitatively different kinds of information storage in some structures of the brain.

Suitable experimental models and reliable interpretation of the results are crucial. On the one hand, the simpler nervous system architectures of mollusks and insects offer several advantages in examining the mechanisms of memory. The behavior of such animals is controlled by relatively few identifiable neurons, and the genomic control of cellular and organismic functions and properties can be investigated with comparative ease. (The complexity of such systems is still much greater than originally expected.) On the other hand, cellular mechanisms, systemic structures, and functions no doubt developed during the evolution of the mammalian nervous system that do not exist in lower animals. Because phylogenetically older principles might be preserved, still meeting evolutionary demands, these two models do not exclude but rather supplement each other. In any case, we should aspire to the thorough examination of a particular model by various interdisciplanary approaches, each methodology compensating for some of the weaknesses and limitations of the others.

Attributing memory to characteristics of the neurophysiological substrate implies the localization of neuronal structures whose connectivity changes, producing new preferred pathways that finally represent a memory trace, the material basis of stored information. This suggestion does not exclude an involvement of several different substructures of the nervous system; but such a "distributed localization of the trace" must be distinguished from a "distributed memory," because in a strict sense the latter denotes a conceptual alternative to connectionist theory. However, even if we assume such a (more or less distributed) localized memory trace, the acquisition and retrieval of information stored at defined places require the involvement of additional functional substructures, if not the activity of most of the nervous system. The location of the trace (i.e. of the changed connectivity) need not be identical with that of the structures and relay stations involved in the entry and readout of information.

Therefore, the identification of the morpho-anatomical sites and a functional implication of their neuronal changes are important contributions to validation of the memory trace. Successful characterization and description of neuronal circuits representing at least necessary sites for storage processes of particular learning tasks were achieved in the last decade in the *Aplysia* model of Kandel's group (Kandel 1987), in *Hermissenda* (Alkon & Woody 1985); and also in mammalian models, as in eyelid conditioning (Thompson 1986). Also hippocampal structures have been shown to reveal intracellular processes attributed to the formation of memory traces (Matthies 1982). I intend to focus here on such mechanisms at the cellular and molecular level without particularly considering in detail the architecture of the particular networks carrying these memory traces.

An old problem in memory research concerns the existence of different kinds of memory. The solution of this problem involves primarily the viewpoint of the observer. Regarding psychological issues, memories are, for instance, distinguished according to semantic aspects, to the sensory input of information, to the functional role in information processing, or to the duration of persistence. It should be clear that these distinctions do not necessarily correspond in any case to different neurobiological mechanisms of memory formation.

Another classification comes from more biologically oriented aspects, distinguishing nonassociative memory, represented by changed responses to repeated or strong stimulation, from associative memory due to experience with particular combinations of events (and thus representing causal, spatial, or temporal relations of the organism and the environment). These two kinds of information storage correspond to different principles of interneuronal signal processing: Nonassociative learning can be regarded as learning in a single modifiable information channel, whereas associative learning represents learning from the modifiable convergence of several specific information channels (see Figure 1). It can be assumed that the neural mechanisms of nonassociative learning evolved first and that associative learning developed later by involvement of additional, but already existing, intracellular signaling systems. However, new neuron-specific mechanisms may have evolved to transform the increased complexity of extracellular signals that occur with associative learning into a corresponding intracellular network of metabolic signals differently controlling the function at diverse spots and with different time course. Such a possibility is supported by references to quantitative and qualitative particularities of neuronal gene expression, gene products, and neuron-specific proteins (Sutcliffe et al 1984).

SHORT-TERM AND LONG-TERM STORAGE IN THE NERVOUS SYSTEM

Another commonly accepted distinction—that between short-term (STM) and long-term memory (LTM)—derives from the classical studies of Ebbinghaus at the end of the last century and from the investigations of Müller & Pilzecker (1900). These researchers suggested that after information was stored in the STM, certain time-dependent processes were necessary to consolidate a long-term trace. They also found that during STM and consolidation of LTM the trace was very sensitive to various interventions; but when memory was consolidated, it is relatively stable and insensitive to disturbance. Numerous studies in animals using different kinds of experimental influences confirmed these suggestions and elucidated more precisely the time course of both STM and the consolidation of LTM (Duncan 1949; Flexner et al 1963; McGaugh 1966; Agranoff et al 1967; Barondes & Cohen 1967; Bennett et al 1977; Flood et al 1986). However, some results also indicated that during consolidation of LTM, retention fluctuates (Kamin 1957, 1963); STM obviously disappears before the final formation of the long-term trace, suggesting the necessity of an intermediate stage of memory (ITM). These observations led to hypotheses of three- or four-stage formation of memory, which were further supported by corresponding experimental data (Matthies 1974; Gibbs & Ng 1976; Ott & Matthies 1978; Frieder & Allweis 1982). These investigations, which also demonstrated the dependence of LTM formation on intact protein systhesis in the brain during a small time window during and after learning, produced the proposal that the time course and sensitivity of the three memory stages may reflect corresponding properties of underlying cellular processes and mechanisms in various neuronal structures and compartments. This view, consonant with the connectionist conception of memory, resulted in the sugges-

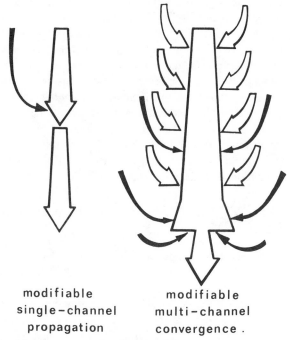

modifiable   modifiable
single-channel   multi-channel
propagation   convergence .

Figure 1   Signal flow in two examples of nonassociative and associative learning, respectively.
Big arrows: specific (sensory) signals; black arrows: modulating or modifying signals (nociception, emotion, motivation, reward, etc).

tion of a synaptic, a synaptosomal or ribosomal, and a nuclear regulation of neuronal connectivity representing mechanisms of STM, ITM, and LTM, respectively (Matthies 1972, 1974).

The dependence of LTM formation on macromolecular synthesis was demonstrated not only by its suppression by inhibitors, but also by numerous experimental data revealing an increase of RNA-, protein, and glycoprotein synthesis during acquisition and for some time after learning (for review see Dunn 1980). Contradictory results showing only limited biochemical changes hardly detectable by the available methods were probably due to unsuitable behavioral models. Careful systematic studies determining the time course of macromolecular changes for several hours after memory acquisition with radiochemical and microautoradiographic methods revealed not only an increased incorporation of RNA-, protein-, and glycoprotein precursors, but the occurrence of two subsequent peaks: one, comprised mainly of soluble proteins very early during and immediately after learning; and a late increase mainly in the formation of insoluble proteins, arising about 5–7 hr after training (Popov et al 1975). The separate inhibition of each phase of increased protein synthesis resulted in a significant loss of long-term memory (Grechsck & Matthies 1980).

A similar biphasic synthesis was observed using labeled ^{3}H-fucose as precursor to determine glycoprotein synthesis (Popov et al 1976). This finding gained further significance, where it was found that such increased glycoprotein formation occurred after learning but not after electrical stimulation of the same structures without behavioral relevance. Protein synthesis increased, however, after both experimental procedures (Jork et al 1978). These results suggest that induction of several stages of macromolecular synthesis and processing depends on the kind of systemic activity, and that control of glycoprotein formation is related to long-term information storage in the nervous system.

INFORMATION STORAGE IN THE NERVOUS SYSTEM OF MOLLUSKS

Both nonassociative and associative memory formation have been extensively investigated in mollusks, taking advantage of the relatively simple architecture of their nervous systems (for review see Farley & Alkon 1985; Byrne 1985; Kandel 1987). In studies on sensitization of sensory synaptic connections, LTM was likewise separated from STM because only the former is prevented by inhibitors of either protein or RNA synthesis. Earlier conclusions from learning experiments on mammals with regard to the involvement of "nuclear regulation" thus gained support (Montarolo et al 1986). Furthermore, this suppression of LTM formation in *Aplysia* requires an inhibition of macromolecular synthesis only during a short period related to acquisition, as already observed in several experiments on mammals (Bennett et al 1977; Flood et al 1986; Grecksch & Matthies 1980). The existence of the intermediate (ITM) stage observed in mammals was either overlooked or not considered in these studies on mollusks. Nevertheless, these investigations provided important data and suggestions of general significance for the understanding of information storage in nervous systems. It was shown that serotonin or other mediators released by facilitating neurons activate a transmitter-sensitive adenylate cyclase in the sensory presynaptic terminal, thus increasing intracellular cAMP. In this way, cAMP-dependent protein kinases become activated that subsequently modify membrane proteins by phosphorylation. It was suggested that their alteration directly or indirectly results in a closure of K^+ channels in the sensory neurons, which leads to an increase of their excitability, to a prolongation of their action potentials, and to a concomitant increase of Ca^{2+} currents. The resulting increase of intracellular free Ca^{2+} could enhance transmitter mobilization and maintain an enhancement of transmitter release, probably by involvement of protein kinase C–dependent reactions. These principal mechanisms elucidated in *Aplysia* (Kandel 1987) represent a presynaptic facilitation underlying both sensitization and associative learning (Figure 2). Several studies had already indicated that second messenger–mediated reactions directly alter ion fluxes and excitability by an interaction with ion channels. A serotonin-dependent increase of cAMP increased the number of functional channels for anomalous rectifier current (Gunning 1987). The K^+-dependent Ca^{2+} influx of PC 12 clonal cells is reduced by calmodulin inhibitors, but not by protein kinase C inhibitors, suggesting a direct or indirect contribution of Ca-calmodulin-dependent events (Greenberg et al 1987). However, in *Aplysia* bag cell neurons, stimulation of protein kinase C seems to unmask covert calcium channels (Strong et al 1987), again indicating the diversity of these intracellular regulatory systems in different cell types and species. It was also shown that phosphorylation and dephosphorylation of ion channels obviously regulates their response to membrane depolarization (Armstrong & Eckert 1987).

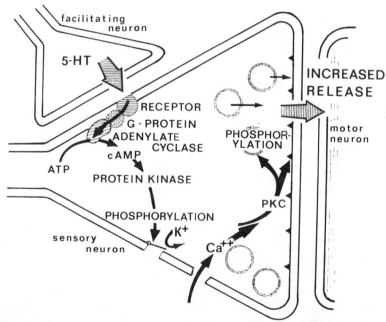

Figure 2 Intracellular processes underlying nonassociative memory formation (according to Kandel 1987).

HIPPOCAMPAL LONG-TERM POTENTIATION AS A MODEL OF MEMORY FORMATION

In mammals, another presumptive mechanism for information storage in the nervous system was found when Bliss & Lomo (1973) discovered hippocampal posttetanic long-term potentiation. This kind of relatively long-lasting synaptic functional change does not represent a presynaptic facilitation, but rather neuronal plasticity at the pre- and postsynaptic level of convergent dendritic inputs. Present knowledge favors a monosynaptic change of glutamatergic transmission, though the contribution of additional aminergic influences to this kind of synaptic potentiation and its maintenance has yet to be elucidated.

There is now agreement about a particular role of N-methyl-D-aspartate (NMDA) receptors in the induction of hippocampal posttetanic long-term potentiation (LTP) (Collingridge & Bliss 1987). This subtype of glutamate receptors seems not to contribute to the production of EPSPs, as the quisqualate and kainate subtypes obviously do. But in Mg^{2+}-free solution, NMDA components can be detected in synaptic transmission (Coan & Collingridge 1987); and further investigations revealed that Mg^{2+} blocks NMDA-receptor-coupled ion channels in a voltage-dependent manner (Novak et al 1984), suggesting that NMDA-mediated responses occur only with coincident depolarization or when the Mg^{2+} blockade is temporarily alleviated during high-frequency stimulation (Herron et al 1986). Therefore, a relatively specific antagonist of NMDA-receptors, D-2-amino-5-phosponovalerate (APV), which does not influence synaptic transmission as does the quisqualate-receptor antagonist γ-D-glutamylglycine (DGG), reversibly blocks the induction of posttetanic LTP (Collingridge et al 1983). It should be mentioned in this connection that NMDA receptors dispose of additional binding sites, also influencing channel functions. Glycin potentiates the NMDA response by a receptor different from the strychnine receptor (Johnson & Ascher 1987), and Phencyclidine, Ketamine, and sigma opiates suppress the NMDA-mediated synaptic transmission and prevent LTP by interaction with particular binding sites (Stringer et al 1983).

It is also commonly accepted that the opening of voltage-dependent channels by NMDA results in further depolarization and in an increase of Ca^{2+} influx, thus initiating and amplifying intracellular signals and finally maintaining LTP. Such a critical role of Ca^{2+} was supported by the observation of the calcium dependency of LTP (Wigström et al 1979), the blockade of LTP by intracellular injection of calcium-chelating EGTA (Lynch et al 1983), the increase of calcium deposits in the dendritic structures after induction of LTP (Kuhnt et al 1985), and the production of LTP-like synaptic enhancement by short pulses of elevated Ca^{2+} concentration in the incubation medium (Turner et al 1982). Even if long-lasting effects were not obtained in each case (Melchers et al 1987), systematic long-term experiments in vitro demonstrated that calcium-induced LTP in CA1 cells can be maintained for longer than 8 hr (Reymann et al 1986). However, the events following the initiation of LTP that maintain the synaptic enhancement are not yet fully understood. Even if some mechanisms and electrophysiological data clearly point to the involvement of postsynaptic processes, the pre- or a postsynaptic location of mechanisms underlying long-term potentiation remains controversial. Dolphin et al (1982) obtained an increased release of glutamate newly synthesized from the preloaded tritium-labeled precursor glutamine. The presence of glutamate antagonists during tetanization prevented the initiation of LTP (Dunwiddie et al 1978; Krug et al 1982), indicating a postsynaptic contribution to LTP, although another study suggested that the blockade of glutamate receptors only masks rather than prevents LTP (Dolphin 1983). The inhibition of both LTP and increased transmitter release by the NMDA antagonist APV (Errington et al 1987) and the increase of transmitter release after induction of LTP by phorbol esters (Malenka et al 1987) also support the assumption that an increased glutamate release is mainly responsible for the maintenance of LTP. However, the augmented release after treatment with phorbol ester seems to last only about 10 min (Aniksztein et al 1987); and other experimental data evidence an increased but gradually diminishing release of glutamate for 3 hr at most, thus not exclusively explaining the much longer duration of LTP, but rather indicating its contribution to an early maintenance. Therefore, postsynaptic events must be considered in any case for an understanding of long-term potentiation.

This consideration as well as the assumed role of LTP as a mnemonic device raised the question of whether sequential changes and stages can be observed during the time course of LTP that are similar to those that occur during memory formation in behavioral experiments. STM and LTM were distinguished by the dependence of the latter on protein synthesis, and a corresponding influence of protein synthesis inhibitors was obtained in LTP experiments. The presence of anisomycin during tetanization of the perforant path did not prevent the initiation of LTP in the rat dentate area, but resulted in a gradual decrease of EPSP- and population spike–potentiation in the course of 3–7 hr after induction (Krug et al 1984). In CA1 cells in vitro, Stanton & Sarvey (1984) obtained an immediate suppression of LTP by emetine but only weak effects of anisomycin. However, they produced only a relatively short LTP of about 5 hr, probably owing to the low frequency of tetanization; thus they did not obtain the induction of the true anisomycin-sensitive late LTP. The relatively early suppression by emetine may not be due to its inhibition of protein synthesis, but rather to side effects of the substance related to mechanisms of an early maintenance of LTP. A gradual suppression by anisomycin was also observed by Otani et al (1988), who further showed that inhibitors of RNA synthesis seem not to impair long-term potentiation. In long-term experiments on CA1 in vitro, using high-frequency tetanization (100 Hz) to produce LTP for more than 10 hr, anisomycin treatment during and some time after induction did not affect initiation and early maintenance of LTP but suppressed both EPSP- and population spike–potentiation in the course of 2–7 hr (Frey et al 1988a). It was also shown that the time course of EPSP-potentiation in CA1 dendrites separated from their cell bodies as the main site of protein synthesis exhibited the same decay as in intact CA1 slices after anisomycin treatment (Frey et al 1988b). These results strongly suggest that a late maintenance of posttetanic LTP requires protein synthesis during a time window after tetanization. This suggestion is supported by the observation of an increased protein synthesis in the rat dentate area after tetanization of the perforant path (Lössner et al 1987). However, this LTP-related increase of protein synthesis did not reveal the biphasic enhancement observed in some hippocampal structures after learning.

Other mechanisms contributing to the maintenance of LTP are obviously related to protein kinase C (PKC). It was shown that PKC is translocated to synaptic membranes in the course of the first hour after induction of LTP in vivo (Akers et al 1986). Redistribution to the cytosolic compartment was related to the persistence of potentiation. The injection of PKC into hippocampal pyramidal cells produces features of long-term potentiation (Hu et al 1987). PKC-activating phorbol esters induce a LTP-like potentiation (Malenka et al 1986). On the other hand, the presence of PKC inhibitors during tetanization does not prevent the initiation, but eliminates the maintenance of LTP in the dentate area in vivo (Lovinger et al 1987) as well as in CA1 cells in vitro (Reymann et al 1988b). The application of the inhibitor 4 hr after tetanization does not affect the potentiation, thus indicating a transient role of PKC as an intraneuronal signal. The PKC inhibitor polymyxin B suppressed EPSP-potentiation in CA1 cells more quickly than did anisomycin; the potentiation of the population spike was also diminished in the course of 1 hr, but the inhibition remained only incomplete during the following 6 hr, probably indicating the involvement of different PKC-dependent processes in the potentiation of EPSP and population spike, respectively. One such pathway seems to result in the phosphorylation of the membrane protein F1 (B50), which is directly related to long-term potentiation (Lovinger et al 1986; Gispen 1986). This protein seems to be involved in presynaptic transmitter availability and release and was found to be identical with a growth-associated protein (Snipes et al 1987).

The observation of a potentiating effect of oleate on long-term potentiation (Linden et al 1987) led to a hypothesis of a PKC-dependent pathway supporting the maintenance of LTP. According to this suggestion, high-frequency stimulation and the resulting increase of intracellular Ca^{2+} triggers phospholipase A–mediated oleate release. The free oleate then could prolong the activation of PKC, thus enabling a long maintenance of LTP. However, because the time courses of the polymyxin B–insensitive and anisomycin-insensitive potentiations are clearly different, a PKC-related stage must exist that is not dependent on protein synthesis. This suggests that a PKC-dependent mechanism supports an intermediate maintenance rather than a persisting LTP. This mechanism could be related to the phosphorylation of the F1 protein, as proposed by Routtenberg; but it would not necessarily support his suggestion that phosphorylation is critical for persistence of LTP; this seems on the contrary to require the synthesis of new proteins and not only the phosphorylation of already existing synaptic membrane constituents. Such a consideration does not exclude an additional role of PKC in the late long-term potentiation. This kinase is a multifunctional enzyme obviously involved not only in the more intensely investigated phosphorylation of synaptic proteins but also in the control of genomic expression and in further processing of proteins at the translational and posttranslational level. With regard to a memory trace that may last for life, the involvement of newly synthesized proteins (a so-to-speak activity-dependent correction of differentiation in reconstructing synaptic functional structures) seems to be more plausible than the more or less reversible phosphorylation of existing macromolecules, although autophosphorylation of kinases and other mechanisms to prolong the phosphorylated state of proteins can be hypothesized. Another hypothesis concerning the modification of proteins as a mechanism of LTP and the formation of memory suggests an activation of proteases due to the increased CA^{2+} influx during tetanization. In this way, glutamate receptors bound to the cytoskeleton in subsynaptic structures become unmasked, thus enhancing subsequent synaptic responses by reason of an increased number of glutamate binding sites (Baudry et al 1981; Lynch et al 1982). Such an increase of glutamate binding, however, was not confirmed by other investigations (Sastry & Goh 1984; Lynch et al 1985). It is not yet clear whether methodological differences account for these controversial results.

The slow onset of phorbol ester–induced LTP (Malenka et al 1986; Reymann et al 1988a) and PKC-translocation after tetanization (Akers et al 1986), as well as the corresponding delayed action of PKC inhibitors, which do not prevent the induction and very early maintenance of LTP, raise the question of whether other signaling systems are involved in these initial processes. For example, calmodulin, too, seems to increase Ca^{2+} influx due to NMDA-receptor activation. It was shown by Mody et al (1984) that neuroleptics inhibit both EPSP- and population spike–potentiation. This effect was explained by an interaction with calmodulin rather than by the dopaminolytic properties to these drugs. Indeed, a complete prevention of EPSP-potentiation and a rapid suppression of a weak initial population spike–potentiation was also obtained in the presence of the more specific inhibitor calmidazolium (Reymann et al 1988b). These results were further supported by the immunochemical determination of a rapid translocation of calmodulin to membranes during the first 30 min after tetanization and of a redistribution to the cytosolic compartment during the following 3–4 hr (Popov et al 1988). It can be assumed that (a) either a Ca^{2+}-calmodulin-dependent kinase or the activation of adenylate cyclase by Ca^{2+}-calmodulin, (b) the subsequent increase of cAMP, and (c), the resulting activation of cAMP-dependent kinases initially phosphorylate ion channels or other membrane constituents, thus enabling the increased responsiveness of postsynaptic neurons or leading to alterations of presynaptic functions.

Reviewing the results on signaling systems and other mechanisms of LTP, there is increasing evidence that posttetanic long-term potentiation is not established by a single process. Rather, it results from the cooperation of various functional principles, probably pre- and postsynaptically localized and revealing different time courses of formation and decay, which produce a sequence of stages similar to those observed in memory formation (Matthies 1988). This suggestion implies that the conditions and properties of LTP observed soon after tetanization are not necessarily those that obtain at later stages. This can be verified only in long-term experiments, just as LTM can only be determined several hours after learning.

A surprising support of this view could be obtained by comparing the time course of LTP after treatment with different inhibitors with the retention curves of a conditioned odor-discrimination task among different *Drosophila* mutants (Tully 1987) (Figure 3). The wild type Can-S exhibits a retention curve that corresponds completely to the decay of LTP after anisomycin treatment (and similarly the retention curve observed after posttrial ECS or anisomycin treatment in several learning experiments on vertebrates). This suggests that *Drosophila* probably do not possess an anisomycin-sensitive, protein synthesis–dependent true long-term memory. The amnesiac and turnip mutants, which do reliably learn the conditioned odor avoidance, show an immediate but not complete loss of retention, thus revealing a time course similar to that of population spike-potentiation after inhibition of protein kinase C by polymyxin B. Indeed, in the turnip mutant, PKC activity is eliminated. On the other hand, in the amnesiac mutant, normal monoamine-stimulated adenylate cyclase and protein phosphorylation could be detected, thus probably indicating their role in initial learning. A very poor learning ability and consequently no retention was observed in the rutabaga and dunce mutants, thus exhibiting a curve similar to that obtained after tetanization in the presence of the calmodulin inhibitor calmidazolium. Actually, the rutabaga mutant shows a deficit in membrane-bound Ca^{2+}-calmodulin-sensitive adenylate cyclase and a reduced stimulation by forskolin, resulting in an abnormally low cAMP level. On the other hand, the dunce mutant is characterized by deficient Ca^{2+}-calmodulin-dependent and cAMP-dependent phosphodiesterases, therefore exhibiting an abnormal high cAMP level. In any case, both mutants seem to have in common disturbances of calmodulin-dependent processes.

While this comparative consideration, along with the results and conclusions of Kandel and his colleagues (Kandel 1987), suggests common roots for information storage in the nervous systems of animals from different phylogenetic branches, it also indicates some diversities between species, which may also exist between different neuronal subsystems of the same animal. Phylogenetically early mechanisms can be conserved when they

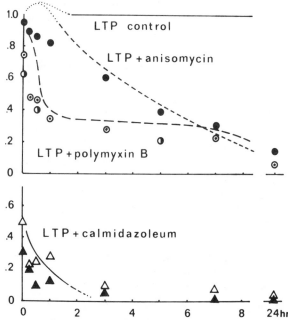

Figure 3   Time courses of long-term potentiation (LTP), shown as fraction of population spike (ordinate), plotted for rat hippocampal CA1 cells in vitro after tetanization in the presence of the protein synthesis inhibitor anisomycin (Frey et al 1988)(- - - - -), of the protein kinase C inhibitor polymyxin B (Reymann et al 1988) (— — — —), and of the calmodulin inhibitor calmidazoleum (Reymann et al 1988) (———, lower graph). These are compared with time courses of retention of conditioned odor avoidance by wild type Can-S *Drosophila* (black circles), and by mutants amnesiac (dotted circles), turnip (half-black circles), and, in the lower graph, rutabaga (open triangles) and dunce (black triangles) (Tully 1987).

continue to meet functional demands, even if selection has favored more efficient principles and functions in other parts of the same system. The existence of such differences have been observed, for instance, when comparing the effect of the NMDA antagonist APV in different experimental models. An inhibition of LTP was obtained in hippocampal granular cells and in CA1 pyramidal cells, as well as in neocortical neurons (Artola & Singer 1987). LTP in CA3 cells from the commissural input can also be blocked by NMDA, but not the potentiation from the mossy fiber input to the same cells (Harris & Cotman 1986). Such differences in LTP mechanisms are also reflected in different effects of antagonists on learning and memory. Morris et al (1986) demonstrated that long-term intraventricular infusion of the NMDA blocker APV selectively impairs place learning on rats without affecting visual discrimination learning.

CELLULAR EVENTS IN A BEHAVIORAL CONTEXT

This study underlines also the necessity to elucidate more precisely the role of LTP in a behavioral context. The assumption that hippocampal long-term potentiation is a mechanism of long-term memory was due mainly to the exceptionally long duration of this functional synaptic change. Most of the innumerable investigations on this experimentally induced phenomenon reiterated this assumption, thus inspiring little by little the impression that it was already a matter of fact. However, relatively few studies have been done to relate LTP and memory formation and to determine its contribution to different kinds of memory.

Some investigations were done to determine the effect of learning procedures or environmental influences on evoked potentials in hippocampal pathways known to produce posttetanic long-term potentiation. An increase of excitability of commissural-CA1 synapses could be observed after continuous reinforcement during bar-press operant conditioning (Jaffard & Jeantet 1981). The changes occurred only in animals that could learn the task, but they were only transient. A longer-lasting increase of the population spike of test potentials in the dentate gyrus of rabbits was observed after conditioning the airpuff response of the nictitating membrane to tone (Thompson 1982). Similar increases of granular-cell responsivity as measured by population spike potentiation also occurred over the course of training in an appetitively motivated discriminated operant task; the increases persisted for some days (Skelton et al 1987). Also, the exposure of rats to a novel complex environment resulted in an enhancement of field potentials in the dentate area (Sharp et al 1985). In hippocampal slices from rats reared for 3–4 weeks in a complex environment, the transmission at perforant path–granular cell synapses was enhanced. This change persisted for a maximum of three weeks, thus corresponding to posttetanic LTP with regard to duration (Green & Greenough 1986).

The increased glutamate release found in stimulated hippocampal slices from rats following classical conditioning of the animals was interpreted in terms of an LTP-like synaptic potentiation occurring with learning and memory formation (Laroche et al 1987). Another indirect evidence for LTP-like events in classical conditioning was obtained with the observation of an increased glutamate receptor binding in hippocampal synaptic membranes after eyelid conditioning in rabbits (Mamounas et al 1984), considering in this case corresponding changes after induction of LTP or after transient exposure to high concentrations of glutamate (Lynch et al 1982; Kessler et al 1986). However, these considerations only demonstrated a correlation between different behavioral changes and functional alterations of hippocampal synapses. Their necessary involvement in the formation of memory or in the underlying long-term trace was not definitively proved, because accompanying alterations may also transiently occur in several other neuronal connections.

A closer relation between learning and LTP-like synaptic changes was obtained in those tasks in which the same stimulating electrode located in the perforant path was used to evoke test potentials in the dentate gyrus as well as to deliver conditioning stimuli in a learning procedure. In this way, functional changes could be determined in a synaptic population that was necessarily involved in the conditioning pathway. This principle was used by Skelton et al (1985) to develop a paradigm with rats, in which single-pulse stimulation of the perforant path could acquire increasing control over operant responses in the course of about 8 days. However, they did not obtain a clear correlation of the induced behavior to the change of the population-spike amplitude. High-frequency prestimulation 2 hr before the first learning session, producing a weak LTP of about 20%, resulted in a considerable delay ($\sim$ 10 days) in the onset of learning, after which the animals clearly exhibited an increase of the discrimination ratio. In rats (serving as controls) with low-frequency prestimulation, no considerable responding occurred even after 17 days of training. It was suggested that LTP-producing prestimulation accelerates acquisition, but this was only true in comparison to low-frequency prestimulation; in controls without any pretreatment, acquisition was delayed and did not correlate in any case with the early increase of the population spike.

It is difficult to explain these conflicting data, but it can be assumed that the single-pulse stimulation as CS is not a reliable signal. Consider the effects of different stimulus parameters observed in the study of Reymann et al (1982). A conditioned active avoidance was developed in rats in a shuttle box using stimulation of the perforant path as CS. This was done not only to investigate synaptic changes during learning, but also to follow the functional alterations during consolidation of memory for several hours after a training session. It was found that stimulation with single impulses (1.7 Hz) did not result in reliable learning, but impulse trains of 15 and 100 Hz, respectively, yielded successful conditioning in sessions of 40 trials. During learning, the population spike of test potentials decreased, whereas the field EPSP increased, but only in good learners (Ott et al 1982). After the training session, the depressed population spike recovered in good learners in the course of 1 hr and then increased beyond baseline in the course of 4 hr, remaining significantly enhanced for more than 24 hr. However, in poor learners, the amplitude of the population spike did not completely return to baseline after learning; a long-term depression occurred in these animals. The field EPSP, not suppressed after learning, increased in the course of 4–6 hr after the learning session in good learners, exhibiting also a significant enhancement for more than 24 hr. On the contrary, poor learners showed a decrease after training and a long-lasting depression of the EPSP component of the evoked test potentials (Matthies et al 1986).

The selective destruction of granular cells after intrahippocampal application of colchicine by an injectrode prevented conditioning by perforant-path stimulation but not by light and tone, thus demonstrating the necessary involvement of the perforant path–granular cell synapses in this conditioning procedure, using perforant-path stimulation as CS (Rüthrich et al 1987). In control animals, conditioning with the sensory cues also resulted in a long-term potentiation of the population spike of test potentials in the dentate area after training, but without changes of the field EPSP. Sessions with corresponding unpaired perforant-path stimulation and sensory cues, respectively, did not influence the test potentials during the following 24 hr.

The individual differences between good and poor learners, corresponding in both learning and posttraining changes of test potentials, were not due to an unreliable location of electrodes, because their implantation sites were determined and controlled by evoked test potentials. It could be shown in another study that these individual differences also corresponded to the degree of posttetanic potentiation. Rats exhibiting a very pronounced potentiation of both EPSP and population spike after tetanization with impulse trains of 200 Hz showed high learning scores and a pronounced postconditioning synaptic enhancement in a learning session performed 3 days later, after disappearance of LTP. However, rats without (or with a weak) posttetanic potentiation could be classified as poor learners according to the criteria used in the previous studies. They exhibited a corresponding depression of postconditioning test potentials (Rüthrich et al 1987).

The results obtained with this experimental paradigm obviously demonstrated close correlations between (a) learning ability and formation of a longer-lasting memory and (b) the ability to change the responsiveness of hippocampal cells. This individual ability obviously corresponds to the power to develop posttetanic LTP. However, potentiation of the field EPSP in the dentate area seems only to occur when the synapses under investigation are carrying the conditioning signal, whereas potentiation of the population spike develops with any other conditioning stimuli in this task. LTP-like postsynaptic changes seem actually to be involved in more or less long-lasting memory traces. However, considering the relatively rapid onset of posttetanic LTP and the slow *gradual* development of postconditioning synaptic enhancement, some differences seem to exist. These became evident also when studying the incorporation of ^{3}H-fucose into hippocampal structures in these conditions: (*a*) after high-frequency stimulation of the perforant path, producing LTP; (*b*) after conditioning with perforant-path stimulation as CS; and (*c*) after corresponding control stimulations (Pohle et al 1987). A significant increase of incorporation occurred in all hippocampal neurons only after the learning procedure; no significant changes (as compared to control stimulation) were observed after LTP-producing tetanization. These results correspond to those obtained with brightness-discrimination learning in comparison to septal stimulation of the hippocampus in rats (Jork et al 1978), which showed an increased incorporation of labeled leucine after both procedures, whereas only after the learning experiment was there an increased incorporation of fucose into hippocampal proteins. Therefore, posttetanic LTP is probably a component of trace formation, but seems not to represent the complete long-term trace. Its duration additionally raises the question of whether LTP contributes to a permanent trace or only to a longer-lasting but nevertheless transient kind of information storage (Racine et al 1983).

THE FURTHER REFINING OF A PREVIOUS MODEL

The observations reviewed above, together with recent results on the genomic control in neuronal cells may allow us to complete a previous model of cellular events underlying the formation of long-term traces in associative learning in mammals (Figure 4). According to this model, specific inputs to an integrating principal cell may mediate CS and UCS inputs by glutamatergic terminals. Additional inputs converge on this neuron, thus enabling the action of such other influences as motivation, emotion, attention, and reward, which are probably mediated by cholinergic, aminergic, or peptidergic fibers. CS activation produces an LTP-like facilitation, if depolarization and action potential of the principal cell are subsequently induced by UCS. Ca-calmodulin-dependent processes seem to be involved in this initiation of synaptic changes. The concomitant increased Ca^{2+}-influx as well as increased cAMP formation and activation of protein kinase C due to the additional inputs may prolong and amplify the facilitation of the CS synapses as well as induce different changes in the genomic control and in processing of proteins

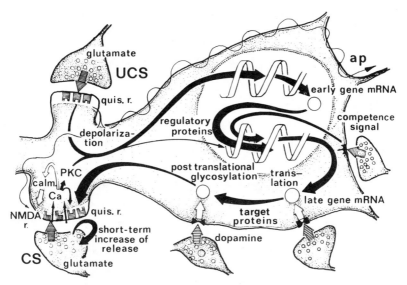

Figure 4   Model of intracellular signaling in an associative neuron with converging specific sensory as well as modifying inputs. ap, action potential; calm., calmodulin; PKC, protein kinase C; quis. r., quisqualate receptors; NMDA r., NMDA receptors

at the translational and posttranslational levels. In this way, the strength and duration of altered neuronal connectivity can be controlled in gating subsequent stages of memory formation according to signal processing during acquisition. The formation of long-term memory traces requires the induction of a transient change of genomic control by a particular set of second messenger–mediated intracellular signals. They may primarily induce an early gene expression of specific proto-oncogenes, as recently observed with the induction of c-fos proteins by chemically produced seizures and after kindling, respectively (Dragunow & Robertson 1987a, b). A transient expression of c-fos proto-oncogene in the rat hippocampus could be recently observed both after tetanization of the perforant path and in a conditioned active avoidance task, but not in the corresponding control experiments (Laszek et al 1988). The translation of these gene products into nuclear regulatory proteins is probably represented by the early wave of soluble protein synthesis after learning (Popov et al 1975; Lössner et al 1987) or after neuronal stimulation. Additional competence signals (e.g. induced by mediation of reward inputs) enable a late gene expression to produce functional or target proteins during the corresponding late wave of protein synthesis after learning. The effective proteins can be finally completed by posttranslational glycosylation under the control of dopaminergic influences (Jork et al 1982a,

b) before finally reaching distal synapses by dendritic transport. The incorporation of these newly synthesized glycoproteins into the structures of those CS synapses that were previously facilitated by LTP-like changes during learning may finally fix this activated state. It could be speculated that such a permanent increase of efficiency can be obtained either by additional incorporation of receptors or other membrane constituents responsible for synaptic response, or by completing such constituents and thus increasing their functional capability. The persistence of such a changed synaptic molecular architecture may be warranted by the common rules of cellular protein renewal. The occurrence of only an early wave of increased protein synthesis after LTP-producing tetanization (Lössner et al 1987) may be explained by the lack of additional convergent signals arising in learning-related signal processing. These may be necessary as competence signals or may induce in another way the increased formation and subsequent processing of macromolecules represented by the second wave of enhanced protein synthesis and glycosylation observed after learning.

This principle of "complex subcellular integration of converging extracellular signals" enables a long-lasting or persisting functional change of single synapses of a neuron without a permanent change of genomic expression. In this way, a pattern of systemic activity is transformed into a corresponding pattern of intracellular metabolic steps controlling macromolecular synthesis, processing, and transport as well as the final localization of resulting synaptic changes. This principle also enables a neuron to be involved either transiently or permanently in numerous different preferred pathways and memory traces.

This concept is sketchy; further experimental research will verify and complete, or falsify, its single components. Nevertheless, that it is possible to outline such a model at present demonstrates the progress made recently in this fascinating field of science.

Literature Cited

Agranoff, B. W., Davis, R. E., Casola, L., Lim, R. 1967. Actinomycin blocks formation of memory of shock-avoidance in goldfish. *Science* 158:1600–1

Akers, R. F., Lovinger, D. M., Colley, P. A., Linden, D. J., Routtenberg, A. 1986. Translocation of protein kinase C activity may mediate hippocampal long-term potentiation. *Science* 231:587–89

Alkon, D. L., Woody, C. D., eds. 1985. *Neural Mechanisms of Conditioning.* New York: Plenum

Aniksztein, L., Roisin, M. P., Gozlan, H., Ben-Ari, A. 1987. Long-lasting potentiation produced by a phorbol ester in the hippocampus of the anaesthetized rat is not associated with a persistent enhanced release of excitatory amino acid. *Neurosci. Lett.* 81:291–95

Armstrong, D., Eckert, R. 1987. Voltage-activated calcium channels that must be phosphorylated to respond to membrane depolarization. *Proc. Natl. Acad. Sci. USA* 84:2518–22

Artola, A., Singer, W. 1987. Long-term potentiation and NMDA receptors in rat visual cortex. *Nature* 330:649–52

Barondes, S. H., Cohen, H. D. 1967. Comparative effects of cycloheximide and puromycin on cerebral protein synthesis and consolidation of memory in mice. *Brain Res.* 4:44–51

Baudry, M., Bundman, M. C., Smith, E. K., Lynch, G. S. 1981. Micromolar calcium stimulates proteolysis and glutamate binding in rat brain synaptic membranes. *Science* 212:937–38

Bear, M. F., Cooper, L. N., Ebner, F. F. 1987. A physiological basis for a theory of synapse modification. *Science* 237:42–48

Bennett, E. L., Rosenzweig, M. R., Flood, J. F. 1977. Protein synthesis and memory studied with anisomycin. In *Mechanisms, Regulation and Special Function of Protein Synthesis in the Brain* ed. S. Roberts, et al. pp. 319–30. Amsterdam Elsevier/North Holland Biomedical Press

Black, I. B., Adler, J. E., Dreyfus, C. F., Friedman, W. F., LaGamma, E. F., Roach, A. H. 1987. Biochemistry of information storage in the nervous system. *Science* 236:1263–68

Bliss, T.V.P., Lomo, T. 1973. Long-lasting potentiation of synaptic transmission in the dentate area of the anaesthetized rabbit following stimulation of the perforant path. *J. Physiol. (London)* 232:331–56

Byrne, J. H. 1985. Neural and molecular mechanisms underlying information storage in Aplysia: implications for learning and memory. *Trends Neurosci.* 8:478–82

Coan, E. J., Collingridge, G. L. 1987. Characterization of an N-methyl-D-aspartate receptor component of synaptic transmission in rat hippocampal slices. *Neuroscience* 22:1–8

Collingridge, G. L., Bliss, T.V.P. 1987. NMDA receptors—their role in long-term potentiation. *Trends Neurosci.* 10:288–93

Collingridge, G. L., Kehl, S. J., McLennan, H. 1983. Excitatory amino acids in synaptic transmission in the Schaffer collateral-commissural pathway of the rat hippocampus. *J. Physiol. (London)* 334:33–46

Dolphin, A. C. 1983. The excitatory amino-acid antagonist γ-D-glutamylglycine masks rather than prevents long-term potentiation of the perforant path. *Neuroscience* 10:377–83

Dolphin, A. C., Errington, M. L., Bliss, T.V.P. 1982. Long-term potentiation of the perforant path in vivo is associated with increased glutamate release. *Nature* 297:496–98

Dragunow, M., Robertson, H. A. 1987a. Generalized seizures induce c-fos protein(s) in mammalian neurons. *Neurosci. Lett.* 82:157–61

Dragunow, M., Robertson, H. A. 1987b. Kindling stimulation induces c-fos protein(s) in granule cells of the rat dentate gyrus. *Nature* 329:441–42

Duncan, C. P. 1949. The retroactive effect of

electroshock on learning. *J. Comp. Physiol. Psychol.* 42:32–44

Dunn, A. J. 1980. Neurochemistry of learning and memory: An evaluation of recent data. *Ann. Rev. Psychol.* 31:343–90

Dunwiddie, T., Madison, D., Lynch, G. 1978. Synaptic transmission is required for initiation of long-term potentiation. *Brain Res.* 150:413–17

Errington, M. L., Lynch, M. A., Bliss, T.V.P. 1987. Long-term potentiation in the dentate gyrus: Induction and increased glutamate release are blocked by D(−)aminophosphonovalerate. *Neuroscience* 20:279–84

Farley, J., Alkon, D. L. 1985. Cellular mechanisms of learning, memory and information storage. *Ann. Rev. Psychol.* 36:419–94

Flexner, I. B., Flexner, L. B., Steller, E. 1963. Memory in mice as affected by intracerebral puromycin. *Science* 141:51–59

Flood, J. F., Smith, G. E., Bennett, E. L., Alberti, M. H., Orme, A. E., Jarrik, M. E. 1986. Neurochemical and behavioral effects of catecholamine and protein synthesis inhibitors in mice. *Pharmacol. Biochem. Behav.* 24:631–45

Frey, U., Krug, M., Reymann, K., Matthies, H. 1988a. Anisomycin, an inhibitor of protein synthesis, blocks late phases of homo- and heterosynaptic long-term potentiation in the hippocampal CA1 region in vitro. *Brain Res.* 452:57–65

Frey, U., Krug, M., Reymann, K., Matthies, H. 1988b. Long-term potentiation induced in dendrites separated from their CA1 pyramidal somata does not establish a late phase. *Neurosci. Lett.* In press

Frieder, B., Allweis, C. 1982. Memory consolidation: further evidence for the four-phase model from the time courses of diethyldithiocarbamate and ethacrinic acid amnesias. *Physiol. Behav.* 29:1071–75

Gibbs, M. E., Ng, K. T. 1976. Memory formation: a new three-phase model. *Neurosci. Lett.* 2:165–69

Gispen, W. H. 1986. Synaptic protein phosphorylation and long-term potentiation. In *Learning and Memory, Mechanisms of Information Storage in the Nervous System.* ed. H. Matthies, pp. 25–33. Oxford: Pergamon

Goelet, P., Castellucci, V. F., Schacher, S., Kandel, E. R. 1986. The long and the short of long-term memory—a molecular framework. *Nature* 322:419–22

Grecksch, G., Matthies, H. 1980. Two sensitive periods for the amnesic effect of anisomycin. Pharmacol. Biochem. Behav. 12:663–65

Green, E. J., Greenough, W. T. 1986. Altered synaptic transmission in dentate gyrus of rats reared in complex environments: evidence from hippocampal slices maintained in vitro. *J. Neurophysiol.* 55:739–50

Greenberg, D. A., Carpenter, C. L., Messing,R. O. 1987. Interaction of calmodulin inhibitors and protein kinase C inhibitors with voltage-dependent calcium channels. *Brain Res.* 404:401–4

Gunning, R. 1987. Increased numbers of ion channels promoted by an intracellular second messenger. *Science* 235:80–81

Harris, E. W., Cotman, C. W. 1986. Long-term potentiation of guinea pig mossy fiber responses is not blocked by N-methyl-D-aspartate antagonists. *Neurosci. Lett.* 70: 132–37

Herron, C. E., Lester, R.A.J., Coan, E. J., Collingridge, G. L. 1986. Frequency-dependent involvement of NMDA-receptors in the hippocampus: a novel synaptic mechanism. *Nature* 322:265–67

Hu, G. Y., Hvalby, Ø., Walaas, S. I., Albert, K. A., Skjeflo, P., et al. 1987. Protein kinase C injection into hippocampal pyramidal cells elicits features of long-term potentiation. *Nature* 328:426–29

Jaffard, R., Jeantet, Y. 1981. Posttraining changes in excitability of the commissural path-CA1 pyramidal cell synapse in the hippocampus of mice. *Brain Res.* 220:167–72

Johnson, J. W., Ascher, P. 1987. Glycine potentiates the NMDA response in cultured mouse brain neurons. *Nature* 325:529–31

Jork, R., Grecksch, G., Matthies, H. 1982a. Apomorphine and glycoprotein synthesis during consolidation. *Pharmacol. Biochem. Behav.* 17:11–13

Jork, R., Lössner, B., Matthies, H. 1978. Hippocampal activation and incorporation of macromolecules precursors. *Pharmacol. Biochem. Behav.* 9:709–12

Jork, R., Schmidt, S., Schulzeck, S., Lössner, B., Popov, N., Matthies, H. 1982b. Mechanisms of dopamine induced changes in hippocampal glycoprotein metabolism. *Pharmacol. Biochem. Behav.* 17:203–7

Kamin, L. J. 1957. The retention of an incompletely learned avoidance response. *J. Comp. Physiol. Psychol.* 50: 457–60

Kamin, L. J. 1963. Retention of the incompletely learned avoidance response: some further analysis. *J. Comp. Physiol. Psychol.* 56:713–18

Kandel, E. R. 1987. The long and short of memory in Aplysia: a molecular perspective. In *Fidia Research Foundation Neuroscience Award Lectures 1986,* ed. E. Costa, pp. 7–47. Padova: Liviana Press

Kessler, M., Baudry, M., Cumming, J. T., Way, S., Lynch, G. 1986. Induction of glutamate binding sites in hippocampal membranes by transient exposure to high concentrations of glutamate or glutamate analogs. *J. Neurosci.* 6:355–63

Krug, M., Brödemann, R., Ott, T. 1982. Blockade of long-term potentiation in the dentate gyrus of freely moving rats by the glutamic acid antagonist GDEE. *Brain Res.* 249:57–62

Krug, M., Lössner, B., Ott, T. 1984. Anisomycin blocks the late phase of long-term potentiation in the dentate gyrus of freely moving rats. *Brain Res. Bull.* 13:39–42

Kuhnt, U., Mihaly, A., Joo, F. 1985. Increased binding of calcium in the hippocampal slice during long-term potentiation. *Neurosci. Lett.* 53:149–54

Laroche, S., Errington, M. L., Lynch, M. A., Bliss, T.V.P. 1987. Increase in [^{3}H] glutamate release from slices of dentate gyrus and hippocampus following classical conditioning in the rat. *Behav. Brain Res.* 25:23–29

Linden, D. J., Sheu, F.-S., Murakami, K., Routtenberg, A. 1987. Enhancement of long-term potentiation by Cis-unsaturated fatty acid: relation to protein kinase C and phospholipase A$_2$. *J. Neurosci.* 7:3783–92

Lössner, B., Schweigert, Chr., Pchalek, V., Krug, M., Frey, S., Matthies, H. 1987. Training and LTP-induced changes of protein synthesis in rat hippocampus. *Neuroscience* 22 (Suppl).:512

Lovinger, D. M., Colley, P. A., Akers, R. F., Nelson, R. B., Routtenberg, A. 1986. Direct relation of long-term synaptic potentiation to phosphorylation of membrane protein F$_1$, a substrate for membrane protein kinase C. *Brain Res.* 399:205–11

Lovinger, D. M., Wong, K. L., Murakami, K., Routtenberg, A. 1987. Protein kinase C inhibitors eliminate hippocampal long-term potentiation. *Brain Res.* 436:177–83

Lynch, G., Halpain, S., Baudry, M. 1982. Effects of high-frequency synaptic stimulation on glutamate receptor binding studied with a modified in vitro hippocampal slice preparation. *Brain Res.* 244:101–11

Lynch, G., Larson, J., Kelso, S., Barrionuevo, G., Schottler, F. 1983. Intracellular injections of EGTA block induction of hippocampal long-term potentiation. *Nature* 305:719–21

Lynch, M. A., Errington, M. L., Bliss, T.V.P. 1985. Long-term potentiation of synaptic transmission in the dentate gyrus: increased release of [^{14}C]-glutamate without increase in receptor binding. *Neurosci. Lett.* 62:123–29

Malenka, R. C., Madison, D. V., Nicoll, R. A. 1986. Potentiation of synaptic transmission in the hippocampus by phorbol esters. *Nature* 321:175–77

Malenka, R. C., Ayoub, G. S., Nicoll, R. 1987. Phorbol esters enhance transmitter release in rat hippocampal slices. *Brain Res.* 403:198–203

Mamounas, L. A., Thompson, R. F., Lynch,

G., Baudry, M. 1984. Classical conditioning of the rabbit eyelid response increases glutamate receptor binding in hippocampal synaptic membranes. *Proc. Natl. Acad. Sci. USA* 81:2548–52

Matthies, H. 1972. Pharmacological influence on teaching and memorization processes (russ.) *Pharmakol. Toxikol.* 35:259–65

Matthies, H. 1974. The biochemical basis of learning and memory. *Life Sci.* 15:2017–31

Matthies, H. 1982. Plasticity in the nervous system—an approach to memory research. In *Neuronal Plasticity and Memory Formation*, ed. C. A. Marson, H. Matthies, pp. 1–15. New York: Raven

Matthies, H., 1988. Long-term synaptic potentiation and macromolecular changes in memory formation. In *Synaptic Plasticity in the Hippocampus*, ed. H. L. Haas, G. Buzsáki, pp. 119–21. Berlin: Springer-Verlag

Matthies, H., Rüthrich, H., Ott, T., Matthies, H.-K., Matthies, R. 1986. Low frequency perforant path stimulation as a conditioned stimulus demonstrates correlations between long-term synaptic potentiation and learning. *Physiol. Behav.* 36:811–21

McGaugh, J. L. 1966. Time dependent processes in memory storage. *Science* 153:1351–58

Melchers, B. P. C., Pennartz, C. M. A., Lopes da Silva, F. H. 1987. Differential effects of elevated extracellular calcium conentrations on field potentials in dentate gyrus and CA1 of the rat hippocampal slice preparation. *Neurosci. Lett.* 77:37–42

Mody, I., Baimbridge, K. G., Miller, J. J. 1984. Blockade of tetanic- and calcium-induced long-term potentiation in the hippocampal slice preparation by neuroleptics. *Neuropharmacology* 23:625–31

Montarolo, P. G., Goelet, P., Castelucci, V. F., Morgan, J., Kandel, E. R., Schacher, S. 1986. A critical time period for macromolecular synthesis in long-term heterosynaptic facilitation in Aplysia. *Science* 234:1249–54

Morris, R. G. M., Anderson, E., Lynch, G. S., Baudry, M. 1986. Selective impairment of learning and blockade of long-term potentiation by an N-methyl-D-aspartate receptor antagonist, AP 5. *Nature* 319:774–76

Müller, G. E., Pilzecker, A. 1900. Experimentelle Beiträge zur Lehre vom Gedächtnis. *Z. Psychol. Physiol. Sinnesorgane Ergänz. Band* 1:1–300

Novak, L., Bregestovski, P., Asher, P., Herbet, A., Prochiantz, A. 1984. Magnesium gates glutamate-activated channels in mouse central neurons. *Nature* 307:462–65

Otani, S., Goddard, G. V., Marshall, C. J., Tate, W. P., Abraham, W. C. 1988. Inhibitors of protein synthesis, but not mRNA synthesis, promote decay of long-term potentiation in rat dentate gyrus. In *Synaptic Plasticity in the Hippocampus*, ed. H. L. Haas, G. Buzsáki, pp. 122–23. Berlin: Springer-Verlag

Ott, T., Matthies, H. 1978. Lernen und Gedächtnis. In *Die Psychologie des 20. Jahrhunderts, Bd. VI, Lorenz und die Folgen*, ed. R. A. Stamm, H. Zeier, pp. 988–1018. Zürich: Kindler

Ott, T., Rüthrich, H., Reymann, K., Lindenau, L., Matthies, H. 1982. Direct evidence for the participation of changes in synaptic efficacy in the development of behavioral plasticity. In *Neuronal Plasticity and Memory Formation*, ed. C. A. Marsan, H. Matthies, pp. 441–52. New York: Raven

Pohle, W., Acosta, L., Rüthrich, H., Krug, M., Matthies, H., 1987. Incorporation of ^{3}H-fucose in rat hippocampal structures after conditioning by perforant path stimulation and after LTP-producing tetanization. *Brain Res.* 410:245–56

Popov, N., Schulzeck, S., Schmidt, S., Matthies, H. 1975. Changes in labeling of soluble and solubilized rat brain proteins using ^{3}H-leucine as precursor during a learning experiment. *Acta Biol. Med. Ger.* 34:583–92

Popov, N., Pohle, W., Rüthrich, H.-L., Schulzeck, S., Matthies, H. 1976. Increased fucose incorporation into rat hippocampus during learning. A biochemical and microautoradiographic study. *Brain Res.* 101:295–304

Popov, N., Reymann, K. G., Schulzeck, K., Schulzeck, S., Matthies, H. 1988. Alterations in calmodulin content in fractions of rat hippocampal slices during tetanic- and calcium-induced long-term potentiation. *Brain Res. Bull.* 21. In press

Racine, R. J., Milgram, N. W., Hafner, S. 1983. Long-term potentiation phenomena in the rat limbic forebrain. *Brain Res.* 260:217–31

Reymann, K. G., Matthies, H. K., Frey, U., Vorobyev, V. S., Matthies, H. 1986. Calcium-induced long-term potentiation in the hippocampal slice: characterization of the time course and conditions. *Brain Res. Bull.* 17:291–96

Reymann, K., Rüthrich, H., Lindenau, L., Ott, T., Matthies, H. 1982. Monosynaptic activation of the hippocampus as a conditioned stimulus: behavioral effects. *Physiol. Behav.* 29:1007–12

Reymann, K., Schnlzeck, K., Kase, H., Matthies, H. 1988a. Phorbol ester-induced hippocampal long-term potentiation is counteracted by inhibitors of protein kinase C. *Exp. Brain Res.* 71:227–30

Reymann, K. G., Frey, U., Jork, R., Matthies, H. 1988b. Polymyxin B, an inhibitor of protein kinase C, prevents the maintenance of synaptic long-term potentiation in hippocampal CA1 neurons. *Brain Res.* 440:305–14

Reymann, K. G., Brödemann, R., Kase, H., Matthies, H. 1988c. Inhibitors of calmodulin and protein kinase C block different phases of hippocampal long-term potentiation. *Brain Res.* In press

Rüthrich, H., Dorochow, W., Pohle, W., Rüthrich, H.-L., Matthies, H. 1987. Colchicine-induced lesion of rat hippocampal granular cells prevents conditioned active avoidance with perforant path stimulation as conditioned stimulus, but not conditioned emotion. *Physiol. Behav.* 40: 147–54

Sastry, B., Goh, J. W. 1984. Long-lasting potentiation in hippocampus is not due to an increase in glutamate receptors. *Life Sci.* 34:1497–1501

Sharp, P. E., McNaughton, B. L., Barnes, C. A. 1985. Enhancement of hippocampal field potentials in rats exposed to a novel, complex environment. *Brain Res.* 339:361–65

Skelton, R. W., Miller, J. J., Phillips, A.G. 1985. Long-term potentiation facilitates behavioral responding to single-pulse stimulation of the perforant path. *Behav. Neurosci.* 99:603–20

Skelton, R. W., Scarth, A. S., Wilkie, D. M., Miller, J. J., Phillips, A. G. 1987. Longterm increases in dentate granule cell responsivity accompany operant conditioning. *J. Neurosci.* 7:3081–87

Snipes, G. J., Chan, S. Y., McGuire, C. B., Costello, B. R., Norden, J. J., Freeman, J. A., Routtenberg, A. 1987. Evidence for the coidentification of GAP-43 a growth-associated protein, and F1, a plasticity-associated protein. *J. Neurosci.* 7:4066–75

Stanton, P. K., Sarvey, J. M. 1984. Blockade of long-term potentiation in rat hippocampal CA1 region by inhibitors of protein synthesis. *J. Neurosci.* 4:3080–88

Stringer, J. L., Greenfield, L. J., Hackett, J. T., Guyenet, P. G. 1983. Blockade of longterm potentiation by phencyclidine and opiates in the hippocampus in vivo and in vitro. *Brain Res.* 280:127–38

Strong, J. A., Fox, A. O., Tsien, R. W., Kaczmarek, L. K. 1987. Stimulation of protein kinase C recruits covert calcium channels in Aplysia bag cell neurons. *Nature* 325:714–17

Sutcliffe, J. G., Milner, R. J., Gottesfeld, J. M., Reynolds, W., 1984. Control of neuronal gene expression. *Science* 225:1308–15

Thompson, R. F. 1982. Increase in the monosynaptic population spike response of the dentate gyrus during classical conditioning. *Neurosci. Res. Prog. Bull.* 20:693–95

Thompson, R. F. 1986. The neurobiology of learning and memory. *Science* 233:941–47

Tully, T. 1987. Drosophila learning and memory revisited. *Trends Neurosci.* 10:330–35

Turner, R. W., Baimbridge, K. G., Miller, J. J. 1982. Calcium induced long-term potentiation in the hippocampus. *Neuroscience* 7:1411–16

Wigström, H., Swann, J. W., Anderson, P. 1979. Calcium dependency of synaptic long-lasting potentiation in the hippocampal slice. *Acta Physiol. Scand.* 105:126–28

Woody, C. D. 1986. Understanding the cellular basis of memory and learning. *Ann. Rev. Psychol.* 37:433–93

Ann. Rev. Psychol. 1989. 40:405–29

AUDITORY PHYSIOLOGY: PRESENT TRENDS

Don C. Teas

Department of Psychology, University of Florida, Gainesville, Florida 32611; and Air Force Office of Scientific Research, Directorate of Life Sciences, Bolling AFB, D.C. 20332–6448

CONTENTS

INTRODUCTION[1]

Auditory physiology has benefited from several summary publications in books, monographs, and symposia during recent years. These include *The*

---

[1] Abbreviations used in this chapter: BF, best frequency; CF, characteristic frequency; CnF, constant frequency; CM, cochlear microphonic; DSCnF, Doppler Shift constant frequency; EM, electron microscopy; EP, endocochlear potential; FM, frequency modulation; HC, hair cells; HRP, horseradish peroxidase; IC, inferior colliculus; IHC, inner hair cells; LOC, lateral olivocochlear component; MOC, medial olivocochlear component; OCB, olivocochlear bundle; OHC, outer hair cells; RW, round window; SR, spontaneous rate; TM, tectorial membrane; TTS, temporary threshold shift

0066–4308/89/0201–0405$02.00

Primary Acoustic Nuclei (Lorente de No 1981), *The Mechanics of Hearing* (de Boer & Viergever 1983), *Peripheral Auditory Mechanisms, Proceedings* (Allen et al 1985), *Neurobiology of Hearing* (Hoffman et al 1986), *Auditory Frequency Selectivity* (Brian et al 1986), and *Directional Hearing* (Yost & Gourevitch 1987). There are also the tutorials and reports of symposia published in the *Journal of the Acoustical Society of America*. These include Saunders et al (1985) on the consequences of acoustic injury, and the report of the CHABA (Committee on Hearing, Bioacoustics, and Biomechanics) Symposium, Basic Research In Hearing (Dolan & Yost 1983).

I have been highly selective in the material included here. I review, first, the exciting results arising from the studies of hair cells. Auditory physiology has been pushed (or perhaps led) to the point where data describing individual isolated hair cells are quickly incorporated into the body of theory on cochlear processing. In vivo studies are now accompanied by anatomical description using contemporary methods that rival the precision of the studies on isolated hair cells. The present state of this work will provide the basis for finally understanding the transduction process.

The second topic chosen for review is relevant to auditory localization. Recent studies, following an ethological orientation, have varied the spatial location of sound sources rather than varying the interaural time and intensitive differences (i.e. using dichotic stimulation that may synthesize spatial locations). These two methods of studying the use of interaural cues by the auditory system should yield similar descriptions of neural processing, but there are discrepancies. These discrepancies must be attributable to different experimental procedures, stimulus deliveries, and anatomical targets.

A second issue buried in the question of auditory localization is shared by all sensory information transmission: How does motor output remain appropriately calibrated with respect to the external world while the sensory information sent to the brain by our receptors is altered? Even though hearing loss occurs and is often unilateral, there is usually little error in assessing the correct location of sound sources. It there a template, containing a map of external space, that must be continually updated? Or is the mapping of auditory space a calculation rather than a matching to a stored representation? How is the auditory resultant used by the visual system, and how is this combined audio-visual information used by the motor system? The sketchy data available on these questions contain exciting hints about how sensory information from different modalities is integrated and used by the organism.

COCHLEAR PROCESSES

The study of cochlear processing began when Wever & Bray (1930) recorded electrical potentials form the cochlear region with gross electrodes. Ingenious studies with round window (RW) electrodes added much information which was, at times, difficult to interpret (Wever & Lawrence 1954). Bekesy's direct observations of displacement at specific locations along the cochlear partition (1960) replaced ambiguity with data and reduced the range of theoretical interpretation. These findings became primary baseline data while electrical recording was considered an indirect assessment of cochlear processing. In the progression of auditory science toward greater precision in structural and functional analysis, the electrical signs of cellular processes have become more closely tied to function than those for the population responses.

The precision of frequency resolution shown by auditory nerve fibers (Kiang et al 1965) was in contrast to that shown by Bekesy's observations (1960) or by electrical measures of displacement of the cochlear partition, the cochlear microphonic (CM) (Tasaki et al 1952; Teas et al 1962). The difference between the two sets of data, mechanical and neural, provided opportunity for theoretical interpretation—e.g. the concept of a "second filter" placed between the mechanical displacement and the neural response. The first filter was in the traveling wave, as reported by Bekesy (1960).

In keeping with the trend toward greater analytic precision, Bekesy's observations on displacement were supplemented by others based on less direct but more accurate measures. The means for measuring displacement, such as capacitive coupling (Wilson & Johnstone 1972) the Mössbauer technique (Johnstone & Boyle 1967; Rhode 1971), and interferometry (Kohloffel 1973), have all exhibited technical uncertainties and limitations. Bekesy's direct visual observations were clearest toward the apex, but the new techniques were more suitable for observations in the basal turn, where the insertion of a radioactive source or small reflective surface can be made through the scala tympani. Over the years the minimal detectable displacements have become smaller. Khanna & Leonard (1982) reported, for one preparation, displacement data on the order of 1 nm. Their interferometry procedure permits acoustic stimulation of the cochlea at intensities within the normal range of hearing. For preparations that met their criteria of normal, the displacement of a small region along the cochlear partition showed frequency resolution comparable to that for an auditory nerve fiber with characteristic frequency appropriate to the location of their measurement. Khanna & Leonard's (1982) data confirmed earlier estimates of mechanical precision (Rhode 1978). Cochlear debilitation was also the cause of the broad tuning found by early applications of other techniques. Sellick et al (1982) showed good agreement between mechanical and neural tuning curves using the Mössbauer technique. There was now no discrepancy between the frequency resolution of cochlear partition displacement and the responses of auditory nerve fibers.

Russell & Sellick (1978) had already demonstrated that single inner hair cells (IHC) produced tuning curves as selective as those of individual auditory nerve fibers. Their study initiated a new level of analysis of cochlear processing. They showed that both the AC (cochlear microphonic, for large electrodes) and the DC potential described by Davis et al (1950) as the summating potential were present in IHC. When Russell & Sellick (1978) plotted the stimulus intensity required to maintain a constant DC potential as frequency was varied, the resulting tuning curve was similar to that for an auditory nerve fiber. Maintaining a constant DC voltage at the IHC was thereby equated to maintaining a constant discharge rate in the auditory nerve fiber. Thus, displacement of the basilar membrane (Khanna & Leonard 1982), the IHC potential (Russell & Sellick (1978), and the discharges of the auditory nerve fibers (e.g. Kiang et al 1965 all show similar frequency resolutions.

SIGNIFICANT QUESTIONS

When frequency resolution was pursued to the level of the IHC, the question of damping arose once again. Bekesy (1960) had showed that the basilar membrane was not quite critically damped. The narrow frequency resolution at the level of the IHC altered the problem so that the focus could no longer be the basilar membrane but must now be the mechanisms associated with stimulating the IHC. Research has tackled three interrelated questions.

Relations Between OHC and IHC

Still uncertain is the relation between the outer hair cells (OHC) and IHC. Spoendlin (1969) had shown that most of the afferent fibers in the auditory nerve terminated on IHC, with only 3–5% reaching out to OHC. There is a complete separation between the afferents to the IHC and the smaller, thinner ones to the OHC (Kiang et al 1982). The relatively few efferent fibers (Rasmussen 1946; Warr 1978) ramify to terminate with large nerve endings on many OHC. Liberman & Brown (1986) found labeled fibers terminating on a range of 7 (radial) columns of OHC. Recent studies (described below) show the subtlety of the efferent system.

The intracellular study of hair cells (HC) has contributed indirectly to the question of OHC/IHC relations. Dallos (1985a) showed that OHC and supporting cells produce AC potentials and both depolarizing and hyperpolarizing DC potentials, much like the IHC. The dependence of the neural response upon the state of the OHC stereocilia has been shown in trauma studies (described below). OHC can change their shape in an alternating electric field or after application of acetylcholine (Brownell 1983). The inference is that the shortening or lengthening of OHC could change the stiffness in local regions of the organ of Corti. This, in turn, could alter the effect of mechanical stimulation at the IHC, via the tectorial membrane or in some other manner. The great sensitivity of normal auditory function is apparently attributable to the OHC; but the mechanism(s) mediating that sensitivity, while becoming less obscure, are still to be specified.

Role of the Efferent System

The anatomical definition of the olivocochlear efferent system by Rasmussen (1946), the functional description by Galambos (1956), the anatomical elaboration by Smith & Rasmussen (1963), the study of gross responses by Desmedt (1962), and the study of individual efferent fibers by Fex (1962) firmly established that centrifugal influences had to be included in cochlear processing. Questions of how the olivo cochlear bundle (OCB) is activated, what it does, and how to measure whatever it does were of great interest. In behavioral studies animals were trained to perform a discrimination task, the OCB was severed, and discrimination acuity was measured again. Dewson (1968) presented signals to be discriminated in both noise and in quiet, then severed the OCB and retested. There was a loss in ability to discriminate signals in a noise background with the OCB severed. In physiological experiments the OCB was stimulated at the floor of the fourth ventricle. Measurements of the endocochlear potential (EP), the gross cochlear response, the cochlear microphonic, and the activity of auditory nerve fibers were made with and without electrical stimulation of the OCB.

Fex (1962) showed that electrical stimulation of the OCB at the floor of the fourth ventricle produced a shift in the endocochlear potential (EP) recorded from the cochlea (see also Konishi & Slepian 1970). The maximum shift occurred for shocks delivered at a rate of 400/sec for about 100 ms. The parameters of OCB stimulation were usually chosen to maximize the inhibitory effect at the periphery. The basic phenomena became well established: The whole-nerve response was decreased by an equivalent of 15–20 dB in signal intensity (Desmedt 1962); the cochlear microphonic (CM) was increased by about 3 dB at its maximum in the upper basal turn (less at other locations); and the discharges of auditory nerve fibers were reduced by varying amounts, with the maximum at about 20 dB SPL (Wiederhold & Kiang 1970; Teas et al 1972). The reduction in the neural response decreased with increasing signal intensity and was strongest for frequencies best for the basal turn and lower second turn (in the guinea pig), and decreased for frequencies appropriate for the more basal hook region and toward the apex.

Warr (1978) described the OCB efferent innervation as arising from medial and lateral superior olivary regions, with each component containing crossed and uncrossed fibers. The lateral and ipsilateral components terminate on afferent fibers beneath the IHC, while the contralateral medial component terminates in large nerve endings at the bases of OHC (Guinan et al 1983). It is the medial component that can modify the micromechanical response of the organ of Corti, since its terminations are upon the OHC. Recent studies have added information about distortion, S/N enhancement, and micromechanical effects due to electrical and acoustic stimulation.

Cochlear Emissions

The OHC/IHC puzzle includes the question of cochlear emissions, the acoustic energy recorded in the external auditory meatus, which arises from within the cochlea (Kemp 1978). Cochlear emissions, both evoked and spontaneous, have often been described (McFadden & Wightman 1983), but as yet it is confirmation of the theoretical basis (Gold 1948) for expecting the emissions that leads researchers to use this window for studying cochlear mechanics. Theoretically, the tuning along the cochlear partition is so narrow that only a local feedback mechanism can achieve it. Such highly tuned feedback systems have a tendency to develop oscillation. In the normal cochlea the hair cells (HC) within a region may be verging on oscillation; when they do oscillate, spontaneous emissions can result. Evoked emissions occur for near-threshold stimuli and are not detected for stimuli above about 40 dB or so re threshold. Subjects with sensorineural hearing loss show no evoked cochlear emissions.

IN VITRO HAIR-CELL STUDIES

Limitations associated with studying hair cells in situ have promoted their study in vitro or in isolated preparations. The frog, turtle, lizard, and fish provide easier access than mammals to cochlear or vestibular HC. The HC can be separated from the excised papilla, maintained, and studied in vitro where the HC environment can be modified. Even though anatomists have shown with electron microscopy (EM) the intriguing detail of stereocilia, mitochondria, and other components of HC, the microanalysis of function to accompany the microscopy has lagged somewhat. The recent physiological studies of HC have provided an analysis similar in analytic level to the EM structural analyses and have contributed greatly to our understanding of cochlear function.

Stereocilia Stiffness

Perhaps the earliest of the recent work focusing on stereocilia is that of Flock and his co-workers, using vestibular HC, showing that the stereocilia are stiff, and that, upon displacement, they bend as a rigid rod, pivoting near their insertion into the cuticular plate of the HC where the diameter of the cilium decreases (Flock 1977). Stereocilia contain oriented actin filaments that provide the stiffness (Tilney et al 1980; Flock et al 1981; Saunders et al 1983). Saunders & Flock (1985) showed that after exposure to noise calculated to produce temporary threshold shift (TTS), stereocilia stiffness decreased. With 15 minutes' recovery time after the exposure, stereocilia stiffness had returned. Restoration of stiffness could be attributed to recovery of actin structure or to some property of the ciliary bundle.

Actin is also found in the cuticular plate and may provide a basis for contractility (Slepecky & Chamberlain 1982). The stiffness of stereocilia on cochlear HC excised from the guinea pig has been reported to be greater for displacement in the excitatory direction than for deflection in the inhibitory direction (Flock & Strelioff 1984; Strelioff & Flock 1984). The IHC stereocilia were reported to be about half as stiff as those in OHC, and their excitatory/ inhibitory stiffness ratio was significantly lower. Stiffness of stereocilia decreases toward the apex of the cochlea, with the range from base to apex greatest for the third row of OHC, from about 9 dyne cm^{-1} at the base to about 2.5 dyne cm^{-1} at the apex. The filamentous crosslinks between rows and between adjacent stereocilia (Pickles et al 1984) also contribute to the stiffness gradient. The authors note that the cross-links among stereocilia distribute the applied force to 7–12 "lateral neighbors" in the bundle, and to the rows as well. Thus, both stereocilia length and the number of cross-links may contribute to the overall gradient of stiffness along the cochlear partition. As an indication of the physiological state of the excised HC in their experiments, Flock & Strelioff (1984) measured the membrane potentials and found values similar to those reported in situ.

Using the measurements of length and stiffness of stereocilia described above, Strelioff et al (1985) calculated the resonant frequencies along the cochlear partition for OHC and IHC. On IHC the stereocilia are considered as freestanding, since they are not attached to the tectorial membrane (see below for an opposing view). The resonant frequencies for IHC ranged from 300 kHz at the base to 128 kHz at the apex, excluding them as determining elements for cochlear frequency selection. The length and stiffness of the OHC stereocilia must be combined with the mass provided by the tectorial membrane (TM) in order to calculate the resonant frequencies. The computed frequencies for the combined OHC-TM system ranged from 22 kHz at the base to 1.2 kHz at the apex. These authors suggest that IHC should be considered as passive responders to the fluid movements passing over them while the OHC-TM system carries the capability for contributing to cochlear tuning. Especially interesting is the possibility that the stiffness of stereociliary bundles might vary owing to the actin in the cuticular plate (Slepecky & Chamberlain 1982) or to changes in HC shape (Brownell 1983). Such variations might be translated into alterations in cochlear micromechanics. The stiffness results based on the combined OHC-TM system calculated by Strelioff et al (1985) are consistent with suggestions by Zwislocki (1980).

Cross-links and Transduction Channels

Hudspeth and his coworkers have studied HC of the frog in vitro. In some studies the entire basilar papilla is removed and placed in a chamber. The basal surface of the papilla can be bathed in synthetic perilymph and the apical surface in synthetic endolymph (Holton & Hudspeth 1983). Isolated single HC can be studied with giga-ohm seal electrodes (Lewis & Hudspeth 1983). The stereociliary bundle can be moved in calibrated steps, the composition of the fluids bathing the HC can be varied (Hudspeth 1982), and responses can be studied under voltage-clamp conditions (Holton & Hudspeth 1986). Hudspeth (1982) showed that moving the stereocilia bundle of a saccular HC from the frog produced an electrical response that was greatest near the bundle's tip. Displacement toward the kinocilium produced depolarization currents, while displacement in the opposite direction, toward the shortest stereocilia, produced hyperpolarization current, but of only about one third the magnitude. The gradation in stereocilia length across the bundle on the saccular HC is also present in HC in the mammalian cochlea. The shear motion between the tectorial membrane and the reticular lamina also produces shear between the rows of stereocilia, as well as their displacement (Hudspeth 1985). The electrical activity, strongest at the tips of the stereocilia bundles, suggested that the transduction elements were located there (Hudspeth 1982).

The cross-links between adjacent stereocilia (Pickles et al 1984; Furness & Hackney 1985) provided anatomical detail of interest for the between-stereocilia shear hypothesis. Stretching of the cross-link filaments or an alteration at the site of attachment of cross-link to stereocilia could be the final mechanical component of transduction. Hudspeth (1985) proposed that near the top of each stereocilium there are 3–7 transduction channels. Analysis of receptor potentials in the saccular HC showed that the entire HC bundle probably contains no more than 100 or so transduction channels (Holton & Hudspeth 1983). Each channel is said to have a gate that randomly opens and closes owing to thermal agitation when the HC bundle is in its resting position (Hudspeth 1985). The gate closes against a spring; thus the tension of the spring is greater for the closed than for the open position. About 20% of the gates spend more time open than closed. Upon displacement of the HC bundle in the excitatory direction, the shear between adjacent stereocilia stretches the cross-links. There is still fluctuation between open and closed states; but now, owing to the excitatory displacement, gates are open more than they are closed; a larger current flows, and depolarization occurs.

The location of molecular gates on stereocilia leaves the HC as the smallest independent element. Without an external stimulus, the transduction gates on one HC might be in a different state from those on another. However, a driving stimulus extending over many HC could drive their gates synchronously. The displacement and therefore the shearing movement will follow the stimulus rate. Since stimulus rates can be quite high, an important criterion for a HC model is its maximum response rate. Holton & Hudspeth (1983) indicate that the kinetics of the ion exchange are in the microsec range.

Hair Cell Membrane and Cytoplasm

HC RESONANCE When HC in the turtle are stimulated with a pulse, their output is an exponentially decaying oscillation at their best frequency. If the pulse is electric and relatively long, the HC resonates at the onset (step) of the pulse and at its offset, in addition to showing a DC shift in output (Crawford & Fettiplace 1983; Lewis & Hudspeth 1983). The frequency of the resonance in the turtle varies with the location of the HC. The resonance has an ionic basis in the interaction between calcium and potassium conductances across the HC membrane. The interaction must be graded along the cochlear partition in order to span the turtle's range of auditory response, from 20 Hz to 600 Hz (Fettiplace 1987). The variation in resonance among HC could be produced by variation in the rate constants for the calcium and the calcium-dependent potassium conductances. Roberts et al (1986) reported a difference in the relation between the two conductances for a saccular cell, which showed the resonance at 224 Hz, and a papillary cell, which showed much greater damping in the response at 341 Hz. Electrical resonance might then be a mechanism supporting frequency resolution in animals with freestanding stereocilia, or it might be contributory (i.e. additive) to resolution provided by a traveling wave.

HC MOTILITY Brownell (1983, 1984; Brownell et al 1985) showed that excised cochlear HC, observed with video microscopy, modify their shape with electrical stimulation. The HC, suspended in a drop of fluid, attached to the cover slip with either end—i.e. ciliary or basal. When the electrode near the free tip of the cell was positive, there was an increase in HC length by as much as 0.5–0.6 μm (Brownell et al 1985). Since the HC attach at either end, the polarity is not associated with its apical or basal end. The authors remind us of the regularity of OHC geometry in situ and of the fluid-filled spaces around them. Brownell (1986) suggested that the motility of the OHC results from the presence of subsurface cisternae, structures unique to the mammalian OHC, located along the cell wall where they are exposed to the fluid-filled spaces of Nuel. The demonstration of HC motility raises the possibility that modifications of cochlear mechanics by changes in HC shape may occur in vivo (Brownell 1986). Shape changes of OHC are reported to occur at kilohertz rates (Brownell 1986a) and in response to iontophoretic delivery of acetylcholine (Brownell 1984). By implication, the OHC might contribute to cochlear sensitivity and emissions.

HC motility provides a way to account for the burden of acute auditory sensitivity. The nonlinear mechanical response at the best frequency location (Rhode 1980) along the cochlear partition prohibits a linear extrapolation from measured displacements to estimates of threshold displacement. The active participation of OHC would add energy to that delivered by the signal, thus amplifying it. At low levels of stimulation the acoustic energy that can be recorded in the external auditory meatus (i.e. the evoked cochlear emissions) might be produced by the oscillations of the OHC. Activity in the OCB could lead to the liberation of acetylcholine from the efferent endings at the base of OHC and alter their state. The shape changes, occurring at the rate of the signal, might then be altered by the change in state of the OHC.

IN VIVO STUDIES

For the last decade or so, Liberman and coworkers have coordinated the use of anatomical and physiological measures in normal and traumatized animals to study cochlear function. These studies have led to an association between loss of function, defined in terms of the responses of auditory nerve fibers, and damage to stereocilia. Well-established functional measures—i.e. spontaneous rate (SR), threshold, characteristic frequency (CF), tuning curve shape, intensity function, and phase function—are determined for each fiber, with standard procedures (Kiang et al 1962). The fibers are then injected with horseradish peroxidase (HRP) so that their anatomical paths can be followed into the organ of Corti (Liberman 1982b) and can also be traced to the cochlear nucleus (Fekete et al 1984). Early in the development of their procedures, functional data on unit responses were obtained from a group of acoustically isolated cats raised in a soundproof chamber (Liberman 1978). These chamber-raised animals provided a normative baseline against which to judge the effects of acoustic or ototoxic trauma (Liberman & Kiang 1978) and the degree to which so-called normal cats were without trauma. The perfection of the series of techniques used in these studies has contributed much to understanding cochlear structure and function.

From such procedures Liberman (1982a) constructed a map relating CF and the locations at which fibers terminated along the cochlear partition. In normal cats the relation between CF and the location at which the fiber terminated was unambiguous and, when expressed as percentage of total length (i.e. in relative terms) showed good agreement among animals (Liberman 1982a). In noise-traumatized animals the CF can be ambiguous owing to distorted tuning curves. However, an HRP-filled fiber can be followed to its termination, and its characteristic frequency (CF) can be determined by matching its location to the frequency map.

For each IHC on which a labeled fiber terminates, there are other endings distributed around the base of the IHC (Spoendlin 1971). Liberman (1982a) showed that the relatively large endings with many mitochondria, located on the pillar-sides of the IHC toward the OHC, are the terminations of fibers with high spontaneous rates (SR). Nerve endings on the modiolar side of the IHC are smaller, have fewer mitochondria, and are the terminations of fibers with low spontaneous rates. The thresholds at CF for fibers with high SR ($>$18 disch sec^{-1}) are the lowest (greatest sensitivity), while those for fibers with low SR ($<$ 0.5 disch sec^{-1}) are the highest. Fibers with intermediate SR have thresholds between the two extreme categories and terminate at the remaining locations around the base of the IHC.

Liberman (1984a) was able to relate these structural differences among nerve endings and the correlated SR to an earlier observation by Kiang et al (1969) that the discharges of many auditory nerve fibers fall abruptly to the SR or very near it at intensities of 80–95 dB SPL. At the critical intensity the phase of the discharges shifts by as much as 180°. With further intensity increases the discharge rate increases again as if the "dip" had not occurred. The intensity range in the "dip" can be quite narrow. Liberman (1985a) named the lower intensity range (below the dip-intensity) Component I and the upper range, Component II. Since a phase change is characteristic of the dip, a low frequency, usually 1 kHz, is used so that phase change is unambiguous. The high-SR units show a Component I and a Component II, with the phase change at the dip. The low-SR units show only a Component II. The prominence of Component I for units with intermediate SRs falls between the two extreme categories.

In other animals structural damage to cochlear components was induced with acoustic trauma (Liberman & Kiang 1978). The same procedures developed for the normal cats were used for the traumatized animals. One difficulty with interpreting trauma experiments lies in assigning specific structural alterations to the change in a functional measure. The effects of acoustic trauma vary widely among animals even though the acoustic exposure is constant (Cody & Robertson 1983). If the trauma damages many structures the relation between the functional loss and its underlying causes is uncertain (Saunders et al 1985). The HRP labeling of single auditory neurons, the use of narrow-band exposures, and the ability to assay the IHC at the termination of the fiber allows each preparation to present both normal and traumatized cochlear regions. Thus, Liberman and his colleagues have been able to relate the state of the rows of stereocilia on the OHC and the IHC at which specific nerve fibers terminate to the alterations in tuning curves and intensity functions (rate and phase of the discharges) in traumatized animals. The joining of anatomical and physiological tools in normal and traumatized animals has provided an elegant and powerful analytic method for studying cochlear processing.

Liberman & Kiang (1984) showed that Components I and II are modified by damage to the stereocilia of IHC. Component I is the more vulnerable to acoustic damage. As the threshold is elevated, the maximum discharge rate decreases. Component II was unaffected by loss of threshold from 0 to 50 dB. In these units the tips and tails of the tuning curves were elevated, and in others with no Component I, no tip was demonstrable—i.e. the tuning curves were shallow. With no Component I there was no phase shift in the intensity function. On anatomical study of these animals, the IHC on which fibers with no Component I terminated showed no tall stereocilia, although the short stereocilia appeared normal. The authors cite Hoshino (1976), who showed indentations in the tectorial membrane from the tall row of stereocilia on the IHC, and suggest that the loss of tall stereocilia on the IHC removes their contribution to transmitter release, thus reducing sensitivity. With sufficient intensity delivered to the cochlea, the short rows of stereocilia are activated and Component II is generated. There are other reports that do not support the IHC stereocilia attachment to the tectorial membrane (Nielsen & Slepecky 1986).

As one might expect from the data on normal animals, a reduction in Component I is correlated with a reduction in SR. Both effects have been traced to a loss of the tall row of stereocilia on the IHC. In the traumatized animals there is a reduction in the range of SR in the region where the stereocilia are damaged or are in disarray. There is no damage to the stereocilia on the OHC (Liberman & Dodds 1984b).

Alterations in the tuning curves of units recorded in traumatized animals were also traceable to damage at the stereociliary level (Liberman & Dodds 1984a). For the tip and the tail of tuning curves to be normal there can be only minimal disarray of the stereocilia on IHC and OHC. It is the first row of OHC that contribute most to the tip. Unit locations that showed loss in the first row of OHC opposite their termination showed tuning curves with decreased tips and hypersensitive tails. This distortion of the tuning curve can produce an apparent CF that is inappropriate to the location at which the fiber terminates. The cochlear map was used to assess the correct CF. The proximity of the tall IHC stereocilia to the first row of OHC suggested that the anatomical arrangement is important for the low thresholds of auditory nerve fibers. In ototoxic antibiotic data, OHC can be lost while IHC remain intact. In these cases the tips are not apparent and the bowl-shaped tuning curves from these units include hypersensitive tail regions. Liberman & Dodds

(1984a) pointed out that the normal complement of OHC may decrease sensitivity at off-CF frequencies.

These authors linked their findings regarding stereocilia to the delivery of neural transmitter. For example, spontaneous discharges presumably arise from the spontaneous release of transmitter between the nerve ending and the IHC. According to the Liberman et al data, the 25 fibers terminating on a single IHC may include a wide range of SR since the nerve endings are distributed around the base of the IHC. Due to the loss of stereocilia and the consequent elimination of transduction channels, the transduction current is reduced, the IHC is hyperpolarized and the release of transmitter is decreased. Since any operation that reduces the rate of transmitter release would be expected to produce similar effects, one must also predict that a decrease in endocochlear potential (EP) that contributes to the transduction current would also produce a decrease in SR, sensitivity, and tuning. Sewell (1984a,b) infused furosemide, a loop diuretic, and measured the responses of auditory units and the magnitude of EP. The magnitude of EP decreased with furosemide and, in other studies, so did the SR and sensitivity.

EFFERENT SYSTEM

The well-demonstrated reduction in the neural response due to OCB stimulation has always seemed mismatched to the profound anatomical elaboration of the relatively few efferent fibers to the many thousands of nerve endings at the bases of OHC and axon-axonal contacts on afferents beneath the IHC. The lateral olivocochlear component (LOC) terminates in axon-axonal contacts on afferent fibers, and the medial olivocochlear component (MOC) terminates in large nerve endings on OHC. It is the function of the latter that is now being integrated with recent work on properties of the OHC—e.g. HC motility and stiffness of the stereocilia. How the OHC influence the responses of IHC may help to elucidate OCB function and will likely provide a rationale for the elaborate divergence of the efferent system.

Mountain (1980) demonstrated that OCB stimulation altered cochlear mechanics as well as the EP—i.e. that the change in EP was concomitant with the alteration in cochlear mechanics. Distortion products are altered by MOC stimulation (Siegal & Kim 1982; Siegal et al 1982). Since OHC are necessary for the production of distortion products (Dallos et al 1980), one can understand that the MOC stimulation alters the state of OHC, consistent with the observations of Mountain (1980). Brown & Nuttall (1984) showed that MOC stimulation altered the response at the best frequency (BF) of the IHC, thus assuring that no circuitous pathway connecting efferent to afferent fibers exists and that efferent effects are mediated mechanically to the IHC. At stimulation intensities no greater than 60 dB or so above a fiber's threshold, the alteration in OHC by MOC stimulation reduces the response of the IHC, provided that the signal is at the BF for that location. The effect is captured in the tuning curve for the IHC, in that the tip is reduced but the tail is altered very little. The interaction between signal frequency and MOC stimulation at the OHC produces a reduction of the response of the IHC at its BF but not at off-BF frequencies.

At this point, it seems that the OHC are important to cochlear processing in the representation of stimulus intensity. At near-threshold intensities the OHC are necessary for the sharply tuned tips of tuning curves and therefore for acute auditory sensitivity. Presumably the evoked and spontaneous cochlear emissions detectable in the auditory canal are by-products of the active participation of OHC in cochlear processing. These characteristics require an active participation of the OHC in the delivery of displacements to the IHC. This feedback is expressed as a force that, at low intensities, is added to the energy present in the acoustic signal. Kim (1985) has discussed the nature of nonlinearities that are required in cochlear theories to account for these cochlear characteristics.

Mountain et al (1983) proposed a feedback model in which a restoring force by the HC is generated from displacement of the basilar membrane. An asymmetric transduction process and an asymmetry in stereocilia displacement (i.e. greater stiffness with displacement in the direction producing depolarization) yield both positive and negative summating potential (McMullen & Mountain 1985). The receptor potential and the HC restoring force vary together. If the receptor potential were to be modified, the restoring force would be exerted and an acoustic emission should be detectable in the external auditory canal. Sinusoidal current injected into scala media produced acoustic outputs in the external meatus at the electric frequency and its harmonics (Hubbard & Mountain 1983). The HC provide a feedback loop. Mountain (1986) described the displacement of the basilar membrane as initiating a foward transduction process that activates a reverse transduction process to exert force on the basilar membrane.

Neely & Kim (1983) incorporated negative damping in their cochlear model to produce mechanical tuning that matches neural data. The basilar membrane was represented by one spring-mass-damper system and the stereocilia on the OHC by another. The two systems were connected by a negative damping component. By varying the negative feedback in the model, its tuning was varied between sharp, as for normal preparations, to broad, similar to that for guinea pigs with decreased cochlear sensitivity (Sellick et al 1982).

With increasing stimulus intensity the near-threshold phenomena are no longer detectable. However, electrical stimulation of the MOC produces a decrease in the neural response to a signal at these intensities. As signal strength is increased, the limited MOC effect at CF is exceeded and the response is no longer reduced. However, if the signal is presented in noise, MOC stimulation improves the recovery of response to the signal. With no signal present, the introduction of broad-band noise increases the rate of unit discharges above the SR. As compared to presentation in the quiet, the stimulus intensity at which the response to the signal is detectable in noise must increase for the higher SR. The elevation of discharge rate leaves a reduced range of discharge rates available for response to the signal. Electrical stimulation of the MOC reduces the rate due to the noise, thus restoring to the nerve fiber a wider range of rates for representing the signal (Winslow 1988). Measurements of receptor potentials in the IHC for signal and signal-in-noise conditions show that noise produces a depolarization of the IHC just as the signal does. If the depolarization due to the signal is less than that for the noise then the signal is "masked" at the IHC (Dolan & Nuttall 1988).

Contralateral acoustic inputs decrease the amount of TTS produced by stimulation at the ipsilateral ear. The interpretation is that contralateral inputs activate the MOC. Rajan et al (1988) showed that stimulating the MOC at the floor of the fourth ventricle could duplicate the contralateral-induced effects but required high rates of electrical stimulation that altered the pre-TTS responses. They moved their electrodes to the lateral surface of the inferior colliculus (IC) and found that substantial reductions of the TTS were produced with low rates of electrical stimulation that left pre-TTS responses unaltered. They suggested that there is an "integration of influences" prior to the output path of the MOC to the OHC.

Robertson & Gummer (1985) recorded from efferents in the intraganglionic spiral bundle in the guinea pig cochlea. Fibers were filled with HRP, which allowed their endings to be followed to the OHC. Audiograms of the N1 potential were done before and after exposure of the experimental ear and during the experiment to provide assurance of normal cochlear status. Efferent neurons were found to have low SR and to produce regular discharges when stimulated. Some fibers responded to ipsilateral, others to contralateral, and still others to binaural stimulation. Latencies were long, with mean values of about 23 msec, with variation of about ± 13 msec. The sensitivity and frequency resolution fell within the range of afferent fibers, as did the CF.

Liberman & Brown (1986) have also reported on labeled MOC fibers in the cat. The posterior fossa approach was modified to enter the cochlea; the integrity of the ipsilateral cochlea is retained. Their descriptions of the discharge characteristics of efferents were similar to those of Robertson & Gummer (1985). Liberman's (1986) classification of efferents into contralateral, ipsilateral, and binaural was modified (Liberman 1988) owing to the finding that low levels of noise in the contralateral ear can facilitate the discharge rate of efferents. Delivery of contralateral noise at an ipsilaterally nonexcitatory level is reported to decrease threshold by 40 dB. The effect of the facilitating noise persisted after its termination for several minutes.

Labeled fibers were followed to the bases of OHC. The range of organ of Corti served by a single efferent was 0.55 to 2.8 mm, and included 23–84 OHC with 4–23 branches. Most of the efferent endings were in the first row of OHC. There was substantial agreement between the findings in the Liberman and in the Robertson & Gummer studies.

SUMMARY, COCHLEAR PROCESSES

Measurements of the displacements along the basilar membrane due to the passage of the traveling wave do not reveal micromechanics—e.g. any movement of structures within the organ of Corti such as the OHC is not specified. The indentations in the "underside" of tectorial membrane that match the locations of the tall rows of stereocilia of OHC are interpreted as indicating stereociliary attachment to the tectorial membrane (Nielsen & Slepecky 1986). The displacement of the tall stereocilia produces a displacement of the entire ciliary bundle due to cross-links. Indentations of the tall stereocilia on the IHC is an attractive hypothesis (Liberman 1984) not uniformly accepted among anatomists.

Stereocilia are stiff, bend at their base, produce an electrical response, are highly structured (until abused by exposure to strong noise, but they can recover), and probably contain 3–7 nonselective transduction channels with pore sizes about 0.7 μm. The stiffness of the stereocilia and the shape of the cuticular plate and lateral walls of the OHC may be altered by changes in the receptor potential or by acetylcholine, the putative efferent transmitter. These alterations are important at near-threshold intensities and for MOC stimulation by either electrical or more natural means. In the first case the micromechanical events return energy to the cochlear system, thus producing a highly sensitive, precisely tuned device. In the second case, the message from the MOC might produce a change in micromechanical state.

The motility of OHC may be of great significance in cochlear mechanics since shape changes could alter the inter-OHC fluid spaces and change the compliance of the organ of Corti, perhaps at the reticular lamina. Alteration of the reticular lamina could, in turn, alter the stiffness of stereocilia at the region where they bend. Alterations in stiffness of stereocilia could change the coupling between tectorial membrane and OHC, perhaps altering the fluid-flow across the stereocilia of the IHC.

The two sets of data that have been generated by recent work on the motility of OHC (i.e. on negative feedback and shape changes) are not mutually exclusive. Brownell (1983) commented that observations of motility do not exclude concomitant alterations in stereocilia stiffness. The alterations of shape occurring at audible frequencies provide the basis for feedback within the cochlea at stimulation frequencies (Davis 1983) and may contribute to cochlear emissions (McFadden & Wightman 1983). Much of the evidence at the HC level of analysis comes from in vitro experiments. The convergence upon the importance of stereocilia in the in vitro and the in vivo studies encourages the thought that the cochlear device may be understood eventually. As a minimum one can now be impressed with the likelihood that stereocilia are of great significance for understanding the mechanics of stimulation in the cochlea.

AUDITORY LOCALIZATION

The review by Phillips & Brugge (1985) included descriptions of the dichotic studies of interaural time and intensitive differences that established the medial and lateral superior olivary and surrounding nuclei as initial sites for the resolution of binaural cues. More recently, Kuwada & Yin (1987) made the case for coincidence detection as the essential neural mechanism underlying azimuth localization. The models they discussed are based on Jeffress's (1948) concept of neural coincidence detection in which nerve impulses from the delayed sound to the more distant ear travel a shorter path than those from the ear nearer the source. Interaural intensity differences can be translated into time via the latency X intensity relation—i.e. stronger inputs produce neural responses with shorter latency; thus interaural intensity differences may be incorporated into the coincidence matrix.

The reduction of intensity differences to time differences is based on dichotic data from the cat. Konishi and coworkers (Konishi 1986; Sullivan & Konishi 1984; Konishi et al 1985) found that in the owl, which presents ears that are not symmetrically located, the interaural intensity differences mediate elevation. These workers treat intensity differences as a dimension to be resolved directly by the auditory system. The discharges of neurons in the *nucleus angularis* of the owl show little variation with interaural time differences but increase with stimulus intensity. In the "companion" nucleus, the *magnocellularis*, neurons show little alteration in discharge rate with variations in intensity but follow the phase of sinusoidal stimuli up to about 8 kHz, higher than in the cat. These neurons project to the *nucleus laminaris*, as do those from the contralateral *magnocellularis*, thus providing the neural substrate for binaural interaction.

The interaural time and intensity cues, for azimuth and elevation, respectively, are said to be brought together in the inferior colliculus. At laminaris the coding of auditory space becomes *place* within the nervous system (Konishi 1986). The rejection of spurious coincidences (responsible for anomalous characteristic delays exceeding psychophysical limits) occurs in the central nucleus of the colliculus. It is the output of the central nucleus that provides the information to be incorporated into the computation to produce movement of the head and eyes to identify the target, and perhaps to initiate the sequence of movements leading to capture of prey.

The stimulus representation identified with binaural studies may subserve functions other than localization in azimuth and elevation. The uses of binaurality may not be the same for all species, even though its presence over a long evolutionary history indicates its survival value (Fay & Feng 1987). One requirement of a sensory system is to maintain correspondence between the environment and its representation. Sensory receptors are vulnerable. Their sensitivity may predispose them to abuse from the ambient levels of stimulation, and the information they transmit can vary due to alterations in receptor capability. Considerations such as these and others have led Merzenich and coworkers (Merzenich et al 1984) to suggest that derived maps, such as that supporting the localization of sound in space, retain the capability for modification into adulthood and are continually updated by experience. In support of their thesis the authors describe the variation in binaural bands within isofrequency planes at the cortex, which contrasts with the relatively fixed locations representing frequencies among animals.

The use of combinations of spectral components by the bat and the projection of binaural bands across isofrequency planes in the cat strengthen the idea that the auditory system processes patterns of activity extending across the audible spectrum. The auditory system of the bat is an illustration of how neurons could process auditory patterns.

The Bat: A Model for Auditory Pattern Recognition

The linking of sensory reception and motor output are closely associated in the bat. Sound production is modified depending on the characteristics of the echo from previously emitted sounds. Suga and coworkers (Suga 1988; Suga & Tsuzuki 1985; Suga et al 1987) have developed a preparation using the moustached bat that has allowed them to develop hypotheses about cortical processing of acoustic information. The characteristic acoustic production of this bat during cruising is a burst of sound (20–30msec) emitted at a rate of $5–10 \sec^{-1}$. The longest segment of the sound is of constant frequency (CnF) and is followed by a short downward frequency modulation (FM). Each segment of the emitted sound contains four harmonics (F1–4) so that there are eight components. Upon detection of a target the duration of the emitted sound decreases and the rate increases so that, upon closing, duration becomes 5–7 ms and the rate is $90–100s^{-1}$. Significant echoes from targets overlap with emitted sounds so that there can be 16 components in the sound complex. The second harmonic is strongest, the third is next (6–12 dB down), the fourth is 12–24 dB down, and the first is 18–36 dB down from the second.

The responses of neurons in the cortex of the bat show an astonishing specificity for particular features of the emitted sound and its echo. About

30% of the cortical area responds to the second harmonic, termed CnF2 (constant frequency), with the range of best frequencies between 61 and 63 kHz. As the bat approaches the target, the frequency of its emitted sound is changed to keep the echo within the 61–63 kHz frequency range; this area is termed the Doppler Shift CnF (DSCnF) area. These neurons form a frequency vs amplitude coordinate system with frequency tuning retaining precision independently of intensity. The other spatial dimension displays amplitude.

Another 30% of the bat's cortex extracts target velocity and range information from the pairs of sounds, emitted and echo, and is called combination sensitive. There are two parts of this area corresponding to the two segments, CnF (constant frequency) and FM (frequency modulated). Suga's designation is CnF/CnF and FM/FM. The occurrence of the echo is facilitative for neurons in this area. Their location in the CnF/CnF area is related to the difference between the F1 (emitted) and F2 (echo)—i.e. to the amount of Doppler Shift, independent of stimulus intensity. The discharges of some of these neurons phase-lock to periodic frequency modulation that can occur with movement of an insect's wings. In the FM/FM section of this area the pulse-echo pair must also have a delay. The spatial organization displays the magnitude of delay between FM1 (emitted) and FM2–4 (echo) components. The neurons are also tuned to echo amplitudes. These neurons are organized to extract range (delay) and size (echo amplitude) of the targets.

Since the bat's behavior depends upon the echoes of its emitted sound received from the target, and since these specify the target's location with respect to the bat, there is some need for the bat to identify the echo of its own signal. The populations of CnF2 resting frequencies in Jamaican moustached bats were found to vary between 59.692 and 63.334 kHz. Within this range, provision must be made for male/female recognition and for individual differences. For males the mean and standard deviation were 61.250 ± 0.534 kHz, and for females 62.290 ± 0.588 kHz. The difference was significant by chi square at $P < 0.001$ (Suga et al 1987). In 5 bats the resting frequency was measured for a duration of 31–38 days and the standard deviation was found to average 91 Hz.

These investigators reported further that the distribution of best frequencies in the DSCnF area of bats in this population was related to the resting frequency. For sample sizes ranging from 20 to 55 among 5 animals the modal best frequencies for DSCnF neurons agreed with the respective resting CnF2 frequencies. On the basis of CnF2 frequencies bats can identify sexual partners with 67% accuracy and recognize their own echoes with less assurance. However, the emitted sound is rich in harmonics, and the additional information may contribute to recognition and identification. The evidence suggests that the content of the pattern analyzed by the bat's cortex is idiosyncratic, but the data do not address the question of whether the origin of the specificity is genetic or experiential.

The Cat: A Model for Auditory Anatomy

In both the owl and the bat there seems to be a match in the precision of behavior and the supporting physiology of the sensory system. In both preparations there is a close relation among the sensory system, predator behavior, and the validity of translating temporal or intensitive cues into spatial representation. In the present literature on the cat there seems to be greater difficulty in translating the precision in physiological data on temporal and intensitive resolution from experiments using dichotic stimulation to equivalent spatial representation. Spatial maps have been reported for superior colliculus in the cat (Middlebrooks & Knudsen 1987) and in the guinea pig (Palmer & King 1982; King & Palmer 1983). In the cat these neurons can be classified into omnidirectional, hemifield, and axial units. The characteristic frequencies of hemifield and axial units are >3 kHz and appear to be representative of interaural intensity differences. Responses to low frequencies appear to be omnidirectional. The auditory fields are commensurate with the visual fields mapped in other layers of the superior colliculus. The fields of axial units are restricted in extent and frontal in location, suggesting that acute spatial resolution is restricted to a small space in front of the cat.

From the viewpoint provided by the data on the bat and the owl, the data from the cat might be considered specious, or at best, limited, since there are no ethological features incorporated into the physiological experiments. The nearest investigators have come to incorporating ethological features is to passively move the cat's pinnae (Middlebrooks & Knudsen 1987). Upon doing so the spatial fields of neurons in the superior colliculus change in the direction in which the pinna was moved—e.g. up and back moves the axial spatial field upward in elevation and laterally in azimuth. The organization of spatial fields changed depending on the position of the two pinnae. It is therefore necessary for the cat to accommodate for the position of the pinnae before combining information from the auditory system with that from the visual system. Kuwada & Yin (1987) cite a result reported by Jay & Sparks (1984) that the position of the auditory field for some cells is taken with respect to eye position—e.g. 10 degrees to the right of the gaze direction whether it be midline or otherwise.

In a study of spatial fields in the inferior colliculus of the cat, Semple et al (1983) found little of the precision shown in previous dichotic studies. Prominent in their results was the finding that the sizes of spatial fields decreased as frequency increased. Low-frequency units were omnidirectional. The authors suggested that the ear contralateral to the sound source may not have received sufficient intensity for stimulation since they reported as much as 28 dB difference between the two ears. An important feature in the cat, and presumably also for other preparations with similar muscular control, is the mobility of the pinnae.

The projection of isofrequency lamina in the medial geniculate body to specific loci in a binaural band (Middlebrooks & Zook 1983) and the projection of binaural bands across iso-frequency planes in AI (Imig & Adrian 1977) may provide the anatomical substrate for the neural display of auditory patterns as well as the representation of binaural differences. At the periphery the study of spectral patterns in auditory nerve fibers is laborious and requires that the identical stimulus conditions be duplicated for each of many units (Sachs & Young 1979). One wishes for an array of small electrodes to sample microscopically over an area sufficient to estimate a pattern of activity. At this point, however, the difficulties of processing such large amounts of data and of interpreting it in anatomical terms seem insuperable. The spatial fields for complex acoustic stimuli might be more restricted than those for tone bursts.

All auditory commerce with the environment occurs via auditory patterns, since pure tones are rare outside our laboratories. In human auditory behavior the spectral patterns called speech are the most significant. Recent psychoacoustic studies of discrimination among complex sounds, such as profile analysis (Green 1988), show that smaller intensity increments of a sinusoid can be discriminated in the company of other sinusoids than when presented in isolation. In another paradigm called comodulation masking, the detection of a signal in noise can be improved by adding a second noise band (Hall 1987). Spectral patterns occur in sequence so there is also analysis of temporal patterns superimposed on the analysis of spectral patterns (Watson & Foyle 1983). These experimental paradigms are likely to be joined by others that incorporate procedures to study the rules by which the auditory system processes spectral patterns.

ACKNOWLEDGMENTS

This review was partially supported by IPA Agreement 002–87–01664A between the Air Force Office of Scientific Research, Life Sciences Directorate and the University of Florida; and also by NIH Grant No. NS 21692.

Literature Cited

Allen, J. B., Hall, J. L., Hubbard, A., Neely, S. T., Tubis, A., eds. 1985. *Peripheral Auditory Mechanisms,* Boston, *Proceedings,* Berlin: Springer-Verlag

Bekesy, G. 1960. *Experiments in Hearing,* New York: McGraw-Hill

Brown, M. C., Nuttall, A. L. 1984. Efferent control of cochlear inner hair cell responses in the guinea pig. *J. Physiol.* 354:625–46

Brown, M. C., Nuttall, A. L., Masta, R. I. 1983. Intracellular recordings from cochlear inner hair cells: effects of stimulation of the crossed olivocochlear efferents. *Science* 222:69–72

Brownell, W. E., 1983. Observations on a motile response in isolated outer hair cells. In *Mechanism of Hearing,* ed. W. R. Web-

ster, L. M. Aitkin. Clayton, Australia: Monash Univ. Press

Brownell, W. E. 1984. Microscopic observations of cochlear hair cell motility. *Scan. Electr. Microsc.* III:1401–6

Brownell, W. E. 1986. Outer hair cell motility and cochlear frequency selectivity. In *Auditory Frequency Selectivity,* ed. B. C. J. Moore, R. D. Patterson, pp. 109–18. New York: Plenum

Brownell, W. E., Bader, C. R., Bertrand, D., de Ribaupierre, Y. 1985. Evoked mechanical responses of isolated cochlear outer hair cells. *Science* 227:194–96

Cody, A. R., Robertson, D. 1983. Variability of noise-induced damage in the guinea pig cochlea: electrophysiological and morphological correlates after strictly controlled exposures. *Hearing Res.* 9:55–70

Crawford, A. C., Fettiplace, R. 1983. Auditory nerve responses to imposed displacements of the turtle basilar membrane. *Hearing Res.* 12:199–208

Dallos, P. 1985a. Response characteristics of mammalian cochlear hair cells. *J. Neurosci.* 5:1591–1608

Dallos, P. 1985b. The role of outer hair cells in cochlear function. *Contemporary Sensory Neurobiology.* New York: Alan R. Liss. pp. 207–30

Dallos, P., Harris, D. M., Relkin, E., Cheatham, M. A. 1980. Two-tone suppression and intermodulation distortion in the cochlea: effect of outer hair cell lesions. In *Psychophysical, Physiological and Behavioral Studies in Hearing,* ed. G. van den Brink, F. A. Bilsen. Delft: Delft Univ. Press

Davis, H. 1983. An active process in cochlear mechanics. *Hearing Res.* 9:79–90

Davis, H., Fernandez, C., McAuliffe, D. R. 1950. The excitatory process in the cochlea. *Proc. Natl. Acad. Sci. USA* 36:580–87

de Boer, E., Viergever, M. A., eds. 1983. *Mechanics of Hearing.* Delft: Delft Univ. Press

Desmedt, J. E. 1962. Auditory evoked potentials from cochlea to cortex as influenced by the activation of the efferent olivo-cochlear bundle. *J. Acoust. Soc. Am.* 34:1478–96

Dewson, J. H. 1968. Efferent olivo-cochlear bundle: some relationships to stimulus discrimination in noise. *J. Neurophysiol.* 31:122–30

Dolan, D. F., Nuttall, A. L. 1988. Inner hair cell responses to tone and noise combinations. *Abstr. 11th Midwinter Res. Meet. Assoc. Res. Otolaryngol.,* Clearwater Beach, Fla.

Dolan, D. F., Nuttall, A. L. 1988. Masked whole-nerve response intensity functions altered by electrical stimulation of the crossed olivocochlear bundle. *J. Acoust. Soc. Am.* 83.

Dolan, T. R., Yost, W. A., eds. 1983. *Basic Research in Hearing. Proceedings of the 1983 CHABA Symposium. J. Acoust. Soc. Am.* 78:295–388

Fay, R. R., Feng, A. S. 1987. Mechanisms of directional hearing among nonmammalian vertebrates. In *Directional Hearing,* ed. W. A. Yost, G. Gourevitch, pp 179–213. New York: Springer-Verlag

Fekete, D. M., Rouiller, E. M., Liberman, M. C., Ryugo, D. K. 1984. The central projections of intracellularly labeled auditory nerve fibers in cats. *J. Comp. Neurol.* 229:432–50

Fettiplace, R. 1987. Electrical tuning of hair cells in the inner ear. *Trends Neural Sci.* 10:421–25

Fex, J. 1962. Auditory activity in centrifugal and centripetal cochlear fibers in cat. *Acta Physiol. Scand.* 55 (Suppl. 189). 68 pp.

Flock, A. 1977. Physiological properties of sensory hairs in the ear. In *Psychophysics and Physiology of Hearing,* ed E. F. Evans, J. P. Wilson. London: Academic

Flock, A., Cheung, H. C., Flock, B., Utter, G. 1981. Three sets of actin filaments in sensory cells of the inner ear. Identification and functional orientation determined by gel electrophoresis, immunofluorescence, and electron microscopy. *J. Neurocytol.* 10:133–47

Flock, A., Strelioff, D. 1984. Studies on hair cells in isolated coils from the guinea pig cochlea. *Hearing Res.* 15:11–18

Furness, D. N., Hackney, C. M. 1985. Crosslinks between stereocilia in the guinea pig cochlea. *Hearing Res.* 18:177–88

Galambos, R. 1956. Suppression of auditory nerve activity by stimulation of efferent fibers to cochlea. *J. Neurophysiol.* 19:424–37

Gold, T. 1957/1948. Hearing. II. The physical basis of the action of the cochlea. *Proc. R. Soc. London Ser. B* 135:492–98

Green, D. M. 1988. *Profile Analysis, Auditory Intensity Discrimination.* London: Oxford Univ. Press. 138 pp.

Guinan, J. J., Warr, W. B., Norris, B. E. 1983. Differential olivocochlear projections from lateral *vs* medial zones of the superior olivary complex. *J. Comp. Neurol.* 221: 358–70

Guth, P. S., Norris, C. H., Bobbin, R. P. 1976. The pharmacology of transmission in the peripheral auditory system. *Ann. Rev. Pharmacol.* 28:95

Hall, J. W. 1987. Experiments on comodulation masking release. In *Auditory Processing of Complex Sounds,* ed. W. A. Yost, C. S. Watson. Hillsdale NJ: Lawrence Erlbaum Assoc. 328 pp.

Hoffman, D. W., Altschuler, R. A., Bobbin, R. P., eds. 1986. *Neurobiology of Hearing.* NY: Princeton Univ. Press

Holton, T. J., Hudspeth, A. J. 1983. A micromechanical contribution to cochlear tuning and tonotopic organization. *Science* 222: 508–10

Hoshino, T. 1976. Attachment of the inner sensory hairs to the tectorial membrane, a scanning electron microscopic study. *Ann. Otol. Rhinol. Laryngol.* 38:11–18

Hubbard, A. E., Mountain, D. C. 1983. Alternating current delivered into the scala media alters sound pressure at the eardrum. *Science* 222:510–22

Hudspeth, A. J. 1982. Extracellular current flow and the site of transduction by hair cells. *J. Neurosci.* 2:1–10

Hudspeth, A. J. 1985. The cellular basis of hearing: the biophysics of hair cells. *Science* 230:745–52

Imig, T. J., Adrian, H. O. 1977. Binaural columns in the primary field (A1) of the cat auditory cortex. *Brain Res.* 138:241–57

Jay, M. F., Sparks, D. L. 1984. Auditory receptive fields in the primate superior colliculus shift with changes in eye position. *Nature* 309:345–47

Jeffress, L. A. 1948. A place theory of sound localization. *J. Comp. Physiol. Psychol.* 41: 35–39

Johnstone, B. M., Boyle, A. J. F. 1967. Basilar membrane vibration examined with the Mössbauer technique. *Science* 158:389–90

Kemp, D. T. 1978. Stimulated acoustic emissions from within the human auditory system. *J. Acoust. Soc. Am.* 65:1386–91

Khanna, S. M., Leonard, D. G. B. 1982. Basilar membrane tuning in the cat cochlea. *Science* 215:305–6

Kiang, N. Y.-S., Watanabe, T., Thomas, E. C., Clark, L. F. 1965. *Discharge Patterns of Single Fibers in the Cat's Auditory Nerve.* Cambridge, Mass: MIT Press

Kiang, N. Y.-S., Baer, T., Marr, E. M., Demont, D. 1969. Discharge rates of single auditory nerve fibers as a function of tone level. *J. Acoust. Soc. Am.* 46:106A

Kiang, N. Y.-S., Rho, J. M., Northrop, C. C., Liberman, M. C., Ryugo, D. K. 1982. Hair cell innervation by spiral ganglion cells in adult cats. *Science* 217:175–77

Kim, D. O. 1985. An overview of non-linear and active cochlear models. In *Peripheral Auditory Mechanisms,* ed. J. B. Allen, J. L. Hall, A. Hubbard, S. T. Neely, A. Tubis, Berlin/Heidelberg/New York/Tokyo: Springer-Verlag, pp. 239–49

King, A. J., Palmer, A. R. 1983. Cells responsive to free-field auditory stimuli in guinea-pig superior colliculus: distribution and response properties. *J. Physiol. (London)* 342:361–81

Kohloffel, L. U. E. 1973. Observations of the mechanical disturbances along the basilar membrane with laser illumination. In *Basic Mechanisms in Hearing,* ed. A. Moller. New York: Academic

Konishi, M. 1986. Centrally synthesized maps of sensory space. *Trends Neurosci.* 9:163–68

Konishi, M., Sullivan, W. E., Takahashi, T. 1985. The owl's cochlear nuclei process different sound localization cues. *J. Acoust. Soc. Am.* 78:360–64

Konishi, T., Slepian, J. Z. 1970. Effects of electrical stimulation of the crossed olivocochlear bundle on cochlear potentials recorded with intracochlear electrodes in the guinea pig. *J. Acoust. Soc. Am.* 49:1762–69

Kuwada, S., Yin, T. C. T. 1987. Physiolog-

ical studies of directional hearing. In *Directional Hearing,* ed. W. A. Yost, G. Gourevitch, pp. 146–76. New York: Springer-Verlag

Lewis, R. S., Hudspeth, A. J. 1983. Voltage- and ion-dependent conductances in solitary vertebrate hair cells. *Nature* 304:538–41

Liberman, M. C. 1978. Auditory nerve responses from cats raised in a low-noise environment. *J. Acoust. Soc. Am.* 63:442–55

Liberman, M. C. 1982a. The cochlear frequency map for the cat: labelling auditory-nerve fibers of known characteristic frequency. *J. Acoust. Soc. Am.* 72:1441–49

Liberman, M. C. 1982b. Single-neuron labeling in the cat auditory nerve. *Science* 216:1239–41

Liberman, M. C. 1984. Single-neuron labeling and chronic cochlear pathology. I. Threshold shift and characteristic-frequency shift. *Hearing Res.* 16:33–41

Liberman, M. C. 1987. Chronic ultrastructural changes in acoustic trauma: serial-section reconstruction of stereocilia and cuticular plates. *Hearing Res.* 26:65–88

Liberman, M. C. 1988. Response properties of olivocochlear neurons in quiet and in noise. Abstr. Midwinter Meet. Assoc. Res. in Otolaryngol.

Liberman, M. C., Brown, M. C. 1986. Physiology and anatomy of single olivocochlear neurons in the cat. *Hearing Res.* 24:17–36

Liberman, M. C., Dodds, L. W. 1984a. Single-neuron labeling and chronic cochlear pathology. II. Stereocilia damage and alterations of spontaneous discharge rates. *Hearing Res.* 16:43–53

Liberman, M. C., Dodds, L. W. 1984b. Single-neuron labeling and chronic cochlear pathology. III. Stereocilia damage and alterations of threshold tuning curves. *Hearing Res.* 16:55–74

Liberman, M. C., Dodds, L. W. 1987. Acute ultrastructural changes in acoustic trauma: serial-section reconstruction of stereocilia and cuticular plates. *Hearing Res.* 26:45–64

Liberman, M. C., Kiang, N. Y.-S. 1978. Acoustic trauma in cats: cochlear pathology and auditory nerve activity. *Acta Otolaryngol. Suppl.* 358:1–63

Liberman, M. C., Kiang, N. Y.-S. 1984. Single-neuron labelling and chronic cochlear pathology. IV. Stereocilia damage and alterations in rate- and phase-level functions. *Hearing Res.* 16:75–90

Lorente de No, R. 1981. *The Primary Acoustic Nuclei.* NY: Raven Press

McFadden, D., Wightman, F. L. 1983. Audition: some relations between normal and pathological hearing. *Ann. Rev. Psychol.* 34:95–128

McMullen, T. A., Mountain, D. C. 1985.

Model of dc potentials in the cochlea: effects of voltage-dependent cilia stiffness. *Hearing Res.* 17:127–41

Merzenich, M. M., Jenkins, W. M., Middlebrooks, J. C. 1984. Observations and hypotheses on special organizational features of the central auditory nervous system. In *Dynamic Aspects of Neocortical Function,* Ch. 12, ed. G. M. Edleman, W. E. Gail, W. M. Cowan. Rockville, Md: Neurosci. Res. Found.

Middlebrooks, J. C., Knudsen, E. I. 1987. Changes in external ear position modify the spatial tuning of auditory units in the cat's superior colliculus. *J. Neurophysiol.* 57: 672–87

Middlebrooks, J. C., Zook, J. M. 1983. Intrinsic organization of the cat's medial geniculate body identified by projections to binaural response-specific bands in the primary auditory cortex. *J. Neurosci.* 3:203–24

Mountain, D. C. 1980. Changes in endolymphatic potential and crossed olivocochlear bundle stimulation alter cochlear mechanics. *Science* 210:71–72

Mountain, D. C. 1986. Electromechanical properties of hair cells. In *Neurobiology of Hearing,* ed. R. A. Altschuler, D. W. Hoffman, R. P. Bobbin. NY: Raven Press

Mountain, D. C., Hubbard, A. E., McMullen, T. A. 1983. Electromechanical processes in the cochlea. In *Mechanics of Hearing,* ed. E. de Boer, M. A. Viergever. Delft: Delft Univ. Press

Neely, S. T., Kim, D. O. 1983. An active cochlear model showing sharp tuning and high sensitivity. *Hearing Res.* 9:123–30

Nielsen, D. W., Slepecky, N. 1986. Stereocilia. In *Neurobiology of Hearing,* ed. D. W. Hoffman, R. A. Altschuler, R. P. Bobbin. NY: Raven Press

Palmer, A. R., King, A. J. 1982. The representation of auditory space in the mammalian superior colliculus. *Nature* 299:248–49

Phillips, D. P., Brugge, J. F. 1985. Progress in neurophysiology of sound localization. *Ann. Rev. Psychol.* 36:245–74

Pickles, J. P., Comis, S. D., Osborne, M. P. 1984. Cross-links between stereocilia of the guinea pig organ of Corti and their possible relation to sensory transduction. *Hearing Res.* 15:103–12

Rajan, R., Robertson, D., Johnson, B. M. 1988. Efferent influences on temporary threshold shift in the guinea pig cochlea. Abstr. Midwinter Meet. Assoc. Res. in Otolaryngol.

Rasmussen, G. L. 1946. The olivary peduncle and their fiber connections of the superior olivary complex. *J. Comp. Neurol.* 84:141–219

Rhode, W. S. 1971. Observations on the vibration of the basilar membrane in squirrel monkeys using the Mössbauer technique. *J. Acoust. Soc. Am.* 49:1218

Rhode, W. S. 1978. Some observations on cochlear mechanics. *J. Acoust. Soc. Am.* 64:158–76

Rhode, W. S. 1980. Cochlear partition vibration—recent views 1980. *J. Acoust. Soc. Am.* 67:1696–1703

Roberts, W. M., Robles, L., Hudspeth, A. J. 1986. Correlation between the kinetic properties of ionic channels and the frequency of membrane-potential resonance in hair cells of the bullfrog. In *Auditory Frequency Selectivity,* ed. B. C. J. Moore, R. D. Patterson, pp. 89–95. NY: Plenum

Robertson, D. 1985. Brainstem location of efferent neurones projecting to the guinea pig cochlea. *Hearing Res.* 20:79–84

Robertson, D., Gummer, M. 1985. Physiological and morphological characterization of efferent neurons in the guinea pig cochlea. *Hearing Res.* 20:63–78

Russell, I. J., Sellick, P. M. 1978. Intracellular studies of hair cells in the mammalian cochlea. *J. Physiol.* 284:261–90

Sachs, M. B., Young, E. D. 1979. Encoding of steady-state vowels in the auditory nerve: representation in terms of discharge rate. *J. Acoust. Soc. Am.* 66:470–79

Saunders, J. C., Flock, A. 1985. Changes in cochlear hair-cell stereocilia stiffness following overstimulation. Abstr. Midwinter Meet. Assoc. in Otolaryngol.

Saunders, J. C., Schneider, M. E., Dear, S. P. 1983. The structure and function of actin in hair cells. *J. Acoust. Soc. Am.* 78:299–311

Saunders, J. C., Dear, S. P., Schneider, M. E. 1985. The anatomical consequences of acoustic injury: a review and tutorial. *J. Acoust. Soc. Am.* 78:833–60

Sellick, P. M., Patuzzi, R., Johnstone, B. M. 1982. Measurement of basilar membrane motion in the guinea pig using the Mössbauer technique. *J. Acoust. Soc. Am.* 72: 131–41

Semple, M. N., Aitkin, L. M., Calford, M. B., Pettigrew, J. D., Phillips, D. P. 1983. Spatial receptive fields in the cat inferior colliculus. *Hearing Res.* 10:203–15

Sewell, W. F. 1984a. The effects of furosemide on the endocochlear potential and auditory nerve fiber tuning curves. *Hearing Res.* 14:305–14

Sewell, W. F. 1984b. Furosemide selectively reduces one component in rate-level functions from auditory nerve fibers. *Hearing Res.* 15:69–72

Siegal, J. H., Kim, D. O. 1982. Efferent neural control of cochlear mechanics? Olivocochlear bundle stimulation affects biomechanical non-linearity. *Hearing Res.* 6:171–82

Siegal, J. H., Kim, D. O., Molnar, C. E. 1982. Effects of altering organ of Corti on cochlear distortion products f2-f1 and 2f1-f2. *J. Neurophysiol.* 47:303–28

Smith, C. A., Rasmussen, G. L. 1963. Recent observations on the olivocochlear bundle. *Ann. Otol. Rhinol. Laryngol.* 72:489–97

Spoendlin, H. 1969. Innervation patterns in the organ of Corti in the cat. *Acta Otolaryngol.* 67:239–54

Spoendlin, H. 1971. Primary ultrastructural changes in the organ of Corti after acoustic overstimulation. *Acta Otolaryngologica* 71:166–76

Slepecky, N., Chamberlain, S. C. 1982. Actin in cochlear hair cells—implications for stereocilia movement. *Arch. Otolaryngol.* 234:131–34

Strelioff, D., Flock, A. 1984. Stiffness of sensory-cell hair bundles in the isolated guinea pig cochlea. *Hearing Res.* 15:19–28

Strelioff, D., Flock, A., Minser, K. E. 1985. Role of inner and outer hair cells in mechanical frequency selectivity of the cochlea. *Hearing Res.* 18:169–75

Suga, N. 1988. What does single-unit analysis in the auditory cortex tell us about information processing in the auditory system? In *Neurobiology of Neo-Cortex,* ed. P. Rakic, W. Finger, London: Wiley pp. 331–49

Suga, N., Niwa, H., Taniguchi, I., Margoliash, D. 1987. The personalized auditory cortex of the mustached bat: adaptation for echolocation. *J. Neurophysiol.* 58:643–54

Suga, N., Tsuzuki, K. 1985. Inhibition and level-tolerant frequency tuning in the auditory cortex of the mustached bat. *J. Neurophysiol.* 53:1109–45

Sullivan, W. E., Konishi, M. 1984. Segregation of stimulus phase and intensity coding in the cochlear nucleus of the barn owl. *J. Neurosci.* 4:1787–99

Tasaki, I., Davis, H., Leguoix, J.-P. 1952. The space-time pattern of the cochlear microphonics (guinea pig) as recorded by differential electrodes. *J. Acoust. Soc. Am.* 24:502–19

Teas, D. C., Eldredge, D. H., Davis, H. 1962. Cochlear responses to acoustic transients: an interpretation of the whole-nerve action potential. *J. Acous. Soc. Am.* 34: 1438–59

Teas, D. C., Konishi, T., Nielsen, D. W. 1972. Electrophysiological studies on the spatial distribution of the crossed olivocochlea bundle along the guinea pig cochlea. *J. Acoust. Soc. Am.* 51:1256–64

Tilney, L. G., De Rosier, D. J., Mulroy, M. J. 1980. The organization of actin filaments in the stereocilia of cochlear hair cells. *J. Cell. Biol.* 86:244

Warr, W. B. 1978. The olivocochlear bundle: its origins and terminations in the cat. In *Evoked Electrical Activity in the Auditory Nervous System,* ed. R. F. Naunton, C. Fernandez. NY: Academic

Watson, C. S., Foyle, D. C. 1983. Central factors in the discrimination and identification of complex sounds. *J. Acoust. Soc. Am.* 78:375–88

Wever, E. G., Bray, C. W. 1930. Action currents in the auditory nerve in response to acoustical stimulation. *Proc. Natl. Acad. Sci. USA* 16:344–50

Wever, E. G., Lawrence, M. 1954. *Physiological Acoustics.* Princeton, NJ: Princeton Univ. Press

Wiederhold, M. L., Kiang, N. Y.-S. 1970. Effects of electrical stimulation of the crossed olivocochlear bundle on single auditory nerve fibers in the cat. *J. Acoust. Soc. Am.* 48:950–65

Wilson, J. P., Johnstone, J. R. 1972. Capacitive probe measures of basilar membrane vibration. In *Hearing Theory,* ed. B. L. Cardozo. Eindhoven, Netherlands: Inst. Perceptie Onderzook

Winslow, R. L. 1988. Effects of electrical stimulation of the COCB on auditory-nerve rate responses to tones in noise. Abstr. 11th *Midwinter Meet. Assoc. Res. Otolaryngol.* Clearwater Beach, Fla.

Yost, W. A., Gourevitch, G., eds. 1987. *Directional Hearing.* NY: Springer-Verlag

Zwislocki, J. J. 1980. Five decades of research on cochlear mechanics. *J. Acoust. Soc. Am.* 67:1679–88

Ann. Rev. Psychol. 1989. 40:431–55
Copyright © 1989 by Annual Reviews Inc. All rights reserved

ENGINEERING PSYCHOLOGY[1]

D. Gopher and R. Kimchi

Industrial Engineering and Management, Technion—Israel Institute of Technology, Haifa 32000, Israel

CONTENTS

INTRODUCTION

Our age is the computer age, and human interaction with an increasing proportion of modern systems entails either direct dialog with a computer system or the use of devices that incorporate artificial intelligence on one level or another. We resolved, however, not to include a separate section on human-computer interaction here. Instead, we concentrate on several problem

[1]Preparation supported in part by a grant from NASA Ames Res. Cent. Aerospace Hum. Factors Div. Thanks to P. Hacock, N. Moray, P. Sanderson, and C. Wickens for comments and suggestions; and to Y. Rubin and M. Olin for help with the bibliographic search. R. Kimchi is now at the Dept. Psychol., Univ. Haifa, Haifa 31999 Israel.

431

0066-4308/89/0201-0431$02.00

areas, in each of which various aspects of computer technology emerge as major instigators of research and modeling of human behavior.

Contemporary work in engineering psychology is marked by a deep interest in high-level cognitive functions and knowledge compilation. Issues include processing and response activities involving encoding, organization, memory represenation, and retrieval of information. Although sometimes subtle, the emphasis on cognition is evident in each of the problem areas discussed here. It is the main scientific force driving current application efforts.

The link between engineering psychology and technology not only affects the content and priorities of research work in this field, but also strongly influences its life cycle and pace. Modern technology is highly dynamic and progresses rapidly. New problems and new perspectives on old problems emerge daily. The current estimate of the duration of a technological generation is about five years (Tadmor et al 1987). What are the implications of such rapid change for our domain? What strategies should be developed to confront new problems at their increasing rate of emergence?

It appears to us that the best strategy engineering psychology can adopt is to slow its response to specific elements of new technology and strengthen its linkage with basic theorectical research. Mathematical control theory of dynamic systems teaches us that when the rate of change of an input function exceeds the point-to-point tracking capabilities of a system, the system can best respond by (a) following higher-order, slow-moving patterns of change, and (b) introducing response lead-time by predicting future inputs. The importance of this analogy is twofold: First, it helps to clarify the need to concentrate on the development of general principles and methods rather than on specific local solutions. Systematic empirical evaluation of human performance in every technological situation is impractical in terms of time, cost, and generalization value. (Think, for example, of the host of text processing programs, or the multiplicity of car instrument panels.) Second, the analogy emphasizes the role of theoretical models in practical work. Only with such models can we generate prinicples and predict the future. If there existed only a limited set of slow-moving technologies, strict empirical approaches could suffice.

We concentrate here on three problem areas that emerge from present technology. We discuss the technological instigators, theoretical foundations, and applied research in the design of visual displays, assessment of mental workload, and training of complex skills. The first illustrates typical issues and problems encountered in the design of engineering systems. The second concerns evaluation of human ability to cope with the demands of tasks. The third involves training operators to master the skills required at a new work station.

We refer the reader to several recent publications that offer a broader and more comprehensive coverage of the field. *The Handbook of Human Factors*

(Salvendy 1987a), which includes 66 chapters written by 104 researchers in the field, is perhaps the most comprehensive recent review of applied work. It is complemented by the 45 chapters of a two-volume *Handbook of Human Perception and Performance* (Boff et al 1986). These chapters review and evaluate human performance theory in topics relevant to engineering psychology. Other recent overviews of traditional and new topics can be found in the 6th edition of Sanders & McCormick's (1987) textbook, in *Trends in Ergonomics/Human Performance II* (Eberts & Eberts 1985), and in *Human Factors Psychology* (Hancock 1987). Two recent volumes on human-computer interaction edited by Salvendy (1987b,c) summarize work in this rapidly growing area.

Also useful are the proceedings of the annual meetings of professional societies in the field: the United States Human Factors Society (1985, 1986, 1987, 1988), the International Ergonomics Association (1985, 1988), and The International IEEE Conference on Systems, Man, and Cybernetics (1986, 1987, 1988). Although less formal, proceedings provide a more recent update of present trends and better pointers to future directions. Given the applied nature of the field, and the fact that field professionals are frequently not pressed to publish regularly in scientific journals, proceedings also better represent the topics of interest.

The primary journals for the core applied work in this area are *Human Factors, Ergonomics, Applied Ergonomics,* and the *International Journal of Man-Machine Studies.*

DISPLAYING AND INTERACTING WITH COMPLEX VISUAL INFORMATION

Efficient ways of displaying information have been a major concern of engineering psychology since its early days. Although each of the previous reviews of the field made brief reference to these issues (e.g. Wickens & Kramer 1985), the last time a large section was devoted to visual displays was in Chapanis's chapter in 1963. Since then, rapid advances in computer technology, increased graphic capabilities, and new display devices have increased interest in this area while introducing new types of problems for research.

Technological Need

The increased complexity of today's dynamic systems entails the presentation of a wealth of information to the human operator. At the same time, the rapid advances in computer and display technology have increased both the capability of presenting multi-element, complex information on a single display and the freedom to select the aspect and mode of presentation. The range of tasks that involve interaction with the new types of displays has increased as well.

While the traditional tasks of detection, identification, and discrimination remain, growing number of more complex, high-level supervisory control and decision-making tasks now require complex evaluations and interpretations (Moray 1986; Sheridan 1987).

A display is a physical device designed to convey information as quickly and accurately as possible. It constitutes a representation of another physical or abstract system. Hence, two major issues are involved in the design of a display: (a) its ability to represent properly the world one wishes to represent, and (b) the physical properties of the display itself.

The physical attributes of the display designed according to psychophysical laws, are critical for the availability of the displayed information to the human opertor. Guidelines for design of displays still focus on the psychophysical qualities of the display, aiming at enhancing readability and legibility (e.g. Helander 1987). There is, however, a growing recognition of the need to consider human perceptual and cognitive processing as well (Foley & Moray 1987; Wickens 1987). Indeed, the human engineering literature of the last five years shows increasing interest in representational and information-processing issues, which brings this discipline closer to central questions in cognitive psychology.

Theoretical Foundation

High-powered computer graphics present a display's designer with many choices about how to present information. In order to exploit this freedom in the best possible way, we need principles of representation design.

Modern cognitive psychology is dominated by the information-processing approach (e.g. Palmer & Kimchi 1986), an attempt to specify the nature of mental representations and the processes that operate upon them (e.g. Palmer & Kimchi 1986; Chase 1986; Treisman 1986). Excellent reviews and analyses of representational systems are provided by Palmer (1978) and Rumelhart & Norman (1988). The problem of representation is one of determining a mapping between the concepts and relations of the represented world and the concepts and relations of the representing world. The distinction between analogical and symbolic (propositional) representations and the distinction between continuous and discrete representations are discussed, and useful ways to view these distinctions are suggested.

Palmer (1978) treats the analogical/symbolic distinction as a distinction between information "intrinsic" to the representation and information "extrinsic" to it. The representation is an analog of the represented world when the relations of interest are intrinsic to the representation. A representation is intrinsic whenever a representing relation has the same inherent constraints as the relation it represents. The continuous/discrete distinction (which is often confused with the analogical/symbolic distinction) is really about the "grain size" or "acuity" that must be captured in the represented world (Rumelhart & Norman 1988).

A representational system consists of both data structures and operations. The data structure can be represented through different representational formats that map best into the set of operations to be performed upon it.

The relevance of this analysis to the design of displays should be readily apparent. If the funciton of a display is to communicate information and to ensure efficient processing of this information, the display's designer must map informaton structure into display attributes in a way that suits both the information to be represented and the operations to be performed on it.

We can learn much about how to organize, access, and manipulate displayed information from current research in cognitive psychology, including studies of pattern recognition, visual search, cognitive maps (Chase 1986), and perceptual organization.

Cognitive psychologists are making serious attempts to go beyond the descriptive laws of the Gestalt psychologists to understand perceptual organization in information-processing terms (e.g. Kubovy & Pomerantz 1981; Boff et al 1986). Particularly relevant are theoretical accounts and empirical studies on grouping, dimensional interactions, analytic and holistic processing, perceptual relations between global and local aspects of visual patterns, top-down processing (Treisman 1986), and the role of spatial-frequency analysis in form and object perception (Ginsburg 1986).

The importance of the Gestalt laws of grouping for organizing display informatin is well recognized (e.g. Helander 1987; Foley & Moray 1987). A better application of these laws can benefit from recent research based on performance measures of grouping (e.g. Pomerantz 1981; Treisman 1985).

How physical dimensions are combined to form perceptual dimensions has been studied extensively by Garner and his colleagues (e.g. Garner 1974, 1978). Garner distinguishes between separable, integral, and configural dimensions. Stimuli varying along integral dimensions are perceived as unitary entities, whereas those varying along separable dimensions are perceived in terms of distinct dimensions or attributes. Configural dimensions interact so that their combination produces a new emergent feature (e.g. closure, symmetry). Integral dimensions facilitate performance when they are perfectly correlated and selective attention to either dimension is impossible. Separable dimensions permit selective attention to either dimension, but they do not facilitate performance when they are redundant. With configural dimensions, performance is dominated by the new emergent feature. It has been suggested that emergent properties are perceived directly (e.g. Pomerantz 1981).

Do the earliest perceptual stages encode unitary wholes, which are later analyzed into parts and properties, or are the parts registered first and then synthesized to form the objects we are aware of? This unsettled issue has generated a wealth of empirical research. The feature-analytic approach provided some evidence for the role played by parts and properties in perception (Treisman 1986). The global superiority phenomenon (Navon 1977, 1981) supported the primacy of holistic or global processing; but other researchers demonstrated important boundary conditions of the phenomenon (e.g. Hoffman 1980; Kinchla & Wolfe 1979; Miller 1981) and provided finer analysis of the perceptual relations between global and local aspects of visual patterns (e.g. Kimchi & Palmer 1985; Kimchi 1988).

The role of prior knowledge or expectations in perception has been studied. Most current models of object and event perception see it as an interactive process between bottom-up (data-driven) processing and top-down (conceptually driven) processing (e.g. Rumelhart 1977; Treisman & Schmidt 1982).

Current Application Research

A major line of application research focuses on representational issues. Typical questions concern selection and evaluation of display symbology, the advantages of one type of format over another, and the benefits of pure vs mixed formats in complex displays.

Analog formats are compared to digital. Analog formats in this context are loosely defined and refer most often to spatial, continuous representation. In many cases analog formats and graphic representations are referred to interchangeably. Traditional analog formats include bar graphs, dot clusters, and dials. Digital formats include alphanumeric coding such as digits, letters, and word names. The relative efficiencies of these formats have been investigated with a variety of tasks. For example, Boles & Wickens (1987) compared analog (bar graphs), digital, and verbal formats in a numerical judgment task and found that analog indicators were responded to more quickly than were digital or verbal indicators. Schwartz & Howell (1985) compared performance in a simulated hurricane-tracking task under conditions in which position information was presented either graphically or digitally. Subjects performed better using graphic displays, particularly under conditions of rapid change. Bauer & Eddy (1986) studied representation of command language syntax. They compared the use of special metacharacters and graphic representations to represent grammatical relations. They found the graphic representation to be superior both during learning and in a reference task.

Boles & Wickens (1987) found that tasks requiring the integration of display elements benefited from pure-format display, while dual tasks benefited from a mixed-format display.

For use in displays one would like to select symbols that represent well and are maximally dissimilar to one another. Graphic symbols, especially pictographs, may be preferred over alphanumeric symbols because the resemblance between the shape of the symbol and that of the object it represents can be exploited. This can be especially beneficial under heavy memory demands. However, intra-set similarity among pictographs can increase search and identification time. For example, Remington & Williams (1986) used a single-target visual task to evaluate a set of CRT symbols for a helicopter situation display. They found numeric symbols superior to graphic symbols. The authors attributed their finding to the familiarity and discriminability of the numeric symbols on the one hand, and to a high degree of intra-set similarity among the graphic symbols on the other. Recently, Workman & Fisher (1987) proposed a new metric of similarity based on the degree of overlap between "fuzzy pictures" of the symbols. The similarity ratings derived from this metric can be used to select the most discriminable subset from a set of meaningful symbols.

A popular solution to the problem of presenting multidimensional correlated information to operators of complex systems has been the integral, object-like display. Integral display formats use several dimensions of a single object to portray system status (e.g. polygons, schematic faces). Separable display formats use separate univariate displays, either in the traditional digital (alphanumeric) formats or by using the same dimension of several objects to display mulitivariate information (e.g. bar graphs). Many studies have found integral displays superior to separable displays when the data variables are highly correlated and/or when integration of data from a number of sources is required by the operator before a decision can be made (e.g. Goldsmith & Schvaneveldt 1984; Carswell & Wickens 1988; Beringer 1985; Beringer & Chrisman 1987; Boulette et al 1987).

The superiority of the integral, object-like display can be attributed to two properties of human perception: (a) The human perceptual system has a limited ability to process a single dimension with multiple objects at the same time, while it is capable of processing in parallel several dimensions of a single object (e.g. Lappin 1967; Kahneman & Treisman 1984). (b) Global or holistic features can be processed faster than local features (e.g. Navon 1977, 1981; Pomerantz 1981). Object-like displays change their global form to convey relations in system states, so such displays may be globally processed (Munson & Horst 1986). However, the advantage of an integral display can be nullified under certain conditions. For example, Coury and associates (1986a) demonstrated that when the system state was certain, the operator was able to classify more quickly integral than separable displays; but when the system state was uncertain, separable displays were superior to the integral ones.

An important determinant of integral display effectiveness is the attentional requirement of the task. For example, Casey (1987) compared integral and separable displays in the detection and diagnosis of failure for systems whose variables were related either by correlation or by causality. For both types of systems separable displays were superior. The diagnosis task required focusing on the components of the display in order to identify the cause of failure. Thus, while holistic processing supported by object-like display is useful for analysis of overall status, it is detrimental when the task requires selective attention, even when the system components are strongly interrelated.

A considerable amount of research effort has been devoted to the relation between the type of display (integral vs separable) and two factors: the structure of the information to be presented (correlated vs noncorrelated) and the nature of the task (integral vs nonintegral). The physical dimensions used to represent the information received much less attention. Granted that there is no one-to-one mapping between physical and perceptual dimensions, it should be important to consider how physical dimensions interact to form perceptual dimensions in terms of their integrality, separability, and configurality (see above). A step in this direction has been taken recently by Barnett & Wickens (1988).

The importance of a compatibility between the format of the displayed information and central processing codes, particularly in working memory, is well recognized (e.g. Wickens 1987). Once visual displays are used to represent complex systems, there is greater concern about the compatibility between the displayed information and the mental model the human operators have of the systems. Displays of complex systems can support or enhance human performance if they match human mental models of the system, or if they help to shape the correct mental models (e.g. Woods 1986; Coury et al 1986b; Eberts & Schneider 1985; Eberts 1986; Sanderson 1986).

A related line of research focuses on representation of spatial information by computer-generated graphics. In natural or even pictorial viewing the viewer can rely on the structure of correlated attributes in the physical world to provide multiple cues about the event and the space in which it occurs (Hochberg 1986). Owing to the synthetic nature of computer-generated graphic representations, such information is missing. In order to communicate spatial information, the designer of such representations must consider both the relevant physical structure (e.g. various perspective cues) and the relevant perceptual processes. One attempt to develop more efficient displays for representing three-dimensional information on two-dimensional screens produced the perspective display for air-traffic control (Ellis et al 1987; McGreevy & Ellis 1986). Use of the perspective display, considered more "natural" than the conventional plan-view, improved decision time and avoidance performance (Ellis et al 1987).

Summary

The most frequent empirical finding is an interaction of displays with tasks. The importance of task requirements in perceptual processing has been manifested in basic research as well (Treisman 1986). How, then, might one go about developing guidelines for the design of complex visual displays? This question brings us back to the representational issues discussed at the beginning of the section, suggesting an answer in the following general terms:

1. Determine which aspects of the represented world (e.g. a complex dynamic system) are to be captured within the representing world (i.e. the visual display).
2. Determine how the selected aspects shall be represented.
3. Recognize that items 1 and 2, above, depend critically upon task domain. This requires a coherent analysis of task requirements in terms of human information processing.

THE STUDY OF MENTAL WORKLOAD

Key books and comprehensive chapters have been published recently on mental processing and response limitations in the performance of tasks (Hancock 1987; Gopher & Donchin 1986; O'Donnell & Eggemeier 1986; Kantowitz 1987; Hart 1986).

Since the review of mental workload by Wickens & Kramer (1985) the need to strengthen the theoretical basis of this research has been increasingly recognized.

Technological Need

Human operators are today required to fulfill monitoring and decision-making roles at the center of highly automated systems. They are confronted with multiple and diversified sources of information, updated at high rates. This state of affairs naturally raises the question of capacity limitations. What are the boundaries of the human ability to attend to sources of information, to process, transform, decide, and carry out the necessary responses? How much information can be provided and in what form? What are the risks and costs of exceeding the limits?

Theoretical Foundations

Contemporary efforts to understand the human processing system follow two major courses: One is an attempt to develop computational models that can mimic basic behavioral phenomena and thus elucidate limitations in terms of the architecture of the underlying psychological processes. A second course studies intensive aspects of behavior and attempts to complement the analysis of structure by introducing considerations of resource scarcity and energy modulation. Both approaches emphasize the development of models linking the findings of behavioral research with those in the physiological and biological sciences.

COMPUTATIONAL APPROACHES   Most significant has been the development of parallel distributed processing (PDP) models (McClelland & Rumelhart 1985, 1986; Rumelhart & McClelland 1986; McClelland 1989). The PDP approach holds that the brain's processing system consists of a collection of simple processing units, each interconnected with many other units. The units take on activation values and communicate wih other units by sending signals modulated by weightings assoicated with the connections between the units. Units are organized into modules that receive input from other modules. The units within a module are richly interconnected. A mental state is a pattern of activation over the units in some subset of modules. Alternative mental states are simply alternative patterns of activation over the modules. Information processing occurs through a series of mental states (McClelland & Rumelhart 1985, pp. 161–62).

This general approach is accompanied by rigorous criteria and construction rules. It has successfully modeled behavior in a variety of tasks, including learning and memory, language understanding and production, and motor behavior.

ENERGETICS   How do energy factors regulate human information processing? This course of research represents a revived and revised interest in one of the classical issues of psychology—accounting for motivational and intensive aspects of behavior, as opposed to structural and directional aspects. A good summary of the present state of knowledge in this area can be found in *Energetics and Human Information Processing* (Hockey et al 1986).

Work in this category covers such topics as: slow and fast phase diurnal fluctuations in response efficiency, sustained attention, effects of voluntary effort, changes in rate as contrasted with quality of responses, mobilization of attention, and response to stress. Behavioral evidence for such changes often correlates with intensity modulations of physiological processes, such as fluctuations in levels of arousal, rhythmicities of activity cycles, event-related brain activity, and responses to pharmacological interventions. Neurobiology has demonstrated evidence of discrete neurotransmitter systems with specifc information-processing functions (Pribram & McGuinness 1975; Pribram 1986; Posner & Rotbart 1986; Peterson et al 1988), and researchers have proposed links between these systems and constructs emerging from information-processing models (Gopher & Sanders 1984; Lavie et al 1987;

Sanders 1986; Van der Molen et al 1987; Coles & Gratton 1986; Posner & Rotbart 1986). Physiological mechanisms may function as separate processing resources (Gopher & Sanders 1984; Friedman & Polson 1981) or act as gain factors to vectors of computational operators (Wickens 1986; Gopher 1986; Posner & Rotbart 1986).

Work in computational structure and work in energetic factors have identified different dimensions of increased task difficulty and different causes of performance deficit. Structural interpretations emphasize the contribution of factors such as the number and type of transformations that must be carried out in sequence, or conflicts and confusions between inputs, throughputs, and outputs of processing activities (Navon 1985; Navon & Miller 1987). Energetic interpretations adopt the term "resources" to define the processing facilities at the disposal of the human "operator." Resources can be invested in shares and actively allocated to the performance of tasks. Resource models emphasize capacity limitations—the scarcity of energy and space—as the cause of performance deficits under increased demands (Norman & Bobrow 1975; Navon & Gopher 1979; Wickens 1984; Gopher 1986).

Most contemporary proponents of the resource approach identify several relatively independent resources (Wickens 1984; Gopher 1986). There is also, however, a modern single-limited-resource approach, which emerges from the distinction between automatic and controlled modes of processing. Controlled processess are postulated to be attention demanding, slow, and effortful, while automatic processes do not require attention and can proceed in parallel. This model was orignally proposed by Shiffrin & Schneider (1977) and has recently been elaborated by Schneider (1985a).

Real-life tasks require processing in both the automatic and the controlled modes. The load is determined by the proportions of the two modes. This approach has been tested in many studies (see Fisk et al 1987 for a recent review). In essence, this model integrates the computational and energetics perspectives. Its basic postulates concern the organization of computational processes. However, operation at different organizational levels has its corresponding energetic costs.

Current Application Research

While basic research is still brooding over the nature of the central limitations and the best approach to modeling them, engineering psychology has launched into development of techniques to assess workload. Apparently, the intuitive appeal of the limited-capacity concept, coupled with the increasing pressure from the field, were strong enough to suppress ambiguities and drive the conduct of a large number of empirical and application-oriented studies. Most of these accept the existence of a central limitation and do not question its general nature. They then consider how to develop standard measurement scales, interpret the obtained values, and compare scales (Hart 1986; O'Donnell & Eggemeier 1986; Wierwille et al 1985).

Three classes of measures have been developed to assess workload: behavioral, physiological, and subjective.

BEHAVIORAL MEASURES   Behavioral measures derive an index of workload from elements of operator performance. The most popular and widely researched behavioral approach has been the "Secondary Task" technique. In this technique the level of performance on one of two concurrently performed tasks is used to index both spare capacity and, by complementary inference, the load imposed on the central processor by the task with which it is time-shared (see Wickens & Kramer 1985). In recent years various types and numbers of secondary tasks have been employed. Types of tasks vary with the researcher's theory about the dominant causes of load. They follow the progress of information-processing models. The number of tasks, or the employment of a battery of different secondary tasks, is a more recent development influenced by the multiple-resource view. It fosters the idea of creating a load profile for tasks to index differential resource loadings of component processes.

Representative studies have employed secondary tasks claimed to provide separate measures of the load share of perceptual, mediational, or response processes (Wierwille et al 1985; Gopher & Braune 1984; Derrick 1988). Other experiments contrasted spatial and verbal tasks, related to right- and left-hemisphere-localized processes (Wickens et al 1984; Carswell & Wickens 1985; Friedman & Polson 1981; Friedman et al 1982). A third group of experiments studies the load consequences of varied versus consistent relationships between S-R components, reflecting controlled or automatic operation modes (Vidulich & Wickens 1986; Fisk & Schneider 1984).

A typical outcome in such studies is a performance interference profile, in which some tasks show larger interference under time-sharing conditions. It is interpreted as revealing the locus of load on the central processor (Wierwille et al 1985; Derrick 1988). A good application of this strategy is the battery of criterion tasks for the measurement of workload, developed by the US Air Force workload branch at Wright Patterson, for use in the design and procurement of systems by the Air Force (Schlegel et al 1987). The selection of tasks in this battery follows the dimensions of resources proposed by Wickens (1984). It includes 9 leading tasks, presented in a total of 25 different configuartions, varying in modality of presentation, temporal structure, type of required transformations, and mode of response.

PHYSIOLOGICAL MEASURES   The study of physiological measures concentrates upon indexes of the physiological activity associated with information-processing tasks. Two factors have influenced the increase of interest in this approach [e.g. see the special issue of *Human Factors* edited by Kramer (April 1987)]: (*a*) the growing emphasis and accumulated knowledge on the relationship between physiological mechanisms and information processing constructs, and (*b*) our enhanced ability to obtain accurate physiological measures in field conditions with little interference to normal operator activity.

Two major classes of physiological measures have been developed: general indexes of arousal and processing effort, and measures locked to specific processing activities. Contemporary studies of general measures focus on cardiovascular activity and pupil dilation. For example, Aasman et al (1987), using spectral analysis of heart-rate variability, have shown correspondence between increased amplitude at 0.10 Hz and increased memory load. Vincente et al (1987) showed correspondence between sinus arrhythmia and demands of manual control. Both cases led to the development of portable measurement equipment for field work. Beatty (1982, 1986) has shown the relationship between pupil dilation and the change of difficulty on a variety of tasks, including memory, perception, and motor control.

Physiological measures of load corresponding to specific processing activity have concentrated primarily on event-related brain evoked potentials (ERP). For example, the amplitude of the P300 component of the ERP varies with the level of encoding and central processing demands in a simulated flight mission (Kramer et al 1987). Mangun & Hillyard (1987) used six ERP components localized at a four scalp regions to describe gradients of visual and spatial attention. Bauer et al (1987) used changes in amplitude of the P1–N1 components to index the selective load of memory and encoding processes. Both ERP measures and general physiological indexes have been included in the workload test battery developed by the US Air Force (Wilson & O'Donnell 1988).

SUBJECTIVE MEASURES   Performers can be asked to indicate the difficulties experienced in the performance of the evaluated task. These estimates are easy to obtain and have high face validity, but they suffer from two major drawbacks. (*a*) The conscious experience they reflect covers only a small portion of the information-processing activity of interest in the assessment of workload. (*b*) Subjective biases as well as intrá and interindividual variability affect how people quantify their experience (Gopher & Braune 1984). Nevertheless, the use of subjective measures increases in popularity, and there have been two recent large-scale research efforts to construct standard workload rating scales based on subjective judgments: the NASA-TLX (*Task Load indeX*: Hart & Staveland 1988) and the US Air Force SWAT (*Subjective Workload Assessment Technique*: Reid & Nygren 1988).

Both TLX and SWAT have been tested on a wide range of laboratory and real-life tasks (primarily in the aviation environment). They correlated highly with each other and were sensitive measures of the subjective experience of load (Vidulich & Tsang 1986).

Summary

Each class of measures has its advantages and disadvantages as an index of workload. Behavioral measures are the final product of the system, the components of which are hard to decompose. Employment of secondary tasks may be obtrusive and introduce spurious consideration of attention policy. Physiological measures are less direct and are influenced by many variables not related to information processing. Subjective measures are influenced by irrelevant variables and reflect only conscious experience.

In absence of a formal model of workload, or a set of decision rules, most of the studies cited above used several measurement classes in conjunction. This strategy has complicated the situation by producing different load estimates of the same task, which have often dissociated. Current research has limited power in resolving dissociation, although several attempts have been made (Gopher & Braune 1984; Vidulich & Wickens 1986; Coles & Gratton 1986; Ye & Wickens 1988).

Which measurement strategy should be used to assessment mental workload? We cannot and should not yet attempt to answer. In spite of the massive research conducted in this area, we remain at the stage of demonstration. We know more about the structure of tasks and the variables that may influence processing difficutly, but we have little ability to estimate and predict limits. We know little about how the different manifestations of load relate to one another, or about how separate elements that influence load interact.

Yet these are the questions engineering phychology must answer. System designers want to know how close is the performer to his limits and how much load can be alleviated by technological innovation. Engineering psychology is now able to give only partial and fragmented answers. Comtemporary applied research has exhausted the degrees of freedom provided by the crude theoretical models that have guided it. Progress now depends on a better theoretical understanding of the human processing system.

TRAINING OF COMPLEX SKILLS

Technological Need

With the advance of automation and robotics the proportion of unskilled jobs diminishes rapidly while that of professional jobs increases. Performers must often acquire advanced knowledge and moderate expertise before entering the operational environment. On-the-job training is either impossible, too time consuming, or too expensive. Moreover, task complexity and the evolution of technology at the work station often require continuous training, reorganization, and upgrading of existing skills.

At the same time, rapid progress in simulation, artificial intelligence, and microprocessor technology paves the way to the development of powerful, inexpensive training devices to meet training objectives.

Theoretical Foundations

The changing roles of human operators at the work station match well the interests of contemporary psychology. Within the general study of cognitive processes is a special focus on knowledge representation and the modeling of expert behavior. Appropriately, the training problem addresses how to develop, maintain, and reformulate expertise in the most efficient way.

Contemporary theories of expert behavior, anchored in the framework of cognitive psychology, concentrate on information-processing concepts (Anderson 1981, 1985; Adams 1987). The focus is on the representation and organization of knowledge in, and methods for its retrieval from long-term memory. Expertise is conjectured to constitute a well-roganized set of schemas in such specific domains of behavior as solving probelms of Physics, computer programming, troubleshooting in mechanical and electrical systems, proficient typing, and piloting airplanes. Interest lies in the final form of representation and in the operation rules of expert knowledge, as well as in the processes of arriving at this stage.

The modern instantiation of the distinction between conscious and nonconscious determinants of skill acquisition manifests itself in the study of top-down strategies of acquisition and represenation (Chase & Ericsson 1981; Anderson 1981; Moray 1986) as compared with new models of bottom-up conditioning through reinforced experience (McClelland & Rumelhart 1985; Schneider 1985b).

Research in top-down processes has shown the influence of encoding strategies, efforts to assimilate new information in exisiting well-organized knowledge bases, and retrieval techniques on the development of expertise. There is also an active interest in the role of mental models developed by the performer in the guidance of efficient behavior (Gentner & Stevens 1983).

Bottom-up processes of acquisition are being investigated by the PDP group, which views the establishment of knowledge bases as a process of emerging patterns of activation and inhibition among multiple interconnected processing modules (McClelland & Rumelhart 1985). Similar priniciples guide the research on the development of automaticity through experience with consistent mappings between stimulus and response (Schneider 1985a). Both types of bottom-up modeling approaches search for physiological counterparts to anchor their constructs and organization rules in the reality of the nervous system.

Implication for Applied Research

Several applications of top-down principles have been studied. One line of investigation focuses on the development of mental models. The mental-model construct has become a key concept in the training of complex skills (Gentner & Stevens 1983; Moray 1987; Eberts & Schneider 1985; Gagne & Glaser 1987). A mental model is loosely defined as an internal representation of the structure of a complex system or the demands of a task, together with a set of heuristics or rules that may guide problem solving and performance. Errors and inefficient performance can be frequently traced to faulty mental models (Moray 1987; Rumelhart & Norman 1981). Gagne & Glaser (1987) identified four tactics for encouraging the use of mental models in the acquisition of skill: (a) discovery, utilization, and elaboration during training of everyday models that trainees may bring to the training environment; (b) tracing the types of models a trainee develops during the acquisition of expertise, and using these in training; (c) deliberate introduction of "good" mental models; and (d) taking advantage of an individual's current model by using examples, counterexamples, and situations in which that model can be tested.

The mental-model concept has been explored in troubleshooting in engineering systems (Morris & Rouse 1985), pilot judgment training (Buch & Diehl 1984), manual control of highly dynamic systems (Eberts & Schneider 1985), spatial ability of air-traffic controllers (Schneider et al 1982), and complex supervisory tasks (Sanderson 1986).

Other applications of top-down cognitive principles attempt to construct training situations that will facilitate encoding, representation, retrieval, and interaction with knowledge bases. Many studies of this type were conducted in the context of human-computer interaction (Bosser 1986). Typical examples are mastering programming languages (Williges et al 1987), carrying on dialogs with computers (Streitz et al 1987; Wood & Wood 1987), operating data entry devices (Gopher & Raij 1988; Gopher 1984, 1987; Gopher et al 1985), using complex software, and interacting with intelligent systems (Grudin & Barnard 1984; Boehm-Davis et al 1987; Bransford et al 1986).

Just as important are the attempts to use the emerging principles of cognition for the development of training-oriented task analysis. Task analysis has always been a major concern of any training program. What are the task's basic components, and what are the best ways to segment them in the course of training? This has been the traditional part-whole issue (Adams 1960; but see also Wightman & Lintern 1985, for a recent discussion). The significance of this question increases as the complexity of tasks advances. In complex tasks the gaps between novice and expert performance are greatly increased and the task in its final form is frequently beyond the capability of the beginner.

Some method of task analysis is either explicitly or implicitly embedded in every training program. The more overt, systematic, and objective it is made, the lower the probabilty of introducing ambiguity and inconsistency to the training situation. Systematic research on this issue is sorely wanting.

The focal point for one proposed approach has been an analysis of the final knowledge base of the expert, which is followed by hierarchical decomposition of the principles, rules, goals, and subgoals of this knowledge (Frederiksen & White 1989; Ryder et al 1987; Nave-Benjamin et al 1986). Another approach concentrates on decomposing task demands in terms of the processing mechanisms involved and the load on each mechanism (Mane et al 1983; Logie et al 1989). Proponents of the distinction between controlled and automatic processes promote a third approach, based on segmentation to components by identifying the consistently vs variably mapped task elements (Schneider 1985b; Fisk et al 1987). A fourth approach proposes decompostion by identifying task elements amenable to being the focus of strategic voluntary shifts of attention (Gopher et al 1989). Research work in all these directions is preliminary. Development of task-decomposition methods for training remains an important challenge for future research.

Training of High-Workload Tasks

While the training research reviewed thus far is primarily concerned with the structure and content of expert behavior, there is also an active interest in the accompanying attention costs to performance. Skilled behavior has been associated with increased automaticity, relegation of authority to peripheral mechanisms, and decreased involvement of high-level, attention-demanding and time-consuming processes. Automaticity may lead, in turn, to an increase in the rate of performance, reduction of attention demands by the task itself, and better ability to attend to secondary or new task elements (Fitts & Posner 1967; Welford 1968).

One approach to this issue follows the theoretical distinction between controlled and automatic processes. Controlled processes are claimed to be attention demanding, sequential, and limited, while automatic processes are argued to be parallel and attention free. According to this approach, reduced costs are concomitants of automaticity developed by repeated exposures to consistent stimulus-response mappings. Tasks that comprise a larger portion of consistent elements will be less limited and less attention demanding. In contrast, tasks that include many elements that vary in their mapping will impose high load even after prolonged periods of training. These arguments have been supported in several empirical studies (Fisk et al 1987; Schnieder (1985b).

An alternative, though not exclusive, approach takes a more active and direct view of the relationship between attention processes and the development of expertise. The theoretical anchors of this approach are the study of workload and the concept of voluntary control of multiple attentional resources (Gopher & Donchin 1986). Processing demands of complex tasks are described by their load vector on different resources and task elements. Proficient performers are hypothesized to develop efficient attention allocation and attention mobilization strategies as part of their expertise. One objective of these strategies is to maximize the match between the demand profile of the task and the individual capabilities of the performer. A second objective is to enable the performer to mobilize efforts and change strategies when task conditions vary. The main arguments of this approach have been summarized in two recent papers (Gopher et al 1985; 1989). A similar view has been proposed by Mane & Wickens (1986). Experiments to test the approach were conducted on subjects practicing complex computer games and on the training of flight skills (Gopher et al 1988).

The Technology of Training

The emphasis on cognition has had interesting influences on the technology of training, most significantly in the arena of complex skills and the design of simulators. Emerging historically from the training of vehicle control skills (piloting airplanes, driving cars, and navigating ships in rough seas), simulators are being employed nowadays in the training of a wide and diversified range of tasks in industrial, military, and office environments (Flexman & Stark 1987). Formal principles for the construction of training simulators have not yet been elaborated. In the absence of sufficient theoretical understanding of skill acquisition and transfer processes, the dominant design rule over the years has been physical fidelity: the greater the similarity between the physical characteristics of the simulator and the operational environment, the larger the training value of the simulator.

As systems and tasks have become more complex and demanding and the operational environments more extreme, so have the challenges and costs of constructing training simulators increased. These developments have made the "physical fidelity" principle impossible or too expensive to achieve. They raise the issue of the cost effectiveness of increased sophistication (see "How much do you want to pay for this box?", C. Hopkins 1975). The situation has generated a growing interest in establishing alternative design principles based on the skill structure and the functional and psychological demands of the task. Such characteristics can be simulated at various levels, even at low levels of physical fidelity (Roscoe 1980).

Initial efforts in this direction lacked the theoretical framework and the technological tools for success; but recent developments in microprocessor technology, on the one hand, and the accumulated knowledge in cognitive psychology, on the other, may soon be joined to develop better designs. Microprocessors are rapidly becoming powerful, inexpensive machines capable of simulating complex situations. Cognitive psychology may supply the tools for the analysis of expertise and delineate the route from novice to expert performance.

Although work in this area is still embryonic, several successful applications have been reported. There is also a growing interest in the potential of part trainers based upon cognitive analysis. Halff et al (1986) review several examples involving the training of military skills. Discussing the cognitive demands of four groups of tasks (maintenance, tactics, piloting, and air-traffic control), Halff et al describe principles and tools developed to train personnel. The cognitive components dealt with included memory and semantic networks, understanding of dynamic systems, perceptual capabilities used to judge relative motion, and synthesis of spatial and orientational components required to perform air-traffic control functions. In all cases, the trainers can be conceived of as part simulators of the skill components and cognitive demands of the represented task. Experience with these trainers led to substantial improvement in task performance.

A forthcomming issue of *Acta Psychologica* (ed. Donchin 1989) is a compendium describing the results of an international collaboration. Headquartered at the University of Illinois and conducted simultaneously at 9 laboratories in the United States, Canada, United Kingdom, and Israel, the project sought to develop learning strategies to be embedded in the algorithms of complex computer games to improve players' acquisition of predetermined skills. The task was a highly complex, dynamic, and difficult computer game, codesigned by all the participant laboratories. It combined difficult manual, visual, attention, memory, and decision-making skills. Laboratories differed in their theoretical emphases, proposed approaches to the decomposition of the complex task, and methods of training.

Representative strategies concentrated on part tasks corresponding to components of the expert knowledge base (Fredriksen & White 1989), on voluntary control of attention (Gopher et al 1989), on training of visual skills (Shapiro & Raymond , 1989) and on improvement of manual control strategies (Newell et al 1989). From several perspectives the project may serve to clarify and underline many of the theoretical and practical issues raised here. More specifically, it indicates the urgent need for a theory-based approach to task analysis, demonstrates the powerful influence of well-designed training, and shows that practice, unless it is properly introduced, does not make perfect.

CONCLUDING REMARKS

The gaps between basic and applied research are narrower than we had expected them to be. Contemporary basic research has grown more attentive to problems raised at the field level. Application efforts have begun to turn more often to theory, in an attempt to increase their influence upon the deveopment of technology. Consequently, there is considerable interest in establishing and maintaining an active dialog between basic and applied research.

In each of the three problem areas reviewed, we detected ongoing shifts in emphasis. The area of visual displays is shifting from an emphasis on basic psychophysical functions to problems of complex perceptual organization and functional representation of multidimensional sources of information. Workload research is marked by increased emphasis on a multitask, multimeasures approaches anchored in multiple-resource theoretical models. There is also a greater focus on physiological and subjective measures than on performance indexes. The training area is undergoing a fundamental reformulation dictated both by the transition from behaviorist to cognitive models of learning and by the new types of skills required at the work station.

Better task analysis methods are needed in each of the problem areas. Task analysis enables the applied worker to relate problems encountered in the field to the knowledge bases of science. Most task analysis methods developed over the years (Fleishman et al 1984) suffer from major drawbacks. They may not be linked explicitly with any theoretical model of performance and/or they may advocate a single generic method for multiple application objectives.

A good task analysis method should be specific to application goals and have clear ties with the constructs of a theory of performance. The dimensions of task analysis relevant to training issues differ considerably from those of interest to workload assessment or to the efficient display of information. Task analysis methods must thus be developed within the context, models, and concerns of a specific problem area. At present, the absence of such methods leaves the field seriously handicapped.

Literature Cited

Aasman, J., Mulder, J., Mulder, L. J. M. 1987. Operator effort and the measurement of heart rate variability. *Hum. Factors* 29:161–70
Adams, J. A. 1960. Part trainers. In *Educational and Training Media: A Symposium,* ed. Finch, G., pp. 129–49. Washington DC: Natl. Acad. Sci., NRC
Adams, J. A. 1987. Historical review and appraisal of research on learning, retention and transfer of human motor skills. *Psychol. Bull.* 101:41–74
Anderson, J. R. 1985. *Cognitive Psychology*

and Its Implications. New York: Freeman. 472 pp. 2nd ed.
Anderson, J. R. ed. 1981. *Cognitive Skills and Their Acquisition.* Hillsdale, NJ: Lawrence Erlbaum
Barnett, B. J., Wickens, C. D. 1988. Display proximity in multicue information integration: the benefits of boxes. *Hum. Factors* 30:15–24
Bauer, D. W., Eddy, J. K. 1986. The representation of command language syntax. *Hum. Factors* 28:1–10
Bauer, L. O., Goldstein, R., Stern, J. A 1987.

Effects of information processing demands on physiological response patterns. *Hum. Factors* 29:213–34

Beatty, J. 1982. Task-evoked pupillary responses, processing load, and the structure of processing resources. *Psychol. Bull.* 91:276–92

Beatty, J. 1986. Computation, control and energetics: a biological perspective. See Hockey et al 1986, pp. 3–21

Beringer, D. B. 1985. A peripheral integrated status display: Is it really giving the "big picture" or is it a miniseries? See Proc. Hum. Factors Soc. 1985, pp. 304–7

Beringer, D. B., Chrisman, S. E. 1987. A comparison of shape/object displays and conventional univariate indicators: integration benefits or the "nearer to thee" effect? See Proc. 31st Ann. Meet. Hum. Factors Soc., pp. 543–47

Boehm-Davis, D., Holr, R., Koll, M. 1987. The effects of different data base formats on information retrieval. See Proc. 31st Ann. Meet. Hum. Factors Soc., pp. 983–86

Boff, K. R., Kaufman, L., Thomas, J. P., eds. 1986. *Handbook of Human Perception and Performance*, Vols. 1, 2. New York: Wiley. 2700 pp.

Boles, B. D., Wickens, C. D. 1987. Display formatting in information integration and nonintegration tasks. *Hum. Factors* 29:395–406

Bosser, T. 1986. Modelling of skilled behavior and learning. See Proc. 16th Int. IEEE Int. Conf., pp. 272–76

Boulette, M. D., Coury, B. G., Bezar, N. A. 1987. Classifiction of multidimensional data under time constraints: evaluating digital and configural display representations. See Proc. 31st Ann. Meet. Hum. Factors Soc., pp. 116–20

Bransford, J. D., Sherwood, R., Vye, N., Reiser, J. 1986. Teaching thinking and problem solving: research foundations *Am. Psychol.* 41:1078–89

Buch, G., Diehl, A. 1984. An investigation of the effectiveness of pilot judgement training. *Hum. Factors* 26:557–64

Carswell, C. M., Wickens, C. D. 1988. Information integration and the object display. *Ergonomics*. In press

Carswell, C. M., Wickens, C. D. 1985. Lateral task segregation and the task-hemispheric integrity effect. *Hum. Factors* 27:695–700

Casey, E. J. 1987. Visual display representation of multidimensional systems: the effect of system structure and display integrality. See Proc. 31st Ann. Meet. Hum. Factors Soc., pp. 112–15

Chapanis, A. 1963. Engineering psychology. *Ann. Rev. Psychol.* 14:285–318

Chase, W. G. 1986. Visual information processing. See Boff et al 1986, pp. 28:1–71

Chase, W. G., Ericsson, A. K. 1981. Skilled memory. See Anderson 1981, pp. 141–89

Coles, M. G. H., Gratton, G. 1986. Cognitive psychophysiology and the study of states and processes. See Hockey et al 1986, pp. 409–24

Coury, B. G., Boulette, M. D., Zubritzky, M. C., Fisher, D. L. 1986a. Classification of multidimensional data: evaluating displays to aid indentification of system states. See Proc. 16th IEEE Int. Conf., pp. 1503–8

Coury, B. G., Zubritzky, M. C., Smith, R. A., Cuqlock, V. G. 1986b. Multidimensional scaling as a method for probing the conceptual structure of state categories. See Proc. 16th IEEE Int. Conf., pp. 593–98

Derrick, W. L. 1988. Dimensions of operator workload. *Hum. Factors* 30:95–110

Donchin, E. ed. 1989. Special interest. *Acta Psychol.* In press

Eberts, R. 1986. Development of mental models of display augmentation. See Proc. 16th IEEE Int. Conf., pp. 262–66

Eberts, R. E., Eberts, C. G. 1985. *Trends in Ergonomics/Human Factors II*. Amsterdam: North Holland

Eberts, R., Schneider, W. 1985. Internalizing the system dynamics for a second-order system. *Hum. Factors* 27:371–93

Ellis, S. R., McGreevy, M. W., Hitchcock, R. J. 1987. Perspective traffic display format and airline pilot traffic avoidance. *Hum. Factors* 29:371–82

Fisk, A. D., Ackerman, P. L., Schneider, W. S. 1987. Automatic and controlled processing theory and its application to human factors problems. See Hancock 1987, pp. 159–97

Fisk, A. D., Schneider, W. 1984. Memory as a function of attention levels of processing, and automation. *J. Exp. Psychol.: Learn. Mem. Cogn.* 19:181–87

Fitts, P. M., Posner, I. M. 1967. *Human Performance*. Belmont, Calif: Brooks Cole. 162 pp.

Fleishman, E. A., Quantaine, M. R., Broedling, L. A. 1984. *Taxonomies of Human Performance*. Orlando, Fla: Academic. 514 pp.

Flexman, R. E., Stark, E. A. 1987. Training simulators. See Salvendy 1987a

Foley, P., Moray, N. 1987. Sensation, perception, and system design. See Salvendy 1987b, pp. 45–71

Frederiksen, J. R., White, B. Y. 1989. An approach to training based upon principled task decomposition. *Acta Psychol.* In press

Friedman, A., Polson, M. C. 1981. The hemispheres as independent resource systems: limited capacity processes and cerebral specialization. *J. Exp. Physchol.: Hum. Percept. Perform.* 7:1031–58

Friedman, A., Polson, M. C., Dafoe, C. D., Gaskill, S. J. 1982. Dividing attention within and between hemispheres: testing a multiple resource approach to limited capacity information processing. *J. Exp. Psychol.: Hum. Percept. Perform.* 8:625–50Gagne, R. M., Glaser, R. 1987. Foundations in learning research. In *Instructional Techniques: Foundations*, ed. R. Glaser, pp. 49–83. Hillsdale, NJ: Laurence Erlbaum

Garner, W. R. 1974. *The Processing of Information and Structure*. Hillsdale, NJ: Erlbaum. 203 pp.

Garner, W. R. 1978. Selective attention to attributes and stimuli. *J. Exp. Psychol.: Gen.* 107:287–308

Gentner, D., Stevens, A. L., eds. 1983. *Mental Models*. Hillsdale, NJ: Lawrence Erlbaum

Ginsburg, A. P. 1986. Spatial filtering and visual form perception. See Boff et al 1986, pp. 34:1–41

Goldsmith, T., Schvaneveldt, R. 1984. Facilitating multi-cue judgments with integral information displays. In *Human Factors in Computer Systems*, ed. J. Thomas, M. Schneider, pp. 243–70. Norwood, NJ: Ablex

Gopher, D. 1984. The contribution of vision based imagery to the acquisition and operation of a transcription skill. In *Cognition and Motor Processes*, ed. W. Printz, A. F. Sanders, pp. 195–208. Berlin: Springer-Verlag

Gopher, D. 1986. In defence of resources: on structures, energies, pools and the allocation of attention. See Hockey et al 1986, pp. 353–72

Gopher, D. 1987. Cognition at your finger tips—a cognitive approach to the design of data entry devices. See Salvendy, 1987a, pp. 233–41

Gopher, D., Braune, R. 1984. On the psychophysics of workload: Why bother with subjective measures? *Hum. Factors* 26: 519–32

Gopher, D., Donchin, E. 1986. Workload: an examination of the concept. See Boff et al 1986, Ch. 41:1–49

Gopher, D. Karis, D., Koenig, W. 1985. The representation of movement schemas in long-term memory: lessons from the acquisition of a transcription skill. *Acta Psychol.* 60:105–34

Gopher, D., Raij, D. 1988. Typing with a two hand chord keyboard—will the QWERTY become obsolete? *IEEE Trans. Syst. Man Cybern.* 18:In press

Gopher, D., Sanders, A. F. 1984. S-Oh-R: Oh stages! Oh resources! In *Cognition and Motor Processes*, ed. W. Printz, A. F. Sanders, pp. 231–54. Berlin: Springer-Verlag

Gopher, D., Weil, M., Bareket, T., Capsi, S. 1988. Using complex computer games as

task simulators in the training of flight skills. See Proc. 18th IEEE Int. Conf., In press

Gopher, D., Weil, M., Siegal, D. 1989. Practice under changing priorities: an approach to the training of complex skills. *Acta Psychol.* In press

Grudin, J., Barnard, P. 1984. The cognitive demands of learning and representing command names for text editing. *Hum. Factors* 26:407–22

Halff, H. M., Hollan, J. D., Hutchins, E. L. 1986. Cognitive science and military training. *Am. Psychol.* 41:1131–39

Hancock, P. A., ed. 1987. *Human Factors Psychology*. Amsterdam: North-Holland

Hancock, P. A., Meshkati, N., eds. 1988. *Human Mental Workload*. Amsterdam: North-Holland

Hart, S. G. 1986. Theories and measures of human workload. In *Human Productivity Enhancement*, ed. J. Zeidner, pp. 496–555. New York: Praeger

Hart, S. G., Staveland, L. H. 1988. Development of NASA TLX (task load index): results of empirical and theoretical research. See Hancock & Meshakati 1988, pp. 139–84

Helander, M. G. 1987. Design of visual displays. See Salvendy 1987b, pp. 507–48

Hochberg, J. 1986. Representation of motion and space in video and cinematic displays. See Boff et al 1986, Ch. 22:1–65

Hockey, G. R., Gaillard, A. W. K., Coles, M. G. H., eds. 1986. *Energetics and Human Information Processing*. Dordrecht: Martinus Nijhoff

Hoffman, J. E. 1980. Interaction between global and local levels of a form. *J. Exp. Psychol.: Hum. Percept. Perform.* 6:222–34

Hopkins, C. D. 1975. How much should you pay for that box? *Hum. Factors* 17:533–41

Kahneman, D., Treisman, A. 1984. Changing views of attention and automaticity. In *Varieties of Attention*, ed. R. Parasuraman, J. Beatty. New York: Academic

Kantowitz, B. H. 1987. Mental workload. See Hancock 1987, pp. 81–122

Kimchi, R. 1988. Selective attention to global and local levels in the comparison of hierarchical patterns. *Percept. Psychophys.* 43:189–98

Kimchi, R., Palmer, S. E. 1985. Separability and integrality of global and local levels of hierarchical patterns. *J. Exp. Psychol.: Hum. Percept. Perform.* 11:673–88

Kinchla, R. A., Wolfe, J. M. 1979. The order of visual processing: "Top down," "bottom up" or "middle-out". *Percept. Psychophys.* 25:225–31

Kramer, A. F., ed. 1987. Cognitive psychophysiology. (Spec. Issue). *Hum. Factors* 29–4:127–235

Kramer, A. F., Sirevaag, E. J., Braune, R. 1987. A psychophysiological assessment of operator workload during simulated flight mission. *Hum. Factors* 29:145–60

Kubovy, M., Pomerantz, J. R., eds. 1981. *Perceptual Organization.* Hillsdale, NJ: Erlbaum. 506 pp.

Lappin, J. S. 1967. Attention in identification of stimuli in complex visual displays. *J. Exp. Psychol.* 75:321–28

Lavie, P., Gopher, D., Wollman, M. 1987. Thirty-six hour correspondence between performance and sleep cycles. *Psychophysiology* 24:430–38

Logie, R., Baddeley, A., Mane, A., Donchin, E., Sheptak, R. 1989. Working memory and the analysis of a complex skill by secondary task methodology. *Acta Psychol.* In press

Mane, A., Coles, M. G. H., Wickens, C. D., Donchin, E. 1983. See Proc. 27th Hum. Factors Soc., Santa Monica, Calif.

Mane, A., Wickens, C. D., 1986. The effects of difficulty and load on training. See Proc. Hum. Factors Soc., 1986, pp. 1124–27

Mangun, G. R. R., Hillyard, S. A. 1987. The spatial allocation of visual attention as indexed by event related brain potentials. *Hum. Factors* 29:195–213

McClelland, J. L., Rumelhart, D. E. 1985. Distributed memory and the representation of general and specific information. *J. Exp. Psychol.: Hum. Percept. Perform.* 114:159–88

McClelland, J. L., Rumelhart, D. E., eds. 1986. Parallel distributed processing: *Explorations in the Microstructure of Cognition.* Vol. 2: *Psychological and Biological Models.* Cambridge, MA: MIT Press

McGreevy, M. W., Ellis, S. R. 1986. The effect of perspective geometry on judged direction in spatial information instruments. *Hum. Factors* 28:439–56

Miller, J. 1981. Global precedence in attention and decision. *J. Exp. Psychol.: Hum. Percept. Perform.* 6:1161–74

Moray, N. 1986. Monitoring behavior and supervisory control. See Boff et al 1986, pp. 40:1–51

Moray, N. 1987. Intelligent aids, mental models and the theory of machines. *Int. J. Man-Mach. Stud.* 27:In press

Morris, N. M., Rouse, W. B. 1985. Review and evaluation of empirical research in troubleshooting. *Hum. Factors* 27:503–30

Munson, R. C., Horst, R. L. 1986. Evidence for global processing of complex visual displays. See Proc. Hum. Factors Soc. 1986, pp. 776–80

Nave-Benjamin, M., McKeachie, W. J., Lin, Y., Tucker, D. G. 1986. Inferring students cognitive structures and their development using the "ordered tree technique". *J. Educ. Psychol.* 78:130–40

Navon, D. 1977. Forest before trees: The precedence of global features in visual perception. *Cognit. Psychol.* 9:353–83

Navon, D. 1981. The forest revisited: More on global precedence. *Psychol. Res.* 43:1–32

Navon, D. 1985. Attention division or attention sharing. In *Attention and Performance 11,* ed. M. I. Posner, S. M. Marin. Hillsdale, NJ: Lawrence Erlbaum

Navon, D., Gopher, D. 1979. On the economy of the human processing system. *Psychol. Rev.* 86:214–55

Navon, D., Miller, J. 1987. Role of outcome conflict in dual task interference. *J. Exp. Psychol.: Hum. Percept. Perform.* 13:435–48

Newell, K. M., Carlton, M. J., Fisher, A. T., Rutter, B. G. 1989. Whole-part training strategies for learning the response dynamics of microprocessors driven simulators. *Acta Psychol.* In press

Norman, D. A., Bobrow, D. G. 1975. On data limited and resource limited processes. *Cognit. Psychol.* 7:44–64

O'Donnell, R. D., Eggemeier, F. T. 1986. Workload Assessement methodology. See Boff et al 1986, pp. 42:1–49

Palmer, S. E. 1978. Fundamental aspects of cognitive representation. In *Cognition and Categorization,* ed. E. Rosch, B. B. Lloyd, pp. 259–303. Hillsdale, NJ: Erlbaum

Palmer, S. E., Kimchi, R. 1986. The information processing approach to cognition. In *Approaches to Cognition: Contrasts and Controversies,* ed. T. J. Knapp, L. C. Robertson, pp. 37–77. Hillsdale, New Jersey/London: Erlbaum. 332 pp.

Petersen, S. E., Fox, M. L., Posner, M. I., Mintum, M., Raichle, M. E. 1988. Positron emission tomographic studies of cortical anatomy of single word processing. *Nature* 331:585–89

Pomerantz, J. R. 1981. Perceptual organization in information processing. See Kubovy & Pomerantz 1981, pp. 141–79

Posner, M. I., Rotbart, M. K. 1986. The concept of energy in psychological theory. See Hockey et al 1986, pp. 23–40

Pribram, K. H. 1986. Matrix and convolution models of brain organization in cognition. See Proc. 16th Int. Conf. IEEE, pp. 5–11

Pribram, K. H., McGuinness, D. 1975. Arousal activation and effort in the control of attention. *Psychol. Rev.* 27:131–42

Proceedings of the Human Factors Society Annual Meetings: **1985,** 29th meet.: Progress for people; **1986,** 30th meet.: A cradle for human factors; **1987,** 31st meet.: Rising to new heights with technology; **1988,** 32nd meet.: Riding the wave of innovation. Santa Monica, Calif: Hum. Factors Soc.

Proceedings of the IEEE International Conference on Systems, Man, and Cybernetics. **1985**, 15th meet., Tucson, Ariz.; **1986**, 16th meet., Atlanta, Ga.; **1987**, 17th meet., Washington, DC.; **1988**, 18th meet., Beijing, China. Piscataway, NJ:IEEE Serv. Cent.

Reid, G. B., Nygren, T. E. 1988. The subjective workload assessment technique: a scaling procedure for measuring mental workload. See Hancock & Meshakati 1988, pp. 185–218

Remington, R., Williams, D. 1986. On the selection and evaluaton of visual display symbology: factors influencing search and identification time. *Hum. Factors* 28:407–20

Roscoe, S. N. 1980. *Aviation Psychology*, Chp. 17, pp. 533–41. Ames, Iowa: Iowa State Univ. Press

Rumelhart, D. E. 1977. Toward an interactive model of reading. In *Attention and Performance VI*, ed. S. Dornic. Hillsdale, NJ: Erlbaum

Rumelhart, D. E., McClelland, J. L., eds. 1986. Parallel distributed processing. In *Explorations in the Microstructure of Cognition*, Vol. 1: *Foundations*. Cambridge, Mass: MIT Press

Rumelhart, D. E., Norman, D. A. 1981. Analogical processes in learning. See Anderson 1981, pp. 335–39

Rumelhart, D. E., Norman, D. A. 1988. Representation in memory. In *Handbook of Experimental Psychology*, ed. R. C. Atkinson, R. J. Herrnstein, G. Lindzey, R. D. Luce. New York: Wiley

Ryder, J. M., Redding, R. E., Beckschi, P. F. 1987. Training development for complex cognitive tasks. See 31st Ann. Meet. Proc. Hum. Factors Soc., pp. 1261–65

Salvendy, G., ed. 1987a. *Handbook of Human Factors*. New York: Wiley

Salvendy, G., ed. 1987b. *Cognitive Engineering in the Design of Human-Computer Interaction and Expert Systems*. Amsterdam: Elsevier

Salvendy, G., Sauler, S. L., Hurrel, J. J., eds. 1987. *Social Ergonomics and Stress Aspects of Work with Computers*. Amsterdam: Elsevier

Sanders, A. F. 1986. Energetical states underlying task performance. See Hockey et al 1986, pp. 139–54

Sanders, M. S., McCormick, E. J. 1987. *Human Factors in Engineering and Design*. New York: McGraw-Hill. 6th ed.

Sanderson, P. 1986. Designing "mental models" for complex worlds. See Proc. 16th IEEE Int. Conf., pp. 267–71

Schlegel, R. E., Gilliland, K., Schlegel, B. 1987. Factor structure of the criterion task

set. See Proc. 31st Ann. Meet. Hum. Factors Soc., pp. 389–93

Schneider, W. 1985a. Toward a model of attention and the development of automatic processing. In *Attention and Performance 11*, ed. M. I. Posner, M. Marin, pp. 475–92. Hillsdale, NJ: Lawrence Erlbaum

Schneider, W. 1985b. Training high performance skills: fallacies and guidelines. *Hum. Factors* 27:285–300

Schneider, W., Vidulich, M., Yeh, Y. Y. 1985. Training spatial skill for air traffic control. See Proc. Hum. Factors Soc., pp. 10–14

Schwartz, D. R., Howell, W. C. 1985. Optional stopping performance under graphic and numeric CRT formatting. *Hum. Factors* 27:433–44

Shapiro, K. L., Raymond, J. E. 1989. Training of efficient oculomotor strategies enhances skill acquisition. *Acta Psychol.* In press

Sheridan, T. B. 1987. Supervisory control. See Salvendy 1987a, pp. 1243–68

Shiffrin, R. M., Schneider, W. 1977. Controlled and automatic human information processing II: Perceptual learning, automatic attending and a general theory. *Psychol. Rev.* 84:127–90

Streitz, N. A., Spijkers, W. A. C., Van Duren, L. L. 1987. From novice to expert user: a transfer of learning experiment on different interaction modes. In *Human Computer Interaction—INTERACT 87*, ed. H. J. Bullinger, B. Schakel, pp. 841–46. Amsterdam: Elsevier

Tadmor, Z., Kohavi, Z., Libai, A., Singer, P., Kohn, 1987. *Engineering Education 2001*. Haifa, Israel: The Neaman Press. 56 pp.

Treisman, A. 1985. Preattentive processing in vision. *Comput. Vision Graph. Image Process.* 31:156–77

Treisman, A. 1986. Properties, parts, and objects. See Boff et al 1986, pp. 35:1–70

Treisman, A., Schmidt, H. 1982. Illusory conjunctions in the perception of objects. *Cognit. Psychol.* 14:107–41

van der Molen, M. W., Somsen, R. J., Jennings, R. J., Nieuwboer, R. T., Orlebeke, J. F. 1987. A psychophysiological investigation of cognitive-energetic relations in human information processing: a heart rate/additive factors approach. *Acta Psychol.* 66:251–89

Vidulich, M. A., Tsang, P. S. 1986. Techniques of subjective workload assesment: a comparison of SWAT and the NASA-Bipolar methods. *Ergonomics* 29:1385–98

Vidulich, M. A., Wickens, C. D. 1986. Causes of dissociation between subjective measures and performance: caveats for the use of subjective assessments. *Appl. Ergon.* 17:291–96

Vincente, K. J., Thornton, D. C., Moray, N. 1987. Spectral analysis of sinus arrhythmia: a measure of mental workload. *Hum. Factors* 29:171–82

Welford, A. T. 1968. *Fundamentals of Skills.* London: Methuen & Co

Wickens, C. D. 1984. Processing resources in attention. In *Varieties of Attention,* ed. R. Parasuraman, D. R. Davis. Orlando, Fla: Academic

Wickens, C. D. 1986. Gain and energetics in information processing. See Hockey et al 1986, pp. 373–90

Wickens, C. D. 1987. Information processing, decision making, and cognition. See Salvendy 1987b, pp. 72–107

Wickens, C. D., Kramer, A. 1985. Engineering psychology. *Ann. Rev. Psychol.* 36:307–48

Wickens, C. D., Vidulich, M., Sandry-Garza, D. 1984. Principles of S-C-R compatibility with spatial and verbal tasks: the role of display control location and voice interactive display control interfacing. *Hum. Factors* 26:533–43

Wierwille, W. W., Rahimi, M., Casali, J. G. 1985. Evaluation of 16 measures of mental workload using a simulated flight task emphasizing mediational activity. *Hum. Factors* 27:489–502

Wightman, D. C., Lintern, G. 1985. Part-training for tracking and manual control. *Hum. Eactors* 27:267–83

Williges, R. C., Williges, B. H., Elkerton, J. 1987. Software interface design. See Salvendy 1987a, pp. 1490–1525

Wilson, G. F., O'Donnell, R. D. 1988. Measurement of operator workload with the neuropsychological workload test battery. See Hancock & Meshakti 1988, pp. 63–100

Wood, W. T., Wood, S. K. 1987. Icons in everyday life. See Salvendy et al 1987, pp. 97–104

Woods, D. D. 1986. Graphic representations of complex worlds. See Proc. 16th IEEE Int. Conf., pp. 259–61

Workman, D., Fisher, D. L. 1987. Selection of display symbology: a new metric of similarity. Proc. 31st Ann. Meet. Hum. Factors Soc., pp. 510–13

Yeh, Y. Y., Wickens, C. D. 1988. Dissociation of performance and subjective measures of workload. *Hum. Factors* 30:111–20

Ann. Rev. Psychol. 1989. 40:457–92

NEUROBEHAVIORAL ASPECTS OF AFFECTIVE DISORDERS

Richard A. Depue and William G. Iacono

Department of Psychology, University of Minnesota, Minneapolis, Minnesota 55455

CONTENTS

A PSYCHOLOGICAL PERSPECTIVE ON THE NEUROBIOLOGY OF AFFECTIVE DISORDERS[*]

Over the past 15 years, biological approaches to affective disorders have shown significant progress that stems, in part, from the revolutionary ad-

---

[*]Abbreviations used in this chapter: ACh, acetylcholine; BFS, behavioral facilitation system; CSF, cerebrospinal fluid; CT, computerized tomography; DA, dopamine; ECS, electroconvulsive shock; 5HT, 5-hydroxytriptamine (serotonin); HVA, homovanillic acid; LA, locomotor activity; LVE, lateral ventricular enlargement; MAOI, monoamine inhibitors; MRI, magnetic resonance imaging; Nacc, nucleus accumbens; NE, norepinephrine; PET, positron emission tomography; TCAs, tricyclic antidepressants; VBR, ventricular brain ratio; VTA, ventral tegmental area.

457

0066-4308/89/0201-0457$02.00

vancements generally observed in the life sciences since World War II. Progress has been particularly evident in two areas: (*a*) the study of functional neurobiology, where neurotransmitters and their major metabolites are studied in body fluids (blood, urine, and cerebrospinal) or in cell systems within these fluids, often under the influence of pharmacologic manipulations or therapies (an approach noticeably fruitful with respect to dopamine functioning in bipolar affective disorders); and (*b*) brain imaging techniques, where the structure and function of tissue in the living human brain are visualized. We focus on these two areas.

There is a serious limitation to much of the neurobiologic research and modelling in psychopathology that can perhaps be best rectified by the attention of psychologists to this area. Neurobiologic models almost invariably focus on the integrity of functioning of a biologic variable *per se;* little attention has been directed to the larger neurobehavioral framework within which the variable operates. In order for neurobiologic models to provide a truly integrative framework for understanding the nature of affective disorders, they must have as their foundation a comprehensive interface between neurobiologic structure and function, on the one hand, and major behavioral systems, on the other. Accordingly, we present a neurobehavioral framework for affective disorders (with an emphasis on bipolar disorders) as a means of integrating the neurobiologic data in a manner meaningful for the psychologically trained reader.

DOPAMINE FUNCTIONING, BEHAVIORAL FACILITATION, AND BIPOLAR AFFECTIVE DISORDERS

As evidenced in several recent reviews (Depue 1988; Jimerson & Post 1984; Silverstone 1985; Swerdlow & Koob 1987; Wood 1985), there has been increasing interest in the role played by dopamine (DA) in bipolar affective disorders. Since most of this work has focused on DA functioning *per se,* we discuss three aspects of a DA-relevant neurobehavioral framework for bipolar affective disorders: (1) the structure of a major behavioral system within which bipolar disorders may be manifested; (2) the neurobiologic structure and function underlying this behavioral system; and (3) implications of this neurobehavioral system for modeling the clinical and neurobiologic features of bipolar disorders.

The Behavioral Facilitation System

Several major systems direct and motivate behavior in response to classes of significant environmental stimuli (Depue 1988; Depue et al 1987; Depue & Spoont 1986; Gray 1982; Iversen 1978, 1984; Milner 1977; Tellegen 1985).

The most relevant of these to the current focus is the behavioral facilitation or activation system (BFS), a very basic behavioral system described in all animals across phylogenetic levels (Schneirla 1959). The BFS mobilizes behavior so that active engagement with the environment occurs under appropriate stimulus conditions. Behavioral facilitation is achieved through stimulus-elicitation of what are believed to be the two major components of the BFS, initiation of locomotor activity and incentive-reward motivation. Thus, the BFS provides a motor/affective (motivational) contribution to the process of active environmental engagement.

As shown in Figure 1, the BFS functions as a generalized system that facilitates a variety of more specific behavioral engagement patterns, grouped into two broad categories: (1) positive engagements with the environment, such as social, sexual, consummatory, and achievement-related patterns; and (2) responses to environmental threat, particularly irritative aggression and active avoidance patterns. Although each engagement pattern is elicited by its own specific external and internal (including cognitive) controlling stimuli,

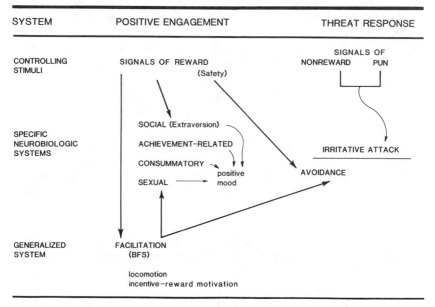

Figure 1 Structure of the behavioral facilitation system (BFS). The BFS is a generalized system, comprised of locomotion and incentive-reward motivation, which facilitates a number of specific environmental engagement patterns in response to signals of reward, including stimuli of safety and of goal-oriented attack. The specific engagement patterns (social, sexual, etc) are associated with their own neurobiology and specific eliciting stimuli, and with traits that provide variation in sensitivity to their controlling stimuli (such as extraversion and aggression). The positive engagement patterns are associated with positive mood.

all patterns are thought to be facilitated by the BFS. This suggests that the BFS is elicited by characteristics common to the specific stimuli eliciting the different engagement patterns.

The BFS appears to facilitate two types of behavior (Crow 1977; Iversen 1978; Milner 1977): (1) unconditioned—i.e. behaviors in an animal's repertoire that occur without specific learning experience, such as eating, drinking, mating, aggression, and spontaneous exploratory locomotion in response to novel stimuli (as long as the novel stimulus context does not induce fear); and (2) conditioned—i.e. voluntary motivated behavior that occurs in response to signals denoting significant stimuli. In both types of behavior, the BFS is thought to be activated mainly by inherently rewarding stimuli (food, social contact, sex, novelty) or conditioned signals of these stimuli. The BFS also facilitates active avoidance responses; in this case, the safe area is conceived of as a reward, thus activating the incentive and locomotor components of the BFS (Gray 1982). Under conditions where reward acquisition is blocked or when avoidance is impossible or unnecessary, the BFS may facilitate irritative aggressive behavior whose goal is removal of stimuli associated with frustrative nonreward. In the latter case the BFS may be elicited by expectations of the reward acquisition that will result from removal of the obstacle to reward (Milner 1977). Thus, the BFS is activated by a broad array of stimulus contexts, all sharing a reward-acquisition component. (The BFS is likely also activated by stimulus contexts not associated with reward—e.g. during stress or defensive aggression—but these are not considered here.)

Recent reviews of research in humans (Tellegen 1985; Watson & Tellegen 1985) indicate that the dimension of positive mood and incentive that correlates with the process of reward acquisition has at its low end an absence of positive mood (a nonreactive, low-incentive, depressed mood) rather than negative mood, a point of considerable theoretical importance (see below).

The relevance of the BFS to bipolar disorders derives in part from the nature of the symptoms. Symptoms of bipolar depression and hypomania/mania appear to represent opposite extremes of normal behavioral dimensions (Post & Uhde 1982), as illustrated in Figure 2. (Depressive features in mania complicate this view, a problem discussed in a subsequent section.) Bipolar depression and mania represent extreme states of engagement with the interpersonal and achievement-related environments. Such pervasive alterations in behavioral engagement raise the possibility that bipolar disorders may involve extreme state alterations in BFS functioning. When the dimensions shown are categorized into behavioral areas (as in Figure 2), core symptoms of bipolar disorders occur in locomotor, incentive-reward, and mood areas (that is, in behavioral areas associated with BFS function).

That the behavioral dimensions of Figure 2 form a behavioral system consistent with a BFS construct is suggested by a diverse literature on normal

MOTOR			INCENTIVE-REWARD ACTIVATION		MOOD	NONSPECIFIC AROUSAL						COGNITIVE	
Locomotion	Speech	Facies	Hedonia (Social, Sex, Food)	Desire for Excitement		Appetite	Energy	Sleep/Wake	Thought	Attention	Sensory Vividness	Optimism	Self-Worth
hyperactivity	rapid, pressured	expressive	excessive interest and pleasure	excessive, creates new activities	elation, euphoria, reactive	decreased	excessive, boundless	< need for sleep	sharper, flight of ideas, witty, > decisional power	distractible	extremely vivid	> self-confidence, < estimation of negative outcomes, grandiosity	increased worth, grandiosity
retardation slowed delayed stupor	retardation slowed delayed mute	unchanging, unexpres-sive	no interest or pleasure (pervasive anhedonia)	avoidance of stimulation	devoid of emotion, depres-sion, lack reactivity	> carbo-hydrate intake	easily fatigued, devoid of energy	hyper-somnia, naps	< decisional power, thoughts "dead", mind dull	poor concen-tration	senses dull, food tastes bland	pessimistic, persistent gloom, brood about past, hopeless about future outcomes, suicidal ideation	totally worthless, delusional

Figure 2 Categorization of the bipolar behavioral dimensions associated with bipolar affective disorder.

human populations. Reviews (Depue et al 1987; Tellegen 1985; Watson & Tellegen 1985; Zevon & Tellegen 1982) of this literature document that, when measured longitudinally on a *state* basis, the behaviors represented in Figure 2 covary cohesively *within individuals across time* and load heavily on one major factor in *intra-* and *inter*-individual factor analyses. This factor has been referred to as a positive-affect/positive-engagement factor. We have also found that the ratings of bipolar patients on these behaviors over 30–60 consecutive days form one major positive-engagement factor (Depue et al 1987; Goplerud & Depue 1985). The strongest behavioral markers of this engagement factor in both normal and bipolar patient samples are locomotion, incentive-reward motivation, and energy, consistent with the notion of a BFS that facilitates the engagement behaviors represented in the dimensions of Figure 2 (Depue et al 1987; Watson & Tellegen 1985). Furthermore, this factor structure derived from behavioral state ratings is stable within individuals over a 10-year period (Costa et al 1980) and correlates highly with personality *traits* that may be viewed as broadly assessing the level of positive engagement with rewarding stimuli, such as extraversion and positive emotionality (Depue et al 1987; Tellegen 1985; Watson & Tellegen 1985). The latter correlation may mean that variation in trait level of BFS activity is manifested in the trait levels of a diverse range of engagement traits.

Neurobiology of the Behavioral Facilitation System

The construct of the BFS as a generalized system that facilitates behavioral engagement is supported by neurobiologic research on the two major components of the BFS: locomotor activity (LA) and incentive-reward motivation. In particular, investigation of the process of LA initiation has led to a general model of BFS facilitation of behavioral engagement. Therefore, we discuss the neurobiology of the two major BFS components first and then consider facilitation of behavioral engagement more generally. An understanding of this discussion is aided by a brief description of particular DA projection pathways.

DOPAMINE PROJECTION PATHWAYS OF THE VENTRAL TEGMENTAL AREA   There are at least nine major DA cell groups, designated A8–A15, plus a retinal system, which are located mainly in the mes- and diencephalon (Fuxe et al 1985). Those of the mesencephalon tend to comprise the ascending DA neuron systems, while those of the diencephalon are descending and local neurons of the hypothalamus and preoptic area having to do with maintenance of the internal milieu (e.g. endocrine and temperature regulation). Because of their apparent involvement in the modulation of motivational processes and in the organization and initiation of goal-directed behavior, the ascending projections of the A10 DA cell group located in the ventral tegmental area (VTA; see Figure 3 for location) of the mesencephalon have been the center of interest with respect to the affective disorders.

VTA A10 DA cells fall into approximately five nuclear groupings, which are the source of various projections to structures of the limbic system and areas of the neocortex (for an extensive review see Oades & Halliday 1987). There are five efferent systems of the VTA, where approximately 70% of the projections are dopaminergic. Two of these systems are most relevant to our discussion, and their points of termination are shown in Figure 3. A general

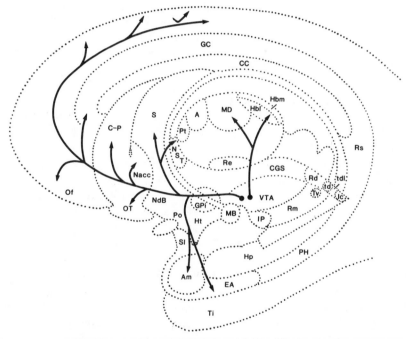

Figure 3 Dopaminergic projections ascending from the ventral tegmental area (shown as one mesolimbic-mesocortical bundle for clarity), as described in the text. A: nucleus anterior thalami; Am: amygdala; CC: corpus callosum; CGS: central grey substance; C-P: caudatoputamen; EA: entorhinal area; GC: gyrus cinguli; GPi: globus pallidus, internal segment; Hbl: lateral habenular nucleus; Hbm: medial habenular nucleus; Hp: hippocampal formation; Ht: hypothalamus; IP: interpeduncular nucleus; lc: locus coeruleus; MB: mammillary body; MD: nucleus mediodorsalis thalami; Nacc: nucleus accumbens; NdB: nucleus of the diagonal band of Broca; NST: bed-nucleus of stria terminalis; OF: orbitofrontal cortex; OT: olfactory tubercle; PH: parahippocampal gyrus; Po: preoptic area; Pt: nucleus parataenialis thalami; Rd: dorsal raphe nucleus; Re: nucleus reuniens thalami; Rm: median raphe nucleus; Rs: retrosplenial cortex; S: septum; SI: substantia innominata; td: dorsal tegmental nucleus of Gudden; tdl: nucleus tegmenti dorsalis lateralis; Ti: inferior temporal cortex. (Adapted from Nauta & Domesick 1981).

point worth noting is that VTA DA projections, which are less diffuse and more restrictively localized than those of other monoamines, innervate mes-, di-, and telencephalic brain regions that receive extraordinarily prolific and diverse input, suggesting that these convergence areas are involved in the association of diverse communications. As discussed below, DA appears to gate sources of input competing for control of output of the convergence areas (Oades 1985).

Mesolimbic system   Mesolimbic DA projections innervate a number of structures of the limbic system or structures closely associated with limbic processes. Perhaps the largest mesolimbic projection is to the nucleus accumbens (Nacc). DA terminals are found throughout this nucleus, particularly moving rostrally, and 85–95% of Nacc DA derives from VTA projections. The Nacc is a major part of the ventral striatum (Nauta 1986), which provides a ventral pathway by which the limbic system and prefrontal areas can influence the initiation of voluntary motor behavior. The VTA DA projection to the Nacc continues by spreading through the olfactory tubercle, medial, lateral, and dorsal olfactory nuclei, and the bed nucleus of the stria terminalis.

VTA DA projections to the amygdala have been traced to several nuclei, including the central, anterior, and posterior lateral, medial, and basal. Approximately 90% of the DA in the amygdala is attributable to the VTA projections. Denser aggregations of DA fibers and terminals are found in the central and basolateral nuclei, the former receiving the highest levels of DA in the amygdala. This is perhaps significant at a functional level because these nuclei are points of convergence of massive sensory input of all modalities, and they may mix these inputs with memories or cues with strongly emotional content (Luiten et al 1985; Sarter & Markowitsch 1985).

There are undisputed VTA DA projections into the substantia innominata (ventral pallidum), which receives input from the ventral striatum, described above. In human substantia innominata, DA levels were only marginally lower than in the amygdala, and homovanillic acid (HVA, a major metabolite of DA) levels were three times higher. One would expect this projection to modulate information related to extrapyramidal motor function.

The major VTA DA projection to the septum is to the lateral nucleus; and, in the medial part of the lateral septum, DA containing fibers form a fine peripheral outline to the fornix. Biochemical lesioning of the VTA depletes septal DA by 90%. There is a massive convergence of input to the lateral septum from many areas (Gray 1982), and the coincidence of this convergence with DA input is so strong that control of input, destined to the hippocampus, may occur via a VTA DA gating mechanism.

Concerning VTA DA projections to the hippocampus, there are projections to the dentate gyrus and to both the anterior and posterior regions of the hippocampus (Haas 1983; Oades & Halliday 1987). Altogether, levels of DA in the human hippocampus approach or surpass those of the entorhinal or prefrontal cortexes, both areas of heavy DA concentration. DA's functional roles in the hippocampus are not clear, although DA appears to modulate hippocampal theta rhythm, which may potentiate information flow in hippocampal circuitry (Larson & Lynch 1986).

Mesocortical system   Recent studies of primate cortex found DA terminals in practically all cortical regions, including primary and association sensory, motor, and limbic (Lewis et al 1986). DA fiber density was particularly high in frontal lobes, which comprise the only neocortical area that allows convergence of information from both internal (e.g. visceral, endocrine) and external sources. Primary motor cortex [Brodmann's (1909) area 4] contained the greatest density of DA terminals, while other motor-related areas, such as premotor and supplemental motor areas, were also densely innervated. Although fiber density decreased in the more rostral prefrontal cortex, among these regions, dorsomedial prefrontal cortex (area 9) and anterior cingulate cortex (area 24) had the greatest density. Dorsolateral prefrontal cortex (area 46) and the frontal pole (area 10) were relatively sparsely innervated, while orbital regions (areas 11 and 12) tended to have an intermediate density of fibers compared to other prefrontal regions. Since all of these areas are involved in the planning, programming, integration of polysensory information relevant to motor programs, and actual sequential initiation of goal-directed motor behavior (Fuster 1985; Roland 1985; Stuss & Benson 1986), DA is likely to play a key role in the development and execution of complex strategies of motor behavior. Indeed, the integrity of DA projections to prefrontal cortex is necessary for the adequate execution of prefrontal functions (Iversen 1984; Oades 1985; Stuss & Benson 1986).

There is a substantial DA projection to primate ventrolateral entorhinal cortex, which is a major site of convergence of information from all sensory modalities via the inferior temporal lobe and from limbic-related structures (Gray 1982). Most of the VTA DA terminals are found in clusters in layers II and III, where hippocampal input also occurs. Perhaps this pattern influences specific inputs, and gates propagation of information to the hippocampus.

In general, the distribution pattern of DA fibers suggests a functional specialization of the DA cortical projections. DA fibers preferentially innervate motor over sensory regions, sensory association (such as inferior parietal—area 39—and temporal) over primary sensory regions, and auditory association (rostral superior temporal gyrus—area 22) over visual association (rostral inferior temporal gyrus—area 21) regions (Lewis et al 1986). In these sensory association areas, laminar innervation patterns suggest that DA modulates the activity of corticocortical rather than thalamocortical projections. This may indicate a role for DA in the advanced information processing that occurs in association regions of cortex.

INITIATION OF LOCOMOTOR ACTIVITY   Processes involved in the generation of volitional locomotion can be divided into three useful, albeit oversimplified, phases: initiation, programming, and execution. Processes involved in LA initiation have received the least attention, but it is specifically
this phase of locomotor generation that relates to the facilitation construct of
the BFS because the initiation process is closely tied to affective/motivational
input to the motor system.

There is a vast literature demonstrating that DA [but not norepinephrine
(NE)] is the primary neurotransmitter in the initiation of LA [see reviews by
Fishman et al (1983), Iversen (1978), and Oades 1985). It is important that
LA initiation occurs via the action of DA and its agonists in the mesolimbic
DA system, in general, and in the VTA A10 DA projection to the Nacc, in
particular. A recent review concluded that, although some role for the
striatum in La appears likely (as some role for the Nacc in stereotypy may
exist), "a formidable number of studies have demonstrated that DA and
its agonists injected into the Nacc induce a greater arousal of LA than equivalent injections in the striatum; there are virtually no studies in the literature
to the contrary" (Fishman et al 1983, p. 61). Moreover, the quantity of spontaneous exploratory LA and magnitude of amphetamine-induced LA are
both positively related to number of DA neurons (including those of the
A10 cell group), the relative density of innervation of DA terminals in target fields, and to DA content in the Nacc in inbred mouse strains, effects perhaps related to the proportionately greater synthesis and release of
DA in high-DA neuron strains (Fink & Reis 1981; Oades 1985; Sved et al
1984, 1985).

Mesolimbic DA projections to the amygdala and olfactory tubercle do not
account in a significant way for initiation of LA (Oades 1985; Oades et al
1986). Results for the VTA DA projection to the prefrontal cortex are
controversial but of clear significance, since these projections may provide
input related to cognitive initiation of goal-directed behavior. The emerging
model suggests that this projection does not *mediate* LA initiation, but rather
modulates it by inhibiting the prefrontal cortex's tonic inhibitory control over
Nacc initiation of LA (Glowinski et al 1984; Iversen 1984; Oades 1985;
Oades et al 1986; Thierry et al 1984).

DA is the primary neurotransmitter involved in LA initiation inasmuch as
LA will not occur to any significant extent in the absence of any central DA
receptor arousal. Although this cannot be said for the receptors of any other
neurotransmitter system (Fishman et al 1983), LA is nevertheless the product
of the mutual interaction of a number of neurotransmitter systems. Much of
this interaction is unknown; but recent neurobiologic models of Nacc circuitry
(Depue & Spoont 1986; Jones et al 1980), and routes for Nacc input to the
motor system, illustrate the basic concepts.

INCENTIVE-REWARD MOTIVATION   Because LA represents the strongest indicator of an incentive motivational state, the second component of the BFS—incentive-reward motivation (the intervening variable invoked to account for the response-enhancing power of reinforcing stimuli)—may have a neurobiology linked to LA. Data indicate that LA and incentive-reward motivation are integrated within VTA A10 DA pathways.

To support the notion that incentive motivation is *elicited* by stimuli of reward, it is necessary to show that VTA A10 DA pathways mediate reward. The experience of reward appears to involve more than one population of axons, with more than one neurotransmitter. One model suggests that first-stage reward fibers, which may be in part muscarinic-cholinergic (see review by Bozarth 1987), descend through the medial forebrain bundle to activate a second-stage reward system, thought to be comprised of VTA A10 DA ascending projections. Indeed, recent reviews (Beninger 1983; Bozarth 1987; Fibiger & Phillips 1987; Goeders & Smith 1983; Mason 1984; Porrino 1987) concluded that DA, but not unequivocally NE, plays a critical role in mediating the effects of reward on behavior, one of the strongest lines of evidence being DA agonist self-administration. Since drug infusion is the only consequence of the emitted response, such infusions are reinforcing as operationally defined (Mason 1984).

That VTA (and nigrostriatal) DA pathways mediate reward is supported by the reviews cited above; by self-administration of cocaine in the Nacc and the medial prefrontal cortex (Goeders & Smith 1983); and by the fact that the distribution of intracranial self-stimulation reward-points, even with micro-mapping techniques, coincides with that of DA terminals in the Nacc and frontal cortex (Mason 1984). [Although unresolved issues remain, recent reviews suggest that intracranial self-stimulation in many but not all sites, but including the A10 cell group, is mediated by DA and not NE (Mason 1984).] Some work suggests that self-administration of cocaine is greatest in VTA DA projections to the medial prefrontal cortex (Goeders & Smith 1983; Porrino 1987), and that self-stimulation with electrodes planted in the VTA leads to much greater DA utilization in prefrontal cortex than in the Nacc (Thierry et al 1984); but this has not been uniformly supported (Fibiger & Phillips 1987). Furthermore, destruction of projections of DA neurons to limbic and cortical areas, and selective lesions of DA terminals in the Nacc, significantly reduce self-administration of cocaine. Since lesions had only slight effects on food responding, this latter effect cannot be explained as a motor deficit (Fibiger & Phillips 1987; Mason 1984).

Although it is not certain that the same reward systems are involved in drug and electrical self-administration as in natural reward [however, recent findings indicate that they are similar (Goeders & Smith 1983; Porrino 1987)], on the basis of these findings, Stein (1983) and others (Bozarth 1987; Fibiger &

Phillips 1987) concluded that DA activity mediates the incentive type of reward that activates goal acquisition, rather than the gratifying type of reward that brings behavior to a satisfying termination. An important distinction is that DA activity may not be necessary to the development of associations between stimuli *per se,* even associations involving reward (Beninger 1983); and no major impairment of memory is found after chemical lesion of ascending DA systems (Mason 1984; Oades 1985). However, in line with Milner's (1977) theoretical notions, DA activity is apparently necessary to link stimulus associations connoting reward to the response-facilitation mechanism in the Nacc (i.e. to observe increased response rates in the presence of the conditioned signal of reward). Milner (1977) suggested that some VTA DA projections to the prefrontal cortex, in being activated by reward (Porrino 1987), serve as this link by facilitating conduction of stimulus associations connoting reward (integrated in the prefrontal cortex) to the Nacc response facilitation mechanism.

FACILITATION OF OTHER BEHAVIORS   The possibility that the BFS plays a generalized role in facilitating behavioral engagement is suggested by DA's initiation or intensification of several behaviors in addition to LA and incentive-reward motivation. Most basic is that DA activity *specifically in the Nacc* (Fishman et al 1983; Oades 1985; Mason 1984) markedly increases frequency and duration of the unconditioned behavior of spontaneous exploratory activity, behavior that is facilitated by incentive-reward motivation elicited by environmental novelty (novelty is thought to have inherent incentive value if the novel stimulus context does not induce fear) (Crow 1977; Iversen 1978; Mason 1984; Milner 1977). Also, an inbred mouse strain (BALB/cJ) with 20–50% more DA neurons in all populations of DA cells investigated, including the A10 group, exhibits significantly increased spontaneous exploratory behavior in novel (but not fearful) environments (Fink & Reis 1981; Sved et al 1984, 1985).

Second, there is a strong relationship between DA activity and, most consistently, irritative aggression, a form of aggression found in humans (for reviews see Depue & Spoont 1986; Mason 1984; Valzelli 1981). DA activity in the VTA A10 projection to the amygdala is believed to provide strong facilitatory effects on irritative aggression in male rats and to slow the habituation of irritative attacks. DA (but not NE) receptor agonists greatly increase foot shock–induced irritative aggression in unrestrained male rats and naturally occurring aggressive behavior in rats and monkeys, although large variabilities exist among animals in relation to social dominance position. Sensitization for eliciting apomorphine aggressiveness in male rats was shown following the supersensitization of DA receptors resulting from withdrawal of chronic neuroleptics. Conversely, acute neuroleptics (but not alpha-NE blockers) counteract apomorphine- and amphetamine-elicited aggressive behavior in male rats. Unfortunately, DA facilitation of other engagement behaviors has not been as thoroughly investigated.

NUCLEUS ACCUMBENS: INTERFACE BETWEEN LIMBIC AND MOTOR SYS-
TEMS   Because LA and incentive-reward motivation represent fundamental components of goal-directed behaviors, a central role for VTA A10 DA projections in the initiation of behavioral engagement is suggested. Thus, these pathways may be viewed conceptually as a generalized system of behavioral facilitation (i.e. the BFS). Research particularly supports a generalized facilitation role of the A10-to-Nacc DA pathway in that DA activity in the Nacc modifies the input of some limbic forebrain projections to neural structures involved in coordinating motor programs. This suggests that the Nacc serves as an interface between limbic and motor systems (for reviews of this notion see Iversen 1984; Mogenson et al 1980; Nauta 1986; Oades & Halliday 1987; Taghzouti et al 1985). The significance of this is that limbic forebrain structures, in interaction with hypothalamic nuclei, are implicated as integrative centers for innate drives and motivational and emotional processes that are prerequisite for the initiation of various goal-directed behaviors, including attack, sex, socializing, drinking, feeding, and other behaviors (Iversen 1984; Mogenson & Huang 1973; Nauta & Domesick 1981).

Two lines of evidence support a limbic interaction with the A10-to-Nacc DA pathway. First, the Nacc receives strong, direct projections from the amygdala, ventral subiculum of the hippocampus, entorhinal cortex, cingulate gyrus, lateral septum, prefrontal cortexes, and other limbic structures (Oades & Halliday 1987; Phillipson & Griffiths 1985). Second, that DA activity in the Nacc modulates input from limbic-Nacc projections has been demonstrated for the ventral subiculum of the hippocampus, amygdala (particularly basolateral nuclei in the rat), and parafascicular nucleus of the thalamus (Louilot et al 1985; Yang & Mogenson 1984; Yim & Mogenson 1982, 1983). Amygdaloid input to the ventral pallidum was modulated by amphetamine injection into the Nacc, suggesting the likelihood of an amygdala-Nacc-ventral pallidal pathway; and other findings suggested that this modulation is due to DA activity in the Nacc (Yim & Mogenson 1983).

The above discussion raises the possibility of a hierarchical organization of neural processes for goal-directed behaviors, where more rostral structures (e.g. limbic and hypothalamic) project directly and indirectly (via the Nacc) to the motor system, on the one hand, and to VTA DA neurons, on the other (Mogenson & Huang 1973). Depending on the sum total effects of all inputs to the VTA A10 DA neurons, DA may modulate the response of Nacc neurons to limbic input, thereby placing the Nacc in a central position to modulate the extent to which some limbic projections influence the motor system, and presumably, the initiation of LA and goal-directed behavior. Put simply, *DA activity in the Nacc appears to modulate the flow of motivational information from the limbic system to the motor system, and thereby contributes to the process of initiating LA, incentive, and goal-directed behavior.*

Of course, this modulation is subject to the overarching control of the prefrontal cortex, which is involved in organizing affective responses (orbital prefrontal) and in establishing and executing a temporal framework for goal-directed behavior (dorsolateral and mesial prefrontal) (Fuster 1985; Nauta & Domesick 1981; Roland 1985; Stuss & Benson 1986). Significantly, this prefrontal control, via strong prefrontal-Nacc projection, is strongly influenced by VTA DA projections to prefrontal cortex, as described above. Indeed, if one focuses on a group of A10 DA cells, an innervation can be mapped to both prefrontal cortex and the Nacc. If one then looks at a prefrontal projection to the Nacc, the termination area of that projection in the Nacc is to the area innervated by the DA projection arising from that very group of A10 DA cells (Iversen 1984; Thierry et al 1984). Thus, the VTA A10 DA cell group plays a crucial role in facilitating motivated behavior via its coordinated modulation of prefrontal and Nacc circuitry, as well as its direct input to limbic structures which affects input to the Nacc at source. The VTA, then, promotes interaction between the mesolimbic and mesocortical systems, where the Nacc serves as a nodal point of input convergence.

A FUNCTIONAL PRINCIPLE OF DOPAMINE ACTIVITY   Central placement of the Nacc in facilitating behavioral engagement suggests that DA activity in the Nacc serves as a gating mechanism that influences whether some signals from limbic structures reach the motor system. This is concordant with the evolving functional principle of DA activity as a switching-initiation mechanism, where DA promotes the switching between alternative sources of information [see the extensive review by Oades (1985)]. DA increases the probability of shutting off ongoing signals to the output, such as in switching or changing response strategies, and of new input influencing the output, where the effect is the initiation of new responses. This principle appears to hold for elements of responses (such as limb movements in walking or lever pressing), for responses of the whole organism (such as feeding, drinking, visits to an alleyway), and for response strategies that require a cognitive plan for their organization (such as searching for food or safety).

A generalized switching-initiation function for DA is consistent with behavioral data. On the basis of studies on behavioral consequences of selective lesions of A 10 DA neurons at the level of cell bodies, and at the level of terminals in the prefrontal cortex, in the Nacc, and in the lateral septum, the A 10 DA neurons do not appear to have a specific behavioral role but rather facilitate or initiate processes in regions they innervate (Louilot et al 1987;

Taghzouti et al 1986). Although animals with DA-system lesions have a broad range of behavioral deficits that would threaten survival, they can be helped to move, eat, or learn discriminations, again suggesting that DA plays a modulatory rather than an all-or-none mediating role in behavior (Oades 1985).

Implications for Bipolar Affective Disorders

MODELING DEPRESSIVE AND MANIC PHASES   The broad diversity of engagement behaviors affected in bipolar disorders suggests that a more generalized functional disturbance in the BFS—and hence in its neurobiologic foundation, the VTA A10 DA projections—may exist in some forms of these disorders. On this view, depressive and hypomanic/manic phases may be viewed as opposite extreme manifestations of a single dimension of BFS functional activity—an activity deficient in depression, and excessively high in hypomania/mania. These divergent symptom patterns are parsimoniously explained by the switch/initiation-incentive principle of DA activity, a principle that must exert its influence on behavior if A10 DA pathways are dysfunctional (for whatever reasons). From the standpoint of this principle, BFS functional activity may be viewed as a dimension of the probability that relevant external and internal (including cognitive) eliciting stimuli will switch-on, initiate, or facilitate motor and affective responses—or, put differently, as a dimension of the propensity to behavioral and affective reactivity to eliciting stimuli. The probability of switching/initiating (or the level of reactivity) would be low in depression and excessively high in hypomania/mania.

Although our goal here is not to account for each symptom, if BFS dysfunction underlies bipolar symptom patterns, then the BFS components of motor and incentive-reward motivation should represent core features of both depression and hypomania/mania. In bipolar depression, psychomotor retardation, where motor and speech responsiveness is delayed and slowed, and a lack of incentive-reward motivation (subjectively, a lack of interest and excitement) to engage with social, sexual, vocational, or recreational stimuli form highly prominent features (Depue & Monroe 1978; Post & Uhde 1982). Furthermore, retarded bipolar depression is often characterized as being devoid of affect and by a lack of affective reactivity to positive stimuli, even stimuli that are highly rewarding—where the depression has a quality distinct from a reactive form of depressed affect found, for instance, in a bereaved state. The literature discussed above on the structure of behavioral states in humans is concordant with this view: The "low" extreme of the major positive engagement dimension is characterized by an absence of positive affect rather than by negative affect (Watson & Tellegen 1985). All of these symptoms may be interpreted (from the standpoint of the functional principle of DA) as a state in which the normal eliciting stimuli of behavioral engagement do not activate BFS function and, hence, do not initiate LA, incentive-reward motivation, and positive mood.

The hypomanic/manic phase also manifests the BFS core components, but the opposite extreme exists. There is an excessively high probability that signals of reward and novelty (including those that are cognitively generated) "switch on" motor behavior (hyperactivity) and initiate a subjective state of excessive incentive-reward motivation and pleasurable (if not too extreme) excitement. Furthermore, as found in animal (Oades 1985) studies (including some with primates, Schultz 1984) where, owing to high DA function, reward and novel stimuli have enhanced power to elicit behavior, positive stimuli appear to more readily initiate behavioral responses in hypomania/mania, such that focused behavioral responding may be difficult to maintain, result-ing in a state of high behavioral-attentional distractibiltiy, where responses are initiated to stimuli that are reward-positive or novel but irrelevant to the task at hand (Belmaker & van Praag 1980; Shopsin 1979).

The occurrence of mixed affect within a single manic episode has long been a theoretical problem for models that integrate depressive and manic phases along a single dimension. The most common meaning of mixed affect (Secun-da et al 1987) concerns the occurrence of elation, depressed mood and cognitions, and irritability in rapid sequence—i.e. affective lability. Although external and internal (cognitive) stimuli elicit concordant affective states, whether these affects and associated motor behavior gain overt expression probably depends on the dual strength of the eliciting stimuli and the reactiv-ity of neurobiologic systems (e.g. the A10 DA system) that facilitate such behavior (Gray 1982). The amygdala, which receives strong projections from VTA DA cells, may play a crucial role in this process because it appears to be involved in loading an affective valence on polysensory information (Sarter & Markowitsch 1985). It is interesting to speculate whether increased DA reactivity in relevant amygdaloid nuclei may promote excessive expression of various affects in response to even mild external and cognitive stimuli in mania.

In mania, stimulus-elicited reactivity is excessively high (Belmaker & van Praag 1980; Post & Uhde 1982; Shopsin 1979), so the nature of the stimulus context becomes a highly potent factor in determining the moment-to-moment mood and cognitive state of the manic individual. Thus, we may hypothesize that stimuli (internal and external) of positive valence (e.g. reward or novelty) would rapidly elicit BFS activity and hence facilitate increased LA, incentive motivation, a desire for excitement, a mood state of euphoria and elation, and active behavioral engagement in manic patients. Similarly, manic patients are notoriously irritable after mild frustration—i.e. any interference with their intended behavior, including the obstruction by others of goal attainment, "seemingly harmless remarks . . . and minor provocations" (Shopsin 1979, p. 59). This raises the dual possibility (*a*) that the A10 DA projection to the amygdala may be highly reactive in mania in initiating irritable mood and aggressive behavior, and (*b*) that this limbic-generated affect is readily facilitated into irritative aggressive motor responses by DA activity in the Nacc. And finally, stimuli of negative valence (e.g. thoughts that one's life is disintegrating) would be expected to elicit "short bursts" (Shopsin 1979, p. 60) of anxious and depressive cognitions and mood. Since all of these classes of stimuli may originate as cognitions, the observation that the manic's "mood is consistent with ideation" (Shopsin 1979, p. 60) and that behavior readily follows cognition is congruent with this formulation. The resulting clinical picture is one of excessive affective and behavioral lability (Post & Uhde 1982; Shopsin 1979), with a mixture of cognitions and moods in rapid sequence, where "rage, delight, irritation, depression, and euphoria appear and disappear inexplicably" (Belmaker & van Praag 1980, p. 8), but in the presence of an activated BFS state.

Concordant with this view is the observation, emphasized by Post & Uhde (1982), that depressive features in mania are not clinically similar to those occurring during bipolar depressive phases. Depressive phases are characterized by an absence of positive affect (an affective void) and a lack of affective reactivity to stimuli, although depressive cognitions and mood are typically present. In mania, the prominent depressive features are *reactive* cognitions and mood (Belmaker & van Praag 1980; Post & Uhde 1982; Secunda et al 1987; Shopsin 1979). That is, motivationally and motorically the two states may be viewed as representing opposite extremes on a single dimension of BFS reactivity, but they each may share depressive cognitions and mood. The depressive features in mania are viewed here as yet another manifestation of excessive reactivity and as different from the deficient motor-motivational-affective state observed in bipolar depression.

DOPAMINERGIC ASPECTS OF FUNCTIONAL INSTABILITY IN THE BE-HAVIORAL FACILITATION SYSTEM   The implication arising from the neurobiology of behavioral engagement is that turnover of DA in depression and mania may be altered, but evidence has not thus far supported this possibility. As thoroughly reviewed (Post 1980), both baseline and probenecid-induced accumulation measures of CSF HVA have not consistently or significantly differentiated manic, depressed (except occasionally retarded depressives), and normal or psychiatric control groups, nor have they distinguished the manic state from the recovered state. CSF HVA may not accurately represent DA turnover in the mesolimbic or mesocortical DA system, since about 80% of all DA in the brain is in the nigrostriatal system (Fishman et al 1983) and since the caudate, which lines the walls of the lateral ventricles, provides a major contribution to the total amount of HVA in CSF (Post 1980). Nevertheless, at this point there is no strong basis for the position that differences in DA turnover characterize either phase of bipolar disorders.

Pharmacologic data reviewed recently (Cookson 1985; Post 1980; Silverstone 1985; Wood 1985) do suggest a role for DA in mania and depression. The efficacy of neuroleptics (and their generally short clinical time course of 1–5 days, which correlates with the rise in DA-inhibited prolactin) and, in some patients, of low-dose DA receptor agonists (such as piribedil, which at low dose preferentially stimulate DA autoreceptors and, thereby, inhibit DA turnover) in the treatment of mania, as well as antidepressant effects in some depressed patients of the DA receptor agonists piribedil and bromocriptine, have all raised the possibility of altered DA function in bipolar disorders. Accordingly, in view of the apparent insensitivity of DA turnover measures, hypotheses that focus more on the functional dynamics of DA activity have been proposed (Bunney et al 1977). We focus here on the behavioral instability that occurs when the regulation of the DA system is challenged or altered in bipolar disorders. To the extent that symptomatic behavioral functioning reflects BFS functioning, the DA literature has implications for evaluating BFS instability in bipolar disorders.

Evidence related to behavioral instability concerns the effects of DA challenges and of unimodal treatments (treatments aimed at one phase of bipolar disorder), both of which are associated with an increased probability of extreme levels of engagement (i.e. hypomania/mania). Since manipulation (Cookson 1985; Jimerson & Post 1984; Post 1980; Silverstone 1985; Wood 1985) and pharmacologic studies (Bunney 1978; Pickar et al 1984; Post 1980; Post & Udhe 1982; Silverstone 1985) were reviewed recently, they are only outlined here. In several studies, enhancement of DA activity by increasing synthesis (L-Dopa), release (amphetamine), or postsynaptic receptor activation (piribedil or bromocriptine) was associated with hypomanic or, less frequently, manic behavioral disturbance, an effect more commonly found in bipolar than in unipolar depressed patients. These studies do not, however, represent a large number of patients, and other studies using amphetamine or piribedil did not observe a manic response (Post & Uhde 1982). Whether a DA-induced vulnerability to hypomania/mania exists in the remitted state has been insufficiently tested, having been found with methylphenidate challenge in euthymic bipolar patients on lithium but not in medication-free (off drugs only two weeks on average) euthymic patients with amphetamine challenge.

As reviewed recently (Bunney 1978; Pickar et al 1984; Post 1980), acute and chronic treatment with tricyclic antidepressants (TCAs) and monoamine oxidase inhibitors (MAOIs) is associated with an increased incidence of hypomanic/manic disturbance, an effect that is much more common in bipolar than unipolar depressed patients and in bipolar 1 vs 2 patients. When assessed from literature review (where patient subtype is not always specified), the proportion of patients experiencing disturbance with TCA usage is approximately 9%, whereas for MAOIs it varies from 11–27% depending on type of MAOI. However, in several double-blind analyses where patient subtype was specified, rates of hypomanic/manic disturbances of 30–60% have been reported for bipolar patients for both treatment and prophylactic studies of TCAs and for treatment studies of MAOIs.

While the relevance of DA-agonist induction of hypomanic/manic behavioral disturbance to BFS function seems clear, TCA and MAOI effects require explanation. In the case of some TCAs (desipramine and iprindole but not fluoxetine), long-term (15 days) but not short-term (1–2 days) treatment enhanced DA-mediated behaviors in rats, such as amphetamine-induced LA [if moderate doses are used (Spyraki & Fibiger 1981)] and intracranial self-stimulation rate-intensity function from the VTA A10 region (a DA-mediated behavior—see above) (Fibiger & Phillips 1981). Neither amphetamine- nor apomorphine-induced stereotypy was enhanced by chronic TCA (Spyraki & Fibiger 1981), suggesting that chronic TCA administration affects the functional properties of the mesolimbic, but not the striatal, DA system. Interestingly, electroconvulsive shock (ECS) also enhances amphetamine- and apomorphine-induced LA in rats (Fink 1984).

Mechanisms responsible for these TCA effects are not known. Both TCAs and newer "atypical" antidepressants are only weak blockers of synaptosomal uptake of DA (Fibiger & Phillips 1981). Some TCAs, as well as MAOIs and ECS, induce progressive subsensitivity of DA autoreceptors, an effect that would potentially enhance release of DA; but contrary evidence exists (Spyraki & Fibiger 1981). Alternatively, on the basis of behavioral evidence, postsynaptic DA-receptor supersensitivity has been proposed as an effect of chronic desipramine (Spyraki & Fibiger 1981) and chronic ECS (Fink 1984). However, DA-receptor binding appears unaffected with chronic TCAs (Snyder & Peroutka 1984), and it is unknown whether effects of chronic TCAs, MAOIs, and ECS on behavior and DA neurons are direct or secondary to actions of NE or 5HT.

Also possibly reflecting BFS instability are effects of the cholinesterase [the degrading enzyme of acetylcholine (ACh) in the synapse] inhibitor physostigmine, which has antimanic properties in some manic patients, especially those without a strong irritable-hostile component (reviewed by Risch & Janowsky 1984). (This strategy is based on the notion that ACh and DA oppose each other in modulating motor behavior and possibly affect, so promotion of ACh may reduce manic or increase depressive behavior.) Centrally active physostigmine has induced depressive symptoms in a subgroup of manic patients and in a majority of remitted bipolar patients on lithium; it has induced rebound hypermania in a limited number of severe manics. Except for very small subgroups, normal and psychiatric controls do not manifest depressive symptoms, but rather show an anergic syndrome that can be antagonized in normal subjects by methylphenidate administration. If physostigmine-induced depression in manic patients is mediated primarily by inhibitory cholinergic effects in the Nacc, rather than in the striatal system and cerebellar tracts, then the cholinergic data are of interest with respect to BFS regulation.

Although responses to amphetamine vary widely in normal controls, most frequently subjects experience elevated mood and arousal in a dose-related manner; affective lability and irritability; insomnia; and increased LA, speech rate, thoughts, and energy (Silverstone 1985)—all of which can be attenuated by pimozide (a DA postsynaptic receptor blocker) administration (Silverstone 1985). Induction of hypomanic/manic disturbance, however, has not been reported. Moreover, cholinergic activation induces an anergic syndrome in normal subjects, but only rarely a depressed state. Thus, DA and ACh challenges to behavioral regulation appear to set in motion a dynamic process that leads to either activation or inhibition of engagement in normal subjects, depending on the type of challenge.

As noted by others (Risch & Janowsky 1984), bipolar patients show a qualitatively similar but quantitatively exaggerated behavioral response to these challenges, where the functional process set in motion may proceed until an extreme behavioral state opposite from the prechallenge level is achieved. This may indicate, as suggested by others (Mandell et al 1984; Sitiram et al 1984), that behavior is inadequately regulated in bipolar disorders, and that this problem is most likely to become manifest under conditions of internal or external regulatory challenge. Concordantly, noting that lithium reduces behavioral instability in remitted bipolar patients, Mandell et al (1984) demonstrated at both enzymatic and behavioral levels that one basic effect of lithium is to increase regulatory stability of variables. We suggest the possibility, particularly on the basis of the clinical DA-challenge and TCA studies and the animal TCA-DA interaction literature, that the inadequate regulation observed in bipolar disorder may be located in the BFS.

BRAIN IMAGING AND THE MAJOR AFFECTIVE DISORDERS

Among the revolutionary developments in the 1970s and 1980s has been the ability to visualize the structure and function of tissue in the living human brain. Among the imaging techniques now common or increasingly becoming available are computerized tomography, positron emission tomography, and magnetic resonance imaging (formerly referred to as nuclear magnetic resonance imaging). Using these procedures, neuroanatomical studies of the brain can be carried out in vivo that previously were feasible only after death. It is now also possible to perform metabolic and neurochemical studies of the central nervous system without the use of indirect, invasive, or potentially life-threatening methods. In this section we introduce imaging techniques, including their relative advantages and limitations, and consider what these procedures have revealed about the major affective disorders, thus providing the first comprehensive review of brain imaging with respect to these disorders. Most of the research using imaging techniques has dealt with schizophrenia and has been adequately summarized elsewhere (Andreasen 1988; Conlon & Trimble 1987; Nasrallah & Weinberger 1986; Smith et al 1988).

Overview of Imaging Techniques

An excellent technical but understandable overview of scanning techniques has been provided by Martin and Burst (1985). A more elementary introduction, complete with an exceptional color pictorial illustrating the images generated by different scanning methods, can be found in a recent issue of *National Geographic* (Sochurek 1987).

COMPUTERIZED TOMOGRAPHY (CT)   Developed in the United Kingdom in the early part of the last decade, the CT scanner generates a series of images, referred to as slices or scans, that depict tissue in a transverse plane through the brain. The procedure involves revolving multiple beams of X rays around one side of the head while scintillation detectors are rotated around the other side in an identical path. A computer sums the many transmission readings associated with all the beams that pass through each point of the head to generate a digital code that represents anatomical features. Because bone, brain tissue, and CSF differ in the extent to which they absorb X rays, the digital code can be translated into a picture in which bone appears white, tissue gray, and CSF black. Each picture represents a slice of the head that is of uniform thickness (e.g. 1 cm thick). By repeating the procedure a dozen or more times, a set of two-dimensional images or tomographs, each representing a different cross-section of the brain, is produced, making it possible to visualize the entire brain through the series of slices.

Because it is difficult to resolve different aspects of brain tissue in a CT film, CT studies of psychopathology have focused on the CSF-filled spaces in and around the brain. The most commonly studied structures have been the lateral ventricles, the third ventricle, and the cortical sulci. Most investigations have determined whether these structures appear enlarged, a phenomenon that suggests brain atrophy.

The lateral ventricles are by far the most studied aspect of brain morphology in psychiatric patients. However, because their structure is complex (each is shaped something like a sickle, with the blade extending toward the frontal and temporal lobes and the handle protruding back into the occiput), they are difficult to measure adequately. Several investigators have used simple linear measures of various aspects of the lateral ventricles. Although these are easy to obtain, they are relatively insensitive to the subtle changes in ventricular size that one might expect to see in psychiatric patients who, after all, do not have gross neurological deficits. They are also difficult to compare across studies because the units of measurement and the nature of the measure are varied and sometimes not specified. Moreover, the best estimate of ventricular size, ventricular volume, does not correlate highly with linear measures (Penn et al 1978).

Although the estimation of ventricular volume is a cumbersome process, an area measurement, referred to as the ventricular brain ratio (VBR; Synek & Reuben 1976), has been found to correlate highly with ventricular volume (Jernigan et al 1982; Penn et al 1978). The VBR has been used in well over 50 investigations of brain morphology in the functional psychoses and is the single, most widely used estimate of lateral ventricle size. To calculate the VBR, the area of the lateral ventricles and the area of the brain are determined from the CT scan that shows the ventricles at their largest (typically, this scan depicts the body of the lateral ventricles). Ventricle area is then divided by brain area and multiplied by 100 to express ventricle size as a percentage of brain area.

The same procedure could be used to estimate third-ventricle size, but more commonly, third-ventricle width has been measured by determining the widest aspect of this structure apparent in the CT films. Bounded by the thalami, the third ventricle appears as a short, narrow slit in the brain. Because there is far less curvature to its shape than is apparent in the lateral ventricles, this linear measurement technique is not as problematic as those associated with the lateral ventricles.

No standard has evolved for the measurement of cortical sulci. In some studies, rating scales are used to quantify the visibility of the sulci, the larger ones being the more visible. Linear measurements of sulcal width are also computed. Specific sulci, such as the Sylvian fissure, may be the target of such measurements, or investigators may choose to sum the measurements made from several of the largest visible sulci.

POSITRON EMISSION TOMOGRAPHY (PET)   Unlike CT, which is used primarily to study brain structure, PET is commonly used to investigate brain pharmacology, blood flow, and metabolism. Emission tomography requires the administration of a compound labeled with an isotope that emits highly unstable particles called positrons (positively charged electrons). After a positron is emitted, it travels away from its source and eventually collides with an electron. This collision results in the annihilation of these two atomic particles and the emission of two gamma rays in opposite directions. A ring of crystal detectors around the subject records an emission only when two coincident events are recorded at opposing detectors. Because the emission of gamma rays depends on the distribution of the labeled compound in the body, this information can be used to form an image that reflects an organ's use or uptake of the compound.

Although hundreds of compounds have been successfully labeled with positron emitters, such as carbon-11 (^{11}C) and fluorine-18 (^{18}F), those compounds of greatest interest to the study of psychopathology are pharmacological agents, such as neurotransmitters, their precursors, and receptor ligand molecules, and analogues of glucose (^{11}C-glucose and ^{18}F-deoxyglucose). The latter are especially relevant to the study of brain function because nerve cell activity is dependent on the utilization of glucose. Hence, if a subject is presented with a task following the intravenous administration of radiolabeled glucose, the glucose will become concentrated in regions of the brain that are activated by the task. With the PET scanner, it is possible to map the location of these regions and identify the brain structures associated with different types of mental processing.

PET scanning is by far the most expensive of the three imaging techniques, the high cost stemming in part from the fact that a cyclotron is needed to prepare the radioactive compounds. There are other limitations to PET scanners as well. At their best, their resolution is poor, on the order of 4–8 mm. Theoretically, it will be difficult to achieve much better spatial resolution than this because positrons may travel several millimeters from their point of generation before colliding with an electron. A consequence of this limitation is that it is not possible to localize precisely the anatomical source of the gamma rays. Another factor that must be considered in PET scanning is the length of time that the radio tracer is active. If a tracer with a long half-life is used, then subjects must engage in a single task for an extended period in order for sufficient gamma radiation to be detected. Any intervening distractions or irrelevant mental effort will also affect neuron metabolism, so care must be taken to control carefully the behavior of subjects undergoing this procedure. It is important to recognize that PET scanning does not provide direct insight into the nature of neurological deficit. PET is a psychophysiological procedure; an identified abnormality in a PET image could stem from a structural or physiological deficit or represent the biological substrate of a dysfunctional psychological process.

Failure to control whether subjects keep their eyes open or closed during the scanning session can have a profound influence on the resulting PET images because the large portion of the brain involved with visual processing will be activated if the eyes are open. It is also possible that a patient's clinical state, determined by such factors as the presence or absence of hallucinations, anxiety, or agitation, could affect glucose uptake in idiosyncratic ways. Finally, interpreting PET scans is complicated by our incomplete understanding of the knowledge and distribution of the radiotracers and their metabolites in different types of tissue.

MAGNETIC RESONANCE IMAGING (MRI)   MRI technology is very complex, both because of the principles of physics on which it is based and in terms of the types of information that can be derived from the procedure. For these reasons, a detailed explication of MRI is beyond the scope of the present review; the interested reader can obtain additional information elsewhere (Conlon & Trimble 1987; Garber et al 1988; Martin & Burst 1985; Coffman & Nasrallah 1986). In principle, MRI combines features of CT and PET and can be used to investigate tissue function, metabolism, pathology, and blood flow as well as brain morphology.

MRI is based on the principle that certain atomic nuclei have magnetic properties and, when placed in a magnetic field, can be made to resonate and produce a radio frequency. Modern MRI is focused largely on hydrogen, a strong resonator that has a single proton in its nucleus and that is found in abundance throughout the human body in the form of water. Subjects are placed in the hollow core of a long, cylindrical magnet that, when activated, causes hydrogen nuclei to align themselves with the static magnetic field. A radio pulse is applied to create a second magnetic field perpendicular to that provided by the magnet, thus causing the protons to change their alignment When the pulse is turned off, the nuclei return to their original orientation, losing energy, which is transmitted as a small electrical voltage. In doing so, they become radio frequency transmitters, resonating at frequencies characteristic for hydrogen in different chemical or physical environments, thereby identifying their presence by their signals. The strength of the transmission is proportional to the density of protons in a given region. By using the magnet to align the nuclei in different directions and adding a magnetic gradient to the static magnetic field, the pattern of frequencies generated by the hydrogen atoms can be translated by computer into two-dimensional images that reveal brain structure. The degree of resolution evident in these images is a function of the strength of the magnet. At its best, the details of structure evident in MRI pictures resemble that of fixed and sectioned brain tissue.

Two different parameters can be measured using this technique, and they can be used to generate different types of images. The rate at which hydrogen nuclei realign themselves after the radio pulse is switched off is called relaxation, a phenomenon described by its time constants, T1 and T2. T1 (spin lattice or longitudinal relaxation) depends on the interaction of nuclei with surrounding molecules, while T2 (spin-spin or transverse relaxation) depends on the interaction of nuclei with each other. Because relaxation times are influenced by tissue composition, images emphasizing one or the other discriminate among various types of tissue. For example, the structure of white matter and water-rich gray matter can best be visualized using T1-weighted images. CSF is best visualized with T2 images.

MRI has a number of advantages over CT for visualizing brain structure. Unlike CT, with MRI white and gray matter are well resolved, and it is easy to generate sagittal and coronal images of the brain, thus making it possible to obtain unique views of nuclei and tracts. It also does not involve exposure to ionizing radiation. Because bone contains little water, it does not appear on MRI scans, thus making it possible to visualize structures such as the posterior fossa and temporal lobes, which may be obscured by bone artifacts with CT imaging. Disadvantages of MRI scanning include its far greater expense, the approximate doubling of the time it takes to scan a subject, its more limited availability, the inability of obese people to fit inside the cylindrical magnet, and the possibility of a claustrophobic reaction from a subject who must lie still inside the magnet for up to 1 hr.

CT Scan Studies

Unfortunately, despite considerable evidence that bipolar disorder and recurrent major depression may be different disorders (Depue & Monroe 1978), CT studies for the most part fail to differentiate between these types of affective disturbance. Consequently, it was not possible to examine thoroughly the morphological correlates of these two affective syndromes separately.

LATERAL VENTRICLES   Do patients with mood disorders have lateral ventricular enlargement (LVE)? To answer this question, we identified 14 studies of lateral ventricle size in affective disorder in which the VBR was calculated and a control group was included. Two studies were unlike the rest in that nonpsychotic psychiatric patients served as the comparison group. One of these investigations reported LVE in affective-disorder patients (Pearlson & Veroff 1981), while the other did not (Owens et al 1985). Of the remaining 12 studies, 7 reported LVE (Dolan et al 1985; Luchins et al 1984; Nasrallah et al 1984; Pearlson et al 1984; Scott et al 1983; Shima et al 1984; Targum et al 1983) and 5 failed to identify significant enlargement (Dewan et al 1988; Iacono et al 1988; Jacoby & Levy 1980; Schlegel & Kretzschmar 1987; Weinberger et al 1982). Hence, these reports are almost evenly split with regard to their finding LVE in mood disorders. Using the information provided in these studies, we were unable to identify systematic procedural differences that could account for the varied outcomes.

In a similar analysis of LVE associated with schizophrenia, Smith & Iacono (1986) found that investigations with positive and negative findings did not differ in the reported mean VBRs associated with schizophrenia. However, they did differ in that the control groups paired with schizophrenic patients in studies with positive results had smaller ventricles than did the control groups in the studies with nonsignificant findings. To determine if a similar relationship holds for studies of affective disorder, we have examined the VBRs associated with patient and control groups as a function of study outcome. As can be seen from Figure 4, there is little difference in the VBRs associated with affective disorder. However, as Smith & Iacono (1986) found for schizophrenia, studies that report LVE use comparison groups that have smaller ventricles than do the control subjects in studies that do not uncover LVE. Using the means and standard deviations (SD) provided for the control subjects in these studies, it is possible to calculate means and SDs across groups of studies and compute a t-statistic to evaluate significant differences. The control subjects from studies reporting LVE (M=5.05, SD=2.67) do indeed have significantly smaller ventricles than the control subjects from investigations that do not find LVE (M=8.02, SD=2.98; t(485)=11.52, p <.001). Although it is unclear how these control groups differ on variables other than ventricle size (cf Smith et al 1988), these findings suggest that control group selection may have an important influence on the outcome of CT investigations of lateral ventricle size.

OTHER STRUCTURES   Investigations of other cerebral structures in affective disorder have yielded a similarly inconsistent picture. Schlegel & Kretzschmar (1987) found a modest but statistically significant enlargement of the

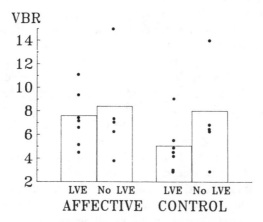

Figure 4   Plot of mean ventricular brain ratios (VBR) for affective disorder and control groups in seven investigations that reported lateral ventricular enlargement (LVE) and five that failed to find enlargement (no LVE).

third ventricle in a heterogeneous group of patients with mood disorders. However, Tanaka et al (1982) did not demonstrate a similar effect, and Iacono and colleagues (1988) failed to find third-ventricle enlargement in either psychotic patients with bipolar disorder or those with major depression. Examinations of sulcal size are also divided between those that do find evidence of cortical atrophy (Dolan et al 1986; Pearlson & Veroff 1981; Tanaka et al 1982) and those that do not (Dewan et al 1988; Iacono et al 1988; Jacoby & Levy 1980; Schlegel & Kretzschmar 1987).

CORRELATES OF STRUCTURAL ABNORMALITIES   An important question concerns the meaning or importance of structural abnormalities when they appear in the brains of individuals with mood disorders. One way to provide an answer to this question is to examine the correlates of these characteristics to determine if they provide any clues or insights as to their significance. Because few studies have explored the correlates of third-ventricle and cortical atrophy, we focus on those variables related to lateral ventricle size that have been studied by more than one investigative team.

A number of factors could logically be expected to be related to ventricular enlargement. Mood-disordered patients with large ventricles might have more treatment with somatic therapies, a stronger genetic liability to develop affective disorder, a greater likelihood of experiencing cognitive impairment, and a more severe form of disorder. For the most part, however, large ventricles do not seem to be related to those variables.

There is uniform agreement in the literature that LVE in affective patients is not associated with prior exposure to electroconvulsive therapy (Dolan et al 1985; Nasrallah et al 1984; Pearlson et al 1984; Standish-Barry et al 1985), medication regimens (Dolan et al 1985; Luchins et al 1984; Pearlson et al 1984; Scott et al 1983), a positive family history of psychopathology (Dolan et al 1985; Jacoby & Levy 1980; Nasrallah et al 1984; Pearlson et al 1984; Standish-Barry et al 1985), or cognitive deficit (Jacoby & Levy 1980; Nasrallah et al 1984). Many clinical features of affective disorders also appear to be unrelated to LVE, including age at onset (Dolan et al 1985; Jacoby & Levy 1980; Nasrallah et al 1984; Pearlson et al 1984; Roy-Byrne et al 1988), duration of disorder (Dolan et al 1985; Nasrallah et al 1984; Roy-Byrne et al 1988; Standish-Barry et al 1985; Tanaka et al 1982), and severity of the most recent episode (Luchins et al 1984; Pearlson et al 1984).

Targum and collaborators (1983) found that although delusional and nondelusional depressed patients did not differ on ventricle size, more delusional than nondelusional patients had values that were greater than the normal control mean plus two SDs. These findings raise the possibility that psychotic depression is associated with LVE. Although Schlegal & Kretzschmar (1987) also uncovered a relationship between LVE and psychotic symptoms in depression, most other investigators have not found such an association (Iacono et al 1988; Luchins et al 1984; Nasrallah et al 1984; Pearlson et al 1984; Standish-Barry et al 1985). Another way to subtype depressive disorder derives from whether or not manic episodes are present. The only two studies directly to contrast unipolar and bipolar patients failed to find a difference between them in ventricle size (Iacono et al 1988; Roy-Byrne et al 1988).

Investigations that have examined how the outcome and course of affective disorder is related to ventricle size have produced mixed results. Jacoby et al (1981) found that outcome three months after hospitalization was not predicted by VBR, but Shima et al (1984) reported that LVE predicted nine-month outcome. In a study of depressed patients over 60, Jacoby et al (1981) found that those with LVE were more likely to die during a two-year follow-up period than those with smaller ventricles. Number of prior hospitalizations was related to ventricle size in one study (Pearlson et al 1984) but not in others (Dolan et al 1985; Roy-Byrne et al 1988). The most comprehensive assessment of the relationship of course of disorder to VBR was undertaken by Roy-Byrne and associates (1988) in a study of 59 patients with affective disorder. No significant correlations were reported between each of 25 course-related variables and VBR measurements.

PET and MRI Studies

Because PET and MRI are more recently deployed developments than CT, and because they are more complicated to apply, far fewer studies have been carried out using these techniques. All the PET studies of affective disorders have examined glucose metabolism; MRI investigations of these disorders are only just beginning to appear in the literature.

All five PET studies of affective disorder have used patients who were not medicated at the time of evaluation. These investigations can be divided into those examining subjects in the "resting state" and those in which participants were stimulated by an experimental manipulation. They can be further differentiated by the requirement that subjects have their eyes open or closed.

The two studies that tested patients at rest with their eyes open found that unipolar depressives did not differ in gross brain metabolism from normal control subjects (Baxter et al 1985; also reported in Phelps et al 1984; Kling et al 1986). One of these reports included patients with bipolar depression and found that overall glucose metabolism in these individuals was lower than normal (Baxter et al 1985). Baxter et al (1985) also examined bipolar manic patients and concluded that their gross metabolic rate was normal. These investigators also noted that activity in the caudate nucleus was depressed in unipolar patients, a finding that was not replicated by Kling et al (1986).

Among studies requiring subjects to close their eyes, two applied painful electrical stimulation to the forearm as a means of activating the frontal lobes

(Buchsbaum et al 1986; Post et al 1987). Buchsbaum et al (1986; also reported in Buchsbaum et al 1984) found global cerebral metabolism to be increased and caudate nucleus activity to be decreased in both unipolar and bipolar depressed patients compared to normal subjects. Bipolar patients showed lower than normal frontal to occipital glucose metabolic rate ratios (relative hypofrontality), while unipolar subjects demonstrated the reverse pattern. Focusing on temporal-lobe function, Post et al (1987) found that glucose utilization in the right temporal lobe was reduced relative to other brain regions in depressed patients. Although they also had subjects close their eyes, Kishimoto et al (1987) did not use electrical stimulation. Unlike all the other PET studies, these investigators used ^{11}C instead of ^{18}F labeled glucose. They reported that glucose uptake was diminished in frontal, temporal, parietal, and occipital cortex in unipolar depressed patients but increased in manic subjects. This pattern of results is unlike that reported by any of the other investigators.

Two of these reports, each using quite different procedures, provide suggestive evidence that altered glucose metabolism is state dependent in affective disorders. Kishimoto et al (1987) found euthymic patients to show normal glucose metabolism, and Baxter et al (1985) found that the low whole-brain metabolic rates evident in depressed bipolar patients increased as these individuals switched to euthymia or mania.

In closing our discussion of PET, it should be noted that unreplicated findings and negative results associated with these studies should be accepted with great caution. Patient sample sizes in these studies range from 3 to 16, with an average of 8 unipolar and 9 bipolar subjects included in any one study. In addition, the potential for Type I error in these studies is high because the number of statistical comparisons between groups is usually greater than sample sizes, in part because there are so many brain regions that can be contrasted across groups.

Few applications of MRI technology to the study of affective disorders exist. Dupont et al (1987) conducted a morphological study of the brains of 14 patients with bipolar disorder and found that 57% of the patients but none of the normal controls showed white-matter abnormalities suggestive of lesions. Examining proton T1 relaxation times in brain tissue rather than brain structure, Rangel-Guerra et al (1983) reported that bipolar patients showed considerably larger T1 times than normal subjects before the patients began lithium therapy. T1 values were normal, however, following lithium therapy. This finding was replicated in a study by Rosenthal et al (1986) that examined T1 relaxation times in the red blood cells rather than in the brain tissue of bipolar depressed patients. They found that proton T1 values in blood samples drawn from these patients were abnormally high preceding lithium therapy but substantially reduced following one week of treatment. Such findings suggest that intracellular hydration is abnormal in bipolar patients and that lithium triggers an apparent return to normal hydration status.

Conclusion

Overall, these provocative and often heralded imaging procedures have yet to generate a clear picture of structural and functional neuroanatomical abnormalities associated with affective disturbance. Although it must be conceded that a structural defect may underlie some subtype of affective disorder, studies employing the most widely used imaging technique, CT, have not convincingly demonstrated the existence of morphological abnormalities. About half the studies report negative results. Even in those investigations that report significant findings, the differences between groups are small (e.g. see Figure 4) and do not suggest substantial atrophy of brain tissue.

No insight has been generated regarding what ventricular and sulcal enlargement signifies if it does characterize these disorders. More systematic study of the correlates of widened CSF spaces are needed. Of the investigations conducted to date, too many use small samples and measures that are not operationally defined and that have unknown reliability. Few studies have searched for biological variables that may be related to brain anomalies.

We have noted how control group selection appears to play an important role in the outcome of CT studies, and Andreasen (1988) has indicated that choice of control group can also affect neuroanatomical studies using MRI. Indeed, one could argue from our analysis of control groups that until a more complete understanding of the normal range of human individual differences in ventricle and cortical size is achieved, it is inappropriate to characterize these spaces as enlarged rather than simply large. To date, no studies have demonstrated that an atrophic process may be affecting patients with mood disorders. To do so would require repeated scanning coupled with evidence that structural change has taken place. Also an open question is whether morphological anomalies antedate disorder onset, are a manifestation of the progression of the disorder, or reflect the consequences of treatment and institutionalization.

It is too soon to draw conclusions from PET and MRI studies. As our understanding of the technical aspects of these procedures improves, our sophistication regarding their use will as well. Both procedures hold considerable promise, MRI in part because of the opportunity it provides to view aspects of brain structure that have as yet gone unexamined, and PET in part because of the unexploited ability to investigate neural transmission and chemistry.

FINAL REMARKS

Assessment of DA functioning in affective, and perhaps especially bipolar, disorders may prove fruitful in learning more about BFS dysfunction and, in the likely event heterogeneity is observed, in possibly defining a DA subtype. Surprisingly, relatively few studies have used a DA-specific neurochemical challenge-protocol to examine the functional characteristics of BFS activity in affective disorders, and most of these focused on response to pharmacologic agents in mania. What is needed is a comprehensive functional assay that examines (a) behavioral and neurochemical response to activation and inhibition of DA synthesis, release, and presynaptic and postsynaptic receptors in depressive and hypomanic/manic phases; (b) the degree to which these responses and clinical symptoms covary across an episode and across phases within patients; and (c) the degree to which these responses are associated with clinical response to DA-active treatments, such as nomifensine in depression and neuroleptics in mania.

Also important to establish is the extent to which any behavioral dysfunction identified in neurochemical challenge studies, presumably mirroring dysfunction in the mesolimbic and mesocortical DA pathways, reflects dysfunction in DA pathways generally. For example, DA functioning peripherally indexed by prolactin secretion (either basal or stimulated) (Jimerson & Post 1984), hypothermic response to heat stress or to apomorphine, and eye-blink rate (Depue et al 1988b) reflect on the functional integrity of different DA cell groups lying outside the A10 group (Depue et al 1988a). The more general the observed dysfunction, the more likely that behavioral disturbance represents a DA-related problem in the BFS or a problem with a factor closely associated with DA function.

A significant advance in understanding the relation between DA and both normal behavior and affective disorder is likely to occur with refinement of brain imaging techniques. For instance, with PET or related strategies, it would be possible to study, in affective disorder subjects, regional cerebral metabolism of specific prefrontal areas during cognitive tasks known to be supported by prefrontal cortex, as in the elegant work of Roland (1985). As noted above, many prefrontal cognitive functions are dependent on the integrity of VTA DA projections to prefrontal cortex. Moreover, the dynamic biochemistry of DA itself may be studied via the PET technique in affective disorders. Further development of the imaging approach to the study of affective disorders is clearly one of the more exciting possibilities for the future.

Nevertheless, what is clear from the extent clinical literature is that much basic research on the manipulation of the DA system in humans is required before clinical studies will yield a consistent picture of the dysfunctional process in affective disorders. That is to say, there is a critical need for basic neurobiologic studies of normal populations. Both the basic and clinical research, however, will require far more sophisticated behavioral and cognitive analysis than has been evident if the effects of DA challenges or if behaviorally relevant imaging studies are to be fully understood. We hope that we have created sufficient interest in the neurobehavioral aspects of affective disorders to encourage psychologists to contribute their unique perspective more fully in interdisciplinary research.

ACKNOWLEDGMENTS

Portions of the research cited within this paper were supported in part by National Institute of Mental Health Research Grant MH-37195 awarded to R. A. Depue.

Literature Cited

Andreasen, N. C. 1988. Brain imaging: Applications in psychiatry. *Science* 239:1381–88

Baxter, L. R., Phelps, M. E., Mazziotta, J. C., Schwartz, J. M., Gerner, R. H., et al. 1985. Cerebral metabolic rates for glucose in mood disorders: Studies with positron emission tomography and fluorodeoxyglucose F18. *Arch. Gen. Psychiatry* 42:441–47

Belmaker, R. H., van Praag, H. M., eds. 1980. *Mania: An Evolving Concept*. New York: Spectrum

Beninger, R. J. 1983. The role of dopamine in locomotor activity and learning. *Br. Res. Rev.* 6:173–96

Bozarth, M. A. 1987. Ventral tegmental reward system. In *Brain Reward Systems and Abuse*, ed. J. Engel, L. Oreland, pp. 1–17. New York: Raven

Brodmann, K. 1909. *Vergleichende Lokalisationlehre der Grosshirnrinde*. Leipzig: Barth

Buchsbaum, M. S., DeLisi, L. E., Holcomb, H. H., Capelletti, J., King, A. C. et al 1984. Anteroposterior gradients in cerebral glucose use in schizophrenia and affective disorders. *Arch. Gen. Psychiatry* 41:1159–66

Buchsbaum, M. S., Wu, J., DeLisi, L. E., Holcomb, H., Kessler, R., et al. 1986. Frontal cortex and basal ganglia metabolic rates assessed by positron emission tomography with 18[F]2-deoxyglucose in affective illness. *J. Affect. Disord.* 10:137–52

Bunney, W. E. 1978. Psychopharmacology of the switch process in affective disorders. In *Psychopharmacology: A Generation of Progress*, ed. M. A. Lipton, A. DiMascio, K. F. Killam, pp. 1249–59. New York: Raven

Bunney, W. E., Post, R. M., Anderson, A. E., Kopanda, R. T. 1977. A neuronal receptor sensitivity mechanism in affective illness (a review of evidence). *Commun. Psychopharmacol.* 1:393–406

Coffman, J. A., Nasrallah, H. A. 1986. Magnetic brain imaging in schizophrenia. See Nasrallah & Weinberger 1986, pp. 251–66

Conlon, P., Trimble, M. R. 1987. Magnetic resonance imaging in psychiatry. *Can. J. Psychiatry* 32:702–12

Cookson, J. C. 1985. The neuroendocrinology of mania. *J. Affect. Disord.* 8:233–41

Costa, P. T., McCrae, R. R., Arenberg, D. 1980. Enduring dispositions in adult males. *J. Pers. Soc. Psychol.* 38:793–800

Crow, T. 1977. Neurotransmitter-related pathways: The structure and function of central monoamine neurones. In *Biochemical Correlates of Brain Structure and Function*, ed. A. Davison, pp. 137–74. New York: Academic

Depue, R. A. 1988. *Neurobehavioral Systems, Personality, and Psychopathology*. New York: Springer-Verlag. In press

Depue, R. A., Arbisi, P., Spoont, M. R., Leon, A., Ainsworth, B. 1988a. Dopamine functioning in the behavioral facilitation system and seasonal variation in behavior: Normal population and clinical studies. In *Seasonal Affective Disorder and Phototherapy*, ed. N. Rosenthal, M. Blehar, New York: Guilford

Depue, R. A., Iacono, W. G., Muir, R., Arbisi, P. 1988b. Effects of phototherapy on spontaneous eye-blink rate in seasonal affective disorder. *Am. J. Psychiatry.* In press

Depue, R. A., Krauss, S., Spoont, M. R. 1987. A two-dimensional threshold model of seasonal bipolar affective disorder. In *Psychopathology: An Interactional Perspective,* ed. D. Magnusson, A. Ohman, pp. 95–123. New York: Academic

Depue, R. A., Monroe, S. 1978. The unipolar-bipolar distinction in the depressive disorders. *Psychol. Bull.* 85:1001–29

Depue, R. M., Spoont, M. R. 1986. Conceptualizing a serotonin trait: A behavioral dimension of constraint. *Ann. NY Acad. Sci.* 487:47–62

Dewan, M. J., Haldipur, C. V., Boucher, M., Major, L. F. 1988. Is CT ventriculomegaly related to hypercortisolemia. *Acta Psychiatr. Scand.* 77:230–31

Dolan, R. J., Calloway, S. P., Mann, A. H. 1985. Cerebral ventricular size in depressed subjects. *Psychol. Med.* 15:873–78

Dolan, R. J., Calloway, S. P., Thacker, P. F., Mann, A. H. 1986. The cerebral cortical appearance in depressed subjects. *Psychol. Med.* 16:775–79

Dupont, R. M., Jernigan, T. L., Gillin, J. C., Butters, N., Delis, D. C., Hesselink, J. R. 1987. Subcortical signal hyperintensities in bipolar patients detected by MRI. *Psychiatry Res.* 21:357–58

Fibiger, H. C., Phillips, A. G. 1981. Increased intracranial self-stimulation in rats after long-term administration of desipramine. *Science* 214:683–85

Fibiger, H. C., Phillips, A. G. 1987. Role of catecholamine transmitters in brain reward systems. In *Brain Reward Systems and Abuse,* ed. J. Engel, L. Oreland, pp. 61–74. New York: Raven

Fink, J. S., Reis, D. J. 1981. Genetic variations in midbrain dopamine cell number: Parallel with differences in responses to dopaminergic agonists and in naturalistic behaviors mediated by central dopaminergic systems. *Br. Res.* 222:335–49

Fink, M. 1984. Theories of the antidepressant efficacy of convulsive therapy (ECT). See Post & Ballenger 1984, pp. 721–30

Fishman, R., Feigenbaum, J., Yanaiz, J., Klawans, H. 1983. The relative importance of dopamine and norepinephrine in mediating locomotor activity. *Prog. Neurobiol.* 20:55–88

Fuster, J. M. 1985. The prefrontal cortex, mediator of cross-temoral contingencies. *Hum. Neurobiol.* 4:169–70

Fuxe, K., Agnati, L. F., Kalia, M., Goldstein, M., Andersson, K., Harfstrand, A. 1985. Dopamine systems in the brain and pituitary. In *The Dopaminergic System,* ed. E. Fluckiger, E. E. Muller, M. O. Thorner, pp. 11–25. New York: Springer-Verlag

Garber, H. J., Weilburg, J. B., Buonanno, F. S., Manschreck, T. C., New, P. F. J. 1988. Use of magnetic resonance imaging in psychiatry. *Am. J. Psychiatry* 145:164–71

Glowinski, J., Tassin, J. P., Thierry, A. M. 1984. The mesocortico-prefrontal dopaminergic neurons. *Trends Neurosci.* 7:415–18

Goeders, N. E., Smith, J. E. 1983. Cortical involvement in cocaine reinforcement. *Science* 221:773–75

Goplerud, E., Depue, R. A. 1985. Behavioral response to naturally-occurring stress in cyclothymes, dysthymes, and controls. *J. Abnorm. Psychol.* 94:128–39

Gray, J. A. 1982. *The Neuropsychology of Anxiety.* New York: Oxford Press

Haas, H. 1983. Amine neurotransmitter actions in the hippocampus. In *Neurobiology of the Hippocampus,* ed. W. Seifert, pp. 139–55. New York: Academic

Iacono, W. G., Smith, G. N., Moreau, M., Beiser, M., Fleming, J. A. E. et al. 1988. Ventricular and sulcal size at the onset of psychosis. *Am. J. Psychiatry.* In press

Iversen, S. D. 1978. Brain dopamine systems and behavior. In *Handbook of Psychopharmacology,* ed. L. Iversen, S. Iversen, S. Snyder, 8:333–84. New York: Plenum

Iversen, S. D. 1984. Cortical monoamines and behavior. In *Monoamine Innervation of Cerebral Cortex,* ed. L. Descarries, T. Reader, H. Jaster, pp. 321–49. New York: Liss

Jacoby, R. J., Levy, R. 1980. Computed tomography in the elderly. 3. Affective disorder. *Br. J. Psychiatry* 136:270–75

Jacoby, R. J., Levy, R., Bird, J. M. 1981. Computed tomography and the outcome of affective disorder: A follow-up study of elderly patients. *Br. J. Psychiatry* 139:288–92

Jernigan, T. L., Zatz, L. M., Moses, J. A., Berger, P. A. 1982. Computed tomography in schizophrenics and normal volunteers. I Fluid volume. *Arch. Gen. Psychiatry* 39:765–70

Jimerson, D. C., Post, R. M. 1984. Psychomotor stimulants and dopamine agonists in depression. See Post & Ballenger 1984, pp. 619–28

Jones, D. L., Mogenson, G. J., Wu, M. 1980. Injections of dopaminergic, cholinergic, serotoninergic and GABAergic drugs into the nucleus accumbens: Effects on locomotor activity in the rat. *Neuropharmacology* 20:29–37

Kishimoto, H., Takazu, O., Ohno, S., Yamaguchi, T., Fujita, H., et al. 1987. 11C-Glucose Metabolism in manic and depressed patients. *Psychiatry Res.* 22:81–88

Kling, A. S., Metter, E. J., Riege, W. H.,

Kuhl, D. E. 1986. Comparison of PET measurement of local brain glucose metabolism and CAT measurement of brain atrophy in chronic schizophrenia and depression. *Am. J. Psychiatry* 143:175–80

Larson, J., Lynch, G. 1986. Induction of synaptic potentiation in hippocampus by patterned stimulation involves two events. *Science* 232:985–88

Lewis, D. A., Campbell, M. J., Foote, S. L., Morrison, J. H. 1986. The monoaminergic innervation of primate neocortex. *Hum. Neurobiol.* 5:181–88

Louilot, A., Simon, H., Taghzouti, K., Le Moal, M. 1985. Modulation of dopaminergic activity in the nucleus accumbens following facilitation or blockade of the dopaminergic transmission in the amygdala. *Br. Res.* 346:141–45

Louilot, A., Taghzouti, K., Deminiere, J. M., Simon, H., Le Moal, M. 1987. Dopamine and behavior: Functional and theoretical considerations. In *Neurotransmitter Interactions in the Basal Ganglia*, ed. M. Sandler, pp. 193–204. New York: Raven

Luchins, D. J., Lewine, R. R. J., Meltzer, H. Y. 1984. Lateral ventricular size, psychopathology, and medication response in the psychoses. *Biol. Psychiatry* 19:29–44

Luiten, P., Koolhaas, J. M., de Boer, S., Koopmans, S. J. 1985. The cortico-medial amygdala in the central nervous system: Organization of agonistic behavior. *Br. Res.* 332:283–97

Mandell, A. J., Knapp, S., Ehlers, C., Russo, P. V. 1984. The stability of constrained randomness: Lithium prophylaxis at several neurobiological levels. See Post & Ballenger 1984, pp. 744–76

Martin, J. H., Burst, J. C. M. 1985. Imaging the living brain. In *Principles of Neural Science*, ed. E. R. Kandel, J. H. Schwartz, pp. 259–83. New York: Elsevier

Mason, S. T. 1984. *Catecholamines and Behavior*. New York: Cambridge

Milner, P. 1977. Theories of reinforcement, drive, and motivation. In *Handbook of Psychopharmacology*, ed. L. Iversen, S. Iversen, S. Snyder, 7:181–200. New York: Plenum

Mogenson, G. J., Huang, Y. H. 1973. The neurobiology of motivated behavior. *Prog. Neurobiol* 1:53–83

Mogenson, G. J., Jones, D. L., Yim, C. Y. 1980. From Motivation to action: Functional interface between the limbic system and the motor system. *Prog. Neurobiol.* 14:69–97

Nasrallah, H. A., McCalley-Whitters, M., Pfohl, B. 1984. Clinical significance of large cerebral ventricles in manic males. *Psychiatry Res.* 13:151–56

Nasrallah, H. A., Weinberger, D. R., eds. 1986. *Handbook of Schizophrenia, Volume 1: The Neurology of Schizophrenia*. Amsterdam: Elsevier

Nauta, W. 1986. Circuitous connections linking cerebral cortex, limbic system, and corpus striatum. In *The Limbic System: Functional Organization and Clinical Disorders*, ed. B. K. Doane, K. E. Livingston, pp. 43–54. New York: Raven

Nauta, W., Domesick, V. B. 1981. Ramifications of the limbic system. In *Psychiatry and the Biology of the Human Brain*, ed. S. Matthysse, pp. 165–88. New York: Elsevier North Holland

Oades, R. D. 1985. The role of noradrenaline in tuning and dopamine in switching between signals in the CNS. *Neurosci. Biobehav. Rev.* 9:261–82

Oades, R. D., Halliday, G. M. 1987. Ventral tegmental (A10) system: Neurobiology. 1. Anatomy and connectivity. *Br. Res. Rev.* 12:117–65

Oades, R. D., Taghzouti, K., Rivet, J-M., Simon, H., Le Moal, M. 1986. Locomotor activity in relation to dopamine and noradrenaline in the nucleus accumbens, septal and frontal areas: A 6-hydroxydopamine study. *Neuropsychobiology* 16:37–42

Owens, D. G. C., Johnstone, E. C., Crow, T. J., Frith, C. D., Jagoe, J. R., Kreel, L. 1985. Lateral ventricular size in schizophrenia: Relationship to the disease process and its clinical manifestations. *Psychol. Med.* 15:27–41

Pearlson, G. D., Garbalz, D. J., Tompkins, R. H., Ahn, H. S., Gutterman, D. F., et al. 1984. Clinical correlates of lateral ventricular enlargement in bipolar affective disorder. *Am. J. Psychiatry* 141:253–56

Pearlson, G. D., Veroff, A. E. 1981. Computerized tomographic scan changes in manic-depressive illness. *Lancet* 2:470

Penn, R. D., Belanger, M. G., Yasnoff, W. A. 1978. Ventricular volume in men computed from CAT scans. *Ann. Neurol.* 3:216–23

Phelps, M. E., Mazziotta, J. C., Baxter, L., Gerner, R. 1984. Positron emission tomographic study of affective disorders: Problems and strategies. *Ann. Neurol.* 15 (Suppl.): S149–56

Phillipson, O. T., Griffiths, A. C. 1985. The topographic order of inputs to nucleus accumbens in the rat. *Neuroscience* 16:275–96

Pickar, D., Cowdry, R. W., Zis, A. P., Cohen, R. M., Murphy, D. L. 1984. Mania and hypomania during antidepressant pharmacotherapy: Clinical and research implications. See Post & Ballenger 1984, pp. 836–45

Porrino, L. J. 1987. Cerebral metabolic changes associated with activation of reward systems. In *Brain Reward Systems and Abuse*, ed. J. Engel, L. Oreland, pp. 51–60. New York: Raven

Post, R. M. 1980. Biochemical theories of mania. In *Mania: An Evolving Concept*, ed. R. H. Belmaker, H. M. van Praag, pp. 217–67. New York: Spectrum

Post, R. M., Ballenger, J. C., eds. 1984. *Neurobiology of Mood Disorders*. Baltimore, Md: Williams & Wilkins

Post, R. M., DeLisi, L. E., Holcomb, H. H., Uhde, T. W., Cohen, R., Buchsbaum, M. S. 1987. Glucose utilization in the temporal cortex of affectively ill patients: Positron emission tomography. *Biol. Psychiatry* 22:545–53

Post, R. M., Uhde, T. W. 1982. Biological relationships between mania and melancholia. *L'Encephale* 8:213–28

Rangel-Guerra, R. A., Perez-Payan, H., Minkoff, L., Todd, L. E. 1983. Nuclear magnetic resonance in bipolar affective disorders. *Am. J. Neuroradiol.* 4:229–31

Risch, S. C., Janowsky, D. S. 1984. Cholinergic-adrenergic balance in affective illness. See Post & Ballenger 1984, pp. 652–63

Roland, P. E. 1985. Cortical organization of voluntary behavior in man. *Hum. Neurobiol.* 4:155–57

Rosenthal, J., Strauss, A., Minkoff, L., Winston, A. 1986. Identifying lithium-responsive bipolar depressed patients using nuclear magnetic resonance. *Am. J. Psychiatry* 143:779–80

Roy-Byrne, P. P., Post, R. M., Kellner, C. H., Joffe, R. T., Uhde, T. W. 1988. Ventricular-brain ratio and life course of illness in patients with affective disorder. *Psychiatry Res.* 23:277–84

Sarter, M., Markowitsch, H. J. 1985. Involvement of the amygdala in learning and memory: A critical review, with emphasis on anatomical relations. *Behav. Neurosci.* 99:342–80

Schlegel, S., Kretzschmar, K. 1987. Computed tomography in affective disorders. Part I. Ventricular and sulcal measurements. *Biol. Psychiatry* 22:4–14

Schneirla, T. 1959. An evolutionary and developmental theory of biphasic processes underlying approach and withdrawal. In *Nebraska Symposium on Motivation*, ed. M. Jones, pp. 27–58. Lincoln: Univ. Nebraska Press

Schultz, W. 1984. Primate dopamine cell activity in relation to behavioral acts. *Clin. Neuropharmacol.* 7 (Suppl. 1):90–91

Scott, M. L., Golden, C. J., Ruedrich, S. L., Bishop, R. J. 1983. Ventricular enlargement in major depression. *Psychiatry Res.* 8:91–93

Secunda, S. K., Swann, A., Katz, M. M.,

Koslow, S. H., Croughan, J., Chang, S. 1987. Diagnosis and treatment of mixed mania. *Am. J. Psychiatry* 144:96–98

Shima, S., Shikano, T., Kitamura, T., Masuda, Y., Tsukumo, T., et al. 1984. Depression and ventricular enlargement. *Acta Psychiatr. Scand.* 70:275–77

Shopsin, B., ed. 1979. *Manic Illness*. New York: Raven

Silverstone, T. 1985. Dopamine in manic depressive illness. *J. Affect. Disord.* 8:225–31

Sitiram, N., Gillin, C., Bunney, W. E. 1984. Cholinergic and catecholaminergic receptor sensitivity in affective illness: Strategy and theory. See Post & Ballenger 1984, pp. 629–51

Smith, G. N., Iacono, W. G. 1986. Lateral ventricular size in schizophrenia and choice of control group. *Lancet* 1:1450

Smith, G. N., Iacono, W. G., Moreau, M., Tallman, K., Beiser, M., Flak, B. 1988. Choice of comparison group and computerized tomography findings in schizophrenia. *Br. J. Psychiatry*. In press

Snyder, S. H., Peroutka, S. J. 1984. Antidepressants and neurotransmitter receptors. See Post & Ballenger 1984, pp. 686–97

Sochurek, H. 1987. Medicines new vision. *Natl. Geogr.* 171:2–41

Spyraki, C., Fibiger, H. C. 1981. Behavioural evidence for supersensitivity of postsynaptic dopamine receptors in the mesolimbic system after chronic administration of desipramine. *Eur. J. Pharmacol.* 74:195–206

Standish-Barry, H. M. A. S., Hale, A. S., Honig, A., Bouras, N., Bridges, P. K., Barlett, J. R. 1985. Ventricular size, the dexamethoasone suppression test and outcome of severe endogenous depression following psychosurgery. *Acta Psychiatr. Scand.* 72:166–71

Stein, L. 1983. The chemistry of positive reward. In *Biological Bases of Sensation Seeking, Impulsivity, and Anxiety*, ed. M. Zuckerman, pp. 151–76. Hillside, NJ: Erlbaum

Stuss, D. T., Benson, D. F. 1986. *The Frontal Lobes*. New York: Raven

Sved, A. F., Baker, H. A., Reis, D. J. 1984. Dopamine synthesis in inbred mouse strains which differ in numbers of dopamine neurons. *Br. Res.* 303:261–66

Sved, A. F., Baker, H. A., Reis, D. J. 1985. Number of dopamine neurons predicts prolactin levels in two inbred mouse strains. *Experientia* 41:644–46

Swerdlow, N. R., Koob, G. F. 1987. Dopamine, schizophrenia, and depression: Toward a unified hypothesis of corticostriato-pallido-thalamic function. *Behav. Br. Sci.* 10:197–208

Synek, V., Reuben, J. R. 1976. The ventricular-brain ratio using planimetric measurement of EMI scans. *Br. J. Radiol.* 49:233–37

Taghzouti, K., Simon, H., Le Moal, M. 1986. Disturbances in exploratory behavior and functional recovery in the Y and radial mazes following dopamine depletion of the lateral septum. *Behav. Neural. Biol.* 45:48–56

Taghzouti, K., Simon, H., Louilot, A., Herman, J. P., Le Moal, M. 1985. Behavioral study after local injection of 6-hydroxydopmaine into the nucleus accumbens in the rat. *Br. Res.* 344:9–20

Tanaka, Y., Hazama, H., Fukuhara, T., Tsutsui, T. 1982. Computerized tomography of the brain in manic-depressive patients-A controlled study. *Folia Psychiatr. Neurol. Jpn.* 36:137–43

Targum, S. D., Rosen, L. N., DeLisi, L. E., Weinberger, D. R., Citrin, C. M. 1983. Cerebral ventricular size in major depressive disorder: Association with delusional symptoms. *Biol. Psychiatry.* 18:329–36

Tellegen, A. 1985. Structures of mood and personality and their relevance to assessing anxiety, with an emphasis on self-report. In *Anxiety and the Anxiety Disorders,* ed. A. H. Tuma, J. D. Maser, pp. 157–84. Hillside, NJ: Erlbaum

Thierry, A-M., Tassin, J-P., Glowinski, J. 1984. Biochemical and electrophysiological studies of the mesocortical dopamine system. In *Monoamine Innervation of Cerebral Cortex,* ed. L. Descarries, T. Reader, H. Jasper, pp. 234–61. New York: Liss

Valzelli, L. 1981. *Psychobiology of Aggression and Violence.* New York: Raven

Watson, D., Tellegen, A. 1985. Toward the structure of mood. *Psychol. Bull.* 92:426–57

Weinberger, D. R., DeLisi, L. E., Perman, G. P., Targum, S., Wyatt, R. J. 1982. Computed tomography in schizophreniform disorder and other acute psychiatric disorders. *Arch. Gen. Psychiatry* 39:778–83

Wood, K. 1985. The neurochemistry of mania. *J. Affect. Disord.* 8:215–23

Yang, C. R., Mogenson, G. J. 1984. Electrophysiological responses of neurones in the nucleus accumbens to hippocampal stimulation and the attenuation of the excitatory responses by the mesolimbic dopaminergic system. *Br. Res.* 324:69–84

Yim, C. Y., Mogenson, G. J. 1982. Response of nucleus accumbens neurons to amygdala stimulation and its modification by dopamine. *Br. Res.* 239:401–15

Yim, C. Y., Mogenson, G. J. 1983. Response of ventral pallidal neurons to amygdala stimulation and its modulation by dopamine projections to nucleus accumbens. *J. Neurophysiol.* 50:148–61

Zevon, M., Tellegen, A. 1982. The structure of mood: An idiographic/nomothetic analysis. *J. Pers. Soc. Psychol.* 43:111–22

Ann. Rev. Psychol. 1989. 40:493–531
Copyright © 1989 by Annual Reviews Inc. All rights reserved

CROSS-CULTURAL PSYCHOLOGY:
Current Research and Trends

Çigdem Kagitçibaşi

Psychology Department, Bogazici University, Istanbul, Turkey

J. W. Berry

Psychology Department, Queen's University, Kingston, Canada, K7L 3N6

CONTENTS

INTRODUCTION

Since the review of Segall (1986) the field of cross-cultural psychology has witnessed none of the major landmarks that identified earlier advances (e.g. *Handbook of Cross-Cultural Psychology*, ed. Triandis et al, 1980), but it has developed new points of view while continuing some established trends.

493

0066-4308/89/0201-0493$02.00

The *Journal of Cross-Cultural Psychology* and the *International Journal of Psychology* have continued as the main outlets for cross-cultural research findings and methodological/theoretical developments, while the *Cross-Cultural Psychology Bulletin* provides a communication network for psychologists involved in cross-cultural research. The first and third are official publications of the International Association for Cross-Cultural Psychology.[1] The biannual conferences of IACCP, as well as its regional conferences, are increasingly well attended and provide a forum for scholarly exchange. Recent publications include those edited by Reyes-Lagunes & Poortinga (1985), Ekstrand (1986), and Kagitcibasi (1987a). A francophone network has been established—L'Association pour la Recherche Interculturelle (ARIC)[2]; conferences were held in 1986 and 1987 (with proceedings planned), and a *Bulletin* is published.

Especially noteworthy among books in cross-cultural psychology is the Sage series on cross-cultural research and methodology, with six volumes published in the 1984–1988 period. Special issues of relevant journals were edited by Lonner (1985) on the impact of television on the developing world, by Mann (1986a) on cross-cultural research in Australia, by Dasen & Jahoda (1986) on cross-cultural human development, and by Landis (1986) on theories and methods of cross-cultural training.

Conception of the Field

Cross-cultural psychology is the study of similarities and differences in individual psychological and social functioning in various cultures and ethnic groups. It attempts to discover systematic relationships between (*a*) psychological variables at the individual level, and (*b*) cultural, social, economic, ecological, and biological variables at the population level. Researchers in the field examine the individual's actual experience of these population variables as they change.[3]

Key terms in this definition signal both continuity and change in the field. Cultural differences in individual psychological and social functioning are of longstanding interest, but similarities have become more central as we search for psychological universals. The inclusion of ethnic groups in the definition represents a virtual explosion of cross-cultural work among peoples whose cultures remain at least partially distinct in plural societies. Sociocultural

---

[1]IACCP address: Dr. Ruth H. Munroe, Secretary-General, IACCP, Pitzer College, 1050 N. Mills Avenue, Claremont, CA 91711-6110, USA

[2]ARIC address: Dr. Pierre Dasen, President ARIC, Institut de Psychologie, Route des Fougères, CH-1700 Fribourg, Suisse

[3]This definition is from an upper-level textbook in cross-cultural psychology in preparation by J. W. Berry, Y. H. Poortinga, M. Segall, and P. Dasen.

variables in behavior remain central to the field, but the broader ecological context (with attendant biological variation) is now often noted. Investigators are increasingly concerned with how individuals experience these population-level variables, no longer content merely to correlate a behavior and certain objective features of a culture. This concern is shown (*a*) by attempts to assess an individual's actual exposure to, and opportunities to learn from particular cultural activities; and (*b*) by attempting to understand the indigenous conceptualization of the phenomenon of interest. Finally, workers analyze the dynamics of behavioral-cultural relationships, examining how individuals adapt to change caused by acculturation and socioeconomic influences.

Focus: Inclusions and Exclusions

Most of the domains we review are the familiar ones. One topic, however, appears here for the first time in an *Annual Review* chapter on the field: Individualism-collectivism as a dimension of both cultural and individual variation.

We do not review separately topics that have declined in importance over the years. For example, perception (once a major area of cross-cultural research) has been merged with cognition; we do not treat environmental psychology, aesthetics, or bilingualism and intercultural communication.

DOMAINS OF CROSS-CULTURAL PSYCHOLOGY

Theory and Method

Cross-cultural psychology, like many other branches, still lacks, and badly needs, a conceptual framework. However, conceptual clarification and theoretical integrations have been achieved in recent years. A volume (van de Koppel 1985) devoted largely to theoretical statements contains Eckensberger's overview of theories used in cross-cultural psychology, while Boesch (1987) argues for the relevance of action theory to cross-cultural psychology. Brislin (1988) and Jahoda (1986a) also present theoretical integrations and critiques. More focused conceptual analyses include those by Goodnow (1986), with an analysis of links between cultural conditions and individual behaviors; by Super & Harkness (1986), who explored the interface of the child and culture in proposing the notion of "developmental niche"; by Cole (1985), who examined the "zone of proximal development"; and by Csikszentmihalyi & Massimini (1985), who explored anew the complex relationships among the psychological, cultural, and biological sciences.

Bridging theory and methods is an ambitious monograph by Retief (1987), who sets his questions and answers in the African context. More concerned with the practical aspects of fieldwork is the volume edited by Lonner &

Berry (1986), which includes information ranging from the theory of comparisons (Poortinga & Malpass 1986; Malpass & Poortinga 1986), through fieldwork (Munroe & Munroe 1986) and observational methods (Bochner 1986a), to formal assessment procedures (Irvine 1986).

Technical papers dealing with bias (Ellis 1986; Thissen et al 1986; Poortinga & van de Vijver 1987; Poortinga & van der Flier 1988) and equivalence (Hui & Triandis 1985; Hulin 1987) are available. Their message is that the field has moved well beyond the simplistic and automatic comparison of mean scores from different cultures. Items, tests, contexts, and behaviors must now be compared using strict, explicit, and critical criteria of validity. Most of these criteria are ignored in virtually all contemporary cross-cultural research, in part because they are relatively new and in part because they stem from a psychometric tradition not accepted by all researchers as the only foundation for valid cross-cultural work.

One theoretical and methodological issue that is only beginning to appear is the place of social class as a variable in cross-cultural psychology. Emphasis on ethnic variation has increased (see below), perhaps because ethnicity is more apparent in the middle-class societies of the Western developed world (e.g. Scandinavia and Western Europe, Canada, the United States, Australia, Israel) than elsewhere, or because ethnicity and (low) social class standing often overlap and are therefore confounded. However, in many parts of the developing world where socioeconomic stratification is sharp, social class variations are salient, and class analysis (in the Marxian tradition) is prevalent, at times undertaken even by psychologists (e.g. in Latin America and Africa).

Clearly cultural (or ethnic) effects must be disentangled from the effects of class and status variation, both of which may determine life-styles and hence psychological variables. For example, Cashmore & Goodnow (1986), in a study of parents' values, found that the significance of differences between Anglo-Australian and Italian parents in Australia decreased when several indicators of socioeconomic status were taken into account. This finding is similar to one on child-rearing values in ten countries (Lambert 1987). Brislin (1988) calls for better understanding and operationalization of four basic concepts: social class and ethnic-, cultural-, and racial-group membership. Because objective indicators of social class vary across societies, exact matching is often not possible. However, contextually relevant indicators of social class must be used in cross-cultural research if comparisons are to make sense. Unless relative social-class standing is known, differences between samples cannot be attributed to ethnic or cultural differences. In other words, culture cannot be assumed to be the main independent variable if social class is not adequately dealt with. Yet research reports often fail to mention the class or status of the participants.

Biology and Evolution

Challenging the emphasis of sociobiology on biological transmission of traits, Boyd & Richerson (1985) proposed a "dual inheritance theory" in which both biological and cultural transmission have their place: The capacity to learn is genetically transmitted, but what is learned is transmitted culturally by a whole range of individuals and institutions. The idea is not novel, but this specification of how cultural transmission can take place and the documentation of population-level and psychological consequences constitute a major advance for the field.

Sociobiological hypotheses about intergroup psychological variations have been numerous, challenging cross-cultural psychology's purely cultural interpretations. Rushton (1985, 1988) has repeatedly proposed that "race" rather than "culture" most effectively categorizes human variation, best accounting for distributions in a wide range of traits and behaviors (personality, sexuality, intellect, etc). Using the biological dimension of r/k reproductive strategies (many offspring with little care of them vs few offspring with much care), Rushton proposes that human races (in the order: Blacks-Whites-Orientals) vary in a way that parallels the infrahuman r/k sequence (from fish to frogs to rabbits to primates). Such assertions are likely to set cross-cultural psychologists scurrying for counter arguments.

In a nonevolutionary framework, the search has continued for biological substrates of psychological universals (see below). Eysenck (1988), for example, continues to search for the biological bases of intelligence, concentrating on evoked potentials as indicators of the underlying processes of cognitive activity. Jensen (1988) is also searching for correlates of general intelligence, but in measures of information processing speed. Both authors are now considering group as well as individual differences.

Using psychophysiological measures, Poortinga & van de Vijver (1988) sought invariance parameters in a series of EEG measures (in response to loud and soft auditory stimuli) with Dutch military conscripts and university students, and members of the Juang tribe in Central India. Only if sufficient similarity exists at such a basic level can valid cross-cultural comparisons be made of (higher-order) cognitive task performance.

Perception and Cognition

Before examining specific areas, it is useful to point out some general cross-cultural treatments of perceptual and cognitive phenomena. First, Irvine and colleagues (Irvine & Newstead 1987; Irvine & Berry 1988; Berry et al 1988) have been attempting to draw two divergent "scientific cultures" together: theoretical and empirical workers from the cross-cultural field, and those from cognitive-process and psychometric laboratories. Second, there have been a number of empirical reviews, theoretical integrations, and proposals for application of cross-cultural work to education, industry, and development (Berry & Irvine 1986; Born et al 1987; Drenth 1987; Laboratory of Comparative Human Cognition 1986; Wagner, 1987). Such overviews supplement the brief presentation possible here.

Investigators have studied the basic character of spatial ability in specific populations (Cohen 1985; Deregowski & Bentley 1986) or its acquisition and development in relation to a variety of environmental experiences (Munroe et al 1985) such as distance from home.

Similarly, findings among Australian Aborigines by Ten Houten (1985), among Bushmen by Deregowski & Bentley (1986) and among Indian and Inuit hunter-gatherer populations by McShane & Berry (1988) provide evidence for high visuo-spatial abilities, relative to verbal performance. These findings suggest an ecological interpretation of this pattern of abilities consistent with the "law of Cultural Differentiation" (Irvine & Berry, 1988). This "law" holds that while all populations likely have the same perceptual and cognitive processes, and the same potential for perceptual and cognitive development, ecological and cultural factors "prescribe what shall be learned and at what age; consequently different cultural environments lead to the development of different patterns of ability" (Ferguson 1956, p. 121).

Cross-cultural research on cognitive style has continued, but at a much reduced rate. Most studies (as in the past) have focused on the Field-Dependent/Field-Independent (FD-FID) cognitive style and increasingly examine specific features of the style and its relationship to ecological and cultural factors (Alvi et al 1986; Griesel & Richter 1987; Yu & Bain 1985). For example, Sinha & Bharat (1985) studied the impact of various family structures (monogamous, polyandrous, polygynandrous) on both child-rearing practices and psychological differentiation.

A second study examined the most valid way to score and interpret performance on the Rod and Frame Test. Jahoda & Neilson (1986) found that relationships among four types of scores differed between white and black samples in Zimbabwe; thus no single score would enable valid intergroup comparisons.

A third study of the FD-FID cognitive style (Berry et al 1986b) was inaugurated in 1973 by the late Hy Witkin. Previous cross-cultural research on cognitive style had shown that hunter-gatherers are generally more field-independent than agriculturalists. However, whereas the previous comparisons had ranged rather broadly across ecological zones (e.g. Arctic vs Africa), this project employed contrasting societies in one zone (the edge of the Central African forest) where hunter-gatherer Pygmies and agricultural Villagers live and interact. There the patterning of test performance resembled, but was not identical to, the FD-FID cognitive style found on the West. Acculturation experience was a more powerful predictor than ecological and cultural factors but did not eliminate their role. Thus, even in this remote area, contact with Western peoples (by way of schooling, economy, media, etc) appears to be a powerful factor in test performance.

Studies have examined both general intelligence and such specific abilities as memory (in Morocco: Wagner 1987), formal thinking (in Surinam and Zambia: van de Vijver et al 1986), learning (in Guatemala: Saco-Pollitt et al 1985), and concrete and abstract thinking (in Senegal: Lalo 1987). One study examined relationships between a number of abilities (tested with indigenous items) and "adaptive competence" (everyday community skills) among Filipino children living in a barrio (Church et al 1985). Traditional psychometric approaches are useful, for when content is local in character, acceptable levels of construct validity, convergent validity, and divergent validity can be achieved for most of the abilities measured.

With respect to general intelligence, IQ scores have been rising over time (Lynn & Hampson 1986; Flynn 1987), although decline and variability have been observed in scholastic tests (Vernon et al 1988). Lynn & Hampson used samples from the United Kingdom, Japan, and the United States and concluded that national mean intelligence is rising. They attributed such a rise to various environmental factors (such as improved health and nutrition, and greater stimulation arising from toys and TV), since the gains were too great and had occurred too fast to have been genetically produced. Flynn documented rising mean IQ scores in a single generation (5–25 IQ points) in 14 nations, using both general and universal military draft samples. Flynn argued that these scores and score changes cannot reflect "intelligence," since there occurred no concomitant increases in such commonsense indicators as the number of geniuses and the introduction of significant inventions. If IQ scores really measured intelligence "the result should be a cultural renaissance too great to be overlooked" (p. 187). According to Flynn the tests measure only "abstract problem solving ability," a correlate "with weak causal link to intelligence" (p. 190). Flynn finds such an interpretation consistent with the decline, over the same period, of scores on academic achievement, particularly in the United States.

This review period has witnessed a veritable flood of work with Oriental groups, perhaps begun by the comprehensive overview prepared by the late Philip Vernon (1982). Two comprehensive edited volumes are available (Bond 1986; Blowers & Turtle 1987), along with specific studies on a wide range of abilities (on Japanese abilities and achievements: Iwawaki & Vernon 1988; on directional preference: Harsel & Wales 1987; on mnemonics in Japan: Higbee & Kunihira 1985; and on simultaneous and successive processing: Leong et al 1985). There have also appeared studies of cognitive processes (on eye movements in reading in Chinese: Sun et al 1985; on digit memory and memory store in Chinese: Stigler et al 1986; on the relationship between the development of the square, and learning to write Japanese with Kanji characters: Yamasaki 1985).

These studies attempt to relate specific features of language (script, word length, direction of writing, etc) or culture (abacus use, training in mental arithmetic, etc) to a range of perceptual and cognitive abilities. The lessons from an earlier generation of cross-cultural studies seem to have been learned well: Take cultural variations seriously (Berry & Irvine 1986), understand their role in daily life (Sternberg & Wagner 1986), and examine how these factors may influence perceptual and cognitive development (Goodnow 1986) during childhood by way of socialization and maturation.

Social Psychology

For close to two decades social psychology has been undergoing a universality crisis caused to a substantial degree by cross-cultural perspectives. Apparently this crisis is not yet over. Pepitone (1987) critically examined the basic metatheoretical features of cognitive social psychology, showing an individualistic natural science bias. He pointed out that intraindividual cognitive process theory with a priori assumptions of unversality prevents falsification of the hypothesized processes. Cross-cultural findings cannot be adequately explained by process theory without taking into account culturally defined meanings. Pepitone & Triandis (1987) emphasized that unless social psychological theories are grounded in the biology of the organism or in features of ecology and social structure common to humanity, claims for their universality are not warranted.

A debate between Jahoda and Gergen (Jahoda 1986a,b; Gergen 1986) further uncovered the metatheoretical assumptions underlying social psychology with regard to nature and culture. Jahoda pointed out that what claims to be the study of natural "laws" or "processes" in social psychology is actually culture-bound (American or Western), as evidenced by failure of cross-cultural replication of experimental findings in an important Israeli study. Amir & Sharon (1987) attempted to replicate in Israel six more or less representative social psychological articles from leading journals. Although main effects held up, interactions did not. The latter were apparently influenced more by culture. Jahoda also took issue with the social constructionist point of view (Gergen & Davis 1985), which allows for multiple interpretations of experiential conditions, producing diversity of meanings and action not readily predictable on the basis of either nature or culture.

Turner & Oakes (1986) further rejected the individualistic metatheory of social psychology and instead proposed social identity theory as an interactionist nonreductionist approach bridging the gap between individual and society. As Tetlock indicates (1986), this is in line with other recent theories in social psychology assigning a key causal role to the self-concept, with group identification as a major part of it. Westen's *Self and Society* (1985) is another important attempt at a nonreductionist social psychology. These views reflect new orientations in social psychology that are congenial to a cultural and cross-cultural perspective.

The Cross-Cultural Challenge to Social Psychology (Bond 1988) contains important contributions by cross-culturalists as well as mainstream social psychologists.

INTERPERSONAL RELATIONS   A number of researchers have studied human relationships from a cross-cultural perspective. Ma (1985) proposed a hierarchy of human relationships in terms of altruism, as supported by data from English and Chinese subjects. Adamopoulos & Bontempo (1986) examined affiliation, dominance, and intimacy as possible universal dimensions of human relations by factor analyses of their frequencies in literary materials from different historical periods. The first two dimensions were found to be invariant over 3000 years, whereas intimacy was found to have evolved systematically through time. Argyle et al (1986) studied rules for human relations in England, Italy, Japan, and Hong Kong. A primary distinction between intimate and nonintimate relations was found, together with a number of culturally relevant differences. The East, especially Japan promulgated more rules regarding conflict avoidance, loss of face, maintaining harmonious relations in groups, and obedience. Foa et al (1987) found cross-cultural support for a resource theory of human interaction with data from the United States, the Philippines, Sweden, and Mexican Americans. Other support was found by Rodrigues & Iwawaki (1986) for the validity of different models of interpersonal balance in Japan, by Pandey & Singh (1986) for Machiavellianism in India, and by Noriyuki (1985) for conformity in Japan.

ATTRIBUTION   Attribution theory continues to be tested and refined cross-culturally. Two key issues are (*a*) whether the basic attribution paradigm works cross-culturally and (*b*) what factors are attended to in making attributions across cultures. Pepitone (1987) referred to Miller's (1984) finding of the contextual attribution to others' behavior in South India, contrasted with dispositional attribution in the United States, showing no "fundamental attribution error" in India. Shweder & Bourn (1984) had also found person descriptions in India involving contextual descriptions rather than abstract traits (see the Personality in Culture section, below). Hortacsu & Karanci (1987), on the other hand, found no cultural specificity in attributional dimensions among Turkish university students; they noted, however, the students' modern outlook. Louw & Potgieter (1986) failed to support categorization in terms of stability and locus of control among South African college students; and Little (1987), comparing Sri Lankan and English children, suggested refinements, such as subdividing ability attributions.

SOCIAL PERCEPTION   Zebrowitz-McArthur's (1988) excellent overview of person perception delineated both culturally specific and universal elements. The specific categories spontaneously used in person perception, the specific qualities ascribed to people, and the basic structures used (i.e. which behaviors and traits are similarly associated) show cross-cultural generality. On the other hand, cultural differences are found in the frequency and salience of the categories used. Furthermore, even though there is impressive evidence of cross-cultural agreement in trait perceptions and impression formation, cultural variations in the contents of contextually bound impressions need to be better understood, for in many cultures people are described in terms of their contextually embedded concrete behaviors and roles, as discussed above. An ecological theory of social perception has been proposed to explain the observed cultural differences (Zebrowitz-McArthur 1988). Hoffman et al (1986) studied the linguistic basis of person perception, and other work (see below) compared person perception in individualistic and collectivistic cultures.

Values and Attitudes

Schwartz & Bilsky (1987), using Rokeach values, proposed a taxonomy of values as cognitive representations of three universal needs: (a) biological, (b) interactional, and (c) societal. From these requirements they derived eight motivational domains of values: enjoyment, security, social power, achievement, self-direction, prosociality, restrictive conformity, and maturity. They also mapped values according to the interest they serve (individualistic vs collectivistic) and the type of goal to which they refer (terminal vs instrumental).

Other work on values has also used the Rokeach value survey. Feather (1986) compared value systems of Australians and Chinese. Though differences in individualism and collectivism were found, there were also significant overlaps, both value orientations being represented in both groups. Similarly, Domino & Hannah (1987) found both different and common factors in Chinese and American children's values. In other exploratory work on values, Munro (1985) developed a free-format values inventory in Africa, Ho (1985) and Chinese Culture Connection (1987) investigated the relationship between values and economic growth, and several studies looked at the meanings of achievement in different sociocultural contexts (Spence 1985; Habteyes & Steinkamp 1985; Jayant et al 1985).

Cross-cultural study of attitudes has been primarily descriptive, though some earlier theoretical frameworks have been used, especially functional theory—e.g. Tyler & Sinha (1988) on religion, and Furnham (1985) on just-world beliefs. Marin & Salazar (1985) found mirror-image stereotyping among conflicting nations and positive attitudes toward highly developed countries in the Americas. Similarly, Aboriginal Australians held positive stereotypes of the (developed) Anglo-Australians whereas the latter held negative stereotypes of the former (Marjoribanks & Jordan 1986). In the United States (Casas et al 1987) less-educated Mexican Americans perceived themselves to be stereotyped more negatively by the larger Anglo society than did more-educated ones. Finally studies of jokes (Gallois & Collon 1985; Toelken 1985) found ethnocentrism especially reflected in jokes where aggression is directed at ethnic victims. These studies indicate a dimension of intergroup power differential in ethnic attitudes and stereotypes, in line with early theoretical views of prejudice as displaced aggression toward vulnerable outgroups.

Personality in Culture

Cultural and cross-cultural analysis has challenged the universality of such concepts as person and selfhood implicitly or explicitly used by theories of personality in psychology. The challenge comes both from critics within psychology and from interpretative anthropologists, both groups adhering to social constructionism. Because the concept of person, like any other concept, is socially constructed, it is a cultural product that shows cross-cultural variation (Kirkpatrick & White 1985). A number of volumes in anthropology elaborate upon and support this point (Shweder & LeVine 1984; Marsella & White 1984; Simons & Hughes 1985; White & Kirkpatrick 1985; Marsella et al 1985). We briefly discuss these anthropological approaches before going on to psychological work.

Many of the assumptions about personality in psychology are considered to be Western cultural products—a Western "folk" psychology (Howard 1985; Lutz 1985). Ethnopsychologies are, therefore, explored to provide alternative perspectives. Psychologists would gain from a better knowledge of interpretive anthropology and from a "symbols and meanings" approach to cultural analysis. For example, Shweder & Bourn (1984) described the sociocentric, holistic conception of individual-society relations among the Oriyas in India where person "units" are believed to be altered by the relations into which they enter. The Oriyas' situational "concrete" thinking describes the individual not in terms of enduring abstract traits but in terms of relations with others. Similar relational concepts of the person are reported widely (e.g. D. Sinha 1986; Ito 1985).

Pursuing a critical stance of close to two decades, Gergen et al (1986) and Sampson (1985, 1987) question the concept of the person in psychology, the former with regard to its noncontextual nature, the latter with regard to its assumptions of centralized equilibrium structure, control, and mastery. Using Rotter's Internal-External Control Scale (I-E), Gergen et al (1986) showed that responses could be used to indicate virtually any common trait and thus are meaningless out of context. Semin & Chassein (1985) found a high level of correspondence between higher-order personality models and everyday conceptions of personality. This finding provides further evidence that the concept of the person in psychology is a cultural product or social construct. From a different perspective, Smith (1987) called for more general, transhistorical and cross-cultural conceptions of identity, such as the ego-ecology approach (Zavalloni & Louis-Guerin 1984).

Cross-cultural work in personality, however, does not appear to have been much affected by these analyses. In South Africa Ochse & Plug (1986) tested Erickson's theory with self-report scales. Because the internal consistency and validity of the scales are likely affected by a language problem when used with Black subjects, the results must be interpreted with caution. Much cross-cultural personality assessment is seen, mostly in validation studies. Several used the Eysenck Personality Questionnaire (EPQ) (e.g. Eysenck & Long 1986; Eysenck et al 1986; Sanyal 1986). A high degree of cross-cultural validity is reported in these studies, conducted in many countries, prompting the researchers to propose universal dimensions of personality (see the section below, Toward Universals).

Katz & Ronen (1986) applied the Wilson conservatism scale to Western- and Eastern-origin Jews in Israel and found for the former the same factor structure as had been established previously for other Western societies. For Eastern-origin Jews, however, instead of ethnocentrism and anti-hedonism, traditionalism and antifeminism were found, a result showing the effects of cultural norms, not "basic personality dynamics." Further support for cultural-social determinants was found in studies of authoritarianism in India (Bushan 1985) and in Australia and South Africa (Heaven 1986). An ambitious study of national character by Peabody (1985) used trait evaluations of foreign nations by student samples, mainly from Europe, separating descriptive and evaluative aspects of traits. Factor analyses of data produced two dimensions: tight vs loose and assertive vs unassertive. Other research in personality studied diverse topics, such as locus of control (Kelly et al 1985; Wheeless et al 1986); and the assumed superiority of internality was questioned (Matthew 1985).

Gender Issues

SEX DIFFERENCES   Sex-related differences on intelligence tests were studied by Born et al (1987) in a major metaanalysis of 189 studies. The statistical significance and the size of sex-related differences in cognitive factors corresponding to Thurstone's intelligence model were investigated. For five large clusters of cultures the researchers further studied the variance in significance and in size of the sex-intelligence relationship. Sex differences in intelligence were found to be small though in general corresponding to previous findings. On some factors of intelligence, differences were found among the African, the Asian, and the Western clusters of cultures, as well as between the minorities and general populations in Western countries. The great heterogeneity in the results, not due purely to methodological factors, makes such metaanalysis difficult, requiring further refinement of the categories and of the ecological and environmental factors.

Other research on sex differences dealt with personal-space needs (Rustemli 1986) and assertive behavior (Florian & Zernitsky-Shurka 1987)

SEX ROLES   Study of sex roles presents a more fertile ground for theoretical/ conceptual advancement. Sex-role socialization has been studied in children (e.g. Lussier et al 1986) and adolescents (e.g. Ostrov et al 1986), but emphasis has shifted to a life-span developmental approach with a focus on later life experiences that show cross-cultural variation. Ward (1987) questioned the cross-cultural validity of the mid-life crisis construct in a study in Singapore. Similarly, a volume of collected papers (Brown & Kerns 1985) reported rich evidence from pretechnological and traditional societies regarding the increasing status of women with age, a situation quite different from the Western experience. Such results call for alternative explanations based on cultural definitions of women's roles and status.

A related conceptual issue is the cross-cultural validity of feminine-masculine sex-role differences and their underlying dimensions. The expressive-instrumental dimension assumed to underlie differential sex-role socialization has been questioned. Hendrix & Johnson (1985) showed that instrumentality and expressiveness are two separate dimensions, not poles of a single dimennsion. Gurbuz (1988) found expressiveness to be equally characteristic of both sexes in Turkey. Thus some societies may routinely socialize children into androgynous patterns.

Other researchers have also reported greater expressiveness of males and more androgyny in general in closely knit traditional cultures of the Third World than in Western cultures (e.g. Ravinder 1987). One explanation would be the socialization in closely knit collectivistic societies of both females and males for greater relatedness, sensitivity to others, and expressiveness. Higher achievement motivation and more egalitarian attitudes have been found among professional women in some developing countries (e.g. Torki 1985).

The apparently paradoxical findings from male-dominant cultures are challenging and call for new conceptualizations of sex roles in non-Western cultural contexts. A provocative hypothesis originally proposed by Papanek (1973) and Fallers & Fallers (1976), based on their work in Pakistan and in

Turkey, respectively, needs to be tested cross-culturally. It asserts the development of greater psychological freedom of women in sex-segregated societies. According to this view, women who are psychologically more independent of men in their segregated contexts are better able to keep separate their gender and professional identities than women freely mixing with men and competing with other women.

Of relevance in this context are studies investigating the validity of the Bem Sex Role Inventory across cultures. While some supported the validity of the BSRI for Italy (DeLeo et al 1986), others either reported mixed results, indicating limited usefulness of the measure (e.g. in Mexico: Reed-Sanders et al 1985; Lara-Cantu & Navarro-Arias 1986, 1987), or found it invalid (in India and Malaysia: Ward & Sethi 1986; in Turkey: Gurbuz 1988). Thus in cultural contexts substantially different from Western patterns, both Western sex-role definitions and measures based on it like the BSRI have limited validity. Cultural variations in sex roles might be better understood if examined in terms of structural-functional linkages common in several societies rather than unique features of any one culture. Multidisciplinary approaches including sociological and anthropological orientations would be especially valuable for this purpose. For example, insights are provided by comparative investigation of women's status in terms of female contribution to subsistence (Schlegel & Barry 1986; Broude 1987), in terms of the interplay between production and reproduction (Schlegel 1986) in pretechnological societies, or in terms of intrafamily dynamics and values as well as urban-rural, social class, and employment characteristics in several nations (Kagitcibasi 1986).

Attitudes and stereotypes about sex roles have continued to be popular topics of research. Williams & Best (1988) report that ideal self-concepts of both men and women in 14 countries were more masculine than their self-concepts; in most countries, men had more traditional sex-role ideology than women. Other research further describes variations in sex-role attitudes (e.g. Rao & Rao 1985; Shapurian & Hojat 1985), the relations between sex-role attitudes and other beliefs [such as just-world and locus-of-control beliefs (Furnham & Karani 1985)], and sex-role stereotyping (Ward 1985; Albert & Porter 1986).

Human Development and Child-Rearing

Cross-cultural research into the family and human development has presented a challenge and corrective to knowledge and theory based mostly on the Western experience.

HUMAN DEVELOPMENT THEORY   A special issue of the *International Journal of Behavioral Development* (edited by Dasen & Jahoda 1986) focused cross-culturally on human development. Jahoda (1986c) noted that in spite of increasing cross-cultural research over the prior two decades, developmental psychology remained parochial; he also noted a convergence of Piagetian and Vygotzgian approaches in a common acceptance of some "local constructivism." Super & Harkness (1986) introduced the concept of the "developmental niche," (by analogy to the "ecological niche" in biology) as a framework for studying the cultural structuring of child development. It comprises three components: the physical and social setting; child care and child rearing; and the psychology of the caretakers. Homeostatic mechanisms are posited that coordinate these subsystems in a way appropriate to the developmental level and individual characteristics of the child. They also interact with the larger cultural and ecological environment.

Following up on this idea, Dasen (1988) proposed a new paradigm in the study of human development, taking as the unit of analysis the interaction of the developing organism and the "milieu." Utilizing this paradigm in observations of child development in Africa, Dasen showed how the third component, parental psychology, in the form of "ethnotheories" (Super & Harkness 1986), "indigenous theories" (Chamoux 1986), or "naive theories" (Sabatier 1986) affects cognitive/social development. An example of such a "theory" is the Baoulé concept of intelligence, which includes a primary social dimension (the readiness to serve) and manual ability, the cognitive dimension being subordinate (Dasen et al 1985). Child rearing and socialization in a niche affected by this theory thus foster the development of social-relational and manual skills.

Rogoff proposed a similar interactionist orientation to cognitive development. This conceptualization holds that (a) culture and behavior (or thought) are not separate variables but are enmeshed, thus rejecting the use of culture as an independent variable, and (b) child socialization is jointly managed by children and adults (cf Vygotzky's concept of the "zone of proximal development") (Rogoff 1986, 1987; Rogoff & Mistry 1985a,b). Using a similar conceptual orientation, Shand and Kosawa (1985) compared Japanese and American infant-mother interactions to test whether maternal behavior shapes infant behavior or whether mutual shaping occurs. Significant differences between the infant populations in motor activity level at birth, and changes in both infant and mother behavior over time supported the interactional model.

Such cross-cultural conceptual models of human development promise to clarify this complex process and provide culturally relevant paradigms to guide policy, a need commonly felt in the Third World (e.g. Wagner 1986; Sinha 1986). For example, a culturally relevant relational model was used in an intervention study to promote the overall development of socioeconomically deprived children in Turkey (Kagitcibasi 1988). The individual child was not aided directly; instead, his/her environment (mainly the mother) was supported to provide continuing support to the child. The impact of mother training on children was impressive. Much cross-cultural work on child development and child rearing uses an interactional/relational framework, especially focusing on the mother (care giver)-child dyad. However, this framework is rarely well spelled out theoretically.

INFANCY AND INFANT CARE   A substantial body of cross-cultural research is devoted to the period of infancy and infant/mother interaction, much of it in Japan (e. g. Shand 1985; Otaki et al 1986; Durrett et al 1986). Early attachment has been studied with the "strange-situation procedure" by a number of researchers who questioned the appropriateness of this procedure in cross-cultural application (Grossman et al 1985; Gardner et al 1986). Takahashi (1986), who used the procedure with Japanese mothers and infants, proposed cultural examination of each behavior as a classificatory cue. For example, the importance of a common behavior, (e.g. in Japan, physical contact between mother and infant) should be somewhat downplayed whereas culturally discouraged rare behaviors (e.g. in Japan, avoiding the mother) should be accorded much diagnostic value. Kermoian & Leiderman (1986), working in East Africa where multiple infant caretaking prevails, described various types of attachments to mother and other caretakers and noted that "when the behavior of the attachment figure varies from that of the prototypic American mother, security of attachment may no longer have the same meaning" (p. 468). Such work has brought conceptual/methodological refinements into the cross-cultural study of attachment behavior, and alternative methodologies have been proposed (e.g. Gardner et al 1986). Other studies have investigated topics such as motor development (Bril & Sabatier 1986).

SOCIAL DEVELOPMENT   Among topics studied in the social development of children are self-concept (Pang et al 1985), help-seeking (Tyler & Verma 1988), factor structures of children/parent dyadic behavior (Bronstein 1986), children's understanding of adult norms (Ekstrand & Ekstrand 1987), maternal strategies for regulating children's behavior (S. R. Sinha 1985), and stability of aggression over time (Eron & Huesmann, 1987, a five-nation extension of a notable longitudinal study of aggression).

Moral development continues to be a topic of much interest. Some studies found a positive role of Israeli kibbutz ideology in promoting sophisticated moral reasoning (Snarey et al 1985; Fuchs et al 1986), while other data from Israel (Zeidner & Nevo 1987) found correlations between principled moral reasoning and aptitude test scores (mainly verbal ability). These results suggest that moral reasoning is affected by ideological training and may reflect verbal sophistication. This is in keeping with lower levels of moral development and conventional morality commonly found in traditional small rural communities (i.e. Tietjen & Walker 1985; Snarey 1985).

In a critical review (45 studies from 27 culture areas), Snarey (1985) provided support for the assumptions of Kohlbergian research. However, he also pointed out major problems regarding the range and general applicability of the stages—specifically, urban and middle-class biases. He suggested adding to the model alternative principled-reasoning criteria based on collective solidarity-relatedness or other indigenous themes at the higher stages (Snarey 1985; Snarey et al 1985). Similarly, Levine et al (1985) described current revisions/additions to the Kohlbergian theory concerning the introduction of higher "soft" stages of ethical awareness, based on ethical-religious thinking, and extension into sociological analysis (group norms, etc). A most serious objection to Kohlbergian theory concerned its male bias (males consistently outscoring females) (Gilligan 1982). Cross-cultural differences had also been noted at the time (subjects from remote rural areas and traditionally closely knit communities scoring lower) but were not deemed objectionable. It has taken longer for cultural correctives to be introduced.

PARENTAL VALUES AND BEHAVIOR   That parental values form the basis of child rearing behavior is the main thesis of Hoffman (1987), who used data from the nine-country "value of children" study. The same data showed that the needs parents expect children to satisfy (e.g. for old-age security) and the value thus accorded to children vary with life-styles, providing a conceptual framework for comparative work on child rearing (Kagitcibasi 1985a). Cultural/familial values with regard to children (e.g. the value of the son for the status of the mother) have influenced theories about South Asian child-rearing practices (Saraswathi & Dutta 1987b; Haque 1987). Two noteworthy volumes (Suvannathat et al 1985; Saraswathi & Dutta 1987a) treat child rearing in Asia.

Perceived parental behavior continues to be an active research topic. Perris et al (1985) and Arrindell et al (1986a,b) applied a retrospective self-report instrument, EMBU, to subjects from five European countries and Australia and identified three cross-nationally constant factors: rejection, emotional warmth, and overprotection. The instrument requires further testing in non-Western cultures.

Rohner combined his and others' extensive work of over 25 years on parental acceptance and rejection (PAR) in his book *The Warmth Dimension* (1986). Using Rohner's instruments, PAR has been studied with young adults in Egypt (Salama 1987) and related to personality dispositions; in Pakistan (Haque 1987) and India (Rohner & Chaki-Sircar 1987), in terms of social class and caste differences, respectively; and in the Sudan (Ahmed et al 1987) in connection with women's workloads. Comparative studies of PAR provide insights into perceived parental control and acceptance-rejection in the context of culturally accepted behavior patterns. In cultural contexts where strict parental discipline is prevalent and therefore perceived as normal by children and adolescents, it is perceived not as rejection but as parental concern—e.g. in Korea (Rohner & Pettengill 1985) and Japan (Trommsdorff 1985a). On the other hand, in contexts where permissive parental behavior is culturally valued, strict parental control is perceived as rejection—e.g. in the United States among Americans and Korean Americans (Pettengill & Rohner 1985; Rohner & Pettengill 1985) and in Germany (Trommsdorff 1985a). Thus cultural factors (and social comparison processes) must be integrated into theories of family functioning.

ADOLESCENT AND LIFE-SPAN DEVELOPMENT   In her studies of the development of values, Keats (1986) identified four stages (assumed to show invariant cross-cultural progression) and supported this concept with data from Malays, Chinese, Indians, and Australians. Tzeng & Everett (1985), in a factor-analytic study using Osgood's *Atlas of Affective Meanings,* identified cross-cultural self-related concepts corresponding to the problem areas of adolescence cited in the literature.

Interest in the cross-cultural study of life-span development is emerging. Study has focused either on life satisfaction in the later years or on attitudes toward the elderly. Are attitudes toward the elderly more favorable in traditional societies? Studies conducted with students showed favorable attitudes in Turkey (Sunar 1988) but not in India (Williams et al 1987), and a holocultural study found very harsh treatment of the elderly in preindustrial societies (Glascock 1987).

FAMILY AND FAMILY CHANGE   Cross-cultural psychological work on the family as a whole is sparse and involves little theory. Spousal (Warner et al 1986) and intergenerational relations (Bankart & Bankart 1985; Cashmore & Goodnow 1986) have been studied. Family change as a result of socioeconomic change has been controversial among social scientists. Modernization theory's assumption that industrialization necessitates family nucleation is commonly accepted by psycholgists, at least implicitly, and some supporting observations have been made (Dadbrook 1985). However, the persistence of familial values of relatedness in industrialized developed countries such as Japan challenges modernization theory and requires more refined analysis incorporating cultural values. Thus Akiyama (1984) studied dependence and independence of the elderly in Japan and the United States respectively, in terms of the types of resources exchanged with younger people. Kagitcibasi (1985a) proposed a model of family change by differentiating two dimensions of intergenerational interdependence: material and emotional. While with urbanization and industrialization material interdependencies in the family decrease and structural nucleation is seen, emotional interdependencies (and their correlate values of relatedness) can continue, and functional nucleation and individuation may not be seen. Imamoglu (1987) pursued the idea toward an interdependent model of human development.

Mental Health and Therapy

Application of cross-cultural psychology to problems of daily life is particularly evident in the area of health. At the same time, academic studies continue in such areas as the relationship between culture and psychopathology (e.g. Draguns 1986; Sartorius et al 1986), and between culture and diagnosis (Tseng et al 1986; Westermeyer 1985; 1987a).

Since the appearance of the successful volume by Pedersen et al (1984), largely concerned with mental health and the care of those who had developed problems, a follow-up volume (Dasen et al 1988) has taken a health promotion/problem prevention orientation, expanding the focus to health generally. In a general re-orientation in the health field, social and behavioral scientists are now being accorded a substantial role in understanding the origins of health problems in the sociocultural and psychological contexts of human activity (Holtzman et al 1987). Among the issues addressed are the health consequences of social and family change (Kagitcibasi 1988; Sinha 1988) and of malnutrition (Dasen & Super 1988); relationships are being sought between health and a variety of cultural factors, such as socialization (Segall 1988), education (Wagner 1988), disability (Serpell 1988) and the organizational structures of health institutions (Garcia-Averasturi 1988). The Dasen et al (1988) volume intends to establish a role for cross-cultural social and behavioral scientists in the field of health promotion and problem prevention in Third World countries. The title ("towards applications") is tentative because principles, policies, and programs developed in one culture may not be applicable in others; substantial local, culturally sensitive work is needed prior to application.

Two volumes have appeared on counseling, one with cross-cultural emphasis (Pedersen 1985), the other with an inter-cultural focus (Samuda & Wolfgang 1985). In the former, considerable attention is paid to work across large cultural differences, while in the latter, work with ethnic and racial groups in culturally plural societies is of central interest. Many of the principles are the same, including the necessity of cultural knowledge and cultural sensitivity, and understanding the role that culture and culture contact play in the origin of the problems presented to the counselor. However, there are important differences, as well as similarities, between these two domains of comparative work (see below).

Culture-bound health issues and problems have been investigated; these intensely rooted phenomena are very much associated with (if not unique to) cultural area, or world view (Simons & Hughes 1985). While much of the literature is concerned with exotic problems in exotic cultures, such as trance and altered states of consciousness (Ward 1988), there is increasing concern with problems that may be peculiar to some Western societies, such as anorexia nervosa (Swartz 1985).

A final area of current activity is that of therapy and services across cultures. While related to counseling (e.g. Folensbee et al 1986), this domain involves some broader issues; the problems dealt with tend to be more substantial, and the cultural ranges crossed tend to be wider. Issues of the transcultural portability of therapeutic (Kakar 1985; Oyewumi 1986; West 1987), preventive (Quah 1985), and epidemiological (Heggenhougen & Shore 1986) models have dominated the discussion. Even after culturally relative adaptations are made, some deep-rooted assumptions in established Western approaches remain inappropriate for cross-cultural use.

Ethnic Psychology and Acculturation

The virtual explosion of psychological research dealing with ethnic groups, immigrants, refugees and native peoples who live in culturally plural societies reflects both political changes in the aspirations of groups in many plural societies and increases in the numbers of immigrants and refugees. Such research tends increasingly to be informed by cross-cultural points of view (Bender-Szymanski & Hesse 1987; Berry 1985; Biesheuvel 1987).

Two volumes of selected conferences proceedings on the topic (Ekstrand 1986; Berry & Annis 1988) have appeared, in addition to book-length reviews (Brislin et al 1986; Furnham & Bochner 1986) and theoretical and methodological integrations (Berry 1986; Berry et al 1986a; Bochner 1986b; Kagitcibasi 1987c; Taft 1985, 1986; Triandis et al 1986a). These materials are diverse but a few central lines of argument are beginning to appear. First, certain groups living in culturally plural societies are coming to be viewed as culturally distinct, in the anthropological sense, rather than as "minority" or "marginal" groups on the fringe of a "mainstream" society (Berry 1986). This theoretical reorientation has methodological implications. Such groups must be studied fully, understood in their own right, and given equal time with all other groups (including the "mainstream") in the research design. Another theoretical development has been the shift from the notion of "assimilation" (in which groups become absorbed) to that of "adaptation" (Kim & Gudykunst 1988), in which a variety of other changes occur (such as integration, separation, and marginalization) as a part of the acculturation process. Thus new research tools must be developed to assess alternatives to assimulation. A final theoretical change has been to consider acculturation as a dynamic process giving rise to different psychological outcomes over time. Methodologically this implies a shift from cross-sectional to longitudinal studies (e.g. Scott & Stumpt 1984) in which changes in an individual's identity, values, and behaviors can be observed, and generalizations can be made about the course of acculturation.

A good deal of the literature on acculturating groups continues to be concerned with mental health issues, particularly with "acculturative stress" (popularly known as "culture shock"). Comprehensive overviews of the field appear in Furnham & Bochner (1986) and Berry & Kim (1988), while a long series of empirical studies has also continued (e.g. Berry et al 1987; Dornic 1986; Kim & Berry 1986). Acculturative stress is a frequent (but not an inevitable) outcome for individuals undergoing acculturation. The degree of stress (indicated by both psychological and social problems, or even break-down) varies with such moderating factors as type of acculturating group (e.g. refugees experience more stress than immigrants), type of larger society (e.g. less stress in multicultural than in monocultural larger societies), mode of acculturation (e.g. separation and marginalization are more stressful than assimilation, but integration is least stressful of all), and a host of psycholog-ical variables (e.g. individual's appraisal of the acculturative arena, coping abilities, identity confusion, and relationship of expectations and aspirations to realistic possibilities). The field is fast developing as an area of both theoretical and applied activity, since a clear understanding is necessary in order to manage the process to the advantage of both acculturating peoples and the larger society.

With the dramatic rise in the number of refugees in recent years, and with the realization that the psychological outcome can be understood and man-aged to some extent, cross-cultural psychologists (along with colleagues in psychiatry and anthropology) have become increasingly active. Two major overview volumes have been published, one dealing largely with the US settlement experience (Williams & Westermeyer 1986) and one with the European experience (Miserez & Horvath 1988). Many review articles and empirical reports have focused on specific aspects of the issue (Kinzie 1985; Westermeyer 1987b; Williams 1985). Although usually greater trauma has been experienced and adaptation problems are more profound for refugee groups than for voluntary immigrants, research-based knowledge can be employed to smooth out the process of acculturation, even for refugees.

Sojourner research is involved with selecting and preparing individuals to work in another culture, evaluating their effectiveness while there, and pre-paring them for their eventual return (Brislin 1986; Heikinhelmo & Shute 1986; Landis 1986; Mendenhall & Oddon 1985). Some experimental work has begun (Landis et al 1985) that should identify the processes involved, and provide the bases for more precise programs in the field of international aid and development, foreign student exchange, and international living by corporate and military families posted abroad.

Last we note studies of ethnic identity during acculturation (e.g. Annis & Corenblum 1986; Blue et al 1987; Keefe & Padilla 1987; Naidoo 1985; Neto 1986; Rosenthal & Hrynerich 1985; Weinreich 1986). Earlier findings of children's preference for and identification with members of the dominant society continue to be supported, but these new studies suggest that the language and ethnicity of the researcher attenuate this cross-identification. Since most adults in plural societies know who they are, and more or less like it, these continuing findings with children demand explanation. While developmental trends have been repeatedly found for making correct categorizations of stimulus objects (such as pictures and dolls), no similar trends exist for group preference or identification. Thus the transition from substantial childhood cross-identification to substantial (but not complete) adult own-group identification, cannot be a simple matter of development; further research is called for.

Ethnic and acculturation studies have a substantial future in cross-cultural psychology. In a sense, this trend respresents a "return" to those societies that originally exported cross-cultural psychology to the far reaches of the world. The lessons learned there, and from making broad cross-cultural comparisons, are now being employed to better understand the relationship between culture and behavior in evolving plural societies.

Work and Organizational Psychology

Especially since Hofstede's study (1980) on work-related values, cultural explanations of organizational behavior have become popular. The concept of corporate culture has replaced earlier social psychological concepts of how organizations function and how they differ (Jabes & Gruere 1987). Many empirical studies have compared widely differing management styles. For example, Adler et al (1986) discussed the East-West cultural differences crucial to business in the Pacific Basin. Trompenaars (1985) contrasted two ideal-typical conceptions of organizational structure: a *Gemeinschaft*-like Right Brain conception based on synthesis, intuition, and emotion, and a *Gesellschaft*-like Left Brain conception stressing analysis and logical reasoning. Of the ten countries studied, Americans were on the extreme Left Brain end, followed closely by the Swedish and Dutch; Venezuelans were at the opposite end, with Singaporeans, Italians, and Spaniards relatively close. (See the discussion below on individualism-collectivism.) Griffeth & Hom (1987), using multivariate clustering techniques with managers' attitudes and perceptions from 15 Western nations, obtained an Anglo cluster (including Holland) and a Latin European one (including Greece).

Henderson & Argyle (1986) studied informal rules from a functional theoretical point of view, differentiating between maintenance and task reward rules. Japanese relationships (followed by those in Hong Kong) differed most from those in other countries, showing greater homogeneity of overall rule structure and more formal work relationships. Hofstede's (1980) results also showed less individualism among the two eastern cultures and greater masculinity in Japan. Other comparative work studied Japanese managers' decision-making styles (Weinberg 1985; Cool & Lengnick-Hall 1985) and perceptions of group performance (Sullivan et al 1986), and conflict management in Hong Kong and Britain (Tang & Kirkbride 1986). A multinational study found that only Japanese and Scandinavian organizations rewarded cooperative manager behavior (Rosenstein 1985).

Gomez-Mejia (1986) found a US based set of scales measuring task-related and contextual work values in 20 countries to be panculturally valid. On the other hand, Spector & Wimalasiri (1986), in a US–Singapore comparison, questioned the stability of job satisfaction dimensionality across cultures. Saiyadain (1985) found the relationship between job satisfaction and personal characteristics in India and Nigeria to be mediated by the level of industrialization. Similarly, J.B.P. Sinha (1985a, 1986) noted the importance of personal relationships in inducing subordinates to work in a culture such as India where work is not intrinsically valued. England & Misumi (1986) found work centrality to be much higher in Japan than in the US. Misra et al (1985) used a measure developed in Canada to suggest the generalizability of a motivational formulation of work involvement in Germany and India. Munro (1986), on the other hand, proposed, as an alternative to instruments developed in Western countries, an unstructured inventory aimed at revealing indigenous value constructs.

NEW DIRECTIONS

Here we highlight trends we believe merit close attention over the next few years. First is the substantive area of individualism-collectivism, where massive amounts of work have been done since 1980. The other trends are the two contrasting fundamental approaches to cross-cultural psychology—indigenous psychologies and the search for universals.

Individualism and Collectivism

Individualistic vs collectivistic tendencies have been variously conceptualized as idiocentric-allocentric at the individual level (Triandis et al 1985; Marin & Triandis 1985), as idiocentric-sociocentric (Shweder & Bourn 1984; Ito 1985), and as individual and group loyalties and culture of relatedness-separateness (Kagitcibasi 1985b; 1987b). Hofstede's work (1980) showed collectivism to be one of the four dimensions along which cultures varied. This idea was extended to organizational cultures (Hofstede & Spangenberg 1987; Jabes & Gruere 1987) and tested extensively. Starting from an Eastern (Chinese) culture's vantage point, another culture-level study in 22 countries found parallels with Hofstede's factors, with collectivism as an underlying dimension (Chinese Culture Connection 1987).

Subjects from individualistic cultures have individualistic values and behaviors, and vice versa for collectivistic cultures; this is reflected in other psychological processes and behaviors as well. For example, studies comparing Americans or Australians with East and South Asian groups (Kim 1986; Sinha & Verma 1987; Forgas & Bond 1985) and with Hispanics (Marin & Triandis 1985), as well as other comparative studies (Triandis et al 1986b, 1987), all showed the expected variations in individualistic and collectivistic orientations in line with the cultural variations.

Overwhelming evidence indicates differences in basic psychological processes between collectivistic and individualistic contexts. Differences have been noted in such basic psychological processes as learning and reinforcement (Haruki et al 1984) and social perception (Bond & Forgas 1984). Perception of social episodes was found to be affected, with Chinese subjects emphasizing communal feelings, social usefulness, and acceptance of authority, and with Australians emphasizing competitiveness, self-confidence, and freedom (Forgas & Bond 1985). Social loafing occurs less in collectivistic than in individualistic cultures owing to "group orientedness" (Gabrenya et al 1985). Kashima & Triandis (1986) showed that an individual coping mechanism (self-serving attribution) was used more by Americans than by the Japanese. Finally, Hui (1988) with his "IndCol" scale found an association in a Chinese but not an American sample, among collectivism, social desirability and sharing others' responsibilities. With respect to a cooperation-competition dimension (e.g. Eliram & Schwarzwald 1987), more cooperative orientations are generally seen among individuals from more closely knit social contexts (e.q. rural areas, less developed countries, cultures that value relatedness).

Other cognitive-behavioral correlates of individualism-collectivism are distributive justice, reward allocation, and conflict resulution. Berman et al (1985) found that in issues of distributive justice Japanese and Indian subjects (but not Australians and Americans) considered (family) need above merit. Several studies with children (Mann et al 1985; Mann 1986b; Mann & Greenbaum 1987) and adults (Kashima et al 1988; Marin 1985; Leung & Lind 1986; Leung 1987) showed that subjects from collectivistic cultures used equality more than equity and preferred conflict avoidance and nonadversary procedures. Triandis et al (1985) found this same difference in reward allocation between idiocentric and allocentric subjects in the same cultural context (United States). They also found the two groups to have different life experiences and values: The allocentrics received more and better social support and valued cooperation, equality and honesty; the idiocentrics exhibited more achievement motivation, alienation, anomie, and loneliness and valued comfort, competition, pleasure, and social recognition.

Other factors complicate the picture. Who the "other" is makes a difference (Triandis et al 1987). Subjects from the collectivistic cultures exhibited the behavior noted above only with members of the in-group; with out-group members their behavior resembled that of subjects from the individualistic cultures. Furthermore, the meaning of the in-group changes culturally (Verma 1985). The tendency to benefit the "other" or to avoid conflict is a reflection of group loyalties and of the desire to maintain group harmony (Triandis et al 1987; see also Argyle et al 1986). Similarly, the stated interaction goal determines reward allocation: When the goal is productivity, equity is preferred; when it is interpersonal harmony, equality is preferred, regardless of culture (Leung & Park 1986). When the goal is not specified, the salience of relatedness and group loyalties for collectivistic subjects apparently orients them more toward maintaining group solidarity than toward productivity.

Though impressive, the evidence summarized above calls for caution and more refined analysis. For example, the assumption that individualistic and collectivistic orientations have a situation-independent trait-like stability is dubious. Perceived situational factors (definition of the situation, ingroup-outgroup targets, trust, identification with the target, goal of interaction, etc) play an important mediating role. Likewise dubious is the assumed uni-dimensionality, and therefore mutual exclusiveness, of individualism and collectivism—an assumption due partly to a methodological bias introduced by forced-choice strategies. In fact, both orientations can be seen in the same person at the same time, or at different times, with different target groups or toward different interaction goals (Kashima 1987; Kagitcibasi 1987b). Factor-analytic work has also suggested that collectivism and individualism should be conceptualized as independent factors, not as opposite poles (Triandis et al 1986b:260).

More cross-cultural work is needed, however, toward valid operationaliza-tion of the basic orientations before further conceptual progress and sophistication can be achieved (Kashima 1987; Triandis et al 1985, 1986b). Better conceptualization at the individual and cultural levels is also called for (Hofstede & Spangenberg 1987), and such work is under way (Leung & Bond 1988). Finally, although the consequences of individualism and collectivism have been studied extensively, their antecedents in socialization and familial values (e.g. intergenerational dependencies and old age security needs, which show cross-cultural variation) require further clarification (Kagitcibasi 1985a, 1987b).

As for the prediction of world trends in individualism and collectivism, the modernization-theory assumption of "progression" toward individualism as "necessitated" by industrialization and economic development has been ques-tioned (Kagitcibasi 1985a, 1987b). Historical-demographic research (e.g. MacFarlane 1987; Hanawalt 1986) showing the existence of individualistic trends and nuclear family living in preindustrial Western Europe and the continuing collectivistic cultural and familial values in highly developed countries such as Japan (Hayashi & Suzuki 1984; Iwawaki 1986) seriously challenge this view. Nevertheless, a key issue is whether nonmaterial close-knit familial and communal relations will continue while greater economic prosperity causes material interdependencies (for example, between generations) to decrease. New syntheses have been called for (J.B.P. Sinha 1985b; Sampson 1987; Kagitcibasi 1985a, 1987b); however, whether such syntheses are emerging or whether cultural diffusion from the West is spreading individualistic ideology in the world (regardless of whether it is adaptive or not) is an empirical question.

Indigenous Psychologies

Two contrasting trends are apparent: On the one hand, the intensive study of psychological phenomena in separate cultures has given rise to the *indigenous psychology* point of view. On the other hand, there is increasing interest in approaching the question of human diversity from a *universalist* point of view. In the former, the *emic* standpoint is adopted, while in the latter the search for underlying regularities in human behavior (*etic* qualities) is of central concern.

The development of indigenous psychologies has been an important movement in recent years, judged both by the number of core publications and by the magnitude of the shift it represents from the earlier approach. Culture-specific histories (Kozulin 1984; Kuo & Liu 1987; Rudmin 1987; Sinha 1986; Whitford 1985) and surveys[4] of current activity in various countries and regions (Angelini 1985; Bond 1986; Blowers & Turtle 1987; Ho 1986; Mauer & Retief 1987; Trommsdorff 1985b) provide broad overviews; more focused treatments are also available (e.g. on indigenous cognition: Mugny & Carugati 1985; Berry et al 1988; on childhood: Okanlawon 1986; on depression: Littlewood 1985). Some would rid all aspects of psychology in a particular culture of external domination (e.g. Enriquez 1982), while others attempt to start from scratch, based upon what a particular culture values (e.g. Dasen et al 1985; Keats 1987).

One major trend in the indigenization of psychology is a search for the relevance of psychology in the Third World, especially with regard to national development (Sinha 1986; Moghaddam 1987; Pandey 1986). Some workers (e.g. Connolly 1985; Moghaddam & Taylor 1986) explicitly state the need for a problem-centered, not theory-driven approach. In this the Third World reacts against domination by Western psychology, with its pure-science emphasis—its quest for universals based on Western theory and data, belittling cultural differences and applied research.

---

[4]Brief histories and surveys of psychology in many countries are provided by Pawlik (1985). A comprehensive look at psychology in 30 countries, and developments since 1945, has been prepared by Gilgen & Gilgen (1987).

The other major trend, apparent mainly among Western researchers and progressing parallel to the first, is theoretically oriented. This theory-driven indigenization is exhibited in the distinct academic orientations of cross-cultural psychology and anthropology. The former holds that emic (indigenous) knowledge is necessary for a truly universal psychology, since universals may simply be the common patterns among various emic realities. Anthropologists, of course, have traditionally used the emic approach, often without an interest in universals. Psychologists have recently sought emic or indigenous knowledge (e.g. Sinha 1986; Saraswathi & Dutta 1987a). Especially in the area of cognition, a rapprochement between psychological and anthropological approaches is apparent (e.g. Dasen et al 1985; Dasen 1988; Super & Harkness 1986; Chamoux 1986; Sabatier 1986; Rogoff 1986, 1987; Dougherty 1985; Holland & Quinn 1987).

Interpretive anthropology and social constructionism (see above) are branches of the emic emphasis. When taken to their logical conclusions, these views lead to radical cultural relativism. They question whether, given the social and cultural construction of reality, any universally valid theory is possible.

Towards Universals

In sharp contrast to the concern of indigenous psychologies is the quest for those features of human psychological functioning that appear to be common across all populations. This trend can be illustrated in four domains.

1. Amir & Sharon (1987) have developed the first empirical research program explicitly directed toward assessing the generalizability and universality of social psychological laws (Pepitone & Triandis 1987). A parallel venture has also been initiated, at the level of critical analysis, by Bond (1988).

2. The Chinese Culture Connection (1987) attempted to establish "culture-free dimensions of culture" that would permit valid description and comparison of values across cultures. They concluded that there exists a basic or underlying dimension, which they called collectivism.

3. Universals are being sought in the area of cognition (Poortinga & van de Vijver 1988; Berry 1984; Verster 1987). Once again, such universals are being sought at the deeper level (that of psychological processes and functions) rather than at the level of behavior (which obviously varies greatly from culture to culture). These "culture-specific manifestations" (Poortinga & van de Vijver 1988; p. 19) are "cultural products" rooted in underlying, probably universal, processes.

4. In the domain of personality, Eysenck (1986) has argued that factor-comparison indexes, if high enough, are valid indicators of universal personality dimensions across the 24 cultures in his studies. However, when Bijnen et al (1986) used the same comparison technique as Eysenck on sets of

random artificial data, they likewise, obtained some high similarity indexes. They argued that if such high values can be obtained from random data, caution is necessary when claiming universality on the basis of similarity indexes between real sample data across cultures. Eysenck rejected these criticisms as unwarranted and faulty.

The dynamics of cross-cultural psychology probably derive from the basic conflict between the emic and the etic approaches, and cross-cultural psychology can progress only through a dialectic of the two. Just as we cannot claim to observe a universal based on a single-culture result or on a behavior pattern common to two or even a few cultures, so we cannot lable a pattern as unique or culture-specific when it is found to differ from patterns in the other cultures we know. The important goal is to discover the structural and functional antecedents of each pattern, to understand how it comes about and how it works, so that we can predict whether and under what conditions it might be seen in another cultural context.

As cross-cultural psychologists pay more attention to the macro characteristics of the sociocultural context, ecology, or social structure and identify their linkages with micro (individual behavioral) variables, they will be in a better position to establish which characteristics are culture-specific, which show commonality in several sociocultural contexts, and which are universal human phenomena.

ACKNOWLEDGMENTS

The authors thank: Cynthia Chataway for assisting in the literature search; Nilgun Saglam and numerous students for helping in preparing the manuscript; Floyd Rudmin and Diane Sunar for their critical reading and helpful comments on a draft of this chapter; and Audrey Bailey, for her skill and patience in assembling material from Turkey and Canada into a readable file. Work by C.K was partially supported by the Bogazici University Research Fund.

Literature Cited

Adamopoulos, J., Bontempo, R. N. 1986. Diachronic universals in interpersonal structures: Evidence from literary structures. *J. Cross-Cult. Psychol.* 17:169–89

Adler, N. J., Doktor, R., Redding, S. G. 1986. From the Atlantic to the Pacific: cross-cultural management reviewed. *J. Manag.* 12:295–318

Ahmed, R. A., Gielen, U. P., Avellani, J. 1987. Perceptions of parental behavior and the development of moral reasoning in Sudanese students. See Kagitcibasi 1987a, pp. 196–206

Akiyama, H. S. 1984. *Resource exchanges in dyadic family relations in the U.S. and Japan: towards a theory of dependence and independence of the elderly.* PhD thesis. Univ. Illinois, Urbana-Champaign

Albert, A. A., Porter, J. R. 1986. Children's gender role stereotypes: a comparison of the United States and South Africa. *J. Cross-Cult. Psychol.* 17:45–65

Alvi, S., Khan, S., Vegeris, S., Ansari, I. 1986. A cross-cultural study of psychological differentiation. *Int. J. Psychol.* 21:659–70

Amir, Y., Sharon, I. 1987. Are social psychological laws cross-culturally valid?

J. Cross-Cult. Psychol. 18:383–470

Angelini, A. 1985. Evolution of psychology in Brazil. In *Cross-Cultural and National Studies in Social Psychology*, ed. R. Diaz-Guerrero, pp. 351–60. New York: Elsevier

Annis, R. C., Corenblum, B. 1986. Self identification and race preference among Canadian Indian children. See Ekstrand 1986, pp. 77–86

Argyle, M., Henderson, M., Bond, M., Ilzuka, Y., Contarello, A. 1986. Cross-cultural variations in relationship rules. *Int. J. Psychol.* 21:287–315

Arrindell, W. A., Perris, C., Eisemann, M., Perris, H., van der Ende, J., et al. 1986a. Cross-national generalizability of patterns of parental rearing behavior: invariance of EMBU dimensional representations of healthy subjects from Australia, Denmark, Hungary, Italy and the Netherlands. *Pers. Indiv. Differ.* 7:103–12

Arrindell, W. A., Perris, C., Eisemann, M., Perris, H., van der Ende, J., et al. 1986b. Cross-national invariance of dimensions of parental rearing behavior: comparison of psychometric data of Swedish depressives and healthy subjects with Dutch target ratings on the EMBU. *Br. J. Psychiatry* 148:305–9

Bankart, C. P., Bankart, B. M. 1985. Japanese children's perception of their parents. *Sex Roles* 13:679–90

Bender-Szymanski, D., Hesse, H.-G. 1987. *Migrantenforschung: Eine Kritische Analyse Deutschsprachiger Empirischer Untersuchungen aus Psychologischer Sicht.* Frankfurt: Deut. Inst. Int. Paedagog. Forsch.

Berman, J. J., Berman, V. M., Singh, P. 1985. Cross-cultural similarities and differences in perception of fairness. *J. Cross-Cult. Psychol.* 16:55–67

Berry, J. W. 1984. Towards a universal psychology of cognitive competence. *Int. J. Psychol.* 19:335–61

Berry, J. W. 1985. Cultural psychology and ethnic psychology: a comparative analysis. See Reyes-Lagunes & Poortinga 1985, pp. 3–15

Berry, J. W. 1986. Multiculturalism and psychology in plural societies. See Ekstrand 1986, pp. 35–51

Berry, J. W., Annis, R. C., eds. 1988. *Ethnic Psychology: Research and Practice with Immigrants, Refugees, Native Peoples, Ethnic Groups and Sojourners.* Lisse: Swets & Zeitlinger

Berry, J. W., Irvine, S. H. 1986. Bricolage: savages do it daily. See Sternberg & Wagner 1986, pp. 271–306

Berry, J. W., Irvine, S. H., Hunt, E. B., eds. 1988. *Indigenous Cognition: Functioning in*

Cultural Context. Dordrecht: Nijhoff. 292 pp.

Berry, J. W., Kim, U. 1988. Acculturation and mental health. See Dasen et al 1988 pp. 207–36

Berry, J. W., Kim, U., Minde, T., Mok, D. 1987. Comparative studies of acculturative stress. *Int. Mig. Rev.* 21:491–511

Berry, J. W., Trimble, J., Olmeda, E. 1986a. Assessment of acculturation. See Lonner & Berry 1986, pp. 291–324.

Berry, J. W., van de Koppel, J. M. H., Sénéchal, C., Annis, R. C., Bahuchet, S., et al. 1986b. *On the Edge of the Forest: Cultural Adaptation and Cognitive Development in Central Africa.* Lisse: Swets & Zeitlinger. 229 pp.

Biesheuvel, S. 1987. Psychology: science and politics. Theoretical developments and application in a plural society. *S. Afr. J. Psychol.* 17:1–8

Bijnen, E. J., van der Net, T. Z. J., Poortinga, Y. H. 1986. On cross-cultural comparative studies with the Eysenck Personality Questionnaire. *J. Cross-Cult. Psychol.* 17:3–17

Blowers, G., Turtle, A., eds. 1987. *Psychology Moving East.* Sydney: Univ. Sydney Press/Boulder: Westview Press. 362 pp.

Blue, A., Corenblum, B., Annis, R. C. 1987. Developmental trends in racial preference and identification in Northern Native Canadian children. See Kagitcibasi 1987a, pp. 311–20

Bochner, S. 1986a. Observational methods. See Lonner & Berry 1986, pp. 165–202

Bochner, S. 1986b. Coping with unfamiliar cultures: adjustment or culture learning? *Aust. J. Psychol.* 38:347–58

Boesch, E. E. 1987. Cultural psychology in action—theoretical perspective. See Kagitcibasi 1987a, pp. 41–51

Bond, M. H., ed. 1986. *The Psychology of the Chinese People.* Hong Kong: Oxford Univ. Press. 354 pp.

Bond, M. H., ed. 1988. *The Cross-Cultural Challenge to Social Psychology.* London: Sage

Bond, M. H., Forgas, J. P. 1984. Linking person perception to behavior intention across cultures: the role of cultural collectivism. *J. Cross-Cult. Psychol.* 15:337–52

Born, M., Bleichrodt, N., van der Flier, H. 1987. Cross-cultural comparison of sex-related differences on intelligence tests: a meta-analysis. *J. Cross-Cult. Psychol.* 18:283–314

Boyd, R., Richerson, P. 1985. *Culture and the Evolutionary Process.* Chicago: Univ. Chicago Press

Bril, B., Sabatier, C. 1986. The cultural context of motor development: postural manipulations in the daily life of Bambara babies

(Mali). *Int. J. Behav. Dev.* 9:153–73

Brislin, R. W. 1988. Expanding students' awareness of class, ethnicity, culture and race by beginning with their own experiences. *The G. Stanley Hall Lecture Series*, Vol 8. Washington, DC: Am. Psychol. Assoc.

Brislin, R. W. 1986. A culture-general assimilator: preparation for various types of sojourns. *Int. J. Intercult. Relat.* 10:215–34

Brislin, R. W., Cushner, K., Cherrie, C., Yong, M. 1986. *Intercultural Interactions: A Practical Guide*. Newbury Park: Sage. 336 pp.

Bronstein, P. 1986. Children's social behavior: a cross-cultural comparison. *Int. J. Behav. Dev.* 9:439–53

Broude, G. J. 1987. A hologeistic study of the patterning of male-female relationships. See Kagitcibasi 1987a, pp. 385–93

Brown, J. K., Kerns, B., eds. 1985. *In Her Prime*. South Hadley, MA: Bergin & Garvey

Bushan, L. I. 1985. Authoritarianism and F-scale in cross-cultural perspective. *Psychol. Stud.* 30:127–33

Carraher, T. N. 1986. From drawings to buildings: working with mathematical scales. *Int. J. Behav. Dev.* 9:527–44

Casas, J. M., Ponterotte, J. G., Sweeney, M. 1987. Stereotyping the stereotyper. *J. Cross-Cult. Psychol.* 18:45–57

Cashmore, J. A., Goodnow, J. J. 1986. Influences on Australian parents' values: ethnicity versus socioeconomic status. *J. Cross-Cult. Psychol.* 17:441–54

Chamoux, M. N. 1986. Apprendre autrement: Aspects des pedagogies dites informelles chez les Indiens du Mexique. In *Demain L'artisanat?*, ed. P. Rossel. Paris: Cahiers I.U.E.D.

Chinese Culture Connection. 1987. Chinese values and the search for culture-free dimensions of culture. *J. Cross-Cult. Psychol.* 18:143–64

Church, A. T., Katigbak, M., Almario-Velazco, G. 1985. Psychometric intelligence and adaptive competence in rural Philippine children. *Intelligence* 9:317–40

Cohen, H. 1985. A comparison of the development of spatial conceptual abilities of students from two cultures. *J. Res. Sci. Teach.* 22:491–501

Cole, M. 1985. The zone of proximal development: where culture and cognition create each other. In *Culture, Communication and Cognition: Vygotskian Perspectives*, ed. J. V. Wertsch. New York: Cambridge Univ. Press

Colomb, E., Dasen, P. R. 1986. La perception des relations spatiales dans le dessin et le developpement des operations concretes. *J. Int. Psychol.* 21:71–90

Connoly, K. 1985. Can there be a psychology of the Third World? *Bull. Br. Psychol. Soc.* 38:249–57

Cool, K. O., Lengnick-Hall, C. A. 1985. Second thoughts on the transferability of the Japanese management style. *Org. Stud.* 16:1–22

Csikszentmihalyi, M., Massimini, F. 1985. On the psychological selection of bio-cultural information. *New Ideas Psychol.* 3:115–38

Dadbrook, D. 1985. The whole sociological aspect of the family. *Ment. Health Aust.* 1:9–13

Dasen, P. R. 1988. Development psychologique et activités quotidiènnes chez des enfants africains. *Enfance*. In press

Dasen, P. R., Berry, J. W., Sartorius, N., eds. 1988. *Cross-Cultural Psychology and Health: Towards Application*. Newbury Park: Sage. 358 pp.

Dasen, P. R., Dembélé, B., Ettien, K., Kamagaté, K., Koffi, D. A., N'Guessan, A. 1985. N'glouèle, l'intelligence chez les Baoulé. *Arch. Psychol.* 53:293–324

Dasen, P. R., Jahoda, G. 1986. Cross-cultural human development. *Int. J. Behav. Dev.* 9:413–16

Dasen, P., Super, C. 1988. The usefulness of a cross-cultural approach in studies of malnutrition and psychological development. See Dasen et al 1988, pp. 112–38

DeLeo, D., Villa, A., Magni, G., Andereotti, A., Gagliardi, A. 1986. Presentation of the Italian version and contribution to the literature of Bem Sex Role Inventory. *Boll. Psicol. Appl.* 175:21–28

Deregowski, J., Bentley, A. 1986. Perception of pictorial space by Bushmen. *Int. J. Psychol.* 21:743–52

Deregowski, J. B., Dziurawiec, S. 1986. Some aspects of comprehension of technical diagrams: an intercultural study. *Travail Humain* 49:43–60

Domino, G., Hannah, M. T. 1987. A comparative analysis of social values of Chinese and American children. *J. Cross-Cult Psychol.* 18:58–77

Dornic, S. 1986. Immigrants, language and stress. See Ekstrand 1986, pp. 149–58

Dougherty, J., ed. 1985. *Directions in Cognitive Anthropology*. Champaign: Univ. Ill. Press

Draguns, J. 1986. Culture and psychopathology: what is known about their relationship? *Aust. J. Psychol.* 38:329–38

Drenth, P.J.D. 1987. Intelligence tests in educational evaluations and selection. See Kagitcibasi 1987a, pp. 293–301

Durrett, M. E., Richards, P., Otaki, M., Pennebaker, J. W., Nyquist, L. 1986. Mother's involvement with infant and her perception of spousal support. Japan and America. *J. Marr. Fam.* 48:187–94

Dziurawiec, S., Deregowski, J. B. 1986. Construction errors as a key to perceptual difficulties encountered in reading technical drawings. *Ergonomics* 29:1203–12

Eckensberger, L. 1985. De Essentie van Theorieën in de cross-culturele Psychologie. See van de Koppel 1985, pp. 71–103

Ekstrand, L., ed. 1986. *Ethnic Minorities and Immigrants in a Cross-Cultural Perspective.* Lisse: Swets & Zeitlinger. 356 pp.

Ekstrand, L., Ekstrand, G. 1987. Children's perception of norms and sanctions in two cultures. See Kagitcibasi 1987c, pp. 171–80

Eliram, T., Schwarzwald, J. 1987. Social orientation among Israeli youth. *J. Cross-Cult. Psychol.* 18:31–44

Ellis, B. 1986. Use of item bias detection in the construction and evaluation of tests administered in more than one culture. See Ekstrand 1986, pp. 315–28

England, G. W., Misumi, J. 1986. Work centrality in Japan and the United States. *J. Cross-Cult. Psychol.* 17:396–416

Enriquez, V. 1982. *Decolonizing the Filipino Psyche.* Quezon City: Philippine Psychol. Res. House. 22 pp.

Eron, L. D., Huesmann, L. R. 1987. The stability of aggressive behavior in cross-national comparison. See Kagitcibasi 1987c, pp. 207–17

Eysenck, H. J. 1986. Cross-cultural comparisons: the validity of assessment by indices of factor comparisons. *J. Cross-Cult. Psychol.* 17:506–15

Eysenck, H. J. 1988. The biological basis of intelligence. See Irvine & Berry 1988, pp. 87–104

Eysenck, S., Barrett, P., Spielberger, C., Evans, F. J., Eysenck, H. J. 1986. Cross-cultural comparisons of personality dimensions: England and America. *Pers. Individ. Differ.* 7:209–14

Eysenck, S., Long, F. Y. 1986. A cross-cultural comparison of personality in adults and children: Singapore and England. *J. Pers. Soc. Psychol.* 50:124–30

Fallers, L., Fallers, M. 1976. Sex roles in Edremit. In *Mediterranean Family Structure,* ed. J. Peristiany. New York: Cambridge Univ. Press

Feather, N. T. 1986. Value systems across cultures: Australia and China. *Int. J. Psychol.* 21:697–715

Ferguson, G. A. 1956. On transfer and the abilities of man. *Can. J. Psychol.* 10:121–31

Florian, V., Zernitsky-Shurka, E. 1987. The effect of culture and gender on self-reported assertive behavior. *Int. J. Psychol.* 22:83–95

Flynn, J. R. 1987. Massive IQ gains in 14 nations: what IQ tests really measure. *Psychol. Bull.* 101:171–91

Foa, U. G., Salcedo, L. N., Tornblom, K. Y., Garner, M., Glaubman, H., et al. 1987. Interrelation of social resources: Evidence of pancultural invariance. *J. Cross-Cult. Psychol.* 18:221–33

Folensbee, R., Draguns, J., Danish, S. 1986. Impact of two types of counselor intervention on Black American, Puerto Rican and Anglo-American analogue clients. *J. Couns. Psychol.* 33:446–53

Forgas, J. P., Bond, M. H. 1985. Cultural influences on the perception of interaction episodes. *Pers. Soc. Psychol. Bull.* 11:75–88

Fuchs, I., Eisenberg, N., Herz-Lazarowitz, R., Shrabang, R. 1986. Kibbutz, Israeli city, and American children's moral reasoning about prosocial moral conflicts. *Merrill-Palmer Q.* 32:37–50

Furnham, A. 1985. Just world beliefs in an unjust society: a cross-cultural comparison. *Eur. J. Soc. Psychol.* 15:363–66

Furnham, A., Karani, R. 1985. A cross-cultural study of attitudes to women, just world, and locus of control beliefs. *Psychologia* 28:11–20

Furnham, A., Bochner, S. 1986. *Culture Shock: Psychological Reactions to Unfamiliar Environments.* London: Methuen. 298 pp.

Gabrenya, W. K., Wang, Y., Latane, B. 1985. Social loafing on an optimizing task: cross-cultural differences among Chinese and Americans. *J. Cross-Cult. Psychol.* 16:223–42

Gallois, C., Collon, V. J. 1985. The influence of ethnocentrism and ethnic label on the appreciation of disparagement jokes. *Int. J. Psychol.* 20:63–76

Garcia-Averasturi, L. 1988. Psychosocial factors in health: The Cuban model. See Dasen et al 1988, pp. 281–97

Gardner, W., Lamb, M. E., Thompson, R. A., Sagi, A. 1986. On individual differences in strange situation behavior: categorical and continuous measurement systems in a cross-cultural data set. *Infant Behav. Dev.* 9:355–75

Gergen, K., Davis, K., eds. 1985. *The Social Construction of the Person.* New York: Springer

Gergen, K. J. 1986. Interpreting the texts of nature and culture: a reply to Jahoda. *Eur. J. Soc. Psychol.* 16:31–37

Gergen, K. J., Fisher, D. C., Hepburn, A. 1986. Hermeneutics of personality develop ment. *J. Pers. Soc. Psychol.* 50:1261–70

Gilgen, A. R., Gilgen, C. K., eds. 1987. *International Handbook of Psychology.* London: Aldwych Press

Gilligan, C. 1982. *In a Different Voice.* Cambridge, MA: Harvard Univ. Press

Glascock, A. P. 1987. The myth of the Golden Isle: the question of old age in preindustrial societies. See Kagitcibasi 1987a, pp. 403–10

Gomez-Mejia, L. R. 1986. The cross-cultural structure of task-related and contextual constructs. *J. Psychol.* 120:5–19

Goodnow, J. J. 1986. Cultural conditions and individual behaviours: conceptual and methodological links. *Aust. J. Psychol.* 38:231–44

Goodnow, J. J., Wilkins, P., Dawes, L. 1986. Acquiring cultural forms: cognitive aspects of socialization illustrated by childrens' drawings and judgments of drawings. *Int. J. Behav. Dev.* 9:485–505

Griesel, R., Richter, L. M. 1987. Cognitive performance and cognitive style among a group of young Bushman children. See Kagitcibasi 1987a, pp. 286–92

Griffeth, R. W., Hom, P. W. 1987. Some multivariate comparisons of multinational managers. *Multiv. Behav. Res.* 22:173–91

Grossmann, K., Grossmann, K. E., Spangler, G., Suess, G., Unzner, L. 1985. Maternal sensitivity and newborns' orientation responses as related to quality of attachment in Northern Germany. *Monogr. Soc. Res. Child Dev.* 50:233–56

Gurbuz, E. 1988. *A measurement of sex-trait stereotypes.* MA thesis. Bogazaci Univ., Istanbul

Habteyes, Y., Steinkamp, M. W. 1985. Sociocultural factors and achievement motivation in the United States Virgin Islands. *Ethos* 13:75–93

Hanawalt, B. A. 1986. *The Ties that Bound: Peasant Families in Medieval England.* Oxford

Haque, A. 1987. Social class differences in perceived maternal acceptance-rejection and personality dispositions among Pakistani children. See Kagitcibasi 1987a, pp. 189–95

Harsel, Y., Wales, R. 1987. Directional preference in problem solving. *Int. J. Psychol.* 22:195–206

Haruki, Y., Shigehisa, T., Nedate, K., Wajima, M., Ogawa, R. 1984. Effects of alienreinforcement and its combined type on learning behavior and efficacy in relation to personality. *Int. J. Psychol.* 19:527–45

Hayashi, C., Suzuki, T. 1984. Changes in belief systems, quality of life issues and social conditions over 25 years in post-

war Japan. *Ann. Inst. Stat. Math.* 36:135–61

Heaven, P. C. L. 1986. Authoritarianism, directiveness and self-esteem revisited: a cross-cultural analysis. *Pers. Individ. differ.* 7:225–28

Heggenhougen, H., Shore, L. 1986. Cultural components of behavioural epidemiology: implications for primary health care. *Soc. Sci. Med.* 22:1235–45

Heikinhelmo, P., Shute, J. 1986. The adaptation of foreign students: student views and institutional implications. *J. Coll. Stud. Personnel* 27:399–406

Henderson, M., Argyle, M. 1986. The informal rules of working relationships. *J. Occup. Behav.* 7:259–75

Hendrix, L., Johnson, G. D. 1985. Instrumental and expressive socialization: a false dichotomy. *Sex. Roles* 13:581–95

Higbee, K. L., Kunihira, S. 1985. Crosscultural application of Yodai mnemonics in education. *Educ. Psychol.* 20:57–64

Ho, D. 1986. Psychology in Hong Kong. *Int. J. Psychol.* 21:213–23

Ho, E. S. 1985. *Values and economic development: Hong Kong and China.* PhD thesis. Univ. Mich., Ann Arbor

Hoffman, C., Lau, I., Johnston, D. R. 1986. The linguistic relativity of person cognition: an English-Chinese comparison. *J. Pers. Soc. Psychol.* 51:1097–1105

Hoffman, L. W. 1987. The value of children to parents and child rearing patterns. See Kagitcibasi 1987c, pp. 159–70

Hofstede, G. 1980. *Culture's Consequences: International Differences in Work-Related Values.* London: Sage

Hofstede, G., Spangenberg, J. 1987. Measuring individualism and collectivism at occupational and organizational levels. See Kagitcibasi 1987a, pp. 113–22

Holland, D., Quinn, N., ed. 1987. *Cultural Models in Language and Thought.* London: Cambridge Univ. Press

Holtzman, W. H., Evans, R., Kennedy, S., Iscoe, I. 1987. Psychology and health: contributions of psychology to the improvement of health and health care. *Int. J. Psychol.* 22:221–67

Hortacsu, N., Karanci, A. N. 1987. Premarital breakways in a Turkish sample: Perceived reasons, attributional dimensions and affective reactions. *Int. J. Psychol.* 22:57–74

Howard, A. 1985. Ethnopsychology and the prospects for a cultural psychology. See White & Kirkpatrick 1985, pp. 401–20

Hui, C. C. H. 1987. Measurement of individualism-collectivism. *J. Res. Pers.* 22:1–16

Hui, H., Triandis, H. 1985. Measurement in cross-cultural psychology: a review and comparison of strategies. *J. Cross-Cult. Psychol.* 16:131–52

Hulin, H. 1987. A psychometric theory of evaluations of item and scale translations: fidelity across languages. *J. Cross-Cult. Psychol.* 18:115–42

Imamoglu, E. O. 1987. An interdependence model of human development. See Kagitcibasi 1987a, pp. 138–45

Irvine, S. H. 1986. Cross-cultural assessment: from practice to theory. See Lonner & Berry 1986, pp. 203–30

Irvine, S. H., Berry, J. W., eds. 1988. *Human Abilities in Cultural Context.* New York: Cambridge Univ. Press, 582 pp.

Irvine, S. H., Newstead, S., eds. 1987. *Intelligence and Cognition: Contemporary Frames of Reference.* Dordrecht: Nijhoff, 460 pp.

Ito, K. L. 1985. Affective bonds: Hawaiian interrelationships of self. See White & Kirkpatrick 1985, pp. 301–11

Iwawaki, S. 1986. Achievement motivation and socialization. In *Human Assessment: Cognition and Motivation*, ed. S. E. Newstead, S. M. Irvine, P. L. Dann. Boston: Martinus Nijhoff

Iwawaki, S., Vernon, P. E. 1988. Japanese abilities and achievements. See Irvine & Berry, pp. 358–82

Jabes, J., Gruere, J. P. 1987. Organization under siege: the onslaught of cultural explanations of organizational behavior. See Kagitcibasi 1987a, pp. 52–59

Jahoda, G. 1986a. Nature, culture and social psychology. *Eur. J. Soc. Psychol.* 16:17–30

Jahoda, G. 1986b. Language games, or as you like it: a reply to Gergen. *Eur. J. Soc. Psychol.* 16:39–42

Jahoda, G. 1986c. A cross-cultural perspective on developmental psychology. *Int. J. Behav. Dev.* 9:417–37

Jahoda, G., Neilson, I. 1986. Nyborg's analytical rod-and-frame scoring system: a comparative study in Zimbabwe. *Int. J. Psychol.* 21:19–29

Jayant, K. R., Karandikar, H. M., Krishnan, L. 1985. Success/failure experiences, achievement motivation, and competition in a scarcity culture. *J. Soc. Psychol.* 125:261–63

Jensen, A. R. 1988. Speed of information processing and population differences. See Irvine & Berry 1988, pp. 105–45

Kagitcibasi, C. 1985a. A model of family change through development: the Turkish family in comparative perspective. See Lagunes & Poortinga 1985, pp. 120–35

Kagitcibasi, C. 1985b. Culture of separateness—Culture of relatedness. *1984: Vision and Reality. Papers in Comparative Studies* 4:91–99

Kagitcibasi, C. 1986. Status of women in Tur-

key: cross-cultural perspectives. *Int. J. Middle East. Stud.* 18:485–99

Kagitcibasi, C. ed. 1987a. *Growth and Progress in Cross-Cultural Psychology.* Lisse: Swets & Zeitlinger. 410 pp.

Kagitcibasi, C. 1987b. Individual and group loyalties: are they compatible? See Kagitcibasi 1987a, pp. 94–104

Kagitcibasi, C. 1987c. Alienation of the outsider: the plight of migrants. *Int. Mig.* 25:195–210

Kagitcibasi, C. 1988. Diversity of socialization and social change. See Dasen et al 1988, pp. 25–47

Kakar, S. 1985. Psychoanalysis and non-western cultures. *Int. Rev. Psycho-Anal.* 12:441–48

Kashima, Y. 1987. Conceptions of person: Implications in individualism/collectivism research. See Kagitcibasi 1987a, pp. 104–12

Kashima, Y., Triandis, H. C. 1986. The self-serving bias in attributions as a coping strategy: a cross-cultural study. *J. Cross-Cult Psychol.* 17:83–97

Kashima, Y., Siegel, M., Tanaka, K., Isaka, H. 1988. Universalism in lay conceptions of distributive justice: a cross-cultural examination. *Int. J. Psychol.* 23:51–64

Katz, Y. J., Ronen, M. 1986. A cross-cultural validation of the conservatism scale in a multi-ethnic society: the case of Israel. *J. Soc. Psychol.* 126:555–57

Keats, D. M. 1986. Using the cross-cultural method to study the development of values. *Aust. J. Psychol.* 38:297–308

Keats, D. M. 1987. Fang Fu-Xi: cultural factors in concepts of intelligence. See Kagitcibasi 1987a, pp. 236–47

Keefe, S., Padilla, A. 1987. *Chicano Ethnicity.* Albuquerque: Univ. New Mexico Press. 238 pp.

Kelly, K., Cheung, F. M., Singh, R., Becker, M. A., Rodriguez-Carrillo, P., et al. 1985. Chronic self-destructiveness and locus of control in cross-cultural perspective. *J. Soc. Psychol.* 126:573–77

Kermoian, R., Leiderman, P. H. 1986. Infant attachment to mother and child caretaker in an East African community. *Int. J. Behav. Dev.* 9:455–69

Kim, U. 1986. *Personality, individualism/collectivism and cognitive style: A preliminary study with Korean-Canadians.* Presented at Int. Assoc. Cross-Cult. Psychol. Confr., 8th, Istanbul

Kim, U., Berry, J. W. 1986. Predictors of acculturative stress: Korean immigrants to Canada. See Ekstrand 1986, pp. 159–70

Kim, Y. Y., Gudykunst. W. B., eds. 1988. *Cross-Cultural Adaptation: Current Approaches.* (Intercultural Commun. Ann., Vol. 11). Newbury Park: Sage. 320 pp.

Kinzie, J. 1985. Cultural aspects of psychiatric treatment with Indochinese refugee. *Am. J. Soc. Psychiatry* 5:47–53

Kirkpatrick, J., White, G. M. 1985. Exploring ethnopsychologies. See White et al, 1985, pp. 3–32

Kozulin, A., ed. 1984. *Psychology in Utopia: Toward a Social History of Social Psychology.* Cambridge: MIT Press. 179 pp.

Kuo, J. F., Liu, E. J., eds. 1987. *History of Chinese Psychology.* Beijing: The People's Education Press. 430 pp. (In Chinese)

Laboratory of Comparative Human Cognition. 1986. Contributions of cross-cultural research to educational practice. *Am. Psychol.* 40:1049–1958

Lalo, A. 1987. Abstractions et apprentissage des quantités physiques. *Int. J. Psychol.* 22:139–64

Lambert, W. 1987. The fate of old country values in a new land: a cross-national study of child rearing. *Can. Psychol.* 28:9–20

Landis, D., Brislin, R. W., Hulgus, J. 1985. Attributional training versus contacts in acculturative learning. *J. Appl. Soc. Psychol.* 15:466–82

Landis, D., ed. 1986. Special issue on theories and methods in cross-cultural orientation. *Int. J. Intercult. Relat.* 10:103–254

Lara-Cantu, M. A., Navarro-Arias, R. 1986. Positive and negative factors in the measurement of sex-roles: findings from a Mexican sample. *Hisp. J. Behav. Sci.* 8:143–45

Lara-Cantu, M. A., Navarro-Arias, R. 1987. Self-descriptions of Mexican college students in response to the Bem sex role inventory and other sex role items. *J. Cross-Cult Psychol.* 18:331–44

Leong, C., Cheng, S., Das, J. P. 1985. Simultaneous-successive synthesis and planning in Chinese readers. *Int. J. Psychol.* 20:19–31

Leung, K. 1987. Some determinants of reactions to procedural models for conflict resolution: a cross-national study. *J. Pers. Soc. Psychol.* 53:898–908

Leung, K., Bond, M. H. 1988. On the search for cultural dimensions: some methodological considerations. *J. Cross-Cult. Psychol.* In press

Leung, K., Lind, E. A. 1986. Procedural justice and culture: effects of culture, gender, and investigator status on procedural preferences. *J. Pers. Soc. Psychol.* 50:1134–40

Leung, K., Park, H. J. 1986. Effects of interactional goal of allocation rule: a cross-national study. *Org. Behav. Hum. Decis. Process* 37:111–20

Levine, C., Kohlberg, L., Hewer, A. 1985. The current formulation of Kohlberg's theory and a response to critics. *Hum. Dev.* 28:94–100

Little, A. 1987. Attributions in a cross-cultural context. *Gen. Soc. Gen. Psychol. Monogr.* 113:61–79

Littlewood, R. 1985. An indigenous conceptualization of reactive depression in Trinidad. *Psychol. Med.* 15:275–81

Lonner, W. J., ed. 1985. Television in the developing world. Special issue. *J. Cross-Cult. Psychol.* 16:259–397

Lonner, W. J., Berry, J. W., eds. 1986. *Field Methods in Cross-Cultural Research.* Newbury Park: Sage. 368 pp.

Louw, J., Potgieter, J. L. 1986. Achievement-related causal attributions: A South African cross-cultural study. *J. Cross-Cult. Psychol.* 17:269–82

Lussier, M. L., Fellers, G. L., Kleinplatz, P. L. 1986. Value orientations of English, French, and Italian Canadian children. *J. Cross-Cult. Psychol.* 17:283–99

Lutz, C. 1985. Ethnopsychology compared to what? Explaining behavior and consciousness among the Ifaluk. See White & Kirkpatrick 1985, pp. 35–79

Lynn, R., Hampson, S. 1986. The rise of national intelligence: evidence from Britain, Japan and the U.S.A. *Pers. Individ. Differ.* 7:23–32

Ma, H. 1985. Cross-cultural study of the hierarchical structure of human relationships. *Psychol. Rep.* 57:967–74

MacFarlane, A. 1987. *The Culture of Capitalism.* Oxford: Blackwell

Malpass, R., Poortinga, Y. 1986. Strategies for design and analysis. See Lonner & Berry 1986, pp. 47–84

Mann, L., ed. 1986a. Contributions to cross-cultural psychology. Special issue. *Aust. J. Psychol.* 38:195–409

Mann, L. 1986b. Cross-cultural studies of rules for determining majority and minority decision rights. *Aust. J. Psychol.* 38:319–28

Mann, L., Greenbaum, C. 1987. Cross-cultural studies of children's decision rules. See Kagitcibasi 1987a, pp. 130–37

Mann, L., Radford, M., Karagawa, C. 1985. Cross-cultural differences in children's use of decision rules: a comparison between Japan and Australia. *J. Pers. Soc. Psychol.* 49:1557–64

Marin, G. 1985. The preference for equity when judging the attractiveness and fairness of an allocator: the role of familiarity and culture. *J. Soc. Psychol.* 125:543–49

Marin, G., Salazar, J. M. 1985. Determinants of hetero and autostereotypes: Distance level of contact and socioeconomic development in seven nations. *J. Cross-Cult. Psychol.* 16:403–22

Marin, G., Triandis, H. C. 1985. Allocentrism as an important characteristic of the behavior of Latin Americans and Hispanics. In *Cross-Cultural and National Studies in*

Social Psychology, ed. R. Guerrero, pp. 85–104. North Holland: Elsevier

Marjoribanks, K., Jordan, D. F. 1986. Stereotyping among Aboriginal and Anglo-Australians: the uniformity, intensity, direction, and quality of auto- and hetero-stereotypes. J. Cross-Cult. Psychol. 17:17–28

Marsella, A. J., White, G. M., ed. 1984. Cultural Conceptions of Mental Health and Therapy. Boston: Reidel

Marsella, A. J., De Vos, G., Hsu, F. L. K., ed. 1985. Culture and Self: Asian and Western Perspectives. New York: Tavistock

Matthew, V. G. 1985. Locus of control: a conceptual analysis. Indian Psychol. Rev. 28:15–18

Mauer, K. F., Retief, A. I., eds. 1987. Psychology in Context: Cross-Cultural Research Trends in South Africa. Pretoria, S. Africa: Hum. Sci. Res. Council. 225 pp.

McShane, D., Berry, J. W. 1988. Native North Americans: Indian and Inuit abilities. See Irvine & Berry 1988, pp. 385–426

Mendenhall, M., Oddon, G. 1985. The dimensions of expatriate acculturation: a review. Acc. Manage. Rev. 20:39–47

Miller, J. 1984. Culture and the development of everyday social explanation. J. Pers. Soc. Psychol. 5:961–78

Miserez, D., Horvath, J., eds. 1988. Psychological Problems of Refugees and Asylum Seekers. Geneva: League of Red Cross and Red Crescent Soc.

Misra, S., Kanungo, R. N., Rosenteil, L., Stuhler, E. L. 1985. The motivational formulation of job and work involvement: a cross-national study. Hum. Relat. 38:501–18

Moghaddam, F. M. 1987. Psychology in the three worlds, as reflected by the crisis in social psychology and the move toward indigenous Third-World psychology. Am. Psychol. 42:912–20

Moghaddam, F., Taylor, D. M. 1986. What constitutes an "appropriate psychology" for the developing world? Int. J. Psychol. 21:253–67

Mugny, G., Carugati, F. 1985. L'intelligence au Pluriel: Les Resprésentations Sociales de L'intelligence et de son Développement. Cousset: Editions Delval

Munro, D. 1985. A free-format values inventory: explorations with Zimbabwean student teachers. S. Afr. J. Psychol. 38:285–95

Munro, D. 1986. Work motivation and values, problems and possibilities in and out of Africa. Aust. J. Psychol. 38:285–95

Munroe, R. H., Munroe, R. L., Brasher, A. 1985. Precursors of spatial ability: a longitudinal study among the Logoli of Kenya. J. Soc. Psychol. 125:23–33

Munroe, R. L., Munroe, R. H. 1986. Field-

work in cross-cultural psychology. See Lonner & Berry 1986, pp. 111–36

Naidoo, J. 1985. A cultural perspective on the adjustment of South Asian women in Canada. See Reyes-Lagunes & Poortinga 1985, pp. 76–92

Neto, F. 1986. Adaptacaco psico-social e regresso ao pais natal dos migrantes portugueses em Franca. Psicologia 5:71–86

Noriyuki, M. 1985. Strong, quasi- and weak conformity among Japanese in the modified Asch procedure. J. Cross-Cult. Psychol. 16:83–87

Ochse, R., Plug, C. 1986. Cross-cultural investigation of the validity of Erikson's theory of personality development. J. Pers. Soc. Psychol. 50:1240–52

Okanlawon, O. L. 1986. Concepts of the child in some Nigerian cultures. J. Black Psychol. 12:61–70

Ostrov, E., Offer, D., Howard, I. K. 1986. Cross-cultural studies of sex differences in normal adolescents' self-image. Hillside J. Clin. Psychiatry. 8:183–92

Otaki, M., Durrett, M. E., Richards, P., Nyquist, L., Pennebaker, J. W. 1986. Maternal and infant behavior in Japan and America: a partial replication. J. Cross-Cult. Psychol. 17:251–68

Oyewumi, L. K. 1986. Psychotherapy in Nigerian psychiatric practice: an overview. Psychiatr. J. Univ. Ottawa 11:18–22

Pandey, J. 1986. Emerging trends in the eighties: psychology in India. In The Third Survey of Research in Psychology. New Delhi: Indian Council Soc. Sci. Res.

Pandey, J., Singh, A. K. 1986. Attribution and evaluation in India. In The Third Survey of Research in Psychology, ed. J. Pandey. New Delhi: Indian Council Soc. Sci. Res.

Pang, V. O., Mizokawa, D. T., Morishima, J. I., Olstad, R. G. 1985. Self-concepts of Japanese-American children. J. Cross-Cult. Psychol. 16:99–109

Papanek, H. 1973. Purdah: separate worlds and symbolic shelter. Comp. Stud. Soc. Hist. 15:289–325

Pawlik, K., ed. 1985. International Directory of Psychologists. Amsterdam: North-Holland. 1181 pp.

Peabody, D. 1985. National Characteristics. New York: Cambridge Univ. Press

Pedersen, P., Sartorius, N., Marsella, A., eds. 1984. Mental Health Services: The Cross-Cultural Context. Newbury Park: Sage. 311 pp.

Pedersen, P., ed. 1985. Handbook of Cross-Cultural Counselling and Therapy. Westport: Greenwood Press. 349 pp.

Pepitone, A. 1987. The role of culture in theories of social psychology. See Kagitcibasi 1987a, pp. 12–21

Pepitone, A., Triandis, H. C. 1987. On the

universality of social psychological theories. *J. Cross-Cult. Psychol.* 18:471–98

Perris, C., Arrindell, W. A., Perris, H., van der Ende, J., Maj, M., et al. 1985. Cross-national study of perceived parental rearing behavior in healthy subjects from Australia, Denmark, Italy, The Netherlands and Sweden: Pattern and level comparisons. *Acta Psychiatr. Scand.* 72:278–82

Pettengill, S. M., Rohner, R. P. 1985. Korean-American adolescents' perceptions of parental control, parental acceptance-rejection and parent-adolescent conflict. See Reyes-Lagunes & Poortinga 1985, pp. 241–49

Poortinga, Y., Malpass, R. 1986. Making inferences from cross-cultural data. See Lonner & Berry 1986, pp. 17–46

Poortinga, Y., van der Flier, H. 1988. The meaning of item bias in ability tests. See Irvine & Berry 1988, pp. 166–83

Poortinga, Y., van de Vijver, F. 1987. Explaining cross-cultural differences: bias analysis and beyond. *J. Cross-Cult Psychol.* 18:249–82

Poortinga, Y., van de Vijver, F. 1988. Culturally invariant parameters of cognitive functioning. See Berry et al 1988, pp. 19–36

Quah, S. 1985. The health belief model and preventive health behaviour in Singapore. *Soc. Sci. Med.* 21:351–63

Rao, V. V. P., Rao, N. 1985. Sex-role attitudes across two cultures: United States and India. *Sex Roles* 13:607–24

Ravinder, S. 1987. Androgyny: Is it really the product of educated, middle class Western societies? *J. Soc. Psycol.* 18:208–20

Reed-Sanders, D., Dodder, R. A., Webster, L. 1985. The Bem Sex Role Inventory across three cultures. *J. Soc. Psychol.* 125:523–25

Retief, A. I. 1987. *Methodological and Theoretical Problems in Cross-Cultural Psychological Assessment.* Pretoria, S. Africa: Hum. Sci. Res. Council. 207 pp.

Reyes-Lagunes, I., Poortinga, Y. H., ed. 1985. *From a Different Perspective: Studies of Behavior Across Cultures.* Lisse: Swets & Zeitlinger. 390 pp.

Rodrigues, A., Iwawaki, S. 1986. Testing the validity of different models of interpersonal balance in the Japanese culture. *Psychologia* 29:123–31

Rogoff, B. 1986. Adult assistance of children's learning. In *The Contexts of School-Based Literacy,* ed. T. E. Raphail, pp. 27–40. New York: Random House

Rogoff, B. 1987. The joint socialization of development by young children and adults. In *Social Influences and Behavior,* ed. M. Lewis, S. Feinman. New York: Plenum

Rogoff, B., Mistry, J. 1985a. A cultural perspective on the development of talent. In *The Gifted and Talented: Developmental Perspectives,* ed. F. D. Horowitz, M. O'Brien. Washington, DC: Am. Psychol. Assoc. Press

Rogoff, B., Mistry, J. 1985b. Memory development in cultural context.. In *Cognitive Learning and Memory in Children,* ed. M. Pressley, C. Brainerd, pp. 117–41. New York: Springer

Rohner, R. P. 1986. *The Warmth Dimension.* Beverly Hills: Sage

Rohner, R. P., Chaki-Sircar, M. 1987. Caste differences in perceived maternal acceptance in West Bengal, India. *Ethos.* 15:406–20

Rohner, R. P., Pettengill, S. A. 1985. Perceived parental acceptance-rejection and parental control among Korean adolescents. *Child Dev.* 56:524–28

Rosenstein, E. 1985. Cooperativeness and advancement of managers: an international perspective. *Hum. Relat.* 38:1–21

Rosenthal, D., Hrynerich, C. 1985. Ethnicity and ethnic identity: a comparative study of Greek-, Italian-, and Anglo-Australian adolescents. *Int. J. Psychol.* 20:723–42

Rudmin, F. 1987. History of cross-cultural psychology: comments on the role of historical research upon cross-cultural psychology. *Cross-Cult. Psychol. Bull.* 21:12–14

Rushton, J. P. 1985. Differential K theory: the sociobiology of individual and group differences. *Pers. Individ. Differ.* 6:441–52

Rushton, J. P. 1988. Race differences in behaviour: a review and evolutionary analysis. *Pers. Individ. Differ.* 9:In press

Rustemli, A. 1986. Male and female personal space needs and escape reactions under intrusion: a Turkish sample. *Int. J. Psychol.* 20:503–11

Sabatier, C. 1986. La mère et son bébé: Variations cultureles. Analyse critique de la litterature. *J. Int. Psychol.* 21:503–11

Saco-Pollitt, C., Pollitt, E., Greenfield, D. 1985. The cumulative deficit hypothesis in the light of cross-cultural evidence. *Int. J. Behav. Dev.* 8:75–97

Saiyadain, M. S. 1985. Personal characteristics and job satisfaction: India-Nigeria comparison. *Int. J. Psychol.* 20:143–53

Salama, M. M. 1987. Perceived parental acceptance-rejection and personality dispositions among college students in Egypt. See Kagitcibasi 1987a, pp. 181–88

Sampson, E. E. 1985. The decentralization of identity: toward a revised concept of personal and social order. *Am. Psychol.* 40:1203–11

Sampson, E. E. 1987. Individualization and domination: undermining the social bond. See Kagitcibasi 1987a, pp. 84–93

Samuda,, R., Wolfgang, A. 1985. *Intercultural Counselling and Assessment*. Toronto: Hogrefe. 408 pp.

Sanyal, K. R. 1986. Socialization and personality variables: a study of two cultural groups. *Indian Psychol. Rev.* 30:17–21

Saraswathi, T. S., Dutta, R. 1987a. *Developmental Psychology in India, 1975–1986: An Annotated Bibliography*. New Delhi: Sage

Saraswathi, T. S., Dutta, R. 1987b. Cross-cultural research in developmental psychology: retrospect and prospects in India. See Kagitcibasi 1987a, pp. 148–58

Sartorius, N., Jablensky, A., Korten, A., Ernberg, G., Anker, M., et al. 1986. Early manifestations and first contact incidence of schizophrenia in different cultures. *Psychol. Med.* 16:909–28

Schlegel, A. 1986. *Cross-cultural Studies of Gender*. Presented at 8th Int. Assoc. Cross-Cult. Psychol. Conf., Istanbul

Schlegel, A., Barry, H. 1986. The cultural consequences of female contribution to subsistence. *Am. Anthropol.* 88:142–50

Schwartz, S. H., Bilsky, W. 1987. Toward a universal psychological structure of human values. *J. Pers. Soc. Psychol.* 53:550–62

Scott, N. A., Stumpt, J. 1984. Personal satisfaction and role performance: subjective and social aspects of adaptation. *J. Pers. Soc. Psychol.* 47:812–26

Seddon, G. M., Nicholson, J. R. 1985. Developmental trends in the ability of primary school children to contruct models from diagrams. *Educ. Psychol.* 5:55–64

Segall, M. H. 1986. Culture and behavior: psychology in global perspective. *Ann. Rev. Psychol.* 37:523–64

Segall, M. H. 1988. Psychocultural antecedents of male aggression: some implications involving gender, parenting and adolescence. See Dasen et al 1988, pp. 71–92

Semin, G. R., Chassein, J. 1985. The relationship between higher order models and everyday conceptions of personality. *Eur. J. Soc. Psychol.* 15:1–15

Serpell, R. 1988. Childhood disability in the sociocultural context. See Dasen et al 1988, pp. 256–80

Shand, N. 1985. Culture's influence in Japanese and American maternal role perception and confidence. *Psychiatry* 48:51–67

Shand, N., Kosawa, Y. 1985. Culture transmission: Caudell's model and alternative hypotheses. *Am. Anthropol.* 87:862–71

Shapurian, R., Hojat, M. 1985. Sexual and premarital attitudes of Iranian college students. *Psychol. Rep.* 57:67–74

Shweder, R. A., Bourn, E. J. 1984. Does the concept of the person vary cross-culturally?

See Shweder & LeVine 1984, pp. 158–99

Shweder, R., LeVine, R., eds. 1984. *Culture Theory*. New York: Cambridge Univ. Press

Simons, R. C., Hughes, C. C., eds. 1985. *The Culture-Bound Syndromes—Folk Illnesses of Psychiatric and Anthropological Interest*. Boston: Reidel

Sinha, D. 1986. *Psychology in a Third World Country: The Indian Experience*. New Delhi: Sage. 160 pp.

Sinha, D. 1988. The family scenario in a developing country, and its implication for mental health: the case of India. See Dasen et al 1988, pp. 48–70

Sinha, D., Bharat, S. 1985. Three types of family structure and psychological differentiation: a study among the Jaunsar-Bawar society. *Int. J. Psychol.* 20:693–708

Sinha, J. B. P. 1985a. Psychic relevance of work in Indian culture. *Dynam. Psychiatry* 2:134–41

Sinha, J. B. P. 1985b. Collectivism, social energy, and development in India. See Reyes-Lagunes & Poortinga 1985, pp. 109–19

Sinha, J. B. P. 1986. Work-related values and climate factors. *Int. Rev. Appl. Psychol.* 35:63–78

Sinha, J. B. P., Verma, J. 1987. Structure of collectivism. See Kagitcibasi 1987, pp. 123–29

Sinha, S. R. 1985. Maternal strategies for regulating children's behavior. *J. Cross-Cult. Psychol.* 16:27–40

Smith, M. B. 1987. *Identity and selfhood in corrosive times*. Presented at Am. Psychol. Assoc., New York.

Snarey, J. R. 1985. Cross-cultural universality of social-moral development: a critical review of Kohlbergian research. *Psychol. Bull.* 97:202–32

Snarey, J. R., Reimer, J., Kohlberg, L. 1985. Development of social-moral reasoning among kibbutz adolescents: a longitudinal cross-cultural study. *Dev. Psychol.* 21:3–17

Spector, P. E., Wimalasiri, J. 1986. A cross-cultural comparison of job satisfaction dimensions in the United States and Singapore. *Int. Rev. Appl. Psychol.* 35:147–58

Spence, J. 1985. Achievement American style: the rewards and costs of individualism. *Am. Psychol.* 40:1285–95

Sternberg, R., Wagner, R., eds. 1986. *Practical Intelligence: Nature and Origins of Competence in the Everyday World*. New York: Cambridge Univ. Press. 386 pp.

Stigler, J., Lee, S.-Y., Stevenson, H. 1986. Digit memory in Chinese and English: evidence for a temporally limited store. *Cognition* 23:1–20

Sullivan, J. J., Suzuki, T., Kondo, Y. 1986. Managerial perceptions of performance. *J. Cross-Cult. Psychol.* 17:379–98

Sun, F., Morita, M., Stark, L. 1985. Comparative patterns of reading eye movement in Chinese and English. *Percept. Psychophys.* 37:502–6

Sunar, D. 1988. Attitudes of Turkish students toward the aged. *J. Cross-Cult. Gerontology.* In press

Super, C. M., Harkness, S. 1986. The developmental niche: a conceptualization at the interface of child and culture. *Int. J. Behav. Dev.* 9:545–70

Suvannathat, C., Bhanthumnavin, D., Bhuapirom, L., Keats, D. M., eds. 1985. *Handbook of Asian Child Rearing Practices.* Bangkok: Srinakharinwirot Univ.

Swartz, L. 1985. Anorexia nervosa as a culture-bound syndrome. *Soc. Sci. Med.* 20:725–30

Taft, R. 1985. The psychological study of the adjustment and adaptation of immigrants in Australia. In *Survey of Australian Psychology,* ed. N. T. Feather. Sydney: Allen & Unwin

Taft, R. 1986. Methodological considerations in the study of immigrant adaptations in Australia. *Aust. J. Psychol.* 38:339–46

Takahashi, K. 1986. Examining the strange-situation procedure with Japanese mothers and 12-month-old infants. *Dev. Psychol.* 22:265–70

Tang, S. F. Y., Kirkbride, P. S. 1986. Developing conflict management skills in Hong Kong: an analysis of some cross-cultural implication. *Manag. Educ. Dev.* 17:287–301

Ten Houten, W. 1985. Right hemisphericity of Australian Aboriginal children. *Int. J. Neurosci.* 28:125–46

Tetlock, P. E. 1986. Is self-categorization theory the solution to the level-of-analysis problem? *Br. J. Soc. Psychol.* 25:255–56

Thissen, D., Steinberg, L., Gerrard, M. 1986. Beyond group mean differences: the concept of item bias. *Psychol. Bull.* 99:118–28

Tietjen, A. M., Walker, L. J. 1985. Moral reasoning and leadership among men in Papua New Guinea society. *Dev. Psychol.* 21:982–92

Toelken, B. 1985. "Turkenrein" and "Turken, Raus!"—Images of fear and aggression in German Gastarbeiterwitze. In *Turkish Workers in Europe,* ed. I. Basgoz, N. Furniss, pp. 151–65. Bloomington: Indiana Univ. Press

Torki, A. M. 1985. Achievement motivation in college women in an Arab culture. *Psychol. Rep.* 56:267–71

Triandis, H. C., Lambert, W. W., Berry, J. W., Lonner, W. J., Heron, A., Brislin, R. W., Draguns, J., eds. 1980. *Handbook of Cross-Cultural Psychology.* Boston: Allyn & Bacon. 6 Vol.

Triandis, H. C., Leung, K., Villareal, N. J.,

Clack, F. L. 1985. Allocentric versus idiocentric tendencies: convergent and discriminant validation. *J. Res. Pers.* 19:395–415

Triandis, H. C., Kashima, Y., Shimada, E., Villareal, M. 1986a. Acculturation indices as a means of confirming cultural differences. *Int. J. Psychol.* 21:43–70

Triandis, H. C., Bontempo, R., Betancourt, H., Bond, M., Leung, K., et al. 1986b. The measurement of the etic aspects of individualism and collectivism across cultures. *Aust. J. Psychol.* 38:257–68

Triandis, H. C., Bontempo, R., Villareal, M. J., Asai, M., Lucca, N. 1987. Individualism and collectivism: cross-cultural perspectives on self-group relationships. *J. Pers. Soc. Psychol.* 54:323–38

Trommsdorff, G. 1985a. Some comparative aspects of socialization in Japan and Germany. See Reyes-Lagunes & Poortinga 1985, pp. 231–40

Trommsdorff, G., 1985b. German cross-cultural psychology. *Ger. J. Psychol.* 10:240–66

Trompenaars, A. M. R. 1985. *The organization of meaning and the meaning of organization: a comparative study on the concepts of organizational structure in different cultures.* PhD thesis. Univ. Penn.

Tseng, W.-S., Xu, D., Keisuke, E., Jing, H., Cui, Y. 1986. Diagnostic patterns for neurosis in China, Japan and the United States. *Am. J. Psychiat.* 143:1010–14

Turner, J. C., Oakes, P. J. 1986. The significance of the social identity concept for social psychology with reference to individualism, interactionism and social influence. *Br. J. Soc. Psychol.* 25:237–52

Tyler, F. B., Sinha, Y. 1988. Psychosocial competence and belief systems. *Gen. Soc. Gen. Psychol. Monogr.* 114:33–49

Tyler, F.B., Verma, M. 1988. Help-seeking and helping behavior in children as a function of psychosocial competence. *J. Appl. Dev. Psychol.* In press

Tzeng, O. C. S., Everett, A. V. 1985. A cross-cultural perspective of self-related conceptions in adolescence. *Int. J. Psychol.* 20:329–48

van de Koppel, J. M. H., ed. 1985. *Verkenningen in de Cross-Culturele Psychologie.* Lisse: Swets and Zeitlinger. 268 pp.

van de Vijver, F., Daal, M., van Zonnonfeld, R. 1986. The trainability of formal thinking: a cross-cultural comparison. *Int. J. Psychol.* 21:589–615

Verma, J. 1985. The ingroup and its relevance to individual behavior: a study of collectivism and individualism. *Psychologia* 28:173–81

Vernon, P. A., Jackson, D. N., Messick, S.

1988. Cultural influences on patterns of abilities in North America. See Irvine & Berry 1988, pp. 208–31

Vernon, P. E. 1982. *The Abilities and Achievements of the Orientals in North America.* New York: Academic. 321 pp.

Verster, J. 1987. Human cognition and intelligence: towards an integrated theoretical perspective. See Irvine & Newstead 1987, pp. 27–139

Wagner, D. A. 1986. Child development research and the Third World. *Am. Psychol.* 41:298–301

Wagner, D. A. 1987. Le développement precoce de la memoirs specialisée. *Eur. J. Congit. Psychol.* 7:57–74

Wagner, D. 1988. "Appropriate education" and literacy in the Third World. See Dasen et al 1988, pp. 93–111

Ward, C. 1985. Sex trait stereotypes in Malaysian children. *Sex Roles* 12:35–45

Ward, C. 1987. Mid-life crisis in women—a cross-cultural phenomenon? See Kagitcibasi 1987A, pp. 218–26

Ward, C., ed. 1988. *Altered State of Consciousness and Mental Health: A Cross-Cultural Perspective.* Newbury Park: Sage. 360 pp.

Ward, C., Sethi, R. R. 1986. Cross-cultural validation of the Bem Sex Role Inventory. *J. Cross-Cult. Psychol.* 17:300–14

Warner, R. L., Lee, G. R., Lee, J. 1986. Social organization, spousal resources and marital power: a cross-cultural study. *J. Marr. Fam.* 48:121–28

Weinberg, S. J. 1985. *Decision making style of Japanese and American managers.* PhD thesis. Calif. Sch. Prof. Psychol., Los Angeles

Weinreich, P. 1986. Identity development: theory and practice. See Ekstrand 1986, pp. 230–39

West, J. 1987. Psychotherapy in the Eastern Province of Saudi Arabia. *Psychotherapy* 24:105–7

Westen, D. 1985. *Self and Society.* New York: Cambridge Univ. Press

Westermeyer, J. 1985. Psychiatric diagnosis across cultural boundaries. *Am. J. Psychiatr.* 142:798–805

Westermeyer, J. 1987a. Cultural factors in clinical assessment. *J. Consult. Clin. Psychol.* 55:471–78

Westermeyer, J. 1987b. Prevention of mental disorder among refugees in the US: lessons from the period 1976–1986. *Soc. Sci. Med.* 25:941–47

Wheeless, L. R., Erickson, K. V., Behrens, S. J. 1986. Cultural differences in disclosiveness as a function of locus of control. *Commun. Monogr.* 53:36–46

White, G. M., Kirkpatrick, J., ed. 1985. *Person, Self, and Experience-Exploring Pacific Ethnopsychologies.* Berkeley: Univ. Calif. Press

Whitford, J. D. 1985. *Historia de la Psicologia en Nicaragua.* Managua: Nicaragua Libre. 109 pp.

Williams, C. 1985. The Southeast Asian refugees and community mental health. *J. Commun. Psychol.* 13:258–69

Williams, C., Westermeyer, J., eds. 1986. *Refugee Mental Health in Resettlement Countries.* Washington: Hemisphere. 267 pp.

Williams, J. E., Pandey, J., Best, D. L., Morton, K. R., Pande, N. 1987. Young adults' views of old adults in India and the USA. See Kagitcibasi 1987a, pp. 227–34

Williams, J. E., Best, D. L. 1988. *Sex and Psyche: Gender Roles and Self Concept Viewed Cross-Culturally.* Newbury Park, CA: Sage

Yamasaki, K. 1985. On development of drawing a square from a cross-cultural point of view. *Percept. Motor Skills* 61:755–60

Yu, A., Bain, B. 1985. *Language, Social Class and Cognitive Style: A Comparative Study of Unilingual and Bilingual Education in Hong Kong and Alberta.* Hong Kong: Teachers' Association. 206 pp.

Zavalloni, M., Louis-Guerin, C. 1984. *Identité social et conscience: Introduction à l'égo-écologie.* Montreal: Presse de l'Université de Montreal.

Zebrowitz-McArthur, L. 1988. Person perception in cross-cultural perspective. See Bond 1988

Zeidner, M., Nevo, B. 1987. The cross-cultural generalizability of moral reasoning research: some Israeli data. *Int. J. Psychol.* 22:315–30

Ann. Rev. Psychol. 1989. 40:533–79

HEALTH PSYCHOLOGY

Judith Rodin and Peter Salovey

Department of Psychology, Yale University, New Haven, Connecticut 06520

CONTENTS

Americans currently spend over $400 billion dollars annually on health care—11% of the Gross National Product (Taylor 1987). This figure does not include such health-relevant expenses as health club memberships, special foods, vitamins, stripping asbestos insulation from the home, or installing air bags in the car. In this social and economic context, behavioral medicine and health psychology have become "buzz words for the 1980s" (Pomerleau & Rodin 1986, p. 483). While some continue to deny the importance of psychosocial variables in health and disease (Angell 1985), most investigators in this area believe that behavioral science knowledge and techniques can contribute to the understanding of physical health and illness (Schwartz & Weiss 1977) by complementing biomedical knowledge and applications.

0066-4308/89/0201-0533$02.00

Behavioral medicine has been defined as the integration of behavioral science approaches with biomedical knowledge and techniques (Schwartz & Weiss 1978) and as the application of behavioral therapies to medical disorders (Pomerleau & Brady 1979). Surwit et al (1983) suggest that behavioral medicine applies to all medical disorders, not just those defined as psychological or psychophysiological in nature. *Health psychology* has been defined as the aggregate of the knowledge base of psychology applied to the understanding of health and illness (Matarazzo 1984). As the disciplines have matured, less attention has been paid to distinguishing one from the other or either from the approach of the medical sciences. Rather, self-defining attention is now paid to practical issues, such as education and training (Taylor 1987), integration with other clinical approaches (Pomerleau & Rodin 1986), and cost-effectiveness (Taylor 1987); and to theoretical issues, such as additive vs interactional models (Cohen & Wills 1985) and the role of applied settings in developing rather than merely testing theory (Rodin 1985).

Another indication of the maturation of the disciplines is reflected in the *Annual Review* chapters covering this area. In the first (Miller 1983), studies were reviewed that attempted to convince the skeptical medical disciplines that psychosocial and behavioral variables influence onset, maintenance, and treatment of disease. Although the skepticism still remained in some quarters (Angell 1985), the second *Annual Review* chapter, appearing in the same year as the Angell editorial in the *New England Journal of Medicine,* presented substantial data indicating not only the role of behavior in health and illness but some mechanisms linking psychosocial variables to these outcomes (Krantz et al 1985). The studies covered in the present review provide further and more detailed evidence for the nature of the physiological mechanisms relating psychosocial and behavioral variables to health and illness, and suggest possible interactions among these variables.

In order to summarize this literature and to highlight further the utility of an approach that emphasizes process models and interactions among variables because of the complex and multiply determined factors that lead to health and illness, we have organized the chapter as follows: First, we describe a group of independent variables shown to correlate most strongly with health and illness outcomes. These include (*a*) dispositional variables, such as the Type A behavior pattern; (*b*) cognitive factors, such as representations and appraisals of illness; (*c*) social environment variables, including social support; and (*d*) sociocultural variables such as age, gender, ethnicity, and poverty. These variables appear to influence health and disease outcomes either directly or because they influence the second category of variables described below.

In the second section, we review specific behaviors that influence health and illness. These include (*a*) coping, (*b*) adherence, (*c*) substance use and abuse, and (*d*) exercise and other health behaviors. This group of health-promoting and health-damaging behaviors is not static. The behaviors fluctuate as a function of motivation, appraisal, social support, and the like. They are also influenced by acute situational variables, such as those covered in the third section. In the third section, we review studies suggesting that the most significant impact of behavioral and psychosocial variables on health and illness may be seen when the system is provoked. The two most widely studied provocative events have been stress in general, whether or not health-relevant, and being sick, in particular.

Finally, in the fourth section we cover the two groups of disease most widely studied in health psychology: cancers and coronary heart disease. We examine studies that consider the direct effects of many behavioral and psychosocial variables, but we emphasize those that posit interactions among them and that focus on explanatory mechanisms.

ANTECEDENT VARIABLES

Dispositional Variables and Health or Illness

Several possible links between personality and disease outcomes have been suggested (Friedman & Booth-Kewley 1987): (a) Certain aspects of personality might *result* from disease processes; (b) personality might cause disease by motivating unhealthy behaviors; (c) personality could affect disease directly through physiological mechanisms; (d) personality might be related to disease through an underlying biological third variable; and (e) a variety of different causal factors and feedback loops might be at work in the relationship between personality and disease. Conceptual distinctions among these alternatives have led to rich theoretical advances in recent years, as noted below.

In research on personality and disease, subjects cannot be randomly assigned a personality and then observed over time. Therefore, no single study can ever prove a causal link. Some of the strongest evidence for causal connections comes from physiological research that identifies disease mechanisms and shows how they are affected by personality variables through prospective studies. For example, the studies of Levy and coworkers (Levy et al 1985, 1987) prospectively consider the effects of personality and other psychosocial variables on a parameter of immune function, natural killer-cell activity, shown to be important in the progression of breast cancer. Problems still exist in the literature, however, because many personality constructs are still not well operationalized. In some efforts, diseases or health-related behaviors are implicitly construed as an external criterion to help anchor or validate current personality constructs (cf Bowers 1987). When these constructs are then used to predict the same or similar diseases or health-relevant behaviors, the logic becomes circular, hampering efforts to identify causal links.

Many methodologists have argued strongly for a trait taxonomy in the study of health and disease. Without a standard framework for identifying traits, two problems arise (Costa & McCrae 1987b). Scales that measure different underlying constructs may be given the same name (e.g. the Jenkins Activity Survey and the Structured Interview to measure Type A behavior). Scales that measure the same construct may also be given different names (e.g. neuroticism and anxiety), violating the requirement for discriminant validity. A variety of purportedly different traits may all essentially converge on the same underlying personality construct (e.g. hardiness, self-efficacy, learned resourcefulness, and internal health locus of control; or repression, denial, defensiveness, and blunting). Both issues continue to plague the field and weaken its conclusions.

TYPE A   The Type A Behavior Pattern (TABP) has been defined as an action-emotion complex (Rosenman et al, in press) involving (a) behavioral dispositions (e.g. ambitiousness, aggressiveness, competitiveness, and impatience), (b) specific behaviors (e.g. muscle tension, rapid and emphatic speech style, and accelerated pace of activities), and (c) emotional responses (e.g. irritation, hostility, and anger). Although many investigators have related the global TABP to chronic heart disease (CHD) end points (see Booth-Kewley & Friedman 1987 for review), in some studies 70–90% of the sample is labeled Type A (Dembroski & MacDougall 1983). Placing such large percentages of individuals in an at-risk category is inconsistent with sound epidemiological practice (Matthews & Haynes 1986).

A first step to resolving this confusion has been to recognize that not all components of the TABP may be coronary prone. A second step, and a more important one to issues of validity of the Type A construct, has been to refine assessment of the empirically different attributes contained in both the conceptual and operational definitions of the TABP (cf Costa et al 1986; Dembroski & Costa 1987). This effort has been problematic because the several different measures of TABP are only modestly correlated (Matthews 1982). In addition to the Structured Interview, based on diagnosis and quantitative assessment of behavior elicited in an interview format, no fewer than ten self-report questionnaires of varying complexity have been used for classifying the TABP (Friedman & Powell 1984). Many of these scales have not been validated as predictors of CHD, and most are distinct from the Structured Interview, which emphasizes behavioral signs indicating the presence of Type A rather than self-report of its consequences. The stability of Type A as measured by the Structured Interview has been high over at least a ten-year period (Carmelli et al in press).

The development of the Structured Interview reflected the belief that Type A is a set of overt behaviors manifested by people in certain situations and not others (Rosenman et al, 1988). Although many investigators have endorsed this perspective theoretically, they have largely ignored it at the level of assessment and intervention (Thoresen & Ohman 1986), a problem with personality typing generally. Ideally, an interactional analysis would require direct observation of the TABP over a range of unconstrained natural situations to determine which situational factors were particularly effective in eliciting Type A behavior (cf Magnussen 1983).

An opposing perspective views the TABP as a fixed personality trait, implying an underlying dimension ranging from Type B personality to Type A. Most current self-report measures share this perspective. A second problem inherent in the dispositional view of Type A is the identification of an appropriate threshold. Classification of Type A becomes tied to some cutoff level (Thoresen & Ohman 1986). This tendency to blur behaviors with traits has pervaded much of the debate about Type A. Nonetheless, as Engel (1986) noted, many investigators of Type A have failed to recognize that traits can be assessed by measuring behaviors.

The most promising avenue for using the TABP to predict CHD in recent years results from componential scoring of the Structured Interview. CHD among individuals under the age of 50 is predicted, for example, by the Structured Interview component score on "potential for hostility" but not by other components (Dembroski & Costa 1987). In fact, recent meta-analyses have suggested that anger generally is an important predictor of CHD (Booth-Kewley & Friedman 1987), and a scale to measure the components of anger has been developed (Spielberger et al 1985). Yet, anger is not measured directly by the scale most frequently employed to study hostility and CHD, the Cook-Medley (1954). The two factors in the Cook-Medley scales, cynicism and alienation, appear intercorrelated, and Costa et al (1986) have concluded that a better label for the two scales combined might be "cynical mistrust," since the total Cook-Medley "hostility" scale correlates .91 with the MMPI cynicism scale. Disappointingly, data from several studies suggest that hostility as measured by the Cook-Medley and behaviorally measured hostility are quite different (Matthews & Haynes 1986).

Children and adolescents have been studied to clarify the Type A syndrome. Most psychophysiologic studies show that Type A children are more reactive to stress than non-Type A children (Matthews & Woodall, in press). In general, boys are more likely than girls to model the Type A behavior of their parents. The competitive aspect of Type A apparently leads to early and important achievements independent of ability, perhaps because caregivers and teachers respond to Type A behaviors in children by encouraging them to continue to strive to achieve (Matthews et al 1986a). Parents of Type A children appear to do the same (Bracke 1985). From these data it appears that Type A develops as an interaction between constitutional predisposition and parenting styles (Matthews & Woodall, in press; Thoresen & Patillo, in press).

BOLSTERING DISPOSITIONS   Several somewhat overlapping personality variables, all focusing on individuals' abilities to respond to difficulties in optimistic, persistent, and flexible ways, have been studied in relation to positive health outcomes. Viewing them together in this broader theoretical framework may have greater heuristic value in predicting health outcomes. One of these constructs—hardiness (Kobasa 1982)—is a composite of commitment, control, and challenge, each measured empirically by several scales. Studies of the stress-buffering role of hardiness are contradictory (Kobasa et al 1983; Ganellen & Blaney 1984; Schmied & Lawler 1986). These inconsistent results may be partly attributable to the construct validity and stability of the factor structure in the hardiness measure (Funk & Houston 1987; Hull et al 1987). Scheier & Carver (1987) have suggested that aspects of hardiness serve as a buffer against stress merely because of the undercurrent of optimism in certain constituents. Alternatively, it may turn out that one or another of the variables presently confounded in the hardiness construct, such as internal/external control, will prove to be a critical mediator (Funk & Houston 1987; Hull et al 1987).

In arguing for a more generic construct of optimism (measured by the LOT; Scheier & Carver 1985), Scheier & Carver (1987) have suggested that differences in well-being between optimists and pessimists could derive from the way individuals select and use the general strategies for coping available to everyone. For example, optimists appear to display coping patterns that involve continued positive striving and making the best of whatever situations they confront. The second possibility is that optimism/pessimism differences directly affect physiological functioning. For example, Van Treuren & Hull (1986) suggested that optimists show less cardiovascular reactivity to stress.

Optimism and pessimism have also been studied from an attribution/ learned-helplessness perspective. Peterson & Seligman (1987) posit that attributional dimensions influence one or more manifestations of helplessness. The emphasis on attributions as a determinant of expectancies is one difference between the theory of optimism/pessimism discussed above and Seligman's view of this construct. In other words, in attribution research, explanatory style is measured rather than expectations per se, and optimistic/ pessimistic expectations are inferred from the explanatory style. Peterson, Seligman, and their colleagues have developed two ways of measuring explanatory style, a self-report questionnaire called the Attributional Style Questionnaire (ASQ; Peterson & Villanova 1988) and a content analysis procedure called the CAVE (Peterson et al 1983). Some studies report inverse correlations between pessimistic explanatory style (the use of causal explanations focusing on internal, stable, and global factors for negative events) and physical well-being (reviewed in Peterson & Seligman 1987).

Other research has emphasized perceived self-efficacy as a mechanism linking psychosocial influences to health (Bandura 1986; O'Leary 1985a), and theoretical developments in efficacy have been advanced by application to the health domain (Litt 1988). There is no generic self-efficacy questionnaire. Rather, a set of specific efficacy judgments is developed for each experimental context regarding the necessary behaviors in a specific domain. For this reason, measures of self-efficacy are typically good predictors of behavior (e.g. Bandura & Schunk 1981).

Perceived self-efficacy may affect physiological systems that mediate health functioning. Bandura et al (1985) found that under conditions of phobic threat, self-doubts regarding coping efficacy produced substantial increases in circulating catecholamines. Catecholamine secretion declined as phobics gained mastery over phobic threats through guided mastery treatment. In arthritic patients, perceived coping efficacy was associated with increases in the number of suppressor T cells, which inhibit production of antibodies (O'Leary 1985b). Others have suggested that perceived self-efficacy may be linked to health-promoting and health-impairing behavior (e.g. Kaplan et al 1984).

DIFFICULTIES WITH EMOTIONAL EXPRESSION   Alexithymia, an inability to use language to describe emotional experiences (Apfel & Sifneos 1979; Ahrens & Deffner 1986), has been linked to a variety of psychosomatic disorders—e.g. chronic pain (Acklin & Bernat 1987) and respiratory disorders (Sifneos 1973). However, a reliable and valid instrument for assessing this deficit has yet to be developed. Some investigators have found alexithymia related to a variety of disease states (e.g. hypertension; Fava et al 1980); others have reported weaker findings (Heiberg 1980; Kleiger & Dirks 1980).

Another aspect of difficulty with emotional expression has been termed the repressive personality style, characterized by avoidance of potentially threatening social encounters or lines of associative thought that might lead to conscious conflict or embarrassing experience (Bonanno & Singer, in press). The repressor style was extensively explored in studies initiated by Byrne et al (1963) and has more recently been revived with greater emphasis on its psychophysiological components by Weinberger, Schwartz, and their collaborators (Weinberger, in press). Weinberger et al (1979) use a combination of the Taylor Manifest Anxiety Scale (Taylor 1953) and the Marlowe-Crowne Social Desirability Scale (Crowne & Marlowe 1964) to measure repression. Repressors on these measures report low anxiety but high defensiveness (i.e. social desirability). The combined method of measuring repression proposed by Weinberger has been criticized on the grounds that the Marlowe-Crowne as originally intended is not a measure of defensiveness but of social desirability [but see the discussion of measurement issues in Weinberger (in press)]. Self-deception or repression is indicated by subjects' refusal to endorse these items. Temoshok (1985) has proposed a Type C behavioral pattern, reflecting inability to express emotion, particularly negative emotion, in an open fashion, and has related it to health end points (Temoshok 1987).

Although the Weinberger et al (1979) study emphasized blood pressure reactivity under stress among repressors, the bulk of the literature in recent years has explored the effects of difficulty in emotional expression on the immune system. Levy and her coworkers have suggested effects on natural killer-cell activity as a function of this constellation of personality variables (Levy et al 1987). This group of investigators and Jensen (1987) have also related the repressive style to breast cancer progression.

It has been suggested that anxiety may underlie all of these difficulties with emotional expression—denial, repression, suppression, and alexithymia (Friedman & Booth-Kewley 1987). Watson & Pennebaker (in press) come to the more general conclusion that a common underlying disposition of somatopsychic distress called negative affectivity accounts for the correlation of physical symptoms and negative emotion.

Cognitive Activities

Individuals' thoughts and beliefs influence their responses to situations in which health is salient. In earlier decades, these beliefs were studied in a framework called the Health Beliefs Model and characterized by dimensions concerning perceived susceptibility, severity, benefits, and barriers (see review by Janz & Becker 1984). More recently, these beliefs have been organized according to strategies suggested by social cognition researchers, allowing the opportunity for researchers in the area of health psychology to benefit from and contribute to the rich theoretical developments in the field of cognition.

MENTAL REPRESENTATIONS OF ILLNESS   According to Leventhal and colleagues, people evaluate a physiological perturbation or symptom against an implicit or "commonsense" cognitive representation of illness, unique to each individual, that includes expectations about illness and examples of particular diseases. Respondents typically construct a mental representation of their physical problems containing four attributes: (a) identity (label and symptoms), (b) cause, (c) consequences, and (d) timeline (Leventhal et al 1980). Lau & Hartman (1983) have added a fifth dimension, cure. A slightly different set of illness attributes was recently suggested by Turk et al (1985), including seriousness, personal responsibility, controllability, and changeability. This approach has been applied to individuals' understanding of hypertension (Baumann & Leventhal 1985; Meyer et al 1985), cancer (Nerenz 1979), and aging (Prohaska et al 1987).

A different method for understanding mental representations of illness has been suggested by Bishop and colleagues (Bishop 1987; Bishop & Converse

1986), who believe that lay people cognitively organize and recall information about physical symptoms according to disease prototypes. The prototype approach differs somewhat from the dimensional approach in that it posits the existence of concrete instances (e.g. specific diseases) rather than generalized abstractions (e.g. illness schemas). Common disease prototypes exist for frequently occurring diseases, for diseases portrayed in the popular media, and for diseases that present clear and obvious symptoms. These disease prototypes may help individuals to understand bodily changes and symptoms because they provide ready-made interpretations for given internal experiences and help the individual to access other information about his or her condition (Bishop & Converse 1986).

Attributions regarding health and illness are another type of mental representation. Attributions here are causal inferences people make about events or states of being (Jones et al 1972). Individuals attribute responsibility for the onset and course of illness to themselves or to the environment (Brickman et al 1982). Studies suggest that these attributions affect health outcomes through a variety of mechanisms. For example, Taylor et al (1984b) found that the belief that one had personal control over the progression of cancer was associated with better adjustment, although attributions of responsibility for the cause of the cancer itself were not associated with more positive outcomes. Attributional processes also affect coping by influencing how individuals understand their role in the illness itself (Tennen et al 1986). Attributional processes also play a role in the interpretation of physical symptoms (Michela & Wood 1986).

PERCEPTIONS OF RISK AND VULNERABILITY   Perhaps as a result of attributional processes, individuals tend to underestimate their own risk relative to other people for illnesses and other negative life events (Kirscht et al 1966; Weinstein 1984). This unrealistic optimism can have important health consequences. Beliefs concerning increased susceptibility to an illness are generally associated with greater interest in prevention and learning prevention behaviors (Cummings et al 1979; Weinstein 1983), although there are exceptions (Joseph et al 1987).

Several factors affect these perceptions of vulnerability. Individuals who have not experienced major negative life events tend to see themselves as especially invulnerable (Perloff & Fetzer 1986). Conversely, sick individuals view their risk of future illness as similar to (rather than less likely than) that of their peers, but they still see themselves as relatively invulnerable to other kinds of negative events (Jemmott et al 1988; Kulik & Mahler 1987). This "false consensus" bias (Ross et al 1977) extends to initiation of health-relevant behaviors. When compared with their nonsmoking peers, adolescents who were smokers or who intended to smoke greatly overestimated the prevalence of adult or peer smoking and greatly underestimated negative adult attitudes toward smoking. Adolescents who intended to smoke believed they would be less likely than others to contract a smoking-related illness if they became smokers (Leventhal et al 1987). Finally, risk estimates are influenced by mood. Dysphoric affect tends to make individuals believe that future victimizations are more likely (Johnson & Tversky 1983; Salovey & Birnbaum 1988).

Awareness and acceptance of information also vary with motivational status. A compelling example is provided by Wagener & Taylor (1986), who discovered that failed renal transplant patients recalled the circumstances of their original decision to have the transplant as involving less personal responsibility than did successful transplant patients. These individuals recalled that they had little choice but to make the decision they had made. Perhaps the emerging interest in motivational influences on social cognition will provide the framework for investigating such mechanisms (Showers & Cantor 1985; Sorrentino & Higgins 1986).

CONTROL   The cognitive activities discussed thus far may all serve to help individuals feel in control of their lives and futures. Control, or perceived mastery over one's circumstances, can be thought of as a basic human motivation (Rodin et al 1986). The presence or absence of a sense of control has a profound influence on individuals' emotional, cognitive, and physical well-being (Rodin 1986a). Efforts to link loss of control and hopelessness to the development of illness were pioneered by Engel and Schmale (Engel 1968; Schmale 1972). More recent work has emphasized a potentially important role for loss of control in cancer (Visintainer et al 1982) and cardiovascular disease (Frankenhaueser 1986a; Matthews 1982).

Numerous mechanisms could mediate the effects of control on health (see Rodin 1986b for review): stress reduction (Lazarus & DeLongis 1983; Rodin et al 1982), increased noticing of symptoms (Pennebaker 1982), direct physiological effects on the immune system (Laudenslager et al 1983; Rodin 1986b; Stein et al 1982) and neuroendocrine system (Frankenhaeuser 1986a), and increased health-enhancing actions (Ewart et al 1984; Manning & Wright 1983).

Many of the health-relevant variables discussed in this review interact with control to influence health and disease outcomes. Lower levels of work stress, for example, result from the ability to exert control (Frankenhaeuser 1986b). Type A individuals appear particularly vulnerable to physiological ill-effects of uncontrollable events, and hypertensives appear relatively unable to profit from the beneficial effects of personal control (Frankenhaeuser 1986a).

Resources from the Social Environment

Health and illness are influenced by resources from the social environment, most notably spouses and close others, family members, and the workplace.

Each of these aspects of the social environment has some impact on the health of the individual, but, reciprocally, an individual's health influences the thoughts and behaviors of significant others and, perhaps, alters the work environment as well.

SOCIAL SUPPORT   For several years, social scientists have noticed that physical and psychological illnesses are more prevalent in communities in which social ties and networks are disrupted by changes in employment patterns, migration, aging, and death. It was felt that something about the social context of the individual had a profound impact on that individual's health and well-being (Caplan 1974; Cassel 1976; Cobb 1976). The process by which the social context influences the individual has been termed "social support," defined as the resources provided by other persons (Cohen & Syme 1985).

It might seem obvious that support from others should improve health and adjustment to illness, but the research literature is mixed. In general, social support provides relief from psychological distress during crises (Holahan & Moos 1986; Sarason & Sarason 1985). Social support may (Berkman & Syme 1979) or may not (Wallston et al 1983) directly inhibit the development of illness. Once an individual is ill, social support plays an important and positive role in promoting adjustment and recovery (DiMatteo & Hays 1981; Wortman 1984).

Theoretical developments have included better specification of the mechanisms by which social support may influence health, either through direct or buffering effects (e.g. Cohen & Syme 1985). By being integrated into a social network, individuals may experience greater positive affect, higher self-esteem, or feel more in control of environmental changes (all direct effects). Each of these cognitive factors might then protect an individual from physical illness through a variety of physiological mechanisms (e.g. immune system functioning; Jemmott & Locke 1984) or by encouraging the individual to make healthy life-style changes. At a more general level, social support via an integrated social network may have direct effects on health by providing the individual with a predictable set of role relationships, a positive social identity, and experiences of mastery and control (Thoits 1983, 1985). In comparison, social support could play a role in buffering the impact of negative events and other stressors by eliminating or reducing the stressor itself, bolstering the ability of the individual to cope with the stressor, or by attenuating the experience of distress after it has already been triggered (Cohen & McKay 1984; Gore 1981; House 1981). Direct effects are more likely to be obtained when support is defined as the degree to which a person is integrated into social networks; buffering effects are typically discovered when support is operationalized as the social resources available to one undergoing stressful events (Cohen & Syme 1985; Kessler & McLeod 1985; Wethington & Kessler 1986).

Social support research, although certainly flourishing, has been hindered by difficulties in measuring support (House et al 1988). Cohen & Syme (1985) concluded that there are "almost as many measures [of social support] as studies" (p. 14). Bruhn & Philips (1984) reported on 14 strategies for measuring social support, but noted that basic psychometric properties for more than half of these have never been investigated. Among the more promising (and reliable) techniques for measuring social support are as-sessment via family and work environment scales (Billings & Moos 1982), social relationship scales (Schaefer et al 1981), and direct self-report (Wilcox 1981).

Kessler et al (1985) note that one of the reasons why the relationship between social support and health may be complicated is that those in greatest need of support from others may be least able to obtain it. Individuals with severe health problems, because they increase others' sense of vulnerability, may be seen as threatening, particularly if others are worried about experienc-ing a similar fate—e.g. when the disease has a poor prognosis (Peters-Golden 1982).

Social support may also play a role in promoting illness or maladaptive behaviors. Adolescent substance abuse, for example, is often encouraged and reinforced by similar behavior among the child's peer group (e.g. Kandel & Maloff 1984). Even in adults, the perception of a supportive community may delay or prevent consultation with medical professionals (Pilisuk et al 1987). Moreover, network size can exert a negative influence on adhering to be-havioral regimens necessary for the management of chronic diseases like diabetes (Kaplan & Hartwell 1987).

MARRIAGE AND FAMILY   Perhaps the most important source of social support is one's spouse and family, and the loss of social support resulting from the death of one's spouse is a significant stressor (Osterweis et al 1984). Adjustment following illness onset is influenced by successful marital adjust-ment and general support by the spouse (Morris 1979; Vess et al 1985a, b). Additionally, a stable and happy marital relationship may have a preventive effect on future illness. Kiecolt-Glaser and her colleagues (1987), for ex-ample, have reported that poor marital quality is associated with poorer immune function. Similarly, chronically ill individuals who have the active support and participation of their spouses in treatment may show better adjustment and faster recovery (Taylor et al 1985).

Although poor marital quality has been associated with negative health outcomes, it has been more difficult to demonstrate that family functioning in general is related to health and illness (Brown et al 1982). More research attention, instead, has been directed toward the consequences of illness for marital relations and family functioning (reviewed below).

WORK ENVIRONMENTS   A variety of aspects of work have an important impact on health, including (*a*) physical, chemical, and biological hazards; (*b*) the physical demands of a given job; (*c*) job security; (*d*) psychosocial demands; (*e*) control and decision latitude; and (*f*) social support.

It has been well demonstrated that unemployment is associated with high levels of stress and significant disease outcomes (Cobb 1974; Kasl & Cobb 1970). More recently, it has been discovered that unemployed individuals differ from employed workers on physiological indicators of stress (such as circulating catecholamine levels) and also perform more poorly on complex tasks, often exhibiting behaviors associated with learned helplessness (Baum et al 1986).

Work, too, can be stressful. Occupational stress is usually associated with employment situations in which multiple competing demands are placed on the individual and in which the individual can exert little authority or control (Singer et al 1986). The perception of these job characteristics seems more closely linked to health behavior and morbidity than are the actual characteristics of the job (House et al 1986). For example, perceived job pressures resulted in a tendency to work longer hours and increase smoking and drinking behaviors.

The workplace can also benefit health. Coworkers can be important sources of social support. They can provide health information and encourage healthy life-style changes. Increasingly, organizations have implemented health-promotion activities for their employees. Because such programs tend to boost company morale (Felix et al 1985), participating individuals may receive both the direct benefit of the program (e.g. weight loss, smoking cessation) and also more positive social interactions with their coworkers. For example, worksite weight-loss programs are as effective as self-help and commercial groups (Brownell et al 1985) and often result in positive changes in morale, better employer/employee relations, and a cost-effective change in participants' life-styles (Brownell et al 1984).

Demographic Variables

GENDER   The effects of gender on health have only recently been explored. Study is urgently needed, however, given epidemiologic demonstrations that women are on the average significantly less vulnerable than men to most modern life-threatening diseases (Bush & Barrett-Connor 1985). Women have until recently been less likely to smoke than men (Waldron 1986), show fewer stress-induced lipid responses (Stoney in press), and have lower numbers and/or density of peripheral vascular adrenergic receptors than men (Freedman et al in press), suggesting several possible reasons for their substantially lower incidence of CHD. Differences in reproductive hormones may also be linked to gender differences in disease epidemiology (Bush &

Barrett-Connor 1985), either directly or as stimuli for other physiological processes.

Because of the high employment rates of women at the present time, it is possible to compare men and women in the same occupation at the same worksite, thus controlling for effects of occupational role on health. Detre et al (1987) studied federal government employees holding high service grades (14 or above). The occupational experience of men and women in similarly responsible and demanding positions appears to reduce the mortality advantage of women, suggesting that variables unrelated to sex-specific hormones may strongly contribute to the overall mortality differences between men and women in national databases. There are also differences in the stress hormone reactivity of males and females. At rest, men and women do not differ in levels of the stress hormones epinephrine, norepinephrine, and cortisol, but when a challenge is applied, males release more epinephrine than females (Frankenhaeuser 1986a). Men also appear to have greater blood pressure responses to many types of stressors than women (Matthews & Stoney 1988). In Western countries, males tend to engage in more risky behaviors than females, particularly those involving physical daring or illegal activities, thus influencing health (Waldron 1986). One important generalization is that gender differences in specific types of health-related behavior are strongly influenced by the compatibility of the behavior with general sex role expectations (Waldron, in press).

In Western countries, women visit physicians more than men (Verbrugge 1985; Waldron 1983). Although many psychological reasons have been posited for this difference, it is important to note that women's more complex and demanding reproductive functions are the major reason for their higher rates of physician visits, at least among young and middle-aged adults (Verbrugge 1985; Waldron 1983). Women may also be more likely to visit physicians because they have more self-reported symptoms and poorer self-rated health. Survey data in the United States suggest that men may put up with more pain than women (Mechanic 1964; Verbrugge 1982). Also women rate the importance of health somewhat higher than do men (Verbrugge 1982). Gender differences in attitudes toward health care are suggested by the findings that women more often than men have a personal physician or a regular source of health care (Cleary et al 1982; NCHS 1985). In the United States, at least, women appear to have greater faith than men in the value of preventive medical care (Cleary et al 1982; Waldron 1983). There is no evidence for the hypothesis that gender differences in employment and other role obligations are the major cause of gender differences in physician visits (Waldron, in press).

Finally, women and men are treated differently by the health-care system. For example, physicians respond less to female patients' requests for information (Todd 1984). However, most evidence suggests little gender difference in physician's recommendations for medical care for a given condition (Verbrugge 1985). In some non-Western societies, females obtain less adequate medical care than males, reflecting sex discrimination and other general sex role differences in these societies.

AGE   Physical health of the aged population reflects both normal biological changes and increased incidence of many major diseases. For example, about 86% of individuals over age 65 living in the community have at least one chronic disease, and 50% have two or more (Jarvik & Perl 1981). Increased vulnerability is additionally reflected in the fact that the impact of acute illness is often more severe in older adults and recovery more protracted (Atchley 1977). Many of the chronic conditions experienced by the elderly result in part from the life-styles and health practices of their youth (Siegler & Costa 1985).

In understanding the effects of age as a variable on health, it is extremely important to note that all data suggest greater interindividual variability with aging (see Rodin 1986b). Second, changes that appear to be related to biological aging may actually result from psychosocial factors associated with being old, such as widowhood. Third, the outcome of the aging process is not always decline. Some diseases (e.g. autoimmune disease) are less likely to occur in old age. Moreover, the impact of many life events, such as the death of a spouse, is often smaller in old age, since these events occur "on time" in old age. Recent theoretical emphasis has shifted to characterization of "successful" vs "usual" aging (Rowe & Kahn 1987).

It has been suggested that the relation between an individual's health and the effects of psychosocial variables might grow stronger in old age (Kasl & Berkman 1981). Rodin (1986b) focused on one psychosocial variable, control, in elaborating further this position, emphasizing that experiences related to control increase markedly in older age and have different social meanings. Further, the association between control and an indicator of health status may be notably altered or conditioned by age, or age may influence the relation between the sense of control and health maintenance behaviors and the seeking of medical care.

There has been substantial attention to changes in social support that occur with aging, which may influence health and well-being. Many of these have focused on bereavement and relocation (see Rowe & Kahn 1987 for review). One outcome of increasing concern is the use of health services. Widowed persons go to the doctor and hospital more often than married persons (Verbrugge 1979). Not being in the labor force any longer has also been considered a cause of the increased use of ambulatory physician services by older adults. However, a recent analysis of data on almost 20,000 individuals aged 55 and over taken from the 1978 Health Interview Survey showed that widowhood and retirement per se are not the issue in utilization of health services among elderly adults. Rather, living alone is the crucial factor (Homan et al 1986), suggesting a theoretically richer set of variables operative. Other suggestions of spurious interpretations of earlier data include the notion that older adults show better rates than younger people of commonly accepted favorable health practices (e.g. abstinence from alcohol use and cigarette smoking; NCHS 1980), leading to suggestions that they are more adherent to health-promoting regimens (Besdine 1981). However, it is reasonable to suggest that people who have engaged in a set of distinctly unfavorable health practices are more likely to have died prior to age 65 (Breslow & Endstrom 1980).

A variety of behaviors relevant to health may be influenced by the fact that older adults are more likely to attribute symptoms to normal and irreversible aging, to underreport symptoms, and to anticipate a health decrement as an expected part of the aging process (Besdine 1981; Brody & Kleban 1981; Rodin 1986b). There are conditions under which this expectation may promote certain forms of health behavior and others where it may inhibit them. Moreover, Leventhal (1984) found few age differences in cognitive representations of various illnesses, but significant age differences in associated emotions. Anger generated by the cancer label decreases with age, as do fear and shame associated with alcoholism and arthritis. These age differences in affective responses to illness could have significant implications for responses to treatment and family relations.

The age of the patient can influence clinical decisions that affect treatment (Riley 1987). Older people are more likely than younger people with identical symptoms to be given a poor prognosis for recovery and more likely to be given palliative rather than intervention treatments (Ciliberto et al 1981). Older people are also less likely to challenge their physicians and more likely to adopt a passive role in health care (Haug 1981). Thus, in viewing all of these data, one must be attentive to the interactive effects of patients' and physicians' expectations and behaviors.

ETHNICITY AND SOCIAL CLASS   Until recently, little of the literature in health psychology focused on racial or ethnic minorities. As noted by Anderson & Jackson (1987), this lack of attention is problematic for at least two reasons. First, sociocultural and socioeconomic differences in behavior and reactions to illness, both among and within racial and ethnic groups, have implications for physical health and illness (Harwood 1981; Hamburg 1982). Second, members of racial and ethnic groups within this society have higher incidence and prevalence rates for many physical illnesses (NCHS 1984; Jackson 1981).

Comparisons of cancer death rates provide evidence of the extra burden of illness experienced by Blacks (NCHS 1984). Blacks (and Hispanics) exhibit a higher incidence of AIDS, and the transmission pattern of this disease in these groups differs from that in Whites [non-Whites are more likely to transmit AIDS through intravenous drug use or sexual contact with drug users (Bakeman et al 1986; Peterson & Bakeman, in press)].

Blacks are roughly twice as likely to develop hypertension as Whites (Saunders & Williams 1975). There is beginning to be evidence with regard to cardiovascular disease that the differences between Blacks and Whites are attributable to biological mechanisms. Most of the research attention has focused on the sympathetic nervous system (see Anderson & Jackson 1987 for a review). There are also striking racial differences in sodium homeostasis (Luft et al 1985). Racial differences in styles of coping with stress have also been implicated in hypertension (James et al 1984).

Racial and ethnic variables are confounded with socioeconomic factors that may influence health and disease. Low socioeconomic status usually results in a less stable physical environment, a less stable and supportive social environment, altered perceptions of oneself and one's group, and altered capacities to adapt psychologically and behaviorally. Inadequate resources, low-status jobs, social stigma, and inadequate education interact with differential physiology, nutrition, environmental risks, and coping styles to create a circle of disadvantage (Kessler et al 1985; Jenkins 1982). These active ingredients of social disadvantage might relate to health risks in a variety of ways including, for example, a noxious environment; lack of knowledge, funds, or availability of early care; economic or cultural barriers to screening or diagnostic services or treatment opportunities; and inadequate follow-through (Jenkins 1982). Differential health behavior is also evident. For example, several surveys indicate that individuals most likely to exercise tend to be younger, more highly educated, and more affluent (Government of Canada 1982).

MEDIATING VARIABLES

Coping Processes

In studying how individuals adapt to stressful life circumstances, coping resources are sometimes distinguished from coping responses. Coping resources are personality, attitudinal, and cognitive factors that provide the psychological context for coping responses (Moos & Billings 1982). Coping responses occur as the result of appraisal processes that may be influenced by coping resources.

A number of investigators have been concerned with the classification of coping responses. Moos & Billings (1982) suggest three primary coping domains can be identified in the literature on coping: (*a*) appraisal-focused coping, attempts to define the meaning of a situation; (*b*) problem-focused coping, trying to modify or eliminate the source of the stress; and (*c*) emotion-focused coping, managing emotions aroused by stressors and trying to maintain affective equilibrium. The distinction between problem-focused and emotion-focused coping has also been suggested by others (e.g. Lazarus & Folkman 1984; Lazarus & Launier 1978). Recently, coping responses have been classified as avoidant and nonavoidant (or attention) types (Suls & Fletcher 1985). Stone et al (in press) argue that current schemes for classifying coping responses are oversimplifications of the way people actually cope with stress. They suggest grouping coping strategies in terms of several general themes: seeking social support, seeking information, religiosity, situation redefinition, behavioral and cognitive avoidance, tension reduction, and problem solving. These themes are similar to those derived empirically by Folkman et al (1986).

Do individuals tend to use the same coping responses across situations or do they select a specific coping response for each stressor? Although more of the variance in coping responses seems attributable to situational differences than to individual differences in coping styles or coping resources (McFarlane et al 1983; Pearlin & Schooler 1978), there is clearly a person × situation interaction (House et al 1988).

Are certain coping responses consistently more efficacious than others? Suls & Fletcher (1985) conducted a meta-analysis of 43 studies of coping efficacy in various domains. Overall, coping strategies involving avoidance were just as effective as those involving active attention, and both types of coping yielded better adjustment than no-coping control conditions. But when the time course of the stressor was considered, avoidant coping responses seemed to be more effective in the short term, unless attentional coping strategies focused on sensory rather than emotional interpretational sets. In terms of longer-term outcome, attention was associated with better adjustment.

Effective coping may play an important role in health promotion, disease prevention, and more rapid recovery from illness (for review see Kessler & Wortman, in press). How individuals cope with stress is an important mediator of the stress-illness relationship (Cohen 1984). Cohen (1984) reviewed several mechanisms by which successful coping can affect the etiology and course of a disease. Coping can influence hormone levels, cause direct tissue changes, or affect the immune system (Jacobs et al 1985; Kielcolt-Glaser et al 1987). Interpersonal coping styles may influence the type of care received (e.g. demanding, task-oriented patients may have their complaints acted upon more quickly). In fact, cancer patients who cope by complaining and expressing high levels of negative affect survive longest (Jensen 1987). Conversely, positive coping, including strong feelings of a "will to live" and high morale, may also have positive physiological consequences (Scheier & Carver 1987; Peterson & Seligman 1987). Effective coping has been linked to quicker recovery from illness, and active participant coping strategies may be especially effective in this regard (Cohen & Lazarus 1979).

Efficacious coping reduces stressor effects, but it also has costs (Cohen et al 1986). Coping processes require effort, and prolonged coping depletes the individual's supply of energy. Successful coping also can result in the over-generalized use of an effective strategy in inappropriate situations. For example, the Type A behavior pattern might be thought of as an overgeneraliza-tion to nearly all life domains of a coping strategy that was effective for coping with competing demands in one domain. Finally, coping may produce pathogenic effects (Contrada et al 1982). Moreover, coping behaviors them-selves can be detrimental to health (e.g. smoking and drinking alcohol; Pomerleau & Pomerleau 1984).

Substance Use and Abuse

Cigarette smoking, excessive use of alcohol, and obesity represent major health risks and therefore continue to be the focus of considerable research attention. For example, the 1982 Surgeon General's Report noted that 30% of all cancer deaths were attributable to tobacco use. Smoking is also a major factor in death from cardiovascular disease (Abbott et al 1986; Dawber 1980). Alcoholism, via its effects on the liver, nutrition, and risk for head and neck cancer, represents one of the three leading causes of death in modern societies (Fourth special report on alcohol and health, 1981). Other health risks include the strong relationship between alcohol abuse during pregnancy and poor fetal outcome (Sokol et al 1980).

Obesity has also been associated with mortality and morbidity. Similarly, there is a small increase in excess mortality with low body weight. The correlates of obesity contributing to excess mortality include non-insulin dependent (Type 2) diabetes, digestive disease, hypertension, cardiovascular diseases, and cancers (Bray 1984).

Over the last several years, models of substance use and abuse have moved away from traditional theories of addiction that focus on pharmacological properties of drugs and their physiological effects (e.g. Lettieri et al 1980; Jellinek 1960). In these theories, the primary emphasis is on uncontrollable endogenous processes as the basis for addiction. The paradigm shift toward a more cognitive-behaviorally based model is most evident in the work of Marlatt and his colleagues on the determinants and prevention of relapse (Marlatt et al 1988 see also Shumaker & Grunberg 1986). These models focus on the cognitions and behaviors that lead to the initiation and maintenance of substance use and abuse.

The field has once again begun to generate biological perspectives, howev-er. Genetic predispositions (for obesity and alcoholism, but not smoking;

Swan et al, 1988b) are now the focus of considerable research, based on new analyses of cohorts of twins and other behavioral-genetics approaches (e.g. Stunkard et al 1986 for obesity; Cadoret et al 1987 and Cloninger 1987 for alcoholism). Recent data for obesity emphasize the possible inheritance of biological parameters such as low metabolic rate (Ravussin et al 1988; Roberts et al 1988). It appears that variability in sensitivity to alcohol among individuals, and in different organ systems within individuals, may also be genetically determined (Straus 1986).

Over the last few years there has also been increasing emphasis on the study of common processes across substance abuse domains. The idea of commonalities was first discussed by Hunt et al (1971), who found nearly identical patterns of relapse in heroin addicts, alcoholics, and cigarette smokers. Adding an analysis of dieters and exercisers, the picture appears the same today (Marlatt & Gordon 1985). Many differences also exist both among the disorders and among persons afflicted with the same disorder. For example, genetic contributions to both alcoholism and obesity suggest separate pathways for their development. There are also key differences in the pharmacology of nicotine and alcohol (Best et al in press; Pomerleau & Pomerleau 1984), and food abuse fits even less neatly with concepts of dependency, withdrawal, and tolerance. Nonetheless, there has been great enthusiasm in the field recently for the study of commonalities.

A National Academy of Sciences report (Levison et al 1984) emphasized common processes at the sociocultural, psychological, and biological levels. There is a strong association between young age and a variety of risk-taking behaviors, including the use of substances such as cigarettes and drugs. Fleming et al (in press) have suggested that cigarettes may be the entry-level drug. Individuals who have tried cigarettes are significantly more likely to use other substances two years later (e.g. coffee, beer, marijuana). This study extended the previous efforts of Kandel (see Kandel & Maloff 1984 for review) demonstrating the tendency for use of illicit drugs to occur in a relatively fixed temporal sequence.

Further commonalities exist in the social influences that underlie the etiology of substance use, such as peer group influence and situational and social contexts. The seminal work of Jessor & Jessor (see Jessor 1984, for review) focuses on adolescence as a relatively high-risk stage of life. Many health risk behaviors in adolescence tend to covary. According to Jessor & Jessor (1982), the term that best captures the content of the dimension underlying psychosocial proneness is conventionality/unconventionality. From their work, it appears that with a permissive environment, unconventionality promotes proneness to at-risk behavior that carries through to adulthood.

Studies of common processes have also focused on the role of learning theory in understanding substance use and abuse. Donegan et al (1984) have identified six properties common to the development of many habitual health-damaging behaviors: (a) the ability of the substance to act as a reinforcer; (b) acquired tolerance—reduced effectiveness of the same dose or exposure over time; (c) physical dependence and withdrawal; (d) affective contrast—often euphoria followed by dysphoria; (e) the capacity of the substance or activity to act as an effective Pavlovian unconditioned stimulus; and (f) the capacity of states like arousal, stress, or pain to influence use.

Lang (1984) has reviewed the evidence for the suggestion that a common personality pattern leads some individuals into the heavy use of recreational drugs. Lang concludes that no unique personality trait or profile is a necessary or sufficient condition for substance abuse, but some personality factors (such as impulsiveness and difficulties in delaying gratification) appear to be predisposing factors that may act in concert with situational and other variables.

Biological commonalities have emphasized the relation of naturally occurring substances and sites in the central nervous system to biological mediators of continued substance use. This work has focused on the body's natural opiate system (e.g. Simon 1984; Bloom 1984). Substances may also alter the bioavailability of several behaviorally active neuroregulators, thus helping to explain the remarkable persistence of substance use behaviors. For example, nicotine alters the bioavailability of acetylcholine, norepinephrine, and dopamine, leading to the suggestion that nicotine is used by smokers to produce temporary improvements in performance and affect (Pomerleau 1986).

The second domain of recent interest in common processes has focused on the relationship between stress and coping and the use of substances. For example, it is a widely held belief that alcohol reduces stress (Sher 1988). Several psychosocial, physiological, and pharmacological variables can influence alcohol's effects on stress, including the amount of alcohol consumed, the person's prior experience with alcohol, individual experiences based on physiological responsiveness to ethanol, learned expectations about alcohol and its effects, the social setting in which drinking occurs, and the specific way stress is measured. Similar proposals have been made for the effects of stress on excessive food intake (Cattanach & Rodin 1988) and on smoking (Pomerleau 1986; Pomerleau & Pomerleau 1984).

Questions about the effects of stress on increasing substance use lead to considerations of the use of these substances as coping strategies (Marlatt & Gordon 1985; Perri et al 1984; Supnick & Colletti 1984). Abrams et al (1987) showed that quitters cope better than nonquitters with relapses involving intrapersonal (negative mood) smoking-specific situations; thus differences in coping skills exist between individuals who are successful and those who are unsuccessful in controlling substance abuse. Substance use may directly affect coping processes by reducing stress. Alternatively, coping processes may involve increases in social skills for dealing with social influences on substance use (Biglan et al 1985). Another possibility is that coping processes are related to third variables, such as self-esteem, and influence substance abuse in this way.

Health-Promoting Behaviors

Individuals may engage in consistent clusters of positive health practices. The belief in a pattern of associations has led to the hypothesis that positive health behavior is part of an overall style of living reflecting the ability to anticipate problems, mobilize to meet them, and cope actively (Mechanic & Cleary 1980). However, in a review of the health behavior literature, Kirscht (1983) concluded that there is little evidence for a health-protective life-style. Studies have examined correlations between the ways people organize their thinking with respect to health and how they ultimately behave to protect their health, with modest findings (e.g. Harris & Guten 1979; Salovey et al 1987). These studies have focused on belief structures and behavioral intentions (Ajzen & Timko 1986), values (Kristiansen 1985, 1986), and current practice (Salovey et al 1987).

In addition to these intrapersonal motivators of health-protective behaviors, interpersonal variables are also important. This view is best illustrated by the impressive data from community based interventions, which combine state of the art communication and educational strategies with community organization and social support to encourage health-protective behaviors across an entire community. The two earliest were the North Karelia project (see Puska 1984 for a review) and the Stanford Three Community Project (see Farquhar 1984 for review). Studies in Rhode Island, Minnesota, and Belgium are still collecting data (see Matarazzo et al 1984).

The role of social support in promoting health behaviors is complex. While some data indicate a relationship between perceived level of support (especially from significant others) and long-term maintenance of positive health behaviors (e.g. Mermelstein et al 1986), several experimental attempts to enhance social support (e.g. by actively involving partners and instructing them in useful supportive skills) have proved unsuccessful (Lichtenstein et al 1986; Colletti & Brownell 1982; Cohen et al 1987).

An entire volume devoted to behavioral health (Matarazzo et al 1984) considered exercise, healthful diet, dental health, and safety. The determinants of these health-promoting practices remain unclear. Nowhere is this truer than about exercise. Only 15% of the general population is highly active, and as much as 70% of the entire population can be characterized as inactive. Fewer than 30% of those volunteering to engage in exercise programs continue to be active over a mean of 3.5 years (see Oldridge 1984 for review). Even less encouraging is the rate of recruitment of subjects into exercise programs. In employee-based exercise programs, approximately 30% or fewer of the potential population actually volunteer (Cox et al 1981). However, as many as 25% of these volunteers report themselves to be regularly active at the time of volunteering (Shephard et al 1981). Participation in employee-based exercise programs has been shown to influence other health-relevant behaviors, resulting in fewer sick days and lower health care costs (Der-Karabetian & Gebharp 1986).

Some have argued that the major problems with poor exercise adherence rates are similar to those for all formal health-behavior programs and stem from poor recruitment, marketing, and motivational strategies (Morgan 1977). Sensenig & Cialdini (1984) suggest that a few basic social psychological principles account for most specific compliance tactics observed in commercial settings, and these could be applied to the health behavior domain to increase adherence. These principles include (a) commitment induced via the pressure for consistency; (b) the use of social evidence to convince target persons to behave in desired ways (social validation); (c) high source credibility; and (d) reciprocation (e.g. rewarding adherence by providing something in return). It is worth noting however, that quite different factors may influence a person's decision to attempt an exercise regimen, determine ongoing participation in the exercise program, and affect the decision to continue to exercise once a formal program is completed (Fontana et al 1986).

Several behaviors believed to be health promoting also have potential health damaging consequences. For example, smoking cessation leads to weight gain (Hall et al 1986; Rodin 1987). This negative consequence is the second most widely cited reason in the Surgeon General's Report that people give for not trying to stop smoking. Rodin & Wack (1984) have reviewed the major pathways by which weight gain may occur, including metabolic changes caused by smoking cessation and increased caloric intake. Rodin (1987) recently demonstrated that ex-smokers are especially responsive to sweet taste, which is consistent with observations in experimental studies with animals (Grunberg et al 1985).

Another example of a paradoxical effect of health-promoting behavior is the recent demonstration that dieting itself may decrease metabolic rate, increase the uptake of fat into storage, and make people generally more food efficient (i.e. able to exist on fewer calories; Brownell et al in press). This phenomenon appears to become increasingly severe with repeated cycles of gaining and losing weight (Brownell et al 1986). After repeated cycles of gaining and losing weight, people and animals may weigh the same as when they started but be significantly fatter (i.e. their fat/lean body mass ratio has increased). In animals, at least, the effect appears stronger for females than for males (Brownell et al, in press).

Adherence

Issues of compliance have long been a focus of attention for medical personnel and health psychologists. One important development has been a shift from use of the term compliance, connoting patient obedience, to the term adherence, implying voluntary effort by the individual (Kristeller & Rodin 1984; Turk et al 1986). This theoretical shift has led to different types of research questions as well, since adherence implies choice and mutuality in the planning and implementation of treatment. Levels of nonadherence vary considerably, depending on the treatment or health recommendation. The highest adherence is for treatments with direct medical procedures (e.g. an injection), high levels of monitoring, and acute onset. For example, Taylor et al (1984a) reported a rate of 94% for cancer patients' adherence to chemotherapy. In contrast, the lowest adherence rates occur with patients who have chronic disorders with no immediate discomfort or evident risk, when lifestyle changes are required, and when prevention instead of symptom reduction or cure is the desired outcome. Treatment nonadherence is not limited to medication. Problems of adherence have been noted for performance of numerous health behaviors such as wearing seat belts, reducing weight, and increasing exercise (cf Brownell et al 1986). In general, level of adherence is difficult to ascertain because adherence may be conceptualized and operationally defined in various ways (Meichenbaum & Turk 1987).

Meichenbaum & Turk (1987) have systematically reviewed research on the determinants of adherence. These include numerous patient variables (e.g. characteristics of the individual, competing ethnic folk concepts of disease and treatment, environments that support nonadherent behavior, and lack of resources). It has also been suggested that nonadherence may represent a person's attempt to gain some control over an illness or treatment. In other circumstances, the decision not to adhere may be based on misunderstanding or inadequate information (Deaton 1985; Janis 1984). In addition, patient beliefs affect adherence (e.g. Buckalew & Sallis 1986).

Characteristics of the disease also affect adherence. For example, the more complex the demands of the treatment, the poorer the rates of adherence (e.g. Glasgow et al 1986). The intrusiveness and duration of the regimen are also important variables in this category (e.g. Meichenbaum & Turk 1987). Issues such as inconvenience of the behavior or treatment, inadequate supervision, and side effects also strongly influence the likelihood of adherence. Finally, relationship variables, particularly in the health-care setting, correlate strongly with rates of adherence (e.g. poor communication or rapport; Janis 1984).

MOTIVATORS

Stress

Stress calls into play dispositional variables, appraisal processes, coping mechanisms, reliance on social support, use of substances, and the like (Elliott & Eisdorfer 1982). In many cases, stress may damage health through a combination of these processes. For example, Type A behavior leads to significantly greater cardiac reactivity under certain kinds of stress that are most meaningful to the Type A individual (Matthews et al 1986b). To take another example, the combination of stress and cigarette smoking may have a greater than additive effect on blood pressure and heart rate responses (Dembroski et al 1985; Pomerleau & Pomerleau, in press). Similarly, consumption of caffeine under conditions of stress affects blood pressure, plasma cortisol level, and serum cholesterol, especially among borderline hypertensives (Pincomb & Lovallo 1987; Goldstein & Shapiro in press).

Controversy has surrounded whether it is useful to define stress in terms of stimuli external to the organism (Selye 1974) or as an interaction among an individual's appraisal processes, reactions, and an external event (Lazarus & Folkman 1984b; see Krantz et al 1985 for a review of this controversy). Large-scale efforts to resolve the issue (Elliott & Eisdorfer 1982) have had little impact (Engel 1986). However, we now know that the objective nature of the stressor is less significant for health outcomes than the person's perceptions of the stress. Reactions to the same stressor (e.g. the death of a spouse; Osterweis et al 1984) vary with the meaning of this stressor for the bereaved.

Another shift in the study of stress is toward the investigation of daily hassles rather than catastrophic life events. Hassles are experiences and conditions of daily living appraised as salient and harmful or threatening to well-being (Lazarus 1984). Lazarus suggested that daily hassles show a stronger relationship to health-relevant variables such as psychological distress and physical symptom reporting than do stressful life events. Major life events may affect health by creating new hassles or increasing the intensity of existing ones (Osterweis et al 1984). However, in such studies subjective stress is often measured in terms of health-relevant annoyances, confounding the operationalization of stress and the health-relevant results of stress (Lazarus et al 1985).

Stress effects on pathophysiological processes have been widely studied (reviewed in Miller 1983). Earlier work focused on corticosteroids and sympathetic nervous system variables; more recent research has examined immune system responses as well (reviewed in Justice 1985; Krantz et al 1985). The controllability of the stressor determines whether or not stress has physiological effects (e.g. Hanson et al 1976; Laudenslager et al 1983). Even variables such as tumor growth and proliferation may be influenced by whether or not a stressor is controllable (Visintainer et al 1982). Use of the triadic design (Seligman 1975) in these newer studies allows separation of the controllability of the stressor from the intensity of the noxious stimulation. Many other physiological systems (including such hormones as testosterone and prolactin, and peptides such as the endorphins and more central immune parameters) also merit further investigation in this context.

Being Sick: The Impact of Illness

The initial illness episode involves the self-evaluation of health status as a reaction to the experience of unusual symptoms (Feist & Brannon 1988). Nerenz & Leventhal (1983) described a theory of how individuals adapt to acute illness episodes, which includes attributional search, potential dysphoria, and preoccupation with bodily experience. Illness-appraisal behaviors include information seeking, social comparison, and even denial. These behaviors contribute to "appraisal delay," the time it takes an individual to determine that new symptoms and sensations indicate illness. Other forms of delay, later in the process, include (a) the time between the recognition that one is ill and the decision to get medical help (illness delay), and (b) the time that elapses between the decision to seek treatment and one's entrance into the medical-care system (utilization delay).

These illness behaviors (determining health status, deciding to seek treatment, and actually obtaining treatment) are related to a variety of variables: gender (Edlin & Golanty 1988; Rosenstock & Kirscht 1979); age (Prohaska et al 1987; socioeconomic status, ethnicity, cultural attitudes toward illness and pain (Mechanic 1978); and the salience of the symptom itself (DiMatteo & DiNicola 1982; Mechanic 1979). The individual's reactions to medical treatment are not well predicted by severity of illness or actual diagnosis, but rather by the individual's stance with regard to the medical system (e.g. positive vs negative affect; perceived physician support) (Ben-Sira 1980; Felton et al 1984).

Once people have an illness, the variables reviewed thus far affect subsequent adjustment. For example, in a study of spinal-cord-injured persons, the psychological well-being of patients who reported high levels of social support and satisfaction with their social contacts was as high as that of healthy individuals (Schulz & Decker 1985). The literature on successful adjustment to cancer is burgeoning. The cancer patient must learn to cope with problems ranging from the side effects of radiation therapy (Andersen 1985; Andersen & Karlsson 1986; to sexual dysfunction (Andersen 1985; Andersen et al 1986). Successful adjustment, at least among breast cancer patients, is often better predicted by prognosis and the invasiveness of treatment than by degree of disability. The impact of prognosis on adjustment seems to be mediated by beliefs about one's current control over the cancer (Taylor et al 1984b), while the effect of surgery seems to be mediated by the patient's sense of disfigurement and by changes in the sexual and affectional patterns in marriage (Taylor et al 1985). Cancer patients often compare themselves to others worse off in order to bolster how they feel about their own progress (Molleman et al 1986; Wood et al 1985).

A growing literature reveals that daily caregiving to a chronically ill person usually depresses and dissatisfies the caregiver (Schulz et al 1987). Much attention has been focused on caregivers of patients with dementing diseases (Maletta & Hepburn 1986; Scott et al 1986). Moreover, family interactions are profoundly affected by the diagnosis of chronic illness in children (Hauser & Jacobson 1986; Walker et al 1987). Family members tend to become overinvolved in the chronically ill person's problem, producing negative consequences for family functioning and the illness itself.

Chronic illness challenges the family. Although the response to this challenge can be dissolution or distress, it is often an increase in cohesiveness (Boss 1988; Leventhal et al 1985). Illness has less impact on well-organized families in which individual goals and ambitions are less important than family goals, a setting that promotes effective problem-solving and coping (Lewis et al 1976; Leventhal et al 1985).

DISEASE END POINTS

Most of the earlier studies in this area (see Krantz et al 1985) were characterized by a "one variable, one outcome" approach in which a single antecedent variable was correlated with the presence or absence of a disease. Investigators then sought to understand the pathophysiological mechanism by which that psychosocial variable influenced the disease process. This approach has been followed most strongly in the area of personality variable effects on disease. For example, Booth-Kewley & Friedman (1987) reviewed the evidence for associations between personality variables (e.g. components of Type A, anxiety, depression, anger, and extraversion) and CHD in a meta-analysis of 83 studies.

Another approach has been to examine interactions among sets of variables. This work is based on several kinds of hypotheses. The most straightforward view holds that since disease is multiply determined, multifactorial approaches are appropriate to the prediction of disease outcome. More interesting models, however, conceptualize interaction effects as the most important predictors. So, for example, recent studies consider the stress-buffering effects of social support or the role of dispositional variables in influencing health practices under certain conditions (e.g. high stress) or in individuals of a certain gender or age.

Cancer

Central nervous, endocrine, and immune systems form a complex regulatory homeostatic network (e.g. Blalock 1984; Roszman et al 1985; Irwin et al 1987; Besedovsky et al 1986). Therefore, for tumors that are also at least partially under hormonal and/or immunological control, known biological pathways make it appropriate to ask whether psychosocial variables can influence tumor outcomes. Levy (1985) has noted that only certain tumors are relevant when considering behavior as a potential modifier of biological responses. The study of indolent tumors with a variable time course for recurrence and subsequent death is most appropriate (e.g. breast cancer and melanoma). More virulent malignancies (e.g. pancreatic or primary lung cancers, with their rapid and aggressive course) leave little time for the host's behavior to play much of a role in progression and outcome.

Levy (1985) noted that behaviors can have both direct and indirect effects on the initiation of cancer and on the progression of the disease. The most important direct behavioral cause of disease initiation is tobacco use. Doll & Peto (1981) estimated that in the United States in 1981, tobacco caused 130,000–140,000 deaths, accounting for 33% of all cancer deaths during the 1980s. Alcohol consumption and occupational exposure to carcinogens also produce direct effects.

Diet and sexual activities indirectly affect the initiation of cancer. Dietary fat may increase cancer risk, and dietary fiber may lower it (Doll & Peto 1981; Boyd 1985; Bright-See & Levy 1985). It has also been suggested (Ames 1983) that even natural foodstuffs expose people to a large variety of naturally derived mutagens and carcinogens.

Nowhere has there been greater attention to the role of behavior in the initiation of disease than in the discussion of the causes and transmission of Acquired Immune Deficiency Syndrome (AIDS). Behaviors involving intravenous drug abuse and unsafe sex practices account for most cases of AIDS (Kelly & St. Lawrence 1988). The incidence of cervical cancer correlates with the character of sexual intercourse (e.g. age of onset, number of sexual partners, etc; American Cancer Society 1985). Moreover, interactions with other psychosocial variables such as race and socioeconomic status are notable. For example, the incidence of cancer of the cervix is highest in low-income groups (Hulka 1982). This social class distinction, of course, may be a proxy for more specific risks generated by particular activities within these groups (Hulka 1982). It is also possible that higher levels of stress accompanied by poverty in this group enhance the risk potential. For example, susceptibility to infectious disease such as herpes simplex virus II has been linked to environmental stress and poor coping ability (Jemmott & Locke 1984). There is strong evidence that cervical cancer is a viral disease with herpes simplex playing a vital role (Graham et al 1982).

Moving next to behavioral and psychosocial variables that may have a direct effect on the progression of disease, social support has been studied in cancer patient samples, and investigators have now begun to suggest a biological advantage of this support (Levy 1982). Second, in an earlier review of this area, Cox & MacKay (1982) concluded that the inability to express emotion was likely the most significant factor related to cancer progression (see also Temoshok 1985, 1987). Jensen (1987), for example, reported that breast cancer patients who reported a repressive, defensive coping style had worse outcomes. A third theme is related to the variable termed helplessness (or hopelessness, a related, but not identical concept; Greer et al 1985; Jensen 1987), although negative findings have also been reported (Cassilith et al 1985, 1987; Jamison et al 1987).

In general, if any or all of these elements—inadequate social support, lack of negative emotional expression, and helplessness or pessimism—play a role in biological vulnerability to cancer or in cancer progression, multiple causal pathways are possible. As Levy (1985) suggests, social support might facilitate stress reduction if homeostatic, regulatory neuroendocrine, and immune function are relatively buffered from severe chronic stress effects. Social factors could also act directly on emotional expressiveness (e.g. Lehman et al 1986).

Finally, there are potential indirect effects of behavior on cancer progression. For example, screening and detection behaviors, and factors relevant to noncompliance and delay, certainly influence cancer progression (Timko & Janoff-Bulman 1985).

CHD

Numerous personality and environmental variables appear involved in the pathogenesis and course of CHD. We attempted to divide this literature into the same four-cell framework suggested by Levy (1985) for cancer and found that while studies could be categorized as specifying the direct versus indirect effects of psychosocial variables, they could not be divided so clearly into those related to the cause versus progression of CHD. It is possible that this distinction has not been made because the pathophysiology of the various forms of CHD depend on the same mechanisms for incidence as they do for progression. In addition, risk factors differ for first CHD episodes vs later events (Matthews, in press). It is also possible that this distinction has not been made as clearly because certain forms of heart disease are risk factors for other forms of heart disease. Alternatively, it may simply be that investigators of behavioral factors relevant to CHD have not distinguished as clearly between etiological factors and those involved in the worsening of the disease.

Behavior can increase the role of physical risk factors. For example, salt intake directly affects blood pressure levels, and diet helps to regulate serum cholesterol levels. There are also, however, indirect effects involving these risk factors. For example, cigarette smoking is a behavioral risk factor itself undoubtedly brought about by psychosocial risk factors (Leventhal & Cleary 1980).

Most work on the role of psychosocial variables in CHD has focused on their indirect effects. Specific psychological factors influence neuroendocrine and autonomic nervous system function. In particular, new situations and tasks that exceed perceptions of self-confidence or elicit intense sustained efforts to cope increase neuroendocrine response (Herd 1986; Rosenman, in press). The most notable examples, of course, come from studies of the TABP. Extremely challenging situations with a component of time urgency elicit sympathetic adrenal medullary responses. Additionally, increased levels of circulating catecholamines, which are elevated in individuals with certain elements of the TABP (Glass et al 1980), may affect coronary atherogenesis through influences on platelet aggregation and on the mobilization of serum lipids (Schneiderman 1983; Haft 1974).

While it has been suggested the aspects of the TABP are related to increased psychophysiological responses (Houston et al, in press; Ward et al 1986), Suls & Sanders (in press) found that studies comparing systolic and diastolic blood pressure in Type A and B individuals obtained various results. Furthermore, Manuck & Krantz (1986) note little evidence that a physiologic hyper-responsivity to behavioral stimuli contributes appreciably to the etiology of CHD or essential hypertension. They argue that it would be premature to consider reactivity as a proven risk factor. More likely, reactivity operates in interaction with stress, personality attributes, and consummatory behaviors in its effects on CHD (Dembroski 1986). For example, smoking, stress, and reactivity may interact in their effects on heart disease. The cardiovascular response is larger when people smoke during stress than when they smoke while relaxed (Epstein & Jennings 1986).

It has also been suggested (Smith & Rhodewalt 1986) that Type As, through their choices, appraisals, and self-evaluations, actively operate on their environments in ways that influence the frequency, duration, and intensity of stressors, and, as a result, episodes of cardiovascular reactivity. Blumenthal et al (1987) show that the presence of social support reduces the risk of significant coronary artery disease among Type A individuals. Since heart rate may be attenuated by social closeness (Manuck et al 1983), Type As who avoid social contact may be deprived of psychological benefits.

Recent meta-analyses (Booth-Kewley & Friedman 1987; Matthews, in press) have focused on the more general relationship between components of the TABP and various types of heart disease. Booth-Kewley & Friedman posit a coronary prone personality that encompasses time urgency, hostility, and competitiveness but also includes aggression and depression. Matthews's more conservative meta-analytic approach finds that Type A/CHD associations are only significant in population-based studies and in studies using the structured interview assessment of Type A.

Despite data suggesting that alteration of the TABP significantly reduces incidence and recurrence of myocardial infarction (MI) (Friedman et al 1986; Powell et al 1984) and possibly serum cholesterol as well (Gill et al 1985), a number of recent studies have failed to find a significant relationship between measures of Type A behavior and new (Shekelle et al (1985) or recurrent (Case et al 1985; Shekelle et al 1985) cases of MI. One reason for the inconsistent pattern is that some components of the TABP may be more pathogenic than others (Dembroski 1986). A second is the potential importance of environmental influences (Blumenthal et al 1987). Finally, the determinants of survival following MI are quite different from the determinants of an initial MI (see Matthews, in press for review). Indeed, while aspects of Type A behavior may increase the risk of heart disease, Type A's are apparently less at risk for mortality after a heart attack (Ragland & Brand 1988).

Finally, many of the behavioral variables that influence disease outcome in individuals with CHD (e.g. changing exercise and diet, smoking cessation) are moderated by psychosocial variables. Changes in perceived efficacy regarding the likelihood of engaging in a new life-style, and social support for making these changes, strongly influence both physical risk factors (e.g. cholesterol) and recurrent MIs (Bandura 1988; Ewart et al 1986; Taylor et al 1985; O'Leary 1985a).

CONCLUSIONS

Despite the demonstration that altering psychosocial and behavioral variables may lessen disease (e.g. Friedman et al 1986), the absence of disease does not necessarily equal good health. In both psychology and medicine, the major focus of research and theory has been on the abnormal; states of normality have been defined as the absence of pathology. This has led to narrow definitions and assumptions about the desirability of encouraging health promoting behaviors that may not in fact be healthy when one takes the whole person into account. For example, elite athletes are often used as examples of outstandingly healthy individuals. However, many such athletes attain excellence in one area by compromising other areas of their bodies or their lives. A notable example is the high incidence of anorexia nervosa and bulimia in athletes for whom low weight is mandated (Striegel-Moore et al 1986). Similarly, longevity has been used as the dependent variable for many studies of health, in part because it is definitive and in part because it was assumed to be a valid outcome. Yet there is much debate over the value that should be placed on the quantity of life compared to the quality. Indeed many variables linked in epidemiological research to longevity—e.g. narcissism and mild paranoia—might not indicate good health by other definitions (Lieberman & Tobin 1983).

Studies both of individuals' subjective perceptions of their own health and of the personal, environmental, and social determinants of these perceptions suggest that people's sense of their own health is not only a reflection of their psychological and physical well-being but also a predictor of subsequent physical health. This relationship holds even when diagnosed illness and major risk factors for illness are statistically controlled (Kaplan & Camacho 1983). How these perceptions and other cognitive processes relate to health and illness remains to be understood.

ACKNOWLEDGMENT

The authors are grateful to Karen Matthews and Camille Wortman for their comments on an earlier draft.

Literature Cited

Abbott, R. D., Yin, Y., Reed, D. M., Yano, K. 1986. Risk of stroke in male cigarette smokers. *New Engl. J. Med.* 315:717–20

Abrams, D. B., Monti, P. M., Pinto, R. P., Elder, J. P., Brown, R. A., Jacobus, S. I. 1987. Psychosocial stress and coping in smokers who relapse or quit. *Health Psychol.* 6:289–303

Acklin, M. W., Bernat, E. 1987. Depression, alexithymia, and pain prone disorder: A Rorschach study. *J. Pers. Assess.* 51:462–79

Ahrens, S., Deffner, G. 1986. Empirical study of alexithymia: methodology and results. *Am. J. Psychother.* 3:430–47

Ajzen, I., Fishbein, M. 1977. Attitude-behavior relations: a theoretical analysis and review of empirical research. *Psychol. Bull.* 84:888–918

Ajzen, I., Timko, C. 1986. Correspondence between health attitudes and behavior. *Basic Appl. Soc. Psychol.* 7:259–76

Ames, B. 1983. Dietary carcinogens and anti-carcinogens. *Science* 221:1256–64

Andersen, B. L. 1985. Sexual functioning morbidity among cancer survivors: Current status and future research directions. *Cancer* 55:1835–42

Andersen, B. L., Anderson, B. 1986. Psychosomatic aspects of gynecologic oncology: present status and future directions. *J. Psychosom. Obstet. Gynaecol.* 5:233–44

Andersen, B. L., Karlsson, J. A. 1986. Radiation therapy and psychological distress in gynecologic oncology patients: outcomes and recommendations for enhancing adjustment. *J. Psychosom. Obstet. Gynaecol.* 5: 283–94

Andersen, B. L., Lachenbruch, P. A., Anderson, B., DeProsse, C. 1986. Sexual dysfunction and signs of gynecologic cancer. *Cancer* 57:1880–86

Anderson, N. B., Jackson, J. S. 1987.

Race, ethnicity, and health psychology: the example of essential hypertension. See Stone 1987, pp. 265–83

Angell, M. 1985. Disease as a reflection of the psyche. *New Engl. J. Med.* 312:1570–72

Atchley, R. C. 1977. *The Social Forces in Later Life: An Introduction to Social Gerontology.* Belmont, Calif: Wadsworth

Apfel, R. J., Sifneos, P. E. 1979. Alexithymia: concept and measurement. *Psychother. Psychosom.* 32:180–90

Bakeman, R., Lumb, J. R., Jackson, R. E., Smith, D. W. 1986. AIDS risk-group profiles in whites and members of minority groups. *New Engl. J. Med.* 315:191–92

Bandura, A. 1986. *Social Foundations of Thought and Action: A Social Cognitive Theory.* Englewood Cliffs, NJ: Prentice-Hall

Bandura, A. 1988. Self-efficacy mechanism in physiological activation and health-promoting behavior. In *Adaptation, Learning and Affect,* ed. J. Madden IV, S. Matthysse, J. Barchas. New York: Raven

Bandura, A., O'Leary, A., Taylor, C. B., Gauthier, J., Gossard, D. 1987. Perceived self-efficacy and pain control: opioid and nonopioid mechanisms. *J. Pers. Soc. Psychol.* 3:563–71

Bandura, A., Schunk, D. H. 1981. Cultivating competence, self-efficacy, and intrinsic interest through proximal self-motivation. *J. Pers. Soc. Psychol.* 41:586–98

Bandura, A., Taylor, C. B., Williams, S. L., Mefford, I. N., Barchas, J. D. 1985. Catecholamine secretion as a function of perceived coping self-efficacy. *J. Consult. Clin. Psychol.* 53:406–14

Baum, A., Fleming, R., Reddy, D. M. 1986. Unemployment stress: loss of control, reactance and learned helplessness. *Soc. Sci. Med.* 22:509–16

Baumann, L. J., Leventhal, H. 1985. I can tell

when my blood pressure is up, can't I? *Health Psychol.* 4:203–18

Belloc, N. B., Breslow, L. 1972. Relationship of physical health status and health practices. *Prev. Med.* 1:409–21

Ben-Sira, Z. 1980. Affective and instrumental components in the physician-patient relationship: an additional dimension of interaction theory. *J. Health Soc. Behav.* 21:170–80

Berkman, L. F. 1985. The relationship of social networks and social support to morbidity and mortality. See Cohen & Syme 1985, pp. 241–62

Berkman, L. F., Syme, S. L. 1979. Social networks, host resistance, and mortality: a nine-year follow-up study of Alameda County residents. *Am. J. Epidemiol.* 109:186–204

Besdine, R. W. 1981. Health and illness behavior in the elderly. In *Health, Behavior and Aging* (IOM Publ. 81–102), ed. D. L. Parron, F. Solomon, J. Rodin. Washington, DC: Inst. Med.

Besedovsky, H., Del Rey, A., Sorkin, E., Dinarello, C. A. 1986. Immunoregulatory feedback between interleukin-1 and glucocorticoid hormones. *Science* 233:652–54

Best, J. A., Wainwright, P. W., Mills, D. E., Kirkland, S. A. 1988. Biobehavioral approaches to smoking control. In *Biological Barriers in Bahavioral Medicine*, ed. W. Linden. New York: Karger. In press

Biglan, A., Weissman, W., Severson, H. 1985. Coping with social influence to smoke. In *Coping and Substance Use*, ed. S. Shiffman, T. A. Wills. New York: Academic

Billings, A. F., Moos, R. H. 1982. Social support and functioning among community and clinical groups. A panel model. *J. Behav. Med.* 5:295–311

Bishop, G. D. 1987. Lay conceptions of physical symptoms. *J. App. Soc. Psychol.* 17:127–46

Bishop, G. D., Briede, C., Cavazos, L., Grotizinger, R., McMahon, S. 1985. Processing illness information: the role of disease prototypes. *Basic Appl. Soc. Psychol.* 8:21–43

Bishop, G. D., Converse, S. A. 1986. Illness representations: a prototype approach. *Health Psychol.* 5:96–114

Blalock, J. 1984. The immune system as a sensory organ. *J. Immunol.* 32:1067–70

Bloom, F. E. 1984. Endorphins: cellular and molecular aspects for addictive phenomena. See Levison et al 1984, pp. 261–95

Blumenthal, J. A., Burg, M. M., Barefoot, J., Williams, R. B., Haney, T., Zimet, G. 1987. Social support, type A behavior, and coronary artery disease. *Psychosom. Med.* 49:331–40

Bonanno, G. A., Singer, J. L. 1988. Repressive personality style: theoretical and methodological implications for health and pathology. In *Repression: Defense Mechanism and Personality Style*, ed. J. L. Singer. Chicago: Univ. Chicago Press. In press

Booth-Kewley, S., Friedman, H. S. 1987. Psychological predictors of heart disease: a quantitative review. *Psychol. Bull.* 101:343–62

Boss, P. 1988. Family stress: perception and context. In *Handbook on Marriage and the Family*, ed. M. B. Sussman, S. Steinmetz. New York: Plenum

Bowers, K. S. 1987. Toward a multidimensional view of personality and health. *J. Pers.* 55:343–49

Boyd, N. 1985. Pilot study of dietary fat reduction in high risk women. In *Cancer, Nutrition, and Eating Behavior: A Biobehavioral Perspective*, ed. T. Burish, S. Levy, B. Meyerwitz. Hillsdale, NJ: Erlbaum

Bracke, P. E. 1985. *Parental childrearing practices and the development of Type A behavior in children.* PhD thesis. Stanford Univ.

Brandt, E. N. Jr. 1982. Statement prepared for the Subcommittee on Health and the Environment, Committee on Energy and Commerce, U.S. Congress, March 11. See Matarazzo et al 1984, pp. 784–85

Bray, G. A. 1984. The role of weight control in health promotion and disease prevention. See Matarazzo et al 1984, pp. 632–56

Breslow, L., Endstrom, J. E. 1980. Persistence of health habits and their relationship to mortality. *Prevent. Med.* 9:469–83

Brickman, P., Rabinowitz, V. C., Krauza, J., Coates, D., Cohn, E., Kidder, L. 1982. Models of helping and coping. *Am. Psychol.* 37:368–84

Bright-See, E., Levy, S. 1985. Dietary intervention in cancer prevention trials and clinical practice: some methodological issues. In *Cancer, Nutrition, and Eating Behavior: A Biobehavioral Perspective*, ed. T. Burish, S. Levy, B. Meyerwitz. Hillsdale, NJ: Erlbaum

Brody, E. M., Kleban, M. H. 1981. Physical and mental health symptoms of older people: Whom do they tell? *J. Am. Geriatr. Soc.* 29:442–49

Brown, J. S., Rawlinson, M. E., Hardin, D. M. 1982. Family functioning and health status. *J. Fam. Issues* 3:91–110

Brownell, K., Greenwood, M. R. C., Blackburn, G., Rodin, J., Stein, L., et al. 1988. Weight cycling, metabolism, and health: a critical review. *J. Nutr.* In press

Brownell, K., Heckerman, C., Westlake, R., Hayes, S., Monti, P. 1978. The effect of couples training and partner cooperativeness in the behavioral treatment of obesity. *Behav. Res. Ther.* 16:323–33

Brownell, K. D., Cohen, R. Y., Stunkard, A. J., Felix, M. R. J., Cooley, N. B. 1984. Weight loss competitions at the work site: impact on weight, morale and cost-effectiveness. *Am. J. Public Health* 74:1283–85

Brownell, K. D., Marlatt, G. A., Lichtenstein, E., Wilson, G. T. 1986. Understanding and preventing relapse. *Am. Psychol.* 41:765–82

Brownell, K. D., Stunkard, A. J., McKeon, P. E. 1985. Weight reduction at the work site: a promise partially fulfilled. *Am. J. Psychiatry* 142:47–52

Bruhn, J. G., Philips, B. U. 1984. Measuring social support: a synthesis of current approaches. *J. Behav. Med.* 7:151–69

Buckalew, L. W., Sallis, R. E. 1986. Patient compliance and medication perception. *J. Clin. Psychol.* 42:49–53

Bush, T. L., Barrett-Connor, E. 1985. Noncontraceptive estrogen used and cardiovascular disease. *Epidemiol. Rev.* 7:80–104

Byrne, D. G., Barry, J., Nelson, D. 1963. Relation of the revised repression-sensitization scale to measures of self-description. *Psychol. Rep.* 13:323–34

Byrne, D. G., Rosenman, R. H. 1986. The Type A behavior pattern as a precursor to stressful life-events: a confluence of coronary risks. *J. Med. Psychol.* 59:75–82

Cadoret, R. J., Cain, C. A., Grove, W. M. 1980. Development of alcoholism in adoptees raised apart from alcoholic biologic relatives. *Arch. Gen. Psychiatry* 78:561–63

Cadoret, R. J., O'Gorman, T. W., Troughton, E., Heywood, E. 1985. Alcoholism and antisocial personality: interrelationships, genetic, and environmental factors. *Arch. Gen. Psychiatry* 42:161–67

Cadoret, R. J., Troughton, E., O'Gorman, T. W. 1987. Genetic and environmental factors in alcohol abuse and antisocial personality. *J. Stud. Alcohol.* 48:1–8

Caplan, G. 1974. *Support Systems and Community Mental Health.* New York: Behavioral Publ.

Carmelli, D., Chesney, M., Rosenman, R., Fabsitz, R., Borhani, N. 1988a. Genetic heritability and shared environmental influences of Type A measures in the NHLBI twin study. Submitted

Carmelli, D., Rosenman, R. H., Chesney, M. A. 1988. Stability of the Type A structured interview and related questionnaires in a 10 year follow-up of an adult cohort of twins. *Behav. Med.* In press

Carmelli, D., Rosenman, R. H., Swan, G. E., Chesney, M. A. 1988b. The Cook and Medley HO scale: a heritability analysis in adult male twins. Submitted

Case, R. B., Heller, S. S., Case, N. B., Moss, A. J. 1985. The multicenter post-infarction research group: type A behavior and survival after acute myocardial infarction. *New Engl. J. Med.* 312:737–41

Cassel, J. 1976. The contribution of the social environment to host resistance. *Am. J. Epidemiol.* 104:107–23

Cassileth, B., Lusk, E., Miller, D., Brown, L., Biller, C. 1985. Psychosocial correlates of survival in advanced malignant disease. *New Engl. J. Med.* 312:1551–55

Cassileth, B., Lusk, E., Walsh, W., Altman, H., Pisano, M. 1987. Psychosocial correlates of unusually good outcome 3 years after cancer diagnosis. *Proc. Am. Soc. Clin. Oncol.* 6:253 (Abstr.)

Cattanach, L., Rodin, J. 1988. Psychosocial components of the stress process in bulimia. *Int. J. Eating Disord.* 7:75–88

Ciliberto, D. J., Levin, J., Arluke, A. 1981. Nurses' diagnostic stereotyping of the elderly: the case of organic brain syndrome. *Res. Aging* 3:299–310

Cleary, P. D., Mechanic, D., Greenley, J. R. 1982. Sex differences in medical care utilization: an empirical investigation. *J. Health Soc. Behav.* 23:106–19

Cloninger, C. R. 1987. Neurogenetic adaptive mechanisms in alcoholism. *Science* 236:410–16

Cobb, S. 1974. Physiological changes in men whose jobs were abolished. *J. Psychosom. Res.* 18:245–58

Cobb, S. 1976. Social support as a moderator of life stress. *Psychosom. Med.* 38:300–14

Cohen, F. 1984. Coping. See Matarazzo et al 1984, pp. 261–74

Cohen, F., Lazarus, R. S. 1973. Active coping processes, coping disposition and recovery from surgery. *Psychosom. Med.* 35:375–88

Cohen, F., Lazarus, R. S. 1979. Coping with the stresses of illness. In *Health Psychology: A Handbook,* ed. G. C. Stone, F. Cohen, N. E. Adler. San Francisco: Jossey-Bass

Cohen, S., Evans, G. W., Stokols, D., Krantz, D. S., eds. 1986. *Behavior, Health, and Environmental Stress.* New York: Plenum

Cohen, S., McKay, G. 1984. Social support, stress and the buffering hypothesis: a theoretical analysis. In *Handbook of Psychology and Health,* ed. A. Baum, J. E. Singer, S. E. Taylor, 4:253–67. Hillsdale, NJ: Erlbaum

Cohen, S., Mermelstein, R., Baer, J. S., Lichtenstein, E., Kingsolver, K., Kamarck, T. W. 1987. Social support interventions for smoking cessation. In *Creating Support*

Groups: Formats, Processes and Effects, ed. B. H. Gottlieb. New York: Sage

Cohen, S., Mermelstein, R., Kamarck, T., Hoberman, H. 1985. Measuring the functional components of social support. See Sarason & Sarason 1985, pp. 73–94

Cohen, S., Syme, S. L. 1985. Issues in the study and application of social support. In *Social Support and Health,* ed. S. Cohen, S. L. Syme. New York: Academic

Cohen, S., Wills, T. A. 1985. Stress, social support, and the buffering hypothesis. *Psychol. Bull.* 98:310–57

Colletti, G., Brownell, K. D. 1982. The physical and emotional benefits of social support: applications to obesity, smoking and alcoholism. In *Progress in Behavior Modification,* ed. M. Hersen, P. M. Miller. New York: Academic

Contrada, R. J., Glass, D. C., Krakoff, L. R., Krantz, D. S., Kehoe, K., et al. 1982. Effects of control over aversive stimulation and Type A behavior on cardiovascular and plasma catecholamine responses. *Psychophysiology* 19:408–19

Contrada, R. J., Wright, R. A., Glass, D. C. 1984. Task difficulty, Type A behavior pattern, and cardiovascular response. *Psychophysiology* 21:638–46

Cook, W., Medley, D. 1954. Proposed hostility and pharisaic virtue scales for the MMPI. *J. Appl. Psychol.* 38:414–18

Costa, P. T. Jr., McCrae, R. R. 1987a. Neuroticism, somatic complaints, and disease: Is the bark worse than the bite? *J. Pers.* 55:299–316

Costa, P. T. Jr., McCrae, R. R. 1987b. Personality assessment in psychosomatic medicine: value of a trait taxonomy. In *Advances in Psychosomatic Medicine,* ed. T. N. Wise. Switzerland: Karger

Costa, P. T. Jr., Zonderman, A. B., McCrae, R. R., Williams, R. B. Jr. 1986. Cynicism and paranoid alienation in the Cook and Medley HO Scale. *Psychosom. Med.* 48:283–85

Cox, M., Shephard, R. J., Corey, P. 1981. Influence of an employee fitness programme upon fitness, productivity and absenteeism. *Ergonomics* 24:795–806

Cox, T., MacKay, C. 1982. Psychosocial factors and psychophysiological mechanisms in the etiology and development of cancers. *Soc. Sci. Med.* 16:381–96

Craig, K. D. 1984. A social learning perspective on pain experience. In *Perspectives on Behavior Therapy in the Eighties,* ed. M. Rosenbaum, C. M. Franks, Y. Jaffe. New York: Springer

Crowne, K. P., Marlowe, D. 1964. *The Approval Motive: Studies in Evaluative Dependence.* New York: Wiley

Cummings, K. M., Jette, A. M., Brock, B.

M., Haefner, D. P. 1979. Psychosocial determinants of immunization behavior in a swine influenza campaign. *Med. Care* 17:639–49

Davis, P., Schwartz, G. 1987. Repression and the inaccessibility of affective memories. *J. Pers. Soc. Psychol.* 52:155–62

Dawber, T. R. 1980. *The Framingham Study: The Epidemiology of Atherosclerotic Disease.* Cambridge, MA: Harvard Univ. Press

Deaton, A. V. 1985. Adaptive noncompliance in pediatric asthma: the parent as expert. *J. Pediatr. Psychol.* 10:1–14

Dembroski, T. M. 1986. Overview of classic and stress-related risk factors: relationship to substance effects on reactivity. See Matthews et al 1986b, pp. 275–89

Dembroski, T. M., Costa, P. T. Jr. 1987. Coronary prone behavior: components of the Type A pattern and hostility. *J. Pers.* 55:211–35

Dembroski, T. M., MacDougall, J. M. 1983. Behavioral and psychophysiological perspectives on coronary-prone behavior. In *Biobehavioral Bases of Coronary Heart Disease,* ed. T. M. Dembroski, T. H. Schmidt, G. Blumchen. New York: Karger

Dembroski, T. M., MacDougall, J. M., Cardozo, S. R., Ireland, S. K., Kurg-Fite, J. 1985. Selective cardiovascular effects of stress and cigarette smoking in young women. *Health Psychol.* 4:153–67

Dembroski, T. M., MacDougall, J. M., Williams, R. B., Haney, T. L., Blumenthal, J. A. 1985. Components of Type A, hostility, and anger in relationship to angiographic findings. *Psychosom. Med.* 47:219–33

Der-Karabetian, A., Gebharp, N. 1986. Effect of physical fitness program in the workplace. *J. Bus. Psychol.* 1:51–57

Detre, K. M., Feinleib, M., Matthews, K. A., Kerr, B. W. 1987. The federal women's study. In *Coronary Heart Disease in Women,* ed. E. Eaker, B. Packard, N. Wenger, et al, pp. 78–82. New York: Haymarket Doyma

DiMatteo, M. R., Hays, R. 1981. Social support and serious illness. In *Social Networks and Social Support in Community Mental Health,* ed. B. H. Gottlieb, pp. 117–47. Beverly Hills, Calif: Sage

DiMatteo, M. R., DiNicola, D. 1982. *Achieving Patient Compliance.* Elmsford, NY: Pergamon

Dimond, M. 1979. Social support and adaptation to chronic illness: the case of maintenance hemodialysis. *Res. Nurs. Health* 2:101–8

Dohrenwend, B. S., Dohrenwend, B. P. 1981. *Stressful Life Events and Their Contexts.* New York: Neale Watson

Doll, R., Peto, R. 1981. *The Causes of Cancer.* New York: Oxford Univ. Press

Donegan, N. H., Rodin, J., O'Brien, C. P., Solomon, R. L. 1984. A learning-theory approach to commonalities. See Levison et al 1984, pp. 111–56

Donovan, J. E., Jessor, R. 1985. Structure of problem behavior in adolescence and young adulthood. *J. Consult. Clin. Psychol.* 53: 890–904

Downey, G., Silber, R. C, Wortman, C. B., Herrmann, C. Reconsidering the attribution-adjustment relation following a major negative event: coping with the loss of a child. Unpublished

Dunkel-Schetter, C., DeLongis, A., Gruen, R. J. 1986. Dynamics of a stressful encounter: cognitive appraisal, coping, and encounter outcomes. *J. Pers. Soc. Psychol.* 50:992–1003

Eagleston, J. R., Kirmil-Gray, K., Thoresen, C. E., Wiedenfeld, S. A., Bracke, P., et al. 1986. Physical health correlates of Type A behavior in children and adolescents. *J. Behav. Med.* 9:341–62

Edlin, G., Golanty, E. 1988. *Health and Wellness.* Boston: Jones & Bartlett

Eiser, J. R. 1982. Addiction as attribution: cognitive processes in giving up smoking. In *Social Psychology and Behavioral Medicine,* ed. J. R. Eiser. New York: Wiley

Elliott, G. R., Eisdorfer, C., eds. 1982. *Stress and Human Health: Analysis and Implications of Research.* New York: Springer

Engel, B. T. 1986. Type A: behavior or trait? In *Biological and Psychological Factors in Cardiovascular Disease,* ed. T. H. Schmidt, T. M. Dembroski, G. Blumchen. Berlin: Springer-Verlag

Engel, B. T. 1985. Stress is a noun! No, a verb! No, an adjective! In *Stress and Coping,* ed. T. McCabe, P. Schneiderman, pp. 3–12. Hillsdale, NJ: Erlbaum

Epstein, L. H., Jennings, J. R. 1986. Smoking, stress, cardiovascular reactivity, and coronary heart disease. See Matthews et al 1986b, pp. 291–309

Ewart, C. K., Stewart, K. J., Gillilan, R. E., Kelemen, M. H., Valenti, S. A., et al. 1986. Usefulness of self-efficacy in predicting overexertion during programmed exercise in coronary artery disease. *Am. J. Cardiol.* 57:557–61

Ewart, C. K., Taylor, C. B., Reese, L. B., De Busk, R. F. 1983. Effects of early postmyocardial infarction exercise testing on self-perception and subsequent physical activity. *Am. J. Cardiol.* 51:1076–80

Eysenck, H. J. 1985. Personality as a predictor of cancer and cardiovascular disease: a causal analysis. *Pers. Indiv. Differ.* 6:535–56

Eysenck, H. J. 1987. Personality as a predictor of cancer and cardiovascular disease, and the application of behaviour therapy in prophylaxis. *Eur. J. Psychiatry* 1:29–41

Farquhar, J. W., Fortmann, S. P., Maccoby, N., Wood, P. D., Haskell, W. L., et al. 1984. The Stanford Five City Project: an overview. See Matarazzo et al 1984, pp. 1154–67

Fava, G. A., Baldaro, B., Osti, R. A. 1980. Towards a self-rating scale for alexithymia. *Psychother. Psychosom.* 34:34–39

Feist, J., Brannon, L. 1988. *Health Psychology.* Belmont, Calif: Wadsworth

Felix, M. R. J., Stunkard, A. J., Cohen, R. Y., Cooley, N. B. 1985. Health promotion at the worksite: a process for establishing programs. *Prev. Med.* 14:99–108

Felton, B. J., Revenson, T. A., Hinrichsen, G. A. 1984. Stress and coping in the explanation of psychological adjustment among chronically ill adults. *Soc. Sci. Med.* 10:889–98

Fields, H. L., Levine, J. D. 1981. Biology of placebo analgesia. *Am. J. Med.* 70:745–46

Fleming, R., Baum, A., Reddy, D., Gatchel, R. J. 1984. Behavioral and biochemical effects of job loss and unemployment stress. *J. Hum. Stress* 10:12–17

Fleming, R., Leventhal, H., Glynn, K., Ershler, J. 1988. The role of cigarettes in the initiation and progression of early substance use. Submitted

Folkman, S. 1984. Personal control and stress and coping processes: a theoretical analysis. *J. Pers. Soc. Psychol.* 46:839–52

Folkman, S., Lazarus, R. S., Gruen, R. J., DeLongis, A. 1986. Appraisal, coping, health status, and psychological symptoms. *J. Pers. Soc. Psychol.* 50:571–79

Fontana, A. F., Kerns, R. D., Rosenberg, R. L., Marcus, J. L., Colonese, K. L. 1986. Exercise training for cardiac patients: adherence, fitness and benefits. *J. Cardiol. Rehabil.* 6:4–15

Frankenhaeuser, M. 1986a. A psychological framework for research on human stress and coping. In *Dynamics of Stress,* ed. M. H. Appley, R. Trumbell, pp. 101–16. New York: Plenum

Frankenhaeuser, M. 1986b. The psychobiology of good health at work. In *Occupational Psychiatry—Current Changes at Work and Their Effects on Mental Health,* ed. L. Levy. Procedures from the WPA Reg. Symp. Copenhagen, August

Freedman, R. R., Sabharwal, S. C., Desai, N. 1988. Sex differences in peripheral vascular adrenergic receptors. *Circ. Res.* In press

Friedman, H. S., Booth-Kewley, S. 1987. The "disease-prone personality": a meta analytic view of the construct. *Am. Psychol.* 42:539–55

Friedman, M., Powell, L. H. 1984. The diagnosis and quantitative assessment of Type A behavior: introduction and description of the videotaped structured interview. *Int. Psychol.* 123–29

Friedman, M., Thoresen, C. E., Gill, J. J., Ulmer, D., Powell, L. H., et al. 1986. Alteration of Type A behavior and its effect on cardiac recurrences in post myocardial infarction patients: summary results of the recurrent coronary prevention project. *Am. Heart J.* 112:653–65

Funch, D., Marshall, J. 1983. The role of stress, social support and age in survival from breast cancer. *J. Psychosom. Res.* 27:177–83

Funch, D., Mettlin, C. 1982. The role of support in relation to recovery from breast surgery. *Soc. Sci. Med.* 16:91

Funk, S. C., Houston, B. K. 1987. A critical analysis of the hardiness scale's validity and utility. *J. Pers. Soc. Psychol.* 53:572–78

Ganellen, R. J., Blaney, P. H. 1984. Hardiness and social support as moderators of the effects of life stress. *J. Pers. Soc. Psychol.* 47:156–63

Gill, J. J., Price, V. A., Friedman, M., Thoresen, C. E., Powell, L. H., et al. 1985. Reduction in Type A behavior in healthy middle-aged American military officers. *Am. Heart J.* 110:503–14

Glasgow, R. E., McCaul, K. D., Schafer, L. C. 1986. Barriers to regimen adherence among persons with insulin-dependent diabetes. *J. Behav. Med.* 9:65–77

Glass, D. C., Contrada, R. 1983. Type A behavior catecholamines: a critical review. In *Norepinephrine: Clinical Aspects*, ed. C. R. Lake, M. Ziegler. Baltimore: Williams & Wilkins

Glass, D. C., Krakoff, L. R., Contrada, R., Hilton, W. C., Kehoe, K., Mannucci, E. G., et al. 1980. Effects of harassment and competition upon cardiovascular and plasma catecholamine responses in Type A and Type B individuals. *Psychophysiology* 17:453–63

Glass, G. V., Singer, J. E. 1972. *Urban Stress: Experiments on Noise and Social Stressors.* New York: Academic

Glasser, W. 1976. *Positive Addiction.* New York: Harper & Row

Goldstein, I. B., Shapiro, D. 1988. The effects of stress and caffeine on hypertensives. *Psychosom. Med.* In press

Gore, S. 1981. Stress-buffering functions of social supports: an appraisal and clarification of research models. In *Stressful Life Events and Their Contexts*, ed. B. S. Dohrenwend, B. P. Dohrenwend. New York: Prodist

Gotay, C. C. 1981. *Causal attributions and coping behaviors in early-stage cervical cancer.* Presented at Am. Psychol. Assoc. Ann. Meet., Los Angeles, Calif.

Government of Canada. 1982. Canada's fitness. In *Fitness Canada*, p. 3. Ottawa, Canada

Graham, S., Rawls, W., Swanson, M.,

McCurtis, J. 1982. Sex partners and herpes simplex virus Type 2 in the epidemiology of cancer of the cervix. *Am. J. Epidemiol.* 115:729–35

Greer, S., Pettingale, K. W., Morris, T., Haybittle, J. 1985. Mental attitudes to cancer: an additional prognostic factor. *Lancet* 1:750

Grunberg, N. E., Bowen, D. J., Maycock, V. A., Nespor, S. M. 1985. The importance of sweet taste and caloric content in the effects of nicotine on specific food consumption. *Psychopharmacology* 87:198–203

Haft, J. I. 1974. Cardiovascular injury induced by sympathetic catecholamines. *Prog. Cardiovasc. Dis.* 17:73–86

Hall, S. M., Ginsberg, D., Jones, R. T. 1986. Smoking cessation and weight gain. *J. Consult. Clin. Psychol.* 54:342–46

Hamburg, D. A., Elliott, G. R., Parron, D. L., eds. 1982. *Health and Behavior: Frontiers of Research in the Biobehavioral Sciences* (IOM Publ. 82-01). Washington, DC: Natl. Acad. Press

Hansen, D. A., Hill, R. 1964. Families under stress. In *Handbook of Marriage and the Family*, ed. H. T. Christensen. Chicago: Rand-McNally

Hanson, J. D., Larson, M. E., Snowdon, C. T. 1976. Effects of control over high-intensity noise on plasma cortisol-levels in rhesus monkeys. *Behav. Biol.* 16:333–40

Harris, D. M., Guten, S. 1979. Health-protective behavior: an exploratory study. *J. Health Soc. Behav.* 20:17–20

Harwood, A., ed. 1981. *Ethnicity and Medical Care.* Cambridge, Mass: Harvard Univ. Press

Haskell, W. L. 1984. Overview: Health benefits of exercise. See Matarazzo et al 1984, pp. 409–23

Haug, M. R. 1981. Age and medical care utilization patterns. *J. Gerontology* 36:103–11

Hauser, S. T., Jacobson, A. M. 1986. Children with recently diagnosed diabetes: interactions within their families. *Health Psychol.* 5:273–96

Haverkos, H., Curran, J. 1982. The current outbreak of Kaposi's sarcoma and opportunistic infections. *Ca-A Cancer J. Clin.* 32:330–39

Haw, M. A. 1982. Women, work and stress: a review and agenda for the future. *J. Health Soc. Behav.* 23:132–44

Haynes, S. G., Feinlieb, M., Kannel, W. B. 1980. The relationship of psychosocial factors to coronary heart disease in the Framingham Study. III. Eight-year incidence of coronary heart disease. *Am. J. Epidemiol.* 107:362–82

Hegsted, D. M. 1984. What is a healthful diet? See Matarazzo et al 1984, pp. 552–74

Heiberg, A. A. 1980. Alexithymic characteristics and somatic illness. *Psychother. Psychosom.* 28:261–66

Hellstrand, K., Hermidsson, S. 1987. Role of serotonin in the regulation of human natural killer cell cytotoxicity. *J. Immunol.* 139: 869–75

Herd, J. A. 1986. Neuroendocrine mechanisms in coronary heart disease. See Matthews et al 1986b, pp. 49–70

Holahan, C. J., Moos, R. H. 1986. Personality, coping, and family resources in stress resistance: a longitudinal analysis. *J. Pers. Soc. Psychol.* 51:389–95

Holmes, T., Rahe, R. 1967. The social readjustment rating scale. *J. Psychosom. Res.* 11:213–18

Homan, S. M., Haddock, C. C., Winner, C. A., Coe, R. M., Wolinsky, F. D. 1986. Widowhood, sex, labor-force participation, and the use of physician services by elderly adults. *J. Gerontol.* 41:793–96

House, J. S. 1981. *Work Stress and Social Support.* Reading, Mass: Addison-Wesley

House, J. S., Kahn, R. L., McLeod, J. D., Williams, D. 1985. Measures and concepts of social support. See Cohen & Syme 1985, pp. 83–108

House, J. S., Strecher, V., Metzner, H. L., Robbins, C. A. 1986. Occupational stress and health among men and women in the Tecumseh Community Health Study. *J. Health Soc. Behav.* 27:62–77

House, J. S., Umberson, D., Landis, K. R. 1988. Structures and processes of social support. *Ann. Rev. Sociol.* 14:293–318

Houston, B. K. 1986. Psychological variables and cardiovascular and neuroendocrine reactivity. See Matthews et al 1986b, pp. 207–29

Houston, B. K., Smith, T. W., Zurawski, R. M. 1988. Principal dimensions of the Framingham Type A scale: differential relationships to cardiovascular reactivity and anxiety. *J. Hum. Stress.* In press

Hulka, B. 1982. Risk factors for cervical cancer. *J. Chronic Dis.* 35:3–11

Hull, J. G., Van Treuren, R. R., Virnelli, S. 1987. Hardiness and health: a critique and alternative approach. *J. Pers. Soc. Psychol.* 53:518–30

Hunt, W. A., Barnett, L. W., Branch, L. G. 1971. Relapse rates in addiction programs. *J. Clin. Psychol.* 27:455–56

Irwin, M. R., Vale, W., Britton, K. T. 1987. Central corticotropin-releasing factor suppresses natural killer cytotoxicity. *Brain Behav. Immunol.* 1:81–87

Jackson, J. J. 1981. Urban black Americans. See Harwood 1981, pp. 37–129

Jacobs, S., Mason, J., Kosten, T., Kasl, S., Ostfeld, A., et al. 1985. Acute bereavement, threatened loss, ego defenses and

adrenocortical function. *Psychother. Psychosom.* 44:151–59

James, S. A., LaCroix, A. Z., Kleinbaum, D. G., Strogatz, D. S. 1984. John Henryism and blood pressure differences among black men. II. The role of occupational stress. *J. Behav. Med.* 7:259–75

Jamison, R. N., Parris, W. C., Maxson, W. S. 1987. Psychological factors influencing recovery from outpatient surgery. *Behav. Res. Ther.* 1:31–37

Janis, I. L. 1984. Improving adherence to medical recommendations: In *Handbook of Psychology and Health*, Vol. 4, ed. A. Baum, S. E. Taylor, J. E. Singer. Hillsdale, NJ: Erlbaum

Janoff-Bulman, R., Frieze, I. H. 1983. A theoretical perspective for understanding reactions to victimization. *J. Soc. Issues* 39:1–17

Janoff-Bulman, R., Lang-Gunn, L. 1988. Coping with disease and accidents: the role of self-blame attributions. In *Social-Personal Interference in Clinical Psychology*, ed. L. Y. Abramson. New York: The Guilford Press

Janz, N. K., Becker, M. H. 1984. The health belief model: a decade later. *Health Educ. Q.* 11:1–47

Jarvik, L. F., Perl, M. 1981. Overview of physiologic dysfunctions related to psychiatric problems in the elderly. In *Neuropsychiatric Manifestations of Physical Disease in the Elderly*, ed. A. J. Levenson, R. C. W. Hall. New York: Raven

Jellinek, E. M. 1960. *The Disease Concept in Alcoholism.* New Brunswick, NJ: Hill House Press

Jemmott, J. B., Croyle, R. T., Ditto, P. H. 1988. Commonsense epidemiology: self-based judgments from laypersons and physicians. *Health Psychol.* 7:55–72

Jemmott, J. B., Locke, S. E. 1984. Psychosocial factors, immunologic mediation, and human susceptibility to infectious diseases: How much do we know? *Psychol. Bull.* 95:78–108

Jenkins, C. D. 1966. The semantic differential for health. *Pub. Health Rep.* 81:549–58

Jenkins, C. D. 1982. Overview: behavioral perspectives on health risks among the disadvantaged. In *Behavior, Health Risks, and Social Disadvantage; from Health and Behavior: A Research Agenda, Interim Rep. 6*, ed. D. L. Parron, F. Solomon, C. D. Jenkins. Inst. Med., Washington, DC: Natl. Acad. Press. IOM Publ. 82-002

Jennings, J. R. 1983. Attention and coronary heart disease. See Krantz et al 1983a, pp. 85–124

Jensen, M. R. 1987. Psychobiological factors predicting the course of breast cancer. *J. Pers.* 55:317–42

Jessor, R. 1984. Adolescent development and behavioral health. See Matarazzo et al 1984, pp. 69–90

Jessor, R. 1987. Problem-behavior theory, psychosocial development, and adolescent problem drinking. *Br. J. Addict.* 82:331–42

Jessor, R., Jessor, S. L. 1982. Adolescence to young adulthood: a twelve year prospective study of problem behavior and psychosocial development. In *Longitudinal Research in the United States*, ed. A. A. Mednick, M. Harway. Boston: Martinus Nijhoff

Johnson, E. H., Broman, C. L. 1987. The relationship of anger expression to health problems among black Americans in national survey. *J. Behav. Med.* 10:103–16

Johnson, E. J., Tversky, A. 1983. Affect, generalization, and the perception of risk. *J. Pers. Soc. Psychol.* 45:20–33

Jones, E. E., Kanouse, D. E., Kelley, H. H., Nisbett, R. E., Valins, S., Weiner, B., eds. 1972. *Attribution: Perceiving the Causes of Behavior.* Morristown, NJ: General Learning Press. 186 pp.

Joseph, J. G., Montgomery, S. B., Emmons, C., Kessler, R. C., Ostrow, D. G., et al. 1987. Magnitude and determinants of behavioral risk reduction: longitudinal analysis of a cohort at risk for AIDS. *Psychol. Health* 1:73–96

Justice, A. 1985. Review of the effects of stress on cancer in laboratory animals: importance of time of stress application and type of tumor. *Psychol. Bull.* 98:108–38

Kamen, L. P., Rodin, J., Seligman, M. E. P. Explanatory style and T-lymphocyte subpopulations: a longitudinal study of the healthy elderly. In draft.

Kandel, D. B., Maloff, D. R. 1984. Commonalities in drug use: a sociological perspective. See Levison et al 1984, pp. 3–27

Kaplan, G. A., Camacho, T. 1983. Perceived health and mortality: A nine-year follow-up of the human population laboratory cohort. *Am. J. Epidemiol.* 117:292–304

Kaplan, R. M., Atkins, C. J., Reinsch, S. 1984. Specific efficacy expectations mediate exercise compliance in patients with COPD. *Health Psychol.* 3:223–42

Kaplan, R. M., Hartwell, S. L. 1987. Differential effects of social support and social network on physiological and social outcomes in men and women with Type II diabetes mellitus. *Health Psychol.* 6:387–98

Kasl, S. V., Beckman, L. F. 1981. In *Aging, Biology, and Behavior*, pp. 345–85. New York: Academic

Kasl, S. V., Cobb, S. 1970. Blood pressure changes in men undergoing job loss: a preliminary report. *Psychosom. Med.* 32:19–38

Kasl, S. V., Cobb, S., Brooks, G. W. 1968. Changes in serum uric acid and cholesterol levels in men undergoing job loss. *J. Am. Med. Assoc.* 206:1500

Kelly, J. A., St. Lawrence, J. S. 1988. AIDS prevention and treatment: psychology's role in the health crisis. *Clin. Psychol. Rev.* 8:255–84

Kessler, R. C., McLeod, J. D. 1985. Social support and mental health in community samples. See Cohen & Syme 1985, pp. 219–40

Kessler, R. C., Price, R. H., Wortman, C. B. 1985. Social factors in psychopathology: stress, social support, and coping processes. *Ann. Rev. Psychol.* 36:531–72

Kessler, R. C., Wortman, C. B. 1988. Social and psychological factors in health and illness. In *Handbook of Medical Sociology*, ed. H. E. Freeman, S. Levine. Englewood Cliffs, NJ: Prentice-Hall. 4th ed. In press

Kiecolt-Glaser, J. K., Fisher, L. D., Ogrocki, P., Stout, J., Speicher, C. E., Glaser, R. 1987. Marital quality, marital disruption, and immune function. *Psychosom. Med.* 49:13–34

Kiecolt-Glaser, J. K., Glaser, R. 1988. Behavioral influences on immune function: evidence for the interplay between stress and health. In *Stress and Coping Across Development*, ed. T. Field, P. M. McCabe, N. Schneiderman. Hillsdale, NJ: Lawrence Erlbaum. In press

Kirscht, J. P. 1983. Preventive health behavior: a review of research and issues. *Health Psychol.* 2:277–301

Kirscht, J. P., Haefner, D. P., Kegeles, S. S., Rosenstock, I. M. 1966. A national study of health beliefs. *J. Health Hum. Behav.* 7:248–54

Kleiger, J. H., Dirks, J. F. 1980. Psychomaintenance aspects of alexithymia: relationship to medical outcome variables in a chronic respiratory illness population. *Psychother. Psychosom.* 34:25–33

Kobasa, S. C. 1982. The hardy personality: toward a social psychology of stress and health. In *Social Psychology of Health and Illness*, ed. G. S. Sanders, J. Suls, pp. 3–32. Hillsdale, NJ: Erlbaum

Kobasa, S. C., Maddi, S. R., Courington, S. 1981. Personality and constitution as mediators in the stress-illness relationship. *J. Health Soc. Behav.* 22:368–78

Kobasa, S. C., Maddi, S. R., Kahn, S. 1982. Hardiness and health: a prospective study. *J. Pers. Soc. Psychol.* 42:168–77

Kobasa, S. C., Maddi, S. R., Zola, M. A. 1983. Type A and hardiness. *J. Behav. Med.* 6:41–51

Korsch, B. M., Negrete, V. F. 1972. Doctor-patient communication. *Sci. Am.* 227:66–74

Krantz, D. S., Baum, A., Singer, J. E. 1983a. *Handbook of Psychology and Health*, Vol.

III: *Cardiovascular Disorders and Behavior*. Hillsdale, NJ: Erlbaum

Krantz, D. S., Baum, A., Singer, J. E. 1983b. Behavior and cardiovascular disease: issues and overview. See Krantz et al 1983a, pp. 1–17

Krantz, D. S., Glass, D. C., Contrada, R., Miller, N. E. 1981. Behavior and health. In *Five Year Outlook on Science and Technology: 1981*. Washington DC: Natl. Sci. Found./US GPO

Krantz, D. S., Grunberg, N. E., Baum, A. 1985. Health psychology. *Ann. Rev. Psychol.* 36:349–83

Kristeller, J., Rodin, J. 1984. The function of attention in cognitive models of behavior change and maintenance. In *Handbook of Psychology and Health*, Vol. 4: *Social Psychological Aspects of Health*, ed. S. E. Taylor, J. E. Singer. Hillsdale, NJ: Erlbaum

Kristiansen, C. M. 1985. Value correlates of preventive health behavior. *J. Pers. Soc. Psychol.* 49:748–58

Kristiansen, C. M. 1986. A two-value model of preventive health behavior. *Basic Appl. Soc. Psychol.* 7:173–83

Kulik, J. A., Mahler, H. I. M. 1987. Health status, perceptions of risk, and prevention interest for health and nonhealth problems. *Health Psychol.* 6:15–27

Lang, A. R. 1984. Addictive personality: a viable construct? See Levison et al 1984, pp. 157–235

Lau, R. R., Hartman, K. A. 1983. Common sense representations of common illnesses. *Health Psychol.* 3:167–86

Laudenslager, M., Ryan, S., Drugan, S., Hyson, R., Maier, S. 1983. Coping and immunosuppression: inescapable but not escapable shock suppresses lymphocyte proliferation. *Science* 221:568–70

Lazarus, R. S. 1966. *Psychological Stress and the Coping Process*. New York: McGraw-Hill

Lazarus, R. S. 1984. Puzzles in the study of daily hassles. *J. Behav. Med.* 7:375–89

Lazarus, R. S., DeLongis, A. 1983. Psychological stress and coping in aging. *Am. Psychol.* 38:245–54

Lazarus, R. S., DeLongis, A., Folkman, S., Gruen, R. 1985. Stress and adaptational outcomes: The problem of confounded measures. *Am. Psychol.* 40:770–79

Lazarus, R. S., Folkman, S. 1984a. Coping and adaptation. In *The Handbook of Behavioral Medicine*, ed. W. D. Gentry, pp. 282–325. New York: Guilford

Lazarus, R. S., Folkman, S. 1984b. *Stress, Appraisal, and Coping*. New York: Springer

Lehman, D. R., Ellard, J. H., Wortman, C. B. 1986. Social support for the bereaved: recipients' and providers' perspectives on what is helpful. *J. Consult. Clin. Psychol.* 54:438–46

Lehman, D. R., Wortman, C. B., Williams, A. F. 1987. Long-term effects of losing a spouse or child in a motor vehicle crash. *J. Pers. Soc. Psychol.* 52:218–31

Lettieri, D. J., Sayers, M., Pearson, H. W., eds. 1980. *Theories on Drug Abuse: Selected Contemporary Perspectives*. NIDA Res. Monogr. 30 Washington, DC: US Gov. Print. Off.

Leventhal, E. A. 1984. Aging and the perception of illness. *Res. Aging* 6:119–35

Leventhal, H., Cleary, P. D. 1980. The smoking problem: a review of research and theory in behavioral risk modification. *Psychol. Bull.* 88:370–405

Leventhal, H., Glynn, K., Fleming, R. 1987. Is the smoking decision an "informed choice"?: Effects of smoking risk factors on smoking beliefs. *J. Am. Med. Assoc.* 257:3373–76

Leventhal, H., Leventhal, E. A., Nguyen, T. V. 1985. Reactions of families to illness: theoretical models and perspectives. In *Health, Illness and Families*, ed. D. C. Turk, R. Kerns, pp. 108–45. New York: Wiley

Leventhal, H., Meyer, D., Nerenz, D. 1980. The commonsense representation of illness danger. In *Contributions to Medical Psychology*, ed. S. Rachman. Oxford: Pergamon

Levine, J. D., Gordon, N. C., Fields, H. L. 1978. The mechanism of placebo analgesia. *Lancet* 2:654–57

Levine, J. D., Gordon, N. C., Jones, R. T., Feilds, H. L. 1978. The narcotic antagonist naloxone enhances clinical pain. *Nature* 272:826–27

Levison, P. K., Gerstein, D. R., Maloff, D. R., eds. 1984. *Commonalities in Substance Abuse and Habitual Behavior*. Lexington, Mass: D. D. Heath. 355 pp. 2nd ed.

Levy, S., Herberman, R., Lippman, M., d'Angelo, T. 1987. Correlation of stress factors with sustained depression of natural killer cell activity and predicted prognosis in patients with breast cancer. *J. Clin. Oncol.* 5:348–53

Levy, S. M., ed. 1982. *Biological Mediators of Behavior and Disease: Neoplasia*. New York: Elsevier Biomed.

Levy, S. M. 1985. *Behavior and Cancer: Life-Style and Psychosocial Factors in the Initiation and Progression of Cancer*. San Francisco: Jossey-Bass. 257 pp.

Lewis, F. M. 1986. The impact of cancer on the family: a critical analysis of the research literature. *Patient Educ. Counsel.* 8:269–89

Lewis, F. M., Beavers, W. R., Gossett, J. T., Phillips, V. A. 1976. *No Single Thread:*

Psychological Health in Family Systems. New York: Brunner/Mazel

Lewis, M., Feiring, C. 1982. Direct and indirect interactions in social relations. In *Advances in Infancy Research,* ed. L. Lipsitt. Norwook, NJ: Ablex

Lichtenstein, E., Glasgow, R. E., Abrams, D. B. 1986. Social support in smoking cessation: in search of effective interventions. *Behav. Ther.* 17:607–19

Lichtman, R. R., Taylor, S. E. 1986. Close relationships and the female cancer patient. In *Women with Cancer: Psychological Perspectives,* ed. B. L. Andersen, pp. 233–56. New York: Springer-Verlag

Lichtman, R. R., Taylor, S. E., Wood, J. V. 1988. Social support and marital adjustment after breast cancer. Submitted

Lieberman, M., Tobin, S. 1983. *The Experience of Old Age: Stress, Coping, and Survival.* New York: Basic Books

Light, K. C., Obrist, P. 1980. Cardiovascular response to stress: effects of opportunity to avoid shock experience, and performance feedback. *Psychophysiology* 17:243–52

Lippman, M. 1982. Interactions of psychic and endocrine factors with progression of neoplastic diseases. See Levy 1982, pp. 55–82

Litt, M. D. 1988. Self-efficacy and perceived control: cognitive mediators of pain tolerance. *J. Pers. Soc. Psychol.* 54:149–60

Luft, F., Gurin, C., Weinberger, M. 1985. Electrolyte and volume hemostasis in blacks. In *Hypertension in Blacks: Epidemiology, Pathophysiology, and Treatment,* ed. W. Hall, E. Saunders, N. Shulman. Chicago: Year Book Medical Publ.

Maddi, S. R., Kobasa, S. C., Hoover, M. 1979. An alienation test. *Hum. Psychol.* 19:73–76

Magnusson, D. 1983. Implications of an interactional paradigm for research on human development. Invited address at the 7th Bienn. Meet. Int. Soc. Study Behav. Dev., Munich, July 31-August 4

Maier, S. F., Davies, S., Grau, J. W., Jackson, R. L., Morrison, D. H., et al. 1980. Opiate antagonist and long-term analgesic reaction induced by inescapable shock in rats. *J. Comp. Physiol. Psychol.* 94:1172–83

Maletta, G. J., Hepburn, K. 1986. Helping families cope with Alzheimer's: the physician's role. *Geriatrics* 41:81–87

Manning, M. M., Wright, T. L. 1983. Self-efficacy expectancies, outcome expectancies, and the persistence of pain control in childbirth. *J. Pers. Soc. Psychol.* 45:421–31

Manuck, S. B., Kaplan, J. R., Clarkson, T. B. 1983. Behaviorally induced heart rate reactivity and atherosclerosis in cynomolgus

monkeys. *Neurosci. Biobehav. Rev.* 7:485–91

Manuck, S. B., Krantz, D. S. 1986. Psychophysiological reactivity in coronary heart disease and essential hypertension. See Matthews et al 1986b, pp. 11–34

Marlatt, G. A. 1985. Coping and substance abuse: implications for research, prevention, and treatment. In *Coping and Substance Abuse,* ed. S. Shiffman, T. A. Wills, pp. 367–86. New York: Academic

Marlatt, G. A., Baer, J. S., Donovan, D. M., Kivlahan, D. R. 1988. Addictive behaviors: etiology and treatment. *Ann. Rev. Psychol.* 39:223–52

Matarazzo, J. D. 1984. Behavioral health: a 1990 challenge for the health sciences professions. See Matarazzo et al 1984, pp. 3–40

Matarazzo, J. D., Weiss, Sh. M., Herd, J. A., Miller, N. E., Weiss, St. M., eds. 1984. *Behavioral Health: A Handbook of Health Enhancement and Disease Prevention.* New York: Wiley. 1292 pp.

Matthews, K. A. 1982. Psychological perspectives on the Type A behavior pattern. *Psychol. Bull.* 91:293–323

Matthews, K. A. 1988. CHD and type A behaviors: update on the alternative to the Booth-Kewley and Friedman quantitative review. *Psychol. Bull.* In press

Matthews, K. A., Haynes, S. G. 1986. Type A behavior pattern and coronary risk: update and critical evaluation. *Am. J. Epidemiol.* 123:923–60

Matthews, K. A., Krantz, D. S., Dembroski, T. M., MacDougall, J. M. 1982. The unique and common variance in the structured interview and the Jenkins Activity Survey measures of the Type A behavior pattern. *J. Pers. Soc. Psychol.* 242:303–13

Matthews, K. A., Stoney, C. M. 1988. Influences of sex and age on cardiovascular responses during stress. *Psychosom. Med.* 50:46–56

Matthews, K. A., Stoney, C. M., Rakaczky, C. J., Jamison, W. 1986a. Family characteristics and school achievements of Type A children. *Health Psychol.* 5:453–67

Matthews, K. A., Weiss, S. M., Detre, T., Dembroski, T. M., Falkner, B., et al. 1986b. *Handbook of Stress, Reactivity, and Cardiovascular Disease.* New York: Wiley

Matthews, K. A., Woodall, K. L. 1988. Childhood origins of overt Type A behaviors and cardiovascular reactivity to behavioral stressors. *Ann. Behav. Med.* In press

McFarlane, A. H., Norman, G. R., Streiner, D., Roy, R. G. 1983. The process of social stress: stable, reciprocal, and mediating relationships. *J. Health Soc. Behav.* 24:160–73

McFarlane, A. H., Norman, G. R., Streiner, D., Roy, R. G., Scott, D. J. 1980. A longitudinal study of the influence of the psychosocial environment on health status: a preliminary report. *J. Health Soc. Behav.* 21:124–33

Mechanic, D. 1964. The influence of mothers on their children's health attitudes and behavior. *Pediatrics* 33:444–52

Mechanic, D. 1979. The stability of health and illness behavior. *Am. J. Public Health* 69:1142–45

Mechanic, D., Cleary, P. D. 1980. Factors associated with the maintenance of positive health behavior. *Prev. Med.* 9:805–14

Meichenbaum, D., Turk, D. C. 1987. *Facilitating Treatment Adherence.* New York: Plenum

Mermelstein, R., Cohen, S., Lichtenstein, E., Baer, J. S., Kamarck, T. 1986. Social support and smoking cessation and maintenance. *J. Consult. Clin. Psychol.* 54:447–53

Meyer, D. 1981. *The effects of patients' representation of high blood pressure on behavior in treatment.* PhD thesis. Univ. Wis.

Meyer, D., Leventhal, H., Gutman, M. 1985. Common-sense models of illness: the example of hypertension. *Health Psychol.* 4:115–35

Michela, J. L., Wood, J. V. 1986. Causal attributions in health and illness. In *Advances in Cognitive Behavior Modification,* ed. P. Kendall. New York: Academic

Miller, N. E. 1983. Behavioral medicine: symbiosis between laboratory and clinic. *Ann. Rev. Psychol.* 34:1–31

Molleman, E., Pruyn, J., Van Knippenberg, A. 1986. Social comparison processes among cancer patients. *Br. J. Soc. Psychol.* 1:1–13

Moos, R. H., Billings, A. G. 1982. Conceptualizing and measuring coping resources and processes. In *Handbook of Stress,* ed. L. Goldberger, S. Breznitz, pp. 212–30. New York: Macmillan

Morgan, W. P. 1977. Involvement in vigorous physical activity with special reference to adherence. In *National College of Physical Education Proceedings,* ed. L. I., Gedvilas, M. E. Knees. Chicago: Univ. Ill. at Chicago, Off. Public Serv.

Morgenstern, H., Gellert, G., Walter, S., Ostfeld, A., Siegel, B. 1984. The impact of a psychosocial support program on survival with breast cancer: the importance of selection bias in program evaluation. *J. Chronic. Dis.* 37:273–82

Morris, L. A., Kanouse, D. E. 1979. Drug-taking for physical symptoms. In *New Approaches to Social Problems,* ed. I. H.

Frieze, D. Bar-Tal, J. S. Carroll. San Francisco: Jossey-Bass

Morris, T. 1979. Psychological adjustment to mastectomy. *Cancer Treat. Rev.* 6:41–61

Moye, T. B., Hyson, R. L., Grau, J. W., Maier, S. F. 1983. Immunization of opiate analgesia: effects of prior escapable shock on subsequent shock-induced and morphine-induced antinociception. *Learn. Motiv.* 14:238–51

Myers, R. D. 1978. Psychopharmacology of alcohol. *Ann. Rev. Pharmacol. Toxicol.* 18:125–44

National Center for Health Statistics. US Depart. H. H. S. 1980. *Advancedata,* No. 64, Nove. 4; HHS Publ. 81-1250

National Center for Health Statistics. US Depart. H. H. S. 1981. *Advancedata,* No. 69, April 1; HHS Publ. (PHS) 81-1250

National Center for Health Statistics. 1984. *Health Indicators for Hispanic, Black and White Americans.* (DHHS Publ. 84-1576). Washington DC: US Depart. Health and Hum. Serv.

National Center for Health Statistics. 1984. Persons with and without a regular source of medical care: United States. *Vital and Health Statistics.* Ser. 10, No. 151. DHHS Publ. (PHS) 85-1579

Nemiah, J. C., Freyberger, H., Sifneos, P. E. 1973. Alexithymia: a view of the psychosomatic process. In *Modern Trends in Psychosomatic Medicine,* ed. O. W. Hill. Butterworth: England

Nerenz, D. R. 1979. *Control of motional distress in cancer chemotherapy.* PhD thesis. Univ. Wis., Madison

Nerenz, D. R., Leventhal, H. 1983. Self-regulation theory in chronic illness. In *Coping with Chronic Disease: Research and Applications,* ed. T. Burish, L. Bradley. New York: Academic

Norman, G. R., McFarlane, A. H., Streiner, D. L., Neal, K. A. 1982. Health diaries: strategies for compliance and relation to other measures. *J. Med. Care* 20:623–29

Oldridge, N. B. 1984. Adherence to adult exercise fitness programs. See Matarazzo et al 1984, pp. 467–87

O'Leary, A. 1985a. Self-efficacy and health. *Behav. Res. Ther.* 23:437–51

O'Leary, A. 1985b. *Psychological factors in rheumatoid arthritis pain and immune function: a self-efficacy approach.* PhD thesis. Stanford Univ.

Osterweis, M., Solomon, F., Green, M., eds. 1984. *Bereavement: Reactions, Consequences, and Care.* Washington DC: Natl. Acad. Press. 312 pp.

Pearlin, L. I., Schooler, C. 1978. The structure of coping. *J. Health Soc. Behav.* 19:2–21

Pennebaker, J. W. 1982. *The Psychology of Symptoms*. New York: Springer-Verlag

Perloff, L. S., Fetzer, B. K. 1986. Self-other judgments and perceived vulnerability to victimization. *J. Pers. Soc. Psychol.* 50: 502–10

Perri, M. G., McAdoo, W. G., Spevak, P. A., Newlin, D. B. 1984. Effect of a multi-component maintenance program on long-term weight loss. *J. Consult. Clin. Psychol.* 52:480–81

Peters-Golden, H. 1982. Breast cancer: varied perceptions of social support in the illness experience. *Soc. Sci. Med.* 16:483–91

Peterson, C., Luborsky, L., Seligman, M. E. P. 1983. Attributions and depressive mood shifts. *J. Abnorm. Psychol.* 92:96–103

Peterson, C., Seligman, M. E. P. 1987. Explanatory style and illness. *J. Pers.* 55:237–65

Peterson, C., Semmel, A., von Baeyer, C., Bramson, L. Y., Metalsky, G. I., Seligman, M. E. P. 1982. The Attributional Style Questionnaire. *Cogn. Ther. Res.* 6: 287–99

Peterson, C., Villanova, P. 1988. An expanded attributional style questionnaire. *J. Abnorm. Psychol.* 97:87–89

Peterson, J., Bakeman, R. 1988. AIDS and IV drug use among ethnic minorities. *J. Drug Issues*. In press

Pilisuk, M., Boylan, R., Acredolo, C. 1987. Social support, life stress, and subsequent medical care utilization. *Health Psychol.* 6:273–88

Pincomb, G. A., Lovallo, W. R. 1987. Caffeine enchances the physiological response to occupational stress in medical students. *Health Psychol.* 6:100–12

Pomerleau, C. S., Pomerleau, O. F. 1988. The effects of psychological stressor on cigarette smoking and subsequent behavioral and physiological responses. *Psychophysiology.* 24:278–85

Pomerleau, O. F. 1986. Nicotine as a psychoactive drug: anxiety and pain reduction. *Psychopharmacol. Bull.* 22:865–69

Pomerleau, O. F., Brady, J. P. 1979. Introduction: the scope and promise of behavioral medicine. In *Behavioral Medicine: Theory and Practice*, ed. O. F. Pomerleau, J. P. Brady. Baltimore: Williams & Wilkins

Pomerleau, O. F., Pomerleau, C. S. 1984. Neuroregulators and the reinforcement of smoking: Towards a biobehavioral explanation. *Neurosci. Biobehav. Rev.* 8:503–13

Pomerleau, O. F., Rodin, J. 1986. Behavioral medicine and health psychology. In *Handbook of Psychotherapy and Behavior Change*, ed. S. L., Garfield, A. E., Bergin, pp. 483–522. New York: Wiley

Powell, L. H., Friedman, M., Thoresen, C.

E., Gill, J. J., Ulmer, D. K. 1984. Can the Type A behavior pattern be altered after myocardial infarction? A second year report from the recurrent coronary prevention project. *Psychosom. Med.* 46:293–313

Prohaska, T. R., Keller, M. L., Leventhal, E. A., Leventhal, H. 1987. Impact of symptoms and aging attribution on emotions and coping. *Health Psychol.* 6:495–514

Puska, P. 1984. Community-based prevention of cardiovascular disease: the North Karelia Project. See Matarazzo et al 1984, pp. 1140–47

Ragland, D. R., Brand, R. J. 1988. Type A behavior and mortality from coronary heart disease. *New Engl. J. Med.* 318:65–69

Ravussin, E., Lillioja, S., Knowler, W. C., Christin, L., Freymond, D., et al. 1988. Reduced rate of energy expenditure as a risk factor for body-weight gain. *New Engl. J. Med.* 318:467–72

Recker, G. T., Wong, P. T. P. 1985. Personal optimism, physical and mental health: the triumph of successful aging. In *Cognition, Stress and Aging*, ed. J. E. Birren, J. Livingston. New York: Prentice-Hall

Redden, E. M., Tucker, R. K., Young, L. 1983. Psychometric properties of the Rosenbaum schedule for assessing self-control. *Psychol. Rec.* 33:77–86

Riley, M. W. 1987. Aging, health, and social change. In *The Aging Dimension*, ed. M. W. Riley, J. D. Matarazzo, A. Baum, Hillsdale, NJ: LEA

Roberts, S. B., Savage, J., Coward, W. A., Chew, B., Lucas, A. 1988. Energy expenditure and intake in infants born to lean and overweight mothers. *New Engl. J. Med.* 318:461–66

Robertson, L. S. 1984. Behavior and injury prevention: whose behavior? See Matarazzo et al 1984, pp. 980–89

Rodin, J. 1985. The application of social psychology. In *The Handbook of Social Psychology*, ed. G. Lindzey, E. Aronson. New York: Ramdom House

Rodin, J. 1986a. Aging and health: effects of the sense of control. *Science* 233:1271–76

Rodin, J. 1986b. Health, control and aging. In *Aging and Control*, ed. M. Baltes, P. Baltes. Hillsdale, NJ: LEA

Rodin, J. 1987. Weight change following smoking cessation: the role of food intake and exercise. *Addict. Behav.* 12:303–17

Rodin, J., Bohm, L., Wack, J. 1982. Control, coping and aging: models for research and intervention. *Appl. Soc. Psychol. Ann.* 3:153–80

Rodin, J., Timko, C., Harris, S. 1986. The construct of control: biological and psychological correlates. In *Annual Review of Gerontology and Geriatrics*, ed. C. Eisdorfer, M. P., Lawton, G. L., Maddox, pp. 3–55. New York: Springer

Rodin, J., Wack, J. T. 1984. A three stage model of treatment continuity: compliance, adherence and maintenance. In *Handbook of Psychology and Health*, ed. A. Baum, S. Taylor, J. E. Singer. Hillsdale, NJ: Erlbaum

Rose, R. J. 1986. Familial influences on cardiovascular reactivity to stress. See Matthews et al 1986b, pp. 259–72

Rosenman, R. H. 1978. The interview method of assessment of the coronary-prone behavior pattern. In *Coronary-Prone Behavior*, ed. T. M. Dembroski, S. M. Weiss, J. L. Shields, S. G. Haynes, M. Feinleib, pp. 55–70. New York: Springer-Verlag

Rosenman, R. H. 1986. Current and past history of Type A behavior pattern. In *Biological and Psychological Factors in Cardiovascular Disease*, ed. T. H. Schmidt, T. M. Dembroski, G. Blumchen, p. 70. New York: Springer-Verlag

Rosenman, R. H. 1988. Type A behavior and hypertension. In *Handbook of Hypertension (Behavioral Factors in Hypertension)*, Vol. 10, ed. S. Julius, D. R. Bassett. Amsterdam: Jaap deVries. In press

Rosenman, R. H., Brand, R. J., Scholtz, R. I., Friedman, M. 1976. Multivariate prediction of coronary heart disease during 8.5 year follow-up in the Western Collaborative Group Study. *Am. J. Cardiol.* 37:903–10

Rosenman, R. H., Swan, G. E., Carmelli, D. 1988. Definition, assessment and evolution of the Type A behavior pattern. In *Type A Behavior Pattern: Current Trends and Future Directions*, ed. B. K. Houston, C. R. Snyder. New York: Wiley. In press

Rosenstock, I. M., Kirscht, J. P. 1979. Why people seek health care. In *Health Psychology: A Handbook*, ed. G. C. Stone, F. Cohen, N. E. Adler. San Francisco: Jossey-Bass

Ross, L., Greene, D., House, P. 1977. The false consensus phenomenon: an attributional bias in self-perception and social perception processes. *J. Exp. Soc. Psychol.* 13: 279–301

Roszman, T. L., Jackson, J. C., Cross, R. J., Titus, M. J., Markesbery, W. R., Brooks, W. H. 1985. Neuroanatomic and neurotransmitter influences on immune function. *J. Immunol.* 135:769s–72s

Rowe, J. W., Kahn, R. L. 1987. Human aging: usual and successful. *Science* 237:143–49

Rozin, P. 1984. The acquisition of food habits and preferences. See Matarazzo et al 1984, pp. 590–607

Salovey, P., Birnbaum, D. The influence of mood on health-relevant cognitions. Unpublished.

Salovey, P., Rudy, T. E., Turk, D. C. 1987.

Preaching and practicing: the structure and consistency of health-protective attitudes and behaviors. *Health Educ. Res.* 2:195–205

Sarason, I. G., Sarason, B. R., eds. 1985. *Social Support: Theory, Research and Applications*. The Hague, The Netherlands: Martinus Nijhof.

Sarrell, P. 1988. Current concepts and applications of medical technologies. In *Effects of Modern Technologies on Women's Health*, ed. J. Rodin, A. Collins. Chicago: Univ. Chicago Press

Saunders, A., Williams, R. 1975. Hypertension. In *Textbook of Black-Related Diseases*, ed. R. A. Williams. New York: McGraw-Hill

Schaefer, C., Coyne, J. C., Lazarus, R. 1981. The health-related functions of social support. *J. Behav. Med.* 4:381–406

Scheier, M. F., Carver, C. S. 1985. Optimism, coping, and health: assessment and implications of generalized outcome expectancies. *Health Psychol.* 4:219–47

Scheier, M. F., Carver, C. S. 1987. Dispositional optimism and physical well-being: the influence of generalized outcome expectancies on health. *J. Pers.* 55:169–210

Schmale, A. H. 1972. Giving up as a final common pathway to changes in health. *Adv. Psychosom. Med.* 8:20–40

Schmied, L. A, Lawler, K. A. 1986. Hardiness, Type A behavior, and the stress-illness relationship in working women. *J. Pers. Soc. Psychol.* 51:1218–23

Schneiderman, N. 1983. Behavior, autonomic function and animal models of cardiovascular pathology. In *Biobehavioral Bases of Coronary Disease*, ed. T. M. Dembroski, T. H. Schmidt, G. Blumchen, pp. 304–64. Basel: Karger

Schulz, R., Decker, S. 1985. Long-term adjustment to physical disability: the role of social support, perceived control, and self-blame. *J. Pers. Soc. Psychol.* 5:1162–72

Schulz, R., Tompkins, C. A., Rau, M. T. 1988. A longitudinal study of the psychosocial impact of stroke on primary support persons. *Psychol. Aging* 3:131–41

Schulz, R., Tompkins, C., Wood, D., Decker, S. 1987. The social psychology of caregiving: the physical and psychological costs of providing support to the disabled. *J. Appl. Soc. Psychol.* 17:401–28

Schunk, D. H., Carbonari, J. P. 1984. Self-efficacy models. See Matarazzo et al 1984, pp. 230–47

Schwartz, G. E., Weiss, S. M. 1977. What is behavioral medicine? *Psychosom. Med.* 36:377–81

Schwartz, G. E., Weiss, S. M. 1978. Behavioral medicine revisited: an amended definition. *J. Behav. Med.* 1:249–51

Scott, J. P., Roberto, K. A., Hutton, J. T. 1986. Families of Alzheimer's victims. Family support to the caregivers. *J. Am. Geriatr. Soc.* 34:348–54

Secretary of Health and Human Services. 1981. Fourth Spec. Rep. to the US Congress on Alcohol and Health (January). Washington DC: Dept. Health Hum. Serv.

Seligman, M. E. P. 1975. *Helplessness: On Depression, Development, and Death.* San Francisco: Freeman

Selye, H. 1974. *Stress Without Distress.* Philadelphia: Lippincott

Sensenig, P. E., Cialdini, R. B. 1984. Social-psychological influences on the compliance process: implications for behavioral health. See Matarazzo et al 1984, pp. 384–92

Shekelle, R. B., Gale, M., Norusis, M. 1985. The Aspirin Myocardial Infarction Study Research Group. Type A score (Jenkins Activity Survey) and risk of recurrent coronary heart disease in the aspirin myocardial infarction study. *Am. J. Cardiol.* 56:221–25

Shekelle, R. B., Hulley, S. B., Neaton, J. D., Billings, J. H., Borhani, N. O., et al. 1985. The MRFIT behavior pattern study II. Type A behavior and incidence of coronary heart disease. *Am. J. Epidemiol.* 122:559–70

Shephard, R. J., Cox, M., Corey, P. 1981. Fitness program participation: its effect on worker performance. *J. Occup. Med.* 23:359–63

Sher, K. J. 1988. Stress response dampening. In *Psychological Theories of Drinking and Alcoholism,* ed. H. T. Blane, K. E. Leonard. New York: Guilford

Shiffman, S., Wills, T. A., eds. 1985. *Coping and Substance Use.* New York: Academic

Showers, C., Cantor, N. 1985. Social cognition: a look at motivated strategies. *Ann. Rev. Psychol.* 36:275–306

Shumaker, S. A., Grunberg, N. E., eds. 1986. Proceedings of the National Working Conference on smoking relapse. *Health Psychology,* Vol. 5(Suppl.). Hillsdale: NJ: Erlbaum

Siegler, I. C., Costa, P. 1985. Health behavior relationships. In *Handbook of the Psychology of Aging,* ed. J. E. Birren, K. W. Schaie. New York: Van Nostrand Reinhold Co. 2nd ed.

Sifneos, P. E. 1973. The prevalence of alexithymic patients in a chronic respiratory illness population. *Psychother. Psychosom.* 22:255–62

Simon, E. J. 1984. Opiate receptors: properties and possible functions. See Levison et al 1984, pp. 239–59

Singer, J. A., Neale, M. S., Schwartz, G. E., Schwartz, J. 1986. Conflicting perspectives on stress reduction in occupational settings: a systems approach to their resolution. In

Health and Industry, ed. M. F. Cataldo, T. J. Coates. New York: Wiley

Sklar, L. S., Anisman, H. 1979. Stress and coping factors influence tumor-growth. *Science* 205:513–15

Slough, N., Klenknecht, R. A., Thorndike, R. M. 1984. The relationship of the repression-sensitization scales to anxiety. *J. Pers. Assess.* 48:378–79

Smith, T. W., Rhodewalt, F. 1986. On states, traits and processes: a transactional alternative to the individual difference assumptions in Type A behavior and physiological reactivity. *J. Res. Pers.* 20:229–51

Sokol, R. J., Miller, S. I., Reed, G. 1980. Alcohol abuse during pregnancy: an epidemiologic study. *Alcohol: Clin. Exp. Res.* 4:2

Sorrentino, R. M., Higgins, E. T. 1986. *Handbook of Motivation and Cognition.* New York: Guilford

Spielberger, C. D., Johnson, E. H., Russell, S. F., Crane, R. J., Jacobs, G. A., Worden, T. J. 1985. In *Anger and Hostility in Cardiovascular and Behavioral Disorders,* ed. M. A. Chesney, R. H. Rosenman. New York: Hemisphere/McGraw-Hill

Stein, M., Schleifer, S., Keller, S. 1982. In *Biological Mediators of Behavior and Disease,* ed. S. Levy, p. 147. North-Holland, Amsterdam: Elsevier

Stone, A. A., Helder, L., Schneider, M. S. 1988. Coping with stressful events: coping dimensions and issues. In *Research on Stressful Life Events: Theoretical and Methodological Issues,* ed. L. H. Cohen. New York: Sage. In press

Stone, G. C., Weiss, S. M., Matarazzo, J. D., Miller, N. E., Rodin, J., et al. 1987. *Health Psychology: A Discipline and a Profession,* p. 547. Chicago: The Univ. Chicago Press

Stoney, C. M., Matthews, K. A., McDonald, R. H., Johnson, C. A. 1988. Sex differences in lipid, lipoprotein, cardiovascular, and neuroendocrine responses to acute stress. *Psychophysiology.* In press

Straus, R. 1986. Alcohol and alcohol problems research 10. The United States. *Br. J. Addict.* 81:315–25

Striegel-Moore, R. H., Silberstein, L. R., Rodin, J. 1986. Toward an understanding of risk factors for bulimia. *Am. Psychologist* 41:246–63

Stunkard, A. J., Sorensen, T. I. A., Hanis, C., Teasdale, T. W., Chakraborty, R., et al. 1986. An adoption study of human obesity. *New Engl. J. Med.* 314:193–98

Suls, J., Fletcher, B. 1985. The relative efficacy of avoidant and nonavoidant coping strategies: a meta-analysis. *Health Psychol.* 4:249–88

Suls, J., Sanders, G. S. 1988. Why do some

behavioral styles place people at coronary risk? In *In Search of Coronary-Prone Behavior*. Hillsdale, NJ: Erlbaum. In press

Supnick, J. A., Colletti, G. 1984. Relapse coping and problem solving training following treatment for smoking. *Addict. Behav.* 9:401–4

Surwit, R. S., Feinglos, M. N., Scovern, A. W. 1983. Diabetes and behavior: a paradigm for health psychology. *Am. Psychol.* 38:255–62

Swan, G. E., Carmelli, D., Rosenman, R. H. 1988a. The Cook and Medley HO scale. Identification of biobehavioral correlates. Submitted

Swan, G. E., Carmelli, D., Rosenman, R. H. 1988b. Psychological characteristics in twins discordant for smoking behavior: a matched-twin-pair analysis. *Addict. Behav.* In press

Taylor, C. B., Bandura, A., Ewart, C. K., Miller, N. H., DeBusk, R. F. 1985. Exercise testing to enhance wives' confidence in their husbands' cardiac capability soon after clinically uncomplicated acute myocardial infarction. *Am. J. Cardiol.* 55:635–38

Taylor, J. A. 1953. A personality scale of manifest anxiety. *J. Abnorm. Soc. Psychol.* 48:285–90

Taylor, S. E. 1987. The progress and prospects of health psychology: tasks of a maturing discipline. *Health Psychol.* 6:73–87

Taylor, S. E., Falke, R. L., Shoptaw, S. J., Lichtman, R. R. 1986. Social support, support groups, and the cancer patient. *J. Consult. Clin. Psychol.* 54:608–15

Taylor, S. E., Lichtman, R. R., Wood, J. V. 1984a. Compliance with chemotherapy among breast cancer patients. *Health Psychol.* 3:553–62

Taylor, S. E., Lichtman, R. R., Wood, J. V. 1984b. Attributions, beliefs about control, and adjustment to breast cancer. *J. Pers. Soc. Psychol.* 46:489–502

Taylor, S. E., Lichtman, R. R., Wood, J. V., Bluming, A. Z., Dosik, G. M., Leibowitz, R. L. 1985. Illness-related and treatment-related factors in psychological adjustment to breast cancer. *Cancer* 55:2506–13

Temoshok, L. 1985. Biopsychosocial studies on cutaneous malignant melanoma: psychosocial factors associated with prognostic indicators, progression, psychophysiology and tumour-host response. *Soc. Sci. Med.* 20:833–40

Temoshok, L. 1987. Personality, coping style, emotion and cancer: towards an integrative model. *Cancer Surv.* 3:546–67

Tennen, H., Affleck, G., Gershman, K. 1986. Self-blame among parents of infants with perinatal complications: the role of self-protective motives. *J. Pers. Soc. Psychol.* 50:690–96

Thoits, P. A. 1983. Multiple identities and psychological well being: a reformulation and test of the social isolation hypothesis. *Am. Sociol. Rev.* 48:174–87

Thoits, P. A. 1985. Social support processes and psychological well-being: Theoretical possibilities. In *Social Support: Theory, Research and Applications*, ed. I. G. Sarason, B. Sarason. The Hague, Holland: Martinus Nijhoff.

Thoresen, C. E., Ohman, A. 1986. The Type A behavior pattern: a person-environment interaction perspective. In *Psychopathology: An Interaction Perspective*, ed. D. Magnusson, A. Ohman. New York: Academic

Thoresen, C. E., Patillo, J. R. 1988. Exploring the Type A behavior pattern in children and adolescents. In *Type A Behavior Pattern: Current Trends & Future Directions*, ed. B. K. Houston, C. R. Snyder. New York: Wiley

Timko, C., Janoff-Bulman, R. 1985. Attributions, vulnerability, and psychological adjustment: the case of breast cancer. *Health Psychol.* 6:521–44

Todd, A. D. 1984. The prescription of contraception: negotiations between doctors and patients. *Discource Process.* 7:2

Turk, D. C., Rudy, T. E., Salovey, P. 1985. Implicit models of illness. *J. Behav. Med.* 9:453–74

Turk, D. C., Salovey, P., Litt, M. D. 1986. Adherence: a cognitive-behavioral perspective. In *Compliance: The Dilemma of the Chronically Ill*, ed. K. E. Gerber, A. M. Nehemkis, pp. 44–72. New York: Springer

US Public Health Service. 1979. *Smoking and Health: A Report of the Surgeon General.* DHEW Publ. (PHS) 79-50066. Washington, DC: US Gov. Print. Off.

US Public Health Service. 1981. *The Health Consequences of Smoking: The Changing Cigarette. A Report of the Surgeon General.* DHHS Publ. (PHS) 81-50156. Washington, DC: US Gov. Print. Off.

Van Treuren, R. R., Hull, J. G. 1986. *Health and Stress: Dispositional Optimism and Psychophysiological Responses.* Presented at the Ann. Meet. Soc. Psychophysiol. Res., Montreal, Canada

Verbrugge, L. M. 1979. Marital status and health. *J. Marr. Fam.* 41:267–85

Verbrugge, L. M. 1982. Sex differences in legal drug use. *J. Soc. Issues* 8:59–76

Verbrugge, L. M. 1985. Gender and health: an update on hypotheses and evidence. *J. Health Soc. Behav.* 26:156–82

Vess, J. D. Jr., Moreland, J. R., Schwebel, A. I. 1985a. An empirical assessment of the effects of cancer on family role functioning. *J. Psychosoc. Oncol.* 3(1):1–16

Vess, J. D. Jr., Moreland, J. R., Schwebel, A. I. 1985b. A follow-up study of role functioning and the psychological environment of families of cancer patients. *J. Psychosoc. Oncol.* 3(2):1–14

Visintainer, M. A., Volpicelli, J. R., Seligman, M. E. P. 1982. Tumor rejection in rats after inescapable or escapable shock. *Science* 216:437–39

Wagener, J. J., Taylor, S. E. 1986. What else could I have done? Patients' responses to failed treatment decisions. *Health Psychol.* 5:481–96

Waldron, I. 1983. Sex differences in illness incidence, prognosis and mortality. *Soc. Sci. Med.* 17:321–33

Waldron, I. 1986. The contribution of smoking to sex differences in mortality. *Public Health Rep.* 101:163–73

Waldron, I. 1988. Gender and health-related behavior. In *Health Behavior: Emerging Research Perspectives*, ed. D. S. Gochman. New York: Plenum. In press

Walker, L. S., Ford, M. B., Donald, W. D. 1987. Cystic fibrosis and family stress: effects of age and severity of illness. *Pediatrics* 79:239–46

Wallston, B. S., Alagna, S. W., DeVellis, B. Mc., DeVellis, R. F. 1983. Social support and physical health. *Health Psychol.* 4:367–91

Ward, M. M., Chesney, M. A., Swan, G. E., Black, G. W., Parker, S. F., Rosenman, R. H. 1986. Cardiovascular responses in Type A and B men to a series of stressors. *J. Behav. Med.* 9:43–49

Watkins, L. O., Eaker, E. 1986. Population and demographic influences on reactivity. See Matthews et al 1986b, pp. 231–57

Watson, D., Pennebaker, J. W. 1988. Health complaints, stress, and distress: exploring the central role of negative affectivity. *Psychol. Rev.* In press

Weinberger, D. A. 1989. The construct validity of the repressive coping style. In *Repression: Defense Mechanisms and Personality Style*, ed. J. L. Singer. Chicago: Univ. Chicago Press. In press

Weinberger, D. A., Schwartz, G. E., Davidson, J. R. 1979. Low-anxious, high-anxious, and repressive coping styles: psychometric patterns behavioral and physiological responses to stress. *J. Abnorm. Psychol.* 88:369–80

Weiner, H. 1977. *Psychobiology and Human Disease*. New York: Elsevier North-Holland

Weiner, H. 1988. *New Directions in Stress Research*. Chicago: Univ. Chicago Press. In press

Weinstein, N. D. 1982. Unrealistic optimism about susceptibility to health problems. *J. Behav. Med.* 5:441–60

Weinstein, N. D. 1983. Reducing unrealistic optimism about illness susceptibility. *Health Psychol.* 2:11–20

Weinstein, N. D. 1984. Why it won't happen to me: perceptions of risk factors and susceptibility. *Health Psychol.* 3:431–57

Wethington, E., Kessler, R. C. 1986. Perceived support, received support, and adjustment to stressful life events. *J. Health Soc. Behav.* 27:78–89

Wilcox, B. L. 1981. Social support, life stress, and psychological adjustment: a test of the buffering hypothesis. *Am. J. Commun. Psychol.* 9:371–86

Williams, R. B., Barefoot, J. C. 1988. Coronary-prone behavior: the emerging role of the hostility complex. In *Type A Behavior Pattern: Current Trends and Future Directions*, ed. B. K. Houston, C. R. Snyder. New York: Wiley. In press

Williams, R. B., Barefoot, J. C., Haney, T. L., Harrell, F. E., Blumenthal, J. A., et al. 1986. Type A behavior and angiographically documented coronary atherosclerosis in a sample of 2,289 patients. Presented at Am. Psychosom. Soc. Meet., Baltimore, Md

Wills, T. A. 1987. Downward comparison as a coping mechanism. In *Coping With Negative Life Events: Clinical and Social-Psychological Perspectives*, ed. C. R. Snyder, C. Ford, pp. 245–70. New York: Plenum

Wood, J. V., Taylor, S. E., Lichtman, R. R. 1985. Social comparison in adjustment to breast cancer. *J. Pers. Soc. Psychol.* 49:1169–83

Wortman, C. B. 1984. Social support and the cancer patient. Conceptual and methodologic issues. *Cancer* 53:2339–60

Wortman, C. B. 1976. Causal attributions and personal control. In *New Directions in Attributional Research*, ed. J. Harvey, W. Ickes, R. F. Kidd. Hillsdale, NJ: Erlbaum

Wortman, C. B., Brehm, J. W. 1975. Responses to uncontrollable outcomes: an integration of reactance theory and the learned helplessness model. *Adv. Exp. Soc. Psychol.* 8:278–332

Ann. Rev. Psychol. 1989. 40:581–602

COMPARATIVE PSYCHOLOGY, ETHOLOGY, AND ANIMAL BEHAVIOR

Donald A. Dewsbury

Department of Psychology, University of Florida, Gainesville, Florida, 32611

CONTENTS

INTRODUCTION: THE STUDY OF ANIMAL BEHAVIOR TODAY

The contemporary study of animal behavior is a dynamic and vigorous enterprise. Recent years have seen continued growth and diversification, as new organizations are formed and new journals are published. The teacher of

581

0066–4308/89/0201-0581$02.00

animal behavior has a wider choice of textbooks and related material than ever before.

Throughout its history, the field has been interdisciplinary and cooperative. The terms "comparative psychology, ethology, and animal behavior" refer to historically different approaches to the study of behavior. Historically, ethology and comparative psychology provided the primary foundation for the development of today's approaches. Core ethology was developed by European zoologists. Led by Konrad Lorenz and Niko Tinbergen, they developed a science that emphasized the study of instinctive behavior and stressed work under natural conditions. Comparative psychology was developed primarily by North American psychologists. There was a more appreciable, though not exclusive, emphasis on mammals and the study of learning. By the 1950s somewhat different theoretical frameworks for the explanation of animal behavior had been developed in the two fields. Many of these differences were resolved by the 1960s. In the 1970s, the "sociobiological" approach had a major impact most systematically elaborated by Wilson (1975). More recently, scientists trained in these, and related, disciplines have cooperated to forge the contemporary science of animal behavior. "Animal behavior" has often been used as the umbrella term.

The differences between ethology and comparative psychology have been exaggerated. Some ethologists studied mammals, did laboratory research, or were interested in learning. Some comparative psychologists studied invertebrates, worked in the field, or studied instinctive behavior (see Dewsbury 1984a). There was considerable concern with similar problems within both traditions.

The two most recent *Annual Review* authors in this field treated the recent interactions among these disciplines differently. Mason & Lott (1976) saw a "new synthesis" and emphasized the common ground of related disciplines. From this synthesis stimulated by the development of sociobiology Snowdon (1983) saw a retreat. For now at least, I adopt the former position. Sociobiology has profoundly influenced the study of animal behavior. As Snowdon noted, it has greatly stimulated interest in animal behavior, both within and outside of the scientific community. However, practitioners of the approach have been prone to excesses, as in simplistic application of some principles to human behavior; these have been exposed to the self-correcting criticisms of the scientific community. The diverse approaches to animal behavior have generally enabled us to sample and juxtapose powerful constructs and to work cooperatively on important problems.

Professional organizations (e.g. The Animal Behavior Society in North America and the Association for the Study of Animal Behaviour in Great Britain) have played an important role in cementing the relationships among disciplines. The 20 biannual International Ethological Conferences have also been critical. Started as a means for communication among closely-knit core ethologists, the conferences have grown and diversified to cover many topics traditionally associated with comparative psychology, sociobiology, and animal science. Many scientific syntheses began with friendly personal interactions at the meetings of these organizations.

Although earlier theoretical and methodological disagreements have been tempered, new signs of fractionation are appearing. The most serious may be organizational. Umbrella organizations, such as the International Ethological Conferences, are losing influence as new specialty groups form. Smaller, more intimate organizations with separate meetings and journals are proliferating. Separate organizations have been established, for example, for those who study aggressive behavior, reproductive behavior, behavior genetics, developmental psychobiology, and behavioral ecology, as well as for specialists on bears, amphibians and reptiles, birds, bats, insects, mammals, and marine mammals. As groups proliferate, the communication that has led to stability in the study of animal behavior may lapse, and new fracture lines may appear. It is to be hoped that the isolation stemming from decreased contact will not lead to unproductive theoretical divergence.

Within comparative psychology, several groups may be distinguished. The International Society for Comparative Psychology (ISCP) was founded in 1983. Its founders, active in publicizing comparative psychology, have been associated with attempts to revive theoretical concepts proposed by T. C. Schneirla. The recent efforts have led to few new insights or substantial data (see also Capitanio 1985; Macphail 1987; Reid 1986). Another group, not well organized, includes active research-oriented psychologists near the forefront of the study of animal behavior, who identify themselves as animal behaviorists rather than comparative psychologists. The ISCP has generally not found favor with the latter group. Still other comparative psychologists work closer to the mainstream of psychology, on problems of learning and cognition. There is thus a split between those who most actively publicize and those who most actively practice comparative psychology. The primary reasons earlier comparative psychology only modestly influenced science as a whole may have been the field's fractionation together with the lack of effective synthesizers and publicists of the stature of Niko Tinbergen or Konrad Lorenz. Comparative psychologists may now be repeating the mistakes of the past.

Among the pervasive trends of recent years has been a swing of the pendulum from theory toward empiricism. In the 1970s, sociobiological theory raced well ahead of empirical testing. The 1980s have seen relatively few fundamental theoretical advances. However, many fine research programs have been stimulated, as animal behaviorists of various disciplines have asked questions not anticipated in earlier years. Excellent edited volumes of research papers, such as those on primate societies (Smuts et al 1986), kin discrimination (Fletcher & Michener 1987), and the ecological aspects of social evolution (Rubenstein & Wrangham 1986) are the fruits of this effort. The 1988 volume of the *Nebraska Symposium on Motivation* is devoted to comparative psychology. In general, the theoretical propositions that have dominated the field have been fruitful, though as always much fine tuning is required.

NEW DEVELOPMENTS IN THE STUDY OF HISTORY

The recent surge in historical scholarship regarding the study of animal behavior may be regarded as beginning with Thorpe's (1979) idiosyncratic and provocative book, *The Origins and Rise of Ethology*. Burghardt (1985) reprinted classical papers in ethology, some of which had not previously been available in English translation. The volume makes accessible papers by authors such as Oskar Heinroth and Bernard Altum, rarely read by English-speaking workers. Shorter histories of ethology were written by Singer (1981) and Durant (1986). Burkhardt (1981, 1983) adopted the externalist approach, prevalent in contemporary work in the history of science, to analyze sociocultural influences on the development of ethological thought.

The history of comparative psychology is also being clarified. The prevailing view has been that after an exciting beginning near the turn of the century, the field became dominated by the study of rat learning for much of the century and only began redevelopment with the influx of European ethology soon after World War II. Somewhat conventional, though insightful, histories were prepared by Gottlieb (1979), Cooper (1985), and Glickman (1985). Dewsbury (1984a) argued that what we now regard as comparative psychology had historical continuity throughout the century and that the differences between European ethology and this part of animal psychology were less profound than portrayed by such earlier historians as Thorpe. It is necessary to separate the tradition of comparative psychology, represented by such workers as Beach, Lashley, Lehrman, Schneirla, Stone, and Yerkes, from other parts of the overall study of animal psychology.

Other work on the history of comparative psychology includes a book of reprinted classical papers (Dewsbury 1984b) and a collection of historically oriented papers with an international emphasis (Tobach 1987).

Two major histories have treated changing conceptions about the evolution of the animal mind. Boakes (1984) examined the development of such ideas between 1870 and 1930. In an ambitious work, Richards (1987) considers similar problems over a longer historical period. Richards emphasizes the role of the study of ethics in the formulation of theories about mind and behavior. He views Darwin and Spencer as key figures in the development of our view of the evolution of the animal mind, with Romanes, Morgan, James, and Baldwin as their intellectual heirs.

Important biographical and autobiographical works have also appeared during this period. A model can be found in Pauly's (1987) study of Jacques Loeb. In a detailed and scholarly treatment, Pauly emphasizes Loeb's concern with the engineering ideal of prediction and control of behavior and considers its antecedents and descendants in psychology. Burkhardt (1988) summarizes the lives and work of Whitman and Craig, presenting the first really thorough treatment of the latter. Scarborough & Furumoto (1987) consider Margaret Floy Washburn in the context of a study of American women psychologists. Other notable papers are those of Banks (1985) on Allee: Chiszar & Wertheimer (1988) on Margaret Altmann: and Cadwallader (1984) on four neglected comparative psychologists: David F. Weinland, T. Wesley Mills, C. L. Herrick, and Charles H. Turner. The latter was an early black psychologist-zoologist, noted for his research on invertebrate behavior. The collection of autobiographical papers published by Dewsbury (1985) included chapters by the likes of Lorenz, Tinbergen, Wilson, and Hess; that of Gandelman (1985) included chapters by Beach and Richter.

ROADS NOT TAKEN

Here, in the interest of perspective, I point to recent trends which, though not reviewed in this chapter, have been summarized elsewhere. Interaction among ecologists, operant conditioners, and comparative psychologists has led to new perspectives related to optimal foraging theory; these are reviewed by Kamil & Roitblat (1985) and in Kamil & Sargent (1981). New perspectives on agonistic interactions are treated by Blanchard & Blanchard (1988). The long-standing interest of comparative psychologists in the ontogeny of behavior is reflected in work on both genetic bases (Wimer & Wimer 1985) and behavioral development (Hall & Oppenheim 1987). Neural correlates of behavior, with an emphasis on neuroethology, have been treated by Ingle & Crews (1985). Information on the evolution of vertebrate brains has been summarized by Jerison (1985). New perspectives on sensory function are emerging as well (e.g. Okanoya & Dooling 1987).

The study of learning has been a focus throughout the history of comparative psychology. Recent work, reviewed elsewhere, has yielded particularly significant results, especially as more workers are studying learning in its natural biological and social contexts (Bitterman 1988; Gould 1986; Domjan & Galef 1983). Representative examples of the placement of learning research in its biological context include studies of learned taste aversions (Garcia et al 1985), song learning in birds (Petrinovich 1988; West & King 1985); foraging and food hoarding in birds (Sherry 1985; Shettleworth 1983), foraging in honeybees (Bitterman 1988), social transmission of food avoidance (Galef 1985), one-trial learning in groups of foraging marmosets (Menzel & Juno 1985), superstitious behavior (Timberlake & Lucas 1985), and territorial defense (Hollis 1984).

THE FOUR QUESTIONS

For a quarter of a century Tinbergen's (1963) "four questions" have provided the primary basis for organizing the study of animal behavior. Tinbergen proposed that we first observe and describe behavior. A complete analysis of behavior then requires analysis of the immediate causation and development (i.e. proximate causation) and the evolution and adaptive significance (i.e. ultimate causation) of behavior. Methodologically, when studying proximate causation, behavior is the dependent variable, studied as a function of the manipulation of independent variables. Questions of immediate causation and development differ mainly with respect to the time span considered. Questions of evolutionary history concern changes with the evolution of species. In studies of adaptive significance, the consequences of behavior provide the focus; behavior becomes the independent variable and the consequences of behavior for survival and reproduction become the dependent variables. Whereas studies of immediate causation and development concern the lives of individual organisms, those of evolutionary history and adaptive significance transcend the lives of individuals.

The Four Questions Today

Historically, individual scientists have tended to focus on one or two of the questions, and communication among workers on the proximate and ultimate has sometimes been restricted. In recent years, however, increasing numbers of workers have combined the study of the proximate and the ultimate in effective synthetic research. Thus, for example, Beecher and his associates have studied not only the ecological significance of parent-offspring recognition in field studies of various species of swallows, but have analyzed its sensory bases as well (e.g. Beecher et al 1986). Studies of hormones and behavior under field conditions have facilitated the integration of the proximate and the ultimate (e.g. Wingfield & Moore 1987). The synthetic effect of the trend for unification, with the conceptual clarity of differentiation, has constituted an important trend in the field. This is brought out in reviewing current research areas, below.

Some Basic Principles of Behavioral Evolution

The contemporary study of behavioral evolution received a great boost from theoretical advances in the 1970s. The cornerstone principles were notions of genetic fitness, the level of action of natural selection, and kin selection. Natural selection works through the differential representation of genes transmitted from one generation to the next. By definition, the organism that has the greatest genetic fitness is that which is most effective in getting copies of its genes into future generations. Fitness is a function only of reproductive success, although obviously organisms must do many things in order to survive and reproduce effectively. To the extent that behavior is a function of genotype, both the gene pools and the behavioral patterns of future generations are shaped by the actions of natural selection.

A crucial problem in this area concerns the level at which natural selection acts. Some (e.g. Wynne-Edwards 1962) have contended that selection often works at the level of the group or species. Thus, organisms might be favored if they sacrifice reproductive effort in the interests of the group. Although this may occur under special conditions, most biologists agree that selection generally works at the level of the individual. Those individuals most effective at getting their genes represented in future generations will have the most impact on future generations and will have the highest fitness.

The notion of kin selection was developed by Hamilton (1964). One shares many genes with close relatives. To the extent that one can enhance the fitness of one's close relatives, one increases the representation of one's own genes in future generations. The concept of inclusive fitness incorporates not only the fitness gained directly from individual reproduction, but, in addition, the increment resulting from increased fitness of close relatives.

These concepts must be applied with care. The prevailing view is that natural selection shapes the genetic structure of individuals and populations and that behavior is the product of the interaction of these genes with environmental variables to produce complete organisms. Although behavior is influenced by genotype, there is no implication that proximate control entails conscious manipulation. Rather, behavioral patterns effective in increasing fitness are ultimately shaped by natural selection but may be proximately blind. Further, one must use care in developing simplistic, untested adaptationist interpretations (Gould & Lewontin 1979); sound methodology should be used to test inferences about adaptive significance.

REPRODUCTIVE BEHAVIOR

The combination of attention to questions of both proximate and ultimate causation, improved technology, consideration of social context, and use of an increasing range of species is yielding new insight into the range of variation, causes, and effects of reproductive behavior. With increasing computerization of data acquisition, finer analyses of behavior become more practical. Increasingly sophisticated endocrine techniques, especially the widespread use of radioimmunoassays, have led to increased knowledge of hormone-behavior relationships. These methods are becoming applicable under field conditions, stimulating a new area of "field endocrinology" (Wingfield & Moore 1987). Hormone assay of primate feces (Risler et al 1987) may soon be possible in the field. With DNA fingerprinting (Hill 1987) it may be possible to identify paternity in many field populations where there is multiple mating.

Hormone-Behavior Relationships

Much attention has been devoted to the study of hormone-behavior relationships in laboratory species (e.g. Adler et al 1985). Hormones appear to have an irreversible organizing action early in development and a reversible activating effect in adults (but see Arnold & Breedlove 1985). The direction of development in mammalian fetuses in the absence of hormones is generally female, with hormones leading to defeminization and masculinization. Thus, if a male or female fetus develops in the absence of gonadal steroid hormones, behavioral patterns will be predominantly female; with hormones there is a shift toward maleness. In birds, however, where males are the homogametic sex (i.e. have two like sex chromosomes), males are the neutral sex; early hormones produce feminization (Adkins-Regan 1985). The comparative approach is necessary for full explication of biological variability. Further, it must be recognized that many factors interact in the development of reproductive behavior; this process is more complex than originally thought (Moore 1985).

Comparative analyses have also shown that the pattern of endocrine control of reproductive behavior elaborated with adults of seasonally breeding, temperate-zone species is not universal. Crews & Moore (1986) term this pattern, with close association of gonadal development and mating activity, the "associated reproductive pattern." By contrast, with a "dissociated" pattern, the gonads develop and gametes form after the breeding season and are stored until the next season. This dissociated pattern appears adaptive for species such as the Canadian red-sided garter snake, which mate in a brief breeding season soon after emerging from hibernation. Mating does not depend on hormones, but is temperature dependent (Crews & Moore 1986). Species with a "constant reproductive pattern," such as zebra finches, breed opportunistically, when environmental conditions appear appropriate. Thus, mating behavior is generally triggered by a signal that coincides with the appropriate time for its occurrence. If hormonal changes do not occur at the appropriate time, other proximate cues are used and copulation may be independent of gonadal hormones. One must be careful in generalizing relationships established on a limited range of species.

Other remarkable examples of hormone-behavior relationship are being revealed. One third of the 45 species of whiptail lizards consist only of females, reproducing parthenogenetically. However, male-like and female-like pseudosexual mounting and receptive behavior occur and are hormonally mediated via mechanisms that appear derived from sexually reproducing ancestors (Crews & Moore 1986; Crews 1987). Female spotted hyenas develop a fully erectile phallus and dominate males. The female virilization appears proximately mediated by androstenedione and ultimately functional in ensuring female access to resources in a highly competitive feeding situation (Frank 1986; Glickman et al 1987). In some species of fishes sex changes occur in adults; males may become females (protandry) or females may become males (protogyny) (Shapiro 1987). Sex reversals are sometimes triggered by social stimuli, such as a female-to-male change following removal of the male from a social group. Field and laboratory studies of several species of sparrows reveal that, as expected, titers of estrogens, androgens, and luteinizing hormone rise during the time of spring breeding. However, male mating behavior appears triggered by female solicitation displays, independent of the male's own endocrine condition; the male endocrine changes appear related primarily to territorial aggressive behavior (Wingfield & Moore 1987).

Copulation in Social Context

Increasingly, copulation is being studied in a broad social and ecological context. Sexual selection, generally interpreted as entailing female choice and male-male competition, has been a focus. Competition at the time of mating can be intense. As many as 20% of male red deer stags may receive permanent injuries during the rut (Clutton-Brock et al 1982); within some species of spiders males may be preyed upon by females (Christenson et al 1985).

Ultimately, selection should favor males behaving in ways that ensure that they, rather than other males, sire offspring. There are various proximate mechanisms of male-male competition. In some species males form dominance hierarchies; the dominant male may or may not copulate more than subordinates and sire a disproportionate number of offspring (Dewsbury 1982a). With a scramble competition system, dominance is a poor predictor of mating success; skill at locating receptive females appears especially important (Schwagmeyer & Woontner 1986). Social influences can affect the timing of copulations; male macaques that ejaculate with a female and see another male mate with the female resume mating sooner than if the female remained unmated, thus protecting genetic investment (Estep et al 1986). The patterning of copulatory activity appears critical in the initiation of pregnancy in some species (see Adler 1983). Sperm are not sufficient for successful pregnancy; vaginal stimulation in the appropriate amount and pattern must also be received. If more than one male mates with a female during a given estrous period, the conditions of sperm competition exist. The patterns of sperm interaction differ across species (see Smith 1984). A male that gains access to a newly pregnant female may block her pregnancy as a result of her exposure to his odors, the Bruce effect (see Marchlewska-Koj 1983). Male-male competition can continue after the birth of litters. Where infanticide occurs, it is often committed by adult males (see Hausfater & Hrdy 1984).

The interests of the two sexes often differ. Phenomena such as the Bruce effect and infanticide raise important issues concerning the adaptiveness of female behavior (Storey 1986; Hrdy 1979). Wasser & Barash (1983) propose that, in general, females can maximize their lifetime reproductive success by deferring reproduction when conditions are suboptimal. Social stimuli can be important in producing synchrony, suppression, and blockage of estrous cyclicity and pregnancy in females under various conditions (McClintock 1983; Wasser & Barash 1983). Olfactory stimuli are generally implicated. Much research is directed at understanding the proximate and ultimate bases of these interactions. The female-choice component of sexual selection is considered below.

PARENTAL BEHAVIOR AND FAMILY STRUCTURE

With respect to ultimate causation, natural selection favors individuals displaying behavioral patterns that maximize reproductive success. The offspring must be viable and fertile if the line is to be continued; parental behavior can have great impact on viability and fertility. Parents are viewed as having limited parental resources; efficient patterns of *parental investment,* generally directed preferentially at one's own offspring, should be favored (Trivers 1972). The interests of the different actors in the drama of parental interactions differ. This is partially because the two parents generally share a limited number of genes with each other and each shares 50% with the offspring. There is reason to expect parent-offspring conflict (Trivers 1974), and examples of such conflicts are given below.

Maternal Behavior

The most pervasive relationship is that between mother and young. Although males may provide some or all parental care in some taxa, maternal care is always present in mammals. As the dynamics of mother-young interactions are explored, proximate correlates of reciprocal costs and benefits are being revealed. In rodents, such as laboratory rats, the mother builds a nest and nurses, transports, and licks the young. Because she engages in other activities, such as mating, during the postpartum period, the female's activities can be conceptualized as a finely balanced time-sharing (Gilbert et al 1980). The young are not passive participants; their behavior helps synchronize the changing mother-young relationship. This relationship can be viewed as partially symbiotic, in that mothers recover substantial volumes of water from licking pup urine (Alberts 1986). Much of the integration of parent-offspring interactions is through olfactory cues (see Leon 1983). It is critical that each developmental stage be viable and adaptive; the young are viewed as passing though a series of developmental stages, each of which is adaptive, rather than simply preparing for adulthood (e.g. Hall & Oppenheim 1987; Henderson 1986).

Analyses of nonhuman primates produce the counterintuitive finding that females often direct their aggressive behavior disproportionately at kin. This is because females use aggressive behavior in the socialization of their young (Bernstein & Ehardt 1986). Mother-daughter relationships are persistent in some primate species; they help each other out in aggressive interactions, thus further revealing the reciprocal nature of mother-young relationships. Young female vervets with a mother in their group reproduce more successfully than those without a mother (Fairbanks & McGuire 1986). Nevertheless, conflicts between mother and young, as at weaning and the development of locomotion, are also apparent (Nicolson 1986).

Parental Care by Individuals Other Than the Mother

Recent work has confirmed the active male role in providing paternal care in a wide range of taxa; findings in arthropods, fishes, birds, rodents, primates, and other taxa were presented at a recent symposium (Brown 1985). Paternal care is well developed in nonhuman primates; male-young interactions range from abuse through tolerance, affiliation, and intensive caretaking in different species and situations (Snowdon & Suomi 1982; Whitten 1986).

Care of young by individuals other than parents has received much attention, because this requires explanation if selection works at the level of the individual. The phenomenon of sterile castes in insects has provided a puzzle since the time of Darwin. Among vertebrates, the phenomenon of helpers at the nest in birds (e.g. Woolfenden & Fitzpatrick 1984) has received the most attention, though similar phenomena occur in other taxa, such as carnivores (Moehlman 1987) and naked mole rats (Jarvis 1981).

Thus, groups of parents, dependent offspring, older offspring, and others may live in an integrated family unit. At the proximate level, the dynamics of the family unit require analysis. The integration of male and female incubation in ring doves, for example, is mediated by circadian clocks in both parents, which determine the onset of incubation bouts (Silver & Norgren 1987). At the ultimate level, males appear to care for young either because male care is necessary for successful rearing or because the distribution of females and resources precludes the acquisition of additional mates (Emlen & Oring 1977). It is generally agreed that helpers, generally close kin, help either because they can profit with respect to their own future reproduction, as in securing territories, or because their inclusive fitness is increased due to kin selection. The phenomenon of male-female "friendship" in baboons, in which bonds may form between males and infants that are not their offspring, may be explained because females mate preferentially with males that were friendly to them and their mothers (Smuts 1985, 1987). Males may thus gain matings with the daughters of their friends.

Considerations of parental behavior in nonhuman animals have important potential implications for human behavior. For example, recent sociobiological analyses have confirmed the risks of child abuse are greater when a child lives with a natural parent and a stepparent than with two natural parents (Daly & Wilson 1988). Although other explanations may be possible, confidence of paternity provides a plausible explanation.

The Genesis of Family Structure

Major differences in behavior and parental investment can be the product of relatively subtle differences in motivational tendencies in different species. Although mating systems may be best analyzed under field conditions, the underlying motivational processes generating such systems may best be analyzed in the laboratory. For example, Mason and his associates have contrasted two primate species, monogamous titi monkeys and polygamous squirrel monkeys. They have found differences in parental behavior, contact proneness, grooming, and psychophysiological responding that differentiate the species (Mason 1974; Mendoza & Mason 1986; Cubicciotti et al 1986). In parallel research with rodents, prairie voles, which are sometimes monogamous (Carter et al 1986), differ from montane voles, which are more polygamous (Jannett 1982), with respect to contact proneness, mate choice, parental behavior, and a whole suite of other traits (Dewsbury 1988a). These suites of motivational traits can drive and create the organized mating and social systems observed in the field.

SOCIAL DISCRIMINATION

As the implications of theories of kin selection and selection working at the level of the individual penetrated the field, the importance of fine discriminations among individuals became apparent. Individuals should be able to maximize their levels of inclusive fitness by behaving differentially toward individuals of differing kinship, genotype, dominance rank, or various other characteristics. The quest for the proximate realization of this statement of ultimate causation has led to an upsurge of research that has revealed capacities for social discrimination in animals not anticipated even a few years ago. There are many bases for social recognition, such as species identity, familiarity, age, size, and genotype (see Colgan 1983). Animals have been found to choose partners on the basis of dominance status (Hoffmeyer 1982), estrous condition (Johnston 1983), and architectural adornment of a bower (Borgia 1986). The topics of kin recognition and mate choice, however, have generated special interest.

Kin Discrimination

Following Hamilton's (1964) development of the notion of kin selection, it became apparent that individuals could benefit by behaving differentially toward kin. In most situations, except mate choice, nepotistic behavior would appear maximally adaptive. There appear to be four potential bases for kin discrimination: (*a*) spatial distribution—when kin are not discriminated individually but are located differentially in space; (*b*) association—differential behavior toward familiar animals, such as nest mates, who often will be kin; (*c*) phenotype matching, in which the characteristics of the target animals are compared to the animal's own phenotype or that of its relatives; and (*d*) recognition alleles—genes that make related individuals distinctive and allow their discrimination by bearers (Sherman & Holmes 1985). There is at least some evidence suggesting the existence of all of these mechanisms in some species (Fletcher & Michener 1987).

Kin discrimination is highly developed among insects and other arthropods (see Fletcher & Michener 1987). For example, the frequency with which female sweat bees guarding a nest entrance permit others to enter is a linear function of their average coefficient of relatedness (Greenberg 1979). Individual honey bee workers reared in total isolation can discriminate between their full sisters and half sisters (Getz & Smith 1986). Families of desert isopods defend a burrow and bear chemical badges that code their identity; contact with alien conspecifics can lead to "alienation" and a rejection by members of the family unit (Linsenmair 1987).

Cascades frog tadpoles are able to discriminate nonkin from kin they have never encountered. The process is chemically mediated, survives metamorphosis, and is mediated by a sensitive mechanism that is not dependent on experience (Blaustein & O'Hara 1986). However, the role of experience in ontogeny differs across species (Waldman 1986). Waldman suggests that the association of kin may be adaptive in that developing tadpoles may regulate rates of growth of kin in a manner consistent with available resources.

Social recognition is not ubiquitous. In a model comparative analysis of recognition of young by parental swallows, Beecher et al (1986) found parental recognition well developed in two colonial species (cliff swallows and bank swallows) but not in two more solitary species (barn swallows or rough-winged swallows). The proximate mechanism appears functional only where there are dense congregations of birds with which young can get confused. The discrimination is mediated via auditory cues, with individual vocalizations being more distinctive in the colonial breeders.

The most extensively studied kin discrimination system in rodents is that in spiny mice (e.g. Porter 1987). If four subadult animals are placed together, kin huddle together preferentially. Recognition requires familiarity; unfamiliar kin are not recognized. Familiarity does not require contact with the individuals to be discriminated but can be mediated by the mother or by other siblings. An olfactory cue is implicated; the effect disappears after the animals are separated from each other for eight days.

Studies of kin discrimination in ground squirrels have shown influences of both genetic relatedness and familiarity (Holmes & Sherman 1982). Pups that share a natal nest are treated as siblings, even if they are unrelated. When sisters are reared apart, however, unfamiliar sister-sister pairs show less aggression than unrelated, unfamiliar female pairs. Further, in Belding's ground squirrels full-sisters treat each other differently from maternal half-sisters despite sharing the same nest. Similar evidence of kin discrimination has been found in other taxa (Hepper 1986).

Recent research has revealed subtle kin discrimination abilities in humans; olfactory discrimination is important in this (e.g. Porter et al 1988). When infants are very young they can use olfactory cues to discriminate their mother from others; mothers can identify their infants using olfactory cues. Similar abilities are present in other adult humans: People can discriminate kin by sniffing soiled T-shirts.

Mate Choice

Mate choice is an integral part of sexual selection; in general, individuals should be favored if they choose mates that are able to provide them and their offspring with resources and that will contribute "good genes." The latter can be either genes that, in interaction with other genes and environmental factors, lead to offspring maximally adapted to the environment in which they live or that are compatible with those of the individual doing the choosing. Active mate choice has been found in many taxa and with many bases for choice (see Bateson 1983a). Indeed, zebra finches have even been found to make choices based on the color bands placed on the birds' legs by experimenters (Burley et al 1982). Although generally studied in females, mate choice also occurs in males (see Dewsbury 1982b).

Kinship appears important in mate choice. However, in contrast to the situation with nepotistic behavior, there is no simple relationship between kinship and mate choice. Breeding with close relatives leads to deleterious effects of "inbreeding depression" on the survival and development of the young (e.g. Ralls et al 1979). However, mating with individuals too different from oneself also has deleterious effects. This has led to the concept of *optimal outbreeding* (Bateson 1983b), according to which individuals should prefer mates optimally different from themselves. Japanese quail appear to do exactly that, preferring to mate with first cousins. The concept of optimal outbreeding is important and appears valid. However, it creates problems in studies of kinship and mate choice because clear-cut predictions are difficult. Unless there is independent determination of what choice is adaptive, only the shape of the curve relating choice to kinship can be predicted for parametric studies. For studies in which just two groups are compared, the theory of optimal outbreeding can be invoked to explain virtually any result (Dewsbury 1988b).

With assortative mating, no single type is consistently preferred; individuals mate preferentially with others depending on their own characteristics. Individuals may prefer mates that are similar to (positive assortative mating) or different from (negative assortative mating) themselves. Assortative mating, generally positive, is common in both nonhuman and human populations (Thiessen & Gregg 1980; Buss 1985); this may relate to optimal outbreeding.

Among the most remarkable instances of mate choice are those based on the Major Histocompatibility Complex (MHC) of house mice (Beauchamp et al 1985; Yamazaki et al 1976). The MHC genes are in the H-2 region of chromosome 17 in house mice and code for individuality in the immune systems of the body. House mice can discriminate among individuals bearing different H-2 types, generally preferring to mate with partners different from themselves. This may be adaptive in providing the offspring with the capacity to respond to a wide range of antigens. Mice appear to make these discriminations based on odors that differ among the different H-2 types. Congenic strains of laboratory rats, differing with respect to MHC, produce urinary odors that can be discriminated by other rats (Brown et al 1987). The MHC region is remarkably variable among different individuals; it may be a primary basis for the characteristic scents of different individuals.

Also on the 17th chromosome of house mice, and linked to the MHC, is the T locus. Some t-alleles that are lethal in homozygotes exist in natural populations, a topic of much interest to evolutionary biologists. Male and female house mice discriminate and mate preferentially with partners bearing the benign wild-type alleles rather than those heterozygous for the deleterious t-alleles. However, whereas the preference in females appears independent of H-2 variability, that is not the case for males (Egid & Lenington 1985; Lenington & Egid 1985).

A premise of much theory concerning the evolution of mate choice is that the preference for mating with individuals of one genotype has a heritable component. Studies of artificial selection in ladybirds indicate that artificial selection over successive generations can increase the level of preference. A relatively simple genetic model for this system has been proposed (Majerus et al 1986).

COGNITION

Although this volume contains a separate review of animal cognition (Gallistel 1989), no treatment of contemporary comparative psychology is complete without at least some brief mention of cognition. The dramatic increase in interest in cognitive processes is viewed by some (e.g. Wasserman 1981) as a return to the roots of comparative psychology.

Cognitive explanations appear appropriate for the behavior of various nonprimate species in complex learning tasks. The research of Olton (1977) on spatial memory by rats in radial mazes has been especially influential in this area. Other representative studies concern chunking in pigeons (Terrace 1987), the learning of natural concepts by pigeons (Herrnstein 1979), the use of phonetic categories by Japanese quail (Kluender et al 1987), and counting behavior in various species (Davis & Memmott 1982). An excellent review of this literature is provided by Roitblat (1987).

A key to the cognitive revival in animal behavior has been the widely publicized studies of language-like behavior, which Wasserman (1981) considers "the most significant single event in delivering comparative psychology from an age of disinterest" (p. 246). Despite this bit of hyperbole, the studies of the Gardners (Gardner & Gardner 1985), Rumbaughs (Savage-Rumbaugh 1986), and Premacks (Premack & Premack 1983) have had great impact, even though the "language learning" there reported may differ in some respects from that in humans (Terrace et al 1979). Recent extensions to other species, such as pygmy chimpanzees (Savage-Rumbaugh et al 1985), dolphins (Herman et al 1984), sea lions (Schusterman & Krieger 1986), and a parrot (Pepperberg 1983) have been impressive. In some cases this research has led to new research on cognitive performance in other situations, such as analogical reasoning in chimpanzees (Premack 1983) and acquisition of a same/different concept in a parrot (Pepperberg 1987).

The cognitive revival has seen the reintroduction of concepts of mind, awareness, intentionality, and consciousness into scientific comparative psychology and cognitive ethology. Mason (1980) views the comparative study of mind as "the central substantive issue for comparative psychology" (p. 964). Woodruff & Premack (1979) provide evidence they believe is indicative of intentional deception in chimpanzees. Dennett (1983) distinguished different orders of intentionality and attempted to place various kinds of animal cognition at appropriate orders. Gallup (1985) develops criteria to improve rigor in making attributions of complex processes and uses studies of self-recognition in mirrors to infer that chimpanzees display self-recognition and mind. Griffin (1976) pushed these directions somewhat further, proposing that studies of animal communication may provide a window to the minds of animals and may reveal evidence of consciousness. The view has not been universally accepted (Mason 1976).

The advances in the study of complex processes have been impressive and demonstrate the heuristic utility of cognitive constructs. Admiration of these achievements need not imply a view that the methodological problems of investigating animal consciousness are near solution.

The question of the adaptive significance of complex cognitive processes remains. Most cognitive abilities have been tested in highly artificial laboratory situations. Surely, some of these cognitive capacities function in the acquisition of food and mates, avoidance of predators, and in related activities. A representative attempt at integrating proximate and ultimate causation appears in a paper on tool use by Candland (1987). A strong case can be made that social contexts were critical for the evolution of many cognitive abilities (Cheney et al 1986). Nonhuman primates live in complex groups, and must make many subtle social discriminations in order to interact effectively with their peers. In these situations there would be strong selective pressures favoring abilities to form complex associations and to predict the behavior of fellow group members.

CONCLUSIONS

Advances in technology, the rich theoretical base of the 1970s, the influx of active young scientists, and times of general prosperity continue to combine to facilitate rapid development of many areas, only a few of which can be considered here. There are also signs of difficulty. As the field grows, signs of fractionation may be reappearing, perhaps counteracting the gains of the recent synthetic trends. Laboratory research may be slowed as new guidelines mandate demands for expenditures that cannot be made in some institutions, especially smaller ones. Continued destruction of animals and their habitats will have an impact on field research. Research on animal behavior can be of great importance for conservation (see Snowdon 1983). Increased conservation efforts are critical to continued progress in the study of animal behavior—to say nothing of the ethical and aesthetic concerns relating to the other organisms with which we share our planet.

ACKNOWLEDGMENT

Preparation of this review was aided by grant BNS-8520318 from the National Science Foundation. I thank J. Bryan, B. Ferguson, J. P. Pierce Jr., A. Salo, and S. A. Taylor for comments on an earlier draft of this paper.

Literature Cited

Adkins-Regan, E. 1985. Nonmammalian psychosexual differentiation. See Adler et al 1985, pp. 43–76

Adler, N. T. 1983. The neuroethology of reproduction. In *Advances in Vertebrate Neuroethology*, ed. J. Ewert, R. Capranica, D. Ingle, pp. 1033–65. London: Plenum

Adler, N. T., Pfaff, D., Goy, R. W., eds. 1985. *Handbook of Behavioral Neurobiology*, Vol. 7. *Reproduction*. New York: Plenum

Alberts, J. R. 1986. New views of parent-offspring relationships. In *Developmental NeuroPsychobiology*, ed. W. T. Greenough, J. M. Juraska, pp. 449–78. New York: Academic

Arnold, A. P., Breedlove, S. M. 1985. Organizational and activational effects of sex steroids on brain and behavior: a reanalysis. *Horm. Behav.* 19:469–98

Banks, E. M. 1985. Warder Clyde Allee and the Chicago school of animal behavior. *J. Hist. Behav. Sci.* 21:345–53

Bateson, P., ed. 1983a. *Mate Choice*. Cambridge: Cambridge Univ. Press

Bateson, P., 1983b. Optimal outbreeding. See Bateson 1983a, pp. 257–77

Beauchamp, G. K., Yamazaki, K., Boyse, E. A. 1985. The chemosensory recognition of genetic individuality. *Sci. Am.* 253(1):86–92

Beecher, M., Medvin, M. B., Stoddard, P. K., Loesche, P. 1986. Acoustic adaptations for parent-offspring recognition in swallows. *Exp. Biol.* 45:179–93

Bernstein, I. S., Ehardt, C. 1986. The influence of kinship and socialization on aggressive behaviour in rhesus monkeys (*Macaca mulatta*). *Anim. Behav.* 34:739–47

Bitterman, M. E. 1988. Vertebrate-invertebrate comparisons. In *Intelligence and Evolutionary Biology*, ed. H. J. Jerison, I. L. Jerison, pp. 251–76. Berlin: Springer-Verlag

Blanchard, D. C., Blanchard, R. J. 1988. Ethoexperimental approaches to the biology of emotion. *Ann. Rev. Psychol.* 39:43–68

Blaustein, A. R., O'Hara, R. K. 1986. Kin recognition in tadpoles. *Sci. Am.* 254(1):108–16

Boakes, R. 1984. *From Darwinism to Behaviourism: Psychology and the Minds of Animals*. Cambridge: Cambridge Univ. Press

Borgia, G. 1986. Sexual selection in bowerbirds. *Sci. Am.* 224(6):92–100

Brown, R. E., ed. 1985. Paternal behavior. *Am. Zool.* 25:779–923

Brown, R. E., Singh, P. B., Rosier, B. 1987. The major histocompatibility complex and the chemosensory recognition of individuality in rats. *Physiol. Behav.* 40:65–73

Burghardt, G. M., ed. 1985. *Foundations of Comparative Ethology*. New York: Van Nostrand Reinhold

Burkhardt, R. W. Jr. 1981. On the emergence of ethology as a scientific discipline. In *Conspectus on History*, ed. D. W. Hoover, J. T. A. Koumoulides, 1:62–81. Muncie, IN: Ball State Univ.

Burkhardt, R. W. Jr. 1983. The development of an evolutionary ethology. In *Evolution from Molecules to Men*, ed. D. S. Bendall, pp. 429–44. Cambridge: Cambridge Univ. Press

Burkhardt, R. W. Jr. 1988. Charles Otis Whitman, Wallace Craig, and the biological study of animal behavior in the United States, 1898–1925. In *The American Development of Biology*, ed. R. Rainger, K. Benson, J. Maienschein. Philadelphia: Univ. Penn. Press. In press

Burley, N., Krantzberg, G., Radman, P. 1982. Influence of colour-banding on the conspecific preferences of zebra finches. *Anim. Behav.* 30:444–55

Buss, D. M. 1985. Human mate selection. *Am. Sci.* 73:47–51

Cadwallader, T. C. 1984. Neglected aspects of the evolution of American comparative and animal psychology. In *Behavioral Evolution and Integrative Levels*, ed. G. Greenberg, E. Tobach, pp. 15–48. Hillsdale, NJ: Erlbaum

Candland, D. K. 1987. Tool use. In *Comparative Primate Biology*. vol. 2B: *Behavior, Cognition, and Motivation*, ed. G. Mitchell, J. Erwin, pp. 85–103. New York: Liss

Capitanio, J. P. 1985. On comparative psychology and sociobiology. *Cont. Psychol.* 30:777–79

Carter, C. S., Getz, L. L., Cohen-Parsons, M. 1986. Relationships between social organization and behavioral endocrinology in a monogamous mammal. *Adv. Stud. Behav.* 16:109–45

Cheney, D., Seyfarth, R., Smuts, B. 1986.

Social relationships and social cognition in nonhuman primates. *Science* 234:1361–66

Chiszar, D., Wertheimer, M. 1988. Margaret Altmann: a rugged pioneer in rugged fields. *J. Hist. Behav. Sci.* 24:102–6

Christenson, T. E., Brown, S. G., Wenzl, P. A., Hill, E. M., Goist, K. C. 1985. Mating behavior of the golden-orb-weaving spider, *Nephila clavipes:* I. Female receptivity and male courtship. *J. Comp. Psychol.* 99:160–66

Clutton-Brock, T. H., Guiness, F. E., Albon, S. D. 1982. *Red Deer: Behavior and Ecology of Two Sexes.* Chicago: Univ. Chicago Press

Colgan, P. 1983. *Comparative Social Recognition.* New York: Wiley

Cooper, J. B. 1985. Comparative psychology and ethology. In *Topics in the History of Psychology,* ed. G. A. Kimble, K. Schlesinger, 1:135–64. Hillsdale, NJ: Erlbaum

Crews, D. 1987. Courtship in unisexual lizards. *Sci. Am.* 257(6):116–21

Crews, D., Moore, M. C. 1986. Evolution of mechanisms controlling mating behavior. *Science* 231:121–25

Cubicciotti, D. D. III, Mendoza, S. P., Mason, W. A., Sassenrath, E. N. 1986. Differences between *Saimiri sciureus* and *Callicebus moloch* in physiological responsiveness: implications for behavior. *J. Comp. Psychol.* 100:385–91

Daly, M., Wilson, M. 1988. The Darwinian psychology of discriminative parental solicitude. *Nebr. Symp. Motiv.* 35:91–144

Davis, H., Memmott, J. 1982. Counting behavior in animals: a critical evaluation. *Psychol. Bull.* 92:547–71

Dennett, D. C. 1983. Intentional systems in cognitive ethology: the "Panglossian paradigm" defended. *Behav. Brain Sci.* 6:343–90

Dewsbury, D. A. 1982a. Dominance rank, copulatory behavior, and differential reproduction. *Q. Rev. Biol.* 57:135–59

Dewsbury, D. A. 1982b. Ejaculate cost and male choice. *Am. Nat.* 119:601–10

Dewsbury, D. A. 1984a. *Comparative Psychology in the Twentieth Century.* New York: Van Nostrand Reinhold

Dewsbury, D. A., ed. 1984b. *Foundations of Comparative Psychology.* New York: Van Nostrand Reinhold

Dewsbury, D. A., ed. 1985. *Leaders in the Study of Animal Behavior: Autobiographical Perspectives.* Lewisburg, PA: Bucknell Univ. Press

Dewsbury, D. A. 1988a. The comparative psychology of monogamy. *Nebr. Symp. Motiv.* 35:1–50

Dewsbury, D. A. 1988b. Kin discrimination and reproductive behavior in muroid rodents. *Behav. Genet.* 18:525–36

Domjan, M., Galef, B. G. Jr. 1983. Biological constraints on instrumental and classical conditioning: retrospect and prospect. *Anim. Learn. Behav.* 11:151–61

Durant, J. R. 1986. The making of ethology: The Association for the Study of Animal Behaviour, 1936–1986. *Anim. Behav.* 34:1601–16

Egid, K., Lenington, S. 1985. Responses of male mice to odors of females: effects of T- and H-2 locus genotype. *Behav. Genet.* 15:287–95

Emlen, S. T., Oring, L. W. 1977. Ecology, sexual selection, and the evolution of mating systems. *Science* 197:215–23

Estep, D. Q., Gordon, T. P., Wilson, M. E., Walker, M. L. 1986. Social stimulation and the resumption of copulation in rhesus *(Macaca mulatta)* and stumptail *(Macaca arctoides)* macaques. *Int. J. Primatol.* 7:507–17

Fairbanks, L. A., McGuire, M. T. 1986. Age, reproductive value, and dominance-related behaviour in vervet monkey females: cross-generational influences on social relationships and reproduction. *Anim. Behav.* 34:1710–21

Fletcher, D. J. C., Michener, C. D., eds. 1987. *Kin Recognition in Animals.* Chichester: Wiley

Frank, L. G. 1986. Social organization of the spotted hyaena *Crocuta crocuta.* II. Dominance and reproduction. *Anim. Behav.* 34:1510–27

Galef, B. G. Jr. 1985. Direct and indirect behavioural pathways to the social transmission of food avoidance. *Ann. NY Acad. Sci.* 443:203–15

Gallistel, C. R. 1989. Animal cognition. *Ann. Rev. Psychol.* 40:155–89

Gallup, G. G. Jr. 1985. Do minds exist in species other than our own? *Neurosci. Biobehav. Rev.* 9:631–41

Gandelman, R., ed. 1985. *Autobiographies in Experimental Psychology.* Hillsdale, NJ: Erlbaum

Garcia, J., Lasiter, P. S., Bermudez-Rattoni, F., Deems, D. A. 1985. A general theory of aversion learning. *Ann. NY Acad. Sci.* 443:8–21

Gardner, B. T., Gardner, R. A. 1985. Signs of intelligence in cross-fostered chimpanzees. *Philos. Trans. R. Soc. London Ser. B* 308:159–76

Getz, W. M., Smith, K. B. 1986. Honey bee kin recognition: learning self and nestmate phenotypes. *Anim. Behav.* 34:1617–26

Gilbert, A. N., Pelchat, R. J., Adler, N. T. 1980. Postpartum copulatory and maternal behaviour in Norway rats under seminatural conditions. *Anim. Behav.* 28:989–95

Glickman, S. E., 1985. Some thoughts on the evolution of comparative psychology. In *A Century of Psychology as Science,* ed. S. Koch, D. E. Leary, pp. 738–82. New York: McGraw-Hill

Glickman, S. E., Frank, L. G., Davidson, J. M., Smith, E. R., Siiteri, P. K. 1987. Androstenedione may organize or activate sex-reversed traits in female spotted hyenas. *Proc. Natl. Acad. Sci. USA* 84:3444–47

Gottlieb, G. 1979. Comparative psychology and ethology. In *The First Century of Experimental Psychology,* ed. E. Hearst, pp. 147–76. Hillsdale, NJ: Erlbaum

Gould, J. L. 1986. The biology of learning. *Ann. Rev. Psychol.* 37:163–92

Gould, S. J., Lewontin, R. C. 1979. The spandrels of San Marco and the Panglossian paradigm: a critique of the adaptationist paradigm. *Proc. R. Soc. London Ser. B* 205:581–98

Greenberg, L. 1979. Genetic component of bee odor in kin recognition. *Science* 206:1095–97

Griffin, D. R. 1976. The *Question of Animal Awareness.* New York: Rockefeller Univ. Press

Hall, W. G., Oppenheim, R. W. 1987. Developmental psychobiology: prenatal, perinatal, and early postnatal aspects of behavioral development. *Ann. Rev. Psychol.* 38:91–128

Hamilton, W. D. 1964. The genetical evolution of social behavior. I and II. *J. Theoret. Biol.* 7:1–52

Hausfater, G., Hrdy, S. B., eds. 1984. *Infanticide.* New York: Aldine

Henderson, N. D. 1986. Predicting relationships between psychological constructs and genetic characters: an analysis of changing influences on activity in mice. *Behav. Genet.* 16:201–20

Hepper, P. G. 1986. Kin recognition: functions and mechanisms a review. *Biol. Rev.* 61:63–93

Herman, L. M., Richards, D. G., Wolz, J. P. 1984. Comprehension of sentences by bottlenosed dolphins. *Cognition* 16:129–219

Herrnstein, R. J. 1979. Acquisition, generalization, and discrimination reversal of a natural concept. *J. Exp. Psychol.: Anim. Behav. Proc.* 5:116–29

Hill, W. G. 1987. DNA fingerprints applied to animal and bird populations. *Nature* 327:98–99

Hoffmeyer, I. 1982. Responses of female bank voles *(Clethrionomys glareolus)* to dominant vs subordinate conspecific males and to urine odors from dominant vs subordinate males. *Behav. Neural Biol.* 36: 178–88

Hollis, K. L. 1984. The biological function of Pavlovian conditioning: the best defense is a good offense. *J. Exp. Psychol.: Anim. Behav. Proc.* 10:413–25

Holmes, W. G., Sherman, P. W. 1982. The ontogeny of kin recognition in two species of ground squirrels. *Am. Zool.* 22:491–517

Hrdy, S. B. 1979. Infanticide among animals: A review, classification, and examination of the implications for the reproductive strategies of females. *Ethol. Sociobiol.* 1:13–40

Ingle, D., Crews, D. 1985. Vertebrate neuroethology: definitions and paradigms. *Ann. Rev. Neurosci.* 8:457–94

Jannett, F. J. Jr. 1982. Nesting patterns of adult voles, *Microtus montanus,* in field populations. *J. Mammal.* 63:495–98

Jarvis, J. U. M. 1981. Eusociality in a mammal: cooperative breeding in naked mole-rat colonies. *Science* 212:571–73

Jerison, H. J. 1985. Issues in brain evolution. *Oxford Surv. Evol. Biol.* 2:102–34

Johnston, R. E. 1983. Chemical signals and reproductive behavior. See Vandenbergh 1983, pp. 3–37

Kamil, A. C., Roitblat, H. L. 1985. The ecology of foraging behavior: implications for animal learning and memory. *Ann. Rev. Psychol.* 36:141–69

Kamil, A. C., Sargent, T. D., eds. 1981. *Foraging Behavior.* New York: Garland

Kluender, K. R., Diehl, R. L., Killeen, P. R. 1987. Japanese quail can learn phonetic categories. *Science* 237:1195–97

Lenington, S., Egid, K. 1985. Female discrimination of male odors correlated with male genotype at the T locus: a response to T-locus or H-2 locus variability? *Behav. Genet.* 15:53–67

Leon, M. 1983. Chemical communication in mother-young interactions. See Vandenbergh 1983, pp. 39–77

Linsenmair, K. E. 1987. Kin recognition in subsocial arthropods, in particular in the desert isopod *Hemilepistus reaumuri.* See Fletcher & Michener 1987, pp. 121–208

Macphail, E. M. 1987. Review of "Behavioral Evolution and Integrative Levels." *Q. J. Exp. Psychol.* 39B:97–98

Majerus, M. E. N., O'Donald, P., Kearns, P. W. E., Ireland, H. 1986. Genetics and evolution of female choice. *Nature* 321: 164–67

Marchlewska-Koj, A. 1983. Pregnancy blocking by pheromones. See Vandenbergh 1983, pp. 151–74

Mason, W. A. 1974. Comparative studies of social behavior in *Callicebus* and *Saimiri:* Behavior of male-female pairs. *Folia Primatol.* 22:1–8

Mason, W. A. 1976. Windows on other minds. *Science* 194:930–31

Mason, W. A. 1980. Minding our business. *Am. Psychol.* 35:964–67

Mason, W. A., Lott, D. F. 1976. Ethology

and comparative psychology. *Ann. Rev. Psychol.* 27:129–54

McClintock, M. K. 1983. Pheromonal regulation of the ovarian cycle: enhancement, suppression, and synchrony. See Vandenbergh 1983, pp. 113–49

Mendoza, S. P., Mason, W. A. 1986. Parental division of labour and differentiation of attachments in a monogamous primate *(Callicebus moloch). Anim. Behav.* 34:1336–47

Menzel, E. M. Jr., Juno, C. 1985. Social foraging in marmoset monkeys and the question of intelligence. *Philos. Trans. R. Soc. London Ser. B* 308:145–58

Moehlman, P. D. 1987. Social organization in jackals. *Am. Sci.* 75:366–75

Moore, C. L. 1985. Another psychobiological view of sexual differentiation. *Dev. Rev.* 5:18–55

Nicolson, N. A. 1986. Infants, mothers, and other females. See Smuts et al 1986, pp. 330–42

Okanoya, K., Dooling, R. J. 1987. Hearing in passerine and psittacine birds: a comparative study of absolute and masked auditory thresholds. *J. Comp. Psychol.* 101:7–15

Olton, D. S. 1977. Spatial memory. *Sci. Am.* 236(6):82–98

Pauly, P. J. 1987. *Controlling Life: Jacques Loeb and the Engineering Ideal in Biology.* New York: Oxford

Pepperberg, I. M. 1983. Cognition in the African grey parrot: preliminary evidence for auditory/vocal comprehension of the class concept. *Anim. Learn. Behav.* 11:179–85

Pepperberg, I. M. 1987. Acquisition of the same/different concept by an African grey parrot *(Psittacus erithacus)*: Learning with respect to categories of color, shape, and material. *Anim. Learn. Behav.* 15:423–32

Petrinovich, L. 1988. The role of social factors in white-crowned sparrow song development. In *Social Learning: A Comparative Approach,* ed. T. Zentall, B. G. Galef Jr., pp. 255–78. Hillsdale, NJ: Erlbaum. In press

Porter, R. H. 1987. Kin recognition: functions and mediating mechanisms. In *Sociobiology and Psychology: Ideas, Issues, and Applications,* ed. C. B. Crawford, M. F. Smith, D. L. Krebs, pp. 175–203. Hillsdale, NJ: Erlbaum

Porter, R. H., Balogh, R. D., Makin, J. W. 1988. Olfactory influences on mother-infant interactions. In *Advances in Infancy Research,* Vol. 5, ed. L. Lipsett, C. Rovee-Collier. Norwood, NJ: Ablex. In press

Premack, D. 1983. The codes of man and beasts. *Behav. Brain Sci.* 6:125–67

Premack, D., Premack, A. J. 1983. *The Mind of an Ape.* New York: Norton

Ralls, K., Brugger, K., Ballou, J. 1979. Inbreeding and juvenile mortality in small populations of ungulates. *Science* 206: 1101–3

Reid, R. L. 1986. Review of "Behavioral Evolution and Integrative Levels." *Anim. Behav.* 34:310

Richards, R. J. 1987. *Darwin and the Emergence of Evolutionary Theories of Mind and Behavior.* Chicago: Univ. Chicago

Risler, L., Wasser, S. K., Sackett, G. P. 1987. Measurement of excreted steroids in *Macaca nemestrina. Am. J. Primatol.* 12: 91–100

Roitblat, H. L. 1987. *Introduction to Comparative Cognition.* San Francisco: Freeman

Rubenstein, D. I., Wrangham, R. W., eds. 1986. *Ecological Aspects of Social Evolution.* Princeton: Princeton Univ. Press

Savage-Rumbaugh, E. S. 1986. *Ape Language: From Conditioned Response to Symbol.* New York: Columbia Univ. Press

Savage-Rumbaugh, S., Rumbaugh, D. M., McDonald, K. 1985. Language learning in two species of apes. *Neurosci. Biobehav. Rev.* 9:653–65

Scarborough, E., Furumoto, L. 1987. *Untold Lives: The First Generation of American Women Psychologists.* New York: Columbia Univ. Press

Schusterman, R. J., Krieger, K. 1986. Artificial language comprehension and size transposition by a California sea lion *(Zalophus californianus). J. Comp. Psychol.* 100:348–55

Schwagmeyer, P. L., Woontner, S. J. 1986. Scramble competition polygyny in thirteen-lined ground squirrels: the relative contributions of overt conflict and competitive mate searching. *Behav. Ecol. Sociobiol.* 19:359–64

Shapiro, D. Y. 1987. Differentiation and evolution of sex change in fishes. *BioScience* 37:490–97

Sherman, P. W., Holmes, W. G. 1985. Kin recognition: issues and evidence. In *Experimental Behavioral Ecology and Sociobiology,* ed. B. Hölldobler, M. Lindauer, pp. 437–60. Sunderland, MA: Sinauer

Sherry, D. F. 1985. Food storage in birds and mammals. *Adv. Stud. Behav.* 15:153–88

Shettleworth, S. J. 1983. Memory in food-hoarding birds. *Sci. Am.* 248(3):102–10

Silver, R., Norgren, R. B. Jr. 1987. Circadian rhythms in avian reproduction. In *Psychobiology of Reproductive Behavior,* ed. D. Crews, pp. 120–47. Englewood Cliffs, NJ: Prentice-Hall

Singer, B. 1981. History of the study of animal behaviour. In *The Oxford Companion to Animal Behaviour,* ed. D. McFarland, pp. 255–72. Oxford: Oxford Univ. Press

Smith, R. L., ed. 1984. *Sperm Competition*

and the Evolution of Animal Mating Systems. Orlando: Academic

Smuts, B. 1985. *Sex and Friendship in Baboons.* New York: Aldine

Smuts, B. 1987. What are friends for? *Nat. Hist.* 96(2):36–45

Smuts, B., Cheney, D. L., Seyfarth, R. M., Wrangham, R. W., Struhsaker, T. T., eds. 1986. *Primate Societies.* Chicago: Univ. Chicago Press

Snowdon, C. T. 1983. Ethology, comparative psychology, and animal behavior. *Ann. Rev. Psychol.* 34:63–94

Snowdon, C. T., Suomi, S. J. 1982. Paternal behavior in primates. In *Child Nurturance,* ed. H. E. Fitzgerald, J. A. Mullins, P. Gage, 3:63–108. New York: Plenum

Storey, A. 1986. Advantages to female rodents of male-induced pregnancy disruptions. *Ann. NY Acad. Sci.* 474:135–40

Terrace, H. S. 1987. Chunking by a pigeon in a serial learning task. *Nature* 325:149–51

Terrace, H. S., Petitto, L. A., Sanders, R. J., Bever, T. G. 1979. Can an ape create a sentence? *Science* 206:891–902

Thiessen, D., Gregg, B. 1980. Human assortative mating and genetic equilibrium: an evolutionary perspective. *Ethol. Sociobiol.* 1:111–40

Thorpe, W. H. 1979. *The Origins and Rise of Ethology.* New York: Praeger

Timberlake, W., Lucas, G. A. 1985. The basis of superstitious behavior: chance contingency, stimulus substitution, or appetitive behavior? *J. Exp. Anal. Behav.* 44:279–99

Tinbergen, N. 1963. On aims and methods of ethology. *Z. Tierpsychol.* 20:410–29

Tobach, E., ed. 1987. *Historical Perspectives and the International Status of Comparative Psychology.* Hillsdale, NJ: Erlbaum

Trivers, R. L. 1972. Parental investment and sexual selection. In *Sexual Selection and the Descent of Man 1871–1971,* ed. B. Campbell, pp. 136–79. Chicago: Aldine

Trivers, R. L. 1974. Parent-offspring conflict. *Am. Zool.* 14:249–64

Vandenbergh, J. G., ed. 1983. *Pheromones and Reproduction in Mammals.* New York: Academic

Waldman, B. 1986. Chemical ecology of kin recognition in anuran amphibians. In *Chemical Signals in Vertebrates. 4. Ecology, Evolution, and Comparative Biology,* ed., D. Duvall, D. Muller Schwarze, R. M. Silverstein, pp. 225–42. New York: Plenum

Wasser, S. K., Barash, D. P. 1983. Reproductive suppression among female mammals: implications for biomedicine and sexual selection theory. *Q. Rev. Biol.* 58:513–38

Wasserman, E. A. 1981. Comparative psychology returns: a review of Hulse, Fowler, and Honig's *Cognitive Processes in Animal Behavior. J. Exp. Anal. Behav.* 35:243–57

West, M. J., King, A. P. 1985. Social guidance of vocal learning by female cowbirds: validating its functional significance. *Z. Tierpsychol.* 70:225–35

Whitten, P. L. 1986. Infants and adult males. See Smuts et al 1986, pp. 343–57

Wilson, E. O. 1975. *Sociobiology: The New Synthesis.* Cambridge, MA: Harvard Univ. Press

Wimer, R. E., Wimer, C. C. 1985. Animal behavior genetics: a search for the biological foundations of behavior. *Ann. Rev. Psychol.* 36:171–218

Wingfield, J. C., Moore, M. C. 1987. Hormonal, social, and environmental factors in the reproductive biology of free-living male birds. In *Psychobiology of Reproductive Behavior: An Evolutionary Perspective,* ed. D. Crews, pp. 148–75. Englewood Cliffs, NJ: Prentice-Hall

Woodruff, G., Premack, D. 1979. Intentional communication in the chimpanzee: the development of deception. *Cognition* 7:333–62

Woolfenden, G. E., Fitzpatrick, J. W. 1984. *The Florida Scrub Jay.* Princeton: Princeton Univ. Press

Wynne-Edwards, V. C. 1962. *Animal Dispersion in Relation to Social Behavior.* Edinburgh: Oliver & Boyd

Yamazaki, K., Boyse, E. A., Miké, V., Thaler, H. T., Mathieson, B. J., et al. 1976. Control of mating preferences in mice by genes in the major histocompatibility complex. *J. Exp. Med.* 144:1324–35

Ann. Rev. Psychol. 1989. 40:603–29

COGNITIVE SCIENCE: Definition, Status, and Questions

Earl Hunt

Department of Psychology, The University of Washington, Seattle, Washington 98195

CONTENTS

Cognitive science is an attempt to unify views of thought developed by studies in psychology, linguistics, anthropology, philosophy, computer science, and the neurosciences (Collins 1977; H. Gardner 1985; Norman 1980). Because cognitive science is a perspective rather than a discipline, it is impossible to review "current findings" in the field; instead, the worth of the overview must be assessed. Since this review is addressed to psychologists, I emphasize the impact of cognitive science upon psychological studies.

I discuss four issues: the overview itself, some of the philosophical questions that it raises, and how the cognitive science overview has been used to

603

0066–4308/89/0201–0603$02.00

bring order into the study of human information processing and reasoning. In the absence of cognitive science concepts, the last two topics, central to modern psychology, have produced notoriously disorganized fields.

THINKING AS THE MANIPULATION OF AN INTERNAL REPRESENTATION

The cognitive science movement has been dominated by the *computational view* of thought, which sees thinking as the manipulation of an internal representation ("mental model") of an external domain.[1] The representation must be expressed in some internal language containing definitions for well-formed structures and operations upon them. The analogy is more to a computer programming language than to a natural language. Following Fodor (1975), the internal language will be called "mentalese." A computational theory of thought must define the mentalese language and describe a hypothetical machine that can execute programs written in it.

Newell (1980) and, in more detail, Pylyshyn (1984) define three distinct levels of psychological theory within a computational view. Information-processing theories attempt to define human mentalese and the machine associated with it. Physical theories explain how the mentalese machine is instantiated by the brain. Representational theories express regularities in the ways that relationships in the external world are captured by mental models.[2]

Representational theories are largely intended to account for our conscious experience of thought. Representational laws can be based upon observation and generalization from those observations. For instance, it is a law of behavior in chess that experienced chess players examine the board to make sure their king is not under attack. This is not of much interest to psychology in general. (It might well be of interest to an anthropologist seeking to understand the game.) The generalization of this observation, not making a move before checking for the existence of vital threats to one's state of being, is a potential regularity of planning in many domains, and could be studied as a psychological regularity in representational thought.

Physical theories are also based on observation, since brain variables are physical variables. One way to study cognition is to try to establish systematic

---

[1]The computational view is sometimes referred to as the "computer metaphor." This is inaccurate, as there is no claim that an electronic computer is a physical model for thought or the brain.

[2]Mandler (1985) has pointed out that the classic mind-body problem disappears when it is stated in terms of computational theories and their physical instantiations. Theories of representation manipulation are coordinated with theories of brain action, instead of coordinating physical observations about the brain with our conscious experiences.

relations between physical and representational observations. The discovery that there are speech-specific areas in the human brain is an example of such an approach. Note the "two-way" nature of this finding. The identification of language with left temporal lobe functioning obviously has important implications for clinical medicine and descriptive biology. The fact that language facilities are associated with a particular part of the brain is evidence that language itself is somehow a modular function, partially dissociated from other aspects of cognition.

Some philosophers of cognition (e.g. Rorty 1979) have argued that theories of thought should be phrased in terms of brain states. The commoner attitude in cognitive science is to assume that information-processing theories must intervene between physical- and representational-level theories (e.g. Fodor 1975, 1985). We are at present unable to state anything more than vague generalizations about the links between physical and representational thought. We can tell from physical measures that the left temporal region of the brain is active when we read, but we cannot discriminate the activity induced by reading Shakespeare from that induced by reading Agatha Christie. Therefore, in order to explain representational-level thought, we must introduce a detailed theory of the functions required to produce such thinking. This is the point at which a computational theory of information processing, in the abstract, becomes essential.

Information-processing studies deal with two somewhat different questions. What sort of language is mentalese, and what problem-solving regularities are expressed in it? For ease of reference, this will be called the syntactic issue. What sort of primitive operations are available to manipulate mentalese data structures, and how do they fit together? This will be called the system architecture issue. The two issues are discussed in more detail below. First, though, I consider some of the philosophic issues raised by the cognitive science view.

PHILOSOPHIC ISSUES

Syntactical and Semantic Models for Thought

Regularities are stated in different ways in information-processing and representational theories. If the regularity is at the information-processing level it should be stated as an operation on structures defined by the syntax of mentalese. If the regularity is at the representational level it should be stated in the semantics of the problem-solving domain. To see the difference between the two types of laws, consider these problem-solving rules, which are paraphrased from J. R. Anderson's (1983, pp. 162–65) discussion of problem solving in plane geometry.

1. IF the goal is to produce an (internal mentalese) structure of type Z, and the current knowledge is a structure of type X, and if there is an operation that changes structures of type Y into type Z,
THEN attempt to solve the problem of transforming the current knowledge structure into a structure of type X.
2. IF the goal is to prove triangle XYZ congruent to triangle ABC,
THEN attempt to prove that one of the angles in triangle XYZ and the lines that form it are congruent to one of the angles of triangle ABC and the lines that form it.

Rule 1 is a syntactic rule for "means-end analysis," a problem-solving method discussed in more detail below. Rule 2 is stated in the semantics of plane geometry. Note that rule 2 is an object that could be used by rule 1.

Even when theories of problem solving are couched semantically they usually contain syntactic rules (Rips 1986). This point is illustrated by the theories of syllogistic reasoning proposed by Johnson-Laird (1980, 1983) and R. J. Sternberg (1980). Verbally both authors describe syllogistic reasoning as if one imagined worlds populated by (in Johnson-Laird's examples) bee-keepers who are all artists and sometimes chemists. Statements are then verified by checking to see if they are consistent with these imagined worlds. In fact, however, Johnson-Laird and Sternberg define "imagining possible worlds" and "examining them for consistency" in terms of the construction and manipulation of symbol structures that might represent beekeepers and chemists, but could equally well represent ice skaters and college students.

The distinction between syntactic and semantic rules is not absolute. Rules defined in terms of the semantics of a known language may be syntactical with reference to problems stated in that language. This is illustrated in the work of Langley et al (1987) on inductive reasoning in science. Langley et al developed programs that were able to recreate some of the classic discoveries in physics and chemistry, such as Kepler's laws of planetary motion, by examining the data available to the scientists of the time. Most of Langley et al's programs could be described as sophisticated rules for exploratory statistical data analysis.[3] Thus the rules were semantic with respect to algebra, and syntactic with respect to the area of science being studied.

---

[3]The three data analysis programs were BACON (which is actually a series of programs), GLAUBER, and STAHL. A fourth program, DALTON, contained some of the semantics of physical chemistry. The principles illustrated in Langley et al's (1987) programs have been used to create programs for multivariate data analysis (Glymour et al 1987). The specific heuristics used in the multivariate programs are much more specialized than those used in the Langley et al work.

Testing System Architecture Theories

Most studies in human experimental psychology are intended to establish facts at the information-processing level, either about mentalese or about its associated machine. To do this, experimental psychologists have tried to define, somewhat intuitively, information-processing functions they believe exist, and then to operationalize their measurement in experimental paradigms. This is how such concepts as "short-term memory scanning" and "visual iconic memory" were developed. Implied is the hope that as regularities of behavior in the experimental paradigms are discovered the conceptual definitions of the hypothesized functions will become clearer.

This approach has been criticized on the grounds that it leads to the study of disconnected paradigms, without the accumulation of a systematic body of knowledge (Newell 1973a). A second criticism is that the knowledge obtained is about behavior forced by the paradigm, and not about the behavior that supports extra-laboratory thinking (Neisser 1976). Quite a few well-known psychologists have acknowledged the force of these complaints (Baars 1986). The cognitive science alternative is to determine the nature of human system architecture by a careful consideration of the constraints placed on possible architectures by observations at the representational and physical levels.

Simon (1969, 1981) has presented an eloquent argument for the study of representational constraints. He points out that intelligent devices must be able to represent the important aspects of their environments in their internal problem solving. When we consider the representational requirements of the problem-solving environments where people function, we find them so severe that only a few information-processing systems can meet them. Therefore a demonstration that a particular information-processing system (including both architectural and syntactical concepts) can support the wide range of representations humans must use would be a powerful argument for that system as the appropriate model of human information processing. This is called the *sufficiency* argument.

The sufficiency argument is used to justify developing computer programs that simulate human thought in a fairly general way, without making detailed comparisons between the behaviors of people and the simulating program. Obviously this approach is a contrast to the concern with model evaluation that characterizes much of experimental psychology. The argument is that the really hard thing to do is to find models that might conceivably approach the complexity of human problem solving—i.e. that plausible theory production is harder than theory verification in a microscopic area of behavior. If computer programs that even approach human capabilities in solving algebra problems, playing chess, and analyzing discourse all require certain information-processing architectures and mentalese structures, then these operations and structures are putative theories of human problem solving. Because there are only a few such programs, representational-level constraints alone are sufficient to restrict our attention to a few plausible computational theories of thought.

Philosophers and linguists have made a somewhat different use of representational-level observations to constrain architectural models. They point out that certain primitive operations at the information-processing level appear to go forward once they are initiated, without any further control at the representational level. Fodor (1983) calls such operations *modules* of thought, which are required at the computational level, and from which representational-level thinking can be constructed.

The study of language provides some of the most striking evidence for modularity. The regularities observed in "slips of the tongue," such as the (apocryphal?) Victorian toast to the "Queer old dean," indicate that there are separate modules for the arousal of words as phoneme clusters and their assembly into articulated words (Fromkin 1973). Experimental studies of slips of the tongue (Baars 1980; Motley 1980) amplify this observation by showing that the articulation plan is subject to an editing process that is itself sensitive to semantic properties. At a higher level of analysis, Perfetti et al (1987) have reported that ambiguous newspaper headlines, such as "Police can't stop gambling" are comprehended more slowly than unambiguous ones, even when the meaning is clear in context. It is as if the syntactic parsing mechanisms for sentence analysis cannot be inhibited once they are engaged. These are only a few of the many linguistic observations used to argue for modularity in speech production and comprehension. However, contradictory evidence exists to suggest that speech is not entirely divorced from cognition in general (Foss 1988).

Architectural theories may also be constrained by physical observations. Establishing a correlation between localized brain damage and the loss of an apparent information-processing function is powerful evidence that the presumed information-processing function does exist. There are several examples of such an argument. The well-known distinction between short-term and long-term memory is a system architecture–level construct that has been supported by observations of selective derangement in short- and long-term memory associated with brain-structural or biochemical damage (Squire 1987). Numerous studies of the effects of brain damage on language competence support the idea that language depends upon several functionally independent modules of thought (Coltheart 1985; Ojemann & Creutzfeldt 1987). Kosslyn (1987) and Farah (1984) offer evidence about derangements in imaging ability as support for the existence of modules used in the normal imaging process.

Because the technology for direct observation of brain structures and processes is advancing rapidly, it seems reasonable to expect that the use of physical observations to constrain theories of information processing will be of great importance in the next 10–15 years.

Reconciling the Emphasis on Constraints versus Experimentation

It has been claimed that the contrast between accepting theories on the basis of experimental testing and accepting theories on the basis of constraints highlights a fundamental philosophical difference between psychologists, on the one hand, and cognitive scientists more generally [especially those whose interest is in the development of artificial intelligence (AI) systems] on the other (L. Miller 1978). This overstates the distinction between the cognitive science and experimental psychology approaches.

Cognitive scientists, many of whom are psychologists, do not categorically reject laboratory studies as sources of data about the mind. Experimental evidence is acceptable if the experimental paradigm can be justified within the framework of a broader theory (Collins 1977). For instance, certain paradigms for studying working memory (but not the classic memory-span paradigm) have been related to performance in reading (Daneman 1985). The cognitive science movement is not suspicious of laboratory studies per se; it demands that their use be justified.

Sufficiency arguments are not as compelling as some of the proponents have maintained. Sufficiency is seldom established by formal proof procedures.[4] It is more common to demonstrate a program's power by example and reasoned argumentation (van Lehn et al 1984). Acceptance of a program as a psychological model then rests on the impressiveness of the demonstration and the subjective feeling that the program solves problems in the way humans appear to do. Many psychologists do not trust this procedure. While they worry that an absolute rejection of intuition can lead to excessively severe restrictions on the study of thought, they are reluctant to accept its unbridled use (Baars 1986).

The issue is not whether to accept intuition or not, but when to do so. Pylyshyn's (1984) concept of cognitive penetrability and Fodor's (1983) notion of modularity are relevant. Cognitively penetrable reasoning is, almost by definition, reasoning at the representational level. There is a startling degree of contextual specificity in such thought (see below). To the extent that representational thought is tied to context and is cognitively penetrable (i.e. to the extent that people are doing exactly what they say they are doing), appeals

---

[4]There is one technique of deductive problem solving, called Resolution Principle problem solving, whose power has been established by formal proof (Hunt 1975; Robinson 1965). This technique has never been considered a realistic candidate theory of human problem solving.

to intuitions are a legitimate form of argument. On the other hand, when dealing with system-architecture concepts, formal experimentation is necessary.

Experimentation, however, is not synonymous with hypothesis testing. What is needed is a broad view of an experiment as a controlled observation of what happens in an important situation; an experiment need not be seen as a contest between theories. In an experimental study of thought the problem solver is, in the most literal sense, the "subject of the study." The experimental situation must elicit those behaviors that *the problem solver* sees as important, regardless of the observer's theory. If the controlling conditions of the study make it difficult for the problem solver to do this, then the conditions, rather than the behaviors, must go.

THE ARCHITECTURE OF INFORMATION PROCESSING

The Production System Model

Since the early 1970s most cognitive science investigations have utilized a computational model known as *production system programming* (Newell & Simon 1972; Newell 1973b). In production system programming there is a privileged symbol structure representing the "current state" of the computation, and a set of rules (productions) of the form "If (pattern) then take (action)." Anderson's rules for solving geometry problems (see above) are examples of this format. The pattern part of a production is some arrangement of symbols that can occur in the privileged symbol structure. The action is any action that the system (i.e. problem solver) can take, including the action of rearranging the privileged symbol structure.

Strictly speaking, production systems are a programming notation without psychological context.[5] However, like all programming languages, production systems imply an architecture for program execution (Hunt 1975). A production-executing machine has a straightforward psychological interpretation. Neches et al (1987), in common with many authors, refer to the privileged structure as "working memory" and to a "long-term memory" containing the production rules. The actions that can be taken within a production are interpreted as operations required to coordinate symbol structures in working and long-term memory. These may be determined logically, by an analysis of the operations required by any symbol manipulating device (Newell 1980), one could also look for evidence of a particular mechanism

---

[5]Unrestricted production systems are equivalent to Turing machines. They can be used to describe an algorithm for any computable function. Therefore the claim that a behavior "can be modeled as a production system" is vacuous unless the definition of a production is restricted in some way.

based upon data from psychological or neuropsychological research (Anderson 1983; Hunt & Lansman 1986; Kosslyn 1987).

The patterns and actions permitted in a production determine the "grain size" of a cognitive model, since they define the primitive elements from which a model of thought can be developed. The geometry problem–solving examples cited earlier exhibit a rather coarse grain size, since they refer to abstract conceptual structures. Finer grain sizes are appropriate if the task to be modeled is an elementary one. Just & Carpenter's (1985) production model of the rotation of mental images is a good example of this approach. The productions in Just's & Carpenter's program contained primitive actions such as focusing attention on parts of a visual image and making slight movements of the fixated image "in the mind's eye."

There are three parts to a production-executing machine: a pattern recognition system that compares the pattern parts of productions to structures in working memory, a set of primitive actions that can be associated with a pattern, and a conflict resolution rule that determines which production is to be executed when two or more productions match the working-memory structure. Production system modeling puts the burden of problem solving upon the pattern recognition system. It is fairly easy to assemble a list of symbol manipulating actions that are sufficient to solve a problem if they are done at the appropriate time. The difficulty is in stating the rules that determine when an action will be taken.

Production-executing machines mix serial and parallel operations. The machines are parallel in the sense that all production patterns are sensed simultaneously, so that the number of production rules in long-term memory does not slow down the conceptual machines' operation.[6] The machines operate in series in the sense that any communication from production to production that takes place via changes in the working-memory structures must be a serial operation.

Production Systems as Models of Psychological Processes

Several different production system architectures have been proposed as psychological models (Anderson 1983; Holland et al 1986; Hunt & Lansman 1986). They differ largely in the assumptions they make about (*a*) the number of working-memory subsystems that can operate in parallel and (*b*) the notations used to code information within each subsystem. The syntactical structures of the systems' mentalese vary from Anderson's use of propositional calculus notation to Hunt & Lansman's use of feature lists and the use of image-like codes by Holland et al and Kosslyn (1980). Since the

---

[6] If a production system is simulated on a conventional (serial) computer the number of productions in the system does affect the program's speed. This is of no conceptual significance.

various investigators have studied different problems there is no way to compare their models directly. Furthermore, there is no need to commit oneself to one or the other representation, because it could well be that there are two (or more) different areas of working memory, each with its own information structures (Baddeley 1986). No one claims that we know in detail what the right model is for the architecture of human cognition. The claim is just that examining production system models gives us a way to talk about the issue.

The emphasis on system architecture as a controlling feature of thought is most explicit in work by Anderson (1983) and Hunt & Lansman (1986). In Anderson's ACT* model, long-term memory contains both facts and productions—i.e. there is both declarative and procedural information in memory. Each fact or production has a level of activation associated with it. Activation can be passed between facts and between productions. The rate at which patterns are matched to facts in declarative memory is a function of the level of activation of the patterns and the facts. As a result, the ACT* model has the interesting feature of defining working memory by level of activation of a statement, so that "being in working memory" is more a matter of degree than an all-or-none state. There is an interesting parallel between this approach and Mandler's (1985) point that conscious experience is constructed from the emerging activation of nonconscious information structures.

The ACT* model has been applied to a wide variety of phenomena, varying from recognition memory experiments to problem solving in geometry and computer programming. The applications are more demonstrations of consistency of the theory with gross observations than demonstrations of detailed, accurate predictions. The breadth of the theory's applications is impressive.

Hunt & Lansman (1986) considered the more circumscribed problem of simulating experimental studies in the attention and performance field. Examples are the simulation of Hick's law relating reaction time in a choice reaction task to the number of targets that may occur, and modeling the deterioration of performance that occurs when attention is split across two or more sensory channels. Hunt & Lansman showed that these phenomena could be produced by the interaction between the trivial production systems required to explain what a participant in an attention and performance study does and the architecture required to execute these trivial productions. As in the case of Anderson's work, emphasis has to be on breadth rather than depth. Taken in isolation, Hunt & Lansman produced complicated explanations for well-known laboratory experiments. The contribution was in applying explanations with common elements to different paradigms.

Two other efforts are worth mention for their concern with architecture, though they are usually considered applications of production systems to specific tasks. Kosslyn and his colleagues (1980, 1983; Kosslyn & Schwartz

1977) have implemented a detailed theory of mental imagery as a production system program. The program utilizes propositional information stored in long-term memory (e.g. "German shepherds are big dogs") to construct appropriate 'visual images' in a working memory in which the data structures are coordinates in a two-dimensional grid. Just & Carpenter (1981, 1987; Thibadeau et al 1982) have developed production system models for reading that extend both to the logical analysis of a text and to the control of eye movements. This is a particularly elegant example of a situation in which the production system approach allows the researcher to combine models of two very different tasks: one under conscious awareness and the other a relatively automatic motor action.

A Note on Learning

The above remarks are directed at production system models of performance. What about learning? In the production system approach learning is the development of new productions. This is thought of as a highly cognitive process. The approach is well illustrated by Anderson's (1986, 1987) treatment of learning within the ACT* framework. Most of the remarks applicable to ACT* apply to other papers on production system models of learning (Klahr et al 1987).

Recall that in ACT* there is a distinction between *declarative* factual information and *procedural* information that is embodied in the pattern parts of productions. Learning is seen as a computation, achieved by production execution, in which procedural and declarative information in long-term memory is used to construct new productions.

If learning is production construction, then transfer of learning from one task to another will be determined by the number of productions the two tasks share, rather than the number of common actions required by the originally learned and transfer tasks. Singley & Anderson (1985) have obtained support for this hypothesis in a clever study in which people learned a computer text editor and then transferred to a second editor that shared either surface features or the underlying production system for solving text editing problems. Positive transfer was related to shared productions based on goal-oriented problem solving.

A second implication of the ACT* view is that learning must compete for computing resources with concurrent problem-solving activities. Nissen & Bullmer (1987) have shown that people's ability to learn a sequence of movements in a serial reaction-time task can be inhibited by the introduction of a concurrent working-memory task. Their work is an elegant test of Anderson's notion in a tightly controlled experimental situation. Reports that eyewitness memory can be disrupted by the occurrence of a dramatic event immediately after the witness has seen the to-be-remembered episode (Loftus & Burns 1982) are also consistent with the ACT* view.

The ACT* learning model contains the strong assumption that all learning must pass through a declarative memory stage en route to being incorporated in productions. In Anderson's terminology, knowledge is moved from the "interpreted" to the "compiled" stage. This assumption is probably too strong. Nissen and her colleagues (Nissen et al 1987) have shown that people suffering from both chronic and temporary physiologically induced amnesias can learn to react to stimulus-response redundancies in a serial reaction-time task, even though they fail to show declarative knowledge of their experiences. These results indicate that learning can occur without problem solving. Other aspects of Nissen's results indicate that cognitively based learning is necessary if the information learned is to be transferred to a new situation.

An Evaluation of the Production System Approach as a Psychological Model of Information Processing

As a broad generality, the production-executing machine seems to be a useful conceptual device for experimental psychology. However, with the exception of studies of learning, developing the model as an explanation for human information processing does not seem to be a high-priority goal in either the cognitive science or experimental psychology community. Even in the case of learning, cognitive science studies focus more on the simulation of "education" (e.g. learning geometry or computer programming) more than they focus on the explanation of data obtained in tightly controlled laboratory situations (Mandler 1985).

The situation is partly due to cognitive scientists' skepticism about experimental psychology's paradigms. A second reason for lack of interest is that attempts to explain observations about human information processing invole studies at a grain size that cognitive scientists find too small to be relevant to extra-laboratory performance. This is particularly the case when a cognitive science study of learning is associated with attempts to build models of human performance in very complex environments, such as medical diagnosis or electronic troubleshooting. In such cases interest focuses on models of representational thought. A system architecture is then something to be assumed as a primitive, rather than being a topic of investigation in its own right.

The trouble with this argument is that short-term concepts of relevance are allowed to guide scientific investigation. The benefits and costs of such guidance need not be repeated here.

Experimental psychologists are disinclined to develop production systems as architectural models for a rather different reason. They value parsimonious explanations, and the overarching explanation of several paradigms is not likely to be a parsimonious explanation for any one of them. The problem with this approach, though, is that parsimony is assessed only for the particular paradigm being studied. Experimental psychologists do not seem to balance local parsimony against global complexity, or vice versa.

Unless cognitive scientists become convinced that experimental psychology's paradigms are interesting, or experimental psychologists become convinced that the paradigms must be related to each other, efforts to understand the system architecture of human cognition may well fall by the wayside. This would be unfortunate, becuase it would contribute to the split between studies of representational and information-processing aspects of thought. Such splits are what cognitive science was supposed to prevent.

STUDIES OF THOUGHT AT THE REPRESENTATIONAL LEVEL: REASONING

Introductory Remarks

Studies of representational thinking cover topics ranging from game playing to text comprehension. The analysis of reasoning has been chosen for discussion, both because it is central to thought and because it illustrates a major issue that has arisen as cognitive science studies have been extended to more and more domains. To what extent are there regularities in representational thought that are general across domains, and that can be developed into a theory of representational-level cognition?

It is worth noting that the various simulation programs to be described here either have been or could be realized as production systems. Thus these representational models are compatible with the system architecture models described previously.

Reasoning is, loosely, the working through of problems so that one can explain either why something happened or what will happen. Philosophers and logicians distinguish between deductive reasoning, which is based upon the application of inference rules to a formal model of a problem, and inductive reasoning, which requires the determination of a model and its associated inference rules. Formal models of how deduction should proceed are well worked out. The rules of induction are much harder to define, since problems typically permit multiple descriptions, and hence the use of several different schemes of inference.

In daily life people move back and forth between induction and deduction. Nevertheless, the distinction has psychological content, for psychometric studies have found that the people who do well on pure deductive problems do not always show superior inductive reasoning, and vice versa (Sternberg 1984). As we progress through various congitive science explanations, though, we see how the two processes are mixed in problem solving.

Deductive Reasoning

Newell & Simon's (1963, 1972; Ernst & Newell 1969) work on a domain-independent deductive reasoning program, the General Problem Solver (GPS), is generally considered the foundation of cognitive science. To use GPS a person provided the program with a set of known statements, rules for deriving new statements from old statements, and the description of a desired (goal) statement. The program contained heuristics for problem solving, defined in its own internal language, that allowed it to use the domain-specific rules to develop a chain of inferences linking the known statements to the goal statement. Three aspects of the GPS approach recur in varying forms in all modern studies of representational thought: searching a problem space, goal-directed problem solving, and reliance on weak (context-free) problem-solving methods.

A problem space is a set of states of knowledge that a problem solver might achieve. A problem is solved when a path is found through this space from the starting state to a goal state. For instance, in chess the problem space is the set of all positions that can be reached from the current position. A game is won (i.e. a problem is solved) if one can find a path from the current position to a position where the opponent is checkmated. Users of GPS implicitly define the problem space by stating the starting state and the rules of inference.

In most interesting cases the problem space is too large to be searched exhaustively. Therefore a problem-solving program must have a way to determine which paths to investigate. One of the major activities in artificial intelligence research is the investigation of algorithms for controlling the search by visiting paths that appear to be on promising lines toward the goal (Stillings et al 1987). Since the method for choosing paths generally involves a guess about whether or not visiting a state is likely to lead to the goal, the algorithms are called *heuristic search* algorithms.[7]

GPS's heuristic procedure was *means-end* (or backward-driven) problem solving. The program compared the goal to the current state, determined the differences between them, and then searched for an operator that would reduce the difference. The method can be illustrated by a simple geographic example: If you wish to move long distances you take an airplane; for intermediate distances you use a car. A slightly different technique, which emphasizes the backward nature of the method somewhat more, is to find those states from which the goal state can be reached, and then establish the

---

[7]In the earlier literature, distinction was made between algorithms that always produced answers and heuristics that might produce a correct answer and did not cost a great deal to execute. In modern computer science an algorithm is any computing procedure that is guaranteed to terminate when given a syntactically correct input. A heuristic is a computing procedure (i.e. an algorithm) that generally terminates quickly with an adequate answer, but that is not guaranteed to do so.

GPS problem of reaching one of those states. Again using a geographic illustration, a traveler who wanted to go from Austin, Texas to Yakima, Washington might first find a way to Seattle, on the grounds that there must be some way to get from Seattle to nearby Yakima.

In forward-driven problem solving, on the other hand, rules of inference are chosen by an examination of the current state of knowledge, without regard for the goal state. To illustrate, consider the problem of proving that $A*C + B*A = A * (B + C)$. Skilled algebraicists will immediately rewrite the left-hand side as $A*B + A*C$, on the grounds that arguments of a commutative operator are normally written in lexical order.

Johnson-Laird's (1983) model for syllogistic reasoning is an example of the use of forward-driven problem solving to simulate human reasoning in area close to those studied using GPS. Syllogistic problems are stated in terms of two premises and a conclusion—e.g. "All Republicans are baseball players; some baseball players are left-handed; therefore, some Republicans are left-handed." The syllogism is invalid. How did you notice?

Johnson-Laird proposes that people construct "mental models," corresponding to the different interpretations of the premises. Model construction is driven by rules that depend only on the premise being read and the current state of the model. Thus Johnson-Laird assumes that on reading "All Republicans are baseball players" people immediately construct a symbol structure in which all terms for "Republican" are attached to "baseball player" but some terms for "baseball player" remain unattached. When the conclusion is read the model(s) previously constructed are examined, to determine whether or not the conclusion is valid in the available models. (In general, a set of premises may be consistent with more than one model. Johnson-Laird's ideas allow for model-construction rules that favor certain interpretations of the premises by giving priority to some models over others.) The problem-solving technique is forward-driven in the sense that the model that is constructed is not determined by the nature of the conclusion. Therefore it is possible that the wrong models will have been constructed, so errors may be made.

A problem-solving model does not have to take an either-or position on the question of whether people use forward- or backward-driven reasoning. The two were mixed in Rips's (1983) ANDS (*A* *N*atural *D*eductive *S*ystem) program, which has produced impressive simulations of human solutions to symbolic logic problems. It is not surprising to find that humans are flexible enough to mix two different forms of problem solving. But when is each method used?

Forward-driven problem solving is riskier than goal-based problem solving, because operations are executed (i.e. new states of the problem space are visited) without first checking to see if these operations are likely to be an advance toward the goal. On the other hand, forward-driven reasoning is cheaper, because operator selection is made without contrasting the present state of knowledge to the goal state. Thus forward-driven problem solving is preferable *if* the problem solver knows enough about the problem-solving domain to recognize when certain actions should be taken. This implies that a rational problem solver would use forward-driven reason in those (limited) domains with which he or she was familiar. This turns out to be true. Before reviewing the evidence, though, another distinction between problem-solving methods must be considered: the distinction between *weak* and *strong* techniques.

A problem solving method is "weak" if it places only weak constraints on the environment in which it is used.[8] GPS is a weak problem solver in this sense, because the rules it used for operator selection can be defined entirely in terms of the syntax of its internal language (Quinlan & Hunt 1968). Therefore the same heuristics (e.g. find an operator whose output state is in the same form as the goal state) could be applied to problems in scheduling airplane travel or problems in solving algebraic equations. By contrast, a "strong" problem solving method is one that is strongly constrained by the environment. "Always protect the king" is a strong rule for the domain of chess.

The distinction between weak and strong problem-solving methods is logically independent of the distinction between forward- and backward-driven problem solving. In practice, however, forward-driven rules tend to be strongly constrained by context. This is reasonable when one considers the risk in forward-driven problem solving (see above). If a rule is to be applied blindly, the situations in which it is applied should be chosen with care. Therefore it is not surprising to find that forward-driven reasoning is characteristic of situations in which people know what they are doing—i.e. situations in which they are expert.

This has been shown in numerous studies contrasting "expert" and "novice" problem solving in domains ranging from physics (Larkin et al 1980; Larkin 1983) to economics (Voss et al 1983) and the law (O'Neil 1987). In all these fields experts appear to utilize forward-driven reasoning. They recognize a situation and "immediately" apply the appropriate rules for extracting information about that situation. The work of Larkin and her colleagues (Larkin et al 1980) is a prototypical case of such research. They contrasted student and professional physicists' ways of attacking problems in physical mechanics. The experts classified problems by the physical laws involved (e.g. balance of

---

[8]The term "weak" could also be interpreted to mean "probably will not work," but that is not the intended meaning. "Context free" would perhaps have been a better term. The terminology is now established.

force problems) and did the appropriate calculations. The students resembled GPS; they reasoned backward from the goal.

In the terminology of cognitive science, the experts seemed to have memorized "schemas" that function like "fill in the blanks" forms for solving certain classes of problems. Once the experts recognized the problem type they could apply a schema to guide further problem solving. It is easy to see that schema-based problem solving is compatible with the production system architecture. A schema can be thought of as a set of productions that are triggered when the schema's preconditions are satisfied. Just as in production execution, thinking is driven by pattern recognition.

Schema-based, forward-driven problem solving seems to be characteristic of experience, and not of the "native intelligence" of the problem solver, at least as assessed on intelligence tests. Scribner (1984) found that experienced dairy workers used visually based schema to pack cartons for delivery. As a result the workers could solve packing problems much more quickly than could students, who used weaker techniques of arithmetical calculation. Similar specialized reasoning schemes have been observed in studies of horse-race handicappers (Ceci & Liker 1986) and grocery shoppers (Lave et al 1984).

The prevalence of domain-specific reasoning raises some serious questions for psychology and education. If virtually all "important" human thought is based on forward-driven, domain-specific reasoning, what is the sense of trying to establish a general theory of problem solving? Is psychology possible? Extending the argument somewhat, to the extent that thinking is domain specific, liberal education must yield to vocational training.

Fortunately this conclusion can be tempered. When one examines in more detail the schemas used by experts, it turns out that they contain within themselves appeals to more general reasoning schemas. In order to develop a generalized physics problem–solving program, Larkin et al (1985) had to include general problem-solving techniques (e.g. the decomposition of a problem into its parts) within the physics program. A v.d.L. Gardner (1987) points out that legal rules are schemas that can be (and have been) programmed, and that they reference generalized reasoning concepts.

Cheng & Holyoak (1985) brought the study of generalized reasoning schemas into the laboratory. They showed that the logical connective "implication" is, psychologically, represented by several different "pragmatic reasoning schemas." One is the permission schema: If A occurs then B is permitted (e.g. "If a traveler is inoculated, then the traveler may enter the country"). Another is obligation: If A has happened, then the actor must do B (e.g. "In order to use the library you must have a card"). Both schemas are examples of implication. Psychologically, however, the conditions indicating the applicability of causal and permission schemas are different. Cheng et al

(1986) have shown that although people have a great deal of trouble learning the formal concept of implication they can easily learn to utilize the pragmatic schemas. Evidently people reason using methods intermediate between the highly context-dependent reasoning implied by study of expert reasoning and the weakly restricted, logically correct operations embedded in programs such as GPS.

Applying a schema is clearly a deductive act. Choosing a schema is an inductive act, because there will typically be many schemas that could fit a given problem. Furthermore, the creation of a schema becomes itself an act of induction, one that is a key part of a cognitive theory of learning. With this observation, we turn to the study of induction.

Inductive Reasoning: Classification

We often treat instances as members of classes, and then use class properties when reasoning about the instance. Research conducted in the 1970s established prototype theory as the dominant psychological theory of classification (Rosch 1978; Rosch & Mervis 1975; Mervis & Rosch 1981; Smith & Medin 1981). Prototype theory is based on the idea that semantic memory contains records of associations between object features and class names. Specific instances are members of a class to the extent that they resemble a "prototypical instance" possessing attributes most closely associated with its class. Therefore it makes sense to say that a robin is a better bird than a penguin. The conclusion that class membership is a matter of degree is critical for a theory of human cognition, for if it is accepted one has to base a psychological theory of reasoning not upon the customary true-false distinction but upon a "fuzzy" logic, where statements can be more or less true (Schmucker 1984; Zadeh 1965).

In fact, there is a large literature indicating that (a) people can indeed rate objects as being members of classes to varying degrees and (b) an object's degree of membership provides an indication of how rapidly the object will be recognized as a category member (Mervis & Rosch 1981). But just what does this mean?

Cognitive scientists have raised several objections to the acceptance of prototype theory as the only basis for human classification decisions, although it is admitted that it may be the basis for some decisions (Neisser 1987). Osherson & Smith (1981) pointed out that prototype theory provides no means for constructing categories based upon combinations of other categories. A very good "brown apple" may be both a poor "apple" and a poor "brown." Somewhat more dramatically, Armstrong et al (1983) showed that people produce reliable prototypical ratings for objects in classes that could not conceivably admit "degree of membership"—e.g. odd numbers. This finding suggests that the experimental evidence used to argue for prototype theory may not be closely related to the way people think about at least some categories. Finally, a number of investigators have shown that category membership is context dependent. Birds like hens and geese, which poorly fit the birds category in general, may fit the category well in the context of a barnyard (Roth & Shoben 1983). Context-appropriate categories may be invented on the spot.

Barsalou (1983, 1987) has independently developed the idea that concepts are not ideas that preexist in our memories. Instead they are classifications that are developed, as needed, to guide our interactions with objects in a particular problem-solving context. People are good at recognizing ad hoc categories, such as "things to take out of the house if there is a fire." Barsalou's idea could be considered the extreme of context-sensitive categorization theories.

Medin and his colleagues (Medin & Wattenmaker 1987; Murphy & Medin 1985) argue that many of the categories people use are based upon theories of the world, in which classifications are formed because there is some purpose for doing so. This, of course, is consistent with Barsalou's position on context-sensitivity. The implicit belief that classes are formed for reasons carries over into laboratory learning. People quickly learn a classification rule based upon what they perceive as reasonable associations between features (e.g. "honest people return lost wallets intact and admit their mistakes") but will not learn classification rules based upon features that do not have a coherent theme (e.g. "the class of people who initiate conversations with people in parks and never go into a park after dark") (Wattenmaker et al 1986; Medin et al 1987).

These arguments against prototype theory are based on the examples of classifications that are difficult to reconcile with the theory. Hintzman (1986) has taken the alternative approach of showing that the evidence offered for prototype theory could be produced without explicit storage of property-class associations. He constructed a computer program that classified an instance as being a member of a class by retrieving records of previously classified items that resembled the current instance, and determining the class membership of the retrieved instances. The program displayed what, in a person, would be called "recall of prototypical information." Note that this changes the nature of the classification act. According to most classification theories the decision rule for classification is developed over time, then applied when an instance is to be classified. In Hintzman's approach, classification rules are developed for the object being classified, using previously classified items as analogies. One can imagine ways of reconciling Hintzman's approach with a model of context-sensitive categorization, although this has not been done to date.

The idea that classificatory behavior is context sensitive can be used to impose some order on the results of the many cognitive science studies of the difference between expert and novice behavior. I noted above that people who are experienced in a particular domain utilize domain-specific schemas as reasoning devices. Accordingly, one would expect domain experts to classify problems according the schemas used to solve them. Novices in a field should use different classification schemas then experts do, simply because they have less sophisticated theories about how the field is organized. This is often the case. For instance, experienced physicists may see both an inclined-plane problem and a pulley problem as examples of balance of force problems, while novices put them in separate categories (Chi et al 1981). Certainly the experts could have distinguished between planes and pulleys, if they had chosen to do so.

Saying that experts see the key relations whereas novices do not, is close to a tautology. What appears to be the case is that the experts have developed ways of describing problems that accentuate what is important. Larkin & Simon (1987) point out that this is what a diagram does in physics. When the diagram is drawn it contains theoretically essential relations but suppresses irrelevant detail. Furthermore, an appropriate diagram makes key relations easy to see, even though they might be difficult to state in propositions. In physics a force diagram can provide a compact representation of a complicated propositional statement. Similar economy of representation can be observed in other problem-solving domains, such as flowcharting in computer programming or causal modeling in multivariate statistics.

A diagram, of course, is only one way of stripping away irrelevancies to focus on cues appropriate for problem solving. O'Neil (1987) observed an experienced lawyer using conversational devices to structure a case so that the legal issues were highlighted. The point is that the expert has learned how to describe a problem so that its key elements are obvious.

Induction and Analogy

An argument by analogy establishes a mapping from objects and relations in an understood field (the *base*) to objects and relations in a field to be understood (the *target*). Known facts about the base are then used to make predictions about yet unobserved relationships in the target problem.

Gentner (1983, 1988) has offered criteria for "true analogies." Objects and relationships in the target domain must be mapped to the base domain without a concomitant mapping of their properties. The mapping must be systematic, in the sense that the relationships mapped must be related to each other in the same way in the target and base domains (e.g. Gallistel 1989). Finally, some known relationship in the base domain must be used to infer something not yet observed about the target domain.

A political analogy, attributed to John Foster Dulles, the US Secretary of State during the Eisenhower administration, illustrates Gentner's criteria. Dulles justified US concern for political events in then "French Indo-China" by saying that the countries in the area were like a row of closely spaced dominoes standing on end: If one fell to the communists, the next would be tipped and tip the next in turn until all had fallen. The analogy maps countries onto dominoes, physical susceptibility onto political susceptibility, and the noncommunist vs communist onto the vertical vs horizontal distinction. The properties of countries, dominoes, and physical and political force are ignored. The analogy depends upon mapping of relationships that enter into a system of relations; in this case a causal chain in which the fall of one domino (or country) causes the adjacent ones to fall. Finally, Dulles used known relations in the base domain, the result of knocking down one domino, to predict an as-yet-unobserved event in the target domain, political events (which did occur!) in Southeast Asia.

Gentner's criteria are not always fulfilled. In "literal similarity" arguments, identical relationships are maintained. An example would be explaining the importance of bowling in cricket by analogy to the importance of pitching in baseball. Gentner believes that such arguments are seen as having less explanatory value than a true analogy. Least convincing of all are "mere appearance analogies", which depend upon surface similarities. Predictions about the 1980s political situation in the Philippines based on the claim that it is analogous to the 1960 situation South Vietnam, for instance, would be rejected because the relationships between different elements of the two societies are not the same, even though (from an American view) the political units themselves are both "fairly large Asian countries."

Gentner's discussion of the psychological appeal of analogical argument is based on a mixture of (*a*) illustrations of analogies, especially in science; (*b*) computational analysis of the effectiveness of AI reasoning systems that comprehend analogies (Falkenhainer et al 1986); and (*c*) experimental study of the generation and acceptance of different types of analogical arguments (Gentner 1988). She maintains that there is both an ontological and historical development in the sophistication of analogical arguments. Forbus & Gentner (1986) suggest that children begin to understand the physical world by "mere appearance" arguments. As they grow older they require more systematic explanations. While this could be a developmental trend, it could also reflect acculturation into a technologically oriented society. Gentner & Jeziorski (1988) point out that the analogical arguments offered by the 16th-century alchemist Paracelsus seem to have been based more on mere-appearance than upon true analogies. These observations could be developed by systematic comparisons of ontological, historical, and cross-cultural differences in analogical reasoning. Such a program would be an excellent illustration of the cognitive science approach to thought.

Before one can evaluate an analogy one has to think of it in the first place. Gentner (1988) argues that surface structure is a powerful, but sometimes misleading, cue for retrieving potential analogs. For instance, naive observers of collegiate lacrosse games may draw an analogy to American football, since both games are exceptionally physical contact sports. A better analogy would be to soccer. Using better-controlled but more artificial examples, Gentner found that when both children and university students read a target (i.e. to-be-understood) story they were more likely to be reminded of a mere-appearance match that was not a good analogy than they were of a true analogy that did not match the surface features of the target (Gentner 1988 Gentner & Toupin 1986).

How do we think of analogies in the first place? It is not always easy. Gick & Holyoak (1980, 1983) had university students try to solve a difficult problem. Those who received no supplementary input hardly ever solved the problem. Of the others, who were given stories to read that were analogs of the target problem, about two thirds were unable to detect the analogy, in spite of its apparent transparency. Hints and diagrams sketching the key elements between the base and target stories were relatively ineffective cues. What did help, however, was reading *two* potential analogs with different surface structures. This led Gick & Holyoak to conclude that the apparent use of an analogy was actually the use of a generalized schema for problem solving.

Gick & Holyoak's argument has been elaborated upon by Holland et al (1986, Ch. 10), who maintain that people form schemas when they encounter two or more problems involving similar causal relations. A schema is less frequently formed if only one problem is encountered, since its utility is then not so apparent. Furthermore, according to Holland et al, schemas are associated with the goals that people perceive when they solve a problem the first time. If the problem solver states the schema abstractly, it is available for use when next a situation with the same goal structure is encountered, again provided that the problem solver has learned to describe problems in a way that makes the goal structure apparent.

Holyoak (1985) has contrasted this approach to Gentner's position, which stresses a direct analogy between base and target situations and does not depend upon the sharing of a common (abstract) goal by base and target situations. Furthermore, while higher-order relations (i.e. relations between relations) are important in Gentner's analysis, they are important for their position in the relationship structure, not because they are causal. The present experimental data cannot distinguish these positions, simply because the higher-order relations in most of the problems studied to date have been causal relations.

AN EVALUATION, A CHALLENGE, AND A PROSPECTUS

The computational model allows us to bring disparate studies of human information processing and reasoning into a common frame of reference. A similar case could be made for the study of language processes (van Dijk &

Kintsch 1983) or for more extensive studies of learning (Klahr et al 1987). The development of a common theme to cover many paradigms is an important event for scientific psychology.

Production system and schema models emphasize the importance of pattern recognition in thinking. They assume that the human mind is organized to take advantage of large memory capacities and to compensate for limited computing capacities, an assumption compatible with what we know of the nervous system.

A second theme in cognitive science is the importance of syntactic structure. In spite of the impressive evidence that people often rely on domain-specific problem solving methods, they do utilize "pragmatic reasoning schemes" that are, in effect, a system of logic. A substantial part of learning and transfer is based on analogy formation—the recognition of structures based not on the properties of their elements, but on the relations between those elements. In other words, people can deal with free variables, a fact that any theory of thought must take into account.

These observations certainly do not prove that the production system architecture now so dominant in cognitive science is "right." That is partly because an overview can't be challenged, it can only be replaced with a better overview. Advocates of the cognitive science approach argue that this is the only known view that might unite the disparate findings of psychology. A challenger has appeared, however: the "connectionist" movement.

The idea behind connectionist modeling is to derive a pattern-recognition system from mathematical idealizations of networks of neuron-like elements. Thus both connectionism and the computational model emphasize pattern recognition. In fact, connectionist systems could be regarded as a way of implementing the pattern recognition part of a production system architecture. Most connectionists argue further that pattern recognition based on idealized networks is sufficient to model all aspects of thought (Rumelhart & McClelland 1986). I believe, however, that something more is required.

People's responses to analogies and schemas must be based upon recognition of abstract symbol structures; they cannot be based upon the physical features of the situation (indeed, it may be necessary to suppress such features). A similar argument can be made for the human ability to respond to linguistic structures (Fodor & Pylyshyn 1988). Whether or not connectionist models and brain-state language should replace computational models and rule-directed problem solving may well depend on whether or not connectionist models can display analogical learning and transfer.

ACKNOWLEDGMENTS

This paper was prepared while I was resident as the visiting Wechsler Professor at the University of Texas at Austin. I thank the University of Texas and the Wechsler Foundation for the opportunity the appointment provided.

The paper has also been partly supported by the Office of Naval Research, Contract N00014-86-C-0065. Gordon Bower made suggestions about the form that the paper should take. The opinions expressed, of course, are my own, and should not be taken as indicative of approval by any of the sponsors or people who have assisted me.

Literature Cited

Anderson, J. R. 1983. *The Architecture of Cognition.* Cambridge, Mass: Harvard Univ. Press

Anderson, J. R. 1986. Knowledge compilation: the general learning mechanism. In *Machine Learning II,* ed. R. Michalski, J. Carbonnell, T. Mitchell, pp. 289–310. Palo Alto, Calif: Tioga Press

Anderson, J. R. 1987. Skill acquisition: compilation of weak-method problem solutions. *Psychol. Rev.* 94: 192–210

Armstrong, S. L., Gleitman, L. R., Gleitman, H. 1983. On what some concepts might not be. *Cognition* 13:263–308

Baars, B. J. 1980. On eliciting predictable speech errors in the laboratory. In *Errors in Linguistic Performance: Slips of the Tongue, Ear, Pen, and Hand,* ed. V. A. Fromkin. New York: Academic

Baars, B. J. 1986. *The Cognitive Revolution in Psychology.* New York: Guilford

Baddeley, A. 1986. *Working Memory.* Oxford: Oxford Univ. Press

Barsalou, L. W. 1983. Ad hoc categories. *Memo. Cognit.* 11:211–17

Barsalou, L. W. 1987. The instability of graded structure. In *Concepts and Conceptual Development: Ecological and Intellectual Factors in Categorization,* ed. U. Neisser. Cambridge: Cambridge Univ. Press

Ceci, S. J., Liker, J. 1986. Academic and nonacademic intelligence: an experimental separation. In *Practical Intelligence: Nature and Origins of Competence in the Everyday World,* ed. R. J. Sternberg, R, K. Wagner. Cambridge: Cambridge Univ. Press

Cheng, P. W., Holyoak, K. J. 1985. Pragmatic reasoning schemas. *Cogn. Psychol.* 17:391–416

Cheng, P. W., Holyoak, K. J., Nisbett, R. E., Oliver, L. M. 1986. Pragmatic versus syntactic approaches to training deductive reasoning. *Cogn. Psychol.* 18:293–328

Chi, M. T. H., Feltovich, P. J., Glaser, R. 1981. Categorization and representation of physics problems by experts and novices. *Cogn. Sci.* 52:121–52

Collins, A. M. 1977. Why cognitive science? *Cogn. Sci.* 1:1–12

Coltheart, M. 1985. Cognitive neuropsychology of reading. In *Attention and Performance XI,* ed. M. I. Posner, O.S.M. Marin. Hillsdale, NJ: Earlbaum Assoc.

Daneman, M. 1985. The measurement of reading comprehension. How not to trade construct validity for predictive power. *Intelligence* 6:331–45

Ernst, G., Newell, A. 1969. *GPS: A Case Study in Generality and Problem Solving.* New York: Academic

Falkenhainer, B., Forbus, K. D., Gentner, D. 1986. The structure-mapping engine. *Univ. Ill. Tech. Rep. No. UIUCDS-R286-1275,* Dept. Comput. Sci. Univ. Ill. Urbana-Champaign

Farah, M. J. 1984. The neurological basis of mental imagery: a componential analysis. *Cognition* 18:245–72

Fodor, J. A. 1975. *The Language of Thought.* New York: Thomas Crowell

Fodor, J. A. 1983. *The Modularity of the Mind.* Cambridge, Mass: MIT Press

Fodor, J. A., Pylyshyn, Z. W. 1988. Connectionism and cognitive architecture: a critical analysis. *Cognition* 28:3–77

Forbus, K. D., Gentner, D. 1986. Learning physical domains: towards a theoretical framework. In *Machine Learning II,* ed. R. Michalski, J. Carbonnell, T. Mitchell, pp. 311–48. Palo Alto, Calif: Tioga Press

Foss, J. 1988. Experimental psycholinguistics. *Ann. Rev. Psychol.* 39:301–48

Fromkin, V. A., ed. 1973. *Speech Errors as Linguistic Evidence.* The Hague: Mouton

Gallistel, C. R. 1989. Animal cognition: the representation of space, time, and number. *Ann. Rev. Psychol.* 40:155–89

Gardner, A. v.d. L. 1987. *An Artificial Intelligence Approach to Legal Reasoning.* Cambridge, Mass: MIT Press

Gardner, H. 1985. *The Mind's New Science. A History of the Cognitive Revolution.* New York: Basic Books

Gentner, D. 1983. Structure mapping: a theoretical framework for analogy. *Cogn. Sci.* 7:155–70

Gentner, D. 1988. Analogical inference and analogical access. In *Analogica: Proceedings of the First Workshop on Analogical Reasoning,* ed. A. Prieditis. London: Pitman

Gentner, D., Toupin, C. 1986. Systematicity and Surface Similarity in the Development of Analogy. *Cogn. Sci.* 10:277–300

Gentner, D., Jeziorski, M. 1988. Historical shifts in the use of analogy in science. In *The Psychology of Science and Metascience*, ed B. Gholson, A. Houts, R. A. Neimayer, W. Shadish. Cambridge: Cambridge Univ. Press

Gick, M. L., Holyoak, K. J. 1980. Analogical problem solving. *Cogn. Psychol.* 12:306–55

Gick, M. L., Holyoak, K. J. 1983. Schema induction and analogical transfer. *Cogn. Psychol.* 12:306–55

Glymour, C., Scheines, R., Spirtes, P., Kelly, K. 1987. *Discovering Causal Structure: Artificial Intelligence, Philosophy of Science, and Statistical Modeling.* New York: Academic

Hintzman, D. L. 1986. "Schema abstraction" in a multiple trace model. *Psychol. Rev.* 93:411–28

Holland, J. H., Holyoak, K. J., Nisbett, R. E., Thagard, P. R. 1986. *Induction: Processes of Inference, Learning, and Discovery.* Cambridge, Mass: MIT Press

Holyoak, K. J. 1985. The pragmatics of analogical transfer. In *The Psychology of Learning and Motivation*, ed. G. H. Bower, Vol. 19. New York: Academic

Hunt, E. 1975. *Artificial Intelligence.* New York: Academic

Hunt, E., Lansman, M. 1986. Unified model of attention and problem solving. *Psychol. Rev.* 93:446–61

Johnson-Laird, P. N. 1980. Mental models in cognitive science. *Cogn. Sci.* 4:71–115

Johnson-Laird, P. N. 1983. *Mental Models.* Cambridge, Mass: Harvard Univ. Press

Just, M. A., Carpenter, P. A. 1981. Cognitive processes in reading: models based on eye fixations. In *Interactive Processes in Reading*, ed. A. M. Lesgold, C. A. Perfetti. Hillsdale, NJ: Erlbaum

Just, M. A., Carpenter, P. A. 1985. Cognitive coordinate systems: accounts of mental rotation and individual differences in spatial ability. *Psychol. Rev.* 92:113–71

Just, M. A., Carpenter, P. A. 1987. *The Psychology of Reading and Language Comprehension.* Boston: Allyn & Bacon

Klahr, D., Langley, P., Neches, R. 1987. *Production System Models of Learning and Development.* Cambridge, Mass: MIT Press

Kosslyn, S. M. 1980. *Image and Mind.* Cambridge, Mass: Harvard Univ. Press

Kosslyn, S. M. 1983. *Ghosts in the Mind's Machine.* New York: Norton

Kosslyn, S. M. 1987. Seeing and imagining in the cerebral hemispheres: a computational approach. *Psychol. Rev.* 94:148–75

Kosslyn, S. M., Schwartz, S. P. 1977. A simulation of visual imagery. *Cogn. Sci.* 1:265–96

Langley, P., Simon, H. A., Bradshaw, G. L., Zytkow, J. M. 1987. *Scientific Discovery: Computational Explorations of the Creative Process.* Cambridge, Mass: MIT Press

Larkin, J. 1983. Problem representation in physics. In *Mental Models*, ed. D. Gentner, A. Stevens. Hillsdale, NJ: Erlbaum Assoc.

Larkin, J. H., McDermott, J., Simon, D. P., Simon, H. A. 1980. Expert and novice performance in solving physics problems. *Science* 208:1335–42

Larkin, J. H., Reif, F., Carbonell, J., Gugliotta, A. 1985. FERMI: a flexible expert reasoner with multi-domain inferencing. *Cogn. Sci.* 12(1):101–38

Larkin, J. H., Simon, H. A. 1987. Why a diagram is sometimes worth ten thousand words. *Cogn. Sci.* 11:65–100

Lave, J., Murtagh, M., de la Roche, O. 1984. The dialect of arithmetic in grocery shopping. In *Everyday Cognition: Its Development in Social Context*, ed. B. Rogoff, J. Lave. Cambridge, Mass: Harvard Univ. Press

Lewis, C. 1987. Composition of productions. In *Production System Models of Learning and Development*, ed. D. Klahr, P. Langley, R. Neches. Cambridge, Mass: MIT Press

Loftus, E. F., Burns, T. E. 1982. Mental shock can produce retrograde amnesia. *Mem. Cognit.* 10:318–23

Mandler, G. 1985. *Cognitive Psychology.* Hillsdale, NJ: Earlbaum Assoc.

Medin, D. L., Wattenmaker, W. D. 1987. Category cohesiveness, theories, and cognitive archeology. See Barsalou 1987

Medin, D. L., Wattenmaker, W. D., Hampson, S. E. 1987. Family resemblance, conceptual cohesiveness, and category construction. *Cogn. Psychol.* 19:242–79

Mervis, C. B., Rosch, E. H. 1981. Categorization of natural objects. *Ann. Rev. Psychol.* 35:113–38

Miller, L. 1978. Has artificial intelligence contributed to an understanding of the human mind? A critique of arguments for and against. *Cogn. Sci.* 2:111–27

Motley, M. T. 1980. Verification of "Freudian Slips" and semantic prearticulatory editing via laboratory-induced Spoonerisms. See Baars 1980

Murphy, G. L., Medin, D. L. 1985. The role of theories in conceptual coherence. *Psychol. Rev.* 92:289–316

Neches, R., Langley, P., Klahr, D. 1987. Learning, development, and production systems. In *Production System Models of Learning and Development*, ed. D. Klahr,

P. Langley, R. Neches. Cambridge, Mass: MIT Press

Neisser, U. 1976. *Cognition and Reality.* San Francisco: Freeman

Neisser, U. 1987. Introduction. See Barsalou 1987

Newell, A. 1973a. You can't play twenty questions with nature and win: projective comments on the papers of this symposium. In *Visual Information Processing,* ed. W. G. Chase, pp. 283–308. New York: Academic

Newell, A. 1973b. Production systems: models of control structures. See Newell 1973a, pp. 463–526

Newell, A. 1980. Physical symbol systems. *Cogn. Sci.* 4:135–83

Newell, A., Simon, H. A. 1963. GPS. A program that simulates human thought. In *Computers and Thought,* ed. E. A. Feigenbaum, J. Feldman. New York: McGraw-Hill

Newell, A., Simon, H. A. 1972. *Human Problem Solving.* Englewood Cliffs, NJ: Prentice-Hall

Nissen, M. J., Bullmer, P. 1987. Attentional requirements of learning: evidence from performance measures. *Cogn. Psychol.* 19:1–32

Nissen, M. J., Knopman, D. S., Schacter, D. L. 1987. Neurochemical dissociation of memory systems. *Neurology* 37:789–94

Norman, D. A. 1980. Twelve issues for cognitive science. *Cogn. Sci.* 4:1–32

Ojemann, G. A., Creutzfeldt, O. D. 1987. Language in humans and animals: contribution of brain stimulation and recording. In *Handbook of Physiology, Section 1, The Nervous System, Vol. V: Higher Functions of the Brain, Part 2,* ed. V. Mountcastle, F. Plum, S. Geiger. pp. 675–99. Baltimore, Md: Am. Physiol. Soc.

O'Neil, D. P. 1987. A process specification of expert lawyer reasoning. *Proc. 1st Int. Conf. Artif. Intell. Law,* pp. 52–59. New York: Assoc. Comput. Mach.

Osherson, D. N., Smith, E. E. 1981. On the adequacy of prototype theory as a theory of concepts. *Cognition* 9:35–58

Perfetti, C. A., Beverly, S., Bell, L., Rodger, K., Faux, R. 1987. Comprehending newspaper headlines *J. Mem. Lang.* 26:692–713

Pylyshyn, Z. W. 1984. *Computation and Cognition: Toward a Foundation for Cognitive Science.* Cambridge, Mass: MIT Press

Quinlan, J. R., Hunt, E. B. 1968. A formal deductive problem solving system. *J. Assoc. Comput. Mach.* 15:625–45

Rips, L. J. 1983. Cognitive processes in propositional reasoning. *Psychol. Rev.* 90:38–71

Rips, L. J. 1986. Mental muddles. In *The*

Representation of Knowledge and Belief, ed. M. Brand, R. M. Harnish. Tucson: Univ. Arizona Press

Robinson, J. A. 1965. A machine oriented logic based on the resolution principle. *J. Assoc. Comput. Mach.* 12:23–41

Rorty, R. 1979. *Philosophy and the Mirror of the Mind.* Princeton: Princeton Univ. Press

Rosch, E. H. 1978. Principles of categorization. In *Cognition and Categorization,* ed. E. Rosch, B. B. Lloyd. Hillsdale, NJ: Earlbaum

Rosch, E. H., Mervis, C. B. 1975. Family resemblances: studies in the internal structure of categories. *Cogn. Psychol.* 7:573–605

Roth, E. M., Shoben, E. J. 1983. The effect of context on the structure of categories. *Cogn. Psychol.* 15:346–78

Rumelhart, D. E., McClelland, J. L. 1986. PDP models and general issues in cognitive science. In *Parallel Distributed Processing: Volume I,* ed. D. E. Rumelhart, J. L. McClelland, and the PDP Res. Group. Cambridge, Mass: MIT Press

Schmucker, K. J. 1984. *Fuzzy Sets, Natural Language, Computations, and Risk Analysis.* Rockville, Md: Computer Science Press

Scribner, S. 1984. Studying working intelligence. In *Everyday Cognition: Its Development in Social Context,* ed. B. Rogoff, J. Lave. Cambridge, Mass: Harvard Univ. Press

Singley, M. K., Anderson, J. R. 1985. The transfer of text-editing skill. *J. Man-Machine Stud.* 22:403–23

Simon, H. A. 1969. *The Sciences of the Artificial.* Cambridge, Mass: MIT Press

Simon, H. A. 1981. *The Sciences of the Artificial.* Cambridge, Mass: MIT Press. 2nd ed.

Smith, E. E., Medin, D. L. 1981. *Categories and Concepts.* Cambridge, Mass: Harvard Univ. Press

Squire, L. 1987. *Memory and Brain.* Oxford: Oxford Univ. Press

Sternberg, R. J. 1980. Representation and process in linear syllogistic reasoning. *J. Exp. Psychol. Gen.* 109:119–59

Sternberg, R. J. 1984. Reasoning, problem solving, and intelligence. In *Advances in the Psychology of Human Intelligence: Vol. II,* ed. R. J. Sternberg. Hillsdale, NJ: Erlbaum Assoc.

Stillings, N. A., Feinstein, M. H., Garfield, J. L., Rissland, E. L., Rosenbaum, D. A., et al. 1987. *Cognitive Science: An Introduction.* Cambridge, Mass: MIT Press

Thibadeau, R., Just, M. A., Carpenter, P. A. 1982. A model of the time course and content of reading. *Cogn. Sci.* 6:157–203

Van Dijk, T. A., Kintsch, W. 1983. *Strategies*

of Discourse Comprehension. New York: Academic

van Lehn, K., Brown, J. S., Greeno, J. 1984. Competitive argumentation in computational theories of cognition. In *Methods and Tactics in Cognitive Science,* ed. W. Kintsch, J. R. Miller, P. G. Polson. Hillsdale, NJ: Erlbaum Assoc.

Voss, J. F., Tyler, S. W., Yengo, L. A. 1983. Individual differences in the solving of social science problems. In *Individual Differences in Cognition, Vol. I,* ed. R. F. Dillon, R. R. Schmeck. New York: Academic

Wattenmaker, W. D., Dewey, G. I., Murphy, T. D., Medin, D. L. 1986. Linear separability and concept learning: context, relational properties, and concept naturalness. *Cogn. Psychol.* 18:158–94

Zadeh, L. A. 1965. Fuzzy sets. *Inf. Control* 8:338–53

Ann. Rev. Psychol. 1989. 40:631–66

LEARNING THEORY AND THE STUDY OF INSTRUCTION

Robert Glaser and Miriam Bassok

Learning Research and Development Center, University of Pittsburgh, Pittsburgh, Pennsylvania 15260

CONTENTS

INTRODUCTION

Instructional psychology has become a vigorous part of the mainstream of research on human cognition and development. The 1980 *Annual Review of Psychology* documented the onset: "It is now difficult to draw a clear line between instructional psychology and the main body of basic research on complex cognitive processes" (Resnick 1981, p. 660). As we move toward the 1990s, the shape of the field is evident in the progress in research on three essential components of a theory of instruction (Glaser 1976): (*a*) description of competent performances (knowledge and skill) that we want students to acquire; (*b*) analysis of the initial state of the learner's knowledge and ability; and (*c*) explication of the process of learning, the transition from initial state to desired state that can be accomplished in instructional settings.

0066–4308/89/0201–0631$02.00

Over the past quarter of a century, cognitive research has focused primarily on the analysis of competence. Studies of memory, language, and problem solving have examined the nature of performance and the outcomes of learning and development. The advances in our understanding of competent performance, including recent studies of expertise, have had formative influence on instructional investigations. Research on the initial state of the learner has received attention more recently in developmental studies that document a priori constraints, principles, and strategies that govern children's learning, in investigations of naive theories and misconceptions that influence the attainment of new knowledge and skill, and in research on processes of intelligence and aptitude. In comparison to our knowledge of attained competences and expertise, the information accumulated on the initial state has only slightly influenced investigations of instruction, but should begin to assume a more significant role.[1] The least developed component of instructional theory is explication of the process of learning—a contrast indeed to behavioral psychology, where learning was of major concern.

Here we consider a set of seminal programs of instructional research in the context of this state of our knowledge. We focus on programs that are grounded in accumulated findings on one of three major aspects of competence: (a) the compiled, automatized, functional, and proceduralized knowledge characteristic of a well-developed cognitive skill; (b) the effective use of internalized self-regulatory control strategies for fostering comprehension; and (c) the structuring of knowledge for explanation and problem solving.

For each program, we show how detailed cognitive task analysis has guided the specification of the objectives of instruction. We attempt also to explicate the principles, theory, and/or assumptions about learning and the principles that underlie the design of instruction. Thus our purpose is to describe the state of the art in applying the cognitive analysis of performance to the design of instruction and to consider current thinking about learning as conceptualized in investigations of instruction.

COGNITIVE ANALYSIS OF PERFORMANCE, LEARNING, AND INSTRUCTION   Learning theory has long been based on analysis of relatively simple performances. Learning theorists have generally expected that principles so gleaned would be extrapolated eventually to explain complex forms of learning. With respect to instruction, this assumption has been strongest in the behavioral tradition spawned by Skinner. Beginning in the 1970s (cf Greeno 1980), however, questions were raised about the nature of what is learned:

[1]For fuller discussions of research on the initial state of knowledge and ability that the learner brings to instruction, see Carey (1985, 1986), Clement (1982), diSessa (1982), Gelman & Brown (1986), Gelman & Greeno (1988), Keil (1981, 1984), McCloskey (1983), McCloskey et al (1980), Nickerson et al (1985), and Sternberg (1985b, 1986).

about the organization of knowledge, the characteristics of understanding, the knowledge and information-processing requirements for solving problems, and the nature of the competences entailed in human performances that require specific knowledge and skills resulting from long-term learning and extended experience. The attempts to answer these questions has brought the study of cognitive performance into prominence and temporarily set aside the study of the learning process.

The scientific decision to tackle performance was explicitly acknowledged by Newell & Simon in the 1972 book, *Human Problem Solving*.

> Turning to the performance-learning-development dimension, our emphasis on performance again represents a scientific bet. We recognize that what sort of information processing system a human becomes depends intimately on the way he develops. . . . Yet, acknowledging this, it still seems to us that we have too imperfect a view of the system's final nature to be able to make predictions from the development process to the characteristics of the structures it produces.
>
> The study of learning, if carried out with theoretical precision, must start with a model of a performing organism, so that one can represent, as learning, the changes in the model. . . .
>
> The study of learning takes its cue, then, from the nature of the performance system. If performance is not well understood, it is somewhat premature to study learning. . . . Both learning and development must then be incorporated in integral ways in the more complete and successful theory of human information processing that will emerge at a later stage in the development of our science. (pp. 7–8)

Over the subsequent years, significant advances have been made in the analysis of puzzle-like laboratory problem-solving tasks, and, more recently, more complex ecologically valid performance has become the object of serious investigation in both cognitive psychology and artificial intelligence (Greeno & Simon 1988). Task analysis and knowledge-engineering approaches to the performance of experts have become prominent activities. In addition, the complex performances inherent in the school subject matters of reading, writing, mathematics, science, and social studies are being productively described (Glaser 1986). Now, research with instructional programs in these areas promises to be a central method for the study of learning (Anderson 1987a).

Concepts that seem essential in the description of complex human behavior are now available for this work. Most impressive is the pervasive influence of structures of knowledge as they interact with sophisticated processes of competent cognition (Feigenbaum 1988; Chi & Ceci 1987). The way knowledge is structured influences its accessibility, and knowledge representation determines understanding and influences problem solving (Greeno & Simon 1988; Gentner & Stevens 1983; Johnson-Laird 1983). We have learned also to appreciate the interplay of general and knowledge-derived processes (Glaser 1984, 1985; Sternberg 1985a), the development of automaticity and the relationships between unconscious and controlled processing (Shiffrin & Schneider 1977; Schneider 1985; Lesgold & Perfetti 1981), the efficiency and functional utility characteristic of a well-developed skill (Anderson 1981, 1987b), and the significance of executive and self-regulatory processes, or metacognition (Brown et al 1983; Bransford et al 1986).

The phenomena captured by these concepts combine to produce the efficiency, judgment, seeming intuition, and outstanding abilities evident in competent performances (cf Chi et al 1988). At various stages of learning, there exist different integrations of knowledge, different degrees of proceduralized and compiled skill, and differences in rapid access to memory— all shaping the representations of tasks and differentiating levels of cognitive attainment. These differences signal advancing expertise or possible blockages in the course of learning. On the basis of this knowledge, dimensions are apparent along which changes in levels of performance occur. These dimensions have become focal objectives for instructional intervention.

Although advances in understanding the outcomes of acquired cognitive performance and, to a lesser degree, of the knowledge and skills brought to learning provide foundations for instructional theory, the study of the transition processes that a theory of learning must account for has been a depressed endeavor until recent years [see the collection edited by Anderson (1981); Rumelhart & Norman (1978)]. Performance and memory are intimately intertwined in learning, but the difference in emphasis is critical. The acquisition of new declarative knowledge, development of a cognitive skill, organization of knowledge into more effective representations, and discovery and inference of new information are differentiated forms of learning, and their characterization varies. Some learning can be characterized as simple accumulation of new information in memory. In the acquisition of complex knowledge and skill over months and years, however, learning appears to involve qualitative restructuring and modification of schemata; it has an emergent quality.

No single set of assumptions or principles pervades the work of investigators who are conducting studies of instructional intervention, and there are as yet no major debates about general learning mechanisms. Rather, scientists are working toward principles of learning by bringing ideas from various areas to bear in different ways. Attempts at instruction are based to a limited extent on explicitly stated theory, on general conceptions of the processes of acquisition for which specific learning mechanisms are unclear, and on observation of the practice of good teachers or tutors. What is common to all the approaches to instruction is grounding in an explicit cognitive task analysis; the objectives of instruction are based upon current knowledge of the characteristics of competent performance on a task. Less consistently, attention is given to shaping the instruction to accommodate the available relevant research on characteristics of the learner's initial state.

The investigators whose work we examine here focus on different forms of competence in separate domains of knowledge. At present, it is not possible to compare several instructional approaches to a particular area of performance and the forms of competence it requires. The domains under investigation span medical diagnosis, reading comprehension, arithmetic skill, geometric proofs, and computer programming. These different domains interact with the researchers' conceptions of learning. As we look toward the development of a theory of instruction, a primary concern is locating points of overlap and disjunction in prototypical work on the acquisition of proceduralized skill, the development of regulatory and monitoring strategies for comprehension and learning, and the acquisition of organized knowledge structures.

FUNCTIONAL, PROCEDURALIZED KNOWLEDGE AND SKILL

Studies of differences between experts' and novices' performances suggest that the course of knowledge acquisition proceeds from a declarative or propositional form to a compiled, procedural, condition-action form (Anderson 1983; Klahr 1984). Novices can know a principle, or a rule, or a specialized vocabulary without knowing the conditions of effective application. In contrast, when experts access knowledge, it is functional or bound to conditions of applicability. Moreover, experts' knowledge is closely tied to their conceptions of the goal structure of a problem space. Experts and novices may be equally competent at recalling specific items of information, but experts chunk these items in memory in cause and effect sequences that relate to the goals and subgoals of problem solution and use this information for further action. The progression from declarative knowledge to well-tuned functional knowledge is a significant dimension of developing competence.

A related aspect of competent performance is the speed of knowledge application. Experts are fast, even though human ability is limited in performing competing attention-demanding tasks (Shiffrin & Schneider 1977; Schneider 1985). This ability is particularly important in integrating basic and advanced components of skill. For example, in reading (as in medical diagnosis or in tennis), attention must alternate between basic skills and higher levels of strategy and comprehension. Even though the component processes may be well executed by the novice when performed separately, they may not be efficient enough to work together (Perfetti & Lesgold 1979). In the development of higher levels of proficiency, therefore, certain component skills need to become compiled and automatized so that conscious processing capacity can be devoted to higher levels of cognition as necessary.

From Declarative Knowledge to a Procedural Skill

A widely discussed instructional program that has proven successful in several domains in which the learning objective is the acquisition of an efficient and functional cognitive skill has been developed at Carnegie-Mellon University (CMU). A group led by John Anderson has designed computer tutoring programs for three complex well-defined skills: programming in LISP (Anderson et al 1984), generating geometry proofs (Anderson et al 1985), and solving algebraic equations (Lewis et al 1988). These programs are unique in their reliance on an explicit learning theory (Anderson 1983, 1987b) and in their use of the instructional setting as a stage for systematically testing hypotheses about mechanisms of learning. Thus, besides its practical contribution to instruction, this work presents a model of the fruitful interaction between cognitive theory and instructional research.

THEORETICAL BACKGROUND   The major learning mechanism posited by the ACT* theory is *knowledge compilation,* which accounts for the transition from declarative knowledge to proceduralized use-oriented knowledge— conversion of "knowing what" into "knowing how." Declarative knowledge encoded in memory (such as the postulate Side-Angle-Side for proving triangles congruent) is assumed to be available for the development of skill. This knowledge is assumed to have been deposited in memory as a product of language comprehension, through reading a text or through oral instruction and lecture, without accompanying knowledge about its use or about conditions of applicability. Procedural knowledge consists of sets of production rules (i.e. condition-action pairs) that define the skill in each domain.

For example, one production rule using the Side-Angle-Side postulate can be:

IF   the goal is to prove Δ XYZ $\cong$ Δ UVW
              and $\overline{XY} \cong \overline{UV}$
              and $\overline{YZ} \cong \overline{VW}$
THEN   set a subgoal to prove $\angle$ XYZ $\cong$ $\angle$ UVW, so SAS can be used.

The theory holds that effective and conditionalized knowledge of procedures can be acquired only through actual use of the declarative knowledge in solving problems. The initial solution is generated by applying the available declarative knowledge, using general problem-solving heuristics or weak methods, such as means-ends search, hill climbing, or analogy to an example. The subsequent process of knowledge compilation creates efficient domain-specific productions from the trace of the initial problem-solving episode. Compilation consists of *proceduralization* and *composition.* Proceduralization results from comparing the problem states before and after generating the solution and creating production rules—the building blocks of the domain-specific skill. Composition, analogous to chunking, results from collapsing a sequence of productions into a single production that has the same effect. Composition reflects meaningful cognitive contingencies as constrained by a hierarchical goal structure for the solution of the problem and results in substantial shortcuts to the solution. Finally, the various productions accumulate strength as a result of practice with successful applications (much as in the strengthening of associative bonds).

The initial interpretative process of solving problems using declarative knowledge by means of weak methods places a high demand on conscious cognitive processing. Knowledge compilation results in automaticity of application and in proficient execution of previously acquired knowledge. It frees the working memory, leaving more capacity for the processing of new knowledge. It also eliminates the relatively undirected search that characterizes early performance.

INSTRUCTIONAL PRINCIPLES   The process of knowledge compilation is assumed to be an automatic learning mechanism, and the major instructional principles that guide the design of the tutors aim to optimize the process using the method of *model tracing*. Each program builds on detailed and explicit analysis in modeling both performance and learning. The performance model explicates how students actually execute the skill that is to be taught; it consists of a set of all the correct and incorrect production rules for performing the skill. Note that the model corresponds to the performance of an ideal student and an array of buggy variations of the ideal student's rules at various stages of skill development, rather than to an expert system. The learner's actual performance is compared in real time to the rules in the model, and the tutoring system tries to keep the student on a correct solution path. The learning model consists of a set of assumptions about how the student's knowledge state changes after each step in solving a problem. Using parameters derived from the ACT* theory, the student's history of correct and incorrect application of productions provides an updated probabilistic estimate of the availability and the strength of the productions comprising the skill [similar to response probability in statistical-learning-theory models for vocabulary instruction (Atkinson 1972)]. Trackings of changes across problems enable the tutor to select problems appropriate to the student's knowledge state in order to optimize learning. Within this general model-tracing paradigm, instruction is guided by several principles.

Learning via problem solving   Learning occurs by doing, by interpretation of declarative knowledge via problem solving. A given problem provides a set of applicability conditions relevant to problem-solving goals. It is assumed that in order for the student to retrieve the learned information in solving other problems, he or she initially has to encode it in a similar problem-solving context during studying. Based on this assumption, the CMU group advocates shortening preliminary instructional texts, and refraining from elaborated explanations. Texts should focus on procedural information, and students should begin actual problem solving as soon as possible. Although textual instructions should be carefully crafted to maximize correct encoding, the inevitable misunderstandings should be corrected during problem solving.

An ideal problem-solving structure for the domain   To accommodate domain variation in problem-solving structures and solution-strategy demands, each tutor communicates a particular problem-solving structure. Carrying out geometry proofs, for example, requires backward and forward search for logical inferences between the givens and what is to be proved. To explicate the search, the tutor uses proof graphs in which a student must link a set of subgoals reached by backward inferences from the to-be-proven statement with a set of subgoals reached by forward inferences from the problem's givens. The proof graphs both represent the actual problem-solving space and explicate the search process for constructing a geometry proof. Constructing a program in LISP is a design activity and has a very different structure, that of problem decomposition. A programming goal has to be decomposed into subgoals until goals are reached that can be achieved with specific code. For instruction, the LISP tutor provides a template organized in a hierarchical goal structure with slots that the student must fill.

Problem specification and immediate error correction   Knowledge compilation and the strengthening of acquired productions result from successful applications of the productions. To ensure maximal correct performance, the tutor monitors the student's learning closely by selecting problems and by displaying and constraining the solution steps. The selection of problems is guided by a *mastery model*—the tutor presents problems involving new rules only when the student has attained a certain threshold level of competence on the current rules. Appropriate additional problems and accompanying instructions provide practice on those production rules that are diagnosed as weak or missing in the student's knowledge state.

During problem solving, the tutor traces the student's performance by matching it to the system's model for a correct solution and intervenes as soon as the student deviates from one of the possible correct solution paths. Errors are corrected immediately, both to avoid lengthy exploration of erroneous paths and to assign blame at actual decision points. The feedback consists of identifying errors and suggesting how to proceed. A complete or a partial solution may be offered, but, in keeping with the principle of learning by doing, wherever possible, the student is required to produce the correct solution.

Minimization of working memory load   Because acquisition of new knowledge places burdens on memory, the tutoring environments aim to minimize the cognitive load. They implement all components accessory to the target skill. For example, when the skill is writing code, the editor of the LISP tutor takes care of such syntactic details as supplying parentheses or the structure of a function. The tutors also maintain relevant contextual information on the screen; for example, the LISP tutor displays the current goal stack to support the student's memory of solution steps.

OVERVIEW AND ANALYSIS   It is worthwhile to consider the scope of the instructional theory and of the learning principles involved in these tutors. First, they are not claimed to be appropriate for learning objectives other than acquisition of proceduralized skill. Furthermore, the learning mechanism that guides the current tutors is the automatic process of knowledge compilation, but other more conscious inferential mechanisms might be involved. For example, as Anderson (1987b) has pointed out, analogical problem solving is fundamental in the skill acquisition domains that the CMU group has been studying. In the course of learning, students resort to examples from the same or another domain that are retrieved from prior experience. The process by which analogous experience helps students solve new problems and its implications for instruction are not yet specified. As the group investigates the mechanisms involved in this and other strategies, instructional recommendations may need to be adjusted. Also, the present view of skill acquisition is minimally adaptive to differences in previous knowledge. Students are assumed to enter the learning situation with only limited declarative information and with an intelligent person's set of general problem-solving heuristics. The appropriateness of this approach for achieving elementary levels of skill proficiency in well-structured tasks, such as learning the syntax and semantics of a new programming language, may not hold for more complex reasoning tasks and for more sophisticated expertise [e.g. program planning and debugging (Soloway & Johnson 1984)], where consideration of understanding and organization of the declarative knowledge may be essential.

Although successfully fostering skill proficiency is, in itself, an important goal, the focus on an automatic learning process of skill acquisition may be further guided by the assumption that acquisition of efficient skill at each level of expertise is a necessary facilitating condition for subsequent depth of understanding and reasoning. The view that understanding and planning ability will emerge as by-products of the basic learning mechanisms for skill acquisition might also be involved. This conceptualization of learning is shared by others (e.g. Anzai & Simon 1979; Neches 1984; Klahr 1984; Siegler 1986) who stress learning by doing and focus on the procedural efficiency achieved with practice. They believe that proceduralization of knowledge results in qualitative changes in knowledge structure and in changes of choice of cognitive strategies. To account for such changes, Siegler (1986), for example, has suggested that extensive practice on such skills as addition, subtraction, reading, and time-telling leads to changes in response distributions that later result in switches of strategy choice (from calculation to retrieval). The theoretical implication is that major metacognitive changes are an unconscious by-product of highly practiced successful performance. Of course, others, like those whose work we discuss below, would disagree with an exclusive focus on skill acquisition. How much learning can be explained by mechanisms such as knowledge compilation and how skill efficiency relates to other aspects of expertise remain open empirical questions.

Anderson supports the view of learning as a domain-independent and relatively simple process. Disparities between domains result from different organization of productions and from differences in the initial usefulness of general heuristics. Because the instructional principles in the tutoring programs derive from a general theory of skill acquisition, Anderson holds that the pedagogical strategies can be decoupled from the domain knowledge. His theory of human skill acquisition reflects belief in generalizable basic learning principles, so the most effective tutoring strategy would simply optimize use of these learning principles (Anderson et al 1988). The assumed generality of the underlying learning theory is to be kept in mind as we review other instructional approaches.

Anderson's theory and work are continuous, to an appreciable extent, with the learning tradition in experimental psychology in which emphasis is placed on the transition of a skill from an initial verbal knowledge phase, to an intermediate associative phase, to a final autonomous phase (Fitts 1962; Fitts & Posner 1967). In that tradition, the component subroutines are acquired and integrated in the intermediate phase, and they become less subject to cognitive control and environmental interference and require less conscious processing in the final phase. In addition, the close control of the learning process, the immediate feedback during problem solving, the focus on minimizing errors, and the gradual approximation to experts' behavior by accumulation of separate parts of the skill are reminiscent of Skinnerian shaping and successive approximation and of the early variations of programmed instruction. The cognitive sophistication of Anderson's theory, however, requires also organizing the productions according to a particular problem-solving structure of goals and subgoals, as well as introducing the intelligent component of the instructional system to trace the student's knowledge and performance.

SELF-REGULATORY SKILLS AND PERFORMANCE CONTROL STRATEGIES

Studies of expert performance, work in developmental psychology, and AI problem-solving models reveal the role that self-regulatory or control strategies play in competent performance. The experience of experts enables them to develop executive skills for monitoring performance; they rapidly check their work on a problem, accurately judge its difficulty, apportion their time, assess their progress, and predict the outcomes of their performance (Simon & Simon 1978; Larkin et al 1980; Brown 1978; Miyake & Norman 1979; Chi et al 1982). These self-regulatory skills vary in individuals and appear to be less developed in those with performance difficulties. Superior monitoring skills both reflect the efficient representational skills of experts in their domains and contribute to the utility of their knowledge. Because knowledge of a rule or procedure is enhanced when one can oversee its applicability and monitor its use, self-regulatory skills are important outcomes of learning.

The investigations of developmental psychologists support the view that the growth of metacognition is a significant dimension of evolving cognitive skills from childhood onward. The emergence of metacognitive processes has been examined in work on children's knowledge of their own abilities (Flavell et al 1970; Brown et al 1983; Bransford et al 1986), their comprehension monitoring (Markman 1985), their allocation of effort and attention, as well as their editing and error correction during problem solving.

In work on artificial intelligence, the design of problem-solving systems requires central strategies for deciding what operator to apply and where and when to apply it, as well as a database describing the task domain and a set of operators to manipulate the database (Barr & Feigenbaum 1981). The control strategies define planning processes that are implemented in a hierarchical database structure or that can be more opportunistic and applied to local decisions as a plan develops. Thus, competent problem solving can be both plan and event driven. In the design of computer models of cognition, researchers have either assumed that a separation between resources and control is not essential, as it is in production system models, or made a distinction between the two, not only as a programming convenience, but as a characterization of human cognitive processes. This distinction becomes especially important in learning and instruction when the learner's strategies for accessing information cannot be assumed to be well developed. Thus, many lines of work force consideration of the development of executive control performances as an important dimension of learning and instruction.

Internalizing Self-Regulatory Strategies for Comprehension

Instructional programs in reading, writing, and mathematics designed to foster the development of self-regulatory skills through supportive modeling of task performance are a major area of research (Collins et al 1988). A program for reading comprehension developed by Brown & Palincsar (1984, 1988) has received sustained analysis and been widely cited. Students in this program acquire specific knowledge and also learn a set of strategies for explicating, elaborating, and monitoring the understanding necessary for independent learning. The knowledge-acquisition strategies they learn in working on a specific text are not acquired as decontextualized skills but as skills instrumental in achieving domain knowledge and understanding. The instructional procedure, called reciprocal teaching—reciprocal in the sense that teacher and a group of students take turns in leading the procedure— specifies strategies for comprehending and remembering text content. Its three major components are (a) instruction and practice with strategies that enable students to monitor their understanding; (b) provision, initially by a teacher, of an expert model of metacognitive processes; and (c) a social setting that enables joint negotiation for understanding. The last two components appear to be ingredients in the success of apprenticeship learning in natural settings (cf Greenfield 1984; Lave 1977; Lave et al 1984).

THEORETICAL BACKGROUND   Two general conceptions in developmental psychology underlie the notions of learning that influence this approach. One is that conceptual change is self-directed, in the sense that humans are intrinsically motivated to understand the world around them. Internal structures, principles, or constraints predispose learners to search for causes and explain events to extend their knowledge. Equipped with initial knowledge (facts, concepts, and rules), the learner tries to impose a causal explanation on the situation at hand. Failure to generate an explanation creates a conflict or dissatisfaction with the existing state of knowledge. Such a conflict triggers mental experimentation (Gelman & Brown 1986) to seek data to test and modify the current explanations. Inquiry proceeds until the learner is able to generate a satisfactory explanation. This new explanation, both the result and the process of generation, is assimilated through restructuring or replacing the initial knowledge organization.

The second general conception derives from theories that emphasize learning's social genesis. Conceptual development in children involves internalizing cognitive activities originally experienced in social settings. Thus, the process of generating explanations, whether enacted by the learner himself, with the help of others, or even completely by others, is believed to be internalized gradually. Internalization [after both Piaget (1926) and Vygotsky (1978)] is considered a key mechanism of learning. (Brown points out that detailed explication of this mechanism and of the processes involved in assimilation and restructuring have yet to receive theoretical and empirical analysis.)

INSTRUCTIONAL PRINCIPLES

Strategies for monitoring comprehension   The program focuses on four strategies: *questioning*, or posing questions about the main content of a paragraph; *clarifying*, or attempting to resolve misunderstandings; *summarizing*, or reviewing the gist of the text; and *predicting*, or anticipating text development. These activities serve to improve comprehension by signaling and monitoring progress toward understanding. Inability to summarize a section, for example, indicates comprehension failure and initiates efforts to clarify the problematic aspect of the text. The application of these strategies structures and constrains the discussion. Thus, the dialog leader, usually first the teacher and later the students, begins by asking a question on the main content and invites clarifications, then summarizes the gist, and, finally, asks for predictions about future content.

The teacher as model and coach   The role of the adult teacher is adapted from principles of guided learning, especially those of expert scaffolding (cf Bruner 1978; Wood 1980) and Socratic tutorial dialogs (cf Collins & Stevens 1982; Davis 1966). First, he or she models mature comprehension activities by explicating use of the target strategies. Students can observe the teacher retelling content in her own words, asking what something means, or posing questions about main points. Watching the teacher model, students become familiar with the strategies and with their utility for penetrating a text to extract central facts or themes. Also, they learn that understanding involves active construction of meaning.

After modeling the techniques, the teacher transfers the leading role to one of the students and assumes the role of a coach, ready to intervene or not, as necessary. For example, when a student is unable to generate a question, the teacher may suggest the content and/or the form of a possible question (e.g. "What would be a good question about the pit vipers that starts with the word *why?*"), or, if necessary, pose the correct question and ask the student to repeat it. When the learner manages the task on his own, the teacher fades out her intervention and primarily supports the ongoing discussion. (The metaphor for such coaching, a scaffold, captures the idea of an adjustable temporary support that can be removed when no longer necessary.)

Shared responsibility for the task   The Vygotskian concept (1978) of thinking as essentially the individual's reenactment of the cognitive processes that were originally experienced in society underlies the program's focus on group learning. The program's provisions for the learning group are adapted from studies that have pointed out the motivational and cognitive variables involved in shared responsibility for thinking that enhance learning in group settings. [See Brown & Palincsar (1988) for a review of relevant studies.]

Cooperative learning provides social support, encouragement, and rewards for individual efforts. From a cognitive perspective, a group serves several additional roles. First, it extends the locus of metacognitive activity by providing triggers for cognitive dissatisfaction outside the individual. An audience monitors individual thinking, opinions, and beliefs, and can elicit explanations that clarify points of difficulty. The learner's exposure to alternative points of view can also challenge his initial understanding. In addition, with the help of a teacher who provides expert scaffolding, the collaborative group maintains a mature version of a target task. Overall, by sharing it, a complex task is made more manageable without simplifying the task itself. The group achieves understanding until such time as its members have acquired the skills themselves. Each learner contributes what she can and gains from the contributions of those more expert. The reciprocal teaching method, with its combination of group discussion and scaffolded instruction, creates a *zone of proximal development* where learners perform within their range of competence while being assisted in realizing their potential levels of higher performance (Vygotsky 1978).

In keeping with the goal-directedness, integrated character, and conditionalized nature of competent performance, programs like this one encourage teaching in the context of problem-solving situations that approximate mature practice. Also, they emphasize comprehension and meaningful outcomes as objectives of learning via the use of cognitive strategies. The learning strategies involved are seen as instrumental to acquisition of content and skill in a domain of knowledge. The strategies employed are not claimed to be heuristics or processes comprising generalized, all-purpose skills of intelligence and general learning ability. Rather, they are designed for and tailored to the specific domain being taught and are learned and practiced while being used for solving problems in that domain. Indeed, within the same general approach, different sets of specific strategies are suggested in programs for teaching other domains.

RELATED WORK   A program of procedural facilitation for teaching written composition shares many features with Reciprocal Teaching (Scardamalia et al 1984). The method involves explicit prompts aimed at supporting student's adoption of the metacognitive activities embedded in sophisticated writing strategies. The prompts help students identify goals, generate new ideas, improve and elaborate existing ideas, and strive for their cohesion. Where students in Reciprocal Teaching take turns in leading the discussion, students in the procedural facilitation program take turns presenting to the group their ideas and their use of prompts in planning to write. The teacher also models the procedures. Thus, this program too involves modeling, scaffolding, and turn taking designed to externalize mental events in a collaborative context.

A program designed by Alan Schoenfeld teaches heuristic methods for mathematical problem solving to college students (1983, 1985, 1988), methods derived, to some extent, from the problem-solving heuristics of Polya (1957). Schoenfeld's program adopts methods similar to reciprocal teaching and procedural facilitation. He teaches and demonstrates control or managerial strategies and makes explicit such processes as generating alternative courses of action, evaluating which course one will be able to carry out and whether it can be managed in the time available, and assessing one's progress. Again, elements of modelling, coaching, and scaffolding, as well as collective problem solving and class and small group discussions are employed. Gradually, students come to ask self-regulatory questions themselves as the teacher fades out. In an interesting variant of teaching tactics, at the end of each of the problem-solving sessions, students and teacher alternate in characterizing major themes by analyzing what they did and why. Those recapitulations highlight the generalizable features of the critical decisions and actions and focus on strategic levels rather than on the specifics of solution.

Furthermore, Schoenfeld directly confronts the issue of imparting an appropriate belief system about the interpretive nature of mathematical problem solving. During the process of learning mathematics, students begin to realize that searches often come to dead ends; exploration of possible heuristics and different paths does not guarantee solution. He challenges his students to find difficult problems for him to solve so they can observe his own struggles and floundering, which legitimate students' floundering as well. Students begin to realize that mathematics requires not merely recognizing principles, nor merely applying procedures, but, rather, a creative interpretive process of exploration and reasoning.

OVERVIEW AND ANALYSIS   In these programs, students do learn to apply the appropriate set of monitoring strategies, and there is improvement in domain skill. The designers, however, have the more ambitious objective in mind that students develop particular attitudes toward their own learning. While learning to apply various cognitive control strategies, students are expected to acquire a conception of learning and problem solving in which skilled cognitive strategies guide their activities. An important question is to what extent students can generalize this attitude and transfer the strategies to other situations and across domains.

It is interesting to note the critical shared assumption in these programs that thinking skills are best cultivated in the context of the acquisition of domain knowledge. The shift in cognitive science and AI from modeling general heuristics to specifying uses of knowledge, and the findings on the knowledge-derived processes of expertise give warrant to that assumption.

We cannot consider here the range of current activity on teaching the processes of general intellectual ability and general problem-solving and thinking skills to support learning (cf Chipman et al 1985; Segal et al 1985; Glaser 1984; Resnick 1987a; Bransford et al 1986; Sternberg 1986; Nickerson et al 1985). It is our judgment that, at present, the research on general intellectual abilities, as they relate to instruction, needs further investigation. As our concluding discussion indicates, however, it is possible to anticipate the eventual synthesis of these findings with detailed analysis of specific domain learning.

There are certain similarities among the instructional principles employed in this group of programs and those in the tutors for procedural skills. For example, in the tutors developed by the CMU group, students are kept on a correct solution path and are not permitted to flounder. When a student chooses an incorrect move, the tutor intervenes to identify the error and promptly suggests an alternative move if the student is off track. When the tutor identifies a bigger problem, it intervenes with several examples. Similarly, in the reciprocal teaching method, Brown & Palincsar stress that the teacher keeps the discussion focused on the content and closely monitors the student leaders, providing feedback or resuming control as necessary. There are further similarities with respect to successive approximation, to gradual fading of support, and to explicit modeling.

However, these two sets of programs present very different views of the learner. The knowledge-compilation approach sees the learner as striving for efficiency in performing a well-defined skill; the metacognitive programs conceive of the learner as motivated to explore and seek explanations. These two views and the instructional environments they prescribe might be taken as complementary: The first would be appropriate for novices' acquisition of basic skills, the latter for advanced students' acquisition of strategic skills in the service of understanding. Nevertheless, the two conceptualizations of the learner and of the process are not easily bridged, regardless of choice of objectives or domains. Those who adhere to the metacognitive approach fault current modes of schooling because students often acquire skills mechanically; although efficient, these skills remain as inert knowledge that is not easily accessible in different situations. So we can expect expanding research on metacognitive approaches to the acquisition of basic skills. The interesting issue is whether the extensive practice required to attain reasonable efficiency and automaticity in basic procedural skills might be achieved not only in highly structured environments in which students practice subcomponent procedures, but also in the context of the mature task format of a reciprocally supportive learning group.

Finally, it is worth repeating that, although the various programs for teaching self-monitoring skills are based on a detailed analysis of strategies used in successful reading, writing, and mathematical problem solving, the assumed learning mechanisms of internalization, assimilation, and restructuring are, as yet, little understood.

KNOWLEDGE ORGANIZATION AND STRUCTURE

As competence is attained, elements of knowledge become increasingly interconnected so that proficient individuals access coherent chunks of information. Beginners' knowledge of a domain is spotty, consisting of isolated definitions and superficial understandings of central terms and concepts. As proficiency develops, these items become structured and are integrated with past organizations of knowledge so that they are retrieved from memory rapidly and in larger units (cf Rumelhart & Norman 1978). The exceptional memory retrieval of experts in a domain is based on the structured content of stored information (Ericsson & Staszewski 1988). These organized structures of knowledge are referred to as schemata (Bartlett 1932; Rumelhart 1980). Such structures evolve and are modified and elaborated to facilitate more advanced thinking, and they enable forms of representation that are correlated with the ability to solve problems.

It is now well known that novices work on the basis of the surface features of a problem and that more proficient individuals make inferences, identify principles, and envision mental models that subsume surface structure. In research by Chi et al (1982), novices and experts were asked to group mechanics problems. Novices put together problems that involved pulleys, inclined planes, and so on. Experts, in contrast, grouped those solvable with Newton's laws of motion, on the one hand, and those solvable using energy equations, on the other. The expert apparently organizes his or her knowledge in terms of schemata not salient to the novice, as is apparent in analyses of the solution processes. Larkin et al (1980) have shown that when solving mechanics problems, novices use painstaking means-ends analysis, working backward from the unknown with equations that they hope are relevant to the problem. Experts, in contrast, apply correct equations in a forward direction, indicating that they have a solution plan in place before they begin. Again, schemata appear to enable experts to grasp the structure of problems and then proceed with quantitative solutions in a way that novices cannot. Such representational ability for fast recognition and perception of underlying principles and patterns and its use in problem solving has been replicated in a variety of domains (e.g. Chi et al 1988). The preeminence of expert pattern recognition is such that the expert virtually sees a different problem than the novice (Charness 1988).

A related line of current research is concerned with qualitative reasoning in the use of mental models that people construct of situations and systems they attempt to understand (Gentner & Stevens 1983; Johnson-Laird 1983). These runnable mental simulations are built, used, and modified as proficiency is acquired. The use of models reveals important aspects of inferencing that facilitates problem solving and comprehension. Access to mental models in familiar domains of knowledge can foster reasoning that is not present in abstract logical problems (Falmagne 1980; Johnson-Laird 1982, 1983). Problem solving is differentially effective depending on the type of mental model employed (Gentner & Gentner 1983). Within an AI framework, de Kleer & Brown (1985) and Forbus (1985) propose formalizations of causal and qualitative models people use when reasoning about physical processes. Within cognitive psychology, Stevens & Collins (1980) have described multiple mental models that students hold for explaining such natural processes as rainfall, and they suggest that learning is a process of adding, replacing, deleting, generalizing, and differentiating parts of the model and of mapping between different models. In related research, Collins & Gentner (1987) have described the use of analogies and their integration in constructing various component models for the process of evaporation. AI and psychological approaches have been combined by Forbus & Gentner (1986), who suggest a progression of mental models in which causal and qualitative models are necessary to the development of expert-like quantitative mathematical models.

In general, structured knowledge enables inference capabilities, assists in the elaboration of new information, and enhances retrieval. It provides potential links between stored knowledge and incoming information, which facilitate learning and problem solving. Two lines of instructional work serve here as examples of programs that are guided by research on structured knowledge. The first has evolved in the AI tradition of knowledge engineering and the construction of expert systems. Its central aim is imparting to the learner the knowledge characteristic of well-developed expertise. The second line of work is newer and originates from research on qualitative reasoning and on the evolution of mental models.

Structuring Knowledge for Problem Solving

The analysis of information structures in the form of knowledge networks is documented as an approach to instruction beginning with Carbonell & Collins's (1973) SCHOLAR program. In this so-called mixed-initiative Socratic tutoring program, the system and the student initiate conversation by asking questions; knowledge about the domain being tutored is represented in a semantic network. Since that time, with the growth of AI and the development of intelligent computer tutors, increasingly advanced attempts at explicit tutoring in the context of expert knowledge structures has forced us to investigate the kinds of knowledge representation that facilitate students' interaction with the domain expert or with the expert teacher.

The GUIDON project, led by Clancey (1986), is a carefully documented attempt to use a model of expert knowledge to design an intelligent tutoring system. The learning objective is the acquisition of (*a*) a well-organized body of knowledge in the complex domain of medical diagnosis and (*b*) the heuristic strategies required to use this knowledge for practical problem solving. The initial base of expertise, modeled in the system's forebearer, MYCIN (Shortliffe 1976), consisted of knowledge in the compiled form that characterizes the expert problem solver. Although excellent in its performance capabilities, it lacked the explicit organization and reasoning strategies necessary for tutoring. This additional expertise was modeled from the explanations generated by a good physician-teacher. Accordingly, the base of expertise was reconfigured (NEOMYCIN, Clancey & Letsinger 1984) into a structure of knowledge that represented the expert's principled understanding of the domain, as well as a large number of problem-solving routines in decompiled form. This new knowledge base was organized into categories of general principles that underlie domain knowledge, definitional and taxonomic relations, causal relations, and heuristic rules and strategies. The reasoning strategies involved revolve around the management of hypotheses—grouping hypotheses into more general cases, refining them into special cases, differentiating them, and so forth. Within the expert model for medical diagnosis, these strategies are represented as general reasoning processes of inference that are separated from the domain knowledge.

The next step in the evolution of the project was construction of a domain-independent expert system that applies the general method of reasoning heuristic classification (HERACLES, Clancey 1984a, 1985). In this system, a predetermined taxonomy is used to relate features of the data to descriptions of candidate categories. The system is general enough to fit such domains as electronic troubleshooting, where one has to recognize known malfunctions from symptoms, as well as other forms of problem solving where a fixed set of solution methods must be selected relevant to specific situations. This evolution in the conceptualization of expert knowledge, from a compiled set of domain-specific rules to a set of general strategies that operate on an organized body of knowledge, was accompanied by a change in the instructional objective and in the conception of the the learning process. In recent developments (GUIDON 2, Clancey 1984b), the instructional objective is not only expertise in medical diagnosis, but also the learning process by which one actively constructs an organized body of functional knowledge. Accordingly, the instructional strategy is no longer to present information to the learner in order to fill a knowledge base; rather, it is to provide an environment for active and self-directed learning in the context of explicit expert knowledge.

THEORETICAL BACKGROUND   The learning process in this approach is characterized as "failure-driven, explanation-based learning for nonformal domains" (Clancey 1987, p. 27). Learning is based on detection and explanation of problem-solving failures. The failure detection as well as the suggested repairs result from the learner's efforts to apply existing partial and incomplete schema to the solution of a specific problem. The learning objective is to acquire new knowledge in the context of generating a causal solution linking conclusions to findings. This conception of learning emphasizes the active role of learners, who direct their own learning by generating plausible conjectures about missing knowledge and by posing focused questions to an expert teacher.

More specifically, the learner is assumed to have background knowledge about the domain to be taught. For instruction with the medical tutor, students' knowledge of fundamental medical terms and concepts and disease processes is assumed. Equipped with this initial knowledge, the learner is introduced to the expert's knowledge representation as organized hierarchically and taxonomically. The learner is also introduced to a set of general heuristic inference rules for grouping, differentiating, and testing hypotheses. To foster generality, these rules are expressed in generic language rather than in terms of diseases and symptoms. Thus, the classifications of disease and symptom type, cause, and location are treated in terms of a general diagnostic reasoning process of clarifying findings, providing data to discriminate between hypotheses, and so on.

The student's prior knowledge about disease processes, together with her initial understanding of the expert knowledge representation and inference procedures for classification, constitute a *partial schema* (or an incomplete general theory) of the diagnostic relations. This schema guides the student's inquiry to a *situation specific model* for a particular case. Given a case, the student acts as a diagnostician, proposing hypotheses about the nature of the disease and gathering data to guide further hypothesis generation and testing. The process of diagnosis builds a coherent argument that causally relates all the findings or symptoms to be explained to the processes that brought them about. The system displays the student's solution as a progressive extension of a graph (similar to the graph representation for constructing a geometry proof in Anderson's tutor) that links conclusions to findings, until the graph represents all the relations for the case.

The student herself directs the diagnosis by implementing inference strategies and by interpreting the evolving solution. Learning is driven by *failure;* the student may be unable to test or to refine a hypothesis, to explain or justify a finding, or to discriminate between two or more hypotheses that explain the same findings. After detecting the failure, which is indicated by the inability to generate a link in the solution graph, the student has to generate possible repairs by reasoning about the additional domain knowledge that, if available, might have prevented the failure. She then articulates the nature of the deficiency by posing a specific question to the system. If the information proves sufficient to generate the desired link, the student updates her knowledge base accordingly.

INSTRUCTIONAL PRINCIPLES   Because the methodology of the knowledge-engineering approach required shaping instruction around an expert model for a domain, it demanded a careful analysis of domain structure and decompilation of expert knowledge. This analysis was followed by construction of a validated model of expertise, which performs the tasks the student is to learn. The instructional system was developed as a separate expert system; ideally, it can be adapted for any domain where heuristic classification methods are appropriate. The following instructional principles are embedded in the approach.

An articulated expert model as an object of study   The student has the opportunity to explore the expert's knowledge organization by browsing through its taxonomies and tables. She can see the expert's reasoning during problem solving and can pose questions or request explanation at any time. An articulated representation of the expert's decompiled knowlege and a simulation of the correct problem-solving process are available to study and emulate as the student constructs her own understanding of the domain.

Explication of the reasoning process   The student is explicitly introduced to the nature of the reasoning process by observing the system diagnosing specific cases using strategies of heuristic classification (The GUIDON WATCH system, Richer & Clancey 1985). Furthermore, students can observe the specific problem representation (a connected graph) and the appropriate vocabulary for applying the strategies and for requesting information. Through the use of a domain-independent representation of reasoning and of domain-independent terminology, it is hypothesized that students will learn strategies applicable to other domains as well.

Construction of a situation-specific model   The student is presented with a realistic problem-solving context that forces the construction of a situation-specific model describing the processes by which the problem features were produced. Because the situation model is intimately tied to the goal of solving a problem, it provides an ideal environment for detecting failures and for hypothesizing and testing new facts. What the student learns is based on acquiring knowledge that arises in solving a particular problem and is directly related to the inference procedure being applied.

Self-directed learning   The learner controls and directs the learning process. First, in generating a situation-specific model in the form of a connected graph, the learner herself can detect a failure. Second, in attempting to repair a failure, the student has to determine what information is needed and to formulate a specific question for the expert teacher. A basic assumption is that learning will be more efficient if the student determines what she needs to know, rather than if the teacher builds and tests a model of her current knowledge.

OVERVIEW AND ANALYSIS   The notion of learning that drives the program focuses on the acquisition of new domain knowledge and inferencing skills, not on the processes of knowledge chunking and compilation. In a sense, the two approaches could be conceived as complementary, assuming that, as the learner acquires new knowledge while diagnosing consecutive cases this knowledge becomes proceduralized and the learner becomes more efficient in applying diagnostic skills. The difference in focus, however, is accompanied by disparate conceptions of the learning process and leads to different instructional principles. Although, as in the knowledge compilation programs, GUIDON 2 assumes that learners begin their problem solving with an initial body of declarative knowledge, the latter strongly implicates the initial organization of that knowledge to serve as a partial schema. This schema allows mindful application of reasoning strategies for locating failures and developing a more coherent representation. GUIDON 2 also focuses explicitly on the acquisition of new declarative knowledge through the conscious processes of error detection and repair. The minimization of errors suggested in the theory of automatic knowledge compilation is a sharp contrast.

In GUIDON 2, there is no control or intervention from the tutor other than responding to the student's requests, no shaping or successive approximation. The programs that focus on teaching metacognitive strategies share with GUIDON 2 the conception of learning as failure driven and motivated by the desire to resolve conflict and to construct an explanation using a set of executive strategies. But the metacognitive skills groups, those working with children as well as adults, rely on careful shaping of learning strategies by the teacher. In implementing his program, Clancey may find that it is insufficient for a student to observe the system in order to learn the various heuristic strategies and that more direct intervention is needed from the tutor.

Although Clancey makes assumptions about learning, so far his instructional program is based principally on the analysis of competent performance. However, his most recent conceptualization (Clancey 1987) tries to tap the learning process directly by building on the analogy between how a knowledge engineer probes the human expert to model expertise and how an ideal learner might observe and interact with expert performance. He plans to develop a learning model of the probing tactics and to design a tutorial program that conveys them to the student. The learner then will be able to emulate the model's efficient learning performance, and the tutorial program will be able to make decisions for guiding the ongoing learning based on the model. The rationale behind this plan is that it is not sufficient to analyze only the target knowledge that comprises expertise; it is necessary also to understand knowledge acquisition, to analyze carefully both the various strategies used to observe and to interrogate the expert and the knowledge updating and restructuring that occur during learning.

It is interesting to compare this approach to the model-tracing approach in Anderson's tutors for procedural knowledge. There, the model of the learning process is used by the tutor for tracing and correcting the student's solution path, but the model's production rules are not presented to the student. Because Clancey deals with learning that requires conscious choice of strategies, conscious self-monitoring of understanding, and systematic interrogation of the expert's knowledge, he intends to present students with an explicit learning model. This conception is similar to that in the apprenticeship programs, which stress the exposition of explicit learning strategies. Emphasizing conscious strategy use may be important to the acquisition of new knowledge, as well as to the creation of a repertoire of backup strategies for future recovery from failure and for coping with unfamiliar situations.

It is interesting also to discuss the work on GUIDON 2 with respect to generality and transferability. First, Clancey points out that he adopts a specific representation of medical knowledge that is tailored to diagnosis. He presents an assimilation model of learning that does not assume any representational changes to the knowledge base. Thus, knowledge is acquired only in the form suitable for diagnosis, not for treatment, say, or research. Accordingly, Clancey does not expect transfer of the knowledge per se. However, because the skill of diagnosis has a structure similar to those of other tasks involving heuristic classification, he believes that the general reasoning involved can be transferred. To stress its generality, he uses a general method for heuristic classification, but it is as yet unclear whether, indeed, students will acquire the method through experience in a single domain. [Clancey (1987) points out that an experienced knowledge engineer, who serves as his model of a good learner, typically develops his expertise by interrogating expert's knowledge in several domains.] Clancey's conception of generality and transfer is compatible with Anderson's (1987b). Anderson compares the skill of proof evaluation to the skill of proof generation in geometry; although they are based on the same declarative knowledge, the production rules do not overlap. According to ACT* theory, transfer will not occur between two different skills based only on the same declarative knowledge. Positive transfer between skills, however, may occur to the extent that they involve the same hierarchical goal structure controlling the behavior (Singley & Anderson, unpublished manuscript).

Progression of Qualitative Mental Models

Instructional work that stems from research on mental models represents an effort to teach understanding of a domain by utilizing possible transitions between the intuitive understanding developed as a result of informal experience and expert conceptualizations. The program developed by White & Frederiksen (1986) for teaching troubleshooting in electric circuits focuses on qualitative causal reasoning as a basis for conceptual understanding. White & Frederiksen assume that experts' knowledge is organized in coordinated mental models. Accordingly, they lead the learner through a progression from simple to advanced models. Each mental model incorporates declarative and procedural knowledge as well as a control structure that determines how this knowledge is used. Declarative knowledge may include a property of a device model, such as the conductivity of a resistor, or a battery as a source of voltage. Procedural knowledge might be the method used to determine the distribution of voltages within a circuit. Control knowledge could include knowing that when one device's conductivity changes, the states of all other devices in the circuit change.

Various mental models can be specified for a domain, each of which represents a different conceptualization of domain phenomena. Within a causal model, a student can predict the behavior of a circuit knowing that a decrease in its resistance causes a decrease in voltage across the component. Within a functional model, she can explain the purpose of a circuit as a whole or as the sum of its components. The mental models can vary in their order of description: A *zero-order* model can reason about binary states of devices, such as "is the light on or off?"; a *first-order* model can reason on the basis of changes, "is the light getting brighter?"; a *second-order* model can reason about the rate at which a variable is changing. Models vary in their degree of elaboration or in the number of rules and constraints taken into account. The objective of learning is to achieve a coordinated set of expert-like mental models, that is, a set of complementary models for the same phenomena, behavioral as well as functional, qualitative as well as quantitative. Each type can be expanded and elaborated.

THEORETICAL BACKGROUND   Learning is viewed as a process of model transformation, as a progression through increasingly sophisticated mental models, each more adequate for a larger set of problems. Transformations entail changes in knowledge and structure. Changes in knowledge may involve adding qualifiers to rules, deleting rules, or adding new rules. Such changes, in turn, may result in restructuring existing knowledge. For example, a new rule learned in the context of a certain device (e.g. a battery) may be encoded as general rather than specific to that device. In this case, all other device models (e.g. switches, resistors, bulbs, transistors) inherit this rule. Model transformations occur in the context of solving problems, in response to demands of more complex problems that cannot be solved with the existing model. Facing an impasse, the student learns from examples and from explanations compatible with the next higher model. The new level of understanding is strengthened by success in solving problems.

The major emphasis in White & Frederiksen's work is *qualitative* models that support *causal* explanations. They argue that students should be initially exposed to qualitative causal reasoning about a domain that connects with their naive intuitive models of physical phenomena. The qualitative models enable students to build upon their naive but accurate intuitions and to override their inaccurate conceptions. The reasoning in their models is compatible with the general intuition that changes in states have precipitating causes. Because causality is directional (cause → effect), the qualitative causal models use directionality by showing, for example, that the voltage applied to a component determines or causes the current through that component. In contrast, if the student is presented only with quantitative expressions, causal relations between current, voltage, and resistance are obscure. Using the algebraic constraints for reasoning precludes a consistent mental model. Accordingly, they advocate that quantitative models of reasoning should be introduced only after the acquisition of a qualitative conception of the domain and should be taught as a logical extension of them.

INSTRUCTIONAL PRINCIPLES   White & Frederiksen have developed, so far, a progression of zero-order qualitative models for troubleshooting. The learning environment enables students to solve problems and to receive explanations and perform experiments while interacting with successive qualitative models. Each model is used to simulate the domain phenomena, to generate articulated explanations, and to provide appropriate problems.

Sequence and choice of models and problems   The models become increasingly complex, yet are constructed to be compatible; early models are designed to enable later transformations with minimum reconsideration. Model choices are guided also by the ease of explanation for a current level of problem solving, although some of the acquired rules will have to be deleted in later, more complex models. Problems are indexed according to models. Particular care is required in choosing the problems that trigger a change of model. In general, these problems should be just beyond the student's level of competence. They must be prototypical to make the model difference clear and should have no distracting causes. (Where this is impossible, extreme cases are used.)

Causal explanation   Causal explanations are provided for each qualitative model. The system can turn any problem into an example and display the reasoning involved while it solves the problem. Also, at any stage during problem solving, the student can call for explanation either about circuit operation or about the logic of troubleshooting. To assure that the task is not too complex, explanations are pruned not to repeat what is known and to refer only to the information necessary at a given model level.

Teaching and supporting multiple learning strategies   The system supports various learning strategies. Students can engage in open-ended explorations and request explanations, they can start by solving problems on their own, or they can request tutorial demonstrations. Within the linear curriculum for troubleshooting, students are free to decide whether, for example, they want to acquire a new concept or to differentiate between two concepts. The authors suggest, on the basis of preliminary findings, that students should be taught explicitly to apply alternative learning strategies.

Minimization of error   White & Frederiksen attempt to minimize error. They assume that, with careful presentations of models and problems and of feedback and explanation, in principle, errorless transition to the desired knowledge state is possible. The system, thus, does not deal with detection of bugs and misconceptions.

As criteria for learning, the authors suggest qualitative components of understanding such as order and level of elaboration of a particular model as well as the integration and coordination of behavioral, functional, and causal models. However, the qualitative measures of understanding are not implemented in the system. It is assumed that the student's understanding is compatible with the latest level of the model mastered within a tutoring period.

OVERVIEW AND ANALYSIS   The mental models that the program attempts to teach are not simply incomplete versions of expert models; rather, they are specifically designed for transition. Construction of models takes into account the initial understanding of the learner (e.g. that beginning students do not have a concept of a circuit or that they do not distinguish between a resistive and a nonresistive path) based on preliminary interviews and on observing students' progress when using the system. Also, although each model is designed to be modifiable to enable progressive upgrading and, ideally, should be compatible with a higher-level version, considerations of learnability ofen demand the introduction of assumptions or rules lacking in expert models, which are later deleted or subsumed. The progression of models is an hypothesis about optimal transitions towards expertise based on articulation of the transition process itself.

The transition to expertise in the mental-models approach differs from that of knowledge engineering. GUIDON 2 provides the learner with an environment that enables exploration of fully developed expertise, albeit in decompiled form. The learner controls his or her own progress, and there is no predetermined and carefully designed transition path. The mental-models mastery model of instruction, by contrast, entails a stricter curriculum, based on an hypothesis about the best transition route. The units of learning are not component productions, but bigger encompassing conceptual units.

In the current sequence of mental models, all models involve qualitative causal reasoning, although the designers acknowledge that explicating causality is insufficient for deep understanding. Thus, important questions are at what point in instruction other conceptualizations (e.g. quantitative and physical) should be introduced, whether these should be initially taught in a separate sequence, and how they should be integrated. Gentner and colleagues (e.g. Collins & Gentner 1987; Forbus & Gentner 1986) have suggested the importance of an analogical mapping process for integrating different models of a domain. Collins, Salter, and Tenney (unpublished manuscript) have indicated, as well, that integration requires monitoring and checking for consistency, comparing the outcome of one line of reasoning to another. They also suggest that consistency checking should be based on central ideas that crosscut the various models.

Finally, it is of interest to note that, although the White & Fredericksen program addresses the issue of the initial state of the learner through preliminary studies of domain relevant pre- and misconceptions, the instruction does not accommodate individual differences on a principled basis. Further, the transition is grounded in a rational analysis rather than in an analysis of conceptual change or in a theory of such change like that formulated in ACT*. Such theories have recently become of major concern for many researchers (e.g. diSessa, unpublished manuscript; Chi 1988; Forbus & Gentner 1986).

COMMENTARY: AN AGENDA FOR THE FUTURE

We have described a set of instructional programs that teach different categories of human performance, deal with different subject matters, and derive from different traditions. At first blush, there is no general view of learning processes or of instructional methods. As gains are made in empirical and theoretical research on learning, one may wonder to what extent such differentiation will be necessary. Is the emphasis on automatic learning mechanisms best suited for acquiring efficient procedural skill, whereas conscious mechanisms, such as monitoring understanding or generating an explanation, must be emphasized for acquiring an organized body of knowledge? Does the choice to focus on learning of specific procedures require individualized instruction where errors can be minimized, whereas a focus on metaconceptual skills prescribes learning within a supportive social context that can encourage error detection? Should we allow, for the time being, that each category of performance warrants a different learning and instructional theory? That conclusion would echo Melton's sense, in 1964, of the conundrum.

> When one is confronted with a decision to use massed or distributed practice, to insist on information feedback or not to insist on it, to arrange training so as to maximize or minimize requirements for contiguous stimulus differentiation, etc, and discovers that the guidance received from experimental research and theory is different for rote learning, for skill learning, and for problem solving, taxonomic issues become critical and taxonomic ambiguities become frustrating, to say the last. (p. 327)

Even if we accept that it will be difficult to achieve a unified theory of learning, we should attempt to discover grounds for integration of the key aspects of human competence in instruction. The apparent fragmentation may be due to each program's attending to one specific aspect of domain competence and neglecting and/or deemphasizing others. The central concern with proceduralization of declarative knowledge in the CMU group's work allows only minimal attention to the structuring of knowledge and does not deal with processes of self-monitoring. The programs on cooperative learning and knowledge restructuring do not attend to issues of efficiency and of automaticity. The mental-models approach does not deal with metacognitive skills, nor do the programs for reading comprehension strategies and heuristics for solving mathematics problems tackle the issue of knowledge structure. It appears to be as yet impossible in research on instruction to attend to the many ingredients of performance. Each of the investigators simplifies objectives by focusing on one aspect or another, choosing the aspect that seems appropriate to the domain and to the values, tradition, and techniques with which he or she is most familiar. It is good science to avoid confounded effects, but the eventual objective in these studies is obviously not isolated phenomena; competence is characterized by both efficiency and principled understanding, by both pattern recognition and conscious monitoring. Accordingly, the process of transition or the various learning mechanisms may not operate in isolation.

As the field of instructional psychology builds from the kinds of research examined here, assessing the potentialities for integrative approaches should be a recurrent theme. To design experimental programs aimed to foster integrated competences, it may be necessary to proceed by teaching relatively separate, yet complementary, components of performance in sequential, spiral, or alternating phases. Under some circumstances, a program might teach a skill to a high degree of efficiency, and then use it in the course of developing higher levels of cognitive processing in that domain. In this way, planning processes, inference, and changes in knowledge structures could take place with memory freed of the demands of an inefficient skill. In other situations, structures of conceptual knowledge and mental models could initially be taught or made available, and practice with complex procedures would follow.

The danger of fragmentation in research is that an isolated focus on certain aspects of performance may explain the frequent findings that students can solve problems but have little ability to explain the underlying principles or why those who can recite or even explain the principles are sometimes unable to recognize the conditions of applicability or to manage the requisite procedures efficiently. A major instructional research task is to design programs that test approaches to the integration of competent performance, and perhaps the most successful approach will be able to test a mix of instructional principles. Evidence, for example, from developmental work (Case & Sandieson 1988a,b) shows that the ability to establish an appropriate conceptual representation constrains acquisition of strategies and procedures, but, at the same time, the degree of procedural efficiency constrains the complexity of children's representations. In other relevant research, training studies show that procedural skill is effectively acquired in the context of a supporting mental model (Kieras & Bovair 1984; Gott 1988). Perhaps, programs aimed at structuring knowledge could be expanded to include the practice required for the acquisition of a procedural skill. Attempts at integration promise to provide new grounds for the development of a more general theory of learning. Such a theory may include subprocesses such as those suggested by the current programs (e.g. knowledge compilation, failure-driven learning) or some other mechanisms that may operate in an integrated setting.

With respect to instruction, there are certain major principles that are shared in the studies discussed, regardless of the aspect of competence or domain on which they focus. All programs advocate learning in the context of working on specific problems—be they those of writing code in LISP, understanding text, diagnosing a medical case, or describing an electric circuit. Thus, all investigators agree that useful knowledge is not acquired as a set of general propositions, but by active application during problem solving in the context of specific goals. Moreover, all programs recommend explication and modeling of the appropriate problem-solving structure and of the procedures or strategies entailed. The investigators also share the view that learning, in the sense of strengthening existing knowledge, results eventually from practice that minimizes error; and, except for the automatic process of knowledge compilation, they agree that failure or conflict triggers new learning. Moreover, categories of performance and related instructional sub-theories may not necessitate different conditions for instruction. Instructional decisions about control, feedback, or the structuring of the curriculum cross-cut approaches. Such principles do seem a basis for studies that promise to inform a more unified theory.

This agreement notwithstanding, in the programs reviewed there seem to be two general stances toward instruction. In the mastery approach, the instructor is responsible for a specific transition path, building a curriculum that carefully fosters a progressive sequence of skills through appropriate tasks. This approach, which resembles behavioral programmed instruction or computer assisted instruction, is characterized by sequenced subgoals of partial or decomposed components of the total target performance. The mastery approach has been adopted for the acquisition of a proceduralized skill, for fostering conceptual evolution with mental models, and for teaching heuristics for mathematical problem solving. The second general approach does not structure transition, but, rather, provides a learning environment that can assist the learner in coping with a complete and mature task. The learner is given certain tools or strategies to apply on his or her own, and where he or she is unable to do so, the tutor, the teacher, or the group provides assistance. Typically, a mastery model implies relatively close control, whereas a less structured curriculum gives the learner more responsibility. Among the approaches, however, there are variations in the amounts of control and freedom. The programs using knowledge compilation, coming from learning theory, exercise more control than the programs for teaching performance control heuristics. Programs for shared learning, coming from a developmental-social tradition, appear to recommend more control and supervision than those coming from knowledge engineering.

This dichotomy may depend, to some extent, on the amount of inherent hierarchical structure or subskill interdependency in subject matters. Cognitive skills, metaconceptual strategies, and procedures for problem solving have different properties as a function of the knowledge domain. Procedural skills that are knowledge lean, those that can be practiced with a minimal or easily acquired knowledge base, might be learned in one way; cognitive skills that entail the constraints offered by an available knowledge schema, those that require inference from knowledge, hypothesis formation, and strategy selection based on emerging information, might be learned in another way.

From another perspective, the dichotomy is a function of research traditions and values. Those who study instruction and learning come to place different values on efficiency, command of factual information, reasoning ability, monitoring skills, and so forth. Designers of instruction may hold that thoughtful problem solving has greater utility than the acquisition of efficient procedural skill, or that procedural skill should precede the development of higher-order processes, or that understanding and appropriate mental models are essential supports for the development of procedural efficiency. In current research, such general assumptions seem to be continuous with a researcher's training, the findings of older learning theories (e.g. Fitts 1962; Vygotsky 1978), cultural beliefs about learning, and commonsense observations of teaching and tutoring. But continued experimental study of phenomena of performance and instructional interventions will provide new information for learning theory. Using available and new tools for detailed description of ongoing cognitive processes, we need to study the phenomena of learning directly, within natural settings as well as within carefully designed instructional settings. Such studies will shed further light on issues raised by the work reviewed here. Research can now be shaped to examine the interplay between conscious mechanisms of inference and the automatic process of knowledge compilation, to explicate the mechanisms of internalization and the conditions that encourage it, and to delineate how failure-driven explanation fosters understanding and how conceptual models evolve and are integrated.

Another basic question is how initial knowledge is acquired. Anderson's and Clancey's programs, for example, assume that a certain amount of declarative knowledge has already been acquired through reading and listening when their instructional procedures are introduced. Such analysis is proceeding in research on reading and text comprehension (Kintsch 1988a,b; Just & Carpenter 1987). In addition, general learning abilities and knowledge-free problem-solving skills need to be further explicated (cf Nickerson et al 1985; Resnick 1987a; Sternberg 1986), particularly individual differences in how they are acquired and guide learning. To some extent, the mental-models approach addresses the introduction of initial structures on which learning can proceed, and programs on cooperative learning address the development of general skills for problem solving and understanding. However, in the main, differences between individuals are left unattended in the programs that have been discussed, differences that are inherent in misconceptions of knowledge in a domain and in the intuitions, theories, principled beliefs, and aptitudes that children and adults bring to subject-matter learning. The accommodation of the array of pertinent findings on the initial competence of the learner (cf Gelman & Brown 1986) will be a significant watershed in attempts to build powerful accounts of learning.[2]

---

[2]Other research areas that should be considered in the development of learning and instructional theory include current work on the analysis of classroom teacher performance (Leinhardt & Greeno 1986); learning in natural settings (Lave 1977; Lave et al 1984; Saxe 1988; Resnick 1987b); motivational processes (Dweck 1988) the technology of instructional design (Gagne 1987; Reigeluth 1983); machine-learning investigations of explanation, discovery, and learning from examples (Michalski et al 1983, 1986); technical training in industrial and military settings (Halff et al 1986; Gott 1988; Lesgold et al 1988); and much work on artificial intelligence and tutoring systems (Wenger 1987).

To conclude, it is apparent that the single most important contribution to date of the knowledge and methodology of cognitive science to instructional psychology has been the analysis of complex human performance. The design of instruction in the studies we have reviewed relies more on models of competent performances in specified areas of knowledge and skill than on models of how this performance is acquired. Anderson's work is the most rigorous in explicitly attempting to use instruction to test a theory of learning. But, in general, assumptions about learning, not well-specified theory, are loosely connected to instructional principles. Indeed, the technology of cognitive task analysis that has emerged is a crucial first step. Over 25 years ago, a major figure in training research offered that "perhaps the most important single contribution to the development of training through research has been the determination of methods for the formulation of objectives of instruction" (Crawford 1962, p. 326). There have since been major improvements in both method and content; the theory underlying task analysis and our understanding of the nature of human competence have been greatly advanced. These advances constitute impressive payoffs on the scientific bet, which we quoted earlier from Newell & Simon, about cognitive science's emphasis in its youth on performance. Now, "both learning and development must be incorporated in integral ways in the more complete and successful theory."

An evolution of instructional theory and the learning theory that underlies it will come about by investigation of questions that emerge from work of the kind we have described here. Progress in an area is often made on the basis of instrumentation that facilitates scientific work, and, at the present time, a significant tool is the design of instructional interventions that operationalize theory in the form of environments, techniques, materials, and equipment that can be carefully studied. These investigations can be testing grounds for new theories of learning and instruction that will benefit both the practice of education and the advance of science.

ACKNOWLEDGMENT

Preparation of this article was sponsored in part by the Center for the Study of Learning (CSL) at the Learning Research and Development Center of the University of Pittsburgh. CSL is funded by the Office of Educational Research and Improvement of the US Department of Education. Additional support was provided by the Cognitive Science Program of the Office of Naval Research and by the Memory and Cognitive Processes Program of the National Science Foundation. The views expressed, however, are solely the responsibility of the authors, who extend thanks to Michelle von Koch for her insightful editorial suggestions and to Susan W. Craft and Anna Marie Schollaert for their copyediting and typing assistance.

Literature Cited

Anderson, J. R. 1981. *Cognitive Skills and Their Acquisition.* Hillsdale, NJ: Erlbaum

Anderson, J. R. 1983. *The Architecture of Cognition.* Cambridge, Mass: Harvard Univ. Press

Anderson, J. R. 1987a. Methodologies for studying human knowledge. *Behav. Brain Sci.* 10(3):467–77

Anderson, J. R. 1987b. Skill acquisition: compilation of weak-method problem solutions. *Psychol. Rev.* 94(2):192–210

Anderson, J. R., Boyle, C. F., Corbett, A., Lewis, M. 1988. Cognitive modelling and intelligent tutoring. *Artif. Intell.* In press

Anderson, J. R., Boyle, C. F., Yost, G. 1985. The geometry tutor. In *Proc. Int. Joint Conf. Artif. Intell. 1985*, pp. 1–7. Los Angeles, Calif: Int. Joint Conf. Artif. Intell.

Anderson, J. R., Farrell, R., Sauers, R. 1984. Learning to program in LISP. *Cogn. Sci.* 8:87–129

Anzai, Y., Simon, H. A. 1979. The theory of learning by doing. *Psychol. Rev.* 86(2): 124–40

Atkinson, R. C. 1972. Optimizing the learning of a second language vocabulary. *J. Exp. Psychol.* 96:124–29

Barr, A., Feigenbaum, E. A., eds. 1981. *The Handbook of Artificial Intelligence,* Vol. 1. Los Altos, Calif: William Kaufmann, Inc.

Bartlett, F. C. 1932. *Remembering.* Cambridge: Cambridge Univ. Press

Bobrow, D. G., ed. 1985. *Qualitative Reasoning about Physical Systems.* Cambridge, Mass: MIT Press

Bransford, J., Sherwood, R., Vye, N., Rieser, J. 1986. Teaching thinking and problem solving: research foundations. *Am. Psychol.* 41(10):1078–89

Brown, A. L. 1978. Knowing when, where, and how to remember: a problem of metacognition. In *Advances in Instructional Psychology,* Vol. 1, ed. R. Glaser, pp. 77–168. Hillsdale, NJ: Erlbaum

Brown, A. L., Bransford, J. D., Ferrara, R. A., Campione, J. C. 1983. Learning, remembering, and understanding. In *Handbook of Child Psychology,* ed. P. H. Mussen, pp. 77–166. New York: Wiley

Brown, A. L., Palincsar, A. S. 1984. Reciprocal teaching of comprehension-fostering and monitoring activities. *Cogn. Instr.* 1(2):175–77

Brown, A. L., Palincsar, A. 1988. Guided, cooperative learning and individual knowledge acquisition. See Resnick 1988. In press

Bruner, J. 1978. The role of dialogue in language acquisition. In *The Child's Conception of Language,* ed. A. Sinclair, R. J.

Jarvella, J. M. Levelt, pp. 241–56. Berlin: Springer-Verlag

Carbonell, J. R., Collins, A. 1973. Natural semantics in artificial intelligence. *Proc. 3rd Int. Joint Conf. Artif. Intell.,* Stanford Univ., pp. 344–51

Carey, S. 1985. *Conceptual Change in Childhood.* Cambridge, Mass: MIT Press

Carey, S. 1986. Cognitive science and science education. *Am. Psychol.* 41(10): 1123–30

Case, R., Sandieson, R. 1988a. A developmental approach to the identification and teaching of central conceptual structures in middle school science and mathematics. In *Research Agenda in Mathematics Education: Number Concepts and Operations in the Middle Grades,* ed. M. Behr, J. Hiebert, pp. 236–59. Hillsdale, NJ: Erlbaum

Case, R., Sandieson, R. 1988b. General conceptual constraints on the acquisition of specific procedural skills (and vice versa). Presented at Ann. Meet. Am. Educ. Res. Assoc., 1988, New Orleans.

Charness, N. 1988. Expertise in chess and bridge. See Klahr & Kotovsky 1988. In press

Chi, M. T. H. 1988. Children's lack of access and knowledge reorganization: an example from the concept of animism. In *Memory Development: Universal Changes and Individual Differences,* ed. F. Weinert, M. Perlmutter, pp. 169–94. Hillsdale, NJ: Erlbaum

Chi, M. T. H., Ceci, S. J. 1987. Content knowledge: its role, representation, and restructuring in memory development. *Adv. Child Dev. Behav.* 20:91–142

Chi, M. T. H., Glaser, R., Farr, M., eds. 1988. *The Nature of Expertise.* Hillsdale, NJ: Erlbaum

Chi, M. T. H., Glaser, R., Rees, E. 1982. Expertise in problem solving. In *Advances in the Psychology of Human Intelligence,* Vol. 1, ed. R. J. Sternberg, pp. 7–75. Hillsdale, NJ: Erlbaum

Chipman, S. J., Segal, J. W., Glaser, R., eds. 1985. *Thinking and Learning Skills: Research and Open Questions,* Vol. 2. Hillsdale, NJ: Erlbaum

Clancey, W. J. 1984a. Classification problem solving. *Proc. Nat. Conf. Artif. Intell.* Austin, Texas, pp. 49–55

Clancey, W. J. 1984b. Teaching classification problem solving. *Proc. Cogn. Sci. Soc. Conf.,* Boulder, pp. 44–46

Clancey, W. J. 1985. Heuristic classification. *Artif. Intell.* 27(3):289–350

Clancey, W. J. 1986. From GUIDON to NEOMYCIN and HERACLES in twenty short lessons: ONR final report 1979–1985. *AI Mag.* 7(3):40–60

Clancey, W. J. 1987. *The Knowledge Engineer as Student: Metacognitive Bases for Asking Good Questions* (Tech. Rep. STAN-CS-87-1183). Stanford, Calif: Dep. Comput. Sci., Stanford Univ.

Clancey, W. J., Letsinger, R. 1984. NEOMY-CIN: reconfiguring a rule-based expert system for application to teaching. In *Medical Artificial Intelligence: The First Decade,* ed. W. J. Clancey, E. H. Shortliffe. Reading, Mass: Addison-Wesley

Clement, J. 1982. Students' preconceptions in introductory mechanics. *Am. J. Phys.* 50:66–71

Collins, A., Brown, J. S., Newman, S. E. 1988. Cognitive apprenticeship: teaching the craft of reading, writing, and mathematics. See Resnick 1988. In press

Collins, A., Gentner, D. 1987. How people construct mental models. In *Cultural Models in Thought and Language,* ed. D. Holland, N. Quinn, pp. 243–65. Cambridge: Cambridge Univ. Press

Collins, A., Stevens, A. 1982. Goals and strategies of inquiry teachers. In *Advances in Instructional Psychology,* Vol. 2, ed. R. Glaser, pp. 65–119. Hillsdale, NJ: Erlbaum

Crawford, M. P. 1962. Concepts of training. In *Psychological Principles in System Development,* ed. R. M. Gagne, pp. 301–42. New York: Holt, Rinehart & Winston

Davis, R. B. 1966. Discovery in the teaching of mathematics. In *Learning by Discovery: A Critical Appraisal,* ed. L. S. Shulman, E. R. Keisler. Chicago: Rand McNally

de Kleer, J., Brown, J. S. 1985. A qualitative physics based upon confluences. See Bobrow 1985, pp. 7–83

diSessa, A. A. 1982. Unlearning Aristotelian physics: a study of knowledge-based learning. *Cogn. Sci.* 6:37–75

Dweck, C. S. 1988. Motivation. In *Cognitive Psychology of Education: Tutorial Essays,* ed. A. Lesgold, R. Glaser. Hillsdale, NJ: Erlbaum. In press

Ericsson, K. A., Staszewski, J. 1988. Skilled memory and expertise: mechanisms of exceptional performance. See Klahr & Kotovsky 1988. In press

Falmagne, R. J. 1980. The development of logical competence: a psycholinguistic perspective. In *Developmental Models of Thinking,* ed. R. H. Kluwe, H. Spada. New York: Academic

Feigenbaum, E. A. 1988. What hath Simon wrought? See Klahr & Kotovsky 1988. In press

Fitts, P. M. 1962. Factors in complex skill training. In *Training Research and Education,* ed. R. Glaser, pp. 177–98. Pittsburgh,

Penn: Univ. Pittsburgh Press. New York: Dover Publications

Fitts, P. M., Posner, M. I. 1967. *Human Performance.* Belmont, Calif: Brooks/Cole

Flavell, J. H., Friedricks, A. G., Hoyt, J. D. 1970. Developmental changes in memorization processes. *Cogn. Psychol.* 1:324–40

Forbus, K. D. 1985. Qualitative process theory. See Bobrow 1985, pp. 85–168

Forbus, K. D., Gentner, D. 1986. Learning physical domains: towards a theoretical framework. In *Machine Learning: An Artificial Intelligence Approach,* Vol. 2, ed. R. M. Michalski, J. Carbonell, T. Mitchell, pp. 311–48. Los Altos, Calif: Morgan Kaufmann

Gagne, R. M., ed. 1987. *Instructional Technology: Foundations.* Hillsdale, NJ: Erlbaum

Gelman, R., Brown, A. L. 1986. Changing competence in the young. In *Behavioral and Social Science: Fifty Years of Discovery,* ed. N. J. Smelser, D. R. Gerstein, pp. 175–209. Washington, DC: Nat. Acad. Press

Gelman, R., Greeno, J. 1988. On the nature of competence: principles for understanding in a domain. See Resnick 1988. In press

Gentner, D., Gentner, D. R. 1983. Flowing waters or teeming crowds: mental models of electricity. See Gentner & Stevens 1983, pp. 99–129

Gentner, D., Stevens, A., eds. 1983. *Mental Models.* Hillsdale, NJ: Erlbaum

Glaser, R. 1976. Components of a psychology of instruction: toward a science of design. *Rev. Educ. Res.* 46(1):1–24

Glaser, R. 1984. Education and thinking: the role of knowledge. *Am. Psychol.* 39(2):93–104

Glaser, R. 1985. All's well that begins and ends with both knowledge and process: a reply to Sternberg. *Am. Psychol.* 40(5):573–74

Glaser, R., ed. 1986. Special issue: Psychological science and education. *Am. Psychol.* 40(10):157 pp.

Gott, S. 1988. Apprenticeship instruction for real world cognitive tasks. In *Review of Research on Education,* ed. E. Z. Rothkopf. Washington, DC: Am. Educ. Res. Assoc. In press

Greenfield, P. M. 1984. A theory of the teacher in the learning activities of everyday life. See Rogoff & Lave 1984, pp. 117–38

Greeno, J. G. 1980. Psychology of learning, 1960–1980: one participant's observations. *Am. Psychol.* 35(8):713–28

Greeno, J. G., Simon, H. A. 1988. Problem solving and reasoning. In *Stevens' Handbook of Experimental Psychology,* ed. R. C. Atkinson, R. Herrnstein, G. Lindzey, R. D.

Luce, pp. 589–672. New York: Wiley. rev. ed. In press

Halff, H. M., Hollan, J. D., Hutchins, E. L. 1986. Cognitive science and military training. *Am. Psychol.* 41(10):1131–39

Johnson-Laird, P. N. 1982. Formal semantics and the psychology of meaning. In *Processes, Beliefs and Questions,* ed. S. Peters, E. Saarinen. Dordrecht: Reidel

Johnson-Laird, P. N. 1983. *Mental Models: Towards a Cognitive Science of Language, Inference, and Consciousness.* Cambridge, Mass: Harvard Univ. Press

Just, M. A., Carpenter, P. A. 1987. *The Psychology of Reading and Language Comprehension.* Boston, Mass: Allyn & Bacon

Keil, F. C. 1981. Constraints on knowledge and cognitive development. *Psychol. Rev.* 88(3):197–227

Keil, F. C. 1984. Mechanisms of cognitive development and the structure of knowledge. See Sternberg 1984, pp. 81–100

Kieras, D. E., Bovair, S. 1984. The role of a mental model in learning to operate a device. *Cogn. Sci.* 8:225–73

Kintsch, W., 1988a. The role of knowledge in discourse comprehension: a construction-integration model. *Psychol. Rev.* 95(2): 163–82

Kintsch, W. 1988b. Learning from text. See Resnick 1988. In press

Klahr, D. 1984. Transition processes in quantitative development. See Sternberg 1984, pp. 101–40

Klahr, D., Kotovsky, K., eds. 1988. *Complex Information Processing: The Impact of Herbert A. Simon.* Hillsdale, NJ: Erlbaum. In press

Larkin, J. H., McDermott, J., Simon, D. P., Simon, H. A. 1980. Models of competence in solving physics problems. *Cogn. Sci.* 4:317–45

Lave, J. 1977. Tailor-made experiences in evaluating the intellectual consequences of apprenticeship training. *Q. Newsl. Inst. Comp. Hum. Dev.* 1:1–3

Lave, J., Murtaugh, M., de la Rocha, O. 1984. The dialectic of arithmetic in grocery shopping. See Rogoff & Lave 1984, pp. 67–94

Leinhardt, G., Greeno, J. G. 1986. The cognitive skills of teaching. *J. Educ. Psychol.* 78(2):75–95

Lesgold, A. M., Lajoie, S., Bunzo, M., Eggan, G. 1988. SHERLOCK: A coached practice environment for an electronics troubleshooting job. In *Computer Assisted Instruction and Intelligent Tutoring Systems: Establishing Communication and Collaboration,* ed. J. Larkin, R. Chabay, C. Scheftic. Hillsdale, NJ: Erlbaum. In press

Lesgold, A. M., Perfetti, C. A. 1981. *Interactive Processes in Reading.* Hillsdale, NJ: Erlbaum

Lewis, M. W., Milson, R., Anderson, J. R. 1988. Designing an intelligent authoring system for high school mathematics ICAI: the teacher apprentice project. In *Artificial Intelligence and Instruction: Applications and Methods,* ed. G. Kearsley. New York: Addison-Wesley. In press

Markman, E. M. 1985. Comprehension monitoring: developmental and educational issues. See Chipman et al 1985, pp. 275–92

McCloskey, M. 1983. Naive theories of motion. See Gentner & Stevens 1983, pp. 299–324

McCloskey, M., Caramazza, A., Green, B. 1980. Curvilinear motion in the absence of external forces: naive beliefs about the motion of objects. *Science* 210:1139–41

Melton, A. W. 1964. The taxonomy of human learning: overview. In *Categories of Human Learning,* ed. A. W. Melton, pp. 325–39. New York: Academic

Michalski, R. S., Carbonell, J. G., Mitchell, T. M., eds. 1983. *Machine Learning: An Artificial Intelligence Approach,* Vol. 1. Palo Alto, Calif: Tioga Publishing Co.

Michalski, R. S., Carbonell, J. G., Mitchell, T. M., eds. 1986. *Machine Learning: An Artificial Intelligence Approach,* Vol. 2. Los Altos, Calif: Morgan Kaufmann

Miyake, N., Norman, D. A. 1979. To ask a question one must know enough to know what is known. *J. Verbal Learn. Verbal Behav.* 18:357–64

Neches, R. 1984. Learning through incremental refinement of procedures. In *Production System Models of Learning and Development,* ed. D. Klahr, P. Langley, R. Neches. Cambridge, Mass: MIT Press/Bradford Books

Newell, A., Simon, H. A. 1972. *Human Problem Solving.* Englewood Cliffs, NJ: Prentice-Hall Inc.

Nickerson, R. S., Perkins, D. N., Smith, E. E. 1985. *The Teaching of Thinking.* Hillsdale, NJ: Erlbaum

Perfetti, C. A., Lesgold, A. M. 1979. Coding and comprehension in skilled reading. In *Theory and Practice of Early Reading,* ed. L. B. Resnick, P. Weaver. Hillsdale, NJ: Erlbaum

Piaget, J. 1926. *The Language and Thought of the Child.* London: Routledge & Kegan Paul

Polya, G. 1957. *How to Solve It: A New Aspect of Mathematical Method.* Princeton, NJ: Princeton Univ. Press. 2nd ed.

Reigeluth, C. M., ed. 1983. *Instructional-Design Theories and Models: An Overview of Their Current Status.* Hillsdale, NJ: Erlbaum

Resnick, L. B. 1981. Instructional psychology. *Ann. Rev. Psychol.* 32:659–704
Resnick, L. B. 1987a. *Education and Learning to Think*. Washington, DC: Nat. Acad. Press
Resnick, L. B. 1987b. Learning in school and out. *Educ. Res.* 16(9):13–20
Resnick, L. B. ed. 1988. *Knowing, Learning, and Instruction: Essays in Honor of Robert Glaser*. Hillsdale, NJ: Erlbaum. In press
Richer, M. H., Clancey, W. J. 1985. GUIDON-WATCH: a graphic interface for viewing a knowledge-based system. *IEEE Comput. Graphics Appl.* 5(11):51–64
Rogoff, B., Lave, J., eds. 1984. *Everyday Cognition: Its Development in Social Context*. Cambridge, Mass: Harvard Univ. Press
Rumelhart, D. E. 1980. Schemata: the building blocks of cognition. In *Theoretical Issues in Reading Comprehension*, ed. R. Spiro, B. Bruce, W. Brewer, pp. 33–58. Hillsdale, NJ: Erlbaum
Rumelhart, D. E., Norman, D. A. 1978. Accretion, tuning, and restructuring: three modes of learning. In *Semantic Factors in Cognition*, ed. J. W. Cotton, R. L. Klatzky. Hillsdale, NJ: Erlbaum
Saxe, G. B. 1988. Candy selling and math learning. *Educ. Res.* 17(6):14–21
Scardamalia, M., Bereiter, C., Steinbach, R. 1984. Teachability of reflective processes in written composition. *Cogn. Sci.* 8:173–90
Schneider, W. 1985. Training high performance skills: fallacies and guidelines. *Hum. Factors* 27(3):285–300
Schoenfeld, A. H. 1983. Problem solving in the mathematics curriculum: a report, recommendations and an annotated bibliography. *Math. Assoc. Am. Notes*, No. 1
Schoenfeld, A. H. 1985. *Mathematical Problem Solving*. Orlando, Fla: Academic
Schoenfeld, A. H. 1988. On mathematics as sense-making: an informal attack on the unfortunate divorce of formal and informal mathematics. In *Informal Reasoning and Education*, ed. D. N. Perkins, J. Segal, J. Voss. Hillsdale, NJ: Erlbaum. In press
Segal, J. W., Chipman, S. F., Glaser, R., eds. 1985. *Thinking and Learning Skills: Relating Instruction to Research*, Vol. 1. Hillsdale, NJ: Erlbaum
Shiffrin, R. M., Schneider, W. 1977. Controlled and automatic human information processing: II. Perceptual learning, automatic attending, and a general theory. *Psychol. Rev.* 84:127–90
Shortliffe, E. H. 1976. *Computer-based Medical Consultations: MYCIN*. New York: American Elsevier
Siegler, R. S. 1986. Unities across domains in children's choices. In *Minnesota Symposium on Child Psychology*, ed. M. Perlmutter, 19:1–48. Hillsdale, NJ: Erlbaum
Simon, D. P., Simon, H. A. 1978. Individual differences in solving physics problems. In *Children's Thinking: What Develops?*, ed. R. S. Siegler, pp. 325–48. Hillsdale, NJ: Erlbaum
Soloway, E. M., Johnson, W. L. 1984. Remembrance of blunders past: a retrospective on the development of PROUST. In *Proc. 6th Cogn. Sci. Soc. Conf.* Hillsdale, NJ: Erlbaum
Sternberg, R. J., ed. 1984. *Mechanisms of Cognitive Development*. New York: W. H. Freeman
Sternberg, R. J. 1985a. All's well that ends well, but it's a sad tale that begins at the end: a reply to Glaser. *Am. Psychol.* 40(5):571–73
Sternberg, R. J. 1985b. *Beyond IQ*. London: Cambridge Univ. Press
Sternberg, R. J. 1986. *Intelligence Applied*. San Diego, Calif: Harcourt Brace Jovanovich
Stevens, A. L., Collins, A. 1980. Multiple conceptual models of a complex system. In *Aptitude, Learning, and Instruction*, ed. R. E. Snow, P. Federico, W. E. Montague, 2:177–98. Hillsdale, NJ: Erlbaum
Vygotsky, L. S. 1978. *Mind in Society: The Development of Higher Psychological Processes*. Cambridge, Mass: Harvard Univ. Press
Wenger, E. 1987. *Artificial Intelligence and Tutoring Systems*. Los Altos, Calif: Morgan Kaufmann
White, B. Y., Frederiksen, J. R. 1986. *Progressions of quantitative models as a foundation for intelligent learning environments*. Tech. Rep #6277, BBN
Wood, D. J. 1980. Teaching the young child: some relationships between social interaction, language, and thought. In *Social Foundations of Language and Thought*, ed. D. R. Olson. New York: Norton

AUTHOR INDEX

SUBJECT INDEX

A

Absenteeism
    expectancy X value and, 338
Abstraction level
    hierarchical representation of,
        287-89
Acculturation
    cross-cultural psychology and,
        512-14
Achievement behavior
    cost-benefit judgments and,
        117
Achievement testing
    criticisms of, 33-38
ACQ Behavior Checklist, 99
Acquired immune deficiency
        syndrome
    behavior and, 560
    ethnicity and, 549
Actin
    stereocilia and, 411
Adherence
    health and illness and, 555-56
Adolescence
    cross-cultural psychology and,
        510
    psychological disturbances in
        taxonomy of, 94
Affect
    category structures and, 51
    control theory and, 342
Affective disorder, 457-88
    behavioral facilitation system
        in, 458-62
    neurobiology of, 462-71
    bipolar, 471-76
    brain imaging and, 476-86
Age
    health and illness and, 547-48
Aggression
    dopamine and, 468-69
Alcohol consumption
    cancer initiation and, 560
Alcoholism
    health and illness and, 551-52
Alexithymia
    psychosomatic disorders and,
        539-40
Amphetamine
    brain stimulation reward and,
        210
    drug reward and, 214-15
Analogy
    cognitive development and,
        365-69
    formation of, 366-69
    induction and, 621-24
Animal behavior

contemporary study of, 581-
        84
Animal cognition, 155-85, 596-
        97
Animal navigation
    representation of space in,
        160-78
Ants
    dead reckoning by, 163-65
Anxiety
    assessment methods for, 102
Apartheid, 68
Assimilation
    color constancy and, 13-14
Associative competition
    cognitive development and,
        359-62
    language development and,
        361-62
Assortative mating, 595
Attention
    motivation and, 109
Attention deficit disorder
    DSM-III and, 91
Attitude
    accessibility of, 294
    ambiguous information and,
        304-5
    cross-cultural psychology and,
        502-3
    feature representativeness and,
        299
    formation of, 307-11
    intergroup bias and, 64
    persuasive communications
        and, 303-4
    as stored evaluation, 285
Attitude theory
    emotional efference and, 254-
        55
Attributional Style Question-
        naire, 235, 242
Attribution theory
    cross-cultural psychology and,
        501-2
    organizational behavior and,
        330, 339-41
Auditory localization, 421-25
Auditory physiology, 405-25

B

Barbiturate
    brain stimulation reward and,
        213
Bargaining
    intergroup relations and, 69-
        70

Basic Personality Inventory, 101
Bat
    auditory pattern recognition
        and, 422-23
    cognitive map of, 173
Beck Depression Inventory,
        102, 235-36
Behavioral evolution
    principles of, 586-87
Behavioral facilitation system,
        458-62
    functional instability in, 473-
        76
    neurobiology of, 462-71
Behavioral medicine, 534
Bem Sex Role Inventory, 506
Benzodiazepine
    brain stimulation reward and,
        213
Biasing
    color constancy and, 14-15
BILOG, 25
Biology
    cross-cultural psychology and,
        497
Bird
    cognitive map of, 173
Blood pressure
    motivational arousal and, 112-
        16
BMDP8V, 30
Brain stimulation reward, 192-
        213
    anatomical studies of, 196-
        206
    neurophysiological studies of,
        206-9
    paradigmatic considerations
        in, 192-96
    pharmacological studies of,
        209-13
Breast cancer
    coping style and, 561
Brief Outpatient Psychopatholo-
        gy Scale, 98
Brief Psychiatric Rating Scale,
        93, 98
Brief Psychiatric Rating Scale
        for Children, 99
Brightness contrast
    color constancy and, 5
Bromocriptine
    antidepressant effects of, 474

C

Caffeine
    brain stimulation reward and,
        213

693

CUMULATIVE INDEXES

CONTRIBUTING AUTHORS, VOLUMES 35–40

A

Achenbach, T. M., 35:227–56
Adelmann, P. K., 40:249–80
Alkon, D. L., 36:419–93
Amir, Y., 37:17–41
Anastasi, A., 37:1–15
Appelbaum, M. I., 40:23–43
Aslin, R. N., 39:435–74

B

Baer, J. S., 39:223–52
Bargh, J. A., 38:369–425
Bassok, M., 40:631–66
Baum, A., 36:349–83
Bednar, R. L., 39:401–34
Beer, M., 38:339–67
Ben-Ari, R., 37:17–41
Berry, J. W., 40:493–531
Bettman, J. R., 37:257–89
Binder, A., 39:253–82
Bjork, R. A., 39:475–544
Blanchard, D. C., 39:43–68
Blanchard, R. J., 39:43–68
Borgen, F. H., 35:579–604
Boynton, R. M., 39:69–100
Brehm, J. W., 40:109–31
Brewer, M. B., 36:219–43
Browne, M. A., 35:605–25
Brugge, J. F., 36:245–74
Burlingame, G. M., 39:401–34

C

Cairns, R. B., 35:553–77
Cantor, N., 36:275–305
Carson, R. C., 40:227–48
Cascio, W. F., 35:461–518
Chaiken, S., 38:575–630
Clark, M. S., 39:609–72
Cohn, T. E., 37:495–521
Cook, T. D., 37:193–232
Cooper, J., 35:395–426
Cross, D. R., 37:611–51
Croyle, R. T., 35:395–426
Cutting, J. E., 38:61–90

D

Dark, V. J., 37:43–75
Datan, N., 38:153–80

Day, R. H., 39:375–400
de Boer, E., 38:181–202
Deaux, K., 36:49–81
Denmark, F., 38:279–98
Depue, R. A., 40:457–92
Dewsbury, D. A., 40:581–602
Diaz-Guerrero, R., 35:83–112
Donovan, D. M., 39:223–52
Dreschler, W. A., 38:181–202
Duncan, C. C., 37:291–319

E

Edelbrock, C. S., 35:227–56

F

Farley, J., 36:419–93
Feder, H. H., 35:165–200
Fischer, K. W., 36:613–48
Foss, D. J., 39:301–348
Fraisse, P., 35:1–36

G

Gallistel, C. R., 40:155–89
Gescheider, G. A., 39:169–200
Gesten, E. L., 38:427–60
Gibson, E. J., 39:1–42
Gibson, W. M., 39:349–74
Glaser, R., 40:631–66
Goldstein, M. J., 39:283–300
Gopher, D., 40:431–55
Gorsuch, R. L., 39:201–22
Gould, J. L., 37:163–92
Green, B. F., 35:37–53
Grunberg, N. E., 36:349–83
Guion, R. M., 39:349–74

H

Hakel, M. D., 37:135–61
Hall, J. A., 35:37–53
Hall, W. G., 38:91–128
Harris, L. C., 35:333–60
Harvey, J. H., 35:427–59
Hasher, L., 38:631–68
Hay, D. F., 37:135–61
Heller, J. F., 38:461–89
Helzer, J. E., 37:409–32
Hendersen, R. W., 36:495–529
Higgins, E. T., 38:369–425

Holahan, C. J., 37:381–407
Honzik, M. P., 35:309–31
Horn, J. M., 39:101–34
Horton, D. L., 35:361–94
House, R., 38:669–718
Hughes, F., 38:153–80
Hunt, E., 40:603–29
Hurvich, L., 40:1–22
Hyman, R., 40:133–54

I

Iacono, W. G., 40:457–92
Ilgen, D. R., 40:327–51
Iscoe, I., 35:333–60

J

Jameson, D., 40:1–22
Jason, L. A., 38:427–60
Johnson, M. K., 38:631–68
Johnston, W. A., 37:43–75
Jones, L. V., 40:23–43
Judd, C. M., 40:281–326

K

Kaas, J. H., 38:129–51
Kagitcibasi, C., 40:493–531
Kamil, A. C., 36:141–69
Keesey, R. E., 37:109–33
Kessler, R. C., 36:531–72
Kihlstrom, J. F., 36:385–418
Kimchi, R., 40:431–55
Kivlahan, D. R., 39:223–52
Klaber, M., 36:115–40
Klein, H. J., 40:327–51
Kolligian, J., Jr., 38:533–74
Kozma, R. B., 37:611–51
Kramer, A., 36:307–48
Kramer, R. M., 36:219–43
Krantz, D. S., 36:349–83

L

Lam, Y. R., 36:19–48
Lanyon, R. I., 35:667–701
Lasley, D. J., 37:495–521
Latham, G. P., 39:545–82
Leventhal, H., 37:565–610

701

CHAPTER TITLES, VOLUMES 35–40

Annual Reviews Inc.

A NONPROFIT SCIENTIFIC PUBLISHER

4139 El Camino Way
P.O. Box 10139
Palo Alto, CA 94303-0897 ● USA

ORDER FORM

ORDER TOLL FREE
1-800-523-8635
(except California)

Telex: 910-290-0275

Annual Reviews Inc. publications may be ordered directly from our office by mail, Telex, or use our Toll Free Telephone line (for orders paid by credit card or purchase order*, and customer service calls only); through booksellers and subscription agents, worldwide; and through participating professional societies. Prices subject to change without notice. ARI Federal I.D. #94-1156476

Individuals: Prepayment required on new accounts by check or money order (in U.S. dollars, check drawn on U.S. bank) or charge to credit card—American Express, VISA, MasterCard.

Institutional buyers: Please include purchase order number.

Students: $10.00 discount from retail price, per volume. Prepayment required. Proof of student status must be provided (photocopy of student I.D. or signature of department secretary is acceptable). Students must send orders direct to Annual Reviews. Orders received through bookstores and institutions requesting student rates will be returned. You may order at the Student Rate for a maximum of 3 years.

Professional Society Members: Members of professional societies that have a contractual arrangement with Annual Reviews may order books through their society at a reduced rate. Check with your society for information.

Toll Free Telephone orders: Call 1-800-523-8635 (except from California) for orders paid by credit card or purchase order and customer service calls only. California customers and all other business calls use 415-493-4400 (not toll free). Hours: 8:00 AM to 4:00 PM, Monday-Friday, Pacific Time. *Written confirmation is required on purchase orders from universities before shipment.

Telex: 910-290-0275

Regular orders: Please list the volumes you wish to order by volume number.

Standing orders: New volume in the series will be sent to you automatically each year upon publication. Cancellation may be made at any time. Please indicate volume number to begin standing order.

Prepublication orders: Volumes not yet published will be shipped in month and year indicated.

California orders: Add applicable sales tax.

Postage paid (4th class bookrate/surface mail) **by Annual Reviews Inc.** Airmail postage or UPS, extra.

ANNUAL REVIEWS SERIES		Prices Postpaid per volume USA & Canada/elsewhere	Regular Order Please send:	Standing Order Begin with:
			Vol. number	Vol. number
Annual Review of ANTHROPOLOGY				
Vols. 1-14	(1972-1985)...............	$27.00/$30.00		
Vols. 15-16	(1986-1987)...............	$31.00/$34.00		
Vol. 17	(1988)	$35.00/$39.00		
Vol. 18	(avail. Oct. 1989)	$35.00/$39.00	Vol(s). _____	Vol. _____
Annual Review of ASTRONOMY AND ASTROPHYSICS				
Vols. 1, 4-14, 16-20	(1963, 1966-1976, 1978-1982)	$27.00/$30.00		
Vols. 21-25	(1983-1987)...............	$44.00/$47.00		
Vol. 26	(1988)	$47.00/$51.00		
Vol. 27	(avail. Sept. 1989)	$47.00/$51.00	Vol(s). _____	Vol. _____
Annual Review of BIOCHEMISTRY				
Vols. 30-34, 36-54	(1961-1965, 1967-1985).......	$29.00/$32.00		
Vols. 55-56	(1986-1987)...............	$33.00/$36.00		
Vol. 57	(1988)	$35.00/$39.00		
Vol. 58	(avail. July 1989)	$35.00/$39.00	Vol(s). _____	Vol. _____
Annual Review of BIOPHYSICS AND BIOPHYSICAL CHEMISTRY				
Vols. 1-11	(1972-1982)...............	$27.00/$30.00		
Vols. 12-16	(1983-1987)...............	$47.00/$50.00		
Vol. 17	(1988)	$49.00/$53.00		
Vol. 18	(avail. June 1989)	$49.00/$53.00	Vol(s). _____	Vol. _____
Annual Review of CELL BIOLOGY				
Vol. 1	(1985)	$27.00/$30.00		
Vols. 2-3	(1986-1987)...............	$31.00/$34.00		
Vol. 4	(1988)	$35.00/$39.00		
Vol. 5	(avail. Nov. 1989)	$35.00/$39.00	Vol(s). _____	Vol. _____

Annual Review of **COMPUTER SCIENCE**

			Vol. number	Vol. number
Vols. 1-2	(1986-1987)................	$39.00/$42.00		
Vol. 3	(1988)	$45.00/$49.00		
Vol. 4	(avail. Nov. 1989)	$45.00/$49.00	Vol(s). _____	Vol. _____

Annual Review of **EARTH AND PLANETARY SCIENCES**

Vols. 1-10	(1973-1982)................	$27.00/$30.00		
Vols. 11-15	(1983-1987)................	$44.00/$47.00		
Vol. 16	(1988)	$49.00/$53.00		
Vol. 17	(avail. May 1989)	$49.00/$53.00	Vol(s). _____	Vol. _____

Annual Review of **ECOLOGY AND SYSTEMATICS**

Vols. 2-16	(1971-1985)................	$27.00/$30.00		
Vols. 17-18	(1986-1987)................	$31.00/$34.00		
Vol. 19	(1988)	$34.00/$38.00		
Vol. 20	(avail. Nov. 1989)	$34.00/$38.00	Vol(s). _____	Vol. _____

Annual Review of **ENERGY**

Vols. 1-7	(1976-1982)................	$27.00/$30.00		
Vols. 8-12	(1983-1987)................	$56.00/$59.00		
Vol. 13	(1988)	$58.00/$62.00		
Vol. 14	(avail. Oct. 1989)	$58.00/$62.00	Vol(s). _____	Vol. _____

Annual Review of **ENTOMOLOGY**

Vols. 10-16, 18	(1965-1971, 1973)			
20-30	(1975-1985)................	$27.00/$30.00		
Vols. 31-32	(1986-1987)................	$31.00/$34.00		
Vol. 33	(1988)	$34.00/$38.00		
Vol. 34	(avail. Jan. 1989)	$34.00/$38.00	Vol(s). _____	Vol. _____

Annual Review of **FLUID MECHANICS**

Vols. 1-4, 7-17	(1969-1972, 1975-1985)	$28.00/$31.00		
Vols. 18-19	(1986-1987)................	$32.00/$35.00		
Vol. 20	(1988)	$34.00/$38.00		
Vol. 21	(avail. Jan. 1989)	$34.00/$38.00	Vol(s). _____	Vol. _____

Annual Review of **GENETICS**

Vols. 1-19	(1967-1985)................	$27.00/$30.00		
Vols. 20-21	(1986-1987)................	$31.00/$34.00		
Vol. 22	(1988)	$34.00/$38.00		
Vol. 23	(avail. Dec. 1989)	$34.00/$38.00	Vol(s). _____	Vol. _____

Annual Review of **IMMUNOLOGY**

Vols. 1-3	(1983-1985)................	$27.00/$30.00		
Vols. 4-5	(1986-1987)................	$31.00/$34.00		
Vol. 6	(1988)	$34.00/$38.00		
Vol. 7	(avail. April 1989)	$34.00/$38.00	Vol(s). _____	Vol. _____

Annual Review of **MATERIALS SCIENCE**

Vols. 1, 3-12	(1971, 1973-1982)...........	$27.00/$30.00		
Vols. 13-17	(1983-1987)................	$64.00/$67.00		
Vol. 18	(1988)	$66.00/$70.00		
Vol. 19	(avail. Aug. 1989)...........	$66.00/$70.00	Vol(s). _____	Vol. _____

Annual Review of **MEDICINE**

Vols. 9, 11-15	(1958, 1960-1964)			
17-36	(1966-1985)................	$27.00/$30.00		
Vols. 37-38	(1986-1987)................	$31.00/$34.00		
Vol. 39	(1988)	$34.00/$38.00		
Vol. 40	(avail. April 1989)	$34.00/$38.00	Vol(s). _____	Vol. _____